Microsoft Exam AZ-800

Guide to Administering Windows Server Hybrid Core Infrastructure

Greg Tomsho

Networking

 Cengage

Australia • Brazil • Canada • Mexico • Singapore • United Kingdom • United States

Microsoft Exam AZ-800: Guide to Administering Windows Server Hybrid Core Infrastructure, First Edition
Greg Tomsho

SVP, Product Management: Cheryl Costantini

VP, Product Management & Marketing, Learning Experiences: Thais Alencar

Sr. Product Director, Portfolio Product Management: Mark Santee

Director, Product Management: Rita Lombard

Portfolio Product Manager: Natalie Onderdonk

Product Assistant: Ethan Wheel

Learning Designer: Carolyn Mako

Senior Content Manager: Brooke Greenhouse

Digital Project Manager: Jim Vaughey

Technical Editor: Danielle Shaw

Developmental Editor: Dan Seiter

VP, Product Marketing: Jason Sakos

Director, Product Marketing: Danae April

Product Marketing Manager: Mackenzie Paine

Portfolio Specialist: Matt Schiesl

Content Acquisition Analyst: Ann Hoffman

Production Service: Straive

Senior Designer: Erin Griffin

Cover Image Source: djero.adlibeshe yahoo.com/ shutterstock.com

For product information and technology assistance, contact us at **Cengage Customer & Sales Support, 1-800-354-9706 or support.cengage.com.**

For permission to use material from this text or product, submit all requests online at **www.copyright.com.**

Library of Congress Control Number: 2023934979

ISBN: 9780357511800
Looseleaf ISBN: 9780357511817

Cengage
200 Pier 4 Boulevard
Boston, MA 02210
USA

Cengage is a leading provider of customized learning solutions. Our employees reside in nearly 40 different countries and serve digital learners in 165 countries around the world. Find your local representative at **www.cengage.com.**

To learn more about Cengage platforms and services, register or access your online learning solution, or purchase materials for your course, visit **www.cengage.com.**

Notice to the Reader

Publisher does not warrant or guarantee any of the products described herein or perform any independent analysis in connection with any of the product information contained herein. Publisher does not assume, and expressly disclaims, any obligation to obtain and include information other than that provided to it by the manufacturer. The reader is expressly warned to consider and adopt all safety precautions that might be indicated by the activities described herein and to avoid all potential hazards. By following the instructions contained herein, the reader willingly assumes all risks in connection with such instructions. The publisher makes no representations or warranties of any kind, including but not limited to, the warranties of fitness for particular purpose or merchantability, nor are any such representations implied with respect to the material set forth herein, and the publisher takes no responsibility with respect to such material. The publisher shall not be liable for any special, consequential, or exemplary damages resulting, in whole or part, from the readers' use of, or reliance upon, this material.

Printed at CLDPC, USA, 04-23

Brief Contents

Introduction x

Before You Begin xvi

Module 1
Dive into Windows Server Hybrid Infrastructure 1

Module 2
Discover Active Directory 38

Module 3
Manage Active Directory Accounts 92

Module 4
Configure Group Policies 171

Module 5
Configure Domains 235

Module 6
Manage Windows Server in a
Hybrid Environment 306

Module 7
Configure DNS 364

Module 8
Manage IP Addressing 418

Module 9
Implement Network Connectivity 487

Module 10
Configure Storage and File Services 547

Module 11
Configure Advanced Storage Solutions 632

Module 12
Implement Virtualization with
Hyper-V and Azure 676

Module 13
Implement Advanced Virtualization 742

Appendix A
Microsoft Exam AZ-800 Objectives
Mapped to Modules 787

Glossary 793

Index 813

Table of Contents

Introduction   x
Before You Begin   xvi

Module 1

Dive into Windows Server Hybrid Infrastructure   1

The Role of a Server Operating System   2
  Server: Hardware or Software?   3
  Server Operating Systems Versus
    Desktop Operating Systems   3
  Windows Server 2022 Roles and Features   4
Windows Server 2022 Core Technologies   5
  Server Manager   6
  NTFS   7
  Microsoft Management Console   7
  Disk Management   9
  File and Printer Sharing   9
  Windows Networking Concepts   9
  Windows Networking Components   9
  Active Directory Domain Services   11
  PowerShell   11
  Hyper-V and Cloud Computing   13
  Storage Spaces   14
Introducing the Windows Server
  Hybrid Infrastructure   25
  Cloud Models   26
  Getting Started with Microsoft Azure   26
  Creating an Azure Virtual Machine   27
  Accessing an Azure Virtual Machine   28
Module Summary   34
Key Terms   34
Review Questions   34
Case Projects   36

Module 2

Discover Active Directory   38

The Role of a Directory Service   39
  Active Directory Domain Services   39
  Overview of the Active Directory Structure 40
Installing Active Directory   44
  Installing Additional Domain Controllers in
    a Domain   48

Installing a New Domain in an Existing Forest   48
Installing Active Directory in Server Core   49
Installing a DC with Install from Media   51
What's Inside Active Directory?   54
  The Active Directory Schema   56
  Active Directory Container Objects   57
  Active Directory Leaf Objects   58
  Recovering Objects with the Active
    Directory Recycle Bin   60
  Locating Active Directory Objects   60
Working with Forests, Trees,
  and Domains   68
  Active Directory Terminology   69
  The Role of Forests   72
  Understanding Domains and Trees   74
Introducing Group Policies   78
  The Computer Configuration Node   79
  The User Configuration Node   80
  How Group Policies Are Applied   80
Module Summary   87
Key Terms   88
Review Questions   88
Case Projects   90

Module 3

Manage Active Directory Accounts   92

Working with Organizational Units   93
  OU Delegation of Control   95
  Active Directory Object Permissions   96
Managing User Accounts   101
  Creating and Modifying User Accounts   103
  Understanding Account Properties   106
  Using Contacts and Distribution Groups   110
Managing Group Accounts   113
  Group Types   113
  Group Scope   114
  Nesting Groups   118
  Converting Group Scope   118
  Default Groups in a Windows Domain   119
Working with Computer Accounts   124
  Creating Computer Accounts   124
  Managing Computer Accounts   127
Working with Service Accounts   129
  Built-in Service Accounts   130

Working with Managed Service Accounts   132
Kerberos Delegation   134

Using Active Directory in a Hybrid Environment   136

Azure Active Directory (AAD)   136
Working with Azure AD Accounts   137
Implementing Azure AD Connect   140
Managing Azure AD Connect Health   148
Azure AD Connect Cloud Sync   149
Implementing Azure AD Cloud Sync   150
Azure AD Domain Services   153

Module Summary   163

Key Terms   164

Review Questions   165

Case Projects   168

Module 4

Configure Group Policies   171

Group Policy Objects   172

Local and Domain Group Policy Objects   173
Group Policy Replication   177
Creating and Linking GPOs   177

Group Policy Settings   188

Software Installation Policies   189
Deploying Scripts   192
Folder Redirection   193

Working with Administrative Templates   196

Computer Configuration Settings   197
User Configuration Settings   198
The ADMX Central Store   199
Working with Filters   199
Using Custom Administrative Templates   200
Migrating Administrative Templates   201

Configuring Group Policy Preferences   204

How Group Policy Preferences Are Applied   205
Creating Group Policy Preferences   206

Group Policy Processing   212

GPO Scope and Precedence   212
Group Policy Inheritance   213
Managing GPO Status and Link Status   214
GPO Filtering   215
Loopback Policy Processing   219

Implementing Group Policy in Azure AD DS   224

Module Summary   227

Key Terms   228

Review Questions   228

Case Projects   232

Module 5

Configure Domains   235

Active Directory Review   236

Configuring Read-Only Domain Controllers   237

RODC Installation   237
Staged RODC Installation   239
RODC Replication   242
Read-Only DNS   243

Understanding and Configuring Sites   246

Site Components   247
The Global Catalog and Universal
Group Membership Caching   250
Configuring Sites   250

Active Directory Replication   254

Active Directory Intrasite Replication   255
Active Directory Intersite Replication   259
SYSVOL Replication   261
Managing Replication   263

Working with Operations Master Roles   268

Operations Master Best Practices   268
Managing Operations Master Roles   270

Configuring Multidomain Environments   273

Reasons for a Single-Domain Environment   273
Reasons for a Multidomain Environment   274
Adding a Subdomain   274
Adding a Tree to an Existing Forest   275
Configuring an Alternative UPN Suffix   276

Configuring Multiforest Environments   281

Active Directory Trusts   283

One-Way and Two-Way Trusts   284
Transitive Trusts   284
Shortcut Trusts   285
Forest Trusts   285
External Trusts and Realm Trusts   287

Configuring Active Directory Trusts   287

Configuring Shortcut Trusts   287
Configuring Forest Trusts   289
Configuring External and Realm Trusts   291
Configuring Trust Properties   291

Working with Domain Controllers in Azure   295

Creating an Azure Domain Controller   296

Module Summary   297

Key Terms   298

Review Questions   299

Case Projects   301

Module 6

Manage Windows Server in a Hybrid Environment   306

Working with Server Roles and Features	307
Managing Server Roles in the GUI	307
Managing Server Roles with PowerShell	312
Managing Servers Remotely	316
Adding Servers to Server Manager	316
Using Server Manager Groups	317
Enabling and Disabling Remote Management	318
PowerShell Remoting	318
Configuring Second-Hop Remoting	319
Configuring Just Enough Administration for PowerShell Remoting	321
Configuring Windows Firewall for Remote Management	324
Using Windows Admin Center	332
Installing Windows Admin Center on Windows 11	333
Installing Windows Admin Center Gateway	335
Managing Windows Servers with Azure Services	340
Azure Arc	341
Just-in-Time Access to VMs	351
Using Runbooks to Manage Azure VMs	353
Managing Servers with Desired State Configuration	354
Implementing DSC on Azure VMs	356
Module Summary	359
Key Terms	359
Review Questions	360
Case Projects	362

Module 7

Configure DNS   364

Introduction to Domain Name System	365
The Structure of DNS	365
The DNS Lookup Process	366
DNS Server Roles	367
Installing and Configuring DNS	370
Creating DNS Zones	371
Configuring DNS with PowerShell	375
Creating DNS Resource Records	376
Host (A and AAAA) Records	377
Canonical Name (CNAME) Records	378
Pointer (PTR) Records	378

Mail Exchanger (MX) Records	378
Service Location (SRV) Records	380
Creating Dynamic DNS Records	382
Creating Static DNS Records	382
Configuring DNS Zones	386
Start of Authority Records	387
Name Server Records	388
Zone Delegation	388
Creating Secondary Zones and Configuring Zone Transfers	389
Configuring DNS Server Settings	392
DNS Forwarders	393
Root Hints	394
Round Robin	395
Recursive Queries	395
PowerShell Commands for Advanced DNS Server Settings	396
Configuring DNS Security	399
Domain Name System Security Extension	400
The DNS Socket Pool	402
DNS Cache Locking	403
Enabling Response Rate Limiting	403
DNS-Based Authentication of Named Entities	404
Azure DNS	405
Creating and Testing an Azure Private DNS Zone	406
Integrating On-Premises DNS with Azure Private DNS Zones	409
Module Summary	411
Key Terms	412
Review Questions	413
Case Projects	415

Module 8

Manage IP Addressing   418

An Overview of Dynamic Host Configuration Protocol	419
The DHCP Address Assignment Process	420
Installing and Configuring DHCP	422
DHCP Server Authorization	422
DHCP Scopes	423
Configuring Superscopes	426
Configuring Multicast Scopes	427
DHCP Options	429
DHCP Server Options	435
Configuring IPv4 Server Properties	437
DHCP Name Protection	440
Configuring Scope Properties	441

Configuring Filters 442
Configuring Policies 442
Configuring DHCP for PXE Boot 443
DHCP Relay Agents 444
Server Migration, Export, and Import 447
Troubleshooting DHCP 447

DHCP High Availability 451
DHCP Split Scopes 452
DHCP Failover 453

IP Address Management 459
The IPAM Infrastructure 459
Deploying IPAM 460
Meeting IPAM Requirements 461
Installing the IPAM Server Feature 462
IPAM Server Provisioning 462
Configuring Server Discovery 464
Provisioning GPOs 466
Selecting Servers to Manage 467
Retrieving Server Data 468

IP Addressing in Hybrid Environments 473
Virtual Networks and IP Addresses 473
IP Address Issues in a Hybrid Environment 475

Module Summary 479

Key Terms 481

Review Questions 481

Case Projects 484

Module 9

Implement Network Connectivity 487

The Remote Access Role 488
Installing and Configuring the Remote
Access Role 489
Virtual Private Networks 489
VPN Configuration 492
Finishing VPN Configuration 494
Configuring Remote Access Options 496
Configuring a Site-to-Site VPN 499

Network Policy Server Overview 505
The RADIUS Infrastructure 505
Installing and Configuring NPS and RADIUS 506
Configuring RADIUS Accounting 508
Using Certificates for Authentication 508
Configuring NPS Policies 515
Managing NPS Templates 517
Importing and Exporting NPS Policies 518

Implementing Web Application Proxy 522
Publishing Web Apps with WAP 524
Publishing Remote Desktop Gateway
Applications 525

Implementing Azure Networking 526
Azure Virtual Network Overview 526
Azure Network Adapter 530
Azure Extended Network 532
Azure Relay 534
Azure Virtual WAN 536
Azure AD Application Proxy 539

Module Summary 540

Key Terms 542

Review Questions 542

Case Projects 545

Module 10

Configure Storage and File Services 547

An Overview of Server Storage 548
What Is Storage? 549
Reasons for Storage 549
Storage Access Methods 550

Configuring Local Disks 552
Disk Capacity and Speed 552
Disk Interface Technologies 553
Volumes and Disk Types 554
Disk Formats 557
The FAT File System 558
The NTFS and ReFS File Systems 558
Preparing a New Disk for Use 559
Managing Disks with PowerShell 559

Working with Virtual Disks 566
VHD versus VHDX Format 566
Dynamically Expanding and Fixed-Size Disks 567

File Sharing 570
Creating Windows File Shares 570
Creating Shares with File and Storage Services 572
Managing Shares with the Shared Folders
Snap-in 575
Creating and Managing Shares at the
Command Line 577
Default and Administrative Shares 578
Accessing File Shares from Client Computers 578
Network File System 579

Securing Access to Files with Permissions 584
Security Principals 585
Share Permissions 586
File and Folder Permissions 587

Using File Server Resource Manager 596
FSRM Quotas 597
Using File Screens 598

Using Distributed File System   605
  Installing and Configuring DFS   607
  Creating a Namespace   607
  Configuring Referrals and Advanced
    Namespace Settings   610
Using BranchCache   614
  Installing and Configuring BranchCache   617
  Configuring Clients to Use BranchCache   619
Module Summary   623
Key Terms   624
Review Questions   625
Case Projects   627

Module 11

Configure Advanced Storage Solutions   632

Storage Spaces   633
  Creating Storage Spaces   635
  Expanding a Storage Pool   638
  Replacing a Failed Physical Disk in a
    Storage Pool   639
  Configuring Enclosure Awareness   642
  Configuring Tiered Storage   643
Implementing Data Deduplication   649
  When to Use Data Deduplication   649
  Installing and Using Data Deduplication   650
  Monitoring Data Deduplication   653
  Backing Up and Restoring with
    Data Deduplication   654
Storage Replica   655
  Storage Replica Use Scenarios   656
  Installing and Configuring Storage Replica 656
  Synchronous and Asynchronous Replication   657
SMB Direct and Storage QoS   658
  Storage Quality of Service   659
Azure File Sync   660
  Azure Storage and File Shares   661
  Configuring Azure File Sync   661
  Configuring Cloud Tiering and Monitoring
    Azure File Sync   666
  Migrating Distributed File System to
    Azure File Sync   669
Module Summary   670
Key Terms   671
Review Questions   671
Case Projects   673

Module 12

Implement Virtualization with Hyper-V and Azure   676

Installing Hyper-V   677
  Installing the Hyper-V Role and
    Management Tools   680
  Managing Hyper-V Remotely   680
  Hyper-V Licensing   680
Creating Virtual Machines in Hyper-V   681
  Basic Virtual Machine Management with
    Hyper-V Manager   682
  Advanced VM Creation Methods   684
  Generation 1 and Generation 2 VMs   686
Managing Virtual Machines   691
  Virtual Machine Hardware Settings   692
  Integration Services   696
  Checkpoints   697
  Automatic Start and Stop Actions   699
  Enhanced Session Mode   700
  Discrete Device Assignment   703
  Managing Windows VMs with PowerShell Direct 703
  Managing Linux VMs with SSH Direct   703
Working with Virtual Hard Disks   704
  Creating and Modifying Virtual Disks   705
  Pass-Through Disks   708
Hyper-V Virtual Networks   711
  External Virtual Switches   712
  Internal Virtual Switches   712
  Private Virtual Switches   713
  Communicating Between Hyper-V Switches   714
  Creating a Virtual Switch   715
  Configuring MAC Addresses   717
  Adding and Removing Virtual Network
    Interface Cards   718
Advanced Virtual Network Configuration   719
  Virtual NIC Hardware Acceleration   720
  Configuring vNICs with Advanced Features   721
  Configuring NIC Teaming   722
  Synthetic Versus Legacy Network Adapters   726
Managing Windows Server VMs on Azure   727
  Managing Azure VMs   727
  Managing Azure VM Data Disks   728
  Resizing an Azure VM   729
  Configuring VM Connections   731
Module Summary   733
Key Terms   734
Review Questions   735
Case Projects   739

Module 13

Implement Advanced Virtualization 742

Nested Virtualization 743

Configuring VM Groups and
Hyper-V Scheduling 744
VM CPU Groups 744
Configuring Hyper-V Scheduler Types 746

Implementing High Availability with
Hyper-V 748
Configuring Highly Available Virtual Machines 748
Implementing Node Fairness 751
Implementing VM Resiliency 752
Configuring Virtual Machine Monitoring 753
Configuring Guest Clustering 755
Configuring Hyper-V Replica 757

Windows Containers 761
Deploying Windows Containers 762
Implementing Containers on
Windows Server 763
Managing Daemon Startup Options 767

Managing Windows Containers 770
Managing Containers with the
Docker Daemon 771
Working with Container Images 772
Implementing Container Networks 774
Working with Container Data Volumes 776
Managing Container Resources 777
Managing Container Images with Dockerfile
and Microsoft Azure 777

Module Summary 781

Key Terms 782

Review Questions 782

Case Projects 784

Appendix A

Microsoft Exam AZ-800 Objectives Mapped to Modules 787

Glossary 793
Index 813

Introduction

Microsoft Exam AZ-800: Guide to Administering Windows Server Hybrid Core Infrastructure gives you in-depth coverage of the AZ-800 certification exam objectives and focuses on the skills you need to administer on-premises Windows Server core technologies and integrate your Windows Server infrastructure with Microsoft Azure services. The text offers more than 80 hands-on activities and dozens of skill-reinforcing case projects, so you'll be well prepared for the certification exam and learn valuable skills to perform on the job.

After you finish this book, you'll have an in-depth knowledge of Windows Server, including installation, local and remote management, file and storage services, and Hyper-V virtualization. You'll also learn how to use a number of Microsoft Azure services, including Azure Active Directory, Azure AD Directory Services, and Azure storage and networking. The AZ-800 and AZ-801 exams are required for earning the Windows Server Hybrid Administrator Associate certification.

This book is written from a teaching and learning point of view, not simply as an exam study guide. The modules guide readers through the technologies they need to master to perform on the job, not just to pass an exam.

Intended Audience

Microsoft Exam AZ-800: Guide to Administering Windows Server Hybrid Core Infrastructure is intended for people who want to learn how to configure and manage Windows Server in a hybrid on-premises and Azure computing environment and earn the Windows Server Hybrid Administrator Associate certification. This book covers in full the objectives of exam AZ-800, one of two exams required for earning the certification. This book serves as an excellent tool for classroom teaching, but self-paced learners will also find that the clear explanations, challenging activities, and case projects serve them equally well. Although this book doesn't assume previous experience with Windows servers, it does assume a familiarity with current Windows operating systems, such as Windows 10. Networking knowledge equivalent to an introductory networking course or Network+ is highly recommended.

A lab setup guide is included in the "Before You Begin" section of this introduction to help you configure a physical or virtual lab environment for doing the hands-on activities. Using a virtual environment is recommended.

Note 1

This text does not include Windows Server software. Windows Server 2022 is used in screen captures and activities. A 180-day evaluation version of Windows Server 2022 is available at no cost from *www.microsoft.com/en-us/evalcenter /evaluate-windows-server-2022*. For more specific instructions, see the section titled "Using an Evaluation Version of Windows Server 2022" later in this introduction.

About the Windows Server Hybrid Administrator Associate Certification

This book prepares you to take one of two exams in the Windows Server Hybrid Administrator Associate certification. The two exams should be taken in order:

- Exam AZ-800: Administering Windows Server Hybrid Core Infrastructure
- Exam AZ-801: Configuring Windows Server Hybrid Advanced Services

Note 2

This text focuses on Exam AZ-800. The companion text, *Microsoft Exam AZ-801: Guide to Configuring Windows Server Hybrid Advanced Services (Cengage 2024)*, focuses on Exam AZ-801.

Module Descriptions

This book is organized to familiarize you with Windows Server features and technologies and then provide in-depth coverage of Windows Server management, storage, and virtualization. The AZ-800 exam objectives are covered throughout the book; you can find a mapping of objectives and the modules in which they're covered in Appendix A. The following list describes this book's modules.

> **Note 3**
>
> Windows Server 2022 is used throughout this book, but Microsoft has made few changes to the core Windows Server technologies since Windows Server 2016, so most of the Windows Server core technology topics that are discussed are applicable to Windows Server 2016 through Windows Server 2022.

- **Module 1**, "Dive into Windows Server Hybrid Infrastructure," describes the role of a server operating system and provides an overview of Windows Server core technologies, such as the NT File System, Active Directory, disk management, Hyper-V, and PowerShell. You are also introduced to Microsoft Azure and the hybrid infrastructure paradigm.

- **Module 2**, "Discover Active Directory," discusses Active Directory, the core component in a Windows domain environment. You learn how to install Active Directory and work with forests, trees, and domains. Additionally, you learn the basics of using the Group Policy tool to set consistent security, user, and desktop standards throughout your organization. You are also introduced to how Active Directory fits in with the Windows Server hybrid infrastructure and Azure Active Directory.

- **Module 3**, "Manage Active Directory Accounts," delves deeper into the Active Directory organizational structure and explains how to design an efficient directory with organizational units. Next, you learn how to create and manage user and group accounts, the primary means of assigning rights and permissions. You examine computer accounts and service accounts, learn how to work with Active Directory accounts in a hybrid infrastructure, and learn how to synchronize information between on-premises AD and Azure Active Directory.

- **Module 4**, "Configure Group Policies," covers the architecture of group policies so that you can understand what a Group Policy Object (GPO) is and how and where it can be applied to your Active Directory structure. In addition, you learn about the myriad policy settings that can be configured through group policies. You also examine how to apply standard security settings throughout your network and work with group policy preferences. This module also discusses GPO scope, precedence, and inheritance so that you can make sure the appropriate objects are configured with the appropriate settings. Finally, you see how Group Policy can be implemented in Azure AD DS.

- **Module 5**, "Configure Domains," discusses domain controllers, the main physical component of Active Directory. You learn how to deploy multiple DCs in both single-site and multisite environments. You also learn how to optimally deploy operations master roles on your DCs and how to best configure your DCs for optimal replication. In addition, you learn when you might need to configure a multidomain or multiforest network. You also learn how to configure trust relationships between domains and forests for efficient operation of Active Directory and how to make these complex environments easier for users. Finally, you see how to deploy and manage domain controllers in a hybrid environment.

- **Module 6**, "Manage Windows Server in a Hybrid Environment," explains how to work with server roles and features and how to manage servers remotely. You also learn how to deploy Windows Admin Center and manage Windows servers with Azure services, including Azure Arc, Azure Policy Guest Configuration, and Azure Security Center. Finally, you learn about Desired State Configuration (DSC), in which both on-premises servers and Azure VMs can be configured and maintained using special PowerShell scripts.

- **Module 7**, "Configure DNS," describes the structure of the worldwide DNS framework and explains how to configure and maintain DNS in a Windows domain environment. In addition, you learn how to manage DNS zones, the main structural component of DNS. Next, you explore several methods to secure and protect DNS. In addition, you learn how to use Azure DNS in a hybrid network environment.

- **Module 8**, "Manage IP Addressing," discusses how DHCP works, and you learn how to install and configure DHCP, including server authorization, scopes, and DHCP options. You also learn about some advanced features, such as reservations and exclusions. In addition, you learn how DHCPv6 works and how to configure a DHCPv6 scope and options. Plus, you learn how to configure high availability, including split scopes, DHCP failover, DHCP server clusters, and hot standby. Next, you learn how to use a DHCP management tool called Internet Protocol Address Management (IPAM) to centrally manage DHCP servers, IP address spaces, and DNS servers and zones. Last, you see how to implement IP addressing in a hybrid network environment with Azure.

- **Module 9**, "Implement Network Connectivity," discusses how to install and configure the Remote Access server role and its three role services. This module also focuses on configuring virtual private networks, Web Application Proxy, and the Network Policy Server role. In addition, you learn about implementing and managing Azure Network Adapter and Azure Extended Network to integrate your on-premises network resources with your Azure resources. Azure Relay, Azure Virtual WAN, and Azure AD Application Proxy are discussed as well.

- **Module 10**, "Configure Storage and File Services," describes the methods available for storage provisioning, including working with local and virtual disks and using disk partition and format options. You learn about the types of volumes you can create on a Windows server and how to work with virtual disks. This module also discusses how Windows implements file sharing and how to secure access to files with permissions. Advanced file system tools and services such as File Server Resource Manager, Distributed File System, and BranchCache are covered.

- **Module 11**, "Configure Advanced Storage Solutions," discusses how to implement Storage Spaces, a method for providing flexible and fault-tolerant storage without using expensive RAID controllers. You also explore data deduplication and Storage Replica. Data deduplication helps reduce storage requirements by eliminating duplicated data, while Storage Replica provides server-to-server and cluster-to-cluster volume replication for high-availability applications. Storage QoS options are described, and you learn how to implement Azure File Sync to synchronize shared files between your on-premises servers and your Azure servers.

- **Module 12**, "Implement Virtualization with Hyper-V and Azure," focuses on how to use the Hyper-V server role for a virtualization platform. You learn the requirements for installing Hyper-V and how to install and configure the Hyper-V role. You learn how to manage Hyper-V both locally and remotely, create virtual machines, and manage and optimize virtual machines. You learn about virtual hard disks and the types of virtual networks you can deploy. Plus, you delve deeper into managing Windows Server VMs in an Azure environment.

- **Module 13**, "Implement Advanced Virtualization," covers nested virtualization, which allows you to run Hyper-V on a virtual machine. In addition, you learn about VM groups and Hyper-V scheduling so you can optimize your computing environment. Next, you learn to configure highly available virtual machines at the Hyper-V host level and at the guest OS level. Last, you see how to implement and manage Windows containers to take virtualization to the next level.

Features

This course includes many features designed to help you fully understand Microsoft Server and Microsoft Azure services and to enhance your learning experience.

- ***Module objectives***—Each module lists the concepts to be mastered within that module. This list serves as a quick reference to the module's contents and as a useful study aid.

- ***Certification objectives***—These lists give you a quick reference for which Microsoft Exam AZ-800 objectives are covered in each major section of the module. See Appendix A for a map of the objectives.

- ***Hands-on activities***—These step-by-step activities walk you through a variety of tasks for using the Windows Server core technologies, such as the NTFS and ReFS file systems, storage options, Active Directory, and Hyper-V virtualization. A number of activities introduce you to working with Windows Server in a Microsoft Azure cloud environment. All activities have been tested by a technical editor.

- ***Self-check questions***—Periodic multiple-choice questions throughout the readings help you mentally complete the "learning cycle" as you practice recalling the information as you learn it. With answers and thorough explanations at the end of each module, you can check your own learning and assess your progress toward mastering each module's objectives.

- *Screen captures, illustrations, and tables*—Numerous screen captures and illustrations help you visualize theories and concepts to see how to use tools and desktop features. In addition, tables provide details and comparison of practical and theoretical information and serve as a quick review.
- *Notes*—Notes draw your attention to helpful material related to the subject being covered.
- *Exam tips*—Exam tips point out specific details about material that is likely to be on Microsoft Exam AZ-800, Administering Windows Server Hybrid Core Infrastructure.
- *Cautions*—Caution icons warn you about potential mistakes or problems and explain how to avoid them.
- *Module summary*—Each module ends with a summary of the concepts introduced in the module. These summaries are a helpful way to review the material covered in each module.
- *Key terms*—All terms introduced with bold text are gathered together in the key terms list at the end of the module. This useful reference encourages a more thorough understanding of the module's key concepts. A definition of each key term is provided in the Glossary.
- *Review questions*—The end-of-module assessment begins with review questions that reinforce the main concepts and techniques covered in each module. Answering these questions helps ensure that you have mastered important topics.
- *Critical thinking case projects*—These case projects require you to apply the concepts and technologies learned throughout the book.

Text and Graphics Conventions

Additional information and exercises help you better understand what's being discussed in the module. Icons and headings throughout the book alert you to these additional materials:

Exam Tip ✔

Exam Tips point out specific details about material that is likely to be covered on the AZ-800 exam.

Note

Notes present additional helpful material related to the subject being discussed.

Caution !

The Caution icon identifies important information about potential mistakes or hazards.

Activity

Each hands-on activity in this book is preceded by a blue Activity heading.

Case Projects

Case Projects headings mark the end-of-module case projects, which are scenario-based assignments that ask you to apply what you have learned in the module.

Microsoft Exam AZ-800

Certification boxes under module headings list exam objectives covered in that section.

Instructor Resources

Instructors, please visit Cengage.com and sign in to access instructor-specific resources, which include the instructor manual, solution and answer guide, Instructor creation tools, and PowerPoint presentations.

- *Instructor's Manual*—The Instructor's Manual that accompanies this course provides additional instructional material to assist in class preparation, including suggestions for discussion topics and additional projects.
- *Solution and answer guide*—Answers to the review questions and case projects are included.
- *Cengage Learning Testing Powered by Cognero*—This flexible, online system allows you to do the following:
  - Author, edit, and manage test bank content from multiple Cengage Learning solutions.
  - Create multiple test versions in an instant.
  - Deliver tests from your LMS, your classroom, or wherever you want.
- *PowerPoint presentations*—This course comes with Microsoft PowerPoint slides for each module. These slides are included as a teaching aid for classroom presentation, to make available to students on the network for module review, or to be printed for classroom distribution. Instructors, please feel at liberty to add your own slides for additional topics you introduce to the class.

MindTap

MindTap for *Microsoft Exam AZ-800: Guide to Administering Windows Server Hybrid Core Infrastructure* is an online learning solution designed to help you master the skills needed in today's workforce. Research shows that employers need critical thinkers, troubleshooters, and creative problem-solvers to stay relevant in our fast-paced, technology-driven world. MindTap helps you achieve this with assignments and activities that provide hands-on practice, real-life relevance, and mastery of difficult concepts. Students are guided through assignments that progress from basic knowledge and understanding to more challenging problems. MindTap activities and assignments are tied to learning objectives. MindTap features include the following:

- *Live virtual machine labs* allow you to practice, explore, and try different solutions in a safe sandbox environment. Each module provides you with an opportunity to complete an in-depth project hosted in a live virtual machine environment. You implement the skills and knowledge gained in the module through real design and configuration scenarios in a practice cloud created with OpenStack.
- *Simulations* allow you to apply concepts covered in the module in a step-by-step virtual environment. The simulations provide immediate feedback.
- *Windows Server for Life* assignments encourage you to stay current with what is happening in the field of Windows Server Hybrid Core Infrastructure.
- *Reflection* activities encourage classroom and online discussion of key issues covered in the modules.
- *Pre and post quizzes* assess your understanding of key concepts at the beginning and end of the course and emulate the text.

For instructors, MindTap is designed around learning objectives and provides analytics and reporting so you can easily see where the class stands in terms of progress, engagement, and completion rates. Use the content and learning path as is or pick and choose how your materials will integrate with the learning path. You control what the students see and when they see it. Learn more at *www.cengage.com/mindtap/*.

Instant Access Code: ISBN: 978-0357-511831

Printed Access Code: ISBN: 978-0357-511848

Acknowledgments

I would like to thank Cengage Portfolio Product Manager Natalie Onderdonk and Content Manager Brooke Greenhouse for their confidence in asking me to undertake this challenging project. I also thank Carolyn Mako, Learning Designer; Mackenzie Paine, Product Marketing Manager; and Jim Vaughey, Digital Project Manager. A special word of gratitude goes to Dan Seiter, the Developmental Editor, who took an unrefined product and turned it into a polished manuscript. Danielle Shaw, the Technical Editor, tested module activities diligently to ensure that they work as intended, and for that I am grateful.

I thank the peer reviewers for their insights: John Geiman of Western Dakota Technical College, Adeleye Bamkole of Passaic County Community College, and Luis Alfonso Lopez Lerma of Southwest University.

Finally, my family: my amazing wife, Julie, lovely daughters, Camille and Sophia, and son, Michael, deserve special thanks and praise for going husbandless and fatherless 7 days a week, 14 hours a day, for the better part of a year. Without their patience and understanding and happy greetings when I did make an appearance, I could not have accomplished this.

About the Author

Greg Tomsho has more than 30 years of computer and networking experience and has earned the CCNA, MCTS, MCSA, Network+, A+, Security+, and Linux+ certifications. Greg is the director of the Computer Networking Technology/Cybersecurity Department and Cisco Academy at Yavapai College in Prescott, Arizona. His other books include *MCSA Guide to Installation, Storage, and Compute with Windows Server 2016, Exam 70-740; MCSA Guide to Networking with Windows Server 2016, Exam 70-741; MCSA Guide to Identity with Windows Server 2016, Exam 70-742; Guide to Operating Systems; MCSA Guide to Installing and Configuring Windows Server 2012/R2, Exam 70-410; MCSA Guide to Administering Windows Server 2012/R2, Exam 70-411; MCSA Guide to Configuring Advanced Windows Server 2012/R2 Services, Exam 70-412; MCTS Guide to Microsoft Windows Server 2008 Active Directory Configuration; MCTS Guide to Microsoft Windows Server 2008 Applications Infrastructure Configuration; Guide to Networking Essentials; Guide to Network Support and Troubleshooting;* and *A+ CoursePrep ExamGuide.*

Contact the Author

I would like to hear from you. Please email me at *greg@tomsho.com* with any problems, questions, suggestions, or corrections. I even accept compliments! Your comments and suggestions are invaluable for shaping the content of future books. You can also submit errata, lab suggestions, and comments via email. I have set up a website to support my books at *http://books.tomsho.com*, where you'll find lab notes, errata, web links, and helpful hints for using my books. If you're an instructor, you can register on the site to contribute articles and comment on articles.

Before You Begin

Working with Windows Server in a hybrid cloud environment requires multiple servers because you work with multidomain Active Directory forests, Hyper-V, storage technologies, and networking, just to name a few technologies. Setting up this lab environment can be challenging; this section was written to help you meet the challenge. Using virtual machines in Hyper-V on Windows 10 or 11 or on Windows Server 2016 or a later version is highly recommended. Other virtual environments work, too, but you'll want to choose one that allows nested virtualization, which means running a virtual machine within a virtual machine, as required by some of the book's Hyper-V activities. Using virtual machines is also highly recommended because it allows you to easily change the storage and network configuration of your servers and allows you to revert your lab to its original state for each module.

Note 4

The MindTap digital online learning platform for this text includes access to live virtual machine labs based on the objectives of the AZ-800 exam. While these labs are not the same as the hands-on activities in the book, they can supplement your learning experience.

Lab Setup Guide

Note 5

If you can't set up a lab environment exactly as described in this section, you might be able to configure a partial lab with just one Windows Server machine and still do many of the hands-on activities. Having two servers is even better, and having three enables you to do the majority of the book's activities. If you can't do an activity, it's important to read the activity steps to learn important information about using Windows Server.

Because of the flexibility and availability of using a virtual environment, the lab setup guide is designed with the assumption that virtualization is used, whether with Hyper-V, VMware, VirtualBox, or some other product. The lab environment is designed so that the initial configuration of the virtual machines will take you through any module. Each module starts with an activity that instructs the reader to revert the virtual machines used in the module to their initial configuration using a saved snapshot/checkpoint.

A total of five virtual machines (VMs) with Windows Server 2022 installed are used throughout the book. However, they are not all used at the same time; some activities use as many as three VMs while some require only one or two. No client OS is used. The decision to use Windows Server 2022 was made primarily on the basis that many readers will be using evaluation versions of Windows on their VMs, and the evaluation period for Windows client OSs such as Windows 10/11 is very short compared to Windows Server 2022's evaluation period. In addition, Windows 10/11 is continually being upgraded, and the upgrades may affect the outcome of some activities. Therefore, any activities that require a client will use a VM that has Windows Server 2022 installed. Readers should see little or no difference between using Windows Server 2022 as a client OS and using Windows 10/11.

Note 6

While Windows Server 2022 is used throughout this book, earlier versions of Windows Server may be used because very few changes have been made to the Windows Server core technologies since Windows Server 2016.

Modules 1 through 11 use four VMs running Windows Server 2022, in which one server is a domain controller (DC) and two servers are domain members. The fourth server is configured as a standalone server that is operating in workgroup mode. Modules 12 and 13 discuss virtualization; for these modules, a Windows Server 2022 VM with Hyper-V installed is required. Nested virtualization must be enabled on the host hypervisor. Instructions are given here for enabling nested virtualization on a Hyper-V host.

Some activities require your VMs to access the Internet. An easy way to accommodate this is to install the Remote Access role on your Hyper-V host (if you're using Hyper-V and Windows Server 2022 for your host computer) and configure NAT so your Hyper-V host can route packets to the physical network and the Internet. After installing the Remote Access role with the Routing role service, configure NAT and then select the interface connected to the physical network as the public interface and the interface connected to the Hyper-V internal switch as the private interface. The interface connected to the Hyper-V internal switch should be configured with the address 172.31.0.250/24. Figure 1 shows a diagram of this network.

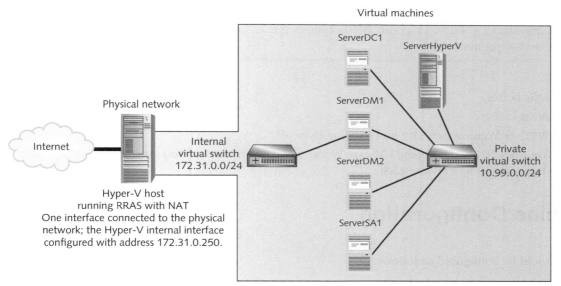

Figure 1   Lab configuration

Note the following in the figure:

- The router address is an example; you can use a different address. You can perform most activities without a router to the Internet, except for the activities that require Internet access.
- ServerDC1 is a domain controller for the AZ800.corp domain and has both the Active Directory Domain Services (AD DS) and DNS server roles installed.
- The host Hyper-V server is the only physical server, and it runs Routing and Remote Access with routing and NAT to allow the VMs access to the physical network and the Internet. You could also do the routing and NAT with a virtual machine.

Specific installation requirements for each server are explained in the following sections.

Working with Microsoft Azure

Some hands-on activities involve working with Microsoft Azure, Microsoft's cloud service. Microsoft Azure is a fee-based service, but students and educators can sign up for a free trial account that provides credit toward the fees. A $100 credit was available for education accounts as of this writing. However, that $100 credit can be used quickly if you are not careful about powering down virtual machines after use and deleting services when you are finished with them.

You can sign up for a free trial student account by going to *https://azure.microsoft.com/en-us/free/students/* and clicking "Start free account." Some services are always free, others are free for 12 months, and others are applied against the $100 credit. No credit card is required to sign up for a student account, so if you exceed the credit amount, you won't be able to use any more fee-based services, but you won't incur more charges. Some services, such as using Azure Bastion and high-resource VMs, are relatively expensive. Whenever feasible, simulations have been created for you to learn the steps of configuring and using selected Azure services so you do not have to use them in Azure. See the book's online learning materials for more information about available simulations.

Host Computer Configuration

The following are recommendations for the host computer when you're using virtualization:

- A multi-core CPU with Intel-VT-x/EPT support.

> **Note 7**
>
> Most activities can be done without a CPU that supports EPT, but you can't install Hyper-V on a VM (for nested virtualization) if the host doesn't support EPT for Intel CPUs.

- 8 GB of RAM; more is better.
- 200 GB of free disk space.
- Windows Server 2022, or Windows 10/11 if you're using Hyper-V.
- Windows 11, or Windows 10 if you're using VMware Workstation or VirtualBox. You may also use Linux with several available hypervisors or VMWare ESXi.

Virtual Machine Configuration

ServerDC1

This virtual machine should be configured as follows:

- Windows Server 2022 Datacenter or Standard – Desktop Experience
- Server name: ServerDC1
- Administrator password: Password01
- Memory: 2 GB or more
- Hard disk 1: 60 GB or more
- Ethernet0 connection – connected to 10.99.0.0/24 network
  - IP address: 10.99.0.220/24
  - Default gateway: 10.99.0.250 (or an address supplied by the instructor)
  - DNS: 127.0.0.1
- Active Directory Domain Services and DNS installed:
  - Domain Name: AZ800.corp
- Windows Update: Configured with most recent updates
- Power Setting: Never turn off display
- Internet Explorer Enhanced Security Configuration: Turned off for Administrator
- User Account Control: Lowest setting
- After the VM is fully configured, create a checkpoint/snapshot named InitialConfig that will be applied at the beginning of each module's activities where this VM is used. Turn off the VM before you create a checkpoint/snapshot.

ServerDM1

This virtual machine should be configured as follows:

- Windows Server 2022 Datacenter or Standard – Desktop Experience
- Server name: ServerDM1
- Administrator password: Password01
- Memory: 2 GB or more
- Hard disk 1: 60 GB or more
- Hard disk 2: 20 GB
- Hard disk 3: 15 GB
- Hard disk 4: 10 GB
- Ethernet0 connection – connected to 10.99.0.0/24 network
  - IP address: 10.99.0.201/24
  - Default gateway: 10.99.0.250 (or an address supplied by the instructor)
  - DNS: 10.99.0.220 (the address of ServerDC1)
- Ethernet1 connection – connected to 172.31.0.0/24 network
  - IP address: 172.31.0.240/24
  - Default gateway: Not configured
  - DNS: Not configured
- Member of domain: AZ800.corp
- Windows Update: Configured with most recent updates
- Power Setting: Never turn off display
- Internet Explorer Enhanced Security Configuration: Turned off for Administrator
- User Account Control: Lowest setting
- After the VM is fully configured, create a checkpoint/snapshot named InitialConfig that will be applied at the beginning of each module's activities where this VM is used.

ServerDM2

This virtual machine should be configured as follows:

- Windows Server 2022 Datacenter or Standard – Server Core
- Server name: ServerDM2
- Administrator password: Password01
- Memory: 2 GB or more
- Hard disk 1: 60 GB or more
- Ethernet0 connection – connected to internal virtual switch
  - IP address: 10.99.0.202/24
  - Default gateway: 10.99.0.250 (or an address supplied by the instructor)
  - DNS: 10.99.0.220 (the address of ServerDC1)
- Member of domain: AZ800.corp
- Windows Update: Configured with most recent updates
- Power Setting: Never turn off display
- Internet Explorer Enhanced Security Configuration: Turned off for Administrator
- User Account Control: Lowest setting
- After the VM is fully configured, create a checkpoint/snapshot named InitialConfig that will be applied at the beginning of each module's activities where this VM is used.

ServerSA1

This virtual machine should be configured as follows:

- Windows Server 2022 Datacenter or Standard – Desktop Experience
- Server name: ServerSA1
- Administrator password: Password01
- Memory: 2 GB or more
- Hard disk 1: 60 GB or more
- Ethernet0 connection – connected to internal virtual switch
  - IP address: 10.99.0.203/24
  - Default gateway: 10.99.0.250 (or an address supplied by the instructor)
  - DNS: 10.99.0.220 (the address of ServerDC1)
- Workgroup: AZ800 (the workgroup name doesn't matter)
- Windows Update: Configured with most recent updates
- Power Setting: Never turn off display
- Internet Explorer Enhanced Security Configuration: Turned off for Administrator
- User Account Control: Lowest setting
- After the VM is fully configured, create a checkpoint/snapshot named InitialConfig that will be applied at the beginning of each module's activities where this VM is used.

ServerHyperV

This virtual machine should be configured as follows (see Figure 2):

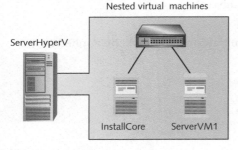

Nested virtual machines

ServerHyperV

ServerHyperV
10.99.0.10/24
Gateway: 10.99.0.250
DNS: 10.99.0.220

ServerVM1
192.168.0.1/24
Gateway: Not configured
DNS: Not configured

InstallCore
No OS installed

InstallCore   ServerVM1

Figure 2   Hyper-V VM with nested VMs

- Windows Server 2022 Datacenter or Standard – Desktop Experience
- Server name: ServerHyperV
- Administrator password: Password01
- Memory: 4 GB or more (dynamic memory disabled)
- Hard disk 1: 100 GB or more
- DVD: Assigned to D: drive and mapped to the Windows Server 2022 installation media ISO file
- Nested virtualization must be configured on this VM before installing the Hyper-V role. If you are using Hyper-V on the host server, take the following steps.

From a PowerShell window, type the following commands:

```
Set-VMProcessor -VMName ServerHyperV -ExposeVirtualizationExtensions $true
Get-VMNetworkAdapter -VMName ServerHyperV | Set-VMNetworkAdapter
    -MacAddressSpoofing On
```

Configure the firewall to allow ping messages:

```
Set-NetFirewallRule FPS-ICMP4-ERQ-In -Enabled True
```

- Ethernet connection – connected to internal virtual switch
  - IP address: 10.99.0.10/24
  - Default gateway: 10.99.0.250 (or an address supplied by the instructor)
  - DNS: 10.99.0.220
- Hyper-V role installed
- Workgroup: AZ800 (the workgroup name doesn't matter)
- Windows Update: Configured with most recent updates
- Power Setting: Never turn off display
- Internet Explorer Enhanced Security Configuration: Turned off for Administrator
- User Account Control: Lowest setting
- After the VM is fully configured and the following VMs are created, create a checkpoint/snapshot named InitialConfig that will be applied at the beginning of each module's activities where this VM is used.

Hyper-V should be configured as follows:

1. Create a private virtual switch named PrivateNet.
2. Create an empty virtual machine named InstallCore with a 40 GB HDD and 1 GB of RAM; the VM should be located in a folder named C:\VMs. This VM will be used to import and export a VM in Module 12. An empty VM will make the process much faster.
3. Create a generation 2 VM named ServerVM1 for use in the Module 12 and 13 activities.

ServerVM1

- Windows Server 2022 Datacenter or Standard – Desktop Experience
- Server name: ServerVM1
- Memory: 1 GB
- Hard disk: 40 GB
- Ethernet connection – connected to PrivateNet
  - IP address: 192.168.0.1/24
  - Default gateway: Not configured
  - DNS: Not configured
  - Configure the firewall to allow ping messages:

    ```
    Set-NetFirewallRule FPS-ICMP4-ERQ-In -Enabled True
    ```

Using an Evaluation Version of Windows Server 2022

You can get a 180-day evaluation copy of Windows Server 2022 from the Microsoft Evaluation Center at *https://www .microsoft.com/en-us/evalcenter/evaluate-windows-server-2022/*. You will need to sign in with your Microsoft account or create a new account. You can download an ISO file that can then be attached to your virtual machine's DVD drive to install Windows Server 2022.

If your evaluation version of Windows Server 2022 gets close to expiring, you can extend the evaluation period (180 days) up to five times. To do so, follow these steps:

1. Open a command prompt window as Administrator.
2. Type **slmgr -xpr** and press **Enter** to see the current status of your license and the number of days left in the evaluation. If the screen shows you're in notification mode, you need to extend the evaluation immediately.
3. To extend the evaluation for another 180 days, type **slmgr -rearm** and press **Enter**. You see a message instructing you to restart the system so the changes will take effect. Click **OK** and restart the system.
4. After you have extended the evaluation period, you should take a new checkpoint/snapshot and replace the InitialConfig checkpoint/snapshot.

Where to Go for Help

Configuring a lab and keeping everything running correctly can be challenging. Even small configuration changes can prevent activities from running correctly. The author maintains a website that includes lab notes, suggestions, errata, and help articles that might be useful if you're having trouble. You can contact the author at these addresses:

- Website: *htttp://books.tomsho.com*
- Email: *greg@tomsho.com*

Module 1

Dive into Windows Server Hybrid Infrastructure

Module Objectives

After reading this module and completing the exercises, you will be able to:

1   Explain the role a server operating system has in a network
2   Explain the core technologies of Windows Server
3   Describe the Windows Server Hybrid Infrastructure

The marriage of on-premises Windows Servers and cloud-based servers running on Microsoft Azure is what Microsoft refers to as Windows Server Hybrid Infrastructure. And what's not to like? As a server administrator, you reap the benefits of both worlds: the high performance and Internet-independent availability of network services in your on-premises datacenter, and the flexibility and fault tolerance of cloud computing, courtesy of Microsoft Azure. The catch is that, as a server administrator, you now must learn how to manage Windows Server roles and services running on your hardware and how to integrate them with complementary services running on Microsoft Azure. The goal is to provide the optimal configuration between on-premises and cloud computing and storage resources and reap the maximum benefits from both. This book, along with *Microsoft Guide to Configuring Windows Server Advanced Services, Exam AZ-801*, aims to help you meet that goal as well as earn the Windows Server Hybrid Administrator Associate certification.

This module takes a shallow dive into the core technologies of on-premises Windows Server, discusses the roles a server operating system plays in a computer network, and discusses the many features in Windows Server designed to fill these roles. This module introduces you to core features such as the NT File System (NTFS), Active Directory, and Hyper-V; later modules will cover them in more detail. Then you are introduced to some of the features and characteristics of an on-premises Windows Server/Microsoft Azure hybrid environment. While much of what this module and the entire book covers is relevant to versions of Windows Server going back to Windows Server 2012 and even Windows Server 2008, this book uses Windows Server 2022, the most recent version of Windows Server as of this writing.

About the Hands-On Activities

Be sure to read and complete the activities in the "Before You Begin" section from the Introduction to this book. The hands-on activities in this module and all that follow require setting up your lab environment so that it's ready to go. The hands-on activities in this module use a Windows Server 2022 Standard or Datacenter Edition computer that's already installed and initially configured. The "Before You Begin" section gives you step-by-step instructions on setting up your lab for use with all activities in this book. (If you are using the MindTap version of this book, you have access to online labs from Practice Labs, which supplement the activities.)

Completing the hands-on activities in this book is important because they contain information about the tools that manage Windows Server 2022 and Microsoft Azure. The proper use of these tools is best understood by hands-on experience. If you can't do some of the activities for some reason, you should at least read through each one to make sure you don't miss important information. Table 1-1 summarizes the requirements of the hands-on activities in this module.

Table 1-1   Activity requirements

Activity	Requirements	Notes
Activity 1-1: Resetting Your Virtual Environment	A server named ServerSA1	You only need to perform this activity if you are using virtual machines with snapshots and you are performing the activities in this module an additional time. If you are using your virtual machines for the first time, they will already be in the initial configuration state.
Activity 1-2: Reviewing System Properties and Exploring Server Manager	ServerSA1	Ensure that Windows Server 2022 Datacenter Edition is installed according to instructions in the "Before You Begin" section of this book's Introduction.
Activity 1-3: Examining NTFS Permissions and Attributes	ServerSA1	
Activity 1-4: Working with MMCs	ServerSA1	
Activity 1-5: Creating a Volume and Sharing a Folder	ServerSA1	
Activity 1-6: Exploring Windows Networking Components	ServerSA1	
Activity 1-7: Working with PowerShell	ServerSA1	
Activity 1-8: Creating a Free Microsoft Azure Account		
Activity 1-9: Creating an Azure Windows Server 2022 VM		

The Role of a Server Operating System

A server or collection of servers is usually at the center of most business networks. The functions a server performs depend on several factors, including the type of business using the server, size of the business, and extent to which the business has committed to using technology to aid operations. The latter factor is the crux of the matter. Technology is designed to help a person or an organization perform everyday tasks more efficiently or more effectively, and a server is technology that provides services a business needs to help its operations. Before you explore these services in more detail, a few definitions are in order.

Server: Hardware or Software?

When most people hear the word "server," they conjure up visions of a large tower computer with lots of hard drives and memory. This image is merely a computer hardware configuration that may or may not be used as a server, however. In short, a computer becomes a server when software is installed on it that provides a network service to client computers. In other words, you could install certain software on an inexpensive laptop computer and make it act as a server. By the same token, a huge tower computer with 6 terabytes of storage and 128 GB of RAM could be used as a workstation for a single user. So, although some computer hardware configurations are packaged to function as a server, and others are packaged as desktop computers, what makes a computer a server or desktop computer is the software installed on it.

Of course, with modern operating systems (OSs), the lines between desktop and server computers are blurred. OSs such as Windows 11 and its predecessors are designed to be installed on desktop computers or workstations (and in the case of Windows 11, tablet computers and phones); to run web browsers, word processors, spreadsheets, and other similar programs; and generally act as a personal computer. However, these OSs can perform server functions, such as file and printer sharing, and even act as a web server. Windows Server 2022 and its predecessors are designed as **server operating systems**, but there's nothing to stop you from installing a word processor or web browser and using Windows Server on your desktop computer. So, what are the differences between a desktop OS, such as Windows 11, and a server OS, such as Windows Server 2022? The following section explains.

Server Operating Systems Versus Desktop Operating Systems

Both Windows Server 2022 and Windows 11 can perform some server functions and some desktop functions, but important differences distinguish them. Windows 11 is configured to emphasize the user interface and is performance-tuned to run desktop applications. Windows Server 2022, on the other hand, deemphasizes many of Windows 11's user interface bells and whistles in favor of a less flashy and less resource-intensive user interface. In fact, Microsoft has made the Server Core version, with no graphical user interface, the default Windows Server installation option since Windows Server 2022. In addition, Windows Server is performance-tuned to run background processes so that client computers can access network services faster. Speaking of network services, most Windows Server editions can run the following network services, among others:

- File and Printer Sharing
- Web Server
- Routing and Remote Access Services (RRAS)
- Domain Name System (DNS)
- Dynamic Host Configuration Protocol (DHCP)
- File Transfer Protocol (FTP) Server
- Active Directory
- Certificate Services
- Fax Server
- Remote Desktop Services
- Distributed File System (DFS)
- Windows Server Update Services
- Hyper-V

Of these services, Windows 11 supports only Hyper-V, File and Printer Sharing, Web Server, and FTP Server in a limited capacity. In addition, Windows 11 is restricted to 20 signed-in network users, whereas on a Windows Server 2022 computer running Standard or Datacenter Edition, signed-in users are limited only by the number of purchased licenses and available resources. In addition, because a server is such a critical device in a network, Windows Server 2022 includes fault-tolerance features, such as redundant array of independent disks (RAID) volumes, load balancing, and clustering, which aren't standard features in Windows 11 or other Windows desktop OSs. Windows Server 2022 is also capable of supporting up to 64 physical processors; Windows 11 supports a maximum of 2.

> **Note** ⓵
>
> Most processors found on client and server computers are multicore processors. The limitations mentioned in the previous paragraph apply to physical processor chips on the computer's motherboard, not processor cores.

Windows Server 2022 Roles and Features

In Windows, a **server role** is a major function or service that a server performs. Probably the best known and most common server role is a file server (called the File Server role in Windows Server 2022), which allows the server to share files on a network. **Role services** add functions to the main role. For example, with the File and Storage Services role, you can install role services such as Distributed File System, Server for NFS, and File Server Resource Manager. Windows server roles and role services are installed in Server Manager by clicking Manage and then clicking Add Roles and Features (see Figure 1-1).

Figure 1-1   Adding roles and features with Server Manager

You can also add **server features**, which provide functions that enhance or support an installed role or add a standalone function. For example, you can add the Failover Clustering feature to provide fault tolerance for a file server or database server. An example of a standalone feature is Internet Printing Client, which enables clients to use Internet Printing Protocol to connect to printers on the Internet. A server can be configured with a single role or several roles, depending on the organization's needs and the load a role puts on the server hardware. Figure 1-2 shows the list of available server roles in Windows Server 2022. Several of these roles, particularly those covered in Exam AZ-800, are explained in detail in later modules.

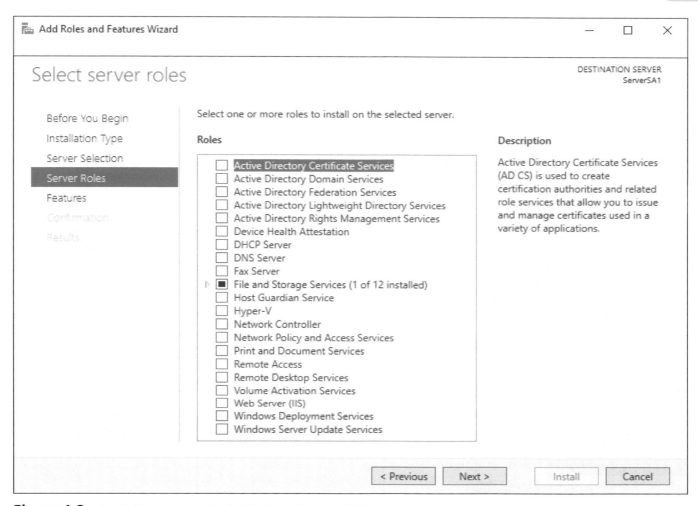

Figure 1-2   Available server roles in Windows Server 2022

Self-Check Questions

1. When Windows Server 2022 is installed on a computer, the computer's role in a network is always as a server. True or False?

    a. True
    b. False

⊙ Check your answers at the end of this module.

Windows Server 2022 Core Technologies

Many of the topics in this book require that you understand the core technologies in Windows Server 2022. Some of these core technologies are discussed in more detail in this book or in *Microsoft Guide to Configuring Windows Server Advanced Services, Exam AZ-801*. This section gives you a brief overview of these technologies so you will be familiar with them when you need to use them later. The following is a list of some of the technologies on which Windows Server 2022 is built:

- Server Manager
- NT File System (NTFS)
- Microsoft Management Console (MMC)

- Disk Management
- File and printer sharing
- Windows networking
- Active Directory
- PowerShell
- Hyper-V and cloud computing
- Storage Spaces

The following sections describe these technologies briefly; some are covered in detail in later modules.

Server Manager

Server Manager provides a single interface for installing, configuring, and removing a variety of server roles and features on your Windows server. It also summarizes your server's status and configuration and includes tools to diagnose problems, manage storage, and perform general configuration tasks. Server Manager can be used to manage all servers in your network and access all the server administration tools from a single console.

When you start Server Manager, you see the Dashboard view, shown in Figure 1-3. The Dashboard shows a list of tasks you can perform, summarizes the installed roles, and shows the servers that are available to manage. The Welcome section can be hidden after you're familiar with Server Manager. This tool is used to access most of the configuration and monitoring tools for administering Windows servers; you learn more about it throughout this book.

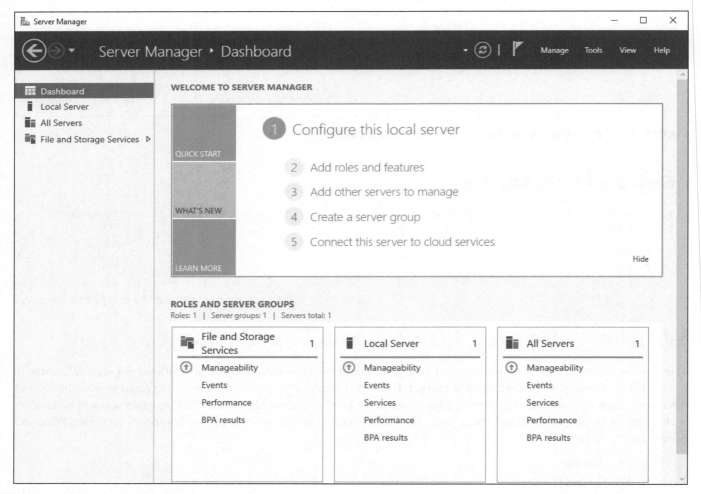

Figure 1-3   Server Manager Dashboard view

The forward and backward arrows near the upper-left corner of the view are used to navigate through recently opened windows. Moving to the right, your current location is displayed, followed by the refresh button and the notifications icon (shaped like a flag) you click to view recent messages from Server Manager. Next is the Manage menu, used to perform major tasks such as adding and removing roles and features and creating server groups. The Tools menu gives you quick access to administrative tools, such as Computer Management, Event Viewer, and Task Scheduler. Management consoles for server roles or features you install are added to this menu. You can use the View menu to choose a magnification option for fonts in Server Manager, and the Help menu is self-explanatory.

The left pane of Server Manager displays the major views: Dashboard (described previously), Local Server, and All Servers. You use the Local Server view to manage just the server where you're running Server Manager and the All Servers view to manage aspects of all servers. To add servers you want to manage, right-click All Servers and click Add Servers or use the Manage menu. Under the All Servers item in the left pane is a node for each installed server role. In Figure 1-3, you see File and Storage Services, which is a preinstalled role. Clicking a server role puts Server Manager into role management mode so that you can manage each role in the Server Manager interface. When you're managing a role, the options for the role are displayed.

NTFS

One of a server's main jobs is to store a variety of file types and make them available to network users. To do this effectively, a server OS needs a robust and efficient file system. **NT File System (NTFS)** was introduced in Windows NT in the early 1990s. Although it has been updated throughout the years, NTFS has remained a reliable, flexible, and scalable file system. Its predecessor was FAT/FAT32, which had severe limitations for a server OS. It lacked features such as native support for long file names, file and folder permissions, support for very large files and volumes, reliability, compression, and encryption. NTFS supports all these features and more.

Perhaps the most important feature of NTFS is the capability to set user and group permissions on both folders and files. With this feature, administrators can specify which users can access a file and what users can do with a file if they're granted access, which increase a server environment's security. FAT/FAT32 has no user access controls.

> **Note 2**
>
> The exFAT file system is similar to FAT/FAT32, except that you can create volumes larger than 32 GB; with FAT32, you are limited to a maximum volume size of 32 GB.

An NTFS volume has a number of advantages over a FAT/FAT32 volume, so what good is a FAT or FAT32 volume? One current reason to use FAT or FAT32 on a Windows computer is that you might have a volume used by another OS that might not support NTFS. In addition, removable drives, USB flash drives, and flash memory cards are often formatted with FAT32, and larger removable drives are often formatted with exFAT. NTFS and other supported file systems are covered in detail in Module 10.

> **Note 3**
>
> A FAT/FAT32 formatted disk can be converted to NTFS without losing existing data by using the `convert` command-line utility.

Microsoft Management Console

A server OS requires a multitude of tools that administrators must use to manage, support, and troubleshoot a server system. One challenge of having so many tools is the numerous user interfaces an administrator has to learn. Microsoft has eased this challenge by including a common framework called the Microsoft Management Console (MMC) for running most administrative tools. The MMC alone isn't very useful; it's just a user interface shell, as you can see in Figure 1-4. What makes it useful is the bevy of snap-ins you can install. Each snap-in is designed to perform a specific administrative task; one example is the Disk Management snap-in shown in Figure 1-5.

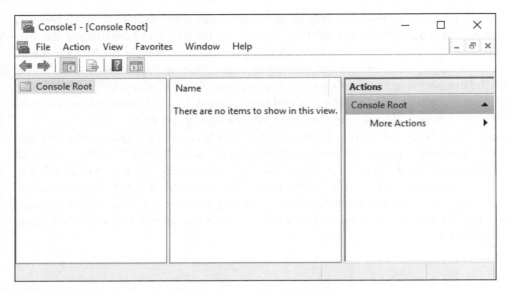

Figure 1-4   The Microsoft Management Console

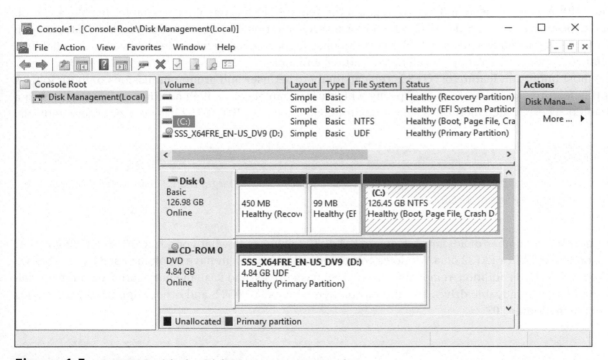

Figure 1-5   An MMC with the Disk Management snap-in

A number of MMCs are available in Server Manager's Tools menu, depending on the roles and features installed on the server. For example, after you install Active Directory, several new MMCs for managing it are created and added to the Tools menu. Not all administrative functions can be accessed from these prebuilt MMCs, however; you might have to create a customized MMC to access some functions or keep an MMC handy on your desktop with the administrative snap-ins you use most often. An important feature of an MMC is the capability to connect to servers remotely. Using this feature, you can install management tools on a Windows 11 workstation, for example, and manage a Windows Server 2022 computer without having to sign in at the server console. (You will still be required to enter credentials that have suitable permissions in order to manage the server.)

Disk Management

To manage the disks and volumes on a Windows Server 2022 computer, you might use the Disk Management snap-in or the File and Storage Services role, which is integrated into Server Manager. With these tools, you can monitor the status of disks and volumes, initialize new disks, create and format new volumes, and troubleshoot disk problems. Both tools enable you to configure redundant disk configurations, such as RAID 1 and RAID 5 volumes. File and Storage Services also lets you create storage pools for Storage Spaces, as discussed later in the Storage Spaces section of this module. These tools are also covered in more detail in Module 10. Activity 1-5 later in this module walks you through using Disk Management.

File and Printer Sharing

Probably the most common reason for building a network and installing a server is to enable users to share files, printers, and other resources. Windows Server 2022 has a full-featured system for file and printer sharing, offering advanced features such as shadow copies, disk quotas, and the Distributed File System (DFS). At its simplest, sharing files or a printer is just a few clicks away. More complex configurations that offer redundancy, version control, and user storage restrictions are also readily available. Windows Server 2022 offers myriad tools and options for configuring file sharing; most are discussed in more detail in Module 10.

Windows Networking Concepts

Administering a Windows server requires extensive knowledge of networking components and protocols as well as a solid understanding of the network security models used in Windows. In a Windows network environment, computers can be configured to participate in one of two network security models: workgroup or domain.

The Workgroup Model

A **Windows workgroup** is a small collection of computers with users who typically have something in common, such as the need to share files or printers with each other. A workgroup is also called a peer-to-peer network sometimes because all participants are represented equally on the network, with no single computer having authority or control over another. Furthermore, logons, security, and resource sharing are decentralized, so users have control over the resources on their computers. This model is easy to configure, requires little expertise to manage, and works well for small groups of users who need to share files, printers, an Internet connection, or other resources. A Windows Server 2022 server that participates in a workgroup is referred to as a **standalone server**.

The Domain Model

A **Windows domain** is a group of computers that share common management and are subject to rules and policies defined by an administrator. The domain model is preferred for a computer network that has several computers and/or requires centralized security and resource management. Unlike the workgroup model, a domain requires at least one computer configured as a domain controller running a Windows Server OS. In the domain model, a computer running a Windows Server OS can occupy one of two primary roles: a domain controller or a member server.

A **domain controller** is a Windows server that has the Active Directory Domain Services (AD DS) role installed and is responsible for authenticating and allowing users and domain member computers access to domain resources. The core component of a Windows domain is Active Directory. A **member server** is a Windows server that's in the management scope of a Windows domain but doesn't have Active Directory installed.

Windows Networking Components

Every OS requires these hardware and software components to participate on a network: a network interface, a network protocol, and network client or network server software. Modern OSs usually have both client and server software installed. In Windows, this collection of networking components working together is called a **network connection**.

Network Interface

A **network interface** is composed of two parts: the network interface card (NIC) hardware and the device driver software, which contains specifics of how to communicate with the NIC. In Windows Server 2022, you configure the network interface in the Network Connections window (see Figure 1-6). To open it from Server Manager, click Local Server and then click the address next to the Ethernet label. Alternatively, right-click Start, click Network Connections, and click Change adapter options.

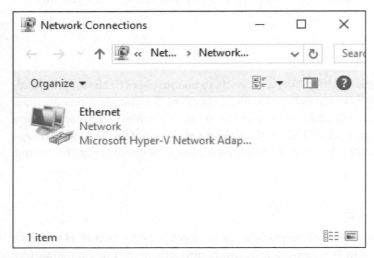

Figure 1-6   The Network Connections window

If you right-click a network connection and click Properties, a dialog box similar to Figure 1-7 opens. The network interface used in this connection is specified in the Connect using text box. You can view details about the interface, including the device driver and configurable settings, by clicking the Configure button.

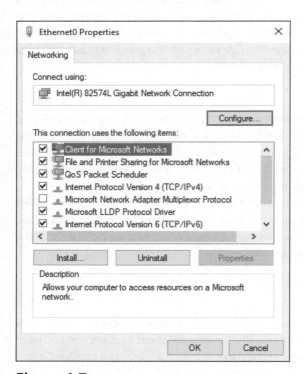

Figure 1-7   Properties of a network connection

Network Protocol

A **network protocol** specifies the rules and format of communication between network devices. Several years ago, network administrators may have had to understand and support two, three, or more protocols on their networks. Today, most administrators need to work with only TCP/IPv4 and more recently, TCP/IPv6. Both versions of TCP/IP are installed by default on Windows computers. To configure a network protocol, select it and click the Properties button.

Network Client and Server Software

Windows systems have both network client and network server software installed. A **network client** is the part of the OS that sends requests to a server to access network resources. So, if you want to access a file shared on a Windows computer, you need to have network client software that can make a request for a Windows file share. In Windows, this software is Client for Microsoft Networks. **Network server software** is the part of the OS that receives requests for shared network resources and makes these resources available to a network client. If you want to share files that other Windows computers can access, you need to have network server software installed that can share files in a format Client for Microsoft Networks can read. In Windows, this server software is File and Printer Sharing for Microsoft Networks.

Windows networking is quite robust, with a number of client and server components and a variety of configuration options. Modules 7 through 9 discuss various aspects of networking with Windows Server 2022 and Microsoft Azure.

Active Directory Domain Services

Active Directory is the foundation of a Windows network environment. With Active Directory, you transform a limited, nonscalable workgroup network into a Windows domain with nearly unlimited scalability. The Active Directory Domain Services (AD DS) role installs Active Directory and turns a Windows Server 2022 computer into a domain controller. The main purpose of AD DS is to handle authentication and authorization for users and computers in a Windows domain environment. Active Directory stores information in a centralized database, giving administrators a tool for deploying user and computer policies, installing software, and applying patches and updates to client computers in the domain. Active Directory is required to operate some server roles and functions, such as certain types of failover clusters and Windows Server Update Services. You will learn about Active Directory and domain controllers in detail in Modules 2 through 5.

PowerShell

PowerShell is a command-line interactive scripting environment that provides the commands for almost any management task in a Windows Server 2022 environment. It can be used much like a command prompt, where you enter one command at a time and view the results, or as a powerful scripting engine that enables you to create and save a series of commands for performing complex tasks. To say PowerShell scripts are like a command-prompt batch file is like saying a two-seat propeller plane is similar to an F-35 fighter jet. Yes, they both fly, but the F-35 is much more powerful.

In a command-prompt environment, commands you type are called simply "commands"; PowerShell uses the term *cmdlets* (pronounced "command-lets"). Hundreds of cmdlets are available in PowerShell, ranging from performing simple tasks, such as displaying the date and time, to managing aspects of Active Directory and every other server role. In addition, new cmdlets can be created and imported as modules for extending the capabilities of PowerShell. PowerShell cmdlets aren't limited to managing the local computer; you can use PowerShell to remotely manage Windows servers and desktops. Remote management using PowerShell is particularly useful when you are managing Server Core computers that have a limited user interface.

Getting the most out of PowerShell requires some effort because the number of available cmdlets is staggering. Learning to use this powerful tool is no longer just an option, however; it's a requirement for enterprise server administrators. PowerShell 1.0 was introduced as a downloadable product in late 2006, and version 2.0 became an important part of Windows 7 and Windows Server 2008 R2. PowerShell 3.0 is an integrated component of Windows Server 2012 and Windows 8, and Windows Server 2012 R2 and Windows 8.1 are equipped with PowerShell 4.0. Microsoft has continued updating PowerShell in Windows Server 2022; version 5.1 of the product includes PowerShell Direct, which manages virtual machines with PowerShell directly from the host computer.

Using PowerShell

The names of PowerShell cmdlets are structured as *verb-noun* pairs with most cmdlets having one or more parameters that are specified after the cmdlet name. For example, the following cmdlet lists the available disks on a computer with the output shown in Figure 1-8:

```
Get-Disk
```

```
PS C:\Users\Administrator> Get-Disk

Number Friendly Name Serial Number                    HealthStatus      OperationalStatus      Total Size Partition
                                                                                                          Style
------ ------------- -------------                    ------------      -----------------      ---------- ----------
0      Intel Raid... OS                               Healthy           Online                  139.73 GB MBR
1      Intel Raid... Volume2                          Healthy           Online                    1.82 TB MBR
4      Samsung SS... S1ATNSAF280691M                  Healthy           Online                  238.47 GB MBR
3      SanDisk SD... 162878405216                     Healthy           Online                  894.25 GB MBR
2      TS128GSSD340  20150307C02837236722             Healthy           Online                  119.24 GB MBR
```

Figure 1-8   Output of the Get-Disk cmdlet

Note that capitalization doesn't matter when you type a cmdlet, but as a convention, cmdlets are written using capital letters at the beginning of recognizable terms in the cmdlet name. If you want to see information about a particular disk, you could use the following cmdlet:

```
Get-Disk –Number 1
```

In the above cmdlet, -Number is called a parameter. A **parameter** is an input to a cmdlet; in this case, the input is the disk number. The 1 that follows –Number is a value for the –Number parameter. Not all parameters require values, but many of them do. In some cases, the value for a parameter can be stored in a variable. A **variable** is a temporary storage location that holds values, whether numeric, strings, or objects. In PowerShell, variables are names that start with a dollar sign ($). For example, the previous cmdlet could be executed using the following PowerShell commands:

```
$DiskNum = 1
Get-Disk –Number $DiskNum
```

The above is not a very useful example of using a variable, but you will see later that variables can make PowerShell easier to use and more powerful.

Some cmdlets and parameters have quite long names. To reduce the amount of typing required, PowerShell has some shortcuts. You can begin typing a cmdlet or parameter and then press the Tab key to have PowerShell complete the name of the cmdlet or parameter. However, you must type enough of the cmdlet for PowerShell to understand what you mean; otherwise, it will complete the name with the first item in alphabetical order that it finds. For example, if you type Get and press Tab, PowerShell will finish the cmdlet with the first cmdlet name that starts with Get, which in this case is Get-Acl. If you type Get-Di and press Tab, the cmdlet will be completed with Get-Disk. That example doesn't save much typing, but if you type Get-NetI and press Tab, the cmdlet will be completed with Get-NetIPAddress, which saves some typing. As with using the command prompt, if you press the up arrow in PowerShell, the last command you typed is repeated and you can edit the command if necessary. This feature comes in handy when you have typed a long cmdlet with several parameters and PowerShell returns an error indicating a typo.

Here are a few more useful tips for using PowerShell:

- To list all the cmdlets that start with Get , type Get-Command Get-*.
- To list all the cmdlets that have the word "disk" in them, type Get-Command *disk*.
- To get help on a cmdlet, type Get-Help *cmdlet*, where *cmdlet* is the name of the cmdlet. PowerShell may display limited help information at first. To update the help files, type Update-Help.
- PowerShell can take the output of one cmdlet and pipe it to another cmdlet. To do this, you use the pipe character (|). For example, if you want to stop all instances of Internet Explorer, type Get-Process iexplore | Stop-Process. You can also use the pipe character to filter the results from a cmdlet. For example, if you want to list all disks that are offline, type Get-Disk | Where-Object IsOffline –eq $True.

This book doesn't aim to make you a PowerShell guru, but given the emphasis on remote administration of servers within the industry and by Microsoft, many of the tasks you learn to do in the GUI are also shown as PowerShell cmdlets and scripts, and some tasks are performed only in PowerShell. You'll learn more PowerShell techniques as you work through the book.

Hyper-V and Cloud Computing

With Microsoft's emphasis on cloud computing and virtualization, it's probably a good idea to define some terms used when talking about these topics. Many of these terms and concepts are expanded on later as you learn about the technologies behind them, but this section should give you a running start.

What exactly is cloud computing? This question isn't as easy to answer as it might seem, and you're likely to get different answers from different people. However, most networking professionals are likely to agree with this definition: **Cloud computing** is a collection of technologies for abstracting the details of how applications, storage, network resources, and other computing services and resources are delivered to users. Why the term *cloud*? It comes from network diagrams that include the Internet (see Figure 1-9), and because the Internet is a vast collection of different technologies, no single networking symbol can be used to represent it. So, a cloud symbol conveys that a lot of complex network services are involved, but the details are unimportant at this time. One goal of cloud computing is to abstract the details of how things get done so that people can get on with their work. For example, do users really care that the X drive is mapped to ServerA by using the SMB protocol over TCP/IP? No, they want to store their files in a place they know is reliable and secure, and do not need to know the details of how this task is done.

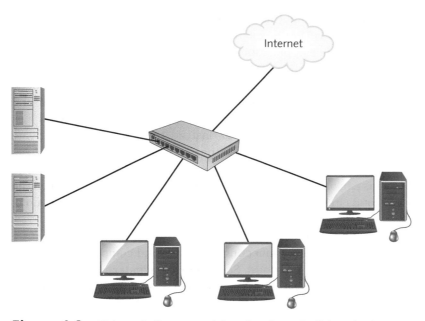

Figure 1-9   Network diagram with a cloud symbolizing the Internet

However, as an IT professional, you do need to know some details because setting up this technology is your job. A core technology of cloud computing is **virtualization**, which uses software (usually aided by specialized hardware) to emulate multiple hardware environments so that multiple operating systems can run on the same physical server simultaneously. Virtualization has its own terms for its operation and components. Some are defined in the following list:

- A **virtual machine (VM)** is the virtual environment that emulates a physical computer's hardware and BIOS. A **guest OS** is the operating system running in a VM.
- A **host computer** is the physical computer on which VM software is installed and VMs run.
- **Virtualization software** is the software for creating and managing VMs and creating the virtual environment in which a guest OS is installed. Microsoft Hyper-V Manager and VMware Workstation are examples of virtualization software.

- The **hypervisor** is the virtualization software component that creates and monitors the virtual hardware environment, which allows multiple VMs to share physical hardware resources. (In some software, this component is called Virtual Machine Monitor, or VMM.) The hypervisor on a host computer acts in some ways like an OS kernel, but instead of scheduling processes for access to the CPU and other devices, it schedules VMs to have that access.

The preceding list covers the basic terms you'll need to know when discussing virtualization. When you learn more about Hyper-V and virtualization in Modules 12 and 13, you'll run across more terms that are particular to Hyper-V.

Hyper-V is virtualization software that can be installed as a server role in Windows Server 2022. It provides services for creating and managing virtual machines running on a Windows Server 2022 computer. As mentioned, a virtual machine is a software environment that simulates the computer hardware an OS requires for installation. In essence, a virtual machine creates in software all the hardware you find on a computer, including BIOS, disk controllers, hard drives, DVD drives, serial ports, USB ports, RAM, network interfaces, video cards, and even processors. An OS can be installed on a virtual machine by using the same methods for installing an OS on a physical machine. Once installed, you can run the OS in the virtual machine and perform all the same tasks as you can with the OS running on a physical server. It's important to note that you can run as many virtual machines in Hyper-V as there are resources available on the host computer. For example, you can set up a virtual environment that includes two Windows Server 2022 VMs, two Windows Server 2019 VMs, and a Windows 11 VM, all running on a Windows Server 2022 host computer.

Public Cloud Versus Private Cloud

There are two broad categories of cloud computing: public and private. The **public cloud** is a cloud computing service provided by a third party, whereas a **private cloud** is a cloud computing service provided by an internal IT department. Examples of public cloud computing are services such as Dropbox and OneDrive, which provide storage as a cloud service, or Google Apps and Office 365, which offer office applications as a cloud service. You don't have to do anything special to have access to these services (some of which are free) other than have access to the Internet.

With a private cloud, a company's IT department provides all services for employees and perhaps customers, but these services aren't generally open to the general public. Typical services include virtual desktops, storage, and applications. **Virtual desktop infrastructure (VDI)** is a rapidly growing sector of private cloud computing. With VDI, users don't run a standard desktop computer to access their data and applications. Instead, they connect to the private cloud with a web browser or downloaded client software. They can then access their desktop and applications from wherever they happen to have an Internet connection, whether it's in their office, from a laptop in a local coffee shop, or even from a tablet computer. The OS and applications run on servers in the company datacenter rather than on the local computer. The key feature for building private clouds in Windows Server 2022 is Hyper-V. All the core technologies in Windows Server 2022, however, are necessary for running a cloud infrastructure.

Where does Microsoft Azure fit in with cloud computing? In the context of a hybrid infrastructure, your private cloud resources in your datacenter can be augmented by seamlessly connecting to storage and computing resources in the publicly available Azure cloud. This is referred to as a **hybrid cloud**. So, if your datacenter needs additional resources, you don't have to add another server or expand memory or storage. Instead, some of the tasks performed by your datacenter can be pushed off to virtual servers in the Azure cloud, and your users won't be aware of whether they are running applications in your datacenter or in the Azure cloud.

Storage Spaces

Software-defined storage (SDS) is one component of the software-defined datacenter (SDDC) paradigm, along with software-defined networking (SDN) and software-defined everything (SDE). Software-defined storage simply decouples the physical storage hardware from the storage requirements of the applications that use it, providing a flexible, software-defined storage solution with advanced features such as deduplication (the ability to store duplicate or repeating data only once), thin provisioning, and replication. In a nutshell, that is what Storage Spaces does.

Storage Spaces is a tool that is designed to make the most of storage on servers. It uses the power of virtual disks to give you a platform for creating volumes from storage pools that can be dynamically expanded and fault tolerant without the usual physical disk restrictions placed on volume creation. Volumes can be created from multiple drive types, including USB, SATA, and SAS. Drives can be internal or external, and RAID volumes don't require same-sized disks. By using virtual disks, Storage Spaces permits **thin provisioning**, which means physical disk space isn't allocated for a volume until it's actually needed. Storage Spaces is covered in detail in Module 11.

Self-Check Questions

2. Which of the following is a server role that is preinstalled on Windows Server 2022?

   a. Active Directory Domain Services   **c.** File and Storage Services
   b. PowerShell   **d.** Hyper-V

3. Which of the following is considered network server software that is preinstalled on Windows Server 2022?

   a. Client for Microsoft Networks
   b. Transport Control Protocol/Internet Protocol
   c. Network interface device driver
   d. File and Printer Sharing for Microsoft Networks

⊙ Check your answers at the end of this module.

Activity 1-1

Resetting Your Virtual Environment

> **Note 4**
>
> The activities in this book are based on the use of virtual machines in a Windows Server 2022 Hyper-V environment. Other virtualization platforms such as VMware and VirtualBox should work for most activities. See the "Before You Begin" section of this book's Introduction for more information about using virtualization.
>
> You only need to perform this activity if you are using virtual machines with snapshots and you are performing the activities in this module an additional time. If you are using your virtual machines for the first time, they will already be in the initial configuration state.

Time Required: 5 minutes
Objective: Reset your virtual environment by applying the InitialConfig checkpoint or snapshot.
Required Tools and Equipment: ServerSA1
Description: Apply the InitialConfig checkpoint or snapshot to ServerSA1.

1. Be sure ServerSA1 is shut down. In your virtualization program, apply the InitialConfig checkpoint or snapshot to ServerSA1.
2. When the snapshot or checkpoint has finished being applied, continue to the next activity.

Activity 1-2

Reviewing System Properties and Exploring Server Manager
Time Required: 10 minutes
Objective: Identify system properties in Windows Server 2022.
Required Tools and Equipment: ServerSA1 with Windows Server 2022 Datacenter or Standard Edition installed according to instructions in the "Before You Begin" section of this book's Introduction
Description: You learn how to find basic information about a Windows Server 2022 installation, such as the server edition, network adapter settings, processors, installed RAM, and disk drives.

1. Start ServerSA1 and sign in as **Administrator** with the password **Password01**. Server Manager starts automatically.
2. In the left pane of Server Manager, click **Local Server**. You see the Properties window for ServerSA1, shown in Figure 1-10.

(continues)

Activity 1-2 Continued

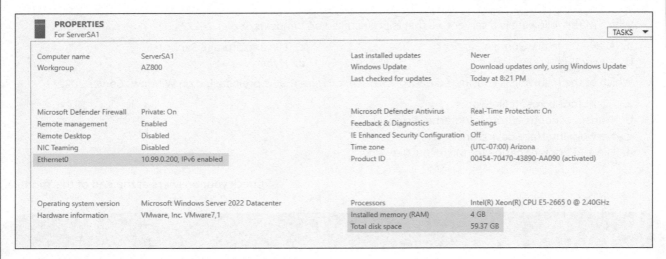

Figure 1-10   The Local Server Properties window

3. Review the fields highlighted in Figure 1-10: Ethernet, Installed memory (RAM), and Total disk space. Your settings may differ depending on your environment.
4. Scroll down to explore other information available in Server Manager, such as a list of recent events, a summary of services, and a list of installed roles and features at the bottom.
5. Click **Dashboard** in the left pane. (Notice the icon next to Dashboard; you'll need it to navigate back to this view later.) The Dashboard is divided into two sections: Welcome and Roles and Server Groups. The Welcome section lists common tasks you can access easily, including adding roles and features, adding other servers to manage, and creating server groups. This section can be hidden if desired.
6. Scroll down, if necessary, to see the Roles and Server Groups section. This section contains a box for each installed role, a box for the local server, and a box for each server group (see Figure 1-11). Each box contains information about manageability, which tells you whether Server Manager can contact the role or server to perform management tasks. You can double-click other items in these boxes to get details about events, services, performance, and Best Practices Analyzer (BPA) results. In the File and Storage Services box, click **Events**. Any events related to this role are then displayed in the resulting dialog box. Click **Cancel** to close the Events Detail View box for File and Storage Services.

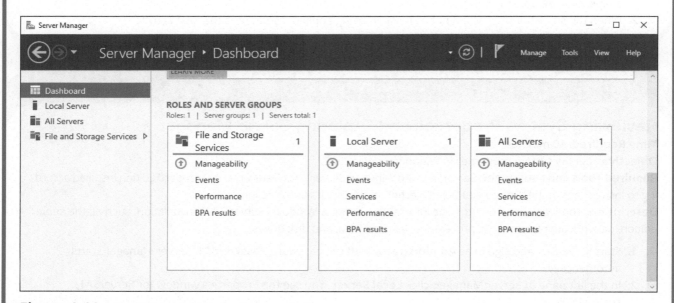

Figure 1-11   The Roles and Server Groups section

(continues)

Activity 1-2 Continued

7. Scroll up to see the Welcome section, if necessary. In the Welcome section, click **Add roles and features** to start the Add Roles and Features Wizard; you use this wizard often in this book's activities. Read the information in the Before you begin window.
8. Note the three tasks that are recommended before installing new roles and features. When you're finished, click **Cancel** to close the Add Roles and Features Wizard window.
9. Click **Local Server** in the left pane. The right pane is then divided into several sections, with the Properties section at the top. Scroll down to the Events section, which shows the most recent warning or error events that have occurred in your system. Clicking an event displays a description of it (see Figure 1-12).

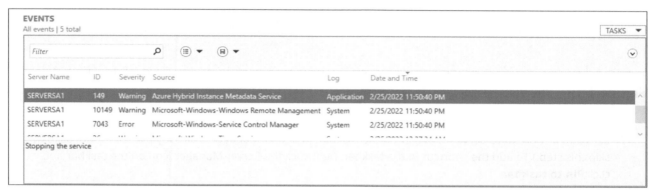

Figure 1-12   The Events section

10. Scroll down to the Services section, which displays a list of services installed on the server along with their status. You can start and stop services by right-clicking them and then selecting an action in the menu.
11. Scroll down to the Best Practices Analyzer section. The Best Practices Analyzer (BPA) is used to make sure a server role is installed in compliance with best practices to ensure effectiveness, trustworthiness, and reliability. Run a BPA scan by clicking the **TASKS** drop-down arrow and then clicking **Start BPA Scan**. After a while, the results and any best practices suggestions will be displayed. There may not be any warnings or errors, which means the server is completely in compliance!
12. Scroll down to the Performance section. You can view and configure performance alerts for CPU and memory use.
13. Scroll down to the Roles and Features section to see a list of roles and features installed on the local server. They're listed in the approximate order in which they were installed. You will see a list of roles and features that are installed by default on Windows Server 2022 because you haven't installed any yet.
14. In the left pane, click **All Servers**. The right pane has the same sections as Local Server, except for the top section, which is labeled Servers instead of Properties. In the Servers section, you can select one or more servers and see information about them in the other sections of this window. As of now, you only have one server that can be managed with Server Manager.
15. In the left pane, click **File and Storage Services**. This server role is installed by default. The window changes to show you specific tools for working with this role. Click **Volumes** to see a summary of the server's volumes (see Figure 1-13). Click **Disks** to see information about the physical disks installed. Click **Storage Pools**. This feature in Windows Server 2022 was explained earlier in the Storage Spaces section of this module and will be discussed in more detail in Module 4.

(continues)

Activity 1-2 Continued

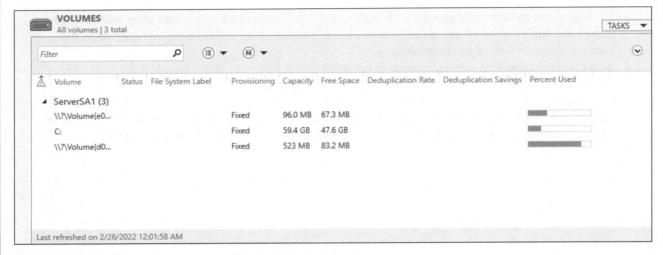

Figure 1-13   The Volumes window in Server Manager

16. Click the **Dashboard** icon in Server Manager to return to the Dashboard view.
17. Let's add a shortcut to Server Manager on the taskbar. (If Server Manager is already pinned to the taskbar, skip this step.) To add the shortcut to the taskbar, right-click the Server Manager icon on the taskbar and click **Pin to taskbar**.
18. Continue to the next activity.

Activity 1-3

Examining NTFS Permissions and Attributes

Time Required: 10 minutes
Objective: Review NTFS file permissions and attributes.
Required Tools and Equipment: ServerSA1
Description: In this activity, you familiarize yourself with the features of NTFS.

1. Sign in to ServerSA1 as **Administrator**, if necessary.
2. Click the **File Explorer** icon on the taskbar, and then click **This PC** in the left pane.
3. Right-click the **(C:)** drive in the right pane and click **Properties**.
4. Click the **General** tab, if necessary. You see that the file system is NTFS, which is the only option for the drive where Windows is installed. FAT/FAT32 lacks the security and features required by Windows.
5. Click the **Security** tab (see Figure 1-14).
6. Click each item in the Group or user names section and view the permission settings for each in the bottom pane.
7. Next, click the **Quota** tab. The quotas feature allows you to set the maximum space a user's files can occupy on a volume. You see that disk quotas are disabled, which is the default configuration.

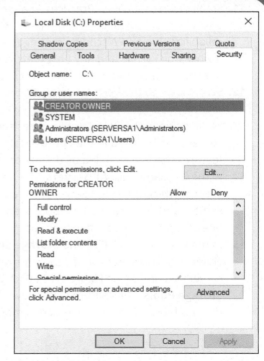

Figure 1-14   The Security tab showing file and folder permissions

(continues)

Activity 1-3 Continued

8. Now click the **Previous Versions** tab. This feature enables you to restore previous versions of a file and must be enabled on each volume on which you want to use the feature.

9. Finally, click the **General** tab again. Note the two check boxes at the bottom for enabling file indexing and compression, which are features of NTFS.

10. Click **Cancel** to close the Properties dialog box.

11. In the left pane, click the **Documents** folder. Right-click in the right pane, point to **New**, and click **Text Document**.

12. Right-click **New Text Document** and click **Properties**. Notice the two check boxes at the bottom labeled Read-only and Hidden. They are common file attributes in both the FAT/FAT32 and NTFS/ReFS file systems. Click **Advanced**.

13. In the Advanced Attributes dialog box, notice four more check boxes for attributes. Only the archiving attribute is available with FAT/FAT32 volumes. The other three, for file indexing, file compression, and encryption, are available only with NTFS volumes. Click **Cancel** and then click **Cancel** again.

14. Close all open windows and continue to the next activity.

Activity 1-4

Working with MMCs

Time Required: 15 minutes
Objective: Use the Tools menu in Server Manager; work with custom MMCs.
Required Tools and Equipment: ServerSA1
Description: Familiarize yourself with the management tools on your server that work with prebuilt MMCs, and create a custom MMC.

1. Sign in to ServerSA1 as **Administrator** and start Server Manager, if necessary.

2. In Server Manager, click **Tools** and then click **Computer Management** from the menu. (You can also access Computer Management by right-clicking Start.) You might notice that some tools in the Computer Management MMC, such as Task Scheduler and Event Viewer, are also available as separate MMCs in the Tools menu.

3. To explore a tool in Computer Management, click the tool name in the left pane. Some tools have an arrow next to them to indicate additional components. Each tool is called a snap-in.

4. Click the arrow next to **Services and Applications** to expand it, and then click the **Services** snap-in. This snap-in is also available as a standalone tool in the Tools menu.

5. In Services, find and double-click **Windows Defender Firewall**. Review the properties for this service, which are typical for most services. Click **Cancel** to close the Windows Defender Firewall Properties window.

6. Explore several snap-ins in the left pane of Computer Management, such as Performance and Disk Management, so you are familiar with the server. Close Computer Management.

7. Now, you'll create a custom MMC. Right-click **Start** and click **Run**. Type **mmc** in the Open text box, and then click **OK**.

8. Click **File** and then click **Add/Remove Snap-in** from the MMC menu.

9. In the Available snap-ins list box (see Figure 1-15), click **Device Manager** and then click **Add**.

(continues)

Activity 1-4 Continued

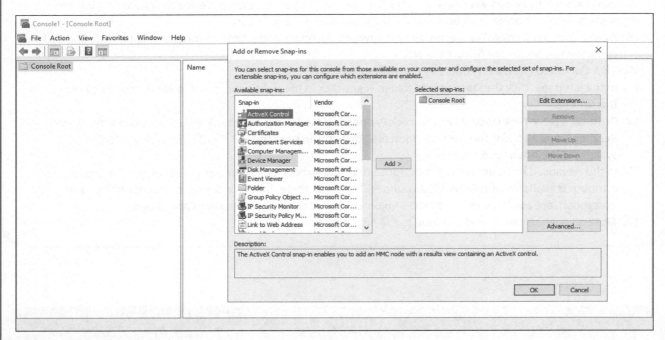

Figure 1-15   Creating a custom MMC

10. Note your choices in the next dialog box. You can decide whether to use the selected snap-in on the local computer or another computer. If you select the "Another computer" option, you can manage this computer remotely with your MMC. Leave the **Local computer** option selected, and then click **Finish**.
11. Repeat Steps 9 and 10, but this time add the **Disk Management** and **Task Scheduler** snap-ins instead of Device Manager. Click **Finish** after adding Disk Management and **OK** after adding Task Scheduler. Then click **OK** to close the Add or Remove Snap-ins dialog box.
12. To name your MMC, click **File** and then click **Save As** from the menu.
13. In the Save As dialog box, click the **Desktop** icon, type **DevDiskTask** for the file name, and then click **Save**. You now have a customized MMC on your desktop. Close the DevDiskTask MMC. When prompted to save the console settings, click **No**.
14. Continue to the next activity.

Note 5

If you are using virtual machines with snapshots, you will be restoring the configuration of all the servers at the beginning of each module, so changes you make, such as adding the custom MMC to the desktop, will be erased when you restore the snapshot for the ServerSA1 server.

Activity 1-5

Creating a Volume and Sharing a Folder

Time Required: 15 minutes
Objective: Create a volume using the Disk Management snap-in; then create and share a folder.
Required Tools and Equipment: ServerSA1
Description: Use the Disk Management snap-in to create a volume. Then create a folder on the new volume and share it.

Note 6

If your server is configured according to instructions in the "Before You Begin" section of the Introduction, you should have four physical disks. Disk 0 has the Windows OS installed, and the others are empty and offline.

1. Sign in to ServerSA1 as **Administrator**, if necessary.
2. From the desktop, open the MMC you created in Activity 1-4. (You can also access Disk Management by right-clicking Start and clicking Disk Management.)
3. Click the **Disk Management** snap-in in the left pane. There are two panes in Disk Management: The upper pane shows a summary of configured volumes and basic information about each volume. The lower pane shows installed disks and how each disk is being used.
4. Right-click the **(C:)** volume in the upper pane and note some of the options you have.
5. In the lower pane, find Disk 1. If its status is online and initialized, skip to the next step; otherwise, right-click **Disk 1** and click **Online**. Right-click it again and click **Initialize Disk** to open the dialog box shown in Figure 1-16. Leave the default option **GPT (GUID Partition Table)** selected and click **OK**.

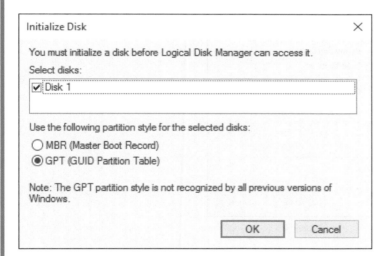

Figure 1-16   Initializing a disk in Disk Management

6. Right-click the unallocated space of **Disk 1** and notice the options for making the unallocated space into a new volume.
7. Click **New Simple Volume** to start the New Simple Volume Wizard. In the welcome window, click **Next**.
8. In the Specify Volume Size window, type **500** to make a 500 MB volume, and then click **Next**.
9. In the Assign Drive Letter or Path window, you have the option to assign a drive letter or mount the new volume into a folder on another volume. Click the drive letter to open the selection box, click drive letter **S**, and then click **Next**.
10. In the Format Partition window, click the **File system** list arrow, and note the available options. Click **NTFS** to select it as the file system. In the Volume label text box, type **DataVol1**, and then click **Next**.

(continues)

Activity 1-5 Continued

11. Review the settings summary, and then click **Finish**. Watch the space where the new volume has been created. After a short pause, the volume should begin to format. When formatting is finished, the volume status should be Healthy (Basic Data Partition).

12. Close the management console; click **No** when prompted to save the settings.

13. Open **File Explorer** and click **This PC** in the left pane to view the available drives.

14. Click the **S:** drive. Click the folder icon near the upper-left corner of the window to create a new folder. Type **DocShare** for the folder name and press **Enter**.

15. Double-click the **DocShare** folder to open it. Create a text file in the folder by right-clicking empty space in File Explorer, pointing to **New**, and clicking **Text Document**. Type **file1** for the file name and press **Enter**.

16. In the left pane, click the **S:** drive so you see DocShare in the right pane again. Right-click the **DocShare** folder, point to **Give access to**, and click **Specific people**.

17. Click the selection arrow, click **Everyone**, and click **Add**. Notice that the default permission level is set to Read (see Figure 1-17), which allows all users with an account on the network to open or copy files in the DocShare folder, but not change them.

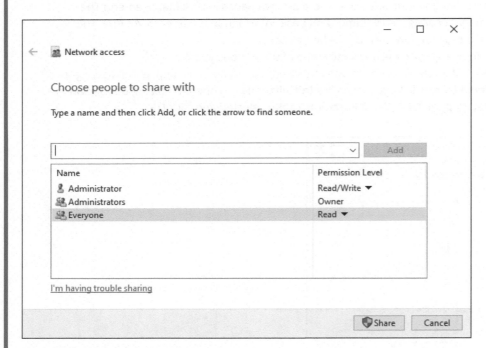

Figure 1-17   Sharing a folder

18. Click **Share**. (If you see a Network discovery and file sharing message, click **No, make the network I am connected to a private network**.) You see a message confirming that the folder is shared and the path to your new share is \\ServerSA1\DocShare. This is called the Universal Naming Convention (UNC) path. Click **Done**.

19. To verify that you can access the share using the UNC path, right-click **Start**, click **Run**, type **\\ServerSA1\DocShare** (note that capitalization is not important), and click **OK** or press **Enter**. A File Explorer window opens and you see the file you created earlier. The UNC path is how someone on another computer would access the shared folder.

20. Close any open **File Explorer** windows and open **Server Manager**, if necessary. Click **File and Storage Services** in the left pane.

(continues)

Activity 1-5 Continued

21. You should see that new tools have been added to the left pane: Shares, iSCSI, and Work Folders. (If you don't see these new tools, press **F5**, click the **Refresh** button at the top of Server Manager, or close and restart Server Manager.) When you created a share, the File Server role service was installed automatically along with additional tools.
22. Click **Shares** to see a list of shares on your server (see Figure 1-18).

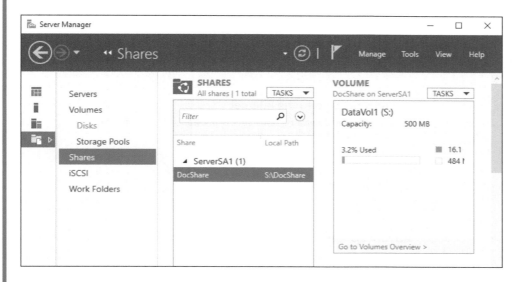

Figure 1-18   Viewing shares in Server Manager

23. Continue to the next activity.

Activity 1-6

Exploring Windows Networking Components
Time Required: 15 minutes
Objective: Identify features of Windows networking components.
Required Tools and Equipment: ServerSA1
Description: Manage various aspects of a network connection on your server.

1. Sign in to ServerSA1 as **Administrator**, if necessary.
2. Right-click the network connection icon in the notification area and click **Open Network & Internet settings**.
3. You see the network status. Depending on your network configuration, your network might have a name or be shown as simply Network or Network 2, as in Figure 1-19.

(continues)

Activity 1-6 Continued

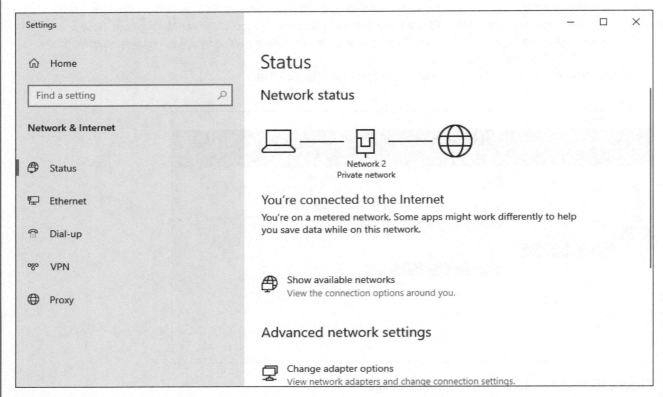

Figure 1-19   The Network status window

4. Click **Change adapter options** under Advanced network settings. Right-click the Ethernet adapter and click **Status** to see connection status and activity information (see Figure 1-20).
5. Click the **Details** button to view address information about TCP/IP and physical address information about your NIC, and then click **Close**.
6. Click the **Properties** button to see details on installed protocols, clients, and services. Each protocol and service has a check box for enabling or disabling it on the connection.
7. Click **Internet Protocol Version 4 (TCP/IPv4)**. (Don't clear the check box, or you'll disable the protocol.) Then click **Properties** to open a dialog box where you can change your server's IP address settings. For now, leave the settings as they are. Click **Cancel**, and then click **Cancel** again. Click **Close**.
8. Close all open windows and continue to the next activity.

Figure 1-20   Viewing the status of a network connection

Activity 1-7

Working with PowerShell

Time Required: 15 minutes
Objective: Use Windows PowerShell cmdlets and features.
Required Tools and Equipment: ServerSA1
Description: Open a PowerShell prompt and work with some cmdlets and features of PowerShell.

1. Sign in to ServerSA1 as **Administrator**, if necessary.
2. Click the Search Windows icon, type **power**, and click **Windows PowerShell** in the search results. A PowerShell window opens. Add PowerShell to the taskbar by right-clicking the PowerShell icon on the taskbar and clicking **Pin to taskbar**.
3. Click in the PowerShell window, type **Get-Verb**, and press **Enter**. You see a list of verbs that PowerShell cmdlet names can begin with.
4. Type **Get-Command** and press **Enter**. You see a list of all PowerShell cmdlets.
5. Press the **up arrow**; Get-Command is repeated. Press the **Backspace** key until you see only **Get-Com**, and then type **p** and press **Tab**. Get-ComputerInfo is displayed. Press **Enter** to see information about the computer. Scroll through the information; a lot of detailed information about your computer is shown.
6. Type **Get-Command *info*** and press **Enter** to see all cmdlets and command prompt commands that have the string "info" as part of their name.
7. Type **Get-Disk** and press **Enter**. You see a list of all disks on the computer. Type **Get-Disk | Where-Object IsOffline –eq $False** and press **Enter** to see a list of disks that are online.
8. Type **Get-Disk | Where-Object IsSystem –eq $True | fl** and press **Enter**. You see information about the system disk. The | fl part of the command means Format-List and provides more details about an object.
9. Type **Get-NetI<Tab> | Where Int<Tab> –like Ethernet*** and press **Enter**. Be sure to press the **Tab** key where the command shows <Tab>, and don't type a space before the Tab key. You see interfaces that have a name starting with "Ethernet."
10. Use a variable to store a value. Type **$interface = "Ethernet*"** and press **Enter**.
11. Press the **up arrow** twice so that the command from step 9 is shown. Press **Backspace** until the word "Ethernet" is erased, then type **$interface** and press **Enter**.
12. Use a variable to store an object. Type **$interfaces = Get-NetIPAddress** and press **Enter**.
13. Type **$interfaces.IPAddress** and press **Enter** to see a list of addresses for all interfaces.
14. This was a brief introduction to PowerShell. Close the PowerShell window.

Introducing the Windows Server Hybrid Infrastructure

In a nutshell, the **Windows Server Hybrid Infrastructure** is the Microsoft paradigm for the hybrid cloud. The hybrid cloud is the marriage of Windows Server running in the on-premises datacenter and Windows Server and other networking services running in the Microsoft Azure cloud. This paradigm provides central management over both on-premises resources and Azure cloud-based resources. Earlier in this module, we defined the various forms of cloud computing, but let's now look at some of the attributes of cloud computing in the context of a hybrid infrastructure:

- Scalable—Perhaps one of the primary reasons organizations turn to the cloud for information technology needs is scalability. **Scalability** is the ability to add storage, computing, or other resources quickly and easily. In an on-premises datacenter, new servers or upgrades are required to add computing power, and new disk drives or storage servers are needed to add storage.

- Agile—Scalability is enhanced by agility. Cloud resources are ready to deploy whenever the customer needs them. There's no need to requisition new hardware and wait for delivery. In many instances, cloud resources can be deployed on a pay-as-you-go basis, so you can add the resources you need immediately and pay for them in the monthly invoice.
- Current—The latest and greatest technology is expensive. It's expensive to acquire and expensive to learn. By leveraging the cloud, even small businesses can benefit from the latest technologies because large cloud providers must offer them to stay competitive. Cloud professionals have already learned how to implement these technologies, so you don't have to. This levels the playing field between your business and larger competitors with deeper pockets.

The attributes of the cloud confer a number of advantages to cloud users. Some of those advantages are realized simply because an organization is housing, powering, and cooling less computing hardware, resulting in physical plant cost savings. Productivity can be improved because less waiting is required when system upgrades are needed to deploy new applications or expand facilities. Plus, IT personnel can focus on big-picture tasks rather than mundane maintenance like operating system updates, backups, hardware upgrades, and operating system installs.

Cloud Models

Cloud computing is divided into distinct services, depending on the needs of the customer. Some cloud providers offer only one or two of the services, while others offer the whole range of cloud services. Briefly, there are three main categories of cloud service:

- Software as a service—With the **software as a service (SaaS)** model, the customer pays for the use of applications that run on a service provider's network. Two well-known examples are Google Apps and Microsoft Office 365.
- Platform as a service—With the **platform as a service (PaaS)** model, the customer develops applications with the service provider's tools and infrastructure. After applications are developed, they can be delivered to the customer's users from the provider's servers.
- Infrastructure as a service—The **infrastructure as a service (IaaS)** model allows companies to use a provider's computing power, storage, and various infrastructure services as needed. IaaS services can be used instead of, or in addition to, a company's own datacenter resources. This model is the focus of Microsoft Azure and the hybrid infrastructure. Other IaaS providers include Amazon Web Services (AWS), Digital Ocean, and Google Cloud Platform.

Note 7

Infrastructure services include networking services such as directory services, domain name services, dynamic address management, and databases. Other "as a service" technologies exist, and most of them fall into one of the three larger categories described above. For example, networking as a service (NaaS) and data as a service (DaaS) fall under the IaaS model, whereas games as a service (GaaS) and banking as a service (BaaS) likely fall under the SaaS category. A general term, anything as a service (XaaS), has sprung up to encompass any type of service that can be delivered via cloud technologies.

Getting Started with Microsoft Azure

To get the most out of this book, you will need a Microsoft Azure account. Thankfully, there are free accounts available for the express purpose of learning Microsoft Azure. If you're using this book as part of a college course, you may already have access to a free education account. Ask your instructor how to get access to an education account if available. The next activity will walk you through how to access and start using a free account.

Once you have an Azure account, you have access to creating various services. With the huge array of services available, it is helpful to go to the Quickstart Center, which is available from the Azure portal home page. From the Quickstart Center, you create new services, including creating web applications, deploying virtual machines, and setting up a database (see Figure 1-21). In this book, you will be working with Azure virtual machines and with various Azure services such as Azure Active Directory, Azure DNS, and Azure file services, in addition to managing network connectivity with Azure network adapters. To start you on that journey, you will begin by creating an Azure virtual machine with Windows Server 2022.

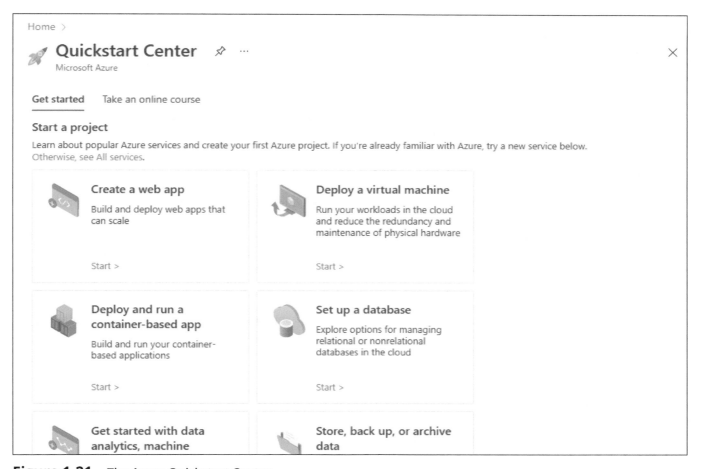

Figure 1-21   The Azure Quickstart Center

Creating an Azure Virtual Machine

Activity 1-9 walks you through the process of creating an Azure VM. Here is a summary of the process. You can deploy an Azure virtual machine by going to the Quickstart Center and clicking Start in the Deploy a virtual machine box. You will be asked what type of VM you want to create (Windows or Linux) and then you will fill out a form specifying the details of the VM. One of the most critical details is the size of the VM, which specifies the number of CPUs, memory, hard disks, and processing power. Some of the VM sizes can cost hundreds of dollars per month, and a few cost less than $50 per month. A Windows Server 2022 VM running the graphical user interface (GUI) requires at least 2 GB of RAM, so your choice must specify 2 GB of RAM or more. A good choice here is the Standard_B2s, which have two virtual CPUs and 4 GB of RAM. The cost is $42/month, but as long as you don't leave your VM running when you're not using it, the cost will be much less.

By default, the VM is configured with Remote Desktop Protocol (RDP), which is available through a public IP address so you can access the VM user interface after the OS is installed. However, after you initially configure the VM, it's best to disable RDP access until you need it again. If you have a Microsoft Windows Server license, you can choose to use the existing license. If you're using an Azure education account, you can get a key from the software downloads area, which you can find by typing "software" in the search bar on any Azure portal page.

After filling out the first part of the form to create a VM, you then select the disk configuration for your VM. The Standard HDD is the least expensive option and is adequate for your purposes while working through this book. You can also choose the encryption type; the default option is sufficient.

Next, you configure networking. Azure will create a new subnet with default options and will create a firewall rule that allows RDP on the standard port. After the networking options, you move on to management options. A key feature here is Enable auto-shutdown. If you select this option, your VM will be automatically shut down each day in the event you leave it on. This option will save on costs because, as mentioned, the bulk of your costs are incurred on running VMs. You can select the time that the VM will be automatically shut down each day.

You can choose some advanced options next or simply click Review + create, and your VM is created for you. On the review screen, you see how much the VM will cost you per hour of runtime. After you review the options, click Create. While the VM is being created, you will see a status screen showing the progress. Once the process is complete, you can click Go to resource and start using your VM.

Accessing an Azure Virtual Machine

You can access your new VM by clicking the VM name you assigned during the creation process, clicking Connect, and then clicking RDP to get a remote desktop connection. You are presented with an option to download an RDP file that you can open on your computer. The RDP file will attempt to start an RDP session with your VM. You will be asked to enter the credentials you created when you created the VM. Once logged in, you will see your Windows Server 2022 desktop. At this point, you can do everything with your Azure VM that you can do with a physical or virtual machine in your own network. Remember, you don't want to use your free account credits too quickly, so don't leave your VM running when you are finished checking it out.

In the upcoming modules, you'll be working with both your local server and your Azure VM as well as other Azure services.

Self-Check Questions

4. Which "as a service" technology best describes the focus of Microsoft Azure?

   a. SaaS   **c.** IaaS

   b. PaaS   **d.** NaaS

5. What protocol is enabled by default on an Azure VM and allows a user to access the VM console via a public IP address?

   a. RDP   **c.** HTTP

   b. SSH   **d.** VNC

● Check your answers at the end of this module.

Activity 1-8

Creating a Free Microsoft Azure Account

Time Required: 20 minutes

Objective: Create a free Microsoft Azure account to use with the labs in this book.

Required Tools and Equipment: Any computer with Internet access

Description: Create a free Microsoft Azure account. If you are not creating a free student account, you will need to submit credit card information to verify your identity. Note that your credit card will not be charged unless you exceed your free credits and choose to continue using Azure with a pay-as-you-go account.

1. Open a web browser and go to azure.microsoft.com/en-us/free. If you are outside the United States, your URL may be different.

Note 8

If you want to understand the process of creating a free Microsoft Azure account before doing it, you can watch the following video: *https://www.youtube.com/watch?v=ExYcSfLlSCk*

2. Click **Start free**; you will be prompted to sign into Microsoft. If you don't already have a Microsoft account, you need to create one. If you are signing in with your student email address, you may be prompted to enter your student credentials or verify your student status. These instructions do not cover creating a new Microsoft account.

3. Once signed in, you will be in the Azure portal. Access the available tasks by clicking the menu icon near the upper-left corner of the browser window (see Figure 1-22). Note that the screenshot shows an education account; yours may differ. Close the menu.

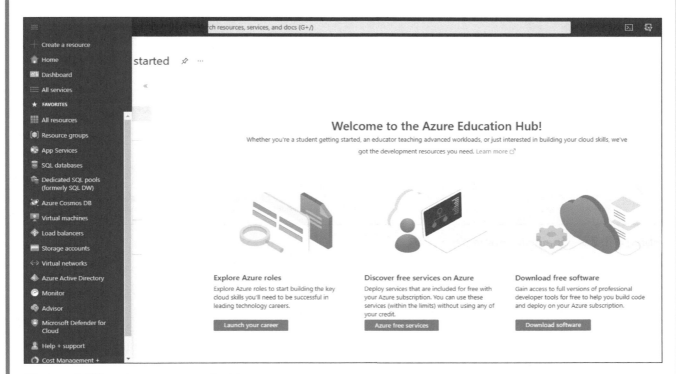

Figure 1-22   The Azure portal with menu

(continues)

Activity 1-8 Continued

4. If you have a student account, you can access benefits available to students, such as downloading Microsoft software and browsing career opportunities in Azure.

> **Note 9**
>
> It's easy to get lost in the Azure portal. You may want to bookmark the education page so you can return to it easily if desired. You can also follow this link: *https://portal.azure.com/#blade/Microsoft_Azure_Education/*

5. Click **Download software** to see the software available for download. The list includes developer tools, Windows 10, Windows 11, and a number of Windows Server versions. Click **Get started** on the left side of the browser to return to the main education page.
6. Click the menu icon and click **Home** to see the portal home page (see Figure 1-23). From this page, you can create virtual machines and access available Azure services.

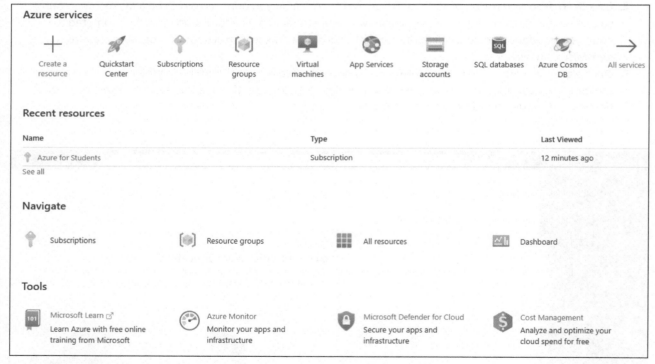

Figure 1-23 The Azure home page

7. Click **Dashboard** to see a summary of resources in use. If you are using a new account, you will see a list of tutorials for working with virtual machines, services, and databases.
8. Click the back button on your browser to return to the portal home page.
9. Explore the Azure portal; you will be using it in the next activity. When you are finished, continue to the next activity, where you create an Azure VM.

Activity 1-9

Creating an Azure Windows Server 2022 VM

Time Required: 20 minutes
Objective: Create an Azure Windows Server 2022 virtual machine.
Required Tools and Equipment: Any computer with Internet access
Description: In this activity, you create an Azure VM with Windows Server 2022 Datacenter installed. You will access the server using RDP.

1. Open a web browser, go to *portal.azure.com*, and sign in if necessary. Click **Quickstart Center** under Azure Services.
2. In the Deploy a virtual machine box, click **Start**. In the Create a Windows virtual machine window, click **Create**.
3. You see the Create a virtual machine page. If you have more than one Azure subscription, be sure the one you want to use is shown in the Subscription box. In Figure 1-24, the subscription is an "Azure for Students" education subscription.

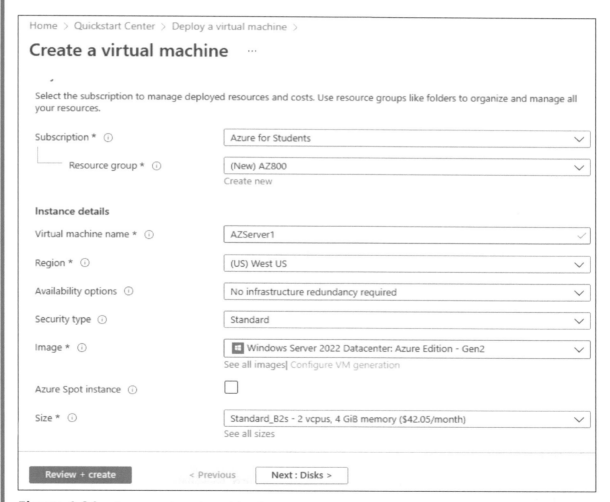

Figure 1-24 Create a virtual machine form

4. Under the Resource group box, click **Create new** to create a resource group. Resource groups are collections of resources that share permissions and policies. All the resources you create in these activities will likely go under the same resource group. Name the resource group **AZ800**.

(continues)

Activity 1-9 Continued ────────────────

5. In the Virtual machine name box, type **AZServer1**. Select the appropriate region for your location. Leave the next two options at their default settings.

6. In the Image box, click **See all images**, then click **Select** in the Windows Server box. Finally, click the down arrow and click **[smalldisk] Windows Server 2022 Datacenter: Azure Edition – Gen2**. The smalldisk option uses a disk for the OS that is smaller and will save on storage costs.

7. Under the Size box, click **See all sizes**, click **B2s** in the list, and click **Select**.

8. In the username box, type the username you want to use to sign in to your VM, along with a password that you will remember. The password must be at least 12 characters and must contain three uppercase characters, three lowercase characters, three numbers, and three special characters.

9. Accept the defaults for Inbound port rules. Under licensing, click the check box if you have an existing license you can use. If you have a student account, you are granted free licenses for Windows Server 2022 under the software download section. If you're not sure what to do here, ask your instructor.

10. Click **Next : Disks >** to move on to the disk configuration page (see Figure 1-25).

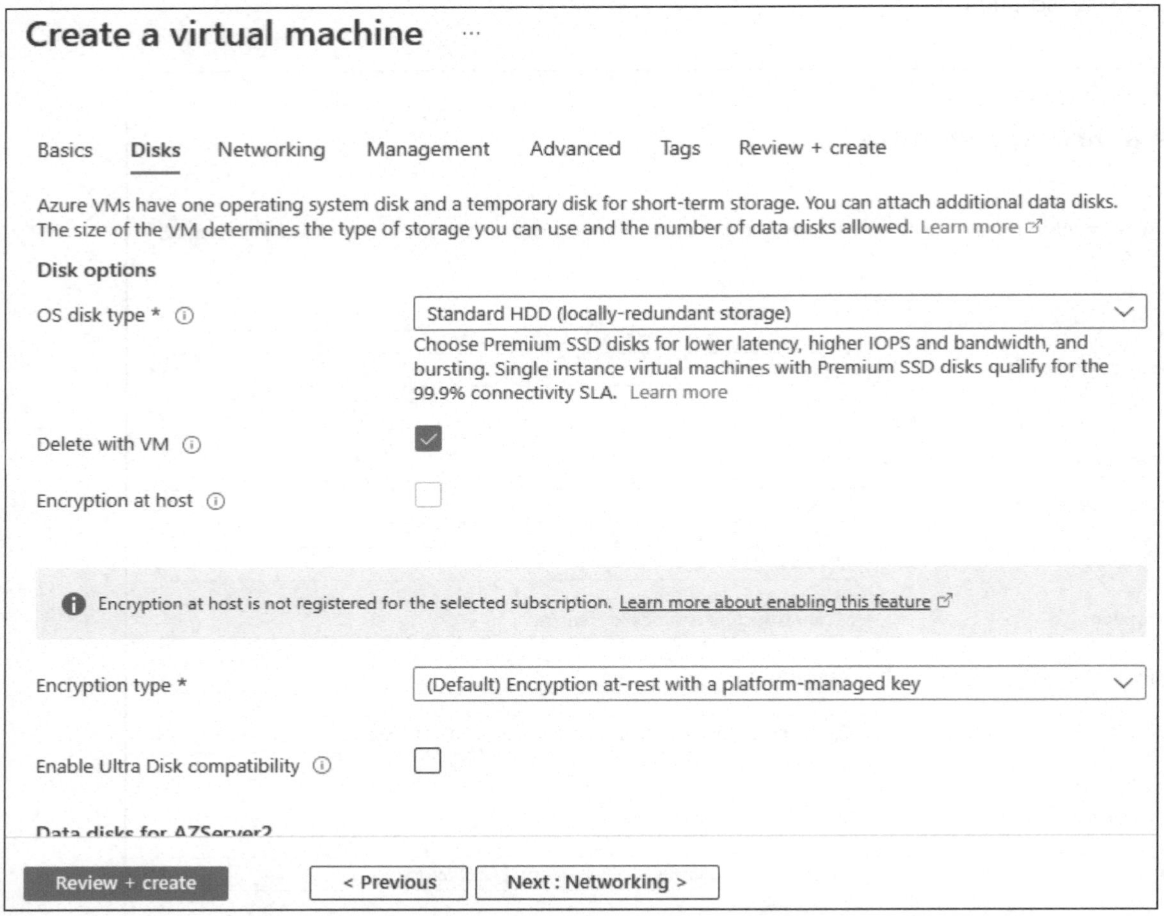

Figure 1-25   Disk configuration options after selecting the OS disk type

11. In the OS disk type box, click the down arrow and select **Standard HDD**. Review the other options and click **Next : Networking >**.

12. On the networking page, accept the defaults and click **Next : Management >**. On the management page, scroll down and click to select **Enable auto-shutdown**. Choose an appropriate time and time zone for your VM to be automatically shut down. It is best to pick a time during which you are unlikely to be working with the VM. Remember, you should always shut down your VM when you are done working with it, so this option is useful in case you forget.

(continues)

Activity 1-9 Continued

13. Enter an email address for notification when your VM is about to be shut down.
14. At this point, you are finished making changes. However, if you like, you can click through the Advanced and Tags screens to see the available options. When you are finished, click **Review + create**.
15. On the Review + Create page, you are shown a summary of the cost of the VM and the options you chose. Click **Create** after reviewing the information.
16. The next page shows the progress of your deployment. When your VM is deployed, you'll see a button labeled Go to resource. Click **Go to resource**. You are now on the AZServer1 Overview page. You'll see the status of the VM, its IP address, and other configuration information. The VM is not yet ready to be accessed. You'll probably see a message like the one in Figure 1-26 indicating that the virtual machine agent status is not ready. Click **Refresh** periodically to see the current status. After the message disappears, you're ready to connect to your VM. It may take quite a while before your VM is ready to access. When it is ready to access, go to the next step.

Figure 1-26   Azure VM status page

17. From your AZServer1's Overview page, make sure your VM is running. If it isn't, click the **Start** button at the top of the page. Next, click **Connect** and click **RDP**. Accept the defaults and click **Download RDP File**.
18. Double-click the downloaded RDP file. When prompted, enter your username and password (click Remember me so you don't need to enter your username in the future) and click **OK**. Click **Yes** when you see the certificate warning. You will see your server desktop after a short time. Congratulations, you've successfully created and accessed an Azure VM!
19. Explore your server. When you finish, shut down the server.

Note 10

You might be prompted to save your public IP address. While it is convenient to do so, it is an extra charge.

Module Summary

- A server is largely defined by the software running on the computer hardware rather than the computer hardware on which the software is running. Although most client OSs now provide some server services, such as file and printer sharing, a true server OS is usually defined as providing these important network services: directory services, DNS, remote access, DHCP, and robust network application services. In addition, current server OSs include hardware support for multiple processors, disk fault tolerance, and clustering.
- Windows Server 2022 includes more than a dozen primary server roles and many supporting role services and features. Administrators can configure a server as a narrowly focused device that provides just one or two specific services, or as a general, do-it-all system that's the center of a Windows network.
- The technologies that make up the core functions of Windows Server 2022 include Server Manager, NTFS, the Microsoft Management Console, disk management, file and printer sharing, Windows networking, Active Directory, PowerShell, Hyper-V, and Storage Spaces.
- The Windows Server Hybrid Infrastructure is the Microsoft paradigm for the hybrid cloud. Cloud computing is scalable, agile, and current. Cloud models include SaaS, PaaS, and IaaS. The focus of Microsoft Azure and the hybrid infrastructure is IaaS.
- You can create a free Azure account or a student account to work with Azure resources for free. You can create a VM with Windows Server 2022 already installed and access it using RDP.

Key Terms

Active Directory
cloud computing
domain controller
guest OS
host computer
hybrid cloud
hypervisor
infrastructure as a service (IaaS)
member server
network client
network connection
network interface

network protocol
network server software
NT File System (NTFS)
parameter
platform as a service (PaaS)
PowerShell
private cloud
public cloud
role services
scalability
server features
server operating system

server role
software as a service (SaaS)
standalone server
thin provisioning
variable
virtual desktop infrastructure (VDI)
virtual machine (VM)
virtualization
virtualization software
Windows domain
Windows Server Hybrid Infrastructure
Windows workgroup

Review Questions

1. Which of the following best defines a computer used as a server?

   a. Computer hardware that includes fast disk drives and a lot of memory
   b. A computer with OS software that has a web browser and Client for Microsoft Networks
   c. A computer with OS software that includes directory services and domain name services
   d. A computer with Linux installed

2. Which of the following best describes a Windows client OS?

   a. Supports up to 64 processors
   b. Includes fault-tolerance features, such as RAID-5 and clustering
   c. Supports network connections based on the number of purchased licenses
   d. Supports a limited number of signed-in network users

3. Which of the following is a service supported by Windows 11? (Choose all that apply.)

    a. File and Printer Sharing
    b. Active Directory
    c. Hyper-V
    d. Distributed File System

4. Which server feature provides fault tolerance?

    a. FTP
    b. Failover clustering
    c. DNS
    d. Internet Printing Protocol

5. Which Windows Server core technology can you use to install, configure, and remove server roles and features?

    a. AD DS
    b. NTFS
    c. Microsoft Management Console
    d. Server Manager

6. With which Windows Server core technology do you use snap-ins?

    a. AD DS
    b. NTFS
    c. Microsoft Management Console
    d. Server Manager

7. You are signed in to a server named Mktg-Srv1 that is part of the Marketing workgroup. What kind of server are you signed in to?

    a. Domain controller
    b. Member server
    c. Standalone server
    d. Cluster server

8. The IT department sent out a memo stating that it will start delivering desktop computer interfaces through the IT datacenter via a web browser interface. What technology is the IT department using?

    a. Public cloud computing
    b. Server clustering
    c. Directory server
    d. Virtual desktop infrastructure

9. Which component of a network connection specifies the rules and format of communication between network devices?

    a. Network protocol
    b. Network interface card
    c. Network client
    d. Device driver

10. Which type of networking component is File and Printer Sharing for Microsoft Networks?

    a. Network interface protocol
    b. Server software
    c. Client software
    d. Device driver

11. Which term describes a computing model in which local datacenter resources are used in conjunction with IaaS resources from a cloud provider?

    a. SaaS
    b. Private cloud
    c. Hybrid cloud
    d. Public cloud

12. You're a consultant for a small business with four computer users. The company's main reason for networking is to share the Internet connection, two printers, and several documents. Keeping costs down is a major consideration, and users should be able to manage their own shared resources. Which networking model best meets the needs of this business?

    a. Domain
    b. Workgroup
    c. Management
    d. Client/server

13. Which networking component includes a device driver?

    a. Network server software
    b. Network client software
    c. Network protocol
    d. Network interface

14. If you want to share files on your computer with other Windows computers, what should you have installed and enabled on your computer?

    a. Client for Microsoft Networks
    b. File and Printer Sharing for Microsoft Networks
    c. Active Directory
    d. Domain Name System

15. If you want to make a computer a domain controller, which of the following should you install?

    a. Client for Microsoft Networks
    b. File and Printer Sharing for Microsoft Networks
    c. Active Directory
    d. Domain Name System

16. Jose is an entrepreneurial software developer who is just starting up a new business for an application he wants to develop. Jose doesn't have the financial resources to purchase the needed development environment for this application, so he turns to a cloud provider. What cloud computing model will Jose most likely need?

    a. SaaS
    b. PaaS
    c. IaaS
    d. XaaS

17. Which of the following is the common framework in which most Windows Server 2022 administrative tools run?

    a. Windows Management Center
    b. Microsoft Management Console
    c. Server Configuration Manager
    d. Windows Configuration Manager

18. You have been asked to advise a business on how to best set up its Windows network. Eight workstations are running Windows 11. The business recently acquired a new contract that requires running a network application on a server. A secure and reliable environment is critical to run this application, and security management should be centralized. There are enough funds in the budget for new hardware and software, if necessary. Which Windows networking model should you advise this business to use?

    a. A Windows domain using Active Directory
    b. A Windows workgroup using Active Directory
    c. A peer-to-peer network using File and Printer Sharing
    d. A peer-to-peer network using Active Directory

19. Which of the following is *not* an attribute typically found in cloud computing?

    a. Scalable
    b. Legacy
    c. Agile
    d. Current

20. Which of the following standard server roles should you install if you want to create and manage virtual machines on Windows Server 2022?

    a. VirtualBox
    b. Server Manager
    c. Hyper-V
    d. DHCP Server

Critical Thinking

The following activities give you critical thinking challenges. Case projects offer a scenario with a problem for which you supply a written solution.

Case Projects

Case Project 1-1: Recommending a Network Model

You're installing a new network for CSM Tech Publishing, a new publisher of technical books and training materials. There will be 10 client computers running Windows 11, and CSM Tech Publishing plans to run a web-based order processing/inventory program that for now is used only by in-house employees while they're on-site. CSM Tech Publishing wants to be able to manage client computer and user policies and allow employees to share documents. Sign-in and security should be centrally managed. What network model—workgroup or domain—should be used? Explain your answer, including any server roles you may need to install.

Case Project 1-2: Preserving Disk Space

CSM Tech Publishing has been operating for six months, and business is good. You do a spot check on server resources and find that RAM use is at 50 percent, which is fine, but the data volume on the server used by employees to store and share documents is approaching 90 percent full. There are two volumes on this server: one for OS and program files and one for data storage. You inspect the data volume and find that some users are storing large amounts of data on the server. You check with the owner and determine that each user should require only about 4 GB of storage on the server for necessary documents. Because some users are clearly exceeding this limit, you're asked to come up with a solution. What file system option can you use, and which file system format must be used with this option?

Case Project 1-3: Explaining the Hybrid Cloud Infrastructure

The owner of CSM Tech Publishing is always thinking about how he can use technology to improve the operation of his business. He read an article about cloud computing and has asked you to explain what cloud computing is and whether he needs it now or in the future for more efficient operations. He doesn't want to lose the investment he has in his current network and server hardware, so he is wondering if he can still leverage the cloud while keeping his investment. Write a memo explaining what cloud computing is and how he can use his on-premises equipment along with the cloud.

Solutions to Self-Check Questions

Section 1-1: The Role of a Server Operating System

1. When Windows Server 2022 is installed on a computer, the computer's role in a network is always as a server. True or False?

   Answer: b. False

   Explanation: While Windows Server 2022 is designed as a server OS, what matters most is how it is used and the software that is installed on it. A user could install Windows Server 2022 and use it as a general-purpose client computer by installing office productivity software, games, and other user- or client-oriented software.

Section 1-2: Windows Server 2022 Core Technologies

2. Which of the following is a server role that is preinstalled on Windows Server 2022?

   Answer: c. File and Storage Services

   Explanation: Only File and Storage Services is a server role that is installed by default on Windows Server 2022. While PowerShell is installed by default, it is not a server role. Active Directory Domain Services and Hyper-V are roles that must be installed manually after Windows Server 2022 is installed.

3. Which of the following is considered network server software that is preinstalled on Windows Server 2022?

   Answer: d. File and Printer Sharing for Microsoft Networks

   Explanation: Only File and Printer Sharing for Microsoft Networks is considered network server software. Client for Microsoft Networks is client software. Transport Control Protocol/Internet Protocol is the primary networking protocol that client and server software run on, and a network interface driver is a software component that communicates with the NIC to read and write network data from and to the media.

Section 1-3: Introducing the Windows Server Hybrid Infrastructure

4. Which "as a service" technology best describes the focus of Microsoft Azure?

   Answer: c. IaaS

   Explanation: While Microsoft Azure can be used to perform other "as a service" technologies, its main focus is on infrastructure as a service, in which users can deploy virtual machines, run infrastructure networking services like Active Directory and DNS, and deploy virtual networks.

5. What protocol is enabled by default on an Azure VM and allows a user to access the VM console via a public IP address?

   Answer: a. RDP

   Explanation: Remote Desktop Protocol (RDP) is enabled by default on a new Azure VM that runs Windows Server 2022, and it can be accessed by a public IP address; however, you can disable it if you prefer.

Module 2

Discover Active Directory

Module Objectives

After reading this module and completing the exercises, you will be able to:

1 Describe the role of a directory service
2 Install Active Directory
3 Describe objects found in Active Directory
4 Create forests, trees, and domains
5 Describe Group Policy

Active Directory is the core component in a Windows domain environment. The Active Directory Domain Services role provides a single point of user identity and authentication as well as client and server administration. To understand Active Directory and its role in a network, you need to know what a directory service is and how it's used to manage resources and access to resources on a network. Before administrators can use Active Directory to manage users, clients, and servers in a network, they need a good understanding of Active Directory's structure and underlying components and objects, which are covered in this module. You also learn how to install Active Directory and work with forests, trees, and domains. Finally, you learn the basics of using the Group Policy tool to set consistent security, user, and desktop standards throughout your organization. You are also introduced to how Active Directory fits in with the Windows Server hybrid infrastructure and Azure Active Directory. In Modules 3 through 5, you will learn how to work with Active Directory in a hybrid environment with Azure.

Table 2-1 summarizes what you need in order to do the hands-on activities in this module.

Table 2-1   Activity requirements

Activity	Requirements	Notes
Activity 2-1: Resetting Your Virtual Environment	A server named ServerSA1	
Activity 2-2: Installing Active Directory Domain Services	ServerSA1	
Activity 2-3: Exploring Active Directory Container Objects	ServerSA1	
Activity 2-4: Viewing Default Leaf Objects	ServerSA1	
Activity 2-5: Creating Objects in Active Directory	ServerSA1	
Activity 2-6: Using the Command Line to Create Users	ServerSA1	
Activity 2-7: Locating Objects in Active Directory	ServerSA1	
Activity 2-8: Publishing a Shared Folder in Active Directory	ServerSA1	
Activity 2-9: Viewing the Operations Master Roles and Global Catalog Server	ServerSA1	
Activity 2-10: Exploring Default GPOs	ServerSA1	
Activity 2-11: Working with Group Policies	ServerSA1	

The Role of a Directory Service

Microsoft Exam AZ-800:
Deploy and manage Active Directory Domain Services (AD DS) in on-premises and cloud environments.

A network **directory service**, as the name suggests, stores information about a computer network and offers features for retrieving and managing that information. Essentially, it's a database composed of records or objects describing users and available network resources, such as servers, printers, and applications. Like a database for managing a company's inventory, a directory service includes functions to organize, search for, add, modify, and delete information. Unlike an inventory database, a directory service can also manage how its stored resources can be used and by whom. For example, a directory service can be used to specify who has the right to sign in to a computer or restrict what software can be installed on a computer.

A directory service is often thought of as an administrator's tool, but users can use it, too. Users might need the directory service to locate network resources, such as printers or shared folders, by performing a search. They can even use the directory service as a phone book of sorts to look up information about other users, such as phone numbers, office locations, and email addresses.

Whether an organization consists of a single facility or has multiple locations, a directory service provides a centralized management tool for users and resources in all locations. This capability does add a certain amount of complexity, so making sure the directory service is structured and designed correctly before using it is critical.

Active Directory Domain Services

Active Directory Domain Services (AD DS) is a Microsoft Windows Server role that provides network directory services based on standards for defining, storing, and accessing directory service objects. A suite of protocols called X.500, developed by the International Telecommunications Union (ITU), is the basis for its hierarchical structure and for how Active Directory objects are named and stored. **Lightweight Directory Access Protocol (LDAP)**, created by the Internet Engineering Task Force (IETF), is based on the X.500 Directory Access Protocol (DAP). DAP required the seldom used, high-overhead Open Systems Interconnection (OSI) protocol stack for accessing directory objects. LDAP became a streamlined version of DAP, using the more efficient and popular TCP/IP—hence the term "lightweight" in the protocol's name.

So, why is knowledge of LDAP important? You run across references to LDAP periodically when reading about Active Directory, and as an administrator, you'll be using tools such as ADSI Edit that incorporate LDAP definitions and objects or running programs that use LDAP to integrate with Active Directory. In addition, integrating other OSs, such as Linux, into an Active Directory network requires using LDAP. In fact, you use a tool that incorporates LDAP terminology used in this module when you run some command-line options for working with Active Directory. LDAP and its syntax are covered in more detail when you work with command-line tools in later modules of this book. For now, you focus on Active Directory and its structure and features.

Active Directory Domain Services, herein referred to as simply Active Directory, became part of the Windows family of server OSs starting with Windows 2000 Server. Before Windows 2000, Windows NT Server had a directory service that was little more than a user manager; it included centralized logon and grouped users and computers into logical security boundaries called domains. The Windows NT domain system was a flat database of users and computers with no way to organize users or resources by department, function, or location. This single, unstructured list made managing large numbers of users cumbersome.

Active Directory's hierarchical database enables administrators to organize users and network resources to reflect the organization of the environment in which it's used. For example, if a company identifies its users and resources mostly by department or location, Active Directory can be configured to mirror this structure. You can structure Active Directory and organize the objects representing users and resources in a way that makes the most sense for the company's structure. Active Directory offers the following features, among others, that make it a highly flexible directory service:

- *Hierarchical organization*—This structure makes management of network resources and administration of security policies easier.

- *Centralized but distributed database*—All network data is centrally located, but it can be distributed among many servers for fast, easy access to information from any location. Automatic replication of information also provides load balancing and fault tolerance. **Active Directory replication** is the transfer of information between all domain controllers to make sure they have consistent and up-to-date information.
- *Scalability*—Advanced indexing technology provides high-performance data access, whether Active Directory consists of a few dozen or a few million objects.
- *Security*—Fine-grained access controls enable administrators to control access to each directory object and its properties. Active Directory also supports secure authentication protocols to maximize compatibility with Internet applications and other systems.
- *Flexibility*—Active Directory is installed with some predefined objects, such as user accounts and groups, but their properties can be modified, and new objects can be added for a customized solution.
- *Policy-based administration*—Administrators can define policies to ensure a secure and consistent environment for users, yet maintain the flexibility to apply different rules for departments, locations, or user classes as needed.

Overview of the Active Directory Structure

As with most things, the best way to understand how Active Directory works is to install it and start using it, but knowing the terms used to describe its structure is helpful. There are two aspects of Active Directory's structure:

- Physical structure
- Logical structure

Active Directory's Physical Structure

The physical structure consists of sites and servers configured as domain controllers. An Active Directory **site** is nothing more than a physical location in which domain controllers communicate and replicate information periodically. Specifically, Microsoft defines a site as one or more IP subnets connected by high-speed LAN technology. A small business with no branch offices or other locations, for example, consists of a single site. However, a business usually needs two sites if it has a branch office in another part of the city that's connected to the main office through a slow WAN link. Typically, each physical location with a domain controller operating in a common domain connected by a WAN constitutes a site. The main reasons for defining multiple sites are to control the frequency of Active Directory replication and to assign policies based on physical location.

Another component of the physical structure is a server configured as a **domain controller**, which is a computer running Windows Server 2022 with the Active Directory Domain Services role installed. Although an Active Directory domain can consist of many domain controllers, each domain controller can service only one domain. Each domain controller contains a full replica of the objects that make up the domain and is responsible for the following functions:

- Storing a copy of the domain data and replicating changes to that data to all other domain controllers throughout the domain
- Providing data search and retrieval functions for users attempting to locate objects in the directory
- Providing authentication and authorization services for users who sign in to the domain and attempt to access network resources

Active Directory's Logical Structure

The logical structure of Active Directory makes it possible to pattern the directory service's look and feel after the organization in which it runs. There are four organizing components of Active Directory:

- Organizational units
- Domains
- Trees
- Forests

These four components can be thought of as containers and are listed from most specific to broadest in terms of what they contain. To use a geographical analogy, an organizational unit represents a neighborhood, a domain is the city, a tree is the state, and a forest is the country. Figure 2-1 shows one of the primary tools used to manage Active Directory, Active Directory Users and Computers. In the figure, you see the domain component and several organizational units. Trees and forests, as you will learn, are defined by the domain name system and are not part of the visual hierarchy.

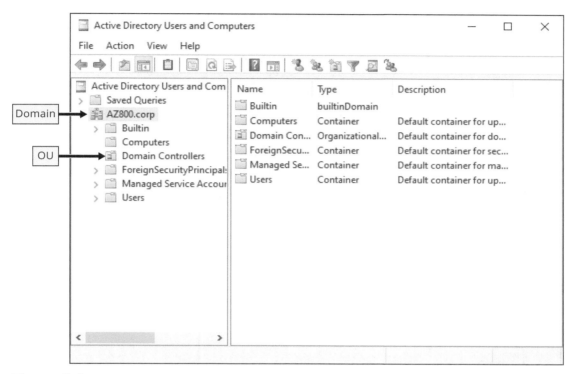

Figure 2-1   Active Directory Users and Computers

An **organizational unit (OU)** is an Active Directory container used to organize a network's users and resources into logical administrative units. An OU contains Active Directory objects, such as user accounts, groups, computer accounts, printers, shared folders, applications, servers, and domain controllers. The OU structure often mimics a company's internal administrative structure, although this structure isn't required. For example, a corporation might create an OU for each department, but an educational institution might create separate OUs for students, faculty, and administration or for campus locations. You can use a combination of structures, too, because OUs can be nested in as many levels as necessary. Besides being an organizational tool, OUs can represent policy boundaries, in which different sets of policies can be applied to objects in different OUs. Figure 2-2 should help you visualize OUs and the types of objects in them.

A **domain** is Active Directory's core structural unit. It contains OUs and represents administrative, security, and policy boundaries (see Figure 2-3). A small to medium-sized company usually has one domain with a single IT administrative group. However, a large company or a company with several locations might benefit from having multiple domains to separate IT administration or accommodate widely differing network policies. For example, a company with major branches in the United States and the United Kingdom might want to divide administrative responsibilities into domains based on location, such as US.csmtech.corp and UK.csmtech.corp domains, each with a separate administrative group and set of policies. This arrangement addresses possible language and cultural barriers and takes advantage of the benefit of proximity.

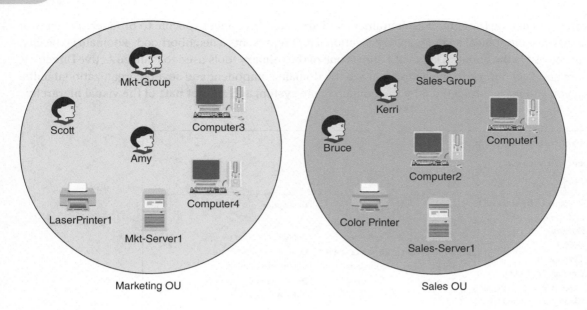

Figure 2-2   Active Directory organizational units

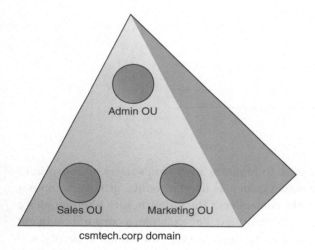

Figure 2-3   An Active Directory domain and OUs

An Active Directory **tree** is less a container than a grouping of domains that share a common naming structure. A tree consists of a parent domain and possibly one or more **child domains** (also called *subdomains*) that have the same second-level and top-level domain names as the parent domain. For example, US.csmtech.corp and UK.csmtech. corp are both child domains of the parent domain csmtech.corp, and all three domains are part of the same Active Directory tree. Furthermore, child domains can have child domains, as in phoenix.US.csmtech.corp. Figure 2-4 depicts domains in an Active Directory tree.

An Active Directory **forest** is a collection of one or more trees. A forest can consist of a single tree with a single domain, or it can contain several trees, each with a hierarchy of parent and child domains. Each tree in a forest has a different naming structure; one tree might have csmtech.corp as the parent, while another tree in the forest might have csmpub.corp as its parent domain. A forest's main purpose is to provide a common Active Directory environment in which all domains in all trees can communicate with one another and share information, yet allow independent

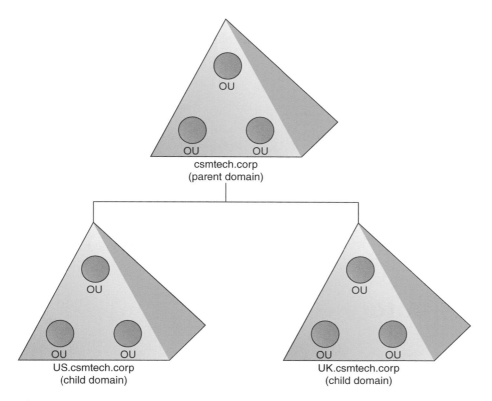

Figure 2-4   An Active Directory tree

operation and administration of each domain. Figure 2-5 shows an Active Directory forest and the trees and domains it contains. Every forest has a forest root domain, which is the first domain created in a new forest. The forest root domain is discussed later in the section titled "The Role of Forests."

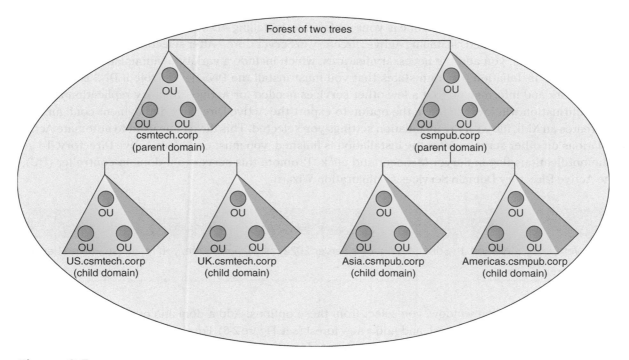

Figure 2-5   An Active Directory forest

This section has given you an overview of Active Directory components. You learn more about Active Directory account objects in Module 3. To understand its features and structure, you install and work with Active Directory in the next section.

Self-Check Questions

1. A directory service provides a centralized management tool for users and resources. True or False?

   a. True   **b.** False

2. Which of the following is part of the physical structure of Active Directory?

   a. Domains   **c.** Organizational units

   b. Domain controllers   **d.** Trees

⊙ Check your answers at the end of this module.

Installing Active Directory

Microsoft Exam AZ-800:

Deploy and manage Active Directory Domain Services (AD DS) in on-premises and cloud environments.
- Deploy and manage AD DS domain controllers
- Configure and manage multisite, multidomain, and multiforest environments

The Windows Active Directory service is commonly referred to as Active Directory Domain Services (AD DS). You must install this role for Active Directory to be part of your network. As with any server role, installing AD DS is straightforward, with the real work in the planning and postinstallation tasks.

To begin installing AD DS in Windows Server 2022 with Desktop Experience, you use Server Manager. Of course, you can also use PowerShell if using the command line is your preference. Installing AD DS using PowerShell is discussed later in this module in the section called "Installing Active Directory in Server Core." After selecting the Active Directory Domain Services role to install, you add the necessary features, which include a variety of administration tools and PowerShell modules. The installation program states that you must install the DNS Server role if DNS isn't already installed on the network and informs you that a few other services needed for Active Directory replication must be installed. In the confirmation window, you have the option to export the Active Directory deployment configuration settings, which creates an XML file with the installation settings you selected. This file can be used to automate Active Directory installations on other servers. After the installation is finished, you must configure Active Directory. To get started, click the notifications flag in Server Manager and click "Promote this server to a domain controller (DC)," which starts the Active Directory Domain Services Configuration Wizard.

Note 1

On a Windows Server Core installation, the default Windows Server 2022 installation mode, you must use PowerShell to install AD DS.

In the Deployment Configuration window, you select from these options: Add a domain controller to an existing domain, Add a new domain to an existing forest, and Add a new forest (see Figure 2-6). For the first DC in the network, you should choose the option to Add a new forest. Next, you're prompted for the **fully qualified domain name (FQDN)** for the new forest root domain. An FQDN is a domain name that includes all parts of the name, including the top-level domain.

> **Note 2**
>
> The first domain in a new forest is also the name of the forest and is called the forest root. The wizard checks to be sure the forest name doesn't already exist.

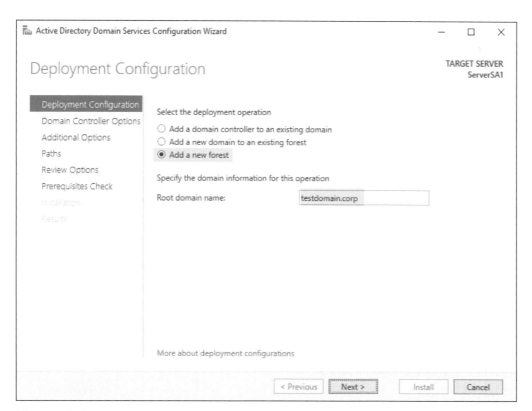

Figure 2-6 The Deployment Configuration window

The next window is Domain Controller Options, where you choose the forest and domain functional levels (see Figure 2-7). Microsoft has expanded Active Directory's functionality with each server OS since Windows 2000. For the most advanced features and security, you should choose the most current functional level, which is Windows Server 2016. For the most backward compatibility with older DCs on the network, you should choose Windows 2008 for the forest functional level. You can't choose a forest functional level earlier than Windows Server 2008. If you choose the Windows Server 2016 forest functional level, you can't run DCs that run an OS version earlier than Windows Server 2016. You can, however, still run older servers as member servers.

You have three options to specify capabilities for the DC:

- *Domain Name System (DNS) server*—For the first DC in a new domain, DNS should be installed unless you will be using an existing DNS server for the domain.
- *Global Catalog (GC)*—For the first DC in a forest, this check box is selected and disabled because the first DC in a new forest must also be a global catalog server.
- *Read only domain controller (RODC)*—This check box isn't selected by default. This option is disabled for the first DC in the domain because it can't be an RODC.

At the bottom of the window, you enter a password for **Directory Services Restore Mode (DSRM)**. This boot mode is used to perform restore operations on Active Directory if it becomes corrupted or parts of it are deleted accidentally.

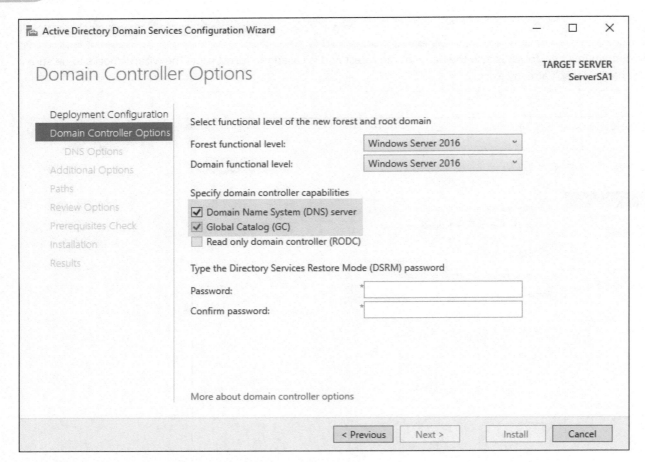

Figure 2-7 Choosing the forest and domain functional levels

The next window, DNS Options, prompts you to create DNS delegation if an existing DNS server for the domain exists, which allows Windows to create the necessary records on the DNS server for the new domain. You must enter valid credentials for the DNS server. If you are installing DNS and there are no other DNS servers for the domain, this option is disabled.

In the next window, Additional Options, you specify a NetBIOS domain name, which is used for backward compatibility with systems that don't use DNS. A default name is entered, but you can change it, if needed. The default name is the first eight characters of the domain name.

In the Paths window, you specify the location of the Active Directory database, log files, and SYSVOL folder (see Figure 2-8). The **SYSVOL folder** is a shared folder containing file-based information that's replicated to other domain controllers. Storing the database and log files on separate disks, if possible, is best for optimal performance. Next, you review your selections in the Review Options window. You can also view and export a PowerShell script with your settings if you want to duplicate them for another Active Directory configuration.

Windows then does a prerequisites check before starting the Active Directory installation and configuration (see Figure 2-9). This check notifies you of anything that could prevent successful installation and configuration of Active Directory. You are likely to see some warnings about some security settings and DNS delegation. You can probably ignore the warnings and continue. You want to locate the green check box at the bottom of the window, indicating that you can proceed. When the installation is finished, the server restarts. Server Manager then includes some new MMCs in the Tools menu for configuring and managing Active Directory.

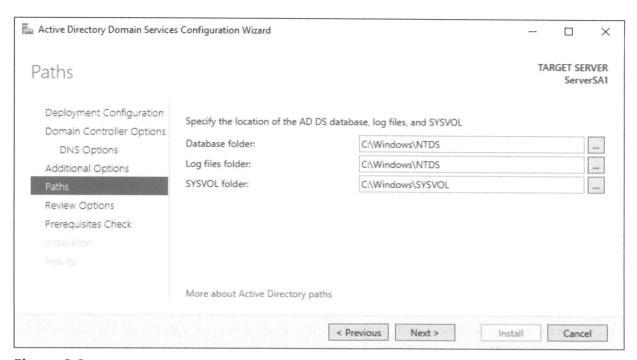

Figure 2-8   Specifying Active Directory paths

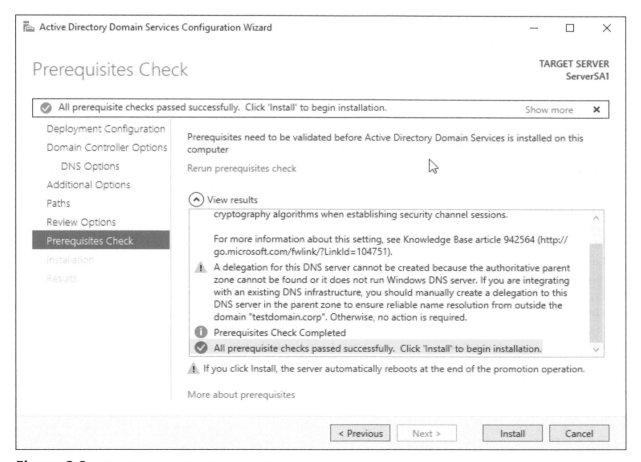

Figure 2-9   The Prerequisites Check window

Installing Additional Domain Controllers in a Domain

Microsoft recommends at least two domain controllers in every domain for fault tolerance and load balancing. Even the smallest domain should have two DCs because a domain controller can disrupt user access to network resources if no backup DC is available. In larger networks, a single DC can become so overwhelmed serving requests for network logons, resource access validation, and the myriad other tasks a DC performs that network performance degrades. Having multiple DCs helps spread the load.

The procedure for installing additional domain controllers in an existing domain is not unlike installing the first domain controller. The biggest difference is that you select the "Add a domain controller to an existing domain" option instead of the "Add a new forest" option. When a new DC is added to an existing domain, you need to know the answers to the following questions:

- *Should you install DNS?* Installing DNS is recommended if you're installing the second DC in a domain because fault tolerance is one reason to install another DC. You need at least two DNS servers as well as two DCs to achieve fault tolerance. If the DC is the only one at a remote site, DNS should also be installed. For DCs beyond the second, DNS installation is optional, and you must weigh the benefit of having an additional DNS server versus the additional load it places on the server.

- *Should the DC be a global catalog (GC) server?* The first DC is always configured as a GC server, but when you're installing additional DCs in a domain, this setting is optional. In most cases, it makes sense to make all your DCs global catalog servers as well, particularly in a single-domain forest. The global catalog and its importance in a network are discussed later in this module in the section titled "Working with Forests, Trees, and Domains."

- *Should this be a read-only domain controller (RODC)?* An RODC is most often used in branch office situations, where ensuring the server's physical security is more difficult. An RODC doesn't store account credentials, so if an RODC is compromised, no passwords can be retrieved. If the DC isn't at a branch office, there's no substantial advantage in making it an RODC.

- *In which site should the DC be located?* If you have more than one site defined for your network, you can choose where you want the DC to be located.

When you are installing an additional DC in a domain, you have the option to use a feature called Install from Media, which is discussed later in the section called "Installing a DC with Install from Media."

Installing a New Domain in an Existing Forest

Another reason to install a new DC is to add a domain to an existing forest. There are two variations to the procedure:

- *Add a child domain*—In this variation, you're adding a domain that shares at least the top-level and second-level domain name structure as an existing domain in the forest. For example, if your current domain is named csmtech.corp and you add a branch office in Europe, your new domain might be named europe.csmtech.corp. The new domain has a separate domain administrator, but the forest administrator has the authority to manage most aspects of both the child and parent domains. Figure 2-10 shows the window in the Active Directory installation where you choose to install a child domain. Notice that Child Domain is selected in the Select domain type list box. The other choice is Tree Domain, which is discussed next. The parent domain is the name of the existing domain you're creating a child domain for. In the figure, the existing domain is csmtech.corp. The new domain name is the name of the new child domain, which in this example is *europe*. The new domain has the FQDN europe.csmtech.corp. You must have the right credentials (a user who's a member of Domain Admins) for the csmtech.corp domain to perform the operation. The new DC must be able to contact a DC from the parent domain, so DNS must be configured correctly. All the other steps are the same as installing a DC in a new forest.

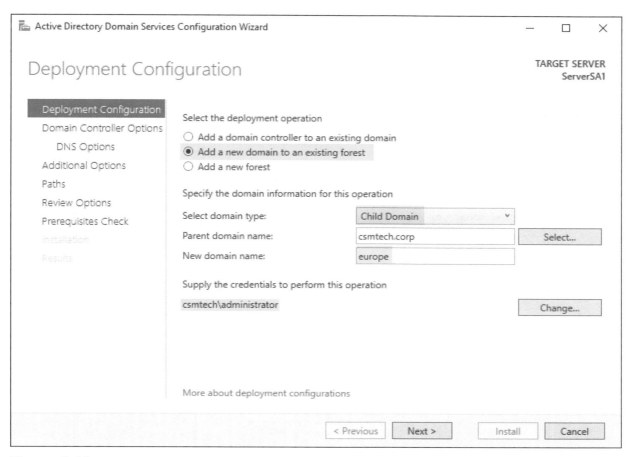

Figure 2-10   Adding a new child domain in an existing forest

- *Add a new tree*—In this variation, you're adding a new domain with a separate naming structure from any existing domains in the forest. So, in a forest named csmtech.corp, you can add a new domain (and therefore a new tree in the forest) named csmpub.corp. Operationally, a new tree is the same as a child domain. Figure 2-11 shows the window in the Active Directory installation where you choose to install a new tree, with Tree Domain selected as the domain type. You need to enter the name of the forest, which is always the name of the first domain installed when the forest was created (the forest root domain); in this example, it's csmtech.corp. As when adding a child domain, you need credentials to add the domain to the forest, but in this case, you need a user who's a member of Enterprise Admins and Schema Admins. The administrator account for the forest root domain is a member of both groups.

Working with multidomain forests and multiforest networks is an advanced topic. Some information you need to know is discussed later in this module in the section titled "Working with Forests, Trees, and Domains." This topic is covered in more detail in Module 5.

Installing Active Directory in Server Core

The preferred method of installing Active Directory in a Windows Server 2022 Server Core installation is to use the PowerShell cmdlets designed for this purpose. Installing Active Directory with PowerShell is a two-step process, just as it is when using Server Manager. First, you install the Active Directory Domain Services role, and then you promote the server to a DC by configuring Active Directory.

Note 3

For server administrators familiar with using `dcpromo.exe` along with an answer file, this option is still available. Just be aware that `dcpromo.exe` is a deprecated command and it may not be available in future Windows versions.

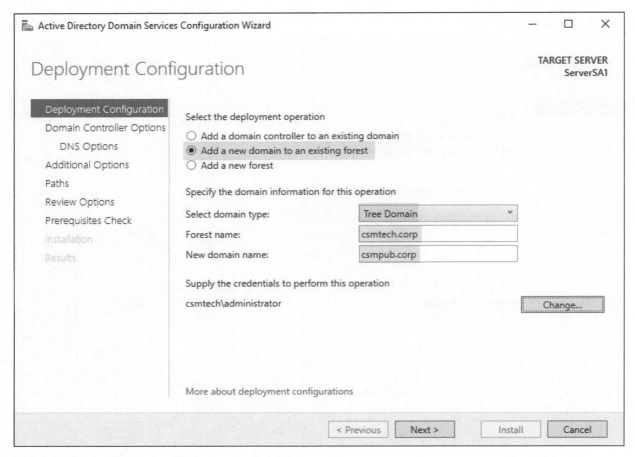

Figure 2-11   Adding a new tree in an existing forest

Use the following command to install the Active Directory Domain Services role, like any other server role:

```
Install-WindowsFeature AD-Domain-Services
```

If you're using PowerShell in a Desktop Experience installation, you should probably include the -IncludeManagementTools parameter in this command. In a Server Core installation, however, you can't use the management tools, because they require the graphical user interface. The preceding command prepares the server for promotion to a DC, but you must enter another command to start the promotion process. Which command you use depends on the type of installation you want:

- Install-ADDSForest—This command creates a new DC in a new forest. You must provide a domain name, which also serves as the forest name. So, for example, to create the csmtech.corp domain in a new forest, use the following command:

```
Install-ADDSForest -DomainName "csmtech.corp"
```

- Install-ADDSDomainController—This command adds a DC to an existing domain. You specify the name of the existing domain as shown:

```
Install-ADDSDomainController -DomainName "csmtech.corp"
```

- Install-ADDSDomain—This command adds a new domain to an existing forest. You need to specify the new domain name, the parent domain, and the type of domain (TreeDomain or ChildDomain). The default is ChildDomain. To add a domain named *europe* to the existing forest named csmtech.corp, use the following command:

```
Install-ADDSDomain -NewDomainName "europe" -ParentDomainName "csmtech.corp"
-DomainType ChildDomain
```

For the preceding commands, you need to specify credentials for an account with the necessary permissions to perform the installation. For each command, you can get detailed help in PowerShell with the Get-Help command, including examples of how to use the command. For instance, to get detailed help on using Install-ADDSDomain, including examples, use the following command:

```
Get-Help Install-ADDSDomain -detailed
```

If you want to see what a PowerShell cmdlet does without actually performing the operation, use the -WhatIf parameter. PowerShell displays the steps needed to perform the command, showing you the default settings and prompting you for other information the command requires.

Installing a DC with Install from Media

When you install a new DC in an existing domain, it must be updated with all existing data in the Active Directory database. Depending on the database's size and the new DC's location in relation to existing DCs, this process could take some time and use considerable bandwidth. If the new DC is the first in a branch office connected via a WAN, the time and bandwidth use might be a concern. Using the **Install from Media (IFM)** option during Active Directory configuration can substantially reduce the replication traffic needed to update the new DC. This utility copies the contents of an existing DC's Active Directory database (and optionally the SYSVOL folder) to disk. These contents are then used to populate the new DC's Active Directory database, thereby reducing the replication needed to bring the new DC's database up to date. The SYSVOL folder contains files that are also replicated, such as Group Policy files and logon scripts, so using IFM to copy SYSVOL can also reduce time and bandwidth consumption.

The procedure for using IFM is as follows:

1. Select a suitable DC from which you'll create the IFM data. If you're creating IFM data for a standard DC (a writeable DC, not an RODC), you must use a standard DC to create this data. If you're creating IFM data for an RODC, you can use an RODC or a standard DC.

2. On the selected DC, run the ntdsutil command-line program at an elevated command prompt. Ntdsutil is an interactive program in which you enter commands, as shown in Figure 2-12. These commands are explained in the following list:

```
C:\Windows\system32>ntdsutil
ntdsutil: activate instance ntds
Active instance set to "ntds".
ntdsutil: ifm
ifm: create full c:\IFMdata
Creating snapshot...
Snapshot set {d4ff2365-d3c2-4a5a-a2e1-4d5b83ca6ca8} generated successfully.
Snapshot {910b49ba-bbe9-4e66-bba9-f5d00e844ab6} mounted as C:\$SNAP_201701281813_VOLUMEC$\
Snapshot {910b49ba-bbe9-4e66-bba9-f5d00e844ab6} is already mounted.
Initiating DEFRAGMENTATION mode...
    Source Database: C:\$SNAP_201701281813_VOLUMEC$\Windows\NTDS\ntds.dit
    Target Database: c:\IFMdata\Active Directory\ntds.dit

              Defragmentation  Status (% complete)

        0    10   20   30   40   50   60   70   80   90   100
        |----|----|----|----|----|----|----|----|----|----|
        ...................................................

Copying registry files...
Copying c:\IFMdata\registry\SYSTEM
Copying c:\IFMdata\registry\SECURITY
Snapshot {910b49ba-bbe9-4e66-bba9-f5d00e844ab6} unmounted.
IFM media created successfully in c:\IFMdata
ifm: _
```

Figure 2-12   Creating IFM data with ntdsutil

- o `ntdsutil`—Starts the command-line program.
- o `activate instance ntds`—Sets the program focus on the Active Directory database.
- o `ifm`—Sets the program to IFM mode.

The next command creates the IFM data and has the following four variations. The `path` parameter specifies where to store IFM data and can be a local drive, a network share, or removable media. A network share is ideal so that the new DC has access to IFM data without having to copy data or transfer removable media. In addition, you can use the network share to create multiple DC installations easily.

- o `create full path`—Creates IFM data for a writeable DC.
- o `create RODC path`—Creates IFM data for an RODC.
- o `create Sysvol Full path`—Creates IFM data for a writeable DC and includes the SYSVOL folder.
- o `create Sysvol RODC path`—Creates IFM data for an RODC and includes the SYSVOL folder.

3. Install the new DC and select the IFM option. If you're using Server Manager, click the Install from media check box in the Additional Options window (see Figure 2-13) of the Active Directory Domain Services Configuration Wizard, and specify the path to the media. If you're using PowerShell, use the `-InstallationMediaPath` parameter and specify the path to the storage location.

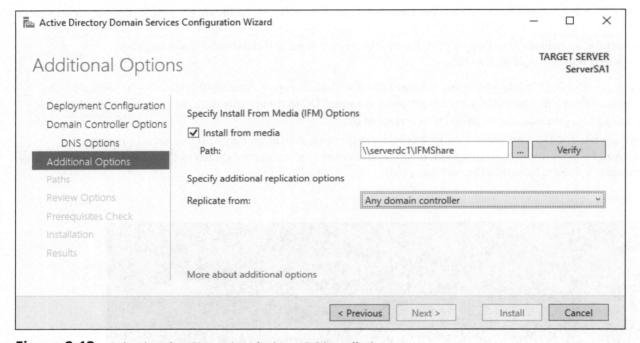

Figure 2-13 Selecting the IFM option during a DC installation

Self-Check Questions

3. When you install Active Directory on the first domain controller in the forest, which other server role should also be installed if it is not already installed on the network?

   a. DHCP

   b. File and Storage Services

   c. DNS Server

   d. ADFS

4. You have an Active Directory forest that consists of a single domain named mydomain.corp. You install Active Directory on another server and create a new domain in the mydomain.corp forest named anotherdomain.corp. Which of the following is true about anotherdomain.corp?

   a. It is the forest root.

   b. It is a new tree.

   c. It is a child domain.

   d. It holds the forest FSMO roles.

🔵 Check your answers at the end of this module.

Activity 2-1

Resetting Your Virtual Environment

Time Required: 5 minutes
Objective: Reset your virtual environment by applying the InitialConfig checkpoint or snapshot.
Required Tools and Equipment: ServerSA1
Description: Apply the InitialConfig checkpoint or snapshot to ServerSA1.

1. Be sure ServerSA1 is shut down. In your virtualization program, apply the InitialConfig checkpoint or snapshot to ServerSA1.
2. When the snapshot or checkpoint has been applied, continue to the next activity.

Activity 2-2

Installing Active Directory Domain Services

Time Required: 15 minutes
Objective: Install AD DS as a new domain controller in a new forest.
Required Tools and Equipment: ServerSA1
Description: You're ready to start working with Active Directory. This server will be the first DC in a new forest. In addition, you install the DNS Server role as part of the installation because DNS is required for Active Directory to function.

1. Start ServerSA1 and sign in as **Administrator**, if necessary.
2. Because this computer will be a domain controller and DNS server, you want to first change the DNS server address so that it references itself. You can do that with the Network Connections control panel or with Power-Shell. To use PowerShell, open a PowerShell window, type **Set-DnsClientServerAddress –InterfaceAlias Ethernet0 –ServerAddresses 127.0.0.1**, and press **Enter**. Close PowerShell. Note that your interface name may be different. To see your interface names, reopen PowerShell, type **Get-Netadapter**, and press **Enter**.
3. In Server Manager, click **Manage** and then click **Add Roles and Features**. The Before You Begin window warns you to be sure that the Administrator account has a strong password, your network settings are configured, and the latest security updates are installed. Click **Next**.
4. In the Installation Type window, click **Role-based or feature-based installation**, and then click **Next**.
5. In the Server Selection window, click **Next**.
6. In the Server Roles window, click the box next to **Active Directory Domain Services**. When you're prompted to add required features, click **Add Features**, and then click **Next**.
7. In the Features window, click **Next**. Read the information in the AD DS window, which explains that having two domain controllers is optimal and DNS must be installed on the network. Click **Next**.
8. In the Confirmation window, click **Install**.
9. The Results window shows the progress of the installation. When the installation is finished, click **Close**.
10. Click the **notifications flag**, and then click **Promote this server to a domain controller**. The Active Directory Services Configuration Wizard starts.
11. In the Deployment Configuration window, click the **Add a new forest** option button, type **TestDomain. corp** in the Root domain name text box, and then click **Next**. You will only use this domain for the purposes of installing and testing some features of Active Directory. It will not be used after this module.
12. In the Domain Controller Options window, verify that the forest and domain functional levels are set to **Windows Server 2016**. Under Specify domain controller capabilities, verify that the **Domain Name System (DNS) server** and **Global Catalog (GC)** check boxes are selected. The Global Catalog (GC) option is always selected for the first DC in a forest and cannot be changed. Notice that the Read only domain controller (RODC) option isn't available because the first DC in a new forest can't be an RODC.

(continues)

Activity 2-2 Continued

13. In the Directory Services Restore Mode (DSRM) password section, type **Password01** in the Password and Confirm password text boxes. You can use a password that's different from the Administrator password if you want, but for this activity, use the same password so that it's easier to remember. Click **Next**.

14. In the DNS Options window, the **Create DNS delegation** check box is disabled because there is no DNS server currently available for the domain. DNS will be installed as part of the AD DS installation. Click **Next**.

15. In the Additional Options window, leave the default NETBIOS domain name as it is. (It may take a few seconds before you see the name.) Click **Next**.

16. In the Paths window, you can choose locations for the database folder, log files, and SYSVOL folder. Specifying different disks for the database and log files is ideal, but leave the default settings for now. Click **Next**.

17. Review your choices in the Review Options window, and go back and make changes if necessary. You can export your options to a Windows PowerShell script by clicking the View script button and saving the resulting text file with a `.ps1` extension; you can then run this file at a PowerShell prompt. To see the script that is created, click **View script**. The list of cmdlets is opened in a Notepad file. Review the script and then close Notepad. Click **Next**.

18. In the Prerequisites Check window, Windows verifies that all conditions for installing Active Directory successfully have been met. If all prerequisites have been met, a green circle with a check is displayed at the top of the window. If they haven't been met, Windows displays a list of problems you must correct before installing Active Directory. You may see some warnings, but these are likely okay. Click **Install**. Watch the messages under Progress and note the steps Windows performs to install Active Directory. After the installation is finished, your computer restarts automatically.

19. After the server restarts, sign in as **Administrator**. (Note that you're now logging on to the TestDomain. corp domain.) In Server Manager, click **Local Server** and verify the domain information shown under Computer name.

20. Click **Tools**. Note the new MMCs that have been added: Active Directory Administrative Center, Active Directory Domains and Trusts, Active Directory Module for Windows PowerShell, Active Directory Sites and Services, Active Directory Users and Computers, ADSI Edit, and DNS.

21. Stay signed in and continue to the next activity.

What's Inside Active Directory?

Microsoft Exam AZ-800:

Deploy and manage Active Directory Domain Services (AD DS) in on-premises and cloud environments.
- Create and manage AD DS security principals
- Deploy and manage AD DS domain controllers

After Active Directory is installed, you can explore it by using the Active Directory Administrative Center (ADAC) or Active Directory Users and Computers MMC; several PowerShell cmdlets are also available for working with Active Directory. ADAC, shown in Figure 2-14, is a central console for performing many Active Directory tasks, including creating and managing user, group, and computer accounts; managing OUs; and connecting to other domain controllers in the same domain or a different domain. You can also change the domain's functional level and enable the Active Directory Recycle Bin.

ADAC is built on PowerShell, so each command you use in ADAC issues a PowerShell command to perform the task. You can take advantage of this feature by using the Windows PowerShell History pane in ADAC (highlighted in Figure 2-15). This pane shows a list of commands generated by creating a new user named Test User. These commands can be copied and edited to make a PowerShell script so that you can handle tasks such as creating users and adding users to groups by running a PowerShell script instead of using the GUI or typing PowerShell commands.

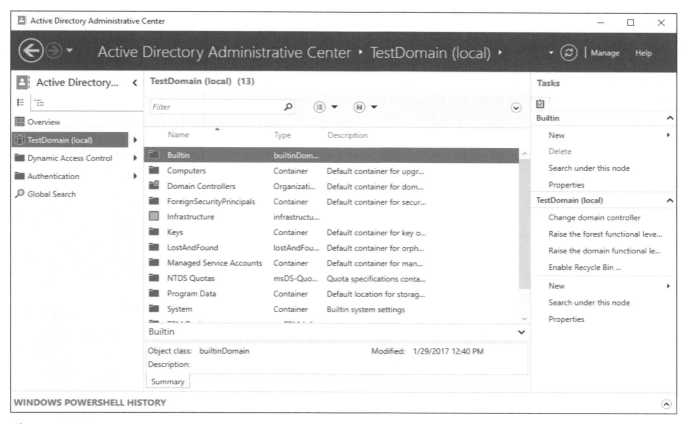

Figure 2-14   Active Directory Administrative Center

Figure 2-15   Viewing the PowerShell history

Active Directory Users and Computers (ADUC) is probably the most popular GUI tool among administrators. As shown in Figure 2-16, Active Directory Users and Computers has two panes. In the left pane, the top node shows the server and domain being managed. The Saved Queries folder contains a list of Active Directory queries you can save to repeat Active Directory searches easily. The third node represents the domain and contains all the objects that make up the domain. In Figure 2-16, the domain being managed is TestDomain.corp. In this figure, the Users container is open, and objects in this container are displayed in the right pane.

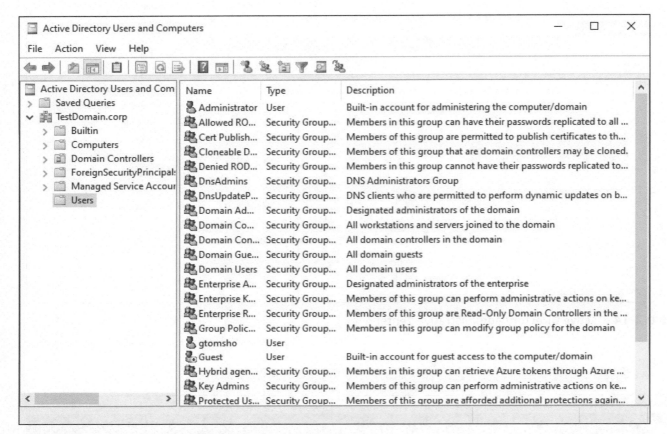

Figure 2-16   Active Directory Users and Computers

Before you continue working with Active Directory, knowing something about the information you find in the database is helpful. Active Directory's contents and the functions it performs in your network are defined by the schema, objects, and Group Policy Objects (GPOs, as discussed later in the "Introducing Group Policies" section).

The Active Directory Schema

All information in the Active Directory database is organized as objects. An Active Directory **object** is a grouping of information that describes a network resource, such as a shared printer; an organizing structure, such as a domain or OU; or an account, such as a user, group, or computer. The **schema** defines the type, organization, and structure of data stored in the Active Directory database and is shared by all domains in an Active Directory forest. The information the schema defines is divided into two categories: schema classes and schema attributes. **Schema classes** define the types of objects that can be stored in Active Directory, such as user or computer accounts. **Schema attributes** define what type of information is stored in each object, such as first name, last name, and password for a user account object. The information stored in each attribute, such as "Mary" in the first name attribute, is called the **attribute value**.

Figure 2-17 shows the relationship between schema classes, attributes, and Active Directory objects. As you can see, some schema attributes, such as the Description attribute used for both objects, can be shared by more than one Active Directory object. When Active Directory is first installed, a default schema describes all available default objects, but you can extend this schema to add attributes to existing object classes or create new object classes.

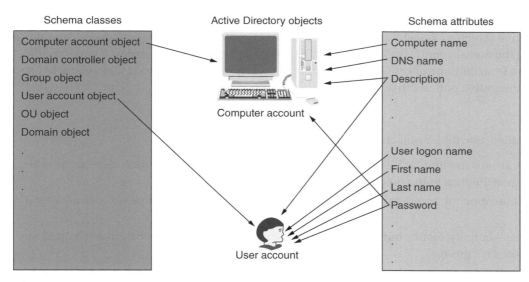

Figure 2-17   Schema classes, schema attributes, and Active Directory objects

This discussion of Active Directory refers to several different object classes in Active Directory. Figure 2-18 shows object classes and their associated icons in Active Directory Users and Computers. Active Directory objects can be organized into two basic groups, as discussed in the next sections: container objects and leaf objects. Similar icons are used in ADAC but are black and white.

Figure 2-18   Icons used to represent Active Directory objects

Active Directory Container Objects

A container object, as the name implies, contains other objects. Container objects are used to organize and manage users and resources in a network. They can also act as administrative and security boundaries or a way to group objects for applying policies. Three container objects, explained in the following sections, are found in Active Directory: OU, folder, and domain.

Organizational Units

An OU is the primary container object for organizing and managing resources in a domain. Administrators can use OUs to organize objects into logical administrative groups, which makes it possible to apply policies to the OU that affect all objects in it. For example, you could apply a policy that prohibits access to Control Panel for all users in an OU. In addition, you can delegate administrative authority for an OU to a user, thereby allowing the user to manage objects in the OU without giving the user wider authority. Object types typically found in an OU include user accounts, group accounts, computer accounts, shared folders, shared printers, published applications, and other OUs. By nesting OUs, administrators can build a hierarchical Active Directory structure that mimics the corporate structure for easier object management.

In Active Directory Users and Computers, an OU is represented by a folder with a book inside, as shown previously in Figure 2-18. When Active Directory is installed, a single OU called Domain Controllers is created; it contains a computer object representing the domain controller. When a new DC is installed in the domain, a new computer object representing it is placed in the Domain Controllers OU by default. A GPO is linked to the Domain Controllers OU and used to set security and administrative policies that apply to all DCs in the domain.

Folder Objects

When Active Directory is installed, five folder objects are created:

- *Builtin*—Houses default groups created by Windows and is mainly used to assign permissions to users who have administrative responsibilities in the domain.
- *Computers*—The default location for computer accounts created when a new computer or server becomes a domain member.
- *ForeignSecurityPrincipals*—Initially empty but later contains user accounts from other domains added as members of the local domain's groups.
- *Managed Service Accounts*—Added to the schema in Windows Server 2008 R2; created specifically for services to access domain resources. In this type of account, the password is managed by the system, alleviating the administrator of this task. This folder is empty initially.
- *Users*—Stores two default users (Administrator and Guest) and several default groups.

These folder objects are represented in Active Directory Users and Computers with the folder icon shown previously in Figure 2-18. You can't create new folder objects, nor can you apply group policies to folder objects. You can delegate administrative control on all folders but the Builtin folder. All objects in a folder are subject to group policies defined at the domain level. You can move objects from the default folders (except the Builtin folder) into OUs you have created. For example, because all computer accounts are created in the Computers folder by default, they're subject to the same policies defined at the domain level. If you want to apply different policies to different computers in your domain, you create one or more OUs, move the computer accounts to the new OUs, and apply group policies to these OUs.

Domain Objects

The domain is the core logical structure container in Active Directory. Domains contain OU and folder container objects but can also contain leaf objects, such as users and groups. A domain typically reflects the organization of the company in which Active Directory is being used, but in large or geographically dispersed organizations, you can create multiple domains, each representing a business unit or location. The main reasons for using multiple domains are to allow separate administration and define policy boundaries. Each domain object has a default GPO linked to it that can affect all objects in the domain. The domain object in Active Directory Users and Computers is represented by an icon with three tower computers (refer back to Figure 2-18).

Active Directory Leaf Objects

A **leaf object** doesn't contain other objects and usually represents a security account, network resource, or GPO. Security account objects include users, groups, and computers. Network resource objects include servers, domain controllers, file shares, and printers. GPOs aren't viewed as objects in the same way as other Active Directory objects. GPOs are managed by the Group Policy Management MMC, as discussed later. The following paragraphs explain some common leaf objects in Active Directory.

User Accounts

A user account object contains information about a network user. Typically, when a user account is created, the administrator enters at least the user's name, logon name, and password. However, the user account object contains much more information, such as group memberships, account restrictions (allowed logon hours and account expiration date, for example), profile path, and dial-in permissions. In addition, administrators can fill in descriptive fields, such as office location, job title, and department. The main purpose of a user account is to allow a user to sign in to a Windows computer or an Active Directory domain to access computer and domain resources. By supplying a user logon name and password, a user is authenticated on the computer or network. **Authentication** confirms a user's identity, and the account is then assigned permissions and rights that authorize the user to access resources and perform certain tasks on the computer or domain.

Active Directory defines three user account types: local user accounts, domain user accounts, and built-in user accounts. A **local user account** is authorized to access resources only on that computer. Local user accounts are mainly used on standalone computers or in a workgroup network with computers that aren't part of an Active Directory domain. Local user accounts aren't defined on domain controllers but can be created on domain member computers. A **domain user account** created in Active Directory provides a single logon for users to access all resources in the domain they're authorized for.

Windows creates two **built-in user accounts** automatically: Administrator and Guest. They can be local user accounts or domain user accounts, depending on the computer where they're created. On a workgroup or standalone Windows computer, these two accounts are created when Windows is installed, and they're local accounts that have access to resources only on the local computer. When Active Directory is installed, these two accounts are converted from local user accounts to domain user accounts. User accounts are discussed in more detail in Module 3.

Groups

A group object represents a collection of users with common permissions or rights requirements on a computer or domain. **Permissions** define which resources users can access and what level of access they have. For example, a user might have permission to open and read a certain document but not to change it. A **right** specifies what types of actions a user can perform on a computer or network. For example, a user might have the right to sign in to and sign out of a computer but not shut down the computer. Groups are used to assign members permissions and rights. This method is more efficient than assigning permissions and rights to each user account separately because you have to perform the assignment task only once, and it applies to all accounts that are members of the group. For example, if all users in the Accounting Department need access to a shared folder, you can create a group containing all users in this department as members and assign permission to access the shared folder to the group as a whole. In addition, if a user leaves the department, you can remove his or her account as a group member, and the user loses all rights and permissions assigned to this group. Groups are explained in more detail in Module 3.

Computer Accounts

A computer account object represents a computer that's a domain controller or domain member and is used to identify, authenticate, and manage computers in the domain. Computer accounts are created automatically when Active Directory is installed on a server or when a server or workstation becomes a domain member. Administrators can also create computer accounts manually if they don't want to allow automatic account creation. By default, domain controller computer accounts are placed in the Domain Controllers OU, and domain member computer accounts are placed in the Computers folder.

The computer account object's name must match the name of the computer that the account represents. Like user accounts, computer accounts have a logon name and password, but a computer account password is managed by Active Directory instead of an administrator. A computer must have a computer account in Active Directory for users to sign in to it with their domain user accounts. You learn about managing computer accounts in Module 3.

Other Leaf Objects

The following list describes other leaf objects that are commonly created in Active Directory:

- *Contact*—A person who is associated with the company but is not a network user. You can think of a contact object as simply being an entry in an address book, used purely for informational purposes.
- *Printer*—Represents a shared printer in the domain. Printers shared on Windows computers that are domain members can be added to Active Directory automatically. If a printer is shared on a nondomain member, you must create the printer object manually and specify the path to the shared printer.
- *Shared folder*—Represents a shared folder on a computer in the network. Shared folder objects can be added to Active Directory manually or by using the publish option when creating a shared folder with the Shared Folders MMC snap-in.

Both printer and shared folder objects enable users to access shared printers and folders on any computer in the domain without knowing exactly which computer the resource was created on. Users can simply do a search in Active Directory to find the type of resource they want. In a large network, shared printers and folders could be located on any one of dozens or hundreds of servers. Publishing these resources in Active Directory makes access to them easier.

> **Note 4**
>
> There are other leaf objects, but the previous sections cover the most common leaf objects you find in Active Directory.

Recovering Objects with the Active Directory Recycle Bin

Working with Active Directory objects is usually straightforward, but what happens if you delete an object by mistake? There's no undo feature, as in word processors, image editors, and other tools you use to create, modify, and delete things. Before Windows Server 2008 R2, the procedure for recovering deleted objects in Active Directory was laborious and required cumbersome command-line syntax. Even worse, the domain controller the object was deleted from had to be taken offline. In Windows Server 2008 R2, Microsoft introduced the Active Directory Recycle Bin to allow easy restoration of deleted objects. Before you see this feature in action, you should be aware of the following:

- Active Directory Recycle Bin is disabled by default; it can be enabled in Active Directory Administrative Center (ADAC).
- After it's enabled, the Recycle Bin can't be disabled without reinstalling all domain controllers in the forest.
- To use the Recycle Bin, all DCs in the forest must be running Windows Server 2008 R2 or later, and the forest functional level must be at least Windows Server 2008 R2.

To enable the Recycle Bin, open ADAC, click the domain node in the left pane, and in the Tasks pane, click Enable Recycle Bin. Click OK in the warning message stating that the Recycle Bin can't be disabled after you enable it. You see a message that the Recycle Bin is being enabled and won't function reliably until all DCs are updated with the change. You need to refresh ADAC to see the new container named Deleted Objects added under the domain node. The Recycle Bin can also be enabled using PowerShell. For example, to enable the Recycle Bin for the TestDomain. corp domain, use the following cmdlet:

```
Enable-ADOptionalFeature –Identity 'CN=Recycle Bin Feature,CN=Optional
Features,CN=Directory Service,CN=Windows NT, CN=Services, CN=Configuration,
DC=TestDomain,DC=local' –Scope ForestOrConfigurationSet –Target 'TestDomain.corp'
```

To undelete an object using ADAC, double-click the Deleted Objects container. All objects that have been deleted since the Recycle Bin was enabled are listed. To restore an object, right-click it and choose one of the following options from the menu: Restore, which restores the object to its original container if it's still available; or Restore To, which restores the object to a container you select. To restore a deleted object using PowerShell, you use a combination of the Get-ADObject and Restore-ADObject cmdlets. For example, if you want to restore a user object named TestUser, use the following cmdlet:

```
Get-ADObject –Filter {displayName –eq "TestUser"} –IncludeDeletedObjects |
Restore-ADObject
```

Locating Active Directory Objects

In a large Active Directory environment with hundreds or thousands of users, groups, computers, and other domain objects, locating objects can be difficult for administrators and users alike. Luckily, Active Directory Users and Computers has a search function for administrators, and File Explorer incorporates an Active Directory search function for users.

You search for Active Directory objects by first selecting the type of object you're searching for. For example, you can search for users, contacts, groups, computers, printers, and shared folders. In a multidomain environment, you can search in a single domain or in the entire directory (all domains). You can also limit your search to a folder or an OU in a domain. The Find dialog box shown in Figure 2-19 is identical whether you're searching for objects with Active Directory Users and Computers or File Explorer. However, not all objects are available to all users, depending on the object's security settings and its container.

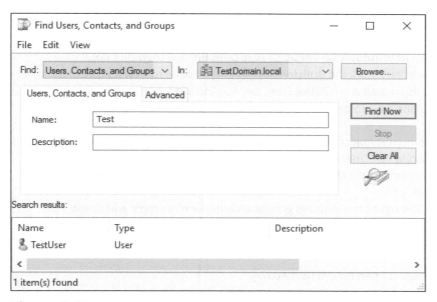

Figure 2-19   The Find Users, Contacts, and Groups dialog box

Now that you've gotten your feet wet using Active Directory, it's time to delve into some details of how Active Directory is structured and how it functions. The next section discusses working with forests, trees, and domains and describes how information from one DC is transferred (replicated) to another DC.

Self-Check Questions

5.   Which Active Directory management tool is built on PowerShell?

 a. Active Directory Users and Computers   **c.** Active Directory Administrative Center

 b. Active Directory Sites and Services   **d.** Group Policy Management Center

6.   Which of the following is the name of a default organizational unit?

 a. Computers   **c.** Builtin

 b. Users   **d.** Domain Controllers

◉ Check your answers at the end of this module.

Activity 2-3

Exploring Active Directory Container Objects

Time Required: 10 minutes
Objective: Locate and identify Active Directory container objects.
Required Tools and Equipment: ServerSA1
Description: After installing Active Directory, you want to view its structure by exploring the default container objects in Active Directory Users and Computers.

1. Sign in to ServerSA1 as **Administrator**.
2. In Server Manager, open Active Directory Users and Computers by clicking **Tools** and selecting **Active Directory Users and Computers** from the menu.
3. Click the domain object (**TestDomain.corp**) in the left pane.
4. Right-click the **TestDomain.corp** object and click **Properties**. Click the **General** tab, if necessary, and verify that both the domain and forest functional levels are Windows Server 2022.

(continues)

Activity 2-3 Continued

5. Enter a description for the domain, such as **Windows Server 2022 Test Domain**, and then click **OK**.
6. Click to expand the domain node, if necessary. Click the **Builtin** folder in the left pane to view its contents in the right pane: a list of group accounts created when Active Directory was installed.
7. Click the **Computers** folder in the left pane. This folder is empty. It will contain the accounts of computers that are joined to the domain.
8. Click the **Domain Controllers** OU. A computer object representing the domain controller is displayed in the right pane. The DC Type column displays GC, meaning the domain controller is a global catalog server. If more servers are added to the domain as domain controllers, the computer accounts will be added here.
9. Click the **Users** folder in the left pane. The right pane displays groups and the Administrator and Guest user accounts that are created by default. Notice that the Guest account has a down arrow, which means the account is disabled. This folder also contains any user accounts that were created before the computer was promoted to a DC.
10. Leave Active Directory Users and Computers open for the next activity.

Activity 2-4

Viewing Default Leaf Objects

Time Required: 15 minutes
Objective: Review the properties of a variety of leaf objects.
Required Tools and Equipment: ServerSA1
Description: You want to learn more about Active Directory objects, so you view the properties of several default leaf objects.

1. If necessary, sign in to ServerSA1 as **Administrator**, and then open Active Directory Users and Computers.
2. In the left pane of Active Directory Users and Computers, click the **Builtin** folder.
3. In the right pane, right-click the **Administrators** group and click **Properties** (or double-click the **Administrators** group).
4. On the General tab, notice that the option buttons under Group scope and Group type are disabled because you can't change this information for built-in groups.
5. Click the **Members** tab. You should see one user and two groups listed as members (see Figure 2-20). The Name column displays the name of the user or group member, and the Active Directory Domain Services Folder column displays the domain and folder or OU where the member is located. Groups can be nested, as shown; the Domain Admins and Enterprise Admins groups are members of the Administrators group.
6. Click the **Member Of** tab. Because built-in groups can't be members of any other group, the Add and Remove buttons are disabled.
7. Click the **Managed By** tab. An administrator can specify another user or group that has the right to manage this group. Click **Cancel**.

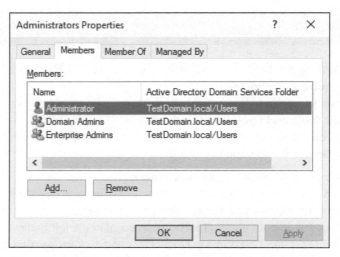

Figure 2-20   Viewing properties of the Administrators group

(continues)

Activity 2-4 Continued

8. In the left pane of Active Directory Users and Computers, click the **Domain Controllers** OU. Double-click the **ServerSA1** computer object in the right pane to open its Properties dialog box.

9. If necessary, click the **General** tab. Notice that only the Description text box can be changed for this object.

10. Click the **Operating System** tab, which displays the name, version, and service pack (if any) installed on the computer this computer object represents.

11. Click the **Member Of** tab. Because this computer object represents a domain controller, it's a member of the Domain Controllers group. (If this computer object represented a domain member, it would be a member of the Domain Computers group.) Click **Cancel**.

12. In the left pane of Active Directory Users and Computers, click the **Users** folder. Double-click the **Administrator** user to open its Properties dialog box.

13. The information on the General tab is optional for user accounts but can be used as part of an employee directory. Type your first name and last name in the corresponding text boxes.

14. Click the **Account** tab. Here you can specify the user logon name, logon restrictions, and account options.

15. Click the **Member Of** tab. Note the groups the Administrator account belongs to, and then click **OK**.

16. Find the Guest user and notice the down arrow on its icon, indicating that it's disabled. Double-click the **Guest** user to open its Properties dialog box.

17. Click the **Account** tab. In the Account options list box, scroll down to view the available account options. You see the Account is disabled option is checked. It's disabled by default because it's created with a blank password, which can pose a security risk. Click **Cancel**.

18. Leave Active Directory Users and Computers open for the next activity.

Activity 2-5

Creating Objects in Active Directory

Time Required: 15 minutes
Objective: Create an OU and add some objects to it.
Required Tools and Equipment: ServerSA1
Description: You want to learn more about Active Directory objects, so you create an OU and add a user object and a group object.

1. If necessary, sign in to ServerSA1 as **Administrator**, and then open Active Directory Users and Computers.

2. Right-click the domain node, point to **New**, and click **Organizational Unit**. In the Name text box, type **TestOU1**. Click to clear the **Protect container from accidental deletion** check box, and then click **OK**.

3. Make sure **TestOU1** is selected in the left pane, and then right-click in the right pane, point to **New**, and click **User** to start the New Object – User Wizard.

4. In the First name text box, type **Test**, and in the Last name text box, type **User1**. Notice that the "Full name" text box is filled in automatically.

5. In the User logon name text box, type **testuser1**. The User logon name (pre-Windows 2000) text box is filled in automatically. (A user logon name longer than 20 characters is truncated to 20 characters in this text box.)

(continues)

Activity 2-5 Continued

6. Click **Next**. In the Password text box, type **mypassword**, and type it again in the Confirm password text box. Click to clear the **User must change password at next logon** check box. Click **Next**, and then click **Finish**. You'll see an error message, but go on to the next step.

7. Read the error message carefully. By default, Windows Server 2022 requires a complex password, meaning one of a minimum length of 7 characters, with at least three characters of the following types: uppercase letters, lowercase letters, numbers, and special symbols (such as # and ?). Click **OK**.

8. In the New Object – User window, click **Back**. In the Password text box, type **Password01**, making sure the P is capitalized and the last two characters are the numbers 0 and 1. Retype the password in the Confirm password text box. Click **Next**, and then click **Finish**.

9. Right-click in the right pane of Active Directory Users and Computers, point to **New**, and click **Group**.

10. Type **TestGroup1** in the Group name text box (see Figure 2-21). Verify that the Group scope setting is **Global** and the Group type setting is **Security**, and then click **OK**.

11. Double-click **Test User1** to open its Properties dialog box, and click the **Member Of** tab. This user account is already a member of the Domain Users group; all new users are members of this group by default.

12. Click the **Add** button to open the Select Groups dialog box. In the "Enter the object names to select" text box, type **TestGroup1**, and then click the **Check Names** button. Active Directory verifies that the group name you entered exists and underlines the name (see Figure 2-22). If the group doesn't exist, a Name Not Found message box is displayed, where you can correct the group name. Click **OK**, and then click **OK** again.

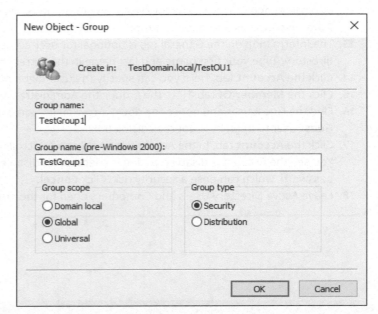

Figure 2-21   Creating a group

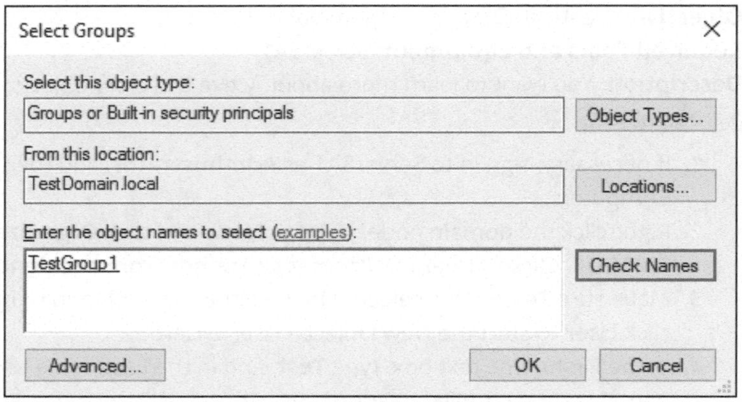

13. Double-click **TestGroup1** to open its Properties dialog box. Click the **Members** tab to verify that Test User1 has been added as a member. Users can be added to groups in the Member Of tab of the user account's Properties dialog box or the Members tab of the group's Properties dialog box. Click **Cancel**.

14. Close Active Directory Users and Computers but stay signed in if you're continuing to the next activity.

Figure 2-22   The Select Groups dialog box

Note 5

Active Directory Users and Computers is a straightforward, easy-to-use tool for managing Active Directory objects, but not every administrator wants to use a graphical utility to create and modify Active Directory objects. Using command-line tools is sometimes easier or even necessary. Although this topic is explored more thoroughly in Module 3, the following activity introduces you to the `dsadd` command-line tool for creating objects in Active Directory and shows you how to use the `New-ADUser` PowerShell cmdlet.

Activity 2-6

Using the Command Line to Create Users

Time Required: 10 minutes
Objective: Create and modify user accounts with command-line tools.
Required Tools and Equipment: ServerSA1
Description: In this activity, you create and modify users using the `dsadd` and `dsmod` command-line tools and PowerShell cmdlets.

1. Sign in to ServerSA1 as **Administrator**, if necessary, and open a command prompt window by right-clicking **Start** and clicking **Command Prompt**.
2. At the command prompt, type **dsadd user "cn=Test User2, ou=TestOU1, dc=TestDomain, dc=corp"** and press **Enter**. This command creates a user named Test User2 and places the user in TestOU1. If you get a response other than "dsadd succeeded: cn=Test User2, ou=TestOU1, dc=TestDomain, dc=corp," check the command for typos and try again.
3. The account you just created is disabled because no password was assigned. You could have assigned a password in the `dsadd` command, but you can also do it with the `dsmod` command. Type **dsmod user "cn=Test User2, ou=TestOU1, dc=TestDomain,dc=corp" –pwd "Password01" –disabled no** and press **Enter**. This command sets the password and enables the account. You can use an asterisk (*) instead of the password; if so, Windows will prompt you to enter a password.
4. To create a user using PowerShell, open a PowerShell window, type **New-ADUser TestUser3**, and press **Enter**. This command creates a new user account and places it in the Users folder. To create a user and place it in the TestOU1 OU, type **New-ADUser TestUser4 –Path "OU=TestOU1, DC=TestDomain, DC=corp"** and press **Enter.**
5. To set the password for TestUser3, type **Set-ADAccountPassword TestUser3** and press **Enter**. You are prompted to enter the current password, so just press **Enter**. You are prompted for the new password, so type **Password01** and press **Enter**. Type **Password01** again and press **Enter**.
6. To enable the TestUser3 account, type **Enable-ADAccount TestUser3** and press **Enter**.
7. Repeat Steps 5 and 6, substituting TestUser4 for TestUser3.
8. Close the command prompt and PowerShell windows.

Activity 2-7

Locating Objects in Active Directory

Time Required: 5 minutes
Objective: Locate user and group objects in Active Directory.
Required Tools and Equipment: ServerSA1
Description: In this activity, you use the search feature in Active Directory Users and Computers and then in File Explorer.

1. If necessary, sign in to ServerSA1 as **Administrator**, and then open Active Directory Users and Computers.
2. Right-click the domain node in the left pane and click **Find**.

(continues)

Activity 2-7 Continued

3. Click the **Find** list arrow and verify that **Users, Contacts, and Groups** is selected. In the In text box, make sure TestDomain.corp is selected. You could click Find Now, but if you do, all users, contacts, and groups in the entire domain are displayed. You want to narrow down the choices first.

4. In the Name text box, type **test**. By specifying this name, all users, groups, and contacts starting with "test" are displayed. Click the **Find Now** button. You should see results similar to those in Figure 2-23.

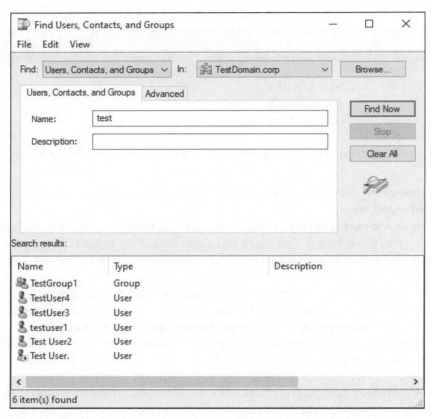

Figure 2-23   Results from an Active Directory find operation

5. In the Search results section, you can double-click any entry to access its properties. Close the Find Users, Contacts, and Groups dialog box and close Active Directory Users and Computers.

6. Open File Explorer, and click **Network** in the left pane.

7. Click **Network** and then click **Search Active Directory** to open the Find Users, Contacts, and Groups dialog box. It's the same as the one in Figure 2-23, shown previously. By default, Entire Directory is set as the search scope.

> ### Note ⑥
> If the Search Active Directory icon is disabled, your network connection did not recognize that it is in a domain. To resolve the problem, open Network Connections, disable the Ethernet interface, and re-enable it. It should show the network as TestDomain.corp. Close File Explorer, open it again, and try Step 7 again.

8. In the Find drop-down list, click **Computers**. In the Role drop-down list, click **All Active Directory Domain Controllers** to specify that you want to search only for computers that are domain controllers.

9. Click the **Find Now** button. You should see ServerSA1 in the search results.

10. Close any windows you opened for this activity and continue to the next activity.

Activity 2-8

Publishing a Shared Folder in Active Directory

Time Required: 25 minutes

Objective: Publish a shared folder in Active Directory and then find the folder.

Required Tools and Equipment: ServerSA1

Description: In this activity, you create a shared folder and then publish it in Active Directory. Then you use the find feature in File Explorer to locate the shared folder in Active Directory.

1. Sign in to ServerSA1 as **Administrator**, if necessary.
2. Open File Explorer. Create a folder named **PubShare** in the root of the C: drive.
3. Share this folder with simple file sharing, giving the Everyone group **Read** permission and leaving the Administrator and Administrators accounts with the default permissions. Close File Explorer.
4. Right-click **Start** and click **Computer Management**. Click to expand the **Shared Folders** node, and then click the **Shares** folder.
5. In the right pane, double-click **PubShare** to open its Properties dialog box. Click the **Publish** tab, and then click the **Publish this share in Active Directory** check box (see Figure 2-24).

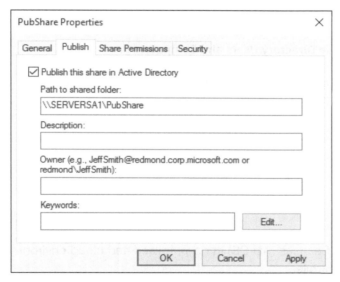

Figure 2-24   The Publish tab of a shared folder's Properties dialog box

6. In the Description text box, type A share to test publishing in Active Directory.
7. Click the **Edit** button. In the Edit Keywords dialog box, type **testing**, and then click **Add**. Click **OK** twice.
8. Close Computer Management. Open File Explorer, and click **Network**.
9. Click Network, and then click Search Active Directory.
10. In the Find drop-down list, click **Shared Folders**. In the Keywords text box, type **test**, and then click **Find Now**.
11. In the Search results section, right-click **PubShare** and click **Explore**. A File Explorer window opens, showing the contents of the PubShare shared folder. It's currently empty.
12. Close the File Explorer and Find Shared Folders windows. Open Active Directory Users and Computers.
13. When you publish a shared folder or printer, the published share appears as a child object of the server where the share is located. To view child objects of servers, click **View**, **Users, Contacts, Groups, and Computers as containers** from the menu.

(continues)

Activity 2-8 Continued

14. Click to expand the **Domain Controllers** OU, and then click the server icon. You see the share you published in the right pane (see Figure 2-25).

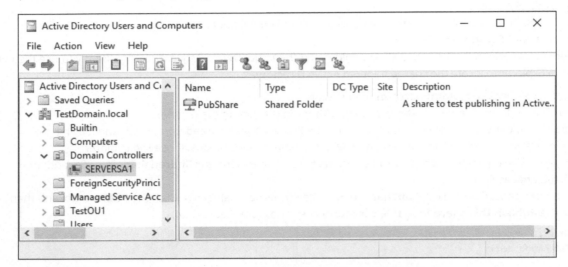

Figure 2-25   A published share in Active Directory Users and Computers

15. Click **View**, **Users, Contacts, Groups, and Computers as containers** from the menu again to disable this feature, and then close Active Directory Users and Computers.

16. Continue to the next activity.

Working with Forests, Trees, and Domains

> **Microsoft Exam AZ-800:**
> Deploy and manage Active Directory Domain Services (AD DS) in on-premises and cloud environments.
> - Deploy and manage AD DS domain controllers
> - Configure and manage multisite, multidomain, and multiforest environments

In the day-to-day administration of an Active Directory domain, most administrators focus on OUs and their child objects. In a small organization, a solid understanding of OUs and leaf objects might be all that's needed to manage a Windows domain successfully. However, in large organizations, it might be necessary to build an Active Directory structure composed of several domains, multiple trees, and even a few forests.

When the first DC is installed in a network, the structure you see in Active Directory Users and Computers—a domain object and some folder and OU containers—isn't all that's created. In addition, a new tree and the root of a new forest are created, along with elements that define a new site. As a business grows or converts an existing network structure to Active Directory, there might be reasons to add domains to the tree, create new trees or forests, and add sites to the Active Directory structure. This section starts by describing some helpful terms for understanding how Active Directory operates and is organized. Next, you learn the forest's role in Active Directory and how to use multiple forests in an Active Directory structure. Then you examine trust relationships and domains, particularly in situations involving multiple domains and multiple trees.

Active Directory Terminology

A number of terms are used to describe Active Directory's structure and operations. In the following sections, you examine terms associated with replication, directory partitions, operations masters, and trust relationships. Although these terms are introduced in this module, many of them are explored in more depth in later modules of this book.

Active Directory Replication

Replication is the process of maintaining a consistent database of information when the database is distributed among several locations. Active Directory contains several databases called partitions that are replicated between domain controllers by using intrasite replication or intersite replication. Intrasite replication takes place between domain controllers in the same site; intersite replication occurs between two or more sites. The replication process differs in these two types, but the goal is the same—to maintain a consistent set of domain directory partitions.

Active Directory uses multimaster replication for replicating Active Directory objects, such as user and computer accounts, which means changes to these objects can occur on any DC and are propagated (replicated) to all other domain controllers. A process called the Knowledge Consistency Checker (KCC) runs on every DC to determine the replication topology, which defines the domain controller path through which Active Directory changes flow. This path is configured as a ring (or multiple rings, if there are enough domain controllers), with each DC in the path constituting a hop. The KCC is designed to ensure that there are no more than three hops between any two domain controllers, which can result in multiple rings, as shown in Figure 2-26.

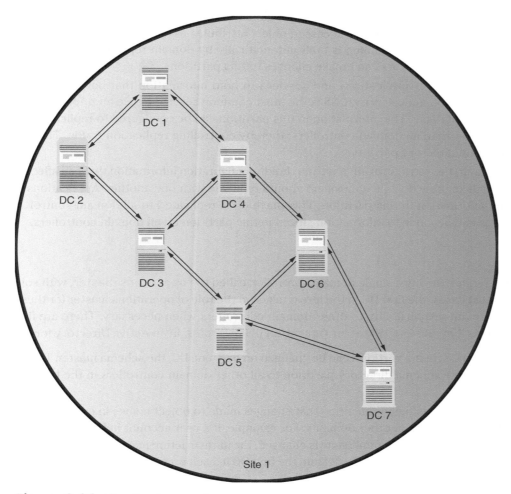

Figure 2-26   Replication topology

Intrasite replication occurs 15 seconds after a change is made on a domain controller, with a 3-second delay between each replication partner. A **replication partner** is a pair of domain controllers configured to replicate with one another. The KCC also configures the topology for intersite replication, but it's different from intrasite replication's topology. Site replication and configuration is discussed more in Module 8.

Directory Partitions

An Active Directory database has many sections stored in the same file on a DC's hard drive. These sections must be managed by different processes and replicated to other domain controllers in an Active Directory network. Each section of an Active Directory database is referred to as a **directory partition**. There are five directory partition types in the Active Directory database:

- *Domain directory partition*—Contains all objects in a domain, including users, groups, computers, OUs, and so forth. There's one **domain directory partition** for each domain in the forest. Changes made to objects in domain directory partitions are replicated to each DC in the domain. Some object attributes are also replicated to global catalog servers (described later in the section titled "The Importance of the Global Catalog Server") in all domains. Changes to the domain directory partition can occur on any DC in the domain except read-only domain controllers.

- *Schema directory partition*—Contains information needed to define Active Directory objects and object attributes for all domains in the forest. The **schema directory partition** is replicated to all domain controllers in the forest. One domain controller in the forest is designated as the schema master domain controller (discussed in the next section) and holds the only writeable copy of the schema.

- *Global catalog partition*—The **global catalog partition** holds the global catalog, which is a partial replica of all objects in the forest. It stores the most commonly accessed object attributes to facilitate object searches and user logons across domains. The global catalog is built automatically by domain replication of object attributes flagged for inclusion. Administrators can't make changes to this partition.

- *Application directory partition*—Used by applications and services to hold information that benefits from automatic Active Directory replication and security. DNS is the most common service to use an **application directory partition** for the DNS database. The information in this partition can be configured to replicate to specific domain controllers rather than all domain controllers, thereby controlling replication traffic. There can be more than one application directory partition.

- *Configuration partition*—By default, the **configuration partition** holds configuration information that can affect the entire forest, such as details on how domain controllers should replicate with one another. Applications can also store configuration information in this partition. This partition is replicated to all domain controllers in the forest, and changes can be made to information stored in this partition on all domain controllers.

Operations Master Roles

A number of operations in a forest require having a single domain controller, called the **operations master**, with sole responsibility for the function. In most cases, the first DC in the forest takes on the role of operations master for these functions. However, you can transfer the responsibility to other domain controllers when necessary. There are five operations master roles, referred to as **Flexible Single Master Operation (FSMO) roles**, in an Active Directory forest:

- *Schema master*—As mentioned, the schema partition can be changed on only one DC, the schema master. This DC is responsible for replicating the schema directory partition to all other domain controllers in the forest when changes occur.

- *Infrastructure master*—This DC is responsible for ensuring that changes made to object names in one domain are updated in references to these objects in other domains. For example, if a user account in Domain A is a member of a group in Domain B and the user account name is changed, the infrastructure master in Domain A is responsible for replicating the change to Domain B. By default, the first DC in each domain is the infrastructure master for that domain.

- *Domain naming master*—This DC manages adding, removing, and renaming domains in the forest. There's only one domain naming master per forest, and the DC with this role must be available when domains are added, deleted, or renamed.

- *RID master*—All objects in a domain are identified internally by a security identifier (SID). An object's SID is composed of a domain identifier, which is the same for all objects in the domain, and a relative identifier (RID), which is unique for each object. Because objects can be created on any DC, there must be a mechanism that keeps two domain controllers from issuing the same RID, thereby duplicating an SID. The RID master is responsible for issuing unique pools of RIDs to each DC, thereby guaranteeing unique SIDs throughout the domain. The RID master must be available when adding a DC to an existing domain. There's one RID master per domain.

- *PDC emulator master*—The PDC emulator master manages password changes to help make sure user authentication occurs without lengthy delays. When a user account password is changed, the change is replicated to all domain controllers but can take several minutes. Meanwhile, the user whose password was changed might be authenticated by a DC that hasn't yet received the replication, so the authentication fails. To reduce this problem, password changes are replicated immediately to the PDC emulator master, and if authentication fails at one DC, the attempt is retried on the PDC emulator master. In addition, this role provides backward compatibility with Windows NT servers configured as Windows NT backup domain controllers or member servers, although it is unlikely you will see Windows NT still in operation in a network today.

Because domain controllers that manage FSMO role data are, by definition, single masters, special attention must be paid to them. When removing domain controllers from a forest, make sure these roles aren't removed from the network accidentally. Domain administrators should keep track of which server holds each role and move the role to another DC if that machine is to be taken offline.

Using PowerShell to View FSMO Roles

You can use PowerShell commands to view the FSMO roles. To view the holder of the three domain-wide roles, use the following PowerShell command:

```
Get-ADDomain
```

This command produces several lines of output (see Figure 2-27). The highlighted lines show the three domain-wide FSMO roles.

```
PS C:\Users\Administrator> Get-ADDomain

ComputersContainer                     : CN=Computers,DC=TestDomain,DC=corp
DeletedObjectsContainer                : CN=Deleted Objects,DC=TestDomain,DC=corp
DistinguishedName                      : DC=TestDomain,DC=corp
DNSRoot                                : TestDomain.corp
DomainControllersContainer             : OU=Domain Controllers,DC=TestDomain,DC=corp
DomainMode                             : Windows2016Domain
DomainSID                              : S-1-5-21-3773442055-3027373140-109070251
ForeignSecurityPrincipalsContainer     : CN=ForeignSecurityPrincipals,DC=TestDomain,DC=corp
Forest                                 : TestDomain.corp
InfrastructureMaster                   : ServerSA1.TestDomain.corp
LastLogonReplicationInterval           :
Name                                   : TestDomain
NetBIOSName                            : TESTDOMAIN
ObjectClass                            : domainDNS
ObjectGUID                             : 8b275d1b-22fb-4b15-8b51-9ca689bc6e67
ParentDomain                           :
PDCEmulator                            : ServerSA1.TestDomain.corp
PublicKeyRequiredPasswordRolling       : True
QuotasContainer                        : CN=NTDS Quotas,DC=TestDomain,DC=corp
ReadOnlyReplicaDirectoryServers        : {}
ReplicaDirectoryServers                : {ServerSA1.TestDomain.corp}
RIDMaster                              : ServerSA1.TestDomain.corp
SubordinateReferences                  : {DC=ForestDnsZones,DC=TestDomain,DC=corp,
```

Figure 2-27   Output of `Get-ADDomain`

To view the folder of the two forest-wide roles, use the following PowerShell command. Figure 2-28 shows its output.

```
Get-ADForest
```

```
PS C:\Users\Administrator> Get-ADForest

ApplicationPartitions : {DC=ForestDnsZones,DC=TestDomain,DC=corp, DC=DomainDnsZones
CrossForestReferences : {}
DomainNamingMaster    : ServerSA1.TestDomain.corp
Domains               : {TestDomain.corp}
ForestMode            : Windows2016Forest
GlobalCatalogs        : {ServerSA1.TestDomain.corp}
Name                  : TestDomain.corp
PartitionsContainer   : CN=Partitions,CN=Configuration,DC=TestDomain,DC=corp
RootDomain            : TestDomain.corp
SchemaMaster          : ServerSA1.TestDomain.corp
Sites                 : {Default-First-Site-Name}
SPNSuffixes           : {}
UPNSuffixes           : {}
```

Figure 2-28   Output of `Get-ADForest`

Exam Tip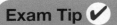

To list all of the FSMO role holders with a single command, type `netdom query fsmo` from a command prompt.

Trust Relationships

In Active Directory, a **trust relationship** defines whether and how security principals from one domain can access network resources in another domain. Trust relationships are established automatically between all domains in a forest. Therefore, when a user authenticates to one domain, the other domains in the forest accept, or trust, the authentication.

Don't confuse trusts with permissions. Permissions are still required to access resources, even if a trust relationship exists. When there's no trust relationship between domains, however, no access across domains is possible. Because all domains in a forest have trust relationships with one another automatically, trusts must be configured only when your Active Directory environment includes two or more forests or when you want to integrate with other OSs. Trusts are discussed in more detail in Module 5.

The Role of Forests

The Active Directory forest is the broadest logical component of the Active Directory structure. Forests contain domains that can be organized into one or more trees. All domains in a forest share some common characteristics:

- *A single schema*—The schema defines Active Directory objects and their attributes and can be changed by an administrator or an application to best suit the organization's needs. All domains in a forest share the same schema, so a change to the schema affects objects in all domains. This shared schema is one reason that large organizations or conglomerates with diverse business units might want to operate as separate forests. With this structure, domains in different forests can still share information through trust relationships, but changes to the schema—perhaps from installing an Active Directory–integrated application, such as Microsoft Exchange—don't affect the schema of domains in a different forest.

- *Forest-wide administrative accounts*—Each forest has two groups defined with unique rights to perform operations that can affect the entire forest: Schema Admins and Enterprise Admins. Members of Schema Admins are the only users who can make changes to the schema. Members of Enterprise Admins can add or remove domains from the forest and have administrative access to every domain in the forest. By default, only the Administrator account for the first domain created in the forest (the forest root domain) is a member of these two groups.

- *Operations masters*—As discussed, certain forest-wide operations can be performed only by a DC designated as the operations master. Both the schema master and the domain naming master are forest-wide operations masters, meaning only one DC in the forest can perform these roles.
- *Global catalog*—There's only one global catalog per forest, but unlike operations masters, multiple domain controllers can be designated as global catalog servers. Because the global catalog contains information about all objects in the forest, it's used to speed searching for objects across domains in the forest and to allow users to sign in to any domain in the forest.
- *Trusts between domains*—These trusts allow users to sign in to their home domains (where their accounts are created) and access resources in domains throughout the forest without having to authenticate to each domain.
- *Replication between domains*—The forest structure facilitates replicating important information between all domain controllers throughout the forest. Forest-wide replication includes information stored in the global catalog, schema directory, and configuration partitions.

The Importance of the Global Catalog Server

The first DC installed in a forest is always designated as a global catalog server, but you can use Active Directory Sites and Services to configure additional domain controllers as global catalog servers for redundancy. The following are some vital functions the global catalog server performs:

- *Facilitates domain and forest-wide searches*—As discussed, the global catalog is contacted to speed searches for resources across domains.
- *Facilitates logon across domains*—Users can sign in to computers in any domain by using their **user principal name (UPN)**. A UPN follows the format *username@domain*. Because the global catalog contains information about all objects in all domains, a global catalog server is contacted to resolve the UPN. Without a global catalog server, users could sign in only to computers that were members of the same domain as their user accounts.
- *Holds universal group membership information*—When a user logs on to the network, all the user's group memberships must be resolved to determine rights and permissions. Global catalog servers are the only domain controllers that hold universal group membership information, so they must be contacted when a user signs in. A universal group is the only type of group that can contain accounts from other domains, which is why this information must be stored in the global catalog.

Because of the critical functions a global catalog server performs, having at least one DC configured as a global catalog server in each location (such as a company's branch offices) is a good idea to speed logons and directory searches for users in all locations.

Forest Root Domain

As discussed, when the first domain is created in a Windows network, the forest root is also created. In fact, the first domain *is* the forest root and is referred to as the **forest root domain**. It has a number of important responsibilities and serves as an anchor for other trees and domains added to the forest. Certain functions that affect all domains in the forest are conducted only through the forest root domain, and if this domain becomes inoperable, the entire Active Directory structure ceases functioning. Figure 2-29 shows the forest root domain with multiple domains and trees. (Figure 2-5 showed the same structure, but for simplicity, it didn't show one of the domains as the forest root.)

What makes the forest root domain so important? It provides functions that facilitate and manage communication between all domains in the forest as well as between forests, if necessary. Some functions the forest root domain usually handles include the following:

- DNS server
- Global catalog server
- Forest-wide administrative accounts
- Operations masters

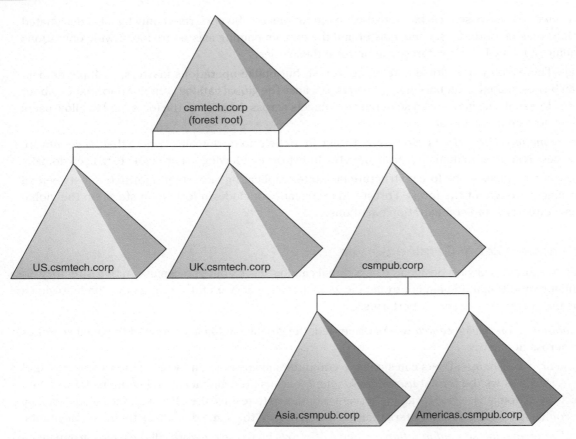

Figure 2-29 The forest root domain

The DNS server and global catalog server functions can be installed on other servers in other domains for fault tolerance. However, the forest-wide operations masters and forest-wide administrative accounts can reside only on a DC in the forest root domain. For these reasons, the forest root domain is a critical component of the Active Directory structure.

Understanding Domains and Trees

As discussed, an Active Directory tree is a group of domains sharing a common naming structure. A tree can consist of a single domain or a parent domain and one or more child domains, which can have child domains of their own. An Active Directory tree is said to have a contiguous namespace because all domains in the tree share at least the last two domain name components: the second-level domain name and the top-level domain name.

Organizations operating under a single name internally and to the public are probably best served by an Active Directory forest with only one tree. However, when two companies merge or a large company splits into separate business units that would benefit from having their own identities, a multiple tree structure makes sense. As you've learned, there's no major functional difference between domains in the same tree or domains in different trees, as long as they're part of the same forest. The only operational difference is the necessity of maintaining multiple DNS zones.

Designing the Domain Structure

A domain is the primary identifying and administrative unit in Active Directory. A unique name is associated with each domain and used to access network resources. A domain administrator account has full control over objects in the domain, and certain security policies apply to all accounts in a domain. Additionally, most replication traffic occurs between domain controllers in a domain. Any of these factors can influence your decision to use a single-domain or multidomain design. Most small and medium-sized businesses choose a single domain for reasons that include the following:

- *Simplicity*—The more complex something is, the easier it is for things to go wrong. Unless your organization needs multiple identities, separate administration, or differing account policies, keeping the structure simple with a single domain is the best choice.

- *Lower costs*—Every domain must have at least one DC and preferably two or more for fault tolerance. Each DC requires additional hardware and software resources, which increases costs.
- *Easier management*—Many management tasks are easier in a single-domain environment:
  - Having a single set of administrators and policies prevents conflicts caused by differing viewpoints on operational procedures and policies.
  - Object management is easier when personnel reorganizations or transfers occur. Moving user and computer accounts between different OUs is easier than moving them between different domains.
  - Managing access to resources is simplified when you don't need to consider security principals from other domains.
  - Placement of domain controllers and global catalog servers is simplified when your organization has multiple locations because you don't need to consider cross-domain replication.
- *Easier access to resources*—A single domain provides the easiest environment for users to find and access network resources. In a multidomain environment, mobile users who visit branch offices with different domains must authenticate to their home domain. If their home domain isn't available for some reason, they can't sign in to the network.

Although a single-domain structure is usually easier and less expensive than a multidomain structure, it's not always better. Using more than one domain makes sense or is even a necessity in the following circumstances:

- *Need for differing account policies*—Account policies that govern password and account lockout policies apply to all users in a domain. If you need to have differing policies for different business units, using separate domains is the best way to meet this requirement. A feature called Passwords Settings Objects can be used to apply different password policies for users or groups in a domain, but this feature can be difficult to manage when many users are involved.
- *Need for different name identities*—Each domain has its own name that can represent a separate company or business unit. If each business unit must maintain its own identity, child domains can be created in which part of the name is shared, or multiple trees with completely different namespaces can be created.
- *Replication control*—Replication in a large domain that maintains several thousand objects can generate substantial traffic. When multiple corporate locations are connected through a WAN, the amount of replication traffic could be unacceptable. Replication traffic can be reduced by creating separate domains for key locations because only global catalog replication is required between domains.
- *Need for internal versus external domains*—Companies that run public web servers often create a domain used only for publicly accessible resources and another domain for internal resources. In fact, Microsoft recommends that all companies have separate domain names for their public presence and their internal network.
- *Need for tight security*—With separate domains, stricter resource control and administrative permissions are easier. If a business unit prefers to have its own administrative staff, separate domains must be created.

Self-Check Questions

7. What process is responsible for determining the replication topology between DCs?

   a. Flexible Single Masters Operation
   b. Knowledge Consistency Checker
   c. Kerberos
   d. PDC emulator master

8. Which of the following is true about forests?

   a. There are three forest-wide FSMO roles.
   b. The last domain installed becomes the forest root.
   c. All domains in a forest share a single schema.
   d. Domains in the same forest do not trust each other.

○ Check your answers at the end of this module.

Activity 2-9

Viewing the Operations Master Roles and Global Catalog Server

Time Required: 15 minutes

Objective: Discover where operations master roles and the global catalog server are configured.

Required Tools and Equipment: ServerSA1

Description: In this activity, you use Active Directory Users and Computers, Active Directory Domains and Trusts, and Active Directory Schema to view the FSMO roles. You also use PowerShell to view these roles. Then, you use Active Directory Sites and Services to see where to configure a DC as a global catalog server.

1. Sign in to ServerSA1 as **Administrator**, if necessary, and then open Active Directory Users and Computers.

2. In the left pane, right-click the top node, Active Directory Users and Computers [ServerSA1.TestDomain.corp], point to All Tasks, and click Operations Masters.

3. The RID tab shows which DC performs the RID master role (see Figure 2-30). Click the **Change** button. The error message tells you that the DC you're connected to is the operations master, and that you must first connect to the DC where you want to transfer the operations master role. You aren't going to transfer the role because there are no other DCs, so click **OK**.

4. Click the **PDC** tab to view the DC that's the PDC emulator master, and then click the **Infrastructure** tab to view the DC that's the infrastructure master. Only one DC per domain performs the three operations master roles you just saw. Click **Close**.

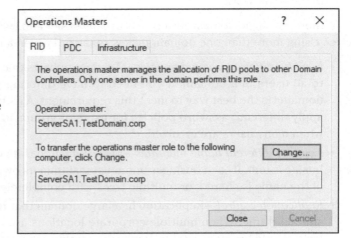

Figure 2-30 Viewing the RID master role

5. Right-click **Active Directory Users and Computers [ServerSA1.410Server2016.corp]** and click **Change Domain Controller**. If your domain had more than one DC, you could connect to any of them here, and then change the operations master role to another DC. Click **Cancel**, and close Active Directory Users and Computers.

6. In Server Manager, click **Tools** and then click **Active Directory Domains and Trusts** from the menu.

7. Right-click **Active Directory Domains and Trusts [ServerSA1.410Server2016.corp]** and click **Operations Master**. Here's where you can find which DC is the domain naming master. Note that only one DC in the entire forest performs this function. Click **Close**, and close Active Directory Domains and Trusts.

8. To view the schema master, you must use a different process because this role isn't shown in any standard MMCs. Right-click **Start**, click **Run**, type **regsvr32 schmmgmt.dll** in the Open text box, and click **OK**. In the message box stating "DllRegisterServer in schmmgmt.dll succeeded," click **OK**.

Note 7

The command in Step 8 is needed to register, or activate, certain commands that aren't normally available in Windows—in this case, the Active Directory Schema snap-in.

9. Right-click **Start**, click **Run**, type **MMC** in the Open text box, and click **OK**.

10. Click **File** and then click **Add/Remove Snap-in** from the MMC menu.

11. In the Available snap-ins list box, click **Active Directory Schema**. Click **Add**, and then click **OK**.

(continues)

Activity 2-9 Continued

12. Click **Active Directory Schema** and then right-click **Active Directory Schema** and click **Operations Master**. As with the domain naming master, only one DC in the entire forest performs the schema master role. Click **Close**, and close the MMC. When prompted to save your console settings, click **No**.

13. Open a PowerShell window. Type **Get-ADDomain** and press **Enter**. You see a list of information about the domain. Look for the following lines: InfraStructureMaster, PDCEmulator, and RIDMaster. Because this is the only domain controller in the domain, it holds all the domain-wide FSMO roles.

14. Type **Get-ADForest** and press **Enter**. You see information about the forest. Look for the following lines: DomainNamingMaster and SchemaMaster. Because this is the only domain controller in the forest, it holds all the forest-wide FSMO roles.

15. To see all the FSMO roles, type **netdom query fsmo** and press **Enter**. You see a list of all the FSMO roles and the server that holds them. This command can also be run from a command prompt.

16. Close the PowerShell window.

17. Now you'll see where the global catalog server can be configured. In Server Manager, click **Tools** and then click **Active Directory Sites and Services** from the menu.

18. Click to expand the **Sites** node. Click to expand **Default-First-Site-Name**, **Servers**, and then **ServerSA1**. Click **ServerSA1**. Your screen should look similar to Figure 2-31.

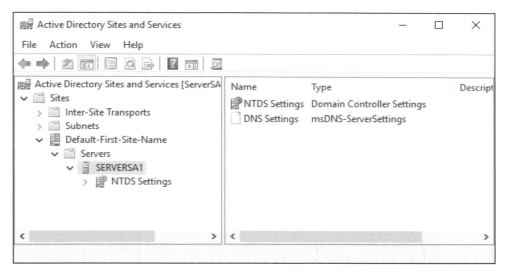

Figure 2-31   Active Directory Sites and Services

19. Right-click **NTDS Settings** under ServerSA1 and click **Properties**. When the Global Catalog check box is selected, the DC is a global catalog server. Because it's the only global catalog server in the forest, clearing the check box generates a warning message that users can't sign in if there's no global catalog server. Click **Cancel**.

20. Right-click **ServerSA1** and click **Properties**. Click the **General** tab, if necessary. Note that Global Catalog is specified in the DC Type text box. Click **Cancel**, and close Active Directory Sites and Services.

21. Continue to the next activity.

Introducing Group Policies

Microsoft Exam AZ-800:
Deploy and manage Active Directory Domain Services (AD DS) in on-premises and cloud environments.
  • Manage Windows Server by using domain-based Group Policies

A **Group Policy Object (GPO)** is a list of settings that administrators use to configure user and computer operating environments remotely. Group policies can specify security settings, deploy software, and configure a user's desktop, among many other computer and network settings. They can be configured to affect an entire domain, a site, and, most commonly, users or computers in an OU. The **GPO scope** defines which objects a GPO affects.

Despite the name, GPOs don't apply to group objects. You can link GPOs to sites, domains, and OUs, and GPOs linked to these containers affect only user or computer accounts in the containers. When Active Directory is installed, two GPOs are created and linked to two containers:

- *Default Domain Policy*—This GPO is linked to the domain object and specifies default settings that affect all users and computers in the domain. The settings in this policy are related mainly to account policies, such as password and logon requirements, and some network security policies.
- *Default Domain Controllers Policy*—This GPO is linked to the Domain Controllers OU and specifies default policy settings for all domain controllers in the domain (provided the computer objects representing domain controllers aren't moved from the Domain Controllers OU). The settings in this policy pertain mainly to user rights assignments, which specify the types of actions users can perform on a DC.

These default policies don't define any user-specific policies; instead, they're designed to provide default security settings for all computers, including domain controllers, in the domain. You can view, create, and manage GPOs by using the Group Policy Management console (GPMC), which is shown in Figure 2-32.

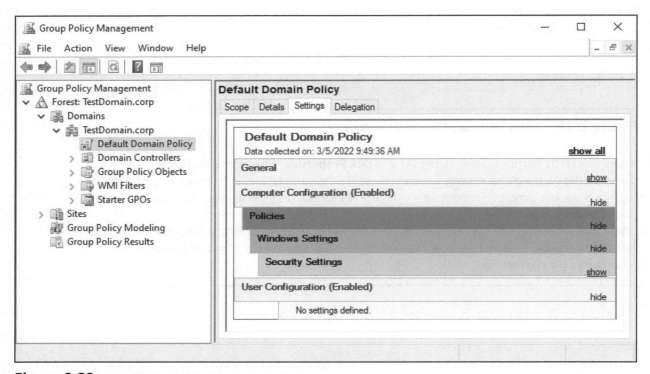

Figure 2-32   The Group Policy Management console

Each GPO has two main nodes in GPMC, as shown in the right pane of Figure 2-32:

- *Computer Configuration*—Used to set policies that apply to computers within the GPO's scope. These policies are applied to a computer when the computer starts.
- *User Configuration*—Used to set policies that apply to all users within the GPO's scope. User policies are applied when a user signs in to any computer in the domain.

Each node contains a Policies folder and a Preferences folder. Settings configured in the Policies folder are applied to users or computers and can't be overridden by users. Settings in the Preferences folder are applied to users or computers but are just that: preferences. Therefore, users can change settings configured in the Preferences folder.

The Policies folder under both the Computer Configuration and User Configuration nodes contains three folders: Software Settings, Windows Settings, and Administrative Templates. They can store different information, depending on whether they're under Computer Configuration or User Configuration.

> **Note 8**
>
> In GPMC, you see only folders that contain configured settings. By default, there are no configured settings in the User Configuration node in the Default Domain Policy, which is why you don't see a Policies folder under User Configuration in Figure 2-32. Likewise, you don't see the Preferences folder in this figure because no preferences have been configured.

To change a GPO's settings, you use the Group Policy Management Editor (GPME, shown in Figure 2-33), which you open by right-clicking a GPO and clicking Edit.

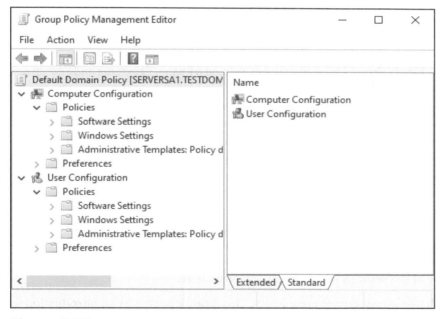

Figure 2-33   The Group Policy Management Editor

The Computer Configuration Node

In the Computer Configuration node, the three folders under the Policies folder contain the following information:

- *Software Settings*—This folder contains an item (**extension**) called Software installation, which enables administrators to install and manage applications remotely. Application installation packages can be configured so that the next time a computer in the GPO's scope starts, the application is installed automatically. This feature is called "assigning" the application to the computer.

- *Windows Settings*—This folder contains the Name Resolution Policy node, Scripts extension, Security Settings node, and Policy-based QoS node. The Name Resolution Policy stores configuration settings for DNS security and DirectAccess. Administrators can use the Scripts extension to create scripts that run at computer startup or shutdown. The Security Settings node contains the lion's share of policies that affect computer security, including account policies, user rights, wireless network policies, Registry and file system permissions, and network communication policies, among others. The Policy-based QoS node can be used to prioritize and control outgoing network traffic from a computer.

- *Administrative Templates*—This folder contains Control Panel, Network, Printers, System, and Windows Components folders. The settings in these folders affect computer settings that apply to all logged-on users. For example, the Network folder contains settings for configuring Windows Firewall, and Windows Components contains settings for configuring Windows Update. You can control hundreds of computer settings with the Administrative Templates folder.

Remember that policies configured in the Computer Configuration node affect all computers in the container (and child containers) to which the GPO is linked. So, a policy set in the Computer Configuration node of a GPO linked to the domain object affects all computers in the domain, including all computers in the Domain Controllers OU and the Computers folder.

The User Configuration Node

In the User Configuration node, the Policies folder contains the same three folders as in the Computer Configuration node. However, the policies defined here affect domain users within the GPO's scope, regardless of which computer the user signs in to. The following list describes other differences from folders under the Computer Configuration node:

- *Software Settings*—This folder also contains the Software installation extension. However, application packages configured here can be assigned or published. An **assigned application** is made available as an icon in the Start screen the next time a user affected by the policy signs in to a computer in the domain. The first time the user tries to run the application or open a document associated with it, the application is installed. A **published application** is made available via Group Policy for a user to install by using Programs and Features in Control Panel.

- *Windows Settings*—This folder contains four items: the Scripts extension, the Security Settings node, the Folder Redirection node, and the Policy-based QoS node. The Scripts extension enables administrators to create scripts that run at user sign-in and sign-out. The Security Settings node contains policies for configuring certificates and controlling what software users can run. Administrators can use the Folder Redirection node to redirect users' profile folders to a network share. The Policy-based QoS node provides the same functions as in the Computer Configuration node, except that the policy is applied to a computer when a user affected by the policy signs in to the computer.

- *Administrative Templates*—This folder contains a host of settings that enable administrators to tightly control users' computer and network environments. For example, Control Panel can be completely hidden from a user, specific Control Panel items can be made available, or items on a user's desktop and Start menu can be hidden or disabled, just to name a few of the settings that can be configured here.

Group Policy is a powerful tool, but with this power comes complexity. This module serves as an introduction to group policies; you learn more about working with their complexities in Module 4.

How Group Policies Are Applied

After reading about group policies and examining the two default policies, you might wonder how the Default Domain Policy can affect all computers in the domain when domain controllers have their own default policy. You might have noticed that the Default Domain Policy defines several account policies, such as password and account lockout settings, but no user rights assignment policies; the Default Domain Controllers Policy defines user rights assignment policies but no account policies. In addition, many policies are left undefined or not configured because GPOs, like Active Directory, work in a hierarchical structure.

GPOs can be applied in four places: the local computer, site, domain, and OU. Policies are also applied in that order. Policies that aren't defined or configured are not applied at all, and the last policy to be applied is the one that takes precedence. For example, a GPO linked to a domain affects all computers and users in the domain, but a GPO linked to an OU overrides the domain policies if there are conflicting settings.

Note 9

You can remember the order in which GPOs are applied with the acronym LSDOU: local computer, site, domain, and OU.

Self-Check Questions

9. Which of the following is the name of a default GPO?

   a. Default Computers Policy
   b. Default Users Policy
   c. Default Domain Controllers Policy
   d. Default Forest Policy

10. Which GPO is applied last and therefore takes precedence if there is a conflict?

   a. GPO linked to an OU
   b. GPO linked to the domain
   c. GPO linked to the forest
   d. GPO linked to a site

⊙ Check your answers at the end of this module.

Activity 2-10

Exploring Default GPOs

Time Required: 30 minutes
Objective: Locate and review the two default GPOs in Active Directory.
Required Tools and Equipment: ServerSA1
Description: In this activity, you familiarize yourself with the default GPOs linked to the domain and the Domain Controllers OU.

1. Sign in to ServerSA1 as **Administrator**, if necessary.
2. Because GPMC uses Internet Explorer to display information, first you'll turn off IE Enhanced Security Configuration to avoid warning messages. In Server Manager, click **Local Server** and click the link next to **IE Enhanced Security Configuration** in the second column. Under Administrators, click **Off** and then click **OK**. Click **Tools** and then click **Group Policy Management** from the menu.
3. In the left pane, click to expand the **Forest** and **Domains** nodes. Click to expand **TestDomain.corp** under the Domains node.
4. Click **Default Domain Policy**. If a Group Policy Management console message is displayed, read the message, click the **Do not show this message again** check box, and then click **OK**.
5. In the right pane, click the **Scope** tab, if necessary (see Figure 2-34). The Links section shows you which container objects are linked to this GPO. In this case, your domain should be the only container linked. All objects in a container linked to the GPO are affected by that GPO.
6. Click the **Settings** tab. (The settings might take a few seconds to be displayed.) You can view GPO settings here, but you can't change them.

(continues)

Activity 2-10 Continued

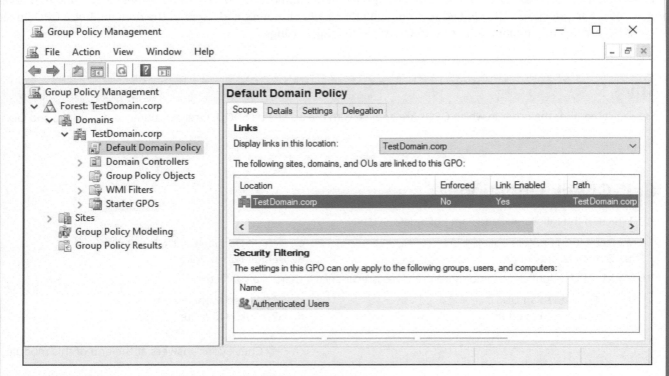

Figure 2-34   The Scope tab in Group Policy Management

7. The two main nodes are highlighted: Computer Configuration and User Configuration. Click the **show all** link to expand the settings and display a screen like the one in Figure 2-35. Only nodes that have config-ured settings are shown.

8. Scroll through the settings for the Default Domain Policy, which pertain to user account settings such as password policies or security. Take some time to see how Windows initially configures security settings for the domain. Notice that no settings are displayed under the User Configuration node because no settings have been configured.

9. Click to expand **Domain Controllers** in the left pane, and then click **Default Domain Controllers Policy**.

10. In the right pane, click the **Settings** tab, if necessary, and then click **show all**. Scroll through the settings for the Default Domain Controllers Policy. Most pertain to user rights assignments, such as which users are allowed to sign in to the computer locally or change the system time. Again, take some time to see how Windows initially configures security settings for domain controllers.

11. Right-click **Default Domain Policy** in the left pane and click **Edit** to open the Group Policy Management Editor.

12. If necessary, click to expand **Computer Configuration** and **User Configuration**. Under Computer Configuration, click to expand the **Policies** folder. You see the three folders described earlier.

13. Click to expand **Windows Settings** and then **Security Settings**. Click to expand the **Account Policies** node, and explore the settings in this node and the nodes under it. Figure 2-36 shows the settings in the Password Policy node. By default, account policies are defined only in the Default Domain Policy, and all domain users are subject to these settings.

14. Click to expand the **Local Policies** node and explore the three nodes under it. Most settings in Local Poli-cies are displayed as Not Defined. In fact, only three policies in the Local Policies node are defined. Can you find them?

15. Browse through some nodes in the Policies folder under User Configuration. No policies are configured in this node. Configuration of user policies is up to the server administrator.

(continues)

Activity 2-9 Continued

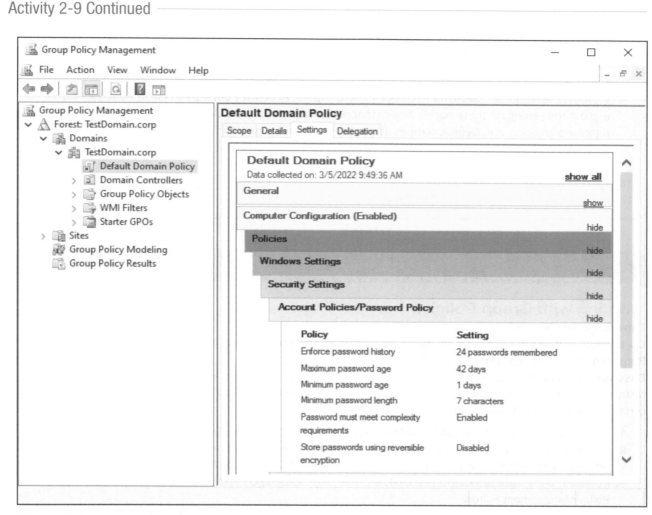

Figure 2-35   The Settings tab in Group Policy Management

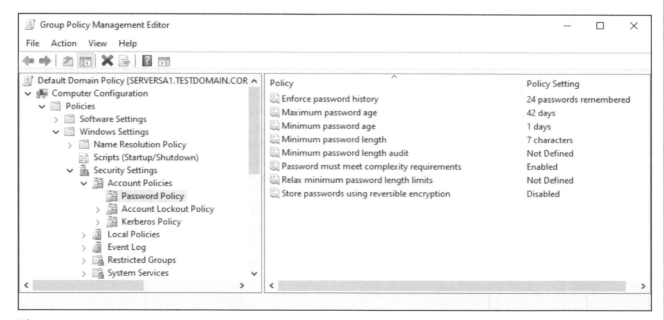

Figure 2-36   Password policies

Activity 2-10 Continued

16. Close the Group Policy Management Editor. In the Group Policy Management console, click to expand **Domain Controllers**, if necessary, and then right-click **Default Domain Controllers Policy** and click **Edit**.

17. Under the Computer Configuration node, click to expand the **Policies** folder, and then click to expand **Windows Settings** and **Security Settings**. Click to expand **Account Policies** and **Local Policies**, and explore the settings in these nodes. Notice that no account policies are defined, but a number of user rights assignments are. Default settings that apply to domain controllers focus on what types of actions users can perform on domain controllers. Most actions are limited to members of the Administrators, Backup Operators, and Server Operators groups.

18. Take some time to explore the GPOs and familiarize yourself with what's available. Leave the Group Policy Management console open for the next activity.

Activity 2-11

Working with Group Policies

Time Required: 30 minutes

Objective: Create a GPO and see how policies you configure affect user objects in the OU to which the GPO is linked.

Required Tools and Equipment: ServerSA1

Description: You want to see how some group policy settings affect users in your domain. You know that you want to restrict some users' access to Control Panel, so you decide to start with this policy. Because you want the policy to affect certain users, you configure it in the User Configuration node.

1. If necessary, sign in to ServerSA1 as **Administrator**, and then open the Group Policy Management console.

2. Under the TestDomain.corp node, right-click **TestOU1** (created earlier) and click **Create a GPO in this domain, and Link it here**. In the New GPO dialog box, type **GPO1** in the Name text box, and then click **OK**.

3. In the left pane, click to expand **TestOU1**, and then right-click **GPO1** and click **Edit** to open the Group Policy Management Editor.

4. Under User Configuration, click to expand **Policies** and then **Administrative Templates**. Click the **Control Panel** node. In the right pane, double-click the **Prohibit access to Control Panel and PC settings** policy to open the dialog box shown in Figure 2-37.

5. Read the description of the policy in the Help box, and then click the **Enabled** option button. Note that there are three possible settings: Enabled, Disabled, and Not Configured. If the policy is enabled, users affected by the policy are prohibited from accessing Control Panel and PC settings. If the policy is disabled, users have normal access to Control Panel. If the policy is not configured, it has no effect on users' access to Control Panel and PC settings. Click **OK**. Notice that the State column in the Group Policy Management Editor for the policy you changed now shows Enabled.

6. Close the Group Policy Management Editor and Group Policy Management console.

7. Sign out of ServerSA1 and sign back in as **testuser1** (which you created earlier). To do so, press **Ctrl+Alt+Delete**, wait a moment, and then click **Other user**. Type **testuser1** in the User name text box and **Password01** in the Password text box, and then press **Enter**. You see an error message, but continue to the next step.

8. You see a message that the sign-in method you're trying to use isn't allowed; a policy prevents regular users from logging on locally to a domain controller. Click **OK**. You'll fix this in the next series of steps.

9. Sign in as **Administrator**. Open the Group Policy Management MMC, and click to expand the **Domain Controllers** OU. Right-click **Default Domain Controllers Policy** and click **Edit** to open the Group Policy Management Editor.

(continues)

Activity 2-11 Continued

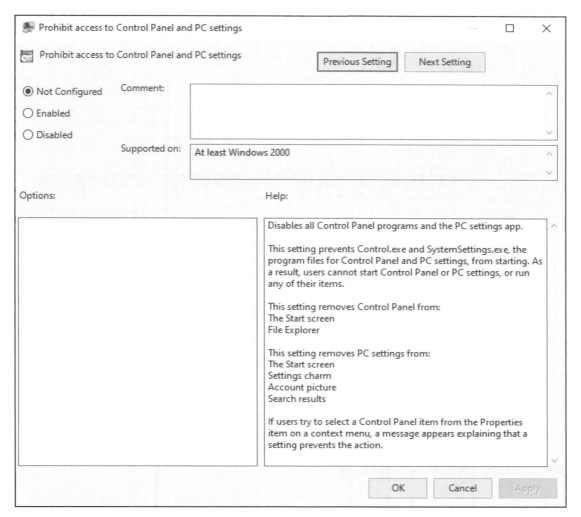

Figure 2-37   Configuring a policy setting

10. Under Computer Configuration, click to expand **Policies**, **Windows Settings**, and then **Security Settings**. Click to expand **Local Policies**, and then click **User Rights Assignment**. You should see a list of User Rights Assignment policies in the right pane (see Figure 2-38).

11. In the right pane, double-click the **Allow log on locally** policy. Notice the list of groups that currently have this right. Click **Add User or Group**. In the Add User or Group dialog box, type **Domain Users**, and then click **OK** twice.

12. Sign out and sign back in as **testuser1**. If you still can't sign in, you might need to wait a few minutes and try again. Group policies could require up to five minutes before they take effect, so keep trying.

13. After you're signed in, right-click **Start** and click **Control Panel**. You see a message indicating that restrictions disallow the operation. In the Restrictions message box, click **OK**.

14. Right-click the desktop and click **Display Settings**. You may see a different message, but you will be unable to change display settings because it is a Control Panel operation. Click **OK**. Your policy has clearly taken effect.

15. Shut down ServerSA1.

(continues)

Activity 2-11 Continued

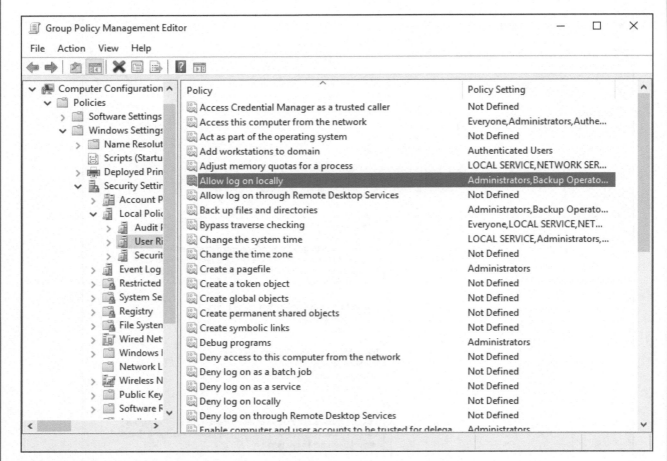

Figure 2-38 The User Rights Assignment node

Note 10

In Activity 2-11, you might have noticed a delay between setting a policy and the policy taking effect. You can run the command-line program gpupdate.exe, which applies group policies immediately to the computer on which gpupdate.exe is running and to the currently logged-on user. This program is an invaluable tool for testing GPOs because it saves considerable time. As mentioned, computer policies are applied when a computer restarts, which can take some time, and user policies are applied when a user logs on. GPOs are also updated on domain controllers every five minutes and on workstations and servers every 90 minutes, even if the computers don't restart.

Note 11

There's a lot more to group policies than the overview in this module. You learn more about managing and configuring GPOs in Module 4.

Module Summary

- A directory service is a database that stores network resource information and can be used to manage users, computers, and resources throughout the network. A directory service provides network single sign-on for users and centralizes management in geographically dispersed networks.
- Active Directory is based on the X.500 standard and LDAP. Active Directory is the Windows directory service and has been part of the Windows Server family since Windows 2000 Server. Active Directory is a hierarchical, distributed database that's scalable, secure, and flexible. Active Directory's physical structure is composed of sites and domain controllers, and the logical structure is composed of organizational units, domains, trees, and forests.
- You use Server Manager to install the Active Directory Domain Services role. After running the wizard in Server Manager, you must finish the Active Directory installation by promoting the server to a domain controller using the Active Directory Domain Services Configuration Wizard. After Active Directory is installed, a number of new MMCs are added to the Administrative Tools folder. The main tools for managing an Active Directory domain are Active Directory Administrative Center and Active Directory Users and Computers.
- Installing the first DC in a network creates a new forest, and the domain is called the forest root domain. Adding domain controllers to a domain or new domains in a forest is similar to creating a new forest. You can use Install from Media (IFM) to install subsequent DCs in a domain. Using IFM reduces the amount of initial replication traffic required to bring the new DC up to date.
- The data in Active Directory is organized as objects. Available objects and their structure are defined by the Active Directory schema, which is composed of schema classes and schema attributes. The data in a schema attribute is called an attribute value.
- There are two types of objects in Active Directory: container objects and leaf objects. Container objects contain other objects and include domains, folders, and OUs. OUs are the primary organizing container in Active Directory. Domains represent administrative, security, and policy boundaries. OUs are organizing and management containers mainly used to mimic a company's structure and apply group policies to collections of users or computers.
- Leaf objects generally represent security accounts, network resources, and GPOs. Security accounts include users, groups, and computers. There are three categories of user account objects: local user accounts, domain user accounts, and built-in user accounts. Groups are used to assign rights and permissions to collections of users. Computer account objects are used to identify computers that are domain members. Other leaf objects include contacts, printers, and shared folders.
- The AD Recycle Bin can be enabled in ADAC, but once enabled, it cannot be disabled. The Recycle Bin feature requires a forest functional level of at least Windows Server 2008 R2.
- Active Directory objects can be located easily with search functions in Active Directory Users and Computers and Windows Explorer. Users can use the Active Directory search function to find network resources (such as shared printers and folders), other users, contacts, and many other items.
- Large organizations might require multiple domains, trees, and forests. Some terms for describing the Active Directory structure include directory partitions, operations master roles, Active Directory replication, and trust relationships.
- Directory partitions are sections of the Active Directory database that hold varied types of data and are managed by different processes. Directory partitions can be replicated from one domain controller to another. FSMO roles are functions carried out by a single domain controller per domain or forest; they perform vital functions that affect Active Directory operations.
- The forest is the broadest logical Active Directory component. All domains in a forest share some common characteristics, such as a single schema, the global catalog, and trusts between domains. The global catalog facilitates several important functions, such as cross-domain logon and forest-wide searching. The forest root domain is the first domain created in a forest.
- A domain is the primary identifying and administrative unit of Active Directory. Each domain has a unique name, and there's an administrative account with full control over objects in the domain. Some organizations can benefit by using multiple domains when different security or account policies are required, among other

reasons. A tree consists of one or more domains with a contiguous namespace. An Active Directory forest might require multiple trees when an organization is composed of companies with a noncontiguous namespace.

- GPOs are lists of settings that enable administrators to configure user and computer operating environments remotely. GPOs have two main nodes: Computer Configuration and User Configuration. Each node contains a Policies folder and a Preferences folder. Under the Policies folder are three additional folders called Software Settings, Windows Settings, and Administrative Templates.
- Policies defined in the Computer Configuration node affect all computers in the Active Directory container to which the GPO is linked. Policies defined in the User Configuration node affect all users in the Active Directory container to which the GPO is linked. Group objects aren't affected by GPOs. GPOs can be applied in the following four places in the following order: the local computer, site, domain, and OU. User policies are applied when a user signs in, and computer policies are applied when a computer restarts.

Key Terms

Active Directory Domain Services (AD DS)	extension	object
Active Directory replication	Flexible Single Master Operation (FSMO) roles	operations master
application directory partition	forest	organizational unit (OU)
assigned application	forest root domain	permissions
attribute value	fully qualified domain name (FQDN)	published application
authentication	global catalog partition	relative identifier (RID)
built-in user account	GPO scope	replication partner
child domain	Group Policy Object (GPO)	right
configuration partition	Install from Media (IFM)	schema
directory partition	intersite replication	schema attribute
directory service	intrasite replication	schema class
Directory Services Restore Mode (DSRM)	Knowledge Consistency Checker (KCC)	schema directory partition
	leaf object	security identifier (SID)
domain	Lightweight Directory Access Protocol (LDAP)	site
domain controller		SYSVOL folder
domain directory partition	local user account	tree
domain user account	multimaster replication	trust relationship
		user principal name (UPN)

Review Questions

1. Which of the following best describes a directory service?

   a. A service similar to a list of information in a text file

   b. A service similar to a database program but with the capability to manage objects

   c. A program for managing the user interface on a server

   d. A program for managing folders, files, and permissions on a distributed server

2. The protocol for accessing Active Directory objects and services is based on which of the following standards?

   a. DNS

   b. LDAP

   c. DHCP

   d. ICMP

3. Which of the following is a feature of Active Directory? (Choose all that apply.)

   a. Fine-grained access controls

   b. Can be distributed among many servers

   c. Can be installed on only one server per domain

   d. Has a fixed schema

4. Which of the following is a component of Active Directory's physical structure?

   a. Organizational units   c. Sites

   b. Domains   d. Folders

5. Which of the following is the responsibility of a domain controller? (Choose all that apply.)

   a. Storing a copy of the domain data

   b. Providing data search and retrieval functions

   c. Servicing multiple domains

   d. Providing authentication services

6. Which of the following is *not* associated with an Active Directory tree?
   a. A group of domains
   b. A container object that can be linked to a GPO
   c. A common naming structure
   d. Parent and child domains

7. Which of the following is *not* part of Active Directory's logical structure?
   a. Tree   c. DC
   b. Forest   d. OU

8. Which of the following is associated with an Active Directory forest? (Choose all that apply.)
   a. Can contain trees with different naming structures
   b. Allows independent domain administration
   c. Contains domains with different schemas
   d. Represents the broadest element in Active Directory

9. Which of the following is associated with installing the first domain controller in a forest?
   a. RODC   c. Global catalog
   b. Child domain   d. DHCP

10. When installing an additional DC in an existing domain, which of the following is an option for reducing replication traffic?
   a. New site   c. GC server
   b. Child domain   d. IFM

11. Which MMC is added after Active Directory installation? (Choose all that apply.)
   a. Active Directory Domains and Trusts
   b. Active Directory Groups and Sites
   c. ADSI Edit
   d. Active Directory Restoration Utility

12. Which of the following is the core logical structure container in Active Directory?
   a. Forest   c. Domain
   b. OU   d. Site

13. Which of the following defines the types of objects in Active Directory?
   a. GPOs   c. Schema attributes
   b. Attribute values   d. Schema classes

14. Which of the following defines the types of information stored in an Active Directory object?
   a. GPOs   c. Schema attributes
   b. Attribute values   d. Schema classes

15. Which of the following specifies what types of actions a user can perform on a computer or network?
   a. Attributes   c. Permissions
   b. Rights   d. Classes

16. Which of the following is considered a leaf object? (Choose all that apply.)
   a. Computer account   c. Domain controller
   b. Organizational unit   d. Shared folder

17. Which of the following is a default folder object created when Active Directory is installed?
   a. Computers   c. Groups
   b. Domain Controllers d. Sites

18. Which type of account is *not* found in Active Directory?
   a. Domain user account   c. Built-in user account
   b. Local user account   d. Computer account

19. Which of the following is a directory partition? (Choose all that apply.)
   a. Domain directory partition
   b. Group policy partition
   c. Schema directory partition
   d. Configuration partition

20. Which of the following is responsible for management of adding, removing, and renaming domains in a forest?
   a. Schema master
   b. Infrastructure master
   c. Domain naming master
   d. RID master

21. All domains in the same forest have which of the following in common? (Choose all that apply.)
   a. Domain name   c. Domain administrator
   b. Schema   d. Global catalog

22. You have an Active Directory forest of two trees and eight domains. You haven't changed any operations master domain controllers. On which domain controller is the schema master?
   a. All domain controllers
   b. The last domain controller installed
   c. The first domain controller in the forest root domain
   d. The first domain controller in each tree

23. To which of the following can a GPO be linked? (Choose all that apply.)
   a. Trees   c. Folders
   b. Domains   d. Sites

24. Which container has a default GPO linked to it?
   a. Users   c. Computers
   b. Printers   d. Domain

25. By default, when are policies set in the User Configuration node applied?
   a. Every five minutes   c. At user logon
   b. Immediately   d. At computer restart

Critical Thinking

The following activities give you critical thinking challenges. Case projects offer a scenario with a problem for which you supply a written solution.

Case Projects

Case Project 2-1: Configuring Active Directory

When CSM Tech Publishing started its Windows network almost a year ago, the network was small enough that you simply used the default Users and Computers containers for the user account and computer account objects you created. However, now that the company has grown to more than 50 users and computers, you decide that some structure is needed. You talk to the owner to understand how the business is organized and learn that there are four main departments: Executive, Marketing, Engineering, and Operations. Draw a diagram of the Active Directory structure based on this information, including the types of objects in each container. Include the objects you know about and where these objects should be located, and state whether you need to move any existing objects. Use triangles and circles to represent container objects in your diagram, as shown in Figures 2-2 through 2-5.

Case Project 2-2: Explaining GPOs

The owner of CSM Tech Publishing has told you he needs to lock down some desktops so that their users can't access certain Windows components, such as Control Panel. He also wants some standardization in the look of users' desktops, such as wallpaper. However, he's not sure how to make these changes without affecting all users and computers. Write a short explanation of how GPOs can be applied to achieve the owner's goals. Include information about how policies defined in one place can take precedence over policies defined elsewhere.

Solutions to Self-Check Questions

Section 2-1: The Role of a Directory Service

1. A directory service provides a centralized management tool for users and resources. True or False?
    Answer: a. True
    Explanation: A directory service like Active Directory allows administrators to manage user accounts and network resources from a centralized tool.

2. Which of the following is part of the physical structure of Active Directory?
    Answer: b. Domain controllers
    Explanation: Domain controllers and sites are the two physical structure components of Active Directory.

Section 2-2: Installing Active Directory

3. When you install Active Directory on the first domain controller in the forest, which other server role should also be installed if it is not already installed on the network?
    Answer: c. DNS Server
    Explanation: DNS must be installed so other computers can locate domain controllers and other domain resources.

4. You have an Active Directory forest that consists of a single domain named mydomain.corp. You install Active Directory on another server and create a new domain in the mydomain.corp forest named anotherdomain.corp. Which of the following is true about anotherdomain.corp?

    Answer: b. It is a new tree.

    Explanation: Each domain in a forest that does not share the first- and second-level domain name is considered a separate tree in the forest.

Section 2-3: What's Inside Active Directory?

5. Which Active Directory management tool is built on PowerShell?

    Answer: c. Active Directory Administrative Center

    Explanation: Active Directory Administrative Center is built on PowerShell. Each task you perform executes one or more PowerShell cmdlets to execute the task.

6. Which of the following is the name of a default organizational unit?

    Answer: d. Domain Controllers

    Explanation: Domain Controllers is the only default OU created when Active Directory is installed. It contains the DC computer account.

Section 2-4: Working with Forests, Trees, and Domains

7. What process is responsible for determining the replication topology between DCs?

    Answer: b. Knowledge Consistency Checker

    Explanation: The Knowledge Consistency Checker communicates with other DCs to determine the best replication topology among DCs in a domain.

8. Which of the following is true about forests?

    Answer: c. All domains in a forest share a single schema.

    Explanation: The schema determines the types of objects and object attributes for all domains in the forest.

Section 2-5: Introducing Group Policies

9. Which of the following is the name of a default GPO?

    Answer: c. Default Domain Controllers Policy

    Explanation: The two default GPOs created when Active Directory is installed are Default Domain Controllers Policy and Default Domain Policy.

10. Which GPO is applied last and therefore takes precedence if there is a conflict?

    Answer: a. GPO linked to an OU

    Explanation: The order in which GPOs are applied is Local, Site, Domain, and OU; the last GPO applied takes precedence when there is a conflict.

Module 3

Manage Active Directory Accounts

Module Objectives

After reading this module and completing the exercises, you will be able to:

1 Use organizational units
2 Manage user accounts
3 Manage group accounts
4 Use computer accounts
5 Use service accounts
6 Use Active Directory in a hybrid environment

A directory service should be thought of as a tool to help administrators manage network resources. Like any tool, the better designed it is, the more useful it will be. In its default configuration, Active Directory is a useful directory service, but its real power is apparent when careful thought has been put into its design and configuration. An efficient Active Directory design that reflects how a business is organized improves the ease and efficiency of managing a Windows network. Likewise, correct configuration of Active Directory is paramount to a smoothly running and secure network. In this module, you learn more about organizational units, how to use them in a hierarchical design, and how to manage access to them.

A major task for an Active Directory domain administrator is managing user, group, and computer accounts. Users are hired, leave the company, change departments, and change their names. Passwords are forgotten and must be reset. New resources become available, and users (or, more likely, groups of users) must be given access to them. New computers are installed on the network and must be added to the domain. All these tasks, particularly in large networks, keep administrators busy.

This module discusses GUI and command-line tools for creating and managing all aspects of Active Directory accounts. You also examine the use of several user account properties. Next, you learn about group account types and group scopes, including how to use groups to maintain secure access to resources. In addition, you learn the purpose of computer accounts and how to work with them.

Services that run on your computer must also be authenticated to the network; traditional methods for configuring service authentication have posed challenges in security, manageability, or both. This module discusses how you can configure service authentication with a variety of methods, allowing you to choose which method fits each service you install.

In a hybrid infrastructure, you must configure secure methods to synchronize information between on-premises domain controllers and Azure domain controllers. In this module, you'll learn how to implement Active Directory in Azure and the tools required to synchronize domain information between the cloud and your datacenter.

Table 3-1 describes what you need in order to do the hands-on activities in this module.

Table 3-1   Activity requirements

Activity	Requirements	Notes
Activity 3-1: Resetting Your Virtual Environment	ServerDC1, ServerSA1	
Activity 3-2: Working with OUs	ServerDC1	
Activity 3-3: Viewing Object Permissions	ServerDC1	
Activity 3-4: Creating User Accounts in Active Directory Users and Computers	ServerDC1, ServerDM1	
Activity 3-5: Creating User Accounts in Active Directory Administrative Center	ServerDC1	
Activity 3-6: Creating Groups with Different Scopes	ServerDC1	
Activity 3-7: Working with Default Groups	ServerDC1	
Activity 3-8: Joining a Computer to the Domain	ServerDC1, ServerSA1	
Activity 3-9: Implementing Azure Active Directory	An Azure subscription and access to the Azure portal	
Activity 3-10: Installing Azure AD Connect	ServerDC1, an Azure subscription, and access to the Azure portal	

Working with Organizational Units

As you learned in Module 2, organizational units (OUs) are the building blocks of the Active Directory structure in a domain. Thoughtful planning of the OU structure eases the process of managing users and computers and applying group policies and makes Active Directory easier for users and technical staff to work with. Here are some benefits of using OUs:

- You can create a familiar hierarchical structure based on the organizational chart that enables users and administrators to locate network users and resources quickly.
- You can delegate administration of network resources to other IT staff without assigning more comprehensive administrative permissions.
- You can change the OU structure easily to accommodate corporate reorganizations.
- You can group users and computers for the purposes of assigning administrative and security policies with the Group Policy tool.
- You can hide Active Directory objects for confidentiality or security reasons by configuring access permissions on OUs.

> **Note 1**
>
> An OU can't be used to assign permissions to objects it contains. Groups, not OUs, are the main Active Directory object for permission assignments, and are discussed in detail later in the section called "Managing Group Accounts."

OUs are containers that hold objects such as user and computer accounts, but they can also contain other OUs. This ability to nest OUs gives you the flexibility to create a hierarchy with as many levels as needed for your organization. Take a look at a fictitious company, csmtech.corp, which has about 40 employees and this top-level organizational structure:

- Administration
- Marketing

- Research and Development (R&D)
- Operations

This organization will likely have a single-level OU structure, as shown on the left in Figure 3-1. Dividing R&D into the Engineering and Research departments and dividing Marketing into Sales and Advertising creates the multilevel OU structure shown on the right in Figure 3-1.

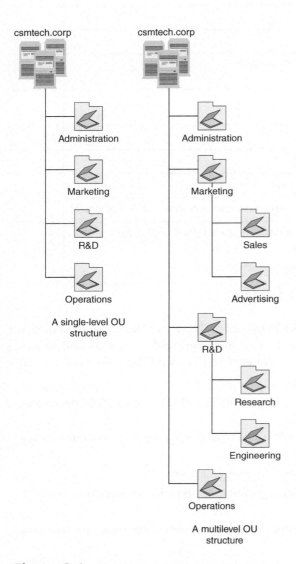

Figure 3-1   Single-level and multilevel OU structures

Now look at a larger organization with departments in different locations. If the company uses departments rather than locations for identification purposes, the OU structure could reflect that focus, as shown on the left in Figure 3-2. The top-level structure remains intact, but under each department is an OU for each location. Conversely, if the business is organized mainly by location, the OU structure looks like the one on the right in Figure 3-2. Notice that some OUs have the same name, which is allowed as long as they're in different parts of the Active Directory hierarchy. For example, the R&D OU is under both the Boston and Seattle OUs.

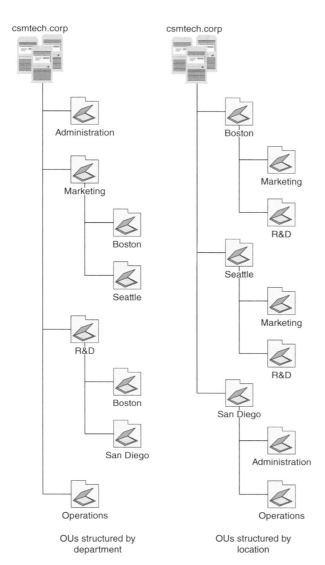

Figure 3-2   A multilocation domain organized by department and location

> **Note 2**
>
> There are other approaches to OU hierarchy design. For example, a current trend is to design OUs based on grouping users and resources according to their security levels.

OU Delegation of Control

As you've learned, one benefit of using OUs is that you can delegate administration of the OU and its contents to other users without giving them broader administrative capability. **Delegation of control**, in the context of Active Directory, means a person with higher security privileges assigns authority to a person of lesser security privileges to perform certain tasks. Delegation of control of an OU is not an all-or-nothing proposition. You can assign specific tasks the user can perform on objects in that OU and even delegate other tasks to different users or groups. The following are the most common tasks that can be delegated:

- Create, delete, and manage user accounts.
- Reset user passwords and force a password change at next logon.
- Read all user information.

- Create, delete, and manage groups.
- Modify the membership of a group.
- Manage group policy links.
- Generate Resultant Set of Policy (Planning).
- Generate Resultant Set of Policy (Logging).

> **Note 3**
>
> Three more predefined tasks can be delegated for the object class `inetOrgPerson`, which is a user and contact class defined in Active Directory for LDAP compatibility.

In addition to these tasks, you can define custom tasks, which allow fine-grained control over the management tasks a user can perform in an OU. When you create a custom task, you must fully understand the nature of objects, permissions, and permission inheritance. Even if you delegate control only by using predefined tasks, your understanding of how permissions and permission inheritance work is important. After all, the Delegation of Control Wizard does nothing more than assign permissions for Active Directory objects to selected users or groups.

After you have delegated control to a user, there's no clear indication that this change has been made. By default, the OU's properties don't show that another user has been delegated control. To verify who has been delegated control of an OU, you must view the OU's permissions, as explained in the following section.

Active Directory Object Permissions

Active Directory object permissions work almost exactly like file and folder permissions. Three types of security principals can be assigned permission to an object: users, groups, and computers. An Active Directory object's security settings are composed of three components, collectively referred to as the object's security descriptor:

- Discretionary access control list (DACL)
- Object owner
- System access control list (SACL)

Like file system objects, every Active Directory object has a list of standard permissions and a list of special permissions that can be assigned to a security principal. For simplicity's sake, the term "users" is used when discussing permissions, but keep in mind that permissions can be assigned to any type of security principal: users, groups, and computers. Each permission can be set to Allow or Deny, and five standard permissions are available for most objects:

- *Read*—Users can view objects and their attributes and permissions.
- *Write*—Users can change an object's attributes.
- *Create all child objects*—Users can create new child objects in the parent object.
- *Delete all child objects*—Users can delete child objects from the parent object.
- *Full control*—Users can perform all actions granted by the previous four standard permissions, and they can change permissions and take ownership of the object.

Different object types have other standard and special permissions. For example, a user object has the Reset password and Read logon information permissions; an OU object has the Create Account objects and Create Printer objects permissions.

Permission Inheritance in OUs

Permission inheritance in OUs works much the same way as it does in the file system. For example, an OU containing other objects is the parent object, and any objects contained in the OU, including other OUs, are considered child objects. All objects in Active Directory are child objects of the domain. By default, permissions applied to the parent OU with the Delegation of Control Wizard are inherited by all child objects of the parent OU. So, if a user has been given permissions to manage user accounts in an OU, these permissions apply to all existing and future user accounts in this OU, including user accounts created in child OUs. For example, look at the OU design structured by department in Figure 3-2. If a user is delegated control to create, delete, and manage user accounts in the R&D OU, the user could perform these actions on users in the R&D OU as well as the Boston and San Diego OUs.

Advanced Features Option in Active Directory Users and Computers

The default display settings in Active Directory Users and Computers hide some system folders and advanced features, but you can display them by enabling the Advanced Features option from the View menu. After you select this option, five new folders are shown under the domain node:

- *LostAndFound*—Contains objects created at the same time their container is deleted, perhaps by another administrator on another domain controller.
- *Program Data*—Initially empty; is available to store application-specific objects.
- *System*—Used by Windows system services that are integrated with Active Directory.
- *NTDS Quotas*—NTDS stands for NT Directory Service; stores quota information that limits the number of Active Directory objects a user, group, computer, or service can create.
- *TPM Devices*—Stores Trusted Platform Module (TPM) information about computer accounts in Windows 8 and later versions.

After Advanced Features is enabled, the Properties dialog box of domain, folder, and OU objects has three new tabs:

- *Object*—Used to view detailed information about a container object, such as the object class, created and modified dates, and sequence numbers for synchronizing replication. It also includes a check box you can select to protect an object from accidental deletion.
- *Security*—Used to view and modify an object's permissions.
- *Attribute Editor*—Used to view and edit an object's attributes, many of which aren't available in standard Properties dialog boxes.

For now, you're most interested in the Security tab of an OU's Properties dialog box (see Figure 3-3). The top section lists all accounts (user, group, and computer) that have an access control entry (ACE) in the DACL. The bottom section lists permission settings for each ACE. In Figure 3-3, the Domain Admins ACE is selected, and the bottom section shows the permissions granted to this group. To view details for permissions, you can click the Advanced button.

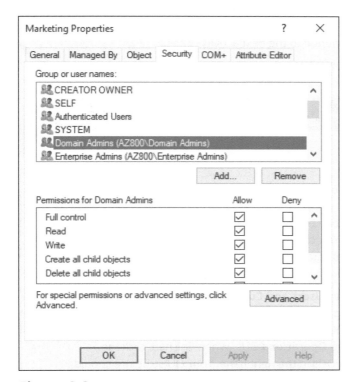

Figure 3-3   The Security tab of an OU's Properties dialog box

Permissions in Active Directory behave like file system permissions, but there are some important differences. Active Directory permissions can become complex with the multitude of inheritance rules and options, so it's best to keep things as simple as possible without compromising security. Until you fully understand permissions in Active Directory, use the Delegation of Control Wizard to assign other users or groups the ability to perform specific functions in Active Directory containers.

Self-Check Questions

1. An OU is a security principal that can be used to assign resource permissions to user and computer accounts in the OU. True or False?

   a. True   **b.** False

2. How can a user that is only a member of the Domain Users group get permission to create and change accounts in an OU?

   a. Link a GPO.   **c.** Delegate control.
   b. Create a trust.   **d.** Inherit permissions.

⊙ Check your answers at the end of this module.

Activity 3-1

Resetting Your Virtual Environment

Time Required: 5 minutes
Objective: Reset your virtual environment by applying the InitialConfig checkpoint or snapshot.
Required Tools and Equipment: ServerDC1, ServerSA1
Description: Apply the InitialConfig checkpoint or snapshot to ServerDC1 and ServerSA1.

1. Be sure the servers are shut down. In your virtualization program, apply the InitialConfig checkpoint or snapshot to ServerDC1 and ServerSA1.
2. When the snapshot or checkpoint has been applied, continue to the next activity.

Activity 3-2

Working with OUs

Time Required: 10 minutes
Objective: Create OUs to reflect a company's departmental structure and then use the Delegation of Control Wizard.
Required Tools and Equipment: ServerDC1
Description: You have been asked to create the OU structure for a business with four main departments: Administration, Marketing, Research and Development, and Operations. You create a single-level OU structure based on these requirements, using Active Directory Users and Computers for this task.

1. Sign in to ServerDC1 as **Administrator**.
2. In Server Manager, click **Tools** and then **Active Directory Users and Computers**.
3. In the left pane, right-click the domain node **AZ800.corp**, point to **New**, and click **Organizational Unit**.
4. In the Name text box, type **Administration** and click **OK**.
5. Repeat Steps 3 and 4 to create the **Marketing**, **R&D**, and **Operations** OUs. When finished, click the domain node in the left pane to display the folders and OUs in the right pane. Your OU structure should be similar to that in Figure 3-4. The OUs you created are highlighted in the figure.

(continues)

Activity 3-2 Continued

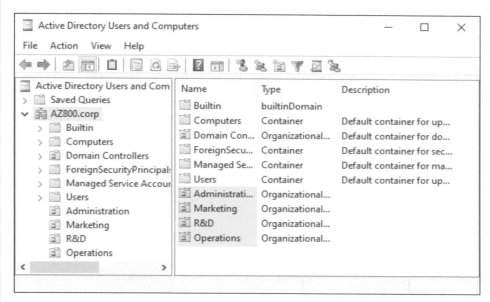

Figure 3-4   The Active Directory structure after creating OUs

6. Right-click the **Operations** OU, point to **New**, and click **User**.
7. Type **Joe** in the First name text box, **Tech1** in the Last name text box, and **jtech1** in the User logon name text box. Click **Next**.
8. Type **Password01** in the Password text box and again in the Confirm password text box. Click to clear the **User must change password at next logon** check box and click to select the **Password never expires** check box. Click **Next**, and then click **Finish**.
9. Right-click the **Marketing** OU and click **Delegate Control** to start the Delegation of Control Wizard. In the welcome window, click **Next**.
10. In the Users or Groups window, click **Add**. In the "Enter the object names to select" text box, type **jtech1**. Click **Check Names**, and then click **OK**. Click **Next**.
11. Click the **Create, delete, and manage user accounts** check box. Click **Next**, and then click **Finish**.
12. Leave Active Directory Users and Computers open and continue to the next activity.

Activity 3-3

Viewing Object Permissions

Time Required: 10 minutes
Objective: View object permissions in Active Directory.
Required Tools and Equipment: ServerDC1
Description: In this activity, you examine the results of delegating control on Active Directory object permissions. To view the settings, you need to enable the Advanced Features option in Active Directory Users and Computers.

1. If necessary, sign in to ServerDC1 as **Administrator**, and open Active Directory Users and Computers.
2. Right-click the **Marketing** OU and click **Properties**. Note the three tabs that are available now: General, Managed By, and COM+. (In the next step, you enable additional tabs.) Click **Cancel**.
3. Click **View** and then **Advanced Features** from the menu. The display changes to include additional folders described previously.

(continues)

Activity 3-3 Continued

4. Right-click the **Marketing** OU and click **Properties**. Click the **Object** tab, where you can find information that's useful in troubleshooting. In addition, when the "Protect object from accidental deletion" check box is selected, the object can't be moved or deleted.

5. Click the **Security** tab. Scroll through the list of groups and usernames so that you know what ACEs are in the DACL. Click each ACE to view its permission settings at the bottom of the tab.

6. Click the **Joe Tech1** ACE and notice in the permissions list that the Special permissions check box is selected. Click the **Advanced** button to open the Advanced Security Settings for Marketing dialog box (see Figure 3-5).

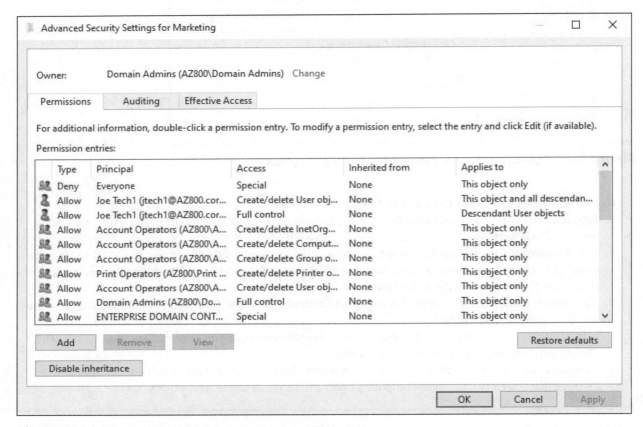

Figure 3-5   An OU's Advanced Security Settings dialog box

7. Double-click the first **Joe Tech1** entry to open the Permission Entry for Marketing dialog box. Scroll down to see that the Create User objects and Delete User objects check boxes are selected, so Joe Tech1 has permission to create and delete users in the Marketing OU (see Figure 3-6). Scroll back to the top of the window. The "This object and all descendant objects" option in the "Applies to" list means Joe Tech1 can create and delete users in the Marketing OU and any child OUs under Marketing.

Note 4

The term *descendant objects* means that all objects underneath the object are also affected by the permission settings.

(continues)

Activity 3-3 Continued

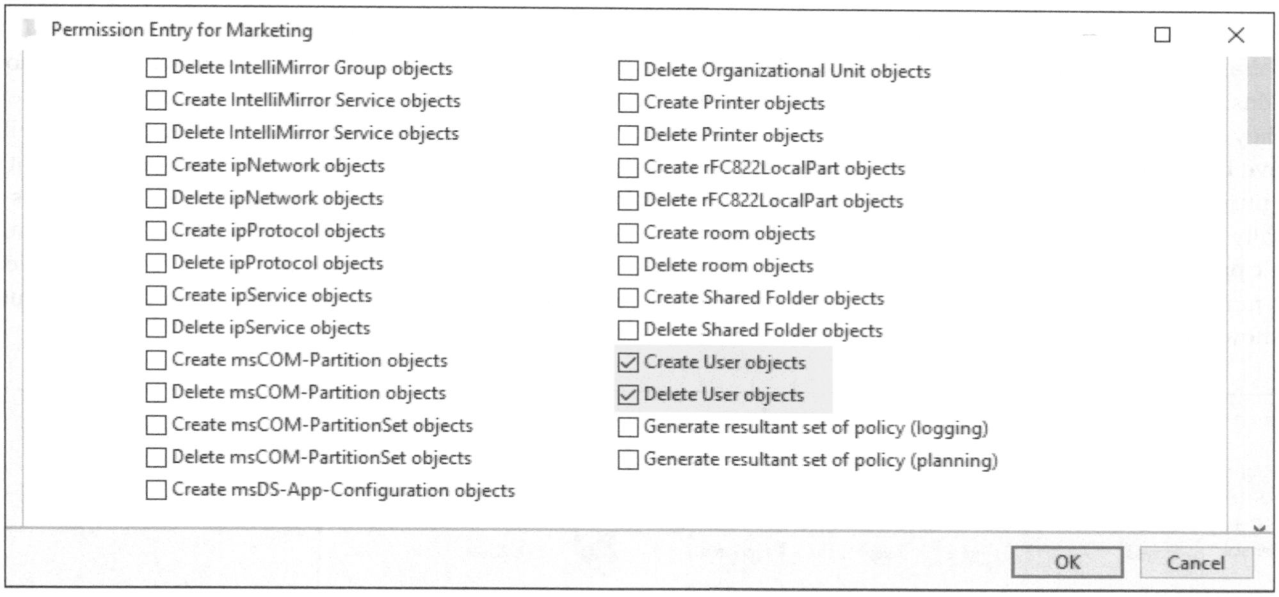

Figure 3-6   The Permission Entry dialog box

8. Click **Cancel**, and then double-click the second **Joe Tech1** entry. Notice that all check boxes in the permissions list are selected. In addition, the "Descendant User objects" option is selected in the "Applies to" list, which means Joe Tech1 has all permissions for all new and existing user objects in the Marketing OU.
9. Click **Cancel** three times, until only Active Directory Users and Computers is open. Leave this window open and continue to the next activity.

Managing User Accounts

Microsoft Exam AZ-800:
Deploy and manage Active Directory Domain Services (AD DS) in on-premises and cloud environments.
  • Create and manage AD DS security principals

Working with user accounts is one of the most important Active Directory administrative tasks. User accounts are the main link between real people and network resources, so user account management requires not only technical expertise, but also people skills. When users can't sign in or access a needed resource, they usually turn to the IT department to solve the problem. Fortunately, an administrator's understanding of how user accounts work and how to best configure them can reduce the need to exercise people skills with frustrated users.

User accounts have two main functions in Active Directory:

• *Provide a method for user authentication to the network*—The user logon name and password serve as a secure method for users to sign in to the network to access resources. A user account can also contain account restrictions, such as when and where a user can sign in or an account expiration date.
• *Provide detailed information about a user*—For use in a company directory, user accounts can contain departments, office locations, addresses, and telephone information. You can modify the Active Directory schema to contain just about any user information a company wants to keep.

As you learned in Module 2, Windows OSs have three categories of user accounts: local, domain, and built-in. Local user accounts are found in Windows client OSs, such as Windows 11, and in Windows Server OSs on systems that aren't configured as domain controllers. These accounts are stored in the **Security Accounts Manager (SAM) database** on local computers, and users can sign in to and access resources only on the computer where the account resides. A network running Active Directory should limit the use of local user accounts on client computers, however, as they can't be used to access domain resources. Local user accounts are mainly used in a peer-to-peer network where Active Directory isn't running. Administrators can also sign in to a computer with a local Administrator account for the purposes of joining the computer to a domain or troubleshooting access to the domain. Local user accounts are usually created in the Accounts section of Settings or the Local Users and Groups snap-in. Because these accounts don't participate in Active Directory, they can't be managed from Active Directory or be subject to group policies. The number of attributes in a local user account pales in comparison with those in Active Directory user accounts, as shown in Figure 3-7.

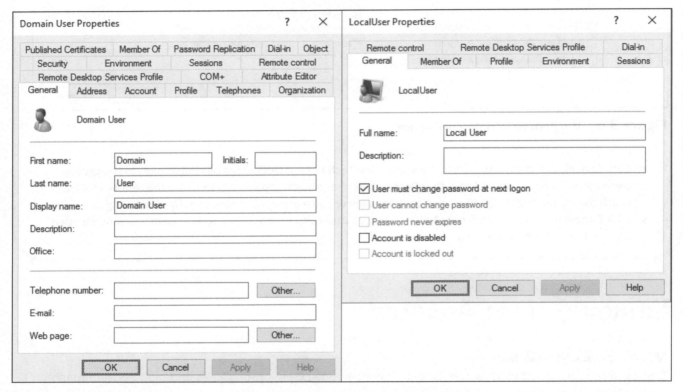

Figure 3-7 A domain user account (left) and local user account (right)

User accounts created in Active Directory are referred to as *domain user accounts*. Generally, these accounts enable users to sign in to any computer that's a domain member in the Active Directory forest. They also provide single sign-on access to domain resources in the forest and other trusted entities to which the account has permission. Domain user accounts can be managed by group policies and are subject to account policies linked to the domain.

Built-in user accounts include the Administrator and Guest accounts created during Windows installation. They can be local or domain user accounts, depending on whether they're stored in the computer's SAM database or in Active Directory. Built-in Active Directory accounts have the same qualities as regular domain accounts, except they can't be deleted. When Active Directory is installed on a Windows Server 2022 computer, the Administrator and Guest accounts, along with any other local accounts, are converted from local user to domain user accounts. The Administrator and Guest accounts require special handling because of their unique role in being the two accounts on every Windows computer. The following guidelines apply to the built-in Administrator account:

- The local Administrator account has full access to all aspects of a computer, and the domain Administrator account has full access to all aspects of the domain.

- The domain Administrator account in the forest root domain has full access to all aspects of the forest. This administrator account is the only default member of the Enterprise Admins group, as discussed later in the section called "Managing Group Accounts."
- Because the Administrator account is created on every computer and domain, it should be renamed and given a very strong password to increase security. With these measures in place, a user attempting to gain unauthorized access must guess not only the administrator's password, but also the logon name.
- The Administrator account should be used to sign in to a computer or domain only when administrative operations are necessary. Network administrators should use a regular user account for signing in to perform nonadministrative tasks.
- The Administrator account can be renamed or disabled but can't be deleted.

The following guidelines apply to the built-in Guest account:

- After Windows installation, the Guest account is disabled by default and must be enabled by an administrator before it can be used to sign in.
- The Guest account can have a blank password, so if you enable this account, be aware that anybody can sign in with it without needing a password. The Guest account should be assigned a password before it's enabled.
- Like the Administrator account, the Guest account should be renamed if it's going to be used.
- The Guest account has limited access to a computer or domain, but it does have access to any resource for which the Everyone group has permission.

Creating and Modifying User Accounts

User accounts can be created with GUI tools, such as **Active Directory Users and Computers (ADUC)** and **Active Directory Administrative Center (ADAC)**, and with command-line tools, such as dsadd and the PowerShell cmdlet New-ADUser. When you create a user account in an Active Directory domain, keep the following considerations in mind:

- A user account must have a unique logon name throughout the domain because it's used to sign in to the domain. However, user accounts in different domains in the same forest can be the same.
- User account names aren't case sensitive. They can be 1 to 20 characters and use letters, numbers, and special characters, with the exception of the following characters:
     \ / " [ ] : ; < > ? * + @ | ^ = , (note that periods are allowed)
- Devise a naming standard for user accounts, which makes creating users easier and can be convenient when using applications, such as email, that include the username in the address. The downside of using a predictable naming standard is that attackers can guess usernames easily to gain unauthorized access to the network. Common naming standards include a user's first initial plus last name (for example, jmartinez for Jose Martinez) or a user's first name and last name separated by a special character (such as Jose.Martinez or Jose_Martinez). In large companies where names are likely to be duplicated, adding a number after the username is common.
- By default, a complex password is required, as described in Module 2. Passwords are case sensitive.
- By default, only a logon name is required to create a user account. If a user is created without a password and the password policy requires a non-blank password, the user is created but disabled. Descriptive information, such as first and last name, should be included to facilitate Active Directory searches.

You have created a few users already, but take a closer look at the process, particularly some of the fields in ADUC and ADAC. Figure 3-8 shows the New Object - User dialog box in ADUC.

As mentioned, the only field required for a valid user is a user logon name—or more specifically, only the User logon name (pre-Windows 2000) field shown in Figure 3-8. However, you can get away with skipping the other fields only when you're using command-line tools. When you use ADUC, you must enter a value for the following attributes:

- *Full name*—This field is normally a composite of the First name, Initials, and Last name fields, but you can enter a name that's different from what's in those three fields.
- *User logon name*—This field isn't actually required, but it's highly recommended. It's called the user principal name (UPN), and the UPN format is *logon name@domain*. The *@domain* part is the UPN suffix. You can fill in the

Figure 3-8 The New Object - User dialog box

logon name and select the domain in the drop-down list, which is set to the current domain controller's domain by default. By using the UPN, users can sign in to their home domains from a computer that's a member of a different domain or from a remote application. In ADAC, this field is called User UPN logon. If you ignore the User logon name field and fill in only the User logon name (pre-Windows 2000) field, the user account is still valid; Windows creates an implicit UPN using the User logon name (pre-Windows 2000) field and the domain name. Microsoft recommends making the UPN the same as the user's email address.

- *User logon name (pre-Windows 2000)*—This field is called the **downlevel user logon name** because of its backward compatibility with older applications and Windows versions. Generally, it's the same as the User logon name, but it doesn't have to be. It consists of the domain name (without the top-level domain), a backslash, and the user logon name. Users running applications that don't recognize the UPN format can use this format to sign in: *domain\user*. Although the User logon name and User logon name (pre-Windows 2000) fields can be different, it's not recommended. This field is required when creating a user account. In ADAC, this field is called User SamAccountName logon.

- *Password and Confirm password*—These fields (see Figure 3-9) are required when creating a user in ADUC because default account policies in a Windows Server 2022 domain don't allow blank passwords. The default password policy requires a minimum length of 7 characters and a maximum of 127, and the password must meet complexity requirements, meaning it must have at least three characters of the following types: uppercase letters, lowercase letters, numbers, and special characters. You can change this password policy by using Group Policy (discussed in Module 4). When creating users with ADAC, `dsadd`, or PowerShell, you have the option of leaving the password blank, but the account is disabled. You must set a suitable password before the account can be enabled.

The four check boxes in Figure 3-9 are as follows:

- *User must change password at next logon*—This option, enabled by default, requires users to create a new password the next time they sign in. Typically, you use this option when users are assigned a generic password at account creation for logging on to the domain for the first time. After the first logon, the user is prompted to change the password so that it complies with the password policy. This option is also used when an existing user's password is reset.

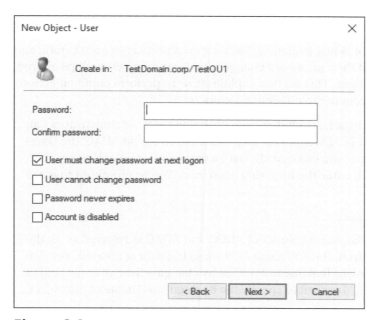

Figure 3-9 Password fields

- *User cannot change password*—This option is useful when multiple users sign in with the same user account, a practice common with part-time employees or guests who need access to the network. However, this option can't be set if "User must change password at next logon" is already selected. If you attempt to set both options, Windows displays a message that only one can be set.
- *Password never expires*—This option overrides the password policy that sets a maximum password age to force users to change their passwords periodically. It applies only to password expiration, not to account expiration, and can't be set when "User must change password at next logon" is already selected. Later, in the "Understanding Account Properties" section, you see how to set an expiration date for a user account.
- *Account is disabled*—This option, which prevents use of the user account, is sometimes set when user accounts are created before users need them, as when you've hired a new employee who hasn't started yet. You can also set this option on existing user accounts, as discussed in the following section.

Disabling User Accounts

You disable a user account to prevent someone from signing in with it. There are a number of reasons you might want to do this:

- *A user has left the company*—You disable the account instead of deleting it so that all the user's files are still accessible and all group memberships are maintained. If the user's position will be replaced, you can rename the account to match the new employee, and the new employee will have the previous user's rights and permissions. Even if a user isn't being replaced, you might want to disable rather than delete the account for auditing purposes.
- *The account is not ready to use*—You might want to create new accounts in anticipation of new hires. You can create these accounts in a disabled state, and when the users are ready to use the system, you can enable the accounts for their first logons.
- *A user goes on extended leave*—For security reasons, it's best to disable an account that will be inactive for an extended period.

Aside from using ADUC and ADAC to enable and disable accounts, you can use the PowerShell cmdlets `Enable-ADAccount` and `Disable-ADAccount` as well as the `dsmod user` command.

Understanding Account Properties

After an account is created, your work as an administrator is just beginning. User account properties aren't static and require modification from time to time. Users might need their password changed, their group memberships altered, their logon restrictions modified, and other account changes. This section explains how to perform common actions on accounts, such as resetting passwords and moving accounts to different containers:

- *Reset a password*—If users forget their passwords or are prohibited from changing them, administrators can reset a password by right-clicking the user account in ADUC and clicking Reset Password. In ADAC, the Overview window has a Reset Password check box so that you can quickly reset a password or unlock an account. To reset a user account password with PowerShell, enter the following command. You're prompted to enter and confirm the new password.

    ```
    Set-ADAccount Password LogonName -Reset
    ```

- *Rename an account*—The object name shown in the Name column of ADUC and ADAC is referred to as the *common name* (CN). A user account's CN is taken from the Full name field when the user is created. You can change the CN by right-clicking the account and clicking Rename in ADUC or by changing the Full name field in ADAC. In PowerShell, enter the following command. You need to specify the distinguished name of the object, the first part of which is the common name:

    ```
    Rename-ADObject DistinguishedName -NewName "NewName"
    ```

> ### Note 5
>
> An object's distinguished name (DN) is used in some commands to identify Active Directory objects. It uses LDAP syntax. For example, `CN=UserOne,OU=Operations,DC=AZ800,DC=corp` identifies a user named UserOne in the Operations OU in the AZ800.corp domain. CN means common name, OU means organizational unit, and DC means domain component.

- *Move an account*—You can move a user account, or any Active Directory object, with any of the following methods:
    - Right-click the user and click Move. (You can also click Action and then Move from the menu.) You're then prompted to select the container to which you're moving the object.
    - Right-click the user and click Cut. Then open a container object and paste the user into the container. This method works only in ADUC.
    - In ADUC, drag the user from one container to another.
    - Use the `Move-ADObject` cmdlet in PowerShell.

This module has covered only a small fraction of the many user account properties that can be configured. The following sections describe some other properties you might need to set on a user account. These sections are organized according to the tabs of an account's properties in ADUC. The same properties are available in ADAC but can be accessed in one place by scrolling down the Properties window.

The General Tab for User Account Properties

The General tab of a user account's Properties dialog box contains descriptive information about the account, none of which affects a user account's logon, group memberships, rights, or permissions. However, some fields in the General tab do bear mentioning:

- *Display name*—The value in this field is taken from the Full name field during account creation and is usually the same as the CN. However, changing the display name doesn't change the CN, and changing the CN doesn't affect the display name. This field can be used in Active Directory searches.
- *E-mail*—You can use the value in this field to send an email to the user associated with the account. If you right-click the user account and click Send Mail, the default mail application starts and the value in this field is entered in the email's To field.

- *Web page*—This field can contain a URL. If this field is configured, you can right-click the user account and click Open Home Page; a web browser opens the specified web page.

The remainder of the fields in the General tab can be used to locate an object with an Active Directory search.

The Account Tab for User Account Properties

The Account tab (see Figure 3-10) contains the information that most affects a user's logon to the domain. Aside from a password reset, this tab is the best place to check when a user is having difficulty with the logon process.

Figure 3-10   The Account tab for user account properties

- *User logon name* and *User logon name (pre-Windows 2000)*—These fields were described previously in the "Creating and Modifying User Accounts" section.
- *Logon Hours*—Clicking this button opens a dialog box (see Figure 3-11) where administrators can restrict days and hours that users can sign in to the domain. By default, all days and all hours are permitted. To exclude hours, click the Logon Denied option button and select the boxes for the hours you want to exclude; each box represents one hour. You can drag over the hour boxes to select several days or hours at a time. In Figure 3-11, logging on is denied to the account every day from 12:00 a.m. to 3:00 a.m. The default behavior of this feature denies new attempts to sign in during denied hours but doesn't affect a user who's already logged on. However, you can set a group policy to force a user to be disconnected when logon hours are denied.
- *Log On To*—Click this button to specify the names of computers that the user account can use to sign in to the domain. By default, a user can use all computers in the domain. However, if an account has access to sensitive information, you might want to limit it to sign in only at designated computers (see Figure 3-12).

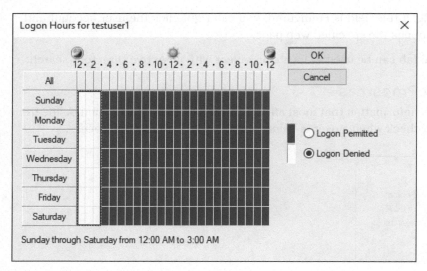

Figure 3-11 Setting logon hours

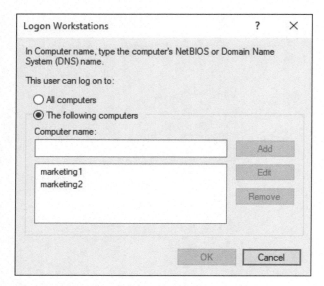

Figure 3-12 Setting logon workstations

- *Unlock account*—If a user's account is locked out due to too many incorrect sign-in attempts, a message next to this check box will indicate that the account is currently locked out. The administrator must click to select the check box and click OK on the Account tab to unlock the user's account.
- *Account options*—Five of these options were described previously. Most account options pertain to the user's password and Kerberos authentication properties, but a few warrant more explanation:
  - Store password using reversible encryption: Allows applications to access an account's stored password for authentication purposes. Enabling this option poses a considerable security risk and should be used only when no other authentication method is available.
  - Smart card is required for interactive logon: Requires a smart card for the user to sign in to a domain member. When this option is enabled, the user's password is set to a random value and never expires.
  - Account is sensitive and cannot be delegated: Used to prevent a service from using an account's authentication credentials to access a network resource or another service. This option increases security and is most often set on administrator accounts.
- *Account expires*—An administrator uses this option to set a date after which the account can no longer sign in. You might set an expiration on a temporary or guest account.

The Profile Tab for User Account Properties

The Profile tab (see Figure 3-13) is used to specify the location of files that make up a user's profile, a logon script, and the location of a home folder:

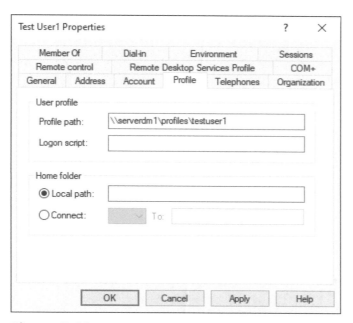

Figure 3-13   The Profile tab for user account properties

- *Profile path*—Used to specify the path to a user's profile. By default, a user's profile is stored on the computer where the user is currently signed in. The profile is stored in the C:\Users*logonname* folder by default, so the Profile path field is blank. It needs to be filled in only if you want to change the profile path. It's most often used when creating roaming profiles, where a user's profile is available from any station the user signs in to. When you're creating a user template, you can use the %username% variable instead of the actual logon name, and the variable is replaced automatically with the user logon name.
- *Logon script*—Used to specify a script that runs when the user signs in. The preferred method for specifying a logon script is with a group policy, so this field is rarely used with domain accounts, but it can be used with local accounts.
- *Local path*—Used to specify the path to a user's home folder. In general, the home folder has been replaced by the Documents folder. Some older applications use this field as the default location for storing user documents, however. You can also use it to specify the location on a terminal server where user documents are stored during Terminal Services sessions. The home folder can be a local path or a drive letter that points to a network share.
- *Connect*—Used to map a drive letter to a network share that's the user's home folder.

The Member Of Tab for User Account Properties

The Member Of tab (see Figure 3-14) lists groups the user belongs to and can be used to change group memberships. Every new user is added to the Domain Users group automatically. You can remove a user from Domain Users, but it's not recommended because membership in this group is a way to give users default rights and permissions. The Set Primary Group button in this tab is needed only when a user is logging on to a macOS, UNIX, or Linux client computer.

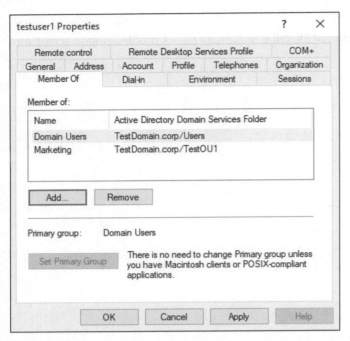

Figure 3-14 The Member Of tab for user account properties

Using Contacts and Distribution Groups

User accounts are security principals, which means permissions and rights can be assigned to them so that users can access network resources and perform certain operations on their computers. You can create two other user-related accounts that aren't security principals: contacts and distribution groups. A **contact** is an Active Directory object that usually represents a person for informational purposes only, much like an address book entry. Like a user account, a contact is created in Active Directory Users and Computers, but a contact isn't a security principal and therefore can't be assigned permissions or rights. The most common use of a contact is for integration into Microsoft Exchange's address book. The Full name field is the only information required to create a contact, but a contact's Properties dialog box has General, Address, Telephones, Organization, and Member Of tabs for adding detailed information about the contact. You use the Member Of tab to add a contact to a group or a distribution group.

A **distribution group** is created in the same way as a group. The only real difference is the group type, which is distribution rather than security, as explained later in the "Managing Group Accounts" section. Like a contact, a distribution group is used mostly with Microsoft Exchange for sending emails, but to several people at once. Both regular user accounts and contacts can be added as members of a distribution group.

> **Note 6**
>
> You can't create contacts and distribution groups in ADAC. You must use ADUC or PowerShell.

Self-Check Questions

3. Where are user accounts stored after they are created on a Windows 11 computer?

   a. SQL database
   b. SAM database
   c. Domain partition
   d. MMC

4. Which of the following is true about the default Administrator account on a Windows domain member computer?

   a. It can be renamed.
   b. It can be deleted.
   c. It cannot be disabled.
   d. It has a default password.

◉ Check your answers at the end of this module.

Activity 3-4

Creating User Accounts in Active Directory Users and Computers

Time Required: 15 minutes
Objective: Create user accounts in ADUC with different account options.
Required Tools and Equipment: ServerDC1, ServerDM1
Description: You want to experiment with some user account options that can be set during account creation. In this activity, you use Active Directory Users and Computers.

1. Sign in to ServerDC1 as **Administrator**, and open Active Directory Users and Computers.
2. Create the following OUs under the domain node: Administration, Marketing, R&D, and Operations. (See Activity 2-5 if you need a reminder of how to create OUs. Also, remember that you need to right-click the domain node each time you create a new OU so the OU will be under the domain).
3. Click **Operations**, and then click the **New User** toolbar icon. (Hover your mouse pointer over toolbar icons to see their descriptions.) Type **testuser1** in the User logon name text box. The User logon name (pre-Windows 2000) text box is filled in automatically. However, the Next button is still disabled, which means you haven't filled in all the required fields. Type **Test** in the First name text box and **User1** in the Last name text box. Now the Full name text box is filled in automatically, and the Next button is enabled. Alternatively, you could just fill in the full name. Click **Next**.
4. In the Password text box, type **p@$$word**. Type **p@$$word** again in the Confirm password text box.
5. Click to select the **User cannot change password** check box. Read the warning message, and then click **OK**. Click to clear the **User must change password at next logon** check box, and then click **User cannot change password**. Click **Next**, and then click **Finish**. Read the error message that's displayed.
6. What can you do to change the password so that it meets complexity requirements? Click **OK**, and then click **Back**.
7. Type **p@$$word1** in the Password and Confirm password text boxes. Adding a number at the end meets complexity requirements, but you could also change one letter to uppercase, such as p@$$Word. Click **Next**, and then click **Finish**.
8. On **ServerDM1**, sign in as **testuser1** with the password you just set (p@$$word1).
9. Press **Ctrl+Alt+Delete**, and then click **Change a password**. Note that in a virtual environment, you probably have to press an alternate keystroke or click a button to execute the Ctrl+Alt+Delete command.
10. In the Old password text box, type **p@$$word1**. In the New password text box, type **p@$$word2**, and then type it again in the Confirm password text box and press **Enter**. You see an "Access denied" message because the account is prohibited from changing the password. Click **OK**, and then click **Cancel** and **Sign out**.
11. On ServerDC1, create a user in the Operations OU with the logon name **testuser2** and the first and last names **Test User2**. Enter an appropriate password, and then click **Account is disabled**. Click **Next**, and then click **Finish**.
12. In Active Directory Users and Computers, notice that Test User2's icon has a down arrow to indicate that the account is disabled. If you open the Users folder, you'll see the Guest user has this icon, too, to indicate its disabled status. Close Active Directory Users and Computers, and stay signed in for the next activity.

Activity 3-5

Creating User Accounts in Active Directory Administrative Center

Time Required: 15 minutes
Objective: Create a user account in Active Directory Administrative Center.
Required Tools and Equipment: ServerDC1
Description: In this activity, you create a test user account with Active Directory Administrative Center (ADAC). You also explore the Windows PowerShell History feature of ADAC.

(continues)

Activity 3-5 Continued

1. On ServerDC1, open Active Directory Administrative Center.
2. Click **AZ800 (local)** in the left pane. In the middle pane, right-click **Operations**, point to **New**, and click **User**.
3. In the Create User window, notice the two fields with asterisks next to them: Full name and User SamAccount-Name logon. In Active Directory Administrative Center, only these two fields are required to create a user. Type **Test User3** in the Full name box and **testuser3** in the User SamAccountName logon box (see Figure 3-15).

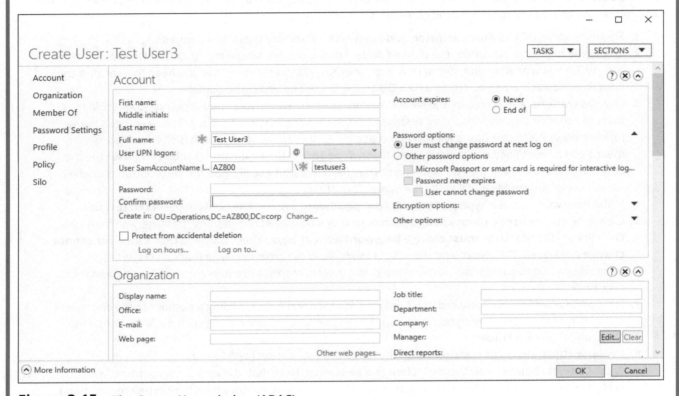

Figure 3-15   The Create User window (ADAC)

4. Click **OK**. In Active Directory Administrative Center, double-click **Operations**. Notice that Test User3 is grayed out and has a down-arrow icon to indicate the account is disabled. (If you don't see Test User3, refresh the view.) Right-click **Test User3** and click **Enable**. In the message stating that the password doesn't meet complexity requirements, click **OK**. You can't enable the account until a suitable password has been set.
5. Right-click **Test User3** and click **Reset password**. In the Reset Password dialog box, type **Password01** in the Password and Confirm password text boxes, and then click **OK**.
6. Right-click **Test User3** and click **Enable**. The account is enabled.
7. At the bottom of Active Directory Administrative Center, you see the Windows PowerShell History. Click the **up arrow** on the right side of the window to expand the Windows PowerShell History Viewer.
8. Scroll to the top of the history, if necessary, to see the `New-ADUser` command. Click to select **New-ADUser** and click **Copy** on the viewer's menu bar.
9. Open Notepad and paste the contents of the Clipboard into Notepad. You see the full PowerShell command that was generated when you created Test User3. Close Notepad without saving the file.
10. Scroll through the PowerShell history to see other commands that were generated for setting the password and other account properties. It isn't obvious which command enables the account. Find the last **Set-ADObject** command in the history. The `userAccountControl=8389120` part of the command is what does the job. This parameter sets account properties that specify the account is a normal user and the password must be changed at next logon.

(continues)

Activity 3-5 Continued

> **Note 7**
>
> You can learn more about the `userAccountControl` parameter at *https://support.microsoft.com/kb/305144*.

11. Although the PowerShell commands generated by Active Directory Administrative Center aren't always the most straightforward way to accomplish a task, they can help you learn how to use these commands for writing scripts. Close Active Directory Administrative Center.
12. If you're continuing to the next activity, stay signed in; otherwise, sign out or shut down the computer.

> **Note 8**
>
> A simpler PowerShell cmdlet for enabling an account is `Enable-ADAccount`. For example, `Enable-ADAccount testuser3` enables the testuser3 account.

Managing Group Accounts

> **Microsoft Exam AZ-800:**
> Deploy and manage Active Directory Domain Services (AD DS) in on-premises and cloud environments.
> - Create and manage AD DS security principals
> - Configure and manage multisite, multidomain, and multiforest environments

Active Directory group objects are the main security principal that administrators use to grant rights and permissions to users. Using groups to assign user rights and permissions is preferable to using separate user accounts, mainly because groups are easier to manage. Users with similar access requirements to resources can be made members of a group, and instead of creating ACEs for each user in a network resource's DACL, you can make a single entry for the group. Furthermore, if a user changes departments or positions in the company, you can remove the user from one group and place the user in another group that meets his or her new access requirements. With a single administrative action, you can completely alter the user's access to resources. If permissions are assigned to a single user account, the administrator must find each resource for which the user has an ACE, make the necessary changes, and then add the user account to the DACL for each resource the new department or position requires. When an administrator creates a group in Active Directory Users and Computers, there are two other settings aside from assigning a name. The settings are group type and group scope, as discussed in the following sections.

Group Types

There are two group types: security groups and distribution groups. As mentioned, a distribution group is used to group users together, mainly for sending emails to several people at once with an Active Directory–integrated email application, such as Microsoft Exchange. Distribution groups aren't security principals and therefore can't be used to assign rights and permissions to their members. A distribution group can have the following objects as members: user accounts, contacts, other distribution groups, security groups, and computers.

Because you can mix user accounts and contacts, you can build useful distribution groups that include people outside your organization. You can also nest groups, which makes organizing users and contacts more flexible. However, because distribution groups aren't used for security and are useful only with certain applications, their use in Active Directory is more limited than security groups.

Security groups are the main Active Directory object administrators use to manage network resource access and grant rights to users. Most discussions about groups focus on security groups rather than distribution groups, and in general, when the term *group* is used without a qualifier, a security group should be assumed. Security groups can contain the same types of objects as distribution groups. However, if a security group has a contact as a member and the security group is granted permission to a resource, the permission doesn't extend to the contact because a contact isn't a security principal. Security groups can also be used as distribution groups by applications such as Microsoft Exchange, so re-creating security groups as distribution groups isn't necessary for email purposes.

Converting Group Type

You can convert the **group type** from security to distribution and vice versa. However, only a security group can be added to a resource's DACL. If a security group is an entry in the DACL for a shared folder, for example, and the security group is converted to a distribution group, the group remains in the DACL but has no effect on access to the resource for any of its members.

The need to convert group type isn't all that common, but when it's necessary, usually a distribution group is converted to a security group. This conversion might be necessary when, for example, a group of users is assigned to collaborate on a project. Distribution groups composed of team members might be created for the purpose of email communication about the project, but later, it might be determined that the project requires considerable network resources to which team members need access. The distribution group could be converted to a security group for the purpose of assigning rights and permissions, and the security group could still be used as an email distribution group.

Group Scope

The **group scope** determines the reach of a group's application in a domain or a forest: which security principals in a forest can be group members and to which forest resources a group can be assigned rights or permissions. Three group scope options are possible in a Windows forest: domain local, global, and universal. A fourth scope—local—applies only to groups created in the SAM database of a member computer or standalone computer. Local groups aren't part of Active Directory. For each group scope, Table 3-2 summarizes possible group members, which groups the scope can be a member of, and to which resources permissions or rights can be assigned.

Table 3-2 Group scope membership and resource assignment

Group scope	Possible members	Can be a member of	Permissions and rights assignments
Domain local	User accounts, computer accounts, global groups from any domain in the forest, and universal groups Other domain local groups from the same domain User accounts, computer accounts, global groups, and universal groups from trusted domains in another forest	Domain local groups in the same domain Local groups on domain member computers; domain local groups in the Builtin folder can be members only of other domain local groups	Resources on any DC or member computer in the domain; domain local groups in the Builtin folder can be added to DACLs only on DCs, not on member computers
Global	User accounts, computer accounts, and other global groups in the same domain	Global groups in the same domain and universal groups Domain local groups or local groups on member computers in any domain in the forest or trusted domains in another forest	Resources on any DC or member computer in any domain in the forest or trusted domains in another forest
Universal	User accounts, computer accounts, global groups from any domain in the forest, and other universal groups	Universal groups from any domain in the forest Domain local groups or local groups on member computers in any domain in the forest or trusted domains in another forest	Resources on any DC or member computer in any domain in the forest or trusted domains in another forest

Domain Local Groups

A **domain local group** is the main security principal recommended for assigning rights and permissions to domain resources. Although both global and universal groups can also be used for this purpose, Microsoft best practices recommend using these groups to aggregate users with similar access or rights requirements. Global and universal groups should then be added as members of domain local groups, which are added to a resource's DACL to assign permissions. The process can be summarized with the abbreviations *AGDLP* and *AGGUDLP*. In single-domain environments or when users from only one domain are assigned access to a resource, use AGDLP:

- **A**ccounts are made members of
- **G**lobal groups, which are made members of
- **D**omain **L**ocal groups, which are assigned
- **P**ermissions to resources

In multidomain environments where users from different domains are assigned access to a resource, use AGGUDLP:

- **A**ccounts are made members of
- **G**lobal groups, which when necessary are nested in other
- **G**lobal groups, which are made members of
- **U**niversal groups, which are then made members of
- **D**omain **L**ocal groups, which are assigned
- **P**ermissions to resources

The repeating theme is that permissions should be assigned to as few different security principals as possible—namely, domain local groups. Using this method to assign permissions keeps the list of ACEs short, making resource access management considerably easier. This rule isn't hard and fast, as there are circumstances in which other group scopes and individual user accounts should be assigned permissions. Whenever possible, however, these rules should be followed.

Some administrators create a domain local group for each level of access to each shared resource. For example, you might have a shared folder called SalesDocs that requires two levels of access by different groups: Read access and Modify access. You could create two domain local groups: one named SalesDocs-Read-DL, with Read permission, and another named SalesDocs-Mod-DL, with Modify permission. By using this group-naming standard, you have identified the resource, access level, and group scope. Next, you need only add the global or universal groups containing users to the correct domain local group. Keep in mind that the "local" in domain local refers to where resources this group scope is assigned can be located. You can't, for example, give a domain local group from Domain A permission to a resource in Domain B.

Global Groups

As mentioned, a **global group** is used mainly to group users from the same domain with similar access or rights requirements. A global group's members can be user accounts, computer accounts, and other global groups from the same domain. However, a global group is considered global because it can be made a member of a domain local group in any domain in the forest or in trusted domains in other forests. Global groups can also be assigned permissions to resources in any domain in the forest or in trusted domains in other forests.

A common use of global groups is creating one for each department, location, or both. In a single-domain environment, global groups are added to domain local groups for assigning resource permissions. You might wonder why user accounts aren't simply added directly to a domain local group, bypassing global groups altogether. In a single-domain environment, you can do this, but the approach has some drawbacks:

- Domain local group memberships can become large and unwieldy, particularly for resources to which many users from several departments must have access. Examine Figure 3-16 and think about which group you would rather manage.
- If the company ever adds a domain, you need to redesign group memberships to grant permissions to cross-domain resources. This task is necessary because a domain local group can't be a member of a group or assigned permission to a resource in another domain.

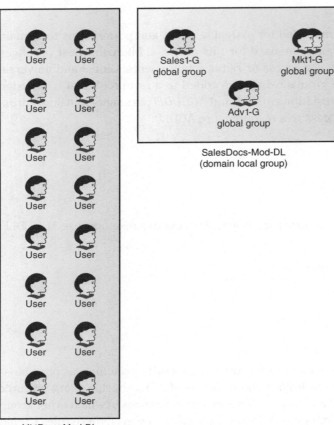

Figure 3-16 Global groups nested inside a domain local group

In multidomain environments where departments are represented in more than one domain, departmental global groups from each domain can be aggregated into a universal group, which is then made a member of a domain local group for resource access. For example, in Figure 3-17, both the U.S. and UK csmtech.corp domains have a global group called Sales. These global groups are added to the universal group Sales-U in the csmtech.corp parent domain; Sales-U is then made a member of the domain local group assigned permissions to the shared folder. Keep in mind that the shared resource could be located in any of the three domains, as long as the domain local group is in the same domain as the shared resource. The universal group in this example can be added to a domain local group in any domain in the forest as well as trusted domains in other forests.

Universal Groups

A **universal group** is special in a couple of ways. First, a universal group's membership information is stored only on domain controllers configured as global catalog servers. Second, they are the only type of group with a truly universal nature:

- User accounts, computer accounts, global groups, and universal groups from any domain in the forest can be a member.
- They can be a member of other universal groups in the forest and of domain local groups and local groups from any domain in the forest and trusted forests.
- They can be assigned permissions to resources in any domain in the forest or in trusted domains in another forest.

Because universal groups' membership information is stored only on global catalog servers, you need to carefully plan the placement of domain controllers configured as global catalog servers in multidomain networks. When users sign in, a global catalog server must be available to determine their memberships in any universal groups. For that

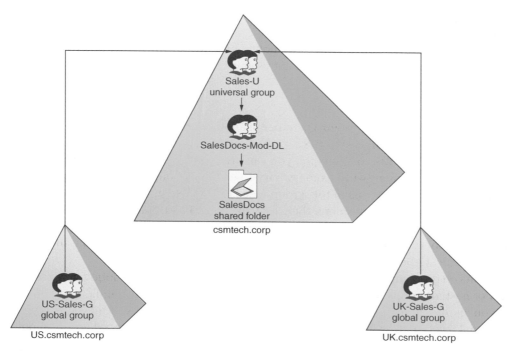

Figure 3-17   Using global and universal groups

reason, a remote office with many users should have at least one domain controller configured as a global catalog server to reduce WAN traffic during user logons.

An alternative to having a global catalog server at each site is to enable universal group membership caching on a remote office's domain controller. With caching enabled, a domain controller queries a global catalog server to determine universal group membership and then keeps a local copy of this information to use for future logons.

Universal group membership changes require replication to all global catalog servers. If you're operating a WAN with global catalog servers in remote locations, extra bandwidth is required to replicate universal group membership changes. Plan your Active Directory group design carefully so that changes to universal groups don't happen often.

Local Groups

A local group is created in the local SAM database on a member server or workstation or a standalone computer. Because groups and users created on a standalone computer can't interact with Active Directory, this discussion focuses on local groups created on computers that are members of an Active Directory domain.

Local groups can be found on any Windows computer that isn't a domain controller, and you manage them with the Local Users and Groups snap-in in the Computer Management MMC. Using local groups to manage resources on a member computer is generally discouraged because it decentralizes resource management. Assigning permissions and rights on member computers to domain local groups is better. However, when a Windows computer becomes a domain member, Windows changes the membership of two local groups automatically:

- *Administrators*—The Domain Admins global group is made a member of this local group, so any Domain Admins group member has administrative access to every member computer in the domain.
- *Users*—The Domain Users global group is made a member of this local group, giving Domain Users group members a set of default rights and permissions appropriate for a regular user on every member computer in the domain.

Local groups can have the following account types as members:

- Local user accounts created on the same computer
- Domain user accounts and computer accounts from any domain in the forest or trusted domains in another forest
- Domain local groups from the same domain (except domain local groups in the Builtin folder)
- Global or universal groups from any domain in the forest or trusted domains in another forest

Local groups can be assigned permissions only to resources on the local computer. The most common use of local groups, besides the Administrators and Users local groups, is in a workgroup environment on nondomain computers. However, when a member computer's user requires considerable autonomy for managing local computer resources, you can grant the user enough rights on the local computer for this autonomy.

Nesting Groups

Nesting groups is exactly what it sounds like: making one group a member of another group. There are few restrictions on group nesting if you follow the group scope's membership rules. Group nesting is often used to group users who have similar roles but work in different departments. For example, you can create a global group for supervisors in each department and place users in each department with a supervisory role in this group. Next, create a SuperAll global group and place the department supervisor groups in this group (see Figure 3-18). In this way, all department supervisors can easily be assigned the rights and permissions their role specifies. Furthermore, in a multidomain environment, a similar group configuration can be developed for each domain. The SuperAll global groups from each domain can then be added to a universal supervisors group for assigning permissions and rights throughout the forest. This example follows the AGGUDLP rule described earlier.

Although there are few restrictions on group nesting, the complexity of tracking and troubleshooting permissions increases as the number of levels of nested groups increases. Like OUs, groups can be nested an unlimited number of levels, but that doesn't mean you should. In most circumstances, one level of nesting groups of the same type is enough, as in Figure 3-18. An additional level, such as aggregating nested global groups into a universal group, should work for most designs. The last step is to put your group of groups, whether global or universal, into a domain local group for resource access.

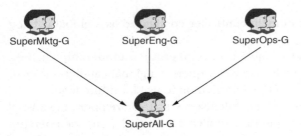

SuperMktg-G   SuperEng-G   SuperOps-G

SuperAll-G

Figure 3-18   Nesting global groups

Exam Tip ✔

The Microsoft AZ-800 exam expects you to know which group types can be members of other group types in a multidomain and multiforest network.

Converting Group Scope

When you create a group, the default setting is a security group with global scope. However, just as you can convert group type from security to distribution and vice versa, you can convert the group scope with some restrictions, as explained in the following list:

- *Universal to domain local*, provided the original universal group isn't a member of another universal group because you would have a domain local group as a member of a universal group, which isn't allowed.
- *Universal to global*, provided no universal group is a member because universal groups can't be members of global groups.
- *Global to universal*, provided the global group isn't a member of another global group because universal groups can't be members of global groups.
- *Domain local to universal*, provided no domain local group is a member because domain local groups can't be members of universal groups.

Group scope conversions not mentioned in the preceding list aren't allowed. Even though you can't do certain group scope conversions directly, however, you can do some conversions with two steps. For example, to convert from domain local to global, first convert the domain local group to universal and then convert the universal group to global.

Default Groups in a Windows Domain

When an Active Directory domain is created, some default groups are created automatically to establish a framework for assigning users rights and permissions to perform common tasks and access default resources. Windows assigns default groups a variety of rights and permissions so that users can carry out certain tasks simply by being added to the appropriate group. For example, the default Backup Operators group is assigned the right to back up all files and directories on all computers in the Domain Controllers OU. To give users this capability, simply add them as members of the Backup Operators group.

There are three categories of default groups in a Windows domain: groups in the Builtin folder, groups in the Users folder, and special identity groups that don't appear in Active Directory management tools and can't be managed. A fourth category, the default local groups in the SAM database on member computers, corresponds roughly to groups in the Builtin folder.

Default Groups in the Builtin Folder

All default groups in the Builtin folder are domain local groups used for assigning rights and permissions in the local domain. Neither the group scope nor type can be converted. Each group in this folder has a brief description in ADUC or ADAC. Table 3-3 describes the most prominent of these groups in more detail.

Table 3-3   Default groups in the Builtin folder

Group	Description
Account Operators	Members can administer domain user, group, and computer accounts, except computers in the Domain Controllers OU and the Administrators, Domain Admins, Enterprise Admins, Schema Admins, and Read-Only Domain Controllers groups. Members can sign in locally and shut down domain controllers in the domain. There are no default members.
Administrators	Members have full control of all DCs in the domain and can perform almost all operations on DCs. Default members are Domain Admins, Enterprise Admins, and the Administrator user account.
Backup Operators	Members can back up and restore all files and directories on DCs in the domain with an Active Directory–aware backup program. Members' ability to access all files and folders doesn't extend beyond their use of backup software. Members can sign in locally to and shut down DCs. There are no default members.
Event Log Readers	Members can read event logs on the local machine. This default group is helpful because you want a technician to be able to read event logs without having broader administrative capabilities. There are no default members.
Guests	This group has no default rights or permissions. The Domain Guests group and Guest user account are default members.
Hyper-V Administrators	Members have full access to all Hyper-V features. A virtualization specialist can be added to this group without giving the user broader administrative capabilities on the server. There are no default members.
IIS_IUSRS	Internet Information Services uses this group to allow anonymous access to web resources.
Network Configuration Operators	Members can change TCP/IP settings and release and renew DHCP-assigned addresses on DCs. There are no default members.

(continues)

Table 3-3 (continued)

Group	Description
Print Operators	Members can manage all aspects of print jobs and printers connected to DCs. Members can sign in locally to and shut down DCs in the domain. There are no default members.
Remote Desktop Users	Members can sign in remotely to DCs with the Remote Desktop client. There are no default members.
Server Operators	Members can sign in locally to DCs, manage some services, manage shared resources, back up and restore files, shut down DCs, format hard drives, and change the system time. There are no default members.
Users	Members can run applications and use local printers on member computers, among other common tasks. Members of this group can't, by default, sign in locally to DCs. Domain Users and the special identity Authenticated Users and Interactive groups are members of the Users group by default. Because all user accounts created in a domain are automatically members of the Domain Users global group, all domain users become members of this group as well.

Exam Tip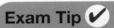

The Microsoft AZ-800 exam expects you to know the capabilities of members of the default groups.

Default Groups in the Users Folder

The default groups in the Users folder are a combination of domain local, global, and, in the forest root domain, universal scope. User accounts are generally added to global and universal groups in this folder for assigning permissions and rights in the domain and forest. Table 3-4 describes several groups in the Users folder.

Table 3-4 Default groups in the Users folder

Group/scope	Description
Allowed RODC Password Replication Group/ domain local	Members can have their passwords replicated to RODCs. There are no default members.
Denied RODC Password Replication Group/ domain local	Members can't have their passwords replicated to RODCs, so this group is a security measure to ensure that passwords for sensitive accounts don't get stored on RODCs. Default members include Domain Admins, Enterprise Admins, and Schema Admins.
DNSAdmins/domain local	This group is created when DNS is installed in the domain. Members have administrative control over the DNS Server service. There are no default members.
Domain Admins/global	Members have full control over domain-wide functions. This group is a member of all domain local and local Administrators groups. The domain Administrator account is a member by default.
Domain Computers/global	All computers that are domain members (excluding DCs) are added to this group by default.
Domain Controllers/global	All DCs are members of this group by default.
Domain Users/global	All user accounts in the domain are added to this group automatically. This group is used to assign rights or permissions to all users in the domain, but it has no specific rights by default. This group is a member of the Users domain local group by default.

(continues)

Table 3-4 (continued)

Group/scope	Description
Enterprise Admins/universal	This universal group is found only on DCs in the forest root domain. Members have full control over forest-wide operations. This group is a member of the Administrators group on all DCs. The Administrator account for the forest root domain is a member by default.
Group Policy Creator Owners/global	Members can create and modify group policies throughout the domain.
Read-only Domain Controllers/global	RODCs are members by default.
Schema Admins/universal	This universal group is found only on DCs in the forest root domain. Members can modify the Active Directory schema. The Administrator account for the forest root domain is a member by default.

Special Identity Groups

Special identity groups, some of which are described in Table 3-5, don't appear as objects in ADUC or ADAC, but they can be assigned permissions by adding them to resources' DACLs. Membership in these groups is controlled dynamically by Windows, can't be viewed or changed manually, and depends on how an account accesses the OS. For example, membership in the Authenticated Users group is assigned to a user account automatically when the user logs on to a computer or domain. No group scope is associated with special identity groups, and users can be members of more than one special identity group at a time. For example, anyone who authenticates to a Windows computer is a member of the Authenticated Users group. In addition, users who sign in remotely with Remote Desktop are members of both the Interactive group and the Remote Interactive Logon group. Special identity groups are also called "well-known groups." You can view all your group memberships, including current membership in special identity groups, by entering `whoami /groups` at a command prompt.

> **Note 9**
>
> For more information on using the `whoami` command, enter `whoami /?` at a command prompt.

Table 3-5 Special identity groups

Group	Description
Anonymous Logon	Users and services that access domain resources without using an account name or a password. Typically used when a user accesses an FTP server that doesn't require user account logon.
Authenticated Users	Members include any user account (except Guest) logging on to a computer or domain with a valid username and password. Often used to specify all users in a forest.
Creator Owner	A user becomes a member automatically for a resource he or she created (such as a folder) or took ownership of. Often assigned Full control permission for subfolders and files only on the root of a drive so that a user who creates a file or folder on the drive has full control of the object automatically.
Dial-up	A user logged on through a dial-up connection is a member.
Everyone	Refers to all users who access the system. Similar to the Authenticated Users group but includes the Guest user.
Interactive	Members are users logged on to a computer locally or through Remote Desktop. Used to specify that only a user sitting at the computer's console is allowed to access a resource on that computer.
Local	Includes all users who have signed in locally.

(continues)

Table 3-5 (continued)

Group	Description
Network	Members are users signed in to a computer through a network connection. Used to specify that only a user who's trying to access a resource through the network can do so.
Remote Interactive Logon	Members include users who sign in to a computer remotely through Remote Desktop.
Owner Rights	Represents the current owner of a folder or file. Permissions set on this group can be used to override implicit permissions granted to the owner of a file, such as Change Permissions and Take Ownership.
Service	Any security principal logged on as a service is a member.
System	Refers to the Windows OS.
Self	Refers to the object whose permissions are being set. If this group is an ACE in the object's DACL, the object can access itself with the specified permissions.

Self-Check Questions

5. Which of the following is *not* a group scope found on a domain controller?

   a. Universal
   b. Global

   c. Forest local
   d. Domain local

6. Which of the following is the acronym used to describe best practices for using groups and assigning permissions in a multidomain forest?

   a. AUUGDLP
   b. ADLGP

   c. AUGDLP
   d. AGGUDLP

○ Check your answers at the end of this module.

Activity 3-6

Creating Groups with Different Scopes

Time Required: 20 minutes
Objective: Create groups with different scopes.
Required Tools and Equipment: ServerDC1
Description: In this activity, you work with groups and see how nesting groups and converting group scope work.

1. On ServerDC1, open Active Directory Users and Computers.
2. Create a new OU named **TestOU1**. Click **TestOU1** and create the following security groups with the indicated scope: **Group1-G** (global), **Group2-G** (global), **Group1-DL** (domain local), **Group2-DL** (domain local), **Group1-U** (universal), and **Group2-U** (universal).
3. In the right pane of Active Directory Users and Computers, double-click **Group1-G** to open its Properties dialog box. In the Group scope section, notice that the Domain local option is disabled because converting from global to domain local isn't allowed.
4. Click the **Members** tab, and then click **Add**. Type **Group2-G**, click **Check Names**, and then click **OK**.
5. Click **Add**. Type **Group1-DL** and click **Check Names**. The Name Not Found message box is displayed because domain local groups can't be members of global groups. Click **Cancel**.
6. Click **Advanced**, and then click **Find Now**. Active Directory displays only valid objects that can be made a group member, so no domain local or universal groups are listed. Click **Cancel** twice, and then click **OK**.

(continues)

Activity 3-6 Continued

7. Double-click **Group2-G** to open its Properties dialog box. In the Group scope section, click the **Universal** option button, and then click **OK**. You should get an error message stating that a global group can't have a universal group as a member. Because Group2-G is a member of Group1-G, attempting to convert it to universal violates that rule. Click **OK**, and then click **Cancel**.

8. Double-click **Group1-DL** to open its Properties dialog box. In the Group scope section, the Global option is disabled because you can't convert a domain local group to a global group.

9. Click the **Members** tab and add **Group1-G** as a member. Adding a global group as a member of a domain local group is in line with the AGDLP best practice. Click **OK** twice.

10. Double-click **Group1-U** to open its Properties dialog box. Add **Group2-U** as a member, and then click **OK** twice. Double-click **Group2-U** to open its Properties dialog box. In the Group scope section, click **Domain local**, and then click **OK**. You get an error message, which reinforces the rule that universal groups can be converted to domain local groups only if they're not already a member of another universal group. Click **OK**, and then click **Cancel**.

11. Double-click **Group1-U** to open its Properties dialog box. Try to add **Group1-DL** as a member. Nesting domain local groups in universal groups isn't permitted. Add **Group1-G** as a member. Success! Global groups can be members of universal groups. Close all open dialog boxes.

12. Leave Active Directory Users and Computers open for the next activity.

Activity 3-7

Working with Default Groups

Time Required: 15 minutes
Objective: View properties of default groups.
Required Tools and Equipment: ServerDC1
Description: In this activity, you examine the properties of default groups to see their scope and default membership.

1. On ServerDC1, open Active Directory Users and Computers, if necessary.

2. Click the **Builtin** folder. Double-click the **Administrators** group to open its Properties dialog box. The options in the Group scope and Group type sections are disabled because you can't change the scope or type of groups in the Builtin folder. Notice that the selected scope is Builtin local. These groups are considered domain local, but there are some differences between Builtin local and other domain local groups, as you'll see.

3. Click the **Members** tab to see this group's members, and then click **Cancel**.

4. Next, view the membership of the **Guests** and **Users** groups. Notice that the Users group has two special identities as members: Authenticated Users and Interactive. In addition, Domain Users is a member. Close both Properties dialog boxes.

5. Click the **Users** folder. Double-click **Domain Admins** to open its Properties dialog box. Notice that you can't change this group's scope or type. Click the **Members** tab to view the group membership, and then click **Cancel**.

6. Next, view the membership of the **Domain Users** group. Notice that all the users you have created became members of this group automatically. Close this Properties dialog box.

7. View the membership of the **Domain Computers** group. Currently, ServerDM1 and ServerDM2 are both members. When a computer is joined to the domain, the computer account is added to this group.

8. To see the groups your currently logged-on account is a member of, open a command prompt window. Type **whoami /groups** and press **Enter**. You see a long list of groups the domain administrator is a member of, including several special identity groups, such as Everyone, Interactive, Authenticated Users, and Local. In the output, these groups are identified as well-known groups. Close the command prompt window.

9. Continue to the next activity.

Working with Computer Accounts

Microsoft Exam AZ-800:
Deploy and manage Active Directory Domain Services (AD DS) in on-premises and cloud environments.
- Create and manage AD DS security principals
- Configure and manage multisite, multidomain, and multiforest environments

Computer accounts are created in Active Directory when a client computer becomes a member of the domain. Like a user account, a computer account is a security principal with a security identifier (SID) and a password, and it must authenticate to the domain. Unlike a user account, an administrator can't manage a computer account's password. The Windows OS changes it automatically every 30 days as long as it can contact a domain controller.

Don't confuse logging on to a computer connected to a computer account in Active Directory with a user's ability to access domain resources. A user can sign in to a workgroup computer with any Windows version installed and still access domain resources. For example, if users sign in to a Windows 10 computer that isn't a domain member, they can access domain resources in the usual way by using the UNC path. However, they must sign in to each domain resource they want to access in the format *domain\username*. From an administrator's standpoint, having users sign in to computers that are domain members has these advantages:

- *Single sign-on*—Users who sign in from domain member computers have access to any permitted resources throughout the forest without needing to authenticate again.
- *Active Directory search*—Users of domain member computers can search Active Directory for objects and resources throughout the forest.
- *Group policies*—Administrators can manage aspects of member computers by using group policies, including security settings and use restrictions.
- *Remote management*—Administrators can right-click a computer object and click Manage to run the Computer Management MMC for member computers.

Creating Computer Accounts

Computer accounts are created in Active Directory in two ways:

- A user changes the computer membership from Workgroup to Domain in the System Properties dialog box of a Windows computer, thereby joining the domain and creating the computer account automatically.
- An administrator creates the account manually in Active Directory.

Usually, computer accounts are created when a computer joins the domain. When a computer account is created in this way, the account is placed in the Computers folder by default. This behavior applies both to client OS computers, such as Windows 11 computers, and server OS computers running a version of Windows Server.

By default, the Authenticated Users group is granted the "Add workstations to domain" right so that users need only a valid username and password to join their computers to the domain if the computer account doesn't already exist. This right permits users to join computers to the domain and create up to 10 computer accounts in the domain. If administrators don't want users to have this right, they can change it through group policies. Other groups that can add workstations to a domain are Domain Admins, Account Operators, and Enterprise Admins.

You can also create computer accounts manually before a computer joins a domain. When a computer attempts to join a domain, Active Directory attempts to find a computer account matching the computer name. If it finds the account, the user is prompted for domain credentials. The computer is joined to the domain if the user has valid credentials. When a computer account is created manually, the administrator chooses which users or groups can join a computer with that account name to the domain. By default, the Domain Admins group has that right (see Figure 3-19). Using this method for creating computer accounts means more work for an administrator but more control over which computers can join the domain.

Figure 3-19   Creating a computer account

Changing the Default Computer Account Location

To gain the full benefit of computer accounts, move them to an OU you have created because the Computers folder can't have a group policy linked to it. Furthermore, because you usually require different policies for servers and user computers, you can move server computer accounts and user computer accounts to separate OUs and link different group policies to these OUs.

You can change the default location for computer accounts that are created automatically when they join the domain by using the `redircmp.exe` command-line program. You might want to do this so that computers joined to the domain are immediately subject to group policies and you don't have to remember to move them later. For example, to change the default location for computer accounts to the MemberComputers OU in the csmtech.corp domain, type the following command on a domain controller:

```
redircmp ou=MemberComputers,dc=csmtech,dc=corp
```

Joining a Domain

The process for joining a domain is straightforward: On the computer joining the domain, go to the Computer Name tab in the System Properties dialog box, click Change, click the Domain option button, and type the name of the domain you want the computer to join. You're prompted for credentials for a domain user account and then prompted to restart the computer to finish the operation. If the computer account doesn't already exist, it's created automatically as long as the domain user account has the "Add workstations to the domain" right. If the computer account already exists, the user account must have been granted the right to join the computer to the domain when the computer account was created.

As with most tasks you perform in the GUI, a command-line program is available to perform the same task. These commands are particularly useful when you're joining a Server Core computer to the domain. To join a domain, enter this command:

```
netdom join ComputerName /Domain:DomainName /UserD:UserName
   /PasswordD:Password
```

In this command, *ComputerName* is the name of the computer you want to join to the domain, and *DomainName* is the name of the domain. *UserName* is the logon name of a user account that has the right to join the computer to the domain. *Password* is the password for *UserName*. You can use * instead of specifying the password so that users are prompted for a password and it is masked when they type it.

To join a domain by using PowerShell, enter this cmdlet:

```
Add-Computer -DomainName DomainName -Restart
```

In this command, *DomainName* is the name of the domain you want to join. You're prompted for credentials for a user account that has the necessary permissions, and then the computer restarts. You can use this cmdlet to join multiple computers to the domain at the same time. For more information and examples on using this cmdlet, type `get-help Add-Computer -detailed`.

Note 10

Use the PowerShell cmdlet `Remove-Computer` to remove a computer from the domain.

Performing an Offline Domain Join

With an **offline domain join**, the computer joining the domain doesn't have to be connected to the network or be able to contact a domain controller when the join occurs. Later, when the computer does communicate with a DC in the domain where the offline join occurred, the computer is authenticated to the domain.

Offline domain joins are useful for large deployments of virtual machines or for mobile device deployments where network connectivity might not be available when the VM or device is deployed. It can also be useful as part of an unattended Windows installation and during setup of branch offices when there's no DC and WAN connectivity hasn't been established. In addition, offline domain joins can be done when regular domain joins can't be performed reliably, as with some WAN connections.

Note 11

Offline domain joins can be done on a running computer or an offline virtual hard drive (VHD or VHDX) image.

To perform an offline domain join, you use the `djoin.exe` command. There are two phases to the process. In the first phase, you run the `djoin.exe` command to create the computer account in the domain and create a file with metadata that's used with the `djoin.exe` command on the computer you're joining. This file is called a blob file. The syntax for this command in the first phase is as follows:

```
djoin /provision /domain DomainName /machine ComputerName
   /savefile filename.txt
```

In this command, the `/provision` option creates the computer account in Active Directory. *DomainName* is the name of the domain you're joining, and *ComputerName* is the computer account name of the computer joining the domain. *Filename.txt* is the name of the blob file where metadata is saved. You transfer this file to the computer joining the domain. The next phase is done on the computer joining the domain or an offline image. The following is the syntax for a running computer:

```
djoin /requestODJ /loadfile filename.txt /windowspath %systemroot% /localos
```

In this command, the `/requestODJ` option requests an offline domain join at the next system start. *Filename.txt* is the name of the blob file created in the first phase. The `/windowspath` option specifies the path to the Windows directory of an offline image. If the `/localos` option is used, the path to the local Windows directory is specified by using `%systemroot%` or `%windir%`. `Djoin.exe` has a number of other optional parameters. To learn more about using them, type `djoin /?` at an elevated command prompt.

Caution !

The metadata file created with the `djoin.exe` command contains very sensitive information, such as the computer account password and the domain's security ID. Take precautions when transferring this file.

Managing Computer Accounts

Computer account objects are, for the most part, a set-it-and-forget-it proposition. After creating them and possibly moving them to another OU, you might not need to do anything with these objects. However, sometimes administrators must attend to computer accounts—usually when something has gone wrong.

As mentioned, a computer account has an associated password and must sign in to the domain. The computer changes this password automatically every 30 days by default. If the password becomes unsynchronized between the computer and the computer account in Active Directory, the computer can no longer access the domain. Sometimes the password can become unsynchronized if a computer has been turned off or is otherwise unable to contact a domain controller for an extended period and therefore can't change its password. In effect, the password expires, and the only solution is to reset the computer account by right-clicking the computer object in Active Directory Users and Computers and clicking Reset Account. After resetting, the computer must leave the domain (by joining a workgroup) and then join it again. You can also use the `netdom` command on member servers with an unsynchronized account. This command resets the password on the local server and the corresponding computer account so the server doesn't have to leave and rejoin the domain.

> ## Note 12
>
> If the computer does become unsynchronized with its account in Active Directory, users get a message that the trust relationship between the workstation and the domain failed.

Another reason for an administrator to access a computer account is to run the Computer Management MMC remotely on a member computer. As mentioned, clicking Manage in the right-click menu of a computer account opens Computer Management on that computer. The Computer Management MMC includes the Task Scheduler, Event Viewer, Shared Folders, Local Users and Groups, Reliability and Performance, Device Manager, Disk Management, and Services and Applications snap-ins—quite a bit of management capability available at a click.

Disabling Computer Accounts

Computer accounts can be deleted or disabled, just as user accounts can be. You might need to delete a computer account if it's no longer a permanent domain member or if resetting the account doesn't solve the problem of a computer not being able to sign in to the domain. In these cases, you can delete the account and re-create it. The computer must also leave and rejoin the domain.

When a computer leaves the domain, its associated computer account is disabled automatically. If the same computer rejoins the domain, the account is enabled again. You might need to disable a computer account manually if the computer (a laptop, for example) won't be in contact with the domain for an extended period. When the computer needs access to the domain again, you can re-enable the computer account. You enable, disable, and reset a computer account by right-clicking it and choosing the option from the shortcut menu in ADUC or ADAC.

You might wonder why you would want to place computer accounts into groups. A common reason for creating groups for computer accounts is to use group policy filtering to configure exceptions for a group of users or computers that would normally be affected by a policy. Group policy filtering is discussed in Module 4.

Self-Check Questions

7. What command is used to change the default location for computer accounts created when the computer joins the domain?

    a. `Add-Computer`   **c.** `netdom`
    b. `redircmp`   **d.** `djoin`

8. Computer accounts that are created by a domain join can be disabled. True or False?

    a. True   **b.** False

● Check your answers at the end of this module.

Activity 3-8

Joining a Computer to the Domain

Time Required: 20 minutes
Objective: Join a computer to a domain using the GUI and PowerShell.
Required Tools and Equipment: ServerDC1 and ServerSA1
Description: In this activity, you join the ServerSA1 computer to the domain using the GUI. Then, you remove the computer from the domain and join it again using PowerShell. Finally, you remove the computer from the domain again.

1. Ensure that ServerDC1 is running. Sign in to ServerSA1. ServerSA1's DNS configuration must point to ServerDC1. Verify that ServerSA1's DNS server is the address of ServerDC1. If it isn't, change it.
2. On ServerSA1, in Server Manager, click **Local Server** and then click **ServerSA1** next to Computer name. The System Properties dialog box opens. In the Computer Name tab, click **Change**.
3. Click the **Domain** option button, type **AZ800.corp**, and then click **OK**. You're prompted for credentials.
4. Type **testuser1** in the User name text box and **p@$$word1** in the Password text box. Click **OK**. (Remember that you created testuser1 earlier, in Activity 3-4.) You see a message welcoming you to the domain. Click **OK**. In the message stating that you need to restart the computer to apply the changes, click **OK** and then click **Close**.
5. When prompted to restart your computer, click **Restart Now**. While ServerSA1 is restarting, sign in to ServerDC1, and open Active Directory Users and Computers.
6. Click the **Computers** folder. You see a computer object named ServerSA1. It was created automatically when you joined ServerSA1 to the domain. (If you don't see the object, click the **Refresh** icon in Active Directory Users and Computers.)
7. When ServerSA1 restarts, click **Other user** on the sign-in screen and sign in to the domain as **az800\ administrator**. Note that when you sign in to the domain as administrator from a member server, you must preface the username with the domain name, as in az800\administrator; to sign in to the domain as any other user, you do not need to enter the domain name.
8. On ServerSA1, in Server Manager, click **Local Computer**. Under Computer name, the entry now reads "Domain" instead of Workgroup.
9. Open a PowerShell window. Type **systeminfo** and press **Enter**. Information about the computer is displayed, including the domain membership and which DC logged you on (see Figure 3-20). Type **Get-ADDomain** and press **Enter** to list information about the domain the computer is a member of.
10. Next, you'll remove the computer from the domain. Type **Remove-Computer** and press **Enter**. Press **Enter** to confirm. Note that the changes only take effect after you restart the computer. Type **Restart-Computer** and press **Enter**.
11. When ServerSA1 restarts, sign in as the local administrator. Open a PowerShell window, type **systeminfo**, and press **Enter**. Notice that the Logon Server is now \\SERVERSA1.
12. On ServerDC1, in ADUC, click the **Computers** folder. Click the **Refresh** icon. You should see that the ServerSA1 computer account has a down arrow, which means it's disabled. Right-click **ServerSA1**, click **Delete**, and then click **Yes** to confirm. Click **Yes** again.
13. Right-click in the **Computers** OU, point to **New**, and click **Computer**. In the New Object – Computer dialog box, type **ServerSA1** in the Computer name box. Notice that the default setting in User or group is Domain Admins, which means only members of that group can join the computer to the domain. Click **OK**.
14. On ServerSA1, in the PowerShell window, type **Add-Computer AZ800.corp –Restart** and press **Enter**. When prompted for credentials, type **testuser1** and **p@$$word1** and click **OK**. You see a message that the computer failed to join the domain because access was denied. That's because when you created the computer account, you specified that only Domain Admins had the right to join the computer to the domain, and testuser1 is not a member of Domain Admins.

(continues)

Activity 3-8 Continued

```
PS C:\Users\administrator.AZ800> systeminfo

Host Name:                     SERVERSA1
OS Name:                       Microsoft Windows Server 2022 Datacenter
OS Version:                    10.0.20348 N/A Build 20348
OS Manufacturer:               Microsoft Corporation
OS Configuration:              Member Server
OS Build Type:                 Multiprocessor Free
Registered Owner:              Windows User
Registered Organization:
Product ID:                    00454-70470-43890-AA090
Original Install Date:         10/5/2021, 2:39:58 AM
System Boot Time:              3/12/2022, 7:11:16 PM
System Manufacturer:           VMware, Inc.
System Model:                  VMware7,1
System Type:                   x64-based PC
Processor(s):                  1 Processor(s) Installed.
                               [01]: Intel64 Family 6 Model 45 Stepping 7 GenuineIntel
BIOS Version:                  VMware, Inc. VMW71.00V.16707776.B64.2008070230, 8/7/2020
Windows Directory:             C:\Windows
System Directory:              C:\Windows\system32
Boot Device:                   \Device\HarddiskVolume1
System Locale:                 en-us;English (United States)
Input Locale:                  en-us;English (United States)
Time Zone:                     (UTC-07:00) Arizona
Total Physical Memory:         4,095 MB
Available Physical Memory:     2,386 MB
Virtual Memory: Max Size:      4,799 MB
Virtual Memory: Available:     3,218 MB
Virtual Memory: In Use:        1,581 MB
Page File Location(s):         C:\pagefile.sys
Domain:                        AZ800.corp
Logon Server:                  \\SERVERDC1
```

Figure 3-20   Output from the `systeminfo` command

15. Type **Add-Computer AZ800.corp –Restart** and press **Enter**. When prompted for credentials, type **administrator** and **Password01** and click **OK**. The computer restarts.
16. When ServerSA1 restarts, click **Other user** and sign in as **az800\administrator**.
17. Now that you know how to add and remove a computer from the domain using ADUC and PowerShell, you will remove ServerSA1 from the domain one more time. Open a PowerShell window, type **Remove-Computer**, and press **Enter**. Press **Enter** to confirm. Type **Stop-Computer** and press **Enter** to shut down ServerSA1.
18. Leave ServerDC1 running for the next activity.

Working with Service Accounts

Microsoft Exam AZ-800:
Deploy and manage Active Directory Domain Services (AD DS) in on-premises and cloud environments.
  • Create and manage AD DS security principals

A **service account** is a user account that Windows services use to log on to a computer or domain with a specific set of rights and permissions. A service needs to log on with a service account if it runs in the background because a user doesn't start it. When a user starts an application that runs interactively, the application uses the user's credentials to access the system, so there's no need for a service account.

In the past, two types of accounts have been used as service accounts: built-in and administrator-created. Built-in service accounts have few options for an administrator to configure different rights and permissions for different services, and the accounts are shared among several services. The OS manages the password for built-in service accounts automatically, much like the password for a computer account.

An administrator can also create a regular user account for use by a service (the administrator-created account) and manage rights and permissions for this account. However, the administrator would also have to manage password changes for each account created for that purpose, a task that can become unwieldy, especially when account policies require periodic password changes.

Starting in Windows Server 2008 R2, Microsoft introduced managed service accounts and group managed service accounts. A **managed service account (MSA)** enables administrators to manage rights and permissions for services but with automatic password management. An MSA can be used on a single server. A **group managed service account (gMSA)** provides the same functions as managed service accounts but can be managed across multiple servers, as in a server farm or a load-balancing arrangement.

> **Note 13**
>
> In this context, a service includes applications that run in the background, such as database or mail server applications.

Built-in Service Accounts

There are three built-in service accounts, each with its own rights and permissions:

- *Local Service*—Intended primarily for services and background applications that need few rights and privileges. This account runs as a member of the local Users group or the Domain Users group in a domain environment. If network access is needed, Local Service runs as an anonymous user.
- *Network Service*—Intended primarily for services that need local and network access. This account runs as a member of the Users or Domain Users group and accesses the network as an Authenticated User member, which provides more privileges than for an anonymous user.
- *Local System*—This account should be used with caution because it has privileges that are in some ways more extensive than the Administrator account when accessing local resources. When accessing network resources, the Local System account uses the local computer account's credentials.

The advantage of using a built-in service account is that no management is needed, and the password is managed automatically. However, if a service requires more privileges than the Local Service or Network Service accounts have, you might need to use the Local System account, which in all likelihood offers more privileges than the service needs. The Services MMC (see Figure 3-21) shows services using all three types of built-in service accounts.

Using Administrator-Created Service Accounts

An administrator-created service account is simply a regular user account that you create for the purpose of assigning a logon account to a service. By using a regular user account, you can assign the service's logon account only the rights and permissions it needs to run correctly. Here are some guidelines to keep in mind when you use a regular user account as a service account:

- Assign only the rights and permissions the service needs.
- Use a very complex password because a user doesn't use this account to sign in.
- Remove the account from the Users or Domain Users group if it doesn't need that group's rights and permissions.
- Set the password to never expire. If you leave the account subject to regular password policies and then fail to change the password when it expires, the service stops working. However, setting this option creates a security risk, which is why using managed service accounts (discussed next) is better.
- Never use the account to log on interactively.
- Use one account per service.

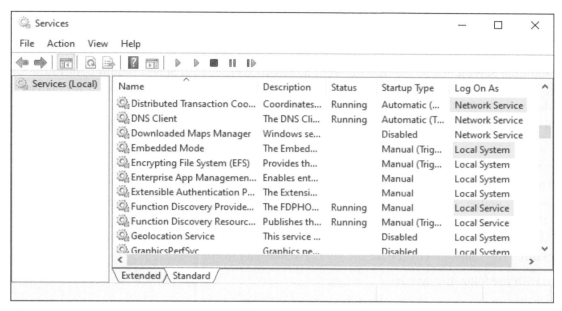

Figure 3-21   Built-in service accounts shown in the Services MMC

To configure a service with a logon account, open the Services MMC, double-click the service, and click the Log On tab. When you configure a service with a user account, you must enter and confirm the password, and then Windows automatically assigns the Log On As A Service right (see Figure 3-22).

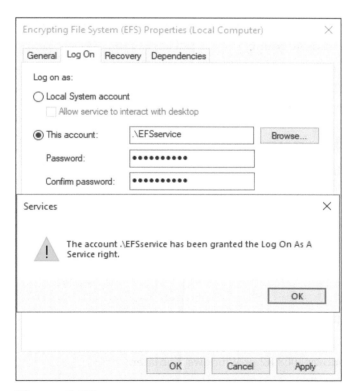

Figure 3-22   Configuring a service with a user account

Service Principal Names

A **service principal name (SPN)** is a name that uniquely identifies a service instance to a client. Multiple instances of a service can be installed in a Windows Active Directory forest, and each instance must have a unique SPN. A service instance can also have multiple SPNs if clients can use different names to access it. An SPN is required for Kerberos authentication; although administrators had to manage SPNs in the past, they're managed automatically for managed service accounts in a Windows Server 2008 R2 or later domain functional level.

When a client wants to connect to a service, it finds the service based on the SPN, which consists of the following elements:

- *Service type*—The service type is usually something like LDAP, MSSQLSvc, or HTTP.
- *Instance name*—This element is usually the hostname or IP address of the host running the service.
- *Port number*—The port number, such as 80 for HTTP or 389 for LDAP. If the service uses the standard port number, you don't need to specify this element.
- *Service name*—This element is usually the DNS name of the host providing the service. The service name and instance name are often the same, in which case the service name isn't needed.

The SPN is specified with the following syntax:

```
service type/instance name:port number/service name
```

As mentioned, the service name can be omitted if it's the same as the instance name, and the port number can be omitted if it's the standard port number for a well-known service. So, an SPN that provides web services on the host www.csmtech.corp, using the standard port, can be specified as follows:

```
HTTP/www.csmtech.corp
```

If you're using user accounts rather than managed service accounts, you might need to manage SPNs, but in most cases they're created automatically. However, if you do have to change an SPN because, for example, a computer name changes or you need clients to be able to connect with a different name, you can use the `setspn.exe` command:

```
setspn.exe -s service/instance name ServiceAccount
```

For example, if you want to set the SPN for a service named LDAP on a server named ldsServ1.cmstech.corp, using port 2300 and a service account called LDAPsvc, use the following command:

```
setspn.exe -s LDAP/ldsServ1.csmtech.corp:2300 LDAPsvc
```

Working with Managed Service Accounts

An MSA is a new type of object in Active Directory that has the following attributes:

- Has a system-managed password
- Has automatic SPN support
- Is tied to a specific computer
- Can be assigned rights and permissions
- Can't be used for interactive logon
- Can't be locked out

The requirements for using an MSA include the following:

- It must be created in an Active Directory domain.
- The computer on which the MSA is used must run Windows 2008 R2 or Windows 7 or later.
- The Active Directory module for PowerShell must be installed.
- For automatic SPN support, you must be using a domain functional level of Windows Server 2008 R2 or later.

You create and manage MSAs with PowerShell; there's no GUI tool for working with them. Follow these steps to use MSAs:

1. Create an MSA in Active Directory in the Managed Service Accounts folder (which can be seen in Active Directory Users and Computers if you enable Advanced Features on the View menu). You can also set one or more SPNs on the account when you create it by using the `-ServicePrincipalNames` option. To create an MSA named LDAPsvc, use the following PowerShell cmdlet on a DC:

   ```
   New-ADServiceAccount -Name LDAPsvc
   ```

2. Associate the MSA with a member computer that will use the MSA. To allow a computer named ldsServ1 to use the service account, run this cmdlet on a DC:

   ```
   Add-ADComputerServiceAccount -Identity ldsServ1 -ServiceAccount LDAPsvc
   ```

3. Install the MSA on the target computer by using the following cmdlet on the computer running the service. If the computer isn't a domain controller, you need to install the Active Directory module for Windows PowerShell.

   ```
   Install-ADServiceAccount -Identity LDAPsvc
   ```

4. Configure the service on the target computer using the MSA. On the computer running the service, open the Services MMC, open the service's properties, and click the Log On tab. Specify the name of the account in the format *domain\MSAname*, or click Browse to select the account. Clear the password fields because the password is managed by the OS, and then stop and start the service.

Other PowerShell cmdlets you can use to work with MSAs include the following:

- `Set-ADServiceAccount`—Change an existing MSA's settings.
- `Get-ADServiceAccount`—Show an MSA's properties.
- `Remove-ADServiceAccount`—Delete an MSA.
- `Reset-ADServiceAccountPassword`—Reset the MSA's password on the computer where the account is installed.
- `UninstallADServiceAccount`—Uninstall the account on the computer where the account is installed.
- `Test-ADServiceAccount`—Test the account to be sure it can access the domain with its current credentials or can be installed on a member computer.

Working with Group Managed Service Accounts

Managed service accounts can be used on only a single server. If a service is running on multiple servers, as in a server farm or load-balancing configuration, you can use a group managed service account (gMSA) and still get all the benefits of an MSA. gMSAs can be used only on computers running Windows Server 2012 or later with a domain functional level of Windows Server 2012 or higher.

gMSAs aren't actually different types of accounts from regular MSAs, but when you create them, you must use an additional option to specify which servers can use the account. You can specify server names or a group the servers are members of. To create a gMSA named LDAPsvc that's available to ldsServ1, ldsServ2, and ldsServ3 (all members of the ldsServers global group), use the following cmdlet:

```
New-ADServiceAccount -Name LDAPsvc

   -PrincipalsAllowedToRetrieveManagedPassword ldsServers
```

Note 14

You can also specify which servers can use the account after it's created by using the `Set-ADServiceAccount` cmdlet.

After the account is created, you need to go to each server using the account and run the `Install-ADServiceAccount` cmdlet, using the same syntax described in the preceding section.

As mentioned, gMSAs can be used in load-balancing situations; for example, if you are running an IIS web application, multiple servers running IIS can handle the load of a heavily used application. One of the advantages of using gMSAs is that the password for the account is changed automatically by the domain controller at periodic intervals. However, to facilitate the changing of the account password, a Key Distribution Services (KDS) root key must first be generated using the PowerShell cmdlet `Add-KdsRootKey`. The `Add-KdsRootKey` cmdlet can be used with timing parameters. The `-EffectiveImmediately` parameter tells the DC that it can begin using the root key immediately. However, if there are multiple DCs (which is usually true), other DCs may not be able to use the key until replication has occurred. You can add a delay to the cmdlet by using the `-EffectiveTime` parameter and specifying a time up to 10 hours in the future.

> ### Exam Tip ✔
>
> The AZ-800 exam expects you to know how to use MSA and gMSA accounts. You should also be aware that for web applications running IIS, the IIS application pool must be configured to run as a Network Service in order to use a gMSA account.

Virtual Accounts

Virtual accounts, introduced in Windows Server 2008 R2, are the simplest service accounts to use because you don't need to create, delete, or manage them in any way. Microsoft refers to them as "managed local accounts." To use them, you simply configure the service to log on as NT Service*ServiceName* with no password (as shown in Figure 3-23) because Windows manages the password. The service name isn't necessarily the name displayed in the Services MMC. You can find the service name in the General tab of the service's Properties dialog box.

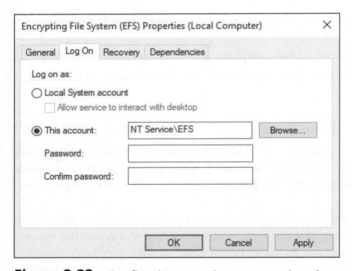

Figure 3-23   Configuring a service to use a virtual account

Virtual accounts access the network with the credentials of the computer account where they're used. If the service needs to access network resources, you give permission for that resource to *ComputerName*$ (replacing *ComputerName* with the name of the computer). In most cases, it's better to use MSAs than virtual accounts if the service must access network resources because giving the computer account permission can be a security risk. For purely local services, however, virtual accounts are simple to use and effective.

Kerberos Delegation

Kerberos delegation is a feature of the Kerberos authentication protocol that allows a service to "impersonate" a client, relieving the client from having to authenticate to more than one service. In other words, if a client has authenticated to a service successfully, the service can then use the user's credentials to authenticate to another service on the client's behalf. For example, say a user signs in to an Outlook Web Access account. The user authenticates with the Outlook Web Access service, but the user's actual mailbox is on another server. Without delegation, the user would then have to authenticate to the server where the mailbox is located. With Kerberos delegation, the Outlook Web Access service can perform the authentication on the user's behalf.

Kerberos delegation is available when you use a domain account as a service account and the account has been assigned an SPN. The Delegation tab is added to the account's Properties dialog box; this tab isn't available for a regular user account that hasn't been assigned an SPN. Figure 3-24 shows the properties of the LDAPsvc user account being used as a service account.

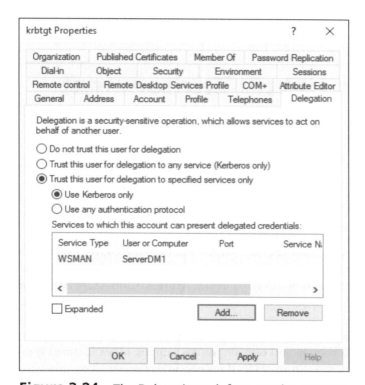

Figure 3-24   The Delegation tab for a service account

The Delegation tab has three main options:

- *Do not trust this user for delegation*—The account can't use Kerberos delegation.
- *Trust this user for delegation to any service (Kerberos only)*—The account can be used for delegation to any service but only by using the Kerberos authentication protocol.
- *Trust this user for delegation to specified services only*—This option is called **constrained delegation** because it limits the delegation to specific services running on specific computers. Constrained delegation can be limited to the Kerberos protocol, or you can specify using any authentication protocol.

Kerberos delegation is a convenient feature, especially when using multitiered applications where users connect only to a front-end interface, such as a web server. It relieves administrators of having to find a way for users to authenticate to servers that might not be directly accessible to them.

Self-Check Questions

9. Which of the following is *not* a built-in service account?

   a. Network System

   b. Local Service

   c. Network Service

   d. Local System

10. Which managed account type is created by specifying NT Service*ServiceName* as the logon account for the service?

    a. Built-in

    b. gMSA

    c. Virtual

    d. Dynamic

⊙ Check your answers at the end of this module.

Using Active Directory in a Hybrid Environment

> **Microsoft Exam AZ-800:**
>
> Deploy and manage Active Directory Domain Services (AD DS) in on-premises and cloud environments.
> - Create and manage AD DS security principals
> - Implement and manage hybrid identities

Now that you are familiar with Active Directory running on a Windows Server (which will be referred to as Windows Active Directory or simply Windows AD), we'll discuss how you can integrate your on-premises server environment with Azure Active Directory services. On Azure, Active Directory comes in two flavors: Azure AD and Azure AD DS. In a nutshell, Azure AD, or **Azure Active Directory (AAD)**, is an Azure service for managing authentication and access to applications and other resources in the Azure cloud. You might say it's an identity and access rights service. **Azure Active Directory DS (AADDS)**, or more simply Azure AD DS, is a close cousin to on-premises Windows Active Directory, with support for Group Policy, organizational units (OUs), Kerberos, and domain joining, among other features typically found on Windows Active Directory. However, as you will see, Azure AD DS does not fully support all on-premises Active Directory features. Azure AD is easier to deploy and is all many organizations will need, so we'll start there.

Azure Active Directory (AAD)

As mentioned, Azure AD is primarily used for authenticating users who want to access Azure cloud resources such as Microsoft 365, cloud storage, and third-party cloud applications. While Windows Active Directory also provides these services, Windows Active Directory does much more with respect to client computer management through domain joining and Group Policy as well as directory organization through OUs. Azure AD focuses only on user accounts and access rights, and sometimes that is all you need.

Azure AD does not use Kerberos authentication, like Windows AD. Instead, because its purpose is cloud identity management, it uses common Internet security protocols such as Security Assertion Markup Language (SAML), OAuth, and OpenID. As such, it is also referred to as a trusted provider for a variety of cloud applications and services, providing single sign-on to ease authentication frustrations that exist with so many cloud apps in use today. **Single sign-on (SSO)** is a process in which you sign in to a network using a set of credentials that are recognized by other entities and applications, so you don't have to enter your credentials multiple times. For example, if you sign in to your work network and then access Microsoft 365 applications using a web browser, SSO will transparently sign you in to those cloud-based applications using your work network credentials.

Azure AD is called a **multitenant** service because all the accounts stored in Azure AD from all Azure customers are part of one very large directory managed by Microsoft. Each customer is referred to as a tenant; their accounts are private and can only be seen by them. Just like apartments in an apartment building are all part of the same structure, each tenant of the apartment has their own private space that is inaccessible by other tenants.

Azure AD can be used by itself, with no connection to an on-premises Active Directory, or it can be used in conjunction with Windows AD using various connection tools, as you'll see. For now, we'll look at how to create Azure AD accounts.

> **Note 15**
>
> The free version of Azure Active Directory is available with an Azure subscription. Compared with a fee-based version, the free version's capabilities are limited in various ways, including multifactor authentication, end-user self-service, logging, and reporting. However, the free version is suitable for testing and for development and production environments that don't need more extensive features.

Working with Azure AD Accounts

Azure AD accounts include user accounts and group accounts. Both account types serve the same purpose as they do in Windows Active Directory—namely, to facilitate authentication and access to network resources.

Unlike Windows Active Directory, which must be installed before you can begin using it, Azure AD is a service available to you with an Azure account and subscription. When you create an Azure AD account, you must specify a domain name for the account to use. Users will sign in to their Azure resources using the syntax *username@domainname*.

Every account is assigned a default domain name that ends in *onmicrosoft.com*. For example, I am signed in to my Azure account using a personal account as opposed to a workplace account. Azure creates a domain name prefix to add to the onmicrosoft.com domain. The prefix for a personal account is usually some part of the email address you used to sign in. The email address I used is greg.tomsho@yc.edu, so my default domain is gregtomshoyc.onmicrosoft.com (see Figure 3-25).

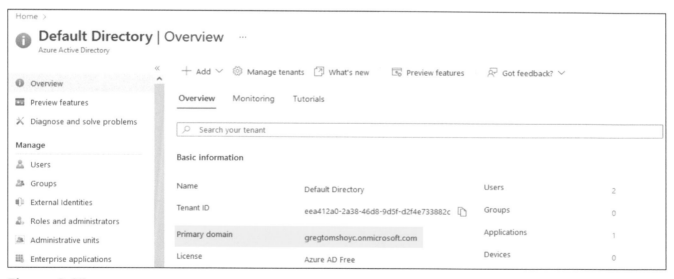

Figure 3-25   The default domain name on Azure AD

If you will only use Azure AD without an on-premises Active Directory, the default domain is fine to use when creating user accounts. However, if you are using Windows Active Directory, it is more convenient for users if you add the Active Directory domain name to Azure, which can be used when creating user accounts. You add an existing domain name using the Custom domain names option (see Figure 3-26). To do so, the domain name must be registered, and you must be able to make changes to DNS records for account verification purposes.

With your on-premises Active Directory domain name added to Azure, you can select it when creating user accounts so users will have the same username on premises and in the Azure cloud. Let's see how to create a user account in Azure AD.

Figure 3-26 Creating a custom domain name

Creating Azure AD User Accounts

When you sign in to the Azure portal, you see a screen similar to that in Figure 3-27. At the top is a list of Azure services. Azure Active Directory may be in the list if you recently used it. If not, you can find it by clicking All services or by clicking the menu button in the upper-left corner and then clicking Azure Active Directory (see Figure 3-27). You can also click in the search bar at the top of the page, start typing in the name of the service, and select it from the results.

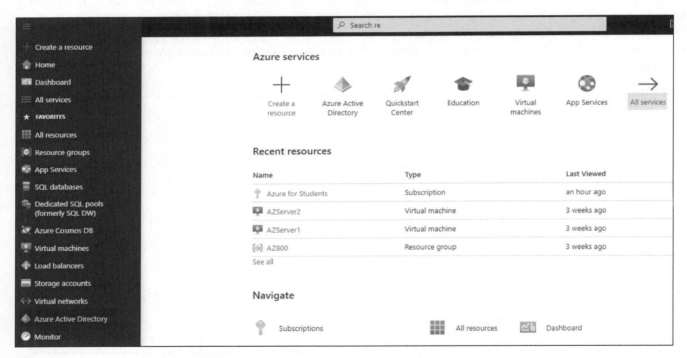

Figure 3-27 Selecting Azure Active Directory

In the Azure Active Directory view, click Add and click User to bring up the New user form (see Figure 3-28). There are two options for creating a new user:

- **Create user**—With this option, you are creating a user that is a member of your organization. You also have the option of uploading a comma separated value (CSV) file that contains a list of users to import into Azure AD. You can download a template for the CSV file that contains the format of the file.
- **Invite user**—When you invite a user, you are adding a user who is not part of your organization but who you want to give access to Azure resources. You simply supply the user's name and email address, and an invitation will be sent to the user. When the user replies and provides a password and other information, their account is added to Azure AD. Guest users can also be invited using a CSV file.

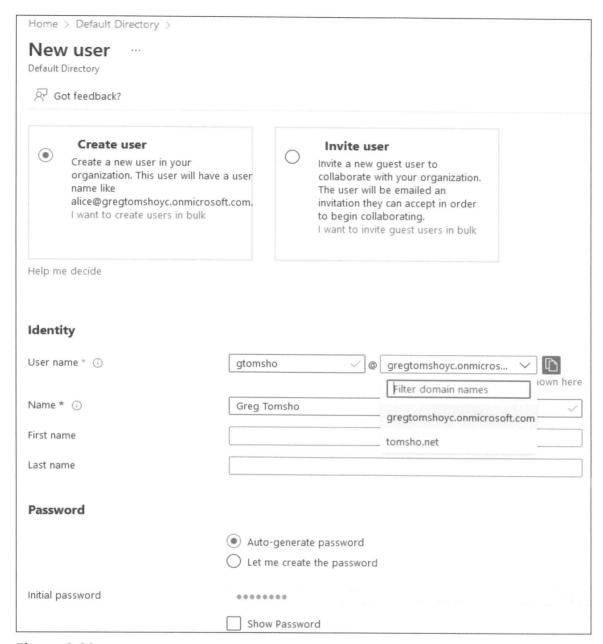

Figure 3-28   Creating a new user in Azure AD

To create a user in your organization (Figure 3-28), you supply a username and select a domain name. If you don't create a custom domain name, the only option is the default onmicrosoft.com domain name. The username and full name are the only required fields, but you can also add the user to groups and assign roles if desired. Basic directory information can also be filled in, such as job title, department, and company name. You can assign a password or let Azure automatically generate the password. If you choose the automatic generation option, you need to copy the password and put it in a safe place because this is the only time you will be able to see it.

Creating Azure AD Groups

There are two types of Azure AD groups: Security and Microsoft 365. A Security group is like a Windows Active Directory security group, meaning that it can be used to assign access to resources. A Microsoft 365 group is like a Windows Active Directory distribution group, which is used only for sending emails to groups of people. An Azure AD group requires only the group type and group name, but you can also add a description. Note that there are no group scopes as there are in Windows Active Directory. Figure 3-29 shows the New Group page.

After you fill in the group information, you can add members. There are two options for adding members to a group:

- Assigned—You manually add users to the group.
- Dynamic—Users are added to the group based on a set of rules you create. The rules specify user attributes such as the user's department, job title, and location. Dynamic membership requires at least an Azure Premium P1 level subscription.

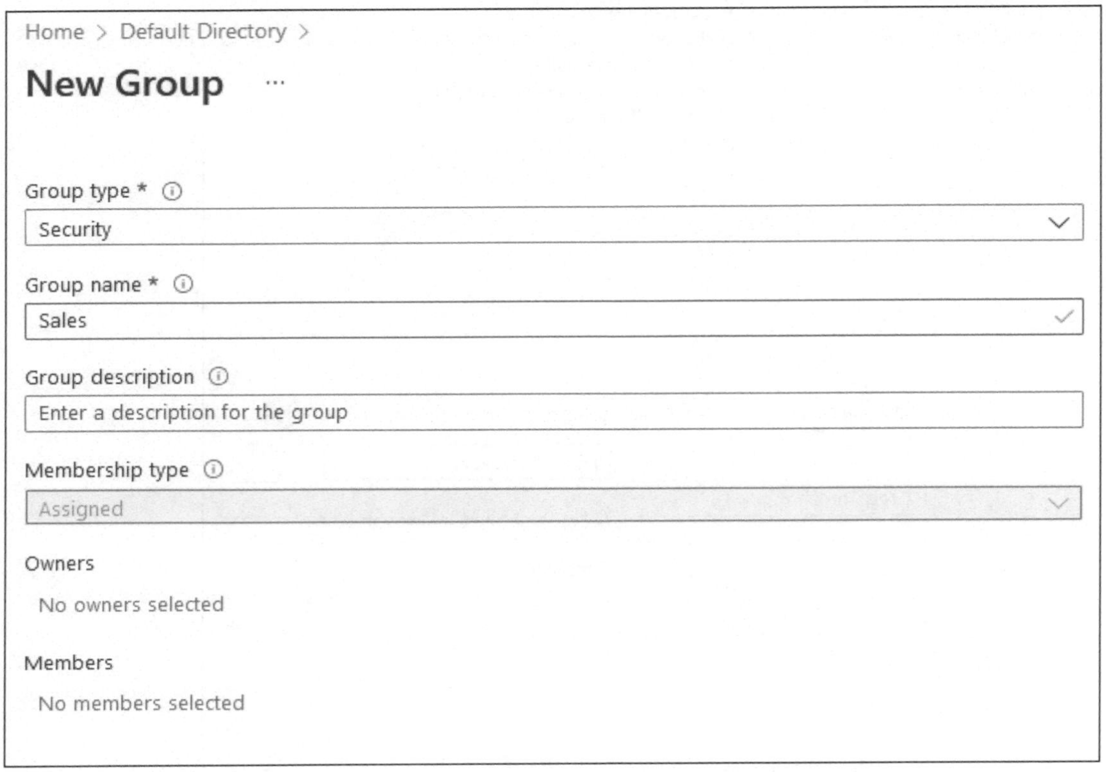

Home > Default Directory >

New Group   ...

Group type * ⓘ

    Security   ⌄

Group name * ⓘ

    Sales   ✓

Group description ⓘ

    Enter a description for the group

Membership type ⓘ

    Assigned   ⌄

Owners

    No owners selected

Members

    No members selected

Figure 3-29   Creating a new group in Azure AD

Implementing Azure AD Connect

Azure AD by itself may be sufficient if you don't have an on-premises Active Directory or if users will only occasionally need to access Azure resources and don't mind having to sign in with different credentials. However, if you want users to be able to sign in to the company network using their on-premises Active Directory account and seamlessly access Azure resources without requiring different sign-in credentials, you can implement Azure AD Connect.

Azure AD Connect is a tool that you install on an on-premises Windows Active Directory domain member or domain controller. The tool synchronizes Windows Active Directory users, groups, and contacts with Azure AD. You can select which object you want to synchronize and choose whether to synchronize user account passwords. With this feature enabled, you don't need to create users and groups on Azure AD, except for accounts that are not part of your on-premises Active Directory.

> **Note 16**
>
> While you can install Azure AD Connect on a domain controller, you should dedicate a member server to run Azure AD Connect for large Active Directory forests.

Azure AD Connect uses the secure HTTPS protocol to synchronize Active Directory objects so you are assured that your user account information is secure. Furthermore, no actual passwords are transferred; only the hash of the account password is transferred if that option is selected. Password changes are also synchronized from the on-premises Active Directory to Azure AD. Optionally, you can enable a feature called **password writeback**, which allows password changes made on Azure AD to be synchronized back to the on-premises Active Directory. Again, only password hashes are transferred, not actual passwords. To be clear, a **hash** is the process that takes a string of characters, such as a password, and runs them through a mathematical formula to create a new string of characters. There is no encryption key involved, so a hash cannot be reverse-encrypted.

Azure AD Connect also has a Health and Analytics feature that allows you to see if there are any problems syncing between your on-premises Active Directory and Azure AD.

Before you install Azure AD Connect, you need to prepare a few prerequisites:

- Select an installation server—As mentioned, you can install Azure AD Connect on a domain member server or a domain controller. However, due to the high level of resources required, you should install it on a dedicated member server in large domains and forests.
- User sign-in method—During installation, you are asked how users will be authenticated by Azure AD. The most common options are password hash synchronization, which allows Azure AD to authenticate users based on the password hash that is synced from the on-premises AD; and pass-through authentication, which requires Azure AD to communicate with your on-premises domain controllers.
- Administrator account on on-premises AD—During the installation process, you will be asked for administrator credentials for the on-premises domain you will be syncing with Azure AD.
- Azure AD Global Administrator account—You need to specify the username and password for an Azure AD user that has been assigned the Global administrator role. Best practices suggest that you should create a new Azure AD user specifically for the purpose of syncing with Azure AD Connect. When you create a user, you can assign the Global administrator role (this is a role, not a group) or you can assign the role after the user is created.
- Custom domain(s) defined in Azure—You need to create custom domains in Azure that match your on-premises domain names for any domains you will be syncing accounts for.
- Accounts to synchronize—During Azure AD Connect installation, you are asked which domains and OUs you want to synchronize. If you want to synchronize all the accounts, just specify the domains or choose all domains. However, in most cases you will want to limit synchronization to one or more OUs that contain user accounts that will have access to Azure resources.
- Password writeback—You specify whether password changes made by users in Azure will be written back to the on-premises Active Directory. If this option is not enabled, and you allow users to change their passwords in Azure, the passwords will be out of sync with their on-premises account. If you allow users to change their passwords in Azure, you should enable password writeback to prevent users from having two sets of credentials.

Installing Azure AD Connect

Azure AD Connect is a free download from the Microsoft download center. Once the application is downloaded to a domain member computer or domain controller, start the installation and continue through the Welcome screen. The Express Settings screen (see Figure 3-30) allows you to use default settings and complete the installation quickly. The default settings will sync all your accounts and use password hash synchronization as the default authentication option; password writeback will be disabled.

If you click Customize on the Express Settings screen, you will see a series of screens that allow you to customize the installation. The next screen (Install required components) allows you to specify the following options:

- Specify a custom installation location—The default location is C:\Program Files.
- Use an existing SQL server—By default, SQL Server Express is installed and used to maintain the synchronization database.
- Use an existing service account—By default, a new account is created that communicates between the SQL Server and the Azure AD Connect service.
- Specify custom sync groups—By default, four local groups are created on the server running Azure AD Connect.
- Import synchronization settings—This option lets you specify a file that contains synchronization settings.

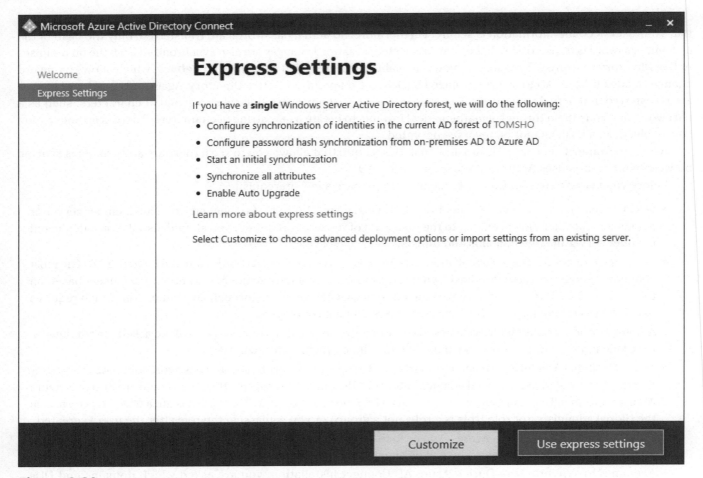

Figure 3-30   Azure AD Connect installation Express Settings screen

After you make any desired changes in the preceding options, click Install to be presented with a series of new screens where you can further customize the installation. On the User sign-in screen (see Figure 3-31), you select the authentication options. The first two options are the most common; any option you choose can include single sign-on if you click the check box at the bottom of the window.

- Password Hash Synchronization—As discussed, this option synchronizes the hashed password of the accounts stored in the on-premises Active Directory with the accounts in Azure AD. Azure AD can directly validate users' sign-ins.

- Pass-through authentication—With this option, password information is not stored in Azure AD. You must install an agent on your on-premises domain controllers to allow Azure AD to communicate with them to verify user sign-ins. Communication is secured using certificate-based authentication between Azure AD and the agent running on your domain controllers. This method has the added benefit of ensuring that passwords are only changed on your on-premises Active Directory and that password policies are adhered to.

- The two federation options shown in Figure 3-31 provide authentication using a federated trust established between the on-premises domain and Azure AD. Configuring federation requires additional servers and is beyond the scope of this discussion.

- The single sign-on option allows users who are signed in to the on-premises network to access Azure AD resources without having to enter their username or password again (provided they are synchronized). When this option is selected, a new account is created in your on-premises Active Directory that is used by Azure AD to authenticate users.

Figure 3-31 Azure AD Connect sign-in options

On the next screen, you are asked for the credentials of an Azure AD global administrator. This should be an account you create in your Azure AD directory that has been assigned the Global Administrator role. Next, you specify which of your on-premises Active Directory domains will be synchronized with Azure AD. Select a directory from the drop-down list and select Add Directory. You will then be asked for your Enterprise Admin credentials. An Enterprise Admin is a user that is a member of the Enterprise Admins Universal security group on the root domain of the forest. Azure AD Connect will create a new account in your on-premises Active Directory that will be used for synchronization. Figure 3-32 shows the screen after you have selected the on-premises directory you want to synchronize and entered valid credentials.

Next, specify the Azure AD domain name (referred to as Active Directory UPN Suffix in Figure 3-33) that you want your user accounts to use when signing in to Azure AD. Normally, this domain name will be a custom domain that you have previously created and verified in Azure AD and that matches the domain name on your on-premises Active Directory. If that's the case, you will see "Verified" next to the domain name, as shown in Figure 3-33. For testing purposes, you can specify a domain that has not been created and verified as a custom domain, but for production purposes you always want to use a verified custom domain so the users' sign-in domain will match between the on-premises Active Directory and Azure AD.

Figure 3-32   Azure AD Connect: Connect your directories

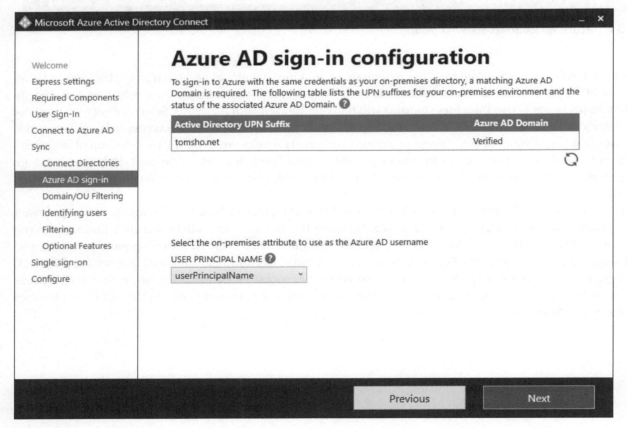

Figure 3-33   Azure AD Connect sign-in configuration

The next screen allows you to specify the domains and OUs you want to synchronize. In Figure 3-34, a single OU named AzureADUsers is selected; only the users and groups in that OU will be synchronized with Azure AD. On the next screen, you can choose how users are identified in your on-premises and Azure AD directories. The default option, which is essentially *username@domainname*, is the most common. Next, you can further filter which accounts are synchronized by specifying members of certain groups, if desired. You can enable optional features such as password writeback, a common choice if you want users to be able to change their password in the cloud and have the change synced with the on-premises Active Directory. Finally, if you selected the single sign-on option, you need to specify credentials of an on-premises domain administrator account so Azure AD Connect can configure the single sign-on feature. By default, Azure AD Connect will perform an initial synchronization after the installation is complete, or you can disable the option and manually start a synchronization later.

Once the synchronization is performed, you should see your on-premises Active Directory accounts in Azure AD, as shown in Figure 3-35. The accounts AAD User1 and AAD User2 were in the AzureADUsers OU in the on-premises Active Directory domain tomsho.net. The Azure AD Connect User account you see in the figure was created in Azure AD before Azure AD Connect was installed and was assigned the Global Administrators role. Groups and contacts in the AzureADUsers OU were also synchronized.

Configuring Azure AD Self-service Password Reset

Self-service password reset (SSPR) is an Azure AD feature that allows Azure users who have accounts in Azure AD to reset or change their password and unlock their account without intervention from an administrator. SSPR also supports password writeback to an on-premises Active Directory. An Azure administrator is required to enable the SSPR option in Azure AD.

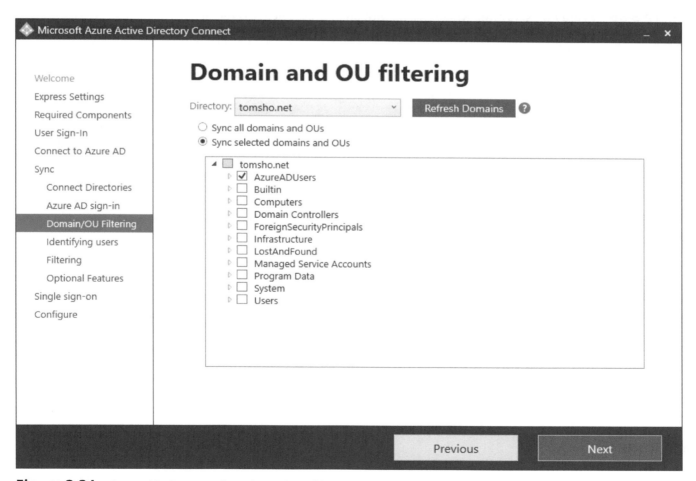

Figure 3-34   Azure AD Connect domain and OU filtering

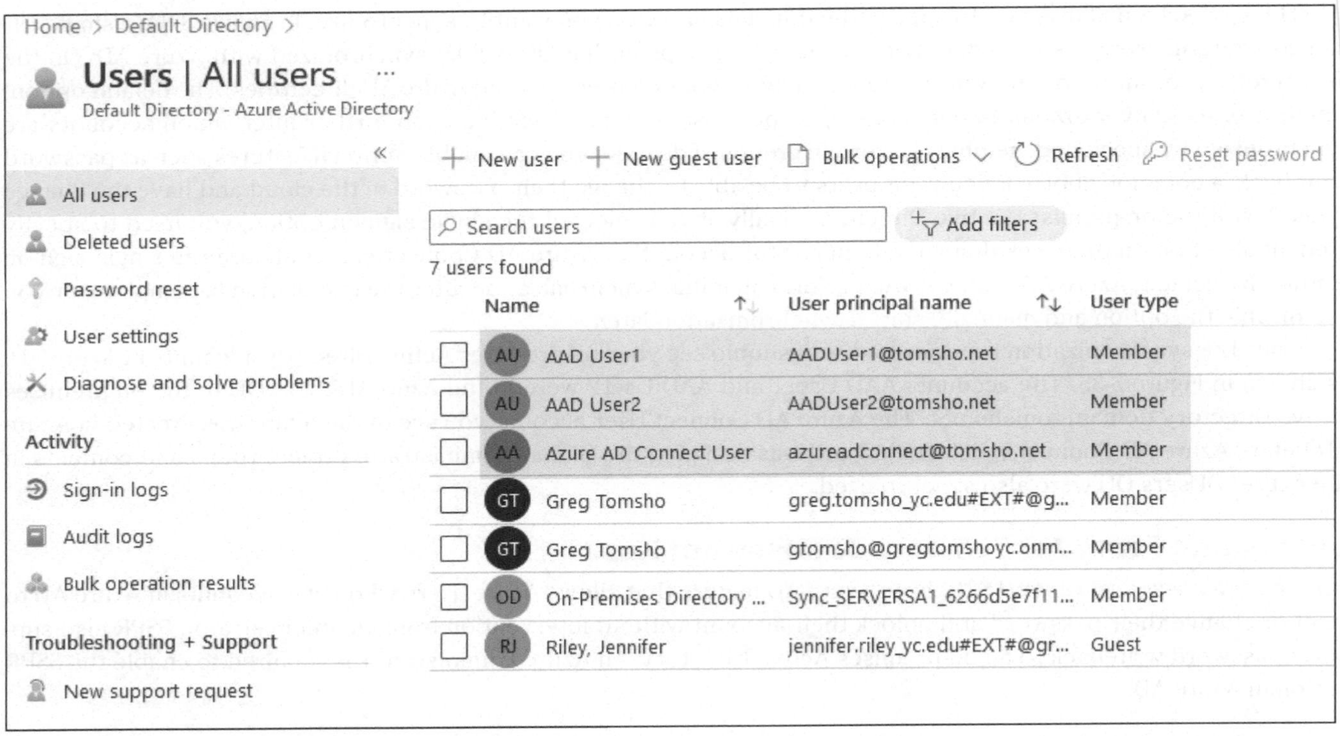

Figure 3-35   Azure AD users after synchronizing with on-premises Active Directory

---

Note 17

SSPR requires a Microsoft 365 Business Standard or Premium account or an Azure AD Premium P1 or P2 license. On-premises password writeback is not supported with the Microsoft 365 Business Standard license. SSPR is a per-user licensed feature, so a license must be assigned for each user that can use SSPR.

To configure SSPR, select Azure Active Directory from the Azure portal and click Password reset. If you don't have the proper Azure AD license, you will be prompted to get a free trial of a supporting license.

Note 18

An Azure AD Premium P2 free trial is active for 30 days and includes 100 licenses that can be used for SSPR and multifactor authentication.

From the Password reset page, you have the option of None, Selected, or All (see Figure 3-36). If you choose Selected, you choose the users that can use SSPR based on group membership. After you save your selection, you can configure the authentication methods available for the selected users by choosing Authentication methods from the menu on the left.

You can specify that users must authenticate using one or two methods, which you select from the list shown in Figure 3-37. You can choose as many methods available to users as you want, and users can choose which method they prefer from the options you select. If you select two as the number of methods required to reset a password, you must enable at least two of the methods available to users.

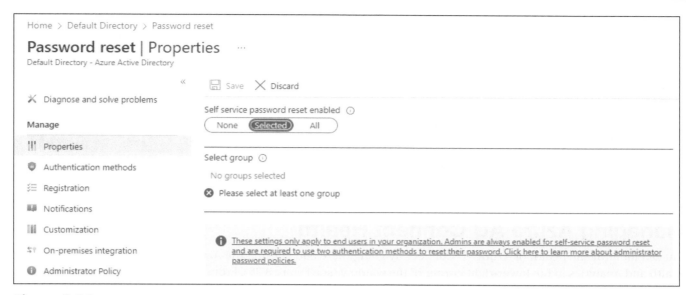

Figure 3-36   Configuring self-service password reset

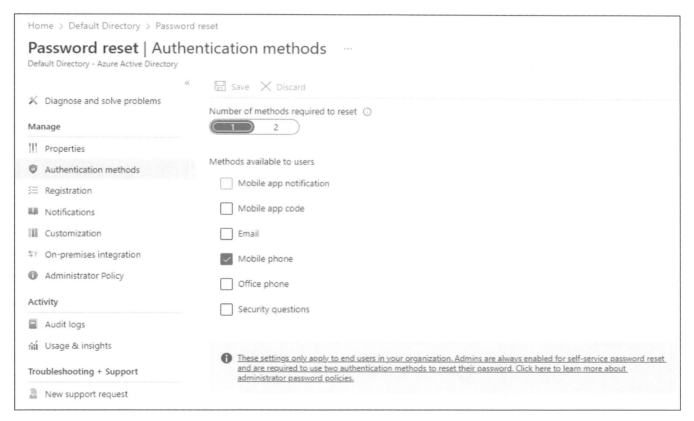

Figure 3-37   Configuring password reset authentication methods

Additional password reset options include the following:

- Notifications—You can enable the option for users to receive an email when their password has been reset using SSPR. This option is enabled by default. You can also enable the option to notify all admins when any admin resets their password.
- On-premises integration—If you enabled password writeback on the Azure AD Connect agent on your on-premises server, you can disable the feature from this page. The option is enabled by default. You also have the option of enabling users to unlock their accounts without resetting their password. The latter option is disabled by default.

Once SSPR is enabled, affected users will be asked to set up one or two of the authentication methods the next time they sign in to the portal. For example, if one of the authentication methods is via mobile phone, the user will be asked to enter their phone number and enter a confirmation code that is sent to the number to verify the method. Once the method is verified, users can choose the "Can't access your account" link on the Azure portal sign-in screen if they need to reset their password.

> **Exam Tip**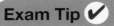
>
> When using SSPR, be sure that password writeback was enabled when installing Azure AD Connect so users that change their password using SSPR will be able to use on-premises domain resources with the changed password.

Managing Azure AD Connect Health

You can monitor the health of Azure AD Connect by going there and clicking the Azure AD Connect Health link under Health and Analytics in the lower-right corner of the window (see Figure 3-38). From the resulting page, you can check for sync errors, verify the status of related services, and configure settings (see Figure 3-39). On the Settings page, you have the option to enable or disable automatic updating of the Azure AD Connect Health agent running on your on-premises servers. The Auto update setting is enabled by default. Other options you can select from the Azure AD Connect Health page include accessing troubleshooting tools and creating a support request.

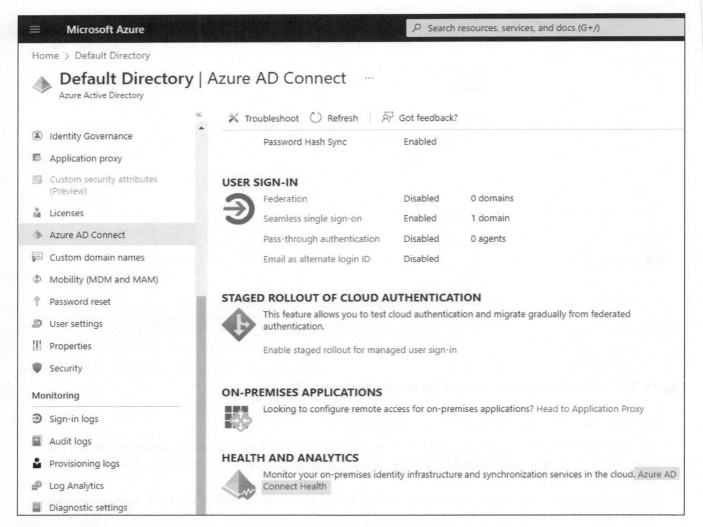

Figure 3-38   Accessing Azure AD Connect Health from the Azure AD Connect page

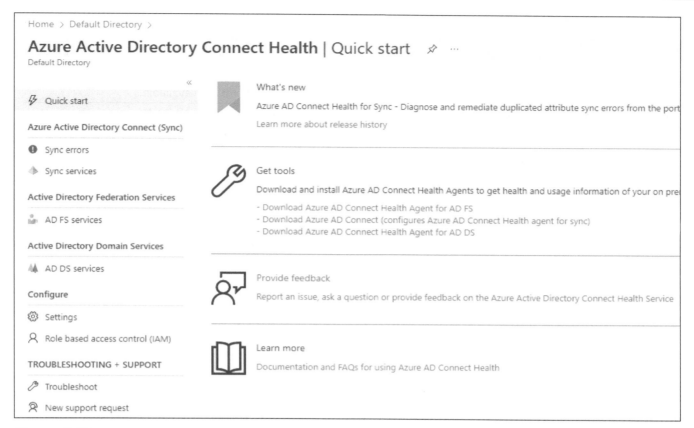

Figure 3-39   Azure AD Connect Health main page

Azure AD Connect Cloud Sync

Azure AD Connect cloud sync is a new offering for Azure AD customers. It is a more lightweight version of Azure AD Connect sync because the configuration and provisioning information is done in the cloud rather than primarily on the on-premises servers. A lightweight agent is installed on the on-premises server(s) that acts as a bridge between Azure AD and on-premises Active Directory. Cloud sync supports the same Active Directory hybrid scenarios as Azure AD Connect sync, with the addition of support for disconnected forests. These forests might be seen, for example, when two companies merge but maintain distinct Active Directory forest structures. Cloud sync requires fewer resources on your on-premises servers and is easier to configure than its predecessor. In most scenarios you can use Azure AD Connect cloud sync instead of Azure AD Connect sync. Table 3-6 shows the features supported exclusively by Azure AD sync and by Azure AD cloud sync, respectively. All other sync features are supported by both services. As you can see from the table, Azure AD Connect sync is the more mature service that provides options for fine-tuning synchronization. However, if those additional features are not needed or support for disconnected forests is required, the newer Azure AD Connect cloud sync is a good option. Keep in mind that cloud sync is a comparatively new feature, and it will probably catch up with the original sync service in offering some of the detailed configuration options.

Table 3-6   Features exclusive to Azure AD Connect Sync and Azure AD Connect cloud sync

Azure AD Connect sync exclusive features	Azure AD Connect cloud sync exclusive features
Connect to LDAP directories	Multiple disconnected on-premises forests support
Device object support	Multiple active agents for high availability
Customer-defined AD attributes	Lightweight agents
Pass-through authentication	
Filter sync on object attributes	
Device writeback	
Group writeback	
Attribute merging	
Azure AD DS support	
Unlimited number of domain objects	
Very large group memberships	

Implementing Azure AD Cloud Sync

Implementing Azure AD cloud sync is a two-step process. First, install the Azure AD Connect cloud sync agent on a member server or domain controller for the forest you want to sync. Second, configure the agent in the Azure portal. As with the Azure AD Connect sync process, you should create any custom domains on Azure AD you want to sync before starting the process. However, for demonstration purposes, the following steps use the default Azure AD domain name instead of a custom domain.

Installing the Azure AD Connect Cloud Sync Agent

Before installing the agent, create a new Azure AD user account that has been assigned the Global administrator role and sign in to the portal as the new user. Figure 3-40 shows the creation of a new account named ADcloudsync in the Azure AD directory named bookstomsho.onmicrosoft.com. This is the default domain name for the Azure account. In a production environment, the actual on-premises Active Directory domain would be created using the Custom domain names option. Once the new account is created, sign out of the Azure portal and sign in using the new account credentials. You will be prompted to change the password the first time you sign in. You should sign in to the portal using a web browser that's running on the domain member server or domain controller on which you want to install the agent.

Once signed in to the portal with the new Global administrator account, go to Azure Active Directory, click Azure AD Connect, and then click Manage Azure AD cloud sync (see Figure 3-41). Click the Download agent link and click the downloaded file to start the installation of the agent. Once the agent is installed, the agent configuration wizard starts. Click through the Welcome screen and click Authenticate. You will be asked for the credentials of the Global administrator account you created earlier. You need to enter the full UPN name, such as ADcloudsync@bookstomsho. onmicrosoft.com. (In a production environment, you would use the custom domain name that matches the domain you will be syncing.)

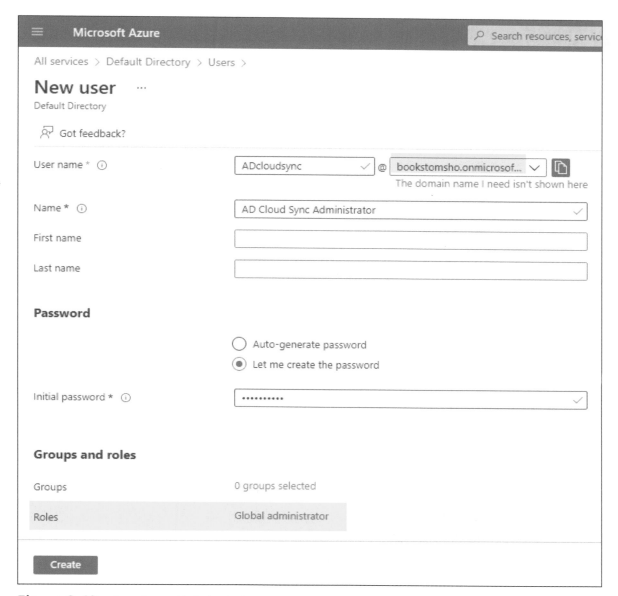

Figure 3-40   Creating a Global administrator account

Next, you are prompted to configure a group managed service account (gMSA). You can select a custom gMSA that you have previously created or allow the wizard to create the gMSA. The latter option is preferable. If you choose to let the wizard create the gMSA, you are prompted to enter Administrator credentials for the domain you are syncing. If you are syncing multiple domains in a forest, use an account that is a member of the Enterprise Admins group.

Next, you select the domain(s) you want to sync with Azure AD. The domain you used for the administrator account on the Configure Service Account page is automatically selected. Any other domains that you add will require Domain Admin or Enterprise Admin credentials. The last screen prompts you to review your choices and confirm the

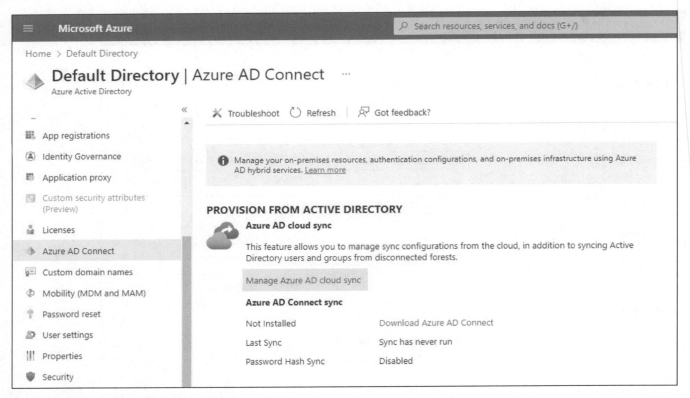

Figure 3-41   Managing Azure AD cloud sync

installation. Once the installation has finished, you can verify that the agent is running by checking the Services control panel. You should find the following two services, and their status should be Running.

- Microsoft Azure AD Connect Agent Updater
- Microsoft Azure AD Connect Provisioning Agent

You are ready to configure Azure AD Connect cloud sync in the Azure portal.

Configuring Azure AD Cloud Sync

Once the agent is installed on your on-premises server, the rest of the configuration takes place in the Azure portal. From the Azure portal, go to Azure Active Directory and then select Azure AD Connect and click the Manage Azure AD cloud sync link. From the Azure AD Connect cloud sync page (see Figure 3-42), click New configuration. If the New configuration option is disabled, verify that the agent is properly installed and running on your on-premises server. You are asked to specify what Active Directory domain you want to sync. You can also choose to enable password hash sync, which is selected by default. Password hashes are synced about every two minutes when this option is selected. You can turn this option off later, for example, after your accounts have been initially synchronized.

Note 19

You can only have one cloud sync configuration per domain. After you have configured cloud sync for a domain, you will not be able to create a new configuration for that domain. You can, however, make changes to the configuration.

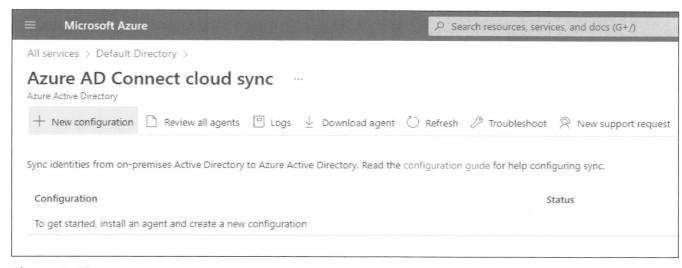

Figure 3-42   Creating a new cloud sync configuration

Next, you choose the synchronization options as follows (see Figure 3-43):

- Scope—Choose the scope of the users you want to synchronize, such as all users, specific security groups, or specific organizational units. You should use organizational units rather than security groups because there are no limitations on OUs, but there are certain limitations for very large groups and nested groups. You can choose as many groups or OUs as you need.

- Manage attributes—In this step, you again have an opportunity to choose whether to sync password hashes. You can also create complex attribute mappings for users, groups, and contacts. Attribute mapping helps ensure that account attributes are transferred in the format you prefer.

- Validate—You have the option to select individual users to sync to validate your configuration. This helps you ensure that your settings are correct before performing a full sync.

- Settings—In the Settings section (not shown in Figure 3-43), you can enter an email address so you can be alerted to any sync issues that may occur. In addition, you can choose an option to prevent accidental deletion.

- Deploy—Finally, in the Deploy section, click Enable to begin the synchronization process. A synchronization cycle occurs about every ten minutes; the initial synchronization may take quite a bit longer than future cycles depending on the number of accounts you are syncing and the frequency of changes to those accounts.

To check the status of cloud sync, you can revisit the Manage Azure AD cloud sync link from Azure AD Connect in the portal and verify that the status is Healthy.

Azure AD Domain Services

Azure AD Domain Services (Azure AD DS or just AADDS) takes Azure AD one step further and implements many of the features of on-premises Active Directory, including organizational units and group policies. Whereas Azure AD is primarily an identity service, Azure AD DS is the right choice when you want many of the same capabilities of on-premises Active Directory in the cloud. Table 3-7 lists some of the key Active Directory features supported by AADDS.

A few notable features not supported by AADDS include schema extensions and domain and forest trusts. Applications that require changes to the schema must use on-premises Active Directory. Multidomain and multiforest environments are somewhat more difficult to implement due to the lack of trusts. However, domain and forest trusts are likely to be added to AADDS in the future. In addition, changes to the directory in AADDS are not written back to the on-premises Active Directory, so in a hybrid environment, changes should occur on the on-premises domain controllers.

Some notable advantages of AADDS compared to on-premises Active Directory include the following:

- Backup of Active Directory is automatic in Azure.
- Domain controller software updates are managed by Azure.
- Domain controllers are highly available, so access to AADDS is maintained even during a partial Azure outage.

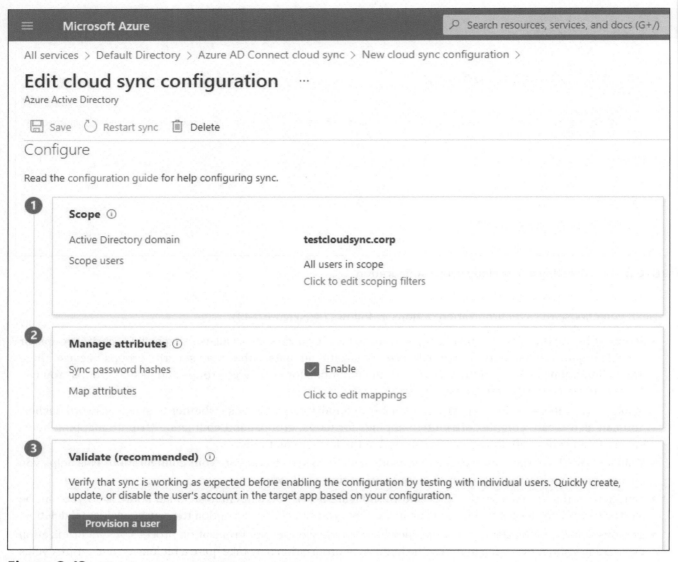

Figure 3-43 Cloud sync synchronization options

Table 3-7 On-premises Active Directory features supported by AADDS

Active directory features supported by AADDS	Notes
Secure deployment	Azure provides a secure Active Directory deployment; with on-premises AD, the administrator must secure the deployment.
DNS Server	As a managed service
Domain join	
Kerberos and NTLM authentication	
Organizational Units	
Group Policy	GPOs from on-premises Active Directory are not synced with AADDS GPOs.
LDAP/Secure LDAP support	

Implementing Azure AD DS

Before you create an Azure AD DS service in Azure, you need to have the Azure AD service running and synchronizing with an on-premises directory. It is also recommended that you have SSPR configured. From the Azure portal, choose Azure AD Domain Services from the list of services or type "domain services" into the search bar and choose Azure AD Domain Services from the search results. From the Azure AD Domain Services page, click Create Azure AD Domain Services. The Create Azure AD Domain Services wizard is launched (see Figure 3-44).

From the wizard, choose the subscription and resource group for which you want to configure AADDS. Next, select the DNS domain name, region, and SKU, which determines the level of service. The domain name can be a built-in domain that ends with onmicrosoft.com or a custom domain name. If you are syncing with on-premises Active

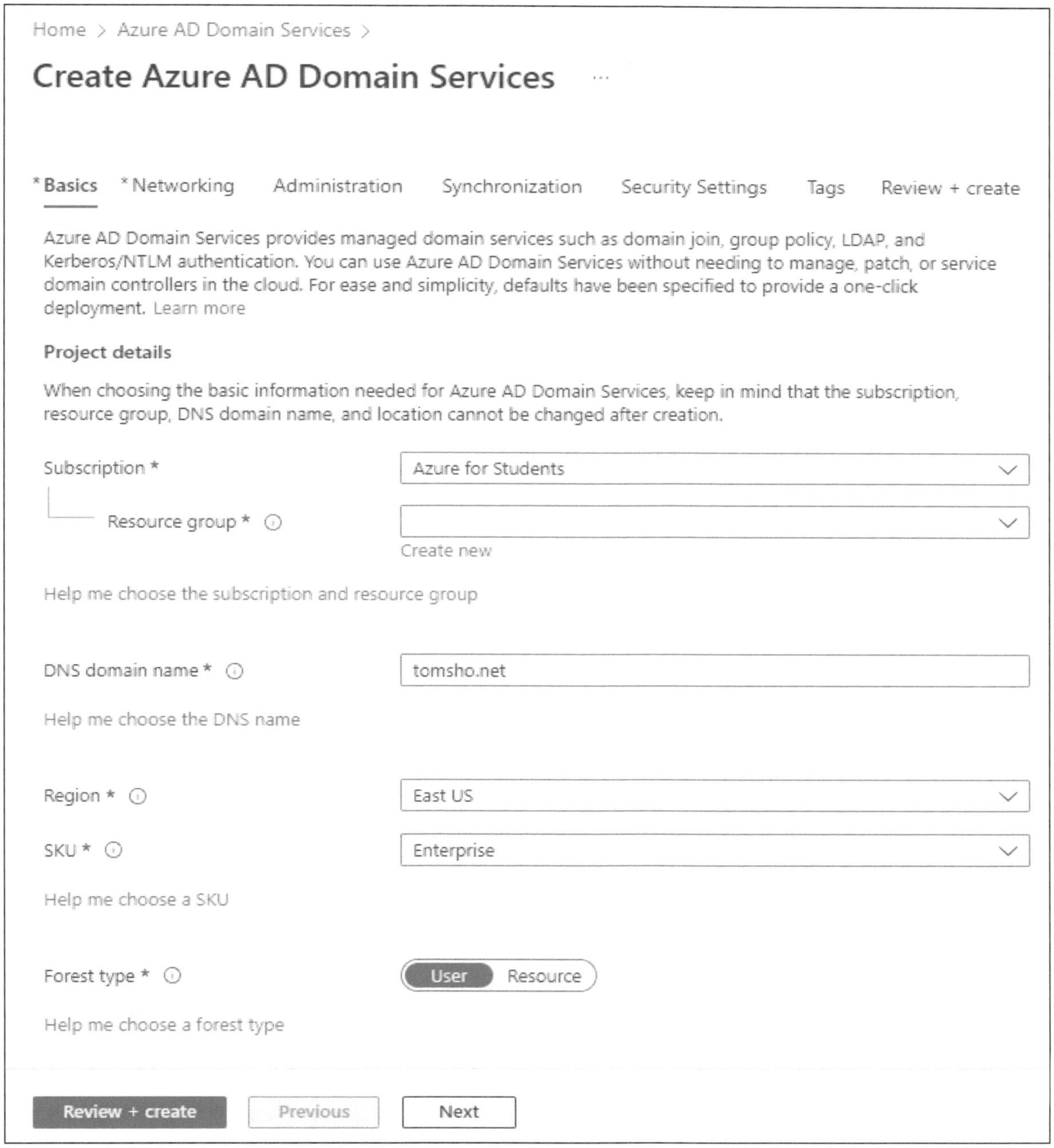

Figure 3-44   The create Azure AD Domain Services configuration wizard

Directory, you should choose a custom domain. The last option is the forest type you want to configure. There are two forest type options:

- User—A **user forest** is the default setting and the recommended choice, in which all objects in Azure AD and all user accounts in on-premises Active Directory are synchronized.
- Resource—A **resource forest** only synchronizes users and groups created in Azure AD and does not include those synced from on-premises Active Directory.

Once the initial page of the wizard is completed, you can accept the default settings for the remaining pages if desired. The remaining pages allow you to configure different network, administration, and synchronization options and change the default authentication and encryption options. For most purposes, the default settings are satisfactory. However, the most likely change you might make is the scope of the synchronization. From the Synchronization page, you can choose to sync all users (the default) or select users based on group membership. When you are finished configuring options, click Review + create; your choices are validated. Click Create to finish the deployment of AADDS. The network and domain are created along with some default objects and an initial synchronization takes place with the on-premises Active Directory. Once the deployment is complete, you'll see a page similar to that shown in Figure 3-45. If you click Go to resource, you'll see a summary of Azure AD DS and any configuration steps still required.

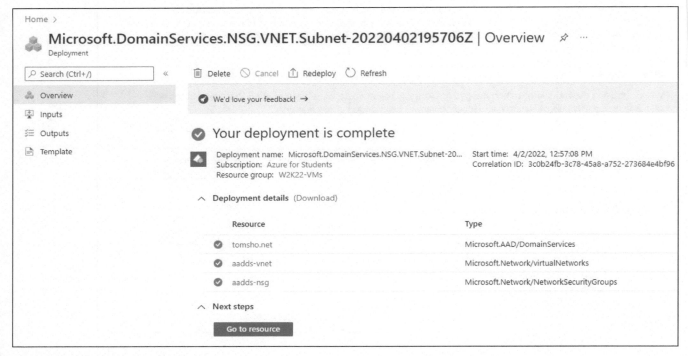

Figure 3-45   Deploying Azure AD DS

If there are any configuration issues, you will see a message at the top of the Overview page. You can click on the message and then click Run to start a detailed diagnosis. A commonly needed step is to add DNS records for the IP addresses of the domain controllers created for your deployment. If this step is necessary, you can click Fix on the configuration diagnostics page to automatically add the records. By doing so, you can join server and client VMs to the Azure AD DS domain.

Default Containers in Azure AD DS

Azure AD DS creates a couple of default OUs that are not found in on-premises Active Directory:

- AADDC Users—This OU contains the synchronized accounts from your Azure AD implementation. This OU is read-only, and these accounts cannot be moved to other OUs; however, new accounts that you create can be put into custom OUs.
- AADDC Computers—This OU contains computer accounts joined to the domain. You can move these accounts to other OUs if desired.

If you want to create custom OUs in Azure AD DS, or deploy GPOs, the Azure account you use must be a member of the AADDC Administrators group in Azure AD.

Exam Tip ✔

The AZ-800 exam expects you to know about the default OUs in Azure AD DS and the AADDC Administrators group membership requirement for creating new OUs and deploying GPOs.

Joining an Azure Windows Server VM to Azure AD DS

The main requirements for joining an Azure Windows Server VM to Azure AD DS are the following:

- A Windows Server VM—The VM must be connected to a virtual network that has access to the Azure AD DS domain. Typically, you will choose the virtual network created when you deployed AADDS and create a new subnet in that network for your domain-joined servers.
- A valid user account and password—You need credentials for a user in the Azure AD DS domain.
- An Azure Bastion host—While not required, using a Bastion host to access your server VM is preferable to using RDP and a public IP address, which has security concerns. A **Bastion host** provides a web-based interface to your Azure VM.

Once the VM is deployed and you're connected to the console, you can join the VM to the Azure AD DS domain in the same way you would join a server to an on-premises Active Directory. You can use the Windows GUI by going to the Computer Name tab in System Properties, clicking Change, and then specifying the Azure AD DS domain name. As an alternative, you can use the PowerShell cmdlet:

```
Add-Computer -DomainName AzureADDomain
```

Whether you use the GUI or PowerShell, you are prompted for credentials. You must enter a username using the UPN format user@domain and a valid password. The account must be a user account in the Azure AD DS domain. If the account you use is a synced account from an on-premises Active Directory, you need to ensure that password hashing sync is enabled for Azure AD DS.

Note 20

The details for enabling password hash sync for Azure AD DS is beyond the scope of this book. You can read a tutorial on the procedure here: *https://docs.microsoft.com/en-us/azure/active-directory-domain-services/tutorial-configure-password-hash-sync*.

Self-Check Questions

11. Azure Active Directory supports group policy. True or False?

    a. True   b. False

12. Which feature in Azure requires at least an Azure Premium P1 level subscription?

    a. Dynamic groups   c. Azure AD
    b. gMSA accounts   d. Password writeback

⊙ Check your answers at the end of this module.

Activity 3-9

Implementing Azure Active Directory

Time Required: 15 minutes

Objective: Examine Azure Active Directory and then create a user and group.

Required Tools and Equipment: An Azure subscription and access to the Azure portal

Description: In this activity, you use the default version of Azure Active Directory and add user and group accounts.

1. Sign in to your Azure portal account. From the home screen, click **Azure Active Directory** if you see it under Azure services. Otherwise, type **Azure Active Directory** in the search box and then click **Azure Active Directory** in the search results.
2. From the Overview page (see Figure 3-46), you see the default domain name assigned to your directory. You also see that one user is already created. The user is the account you used to sign in to the Azure portal.
3. Click the number **1** next to Users or click **Users** in the left pane to see the account information.

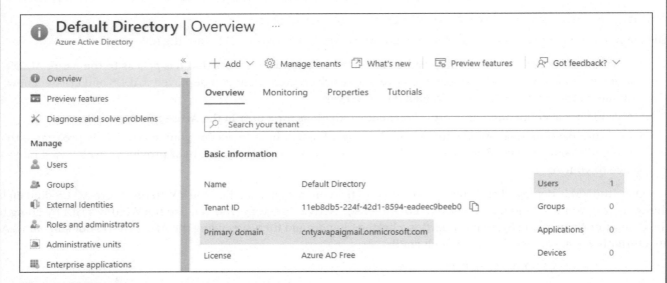

Figure 3-46   Azure Active Directory Overview page

4. From the user page, click **Assigned roles** in the left pane. You'll see that the default user is the Global administrator for Azure AD and services that use Azure AD.
5. Click the browser's **back arrow** until you get back to the Default Directory | Overview page, or click **Home** on the upper-left side of the page and click **Azure Active Directory** on the home page.
6. If you have on-premises Windows Active Directory, you can create a custom domain name in Azure Active Directory and use the same name as your on-premises Active Directory. However, the domain name must be registered, and you must be able to add DNS records to verify ownership. To see where to add a custom domain, click **Custom domain names** in the left pane of the Overview page.
7. You'll see the default domain name listed. Click **Add custom domain** at the top of the page. You'll be prompted to type the name of the custom domain. Click the information circle above the text box to see the message about updating the DNS records of the registered domain. You won't create a custom domain name in this activity, so click **Overview** in the left pane to get back to the Overview page.
8. To create a user account, click **Users** in the left pane. Click **New user** and then **Create new user**.
9. From the New user page, you can choose to create a new user or invite a user that will be added as a guest. Guest users are usually users from other organizations that you want to collaborate with using Azure services and applications. Click **Create user** if necessary.
10. Type **AZGlobal** in the User name box. The box after the @ is the domain name you want to use for the user. If you created a custom domain name, it would be available in the drop-down list.

(continues)

Activity 3-9 Continued

11. Type **Azure Global Admin** in the Name box. Note that you aren't required to enter a first name and last name; only the fields marked with an asterisk are required.

12. Under Password, click **Let me create the password** and type **Password1** in the Initial password box. The user will be required to change the password at the first login. The password has complexity requirements that are the same as Windows complexity requirements. Click the information circle next to Initial password for more information.

13. You can assign the user group memberships and roles if desired. The default role is User. If desired, you can block the user from signing in and choose a country where the user is located. Additionally, you can fill in the user's job information. This information will be used to install the Azure AD Connect software in the next activity, which requires the Azure AD Global Administrator role. Click **User** next to Roles to open the Directory roles dialog box and click to select **Global administrator** (see Figure 3-47). Click **Select**.

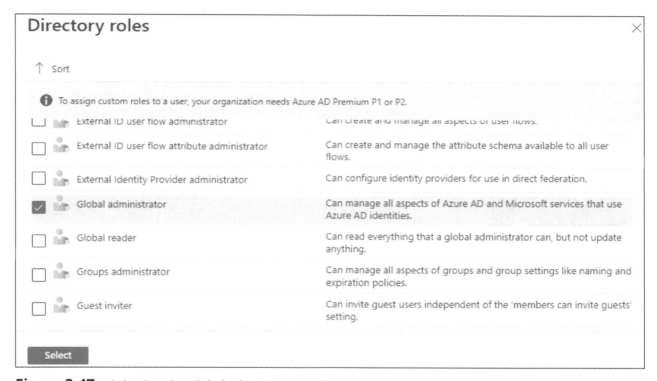

Figure 3-47   Selecting the Global administrator role

14. Figure 3-48 shows the New user page filled out. Scroll to the bottom of the page, if necessary, and click **Create**. You are brought back to the Users page. Click **Refresh** to see the new user, if necessary.

15. Click **Default Directory** at the top of the page. Click **Groups**. On the Groups page, click **New group**.

16. On the New Group page, leave the default Group type of **Security** selected. The other option is Microsoft 365. If you choose Microsoft 365, a group email address field is added to the page. Type **TestGroup** in the Group name box; you can also enter a description if you want. The Membership type can be Assigned or Dynamic. The Dynamic option is only available if you have an Azure AD Premium P1 license for each user that will use the option. With the Dynamic option, users are automatically added or removed from the group based on rules that you create.

(continues)

Activity 3-9 Continued

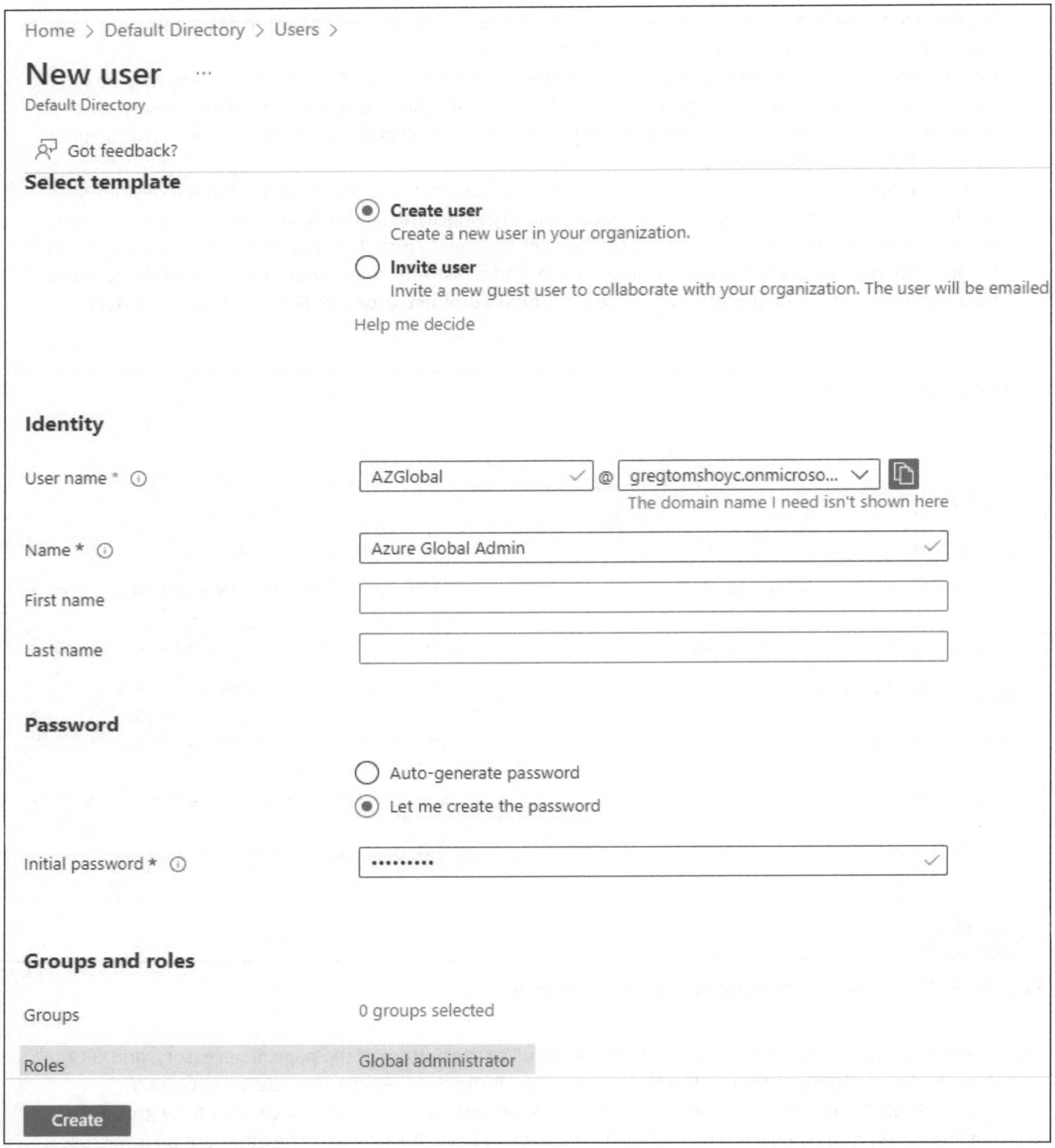

Home > Default Directory > Users >

New user   ···
Default Directory

  ⟨⟩ Got feedback?

Select template

◉ **Create user**
Create a new user in your organization.

◯ **Invite user**
Invite a new guest user to collaborate with your organization. The user will be emailed

Help me decide

Identity

| User name * ⓘ | AZGlobal ✓ | @ | gregtomshoyc.onmicroso... ⌄ | ⧉ |

The domain name I need isn't shown here

Name * ⓘ   Azure Global Admin ✓

First name

Last name

Password

◯ Auto-generate password
◉ Let me create the password

Initial password * ⓘ   ·········· ✓

Groups and roles

Groups   0 groups selected

Roles   Global administrator

Create

Figure 3-48   Creating a new user

17. If you want other users to be able to manage the group, you can make them owners. Click **No members selected** to add members to the group. In the dialog box on the right, click the **Azure Global Admin** option that you just created and click **Select**. You can also add users later, after creating the group. Figure 3-49 shows the New Group page after the user has been added.

(continues)

Activity 3-9 Continued

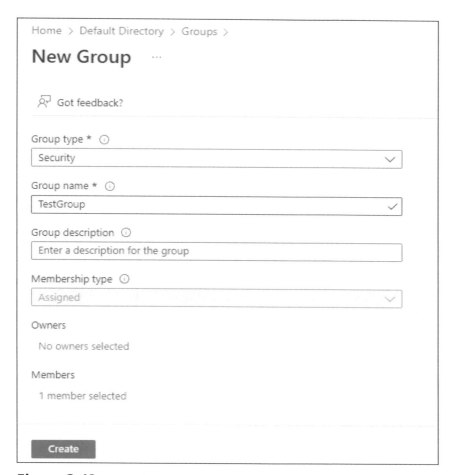

Figure 3-49   Creating a new Azure AD group

18. Click **Create**. Click **Refresh** on the Groups page to see the new group.
19. Next, you'll sign out of Azure and sign in as the new user you created. Click your username in the upper-right section of the browser and click **Sign out**. After you are signed out, you are prompted to pick an account to sign in with. Click **Use another account** and use the account name you just created. Your sign-in information will look something like AZGlobal@*yourdomain*.onmicrosoft.com. The *yourdomain* part of the domain name is automatically created by Azure. Type **Password1** when prompted for the password.
20. When prompted to change your password, change it to **AZ800Pass** or a password of your choice.
21. Stay signed in to the Azure portal if you are continuing to the next activity.

Activity 3-10

Installing Azure AD Connect

Time Required: 15 minutes

Objective: Install Azure AD Connect.

Required Tools and Equipment: ServerDC1, an Azure subscription, and access to the Azure portal

Description: In this activity, you install Azure AD Connect and synchronize Active Directory accounts with Azure AD.

1. Start ServerDC1 and sign in as **Administrator**. Open a web browser, go to *portal.azure.com*, and sign in to the Azure portal.
2. Open a web browser (most likely Edge is installed) and search for "Azure AD Connect download" or go to *www.microsoft.com/en-us/download/details.aspx?id=47594*.
3. Click **Download** to start the download. When the download is complete, click **Open file** in the pop-up box or double-click the file name in File Explorer. The Azure AD Connect setup wizard starts.
4. Click the box to agree to the license terms and click **Continue**.
5. From the Express Settings page, you see a message indicating that AZ800.corp is not a routable domain (it is not registered on the Internet). You can still install Azure AD Connect, but users will not have single sign-on capability because the on-premises domain will be different from the Azure AD domain. Click **Use Express Settings**.
6. On the Connect to Azure AD page, type the global administrator account name you just created in the following format: AZGlobal@*yourdomain*.onmicrosoft.com. Type the password **AZ800Pass** or the password you created (see Figure 3-50). Click **Next**.

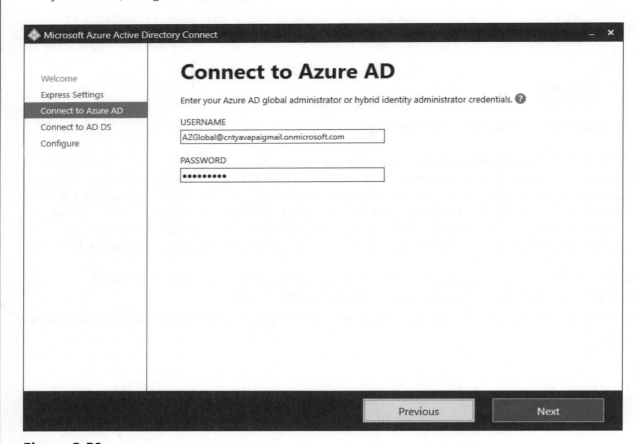

Figure 3-50 Connect to Azure AD

(continues)

Activity 3-10 Continued

7. On the Connect to AD DS page, type **AZ800\Administrator** for the username and **Password01** for the password. Click **Next**.
8. On the Azure AD sign-in configuration page, click the check box at the bottom: **Continue without matching all UPN suffixes to verified domains**. If you created a custom domain name, you would not need to select this box.
9. Azure AD Connect begins the configuration process, which may take several minutes. When you see the Configuration complete page, click **Exit**. An initial synchronization occurs. Any users you created in your AZ800.corp domain will be synchronized with Azure AD, but users will be required to use the @*yourdomain*.onmicrosoft.com suffix in order to sign in to Azure.
10. In the Azure portal, go to the Azure AD page and click **Users** to see the synchronized users. If you don't see the user accounts from AZ800.corp, wait a few minutes and click the **Refresh** button on the Users page.
11. Sign off all accounts and close all windows.

Module Summary

- OUs, the building blocks of the Active Directory structure in a domain, can be designed to mirror a company's organizational chart. Delegation of control can be used to give certain users some management authority in an OU. You need to be familiar with OU permissions and permission inheritance to understand delegation of control.
- OU permissions and permission inheritance work much the same way as they do in the file system. You must enable the Advanced Features option in Active Directory Users and Computers (ADUC) to view an object's Security tab and other folders and tabs.
- User accounts provide a way for users to authenticate to the network and contain user information that can be used in a company directory. There are three categories of users in Windows: local, domain, and built-in. The two built-in accounts are Administrator and Guest.
- ADUC and Active Directory Administrative Center (ADAC) are GUI tools for creating and maintaining user accounts. User account names must be unique in a domain, aren't case sensitive, and must be 20 or fewer characters. A complex password is required by default. A naming standard should be devised before creating user accounts. At the very least, the user's full name, logon name, and password are required to create a user account in ADUC.
- This module covers the user account properties in the General, Account, Profile, and Member Of tabs. The Account tab contains information that controls many aspects of logging on to the domain, such as logon name, logon hours, logon locations, account lockout, and account expiration. The Profile tab contains information about where a user's profile data is stored and can specify a logon script. The Member Of tab lists groups the user belongs to and can be used to change group memberships. Every new user is added to the Domain Users group automatically.
- Groups are the main security principal used to grant rights and permissions. The two group types are security and distribution, but only security groups are used to assign permissions and rights. The group type can be converted from security to distribution and vice versa.
- The group scope determines the reach of a group's application in a domain or a forest: which security principals in a forest can be group members and to which forest resources a group can be assigned rights or permissions.
- There are three group scopes in Active Directory: domain local, global, and universal. (Local groups are found on domain member computers and standalone computers.) The recommended use of groups can be summarized

with the acronyms AGDLP and AGGUDLP. Groups can be nested, as long as the rules for group membership are followed. Group scope can be converted, with some restrictions. There are default groups in the Builtin and Users folders, and there are special identity groups with dynamic membership that can't be managed.

- Computers that are domain members have computer accounts in Active Directory. Domain users logging on to member computers can use single sign-on forest-wide and perform Active Directory searches. Computers can be managed by using group policies and remote MMCs.

- Computer accounts are created automatically when a computer joins a domain or manually by an administrator. By default, computer accounts are created in the Computers folder, but to use group policies, they must be moved to an OU that has a group policy linked to it.

- Computer accounts can be deleted or disabled, just as user accounts can be. When a computer leaves the domain, its associated computer account is disabled automatically. If the same computer rejoins the domain, the account is enabled again. When the computer needs access to the domain again, you can re-enable the computer account.

- A service account is a user account that Windows services use to log on with a specific set of rights and permissions. A service needs to log on with a service account if it runs in the background because a user doesn't start it.

- A managed service account enables administrators to manage rights and permissions for services with automatic password management. A group managed service account provides the same functions but can be managed across multiple servers.

- There are three built-in service accounts, each with its own rights and permissions: Local Service, Network Service, and Local System. The advantage of using a built-in service account is that no management is needed, and the password is managed automatically.

- Virtual accounts are the simplest service accounts to use because you don't need to create, delete, or manage them in any way. Microsoft refers to them as "managed local accounts." They access the network with the credentials of the computer account where they're used.

- Kerberos delegation is a feature of the Kerberos authentication protocol that allows a service to impersonate a client, relieving the client from having to authenticate to more than one service. Kerberos delegation is available when you use a domain account as a service account and the account has been assigned an SPN.

- Azure AD is primarily used for authenticating users who want to access Azure cloud resources such as Microsoft 365, cloud storage, and even third-party cloud applications.

- Azure AD is called a multitenant service because all the accounts stored in Azure AD from all Azure customers are part of one very large directory managed by Microsoft.

- Azure AD Connect is a tool that you install on an on-premises Windows Active Directory domain member or domain controller and that synchronizes Windows Active Directory users, groups, and contacts with Azure AD.

- Self-service password reset (SSPR) is an Azure AD feature that allows Azure users who have accounts in Azure AD to reset or change their password and unlock their account without intervention from an administrator.

- You can monitor the health of Azure AD Connect by going there and clicking the Azure AD Connect Health link under Health and Analytics. From the resulting page, you can check for sync errors, verify the status of related services, and configure settings.

- Azure AD Connect cloud sync is a more lightweight version of Azure AD Connect sync because the configuration and provisioning information is done in the cloud rather than primarily on the on-premises servers.

- Azure AD Domain Services takes Azure AD one step further and implements many of the features of on-premises Active Directory, including organizational units and group policies. Whereas Azure AD is primarily an identity service, Azure AD DS is the right choice when you want many of the same capabilities of on-premises Active Directory in the cloud.

Key Terms

Active Directory Administrative Center (ADAC)

Active Directory Users and Computers (ADUC)

Azure Active Directory (AAD)

Azure Active Directory DS (AADDS)

Azure AD Connect

Azure AD Connect cloud sync

Bastion host

constrained delegation

contact

delegation of control

distribution group
domain local group
downlevel user logon name
global group
group managed service account
   (gMSA)
group scope
group type
hash
Kerberos delegation

local group
managed service account (MSA)
multitenant
offline domain join
password writeback
resource forest
Security Accounts Manager (SAM)
   database
security group
self-service password reset (SSPR)

service account
service principal name (SPN)
single sign-on (SSO)
special identity group
universal group
universal group membership caching
user forest
virtual account

Review Questions

1. Which of the following are true about organizational units? (Choose all that apply.)

   a. OUs can be added to an object's DACL.
   b. OUs can be nested.
   c. A GPO can be linked to an OU.
   d. Only members of Domain Administrators can work with OUs.

2. You want to see the permissions set on an OU, so you open Active Directory Users and Computers, right-click the OU, and click Properties. After clicking all the available tabs, you can't seem to find where permissions are set in the Properties dialog box. What should you do?

   a. Log on as a member of Enterprise Admins and try again.
   b. In the Properties dialog box, click the Advanced button.
   c. Right-click the OU and click Security.
   d. In Active Directory Users and Computers, click View and then click Advanced Features.

3. You have hired a new junior administrator and created an account for her with the logon name JrAdmin. You want her to be able to reset user accounts and modify group memberships for users in the Operations department whose accounts are in the Operations OU. You want to do this with the least effort and without giving JrAdmin broader capabilities. What should you do?

   a. In Active Directory Administrative Center, right-click the Operations OU, click Properties, and click Managed By.
   b. In Active Directory Users and Computers, right-click the Operations OU and click Delegate Control.
   c. Open the Operations Security tab and add JrAdmin to the DACL.
   d. Add JrAdmin to the Password Managers domain local group.

4. Which of the following are user account categories? (Choose all that apply.)

   a. Local
   b. Global
   c. Domain
   d. Universal

5. Which of the following is a built-in user account? (Choose all that apply.)

   a. Administrator
   b. Operator
   c. Anonymous
   d. Guest

6. Which of the following is *not* a valid user account name?

   a. Sam$Snead1
   b. Sam*Snead35
   c. SamSnead!24
   d. Sam23Snead

7. Which of the following are true about user accounts in a Windows Server 2016 domain? (Choose all that apply.)

   a. The name can have 1 to 20 characters.
   b. The name is case sensitive.
   c. The name can't be duplicated in the domain.
   d. Using default settings, PASSWORD123 is a valid password.

8. Which of the following account options can't be set together? (Choose all that apply.)

   a. User must change password at next logon
   b. Store password using reversible encryption
   c. Password never expires
   d. Account is disabled

9. Which of the following members can belong to a global group? (Choose all that apply.)

   a. Computer accounts
   b. Global groups from any domain
   c. User accounts
   d. Universal groups

10. Jada has left the company. Her user account is a member of several groups, and it has permissions and rights to a number of forest-wide resources. Jada's replacement will arrive in a couple of weeks, and the replacement will need access to the same resources. What's the best course of action?

   a. Find all groups that Jada is a member of and make a note of them. Delete Jada's user account and create a new account for the new employee. Add the new account to all the groups that Jada was a member of.

   b. Copy Jada's user account and give the copy another name.

   c. Disable Jada's account. When the new employee arrives, rename Jada's account, assign it a new password, and enable it again.

   d. Export Jada's account and then import it when the new employee arrives. Rename the account and assign it a new password.

11. Tom has access to sensitive company information. Over the past few months, he has signed in to computers in other departments and left them without signing out. You have discussed the matter with him, but the problem continues to occur. You're concerned that someone could access these sensitive resources easily. What's the best way to solve this problem?

   a. On all computers that Tom is signing in to, have screen savers set to lock the computer after 15 minutes of inactivity.

   b. Specify which domain computers Tom can sign in to by using the "Log On To" option in his account's properties.

   c. Move Tom's account and computer to another domain, thereby making it impossible for him to sign in to computers that are members of different domains.

   d. Disable local logon for Tom's account on all computers except Tom's.

12. You have noticed the inappropriate use of computers for gaming and Internet downloads by some employees who come in after hours and on weekends. These employees don't have valid work assignments during these times. You have been asked to devise a solution for these employees that doesn't affect other employees or these employees' computers during working hours. What's the best solution?

   a. Install personal firewall software on their computers in an attempt to block the gaming and Internet traffic.

   b. Request that the Maintenance Department change the locks on the employees' office doors so that they can enter only during prescribed hours.

   c. Set the Logon Hours options for their user accounts.

   d. Before you leave each evening and before the weekend, disable these employees' accounts and re-enable them the next working day.

13. You have decided to follow Microsoft's best practices to create a group scope that will allow you to aggregate users with similar rights requirements. Which group scope should you create and then use to assign permissions to a resource?

   a. Global   c. Local
   b. Domain local   d. Universal

14. Which of the following are considered security principals? (Choose all that apply.)

   a. Contacts   c. User accounts
   b. Computer accounts d. Distribution groups

15. Which of the following are valid group scopes? (Choose all that apply.)

   a. Global   c. Forest
   b. Domain local   d. Domain global

16. What happens if a security group that's an ACE in a shared folder is converted to a distribution group?

   a. A security group can't be converted to a distribution group if it has already been assigned permissions.

   b. The group is removed from the DACL automatically.

   c. The group remains in the DACL, but the ACE has no effect on members' access to the resource.

   d. The group remains in the DACL, and permissions assigned to the group affect access to the resource as though it were still a security group.

17. Which of the following can be a member of a universal group? (Choose all that apply.)

   a. User accounts from the local domain only
   b. Global groups from any domain in the forest
   c. Other universal groups
   d. Domain local groups from the local domain only

18. Which direct group scope conversion is allowed?

   a. Domain local to universal, provided no domain local group is already a member

   b. Global to domain local, without restriction

   c. Domain local to global, provided no domain local group is already a member

   d. Universal to global, without restriction

19. Which of the following is true about the Users domain local group?

   a. It's in the Users folder.
   b. It can be converted to a global group.
   c. Domain Users is a member.
   d. Its members can log on locally to a domain controller.

20. A domain user signing in to the domain becomes a member of which special identity group?

   a. Creator Owner   c. Authenticated Users
   b. System   d. Anonymous Logon

21. A user is having trouble signing in to the domain from a computer that has been out of service for several months, and nobody else can seem to sign in from the computer. What should you try first to solve the problem?

   a. Reinstall Windows on the workstation and create a new computer account in the domain.
   b. Rename the computer and create a new computer account with the new name.
   c. Reset the computer account, remove the computer from the domain, and rejoin it to the domain.
   d. Disable the computer account, remove the computer from the domain, and rejoin it to the domain.

22. Which of the following service accounts can be managed across multiple servers?

   a. AD managed service account
   b. Group managed service account
   c. Multimanaged service account
   d. Managed service account

23. Which of the following are built-in service accounts? (Choose all that apply.)

   a. Anonymous Logon
   b. Local System
   c. Network Service
   d. Authenticated Users

24. Which of the following are advantages of using a managed service account instead of a regular user account for service logon? (Choose all that apply.)

   a. The system manages passwords.
   b. You can assign rights and permissions precisely.
   c. You can use the account to log on interactively.
   d. You can't be locked out.

25. Which of the following is used to uniquely identify a service instance to a client?

   a. SPN   c. Service ticket
   b. KDC   d. TGT

26. You have created an MSA on DC1 to run a service on the ldsServ1 server. What's the last thing you should do before using the Services MMC to configure the service to use the new MSA?

   a. On DC1, run the `Install-ADServiceAccount` cmdlet.
   b. On ldsServ1, run the `Install-ADServiceAccount` cmdlet.

   c. On DC1, run the `Add-ADComputerServiceAccount` cmdlet.
   d. On ldsServ1, run the `Add-ADComputerServiceAccount` cmdlet.

27. You have four servers running a service in a load-balancing configuration, and you want the services on all four servers to use the same service account. What should you do?

   a. Create a group and add the servers' computer accounts to it. Run the `New-ADServiceAccount` cmdlet.
   b. Run the `New-ADServiceAccount` cmdlet and configure constrained Kerberos delegation.
   c. Run the `New-gMSAServiceAccount` cmdlet and specify the four servers in the SPN.
   d. Move the four servers' computer accounts to the Managed Service Accounts folder in Active Directory.

28. In your Windows Server 2022 domain, you have a member server that is also running Windows Server 2022. You want to install the LocSvc service, which will access only local resources. You need to configure authentication for this service but don't want to use one of the built-in service accounts; also, you want to use the least administrative effort. What should you do?

   a. Create a local user on the server and configure the service to log on as that user.
   b. Create an MSA with PowerShell and configure the service to log on as the MSA.
   c. Create a domain user, and in the Delegation tab, select LocSvc.
   d. Configure the service to log on as NT Service\LocSvc.

29. You are considering integrating Azure with your on-premises datacenter and you want to start with identity. You want a lightweight footprint on your on-premises servers. At the moment, you are only concerned with making sure your users can authenticate to the cloud without having to enter their credentials again after they have authenticated to the on-premises Active Directory. You also want to be sure that when users change their password, they are subject to on-premises policies. Which collection of Azure services should you deploy?

   a. Azure AD, Azure AD Connect cloud sync, SSPR
   b. Azure AD, Azure AD Connect sync
   c. Azure AD DS, Azure AD Connect sync, SSPR
   d. Azure AD Connect cloud sync, SSO, Azure AD

30. Which of the following is a process that allows users to sign in using one set of credentials without having to enter credentials again to access remote services and applications?

    a. SSPR
    b. SSO
    c. MFA
    d. AADDS

31. Which of the following is a characteristic of Azure AD?

    a. Multitenant
    b. On-premises
    c. Support GPOs
    d. Lightweight agents

32. You have deployed Azure AD, installed Azure AD Connect, and configured synchronization. However, some users are complaining that they can no longer sign in to the on-premises Active Directory after changing their password in the cloud. They are able to sign in to the Azure cloud, however. What should you do?

    a. Configure SSPR.
    b. Use Azure AD Connect sync.
    c. Configure password writeback.
    d. Disable password hash sync.

33. Which of the following Azure AD Connect sign-in options requires an agent to be installed on-premises to allow users to authenticate with Azure services?

    a. Password Hash Synchronization
    b. Pass-through authentication
    c. Federation with AD FS
    d. Federation with PingFederate

34. You are deploying Azure AD DS and are on the option to configure the forest type. You want to sync all objects in Azure AD and all user and group accounts in your on-premises Active Directory. Which forest type should you choose?

    a. User forest
    b. Trusted forest
    c. Resource forest
    d. Global forest

35. You have just deployed a Windows Server VM in Azure. You want to connect to the server's console to further configure the VM via Server Manager. You want the connection to be secure via a web browser. Which type of connection should you configure?

    a. Remote Desktop Protocol
    b. Hypertext Transport Protocol
    c. Bastion host
    d. Secure shell

Critical Thinking

The following activities give you critical thinking challenges. Case projects offer a scenario with a problem for which you supply a written solution.

Case Projects

Case Project 3-1: Working with Service Accounts

You're installing six new servers as members of a Windows Server 2022 domain. All existing servers are also running Windows Server 2022. Server 1 is running the NetServ1 network service, Server 2 is running the Loc-Serv2 local service, and Servers 3 through 6 are a server farm, each running the LBServ service. Security policies forbid using built-in service accounts for configuring authentication on new services. You don't want to have to manage service account passwords, and you want to perform this task with the least administrative effort. Describe what type of service account you should use for each server and explain your reasons.

Case Project 3-2: Deploying Azure AD

Your company has an on-premises datacenter with four domain controllers running Active Directory. Your domain, csmpub.corp, is a registered domain name and you have a public presence on the Internet, including a web server and DNS servers. You are considering extending your network to the cloud to take advantage of some network applications that were designed to run in an Azure environment. You want your employees to take advantage of single sign-on features in Azure so they can sign in to the on-premises domain and access Azure resources using the same credentials, and vice versa. You also want employees to be able to change their password while signed in to Azure and have the changes reflected in the on-premises Active Directory. What are some of the steps you need to take to make this happen, and which features do you need to use in Azure Active Directory? Is there a reason you should consider deploying Azure AD DS at this time?

Solutions to Self-Check Questions

Section 3-1: Working with Organizational Units

1. An OU is a security principal that can be used to assign resource permissions to user and computer accounts in the OU. True or False?

   Answer: b. False

   Explanation: An OU is not a security principal and cannot be used to assign permissions or rights to accounts; a security group is used for that purpose.

2. How can a user that is only a member of the Domain Users group get permission to create and change accounts in an OU?

   Answer: c. Delegate control.

   Explanation: A user account with administrative permissions to an OU can delegate control of the OU to another user account, which confers selected permissions to the OU to the delegated user account.

Section 3-2: Managing User Accounts

3. Where are user accounts stored after they are created on a Windows 11 computer?

   Answer: b. SAM database

   Explanation: User and group accounts on a standalone or member Windows computer are stored in the Security Accounts Manager (SAM) database.

4. Which of the following is true about the default Administrator account on a Windows domain member computer?

   Answer: a. It can be renamed.

   Explanation: The built-in Administrator and Guest accounts can be disabled and renamed, but they cannot be deleted.

Section 3-3: Managing Group Accounts

5. Which of the following is *not* a group scope found on a domain controller?

   Answer: c. Forest local

   Explanation: Valid group scopes on a domain controller are Universal, Global, and Domain local. Member computers and standalone computers have Local groups.

6. Which of the following is the acronym used to describe best practices for using groups and assigning permissions in a multidomain forest?

   Answer: d. AGGUDLP

   Explanation: Best practices for using groups and assigning permissions in a multidomain environment can be summarized as: **A**ccounts are members of **G**lobal groups, and nest **G**lobal groups in other Global groups, if necessary; Global groups are members of **U**niversal groups, if necessary; and Universal groups are members of **D**omain **L**ocal groups. Finally, **P**ermissions to resources are assigned to Domain local groups (AGGUDLP). Note that the use of Universal groups is not always necessary, so Global groups would be made members of Domain local groups.

Section 3-4: Working with Computer Accounts

7. What command is used to change the default location for computer accounts created when the computer joins the domain?

   Answer: b. `redircmp`

   Explanation: Use `redircmp` to change the default location for computer accounts created during a domain join. The syntax is: `redircmp ou=MemberComputers,dc=csmtech,dc=corp`

8. Computer accounts that are created by a domain join can be disabled. True or False?

   Answer: a. True

   Explanation: Computer accounts can be disabled using Active Directory Users and Computers by right-clicking the account and clicking Disable. It doesn't matter how the account was created.

Section 3-5: Working with Service Accounts

9. Which of the following is *not* a built-in service account?

   Answer: a. Network System

   Explanation: The three built-in service accounts are Local Service, Network Service, and Local System.

10. Which managed account type is created by specifying NT Service*ServiceName* as the logon account for the service?

    Answer: c. Virtual

    Explanation: Virtual accounts are created when you configure a service's logon account with the name NT Service*ServiceName*, where *ServiceName* is the name of the service.

Section 3-6: Using Active Directory in a Hybrid Environment

11. Azure Active Directory supports group policy. True or False?

    Answer: b. False

    Explanation: Azure Active Directory (Azure AD) does not support group policy; however, Azure Active Directory Domain Services (Azure AD DS) does support group policy.

12. Which feature in Azure requires at least an Azure Premium P1 level subscription?

    Answer: a. Dynamic groups

    Explanation: Dynamic groups, a feature that adds accounts to groups based on rules an administrator creates, are only available with at least an Azure Premium P1 level subscription. The other features are available with a basic or trial subscription.

Module 4

Configure Group Policies

Module Objectives

After reading this module and completing the exercises, you will be able to:

1 Describe the architecture and processing of group policies

2 Configure group policy settings

3 Configure and manage administrative templates

4 Configure group policy preferences

5 Describe group policy processing

6 Implement Group Policy in Azure AD DS

Group Policy is a powerful tool for network administrators to manage domain controllers, member servers, member computers, and users. It allows administrators to manage most aspects of computer and user environments centrally through Active Directory. An administrator's solid understanding of how to get the most out of group policies can relieve some of the burden of user and computer management. Even more important, designing and applying group policies correctly results in a more secure network.

This module covers the architecture of group policies so that you understand what a Group Policy Object (GPO) is and how and where GPOs can be applied to your Active Directory structure. In addition, you learn about the myriad security settings and user and computer environment settings that can be configured through group policies and group policy preferences.

Once you have a solid understanding of how Group Policy works in an on-premises Active Directory environment, you look at how Group Policy can be deployed and configured in a hybrid environment using Azure AD DS Group Policy.

Table 4-1 describes what you need in order to do the hands-on activities in this module.

Table 4-1 Activity requirements

Activity	Requirements	Notes
Activity 4-1: Resetting Your Virtual Environment	ServerDC1, ServerDM1, ServerSA1	
Activity 4-2: Working with Local GPOs	ServerDC1, ServerDM1	
Activity 4-3: Browsing GPTs and GPCs	ServerDC1	
Activity 4-4: Creating, Linking, and Unlinking GPOs	ServerDC1	
Activity 4-5: Configuring and Testing a GPO	ServerDC1, ServerDM1	
Activity 4-6: Creating and Using Starter GPOs	ServerDC1	
Activity 4-7: Deploying a Shutdown Script to a Computer	ServerDC1, ServerDM1	

(continues)

Table 4-1   (continued)

Activity	Requirements	Notes
Activity 4-8: Configuring a Folder Redirection Policy	ServerDC1, ServerDM1	
Activity 4-9: Working with Computer Administrative Template Settings	ServerDC1, ServerDM1	
Activity 4-10: Working with User Administrative Template Settings	ServerDC1, ServerDM1	
Activity 4-11: Viewing Policy Settings with Filter Options	ServerDC1	
Activity 4-12: Configuring and Testing Preferences	ServerDC1, ServerDM1	
Activity 4-13: Configuring Item-Level Targeting	ServerDC1, ServerDM1	
Activity 4-14: Working with GPO Inheritance Blocking and Enforcement	ServerDC1, ServerDM1	
Activity 4-15: Using GPO Security Filtering	ServerDC1, ServerDM1	
Activity 4-16: Using GPO Security Filtering for a Computer Account	ServerDC1, ServerDM1	
Activity 4-17: Configuring Loopback Policy Processing	ServerDC1, ServerDM1	

Group Policy Objects

Microsoft Exam AZ-800:
Deploy and manage Active Directory Domain Services (AD DS) in on-premises and cloud environments.
- Manage Windows Server by using domain-based Group Policies

The processes of centrally maintaining lists of computer and user settings, replicating these settings to all domain controllers (DCs), and applying these settings to users and computers are complex. The architecture of group policies is equally complex, at least when you're trying to envision the architecture as a whole. When broken down into its constituent parts, however, the architecture is easier to grasp. Group policy architecture and functionality involve the following components:

- *GPOs*—A GPO is an object containing policy settings that affect user and computer operating environments and security. GPOs can be local (stored on users' computers) or they can be Active Directory objects linked to sites, domains, and organizational units (OUs).
- *Replication*—Replication of Active Directory–based GPOs ensures that all DCs have a current copy of each GPO. Changes to GPOs can be made on any DC and are replicated to all other DCs.
- *Creating and linking*—GPOs are created in the Group Policy Management console and can then be linked to one or more Active Directory containers. Multiple GPOs can be linked to the same container. This module discusses the basics of creating and linking GPOs and managing GPO links.
- *Scope and inheritance*—The scope of a group policy defines which users and computers are affected by its settings. The scope can be a single computer (in the case of a local GPO), an OU, a domain, or a site. Like permissions, policy settings applied to users and computers are inherited from parent containers, and like permission inheritance, an administrator can override the default behavior of group policy inheritance.

Local and Domain Group Policy Objects

A GPO, the main component of group policies, contains policy settings for managing many aspects of domain controllers, member servers, member computers, and user accounts. There are two main types of GPOs: local GPOs and domain GPOs.

Local GPOs

Local GPOs are stored on local computers and can be edited with the Group Policy Object Editor snap-in (see Figure 4-1). To use this tool, you add the Group Policy Object Editor snap-in to a custom MMC or enter `gpedit.msc` at the command line to open an already configured MMC called Local Group Policy Editor. You use one of these tools to manually edit local GPOs on computers that are not domain members or to edit policies that are not configured by Active Directory GPOs. The policy settings on domain member computers can be affected by domain GPOs linked to the site, domain, or OU in Active Directory. Settings in local GPOs that are inherited from domain GPOs can't be changed on the local computer; only settings that are undefined or not configured by domain GPOs can be edited locally.

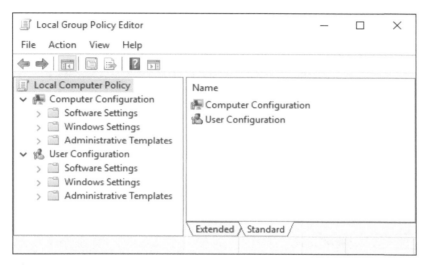

Figure 4-1   The Local Group Policy Editor

When you run `gpedit.msc`, you open a local GPO named Local Computer Policy that contains Computer Configuration and User Configuration nodes. The policies defined in this GPO, when configured on nondomain member computers, apply by default to all users who sign in to the computer. For example, a computer used in a public environment, such as a kiosk, might have policies that severely restrict what users can do on the computer.

> **Note 1**
>
> Windows has a preconfigured MMC called Local Security Policy that enables you to edit policies in just the Security Settings node of the local GPO. You access this MMC via Administrative Tools in Control Panel or by entering `secpol.msc` at the command line.

In addition to the Local Computer Policy GPO, there are local GPOs, described in the following list, that allow different policy settings depending on who signs in to the computer. The policies in these GPOs aren't configured, so they have no effect on users until they're configured. In addition, these GPOs have only a User Configuration node, so policies are limited to user-related settings:

- *Local Administrators GPO*—Members of the local Administrators group are affected by settings in this GPO. The default membership includes the local Administrator account and the Domain Admins global group when the computer is a domain member.

- *Local Non-Administrators GPO*—All users who sign in to the computer but aren't members of the local Administrators group are affected by settings in this GPO, including domain users when the computer is a domain member.
- *User-specific GPO*—A user-specific GPO is created for each account (except Guest) created in the local Security Accounts Manager (SAM) database.

To access these GPOs, first add the Group Policy Object Editor snap-in to an MMC. Instead of accepting the default Local Computer Policy when asked to select a GPO, click Browse to open the dialog box shown in Figure 4-2, click the Users tab, and select one of the GPOs. Local GPOs are intended to be configured on nondomain computers because domain GPOs take precedence over local GPOs, and administration is centralized by using domain GPOs. Configuring the domain-based group policy "Turn off Local Group Policy objects processing" causes member computers to ignore local GPOs. Doing so is a good idea to ensure that all policies are controlled from the domain.

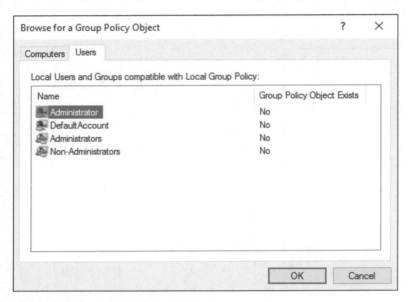

Figure 4-2   Viewing local GPOs

Three of the four local GPOs can contain settings that affect a particular user signing in to a Windows computer. The Local Computer Policy object is processed first for all users and is the only local GPO that affects the computer configuration. The local Administrators or local Non-Administrators GPO is processed next, if configured, and the user-specific GPO is processed last, if configured. Any conflicting settings are resolved in the same order. In other words, the last configured policy setting that's applied takes precedence.

Here's an example: User MSmith has an account on a computer that's not a domain member. The Local Computer Policy is configured to prohibit access to Control Panel, and the Control Panel policy isn't configured in the Non-Administrators GPO. MSmith has a user-specific GPO that enables access to Control Panel. When MSmith signs in, the Local Computer Policy is processed first, which disables access to Control Panel; next, the Non-Administrators policy is processed, which has no effect on the Control Panel policy because it's not configured. Finally, the user-specific MSmith GPO is processed, which allows Control Panel access, so MSmith has Control Panel access.

Note 2

Local GPOs (except for the Local Computer Policy) were introduced in Windows Server 2008 and Vista, so they aren't available in Windows XP and earlier versions.

Domain GPOs

Domain GPOs are stored in Active Directory on domain controllers. They can be linked to a site, a domain, or an OU, and they affect users and computers whose accounts are stored in these containers. A domain GPO is represented by an Active Directory object, but it's composed of two separate parts: a Group Policy Template (GPT) and a Group Policy Container (GPC). The GPT and GPC have different functions and hold very different information, but they do have these things in common:

- *Naming structure*—Each GPO is assigned a globally unique identifier (GUID), a 128-bit value represented by 32 hexadecimal digits that Windows uses to ensure unique object IDs. The GPT and GPC associated with a GPO are stored in a folder with the same name as the GPO's GUID. This naming structure makes associating each GPO with its GPT and GPC easier.
- *Folder structure*—Each GPT and GPC has two subfolders: Machine and User. The Machine folder stores information related to a GPO's Computer Configuration node, and the User folder stores information about the User Configuration node.

One reason administrators must understand the structure of GPOs is so they know where to look when problems happen, particularly with replication of GPOs (which is covered later in this module in the "Group Policy Replication" section). To that end, you examine GPT and GPC components more closely in the following sections.

Group Policy Templates

A **Group Policy Template (GPT)** isn't stored in Active Directory but in a folder in the SYSVOL share on a domain controller. It contains all the policy settings that make up a GPO as well as related files, such as scripts. Every GPO has a GPT associated with it. The local path to GPT folders on a domain controller is %*systemroot*%\SYSVOL\sysvol*domain*\Policies; %*systemroot*% represents the drive letter and folder name where the Windows OS is stored, usually C:\Windows, and *domain* is the domain name. Each GPT is actually a series of folders and files, but the root folder has the name of the GPO's GUID. Figure 4-3 shows the Policies folder with four GPT folders.

The names of GPT folders look random, but two folders have the same name on every domain controller. The folder starting with 6AC1 is the GPT for the Default Domain Controllers Policy, and the folder starting with 31B2 is the GPT for the Default Domain Policy. The other folders are for GPOs created by the administrator.

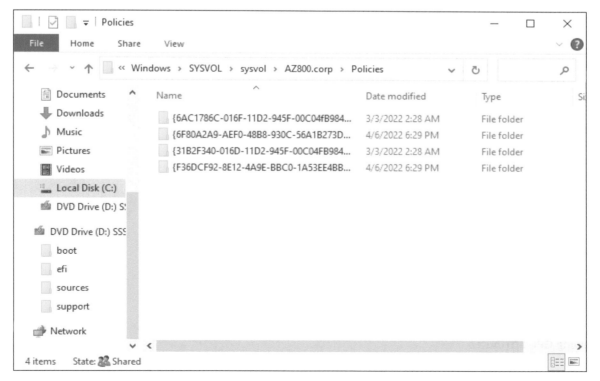

Figure 4-3   GPT folders

When a GPO is created, files and subfolders are created under the root folder. The number of files and subfolders in each GPT folder varies depending on which policies have been configured, but each one has at least these three items:

- GPT.ini—This file contains the version number used to determine when a GPO has been modified. Every time a GPO changes, the version number is updated. When GPO replication occurs, DCs use this version number to determine whether the local copy of the GPO is up to date.
- *Machine*—This folder contains subfolders that store policy settings related to the Computer Configuration node.
- *User*—This folder contains subfolders that store policy settings related to the User Configuration node.

A GPO with few policy settings defined or configured has only a few other subfolders and files under the root folder. For example, only a few policies are configured on the Default Domain Controllers GPO, which is in the folder starting with 6AC1. If you browse the Machine folder, you'll likely find only one additional file, GptTmpl.inf. This file contains settings configured in the Security Settings node under Computer Configuration. If you browse the User folder, you won't find any files because no policy settings are configured in the User Configuration node of the Default Domain Controllers GPO.

Group Policy Containers

A **Group Policy Container (GPC)** is an Active Directory object stored in the System\Policies folder; it can be viewed in Active Directory Users and Computers with the Advanced Features option enabled. A GPC stores GPO properties and status information but no actual policy settings. Like a GPT, the folder name of each GPC is the same as the GPO's GUID.

A GPC is composed of several attributes you can view in the Attribute Editor tab of the GPC's Properties dialog box, as shown in Figure 4-4. Although deciphering the purpose of each attribute isn't always easy, some information the GPC provides includes the following:

- *Name of the GPO*—The displayName attribute tells you the name of the GPO the GPC is associated with.
- *File path to GPT*—The gPCFileSysPath attribute specifies the Universal Naming Convention (UNC) path to the related GPT folder.

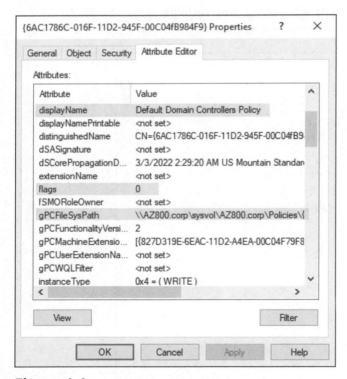

Figure 4-4 Viewing GPC attributes

- *Version*—The versionNumber attribute (not shown in Figure 4-4) should have the same version number as the GPT.ini file in the GPT folder.
- *Status*—The flags attribute contains a value that indicates the GPO's status. In Figure 4-4, it has the value 0, which indicates that the GPO is enabled. The value 3 means the GPO is disabled.

A GPC might seem less interesting than a GPT, but it's just as important. This Active Directory object links the GPO to Active Directory, which is critical for GPO replication to all domain controllers.

Group Policy Replication

Because the two components of a GPO are stored in different places on a DC, different methods are required to replicate GPOs to all domain controllers. GPCs, which are Active Directory objects, are replicated during normal Active Directory replication. GPTs, located in the SYSVOL share, are replicated by using one of these methods:

- *File Replication Service (FRS)*—FRS is used if you have DCs in your domain that are running versions of Windows Server earlier than Windows Server 2008.
- *Distributed File System Replication (DFSR)*—DFSR is used when all DCs are running Windows Server 2008 or later versions.

Of these two replication methods, DFSR is the more efficient and reliable. It's efficient because it uses an algorithm called remote differential compression (RDC) in which only data blocks that have changed are compressed and transferred across the network. DFSR is more reliable because of improvements in handling unexpected service shutdowns that could corrupt data and because it uses a multimaster replication scheme.

Because GPCs and GPTs use different replication methods, they can become out of sync. As mentioned, GPCs are replicated when Active Directory replication occurs. Between DCs in the same site, this interval is about 15 seconds after a change occurs. Between DCs in different sites, the interval is usually much longer—minutes or even hours. DFSR of the SYSVOL share (and therefore the GPT) occurs immediately after a change is made. Strange and unpredictable results could occur when a client computer attempts to apply a GPO when the GPC and GPT aren't synchronized. However, starting with Windows XP, the client computer checks the version number of both components before applying GPO settings.

As long as replication services are running correctly, the most likely problem with GPO replication is a delay in clients receiving changes in policy settings. This problem usually occurs when multiple sites are involved. When you open the Group Policy Management console and then click the domain node in the left pane and the Status tab in the right pane, you see a summary of Active Directory and SYSVOL replication. Click Detect Now to gather replication information and to see a report similar to that in Figure 4-5.

Creating and Linking GPOs

Module 2 introduced you to the Default Domain Policy and Default Domain Controllers Policy, but as you work with Active Directory, you'll need to create additional GPOs, configure settings, and link them to Active Directory containers. Creating new GPOs and linking them to containers is recommended instead of editing the two default GPOs.

As you have learned, the main tools for managing, creating, and editing GPOs are the Group Policy Management console (GPMC) and the Group Policy Management Editor (GPME). The purpose of using these tools is to carry out changes to security and the working environment for users or computers. There are several ways to go about this task:

- Edit an existing GPO that's linked to an Active Directory container.
- Link an existing GPO that's already been configured to an Active Directory container.
- Create a new GPO for an Active Directory container.
- Create a new GPO in the Group Policy Objects folder, which isn't linked to an Active Directory object.
- Create a new GPO by using a Starter GPO.

If you edit an existing GPO that's already linked to an Active Directory container, keep in mind that changes in policy settings take effect as soon as client computers download them. In other words, there's no Save option in the GPME; changes are saved immediately. By default, computers download and apply GPOs when the computer is started, and

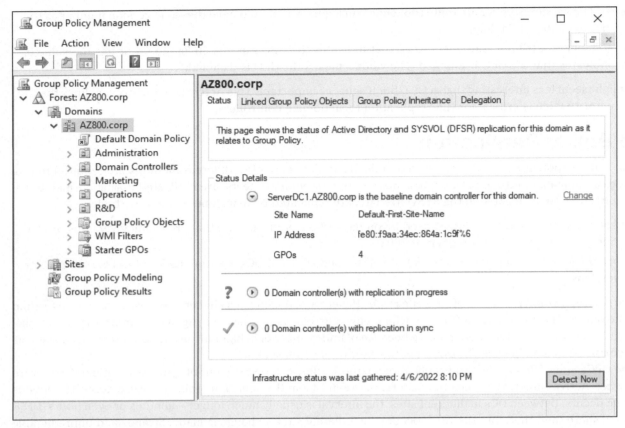

Figure 4-5   Viewing replication status in GPMC

user policies are downloaded and applied at the next logon. Therefore, the best practice is usually creating GPOs in the Group Policy Objects folder, and then linking them to the target Active Directory container after all changes have been made and tested. When you're changing several policy settings at once or are unsure of the effect policy changes will have, you should test policies before enabling them by using the following method:

1. Set up at least one test computer per OS used in the organization.
2. Join test computers to the domain and place their accounts in a test OU.
3. Create one or more test user accounts in the test OU.
4. Create the new GPO in the Group Policy Objects folder and set the policies you want.
5. Link the GPO to the test OU.
6. Restart and sign in to the test computers with the test user accounts to observe the policy effects.
7. Make changes to the GPO, if necessary, and repeat Step 6 until the policy has the desired effect.
8. Unlink the policy from the test OU and link it to the target Active Directory container.

Editing an Existing GPO

To edit an existing GPO, right-click it in the GPMC and click Edit, which opens the GPO in the GPME. In the GPMC, all GPOs are stored in the Group Policy Objects folder; you can also find GPOs linked to an Active Directory container displayed as shortcut objects in the container to which they're linked. Checking whether and where a GPO is linked is a good idea before editing. To do this, select the GPO in the left pane of the GPMC and view the Scope tab in the right pane (see Figure 4-6). All Active Directory objects the GPO is linked to are listed for the selected location. In this figure, the domain is selected as the location; you can also select Entire forest or All sites in the "Display links in this location" list box.

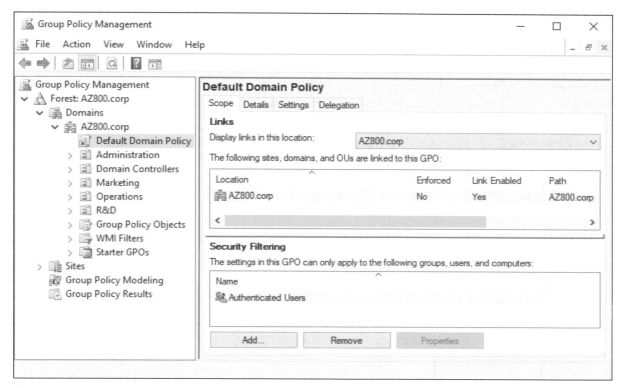

Figure 4-6   The Scope tab for a GPO

As mentioned, editing the two default GPOs is not advisable. One reason is that you can't test the GPO adequately because it's already linked to the domain or the Domain Controllers OU. Another reason is that you might want to revert to the default settings, and you could have difficulty determining what was changed. The recommended method for making changes to domain policies is creating a new GPO and linking it to the domain. Remember: You can have multiple GPOs linked to the same container. The steps for making policy changes that affect the whole domain are as follows, assuming you already have the test computers, users, and OU set up as described previously:

1. Create the new GPO in the Group Policy Objects folder and set the policies you want.
2. Link the GPO to the test OU, making sure to unlink any GPOs that are linked there from previous tests.
3. Test your policies by restarting and signing in to the test computers with the test user accounts to observe the policy effects.
4. Make changes to the GPO, if necessary, and repeat testing until the policy has the effect you want.
5. Unlink the policy from the test OU and link it to the domain.

You might wonder how this procedure tests domain-wide settings. Because a GPO can be linked to multiple containers, you could have linked the Default Domain Policy to the test OU as well. However, by default, policy settings are inherited by child objects, so settings in the Default Domain Policy affect objects in all Active Directory containers in the domain, including containers with another GPO linked. If you have two or more GPOs linked to the domain, as in Figure 4-7, GPOs are applied to objects in reverse of the specified link order. In this example, the NewSample GPO is applied, and then the Default Domain Policy GPO is applied. If any settings conflict, the last setting applied takes precedence. GPO processing and inheritance are discussed later in this module.

Creating a New GPO

There are two ways to create a new GPO in the GPMC. You can right-click the container you're linking the GPO to and select "Create a GPO in this domain, and Link it here," or you can right-click the Group Policy Objects folder and click New. The latter method is preferable for the reasons stated earlier. After creating a GPO, you can edit it and link it to an Active Directory container, if necessary. Because several GPOs can be linked to the same container, the best practice

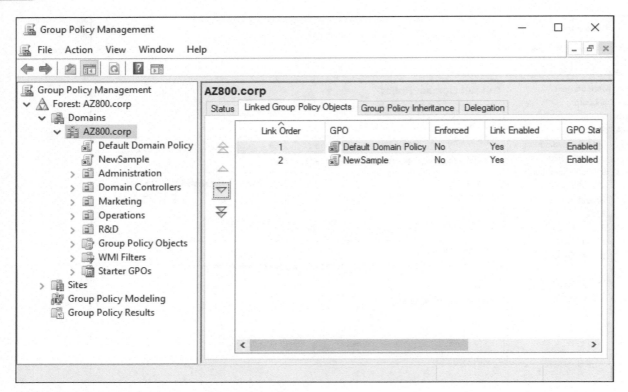

Figure 4-7 Multiple GPOs linked to a container

is to create GPOs that set policies narrowly focused on a category of settings, and then name the GPO accordingly. For example, if you need to configure policy settings related to the Network node under Computer Configuration, create a GPO named CompNetwork. If this policy will apply only to a certain container, you could include the container name in the GPO name—for example, CompNetwork-MarketingOU. Creating and naming GPOs in this manner makes it easier to identify the GPO that sets a particular policy and to troubleshoot GPO processing problems.

Using Starter GPOs

A **Starter GPO** is a GPO template, for lack of a better word, and is not to be confused with the GPTs discussed earlier. An administrator creates a Starter GPO to be used as a baseline for new GPOs.

When you create a GPO, the New GPO Wizard includes an option to use a Starter GPO. Starter GPOs are stored in the Starter GPOs folder in the GPMC. As discussed, creating GPOs that focus on a narrow category of settings is a best practice. Starter GPOs can be used to specify a baseline for certain settings categories and then modified when the Starter GPO is used to create the new GPO.

To use a Starter GPO to create a new GPO, select one in the Source Starter GPO list box in the New GPO Wizard, or right-click a Starter GPO in the Starter GPOs folder and click New GPO From Starter GPO. To create a Starter GPO, right-click the Starter GPOs folder and click New. After creating a Starter GPO, you can edit it just like any GPO. However, Starter GPOs don't contain all the nodes of a regular GPO; only the Administrative Templates folder in both Computer Configuration and User Configuration is included.

Starter GPOs can be useful for making sure your policies are consistent throughout the domain by defining a baseline for group policy setting categories. You can change the baseline settings as needed in the GPO created from the Starter GPO. However, after a new GPO is created from a Starter GPO, changes to the Starter GPO aren't propagated to existing GPOs created from it.

Starter GPOs can also be shared with other administrators by placing them in cabinet (CAB) files. If you click the Starter GPOs folder in the GPMC (see Figure 4-8), all Starter GPOs are listed in the right pane. You can use the Load Cabinet and Save as Cabinet buttons to load a Starter GPO from a CAB file or save a Starter GPO as a CAB file. The two Starter GPOs you see in Figure 4-8 come pre-installed on Windows Server 2022.

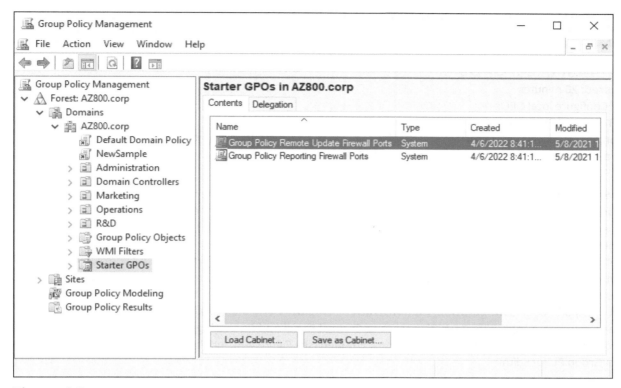

Figure 4-8 Saving Starter GPOs as CAB files

Self-Check Questions

1. The scope of a group policy defines which users and computers are affected by its settings. True or False?

   a. True   **b.** False

2. What component of Group Policy is an Active Directory object stored in the System\Policies folder?

   a. GPO   **c.** GPT
   b. GPC   **d.** GUID

◉ Check your answers at the end of this module.

Activity 4-1

Resetting Your Virtual Environment
Time Required: 5 minutes
Objective: Reset your virtual environment by applying the InitialConfig checkpoint or snapshot.
Required Tools and Equipment: ServerDC1, ServerDM1, ServerSA1
Description: Apply the InitialConfig checkpoint or snapshot to ServerDC1, ServerDM1, and ServerSA1.

1. Be sure the servers are shut down. In your virtualization program, apply the InitialConfig checkpoint or snapshot to ServerDC1, ServerDM1, and ServerSA1.
2. When the snapshot or checkpoint has been applied, continue to the next activity.

Activity 4-2

Working with Local GPOs

Time Required: 20 minutes

Objective: Configure local GPOs.

Required Tools and Equipment: ServerDC1, ServerDM1

Description: In this activity, you sign in to ServerDM1 with the *local* Administrator account, configure some local GPOs, and create a local user account. Then you see how local GPOs can affect different users.

1. Turn on ServerDC1 and ServerDM1. Sign in to ServerDM1 with the **adminuser1** account. To do so, click **Other user** on the sign-in screen and then type **serverdm1\adminuser1** in the User name box and **Password01** in the Password box. You must specify that you are signing in to the local computer instead of the domain by prefacing the user name with the name of the computer, unless you are signing in as Administrator.
2. Right-click **Start** and click **Control Panel** to verify that you have access to it, and then close Control Panel. Right-click **Start**, click **Run**, type **gpedit.msc** in the Open text box, and press **Enter** to open the Local Group Policy Editor for the Local Computer Policy GPO.
3. Click to expand **User Configuration**, **Administrative Templates**, and then click the **Control Panel** node.
4. In the right pane, double-click **Prohibit access to Control Panel and PC settings**. In the Prohibit access to Control Panel and PC settings dialog box, click **Enabled** (see Figure 4-9) and then click **OK**. Close the Local Group Policy Editor.

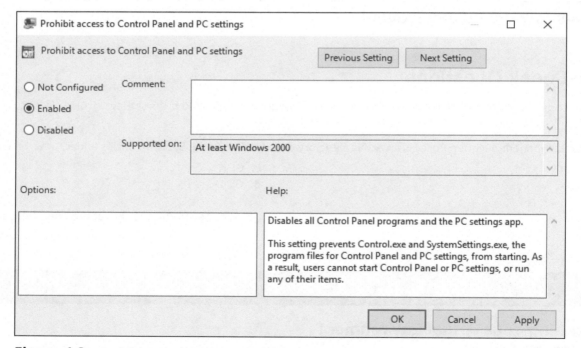

Figure 4-9 Prohibit access to Control Panel

5. Right-click **Start** and click **Control Panel**. You see a message indicating that the action has been canceled because of restrictions in effect on the computer. Click **OK**.
6. Right-click **Start**, click **Run**, type **mmc** in the Open text box, and press **Enter**.
7. In the MMC window, click **File** and then select **Add/Remove Snap-in** from the menu. In the Available snap-ins list box, click **Group Policy Object Editor**, and then click **Add**. The Group Policy Wizard starts.

(continues)

Activity 4-2 Continued

8. In the Select Group Policy Object window, click **Browse**. In the Browse for a Group Policy Object dialog box, click the **Users** tab. Click **Administrators** (make sure you click the Administrators group, not the Administrator user account), and then click **OK**. Click **Finish** and then **OK**.

9. Click to expand **Local Computer\Administrators Policy**. Click to expand **User Configuration** and **Administrative Templates**, and then click the **Control Panel** node. (You might want to click the Standard tab at the bottom so that you can see the policy setting descriptions better.)

10. In the right pane, double-click **Prohibit access to Control Panel and PC settings**. In the dialog box for configuring the policy, click **Disabled**, and then click **OK**. Close the MMC window and click **No** when prompted to save the console settings.

11. Right-click **Start** and click **Control Panel**, which opens. The Administrators local GPO overrode the Local Computer Policy (because you're signed in as adminuser1, which is a member of the Administrators group). Close Control Panel.

12. Sign out of ServerDM1 and sign back in as **reguser1** with **Password01**. Be sure to enter the user name as **serverdm1\reguser1** so that Windows knows you're signing in to the local computer.

13. Right-click **Start** and click **Control Panel**. You see the same message as in Step 5. Click **OK**. Because reguser1 isn't an administrator and doesn't have a user-specific GPO configured, the default Local Computer Policy takes effect, which prohibits access to Control Panel.

14. Sign out of ServerDM1 and sign in to the domain as **domuser1** using password **Password01**.

15. Right-click **Start** and click **Control Panel**. You see the same message as in Steps 5 and 13, which demonstrates that the Local Computer Policy affects domain users as well as local users. The only local GPO that doesn't affect domain users is the user-specific GPO. Click **OK**.

16. Sign out and sign in to ServerDM1 as **adminuser1**. (Remember to sign in as ServerDM1\adminuser1.) Open the Group Policy Object Editor for the Local Computer Policy (gpedit.msc). Change the Prohibit access to the Control Panel policy back to **Not Configured**, and then click **OK**. Close the Local Group Policy Editor. Sign out of ServerDM1.

17. Continue to the next activity.

Activity 4-3

Browsing GPTs and GPCs
Time Required: 15 minutes
Objective: Browse subfolders and files in a GPT folder.
Required Tools and Equipment: ServerDC1
Description: In this activity, you explore the folders where the GPT component of GPOs is located and then you investigate the GPC component in Active Directory.

1. On ServerDC1, open File Explorer and navigate to **C:\Windows\SYSVOL\sysvol\AZ800.corp\Policies**, where you should see a list of folders similar to those in Figure 4-3, shown previously.

2. Double-click the folder starting with **6AC1**, which is the Default Domain Controllers Policy GPT. Double-click the **GPT.ini** file to open it in Notepad. Notice the version number, which changes each time the GPO is modified. Exit Notepad.

3. Click to expand the **MACHINE\Microsoft\Windows NT\SecEdit** folder, and double-click the **GptTmpl.inf** file to open it in Notepad. Knowing the details of what's in this file or other GPT files isn't important; you just need to know that they exist and how to find them. Exit Notepad.

4. Open Active Directory Users and Computers. Click **View** on the menu bar and click **Advanced Features** to enable the advanced features option for Active Directory Users and Computers. You'll see a few more folders.

5. Click to expand the **System** folder and then click the **Policies** folder to see the list of GPC folders, as shown in Figure 4-10.

(continues)

Activity 4-3 Continued

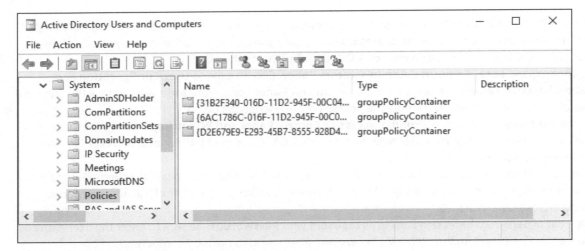

Figure 4-10 GPC folders in Active Directory

6. In the right pane, right-click the GPC folder associated with the Default Domain Controllers GPO (the one that starts with 6AC1) and click **Properties**. In the Properties dialog box, click the **Attribute Editor** tab. Scroll down to view some attributes of the GPC; attributes are listed in alphabetical order. Although you can edit attributes here, it isn't recommended unless you're sure of the results.
7. Find the **versionNumber** attribute. It should have the same value you noted for the GPT.ini file in Step 2.
8. Find the **flags** attribute. Its value should be 0, indicating that the GPO is enabled. Click **Cancel**.
9. Open the Group Policy Management console from the Tools menu in Server Manager. In the left pane, navigate to the **Group Policy Objects** folder. Right-click the **Group Policy Objects** folder and click **New**.
10. In the New GPO dialog box, type **TestGPO** in the Name box and click **OK**.
11. Click **TestGPO** in the left pane. In the right pane, click the **Details** tab.
12. Click the **GPO Status** list arrow, click **All settings disabled** (see Figure 4-11), and then click **OK**.

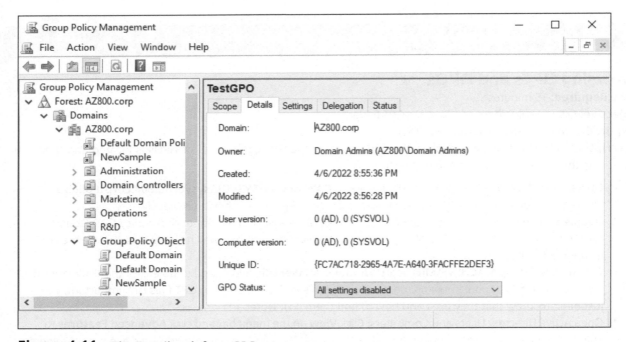

Figure 4-11 The Details tab for a GPO

(continues)

Activity 4-3 Continued

13. In Active Directory Users and Computers, click the Refresh icon to see that a new folder has been added under Policies. Open the Properties dialog box of the GPC folder associated with TestGPO (the folder that does *not* start with 6AC1 or 31B2). Click the **Attribute Editor** tab, and then view the value of the flags attribute. It's 3, indicating that the GPO is disabled.
14. Click the **flags** attribute and click the **Edit** button. Type **0**, and then click **OK** twice. Close Active Directory Users and Computers.
15. In the Group Policy Management console, click the **Refresh** icon. The GPO status changes to Enabled because you changed the flags attribute to 0. Close the Group Policy Management console.
16. Continue to the next activity.

Activity 4-4

Creating, Linking, and Unlinking GPOs

Time Required: 15 minutes
Objective: Create, link, and unlink GPOs.
Required Tools and Equipment: ServerDC1
Description: In this activity, you create an OU and GPO and work with GPO links.

1. On ServerDC1, open Active Directory Users and Computers, and create an OU named **TestOU1** under the domain node.
2. Open the Group Policy Management console. Right-click **TestOU1** and click **Create a GPO in this domain, and Link it here**. In the New GPO dialog box, type **GPO1** in the Name text box, and then click **OK**.
3. In the right pane, notice that GPO1 is listed as Enabled. Changes you make to GPO1 affect any user or computer accounts that might be in TestOU1. Right-click **GPO1** and click **Delete**. Click **OK**. This action deletes only the link to the GPO, not the GPO itself.
4. Click the **Group Policy Objects** folder to see all your GPOs, including the default GPOs.
5. Right-click **GPO1** and point to **GPO Status**. You can enable or disable a GPO or just disable the Computer Configuration or User Configuration settings.
6. Right-click the **TestOU1** OU and click **Link an Existing GPO**. In the Select GPO dialog box, click **GPO1**, and then click **OK**.
7. To link another GPO to test **TestOU1**, right-click **TestOU1** and click **Link an Existing GPO**. Click **TestGPO** and click **OK**.
8. Click **TestOU1**. Notice that both GPO1 and TestGPO are linked to TestOU1. If both GPOs had the same policy setting configured but with different values, the value of the policy setting in GPO1 would take precedence because it would be applied last.
9. Click **TestGPO** in the right pane and click the **up arrow** to the left of the Link Order column. TestGPO now has link order 1 and GPO1 has link order 2, so TestGPO takes precedence if any settings conflict.
10. Right-click **TestGPO** and click **Delete**. Click **OK** in the message box asking you to confirm the deletion. Next, right-click **GPO1** and click **Delete**, and then click **OK**. No policies should be linked to TestOU1 now.
11. Continue to the next activity.

Activity 4-5

Configuring and Testing a GPO

Time Required: 25 minutes

Objective: Configure and test a GPO.

Required Tools and Equipment: ServerDC1 and ServerDM1

Description: In this activity, you move the ServerDM1 computer account to TestOU1 and test some computer settings by configuring GPO1.

1. Start ServerDM1. On ServerDC1, open Active Directory Users and Computers, if necessary.
2. Click the **Computers** folder and drag the **ServerDM1** computer account to the **TestOU1** OU. If necessary, click **Yes** in response to the warning message about moving Active Directory objects.
3. Open the Group Policy Management console, if necessary. Right-click **TestOU1** and click **Link an Existing GPO**. Click **GPO1** and click **OK**. Right-click **GPO1** and click **Edit** to open it in the Group Policy Management Editor.
4. Click to expand **Computer Configuration**, **Policies**, **Windows Settings**, **Security Settings**, and **Local Policies**, and then click **User Rights Assignment**.
5. In the right pane, double-click **Allow log on locally** to open the setting's Properties dialog box. Notice that the policy setting is currently not defined. Click the **Define these policy settings** check box, and then click **Add User or Group**. In the Add User or Group dialog box, click **Browse**. Type **Administrators** in the "Enter the object names to select" text box, and click **Check Names**. Click **OK** three times.
6. On ServerDM1, sign in to the domain as **Administrator**. To update the policies on ServerDM1, open a command prompt, type **gpupdate**, and press **Enter**. Close the command prompt.

Exam Tip ✔

In this module's activities, if `gpupdate.exe` doesn't seem to update policies on the local computer, try using `gpupdate /force`, which reapplies all policy settings, even those that haven't changed.

7. Right-click **Start**, click **Run**, type **secpol.msc** in the Open dialog box, and press **Enter** to open the Local Security Policy console. The Local Security Policy console contains only the security settings for the local computer.
8. Click to expand **Local Policies** and then click **User Rights Assignment**. Notice in Figure 4-12 that the icon next to the "Allow log on locally" policy looks like two towers and a scroll instead of the torn-paper icon next to the other policies. This icon indicates that the policy is defined by a domain GPO.
9. In the right pane, double-click **Allow log on locally**. In the list box of users and groups, click **Administrators**. Neither the Add User or Group button nor the Remove button is active because no users, not even administrators, can override domain polices on the local computer. Click **Cancel**.
10. Sign out of ServerDM1, and then try to sign back in as **domuser1** using **Password01**. Because you have restricted local logon to Administrators only, you'll see the following message: "The sign-in method you're trying to use isn't allowed. For more info, contact your network administrator." The sign-in method referred to in the message is interactive logon or local logon. Click **OK**.
11. On ServerDC1, change the **Allow log on locally** policy on GPO1 to Not Defined by clearing the **Define these policy settings** check box, and then click **OK.** Close the Group Policy Management Editor.
12. On ServerDM1, try again to sign in as **domuser1**. You'll probably get the same message about not being able to sign in because the policy hasn't been updated yet. Click **OK**. Sign in as administrator, run **gpupdate** at a command prompt, and sign out again.
13. Sign in to ServerDM1 as **domuser1**. Only an administrator can run the Local Security Policy MMC, but there's a workaround if you start it from an elevated command prompt. Right-click **Start** and click **Command Prompt (Admin)**. When prompted, type the Administrator account credentials, and click **Yes**.

(continues)

Activity 4-5 Continued

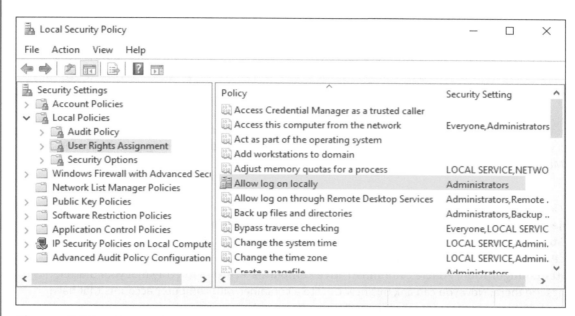

Figure 4-12   The Local Security Policy MMC with a policy set by a domain GPO

14. At the command prompt, type **secpol.msc** and press **Enter**.
15. In the Local Security Policy console, click to expand **Local Policies** and **User Rights Assignment**. In the right pane, double-click **Allow log on locally** to view the list of users and groups assigned this permission. Notice that this right is now assigned from a local GPO rather than a domain GPO, so you can make changes if needed. Click **Cancel**.
16. On ServerDC1, from the Group Policy Management console, unlink **GPO1** from **TestOU1** by right-clicking **GPO1** under TestOU1 and clicking **Delete**. Click **OK**.
17. Sign out of ServerDM1. Continue to the next activity.

Activity 4-6

Creating and Using Starter GPOs

Time Required: 20 minutes
Objective: Create Starter GPOs to be used to create new GPOs.
Required Tools and Equipment: ServerDC1
Description: In this activity, you create some Starter GPOs for creating new GPOs. You create two: one in the Computer Configuration node for configuring printers and one in the User Configuration node for configuring Start menu options.

1. On ServerDC1, open the Group Policy Management console. Right-click the **Starter GPOs** folder and click **New**.
2. In the New Starter GPO dialog box, type **StartPrintersC** in the Name text box. (*Start* stands for Starter GPO, *Printers* refers to the Printers node, and *C* refers to the Computer Configuration node of the GPO.) In the Comment text box, type **Starter GPO for the Printers node of Computer Configuration**, and then click **OK**.
3. Right-click the **StartPrintersC** GPO and click **Edit**. In the Group Policy Starter GPO Editor, click to expand **Computer Configuration** and **Administrative Templates**, and then click **Printers**.

(continues)

Activity 4-6 Continued

4. In the right pane, double-click **Automatically publish new printers in Active Directory**. In the Properties dialog box, click **Enabled**. Read the explanation of this policy setting, and then click **OK**.
5. Double-click **Always render print jobs on the server**. In the Properties dialog box, click **Enabled**. Read the explanation of this policy setting, and then click **OK**.

Note 3

To list the policy settings in alphabetical order so you can find them easier, click the Setting column header in the Group Policy Management Editor.

---

6. Close the Group Policy Starter GPO Editor. In the Group Policy Management console, right-click the **Group Policy Objects** folder and click **New**. In the New GPO dialog box, type **PrintConfigGPO** in the Name text box, click **StartPrintersC** in the Source Starter GPO list box, and then click **OK**.
7. Right-click **PrintConfigGPO** and click **Edit**. In the Group Policy Management Editor, expand and navigate to **Computer Configuration**, **Policies**, **Administrative Templates**, **Printers** to verify that your Starter GPO settings are there. Now you can link this new GPO to a container with computer accounts that have print servers installed, and the printer policies will be in effect on these servers. Close the Group Policy Management Editor.
8. To see the other method of using Starter GPOs to create new GPOs, click the **Starter GPOs** folder in the Group Policy Management console. Right-click **StartPrintersC** and click **New GPO From Starter GPO**. The New GPO Wizard starts. Click **Cancel**.
9. Create another Starter GPO named **StartU**, which is used as a baseline for Start screen options in a later activity.
10. Right-click the **StartU** GPO and click **Edit**. In the Group Policy Management Editor, click to expand **User Configuration** and **Administrative Templates**, and then click **Start Menu and Taskbar**.
11. Configure the following policies as shown:
    - Lock the Taskbar: **Enabled**
    - Remove the networking icon: **Enabled**
12. Continue to the next activity.

Group Policy Settings

Microsoft Exam AZ-800:
Deploy and manage Active Directory Domain Services (AD DS) in on-premises and cloud environments.
- Manage Windows Server by using domain-based Group Policies

As you have learned, GPOs have a Computer Configuration node, affecting all computer accounts in a GPO's scope, and a User Configuration node, affecting all user accounts in a GPO's scope. Computer Configuration policies are downloaded by a computer when the OS starts, and User Configuration policies are downloaded when a user signs in to a domain. All policies are updated every 90 minutes thereafter. Although many policies take effect when the GPO is updated, some might require a computer restart. Most policies in these two nodes affect different aspects of the working environment, but a few policies are the same. If the same policy is configured in both nodes and the settings conflict (for example, one disables a policy and the other enables it), the setting in Computer Configuration takes precedence.

Both nodes have a Policies folder and a Preferences folder. Under the Policies folder are these three folders: Software Settings, Windows Settings, and Administrative Templates. The Software Settings and Windows Settings folders include items called *extensions* because they extend the functionality of Group Policy beyond what was available in Windows

2000. The Administrative Templates folder contains categorized folders or nodes with settings that affect users' or computers' working environments, mainly by changing Registry settings.

Policy settings can be managed or unmanaged. A **managed policy setting** is applied to a user or computer when the object is in the scope of the GPO containing the setting. When the object is no longer in the GPO's scope or the policy is set to Not configured, however, the setting on the user or computer reverts to its original state. An **unmanaged policy setting** is persistent, meaning it remains even after the computer or user object falls out of the GPO's scope and until it is changed by another policy or manually. The policies already loaded in Active Directory are managed policies, but you can customize Group Policy by adding your own policies, which are unmanaged.

You learned about user account policies in Module 3. Administrative Templates are discussed later in the "Working with Administrative Templates" section. The following sections focus on these categories of settings:

- *Software installation*—In the Software Settings folder under both the Computer Configuration and User Configuration nodes.
- *Scripts*—In the Windows Settings folder under both the Computer Configuration and User Configuration nodes.
- *Folder redirection*—In the Windows Settings folder under the User Configuration node.

Software Installation Policies

The Software installation extension (see Figure 4-13) is used to install software packages remotely on member computers. If it's configured under the Computer Configuration node, the software package is installed regardless of who signs in to the targeted computers. When it's configured under User Configuration, the software package is available to targeted users when they sign in to any domain computer.

Applications are deployed with the Windows Installer service, which uses installation packages called *MSI files*. A **Microsoft Software Installation (MSI) file** is a collection of files gathered into a package with an `.msi` extension that contains the instructions Windows Installer needs to install an application.

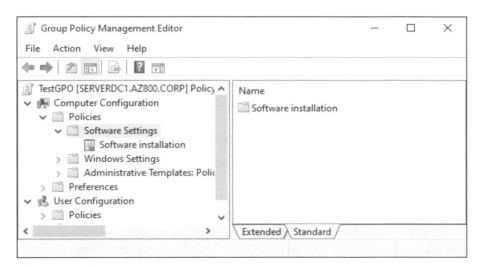

Figure 4-13   The Software installation extension

> ### Note 4
>
> You might want to install a software package that's available only as an executable (`.exe`) file. Depending on the software developer, an `.exe` file might contain an MSI file that you can extract with the command `filename.exe /extract` (replacing `filename` with the `.exe` file's name). If that's not possible, you might need to convert the `.exe` file to an MSI file. Although there's no Windows utility for this purpose, third-party programs are available, such as Advanced Installer (*www.advancedinstaller.com*) and Exe to MSI Converter Pro (*www.exetomsi.com*).

Configuring Software Installation for Computers

In the Computer Configuration node, software packages are assigned to target computers, meaning that installation of the software is mandatory, and assigned packages are installed the next time the computer starts. To assign a software package to a computer, you must create a shared folder on a server that gives the computer the Read & execute permission. Typically, you do this by assigning the necessary permissions to the Authenticated Users special identity group. If you're deploying several applications through Group Policy, you can create a separate folder in the share for each package.

After creating the shared folder and copying the installation package to it, you can create the deployment policy by using the Software installation extension. To do so, follow these steps from the Group Policy Management Editor:

1. Right-click Software installation, point to New, and click Package.
2. Browse to and select the application installation file using the UNC path of the shared folder.
3. Select the deployment method (see Figure 4-14). If you choose Assigned, the application will be deployed the next time any computer in the scope of the policy restarts. If you choose Advanced, you can choose additional deployment options, as discussed in the following section.

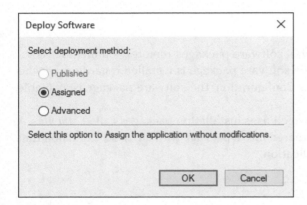

Figure 4-14   Choosing a deployment method

Advanced Application Deployment Options

To access options for deploying applications, click the Advanced option button in the Deploy Software dialog box or open the Properties dialog box for a package you've already added to the Software installation node. The Properties dialog box has several tabs with options for changing how the application is deployed:

- *General*—This tab contains information about a package, including the name, version, language, publisher, and hardware platform. You can change the package name here.
- *Deployment*—You can select whether a package is published or assigned. In the Computer Configuration node, software packages can only be assigned, so the Published option is disabled (see Figure 4-15). The Deployment type selection determines what's available in the Deployment options section, including when and how an application is deployed. For example, an application can be installed at user logon or when a document used by the application is opened. Another deployment option uninstalls the application automatically if the user or computer falls out of the GPO's scope. In the Computer Configuration node, the only two deployment options are Auto-install and Uninstall. At the bottom of this tab, you can choose user interface options (Basic or Maximum), but this option is available only in the User Configuration node. Clicking the Advanced button shows options for ignoring the language when deploying the package and making a 32-bit application available on 64-bit machines (enabled by default).
- *Upgrades*—You can deploy a package upgrade by specifying which existing packages should be upgraded by the new package and which packages can upgrade the current package.
- *Categories*—You use this tab to associate a published package with a category. Control Panel's Programs applet lists available applications under the specified categories. This option is used only for packages published in the User Configuration node.

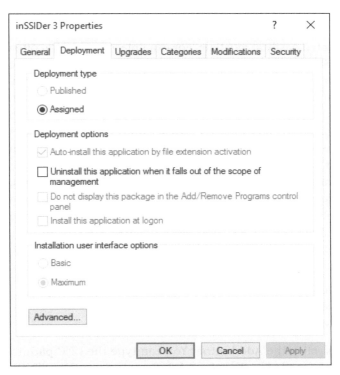

Figure 4-15   Settings for installing a software package

- *Modifications*—You can use this tab to customize a package installation by using a transform file (.mst extension). Select transform files for customizing the installation of an MSI file. A transform file contains information about features and components that can be used to customize an application installation. For example, if you're installing Microsoft Office, you can use the Office Resource Kit to create a transform file that overrides the default installation path or specifies which Office components should be installed.
- *Security*—This is a standard permissions dialog box for the package object. By default, Authenticated Users have Read permission, and Domain Admins have Full control.

After a package is deployed to a computer, by default it's not installed again. However, if changes have been made to the original package, right-click the package in the Software installation extension, click All Tasks, and then click Redeploy application. This action reinstalls the package on target computers. To remove a deployed package, right-click the package, click All Tasks, and then click Remove. You have the option to uninstall the software immediately or simply prevent new installations yet allow users to use already deployed packages.

Configuring Software Installation for Users

The Software installation extension performs the same function in the User Configuration node as in the Computer Configuration node—deploying software to remote destinations—but has important differences in options and execution. A software package can only be assigned to a computer, but there are two options for deploying software to users:

- *Published*—A **published application** isn't installed automatically; instead, a link to install the application is available in Control Panel's Programs and Features by clicking the "Install a program from the network" link. Published applications can also be configured to install when the user opens a file type associated with the application.
- *Assigned*—An **assigned application** can be installed automatically when the user logs on to a computer in the domain, or it can be set to install automatically if a user opens a file associated with the application.

Deploying Scripts

A **script** is a series of commands saved in a text file to be repeated easily at any time. For example, suppose you often use PowerShell to perform certain tasks. As you know, PowerShell commands can be long and complex. You can type the commands in a text file and save the file with a `.ps1` extension, such as `myscript.ps1`. To run this string of commands, type `PowerShell myscript.ps1` at a command prompt or just `myscript.ps1` at a PowerShell prompt. In addition to PowerShell scripts, you can create command scripts, which consist of a series of commands saved in a file with a `.bat` extension, also known as a **batch file**. You can also create scripts with scripting languages such as VBScript and JScript. For the purposes of this section, you focus on deploying scripts with Group Policy that run when a computer starts up or shuts down or when a user logs on or logs off.

There's a Scripts extension in both the Computer Configuration and User Configuration nodes in the path Policies, Windows Settings, Scripts. In the Computer Configuration node, you configure startup or shutdown scripts, and in the User Configuration node, you configure logon and logoff scripts. For example, to configure a logon script, navigate to User Configuration, Policies, Windows Settings, Scripts, and then right-click Logon and click Properties (see Figure 4-16). The properties of a logon script are the same as for the other three script types.

This dialog box has two tabs:

- *Scripts*—This tab is used for command scripts (batch files) and scripts that can be run by Windows Scripting Host (WSH). WSH is used to run VBScript and JScript files.
- *PowerShell Scripts*—To run PowerShell scripts, the target computer must be running Windows 7 or later versions.

To add a script in the Scripts or PowerShell Scripts tabs, click the Add button. You can type the UNC path to a share where the script file is located or click Browse to search for the file. By default, Windows looks in the SYSVOL share on the DC in the folder containing the GPO where you're creating the script. The advantage of using the SYSVOL share is that scripts are replicated automatically and can be retrieved by clients from a DC in the domain. If you use a regular shared folder, the server hosting the share must always be available; the script might have to run across a WAN link if the server is in a remote site.

If you want to store scripts in the SYSVOL folder with your GPO, you need the GUID of the GPO to locate the correct folder. You can find the GUID by looking in the System\Policies folder in Active Directory Users and Computers.

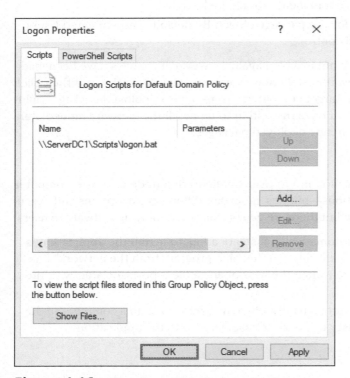

Figure 4-16   The properties of a logon script

Folder Redirection

Folder redirection enables an administrator to set policies that redirect folders in a user's profile directory. This feature is useful when you want users to store documents on a server for centralized backup, but you don't want to change the way they access their document folders. It's also quite useful when roaming profiles are used because it decreases the network bandwidth needed to upload and download a user's roaming profile.

Folder redirection applies strictly to user accounts and is found only under the User Configuration node in Policies, Windows Settings, Folder Redirection. There are 13 folders you can redirect, as shown in Figure 4-17.

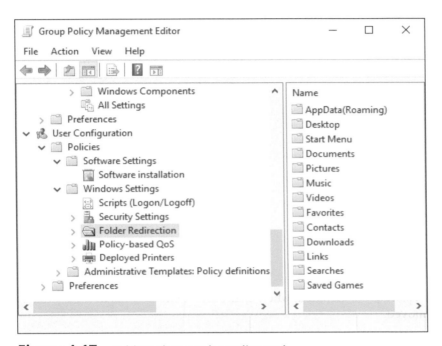

Figure 4-17   Folders that can be redirected

To redirect a folder, right-click the folder in the Folder Redirection node and click Properties. In the Target tab of a folder's Properties dialog box, you have the following options (see Figure 4-18):

- *Setting*—In this list box, you have the following options:
  - ○ Not configured: This default option means folder redirection isn't enabled for the folder.
  - ○ Basic - Redirect everyone's folder to the same location: This option redirects the selected folder to the same location for all user accounts in the GPO's scope.
  - ○ Advanced - Specify locations for various user groups: With this option, you can redirect folders to different locations based on group membership.
- *Target folder location*—In this list box, you have the following options:
  - ○ Create a folder for each user under the root path: This is the default setting; you specify the UNC path to a share in the Root Path text box. Each user has a folder under the root path. For example, the Documents folder for a user with the logon name jsmith is at \\ServerDM1\UserDocs\jsmith\Documents.
  - ○ Redirect to the user's home directory: If home directories are defined, the folder is redirected to the specified location.
  - ○ Redirect to the following location: The folder is redirected to the path you specify in the Root Path text box. If you use this option, multiple users have the same location for the folder.
  - ○ Redirect to the local userprofile location: The folder is located wherever the user's local profile is stored, which is usually in the C:\Users folder.

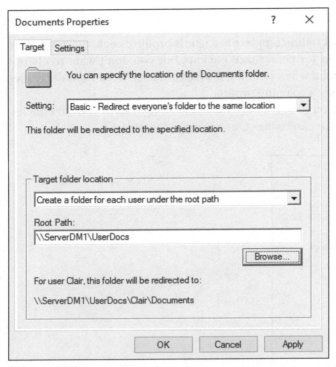

Figure 4-18   Configuring folder redirection for the Documents folder

In the Settings tab, you specify options for redirection, including whether the folder should remain redirected or revert to its original location if the policy is removed.

Grow with Cengage Unlimited

There are many security settings in Group Policy that can be configured to secure the Windows OS. These settings are covered in *Microsoft Guide to Configuring Windows Server Hybrid Advanced Services, Exam AZ-801*.

Self-Check Questions

3. An unmanaged policy setting reverts to its original state when the object is no longer in the GPO's scope. True or False?

   a. True   b. False

4. What kind of file can be used with the Software installation extension?

   a. .exe   c. .ini
   b. .com   d. .msi

◉ Check your answers at the end of this module.

Activity 4-7

Deploying a Shutdown Script to a Computer

Time Required: 15 minutes

Objective: Create and deploy a shutdown script.

Required Tools and Equipment: ServerDC1, ServerDM1

Description: In this activity, you write a shutdown script that deletes all files with a `.temp` extension, and then you deploy this script using group policies.

1. On ServerDC1, start Notepad and type **del /F /S c:*.temp**. The `/F` option forces deletion of read-only files, and the `/S` option deletes the file in the current directory and all subdirectories.
2. Click **File** and then **Save As** from the menu. Choose the desktop as the location for saving your file. In the Save as type list box, click **All Files (*.*)**. Type **deltemp.bat** in the File name text box and click **Save**. Exit Notepad.
3. Right-click **deltemp.bat** on your desktop and click **Copy**. (You paste the script into the SYSVOL share in a later step.)
4. Open the Group Policy Management console. Click the **Group Policy Objects** folder and create a GPO named **Scripts**.
5. Right-click the **Scripts** GPO and click **Edit**. In the Group Policy Management Editor, click to expand **Computer Configuration**, **Policies**, and **Windows Settings**, and then click **Scripts (Startup/Shutdown)**. Right-click **Shutdown** in the right pane and click **Properties**. In the Shutdown Properties dialog box, click **Show Files**. In the File Explorer window that opens, right-click the right pane and click **Paste**. Note the path where the script is stored—a folder in the SYSVOL share on your DC. Close the File Explorer window.
6. In the Shutdown Properties dialog box, click **Add**. In the Add a Script dialog box, click **Browse**. Click **deltemp**, and then click **Open**. Click **OK** twice.
7. Close the Group Policy Management Editor. Link **Scripts** to the **TestOU1** OU, which is where you moved the ServerDM1 account earlier.
8. Sign in to ServerDM1 as **domadmin1**. You're going to create a few files on your desktop that have the `.temp` extension. Open a command prompt window, type **cd desktop**, and press **Enter**. Type **copy nul > file1.temp** and press **Enter** to create an empty file. Repeat the command two more times, changing `file1` to **file2** and then **file3**. You see the files on your desktop. (You may have to minimize Server Manager and the command prompt to see the files.)

> **Note 5**
>
> In the `copy nul > file1.temp` command, `nul` is a system device that's just an empty file, and the `>` redirects the empty file to a new file named `file1.temp`.

9. Type **gpupdate** and press **Enter**. After `gpupdate` is finished, restart ServerDM1. (If you don't run `gpupdate`, you have to restart the computer to load the policy, and then shut it down again to make the shutdown script run.) The shutdown process will probably take a little longer than usual because the script has to run.
10. Sign in to ServerDM1 as **domadmin1** again and verify that the `.temp` files have been deleted. Sign out of ServerDM1.
11. On ServerDC1, unlink the **Scripts** GPO from the **TestOU1** OU. Continue to the next activity.

Activity 4-8

Configuring a Folder Redirection Policy

Time Required: 15 minutes

Objective: Redirect the Documents folder.

Required Tools and Equipment: ServerDC1 and ServerDM1

Description: In this activity, you configure a folder redirection policy for the Documents folder and apply it to ServerDM1.

1. On ServerDC1, open File Explorer and create a folder named **Redirected** in the **C:** volume. Share the folder, giving the **Everyone** group **Read/Write** sharing permission, and leave the remaining permissions at their default settings. Close File Explorer.

2. Open the Group Policy Management console, and create a GPO named **FolderRedir** in the Group Policy Objects folder. Open **FolderRedir** in the Group Policy Management Editor. Expand **User Configuration**, **Policies**, **Windows Settings**, and **Folder Redirection**. Right-click the **Documents** folder and click **Properties**.

3. In the Documents Properties dialog box, click **Basic - Redirect everyone's folder to the same location** in the Setting drop-down list. Click the **Target folder location** list arrow to view the available options, and then, if necessary, click **Create a folder for each user under the root path** in the list. In the Root Path text box, type **\\ServerDC1\Redirected**.

4. Click the **Settings** tab and review the available options. Click to clear the **Grant the user exclusive rights to Documents** check box. Click **Redirect the folder back to the local userprofile location when policy is removed**, click **OK**, and in the warning message box, click **Yes**. Close the Group Policy Management Editor.

5. In the Group Policy Management console, link the **FolderRedir** GPO to **TestOU1**.

6. Open Active Directory Users and Computers and move the user **domadmin1** (located in the Users folder) to TestOU1 by dragging and dropping the user account.

7. On ServerDM1, sign in as **domadmin1**, and run **gpupdate** from a command prompt. Then sign out of ServerDM1, and sign in again as **domadmin1**. You might see a message indicating that folder redirection is occurring.

8. On ServerDC1, open File Explorer and navigate to C:\redirected. You see a folder there named domadmin1. In that folder is a folder named Documents.

9. Unlink the **FolderRedir** GPO from **TestOU1**. Continue to the next activity.

Working with Administrative Templates

Microsoft Exam AZ-800:

Deploy and manage Active Directory Domain Services (AD DS) in on-premises and cloud environments.

- Manage Windows Server by using domain-based Group Policies

Both the Computer Configuration and User Configuration nodes have an Administrative Templates folder. In the Computer Configuration node, the settings in Administrative Templates affect the HKEY_LOCAL_MACHINE Registry key. Settings in the User Configuration node affect the HKEY_LOCAL_USER Registry key.

Hundreds of settings are defined in the Administrative Templates nodes, and many more can be added through customization. The Administrative Templates folder uses policy definition files, called **administrative template files**, in XML format (with an .admx extension), which makes creating your own policies fairly easy if you need to control a setting not provided by default. The following sections cover topics related to administrative templates:

- Computer Configuration settings
- User Configuration settings

- The ADMX central store
- Administrative Templates property filters
- Custom administrative templates
- Migrating administrative template files

Computer Configuration Settings

This section doesn't attempt to cover all the settings in Administrative Templates, but it gives you a brief explanation of the types of settings in each folder under Administrative Templates. You're encouraged to spend some time browsing through the settings with the Group Policy Management Editor so that you have a good idea where to look when you need to configure a particular type of policy setting. To see an explanation of a setting, double-click it and read the Help section of the dialog box for the policy's settings (see Figure 4-19).

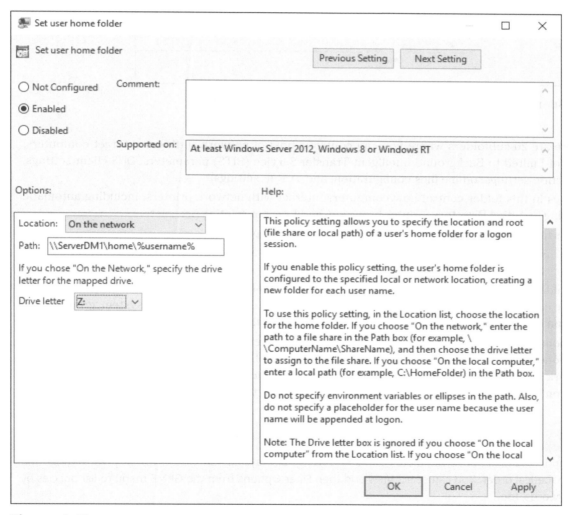

Figure 4-19   Configuring settings for a policy

Administrative Templates in the Computer Configuration node, where many aspects of the computer working environment are controlled, contains the following folders (see Figure 4-20), most with additional subfolders:

- *Control Panel*—This folder has three subfolders: Personalization, Regional and Language Options, and User Accounts. Personalization has settings that affect the look of Windows, particularly the lock screen and background. Settings in Regional and Language Options allow administrators to set and restrict the language in the Control Panel user interface. The single policy in User Accounts configures a default user logon picture for all users on target computers.

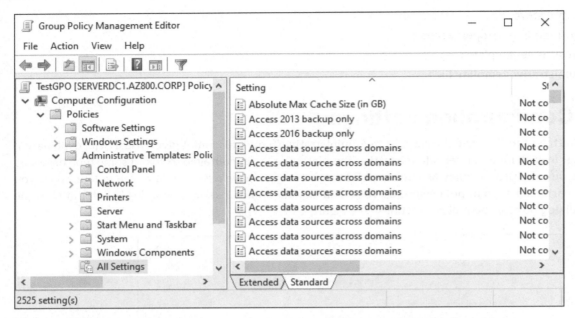

Figure 4-20   The Administrative Templates folders under Computer Configuration

- *Network*—There are 20 subfolders where you can control a host of network settings on target computers, including but not limited to Background Intelligent Transfer Service (BITS) parameters, DNS client settings, network connection settings, offline files configuration, and TCP/IP settings.
- *Printers*—Settings in this folder control how computers interact with network printers, including automatic printer publishing in Active Directory, printer browsing, and Internet printing parameters.
- *Server*—Settings in this folder control options for backing up a computer.
- *Start Menu and Taskbar*—Settings in this folder allow you to specify a Start screen layout and pin apps to the Start screen.
- *System*—This folder contains more than 35 subfolders with settings for controlling general computer system operation. Some computer functions that can be controlled include disk quotas, the file system, group policy processing, logon and shutdown, power management, and user profiles.
- *Windows Components*—This folder contains more than 50 subfolders with settings for configuring specific Windows components, such as app deployment, Event Viewer, File Explorer, Windows PowerShell, Windows Update, and Work Folders. Some settings in this folder have an identical counterpart in the User Configuration node. When a conflict exists, the setting in Computer Configuration takes precedence.

Note 6

An additional node under Administrative Templates called All Settings displays all Administrative Template settings and can be sorted in alphabetical order. You can select View and then Filter Options from the GPME menu to list policies by certain criteria or keywords, too.

User Configuration Settings

Most of the previous information about Administrative Templates in the Computer Configuration node applies to the User Configuration node, too. Administrative Templates in User Configuration also contains the Control Panel, Network, Start Menu and Taskbar, System, and Windows Components subfolders, although most of the settings are different because they apply to specific users rather than all users who log on to a computer. With Administrative Templates in the User Configuration node, you can customize many aspects of a user's working environment. Policies in this node add the following subfolders to the previous list for the Computer Configuration node:

- *Desktop*—Controls the look of users' desktops, determines which icons are available, and can limit actions users can take on the desktop.
- *Shared Folders*—Controls whether a user can publish shared folders and Distributed File System (DFS) root folders in Active Directory.

The ADMX Central Store

ADMX files, as discussed, contain the settings in the Administrative Templates folder. The **ADMX central store** is a centralized location for maintaining ADMX files so that when an ADMX file is modified from one domain controller, all DCs receive the updated file. You can also create custom ADMX files that are available to all administrators to use without having to copy the files from one location to another.

The default location of ADMX files is in the *%systemroot%*\PolicyDefinitions folder. Without a central store, any ADMX file you customize or create would have to be copied manually to all other systems where group policies are being configured and managed. In a large network with many people working with group policies, ADMX files would get out of sync rapidly without a central store.

To create a central store, simply create a folder named PolicyDefinitions in the *%systemroot%*\SYSVOL\ sysvol*domainname*\Policies folder (the same folder where GPTs are stored). Under the PolicyDefinitions folder, create a language-specific folder that uses the two-character ISO standard for worldwide languages. Variations of some languages use an additional two characters to specify the country. For example, English is en-us for U.S. English or en-GB for Great Britain English. In a network with multiple domain controllers, the central store should be created on the DC that controls the PDC emulator role.

After creating folders for the central store, you just need to copy the ADMX files from their current location to the central store location. If you're managing ADMX files from a computer other than where you created the central store, the process is easy—simply copy the ADMX files to the SYSVOL share (*server*\SYSVOL*domainname*\Policies\PolicyDefinitions). Because the SYSVOL share is replicated, the files and folders in the PolicyDefinitions folder are, too.

Working with Filters

The number of settings in the Administrative Templates section of a GPO can be daunting when you're trying to find a particular policy to configure. There are several hundred policy settings under both Computer Configuration and User Configuration. If you know the name of the setting you need to configure or at least know the first word of the name, you can sort the settings alphabetically under All Settings and find it that way. However, if you don't know the name and perhaps know only the policy's general function, you could be searching a while. Thankfully, you can narrow the search by using a filter in the Group Policy Management Editor:

1. Open a GPO in the GPME, click Policies, and then click Administrative Templates under Computer Configuration or User Configuration. You see the filter icon on the toolbar.
2. Click Action and then click Filter Options from the menu to open the Filter Options dialog box (see Figure 4-21).
3. You can configure a filter with the following criteria:
   - *Managed*—Select Any, Yes, or No. If you select Any, both managed and unmanaged policies are included in the filter criteria. If you select Yes, only managed policies are included, and if you select No, only unmanaged policies are included.
   - *Configured*—Select Any, Yes, or No to see only configured policies, unconfigured policies, or both.
   - *Commented*—You can add a comment to any policy setting in Administrative Templates by double-clicking it and typing a comment in the Comment text box. This filter option allows you to view only policy settings with a comment, those without a comment, or both. By default, policy settings don't have a comment.
   - *Enable Keyword Filters*—Select this check box, if needed, and in the Filter for word(s) text box, type one or more words that are part of the policy setting's title, help text, or comment field. You can specify how the words match by selecting Exact, All, or Any.

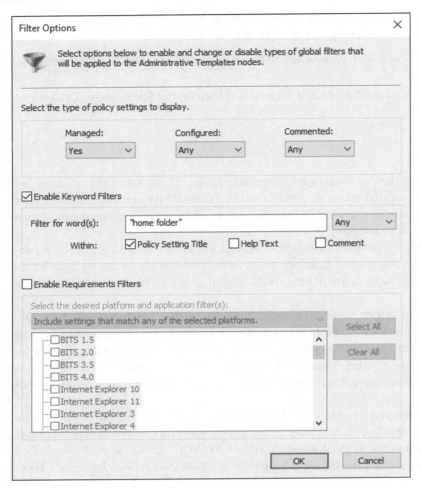

Figure 4-21   Configuring an Administrative Templates filter

- *Enable Requirements Filters*—Narrow the search by OS or application platform. For example, you might want to see only policy settings that work with Windows Server 2022.

> **Note 7**
>
> Filters work only with settings in the Administrative Templates folders; you can't filter settings in the Software Settings or Windows Settings folders.

After you have configured filter options, you apply the filter by clicking Action and then Filter On from the menu or by clicking the Filter toolbar icon. Only policies matching the criteria are displayed in the GPME.

Using Custom Administrative Templates

Administrative templates are a collection of policy definition files in XML format. These XML files, referred to as "ADMX files" because of their .admx extension, specify Registry entries that should be controlled and the type of data the entries take. Many software vendors provide administrative template files for controlling their applications' settings through group policies. For example, Microsoft offers administrative template files for the Microsoft Office suite.

Windows versions before Vista and Server 2008 used .adm files. This format can still be used on the same system as ADMX files, but you can create and edit ADMX files only on Windows Vista or later computers. ADMX files can also have an .adml extension, which provides a language-specific user interface in the Group Policy Management Editor. You can find all ADMX and ADML files under %systemroot%\PolicyDefinitions and open them in Notepad or an XML editor. However, you don't usually edit the standard ADMX files that ship with Windows.

Adding a Custom Administrative Template to Group Policy

If you create your own ADMX file or download one for configuring settings on an installed application, you can simply add the ADMX file to the %*systemroot*%\PolicyDefinitions folder. The next time you open the GPME, the file is loaded. Any language-specific files (.adml) should be placed in the corresponding language folder. For example, if there's a U.S. English file, place it in the en-US folder under the PolicyDefinitions folder.

If you have created a central store for policy definition files, place your custom ADMX files in this location so that they're replicated to all domain controllers. It's a folder named PolicyDefinitions on the SYSVOL share of a DC that makes sure all policy definitions are replicated to other DCs.

> **Note 8**
>
> Learn more about ADMX files at *https://docs.microsoft.com/en-us/troubleshoot/windows-client/group-policy/create-and-manage-central-store*.

Working with Older Administrative Templates

If you're using older ADM administrative templates, which were used in Windows Server 2008 and earlier versions, you can add them manually by following these steps:

1. In the GPMC, open a GPO in the GPME. Right-click the Administrative Templates folder under Computer Configuration or User Configuration and click Add/Remove Templates.
2. In the Add/Remove Templates dialog box, click Add.
3. In the Policy Templates window in File Explorer, browse to the ADM file's location. Select the ADM file and click Add.
4. In the Add/Remove Templates dialog box, click Close.

Migrating Administrative Templates

If you're running a Windows Server 2008 or later domain but still have to support clients that run operating systems older than Vista or older applications that use ADM files, you might want to migrate the older ADM files to ADMX format so that you can make use of the central store. As mentioned, the central store ensures that all policy definitions are replicated to other DCs. Because the central store can't work with ADM files, you need to convert the ADM files to ADMX files with ADMX Migrator, a snap-in tool available for free from the Microsoft Download Center. To use this tool, follow these steps:

1. Download ADMX Migrator from the Microsoft Download Center.
2. Install ADMX Migrator on the computer with the ADM files; in most cases, it's a domain controller.
3. Navigate to the folder where you installed ADMX Migrator and double-click the faAdmxEditor.msc file. An MMC opens with the ADMX Migrator snap-in.
4. Click Generate ADMX from ADM.
5. After the ADMX file is generated, move it to the %*windir*%\PolicyDefinitions folder or the central store.

Self-Check Questions

5. What is the name of the folder that is the default location for ADMX files?

   a. GroupPolicy
   b. ADMXFiles
   c. SYSVOL
   d. PolicyDefinitions

6. Which subfolder is found under the User Configuration node but not in the Computer Configuration node?

   a. Control Panel
   b. Network
   c. Desktop
   d. System

Check your answers at the end of this module.

Activity 4-9

Working with Computer Administrative Template Settings

Time Required: 15 minutes

Objective: Become familiar with Administrative Templates settings in Computer Configuration.

Required Tools and Equipment: ServerDC1, ServerDM1

Description: In this activity, you explore Administrative Templates settings under Computer Configuration and configure some settings to see the effect they have on the computer operating environment.

1. On ServerDC1, open **GPO1** in the Group Policy Management Editor.
2. Under Computer Configuration, click to expand **Policies** and **Administrative Templates**. Browse through the folders under Administrative Templates to see the settings and subfolders under each one. Take your time to get a good feel for the types of settings available in each main folder.
3. Click the **All Settings** folder to see the full list of settings in Administrative Templates. The settings are arranged in alphabetical order by default. Click the **State** column to view the settings according to their state, which is Not configured, Enabled, or Disabled. Because GPO1 has no configured settings, the view doesn't change.
4. In the left pane, click to expand the **System** folder, and then click **Logon**. In the right pane, click the **Setting** column header to arrange the setting in alphabetical order and then double-click **Run these programs at user logon**. This policy can be used in place of a logon script if you want more programs to run when any user logs on to certain computers.
5. In the Run these programs at user logon window, click **Enabled**, and then click **Show**. In the first row of the Show Contents dialog box, type **explorer.exe**, and in the second row, type **notepad.exe** (see Figure 4-22). Now all target computers run File Explorer and Notepad when a user logs on. Click **OK** twice and close the Group Policy Management Editor.

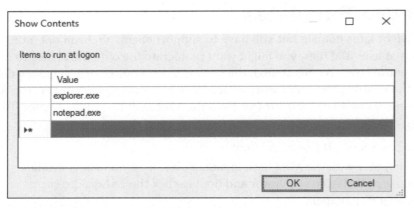

Figure 4-22 Configuring programs to run at user logon

6. Link **GPO1** to the **TestOU1** OU.
7. On ServerDM1, sign in as **domadmin1** and run **gpupdate**. Then sign out of ServerDM1, and sign in again as **domadmin1**. After a few moments, File Explorer and Notepad open. Close File Explorer and Notepad.
8. On ServerDC1, unlink **GPO1** from **TestOU1** and link it to the domain node. Open **GPO1** in the Group Policy Management Editor. Navigate to **Run these programs at user logon policy** and set it to **Not Configured**.
9. Navigate to **Computer Configuration**, **Policies**, **Administrative Templates**, and **Windows Components**, and click **Windows Logon Options**. In the right pane, double-click **Display information about previous logons during user logon**. Read the Help information about this policy setting. Click **Enabled**, and then click **OK**.

(continues)

Activity 4-9 Continued

10. On ServerDM1, run **gpupdate**, and then sign out and sign in again as **domadmin1**. You see a message stating that it's the first time you have signed in to the account. That's because this is the first time you have signed in since the policy was enabled. Click **OK**.

11. Sign out of ServerDM1, and then try to sign in again, but with an incorrect password. Then sign in with the correct password. A window opens to show the last successful sign-in and an unsuccessful sign-in attempt. This information is intended to let users know whether somebody has been trying to use their accounts to log on. Click **OK**.

12. Sign out of ServerDM1. On ServerDC1, in the Group Policy Management Editor, set the **Display information about previous logons during user logon** policy to **Not Configured**. Unlink GPO1 from the domain node.

13. Continue to the next activity.

Activity 4-10

Working with User Administrative Template Settings

Time Required: 10 minutes
Objective: Become familiar with Administrative Templates settings in User Configuration.
Required Tools and Equipment: ServerDC1, ServerDM1
Description: In this activity, you explore Administrative Templates settings under User Configuration and then configure some settings to see the effect they have on a user's environment.

1. On ServerDC1, open **GPO1** in the Group Policy Management Editor.

2. Under User Configuration, click to expand **Policies** and **Administrative Templates**. Browse through the folders under Administrative Templates to see the settings and subfolders under each one. Take your time to get a good feel for the types of settings available in each main folder.

3. In the left pane, click to expand the **System** folder, and then click to select the **System** folder. In the right pane, double-click **Prevent access to the command prompt**.

4. Read the policy help information. Click **Enabled**, and then click **OK**. Close the Group Policy Management Editor.

5. In Group Policy Management, link **GPO1** to **TestOU1**.

6. On ServerDM1, sign in as **domadmin1**. Right-click **Start** and click **Command Prompt**. A command prompt window opens, but you see a message stating that the administrator has disabled it. Press any key to close the command prompt window.

7. On ServerDC1, unlink **GPO1** from **TestOU1**.

8. Sign off ServerDM1. Continue to the next activity.

Activity 4-11

Viewing Policy Settings with Filter Options

Time Required: 10 minutes
Objective: Configure filter options to find a policy setting in Administrative Templates.
Required Tools and Equipment: ServerDC1
Description: In this activity, you want to configure the setting that displays the desktop instead of the Start screen when users sign in to Windows 8 computers. You can't remember the exact setting name, but you know it's in the User Configuration node of a GPO. You configure a filter to narrow down the search. (You don't actually configure the policy; you only use the filter option to find the policy.)

(continues)

Activity 4-11 Continued

1. On ServerDC1, open **GPO1** in the Group Policy Management Editor.
2. Under User Configuration, click to expand **Policies**, and click **Windows Settings**. Notice that there's no Filter icon on the toolbar because you can't filter settings in Windows Settings. Click **Administrative Templates**. You see the Filter icon now.
3. Click **Action** and then **Filter Options**. In the Filter Options window, click the **Enable Keyword Filters** check box. You remember that the policy setting title has the word "desktop" in it, so type **desktop** in the Filter for word(s) text box. If necessary, click **Any** in the list box next to the Filter for word(s) text box.
4. Click the **Policy Setting Title** check box, and if necessary, click to clear the **Help Text** and **Comment** check boxes. Click **OK**. You see a filter icon on the Administrative Templates folder.
5. Under User Configuration, click to expand **Administrative Templates**, and click **All Settings**. You see a list of policy settings with the word *desktop* in the title. That's still quite a few settings to sift through.
6. Click **Action** and then **Filter Options**. You remember that the word "start" was also in the title. In the Filter for word(s) text box, type the word **start** next to "desktop," making sure to leave a space between them. In the list box, click **All** so that the filter shows only policy settings with both words in them. Click **OK**.
7. Now you see only one policy setting, and it's the one you are looking for. Click the filter icon on the toolbar to remove the filter. You see all settings again. Close the Group Policy Management Editor.
8. Continue to the next activity.

Configuring Group Policy Preferences

Microsoft Exam AZ-800:
Deploy and manage Active Directory Domain Services (AD DS) in on-premises and cloud environments.
- Manage Windows Server by using domain-based Group Policies

Unlike user or computer policies that can't be changed by users, **group policy preferences** enable administrators to set up a baseline computing environment yet still allow users to make changes to configured settings. Both the Computer Configuration and User Configuration nodes have a Preferences folder with two subnodes—Windows Settings and Control Panel Settings—that contain settings organized into categories (see Figure 4-23).

With group policy preferences, you can perform many useful tasks, including the following:

- Create and modify local users and groups.
- Enable and disable devices on a computer, such as USB ports, DVD drives, and removable media.
- Create drive mappings.
- Manage power options.
- Create and manage files, folders, and shortcuts.
- Create and modify printers.
- Configure custom Registry settings.
- Configure custom application settings.
- Configure Control Panel settings.
- Configure Internet settings.

Many of these tasks were managed by complex logon scripts in the past, but using group policy preferences should reduce the need for scripts substantially. In addition, new preferences can be created. For example, software vendors can create ADMX files for managing settings in their applications.

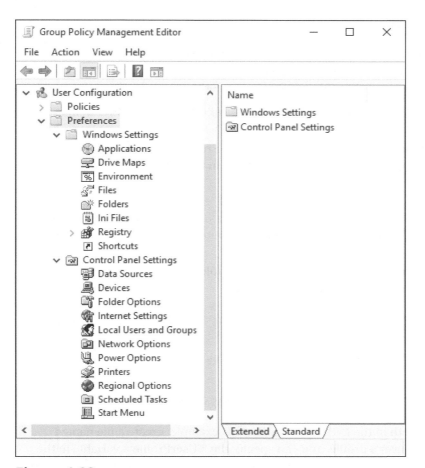

Figure 4-23   Categories for preference settings

Computers need the Group Policy Preferences Client Side Extensions (GPP CSE) package installed to recognize and download settings in the Preferences folder when processing group policies. This package is already installed in Windows Server 2008 and later versions. For older clients (such as Windows XP, Windows Vista, and Windows Server 2003), you can download the client-side extensions package by going to *www.microsoft.com/download* and searching for "client-side extensions."

How Group Policy Preferences Are Applied

As mentioned, group policy preferences are simply preferences, which means users can usually change these settings as long as they have the permission to do so. However, preferences are refreshed on the same schedule as policies by default. This means Computer Configuration preferences are refreshed when the computer restarts and every 90 minutes thereafter, and User Configuration preferences are refreshed when the user signs in and then every 90 minutes. You can change this behavior by setting preferences to be applied only once. That way, preferences are used as a baseline configuration for the settings they affect, but users can still change them. Another difference between policies and preferences is management. If a managed policy setting is removed, unconfigured, or disabled, the original setting is restored on target users or computers. With preferences, the settings aren't restored by default, but you can change this behavior to make preferences act more like managed policies.

Creating Group Policy Preferences

There aren't hundreds of built-in preference settings to configure, as there are with policies. In fact, there aren't any preferences at all—just preference categories. You must create each preference you want to deploy. The process of creating most preferences is similar. This example creates a folder preference under the User Configuration node:

1. Open the GPO in the Group Policy Management Editor, and navigate to User Configuration, Preferences, Windows Settings.
2. Right-click Folders, point to New, and click Folder to open the New Folder Properties dialog box.
3. In the New Folder Properties dialog box, select from the following actions in the General tab (which are common to most preferences categories):
   - *Create*—Creates a new folder.
   - *Replace*—Deletes and re-creates a folder. If the folder already exists, it's deleted along with its contents, and a new folder with the same name is created with the specified attributes. If the folder doesn't already exist, a new folder is created.
   - *Update*—Updates a folder's properties. If the folder doesn't exist, a new folder is created.
   - *Delete*—Deletes a folder.

> **Note 9**
>
> The General tab has different settings depending on the type of preference you're creating.

4. In this case, select Update. If the folder already exists, it's updated with any changes; otherwise, the folder is created.
5. Select the path of the folder or type the path in the Path text box. For this example, create a file named `TestPrefs` in the Documents folder of a user's profile. You can specify the %UserProfile% variable in the path. For example, if the user is testuser1, the %UserProfile% variable has the value C:\Users\testuser1, so the full path is %UserProfile%\Documents\TestPrefs (see Figure 4-24).
6. Select attributes for the folder. You can choose from Read-only, Hidden, and Archive (the default setting).

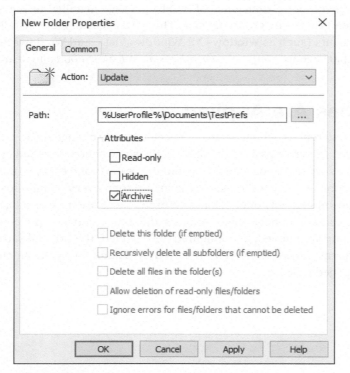

Figure 4-24 Creating a folder preference

7. If you choose Delete or Replace, you have additional options for deleting the folder. When the action is Create or Update, the delete options are grayed out.

8. Click the Common tab to see additional properties that are common to all preferences (see Figure 4-25):

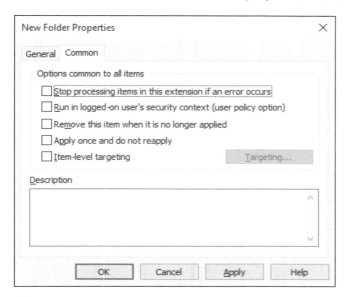

Figure 4-25   Common preferences properties

- *Stop processing items in this extension if an error occurs*—If there's more than one preference in the extension (for example, you create two folder preferences) and this option is selected, no additional preferences are processed in the extension in case of an error.

- *Run in logged-on user's security context (user policy option)*—By default, preferences are processed with the SYSTEM account security context. Enable this option to have preference processing use the logged-on user's security context. This option ensures availability of resources the user has permission to and makes sure environment variables are set for the logged-on user.

- *Remove this item when it is no longer applied*—Select this option if you want preferences to be restored to their original values when the user or computer account falls out of the GPO's scope. For example, if you select this option and the user account falls out of the GPO's scope, the folder is removed. This option isn't available when the action in the General tab is set to Delete.

- *Apply once and do not reapply*—By default, preferences are applied on the same schedule as policies. Enable this option if you want users to be able to change the preference setting without their changes being overridden by the next Group Policy refresh.

- *Item-level targeting*—**Item-level targeting** enables you to target specific users or computers based on criteria, as described next in the "Item-Level Targeting" section.

There are too many preference types to cover thoroughly in one module, but some of the activities in this module walk you through creating a few types of preferences. You should explore the Preferences folders and try creating different preferences in a lab environment to get a good idea of what you can do with them.

Item-Level Targeting

Preferences operate the same way as policies for default inheritance and scope. However, you can target users or computers for each preference based on certain criteria. For example, you can specify that only portable computers that are docked have a preference applied. Select the "Item-level targeting" option in the Common tab of the preference's Properties dialog box, and then click the Targeting button to define criteria that a computer or user must meet before the preference is applied. Figure 4-26 lists the properties that can be selected to define criteria.

Criteria can be combined with the AND and OR operators. For example, if you want to target only mobile computers running Windows 10, you can create an item-level targeting statement that effectively says "If the operating system is Windows 10 AND a battery is present, apply this preference" (see Figure 4-27).

Figure 4-26 List of criteria for item-level targeting

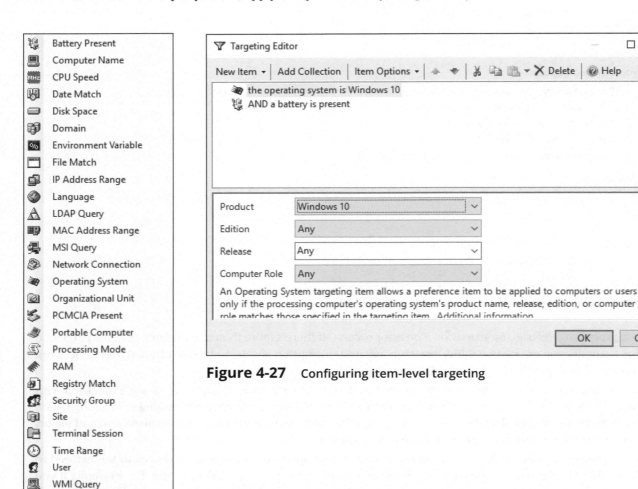

Figure 4-27 Configuring item-level targeting

Self-Check Questions

7. Users can usually change settings that are configured with a group policy preference. True or False?
   - a. True
   - b. False
8. What feature allows preferences to target users or computers based on criteria such as whether the computer is portable?
   - a. Item-level targeting
   - b. Policy inheritance
   - c. Central store
   - d. Client-side extensions

Check your answers at the end of this module.

Activity 4-12

Configuring and Testing Preferences

Time Required: 20 minutes
Objective: Configure and test preferences.
Required Tools and Equipment: ServerDC1 and ServerDM1
Description: In this activity, you configure a number of Group Policy Preferences. You create a file preference, deploy a VPN connection, and configure local groups.

1. To create a file preference in which a folder with files is distributed to all computers, first you create a share for the files to be copied in a preference. On ServerDC1, open **File Explorer**.
2. Create a folder named **PandP** on the **C:** volume. Share this folder and give the **Everyone** group **Read** permission.
3. In the PandP folder, create two text files: Name the first file **Policy.txt** and the second one **Procedure.txt**. Close File Explorer.
4. Open the Group Policy Management console, if necessary. Create a GPO named **Prefs** in the Group Policy Objects folder and open it in the Group Policy Management Editor.
5. Under User Configuration, click to expand **Preferences** and **Windows Settings**. Right-click **Files**, point to **New**, and click **File**.
6. In the Action list box, click **Create**.
7. In the Source file(s) text box, type **\\ServerDC1\PandP*.***. Using a wildcard copies all files in the PandP folder. In the "Destination folder" text box, type **%UserProfile%\Documents\PandP**. The PandP folder is created automatically when the policy is applied. Leave the default **Archive** attribute selected (see Figure 4-28).

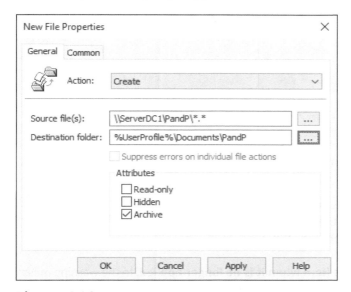

Figure 4-28   Creating a file preference

8. Click the **Common** tab. Review the available options, and then click **OK**. Note that you can change the processing order of preferences, so if you need one preference to be processed before another, you can arrange them in the order you want. Close the Group Policy Management Editor.
9. In the Group Policy Management console, link the **Prefs** GPO to the domain object.
10. Sign in to ServerDM1 as **domadmin**. Open File Explorer, and in the left pane, click **Documents** under This PC. Double-click the **PandP** folder; you should see the two files you created. Sign out of ServerDM1.
11. Next, you'll create a Control Panel preference in which you deploy a VPN connection. On ServerDC1, open the **Prefs** GPO in the Group Policy Management Editor. Under Computer Configuration, click to expand **Preferences** and **Control Panel Settings**. Right-click **Network Options**, point to **New**, and click **VPN Connection**.

(continues)

Activity 4-12 Continued

12. In the Action drop-down list, leave the default setting, **Update**. Click the **All users connection** option button so that all users logging on to target computers have access to the connection. In the Connection name text box, type **WorkVPN**. In the IP Address text box, type **192.168.0.1** (see Figure 4-29).

> ### Note 10
> If the VPN connection was already created on the server, you could select it by clicking the browse button, and the preferences settings would be populated from the existing connection.

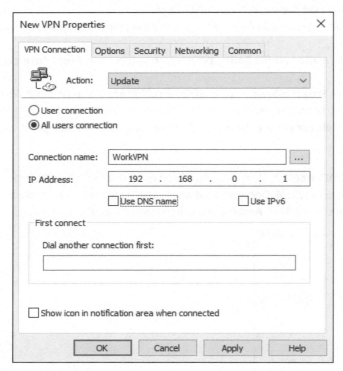

Figure 4-29   Creating a VPN connection preference

13. Click the **Options** tab and review the available settings. Click the **Security** tab, which is where you set authentication options. Leave the settings at their defaults.
14. Click the **Networking** tab, where you can choose the VPN tunnel type. Leave the default setting at **Automatic**.
15. Click the **Common** tab and click **Remove this item when it is no longer applied**. In the warning message stating that the preference will be set to Replace mode, click **OK**. Click **OK** again.
16. Link the **Prefs** GPO to the **Desktops** OU. Sign in to ServerDM1 as **domadmin1**. Because it's a Computer Configuration policy, you have to restart the computer or run gpupdate for the policy to be applied. Open a command prompt window, type **gpupdate**, and press **Enter**.
17. Right-click **Start** and click **Network Connections**. You see the WorkVPN connection.
18. Because you selected the "Remove this item when it is no longer applied" option, you should test that functionality. On ServerDC1, unlink **Prefs** from the domain. On ServerDM1, run **gpupdate** again.
19. Look in the Network Connections window to verify that the VPN connection has been removed. Sign out of ServerDM1.

(continues)

Activity 4-12 Continued

20. Next, you'll create a preference that configures local groups on member computers. On ServerDC1, open Active Directory Users and Computers. Click the **Users** folder, and then create a global security group named **Local_Admins** in this folder. Add **domuser1** to this group.

21. Open the Group Policy Management console and open the **Prefs** GPO in the Group Policy Management Editor. Delete the **Network Options** preference under Computer Configuration\Control Panel Settings.

22. Next, right-click **Local Users and Groups**, point to **New**, and click **Local Group**.

23. Make sure **Update** is the selected action. Click the **Group name** list arrow and click **Administrators (built-in)** in the list.

24. Click the **Add** button, and then click the browse button next to the Name text box. In the Select User, Computer, or Group dialog box, type **Local_Admins**, click **Check Names**, and then click **OK**. Make sure the action is **Add to this group**, and then click **OK** twice. Close the Group Policy Management Editor.

25. Link the **Prefs** GPO to the **TestOU1** OU.

26. Sign in to the domain from ServerDM1 as **domadmin1**. Open a command prompt window, type **gpupdate**, and press **Enter**. Close the command prompt window.

27. Right-click **Start** and click **Computer Management**. Click to expand **Local Users and Groups**, click **Groups**, and then double-click **Administrators** to open the Properties dialog box. You should see Local_Admins in the Members text box. Click **OK**. Now any domain user you add to the Local_Admins group has local administrator access to all computers in the scope of the Prefs GPO. Sign out of ServerDM1.

28. On ServerDC1, unlink the **Prefs** GPO from the **TestOU1** OU. Continue to the next activity.

Activity 4-13

Configuring Item-Level Targeting

Time Required: 10 minutes
Objective: Configure a preference with item-level targeting.
Required Tools and Equipment: ServerDC1 and ServerDM1
Description: In this activity, you configure item-level targeting for the file preference so that you can still have the policy linked to the domain, and other preferences affect all users.

1. On ServerDC1, open the **Prefs** GPO in the Group Policy Management Editor. Under User Configuration, expand **Preferences** and **Windows Settings**, and then click **Files**.

2. Double-click the **PandP** file preference in the right pane. In the Properties dialog box, click the **Common** tab.

3. Click the **Item-level targeting** check box, and then click the **Targeting** button.

4. In the Targeting Editor window, click **New Item**, and then click **Organizational Unit**.

5. In the Organizational Unit text box, click the browse button, click **TestOU1**, and then click **OK**. Click **OK** twice to get back to the Group Policy Management Editor. This will limit the preference to only the users in the TestOU1 organization unit, which in this case is only domadmin1.

6. Close the Group Policy Management Editor. Link the **Prefs** GPO to the domain.

7. Sign in to ServerDM1 as **domadmin1**. Open File Explorer, click Documents in the left pane, and delete the **PandP** folder. Sign out of ServerDM1.

8. Sign in again to ServerDM1 as **domadmin1** and verify that the PandP folder and the two files were created again.

9. Sign out of ServerDM1 and sign in as **domuser1**. (This user account is in the Users folder in Active Directory.) Open File Explorer, and in the left pane, click **Documents** under This PC. You don't see the PandP folder because item-level targeting limited this preference to user accounts in TestOU1. Sign out of ServerDM1.

10. On ServerDC1, unlink the **Prefs** GPO from the domain.

Group Policy Processing

> **Microsoft Exam AZ-800:**
> Deploy and manage Active Directory Domain Services (AD DS) in on-premises and cloud environments.
> - Manage Windows Server by using domain-based Group Policies

Group policy processing can be confusing because there are so many exceptions to normal processing and inheritance behavior. When you configure and link a GPO to an Active Directory container, you need to be aware of how that GPO affects objects in the container and subcontainers. To do so, you need to have a solid understanding of how GPOs are processed, how settings are inherited, and the exceptions to normal processing and inheritance. This section discusses the following topics related to group policy processing:

- *GPO scope and precedence*—Defines which objects are affected by settings in a GPO and which settings take precedence if conflicts exist
- *GPO inheritance*—Defines how settings are applied to objects in subcontainers
- *GPO status and link status*—Determines if a GPO is disabled or enabled and whether the link to the container is enabled or disabled
- *GPO filtering*—Creates exceptions to the normal scope by using security and WMI filtering
- *Loopback processing*—Changes how settings in the User Configuration node are applied

GPO Scope and Precedence

GPO scope defines which objects are affected by settings in a GPO. As you've learned, policies and preferences defined in a GPO's Computer Configuration node affect computer accounts, and policies and preferences in the User Configuration node affect user accounts. In addition, GPOs are applied in the following order:

1. Local policies
2. Site-linked GPOs
3. Domain-linked GPOs
4. OU-linked GPOs

Policies that aren't defined or configured are not applied at all, and the last policy applied is the one that takes precedence. For example, a GPO linked to a domain affects all computers and users in the domain, but settings in a GPO linked to an OU override the settings in a GPO linked to the domain if there are conflicts.

When OUs are nested, the GPO linked to the OU nested the deepest takes precedence over all other GPOs. When a policy setting isn't configured, its status is Not defined or Not configured. When a GPO is applied to an object, only the configured settings have any effect on that object. If two GPOs are applied to an object, and a certain setting is configured on one GPO but not the other, the configured setting is applied.

Understanding Site-Linked GPOs

GPOs linked to a site object affect all users and computers physically located at the site. Because sites are based on IP address, GPO processing determines where a user is signing in and from what computer, based on that computer's IP address. So, users who sign in to computers at different sites might have different policies applied to their accounts. In addition, mobile computers can have different policies applied, depending on the site where the computer connects to the network. Keep in mind that if a site contains computers and domain controllers from multiple domains, a site-linked GPO affects objects from multiple domains. For simplicity, when you have only one site and one domain, domain GPOs should be used rather than site-linked GPOs. As you might imagine, using site-linked GPOs can be confusing for users, particularly if there is a lot of user mobility between sites, so site-linked GPOs should be used with caution and only when there are valid reasons for different sites to have different policies.

Understanding Domain-Linked GPOs

GPOs set at the domain level should contain settings that you want to apply to all objects in the domain. The Default Domain Policy is configured and linked to the domain object by default and mostly defines user account policies. Account policies that affect domain logons can be defined only at the domain level, as you learned in Module 3. Default account policies are configured in the Default Domain Policy, but you can change them by creating a new GPO, configuring account policies, and linking the GPO to the domain object.

Active Directory folders, such as Computers and Users, are not OUs and therefore can't have a GPO linked to them. Only domain-linked GPOs and site-linked GPOs affect objects in these folders. If you need to manage objects in these folders with group policies, moving the objects to OUs is recommended instead of configuring domain or site GPOs to manage them.

It might be tempting to define most group policy settings at the domain level and define exceptions at the OU level, but in a large Active Directory structure, this strategy could become unwieldy. Best practices suggest setting account policies and a few critical security policies at the domain level and setting the remaining policies on GPOs linked to OUs.

Understanding OU-Linked GPOs

Most fine-tuning of group policies, particularly user policies, should be done at the OU level. Because OU-linked policies are applied last, they take precedence over site and domain policies (with the exception of account policies, which can be applied only at the domain level). Because the majority of policies are defined at the OU level, a well-thought-out OU design is paramount in your overall Active Directory design. Users and computers with similar policy requirements should be located in the same OU or have a common parent OU when possible.

Because OUs can be nested, so can the GPOs applied to them. When possible, your OU structure should be designed so that policies defined in GPOs linked to the top-level OU apply to all objects in that OU. GPOs applied to nested OUs should be used for exceptions to policies set at the higher-level OU or when certain computers or users require more restrictive policies. For example, suppose you have a scenario in which all full-time employees in the Engineering Department need complete access to Control Panel, but part-time employees should be restricted from using it. You can configure a policy allowing Control Panel access in a GPO linked to the Engineering OU. Then you create an OU under the Engineering OU that contains part-time employees' accounts and link a GPO to it that restricts use of Control Panel.

Group Policy Inheritance

By default, GPO inheritance is enabled and settings linked to a parent object are applied to all child objects. Therefore, settings in a GPO linked to the domain object are inherited by all OUs and their child objects in the domain. Settings in a GPO linked to the site are inherited by all objects in that site. To see which policies affect a domain or OU and where the policies are inherited from, select a container in the left pane of the Group Policy Management console and click the Group Policy Inheritance tab in the right pane. There are two main ways to change default GPO inheritance:

- Blocking inheritance
- GPO enforcement

Blocking Inheritance

Although the default inheritance behavior is suitable for most situations, as with file permissions inheritance, sometimes you need an exception to the default. One method is blocking inheritance, which prevents GPOs linked to parent containers from affecting child containers. To block inheritance, open the GPMC, right-click the child domain or OU, and click Block Inheritance (see Figure 4-30). You can enable this setting on a domain or an OU. On a domain object, this setting blocks GPO inheritance from a site, and on an OU, it blocks inheritance from parent OUs (if any), the domain, and the site. If inheritance blocking is enabled, the OU or domain object is displayed with an exclamation point in a blue circle. Inheritance blocking should be used sparingly; if you find that you need to block GPO inheritance frequently, it's an indication that your OU design is probably flawed and should be reexamined.

What happens if you have a nested OU and want to block GPO inheritance from its parent OU, but you still want domain- and site-linked GPOs to apply? This is where GPO enforcement comes in, as discussed next.

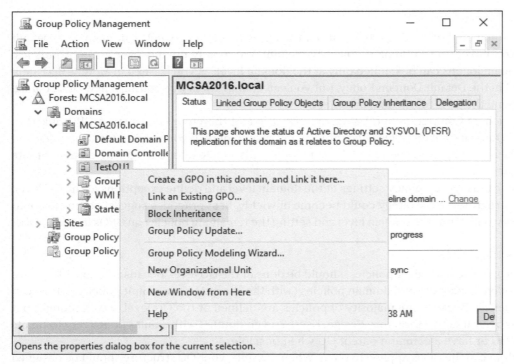

Figure 4-30   Blocking GPO inheritance

GPO Enforcement

GPO enforcement forces inheritance of settings on all child objects in the GPO's scope, even if a GPO with conflicting settings is linked to a container at a deeper level. In other words, a GPO that's enforced has the strongest precedence of all GPOs in its scope. If multiple GPOs have the Enforced option set, the GPO that's highest in the Active Directory hierarchy has the strongest precedence. For example, if both a GPO linked to an OU and a GPO linked to a domain have the Enforced option set, the GPO linked to the domain has stronger precedence. GPO enforcement also over-rides GPO inheritance blocking, so using inheritance blocking will not block inheritance of settings in a GPO that has enforcement configured.

GPO enforcement is configured on the GPO, not the Active Directory container. To configure enforcement in the GPMC, right-click the shortcut to a linked GPO and click Enforced (see Figure 4-31).

> **Exam Tip** ✔
>
> Remember that the Block Inheritance option is set on a domain or OU, and the Enforced option is set on a GPO that is linked to a site, domain, or OU.

Managing GPO Status and Link Status

After a GPO is created, it can be in one of the following states:

- *Link status: unlinked*—The GPO is in the Group Policy Objects folder but hasn't been linked to any container objects.
- *Link status: enabled*—The GPO is listed under the container object, and the link is enabled. This status is set by right-clicking a container, clicking Link an Existing GPO, and choosing a GPO from the Group Policy Objects folder or by right-clicking a container and clicking "Create a GPO in this domain, and Link it here."
- *Link status: disabled*—The GPO is listed under the container object and the link is disabled. Link status can be toggled between enabled and disabled by right-clicking a GPO linked to a container and clicking Link Enabled.

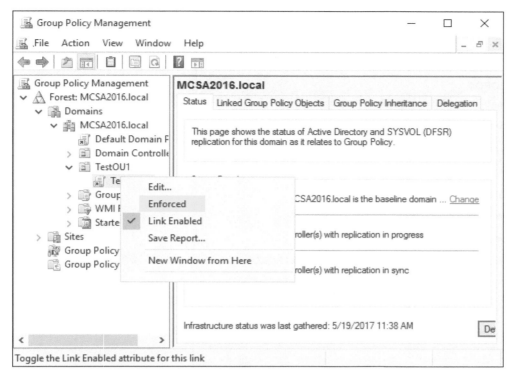

Figure 4-31   Configuring GPO enforcement

- *GPO status: Enabled*—The GPO is fully functional. In the Group Policy Objects folder, right-click a GPO, point to GPO Status, and click Enabled.
- *GPO status: User configuration settings disabled*—The User Configuration node isn't processed by computers running the group policy client. In the Group Policy Objects folder, right-click a GPO, point to GPO Status, and click User Configuration Settings Disabled.
- *GPO status: Computer configuration settings disabled*—The Computer Configuration node isn't processed by computers running the group policy client. In the Group Policy Objects folder, right-click a GPO, point to GPO Status, and click Computer Configuration Settings Disabled.
- *GPO status: All settings disabled*—The GPO is disabled. In the Group Policy Objects folder, right-click a GPO, point to GPO Status, and click All Settings Disabled.

You can view and modify the GPO status by clicking the GPO in the left pane of Group Policy Management and clicking the Details tab (see Figure 4-32).

GPO Filtering

Blocking inheritance excludes all objects in an OU from inheriting GPO settings (unless they're enforced), but what if you want to exclude only some objects in the OU? This is where GPO filtering comes into play. There are two types of **GPO filtering**: security filtering and Windows Management Instrumentation (WMI) filtering.

Security filtering uses permissions to restrict objects from accessing a GPO. Like any object in Active Directory, a GPO has a discretionary access control list (DACL) that contains lists of security principals with assigned permissions to the GPO. User and computer accounts must have the Read and Apply Group Policy permissions in order for a GPO to apply to them. By default, the Authenticated Users special identity is granted these permissions for every GPO; Authenticated Users applies both to logged-on users and computers. You can see a GPO's DACL in Active Directory Users and Computers in the System\Policies folder and in the Delegation tab in the GPMC, but for basic GPO filtering, you can use the Scope tab in the GPMC. To view the current security filtering settings, click a GPO in the GPMC and click the Scope tab in the right pane (see Figure 4-33).

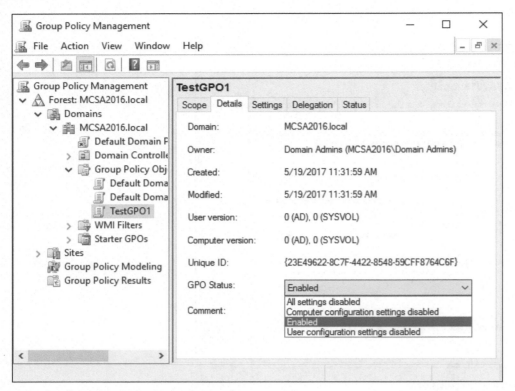

Figure 4-32　The status of a GPO

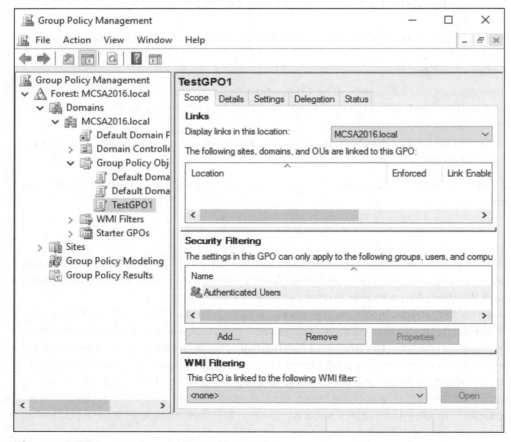

Figure 4-33　Viewing security filtering settings

You use the Security Filtering dialog box in the GPMC to add or remove security principals from the GPO access list. For example, if you want a GPO to apply to all users in a domain or OU except a few, follow these steps:

1. Create a security group in Active Directory Users and Computers.
2. Add all the users who should be subject to the GPO as members of the new group.
3. In the GPMC, click the GPO, and click the Scope tab in the right pane.
4. Use the Security Filtering dialog box to add the new group to this GPO.
5. In the Security Filtering dialog box, remove the Authenticated Users special identity from this GPO.

Remember that computer accounts are also affected by GPOs. So, if the GPO you're filtering contains computer settings, you must add a group containing the computer accounts that should be subject to the GPO's policies.

Another way to use security filtering is to edit the GPO's DACL directly. This method is often easier when the GPO must be applied to many users or computers with just a few exceptions. In the GPMC, click the GPO in the Group Policy Objects folder, and click the Delegation tab in the right pane to see the complete list of access control entries (ACEs) for the GPO, as in Figure 4-34. You can add security principals to the DACL or click the Advanced button to open the Advanced Security Settings dialog box.

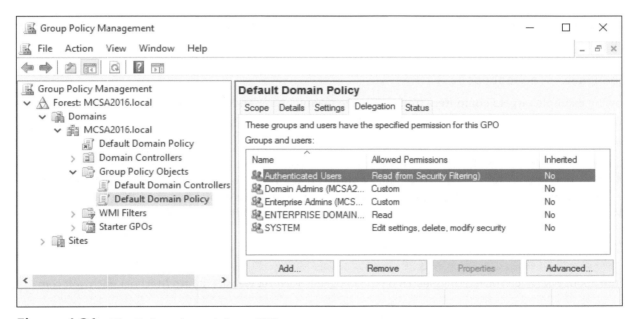

Figure 4-34   The Delegation tab for a GPO

By using the Advanced Security Settings dialog box, you can assign Deny permissions as well as Allow permissions. Assigning the Deny Read permission, for example, enables you to create exceptions to normal GPO processing. You can add a single user account, a computer account, or a group to the DACL and prevent these security principals from being affected by the GPO.

For example, suppose you have a GPO that has some Microsoft Edge browser settings in the Computer Configuration node that restrict access to advanced features. You have more than 500 computer accounts in different OUs, so you want to link the GPO to the domain so that it affects all computers in the domain. However, you have a dozen or so power users whose computers you want to exempt from these policies. You can create a group, add the power users' computers as members, add the group to the GPO's DACL, and then configure Deny Read permission.

WMI Filtering

The second type of filtering is **WMI filtering**. Windows Management Instrumentation (WMI) is a Windows technology for gathering management information about computers, such as the hardware platform, the OS version, available disk space, and so on. WMI filtering uses queries to select a group of computers based on certain attributes, and then applies or doesn't apply policies based on the query results. It's similar to the preference item-level targeting you learned about in a previous section. You need to have a solid understanding of the complex WMI query language before you can create WMI filters. Here's an example of using a WMI query to select only computers running Windows 10 Enterprise:

```
Select * from Win32_OperatingSystem where Caption =
   "Microsoft Windows 10 Enterprise"
```

The next example uses the OS version number. Windows 8.1 and Windows Server 2012 R2 have version numbers beginning with 6.3, and Windows 10 and Windows Server 2016 have version numbers beginning with 10. This command selects computers running an OS with a version number beginning with 10:

```
Select * from Win32_OperatingSystem where Version
   like "10%"
```

The next example uses Version and ProductType. ProductType differentiates between client and server OSs. A client OS, such as Windows 10, has a ProductType of 1, and a server OS, such as Windows Server 2016, has a ProductType of 3. This example selects Windows 10 systems:

```
Select * from Win32_OperatingSystem where Version
   like "10%" and ProductType = "1"
```

Suppose you want a policy that installs a large application on target machines with at least 20 GB of disk space available. You can use the following command:

```
Select * from Win32_LogicalDisk where
   FreeSpace > 20000000000
```

The following example targets computers from a specific manufacturer and model:

```
Select * from Win32_ComputerSystem where
   Manufacturer = "Dell" and Model = "Optiplex 960"
```

You create WMI filters in the WMI Filters node of the GPMC. Right-click in the right pane and click New to open the New WMI Filter dialog box. You assign a name and optional description to the WMI filter and then click Add to create a new query (see Figure 4-35). After creating a WMI filter, select it in the Scope tab of a GPO (see Figure 4-36). Only one WMI filter can be selected per GPO, but you can use the same WMI filter in multiple GPOs.

Note 11

To learn more about WMI and WMI filtering, search on the Microsoft TechNet website at http://technet.microsoft.com.

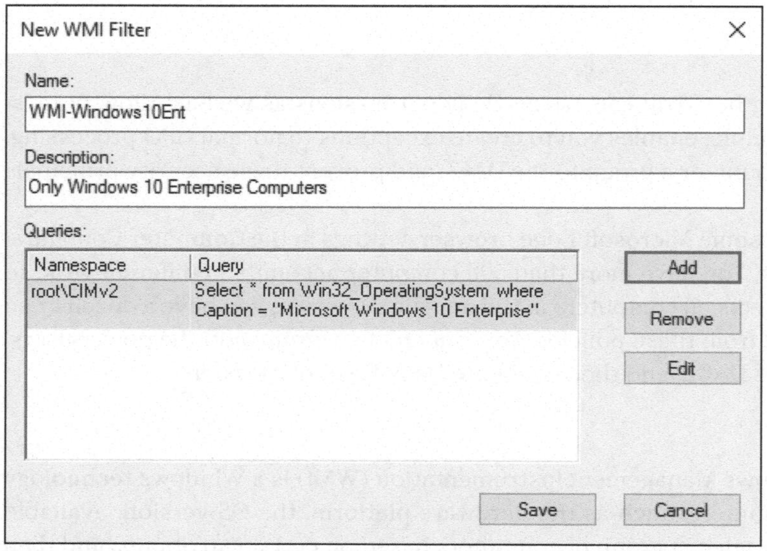

Figure 4-35   Creating a new WMI filter

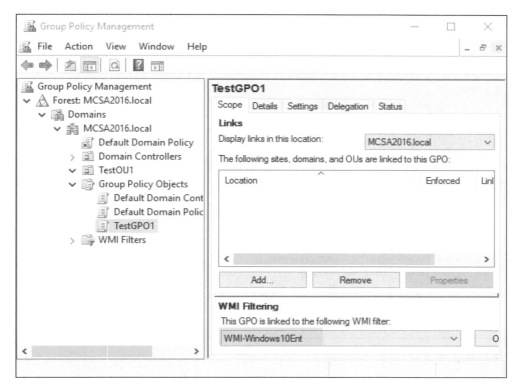

Figure 4-36   Linking a WMI filter to a GPO

Loopback Policy Processing

By default, users are affected by policies in the User Configuration node, and computers are affected by policies in the Computer Configuration node. Furthermore, users are affected by GPOs whose scope they fall within, and the same goes for computers.

Normally, the policies that affect user settings follow users to whatever computer they sign in to. However, you might want user policy settings to be based on the GPO within whose scope the computer object falls. To do this, you can use loopback policy processing. For example, suppose you have an OU named ConfRoomComputers containing all computer accounts of computers in conference rooms. Perhaps you want standardized desktop settings, such as wallpaper, screen savers, Start screen, and so forth, so that these computers have a consistent look for visitors. All these settings are in the User Configuration node, however, so they can't apply to computer accounts. You don't want all users in the organization to be restricted to these settings when they sign in to their own computers. The solution is to enable the "Configure user Group Policy loopback processing mode" policy setting under the Computer Configuration node. After this setting is enabled, all settings in the User Configuration node of the GPO apply to all users who sign in to the computer. If you enable loopback policy processing, you have the option to replace the settings normally applied to the user or merge the settings in the GPO with settings normally applied to the user. If there's a conflict, the settings in the GPO take precedence.

To use loopback policy processing in the conference room computers example, you take the following steps:

1. Create a GPO (or edit an existing one) and enable the "Configure user Group Policy loopback processing mode" policy setting in the Computer Configuration\Policies\Administrative Templates\System\Group Policy node (see Figure 4-37).
2. In the User Configuration node of the GPO, edit policies to set wallpaper, screen saver, and Start screen options.
3. Link the GPO to the ConfRoomComputers OU.

When users sign in to a computer in a conference room, they're now subject to the User Configuration policies you set in the GPO linked to the ConfRoomComputers OU. When users sign in to any other computer, they're subject to whatever policies normally affect their user accounts.

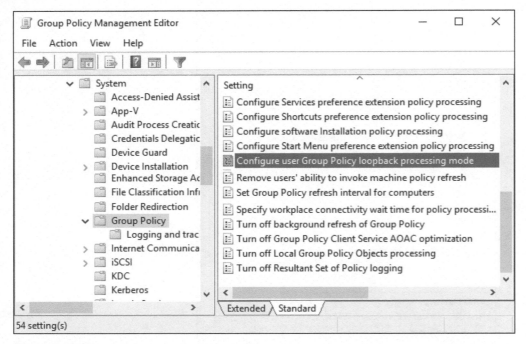

Figure 4-37 The loopback processing policy

Self-Check Questions

9. Which aspect of Group Policy processing defines how settings are applied to objects in subcontainers?

   a. Scope and precedence
   b. Inheritance

   c. Filtering
   d. Loopback processing

10. What feature of GPO processing should you use if you want to ensure that all child objects in the GPO's scope are subject to the GPO's settings even if a lower-level GPO has a conflicting setting?

    a. Item-level targeting
    b. GPO filtering

    c. GPO enforcement
    d. Inheritance blocking

⊙ Check your answers at the end of this module.

Activity 4-14

Working with GPO Inheritance Blocking and Enforcement

Time Required: 20 minutes

Objective: Use the Block Inheritance option on an OU and the Enforcement option on a GPO.

Required Tools and Equipment: ServerDC1, ServerDM1

Description: In this activity, you configure a policy to prohibit access to Control Panel. Then you block inheritance to see that the policy doesn't affect objects below where inheritance blocking is enabled. Next, you configure the enforcement option on the GPO to see that the GPO enforcement option overrides the block inheritance option.

1. Sign in to ServerDC1 as **Administrator** and open the Group Policy Management console.
2. Create a GPO named **GPO1** in the Group Policy Objects folder. Open GPO1 in the Group Policy Management Editor.
3. Navigate to **User Configuration\Policies\Administrative Templates\Control Panel**. In the right pane, double-click the **Prohibit access to Control Panel and PC settings** policy. Click **Enabled** to enable the policy. Read the Help information so you know what the policy does. Click **OK**. Close the Group Policy Management Editor.

(continues)

Activity 4-14 Continued

4. Link GPO1 to the domain by right-clicking **MCSA2016.local** and clicking **Link an Existing GPO**. Click **GPO1** and click **OK**.
5. Open Active Directory Users and Computers. Right-click **MCSA2016.local**, point to **New**, and click **Organizational Unit**. Type **TestOU1** and click **OK**.
6. Click the **Users** folder and then drag and drop **domuser1** to **TestOU1**. Click **Yes** to confirm. Close Active Directory Users and Computers.
7. On ServerDM1, sign in as **domuser1**. Right-click **Start** and click **Control Panel**. You should see a message that the operation has been cancelled due to restrictions (see Figure 4-38). Click **OK**. As you can see, domuser1 is restricted from using Control Panel. Sign out of ServerDM1.

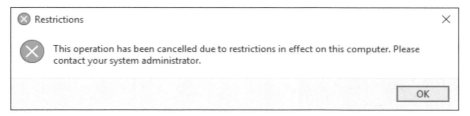

Figure 4-38   The message indicating that Control Panel is restricted

8. On ServerDC1, in Group Policy Management, right-click **TestOU1** and click **Block Inheritance**. You see a blue circle with a white exclamation point, indicating that inheritance is blocked. Now users in TestOU1 aren't affected by GPOs linked to the domain.
9. On ServerDM1, sign in again as **domuser1**. Right-click **Start** and click **Control Panel**. Control Panel opens normally because the policy setting in GPO1 is being blocked. Sign out of ServerDM1.
10. On ServerDC1, in Group Policy Management, right-click **GPO1** under the domain node and click **Enforced**.
11. Sign in to ServerDM1 as **domuser1**. Right-click **Start** and click **Control Panel**. You should see the message that the operation has been cancelled due to restrictions. Click **OK**. As you can see, domuser1 is once again restricted from using Control Panel because enforcement overrides block inheritance. Sign out of ServerDM1.
12. On ServerDC1, right-click **GPO1** under the domain node and click to uncheck **Enforced**. Right-click **TestOU1** and click to uncheck **Block Inheritance**.
13. Continue to the next activity.

Activity 4-15

Using GPO Security Filtering

Time Required: 15 minutes
Objective: Examine the results of changing the default security filtering on a GPO.
Required Tools and Equipment: ServerDC1, ServerDM1
Description: In this activity, you use GPO filtering to change the default inheritance behavior of GPO processing.

1. On ServerDC1, in the Group Policy Management console, click to expand the **Group Policy Objects** folder, and then click **GPO1**. In the right pane, click the **Scope** tab, if necessary.
2. In the Security Filtering dialog box, click the **Add** button in the right pane. Type **domuser2**, click **Check Names**, and then click **OK**.
3. Click the **Delegation** tab. Click **Advanced**. In the top pane of the GPO1 Security Settings dialog box, click **Authenticated Users**. In the bottom pane, scroll down and click to clear **Apply group policy** (see Figure 4-39). Click **OK**.

(continues)

Activity 4-15 Continued

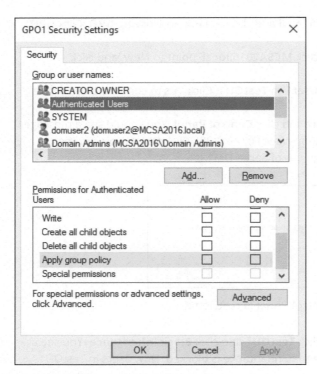

Figure 4-39   Setting GPO security

4. Click the **Scope** tab again; domuser2 is now the only security principal with Read and Apply Group Policy permissions for GPO1.

> ### Note 12
>
> Authenticated Users must have the Read permission in order for other users to access a GPO. This is unexpected but a known issue.

5. GPO1 is still linked to the domain object, so there's no need to link it to a container. On ServerDM1, sign in as **domuser1**. Right-click **Start** and click **Control Panel**. Control Panel opens normally because only domuser2 has permission to read the GPO1 Group Policy object that restricts access to Control Panel.
6. Sign off ServerDM1 and sign in as **domuser2**. Right-click **Start** and click **Control Panel**. You should see the message that the operation has been cancelled due to restrictions because domuser2 has permission to read and apply the GPO that restricts access to the control panel. Sign out of ServerDM1.
7. On ServerDC1, click to select GPO1 if necessary, and click the Scope tab if necessary. Click **Add**, type **Authenticated Users**, and click **Check Names**. Click **OK**. Click **domuser2**, click **Remove**, and click **OK**.
8. Right-click **GPO1** under the domain node and click **Delete** to unlink it.
9. Continue to the next activity.

Activity 4-16

Using GPO Security Filtering for a Computer Account
Time Required: 15 minutes
Objective: Examine the results of changing the security filtering on a GPO.
Required Tools and Equipment: ServerDC1, ServerDM1
Description: In this activity, you change the security filtering on a GPO for a computer account.

1. On ServerDC1, open the Group Policy Management console, if necessary. Right-click the **Group Policy Objects** folder and click **New**. Type **GPO2** in the Name text box and click **OK**.
2. Click **GPO2** in the left pane. In the right pane, click the **Scope** tab, if necessary.
3. In the Security Filtering dialog box, click the **Add** button in the right pane. Click the **Object Types** button. By default, computer accounts aren't recognized in this dialog box. In the Object Types dialog box, click to select **Computers**. Click **OK**.
4. Type **ServerDM1**, click **Check Names**, and click **OK**.
5. Click the **Delegation** tab. Click **Advanced**. In the top pane of the GPO2 Security Settings dialog box, click **Authenticated Users**. In the bottom pane, scroll down and click to clear **Apply group policy**. Click **OK**. ServerDM1 is now the only security principal with Read and Apply Group Policy permissions for GPO2.
6. Open GPO2 in the Group Policy Management Editor. Navigate to **Computer Configuration\Policies\ Windows Settings\Security Settings\Local Policies\Security Options**.
7. Find and double-click **Interactive logon: Message text for users attempting to log on**. Click **Define this policy setting in the template**. In the text box, type **Authorized users only may attempt to sign in to this computer!** Click **OK**.
8. Double-click **Interactive logon: Message title for users attempting to log on**. Click **Define this policy setting** and then type **Sign in Warning** in the text box. Click **OK**.
9. Close the Group Policy Management Editor. Link GPO2 to the domain.
10. Sign in to ServerDM1 as domuser1. Because the policy you configured is a Computer policy, it is only applied when the computer restarts or if you run `gpupdate`. Open a command prompt and run **gpupdate**, then sign out of ServerDM1.
11. Attempt to sign in again to ServerDM1. (You usually need to press Ctrl+Alt+Delete to sign in, and with a virtual machine, you probably need to press the Ctrl+Alt+Delete toolbar icon or use an alternate key sequence.) You see the sign-in warning you just created. Click **OK**. You don't need to sign in right now.
12. On ServerDC1, run **gpupdate**. Because you linked the policy to the domain, it would normally affect ServerDC1 as well as ServerDM1. Sign out of ServerDC1 and try to sign in again as **Administrator**. You don't see the warning message because only ServerDM1 has permission to read and apply GPO2. Sign in to ServerDC1.
13. On ServerDC1, open Group Policy Management. Navigate to the **Group Policy Objects** folder and click **GPO2** in the left pane. Under Security Filtering, click **Add**. Type **Authenticate Users**, click **Check Names**, and click **OK**. Click **ServerDM1$ (MCSA2016\ServerDM1$)**, click **Remove**, and click **OK** to set Security Filtering back to the default.
14. Continue to the next activity.

Activity 4-17

Configuring Loopback Policy Processing
Time Required: 20 minutes
Objective: Configure loopback policy processing.
Required Tools and Equipment: ServerDC1, ServerDM1
Description: In this activity, you configure loopback policy processing.

(continues)

Activity 4-17 Continued

1. On ServerDC1, open Active Directory Users and Computers. Create an OU under the domain node named **MemberServers**. Click the **Computers** folder and drag and drop **ServerDM1** to the **MemberServers** OU. Click **Yes** to confirm. Close Active Directory Users and Computers.

2. Open the Group Policy Management console, if necessary. Create a GPO named **GPO3** and open it in the Group Policy Management Editor.

3. Expand **User Configuration**, **Policies**, **Administrative Templates**, and configure the following settings:
   Desktop\Remove Recycle Bin icon from desktop: **Enabled**
   Desktop\Desktop\DesktopWallpaper: **Enabled**
   Wallpaper Name: **C:\windows\web\wallpaper\theme2\img7.jpg** (or another image file if you don't have img7.jpg)
   Wallpaper Style: **Fill**

4. Link **GPO3** to the **MemberServers** OU. (If you don't see the MemberServers OU, click the Refresh icon.) Remember that these settings are User Configuration settings, so they don't normally have an effect on computer accounts, which is the only type of account in MemberServers.

5. Sign in to ServerDM1 as **domuser1**. Run **gpupdate**, sign out, and sign in again. The changes you made in GPO3 don't have any effect. The Recycle Bin is still on the desktop, and the wallpaper hasn't changed. Stay signed in to ServerDM1.

6. On ServerDC1, open **GPO3** in the Group Policy Management Editor, if necessary.

7. Expand **Computer Configuration**, **Policies**, **Administrative Templates**, **System**, and **Group Policy**. Double-click **Configure user Group Policy loopback processing mode**. Click **Enabled**, and in the Mode drop-down list box, click **Merge**. This option allows existing user settings that are normally applied to be applied as long as there's no conflict. Click **OK**.

8. On ServerDM1, run **gpupdate**. Sign out, and sign in again as **domuser1**. The settings made in the User Configuration node of GPO3 should now be applied. The wallpaper has changed, and the Recycle Bin is no longer on the desktop. Sign out of ServerDM1.

9. On ServerDC1, unlink **GPO3** from the **MemberServers** OU. Close the Group Policy Management Editor.

10. Close all windows, and then sign off and shut down all running servers.

Implementing Group Policy in Azure AD DS

Microsoft Exam AZ-800:
Deploy and manage Active Directory Domain Services (AD DS) in on-premises and cloud environments.
- Manage Windows Server by using domain-based Group Policies

Group Policy in Azure AD DS is not unlike Group Policy in on-premises Active Directory. Once your Azure AD DS domain is set up, you can manage Group Policy from an Azure VM that has been joined to the Azure AD DS domain. Be aware that in a hybrid environment in which you are running on-premises Active Directory and Azure AD DS, GPOs are not synced between the two environments.

To begin working with Azure AD DS Group Policy, follow these steps:

- Configure Azure AD DS—Group Policy only works with Azure AD DS; Azure AD does not support Group Policy.
- Create a Windows Server VM in Azure—You can use an existing VM if it is connected to the same virtual network you configured for Azure AD DS or you can create a new VM. If you create a new VM, you must select the same region that Azure AD DS is running in so you can select the same virtual network. Select an existing subnet that is different from the Azure AD DS subnet or create a new subnet if necessary.

- Join the Azure VM to the Azure AD DS domain—You follow the same procedure as joining a computer to on-premises Active Directory. When prompted for credentials, you must use the credentials for an account in the Azure AD DS domain.
- Install Group Policy Management tools—From Server Manager, click Manage and Add Roles and Features. Click Next until you see the Select Features page, and then click Group Policy Management. If you have not already configured a server with AD DS tools, you can install those as well (see Figure 4-40).

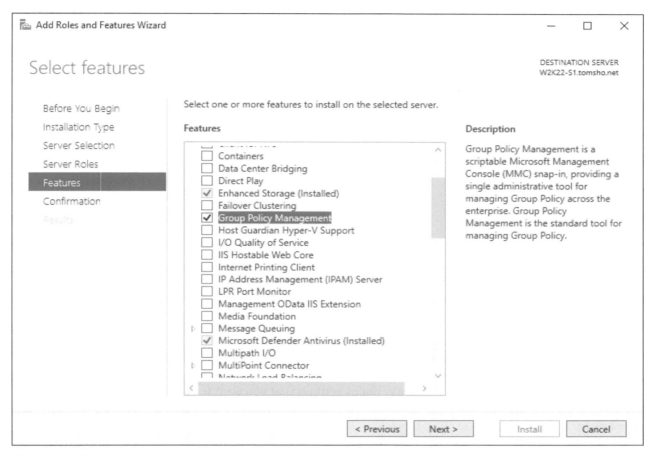

Figure 4-40   Installing Group Policy Management tools

Once the GPMC is installed, you will see that the available policies are similar to those in on-premises Active Directory. There is a Default Domain Policy GPO and a Default Domain Controllers Policy GPO. These GPOs are read-only and are managed by Azure. In addition, there are three other default GPOs that are not found in on-premises Active Directory (see Figure 4-41):

- AADDC Computers GPO—Linked to the AADDC Computers OU, this GPO sets policies on computers that have been joined to the Azure AD DS domain. The only policy configured by default is a Group Policy Preference, which automatically adds the AADDC Administrators group to the local Administrators group on any computer account in the AADDC Computers OU.
- AADDC Users GPO—Linked to the AADDC Users OU, this GPO sets policies on user accounts in the Azure AD DS domain. By default, all users synced from an on-premises Active Directory or created in Azure AD are placed in this OU. There are no policies configured by default in this GPO.
- Event Log GPO—This is another read-only GPO; it is managed by Azure. The only setting configured is a startup PowerShell script that sets the Event Log retention policy on the Azure DCs.

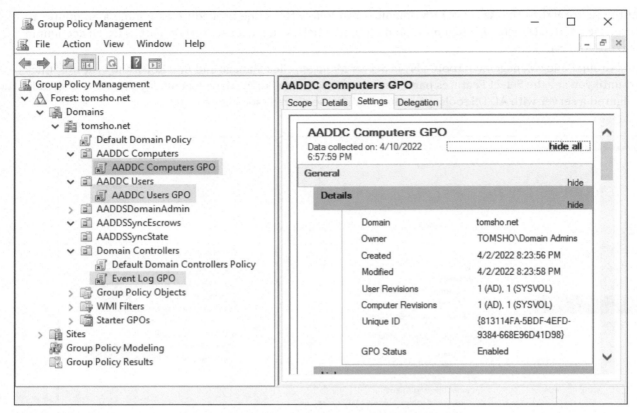

Figure 4-41 Group Policy Management Console with Azure AD DS default GPOs

You can create new GPOs as desired or edit the two existing GPOs (AADDC Computers GPO and AADDC Users GPO). You can also create new OUs using Active Directory Users and Computers, Active Directory Administrative Center, or PowerShell, and you can link new GPOs to OUs you create. You cannot link a GPO to the Azure-managed Domain Controllers OU or the domain object. So, any policy settings that you want to configure must be in the AADDC Computers GPO, AADDC Users GPO, or a new GPO that you create and link to one of the Azure AD DS OUs or a new OU that you create.

Exam Tip ✔

You must sign in to the Azure AD DS domain using an account that is a member of the AADDC Administrators group to manage group policy on Azure AD DS.

Self-Check Questions

11. Which of the following is true about using Group Policy with Azure AD DS?

    a. You can use an on-premises VM joined to Azure AD DS.
    b. You can link a GPO to an OU in Azure AD.
    c. You can make changes to the Default Domain Policy GPO.
    d. The VM that will run Group Policy Management must be connected to the AD DS virtual network.

◉ Check your answers at the end of this module.

Module Summary

- Group Policy is a powerful tool for network administrators to manage domain controllers, member servers, member computers, and users. It allows administrators to manage most aspects of computer and user environments centrally through Active Directory.

- Group policy architecture and function involve these components: GPOs, replication, scope and inheritance, and creating and linking GPOs. The main component of group policies contains policy settings for managing many aspects of domain controllers, member servers, member computers, and user accounts. GPOs can be local or domain.

- GPO replication is handled by Active Directory replication for GPCs and by FRS or DFSR for GPTs. DFSR is used only when all DCs are running Windows Server 2008 and later versions.

- You use the Group Policy Management console to create, link, and manage GPOs, and you use the Group Policy Management Editor to edit GPOs.

- GPOs can be linked to sites, domains, and OUs. Policies are applied in this order, and the last policy setting applied takes precedence when conflicts exist. Local policies are applied before domain policies, so when conflicts exist, domain policies take precedence over local policies.

- Starter GPOs are like template files for GPOs. You can create a new GPO by using a Starter GPO as a baseline. Starter GPOs contain only the Administrative Templates folder in the Computer Configuration and User Configuration nodes.

- A script is a series of commands saved in a text file to be repeated easily at any time. There's a Scripts extension in both the Computer Configuration and User Configuration nodes in the path Policies, Windows Settings, Scripts. In the Computer Configuration node, you configure startup or shutdown scripts, and in the User Configuration node, you configure logon and logoff scripts.

- Folder redirection enables administrators to set policies that redirect folders in a user's profile directory. This feature is useful when you want users to store documents on a server for centralized backup, but you don't want to change the way they access their document folders.

- There are over 100 policies under Security Settings. Some of the most important are under Account Policies and Local Policies because they contain baseline security options for your computers.

- Both the Computer Configuration and User Configuration nodes have an Administrative Templates folder. In the Computer Configuration node, the settings in Administrative Templates affect the HKEY_LOCAL_MACHINE Registry key. Settings in the User Configuration node affect the HKEY_LOCAL_USER Registry key.

- Administrative templates are a collection of policy definition files in XML format. These XML files, referred to as ADMX files because of their .admx extension, specify Registry entries that should be controlled and the type of data the entries take.

- The ADMX central store can be created to ensure that ADMX files are synchronized among all computers where group policies are managed.

- The number of settings in the Administrative Templates section of a GPO can be daunting when you're trying to find a policy to configure. You can narrow the search by using a filter in the Group Policy Management Editor.

- If you're running a Windows Server 2008 or later domain but still must support clients older than Vista, or if you're running older applications that use ADM files, you might want to migrate the older ADM files to ADMX format so that you can make use of the central store.

- Unlike user or computer policies that can't be changed by users, group policy preferences enable administrators to set up a baseline computing environment yet still allow users to make changes to configured settings. You must create each preference you want to deploy.

- Preferences operate the same way as policies for default inheritance and scope. However, you can target users or computers for each preference based on a set of criteria; this feature is called item-level targeting.

- Group policy processing can be confusing because there are so many exceptions to normal processing and inheritance behavior. When you configure and link a GPO to an Active Directory container, you need to be aware of how that GPO will affect the objects in the container and subcontainers.

- GPO scope defines which objects are affected by the settings in a GPO. GPOs are applied in this order: local computer, site, domain, and OU. When OUs are nested, the GPO linked to the OU that's nested the deepest takes precedence over all other GPOs.

- There are two main ways to change default GPO inheritance: blocking inheritance and using GPO enforcement.
- After a GPO is created, it can be in a specific state. You can view and modify the GPO status by clicking the GPO in the left pane of Group Policy Management and clicking the Details tab.
- There are two types of GPO filtering: security filtering and Windows Management Instrumentation (WMI) filtering. Security filtering uses permissions to restrict objects from accessing a GPO. WMI filtering uses queries to select a group of computers based on certain attributes, and then applies or doesn't apply policies based on the query's results.
- If you enable loopback policy processing, all settings in the User Configuration node of the GPO apply to all users who sign in to the computer.
- Group Policy in Azure AD DS is not unlike Group Policy in on-premises Active Directory. Once your Azure AD DS domain is set up, you can manage Group Policy from an Azure VM that has been joined to the Azure AD DS domain.
- Once you have a suitable VM joined to the domain, install the Group Policy Management tools using Server Manager. Once the GPMC is installed, you will see two new GPOs linked to the Azure AD DS OUs. AADDC Computers GPO is linked to the AADDC Computers OU and AADDC Users GPO is linked to the AADDC Users OU.

Key Terms

administrative template files	GPO scope	Microsoft Software Installation (MSI)
ADMX central store	Group Policy Container (GPC)	file
assigned application	group policy preferences	published application
batch file	Group Policy Template (GPT)	script
domain GPO	item-level targeting	security filtering
folder redirection	local GPO	Starter GPO
GPO enforcement	loopback policy processing	unmanaged policy setting
GPO filtering	managed policy setting	WMI filtering

Review Questions

1. Which of the following is a local GPO on a Windows 10 computer? (Choose all that apply.)

   a. Local Administrators
   b. Local Default User
   c. Local Default Domain
   d. Local Non-Administrators

2. Which of the following is true about GPOs? (Choose all that apply.)

   a. Local GPOs override domain GPOs.
   b. Domain GPOs are stored on member servers.
   c. Domain GPOs can be linked to Active Directory sites.
   d. The `gpedit.msc` tool can be used to edit local GPOs.

3. Where is a GPT stored?

   a. In a folder with the same name as the GPO in the SYSVOL share
   b. In a folder with the same name as the GUID of the GPO in Active Directory
   c. In a folder with the same name as the GUID of the GPO in the SYSVOL share

   d. In a folder with the same name as the GPO in Active Directory

4. You're having replication problems with your GPOs and suspect that the version numbers have somehow gotten out of sync between the GPT and the GPC. What can you do to verify the version numbers on a GPO?

   a. Check the versionNumber attribute of the GPC and open the `GPT.ini` file.
   b. Check the versionNumber attribute of the GPT and open the `GPC.ini` file.
   c. Right-click the GPO in the Group Policy Management console, click Properties, and view the version in the General tab.
   d. Right-click the GPO in the Group Policy Management Editor, click Properties, and view the version in the General tab.

5. Which of the following are methods for linking a GPO to a container? (Choose all that apply.)

   a. In ADUC, right-click the container and then select "Create a GPO in this domain and link it here."

b. In the GPMC, right-click the container and then select "Create a GPO in this domain and link it here."

c. In the GPMC, right-click a container and select Link an Existing GPO.

d. In ADAC, right-click a container and select Link an Existing GPO.

6. You have configured a policy setting in the User Configuration node of a domain GPO and linked the GPO to OU-X. Later, you discover you linked it to the wrong OU, so you unlink it from OU-X and link it to OU-Y, which is correct. A few days later, you find that users in OU-X still have the policy setting applied to their accounts. What's the most likely cause of the problem?

a. Group policy settings haven't been refreshed.

b. The policy setting is unmanaged.

c. Users in OU-X have an item-level target filter configured.

d. The GPO is disabled.

7. All your domain controllers are running Windows Server 2022. You're noticing problems with GPT replication. What should you check?

a. Verify that Active Directory replication is working correctly.

b. Verify that FRS is operating correctly.

c. Verify that DFSR is operating correctly.

d. Check the GPOReplication flag for the GPT in the Attribute Editor.

8. You want to deploy a software package that's available to all users in the domain if they want to use it, but you don't want the package to be installed unless a user needs it. How should you configure the software installation policy?

a. Publish the package under the Computer Configuration node.

b. Assign the package under the Computer Configuration node.

c. Publish the package under the User Configuration node.

d. Assign the package under the User Configuration node

9. You want to deploy a logon script by using Group Policy. You have several sites connected via a WAN with a DC at each site. You want to make sure the script is always available when users log on from any computer at any location. What should you do?

a. Create a share on the fastest DC in the network and save the script there.

b. Send the script via email to all users and have them save it locally.

c. Save the script in the SYSVOL share.

d. Copy the script to cloud storage.

10. You want to centrally back up the files that users store in the Documents folder in their user profiles, but you don't want users to have to change the way they access their files. What's the best way to go about this?

a. Deploy a script that copies files from the Documents folder to a share on a server.

b. Configure folder redirection in the User Configuration node of a GPO.

c. Deploy a Mapped Drive preference and tell users to save their files to the mapped drive.

d. Configure a backup policy in the Computer Configuration node of a GPO.

11. Which of the following is best described as policy definition files saved in XML format?

a. Administrative templates

b. Security templates

c. Group Policy objects

d. Group Policy templates

12. Which of the following is a subfolder in the User Configuration node but not the Computer Configuration node of a GPO?

a. Network

b. Windows Components

c. System

d. Desktop

13. You have been working with ADMX files to modify existing Administrative Templates and create new templates. You work on different domain controllers, depending on your location. Despite a concerted effort, your ADMX files are getting out of sync. How can you solve this problem?

a. Remove Group Policy Management tools from all but one domain controller so that policies can be managed from only one computer.

b. Create an ADMX store in the SYSVOL share and copy the ADMX files to the ADMX store.

c. Create an ADMX store in Active Directory and move all your ADMX files to Active Directory.

d. Share the %*systemroot*%\PolicyDefinitions folder on all your domain controllers and set up Task Scheduler to copy ADMX files automatically from one system to all other systems.

14. You need to find a policy related to an application that was installed a couple years ago. You know that the policy is persistent when the computer it's applied to falls out of scope, but you can't

remember its name. You remember a word or two that might be in the policy name or comments. What can you do to find this policy quickly?

a. In the Group Policy Management console, create a policy search term; set Persistent to Any, and enable Full Text search.

b. In the Group Policy Management Editor, configure a filter; set Managed to No, and enable Keyword Filters.

c. In the Group Policy Management console, configure a search script; set Managed to Yes, and enable Requirements Filters.

d. In the Group Policy Management Editor, configure a policy screen; set Persistent to Yes, and enable Title and Comments.

15. You have created a custom administrative template. You want this template to be available to all DCs so that policies can be configured with it from any DC. Where should you save it?

a. In %*systemroot*%\PolicyDefinitions

b. In the central store

c. In the root of the C drive

d. In ADUC

16. You have installed an application that can be configured with Group Policy. The application came with a custom ADM file that must be replicated to all DCs. What should you do first?

a. Copy the file to %*windir*%\PolicyDefinitions.

b. Open the file with an XML editor and save it.

c. Open the file with ADMX Migrator.

d. Change the extension to .inf.

17. You want to set a group policy preference that affects only computers with a CPU speed of at least 4.0 GHz. What's the best way to do this?

a. Configure item-level targeting.

b. Move all computers meeting the criteria to a separate OU.

c. Configure the group policy client on each computer with this type of CPU.

d. Create a WMI filter with the Group Policy Management Editor.

18. You have configured a group policy preference that creates a VPN connection for all computers in the GPO's scope. One user says the connection was there yesterday, but it's no longer showing in his Network Connections window. You suspect he might have deleted the connection accidentally. What can you do to make sure the VPN connection is re-created even if a user deletes it?

a. Disable the "Remove this item when it is no longer valid" option.

b. Configure the Read-only option.

c. Configure item-level targeting.

d. Disable the "Apply once and do not reapply" option.

19. You want all users to have the company home page and two other web sites loaded in tabs when they start the Microsoft Edge browser, but you want them to be able to change their home pages if they like. What should you do?

a. Configure an IE policy and set it to unmanaged.

b. Configure an Internet Options preference and accept the default options in the Common tab.

c. Configure an IE policy and enable the Allow user changes option.

d. Configure an Internet Options preference and change the default options in the Common tab.

20. Which of the following represents the correct order in which GPOs are applied to an object that falls within the GPO's scope?

a. Site, domain, OU, local GPOs

b. Local GPOs, domain, site, OU

c. Domain, site, OU, local GPOs

d. Local GPOs, site, domain, OU

21. After a GPO is created, which of the following is a possible state for the new GPO? (Choose all that apply.)

a. GPO status: Enabled

b. GPO status: Unlinked

c. Link status: enabled

d. GPO status: All Settings Disabled

22. You have created a GPO named RestrictU and linked it to the Operations OU (containing 30 users) with link order 3. RestrictU sets several policies in the User Configuration node. After a few days, you realize the Operations OU has three users who should be exempt from the restrictions in this GPO. You need to make sure these three users are exempt from RestrictU's settings but that all other policy settings are still in effect for them. What's the best way to proceed?

a. Move the three users to a new OU. Create a GPO with settings suitable for the three users and link it to the new OU.

b. Create an OU under Operations and move the three users to this new OU. Create a GPO and link it to this new OU. Configure the new OU to block inheritance of the RestrictU GPO.

c. Create a global group and add the three users as members. Configure GPO security filtering so that the global group is denied access to the GPO.

d. Set the Enforced option on RestrictU with a WMI filter that excludes the three user accounts.

23. None of the computers in an OU seem to be getting computer policies from the GPO linked to the OU, but users in the OU are getting user policies from this GPO. Which of the following is a possible reason that computer policies in the GPO aren't affecting the computers? (Choose all that apply.)

   a. The GPO link is disabled.
   b. The Computer Configuration settings are disabled.
   c. The computer accounts have Deny Read permission.
   d. The OU has the Block Inheritance option set.

24. You don't have policies that force settings for the look of users' computer desktops. Each user's chosen desktop settings are applied from the user's roaming profile to any computer the user signs in to. You think it's important for users to have a choice, but you'd like a consistent look for computers used for product demonstrations to customers. What's the best way to do this without affecting users when they sign in to other computers?

   a. Configure desktop policies in the Computer Configuration node of a GPO and link this GPO to the OU containing the demonstration computers.
   b. Configure loopback policy processing in Computer Configuration. Configure the desktop settings in User Configuration and link the GPO to the OU containing the demonstration computers.
   c. Create a user named Demo. Configure Demo's desktop settings and use only this user account to sign in to demonstration computers.
   d. Create a GPO with a startup script that configures desktop settings suitable for demonstration computers when these computers are started. Link the GPO to the OU containing the demonstration computers. Instruct users to restart demonstration computers before using them.

25. You want to create policies in a new GPO that affect only computers with Windows 8 installed. You don't want to reorganize your computer accounts to do this, and you want computers that are upgraded to Windows 10 to fall out of the GPO's scope automatically. What can you do?

   a. For each policy, use selective application to specify Windows 8 as the OS.

b. Create a new OU, place all computer accounts representing computers with Windows 8 installed in this OU, and link the GPO to this OU.

c. Create a group called Win8Computers. Place all computer accounts representing computers with Windows 8 installed in this group, and use this group in a security filter on the GPO. Link the GPO to the domain.

d. Configure a WMI filter on the GPO that specifies Windows 8 as the OS. Link the GPO to the domain.

26. An OU structure in your domain has one OU per department, and all the computer and user accounts are in their respective OUs. You have configured several GPOs defining computer and user policies and linked the GPOs to the domain. A group of managers in the Marketing Department need different policies from the rest of the Marketing Department users and computers, but you don't want to change the top-level OU structure. Which of the following GPO processing features are you most likely to use?

   a. Block inheritance
   b. GPO enforcement
   c. WMI filtering
   d. Loopback processing

27. You have created a GPO that sets certain security settings on computers. You need to make sure these settings are applied to all computers in the domain. Which of the following GPO processing features are you most likely to use?

   a. Block inheritance
   b. GPO enforcement
   c. WMI filtering
   d. Loopback processing

28. You have just finished configuring a GPO that modifies several settings on computers in the Operations OU and linked the GPO to the OU. You check on a few computers in the Operations Department and find that the policies haven't been applied. On one computer, you run `gpupdate`, and the policies are applied correctly. What's a likely reason the policies weren't applied to all computers when you tried to update them remotely?

   a. The Computer Configuration node of the GPO is disabled.
   b. A security filter that blocks the computer accounts has been set.
   c. The Operations OU has Block Inheritance set.
   d. Computers only apply GPO settings every 90 minutes or when the computer reboots.

29. Which of the following do you need to do before you can start working with Group Policy on Azure accounts? (Choose all that apply.)

   a. Configure Azure AD.
   b. Create a Windows Server VM in Azure.
   c. Join an Azure VM to the Azure AD DS domain.
   d. Install Azure AD Connect on the Azure VM.

30. Which of the following is true about administering Group Policy on Azure AD DS?

   a. You can modify the Default Domain Policy GPO.
   b. There is no Default Domain Controllers Policy GPO.
   c. The administering account must be a member of the AADDC Administrators group.
   d. The administering account must be a member of the Enterprise Admins group.

Critical Thinking

The following activities give you critical thinking challenges. Case projects offer a scenario with a problem for which you supply a written solution.

Case Projects

Case Project 4-1: Configuring Users' Working Environments

You have been told that all users in the Marketing Department must have a computer working environment that meets certain criteria. Marketing Department users don't always sign in to the same computer every day, so these requirements should apply wherever they sign in. You have a Windows Server 2022 domain, and all computers are domain members. All Marketing Department user and computer accounts are in the Marketing OU. All desktops run Windows 11.

- Marketing users must be able to access documents they save in the Documents folder in their profiles from any computer they sign in to.
- A company marketing application must be installed automatically whenever users sign in if it's not already installed.
- The marketing application they run leaves behind temporary files named mktapp.tmp*X* in the C:\MktApp folder (with the *X* representing a number). These files contain sensitive information and must be deleted when the user signs out.

How can you make sure all these criteria are met? What should you configure to meet each criterion? Be specific about any options that should be enabled or disabled and how the configuration should be applied.

Case Project 4-2: Configuring Preferences

Users in the Engineering Department need a higher level of access on their local computers than other users do. In addition, you want to set power options on the mobile computers of Engineering users. All Engineering Department user and computer accounts are in the Engineering OU. What should you configure to meet the following criteria?

- When an Engineering user signs in to a computer, the user account is added to the local Administrators group on that computer.
- Enable the hibernation power mode, but only if the user's computer is identified as a portable computer. Set the power scheme to hibernate mode if the laptop's lid is closed or the power button is pressed.

Case Project 4-3: Dealing with GPOs and Nested OUs

You have an OU structure like the following:
- Domain
  - AllUsers
    - Managers
    - Engineers

Your GPOs are applied as follows:

AllUsers ← AllUsersGPO and CPanelRestrictionsGPO

Managers ← ManagersGPO

Engineers ← EngineersGPO

The AllUsersGPO has settings that should apply to all users in the AllUsers OU as well as the users in the Managers and Engineering OUs, even if someone configures settings in the GPOs linked to Managers and Engineers that conflict with the settings. However, the CPanelRestrictionsGPO settings can be overridden by settings in the ManagersGPO and EngineersGPO.

What is the best way to meet these requirements using the minimal amount of administrative effort?

Solutions to Self-Check Questions

Section 4-1: Group Policy Objects

1. The scope of a group policy defines which users and computers are affected by its settings. True or False?

   Answer: a. True

   Explanation: The scope of a group policy specifies which objects are affected by the GPO. With GPO inheritance, by default all child objects and subcontainers and their objects are affected by a GPO linked to a higher-level container.

2. What component of Group Policy is an Active Directory object stored in the System\Policies folder?

   Answer: b. GPC

   Explanation: A Group Policy Container (GPC) is an Active Directory object stored in the System\Policies folder. A GPC stores GPO properties and status information but no actual policy settings.

Section 4-2: Group Policy Settings

3. An unmanaged policy setting reverts to its original state when the object is no longer in the GPO's scope. True or False?

   Answer: b. False

   Explanation: An unmanaged policy retains its setting if the object is no longer in the GPO's scope, unless the setting is changed by some other means.

4. What kind of file can be used with the Software installation extension?

   Answer: d. .msi

   Explanation: Microsoft Installation (MSI) files have an .msi extension and are used to install software via Group Policy.

Section 4-3: Working with Administrative Templates

5. What is the name of the folder that is the default location for ADMX files?

   Answer: d. PolicyDefinitions

   Explanation: ADMX files are stored by default in the %*windir*%\PolicyDefinitions folder.

6. Which subfolder is found under the User Configuration node but not in the Computer Configuration node?

   Answer: c. Desktop

   Explanation: The Desktop folder is only found under the User Configuration node, not the Computer Configuration node. Control Panel, Network, and System are found under both nodes.

Section 4-4: Configuring Group Policy Preferences

7. Users can usually change settings that are configured with a group policy preference. True or False?

   Answer: a. True

   Explanation: Group Policy preference settings can be changed by the user in most cases. Group Policy policies, however, cannot be changed by users, including administrative users.

8. What feature allows preferences to target users or computers based on criteria such as whether the computer is portable?

   Answer: a. Item-level targeting

   Explanation: Item-level targeting allows you to create criteria based on properties of computers and users to target where preferences should be applied.

Section 4-5: Group Policy Processing

9. Which aspect of Group Policy processing defines how settings are applied to objects in subcontainers?

   Answer: b. Inheritance

   Explanation: By default, GPO inheritance is enabled and settings linked to a parent object are applied to all child objects, including objects in subcontainers, such as with nested OUs. For example, settings in a GPO linked to the domain object are inherited by all OUs and their child objects in the domain.

10. What feature of GPO processing should you use if you want to ensure that all child objects in the GPO's scope are subject to the GPO's settings even if a lower-level GPO has a conflicting setting?

    Answer: c. GPO enforcement

    Explanation: GPO enforcement forces inheritance of settings on all child objects in the GPO's scope, even if a GPO with conflicting settings is linked to a container at a deeper level.

Section 4-6: Implementing Group Policy in Azure AD DS

11. Which of the following is true about using Group Policy with Azure AD DS?

    Answer: d. The VM that will run Group Policy Management must be connected to the AD DS virtual network.

    Explanation: The VM that will run Group Policy Management must be in the same region and on the same virtual network as the Azure AD DS installation.

Module 5

Configure Domains

Module Objectives

After reading this module and completing the exercises, you will be able to:

1 Describe Active Directory key concepts and components
2 Configure a read-only domain controller
3 Configure sites
4 Manage Active Directory replication
5 Manage operations master roles
6 Configure multidomain environments
7 Support multiforest environments
8 Describe Active Directory trusts
9 Configure Active Directory trusts
10 Use domain controllers in Azure

Domain controllers are the main physical component of Active Directory and must be used strategically to get the best performance and reliability from your domain. A single DC is rarely enough, even for a small domain. To provide fault tolerance and load balancing for the functions that DCs offer, inevitably you need to install two or more DCs in your network. In a multisite domain, you might want to use read-only domain controllers. If you have multiple sites, it's important to understand how replication works between sites. When new DCs are deployed or DCs are taken offline, you need to be aware of the function and placement of DCs that hold operations master roles. This module covers all these topics so that you can manage domain controllers safely and efficiently in a variety of domains.

Once you have a solid understanding of domain controllers, you'll be able to configure and manage larger Active Directory environments that can include multiple domains, multiple sites, and multiple forests. This module covers multidomain and multiforest environments, including how to configure trusts, sites, and efficient replication of Active Directory data between domain controllers. You'll also explore how to use domain controllers in an Azure environment for a hybrid configuration or in an Azure-only Active Directory environment.

Table 5-1 summarizes the requirements for the hands-on activities in this module.

Table 5-1 Activity requirements

Activity	Requirements	Notes
Activity 5-1: Resetting Your Virtual Environment	ServerDC1, ServerDM1, ServerSA1	
Activity 5-2: Installing an RODC with Staging	ServerDC1, ServerSA1	
Activity 5-3: Configuring the Password Replication Policy	ServerDC1, ServerSA1	
Activity 5-4: Creating a Subnet in Active Directory Sites and Services	ServerDC1	
Activity 5-5: Viewing Site Properties	ServerDC1	
Activity 5-6: Working with Connection Objects	ServerDC1, ServerSA1	
Activity 5-7: Creating a Site Link	ServerDC1, ServerSA1	
Activity 5-8: Managing Replication	ServerDC1, ServerSA1	
Activity 5-9: Changing an RODC to a Standard DC	ServerDC1, ServerSA1	
Activity 5-10: Transferring FSMO Roles	ServerDC1, ServerSA1	
Activity 5-11: Resetting Your Virtual Environment	ServerDC1, ServerSA1	
Activity 5-12: Installing a Subdomain	ServerDC1, ServerSA1	
Activity 5-13: Removing a Subdomain and Creating a New Tree	ServerDC1, ServerSA1	
Activity 5-14: Creating a New Forest	ServerDC1, ServerSA1	
Activity 5-15: Creating and Testing a Forest Trust	ServerDC1, ServerSA1	

Active Directory Review

As you have learned, domain controllers (DCs) are the heart of the physical structure of a Windows Active Directory domain. The other physical component of Active Directory is a site. The logical components of Active Directory are forests, domains, and OUs. Before you learn about new topics related to DCs and Active Directory, review the following list of key points to keep in mind:

- DCs are servers that have a Windows Server OS installed with the Active Directory Domain Services server role installed and configured.
- DCs depend on Domain Name System (DNS) as part of the Active Directory infrastructure, and there must be at least one DNS server in a domain.
- One DC per domain is required, but having two DCs for each domain is recommended for reliability and availability. A DC can support only a single domain.
- DCs maintain data consistency in Active Directory with other DCs in the domain by using multimaster replication.
- A **read-only domain controller (RODC)** is a DC that stores a read-only copy of the Active Directory database but no password information. Changes to the domain must be made on a writeable DC, and then replicated to an RODC, which is called *unidirectional replication.*
- Some functions related to maintaining the Active Directory infrastructure are stored in certain DCs referred to as operations masters. These DCs are assigned the Flexible Single Master Operation (FSMO) role, which uses single master replication.
- A **global catalog (GC) server** is a DC configured to hold the global catalog. Every forest must have at least one GC server. GC servers facilitate domain-wide and forest-wide searches and logons across domains, and they hold universal group membership information. Each site should have at least one GC server to speed logons and directory searches.
- Active Directory is based on the Lightweight Directory Access Protocol (LDAP) standard for accessing directory objects.

- An Active Directory tree is made up of one or more domains that share a common top-level and second-level domain name.
- An Active Directory forest consists of one or more trees with domains that share a common trust relationship and schema yet allow independent policies and administration.
- An Active Directory site is a physical location in which DCs communicate and replicate information frequently. A site is composed of one or more IP subnets connected by high-speed LAN technology. Replication between DCs in separate sites can be configured according to the available bandwidth.

Now that you're refreshed on the basics of DCs and Active Directory, turn your attention to configuring RODCs.

Self-Check Questions

1. Changes on RODCs are replicated to other DCs. True or False?

   a. True   **b.** False

2. Which of the following facilitates forest-wide Active Directory searches?

   a. GC   **c.** GPT
   b. RODC   **d.** GUID

○ Check your answers at the end of this module.

Configuring Read-Only Domain Controllers

Microsoft Exam AZ-800:
Deploy and manage Active Directory Domain Services (AD DS) in on-premises and cloud environments.
  - Deploy and manage AD DS domain controllers.
  - Configure and manage multisite, multidomain, and multiforest environments.

An RODC is simply an installation option of a server role you're already familiar with: Active Directory Domain Services. The RODC role was developed to address the need to have a domain controller in a branch office where server expertise and physical security are often lacking. An RODC performs many of the same tasks as a regular DC, but changes to Active Directory objects can't be made on an RODC. An RODC maintains a current copy of Active Directory information through replication. However, there are some important differences in the information an RODC keeps that make it more secure than writeable DCs. These differences are discussed later in the section called "RODC Replication." In addition, you should be aware of some factors before installing an RODC in your network. This section discusses the following aspects of using RODCs in a Windows network:

- RODC installation
- RODC replication
- The Password Replication Policy
- Read-only DNS

RODC Installation

Before you can install an RODC, you must meet these prerequisites:

- A writeable DC running Windows Server 2008 or later must be operating in the domain. RODCs were introduced in Windows Server 2008, and they can't replicate with DCs running earlier versions of Windows Server.
- The forest functional level must be at least Windows Server 2003.

Installing an RODC isn't much different from installing a regular DC. You still install the Active Directory Domain Services role and run the Active Directory configuration wizard. In the Domain Controller Options window (see Figure 5-1), you select the "Read only domain controller (RODC)" check box.

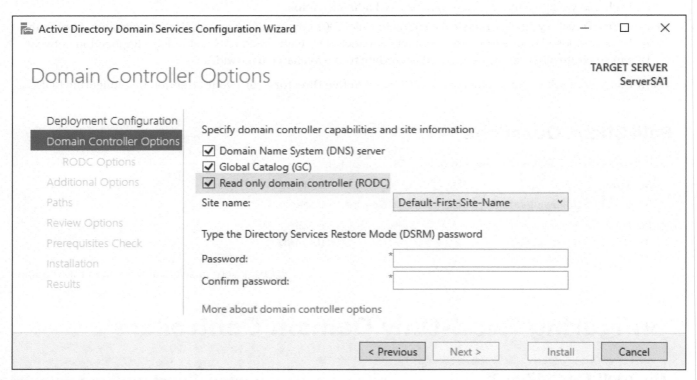

Figure 5-1   The Domain Controller Options window

If you select the RODC option, you move to the RODC Options window (shown in Figure 5-2), where you can select a **delegated administrator account**. A delegated administrator account has local administrative rights and permissions to the RODC, similar to members of the local Administrators group on a member computer or standalone computer.

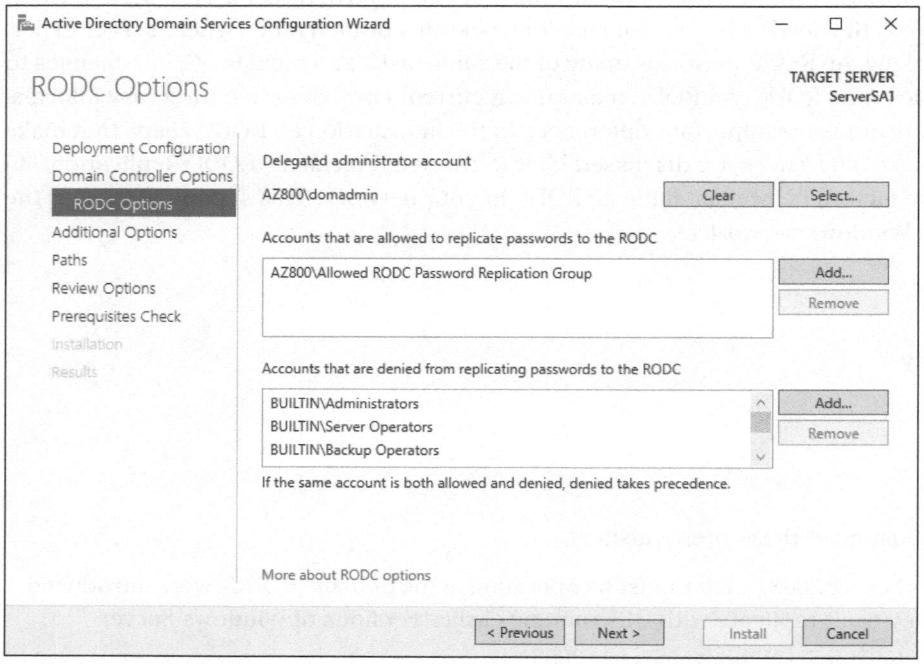

Figure 5-2   The RODC Options window

A delegated administrator account for an RODC doesn't have domain administrative rights and permissions, so the scope of the delegated permissions is limited to just the RODC computer. Delegated administration is useful if you need someone in a branch office to perform tasks on an RODC that require administrative capability without giving that user broader domain authority. Delegated administrators can perform tasks such as installing drivers and software updates, managing disk drives, installing devices, and starting and stopping Active Directory Domain Services.

In Figure 5-2, notice the two boxes listing group accounts:

- *Accounts that are allowed to replicate passwords to the RODC*—Contains the Allowed RODC Password Replication group, which has no members by default. You add accounts to this box or the Allowed RODC Password Replication group if you want account passwords to be replicated to the RODC.

- *Accounts that are denied from replicating passwords to the RODC*—You add accounts to this box or the Denied RODC Password Replication group to specifically deny replication of account passwords. By default, members of the Administrators, Server Operators, Backup Operators, and Account Operators are denied password replication. This ensures that users who have substantial authority in the domain do not have their password replicated to the RODC, which could pose a security risk.

Password replication is discussed more in the section called "Password Replication Policy."

Staged RODC Installation

Another option for installing an RODC that isn't available with a regular DC is a **staged installation** or *delegated installation*. With staged installation, a domain administrator creates the RODC computer account in Active Directory, and then a regular user can perform the installation at a later time. To use this feature, you create a computer account for the server performing the RODC role in the Domain Controllers OU before installing the RODC. You use Active Directory Administrative Center (ADAC) for this task; the option is not available in Active Directory Users and Computers (ADUC). In ADAC, click the Domain Controllers OU and click "Pre-create a Read-only domain controller account" in the Tasks pane to start the Active Directory Domain Services Installation Wizard (see Figure 5-3).

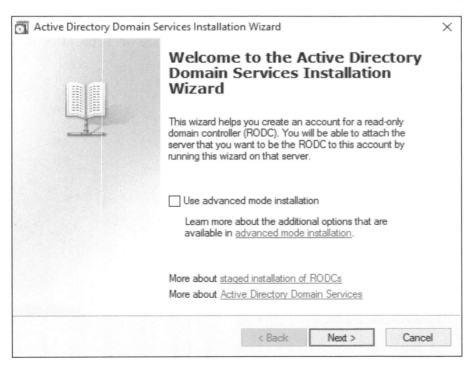

Figure 5-3   The Active Directory Domain Services Installation Wizard

In the next window, you enter credentials if you aren't already signed in as an administrator. In the Specify the Computer Name window, you enter the name of the new RODC computer account (see Figure 5-4). The target server must not be a domain member before you install Active Directory Domain Services on it.

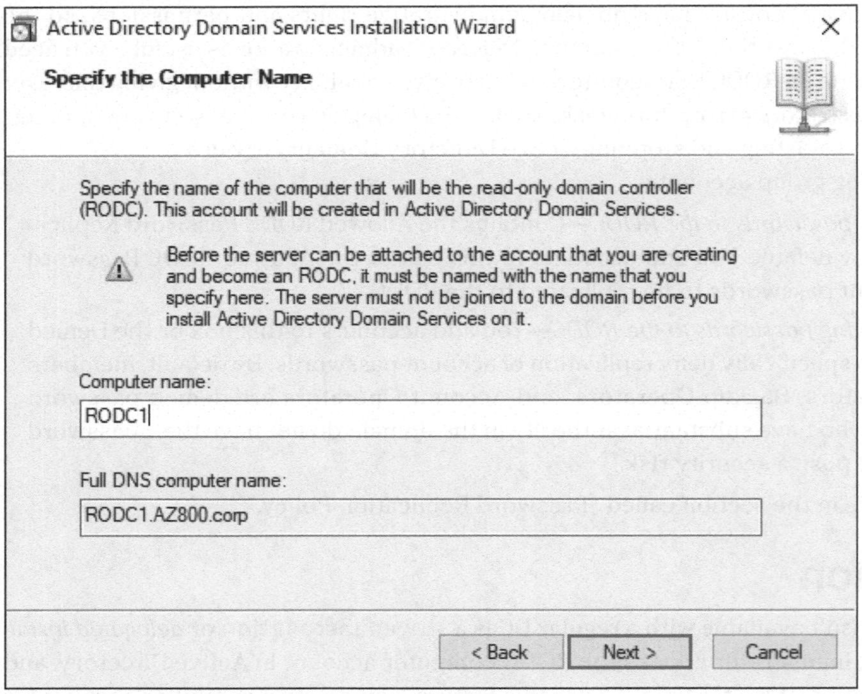

Figure 5-4 Specifying the computer name

Next, you select a site for the new RODC. The target server must have an IP address configuration that's suitable for the site. The next window looks much like Figure 5-1, where you specify whether the RODC should also be a DNS server or GC server. The "Read only domain controller (RODC)" option is selected and grayed out. In the Delegation of RODC Installation and Administration window, you specify the user or group who can perform the RODC installation (see Figure 5-5). This account should represent a user or users who are physically at the place where the RODC is to be installed. Administration of the RODC is also delegated to this account.

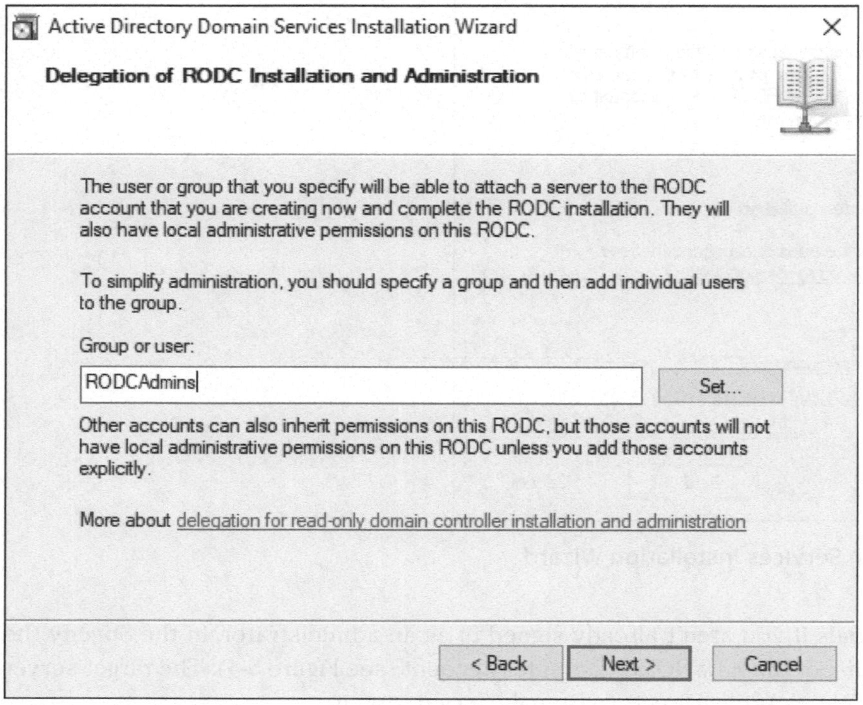

Figure 5-5 Delegating RODC installation and administration

Finally, you review your selections and finish the wizard. A computer account is created in the Domain Controllers OU, and ADAC shows the Domain Controller Type as Unoccupied Domain Controller until the RODC installation is finished. The rest of the process is done on the target server that will be the RODC. Make sure the target server's computer name is the name specified in the wizard and the server isn't currently a domain member.

> **Note 1**
>
> The procedure for staging RODC installation can also be done in Active Directory Users and Computers by right-clicking the Domain Controllers OU and clicking "Pre-create Read-only Domain Controller account."

Staged RODC Installation with PowerShell

As you might expect, the procedure for staging an RODC installation can be done with a PowerShell cmdlet. At an elevated PowerShell prompt, use the following command to create an RODC computer account named RODC1 in the csmtech. corp domain in a site named BranchOffice with a group named BranchOff-G as the delegated administrator account:

```
Add-ADDSReadOnlyDomainControllerAccount
  -DomainControllerAccountName RODC1 -DomainName
  csmtech.corp -SiteName BranchOffice
  -DelegatedAdministratorAccountName BranchOff-G
```

> **Note 2**
>
> Some PowerShell commands are lengthy. Remember, you can type them more easily by using the Tab key shortcut. Type a few letters of the command (enough letters to make it unique) and press the Tab key. PowerShell finishes the command for you. This method also works for options in the command. For example, you could type `Add-ADDSR<Tab> -DomainC<Tab>` for the first part of the preceding command.

Staged RODC Installation on the Target Server

To do the RODC installation on the target server, follow these steps:

1. Sign in to the server as a local administrator.
2. Change the computer name to match the RODC account name, if necessary.
3. Install the Active Directory Domain Services role.
4. To configure the Active Directory Domain Services role, start the Active Directory Domain Services Installation Wizard by clicking the Alert flag and clicking Promote this server to a domain controller.
5. Next, click "Add a domain controller to an existing domain." In this window, you specify the domain name and the credentials of an account that can perform the operation. Use the account credentials for an account that was delegated installation and administration for the RODC.
6. The Domain Controller Options window displays a message that a pre-created RODC account exists. The options are grayed out because they were specified when the computer account was created. However, you must supply a Directory Services Restore Mode (DSRM) password. The "Reinstall this domain controller" option can be used if a DC is being replaced by another server because of hardware failure.

The remainder of the installation is the same as installing a regular DC or RODC.

To use PowerShell to complete the staged RODC installation, first install the AD DS server role. Then type the following command at an elevated PowerShell prompt to configure RODC1 as an RODC in the csmtech.corp domain, using credentials from BranchUser1:

```
Install-ADDSDomainController -DomainName csmtech.corp
  -UseExistingAccount -credential (get-credential)
```

After you enter this command, you're prompted for the user name and password of the delegated account and for the DSRM password.

Note 3

Because an RODC is meant to address the needs of a branch office, administrators can combine the RODC installation with another one that's designed for branch office installation: Server Core. This configuration often goes together because both optimize security and both are meant for remote management.

RODC Replication

Replication on an RODC is unidirectional, meaning the Active Directory database is replicated from a writeable DC to an RODC, but data is never replicated from an RODC to another DC. RODCs can replicate only with Windows Server 2008 and later writeable DCs. **Unidirectional replication** provides an extra level of security for networks with branch office locations. Even if a server is compromised and someone is able to make malicious changes to Active Directory on the RODC, the changes can't be propagated to DCs in the rest of the network.

You already learned that you can limit which accounts' passwords are replicated to an RODC. To increase security of the Active Directory data stored on an RODC, administrators can configure a **filtered attribute set**, which specifies domain objects that aren't replicated to RODCs. The type of data to filter usually includes credential information that might be used by applications using Active Directory as a data store. Any data that might be considered security sensitive can be filtered, except objects required for system operation. Filtered attribute sets are configured on the schema master.

RODC placement in your site topology is important to ensure that replication occurs between an RODC and a writeable DC. A writeable DC is usually placed in the site nearest in the replication topology to the RODC's site. The nearest site is defined as the site with the lowest-cost site link. If this placement isn't possible, you must create a site link bridge between the RODC site and a site with a writeable DC. Site links and site link bridges are discussed later in this module in the "Understanding and Configuring Sites" section.

Password Replication Policy

As discussed, account passwords are not stored by default on an RODC, which includes both user and computer account passwords. This arrangement makes the RODC more secure in case an attacker tries to crack locally stored passwords. However, it also negates some advantages of having a domain controller on the local network. If the RODC stores no passwords, each user and computer authentication must be referred to a writeable DC, most likely located across a WAN link. To prevent this problem, as you learned, you can specify accounts for which passwords will be replicated. When an account password is replicated, its password is retrieved from a writeable DC the first time the account logs on, and thereafter the password is retrieved from the RODC.

Note 4

Password replication is also known as *credential caching*.

Password replication is controlled by the Password Replication Policy (PRP), which is accessed in the Properties dialog box of the RODC computer account (see Figure 5-6) in Active Directory. A PRP lists users and groups along with a setting of Allow or Deny. Account Operators, Administrators, Backup Operators, and Server Operators are built-in domain local groups added to the PRP with the Deny setting by default. Passwords of these groups' members aren't stored on the RODC.

The PRP also contains groups named Allowed RODC Password Replication Group and Denied RODC Password Replication Group. These two groups are added to the PRP of all RODCs. These groups have no members at first, but administrators can add users or groups to them to centrally control password caching on all RODCs. If a user is a member of a group with the Allow setting and a group with the Deny setting, the Deny setting takes precedence. Generally, groups or users with permission to sensitive information should be added to the Denied RODC Password Replication group. Users who often visit where RODCs are used might be candidates for membership in the Allowed RODC Password Replication group.

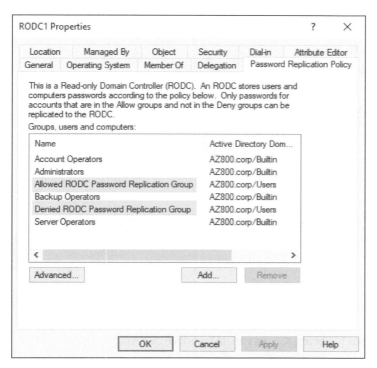

Figure 5-6   Viewing the Password Replication Policy

Besides the default groups added to the PRP for all RODCs, an administrator can customize each RODC's PRP. For example, a group can be created for all users located at a branch office, and this group can be added to the PRP of the RODC at the branch office with an Allow setting. In addition, you can create a group for the computer accounts in the branch office and add this group to the PRP. Adding computer accounts to the PRP speeds up computer boot times and other actions that require the computer account to authenticate to the domain.

Exam Tip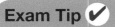

The AZ-800 certification exam expects you to understand Active Directory replication, including RODC replication.

Read-Only DNS

If you install DNS on an RODC, all Active Directory-integrated DNS zones are read only on the RODC. This is a departure from standard terminology because the zone is still considered a primary zone, even though it is read only. Zone information is replicated from other DNS servers, but zone changes can't be made on the RODC. Client workstations can still make name resolution queries to the RODC, but workstations in the branch office using Dynamic DNS can't create or update their DNS records on the RODC. Instead, the RODC sends a referral record to the client with the address of a DNS server that can handle the update. To maintain a current DNS database, the RODC requests a single-record replication from the DNS server that updated the client record. Note that if you attempt to create a new DNS zone on an RODC, you can create only a standard primary, secondary, or stub zone. You can't create a new Active Directory-integrated zone on an RODC.

Note 5

If theft of an RODC is a likely risk, you can take further precautions to secure its sensitive data by using BitLocker Drive Encryption, which is installed as a server role in Server Manager. With BitLocker, you can secure data on the volume containing the Windows OS and Active Directory as well as on additional volumes.

Self-Check Questions

3. A delegated administrator has administrative privileges only on the RODC. True or False?

   a. True
   b. False

4. What can you configure on an RODC to limit replication of objects for security purposes?

   a. Unidirectional replication
   c. Filtered attribute set
   b. Read-only DNS
   d. Delegated installation

   ⊙ Check your answers at the end of this module.

Activity 5-1

Resetting Your Virtual Environment
Time Required: 5 minutes
Objective: Reset your virtual environment by applying the InitialConfig checkpoint or snapshot.
Required Tools and Equipment: ServerDC1, ServerDM1, ServerSA1
Description: Apply the InitialConfig checkpoint or snapshot to ServerDC1, ServerDM1, and ServerSA1.

1. Be sure all servers are shut down. In your virtualization program, apply the InitialConfig checkpoint or snapshot to ServerDC1, ServerDM1, and ServerSA1.
2. When the snapshot or checkpoint has been applied, continue to the next activity.

Activity 5-2

Installing an RODC with Staging
Time Required: 20 minutes
Objective: Install an RODC with staging.
Required Tools and Equipment: ServerDC1, ServerSA1
Description: In this activity, you use RODC staging with PowerShell. First you create a group and an account to which you delegate administration. ServerSA1 will be the RODC.

1. Start ServerDC1 and ServerSA1 and sign in to both as **Administrator**.
2. On ServerDC1, open Active Directory Users and Computers. Create a new OU named **BranchOffice** under the domain node. In the BranchOffice OU, create a global group named **BranchOff-G** and a user named **BranchUser1** with **Password01**. Make sure to set the password to never expire. Make BranchUser1 a member of the BranchOff-G group.
3. Right-click the **Domain Controllers** OU. Notice the option to "Pre-create" an RODC account. You can use this wizard to stage the RODC account, but for this activity, you'll use PowerShell.
4. On ServerDC1, open a PowerShell window. Type **Add-ADDSReadOnlyDomainControllerAccount -DomainControllerAccountName ServerSA1 -DomainName az800.corp -SiteName Default-First-Site-Name -DelegatedAdministratorAccountName BranchOff-G** and press **Enter**. You might note a warning message about default security settings, which you can ignore. The last part of the output should read "Operation completed successfully."
5. In Active Directory Users and Computers, make sure the **Domain Controllers** OU is selected and click the **Refresh** button. You should note ServerSA1 in the right pane with the Domain Controller (DC) Type showing Unoccupied DC Account (see Figure 5-7).

(continues)

Activity 5-2 Continued

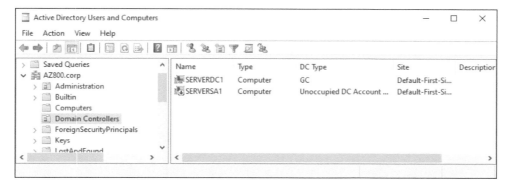

Figure 5-7   The staged RODC account in Active Directory Users and Computers

6. On ServerSA1, open a PowerShell prompt. First you need to install the Active Directory server role. Type **Install-WindowsFeature AD-Domain-Services -IncludeManagementTools** and press **Enter**. This installation takes some time.
7. At the PowerShell prompt, type **Install-ADDSDomainController -DomainName az800.corp -UseExistingAccount -credential (get-credential)** and press **Enter**.
8. In the credentials dialog box, type **az800\BranchUser1** in the User name text box, type **Password01** in the Password text box, and then click **OK**.
9. When you're prompted for the SafeModeAdministratorPassword (which is the DSRM password), type **Password01**, press **Enter**, type it again, and press **Enter**.
10. When you're prompted to continue with the operation, press **Enter**.
11. The installation takes a while. When it's finished, a message states that you'll be signed out. Click **Close** or just wait for Windows to restart.
12. While ServerSA1 is restarting, refresh the screen in Active Directory Users and Computers on ServerDC1 to see that ServerSA1 is now listed as a read-only, global catalog (GC) domain controller.
13. Continue to the next activity.

Activity 5-3

Configuring the Password Replication Policy

Time Required: 15 minutes
Objective: Add a group to the PRP of the ServerSA1 computer account.
Required Tools and Equipment: ServerDC1, ServerSA1
Description: In this activity, you create a group and add it to the Allowed RODC Password Replication group.

1. On ServerDC1, open Active Directory Users and Computers, click **Domain Controllers** in the left pane, and in the middle pane, double-click **ServerSA1** to open its Properties dialog box. Click the **Password Replication Policy** tab.
2. Click the **Advanced** button. The Advanced Password Replication Policy for ServerSA1 dialog box shows you which account passwords are stored on the RODC. By default, the RODC computer account is replicated, as is a special account used by the Kerberos authentication process. Click **Close** and then **Cancel**.
3. Open a PowerShell prompt. Add the BranchOff-G group to the Allowed RODC Password Replication Group by typing **Add-ADGroupMember "Allowed RODC Password Replication Group" BranchOff-G** and pressing **Enter**.

(continues)

Activity 5-3 Continued

4. Sign in to ServerSA1 as **BranchUser1**.
5. On ServerDC1, open the Properties dialog box for the ServerSA1 account again, and click the **Password Replication Policy** tab. Click **Advanced** to see that BranchUser1 is now among the accounts whose passwords are stored on the RODC. Click **Close** and then **Cancel**.
6. Sign out of ServerSA1. Continue to the next activity.

Understanding and Configuring Sites

Microsoft Exam AZ-800:
Deploy and manage Active Directory Domain Services (AD DS) in on-premises and cloud environments.
- Deploy and manage AD DS domain controllers.
- Configure and manage multisite, multidomain, and multiforest environments.

In Module 2, you learned what an Active Directory site is and some of the differences in how replication occurs between DCs in different sites. As you know, a site is one of Active Directory's physical components, along with a domain controller. An Active Directory site represents a physical location where DCs are installed and group policies can be applied. When you're designing the logical components of Active Directory, such as domains and OUs, you don't need to consider the physical location of objects. In other words, an OU named Accounting could contain user accounts from both Chicago and New Orleans, and the DCs holding the Active Directory database could be located in San Francisco and New York. As long as there's a network connection between the location where a user logs on and the location of the DC, the system works.

Having said that, having a DC near the accounts using it makes sense. Authentication and resource access usually work fine across a reliable WAN link, but if a company location contains several users, placing DCs in that location is more efficient. Performance and reliability are less predictable on slower WAN links than on LAN links. So, the extra cost of additional DCs can be outweighed by the productivity gained from faster, more reliable network access.

When the first DC of a forest is installed, a site is created named Default-First-Site-Name, but you can rename the site as something more descriptive. Any additional DCs installed in the forest are assigned to this site until additional sites are created. Figure 5-8 shows a single-site domain in two locations at the top and the same domain defined as two sites at the bottom.

There are three main reasons for establishing multiple sites:

- *Authentication efficiency*—When a user logs on to a domain, the client computer always tries to authenticate to a DC in the same site to ensure that logon traffic is kept in the same site and off slower WAN links.

- *Replication efficiency*—A DC in every branch office facilitates faster and more reliable network access, but DCs must communicate with one another to replicate the Active Directory database. Using the default replication schedule, however, can create considerable replication traffic. Replication between DCs occurs within 15 seconds after a change is made and once per hour when no changes have occurred. In databases with several thousand objects, this schedule can take a toll on available bandwidth for other network operations. With multiple sites, intersite replication can be scheduled to occur during off-peak hours and at a frequency that makes the most sense. For example, a small branch office site with a limited bandwidth connection to the main office can be configured to replicate less often than a larger branch office that requires more timely updates.

- *Application efficiency*—Some distributed applications, such as Exchange Server (an email and collaboration application) and Distributed File System (DFS), use sites to improve efficiency. These applications ensure that client computers always try to access data in the same site before attempting to access services in remote sites by using the WAN link.

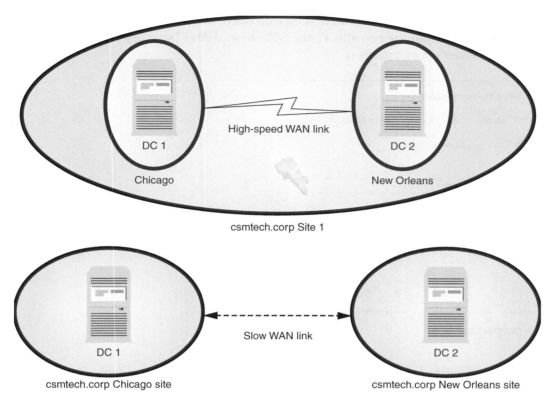

csmtech.corp Site 1

csmtech.corp Chicago site   csmtech.corp New Orleans site

Figure 5-8   Active Directory sites

Sites are created by using Active Directory Sites and Services. A site is linked to an IP subnet that reflects the IP addressing scheme used at the physical location the site represents. A site can encompass one or more IP subnets, but each site must be linked to at least one IP subnet that doesn't overlap with another site. When a DC is created and assigned an IP address, it's assigned to a site based on its address automatically. Figure 5-9 shows the relationship between sites and IP subnets.

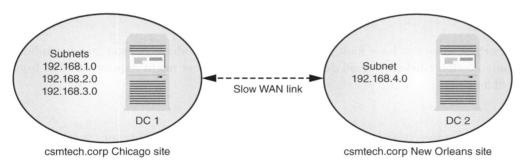

csmtech.corp Chicago site   csmtech.corp New Orleans site

Figure 5-9   The relationship between sites and subnets

Site Components

Sites and connections between sites are defined by several components that can be created and configured in Active Directory Sites and Services. They include subnets, site links, and bridgehead servers, as discussed in the following sections.

Subnets

As discussed, each site is associated with one or more IP subnets. An IP subnet is a range of IP addresses in which the network ID is the same. All computers assigned an address in the subnet can communicate with one another without requiring a router. By default, no subnets are created in Active Directory Sites and Services. When a new site is created, all subnets used by the default site should be created and associated with the default site. Then the subnets for the new site should be created and associated with the new site. Figure 5-10 shows Active Directory Sites and Services with the Default-First-Site-Name Properties dialog box open.

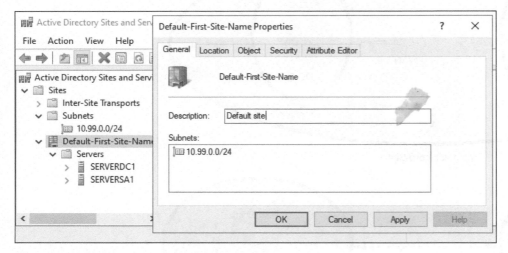

Figure 5-10   Viewing site properties

After creating a site, you must associate one or more subnets with it. Active Directory uses this information in two important ways:

- *Placing new domain controllers in the correct site*—Correct placement is necessary to determine the optimum intrasite and intersite replication topology and to associate clients with the nearest domain controllers. When a new DC is installed, it's automatically placed in the site corresponding with its assigned IP address. If the DC existed before the site was created, you need to move the DC manually from its existing site to the new site.

- *Determining which site a client computer belongs to*—When a client requests a domain service, such as logging on to the domain or accessing a Distributed File System resource, the client request can be directed to a DC or member server in the same site. A local resource is usually preferable, especially when remote sites are connected via slower WAN links.

Defining your subnets is important when you have multiple sites. If a client's IP address doesn't match a subnet in any of the defined sites, communication efficiency could degrade because the client might request services from servers in remote sites instead of locally.

Site Links

A **site link** is needed to connect two or more sites for replication purposes. When Active Directory is installed, a default site link called DEFAULTIPSITELINK is created. Until new site links are created, all sites that are added use this site link. Site links determine the replication schedule and frequency between two sites. If all locations in an organization are connected through the same WAN link or WAN links of equal bandwidth, one site link might be suitable. If the locations use different WAN connections at differing speeds, however, additional links can be created to configure differing replication schedules. You access the properties of a site link in Active Directory Sites and Services by expanding Sites and Inter-Site Transports and then clicking IP. Site links have three configuration options, as shown in Figure 5-11.

The Cost field is an administrator-assigned value that represents the bandwidth of the connection between sites. The default value is 100. An administrator can alter this value to influence which path is chosen when more than one path exists between two sites. As shown in Figure 5-12, Site A replicates with Site B and Site C through the corresponding site links, but Site A has two options for replicating with Site D: the link with Site B or the link with Site C. The site link cost determines that Site A will use the link with Site B. Site link costs are additive, so the total cost for Site A to replicate with Site D through Site C is 400; the total cost to replicate with Site D via Site B is only 300. When you have

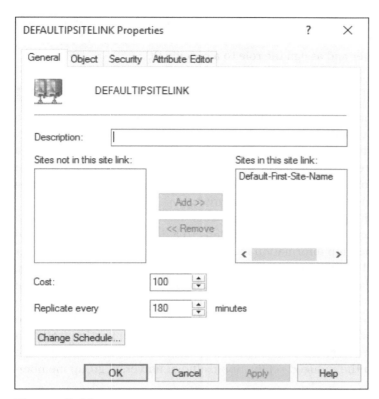

Figure 5-11   The Properties dialog box for DEFAULTIPSITELINK

more than one path option between two sites, the lower-cost path is always used unless links in the path become unavailable. In this case, the replication process reconfigures itself to use the next lower-cost path, if available. Site links are transitive by default, which means Site A can replicate directly with Site D and Site C can replicate directly with Site B without creating an explicit link between the two sites.

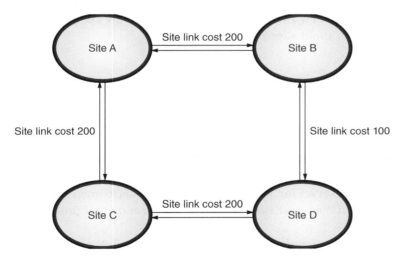

Figure 5-12   Site replication topology

Bridgehead Servers

Intrasite replication occurs among several domain controllers after the Knowledge Consistency Checker (KCC) creates the topology. Intersite replication occurs between bridgehead servers. When the KCC detects that replication must occur between sites, one DC in each site is designated as the Inter-Site Topology Generator (ISTG). The ISTG then designates a bridgehead server to handle replication for each directory partition. Because bridgehead servers perform such a vital function in multisite networks and the function can consume a lot of server resources, the administrator can override automatic assignment of a bridgehead server and assign the role to a specific DC.

The Global Catalog and Universal Group Membership Caching

As you've learned, the global catalog is a critical component for many Active Directory operations. It's the only place where universal group membership information is maintained, and it contains a partial replica of all domain objects. Access to a global catalog server must be considered when designing sites and configuring site replication. Having a global catalog server used to be critical in sites with more than a few users because it speeded logons and forest-wide searches for Active Directory objects. However, replication traffic is increased considerably in sites with global catalog servers, particularly if there are several large domains in your Active Directory forest.

Universal group membership caching handles the potential conflict between faster logons and increased replication traffic. When this feature is enabled and a user logs on for the first time to a domain in the site with no global catalog server, the user's universal group membership information is retrieved from a global catalog server in a different site. Thereafter, the information is cached locally on every DC in the site and updated every 8 hours, so there's no need to contact a global catalog server. Having this feature available, however, doesn't mean a global catalog server should never be placed in a site. Microsoft recommends placing a global catalog server in the site when the number of accounts (user and computer) exceeds 500 and the number of DCs exceeds 2. With 500 cached accounts, the traffic created by refreshing every 8 hours might be higher than global catalog replication traffic. In addition, you need to determine whether the other benefits of having a global catalog server (faster forest-wide searches, faster updates of universal groups) outweigh the reduced replication traffic of universal group membership caching.

To configure universal group membership caching, expand the site object in Active Directory Sites and Services, and then open the Properties dialog box of the NT Directory Service (NTDS) Site Settings object. In the Site Settings tab, click the Enable Universal Group Membership Caching check box. In addition, you can select which site is used for refreshing the cache.

Configuring Sites

In the previous sections, you learned about basic site components and the reasons for creating additional sites, and you learned how to create subnets in preparation for creating new sites. You also learned about the components of intersite replication. This section covers the following topics about sites:

- Registering SRV records
- Working with automatic site coverage
- Moving DCs between sites

SRV Record Registration

Domain controllers advertise themselves by registering service (SRV) records with DNS servers so that clients can find DCs that offer services related to Active Directory. When a client needs the services of a DC (for example, to authenticate to the domain or join a domain), it queries a DNS server for SRV records for all DCs. It also queries for SRV records for DCs in its own site and uses these records first, if they exist, so that authentication and other procedures don't travel across a WAN.

The Netlogon service on the DC handles registration of SRV records for the Lightweight Directory Access Protocol (LDAP) and Kerberos services. These records are stored on the DNS server in folders in a subdomain named _msdcs, which is located in the zone for the DC's domain. A folder for each site is maintained so that determining which sites offer these services is easier. For example, a DC in the Headquarters site for domain AZ800.corp registers SRV records under Forward Lookup Zones in _msdcs.AZ800.corp\dc_sites\Headquarters_tcp and _msdcs.AZ800.corp\dc_tcp (see Figure 5-13).

Figure 5-13   SRV records in DNS

If a DC fails to register its SRV records, you can force it to attempt to register the records by stopping and starting the Netlogon service in the Services MMC or with one of the following commands:

- At a command prompt: Type `net stop netlogon` and press Enter, and then type `net start netlogon` and press Enter.
- At a PowerShell prompt: Type `Restart-Service -Name netlogon` and press Enter.

Exam Tip ✔

The AZ-800 exam expects you to know how to configure DCs and sites for efficient user authentication—that is, to prevent authentication requests from having to travel across WAN links.

Working with Automatic Site Coverage

Having a DC in each site is usually preferable so that authentication of clients occurs on the local LAN instead of having to traverse the WAN. However, having a DC at each site isn't always necessary or practical if you have a remote site with few users, an environment that isn't secure enough, or inadequate environmental controls for a DC.

When a site doesn't have a DC, other DCs in other sites in the domain can provide the services clients need. **Automatic site coverage** is a feature in which each DC advertises itself by registering SRV records in DNS in sites that don't have a DC if the advertising DC has the lowest-cost connection to the site. When a client in the site attempts to contact a DC for authentication and other purposes, it performs a DNS lookup to request the closest DC. The SRV record for the advertising DC is returned. This process prevents clients from using DCs located across higher-cost links. Generally, you want automatic site coverage enabled for efficient domain operation.

Moving DCs Between Sites

When a Windows server is first promoted to a DC, it's assigned to a site based on its IP address settings, or you can choose the site to install the DC during the promotion process. If there's only one site, the DC is placed in it. If you later change a DC's IP subnet address or change subnet assignments for sites, the affected DCs aren't moved to a different site automatically. You need to move DCs to new sites manually if changes in your site design or IP addressing warrant it. Here's the basic procedure for moving a DC to a new site:

1. Verify that the target site is created and has the right subnets assigned to it.
2. Change the DC's IP address, subnet mask, and default gateway as needed for the target site. If necessary, change the DC's DNS server addresses.
3. If the DC is used as a DNS forwarder, make the necessary changes in the forwarder configuration on other DNS servers.
4. If the DC hosts a delegated DNS zone, update the NS record in the parent domain's DNS zone to the new IP address of the DC.

5. If the DC being moved is a preferred bridgehead server, you must make the necessary adjustments in both the current site and the target site. In most cases, it's better to configure the DC so that it's not a preferred bridgehead server and ensure that no DCs in the current and target site are configured as bridgehead servers. By doing so, the ISTG assigns bridgehead servers automatically as needed when the DC is moved. After the move, you can then assign preferred bridgehead servers again, if necessary.

6. Move the server to the target site in Active Directory Sites and Services. To do so, right-click the server object in Active Directory Sites and Services, click Move, and then click the destination site name. If necessary, physically move the server to the new site location.

7. In DNS Manager, verify that SRV records are created for the DC in the target site folder. It could take up to an hour for these records to be created. The System event log contains any errors related to SRV record creation.

Self-Check Questions

5. Having a single IP subnet is a reason for establishing multiple sites. True or False?

   a. True   **b.** False

6. What creates the topology used for intrasite replication?

   a. Bridgehead server   **c.** Global catalog

   b. Knowledge Consistency Checker   **d.** ISTG

⊙ Check your answers at the end of this module.

Activity 5-4

Creating a Subnet in Active Directory Sites and Services

Time Required: 5 minutes

Objective: Create a subnet in Active Directory Sites and Services and associate it with a site.

Required Tools and Equipment: ServerDC1

Description: In this activity, you configure the default site to use the subnet already in use in your network. In addition, you rename the default site.

1. On ServerDC1, in Server Manager, click **Tools** and then click **Active Directory Sites and Services** from the menu.

2. Double-click to expand **Sites**, if necessary. Right-click **Subnets**, point to **New**, and click **Subnet**.

3. In the Prefix text box, type **10.99.0.0/24** (assuming that you're following the IP address scheme used in this book; otherwise, ask your instructor what to enter).

4. In the "Select a site object for this prefix" list box, click **Default-First-Site-Name**, and then click **OK**.

5. In the left pane, click **Subnets**. Right-click **10.99.0.0/24** and click **Properties**. In the General tab, you can give the subnet a description and change the site the subnet is associated with. For now, leave it as is. Click **Cancel**.

6. In the left pane, right-click **Default-First-Site-Name** and click **Rename**. Type **Headquarters** and press **Enter**.

7. In the left pane, right-click **Headquarters** and click **Properties**. In the Description text box, type **AZ800 Headquarters site for the 10.99.0.0/24 subnet**, and then click **OK**.

8. Right-click the **Sites** folder and click **New Site**. In the New Object – Site dialog box, type **BranchOffice** in the Name text box. Notice that you're prompted to select a site link object for the site. Click **DEFAULTIPSITELINK**, and then click **OK**.

9. You should see a message from Active Directory Domain Services that more steps are needed to finish configuring the site: making sure site links are suitable, adding subnets for the site in the Subnets folder, and adding a domain controller to the site. Click **OK**.

10. Continue to the next activity.

Activity 5-5

Viewing Site Properties

Time Required: 10 minutes
Objective: View site properties.
Required Tools and Equipment: ServerDC1
Description: In this activity, you explore the properties of NTDS site settings, server NTDS settings, and connection objects.

1. On ServerDC1, open Active Directory Sites and Services, if necessary. Click to expand **Sites**, **Headquarters**, **Servers**, and **ServerDC1**. Under ServerDC1 in the left pane, right-click **NTDS Settings** and click **Properties**.
2. In the General tab, you can select or clear the Global Catalog option to configure whether the server is a global catalog server. Click the **Connections** tab. Note that ServerSA1 appears in the Replicate To list box (see Figure 5-14). Click **Cancel**.

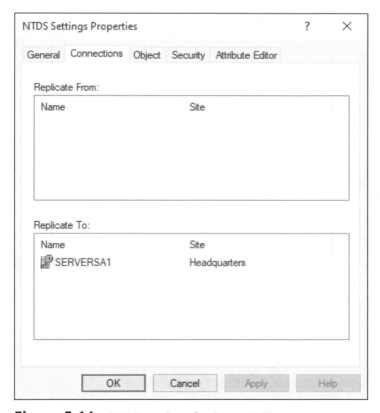

Figure 5-14   NTDS settings for ServerDC1

3. In the left pane, click **Headquarters**. In the right pane, right-click **NTDS Site Settings** and click **Properties** to open the dialog box shown in Figure 5-15. There are NTDS settings associated with server objects and NTDS site settings associated with site objects.
4. Click the **Change Schedule** button to open the Schedule for NTDS Site Settings dialog box. As you can see, the regular schedule for intersite replication is once per hour. Click **Cancel**.
5. Notice the Enable Universal Group Membership Caching check box, which is where you enable this feature if the DC isn't a global catalog server. Because it is, enabling this feature has no effect. In the "Refresh cache from" list box, you can select a site for refreshing the cache. Click **Cancel**.

(continues)

Activity 5-5 Continued

Figure 5-15   The NTDS Site Settings Properties dialog box

6. Close Active Directory Sites and Services and continue to the next activity.

Active Directory Replication

Microsoft Exam AZ-800:
Deploy and manage Active Directory Domain Services (AD DS) in on-premises and cloud environments.
   • Configure and manage multisite, multidomain, and multiforest environments.

Timely and reliable replication of data between domain controllers is paramount to a functioning Active Directory domain and forest. Active Directory replication includes the following types of information:

- Active Directory objects, such as OUs and user, group, and computer accounts
- Changes to data held in partitions maintained by FSMO role holders
- Trust relationships
- Global catalog data
- Group policy information
- Files located in SYSVOL, such as group policy templates and scripts

Most replication data is generated by changes to Active Directory objects and group policies. Active Directory replication occurs within sites (called "intrasite replication") and between sites (called "intersite replication"). The following sections cover managing both types of replication along with RODC replication and SYSVOL replication, as well as tools to help you monitor and troubleshoot replication.

Active Directory Intrasite Replication

Efficient and accurate replication of changes made to the Active Directory database is critical in a Windows domain. Intrasite and intersite replication use the same basic processes to replicate Active Directory data; the main goal is to balance replication timeliness and efficiency. To that end, the replication strategy between DCs within a site (intrasite) is optimized for high-speed, low-latency LAN links. Intersite replication involves two main components—the KCC and connection objects—and is optimized to take slower WAN links into account. It can be initiated in one of two ways:

- *Notification*—When a change is made to the Active Directory database, the DC on which the change was made notifies its replication partners. The partners then request replication from the notifying DC.
- *Periodic replication*—To account for missed updates, DCs request replication from their partners periodically. The interval can be configured in the connection object's Properties dialog box (as explained later in the "Connection Objects" section).

Knowledge Consistency Checker

For intrasite replication, the KCC builds a replication topology for DCs in a site and establishes replication partners. As shown in Figure 5-16, each DC in a site has one or more replication partners. For example, DC3 is partners with DC2, DC4, and DC5. The topology is designed to ensure that no more than two DCs lie in the replication path between two domain controllers. To put it another way, data in a replication transfer doesn't have to travel more than three hops to reach its destination DC. For example, if Active Directory data on DC1 changes, the changes have to hop through DC4 and DC6 to reach DC7. A domain controller waits 15 seconds after an Active Directory change before replicating with its partners, with a 3-second delay between partners. This arrangement guarantees that all DCs in a site receive changes in less than a minute.

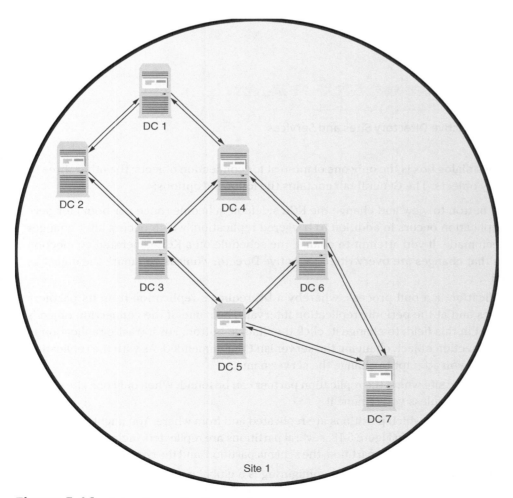

Figure 5-16   Intrasite replication partners

The KCC on each DC uses data stored in the forest-wide configuration directory partition to create the replication topology. The configuration directory partition is replicated to all DCs in the forest, so the KCCs don't need to communicate with one another. Because they all run the same algorithm on the same data, the KCCs on domain controllers create the same replication topology. The KCC recalculates the replication topology every 15 minutes by default to make sure the topology accurately reflects DCs that come online or go offline. If necessary, the replication topology can be recalculated manually in Active Directory Sites and Services. You might need to do this after you have added, changed, or removed connection objects, for example. To do so, right-click the NTDS Settings node under a domain controller, point to All Tasks, and click Check Replication Topology. The partnership between DCs is controlled by a connection object, which the KCC creates automatically for intrasite replication.

Connection Objects

A **connection object** defines the connection parameters between two replication partners. The KCC generates these parameters automatically between intrasite DCs. Generally, you don't need to make changes to intrasite connection objects, but if you do, you can change them in Active Directory Sites and Services. Figure 5-17 shows connection objects in Active Directory Sites and Services, and Figure 5-18 shows the Properties dialog box for one of the objects.

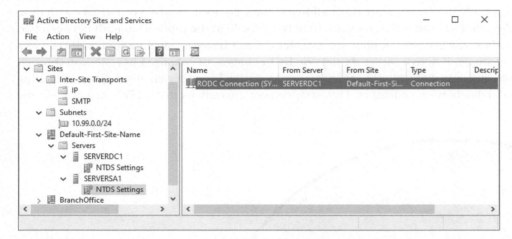

Figure 5-17   Connection objects in Active Directory Sites and Services

The General tab in the Properties dialog box is the only one of interest for connection objects; the other three tabs are the same for all Active Directory objects. The General tab contains the following options:

- *Change Schedule*—Click this button to view and change the KCC's default schedule (once per hour) for periodic replication. Periodic replication occurs in addition to triggered replication, which occurs after changes to Active Directory have been made. If you attempt to change the schedule on a KCC-generated connection object, Windows warns you that changes are overwritten by Active Directory unless you mark the object as not automatically generated.

- *Replicate from Server*—Replication is a pull process, whereby a DC requests replication from its partners after being notified of changes and at the periodic replication interval. The name of the connection object's replication partner is specified in this field; to change it, click the Change button. For intrasite replication in which the KCC creates the connection object, changing the server isn't recommended. As with the replication schedule, Windows warns you if you attempt to change the server name.

- *Replicate from Site*—The name of the site where the replication partner can be found. When only one site exists, this name is Default-First-Site-Name unless you rename it.

- *Replicated Naming Context(s)*—Specifies which partitions are replicated and from where. You might not see the full list because the text box isn't very wide. In Figure 5-18, several partitions are replicated, including the forest-wide and domain-wide DNS partitions, the domain partition, the schema partition, and the configuration partition.

- *Partially Replicated Naming Context(s)*—If the DC you're configuring is a global catalog server, a list displays other domains from which partial Active Directory data is replicated; "All other domains" appears if there are no additional domains in the forest. This text box is usually empty if the DC isn't a global catalog server.

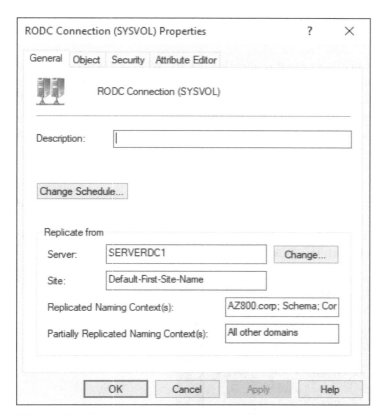

Figure 5-18   The Properties dialog box for a connection object

Creating Connection Objects

You can create connection objects for intrasite replication if you want to alter the replication topology manually. You might want to alter the topology if a site includes WAN links that could benefit from a different replication schedule. To create a connection object, right-click NTDS Settings under the applicable server and click New Active Directory Domain Services Connection. You're asked to select a DC as a replication partner, and the connection object is named after this server by default. By default, the schedule for a new connection object is set to every 15 minutes, but you can change this value.

Creating a connection object is usually unnecessary, but it can be useful for troubleshooting replication problems or for creating special replication schedules between DCs. The KCC uses the new connection object in its topology calculations and might alter the topology as a result. You must be sure of what you're doing before making manual changes to the intrasite replication topology or you could break replication.

If you do make changes, right-click the NTDS Settings node, point to All Tasks, and click Check Replication Topology to run the KCC algorithm. If you created a connection manually to a server that already exists, the KCC deletes the automatically generated connection and leaves the manually created connection. If you remove the manually created connection, the KCC generally re-creates the original topology.

Special Replication Scenarios

Some changes to Active Directory objects require special handling, called **urgent replication**. This event triggers immediate notification that a change has occurred instead of waiting for the normal 15-second interval before replication partners are notified. Urgent replication events include the following:

- Account lockout changes sent immediately to the primary domain controller (PDC) emulator, which then replicates the event to other DCs
- Changes to the account lockout policy
- Changes to the password policy
- Changes to a local security authority secret, such as a trust relationship password

- Password changes to DC computer accounts
- Changes to the relative identifier (RID) master role holder

Password changes are handled slightly differently from other urgent replication events. When a password change occurs, the DC handling the change immediately transmits the new password to the PDC emulator, and the PDC emulator uses normal intrasite replication procedures. If a user attempts to log on to a DC with an incorrect password, the DC contacts the PDC emulator to see whether a password change has occurred before denying the authentication attempt. This process allows users to log on immediately after a password change, even if not all DCs have been updated with the change.

Checking Replication Status

You can use Active Directory Sites and Services to force the KCC to check the replication topology, but if you want to view detailed information about connections and replication status, use the command-line program repadmin. exe. Many arguments can be used with this command, but to view replication status, use repadmin /showrepl. Figure 5-19 shows the output of this command in a domain with two DCs. Each replication partner is listed.

```
C:\Users\Administrator>repadmin /showrepl

Repadmin: running command /showrepl against full DC localhost
Default-First-Site-Name\SERVERDC1
DSA Options: IS_GC
Site Options: (none)
DSA object GUID: b44b9568-0661-41e7-99d9-533540293934
DSA invocationID: c81d103a-8bbd-4fc5-8526-03c4e5a6f185

==== INBOUND NEIGHBORS ======================================

DC=AZ800,DC=corp
    Default-First-Site-Name\SERVER19DM1 via RPC
        DSA object GUID: f0d450f6-97ef-4f84-aaa2-60847970c17b
        Last attempt @ 2022-10-12 19:02:03 was successful.

CN=Configuration,DC=AZ800,DC=corp
    Default-First-Site-Name\SERVER19DM1 via RPC
        DSA object GUID: f0d450f6-97ef-4f84-aaa2-60847970c17b
        Last attempt @ 2022-10-12 19:01:48 was successful.

CN=Schema,CN=Configuration,DC=AZ800,DC=corp
    Default-First-Site-Name\SERVER19DM1 via RPC
        DSA object GUID: f0d450f6-97ef-4f84-aaa2-60847970c17b
        Last attempt @ 2022-10-12 19:01:19 was successful.
```

Figure 5-19 Output of the repadmin /showrepl command

Each section of the output lists a directory partition followed by the DCs from which the partition is replicated. For example, the first line under INBOUND NEIGHBORS specifies the domain partition, and the second line shows that a server domain controller is a replication partner for this partition. The next two lines show the connection object's GUID and the status of the last replication attempt. Each replication partner is listed, along with the status of the last replication attempt. Other partitions are represented in the subsequent lines of output. You can also use repadmin to show the partitions being replicated by each connection object, to force replication to occur, to force the KCC to recalculate the topology, and other actions.

> **Note** 6
>
> Entering `repadmin /?` doesn't show all the available parameters. To learn more about this command and see the full list of parameters, visit *https://learn.microsoft.com/en-us/previous-versions/windows/it-pro/windows-server-2012-r2-and-2012/cc770963(v=ws.11)*.

Active Directory Intersite Replication

You've learned that intrasite replication occurs among several domain controllers after the KCC creates the topology. Intersite replication, however, occurs between bridgehead servers. When the KCC detects that replication must occur between sites, one DC in each site is designated as the ISTG, which assigns a bridgehead server to handle replication for each directory partition. Because bridgehead servers perform such a vital function in multisite networks, and this function can consume considerable server resources, the administrator can override automatic assignment of a bridgehead server and assign the role to a specific DC.

You might need to designate bridgehead servers manually. Perhaps you've identified a DC in a site that's less burdened by other server tasks and is better able to handle the task than the server the ISTG identified. You can use the `repadmin /bridgeheads` command to list which DCs in a site are acting as bridgehead servers to other sites.

After determining which DCs are currently acting as bridgehead servers, you can designate preferred bridgehead servers in Active Directory Sites and Services. Find the server in the Servers folder under the site, right-click the server object, and click Properties. Select the intersite transport protocol on the left (see Figure 5-20) and add it to the "This server is a preferred bridgehead server for the following transports" list box. You need to make sure all directory partitions in the site are contained on the bridgehead servers you configure. If you don't, Windows warns you about which partitions the configured bridgehead servers won't replicate. Replication still takes place for these partitions because Windows configures the necessary bridgehead servers automatically, but relying on this automatic configuration defeats the purpose of assigning bridgehead servers manually.

Figure 5-20   Configuring a bridgehead server

> **Caution** ⓘ
>
> If a manually configured bridgehead server fails, replication stops for the partitions it contains. The ISTG doesn't configure a new bridgehead server automatically if a manually configured bridgehead server fails. However, if the ISTG assigns a bridgehead server and it fails, the ISTG attempts to assign a new one automatically.

Intersite Transport Protocols

Two protocols can be used to replicate between sites: IP and Simple Mail Transport Protocol (SMTP). By default, IP is used in the DEFAULTIPSITELINK site link and is recommended in most cases. To be precise, when you choose IP as the intersite transport protocol, you're choosing Remote Procedure Call (RPC) over IP. RPC over IP uses synchronous communication, which requires a reliable network connection with low latency. With synchronous communication, a reply is expected immediately when a request is made, and the entire process of replication with one DC finishes before the process can begin with another DC.

If your network connections don't lend themselves to RPC over IP, you can use SMTP, which is used primarily for email. It's an asynchronous protocol that works well for slower, less reliable, or intermittent connections. The advantage of SMTP is that a DC can send multiple replication requests simultaneously without waiting for a reply; the reply can occur sometime later. So, if you think of SMTP as an email conversation, you can liken RPC over IP to a chat session.

SMTP requires fairly complex configuration and the administrative effort is rarely worth it, particularly with today's fast and reliable WAN connections. In addition, SMTP can't be used to replicate domain directory partitions, so it can't be used in domains spanning multiple sites. It can be used only to replicate the schema, global catalog, and configuration partitions. In a nutshell, here are the requirements for the bridgehead servers on both ends of an SMTP-configured site link:

- The SMTP feature must be installed on both servers.
- An enterprise certification authority must be configured on the network.
- The site link path must have a lower cost than an RPC over IP site link.
- You can't have DCs from the same domain in both sites.
- DCs must be configured to receive email.

> **Note** ⑦
>
> RPC over IP is the only replication protocol used in intrasite replication.

Site Link Bridges

As mentioned, site link bridging is a property of a site link that makes the link transitive. Site link bridging is enabled by default; however, in some circumstances, you don't want all site links to be transitive, as when some WAN links are slow or available only sporadically (with a dial-up connection, for example). To change the transitive behavior of site links, turn off site link bridging and create site link bridges manually, which enables you to manage replication traffic between sites more efficiently with some network topologies.

Figure 5-21 shows a network with a hub-and-spoke WAN topology. Because of the transitive nature of site links, Site1 replicates with bridgehead servers in Site2 and can also replicate with bridgehead servers in Site2A, Site2B, and Site2C. If WAN connections between all sites are fast and reliable, with plenty of bandwidth for replication traffic, this default behavior works well.

Keep in mind, however, that the same replication traffic is crossing WAN links four times, one for each site. On slower or heavily used WAN links between Site1 and Site2, this extra traffic could be excessive. To control the flow of replication traffic better, disable automatic site link bridging and create site link bridges between Site1 and Site2 and between Site2 and its satellites. Replication traffic still flows between Site1 and Site2, but Site2 distributes the traffic to satellite sites, so replication traffic crosses the Site1–Site2 WAN link only one time. You would probably want to create site link bridges in the opposite direction, too.

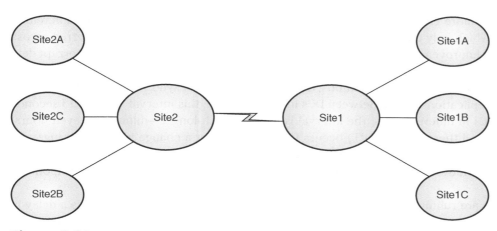

Figure 5-21   A hub-and-spoke topology

Other reasons to create site link bridges manually include the following:

- *Control traffic through firewalls*—You might want to limit which DCs can communicate with one another directly through firewalls. You can configure firewalls to allow traffic between DCs at specific sites and create site link bridges as needed.
- *Accommodate partially routed networks*—Normally, the KCC considers all possible connections when determining the replication topology. If sites are connected only intermittently, you can configure site link bridges between only the sites that map to full-time network connections, which bypasses intermittent links.
- *Reduce confusion of the KCC*—A complex network involving many alternative paths between sites can cause confusion when the KCC and ISTG create the replication topology. You can force what kind of topology is created by using custom site link bridges and disabling transitivity.

To disable transitivity of site links, right-click the IP or SMTP folder under Inter-Site Transports and click Properties, and then click to clear the "Bridge all site links" check box. To create a site link bridge, right-click the IP or SMTP folder and click New Site Link Bridge. Give a descriptive name to the site link bridge, and then add at least two site links to it.

Exam Tip ✔

The Microsoft exam expects you to understand how to manage replication in multiple sites using connection objects and site links.

SYSVOL Replication

Not all Active Directory–related data is stored on Active Directory partitions. Some crucial information for domain operation is stored as files in the SYSVOL share on domain controllers, including group policy template files, the ADMX central store, and logon scripts. SYSVOL replication uses the same replication service as Distributed File System (DFS), called Distributed File System Replication (DFSR). Versions of Windows Server before Windows Server 2008 used File Replication Service (FRS).

Group Policy Replication

A Group Policy object (GPO) is composed of a group policy template (GPT) and a group policy container (GPC). A GPC is an Active Directory object stored in the Active Directory domain partition, and a GPT is a collection of files stored in the SYSVOL share. Because these two components are stored in different places on a DC, different methods are required to replicate GPOs to all domain controllers. GPCs are replicated during normal Active Directory replication, and GPTs are replicated with one of these methods:

- *File Replication Service*—FRS is used with DCs running Windows Server 2003 and Windows 2000 Server.
- *Distributed File System Replication*—DFSR is used when all DCs are running Windows Server 2008 and later.

Of these two methods, DFSR is more efficient and reliable. It's efficient because it uses the remote differential compression (RDC) algorithm, in which only data blocks that have changed are compressed and transferred across the network. It's reliable because of improvements in handling unexpected service shutdowns that could corrupt data and because it uses a multimaster replication scheme.

Because the GPC and GPT use different replication methods, they can become out of sync. As mentioned, GPCs are replicated when Active Directory replication occurs. Between DCs in the same site, this interval is about 15 seconds after a change occurs. Between DCs in different sites, the interval is usually much longer—minutes or even hours. Replication of the SYSVOL share (and therefore the GPT) occurs immediately after a change is made. Strange and unpredictable results could occur when a client computer attempts to apply a GPO and the GPC and GPT aren't synchronized. However, starting with Windows XP, the client computer checks the version number of both components before applying GPO settings.

As long as replication services are running correctly, the most likely problem with GPO replication is a delay in clients receiving changes in policy settings. This problem usually occurs when multiple sites are involved. Replication problems can be diagnosed with the Group Policy Management console (GPMC) by selecting the GPO in the left pane, clicking the Status tab in the right pane, and clicking the Detect Now button (see Figure 5-22).

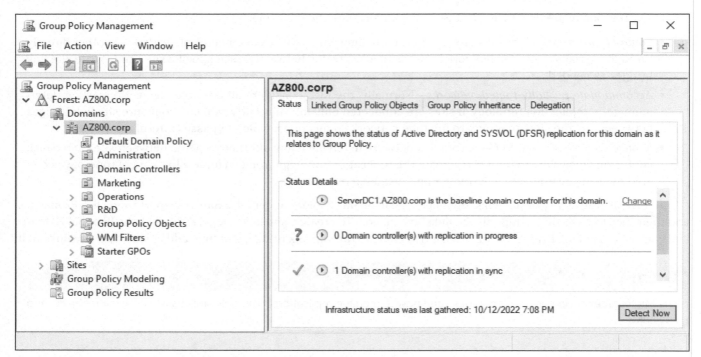

Figure 5-22   Checking the status of Group Policy replication

Upgrading to DFSR

If your domain includes Windows Server 2003 or older DCs, it's using FRS to replicate SYSVOL, and you should migrate to the more reliable DFSR as soon as possible. Even if you have upgraded all servers to Windows Server 2008 and later versions, FRS might still be running if your domain once contained older DCs and you haven't migrated to DFSR. Before migrating from FRS to DFSR, you need to understand the four phases of migration, referred to as "migration states":

- *State 0 - Start*—The C:\Windows\SYSVOL folder is present and mapped to the SYSVOL share, and is being replicated with FRS.
- *State 1 - Prepared*—The SYSVOL share continues to be replicated with FRS. A new folder named SYSVOL_DFSR has been created; it contains a copy of the SYSVOL share and is being replicated with DFSR.
- *State 2 - Redirected*—The SYSVOL_DFSR folder is mapped to the SYSVOL share and is being replicated with DFSR. FRS continues to replicate the old C:\Windows\SYSVOL folder, which is no longer mapped to the SYSVOL share.
- *State 3 - Eliminated*—The SYSVOL_DFSR folder is mapped to the SYSVOL share and continues to be replicated with DFSR. The original C:\Windows\SYSVOL folder is deleted, and FRS replication no longer occurs.

Note 8

You can use `dfsrmig /getmigrationstate` to see whether you need to perform DFSR migration. If you don't, the following message is displayed: "All domain controllers have migrated successfully to the Global state ('Eliminated'). Migration has reached a consistent state on all domain controllers."

Migrating from FRS to DFSR is done with the `dfsrmig` command-line tool on a writeable DC (not an RODC). Before beginning, do a system state backup on domain controllers with the command `wbadmin start systemstatebackup`. The steps for FRS-to-DFSR migration are as follows:

1. To verify that all DCs are operating in at least the Windows Server 2008 functional level, open Active Directory Domains and Trusts, right-click the domain, and then click Raise domain functional level. The current domain functional level is shown. Raise it to at least Windows Server 2008, if necessary.

2. To migrate the domain to the Prepared state, open a command prompt window, type `dfsrmig /setglobalstate 1`, and press Enter. To verify that all DCs have migrated to the Prepared state, type `dfsrmig /getmigrationstate` and press Enter. Output similar to the following appears:

```
All Domain Controllers have migrated successfully to Global state ('Prepared').
Migration has reached a consistent state on all Domain Controllers.
Succeeded.
```

3. To migrate the domain to the Redirected state, type `dfsrmig /setglobalstate 2` and press Enter. To verify that all DCs have migrated to the Redirected state, type `dfsrmig /getmigrationstate` and press Enter. Output similar to the following appears:

```
All Domain Controllers have migrated successfully to Global state ('Redirected').
Migration has reached a consistent state on all Domain Controllers.
Succeeded.
```

4. Before migrating the domain to the Eliminated state, verify that replication is working correctly by typing `repadmin /replsum` and pressing Enter. There should be no errors reported. After this final step, you can't revert to FRS replication. Type `dfsrmig /setglobalstate 3` and press Enter. To verify that all DCs have migrated to the Eliminated state, type `dfsrmig /getmigrationstate` and press Enter. Output similar to the following appears:

```
All Domain Controllers have migrated successfully to Global state ('Eliminated').
Migration has reached a consistent state on all Domain Controllers.
Succeeded.
```

5. To verify the migration, type `net share` and press Enter on all DCs. The NETLOGON share should be mapped to the C:\Windows\SYSVOL_DFSR\sysvol*DomainName*\SCRIPTS folder, and the SYSVOL share should be mapped to the C:\Windows\SYSVOL_DFSR\sysvol folder.

6. Unless you're using FRS for some other purpose, stop and disable the service by typing `sc stop ntfrs` and pressing Enter on each DC. Then type `sc config ntfrs start=disabled` and press Enter on each DC.

Managing Replication

Active Directory and SYSVOL replication usually work fine with the built-in scheduling and processes. However, you might want to force replication to occur for troubleshooting or testing purposes or just so that you don't have to wait for the normal replication schedule between sites. The main tool for controlling Active Directory replication is the `repadmin` command-line program. Some commonly used variations of the `repadmin` command are shown in the following list:

- `repadmin /replicate`—This command causes replication of a specified partition from one DC to another. For example, to replicate the domain directory partition from ServerDC1 to ServerSA1, use the following command. Note that the destination DC (the DC you're replicating to) is listed first, followed by the source DC (the DC you're replicating from).

  ```
  repadmin /replicate ServerSA1 ServerDC1 dc=AZ800,dc=local
  ```

If one of the servers is an RODC, add the /readonly switch to the end of the command.

- repadmin /syncall—This command forces replication to occur between the specified DC and all its replication partners. All partitions are synchronized unless you specify a partition. For example, the following command synchronizes all partitions on ServerDC1 with all its replication partners:

```
repadmin /syncall ServerDC1
```

- repadmin /kcc—This command causes the KCC to check the replication topology and update it, if necessary. You should use it if you have recently made changes to the domain or forest, such as adding or removing domains or domain controllers, or if you have recently upgraded older DCs to Windows Server 2012/R2.

Managing Replication with Active Directory Sites and Services

With Active Directory Sites and Services, you can force replication to occur and force the KCC to check the replication topology. To cause replication to occur, expand the site node where the server on which you want to force replication is located. Expand the Servers node, click the target DC, and then click the NTDS Settings object. Right-click the connection object connecting the server on which you want to force replication and click Replicate Now (see Figure 5-23). In the figure, ServerDC1 replicates immediately with ServerSA1.

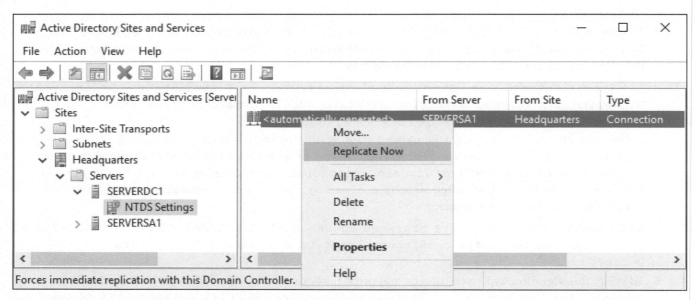

Figure 5-23   Forcing replication in Active Directory Sites and Services

To force the KCC to check the replication topology, right-click the NTDS Settings object under a DC, point to All Tasks, and click Check Replication Topology.

Note 9

The Sync-ADObject PowerShell cmdlet forces replication of a single specified Active Directory object between two specified DCs.

Self-Check Questions

7. The ISTG defines the connection parameters between two replication objects. True or False?

   a. True   b. False

8. What should you configure if you want to alter the Active Directory intrasite replication topology manually?

   a. Bridgehead server   c. Site link bridge
   b. Intersite topology generator   d. Connection object

⊙Check your answers at the end of this module.

Activity 5-6

Working with Connection Objects

Time Required: 15 minutes
Objective: View and change properties of connection objects.
Required Tools and Equipment: ServerDC1 and ServerSA1
Description: In this activity, you explore the properties of NTDS Site Settings, server NTDS Settings, and connection objects.

1. On ServerDC1, open **Active Directory Sites and Services**.
2. Click to expand **Sites**, and then click **Headquarters**. Two objects are displayed in the right pane: the Servers folder, which lists the DCs in the site, and NTDS Site Settings.
3. In the right pane, double-click to expand the **Servers** folder and then double-click **ServerDC1**. Right-click **NTDS Settings** and click **Properties** to open the dialog box shown in Figure 5-24. (Notice that there are NTDS settings associated with server objects and site objects.)

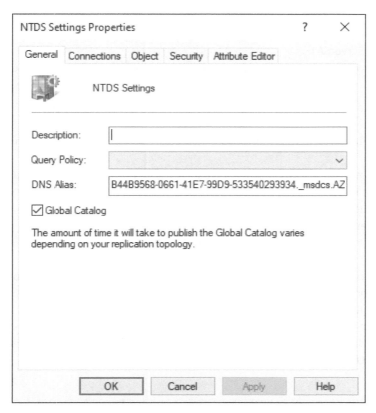

Figure 5-24   The NTDS Settings Properties dialog box

(continues)

Activity 5-6 Continued

4. In the General tab, you can configure the server as a global catalog server. Click the **Connections** tab. You should see ServerSA1 in the Replicate To text box. Because ServerSA1 is an RODC, it is not shown in the Replicate From box. Click **Cancel**.

5. In the left pane, click **NTDS Settings** under ServerSA1. In the right pane, right-click the connection object. Notice that Replicate Now is an option, which you can use to force replication to occur immediately. Click **Properties**.

6. Click the **Change Schedule** button. The regular schedule for intrasite replication is once per hour. Click **Cancel**, and then click **Cancel** again.

7. In the left pane, click **Headquarters**. In the right pane, right-click **NTDS Site Settings** and click **Properties**.

8. In the Site Settings tab, click **Change Schedule**. In the Schedule for NTDS Site Settings dialog box, click **All**, and then click the **Four Times per Hour** option button. Changing the replication schedule here changes it for all automatically generated connections in the site. Click **OK** twice.

9. To verify that the schedule has changed, click **NTDS Settings** under ServerSA1 again. Double-click the connection object to open its Properties dialog box and then click the **Change Schedule** button. (The schedule change might take a while to occur under each server. Eventually, the change at the site level overwrites the server settings.) Click the **All** button on the upper-left side of the day/time table, click the **Once per Hour** option button, and then click **OK** twice.

10. Continue to the next activity.

Activity 5-7

Creating a Site Link

Time Required: 10 minutes
Objective: Create a site link.
Required Tools and Equipment: ServerDC1, ServerSA1
Description: In this activity, you create a site link to configure replication between the Headquarters and BranchOffice sites.

1. On ServerDC1, in Active Directory Sites and Services, click to expand **Sites** and **Inter-Site Transports**, if necessary. Click the **IP** folder.

2. Right-click the **IP** folder and click **New Site Link**. In the Properties dialog box, type **SiteLinkHQ-BO** in the Name text box.

3. Because only two sites are defined and a site link must contain at least two sites, both BranchOffice and Headquarters are added to the "Sites in this site link" list box. If there were more than two sites, you would choose two or more sites to include in the site link. Click **OK**.

4. In the right pane of Active Directory Sites and Services, right-click **SiteLinkHQ-BO** and click **Properties**. Click the **Change Schedule** button. Notice that replication takes place all day every day, which is the default setting for site links.

5. Drag to form a box around Monday through Friday from 8 a.m. to 3 p.m., and then click **Replication Not Available**. Now Headquarters and BranchOffice won't attempt to replicate during these times. Click **OK**.

6. Click in the Cost text box and type **200**. Recall that the higher the cost of the link, the less attractive it is when the topology is generated. If there are multiple paths between destinations, the lower-cost path is selected. In this case, DEFAULTIPSITELINK also contains Headquarters and BranchOffice and has a cost of 100, so it's the preferred site link. Click **OK**.

7. Continue to the next activity.

Activity 5-8

Managing Replication

Time Required: 10 minutes
Objective: Manage replication with Active Directory Sites and Services and with the command line.
Required Tools and Equipment: ServerDC1 and ServerSA1
Description: In this activity, you learn how to force replication to occur and how to check the replication topology by using Active Directory Sites and Services and command-line tools.

1. Sign in to **ServerSA1** as Administrator, open **Active Directory Sites and Services**, and navigate to ServerSA1 under Headquarters. Click to expand **ServerSA1** and click **NTDS Settings** in the left pane.
2. In the right pane, right-click the connection object and click **Replicate Now**. Click **OK** in the message box.
3. Open a command prompt window, type **repadmin /showrepl**, and press **Enter**. Detailed information appears regarding partitions that were replicated, the date and time of the last attempt, and whether it was successful. The information should show that the last attempt just occurred and was successful.
4. Type **repadmin /replsum** and press **Enter**. A less detailed summary of the most recent replication appears (see Figure 5-25). There are two parts to the display: Source DSA and Destination DSA. The Source DSA indicates the server that data is being transferred from, and the Destination DSA indicates the server to which data is being transferred. The "largest delta" column shows the last time replication occurred. Notice that for ServerDC1, under Source DSA, the time shows just a few seconds or minutes; under Destination DSA, the times are reversed.

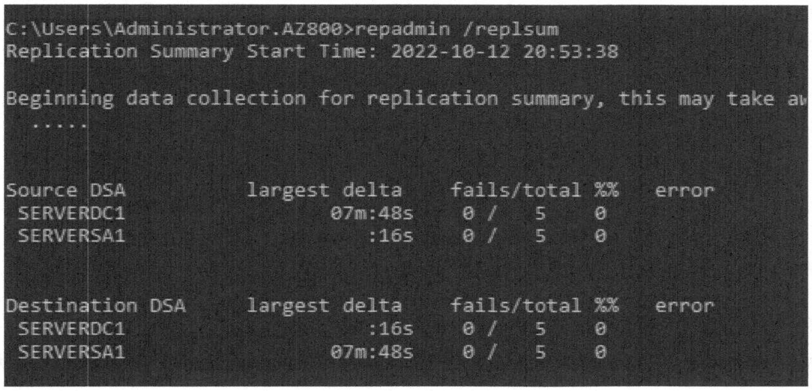

```
C:\Users\Administrator.AZ800>repadmin /replsum
Replication Summary Start Time: 2022-10-12 20:53:38

Beginning data collection for replication summary, this may take aw
    .....


Source DSA          largest delta     fails/total %%    error
  SERVERDC1                 07m:48s     0 /    5      0
  SERVERSA1                    :16s     0 /    5      0


Destination DSA     largest delta     fails/total %%    error
  SERVERDC1                    :16s     0 /    5      0
  SERVERSA1                 07m:48s     0 /    5      0
```

Figure 5-25   Output of `repadmin /replsum`

5. In Active Directory Sites and Services, right-click the **NTDS Settings** object under ServerSA1, point to **All Tasks**, and click **Check Replication Topology**. Read the message. Click **OK** in the message box. Because no changes have been made to the domain, the topology won't change.
6. On ServerSA1, at the command prompt, type **repadmin /replicate ServerSA1 ServerDC1 dc=AZ800,dc=corp** and press **Enter**. A message states that the sync was completed successfully. In this command, the source DC is ServerDC1, and the destination DC is ServerSA1. Recall that this command replicates only the domain partition unless additional partitions are specified.
7. Type **repadmin /replsum** and press **Enter**. You'll probably see that the replication doesn't seem to have happened because the timers weren't reset. However, `repadmin /replicate` replicates only changes; if no changes occurred since the last replication, no replication takes place.
8. Type **repadmin /syncall** and press **Enter**. This command replicates all partitions as needed.
9. Type **repadmin /showrepl** and press **Enter**. The most likely partition to have changed that requires replication is the Configuration partition.

(continues)

Activity 5-8 Continued

10. Type **dcdiag /test:replications** and press **Enter**. The output indicates whether a connection can be made and the results of tests run on each Active Directory partition. Any replication errors are shown in the output.

11. Shut down ServerDC1. After ServerDC1 is shut down, type **dcdiag /test:replications** and press **Enter**. Because ServerSA1 was shut down, the command takes a while to time out. The output indicates that replication failed.

12. Type **repadmin /replicate ServerSA1 ServerDC1 dc=AZ800,dc=local corp** and press **Enter**. Because ServerDC1 was shut down, the command takes a while to time out. After it does, type **repadmin /showrepl** and press **Enter**. You should see that there was an error replicating the domain partition because it's the partition you attempted to replicate.

13. Type **repadmin /replsum** and press **Enter**. The output indicates that errors occurred in replication. A message states, "The RPC server is unavailable."

14. Shut down ServerSA1.

Working with Operations Master Roles

Microsoft Exam AZ-800:
Deploy and manage Active Directory Domain Services (AD DS) in on-premises and cloud environments.
- Deploy and manage AD DS domain controllers.
- Configure and manage multisite, multidomain, and multiforest environments.

Active Directory uses a multimaster replication scheme to synchronize copies of most information in the Active Directory database. However, some critical information is subject to a single master replication scheme to avoid any possibility of the information becoming unsynchronized. The servers that keep this critical information are assigned a **Flexible Single Master Operation (FSMO) role**. FSMO roles can be summarized as follows:

- *Forest-wide FSMO roles*—Only one DC per forest performs these roles: domain naming master and schema master.
- *Domain-wide FSMO roles*—Only one DC per domain performs these roles: PDC emulator, RID master, and infrastructure master.

This section discusses best practices for locating these DCs in your network for optimal reliability and replication efficiency and explains how to transfer and seize FSMO roles when you need to assign a role to a different DC.

Operations Master Best Practices

The decision of where to place an FSMO role holder is part of your overall Active Directory design strategy. If you create a new forest, the first DC installed performs all five FSMO roles listed in the following sections. When a new domain is created after the forest root domain, the first DC performs all three domain-wide FSMO roles for that domain, and a DC in the forest root domain handles the forest-wide roles. In a smaller network, having all these critical roles on a single server can work, but in a large network with multiple domains and sites, you might need to transfer some roles to different servers. Placement of the DCs functioning in these roles can affect replication and the capability to recover from a server failure. In addition, being able to restore the functioning of FSMO roles quickly after a server failure is critical. However, not all FSMOs have equal importance; some roles must be functioning almost continuously for correct domain operation, but other roles can be offline for a while with little disturbance to the network. Here are some common rules for operations masters:

- Unless your domain is very small, transfer some operations master roles from the first DC installed in the forest to other DCs because some FSMO roles require a lot of resources.

- Place the servers performing these roles where network availability is high.
- Designate an alternate DC for all roles. The alternate assumes the role if the original server fails, and it should be a direct replication partner with the original FSMO role holder. Document your plan to make sure alternate DCs aren't burdened with other services that could impede their performance as an FSMO role holder.

The following sections explain best practices with FSMO roles in more detail.

Domain Naming Master

The **domain naming master** manages adding, removing, and renaming domains in the forest. There's only one domain naming master per forest, and the DC with this role must be available when domains are added, deleted, or renamed. In most cases, neither users nor administrators notice its absence until one of these operations is attempted. If the DC performing this role goes offline, you should probably wait until it comes back online before attempting to add or remove a domain or DC. The exception, of course, is if you need to add a domain to the network immediately. If you decide to install this role on another DC, the original domain naming master server must not be put back into service unless you uninstall Active Directory.

When possible, the domain naming master should be a direct replication partner with another DC that's also a global catalog server in the same site. Ideally, the domain naming master should also be a global catalog server. If the role must be moved, the direct replication partner is the preferred choice because it should be most fully replicated with the original FSMO. The domain naming master and the other forest-wide FSMO role, the schema master, can be on the same server but need not be.

Schema Master

The **schema master** is responsible for replicating the schema directory partition to all other domain controllers in the forest when changes occur. It is needed when the Active Directory schema is changed, including raising the forest functional level. Its absence isn't apparent to users or administrators unless a schema change is attempted. Generally, the schema master should be transferred to another server only when you're certain the original server will be down permanently.

PDC Emulator

The **PDC emulator** processes password changes for older Windows clients (Windows 9x and NT) and is used during sign-in authentication. The DC performing this role should be centrally located where there's a high concentration of users to facilitate logons. The PDC emulator is the most heavily used of the FSMO roles and should be placed on a suitable DC. Unless your forest configuration has all DCs configured as GC servers, the PDC emulator should be on a DC that's not a global catalog server because global catalog servers are also used heavily. If the PDC emulator role fails, you might want to move the role to another server immediately. After the original server returns to service, the role can be transferred back to it.

RID Master

All objects in a domain are identified internally by a **security identifier (SID)**. An object's SID is composed of a domain identifier, which is the same for all objects in the domain, and a **relative identifier (RID)**, which is unique for each object. Because objects can be created on any DC (except RODCs), there must be a mechanism that keeps two DCs from issuing the same RID, thereby duplicating an SID. The **RID master** is responsible for issuing unique pools of RIDs to each DC, thereby guaranteeing unique SIDs throughout the domain. The RID master must be available when adding a DC to an existing domain and should be placed in an area where Active Directory objects are created most often, such as near the server administrator's office. This FSMO role must be highly available to other DCs and is ideally placed with the PDC emulator because the PDC emulator uses the RID master's services frequently. Because the RID master doles out RIDs to DCs in blocks of 500, temporary downtime might not be noticed. However, if a DC has exhausted its pool of RIDs, and the RID master isn't available, new objects can't be created in Active Directory on that DC. If the RID master fails, moving this role to another server should be considered only when the original RID master is down permanently.

Infrastructure Master

This DC is responsible for ensuring that changes made to object names in one domain are updated in references to these objects in other domains. A temporary interruption of this role's services probably won't be noticed. This role is most needed when many objects have been moved or renamed in a multidomain environment. The **infrastructure master** role shouldn't be performed by a DC that's also a global catalog server unless all servers in the forest have been configured as global catalog servers or there's only one domain in the forest. However, a global catalog server should be in the same site as the infrastructure master because there's frequent communication between these two roles. If an infrastructure master fails, the role can be moved to another DC, if necessary, and returned to the original server when it's back in service.

> **Caution !**
>
> The only time the infrastructure master and global catalog can be on the same DC is when there's only one domain in the forest or all DCs are configured as global catalog servers. If neither is the case, and the infrastructure master is also a global catalog server, the infrastructure master never finds out-of-date data, so it never replicates changes to other DCs in the domain.

Managing Operations Master Roles

Because of the critical nature of the functions FSMO role holders perform, administrators should be familiar with two important FSMO management operations: transferring and seizing. These two functions enable administrators to change the DC performing the FSMO role to make the Active Directory design more efficient and to recover from server failure. Of course, system backups should always be part of managing disaster recovery.

Transferring Operations Master Roles

Transferring an operations master role means moving the role's function from one DC to another while the original DC is still in operation. This transfer is generally done for one of the following reasons:

- The DC performing the role was the first DC in the forest or domain, and therefore holds all domain-wide or domain- and forest-wide roles. Unless you have only one DC, distributing these roles to other servers is suggested.
- The DC performing the role is being moved from a location that isn't well suited for the role.
- The current DC's performance is inadequate because of the resources the FSMO role requires.
- The current DC is being taken out of service temporarily or permanently.

Aside from the best practices discussed previously, there's one restriction when transferring FSMO roles: An RODC can't be an FSMO role holder. Table 5-2 lists each FSMO role and its corresponding scope, the MMC used to work with the role, and the PowerShell command used to transfer the role to another DC.

In Table 5-2, you can replace the role name with a number to shorten the PowerShell command, as shown in the following list:

- PDC emulator: 0
- RID master: 1
- Infrastructure master: 2
- Schema master: 3
- Domain naming master: 4

> **Note 10**
>
> To seize the role by using PowerShell, add the `-Force` parameter to the command.

You can also use PowerShell or netdom to see which servers carry the FSMO roles:

- `Get-ADForest`—Shows which servers carry forest-wide roles and other forest information.
- `Get-ADDomain`—Shows which servers carry domain-wide roles and other domain information.
- `netdom /query fsmo`—Run this command from a command prompt to list all the FSMO role holders.

Before you begin to work with FSMO roles, you need another writeable DC. In the next activity, you demote your RODC to a member server and then promote it again to a standard DC.

Table 5-2   The MMCs and PowerShell cmdlets for transferring FSMO roles

FSMO role/scope	MMC	PowerShell cmdlet
Schema master/ forest	Active Directory Schema	`Move-ADDirectoryServerOperationMasterRole -Identity "TargetDC" -OperationMasterRole SchemaMaster`
Domain naming master/forest	Active Directory Domains and Trusts	`Move-ADDirectoryServerOperationMasterRole -Identity "TargetDC" -OperationMasterRole DomainNamingMaster`
RID master/ domain	Active Directory Users and Computers	`Move-ADDirectoryServerOperationMasterRole -Identity "TargetDC" -OperationMasterRole RIDMaster`
PDC emulator master/domain	Active Directory Users and Computers	`Move-ADDirectoryServerOperationMasterRole -Identity "TargetDC" -OperationMasterRole PDCEmulator`
Infrastructure master/domain	Active Directory Users and Computers	`Move-ADDirectoryServerOperationMasterRole -Identity "TargetDC" -OperationMasterRole InfrastructureMaster`

Exam Tip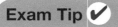

The AZ-800 exam expects you to know the various methods you can use to see which DCs hold the FSMO roles.

Seizing Operations Master Roles

An operations master role is seized when the current role holder is no longer online because of some type of failure. Seizing should never be done when the current role holder is accessible and should usually be done only when it's unlikely the original server can be restored to service. If a DC is scheduled to be decommissioned, you should transfer the role while the DC is still online. If the operations master DC becomes inaccessible because of network failure or a temporary hardware failure, you should wait until this server is back online rather than seize the operations master role.

An exception might be the PDC emulator role, which can affect user logons, or the RID master, which might be needed to create Active Directory objects. If either role holder is going to be offline for an extended period, seizing the role and then transferring it to the original DC when it's back online might be best for continued Active Directory operation. You can't use MMCs to seize a role. You must use the PowerShell cmdlets in Table 5-2 with the `-Force` option or use `ntdsutil` from the command line, as shown in these steps:

1. Open a command prompt window, type `ntdsutil`, and press Enter.
2. Type `roles` and press Enter to get the FSMO Maintenance prompt.
3. Type `connections` and press Enter to get the Server Connections prompt.
4. Type `connect to server` *DCName*, replacing *DCName* with the domain controller where you're transferring the FSMO role.
5. Type `quit` to get back to the FSMO Maintenance prompt.
6. Type `seize` *RoleName* and press Enter, replacing *RoleName* with the name of the role you want to seize. Possible role names are domain naming master, schema master, PDC emulator, RID master, and infrastructure master.
7. Windows attempts to transfer the role first; if a transfer fails, the role is seized. Type `quit` and press Enter to exit `ntdsutil`.

Self-Check Questions

9. The schema master is a domain-wide FSMO role. True or False?

   a. True   **b.** False

10. Which FSMO role is responsible for issuing unique pools of values that are used when creating Active Directory objects?

   a. Schema master   **c.** RID master
   b. PDC emulator   **d.** Infrastructure master

⊙Check your answers at the end of this module.

Activity 5-9

Changing an RODC to a Standard DC

Time Required: 20 minutes
Objective: Change an RODC to a standard writeable DC.
Required Tools and Equipment: ServerDC1, ServerSA1
Description: You want to transfer some FSMO roles from ServerDC1 to ServerSA1, but first you must change ServerSA1 from an RODC to a standard DC. You use PowerShell for this task.

1. Start ServerDC1 and ServerSA1, if necessary. Sign in to ServerSA1 as **Administrator**. On ServerSA1, open a PowerShell prompt. First, uninstall DNS because it's also read-only. Type **Remove-WindowsFeature DNS -Restart** and press **Enter**. DNS is removed, and the server restarts. Sign in to ServerSA1 as **Administrator** after it restarts.

2. Next, uninstall the domain controller function. The following command doesn't remove the role; it just demotes ServerSA1 back to being a member server. From a PowerShell window, type **Uninstall-ADDSDomainController** and press **Enter**.

3. When you're prompted for the local administrator password (which you need to sign in to the server when it's no longer a DC), type **Password01**, press **Enter**, type **Password01** to confirm, and press **Enter**.

4. A message states that the server restarts automatically. When you're prompted to continue, press **Enter**. When the operation is finished, ServerSA1 restarts.

5. Sign in to ServerSA1 as **Administrator**. When you installed Active Directory and DNS, the DNS server address in the IP address configuration was set to 127.0.0.1 because this server was a DNS server. You need to set it back to the address of ServerDC1. Open a PowerShell window, type **Set-DnsClientServerAddress -InterfaceAlias Ethernet0 -ServerAddresses 10.99.0.220**, and press **Enter**.

6. Type **Install-ADDSDomainController -DomainName az800.corp -credential (get-credential)** and press **Enter**. When you're prompted for credentials, type **az800\administrator** and **Password01**.

7. When you're prompted for the safe mode administrator password, type **Password01**, press **Enter**, type **Password01** to confirm, and press **Enter**. Press **Enter** to confirm. The rest of the settings are the defaults for new DCs, which include installing DNS and configuring the paths to C:\Windows. The site is chosen based on the server's IP address; if no subnets are defined, the default site is used.

8. Warning messages appear regarding default security settings, dynamic IP addresses, and DNS delegation. You can ignore these messages. When the configuration is finished, the server restarts. Continue to the next activity.

Activity 5-10

Transferring FSMO Roles

Time Required: 15 minutes

Objective: Transfer the schema master and infrastructure master roles.

Required Tools and Equipment: ServerDC1, ServerSA1

Description: In this activity, you transfer the schema master and infrastructure master roles to ServerSA1 using PowerShell.

1. On ServerDC1, open a PowerShell prompt. Type **Get-ADForest** and press **Enter**. Find the output lines listing "DomainNamingMaster" and "SchemaMaster." Both indicate that ServerDC1 is the FSMO role holder for the two forest-wide roles.
2. Type **Get-ADDomain** and press **Enter**. Find the FSMO roles and verify that ServerDC1 is shown as the FSMO role holder for all three domain-wide roles.
3. To see what roles a server holds, if any, type **Get-ADDomainController** and press **Enter**. Look for the output line "OperationMasterRoles," which lists the roles held by the current DC.
4. Now move the schema master role to ServerSA1 by typing **Move-ADDirectoryServerOperationMasterRole -Identity ServerSA1 -OperationMasterRole 3** and pressing **Enter**. The number 3 is the role number for the schema master.
5. When prompted to confirm, press **Enter**. When the operation is finished (there's no confirmation message, but the PowerShell prompt returns), type **Get-ADForest** and press **Enter**. Verify that the schema master role is now held by ServerSA1. Another way to confirm is to type **Get-ADDomainController -Server ServerSA1** and press **Enter**. It might take a while to display the results.
6. Next, transfer the infrastructure master role by typing **Move-ADDirectoryServerOperationMasterRole -Identity ServerSA1 -OperationMasterRole 2** and pressing **Enter**.
7. Press **Enter** to confirm. To view the domain-wide FSMO role holders in an easier-to-read format, type **Get-ADDomain | Format-Table PDCEmulator, RIDMaster, InfrastructureMaster** and press **Enter**. This command displays information about only these three items.
8. You'll need the schema master back on ServerDC1 to enable the Active Directory Recycle Bin in a future activity, so transfer it back by typing **Move-ADDirectoryServerOperationMasterRole -Identity ServerDC1 -OperationMasterRole 3** and pressing **Enter**. Press **Enter** to confirm.
9. Continue to the next activity.

Configuring Multidomain Environments

Microsoft Exam AZ-800:

Deploy and manage Active Directory Domain Services (AD DS) in on-premises and cloud environments.
- Deploy and manage AD DS domain controllers.
- Configure and manage multisite, multidomain, and multiforest environments.

In the day-to-day administration of an Active Directory domain, most administrators focus on OUs and their child objects, along with Group Policy. In a small organization, a solid understanding of OUs, leaf objects, and Group Policy might be all that's needed to manage a Windows domain successfully. However, in large organizations, building an Active Directory structure composed of several domains, multiple trees, and even a few forests might be necessary.

Reasons for a Single-Domain Environment

A domain is the primary identifying and administrative unit in Active Directory. A unique name is associated with each domain and used to access network resources. A domain administrator account has full control over objects in the domain, and certain security policies apply to all accounts in a domain. Additionally, most replication traffic occurs between DCs in a domain. Any of these factors can influence your decision to use a single-domain or multidomain design. Most small and medium-sized businesses choose a single domain for reasons that include the following:

- *Simplicity*—The more complex something is, the easier it is for things to go wrong. Unless your organization needs multiple identities, separate administration, or differing account policies, keeping the structure simple with a single domain is the best choice.
- *Lower costs*—Every domain must have at least one DC and preferably two or more for fault tolerance. Each DC requires additional hardware and software resources, which increase costs.
- *Easier management*—Many management tasks are easier in a single-domain environment:
  - Having a single set of administrators and policies prevents conflicts caused by differing viewpoints on operational procedures and policies.
  - Object management is easier when personnel reorganizations or transfers occur. Moving user and computer accounts between different OUs is easier than moving them between different domains.
  - Managing access to resources is simplified when you don't need to consider security principals from other domains.
  - Placement of DCs and global catalog servers is simplified when your organization has multiple locations because you don't need to consider cross-domain replication.
- *Easier access to resources*—A single domain provides the easiest environment for users to find and access network resources. In a multidomain environment, mobile users who visit branch offices with different domains must authenticate to their home domain. If their home domain isn't available for some reason, they can't log on to the network.

Reasons for a Multidomain Environment

Although a single-domain structure is usually easier and less expensive than a multidomain structure, it's not always better. Using more than one domain makes sense or is even a necessity in the following circumstances:

- *Need for differing account policies*—Account policies that govern passwords and account lockouts apply to all users in a domain. If you need differing policies for different business units, using separate domains is the best way to meet this requirement. Although you can use a password settings object (PSO) to apply different password policies for users or groups in a domain, this feature can be difficult to manage when many users are involved.
- *Need for different name identities*—Each domain has its own name that can represent a separate company or business unit. If each business unit must maintain its own identity, child domains can be created in which part of the name is shared, or multiple trees with completely different namespaces can be created.
- *Replication control*—Replication in a large domain maintaining several thousand objects can generate substantial traffic. In addition, when multiple business locations are connected through a WAN, the amount of replication traffic could be unacceptable. Replication traffic can be reduced by creating separate domains for key locations because only global catalog replication is required between domains.
- *Need for internal versus external domains*—Companies often create a domain name used only for publicly accessible resources, such as web servers and Internet apps, and another domain for internal resources.
- *Need for tight security*—With separate domains, stricter resource control and administrative permissions are easier, especially when dealing with hundreds or thousands of users in multiple business units. If a business unit prefers to have its own administrative staff, separate domains must be created.

The following sections discuss several aspects of multidomain environments, including adding subdomains, adding a tree to an existing forest, and configuring user accounts in multidomain environments.

Adding a Subdomain

Adding a subdomain is a common reason for expanding an Active Directory forest. A subdomain maintains a common naming structure with the forest root, so the top-level and second-level domain names remain the same. What makes a subdomain name different from the forest root's name is the third-level domain name. For example, if the forest root domain is csmtech.corp, you might create subdomains named US.csmtech.corp and Europe.csmtech.corp to represent company branches organized by geography. A company might also create subdomains for different business units, such as widgets.csmtech.corp and publishing.csmtech.corp.

When you create a subdomain, you must consider a few questions before beginning:

- *What server will be the first DC for the new domain?* You can use an existing server or put a new computer into service. If you use an existing server that's currently a member of the forest root domain or a standalone server, you can just install the AD DS role and promote the server to a DC. If you use an existing DC, you must demote it and promote it again as the first DC in a new domain.

- *What are the names of the subdomain and the new DC?* You should have a naming convention established so that this question is easy to answer.

- *What Active Directory–related roles will the new DC fill?* Will the DC be a global catalog server, a DNS server, or another type?

- *In which site will the new DC be located?* Do you need to create a new site or add this DC to an existing site? Be sure the DC's IP addressing matches the site location.

- *Are you going to install a second DC for the subdomain immediately?* Remember that each domain should have a minimum of two DCs for fault tolerance and load balancing. In addition, you might want to offload FSMO roles to a second DC.

- *Who will administer the new domain?* Each domain or subdomain has a Domain Admins global group. Aside from the local administrator account, what other users should be a member of this group, if any?

These are some of the questions you should answer before you create a subdomain, and there might be others, depending on the circumstances.

Adding a Tree to an Existing Forest

Recall that an Active Directory tree is a grouping of domains sharing a common naming structure. A tree can consist of a single domain or a parent domain and child domains, which can have child domains of their own. An Active Directory tree is said to have a contiguous namespace because all domains in the tree share at least the second-level and top-level domain names. For example, csmtech.corp has a second-level domain name of csmtech and a top-level domain name of corp.

Organizations operating under a single name internally and to the public are probably best served by an Active Directory forest with only one tree. However, when two companies merge or a large company splits into separate business units that would benefit from having their own identities, a multiple tree structure makes sense. There's no functional difference between domains and subdomains in the same tree or domains in different trees, as long as they're part of the same forest. The only operational difference is the necessity of maintaining multiple DNS zones. Figure 5-26 shows a forest with two trees, each with two subdomains.

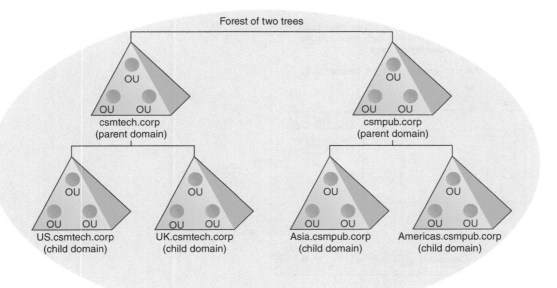

Figure 5-26   A forest with two trees

Adding a tree to an existing Active Directory forest isn't much different from adding a subdomain to an existing tree. Most of the same questions you should answer for adding a subdomain apply to adding a new tree, except you need a name for the new tree that includes the top-level and second-level domain names.

Configuring an Alternative UPN Suffix

When a user is created in a domain, the account is assigned a **UPN suffix** that's the same as the domain name. The UPN suffix is the part of the user principal name (UPN) that comes after the @. For example, in the UPN gbethany@csmtech.corp, csmtech.corp is the UPN suffix. In a multidomain environment, you might want to configure multiple UPN suffixes to make logons easier. For example, suppose you have a domain structure with multiple levels of subdomains, such as csmtech.corp, development.csmtech.corp, and us.development.csmtech.corp. A user named gbethany in us.development.csmtech.corp would have to enter gbethany@us.development.csmtech.corp whenever the full UPN was required for authentication. To simplify logons, an alternative UPN suffix, such as csmtech.corp, can be created and assigned to the gbethany account.

> **Note 11**
>
> A user account assigned an alternative UPN suffix can still use the original domain name when entering credentials. So, even though gbethany is assigned the csmtech.corp UPN suffix, gbethany can enter credentials by using gbethany@us.development.csmtech.corp or gbethany@csmtech.corp.

To create alternative UPN suffixes, follow these steps:

1. Using enterprise administrator credentials, sign in to the domain controller where you want to create the alternative suffix. The account you sign in with must be a member of Enterprise Admins.
2. In Server Manager, open Active Directory Domains and Trusts.
3. Right-click Active Directory Domains and Trusts [*server name*] and click Properties to open the dialog box shown in Figure 5-27.

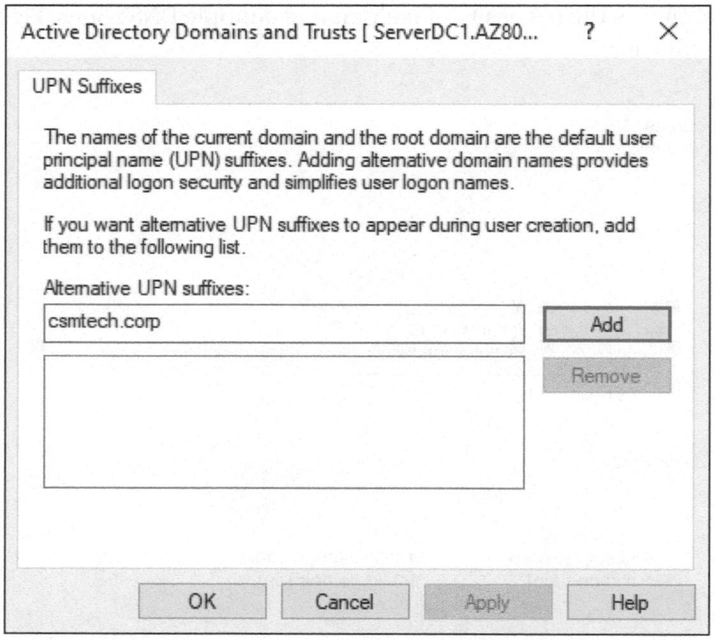

Figure 5-27 Creating an alternative UPN suffix

4. Type the suffix in the Alternative UPN suffixes text box, click Add, and then click OK. Close Active Directory Domains and Trusts.

5. In Active Directory Users and Computers, open the Properties dialog box for the user to whom you want to assign the UPN suffix and click the Account tab. Click the User logon name list arrow, and click the UPN suffix you want this user to use (see Figure 5-28). You can also assign a UPN suffix when you create a user.

Figure 5-28   Assigning a UPN suffix to a user account

The UPN suffix doesn't need to have the same domain-naming structure as the account's actual domain. Although you should follow DNS naming rules when creating an alternative UPN suffix, the suffix name isn't required to be an actual DNS domain name. For example, you could create a single-level suffix named *csm* so that users assigned this suffix enter their user names as *username*@csm.

Self-Check Questions

11. You should have multiple domains if you require differing account policies. True or False?

   a. True   b. False

12. What can you do to make logons for users easier when you have multiple levels of subdomains?

   a. Install multiple global catalog servers.   c. Install a second domain naming master.
   b. Configure the infrastructure master.   d. Create an alternate UPN suffix.

○ Check your answers at the end of this module.

Activity 5-11

Resetting Your Virtual Environment

Time Required: 5 minutes

Objective: Reset your virtual environment by applying the InitialConfig checkpoint or snapshot. You are taking these steps again because you will create a new Active Directory environment.

Required Tools and Equipment: ServerDC1, ServerSA1

Description: Apply the InitialConfig checkpoint or snapshot to ServerDC1 and ServerSA1.

1. Be sure all servers are shut down. In your virtualization program, apply the InitialConfig checkpoint or snapshot to ServerDC1 and ServerSA1.
2. When the snapshot or checkpoint has been applied, continue to the next activity.

Activity 5-12

Installing a Subdomain

Time Required: 25 minutes or longer

Objective: Install a subdomain in an existing forest.

Required Tools and Equipment: ServerDC1, ServerSA1

Description: In this activity, you install the AD DS role on ServerSA1 and promote ServerSA1 to a domain controller, creating a subdomain named SubA.AZ800.corp in the AZ800.corp forest.

Note 12

It's important that ServerSA1's IP address settings are correct. In particular, the Preferred DNS Server option must be set to 10.99.0.220 (the address of ServerDC1).

1. Start ServerDC1. Start ServerSA1 and sign in as **Administrator** with the password **Password01**.
2. On ServerSA1, you'll install the Active Directory Domain Services role. Open a PowerShell window, type **Add-WindowsFeature AD-Domain-Services -IncludeManagementTools**, and press **Enter**.
3. After the role is installed, you need to promote the server to a domain controller. You will add a new domain named SubA to the AZ800.corp domain. Type **Install-ADDSDomain –Credential (Get-Credential az800\administrator) -NewDomainName SubA -ParentDomainName az800.corp -DomainType ChildDomain** and press **Enter**.
4. When prompted for your credentials, type **Password01** in the Password text box. When prompted for the SafeModeAdministratorPassword, type **Password01** and then type it again and press **Enter** to confirm it. Press **Enter** to confirm the operation. You will see a few warnings that you can safely ignore as long as there are no errors.
5. After the installation is finished, the server restarts automatically. After the server restarts, sign in as **Administrator**. (Note that you're now signing in to the SubA.AZ800.corp domain.) In Server Manager, click **Local Server** and verify the domain information shown under Computer name (see Figure 5-29).
6. Click **Tools** and then click **Active Directory Domains and Trusts** from the menu. In the left pane, click to expand **AZ800.corp**. The new subdomain appears. Right-click **AZ800.corp** and click **Properties**. Click the **Trusts** tab to display an outgoing and incoming trust with SubA.AZ800.corp. Trusts are discussed later in the "Configuring Active Directory Trusts" section. Click **Cancel**, and close Active Directory Domains and Trusts.
7. Click **Tools** and then click **DNS** to open DNS Manager. (DNS was automatically installed when you installed Active Directory on ServerSA1.) Click to expand **ServerSA1**, **Forward Lookup Zones**, and click **SubA.AZ800.corp** to see the records that were created automatically, including an A record for ServerSA1 and the folders holding Active Directory–related records.

(continues)

Activity 5-12 Continued

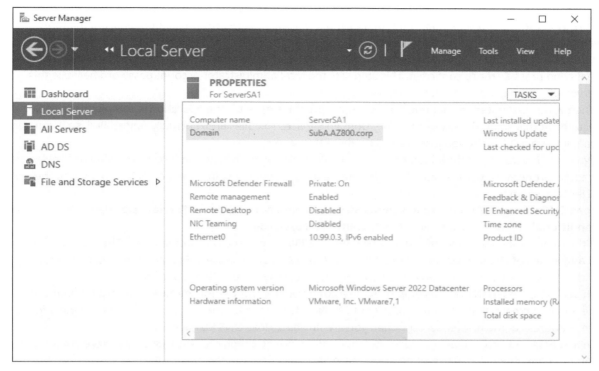

Figure 5-29   ServerSA1 is now in SubA.AZ800.corp

8. Sign in to ServerDC1, open Server Manager, click **Tools**, and then click **DNS**. In DNS Manager, click to expand **ServerDC1**, **Forward Lookup Zones**, and **AZ800.corp**. The SubA folder is grayed out because the zone was automatically delegated to ServerSA1 when ServerSA1 was promoted to a DC for the SubA subdomain. Click **SubA** to see that there is only an NS record pointing to ServerSA1, which means ServerSA1 will handle queries for the SubA subdomain. Close DNS Manager.
9. Continue to the next activity.

Activity 5-13

Removing a Subdomain and Creating a New Tree
Time Required: 15 minutes
Objective: Remove a subdomain.
Required Tools and Equipment: ServerDC1 and ServerSA1
Description: In this activity, you demote ServerSA1, which removes the SubA subdomain. Note that you aren't uninstalling the Active Directory Domain Services role because you'll need it again to create a new tree. Next, you create a new domain tree in the AZ800.corp forest. You will use PowerShell to demote ServerSA1 and then use the GUI to promote it as a DC for a new tree.

1. On ServerSA1, open a PowerShell window. Type **Uninstall-ADDSDomainController -LastDomainControllerInDomain -RemoveApplicationPartitions -Credential (get-credential)** and press **Enter**. The `-RemoveApplicationPartitions` parameter is needed to confirm that you want to delete the DNS data for the SubA subdomain. Note that the DNS Server role is still installed, but the zone data will be deleted.

(continues)

Activity 5-13 Continued ────────────────────────────

2. In the Enter your credentials dialog box, type **AZ800\administrator** in the User name text box and **Password01** in the Password text box, and then click **OK**. Because you're removing a domain from the forest, you must enter the forest root administrator's credentials.

3. When prompted for the local administrator password, type **Password01** and press **Enter**, and then type it again and press **Enter** to confirm it. This step sets the local administrator account password because this server will no longer be a domain controller.

4. When you're prompted to continue the operation, press **Enter**. After the operation is complete, the server restarts. At this point, the Active Directory Domain Services role files aren't actually uninstalled, so if you want it to be a DC again, you just need to promote this server.

5. Sign in to ServerSA1 as **Administrator**. Before you can add a new tree to the forest, you need to configure DNS properly on both servers. First, you create a conditional forwarder on ServerSA1 to point to the AZ800.corp domain.

6. Open DNS Manager. Click to expand **ServerSA1** and then click **Conditional Forwarders**. Right-click **Conditional Forwarders** and click **New Conditional Forwarder**.

7. In the New Conditional Forwarder dialog box, type **AZ800.corp** in the DNS Domain box. Then click in the **IP addresses of the master servers** text box, type **10.99.0.220**, and press **Enter**. You may see an error under the Validated column; you can ignore this error. Click **OK**. Close DNS Manager.

8. On ServerDC1, open DNS Manager and create a conditional forwarder for the NewTree.corp domain you are about to create. Repeat Steps 6 and 7 but use **NewTree.corp** for the domain name and **10.99.0.3** for the IP address of the master server. When you are finished, close DNS Manager.

9. On ServerSA1, in Server Manager, click the notifications flag and then click **Promote this server to a domain controller**. The Active Directory Domain Services Configuration Wizard starts.

10. In the Deployment Configuration window, click the **Add a new domain to an existing forest** option button. In the Select domain type list box, click **Tree Domain**. Type **AZ800.corp** in the Forest name text box and **NewTree.corp** in the New domain name text box (see Figure 5-30).

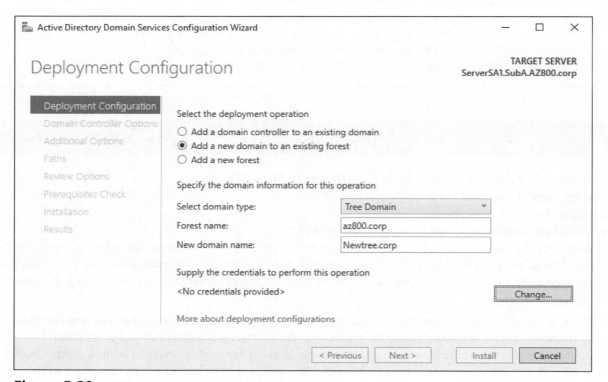

Figure 5-30   Adding a tree to an existing forest

Activity 5-13 Continued

11. Click **Change** to enter credentials. In the Windows Security dialog box, type **AZ800\Administrator** for the user name and **Password01** for the password, and then click **OK**. Click **Next**.

12. In the Domain Controller Options window, verify that the **Domain Name System (DNS) server** and **Global Catalog (GC)** check boxes are selected. You should have a DNS server in each domain tree in the forest. Configuring this DC as a global catalog server is optional.

13. In the "Directory Services Restore Mode (DSRM) password" section, type **Password01** in the Password and Confirm password text boxes, and then click **Next**.

14. In the DNS Options window, a warning message about DNS delegation appears. This is okay and expected. Click **Next**.

15. In the Additional Options window, leave the default NetBIOS domain name, and then click **Next**.

16. In the Paths window, leave the default settings, and then click **Next**.

17. Review your choices in the Review Options window and go back and make changes if necessary. When you're finished, click **Next**.

18. In the Prerequisites Check window, verify that all prerequisites have been met. You may see some warning messages, which is okay as long as there are no error messages. Click **Install**.

19. Watch the progress message at the top of the window to see the tasks being performed to install Active Directory. After the installation is finished, your computer restarts automatically. After the server restarts, sign in as **Administrator**. (Note that you're now signing in to the NewTree.corp domain, which is part of the AZ800.corp forest.)

20. In Server Manager, click **Tools** and then click **Active Directory Domains and Trusts** from the menu. In the left pane, both AZ800.corp and NewTree.corp are displayed. Right-click **AZ800.corp** and click **Properties**. Click the **Trusts** tab to display an outgoing and incoming trust with NewTree.corp. Click **Cancel**. Right-click **NewTree.corp** and click **Properties**. Click the **Trusts** tab to display an outgoing and incoming trust with AZ800.corp. Click **Cancel**. Close Active Directory Domains and Trusts.

21. In Server Manager, click **Tools** and then click **DNS** to open DNS Manager.

22. In DNS Manager, click to expand **Forward Lookup Zones**, and click **NewTree.corp**. The records that were created automatically are displayed, including an A record for ServerSA1 and the folders containing Active Directory–related records. Close DNS Manager.

23. Continue to the next activity.

Configuring Multiforest Environments

> **Microsoft Exam AZ-800:**
> Deploy and manage Active Directory Domain Services (AD DS) in on-premises and cloud environments.
> - Deploy and manage AD DS domain controllers.
> - Configure and manage multisite, multidomain, and multiforest environments.

An Active Directory forest is the broadest logical component of the Active Directory structure. Forests contain domains that can be organized into one or more trees. All domains in a forest share some common characteristics:

- *A single schema*—The schema defines Active Directory objects and their attributes and can be changed by an administrator or an application to suit an organization's needs. All domains in a forest share the same schema, so a change to the schema affects objects in all domains. This shared schema is one reason that large organizations or conglomerates with diverse business units might want to operate as separate forests. With this structure, domains in different forests can still share information through trust relationships, but changes to the schema—perhaps from installing an Active Directory–integrated application, such as Microsoft Exchange—don't affect the schema of domains in a different forest.

- *Forest-wide administrative accounts*—Each forest has two groups with unique rights to perform operations that can affect the entire forest: Schema Admins and Enterprise Admins. Members of Schema Admins are the only users who can make changes to the schema. Members of Enterprise Admins can add or remove domains from the forest and have administrative access to every domain in the forest. By default, only the Administrator account for the first domain created in the forest (referred to as the forest root domain) is a member of these two groups.

- *Operations masters*—As discussed, certain forest-wide operations can be performed only by a DC designated as the operations master. Both the schema master and the domain naming master are forest-wide operations masters, meaning only one DC in the forest can perform these roles.

- *Global catalog*—There's only one global catalog per forest, but unlike operations masters, multiple DCs can be designated as global catalog servers. Because the global catalog contains information about all objects in the forest, it's used to speed searching for objects across domains in the forest and to allow users to log on to any domain in the forest.

- *Trusts between domains*—These trusts allow users to log on to their home domains (where their accounts are created) and access resources in domains throughout the forest without having to authenticate to each domain.

- *Replication between domains*—The forest structure facilitates replicating important information among DCs throughout the forest. Forest-wide replication includes information stored in the global catalog, schema directory, and configuration partitions.

With the preceding concepts in mind, you might need an additional forest for the following reasons:

- *Schema changes*—Business units in a large organization might require different schemas because of language or cultural differences or application differences. The schema controls the objects you can create in Active Directory and the attributes of these objects. If a new object or object attribute needs to be defined for language or cultural reasons, the schema must be changed. Likewise, an Active Directory–integrated application can make schema changes to accommodate its needs. Creating a separate forest isolates schema changes to the business unit requiring them.

- *Security*—Many industries and government entities have strict security requirements for access to resources. Domains in the same forest have a built-in trust, and members of the Enterprise Admins group have access to all domains, so the only way to have a true security boundary is with separate forests. Administrators in each forest can develop their own forest-wide security policies to ensure the degree of security suitable for the forest's assets. If necessary, a trust can be created between the forests to allow users in one forest to access resources in the other.

- *Corporate mergers*—Two businesses that merge might have their own established Active Directory forests and forest administrators. When the forests have different schemas or different security policies, merging them could be difficult or undesirable. Maintaining separate forests, with trusts for cross-forest access, is sometimes the best approach.

To create a forest, you simply choose the option to create a domain in a new forest when promoting a server to a domain controller. After the forest is created, you can choose whether to allow accounts in one forest to access resources in the other forest. You do that by creating a trust relationship, which is discussed next.

Activity 5-14

Creating a New Forest
Time Required: 25 minutes or longer
Objective: Create a new forest.
Required Tools and Equipment: ServerDC1 and ServerSA1
Description: In this activity, you create a new forest, using ServerSA1 as the DC for the new forest root. First, you demote ServerSA1, and then you promote it, choosing the option to add a new forest. You name the new forest NewForest.corp.

1. On ServerSA1, in Server Manager, click **Manage** and then click **Remove Roles and Features** from the menu to start the Remove Roles and Features Wizard.

(continues)

Activity 5-14 Continued

2. In the Before You Begin window, click **Next**. In the Server Selection window, click **Next**.

3. In the Server Roles window, click to clear **Active Directory Domain Services**, and then click **Remove Features**. The Validation Results message box states that you must first demote the domain controller. Click **Demote this domain controller**.

4. In the Credentials window, you must enter enterprise administrator credentials. Click **Change**. In the Windows Security dialog box, type **AZ800\Administrator** in the User name text box and **Password01** in the Password text box. Click **OK**.

5. Click the **Last domain controller in the domain** check box, and then click **Next**. In the Warnings window, click the **Proceed with removal** check box, and then click **Next**.

6. In the Removal Options window, click the **Remove this DNS zone (this is the last DNS server that hosts the zone)** check box, click the **Remove application partitions** check box, and then click **Next**.

7. Type **Password01** in the Password and Confirm password text boxes. (It's the password for the local Administrator account when the server is no longer a DC.) Click **Next**.

8. In the Review Options window, click **Demote**. When the demotion is finished, the server restarts.

9. After ServerSA1 restarts, sign in as **Administrator**.

10. You need to ensure that all metadata is cleaned up after the demotion of ServerSA1. On ServerDC1, from Server Manager, open Active Directory Sites and Services. Navigate to **Sites\Default-First-Site-Name\ Servers**. If ServerSA1 is listed, right-click it and click **Delete**. Click **Yes** to confirm. Close Active Directory Sites and Services.

11. On ServerSA1, in Server Manager, click the notifications flag, and then click **Promote this server to a domain controller**. The Active Directory Domain Services Configuration Wizard starts.

12. In the Deployment Configuration window, click the **Add a new forest** option button. Type **NewForest.corp** in the Root domain name text box, and then click **Next**.

13. In the Domain Controller Options window, type **Password01** in the Password and Confirm password boxes. Click **Next**.

14. In the DNS Options window, click **Next**. In the Additional Options window, click **Next**.

15. In the Paths window, click **Next**. In the Review Options window, click **Next** and then click **Install**. The server will restart.

16. After the server restarts, sign in and verify the installation.

17. Continue to the next activity.

Active Directory Trusts

Microsoft Exam AZ-800:

Deploy and manage Active Directory Domain Services (AD DS) in on-premises and cloud environments.
- Configure and manage multisite, multidomain, and multiforest environments.

In Active Directory, a **trust relationship** (or simply "trust") defines whether and how security principals from one domain can access network resources in another domain. Active Directory trust relationships are established automatically between all domains in a forest. Therefore, when a user authenticates to one domain, the other domains in the forest accept, or trust, the authentication. Because all domains in a forest have trust relationships with one another automatically, trusts must be configured only when an Active Directory environment includes two or more forests or when you want to integrate with other OSs.

Note 13

Don't confuse trusts with permissions. Permissions are still required to access resources, even if a trust relationship exists.

Active Directory trusts can exist between domains and between forests. With a trust relationship between domains in the same forest or in different forests, users can access resources across domains without having to sign in more than once. Moreover, a user account needs to exist in only one domain, which simplifies user management.

To say that Domain A trusts Domain B means that users in Domain B can be given permission to access resources in Domain A. Domain A is referred to as the "trusting domain," and Domain B is referred to as the "trusted domain." In Active Directory design documentation, a trust relationship is drawn with an arrow pointing from the trusting domain to the trusted domain, as shown in Figure 5-31. Trust relationship types are explained in the following sections.

> ### Note 14
>
> Although configuring trusts in a single-forest environment might not be necessary, it can be a benefit in some configurations, as you learn later in the "Shortcut Trusts" section.

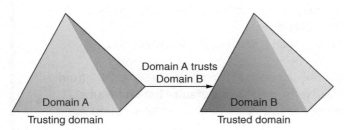

Figure 5-31   A trust relationship

One-Way and Two-Way Trusts

A **one-way trust** exists when one domain trusts another, but the reverse is not true, as shown in Figure 5-31. Domain A trusts Domain B, but Domain B doesn't trust Domain A. This means Domain B's users can be given access to Domain A's resources, but Domain A's users can't be given access to Domain B's resources. More common is the **two-way trust**, in which users from both domains can be given access to resources in the other domain. The automatic trusts configured between domains in an Active Directory forest are two-way trusts. Both one-way and two-way trusts can be transitive or nontransitive, depending on the type of trust being created.

Transitive Trusts

A **transitive trust** is named after the transitive rule of equality in mathematics: If A = B and B = C, then A = C. When applied to domains, if Domain A trusts Domain B and Domain B trusts Domain C, then Domain A trusts Domain C. The automatic trust relationships created between domains in a forest are transitive two-way trusts. These trusts follow the domain parent–child relationship in a tree and flow from the forest root domain to form the trust relationship between trees. Figure 5-32 shows two-way transitive trusts between all domains in a forest. The trust relationship between branches of the tree (US.csmtech.corp and UK.csmtech.corp) and between trees flows through the forest root domain.

Referring to Figure 5-32, the transitive nature of these trust relationships means that R&D.us.csmtech.corp trusts Asia.csmpub.corp because R&D.us.csmtech.corp trusts US.csmtech.corp, which trusts csmtech.corp, which trusts csmpub.corp, which trusts Asia.csmpub.corp. Because the trusts are two-way, the reverse is also true.

Note that for Asia.csmpub.corp to authenticate a user account in the R&D.us.csmtech.corp domain, the authentication must be referred to a DC in each domain in the path from R&D.us.csmtech.corp to Asia.csmpub.corp. A **referral** is the process of a DC in one domain informing a DC in another domain that it doesn't have information about a requested object. The DC requesting the information is then referred to a DC in another domain and on through the chain of domains until it reaches the domain holding the object. This referral process can cause substantial delays when a user wants to access resources in a domain that's several referrals away. Fortunately, you can reduce the delays caused by the referral process by implementing a shortcut trust.

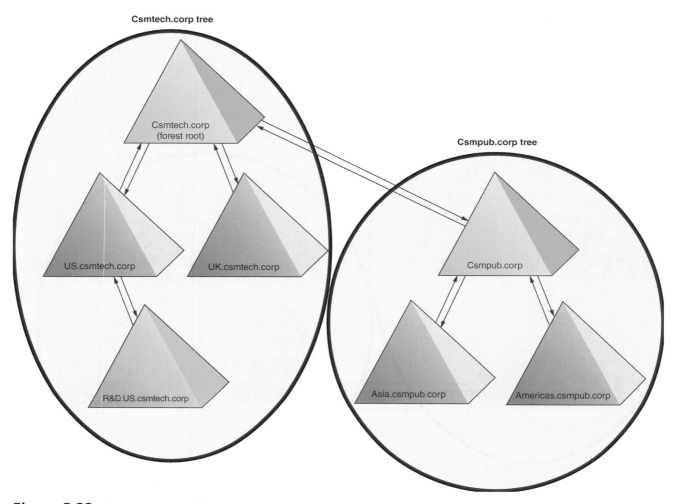

Figure 5-32   Two-way transitive trusts

Shortcut Trusts

A **shortcut trust** is configured manually between domains in the same forest to bypass the normal referral process. Figure 5-33 shows the same forest as Figure 5-32 but with a manually configured two-way shortcut trust between R&D.us.csmtech.corp and Asia.csmpub.corp.

Shortcut trusts are transitive and can be configured as one-way or two-way trusts. Generally, they're configured when user accounts often need to access resources in domains that are several referrals away. Shortcut trusts can be used only between domains in the same forest. If users need access to resources in a different forest, you use a forest trust or an external trust.

Forest Trusts

A **forest trust** provides a one-way or two-way trust between forests that allows security principals in one forest to access resources in any domain in another forest. It's created between the forest root domains of Active Directory forests running Windows Server 2003 or later versions. Forest trusts aren't possible in Windows 2000 forests. A forest trust is transitive to the extent that all domains in one forest trust all domains in the other forest. However, the trust isn't transitive from one forest to another. For example, if a forest trust is created between Forest A and Forest B, all domains in Forest A trust all domains in Forest B. If there's a third forest, Forest C, and Forest B trusts Forest C, a trust relationship isn't established automatically between Forest A and Forest C. A separate trust must be configured manually between these two forests. In Figure 5-34, a two-way trust exists between Forest A and Forest B and between Forest B and Forest C, but there's no trust between Forest A and Forest C.

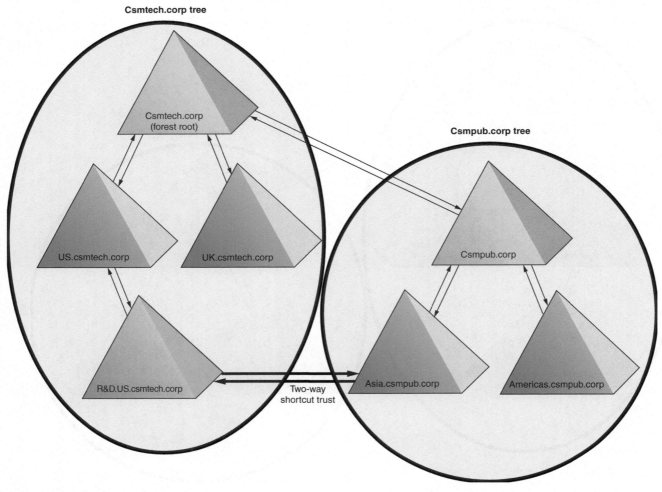

Figure 5-33 A shortcut trust

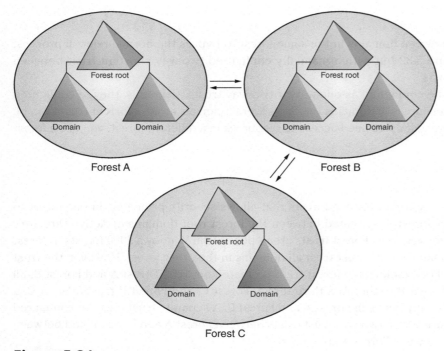

Figure 5-34 A forest trust

External Trusts and Realm Trusts

A forest trust is a powerful tool when having a trust relationship between all domains in two separate forests is an advantage. If the need for a trust relationship is limited to just a few domains in different forests, however, an external trust is a better option. An **external trust** is a one-way or two-way nontransitive trust between two domains that aren't in the same forest. External trusts are generally used in these circumstances:

- *To create a trust between two domains in different forests*—If no forest trust exists, an external trust can be created to allow users in one domain to access resources in another domain in a different forest. If a forest trust does exist, an external trust can still be used to create a direct trust relationship between two domains. This option can be more efficient than a forest trust when access between domains is frequent, much like a shortcut trust is used within a forest.
- *To create a trust with a Windows 2000 or Windows NT domain*—You probably won't run across many Windows 2000 or Windows NT domains, but if you do, an external trust is needed to create the trust relationship between a Windows Server 2003 or later forest and these older domains.

Networks are often composed of systems running different OSs, such as Windows, Linux, UNIX, and macOS. A **realm trust** can be used to integrate users of other OSs into a Windows domain or forest. It requires the OS to be running the Kerberos v5 or later authentication system that Active Directory uses.

Configuring Active Directory Trusts

Microsoft Exam AZ-800:
Deploy and manage Active Directory Domain Services (AD DS) in on-premises and cloud environments.
- Configure and manage multisite, multidomain, and multiforest environments.
- Implement and manage an on-premises and hybrid networking infrastructure.
- Implement on-premises and hybrid name resolution.

One important requirement before creating any trust is that DNS must be configured so that the fully qualified domain names (FQDNs) of all participating domains can be resolved. DNS configuration might require Active Directory–integrated forest-wide replication of zones, conditional forwarders, or stub zones, depending on the type of trust being created and the OSs involved. Before you attempt to create a trust, make sure you can resolve the FQDNs of both domains from both domains by using `nslookup` or a similar tool.

Configuring Shortcut Trusts

You usually create a shortcut trust between subdomains of two domain trees. To create a shortcut trust, open Active Directory Domains and Trusts, and then open the Properties dialog box of the domain node. Follow these steps:

1. In the Trusts tab, click the New Trust button to start the New Trust Wizard, and then click Next.
2. In the Trust Name window, type the DNS name of the target domain, and then click Next.
3. In the Direction of Trust window, leave the default setting, Two-way, selected, and then click Next.
4. In the Sides of Trust window, specify whether to create the trust only in the local domain or in both the local domain and the target domain specified in Step 2. If you choose the latter, you must have the credentials to create a trust in the target domain. If you choose to create the trust only in the local domain, an administrator in the target domain must create the other side of the trust. Click Next.
5. The User Name and Password window appears. If you choose to create the trust in both domains, you're prompted for credentials for an account in the target domain that can create the trust. You must be an administrator in the target domain and enter your credentials with the *username@domain* or *domain\username* syntax. If you're creating only the local side of the trust, you're prompted to enter a trust password. This password must also be used when creating the other side of the trust, so it must be communicated to the administrator who creates the trust in the other domain.

6. In the Trust Selections Complete window, you can review your choices. This window is the only place in the wizard where you actually see the word "shortcut" describing the trust type. After reviewing your choices, click Next to create the trust.

7. The next window shows the status of the created trust and summarizes the trust settings again. After reviewing the information, click Next.

8. Next, you can confirm the trust, which you should do if you created both sides of the trust.

After the wizard is finished, the Trusts tab shows the trust relationship and trust type. In Figure 5-35, the Trusts tab for the Sub1.ForestRoot.local domain shows an automatic parent trust with ForestRoot.local and a shortcut trust with Tree2.local, a domain in another tree in the forest. Figure 5-36 shows the entire forest and its trust relationships.

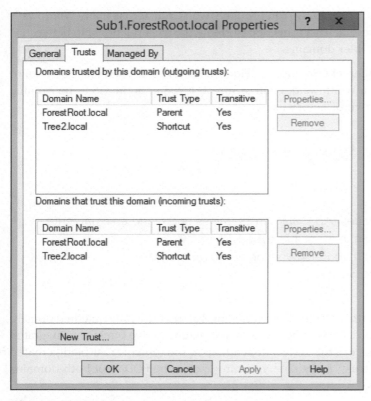

Figure 5-35   Reviewing a trust relationship

The forest in Figure 5-36 is a small forest of only two trees and three domains. The path between Sub1.ForestRoot.local and Tree2.local is only two referrals away, and normally you don't need to create a shortcut trust for such a small forest. However, if four or five other domains were along the path between these two domains, a shortcut trust makes sense when users from these domains access each other's resources frequently.

In the preceding example, because all the domains are in the same forest, the DNS domains could be configured as Active Directory–integrated zones, and zone replication could be configured so that zones are replicated to all DNS servers in the forest. No further DNS configuration is necessary because the DNS servers in ForestRoot.local store the zone for Tree2.local, and vice versa. Trusts between forests and external trusts require additional DNS configuration.

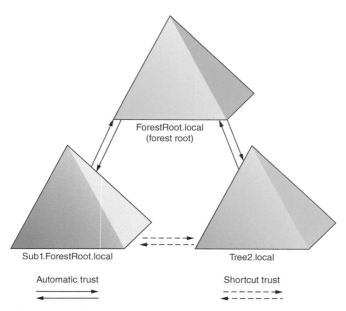

Figure 5-36   A forest with automatic trusts and a shortcut trust

Configuring Forest Trusts

Configuring a forest trust is similar to creating a shortcut trust. The main consideration before you begin is making sure DNS is configured correctly in both forest root domains. The following are the three most common ways to configure DNS for a forest trust:

- *Conditional forwarders*—They forward all DNS requests for a domain to a DNS server specified in the conditional forwarder record. With this method, you create a conditional forwarder in the forest root domain pointing to a DNS server in the other forest root domain. Do this in both forests involved in the trust.
- *Stub zones*—They're much like conditional forwarders, except they're updated dynamically if DNS servers' addresses change. To use this method, create a stub zone in the forest root domain of each forest pointing to the forest root domain of the other forest.
- *Secondary zones*—Creating a secondary zone for the purpose of configuring forest trusts is probably overkill. With secondary zones, you need to configure zone transfers, which causes more network traffic than stub zones do, especially if the primary zone's forest root domain contains a lot of records. However, you might want to use secondary zones as fault tolerance for the primary zone and to facilitate local hosts' name resolution for hosts in the primary domain.

You can also configure a DNS server to act as the root server for the DNS namespaces of both forests. On the root server, you must delegate the namespaces for each forest, and then configure root hints on DNS servers in the two forests to point to the root server.

After DNS is configured and you can resolve the forest root domain of both forests from both forests, you're ready to create the forest trust. This procedure is essentially the same as creating a shortcut trust, but there are a few important differences. You must initiate the forest trust in Active Directory Domains and Trusts from the forest root domain by following these steps:

1. In Active Directory Domains and Trusts, right-click the forest root domain and click Properties. In the root domain's Properties dialog box, click the Trusts tab. In this example, a two-way forest trust is created between one forest root domain named Forest1.local and another named Forest2.local.
2. Click the New Trust button to start the New Trust Wizard, and then click Next.
3. In the Trust Name window, specify the forest root domain of the target forest, which is Forest2.local.

4. In the Trust Type window, Windows recognizes that the specified domain is a forest root domain and gives you the option of creating an external trust or a forest trust, as shown in Figure 5-37. (Note that the forest trust option is available only from the forest root domain.) Click the Forest trust option button, and then click Next.

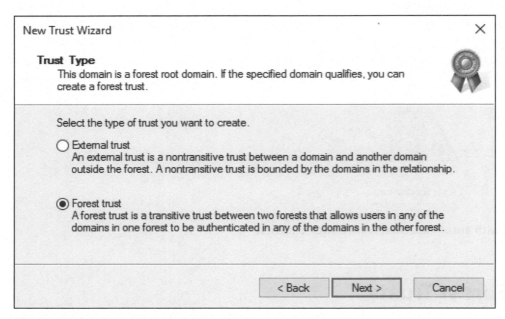

Figure 5-37   Selecting the trust type

5. In the Direction of Trust window, select Two-way, One-way: incoming, or One-way: outgoing, based on whether you need a two-way trust or just a one-way trust.
6. In the Sides of Trust window, specify whether you're creating the trust for the local domain only or for both domains. You need enterprise administrator credentials in both forests if you want to create both sides of the trust. If you create the trust for both domains, you're prompted for credentials for the other forest in the next window. Click Next.
7. In the Outgoing Trust Authentication Level window for the local forest, the choices are forest-wide authentication or selective authentication (see Figure 5-38). **Forest-wide authentication** means Windows should authenticate all users in the specified forest for all resources in the local forest. With **selective authentication**, you can choose which local forest resources the users in the specified forest can be authenticated to. Authenticating a user for a resource doesn't grant the user access; permissions must also be set. Microsoft recommends forest-wide authentication when both forests belong to the same company and selective authentication when the forests belong to different organizations. Select the authentication level, and then click Next. If you're creating both sides of the trust, you're prompted to specify the trust authentication level for the other forest.
8. If multiple trees exist in one of the forests, the Routed Name Suffixes—Specified forest window appears. You're asked whether you want to prevent authentication requests from any of the name suffixes. Name suffix routing is discussed later in the "Configuring Trust Properties" section.
9. Finally, you can confirm the trust if you created both sides of it, and you can confirm both the incoming and outgoing trusts if you created a two-way trust.

Figure 5-38   Selecting the trust authentication level

Configuring External and Realm Trusts

External trusts and realm trusts are configured in Active Directory Domains and Trusts. An external trust involves Windows domains on both sides of the trust, but a realm trust is created between a Windows domain and a non-Windows OS running Kerberos v5 or later. Unlike a forest trust, an external trust isn't transitive and need not be created between the forest root domains of two forests. In addition, SID filtering (discussed later in the "SID Filtering" section) is enabled by default for external trusts. Aside from these differences, configuring an external trust is nearly identical to creating a forest trust.

The only real consideration when creating a realm trust is whether it should be transitive. If it's transitive, the trust extends to all child domains and child realms. Otherwise, the procedure is much the same as configuring other trust types.

Configuring Trust Properties

After creating a trust, you might need to view or change its settings. To do this, open Active Directory Domains and Trusts, open the domain's Properties dialog box, and click the Trusts tab. Select the trust you want to configure and click the Properties button. The Properties dialog box of a forest trust contains three tabs—General, Name Suffix Routing, and Authentication—as discussed in the following sections.

> **Note 15**
>
> A trust's Properties dialog box varies depending on the type of trust you're configuring. For example, an automatic trust has only a General tab.

The General Tab

The General tab, shown in Figure 5-39, contains the following fields and information:

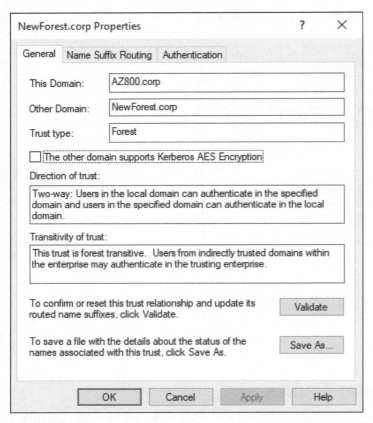

Figure 5-39   The General tab of a trust's Properties dialog box

- *This Domain*—The domain you're currently configuring.
- *Other Domain*—The domain a trust has been created with.
- *Trust type*—The type of trust, such as shortcut, forest, or external.
- *The other domain supports Kerberos AES Encryption*—Kerberos AES encryption enhances authentication security and is supported by Windows Server 2008 and later versions. If the forest trust is between two Windows Server 2008 or later domains, you can select this option for better security.
- *Direction of trust*—This field is for informational purposes only. You can't change the trust direction without deleting and re-creating the trust.
- *Transitivity of trust*—This field is for informational purposes only. You can't change the transitivity without re-creating the trust. Some trusts, such as forest and shortcut trusts, are always transitive.
- *Validate*—Click this button to confirm the trust. It performs the same action as the confirmation process at the end of the New Trust Wizard. If you didn't create both sides of the trust with the wizard, you should validate the trust with this option after both sides have been created.
- *Save As*—Click this button to create a text file containing details of the trust.

The Name Suffix Routing Tab

In the Name Suffix Routing tab, you can control which name suffixes used by the trusted forest are routed for authentication. For example, the csmtech.corp forest contains multiple trees—csmtech.corp and csmpub.corp—and csmtech.corp is trusted by a second forest, csmAsia.corp. Only users from the csmtech.corp domain should have access to csmAsia.corp resources, however. To do this, the csmAsia administrator can disable authentication requests containing the name suffix csmpub.corp. The Name Suffix Routing tab displays all available name suffixes in the trusted forest, and you can disable or enable them. In Figure 5-40, only one name suffix is listed because there's only one domain tree in NewForest.corp.

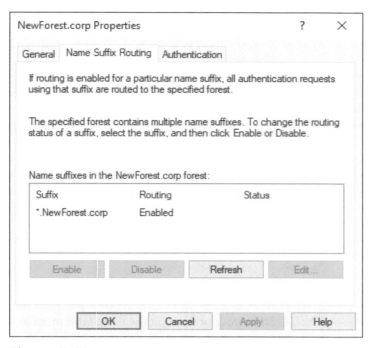

Figure 5-40   The Name Suffix Routing tab

The Authentication Tab

The Authentication tab has the same options as the Outgoing Trust Authentication Level window shown previously in Figure 5-38: forest-wide or selective authentication. As discussed, forest-wide authentication is recommended for forest trusts when both forests belong to the same organization. Selective authentication, recommended for forests in different organizations, enables you to specify users who can authenticate to selected resources in the trusting forest. After selecting this option, you add users and groups from the trusted forest to the DACL of computer accounts in the trusting forest and assign the "Allowed to authenticate" permission to these computer accounts. When selective authentication is enabled, users from the trusted forest (by default) can't authenticate to the trusting forest. If users try to authenticate to a computer in the trusting domain and haven't been granted authentication permission, they see an error message indicating a logon failure.

SID Filtering

Every account has an sIDHistory attribute that's used when migrating accounts from one domain to another to determine the account's rights and permissions in both the new and old domains. This attribute can also be used for nefarious purposes to gain administrative privileges in a trusting forest. Suppose ForestA is trusted by ForestB. An administrator in ForestA can edit the sIDHistory attribute of a user in ForestA to include the SID of a privileged account in ForestB. When this user logs on to a domain in ForestB, the user has the same access as the privileged account.

To counter this security risk, Windows has a feature called **SID filtering** (also called "SID filter quarantining") that's enabled by default on external trusts but is disabled on forest trusts. It causes the trusting domain to ignore any SIDs that aren't from the trusted domain. Essentially, the trusting domain ignores the contents of the sIDHistory attribute. SID filtering should be enabled or disabled from the trusting side of the domain and should be used only between forests or with external domains. It shouldn't be used between domains in the same forest because it would break Active Directory replication and automatic transitive trusts.

For Active Directory migration purposes, SID filtering can be disabled but should be reenabled after the migration. To disable SID filtering, use the following command:

```
netdom trust TrustingDomainName /domain:TrustedDomainName
  /quarantine:No
```

To enable SID filtering, simply change the No to Yes. To check the status of SID filtering, omit the Yes or No at the end of the command.

Note 16

You can view and clear the contents of sIDHistory in Attribute Editor and ADSI Edit, but you can't add or change existing values. If you attempt to do so, you get an access denied error.

Self-Check Questions

13. A transitive trust means if domain A trusts domain B, then domain B must trust domain A. True or False?

    a. True   **b.** False

14. What must be configured correctly before you can create trusts between domains or forests?

    a. GC   **c.** KCC

    b. DNS   **d.** UPN

◉Check your answers at the end of this module.

Activity 5-15

Creating and Testing a Forest Trust

Time Required: 15 minutes
Objective: Create a forest trust.
Required Tools and Equipment: ServerDC1 and ServerSA1
Description: In this activity, you create a forest trust between AZ800.corp and NewForest.corp. Then, you will test the trust by accessing resources in the NewForest.corp domain from the AZ800.corp domain, using credentials for the AZ800.corp domain.

    1. Sign in to ServerDC1 as **Administrator**, and from Server Manager, open Active Directory Domains and Trusts.

    2. Right-click **AZ800.corp** and click **Properties**.

    3. Click the **Trusts** tab and then click the **New Trust** button to start the New Trust Wizard. Click **Next** in the wizard's welcome window.

    4. Type **NewForest.corp** in the Name text box, and then click **Next**.

    5. In the Trust Type window, click the **Forest trust** option button. (Note that you can create an external trust in this window, but an external trust creates a trust only between two domains, whereas all domains in the forest are included in a forest trust.) Click **Next**.

    6. In the Direction of Trust window, verify that the default **Two-way** option is selected, and then click **Next**.

    7. In the Sides of Trust window, click **Both this domain and the specified domain**. If you're creating only one side of the trust, you're asked to enter a trust password, which must be used to create the second side of the trust. Click **Next**.

    8. You need to specify credentials for the NewForest.corp domain to create the other side of the trust. Type **Administrator** in the User name text box and **Password01** in the Password text box, and then click **Next**.

(continues)

Activity 5-15 Continued

9. In the Outgoing Trust Authentication Level window for the local forest, verify that **Forest-wide authentication** is selected for the authentication level, and then click **Next**.

10. In the Outgoing Trust Authentication Level window for the specified forest, verify that **Forest-wide authentication** is selected, and then click **Next**.

11. Review your settings in the Trust Selections Complete window, and then click **Next**.

12. In the Trust Creation Complete window, the status of the trust creation and a summary of your choices are displayed. Click **Next**.

13. In the Confirm Outgoing Trust window, click **Yes, confirm the outgoing trust**, and then click **Next**.

14. In the Confirm Incoming Trust window, click **Yes, confirm the incoming trust**, and then click **Next**.

15. Click **Finish**. The Trusts tab should list NewForest.corp in both the outgoing trusts and incoming trusts lists. Click **OK**, and close Active Directory Domains and Trusts.

16. Sign in to ServerSA1 as **Administrator**, and open **Active Directory Domains and Trusts**. Verify that the trust relationship with AZ800.corp was created successfully by right-clicking **NewForest.corp**, clicking **Properties**, and clicking the **Trusts** tab. You should see AZ800.corp in the outgoing and incoming trusts boxes. Close Active Directory Domains and Trusts.

17. Now, you will set up a share on ServerSA1 and access that share from ServerDC1 to test the trust. On ServerSA1, open File Explorer. On the root of the C drive, create a folder named **Share1**. Right-click the **Share1** folder, click **Give access to**, and click **Specific people**. Add **Everyone** with **Read/Write** permission. Click **Share**, and then click **Done**.

18. Repeat the previous step, this time creating a share named **Share2** and leaving the default sharing permissions as they are. (Don't add the Everyone group to the list of users who can access the share.) Close File Explorer.

19. On ServerDC1, right-click **Start**, click **Run**, type **\\ServerSA1.NewForest.corp** in the Open text box, and press **Enter**. A File Explorer window opens and lists all shares on ServerSA1.

20. Double-click the **Share1** share to open it. Notice that you weren't prompted for credentials because a trust exists between the two forests. Create a text file named **doc1.txt** to show that you can write files to the share across the forest. Share1 has Read/Write permission assigned to the Everyone group, which includes authenticated users from other forests.

21. In File Explorer, click the **back arrow** to see the list of shared folders on ServerSA1. Double-click **Share2**. A "Windows cannot access" message appears. You can't access this share because the default share permissions don't include users from other forests. Click **Close**. Close File Explorer.

22. Shut down ServerDC1 and ServerSA1.

Working with Domain Controllers in Azure

Microsoft Exam AZ-800:
Deploy and manage Active Directory Domain Services (AD DS) in on-premises and cloud environments.
  • Deploy and manage AD DS domain controllers.

Deploying a domain controller in Azure is not too different from deploying a domain controller on-premises. However, there are a few important considerations to keep in mind:

  • When you select the path for where Active Directory should store Active Directory database files, you must select a data disk rather than the OS disk. This is due to caching settings on the OS disk in Azure, which could cause data corruption.

  • If you are creating a hybrid Active Directory environment, you need to configure intersite connectivity between the on-premises DCs and the Azure DC and configure replication based on the frequency with which you want Active Directory objects to be updated between on-premises and Azure. Intersite connectivity requires a secure connection that can be accomplished with a VPN or ExpressRoute. **ExpressRoute** is a technology that provides a secure connection between your on-premises datacenter and the Microsoft Azure virtual network to which your Azure DC is connected. ExpressRoute does not use the public Internet and therefore requires a third-party provider that supports ExpressRoute. Also, there's an additional monthly fee for the Azure ExpressRoute service. The fee depends on the service level you choose and ranges from $55 per month to over $6000 per month.

- All Azure DCs should be configured as GC servers. Otherwise, global catalog lookups (for example, universal group membership queries) in Azure will have to traverse the link to an on-premises GC server.
- Even if you already have two or more DCs on-premises, you should configure at least two DCs in Azure for high availability.
- Azure DCs should never be shut down using the Azure portal controls; they should always be shut down using the OS shutdown command. Using the portal controls causes the VM to be deallocated and causes the relative identifier (RID) pool held by the DC to be discarded. The RID pool is used to assign Active Directory objects a unique identifier.

If you are deploying an Azure domain controller for an existing on-premises domain, it makes sense to deploy an RODC. Because changes to Active Directory can't be made on an RODC, you won't incur any replication traffic from the Azure RODC to your on-premises network, thereby saving on network bandwidth and Azure service charges.

Creating an Azure Domain Controller

The steps required for deploying an Azure DC with VPN connectivity to an on-premises Active Directory are as follows:

- Create an Azure virtual network (Vnet) with site-to-site VPN to the on-premises network.
- Create a storage account for the data disk that will hold the Active Directory database.
- Create the VM that will be the DC and assign a static IP address.
- Install the Active Directory Domain Services (AD DS) server role on the VM and include the DNS server role.
- Promote the server to a domain controller.

As with an on-premises DC, you need to decide if the Azure DC will be an additional domain controller for an existing domain, a domain controller for a new domain in the existing on-premises forest, or a domain controller for a new forest. If you are creating a new forest, you don't need to first establish connectivity with an on-premises DC. However, if you want to implement a forest trust between the on-premises forest and the Azure forest, connectivity will be required.

> ## Note 17
>
> Azure VMs configured as domain controllers and providing other services such as DNS are frequently referred to as infrastructure as a service (IaaS) VMs because they are providing network infrastructure services.

Self-Check Questions

15. Before you can install a DC in Azure, you must acquire the Azure Domain Controller installation media. True or False?

   a. True   **b.** False

16. Which of the following is true about DCs in Azure?

   a. All DCs should be GC servers.

   b. DCs must be shut down using the Azure portal.

   c. RODCs are not supported.

   d. The Active Directory database should be on the OS disk.

⦿Check your answers at the end of this module.

Module Summary

- DCs and sites are the physical components of Active Directory, and forest, domains, and OUs are the logical components. DCs use multimaster replication, but read-only domain controllers (RODCs) use unidirectional replication.
- A global catalog (GC) server is a DC configured to hold the global catalog. Every forest must have at least one GC server. GC servers facilitate domain-wide and forest-wide searches, enable logons across domains, and hold universal group membership information. Each site should have at least one GC server to speed logons and directory searches.
- RODCs were developed to provide secure Active Directory support in branch office installations where physical server security is lax and there are no on-site server administrators. Before installing an RODC, make sure there's a writeable Windows Server 2008 DC or later version the RODC can replicate with. The forest functional level must be at least Windows Server 2003.
- Replication on an RODC is unidirectional, and user passwords aren't stored on the RODC by default. You can configure credential caching if you want the RODC to store passwords of selected users locally.
- With staged RODC installation, a domain administrator creates the RODC computer account in Active Directory, and a regular user can then perform the installation.
- An Active Directory site represents a physical location where domain controllers reside. Multiple sites are used for authentication efficiency, replication efficiency, and application efficiency. Site components include subnets, site links, and bridgehead servers.
- Universal group membership caching handles the potential conflict between faster logons and additional replication traffic.
- Configuring sites may involve registering SRV records, working with automatic site coverage, and moving DCs between sites.
- Domain controllers advertise themselves by registering service (SRV) records with DNS servers so that clients can find DCs that offer services related to Active Directory. The Netlogon service on the DC handles registration of SRV records for the Lightweight Directory Access Protocol (LDAP) and Kerberos services.
- Having a DC in each site is usually preferable so that authentication of clients occurs on the local LAN instead of having to traverse the WAN. However, having a DC at each site isn't always necessary or practical. Automatic site coverage is a feature in which each DC advertises itself by registering SRV records in DNS in sites that don't have a DC if the advertising DC has the lowest-cost connection to the site.
- Timely and reliable replication of data between domain controllers is paramount to a functioning Active Directory domain and forest. Active Directory replication information includes Active Directory objects, such as OUs and user, group, and computer accounts; changes to data held in partitions maintained by FSMO role holders; trust relationships; global catalog data; group policy information; and files located in SYSVOL, such as group policy templates and scripts.
- The KCC is a process that runs on every DC and, for intrasite replication, builds a replication topology among DCs in a site and establishes replication partners.
- A connection object defines the connection parameters between two replication partners. The KCC generates these parameters automatically between intrasite DCs. You can create connection objects for intrasite replication if you want to alter the replication topology manually.
- Two protocols can be used to replicate between sites: IP and SMTP. By default, IP is used in the DEFAULTIP-SITELINK site link and is recommended in most cases.
- GPTs are replicated by using FRS or DFSR. Of these two methods, DFSR is the more efficient and reliable. If your domain includes Windows Server 2003 or older DCs, it uses the older FRS to replicate SYSVOL, and you should migrate to the more reliable DFSR as soon as possible.
- Deciding where to place the FSMO role holder is part of the overall Active Directory design strategy. Two important operations for managing FSMOs are transferring and seizing operations master roles.
- A domain is the primary identifying and administrative unit in Active Directory. A unique name is associated with each domain and used to access network resources. A domain administrator account has full control over objects in the domain, and certain security policies apply to all accounts in a domain.

- Most small and medium-sized businesses have a single domain, but using more than one domain makes sense when there's a need for differing account policies, different name identities, replication control, internal and external domains, and tighter security.
- Adding a subdomain is a common reason for expanding an Active Directory forest. A tree can consist of a single domain or a parent domain and child domains, which can have child domains of their own.
- When a user is created in a domain, the account is assigned a UPN suffix that's the same as the domain name. To simplify logons, an alternative UPN suffix can be created and assigned to user accounts.
- The Active Directory forest is the broadest logical component of the Active Directory structure. Forests contain domains that can be organized into one or more trees. All domains in a forest share some common characteristics: a single schema, forest-wide administrative accounts, operations masters, global catalogs, trusts between domains, and replication between all domains.
- A trust relationship defines whether and how security principals from one domain can access network resources in another domain. Trust relationship types include one-way and two-way trusts, transitive trusts, shortcut trusts, forest trusts, external trusts, and realm trusts. You configure trusts with Active Directory Domains and Trusts.
- The Properties dialog box for a forest trust has three tabs: General, Name Suffix Routing, and Authentication. In the Name Suffix Routing tab, you can control which name suffixes used by the trusted forest are routed for authentication. In the Authentication tab, you choose forest-wide or selective authentication. SID filtering, which is enabled by default on external trusts but disabled on forest trusts, causes the trusting domain to ignore any SIDs that aren't from the trusted domain.
- Deploying a domain controller in Azure is not too different from deploying a domain controller on-premises. However, the Active Directory database files should be stored on a separate disk from the OS due to Azure caching.
- Deploying a DC on Azure that will communicate with on-premises Active Directory requires connectivity using either a VPN or ExpressRoute.
- All Azure DCs should be configured as GC servers to prevent global catalog lookups from traversing the link to an on-premises GC server.
- If you are deploying an Azure domain controller for an existing on-premises domain, deploying an RODC saves bandwidth and Azure costs.

Key Terms

automatic site coverage	global catalog (GC) server	shortcut trust
bridgehead server	infrastructure master	SID filtering
connection object	one-way trust	site link
delegated administrator account	PDC emulator	staged installation
domain naming master	read-only domain controller (RODC)	transitive trust
ExpressRoute	realm trust	trust relationship
external trust	referral	two-way trust
filtered attribute set	relative identifier (RID)	unidirectional replication
Flexible Single Master Operation (FSMO) role	RID master	universal group membership caching
	schema master	UPN suffix
forest trust	security identifier (SID)	urgent replication
forest-wide authentication	selective authentication	

Review Questions

1. Which of the following is *not* a function of the global catalog?
   a. Facilitates forest-wide searches
   b. Keeps universal group memberships
   c. Facilitates intersite replication
   d. Facilitates forest-wide logons

2. You have an Active Directory forest of two trees and eight domains. You haven't changed any of the operations master domain controllers. On which domain controller is the schema master?
   a. All domain controllers
   b. The last domain controller installed
   c. The first domain controller in the forest root domain
   d. The first domain controller in each tree

3. Which of the following is a reason for establishing multiple sites? (Choose all that apply.)
   a. Improving authentication efficiency
   b. Enabling more frequent replication
   c. Reducing traffic on the WAN
   d. Having only one IP subnet

4. Users of a new network subnet have been complaining that logons and other services are taking much longer than they did before being moved to the new subnet. You discover that many logons and requests for resources from clients in the new subnet are being handled by domain controllers in a remote site instead of local domain controllers. What should you do to solve this problem?
   a. Create a new site and add the clients and new GC server to the new site.
   b. Change the IP addresses of the clients to correspond to the network of the DCs that are handling the logons.
   c. Compact the Active Directory database because fragmentation must be causing latency.
   d. Create a new subnet and add the subnet to the site that maps to the physical location of the clients.

5. You want to decrease users' logon times at SiteA but not increase replication traffic drastically. You have 50 users at this site with one domain controller. Overall, your network contains 3000 user and computer accounts. What solution can decrease logon times with the least impact on replication traffic?
   a. Configure the domain controller as a domain naming master.
   b. Configure the domain controller as a global catalog server.

   c. Configure multiple connection objects between the domain controller in SiteA and a remote global catalog server.
   d. Enable universal group membership caching.

6. In a multidomain forest in which only some DCs are GC servers, which of the following configurations should you avoid?
   a. Domain naming master and schema master on the same domain controller
   b. PDC emulator and RID master on the same computer
   c. Infrastructure master configured as a global catalog server
   d. Schema master configured as a global catalog server

7. User authentications are taking a long time. The domain controller performing which FSMO role will most likely decrease authentication times if it's upgraded?
   a. RID master
   b. PDC emulator
   c. Infrastructure master
   d. Domain naming master

8. An older server that's performing the RID master role is being taken out of service, and you will be replacing it with a new server configured as a domain controller. What should you do to ensure the smoothest transition?
   a. Transfer the RID master role to the new domain controller, and then shut down the old server.
   b. Shut down the current RID master and seize the RID master role from the new domain controller.
   c. Back up the domain controller that's currently the RID master, restore it to the new domain controller, and then shut down the old RID master.
   d. Shut down the current RID master, and then transfer the RID master role to the new domain controller.

9. Which of the following is true about an RODC installation?
   a. A Windows server running at least Windows Server 2012 is required.
   b. The forest functional level must be at least Windows Server 2003.
   c. An RODC can be the first DC in a forest.
   d. Another RODC must be available as a replication partner.

10. You need to install an RODC in a new branch office and want to use an existing workgroup server running Windows Server 2019. The office is a plane flight away and is connected via a WAN. You want an employee at the branch office, Michael, to do the RODC installation because he's good at working with computers and following directions. What should you do?

    a. Add Michael to the Domain Admins group and give him directions on how to install the RODC.

    b. Add Michael's domain account to the Administrators group on the server and give him directions on how to install the RODC.

    c. Create the computer account for the RODC in the Domain Controllers OU and specify Michael's account as one that can join the computer to the domain.

    d. Create a group policy that specifies that Michael's account can join RODCs to the domain. Then use the Delegation of Control Wizard on the Domain Controllers OU.

11. You have an application integrated with AD DS that maintains Active Directory objects containing credential information, and there are serious security implications if these objects are compromised. An RODC at one branch office isn't physically secure, and theft is a risk. How can you best protect this application's sensitive data?

    a. Configure the PRP for the RODC and specify a Deny setting for the application object.

    b. Configure a filtered attribute set and specify the application-related objects.

    c. Use EFS to encrypt the files storing the sensitive objects.

    d. Turn off all password replication on the RODC.

12. You maintain an RODC running Windows Server 2022 at a branch office, and you want one employee with solid computer knowledge to perform administrative tasks, such as driver and software updates and device management. How can you do this without giving the employee broader domain rights?

    a. Assign the employee's account as a delegated administrator in the RODC's computer account settings.

    b. Create a local user on the RODC and add it to the Administrators group. Have the user log on with this account when necessary.

    c. Create a script that adds the user to the Domain Admins group each day at a certain time and then removes the user from the group one hour later. Tell the user to log on and perform the necessary tasks during the specified period.

    d. Send the user to extensive Windows Server 2022 training, and then add the user to the Domain Admins group.

13. Which of the following is true about installing a DC in Azure?

    a. All Azure DCs should be configured as PDC emulators.

    b. The Active Directory database files should be installed on a data disk.

    c. You can't install a read-only domain controller in Azure.

    d. You should never configure an Azure DC as a global catalog server.

14. You have installed an RODC at a branch office that also runs the DNS Server role. All DNS zones have Active Directory integrated. What happens when a client computer attempts to register its name with the DNS service on the RODC?

    a. The DNS service rejects the registration. The client must be configured with a static DNS entry.

    b. The DNS service passes the request to another DNS server. After registration is completed, the DNS server that performed the registration sends the record to the DNS service on the RODC.

    c. The DNS service creates a temporary record in a dynamically configured primary zone. The record is replicated to other DNS servers and then deleted on the RODC.

    d. The DNS service sends a referral to the client. The client registers its name with the referred DNS server.

15. You have four users who travel to four branch offices often and need to log on to the RODCs at these offices. The branch offices are connected to the main office with slow WAN links. You don't want domain controllers at the main office to authenticate these four users when they log on at the branch offices. What should you do that requires the least administrative effort yet adheres to best practices?

    a. Create a new global group named AllBranches. Add the four users to this group and add the AllBranches group to the Allowed RODC Password Replication group.

    b. Add the four users to a local group on each RODC. Add the local groups to the PRP on each RODC with an Allow setting.

    c. Add each user to the PRP on each RODC with an Allow setting.

    d. Create a group policy and set the "Allow credential caching on RODCs" policy to Enabled. Add the four users to the policy and link the policy to the Domain Controllers OU.

16. Which of the following is the term for a DC in a site that handles replication of a directory partition for that site?

a. Inter-Site Topology Generator
b. Knowledge Consistency Checker
c. Bridgehead server
d. Global catalog server

17. Where would you find files related to logon and log-off scripts in an Active Directory environment?
    a. C:\Windows\NTDS
    b. %*systemroot*%\SYSVOL
    c. %Windir%\ntds.dit
    d. C:\Windows\edb.log

18. Which of the following best describes the first domain installed in a forest?
    a. Forest root
    b. Global catalog
    c. Master domain
    d. Primary tree

19. Which of the following is responsible for facilitating forest-wide Active Directory searches?
    a. Knowledge Consistency Checker
    b. Infrastructure master
    c. Domain naming master
    d. Global catalog server

20. In intrasite replication, which of the following is responsible for building a replication topology for DCs in a site and establishes replication partners?
    a. GPO
    b. PDC
    c. RID
    d. KCC

21. Your company has merged with another company that also uses Windows Server 2022 and Active Directory. You want to give the other company's users access to your company's forest resources and vice versa without duplicating account information and with the least administrative effort. How can you achieve this goal?
    a. Transfer your global catalog to one of their servers.
    b. Create a two-way forest trust.
    c. Configure an external trust.
    d. Configure selective authentication.

22. You have three sites: Boston, Chicago, and Los Angeles (LA). You have created site links between Boston and Chicago and between Chicago and LA with the default site link settings. What do you need to do to make sure replication occurs between Boston and LA?
    a. Do nothing; replication will occur between Boston and LA with the current configuration.
    b. Create a new connection object between Boston and LA.
    c. Create a site link bridge between Boston and LA.
    d. Configure a site link between Boston and LA with SMTP.

23. Which of the following is a valid reason for using multiple forests?
    a. Centralized management
    b. Need for different schemas
    c. Easy access to all domain resources
    d. Need for a single global catalog

24. What can you do to reduce the delay caused by authentication referral?
    a. Create a forest trust.
    b. Create an external trust.
    c. Create a shortcut trust.
    d. Create a transitive trust.

25. You are deploying a domain controller in Azure for an on-premises domain for which you already have several DCs configured in your datacenter. You want to minimize the bandwidth used for traffic coming from the Azure DC to your on-premises network and minimize Azure costs. What should you do?
    a. Deploy a DC in Azure that is not a GC server.
    b. Make sure the DC is running on Server Core.
    c. Create a new child domain.
    d. Deploy the DC as an RODC.

Critical Thinking

The following activities give you critical thinking challenges. Case projects offer a scenario with a problem for which you supply a written solution.

Case Projects

Case Project 5-1: Devising a DC Strategy

You're the administrator of a network of 500 users and three Windows Server 2022 DCs. All users and DCs are in a single building. Your company is adding three satellite locations that will be connected to the main site via a WAN link. Each satellite location will house between 30 and 50 users. One location has a dedicated server room where you can house a server and ensure physical security. The other two locations don't have a dedicated room for network equipment. The WAN links are of moderate to low bandwidth.

Further, you have recently deployed an application in Azure that will need Active Directory services and you have decided to deploy a DC in Azure. The deployment of the DC should cost as little as possible in Azure service fees.

Design an Active Directory structure, taking into account global catalog servers, FSMO roles, sites, and domain controllers. What features of DCs and Active Directory discussed in this module might you use in your design?

Case Project 5-2: Working with Trusts

Examine the network in Figure 5-41. You need to configure this network to meet the following requirements:

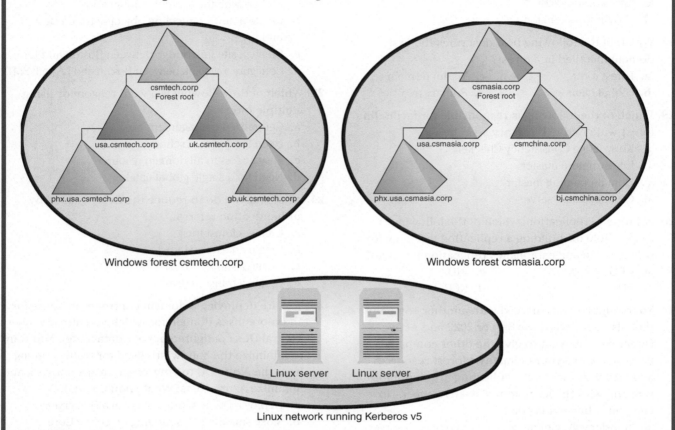

Figure 5-41   The network for Case Project 5-2

- Requirement 1: All users in the csmtech.corp forest should be authenticated to all resources in the csmasia. corp forest.
- Requirement 2: Selected users in the csmasia.corp domains should be authenticated to selected resources in the csmtech.corp forest.
- Requirement 3: No users in the csmchina.corp domain tree should be authenticated to the csmtech.corp forest.
- Requirement 4: Users in the bj.csmchina.corp domain access resources in the phx.usa.csmtech.corp domain frequently. Latency should be kept to a minimum.
- Requirement 5: Users in the phx.usa.csmtech.corp domain access resources in the gb.uk.csmtech.corp domain frequently. Latency should be kept to a minimum.
- Requirement 6: Users in the Linux network need to access resources in the csmasia.corp forest frequently.

Given the preceding requirements, write a report describing how to configure trust relationships and listing configuration options, such as one-way or two-way, transitivity, and authentication.

Case Project 5-3: Designing Sites

You're called in as a consultant to create a site design. The company has a network consisting of four hub sites and six satellite sites (see Figure 5-42). There are four domains, one for each city. Note the following facts about the company's site requirements:

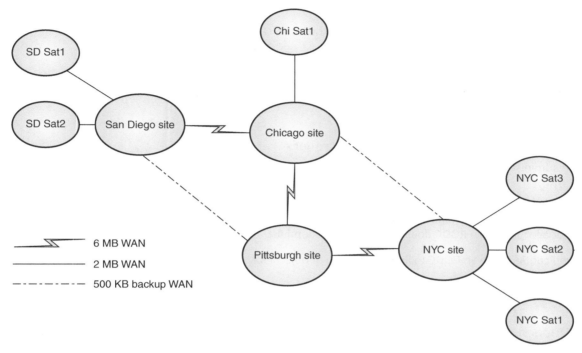

Figure 5-42   The site design for Case Project 5-3

- The satellite sites are in the same domain as the city to which they're connected.
- No sites contain domain controllers from outside their domain.
- Each hub site has 750 to 1000 users and 10 to 15 domain controllers.
- Each satellite site has 50 to 100 users and 2 to 4 domain controllers.

Write a memo of one to two pages describing some factors to consider when designing this site, and take the following into account:

- Site links
- Intersite transport protocols
- Site link bridges
- Bridgehead servers
- FSMO role holders
- Global catalog servers

What additional information do you need to choose an efficient site design for this network?

Solutions to Self-Check Questions

Section 5-1: Active Directory Review

1. Changes on RODCs are replicated to other DCs. True or False?

    Answer: b. False

    Explanation: Changes cannot be made on RODCs and therefore cannot be replicated to other DCs.

2. Which of the following facilitates forest-wide Active Directory searches?

    Answer: a. GC

    Explanation: The Global Catalog (GC) contains a partial replica of all forest objects' attributes and facilitates searches across domains in the forest.

Section 5-2: Configuring Read-Only Domain Controllers

3. A delegated administrator has administrative privileges only on the RODC. True or False?

    Answer: a. True

    Explanation: A delegated administrator account has local administrative rights and permissions to the RODC, similar to members of the local Administrators group on a member computer or standalone computer. A delegated administrator account for an RODC doesn't have domain administrative rights and permissions.

4. What can you configure on an RODC to limit replication of objects for security purposes?

    Answer: c. Filtered attribute set

    Explanation: A filtered attribute set specifies domain objects that aren't replicated to RODCs.

Section 5-3: Understanding and Configuring Sites

5. Having a single IP subnet is a reason for establishing multiple sites. True or False?

    Answer: b. False

    Explanation: Each site is associated with one or more subnets. If a network has only one subnet, there is no reason to create additional sites beyond the default site.

6. What creates the topology used for intrasite replication?

    Answer: b. Knowledge Consistency Checker

    Explanation: For intrasite replication, the KCC builds a replication topology for DCs in a site and establishes replication partners.

Section 5-4: Active Directory Replication

7. The ISTG defines the connection parameters between two replication objects. True or False?

    Answer: b. False

    Explanation: A connection object defines the connection parameters between two replication partners. The ISTG designates a bridgehead server to handle replication for each directory partition.

8. What should you configure if you want to alter the Active Directory intrasite replication topology manually?

    Answer: d. Connection object

    Explanation: You can create connection objects for intrasite replication if you want to alter the replication topology manually.

Section 5-5: Working with Operations Master Roles

9. The schema master is a domain-wide FSMO role. True or False?

    Answer: b. False

    Explanation: The schema master and the domain naming master are forest-wide FSMO roles. The PDC emulator, RID master, and infrastructure master are domain-wide FSMO roles.

10. Which FSMO role is responsible for issuing unique pools of values that are used when creating Active Directory objects?

    Answer: c. RID master

    Explanation: The RID master is responsible for issuing unique pools of RIDs to each DC, thereby guaranteeing unique SIDs throughout the domain.

Section 5-6: Configuring Multidomain Environments

11. You should have multiple domains if you require differing account policies. True or False?

    Answer: a. True

    Explanation: Account policies are established at the domain level, so if differing account policies are needed for different parts of the organization, you should create multiple domains.

12. What can you do to make logons for users easier when you have multiple levels of subdomains?

    Answer: d. Create an alternate UPN suffix.

    Explanation: The UPN suffix is the part of the user principal name (UPN) that comes after the @. For example, in the UPN bab@csmtech.corp, csmtech.corp is the UPN suffix. In a multidomain environment, you might want to configure multiple UPN suffixes to make logons easier.

Section 5-7: Configuring Active Directory Trusts

13. A transitive trust means if Domain A trusts Domain B, then Domain B must trust Domain A. True or False?

    Answer: b. False

    Explanation: A transitive trust is named after the transitive rule of equality in mathematics: If A = B and B = C, then A = C. When applied to domains, if Domain A trusts Domain B and Domain B trusts Domain C, then Domain A trusts Domain C.

14. What must be configured correctly before you can create trusts between domains or forests?

    Answer: b. DNS

    Explanation: DNS must be configured so that domains or forests can find each other by name when creating the trust relationship.

Section 5-8: Working with Domain Controllers in Azure

15. Before you can install a DC in Azure, you must acquire the Azure Domain Controller installation media. True or False?

    Answer: b. False

    Explanation: There are no media for an Azure Domain Controller. You install an Azure Domain Controller by creating a VM with Windows Server and then installing the AD DS server role.

16. Which of the following is true about DCs in Azure?

    Answer: a. All DCs should be GC servers.

    Explanation: All Azure DCs should be configured as GC servers. Otherwise, global catalog lookups (for example, universal group membership queries) in Azure will have to traverse the link to an on-premises GC server.

Module 6

Manage Windows Server in a Hybrid Environment

Module Objectives

After reading this module and completing the exercises, you will be able to:

1   Use server roles and features
2   Manage servers remotely
3   Deploy Windows Admin Center
4   Manage Windows servers with Azure services
5   Manage servers with Desired State Configuration

After you have installed a server and performed initial configuration tasks, next comes the task of configuring the server. This module covers how to add and remove server roles and features on both local and remote servers. You also learn how to add servers to Server Manager, configure PowerShell remoting, and configure firewall rules to allow remote management.

Windows Admin Center is a newer management tool available to remotely manage servers with just a web browser. You can manage on-premises physical and virtual Windows servers, client OSs, server clusters, and Azure VMs. While it may be convenient to manage Azure VMs with a tool you can install on-premises, you can also use many of the Azure management and monitoring tools to manage on-premises servers with Azure Arc. Both of these tools and other Azure management tools are discussed in this module.

Finally, you'll learn about a powerful feature called Desired State Configuration (DSC), in which both on-premises servers and Azure VMs can be configured and maintained using special PowerShell scripts. DSC can configure servers and prevent inadvertent changes to their configuration so that you can be assured your servers are always in a consistent state.

Table 6-1 describes what you need in order to do the hands-on activities in this module.

Table 6-1   Activity requirements

Activity	Requirements	Notes
Activity 6-1: Resetting Your Virtual Environment	ServerDC1, ServerDM1, ServerDM2, ServerSA1	
Activity 6-2: Installing and Removing Server Roles with Server Manager	ServerDC1, ServerDM1	
Activity 6-3: Installing and Uninstalling a Server Role with PowerShell in Server Core	ServerDC1, ServerDM2	
Activity 6-4: Adding Servers to Server Manager and Creating Server Groups	ServerDC1, ServerDM1, ServerDM2	
Activity 6-5: Deploying JEA for PowerShell Remoting	ServerDC1, ServerDM1	
Activity 6-6: Deploying Windows Admin Center	ServerDC1, ServerSA1	

Working with Server Roles and Features

Microsoft Exam AZ-800:

Manage Windows servers and workloads in a hybrid environment.
- Manage Windows servers in a hybrid environment

Windows Server without roles and features installed is like an iPhone without apps installed. The basic installation does have some limited functions, such as basic file and printer sharing, but not much beyond that. You need to add server roles and features to take advantage of the power that Windows Server 2022 offers. This section covers how to work with server roles and features in both a GUI installation and a Server Core installation and how to update roles and features installed in offline images.

In Module 1, you learned the difference between server roles and features and explored the Add Roles and Features Wizard in Server Manager. In this module, you look more closely at the process of adding and removing roles and features.

Managing Server Roles in the GUI

In Server Manager, you can start the Add Roles and Features Wizard in the Welcome window or by clicking Manage and then Add Roles and Features from the menu (see Figure 6-1).

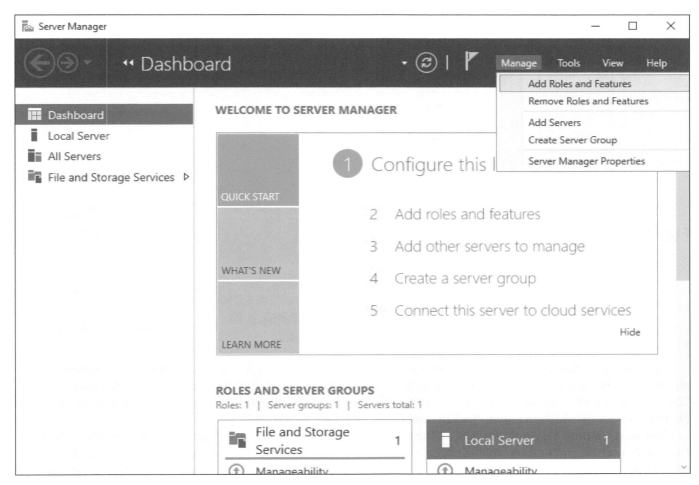

Figure 6-1   Starting the Add Roles and Features Wizard

In either case, the Add Roles and Features Wizard opens to the Before You Begin window, as shown in Figure 6-2. You can bypass this window in the future by selecting the option to skip it. If you're new to Windows Server, however, reading the information in this window is a good idea so that you can make sure you have performed the following crucial tasks before installing server roles and features:

- The administrator has a strong password.
- Static IP addresses have been configured. Some server roles, such as DHCP and Active Directory, don't work correctly with dynamically assigned addresses. Although not all roles require static IP addresses, using them on servers is a recommended practice.
- Security updates are current.

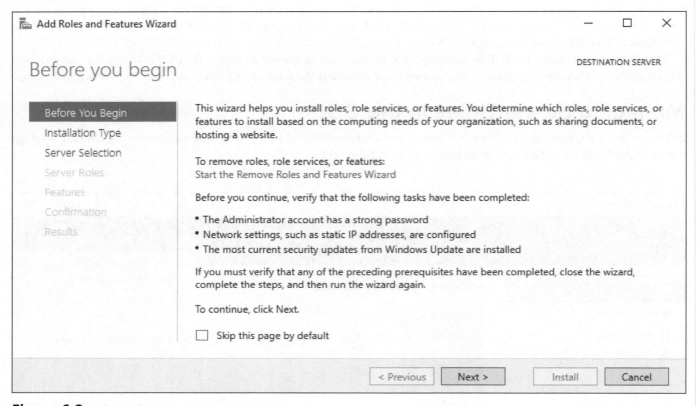

Figure 6-2   The Before You Begin window

The next window, Installation Type (see Figure 6-3), has two options:

- *Role-based or feature-based installation*—Use this default option to install a role or feature on a single server or an offline virtual hard disk. In most cases, you choose this option.
- *Remote Desktop Services installation*—Use this option to distribute components of the Remote Desktop Services role across different servers for use in a virtual desktop infrastructure.

In the next window, Server Selection (see Figure 6-4), you choose a server from the server pool for installing roles and features. You learn how to add servers to this list later in the module in the "Managing Servers Remotely" section. You can also install roles and features on a virtual hard disk (VHD). If you choose this option, you're prompted to choose a server on which to mount the VHD and specify the path to the VHD file.

The next window, Server Roles, lists all the server roles you can install (see Figure 6-5). Underneath each server role, there may be one or more role services. Next to each role or role service is a box. If it's selected, that role or role service and any subordinate role services are installed. If the box is shaded, one or more role services or subordinate role services are installed. Figure 6-5 shows "File and Storage Services (1 of 12 installed)," which means one of the 12 role services (and subordinate role services) under File and Storage Services is installed. When you click the box next to a server role, Windows prompts you to include additional features and management tools, if necessary.

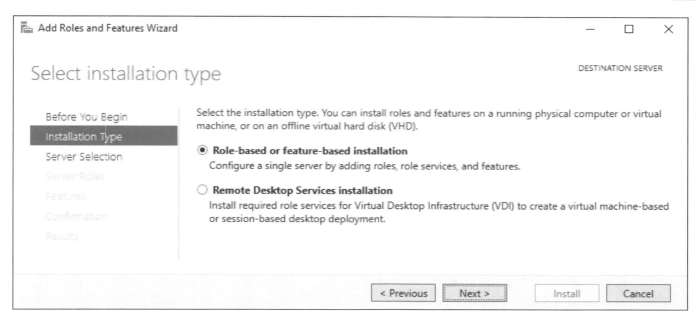

Figure 6-3 Selecting an installation type

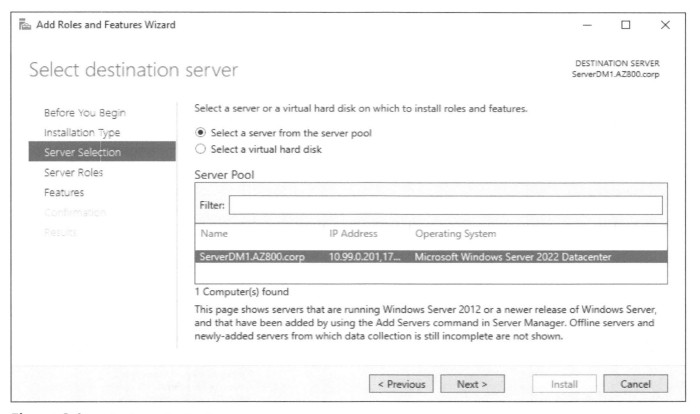

Figure 6-4 Selecting a destination server

The next window, Features, lists available features and works like the Server Roles window. If you select a server role with multiple associated role services, the next step is selecting which role services you want. For example, the Remote Access server role has three role services associated with it (see Figure 6-6). If a role service requires installing other roles and role services, you're prompted to confirm their installation, too.

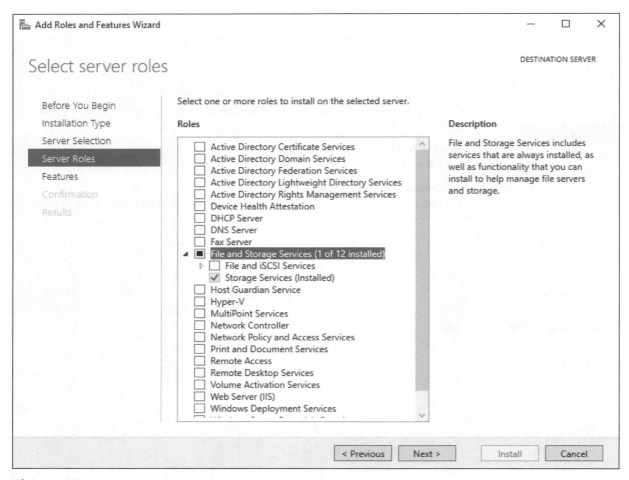

Figure 6-5 Selecting roles to install on a server

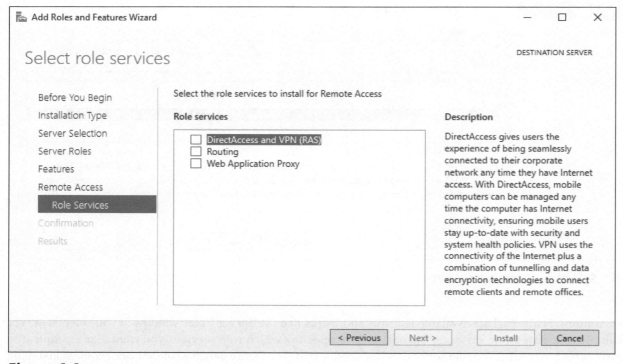

Figure 6-6 Selecting role services

In the Confirmation window, shown in Figure 6-7, you can review your selections. Selecting the check box at the top ensures that the server restarts automatically, if needed, during installation. At the bottom of this window are links to two options:

- *Export configuration settings*—Select this option if you want to generate an XML script for installing the selected roles and features on another server using the PowerShell command `Install-WindowsFeature -ConfigurationFilePath XMLscript.xml`.
- *Specify an alternate source path*—If the files aren't available locally, select this option to specify a path to an image file containing the installation files for roles and features.

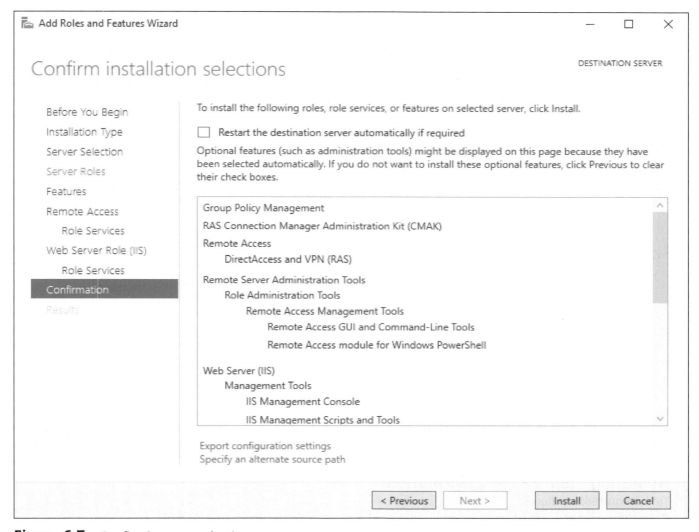

Figure 6-7   Confirming your selections

Clicking the Install button starts installing the server roles or features you've selected. The Results window shows the progress of the installation.

The procedure for removing roles and features is similar. In Server Manager, click Manage and then click Remove Roles and Features from the menu to start the Remove Roles and Features Wizard. The main difference between this wizard and the installation wizard is that you clear the box for the role or feature you want to remove. Roles and features that aren't installed are grayed out and can't be selected.

Managing Server Roles with PowerShell

You can use PowerShell to add and remove server roles from a Server Core or Desktop Experience server if you don't want to use Server Manager. To start PowerShell, type `powershell` at an elevated command prompt or right-click the PowerShell icon and click Run as Administrator. The following PowerShell commands are used to work with server roles and features:

- `Get-WindowsFeature`—Displays a list of available roles and features. You can also use `Get-WindowsFeature | where Installed` to display a list of installed roles and features or `Get-WindowsFeature | where InstallState -eq Available` to display roles and features that are available to be installed.
- `Install-WindowsFeature` *RoleOrFeatureName*—Installs the server role or feature specified by *RoleOrFeatureName*. To specify multiple roles and features, separate the names with a space. Variations on this command include `Install-WindowsFeature` *RoleOrFeatureName* `-IncludeAllSubFeature -IncludeManagementTools`, which installs the specified role or feature and includes necessary subfeatures and management tools, and `Uninstall-WindowsFeature` *RoleOrFeatureName* `-IncludeManagementTools`, which uninstalls the specified role or feature along with management tools. Separate the names of multiple roles and features with a space.

Note 1

Remember, PowerShell commands aren't case sensitive. They're shown with selective capitalization to make them more readable, but you can use all lowercase (or uppercase) letters when typing commands at a PowerShell prompt.

Self-Check Questions

1. Which PowerShell cmdlet lists all roles and features that are both installed and available to be installed?

   a. `List-AllFeatures`
   b. `Get-WindowsFeature`
   c. `Show-Features -All`
   d. `Add-WindowsFeature -ListOnly`

◉ Check your answers at the end of this module.

Activity 6-1

Resetting Your Virtual Environment

Time Required: 5 minutes

Objective: Reset your virtual environment by applying the InitialConfig checkpoint or snapshot.

Required Tools and Equipment: ServerDC1, ServerDM1, ServerDM2, ServerSA1

Description: Apply the InitialConfig checkpoint or snapshot to ServerDC1, ServerDM1, ServerDM2, and ServerSA1.

1. Be sure the servers are shut down. In your virtualization program, apply the InitialConfig checkpoint or snapshot to ServerDC1, ServerDM1, ServerDM2, and ServerSA1.
2. When the snapshot or checkpoint has been applied, continue to the next activity.

Activity 6-2

Installing and Removing Server Roles with Server Manager

Time Required: 15 minutes

Objective: Install a server role with Server Manager.

Required Tools and Equipment: ServerDC1, ServerDM1

Description: You've done the initial configuration on your server, so now it's time to install some roles and features. In this activity, you will install the Print and Document Services role using Server Manager.

1. Start ServerDC1. Start ServerDM1 and sign in to it as the domain administrator, **AZ800\Administrator**.
2. On ServerDM1, in Server Manager, click **Manage** and then click **Add Roles and Features** from the menu to start the Add Roles and Features Wizard.
3. In the Before You Begin window, read the information to make sure you have completed the prerequisite tasks, and then click **Next**.
4. In the Installation Type window, accept the default option **Role-based or feature-based installation**, and then click **Next**.
5. In the Server Selection window, the only option is ServerDM1 because you haven't added any other servers to be managed from this server. If you were installing the feature on an offline VHD file, you would click the "Select a virtual hard disk" option button. Accept the default setting **Select a server from the server pool**, and then click **Next**.
6. In the Server Roles window, click the box next to **Print and Document Services**. In the Add Roles and Features Wizard dialog box, which asks you to confirm the additional features needed for this role (see Figure 6-8), click the **Add Features** button.

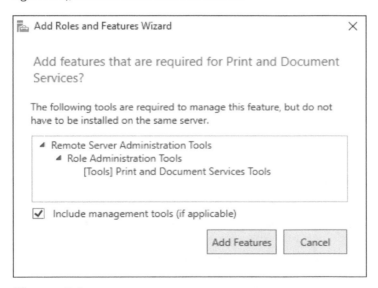

Figure 6-8   Adding features for a role service

7. Click **Next**. In the Features window, scroll through the list of features to review what's available, and then click **Next**.
8. Read the description of the Print and Document Services role in the next window, and then click **Next**.
9. In the Role Services window, you can choose other role services that work with this role, such as Internet Printing. Accept the default option **Print Server** and click **Next**.
10. In the Confirmation window, click **Install**. The Results window shows the progress of the installation. You can close this window without interrupting the installation; if you close the window, you can restore it to view your progress by clicking Notifications. Wait until the installation is finished, and then click **Close**.

(continues)

Activity 6-2 Continued

11. A new icon named Print Services is added to Server Manager in the left pane. As shown in Figure 6-9, Print Services is also added in the Roles and Server Groups section.

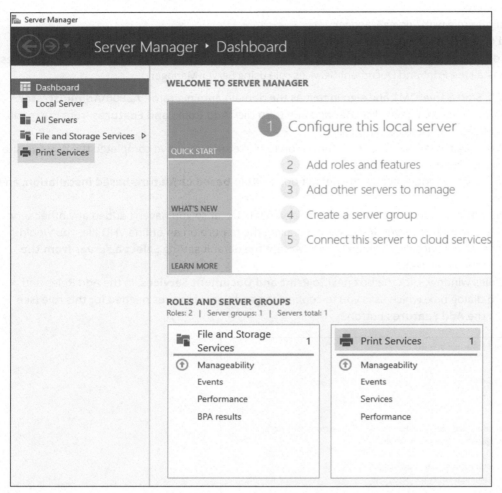

Figure 6-9 Adding Print Services to Server Manager

12. Now you will remove the role. On ServerDM1, in Server Manager, click **Manage** and then **Remove Roles and Features** from the menu.
13. In the Before You Begin window, click **Next**. In the Server Selection window, click **Next**.
14. In the Server Roles window, click the box next to **Print and Document Services**.
15. In the Remove Roles and Features Wizard dialog box, click **Remove Features**, and then click **Next**. In the Features window, click **Next**.
16. In the Confirmation window, click **Remove**.
17. In the Results window, wait until the process is finished, and then click **Close**. Notice that Print Services has been removed from Server Manager.
18. Stay signed in if you are going to the next activity.

Activity 6-3

Installing and Uninstalling a Server Role with PowerShell

Time Required: 10 minutes

Objective: Install and uninstall a server role with PowerShell.

Required Tools and Equipment: ServerDC1, ServerDM1

Description: For practice using PowerShell cmdlets to install and remove server roles, you install Print and Document Services with PowerShell and then uninstall it.

1. Sign in to ServerDM1 as the domain **Administrator**, if necessary.
2. Open a PowerShell window.
3. To see what roles and features are available to install, type **Get-WindowsFeature** and press **Enter**. You see a list of server roles, role services, and features (see Figure 6-10). Installed roles, role services, and features are preceded with an X. The left column shows the display name of the server role, role service, or feature, and the right column is the name you use in PowerShell commands.

Figure 6-10   Output of `Get-WindowsFeature`

4. Scroll up to Print and Document Services. Notice that the name in the right column is `Print-Services`.
5. Type **Install-WindowsFeature Print-Services -IncludeManagementTools** and press Enter.
6. Your progress is shown at the top of the PowerShell window. When the installation is finished, type **Get-WindowsFeature | where Installed** and press **Enter** to see a list of installed roles and features.
7. To uninstall Print and Document Services, type **Uninstall-WindowsFeature Print-Services -IncludeManagementTools** and press Enter.
8. When the role has been removed, you see a status message indicating success. Type **Get-WindowsFeature | where Installed** and press **Enter**. You no longer see Print and Document Services in the list of installed features.
9. Continue to the next activity.

Managing Servers Remotely

> **Microsoft Exam AZ-800:**
> Manage Windows servers and workloads in a hybrid environment.
> * Manage Windows servers in a hybrid environment

The server management and configuration tools you have used so far perform tasks on the local server. Most networks have more than one server, and although you can perform a task by signing in to the console at each server or using Remote Desktop, there are more convenient ways to manage a multiserver environment remotely, as you learn in the following sections. By managing servers remotely, you can take advantage of the benefits of Server Core yet still be able to use a GUI on a remote machine. In addition, remote management reduces the need for a physical keyboard and monitor for each server. Most remote management tasks are handled by using Server Manager, MMCs, or the PowerShell command line.

Adding Servers to Server Manager

In Windows Server 2022, you can manage all your servers from a single Server Manager interface. In Server Manager, you can manage all roles and features installed on any server and view the status of all servers, including events and performance data. To do this, you must add servers to Server Manager. To start the process, click Manage and then Add Servers from the Server Manager menu. If the server where you're running Server Manager is a member of a domain and the server you want to add is also a domain member, you can add it by using any of these methods:

* *Searching Active Directory*—This method is probably the easiest. You can type the first few characters of the server name in the Name text box (see Figure 6-11) and click Find Now, or just click Find Now to see all computers in the domain. Then select one or more servers to manage. (Note that you can't manage computers running a client OS.)
* *Searching DNS*—Type the server name or IP address in the Search text box on the DNS tab and then select the servers you want to add.
* *Importing a text file*—Browse for and select a text file that contains a list of server names or IP addresses on the Import tab, one per line; all the servers listed in the file are added.

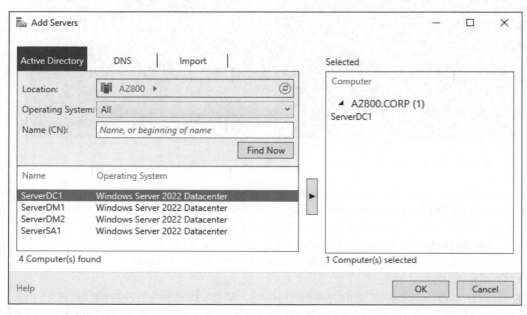

Figure 6-11   Adding a server to Server Manager

In Windows Server 2022, you can manage servers running Windows Server 2003 and later versions. However, you can't manage a more recent version of Windows Server than the version on which Server Manager is running. For example, you can't manage a Windows Server 2022 server from a Windows Server 2019 server, but you can manage a Windows Server 2019 server from a Windows Server 2022 server.

If the server where you're running Server Manager is a member of a workgroup rather than a domain, or the server you want to manage is a workgroup member, first you need to add the remote server to the TrustedHosts list on the computer running Server Manager. To do this, use the following PowerShell cmdlet while signed in as Administrator:

```
Set-Item wsman:\localhost\Client\TrustedHosts RemoteServerName
  -Concatenate -Force
```

RemoteServerName is the name or IP address of the remote server you want to manage. The -Concatenate option adds the entry to the list instead of overwriting the existing list. After adding the remote server to the Trusted-Hosts list, you can add the server to Server Manager by using the previously described methods of searching DNS or importing a text file.

> **Note 2**
>
> If you try to add a standalone server that's not in the TrustedHosts list to Server Manager, Server Manager reports this error: "WinRM Negotiate authentication error."

Using Server Manager Groups

If you have only a few servers to manage, you can add them as described previously and access them by clicking All Servers in Server Manager. If you have dozens or even hundreds of servers to manage, however, you might want to organize them in groups, such as by department, location, or function. For example, you can group all servers related to the Operations Department, all servers in the Phoenix office, or all DNS servers. By organizing servers in this manner, you can see a group's status at a glance. Servers can be a member of more than one group, so you can place a domain controller in the Phoenix office in both the Domain Controllers group and the Phoenix group, for example.

To create a server group in Server Manager, click Manage and then Create Server Group from the menu. Give the group a name, and then add servers to the group (see Figure 6-12). You can add servers from the existing list of servers managed by Server Manager, or you can add other servers to manage by using the methods described earlier. After you create a server group, the group name is added to the left pane of Server Manager and can be used just like the All Servers node.

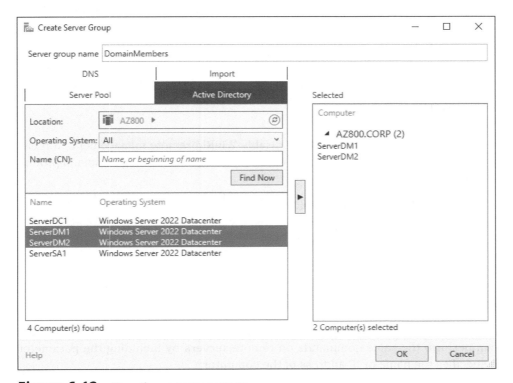

Figure 6-12   Creating a server group

Enabling and Disabling Remote Management

By default, Windows Server remote management is enabled via **Windows Remote Management (WinRM)**. WinRM provides a command-line interface for performing a variety of remote management tasks. Running in the background, it allows commands or applications that require Windows Management Instrumentation (WMI) or PowerShell to access the server remotely. To change the remote management setting, click the setting next to the label "Remote management" in the Local Server Properties window (see Figure 6-13).

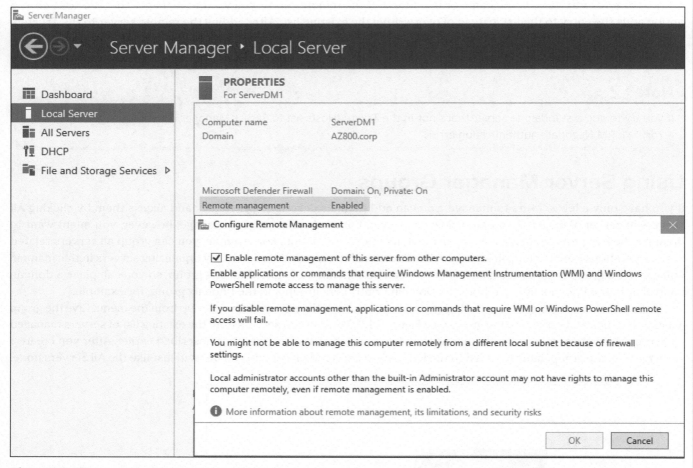

Figure 6-13 Configuring remote management

You can select or clear the check box in Figure 6-13 to enable or disable WinRM remote management. You can enable or disable WinRM and PowerShell remoting on Windows 10 or 11 clients by using the following command-prompt commands, which also work on Windows Server:

- `winrm quickconfig`—Starts the WinRM service and configures the firewall for remote management
- `Configure-SMRemoting.exe -Get`—Displays the current status of WinRM (enabled or disabled)
- `Configure-SMRemoting.exe -Enable`—Enables WinRM
- `Configure-SMRemoting.exe -Disable`—Disables WinRM

PowerShell Remoting

All the PowerShell commands discussed in the previous section can be used to install or remove server roles and features on remote servers. You can perform the same commands on remote servers by including the parameter -ComputerName *string*, which specifies the name or IP address of the computer:

`-ComputerName` *string*

For example, if you're on Server1 and want to install the Windows Server Backup feature on a server named Server2, use this command:

```
Install-WindowsFeature Windows-Server-Backup -ComputerName Server2
 -IncludeAllSubFeature -IncludeManagementTools
```

For this command to work, Server2 must be in the same domain as the server where you entered the command. If the remote server isn't in the same domain, it must be added to the TrustedHosts setting, as explained previously in the "Adding Servers to Server Manager" section.

You can see the full list of PowerShell cmdlets that support the -ComputerName parameter, and therefore PowerShell remoting, by using the following command:

```
Get-Command -ParameterName ComputerName
```

Exam Tip ✔

The Microsoft AZ-800 exam expects you to know how to remotely manage workgroup servers as well as domain members. If you are remotely managing workgroup servers, either through Server Manager or with PowerShell remoting, you need to add the server name to the TrustedHosts file.

To configure remote management using PowerShell, use the following cmdlets from a PowerShell prompt with the Run as Administrator option:

- Enable-PSRemoting—Enables WinRM
- Disable-PSRemoting—Disables WinRM
- Test-WSMan –ComputerName *computer*—Tests whether the WinRM service is running on *computer*

Aside from using the -ComputerName parameter to execute a PowerShell cmdlet on a remote computer, you can establish a PowerShell session with the remote computer and get a PowerShell prompt as if you were on the remote computer's console, as in the following example:

```
Enter-PSSession -ComputerName ServerDC1
```

If you are signed in to ServerDM1, for example, the preceding cmdlet establishes a PowerShell session with ServerDC1 using your current credentials, as long as those credentials are sufficient to give you access to ServerDC1. You can also use a version of the command that specifies different credentials:

```
Enter-PSSession -ComputerName ServerDC1 -Credential (Get-Credential)
```

In the preceding cmdlet, you will be prompted for a username and password to connect to ServerDC1, and the resulting PowerShell session will have the rights and permissions of the account entered. To leave a PowerShell remoting session, simply type exit.

Configuring Second-Hop Remoting

If you use PowerShell remoting from ServerDC1 to ServerDM1 and then use a command from ServerDM1 that accesses ServerDM2, ServerDM2 is the second hop, and the process is called **second-hop remoting**. The problem is that your credentials aren't passed from ServerDM1 to ServerDM2, so the command fails. In this section, we examine three of the most common methods for supporting second-hop remoting:

- *CredSSP*—**Credential Security Support Provider (CredSSP)** is an authentication provider tool that caches credentials on the remote server (in this example, ServerDM1) so they can be used to connect to the second-hop server (in this example, ServerDM2).
- *Kerberos delegation*—There are two types of Kerberos delegation: constrained and unconstrained. While both types can solve the second-hop remoting problem, only constrained delegation is recommended.
- *Just Enough Administration (JEA) for PowerShell remoting*—This method involves substantial configuration on the server(s) to be managed and is discussed in the next section.

CredSSP

CredSSP allows an application to delegate authentication for remote authentication using the user's credentials. The configuration requires just a few PowerShell cmdlets on the client station (the computer from which the user initiates the remote connection) and the server to which the user connects. Here is the scenario we will use as an example: The user is signed in to ServerDC1 and wants to start a remote PowerShell session with ServerDM1. As part of the remote PowerShell session, one or more PowerShell cmdlets will be executed that target ServerDM2.

On the client station, ServerDC1, run the following PowerShell cmdlet:

```
Enable-WSManCredSSP -Role client -DelegateComputer ServerDM1
```

On the remote server, ServerDM1, run the following cmdlet:

```
Enable-WSManCredSSP -Role server
```

Then, when you make the remote connection to ServerDM1 using the `Enter-PSSession` cmdlet, use the `-Authentication CredSSP` option, such as:

```
Enter-PSSession -ComputerName ServerDM1 -Authentication CredSSP
```

As long as your credentials have access to ServerDM2, you'll be able to execute commands that use ServerDM2 in the `-ComputerName` parameter.

CredSSP is effective and convenient, but it comes with some security risks due to the caching of credentials on the intermediate server (in this case, ServerDM1). For this reason, CredSSP should only be used on highly trusted servers such as domain controllers. CredSSP works with servers starting with Windows Server 2008, so it's a good option if you have older servers in the environment.

Kerberos Constrained Delegation

Kerberos constrained delegation is a feature that allows an application running on one server to access resources hosted on a remote server. For example, an IIS web server may need to access a database running on another server. As you know, all services running in Windows run with the credentials of a service account. You could give the service account permission to access the database, but if the service account is compromised, the attacker will have access to the database. With Kerberos delegation, the service account running the web server is delegated to the service account running the database. In this scenario, when a user signs in to the website, the service account running the web service requests access to the database service on behalf of the user. To configure constrained delegation, you can access the properties of the computer account that will be configured for delegation; in our example, this is ServerDM1. From the Delegation tab, select "Trust this computer for delegation to specified services only" and then choose the authentication protocol option. Next, select the computer and service(s) to which the account can delegate credentials.

While this type of delegation works for many types of services, it doesn't work with the WinRM service, which is necessary for PowerShell remoting. To facilitate second-hop remoting using Kerberos constrained delegation, you must configure resource-based constrained delegation.

Resource-based Constrained Delegation

Resource-based constrained delegation was introduced in Windows Server 2012. With this type of delegation, you need to configure delegation on the computer that will be the second hop; in our scenario, that's ServerDM2. One of the advantages of resource-based constrained delegation over CredSSP is that credentials are not stored on any of the servers, and it only takes a single PowerShell command to configure. In addition, resource-based constrained delegation, unlike standard constrained delegation, works across domains and even forests.

To configure resource-based constrained delegation, you need to install the Active Directory remote server administration tools (RSAT) for PowerShell on the second-hop computer. (These tools are already installed on domain controllers.) Then, enter the following PowerShell cmdlet. In this scenario, you enter the cmdlet on ServerDM2, and ServerDM1 is the server that will be configured for delegation.

```
Set-ADComputer -identity (Get-ADComputer ServerDM2)
  -PrincipalsAllowedToDelegateToAccount (Get-ADComputer ServerDM1)
```

In the preceding cmdlet, which is run on ServerDM2, you are specifying that ServerDM1 is allowed to delegate credentials to ServerDM2. For the purposes of PowerShell remoting, this configuration allows a user to start a

PowerShell remote session from ServerDC1 to ServerDM1. From the ServerDM1 PowerShell session, cmdlets that target ServerDM2 can be executed. For example, from the remote PowerShell session to ServerDM1, you can enter the cmdlet `Get-WindowsFeature -ComputerName ServerDM2` to see a list of Windows features available on ServerDM2. Any PowerShell cmdlet that supports the `-ComputerName` parameter can be used in this manner.

Configuring Just Enough Administration for PowerShell Remoting

Just Enough Administration (JEA) is a technology that allows administrators to delegate administrative tasks to other personnel without granting excessive privileges. JEA leverages the concept of the **principle of least privilege**, which states that users and administrators should be given sufficient rights and permissions to perform their jobs, but no more than that.

An account with a high level of rights and permissions on a network poses a serious security risk if the account is compromised. Many administrative tasks require membership in the highly privileged Domain Admins security group, and members of the Domain Admins group have nearly unlimited privileges in the entire domain. JEA addresses this problem by allowing you to configure management endpoints that give accounts access to the PowerShell cmdlets necessary to perform specific administrative tasks, such as administering DNS or DHCP, without the need to make the account a member of the Domain Admins group.

JEA Deployment Requirements

JEA requires PowerShell 5.0 or a later version. The PowerShell version can be checked by typing the variable `$PSVersionTable`. Simply type `$PSVersionTable.PSversion` in a PowerShell prompt to see the PowerShell version. PowerShell version 5.0 or later is installed on updated Windows 10 installations (1607 and above) and on Windows Server 2016 and later versions. For older OSs, you can install Windows Management Framework (WMF) 5.1 to get a compatible PowerShell version.

Although it's not necessary, it is recommended that you enable PowerShell logging to verify your JEA configuration. Logging will tell you what commands users are running. PowerShell Module Logging can be enabled using Group Policy. The policy is located in Computer Configuration\Administrative Templates\Windows Components\Windows PowerShell and should be applied to OUs that contain the computer accounts you want to monitor.

Configuring JEA

Configuring JEA for PowerShell remoting involves creating a PowerShell data file called a **PowerShell role capability file** that specifies which cmdlets and functions users can run. You can create one data file for each set of administrative tasks performed by users. For example, if a user or group of users will manage aspects of your DNS environment, you can create a PowerShell data file related to DNS tasks. If a different user or group of users will manage aspects of your DHCP environment, you can create a PowerShell data file related to DHCP tasks. The file must be placed on each computer that will be managed remotely using JEA for PowerShell remoting. Before you create the file, you need to determine which cmdlets are needed to perform a specific task or group of tasks. You can also limit which parameters or parameter values can be used on cmdlets to limit the scope of the cmdlets. You need to be careful to restrict the use of cmdlets and executables that allow users to elevate their own privileges. Commands that start processes and services, as well as commands that change group memberships, are examples of these types of commands.

When you have determined what cmdlets and functions are necessary for the administrative tasks you are delegating to other users, you are ready to create a PowerShell data file. Use the `New-PSRoleCapabilityFile` cmdlet to create the file using the following syntax:

```
New-PSRoleCapabilityFile -Path path\filename.psrc
```

The file must have a .psrc extension, which stands for "PowerShell role capability." The file created is a text file that can be edited with any text editor, such as Notepad. The file contains a template with examples of how to use the various sections of the file. Figure 6-14 shows the relevant parts of the file with example syntax.

The following list explains some of the sections you will most likely need to configure:

- *VisibleCmdlets*—In this section, you list the cmdlets that are available to the accounts you want to restrict. You can specify just the cmdlet name if all parameters and parameter values are allowed, or you can specify a list of parameters and allowed values. The allowed values can include wildcard syntax.

- *VisibleFunctions*—This section is used with the same syntax as the VisibleCmdlets section but applies to Power-Shell functions. It's not always easy to know if a PowerShell command is a cmdlet or function, so you can use the `Get-Command` cmdlet in PowerShell, which shows the command type (cmdlet, function, alias, etc.) in the output.
- *VisibleExternalCommands*—This section specifies which external commands, such as executables or scripts (including PowerShell scripts), are available to the user. The full path to the external command should be specified so that a command with the same name but a different function cannot be used instead. Parameters and parameter values can't be specified for external commands, so use this section with caution. For example, certain commands like net.exe and dsadd.exe can be used to elevate a user's own privileges. Microsoft recommends allowing access to external commands only if there is not a PowerShell alternative.
- *VisibleProviders*—A provider is a resource available to PowerShell, such as the Windows registry, file system, and certificate store. If necessary, you can provide users with access to such resources in this section, but best practices suggest that you write a custom function that accesses the resource on the user's behalf. You can see a list of providers by using the `Get-PSProvider` cmdlet.

The resulting file should be placed in a folder under the PowerShell modules folder on the target computer(s) to be managed. This folder is usually found at C:\Program Files\WindowsPowerShell\Modules. For example, you can create a folder named JEARoleCapability under C:\Program Files\WindowsPowerShell\Modules and put the role capability file in that folder.

```
# Cmdlets to make visible when applied to a session
# VisibleCmdlets = 'Invoke-Cmdlet1', @{ Name = 'Invoke-Cmdlet2'; Parameters = @{ Name =
'Parameter1'; ValidateSet = 'Item1', 'Item2' }, @{ Name = 'Parameter2'; ValidatePattern =
'L*' } }

# Functions to make visible when applied to a session
# VisibleFunctions = 'Invoke-Function1', @{ Name = 'Invoke-Function2'; Parameters = @{ Name
= 'Parameter1'; ValidateSet = 'Item1', 'Item2' }, @{ Name = 'Parameter2'; ValidatePattern =
'L*' } }

# External commands (scripts and applications) to make visible when applied to a session
# VisibleExternalCommands = 'Item1', 'Item2'

# Providers to make visible when applied to a session
# VisibleProviders = 'Item1', 'Item2'
```

Figure 6-14   A PowerShell role capability file

Creating a JEA Endpoint and Session Configuration

After you have created a PowerShell data file, the last step in JEA for PowerShell remoting is to register a JEA endpoint. A **JEA endpoint** is an administrative paradigm that represents a set of users, a list of tasks they can perform, and resources to which they have access. A JEA endpoint is defined by creating a PowerShell session configuration file that specifies who can use the endpoint and the roles to which they have access.

To register a JEA endpoint, you create a session configuration file, which is a PowerShell data file with a .pssc extension (PowerShell session configuration). In this file, you will define a variety of options that determine the specifics of the endpoint:

- The JEA endpoint name
- Accounts that are granted access
- The roles of the granted accounts
- The identity under which the endpoint runs

The last item in the previous list requires explanation. One of the ways that JEA maintains security is that when a user enters a JEA session, the performed tasks are executed with an identity that is specified in the configuration file rather than with the user's identity.

Like the PowerShell role capability file (.psrc) discussed earlier, the PowerShell session configuration file is a template with various sections that you fill out to define the details of the JEA session. You create the file using the following cmdlet:

```
New-PSSessionConfigurationFile -Full -SessionType RestrictedRemoteServer -Path
    path\filename.pssc
```

In the preceding cmdlet, the SessionType parameter of RestrictedRemoteServer specifies that this is a JEA PowerShell remoting session configuration. The -Full option creates a template file with more options included. Some of the key sections of this file are explained next (see Figure 6-15):

- *TranscriptDirectory*—Specify a path to a transcript directory. When enabled, a transcript of the PowerShell session is created that specifies the actual user account connecting to the session, the identity used to run the session, and which commands were executed.

- *RunAsVirtualAccount*—This option is specified as either true or false. If this option is set to true ($true is the built-in PowerShell variable that contains the value true), a temporary virtual account is used for the duration of the PowerShell session. On a domain member computer, this virtual account is assigned as a member of the local Administrator's group; on a domain controller, it is assigned as a member of the Domain Admins group.

- *RunAsVirtualAccountGroups*—If the roles assigned in the session don't require administrative access, you can specify this option and list the groups to which the virtual account should be assigned instead of an administrator group.

- *GroupManagedServiceAccount*—If JEA users require network resources, this identity should be used instead of a virtual account. A GMSA allows the user to authenticate to any computer in the domain with rights that are determined by the resource being accessed. This identity option gives users broad access and should only be used when necessary. Furthermore, the user account that connects to the session is not included in the session transcript, which makes auditing somewhat more difficult.

- *RoleDefinitions*—This is where you specify the role capability file (.psrc file). This section maps users or groups to the role capability file for the user or group using a hash table. (Groups are preferred over specifying individual user accounts.) In the hash table shown in Figure 6-15, the item to the left of the first equal sign is the user or group name, and the items following RoleCapabilities are the names of the role capability file(s) without the .psrc extension. Users and groups can be assigned multiple roles, but you can only specify the user or group one time in the hash table. Role capabilities can be specified multiple times in the hash file. Instead of specifying a role capability file, you can include a list of visible cmdlets, functions, or external commands directly in the hash table; however, a role capability file is preferred.

Typically, you place the session configuration file in a folder named JEAConfiguration, which you create in the C:\ProgramData folder. You must place the JEA session configuration file on each computer that must be managed using JEA for PowerShell remoting.

```
# Directory to place session transcripts for this session configuration
# TranscriptDirectory = 'C:\Transcripts\'

# Whether to run this session configuration as the machine's (virtual) administrator account
# RunAsVirtualAccount = $true

# Groups associated with machine's (virtual) administrator account
# RunAsVirtualAccountGroups = 'Remote Desktop Users', 'Remote Management Users'

# Group managed service account name under which the configuration will run
# GroupManagedServiceAccount = 'CONTOSO\GroupManagedServiceAccount'

# User roles (security groups), and the role capabilities that should be applied to them
when applied to a session
# RoleDefinitions = @{
'CONTOSO\SqlAdmins' = @{ RoleCapabilities = 'SqlAdministration' };
'CONTOSO\SqlManaged' = @{ RoleCapabilities = 'SqlManaged' };
'CONTOSO\ServerMonitors' = @{ VisibleCmdlets = 'Get-Process' } }
```

Figure 6-15   JEA session configuration file

The last step for configuring JEA PowerShell remoting is to register the new configuration on the target computer using the following PowerShell cmdlet:

```
Register-PSSessionConfiguration -Name <SessionName> -Path <PathTo_pssc_file>
```

You must run this cmdlet on each computer that must be managed. The `-Name` parameter is a friendly name for the session, such as `DNS_Operators_Session`, and will be used by users when they connect to a session.

Users can connect to a JEA session from their domain member computers using the following cmdlet:

```
Enter-PSSession -ComputerName <targetcomputer> -ConfigurationName <Session Name>
  -Credential (Get-Credential)
```

In the preceding cmdlet, a new PowerShell session is started on the computer indicated by the `-ComputerName` parameter. The `-ConfigurationName` parameter is the session name assigned with the `Register-PSSessionConfiguration` cmdlet on the target computer. You will be prompted for your credentials, and you will be granted access to PowerShell features based on the session configuration file and role capability file.

> **Note ③**
>
> Be sure to enter the `Enable-PSremoting` cmdlet on any target computers that will be accessed remotely with PowerShell.

Configuring Windows Firewall for Remote Management

Adding a server to Server Manager and enabling WinRM gives you only a few remote management capabilities. You can view the status of a remote server, run PowerShell, add and remove server roles, restart a server, and perform some additional tasks. However, to use an MMC to manage a remote server, you need to make some firewall rule changes on the remote server. To further complicate matters, different MMCs require different firewall rule changes. If you right-click a remote server in Server Manager and click Computer Management, for example, you get an error message that you must enable some firewall rules on the remote server (see Figure 6-16).

Figure 6-16   An error when trying to manage a server remotely

Configuring Firewall Rules with Desktop Experience

If the remote server you want to manage is running the Desktop Experience, you can use the Windows Firewall with Advanced Security MMC to configure firewall rules. You need to sign in to the remote server and open the Windows Firewall with Advanced Security console. In the Inbound Rules section, enable the following rules (see Figure 6-17):

- COM+ Network Access (DCOM-In)
- Remote Event Log Management (NP-In)
- Remote Event Log Management (RPC)
- Remote Event Log Management (RPC-EPMAP)

Enabling the preceding rules makes it possible to run most MMCs and snap-ins for managing a remote server.

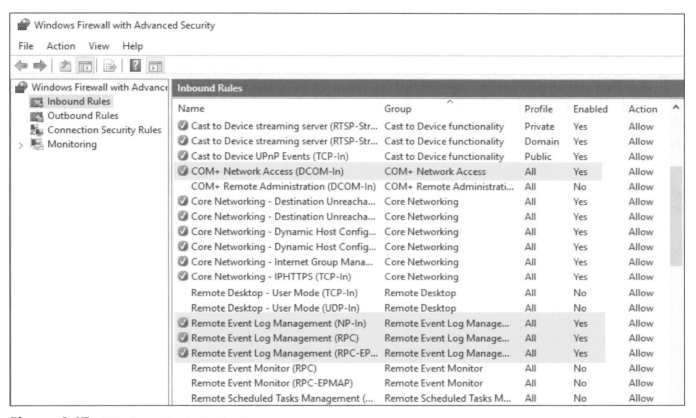

Figure 6-17   Windows Firewall rules for remote management

Configuring Firewall Rules with the Command Line

You can configure the firewall with the `netsh` command or the `Set-NetwFirewallRule` cmdlet in PowerShell. To enable the four rules highlighted in Figure 6-17 with `netsh`, use the following commands:

```
netsh advfirewall firewall set rule group = "COM+ Network Access" new enable=yes
netsh advfirewall firewall set rule group = "Remote Event Log Management" new enable=yes
```

Note 4

Using the `group` keyword in these commands sets all three Remote Event Log Management rules at the same time.

The `netsh` command can be used to configure the firewall remotely, but *first* the Windows Firewall Remote Management group rules must be enabled on the remote computer, and they're disabled by default. To specify a remote computer in the `netsh` command, use the `-r RemoteComputer` parameter (replacing `RemoteComputer` with the name or IP address of the computer you're configuring).

To use PowerShell to configure the firewall, open a PowerShell command prompt window and enter the following commands:

```
Set-NetFirewallRule -DisplayGroup "COM+ Network Access" -enabled True
Set-NetFirewallRule -DisplayGroup "Remote Event Log Management" -enabled True
```

You can issue these commands while signed in to the remote computer or by opening a PowerShell command prompt remotely, as shown in Activity 6-3.

Special Considerations for Server Core

Server Core doesn't have the COM+ Network Access firewall group, and firewall rules for several MMC snap-ins might need to be enabled separately. You might want to enable the necessary firewall rules on the Server Core computer first so that you can manage the firewall remotely using the Windows Firewall with Advanced Security snap-in. To do so, open a PowerShell command prompt window on the Server Core computer and enter the following command:

```
Set-NetFirewallRule -DisplayGroup "Windows Firewall Remote Management" -enabled True
```

After you have enabled the firewall rule, you can create a Windows Firewall with Advanced Security MMC snap-in on a client computer or another server to manage the Server Core computer's firewall. Here are some other firewall rule groups you might want to enable on the Server Core computer for remote management with MMCs:

- *File and Printer Sharing*—Enables use of the Shared Folders snap-in and most of the other snap-ins in Computer Management, with the exception of Event Viewer and Device Manager.
- *Remote Event Log Management*—Allows use of the Event Viewer snap-in.
- *Remote Volume Management*—Enables you to use the Disk Management snap-in to manage disks remotely. This firewall rule group must be enabled on both the Server Core computer and the computer where you're running Disk Management.
- *Remote Service Management*—Allows use of the Services snap-in.
- *Performance Logs and Alerts*—Enables use of the Performance Monitor snap-in.
- *Remote Scheduled Tasks Management*—Allows use of the Task Scheduler snap-in.

Note 5

You can't access Device Manager remotely on Windows Server 2022 systems.

Self-Check Questions

2. If you want to manage servers remotely using Server Manager on a workgroup computer, what do you need to do for each remote server?

   a. Disable the firewall on each remote server.

   b. Enable the SSH protocol.

   c. Add each server to a Server Manager group.

   d. Add the server name to the TrustedHosts file.

3. Which of the following is a reason to configure CredSSP?

   a. To use Server Manager on a remote computer

   b. To use PowerShell second-hop remoting

   c. To connect to a remote server using the command prompt

   d. To manage Azure VMs with Server Manager

Check your answers at the end of this module.

Activity 6-4

Adding Servers to Server Manager and Creating Server Groups

Time Required: 15 minutes
Objective: Add a server to Server Manager and create a server group.
Required Tools and Equipment: ServerDC1, ServerDM1, ServerDM2
Description: You have one server running the Desktop Experience and one running Server Core. You want to manage the server running Server Core with Server Manager, so you add it to Server Manager on the server running the Desktop Experience. Next, you create a server group and place both servers in the group.

1. Start all three servers, if necessary: ServerDC1, ServerDM1, and ServerDM2.
2. Sign in to ServerDM1 as the **domain Administrator** (AZ800\administrator).
3. In Server Manager, click **Manage** and then **Add Servers** from the menu to open the Add Servers window (see Figure 6-18).

> ### Note 6
>
> If the servers you plan to manage aren't domain members, you must add them to the TrustedHosts list. In PowerShell, type `Set-Item wsman:\localhost\Client\TrustedHosts` *ServerName* `-Concatenate -Force`. (The *ServerName* must be the fully qualified domain name or the IP address of the server.)

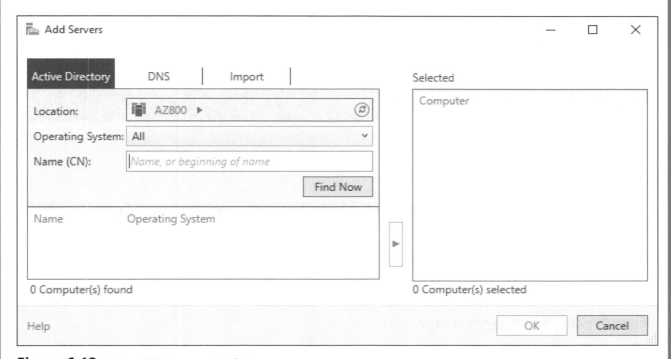

Figure 6-18   The Add Servers window

4. Be sure the Active Directory tab is selected and click the **Find Now** button. Click **ServerDM2** and then click the right-pointing arrow to move ServerDM2 to the Selected box (see Figure 6-19). Click **OK**.
5. In Server Manager, click **Dashboard** in the left pane, if necessary. Scroll down to the Roles and Server Groups section. Notice that the File and Storage Services box displays the number 2, indicating that two servers are running the File and Storage Services role. The All Servers box also displays a 2.
6. In the left pane of Server Manager, click **All Servers**. You should see both ServerDM1 and ServerDM2 in the list of servers (see Figure 6-20).

(continues)

Activity 6-4 Continued

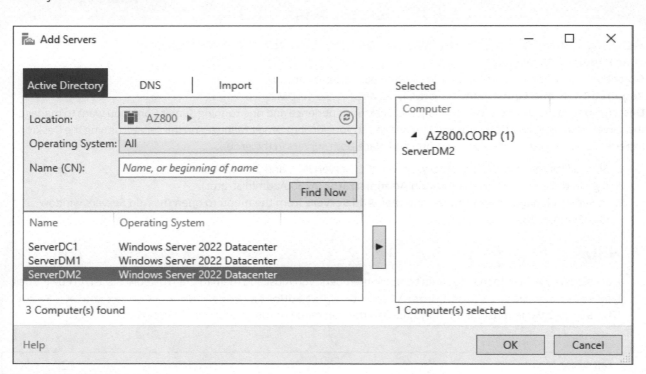

Figure 6-19 Adding a server

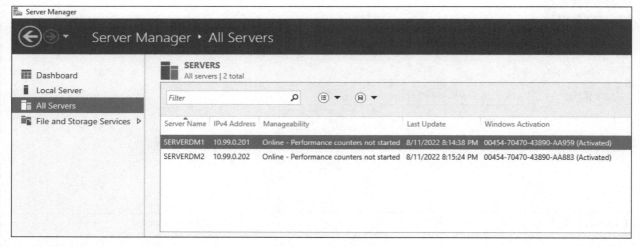

Figure 6-20 The All Servers window

7. Click **ServerDM2**. The Events box changes to show recent events generated on the ServerDM2 server. Scroll down to view the Services box, which shows the status of services running on ServerDM2.

8. Scroll back up to the list of servers and right-click **ServerDM2**. You see a number of management options you can perform on the server, including Add Roles and Features, Restart Server, and Computer Management. Click **Computer Management**. Before you can use MMCs to manage a remote server, you need to configure Windows Firewall on the remote server, but if the virtual machines were preconfigured with the correct firewall settings, Computer Management will open without error. In either case, the following steps help you configure the firewall for remote management. Close the Computer Management window.

(continues)

Activity 6-4 Continued

9. Right-click **ServerDM2** and click **Windows PowerShell**. Notice that the prompt is prefaced with [ServerDM2.AZ800.corp], indicating you are connected to ServerDM2. To set the firewall for remote management with the Computer Management MMC, type **Set-NetFirewallRule -DisplayGroup "Remote Event Log Management" –Enabled True** and press **Enter**. Close the PowerShell window.

10. In Server Manager, right-click **ServerDM2** and click **Computer Management**. The Computer Management MMC opens successfully. Click each snap-in to see which you can use; it may take a while to open each snap-in after you click it. You should be able to use all of them except Device Manager, which can't be remotely managed, and Disk Management, which requires additional firewall configuration. Close Computer Management.

11. In Server Manager, click **Manage** and then **Create Server Group** from the menu to open the dialog box shown in Figure 6-21.

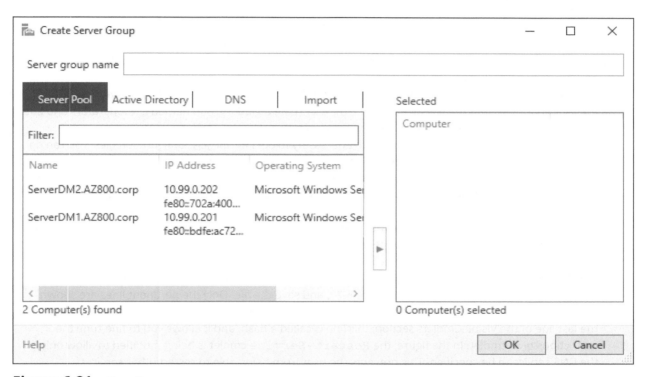

Figure 6-21   Creating a server group

12. In the Server group name text box, type **Domain Members**.

13. In the list of servers, click **ServerDM1**, and then click the right-pointing arrow to move the server to the Selected list box. Next, add **ServerDM2** to the Selected box. Click **OK**.

14. In Server Manager, click **Domain Members** in the left pane. You see the two servers ServerDM1 and ServerDM2 listed.

15. Next, you'll delete the server group. In the left pane of Server Manager, right-click **Domain Members** and click **Delete Server Group**. When prompted to confirm the deletion, click **OK**.

16. In the left pane of Server Manager, click **All Servers**. Right-click **ServerDM2** and click **Remove Server**. When prompted to confirm the deletion, click **OK**.

17. Shut down all three servers before continuing to the next activity.

Activity 6-5

Deploying JEA for PowerShell Remoting

Time Required: 45 minutes
Objective: Configure JEA for PowerShell remoting.
Required Tools and Equipment: ServerDC1, ServerDM1
Description: You want to delegate some of the DNS management tasks to a junior administrator. You will apply the principle of least privilege; the junior administrator doesn't have administrative capabilities in the domain, so you will configure JEA for PowerShell remoting and allow your colleague to perform DNS tasks that otherwise would require administrator privileges.

1. Start both servers, if necessary: ServerDC1 and ServerDM1.
2. Sign in to **ServerDC1** as the **domain Administrator**. The first thing you'll do is create a user account to perform DNS administrative tasks and create a regular user that will pose as the junior administrator.
3. Open Active Directory Users and Computers. Create a new OU named JEAUsers under the domain node. Next, create a new OU named JRAdmins, also under the domain node.
4. In the JRAdmins OU, create a user account named **JrAdmin1** with the password **Password01**. Set the account options so that the password never expires.
5. In the JEAUsers OU, create a user account named **DNSoper1** with the password **Password01**. Set the account options so that the password never expires. Create a global group named DNSoperators and add DNSoper1 to the DNSoperators group. Close Active Directory Users and Computers.
6. Open a PowerShell window. You will create the necessary folders for the JEA configuration files. You can do this in File Explorer or at a command prompt if you prefer, but the instructions here use PowerShell cmdlets. Remember to use the Tab key while typing in the commands, including path names, to decrease the amount of typing required. Type **New-Item "C:\Program Files\WindowsPowerShell\Modules\JEA\RoleCapabilities"** **-ItemType Directory** and press **Enter**. This is the folder where you will place the role capability file.
7. Create the role capability file. Type **New-PSRoleCapabilityFile "C:\Program Files\WindowsPowerShell\Modules\JEA\RoleCapabilities\DNSOperator.psrc"** and press **Enter**.
8. Next, edit the file you just created. You can use Notepad. Type **Notepad "C:\Program Files\WindowsPowerShell\Modules\JEA\RoleCapabilities\DNSOperator.psrc"** and press **Enter**.
9. Edit the highlighted lines, as shown in Figure 6-22, and save the file. Only the pertinent lines are shown in the figure. Notice that all the other sections of the file have a comment in front of each line. Look at the last line of the VisibleCmdlets section; this line is called a hash, and it allows you to fine-tune the restrictions on a cmdlet. In the figure, the `Restart-Service` cmdlet is being modified to allow only the DNS service to be specified. This prevents the user from being able to restart other services.

```
*DNSOperator - Notepad

File  Edit  Format  View  Help

# Description of the functionality provided by these settings
Description = 'DNS operators role capabilities file'

# Cmdlets to make visible when applied to a session
VisibleCmdlets = 'Add-DnsServerResourceRecord', 'Add-DnsServerForwarder',
'Clear-DnsServerCache', 'Clear-DnsServerStatistics', 'Get-DnsServer',
'Get-DnsServerCache', 'Get-DnsServerSetting', 'Get-DnsServerStatistics',
@{ Name = 'Restart-Service'; Parameters = @{ Name = 'Name'; ValidateSet = 'DNS' } }
```

Figure 6-22   Editing the role capability file

(continues)

Activity 6-5 Continued

10. Now you need to create the PowerShell session configuration file. This file is traditionally placed in the ProgramData folder. Create a new folder: Type **New-Item C:\ProgramData\JEAConfiguration -ItemType Directory** and press **Enter**.
11. Create the session configuration file: Type **New-PSSessionConfigurationFile C:\ProgramData\ JEAConfiguration\JEADnsSession.pssc** and press **Enter**.
12. Open the file in Notepad: Type **notepad C:\ProgramData\JEAConfiguration\JEADnsSession.pssc** and press **Enter**. Edit the highlighted lines, as shown in Figure 6-23, and save the file. In the RoleDefinitions section, the hash first specifies the group that the role capabilities apply to (az800\DNSOperators), followed by the name of the role capability file without the .psrc extension.

```
# Session type defaults to apply for this session configuration. Can be 'RestrictedRemoteServer'
SessionType = 'RestrictedRemoteServer'

# Directory to place session transcripts for this session configuration
TranscriptDirectory = 'C:\ProgramData\JEAConfiguration\Transcripts\'

# Whether to run this session configuration as the machine's (virtual) administrator account
RunAsVirtualAccount = $true

# User roles (security groups), and the role capabilities that should be applied to them when ap
RoleDefinitions = @{ 'az800\DNSOperators' = @{ RoleCapabilities = 'DNSOperator' }}
```

Figure 6-23   Editing the session configuration file

13. Register the session configuration. In PowerShell, type **Register-PSSessionConfiguration -Name DNSSession -Path C:\ProgramData\JEAConfiguration\JEADnsSession.pssc** and press **Enter**. You should see output similar to that in Figure 6-24.

```
PS C:\Users\Administrator> Register-PSSessionConfiguration -Name "DNSSession" -path C:\ProgramData\JEAConfiguration\JEAD
nsSession.pssc
WARNING: Register-PSSessionConfiguration may need to restart the WinRM service if a configuration using this name has
recently been unregistered, certain system data structures may still be cached. In that case, a restart of WinRM may be
 required.
All WinRM sessions connected to Windows PowerShell session configurations, such as Microsoft.PowerShell and session
configurations that are created with the Register-PSSessionConfiguration cmdlet, are disconnected.


   WSManConfig: Microsoft.WSMan.Management\WSMan::localhost\Plugin

Type          Keys                    Name
----          ----                    ----
Container     {Name=DNSSession}       DNSSession
```

Figure 6-24   Output from the `Register-PSSessionConfiguration` cmdlet

14. Next, type **Get-PSSessionConfiguration DNSSession** and press **Enter** to see the session settings.
15. Sign in to **ServerDM1** as **JrAdmin1** using the password **Password01**. Open a PowerShell window. First, let's see what happens if you attempt to use PowerShell remoting without using JEA. Type **Enter-PSSession -ComputerName ServerDC1** and press **Enter**. The command uses your current username for credentials. You will see an error message that access is denied because user Jradmin1 doesn't have permissions for PowerShell remoting to ServerDC1. If you had signed in to ServerDM1 as the domain administrator, you would have been given access with full administrative capabilities in the PowerShell prompt.

(continues)

Activity 6-5 Continued

16. Now, enter the JEA session: Type **Enter-PSSession -ComputerName ServerDC1 -ConfigurationName DNSSession -Credential (Get-Credential)** and press **Enter**. When prompted, enter **DNSOper1** for the username and **Password01** for the password.

17. You should get a new prompt that looks like [ServerDC1]: PS>. You are connected to ServerDC1 with PowerShell. To see the list of cmdlets that are available, type **Get-Command** and press **Enter**. You should see output similar to that in Figure 6-25. Note that you will see a few other cmdlets listed besides the DNS-related cmdlets specified in the role capability file. These additional cmdlets are available by default in every PowerShell remoting session.

```
PS C:\Users\JrAdmin1> Enter-PSSession -ComputerName ServerDC1 -ConfigurationName DNSSession -Credential (Get-Credential)

cmdlet Get-Credential at command pipeline position 1
Supply values for the following parameters:
Credential
[ServerDC1]: PS>get-command

CommandType     Name                                Version    Source
-----------     ----                                -------    ------
Function        Add-DnsServerResourceRecord         2.0.0.0    DnsServer
Function        Clear-DnsServerCache                2.0.0.0    DnsServer
Function        Clear-Host
Function        Exit-PSSession
Function        Get-Command
Function        Get-DnsServer                       2.0.0.0    DnsServer
Function        Get-DnsServerCache                  2.0.0.0    DnsServer
Function        Get-DnsServerSetting                2.0.0.0    DnsServer
Function        Get-FormatData
Function        Get-Help
Function        Measure-Object
Function        Out-Default
Function        Restart-Service
Function        Select-Object
```

Figure 6-25   The `Enter-PSSession` **cmdlet and output from the** `Get-Command` **cmdlet**

18. Close all windows and continue to the next activity.

Using Windows Admin Center

Microsoft Exam AZ-800:
Manage Windows servers and workloads in a hybrid environment.
- Manage Windows servers in a hybrid environment

Windows Admin Center provides another way to remotely manage both on-premises and Azure VM servers and client stations. It is a browser-based application that can be downloaded free from the Microsoft Evaluation Center. You can install Windows Admin Center on a client workstation running Windows 10 or 11, or you can install the Windows Admin Center Gateway on a Windows Server computer to allow all the computers in the network to use it without any locally installed software except a web browser. Windows Admin Center has been tested to work with Microsoft Edge and Chrome.

Windows Admin Center can be installed using four different methods, depending on your needs:

- *Local client*—Installed on a Windows 10 or 11 computer to manage local servers in a small environment or for testing.
- *Gateway server*—Installed on a Windows Server computer to allow any client machine that has access to the gateway server to manage all the servers in your enterprise.

- *Managed server*—Installed on a Windows Server computer so you can manage the server from a client web browser.
- *Failover cluster*—Installed as a gateway server in a Windows failover cluster, providing high availability to Windows Admin Center.

This section covers the local client and gateway server installation options.

Grow with Cengage Unlimited

Using Windows Admin Center in a failover cluster is covered in the *Microsoft Guide to Configuring Windows Server Advanced Services, Exam AZ-801*, which is also published by Cengage.

Installing Windows Admin Center on Windows 11

You can install Windows Admin Center on Windows 10 or Windows 11, which gives you a web-based interface to manage the local computer, PCs, and servers in your network, and Azure VMs. To install Windows Admin Center, do an Internet search for "Windows Admin Center download" and find a download link, or use this link to download it directly: *https://aka.ms/wacdownload*. After you install Windows Admin Center, you can start it from a shortcut on the desktop or from the Start menu. Windows Admin Center will open in a browser window with the address *https://localhost:6516*. You will see a page similar to that in Figure 6-26, except you will only see a link for the local PC. In the figure, three servers have been added by clicking the Add button on the upper-left side of the page.

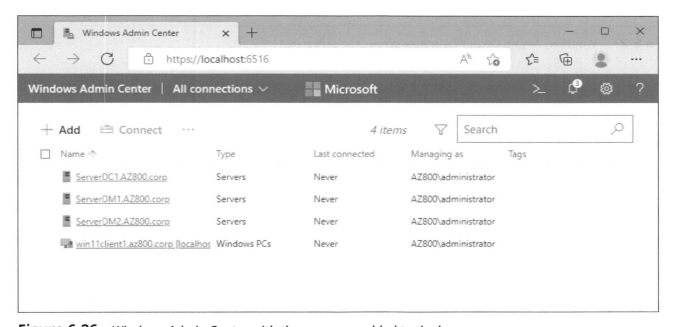

Figure 6-26 Windows Admin Center with three servers added to the home screen

To manage a server or PC, click the link for the desired device; Windows Admin Center will connect to the specified device. Figure 6-27 shows the web page after the ServerDC1.AZ800.corp link is selected. When you connect to a Windows 10 or 11 computer, you see the web-based Computer Management interface. When you connect to a server, you see the web-based Server Manager interface, as shown in Figure 6-27.

The left side of the page shows the tools available for managing the server.

As you can see in Figure 6-27, there are several tools that integrate with Azure. Some of the tools available include Performance Monitor, Scheduled Tasks, Firewall, Storage, Services, and PowerShell. If you click PowerShell, a PowerShell prompt opens in the right pane, allowing you to execute PowerShell cmdlets on the selected server (see Figure 6-28).

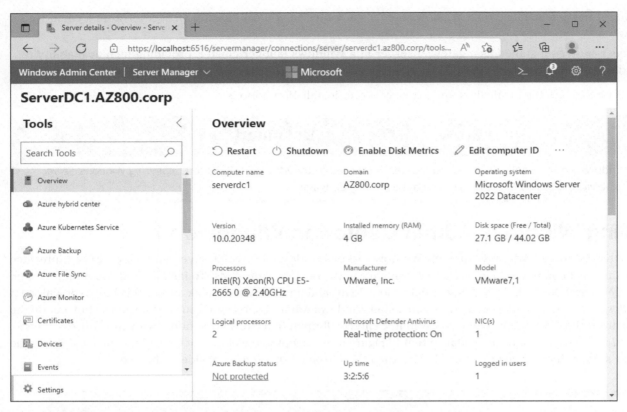

Figure 6-27 Windows Admin Center Overview screen for ServerDC1

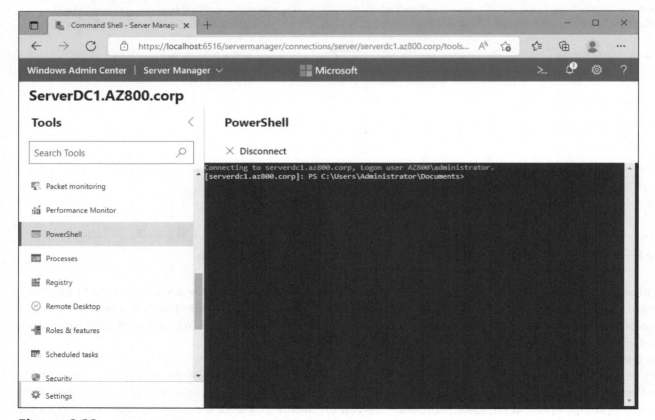

Figure 6-28 Windows Admin Center PowerShell tool

Installing Windows Admin Center Gateway

As mentioned, Windows Admin Center Gateway can be installed on Windows Server; it allows you to manage multiple servers using that server as a gateway. The advantage of this type of installation is that you only need to install Windows Admin Center on one computer. Any other computer in your network can then access it to manage all the servers in your network.

When you install Windows Admin Center on a Windows Server computer, the installation program detects that you are running Windows Server and installs it as a service. During installation, you are asked if you want Windows Admin Center to modify the trusted hosts settings. This option allows you to manage servers if the installation server is not in the same domain as the managed servers, without you having to manually add the servers to the trusted hosts file. You are also prompted for the port number (see Figure 6-29). The default port is 443 (HTTPS); the server will use a self-signed certificate by default. Or, you can use a certificate that is already installed on the server.

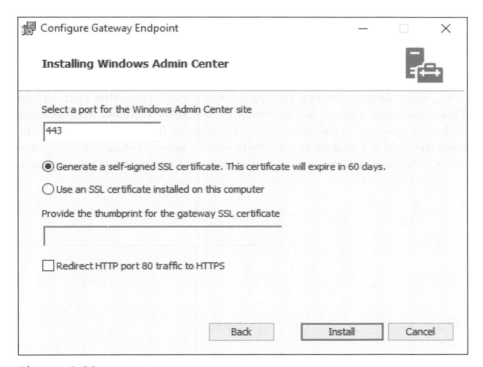

Figure 6-29   Installing Windows Admin Center

After installation, you can connect to Windows Admin Center from another computer using the IP address or DNS name of the installation server. You are prompted for credentials. You can use domain credentials if the installation server is in the domain, or you can use a local account. Once signed in, you see a screen similar to that in Figure 6-26 shown earlier, with a link to the installation server. Now you can add more servers to manage by clicking the Add button. You are prompted to choose what type of system you want to add, as shown in Figure 6-30. You can add local servers, PCs, clusters, or Azure VMs. Just click on a category and type the name of the computer or cluster to add it to the connections page.

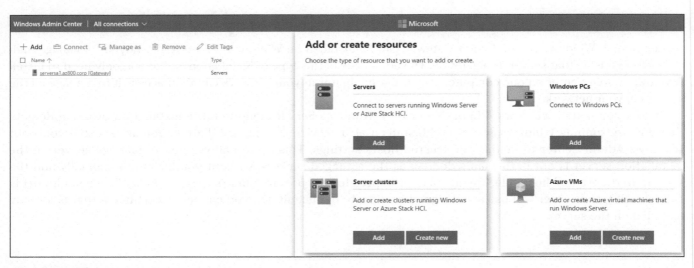

Figure 6-30   Adding servers to Windows Admin Center

Managing Azure VMs with Admin Center Gateway

If you want to manage your Azure VMs with Admin Center Gateway, choose the Azure VMs option after clicking Add on the connections page. When you add your first Azure VM, you will be prompted to register Windows Admin Center with Azure. Azure Active Directory must already be set up in the portal. You'll see a dialog box similar to Figure 6-31; after you copy the code, you click the Enter the code link and paste it in the browser window that opens. Then, sign in to the Azure portal and close the browser window. Finish the registration by clicking Connect, and then click Sign in and provide your Azure credentials.

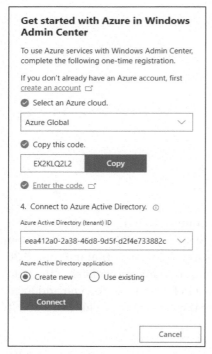

Figure 6-31   Registering Windows
Admin Center as an Azure AD app

You can now add Azure VMs to Windows Admin Center. You can connect to Azure VMs that have a public IP address as long as WinRM is enabled on the target VM and TCP port 5985 is open for inbound connections from the gateway to the target VM.

If you want to manage a VM that does not have a public IP address, you must establish a connection to the Azure network using ExpressRoute or a VPN.

Self-Check Questions

4. Which Windows Admin Center installation option should you use to manage a single server from a client web browser?

    a. Failover cluster   **c.** Gateway server
    b. Managed server   **d.** Local client

5. If you want to install Windows Admin Center on an on-premises Windows Server 2022 computer, and you want to manage Azure VMs from a web browser running on Windows 11, what type of installation should you use?

    a. Gateway server   **c.** Managed server
    b. Local client   **d.** Azure Arc server

◉Check your answers at the end of this module.

Activity 6-6

Deploying Windows Admin Center
Time Required: 45 minutes
Objective: Install Windows Admin Center Gateway on a server.
Required Tools and Equipment: ServerDC1, ServerSA1
Description: In this activity, you install Windows Admin Center Gateway on a server, which allows you to manage multiple servers using the gateway server.

1. Start both servers, if necessary: ServerDC1 and ServerSA1.
2. Sign in to **ServerSA1** as the local Administrator. Open a web browser and go to **https://www.microsoft.com/en-us/evalcenter/download-windows-admin-center**. If the link no longer works, do a search for "Windows Admin Center download" and find the download link.
3. Download the current version of Windows Admin Center, which is 2110.2 as of this writing. Open the installation file and start the installation process. Follow the installation wizard, accepting the default options. You will be installing the Gateway version of Windows Admin Center, which is the default option when installing on Windows Server. The default port when installing the gateway is 443, which is suitable in most instances. On the port selection page, you can also choose to redirect port 80 to 443 so users that use HTTP (port 80) in the URL will be redirected to HTTPS (port 443).
4. When the installation is finished, point your browser to *https://serversa1*; you should see a window indicating that Windows Admin Center was successfully installed. After you close the window, you'll see that the All connections window lists serversa1 (see Figure 6-32).

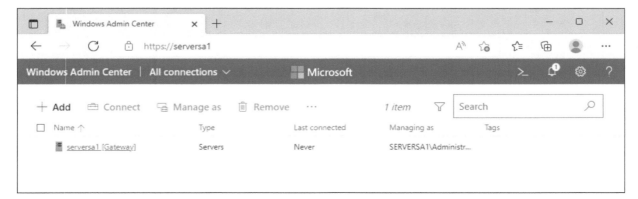

Figure 6-32   Windows Admin Center: All connections page

(continues)

Activity 6-6 Continued

5. Click **Add** to add servers to manage. You'll see links to resources you can add. Click **Add** in the Servers box. You are prompted to enter a server name. Type **serverdc1**. Alternatively, you can import a list of servers that you have in a .txt or .csv file, or you can search Active Directory. When ServerDC1 is found, click **Add** (see Figure 6-33). ServerDC1 is added to the connections page.

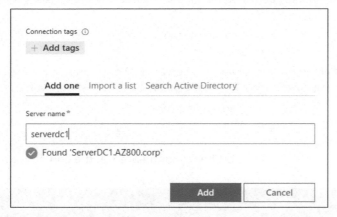

Figure 6-33 Windows Admin Center: Add a server

6. Click the **ServerDC1** link to see the Overview page. Scroll through the tools on the left to see what you can manage. You can add capabilities to Windows Admin Center by adding extensions.
7. If you want to manage Active Directory from Windows Admin Center, click the **Settings** icon on the upper-right side of the page. From the Settings page, click **Extensions** from the menu in the left pane and click **Active Directory** in the middle pane (see Figure 6-34).

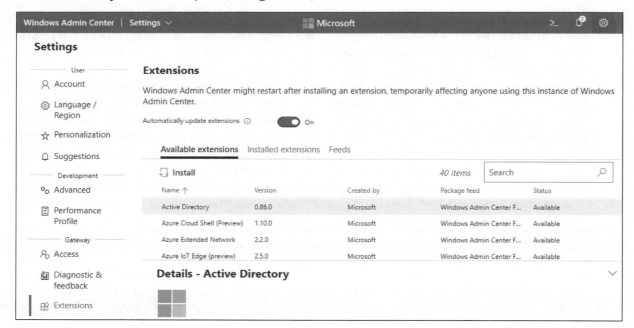

Figure 6-34 Windows Admin Center: Extensions

8. Click **Install** to install the extension. When installation is complete, click **Windows Admin Center** at the top of the page and click **ServerDC1**. You'll see the Active Directory tool in the left pane; after the Overview tool, the tools are listed in alphabetical order. Click **Active Directory**. In the middle pane, click **Browse** to see the contents of Active Directory. Note that as of this writing, the Active Directory extension is a preview version (see Figure 6-35).

(continues)

Activity 6-6 Continued

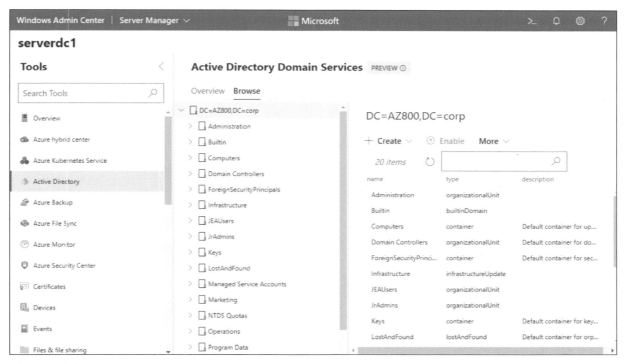

Figure 6-35   Windows Admin Center: The Active Directory extension

9. Click Windows Admin Center to go back to the connections page. Now you will add an Azure VM to Windows Admin Center. Click **Add**. In the Azure VMs box, click **Add**. Before you can add an Azure VM to Windows Admin Center, you need to register the Windows Admin Center app with Azure. Click **Register**.

10. In the Get started with Azure in Windows Admin Center page, click **Copy this code** to copy the code and then click the **Enter the code** link (see Figure 6-36).

11. A web page opens, and you are prompted to enter the code. Press **Ctrl+V** to paste the code you copied. Click **Next**. Provide your Azure portal account credentials. You will be prompted to close the browser window after you have entered your credentials.

12. From the Windows Admin Center browser window, click **Connect**. Then click **Sign in**. You see a Permissions requested window. Click the check box to give your consent and then click **Accept** (see Figure 6-37).

13. You see the Add an Azure VM window. Click **Sign in**. You are prompted for your subscription name, resource group, virtual machine name, and the public IP address of your VM. Click the **Subscription** drop-down box to select your subscription. Then do the same for **Resource Group**, **Virtual Machine**, and **IP Address** (see Figure 6-38). Click **Add** to add the selected VM to Windows Admin Center.

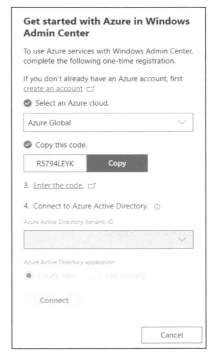

Figure 6-36   Windows Admin Center: Get started with Azure

(continues)

Activity 6-6 Continued

Figure 6-37   Windows Admin Center: Permission requested

Figure 6-38   Windows Admin Center: Add an Azure VM

> **Note 7**
>
> Your VM must have a public IP address, or you must connect to the Azure portal through a VPN/ExpressRoute to manage an Azure VM that has a private IP address. In addition, for a public IP address, TCP port 5985 must be open for inbound connections from the Windows Admin Center gateway to the target VM. If the VM you are trying to manage is configured for just-in-time VM access, you need to request access using the portal before you can manage it with Windows Admin Center.

14. The Azure VM is added to Windows Admin Center using its IP address. The VM must be powered on in order to manage it with Windows Admin Center. Click the IP address to manage the Azure VM like any other server in Windows Admin Center.
15. Close all windows.

Managing Windows Servers with Azure Services

Microsoft Exam AZ-800:

Manage Windows servers and workloads in a hybrid environment.
- Manage Windows servers and workloads by using Azure services

Microsoft Azure provides a host of services for managing Windows servers running in Azure and in your on-premises datacenter. In this section, we'll take a look at a number of these services, including the following:

- Azure Arc
- Just-in-time access to VMs
- Runbooks for VM task automation

Azure Arc

Azure Arc is a management platform that allows you to run Azure services on on-premises servers and even other public clouds and manage all of it using Azure-based tools. Manageable resources include both Windows and Linux servers, Kubernetes clusters, Azure data services, SQL Server and VMs hosted on VMware vSphere and Hyper-V, and third-party cloud providers.

Azure Arc was introduced by Microsoft to allow organizations with substantial datacenters to leverage their existing computing investment and seamlessly use the resources and management tools available in Azure. In other words, Azure Arc offers a truly hybrid infrastructure you can manage using common tools, rather than a disjointed situation where you have to manage your on-premises, third-party cloud, and Azure resources separately.

> **Exam Tip** ✔
>
> The objectives of the AZ-800 exam specify using Azure Arc to manage Windows servers, so that is the focus of this section.

Azure Arc is supported on a variety of OSs, and more are being added. As of this writing, Azure Arc allows you to manage Windows Server 2008 R2, Windows Server 2012 R2, and newer versions. A variety of Linux distributions are supported, including CentOS, SUSE, Ubuntu, Amazon, Oracle, and Red Hat Enterprise.

Before you can start managing physical or virtual servers with Azure Arc, you need to "onboard" them with the Connected Machine agent. **Onboarding** is a process that brings a device under a management system; in this case, by installing the Connected Machine agent, you will be able to manage the server using the Azure portal.

Onboarding Windows Servers for Azure Arc

There are several ways to onboard a server, including using individual PowerShell cmdlets, a Microsoft-provided PowerShell script, Desired State Configuration, and Windows Admin Center. For individual servers, using the Microsoft-provided PowerShell script is simple and straightforward; the procedure is described next.

Here are the steps to onboard a Windows server. The steps for onboarding a Linux server are nearly identical:

1. Sign in to the Azure portal and select Servers – Azure Arc in the services. The fastest way to find the service is to enter "Arc" in the search bar and select Servers – Azure Arc from the search results.

2. Click the Add button to see the options for adding servers. Click Generate script in the Add a single server box (see Figure 6-39).

3. You are shown a list of prerequisites. The server you are onboarding must be able to connect to port 443 outbound. Also, you must have local administrator permission and a way for the server to connect to the Internet to access the Azure portal. After reviewing the prerequisites, click Next.

4. The next page is Resource details, where you select the subscription, resource group, region, operating system, and connectivity method (see Figure 6-40). Under Operating system, you can choose a Windows or Linux server and the script will be modified appropriately. Click Next and create tags for custom views of your resources. Tags are optional. Click Next.

5. On the last page, click Register to register your subscription. You can download the script or copy and paste it into a file. You will be executing the script on the server you want to onboard.

6. Save the script file on the server you want to onboard, and then open a PowerShell window as Administrator and run the script. You may need to change the PowerShell execution policy settings before you can run the script by using the `Set-ExecutionPolicy Bypass` cmdlet.

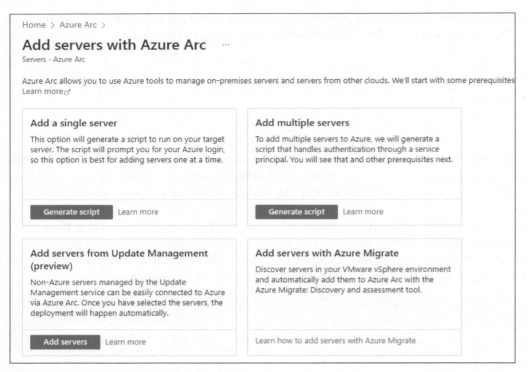

Figure 6-39 Arc onboarding options

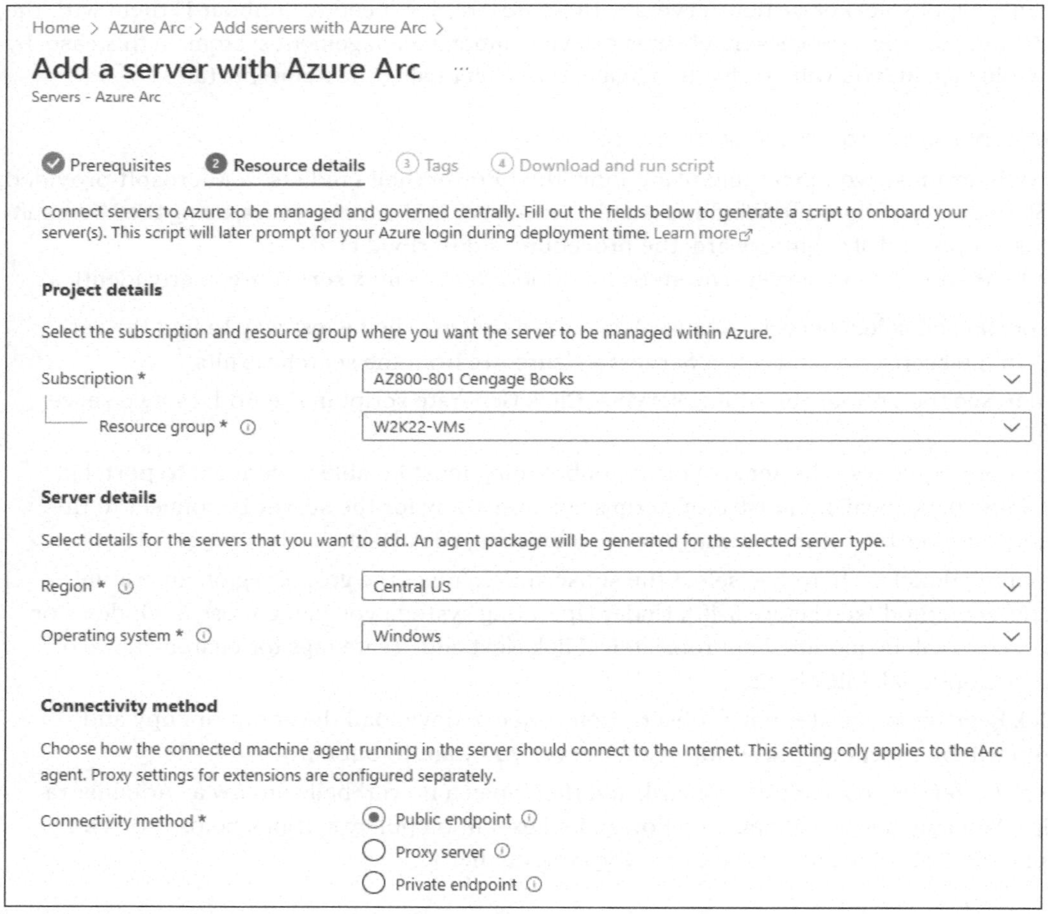

Figure 6-40 Arc onboarding resource details

7. When you run the script, you will be prompted to sign in to *https://microsoft.com/devicelogin* and enter the code provided (see Figure 6-41). When you have been authenticated, the onboarding process completes, and you see a success message. You can now sign in to the Azure portal and go to Servers – Azure Arc to see the onboarded server listed.

```
PS C:\Users\administrator.AZ800\desktop> .\OnboardingScript.ps1
VERBOSE: Installing Azure Connected Machine Agent
VERBOSE: Downloading agent package
VERBOSE: Installing agent package
Installation of azcmagent completed successfully
time="2022-05-23T20:00:35-07:00" level=info msg="Onboarding Machine. It usually takes a few minutes to complete. Sometim
es it may take longer depending on network and server load status."
To sign in, use a web browser to open the page https://microsoft.com/devicelogin and enter the code EB7GRP3QM to authent
icate.
time="2022-05-23T20:03:12-07:00" level=info msg="Successfully Onboarded Resource to Azure" VM Id=87d85728-0733-4a91-b25c
-e6a20568991a
To view your onboarded server(s), navigate to https://portal.azure.com/#blade/HubsExtension/BrowseResource/resourceType/
Microsoft.HybridCompute%2Fmachines
PS C:\Users\administrator.AZ800\desktop> _
```

Figure 6-41   Output from the Arc onboarding script

Managing Windows Servers with Azure Arc

After the Connected Machine agent is installed, you will find your onboarded server in the Azure portal in Servers – Azure Arc. Click the server name to see the Overview page for the server, as shown in Figure 6-42. The overview page shows the connection status, computer name, OS, and other identifying information about the managed server. You can access a number of management features by clicking the options on the left side of the screen. Specifically, we will look at the following Azure Arc management features:

- Policies
- Extensions
- Logs
- Update management
- Security

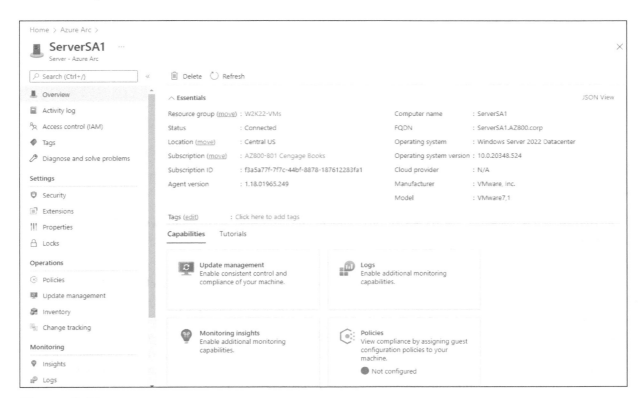

Figure 6-42   Arc-enabled server Overview page

The Policies page allows you to configure the Azure Policy Guest Configuration agent. Azure Policy is an Azure feature that helps to enforce configuration compliance for your Azure resources, such as Azure VMs. It provides both reporting and remediation for out-of-compliance resources. Azure Policy Guest Configuration provides the same service for Arc-enabled non-Azure servers. Azure Policy and Azure Policy Guest Configuration do their job by examining the properties of specified resources and comparing them to rules you create or those that are pre-built and available to you on Azure. These rules are referred to as policy definitions. Azure Policy uses PowerShell Desired State Configuration to perform policy evaluation and remediation. Desired State Configuration is discussed in the next section.

After you install the Connected Machine agent on your onboarded server and select it in Azure Arc in the Azure portal, click Policies from the left menu. You might see that your server is considered noncompliant because a default policy is being applied and your server doesn't meet all the requirements (see Figure 6-43). You can remove the default policy, if desired, or click on the policy name and see which rules are not in compliance.

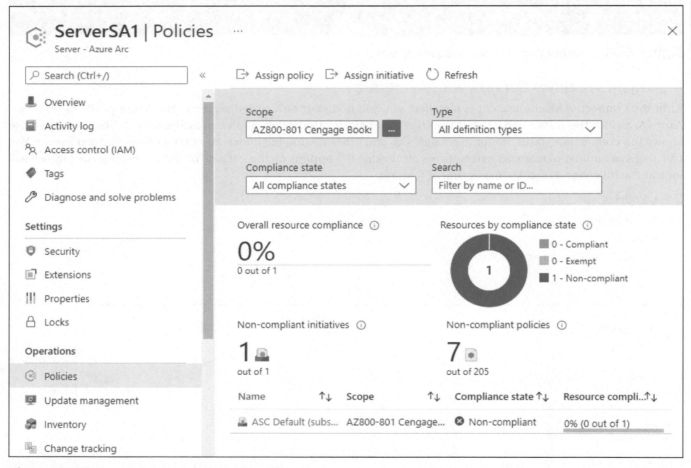

Figure 6-43   Azure Arc server Policies page

We'll add a policy to our server to see the effect it has. Specifically, we'll add Audit Windows machines that do not have a policy of requiring a minimum password age of 1 day. Here are the steps to add a policy definition.

1. From the Server – Azure Arc Overview page, click Policies. Then click Assign policy.
2. From the Assign policy page, select the Scope (Subscription/Resource Group). The Exclusions field can be left blank. The Exclusions field allows you to exclude specific resources from the policy assignment.
3. Click the box next to Policy definition to see a list of available policies. Here you will see the built-in policies and any custom policies you have created. Type Audit in the Search bar to only see policy definitions that include the word *audit*. Scroll down until you find "Audit Windows machines that do not have a minimum password age of 1 day." Click the policy and then click Select (see Figure 6-44). After you select the policy, you can give it a new name and add a description if desired.

Figure 6-44   Azure Arc Policy Definitions

4. Click Next. On the Parameters page, in the Include Arc connected servers box, select "true" and click Next.

5. Accept the default settings on the Remediation page. Because this is an audit policy, no remediation is possible. Policies that deploy or change settings will have remediation parameters. Click Next.

6. On the Noncompliance messages page, you can add a message that explains to users why a resource is not in compliance. For example, for the policy we are adding, you could add the message: Server minimum password age must be at least 1 day.

7. Click Review + create and then click Create. After the policy is applied, you are brought back to the Policies page.

Initially, the Compliance state will be "Not-started." After refreshing the screen a few times (it could take up to 30 minutes), you will see the compliance state. If the server is noncompliant, you can click the policy name and then click Details under Compliance reason on the resulting page to see more information that explains the problem.

Policy compliance is checked twice per day on Windows machines and once per hour on Linux machines. So, if a machine is noncompliant and you make changes to bring it into compliance, it might take a while before you see the results of your changes. Figure 6-45 shows the Policies page after the audit policy is evaluated.

Azure VM Extensions provide additional functions for Arc-enabled VMs. Some of the additional capabilities include running custom scripts, log analytics, Azure Monitor for VM, and Azure Automation using runbooks. Azure VM extensions on Arc-enabled servers can be managed using the Azure portal, Azure CLI, Azure PowerShell, and resource management templates. We'll look at using Azure PowerShell to manage and install Azure VM extensions.

Figure 6-45 Policies page showing compliance

The Azure PowerShell module must be installed on the Azure Arc-enabled server before you can begin managing extensions. To install the module, use the following PowerShell cmdlet on the Arc-enabled server:

```
Install-Module Az-ConnectedMachine
```

The module is probably installed already because it was installed by default when the Connected Machine agent was installed. If it is, you will see a message.

With the Az-ConnectedMachine module installed, you can enable extensions. To create new extensions on an Arc-enabled server, use the following PowerShell cmdlet:

```
New-AzConnectedMachineExtension -Name "ExtensionName" -ResourceGroupName
"ResourceGroupName" -MachineName "MachineName" -Location "RegionName" -Publisher
"ExtensionPublisher" -Settings "SettingsParameters" -ExtensionType "TypeofExtension"
```

The details of adding various extensions using PowerShell are beyond the scope of this book. Many extensions can be added using the Azure portal by selecting the Extensions option on the Azure Arc – Servers page. You can enable log analytics, a key extension that other server monitoring and management features rely on, by enabling the Insights feature. To do so, select the server from Azure Arc – Servers and click Insights in the left column. Click the Enable button to enable the Insights feature (see Figure 6-46).

Figure 6-46 Enabling Azure Insights

Next, choose an Azure Workspace subscription and a Log Analytics workspace. If you don't already have a Log Analytics workspace, a default workspace will be created. Click Enable and wait until deployment is complete; the process could take 10 minutes or longer.

After Insights is enabled, you have several Azure server management and monitoring tools available to you, including Log Analytics, Update management, Inventory, and Change tracking. We'll look a little more at Log Analytics and Update management.

Access Log Analytics by clicking Logs under Monitoring from the Azure Arc – Servers page for the selected server. You will see a Queries page that contains a number of pre-built queries you can run to get information on a host of topics (see Figure 6-47).

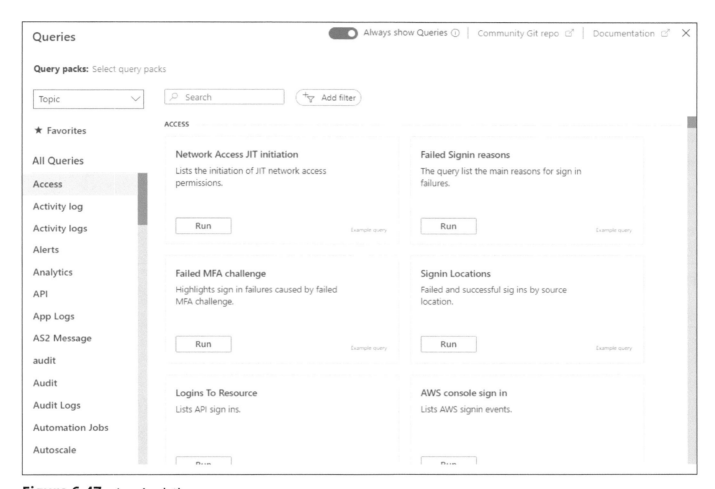

Figure 6-47   Log Analytics

With the Azure Arc Update management feature, you can manage patches and system updates to both Windows and Linux computers. To use Update management, you must have a Log Analytics workspace. The workspace created if you enable Insights is satisfactory, or you can create an additional workspace. You also need an Azure Automation account. To enable Update management, go to your Automation account or create a new one if necessary. From the Automation account, click Update management. If your Automation account was created in a different region from your existing Log Analytics workspace, you'll need to create a new workspace (see Figure 6-48).

After Update management is installed, you will be prompted to add any servers that are linked to the Log Analytics workspace by Update management (see Figure 6-49).

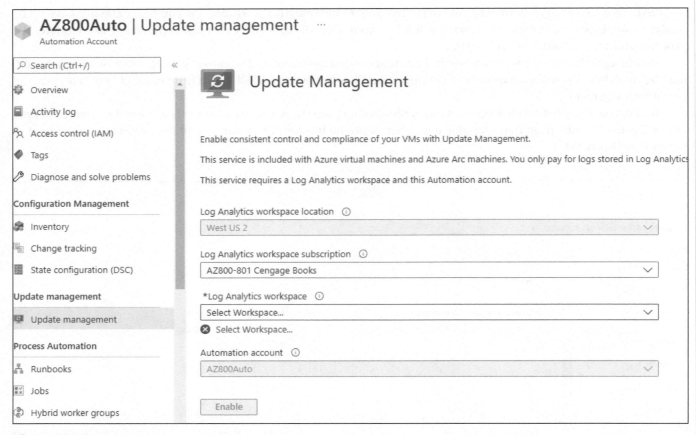

Figure 6-48   Update management

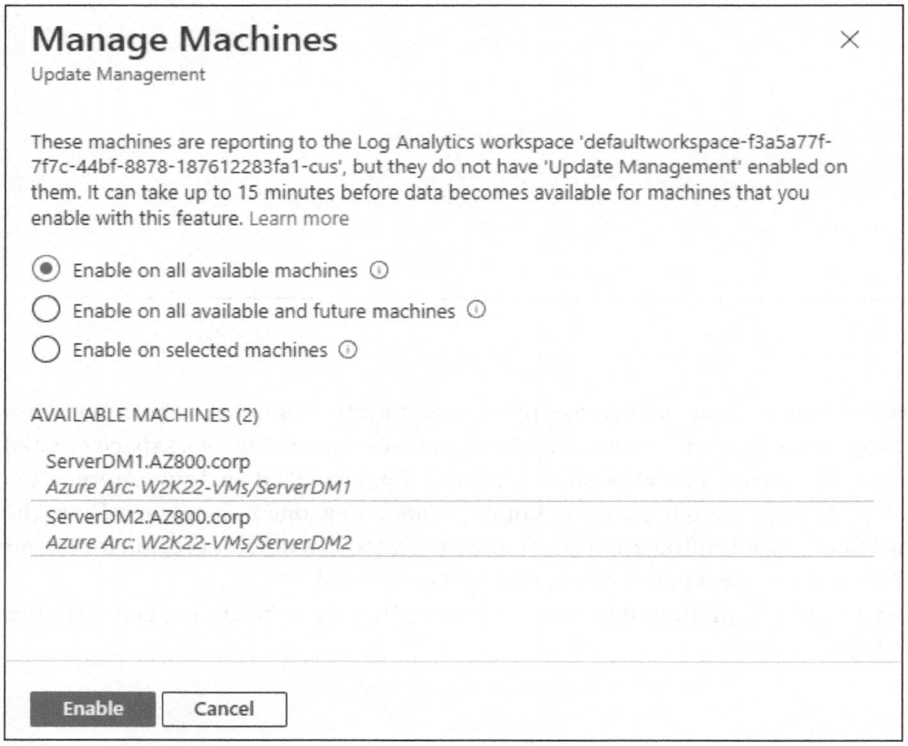

Manage Machines ✕
Update Management

These machines are reporting to the Log Analytics workspace 'defaultworkspace-f3a5a77f-
7f7c-44bf-8878-187612283fa1-cus', but they do not have 'Update Management' enabled on
them. It can take up to 15 minutes before data becomes available for machines that you
enable with this feature. Learn more

◉ Enable on all available machines ⓘ

○ Enable on all available and future machines ⓘ

○ Enable on selected machines ⓘ

AVAILABLE MACHINES (2)

ServerDM1.AZ800.corp
Azure Arc: W2K22-VMs/ServerDM1

ServerDM2.AZ800.corp
Azure Arc: W2K22-VMs/ServerDM2

[Enable]   [Cancel]

Figure 6-49   Update management: Enable servers

After Update management is enabled on the Arc-enabled servers, it may take several minutes before you see the servers on the Update management page. (Figure 6-50 shows servers ready to be assessed.) The update assessment may take several hours, so Microsoft recommends that you let the assessment process run overnight. After the assessment has run, a report details any updates required for the selected servers.

> **Note 8**
>
> You may need to deselect the Update management page and reselect it several times before you see the results of any changes you make on the page. You can see Update management information from the Update management selection under the Azure Automation workspace or the Azure Arc – Servers page.

Figure 6-50   Update management page with two servers ready to be assessed

Azure Security Center

Azure Security Center is a tool that centralizes security configuration and reporting for both Azure-based and Arc-enabled resources. It provides security scanning, notifications, and recommendations for improving your overall security posture. As with Log Analytics and Update management, the Arc-enabled servers must be onboarded before they can participate in Security Center. To onboard the servers, you need to enable Microsoft Defender for Cloud's enhanced security features. A 30-day trial is available if your subscription doesn't include it. To enable Azure Security Center, select your server in Azure Arc – Servers and click Security in the left pane. You'll see a link to upgrade your subscription to the Microsoft Defender for Cloud plan, which brings you to the Getting started page (see Figure 6-51).

On the Getting started page, you'll see pricing for various resources. You can click Upgrade or the Get started tab. If you click Get started, you'll see a page that gives you the option to add non-Azure servers. Click Configure to add Defender for Cloud to Arc-enabled servers. On the Onboard servers to Defender for Cloud page (see Figure 6-52), click Upgrade to add Defender for Cloud to your subscription. You can create a new workspace or use an existing workspace. Next, click Add Servers and select the servers you want to onboard.

Once onboarded, you can see detailed security information about your resources. To see a list of all resources and their status, go to Microsoft Defender for Cloud from the portal home page and click Inventory in the left pane (see Figure 6-53). Click on the server or other resources you want to see information about; a page appears with recommendations and alerts. To get the most out of Microsoft Defender for Cloud, your servers should have the monitoring agent installed; however, you can still get security recommendations without it.

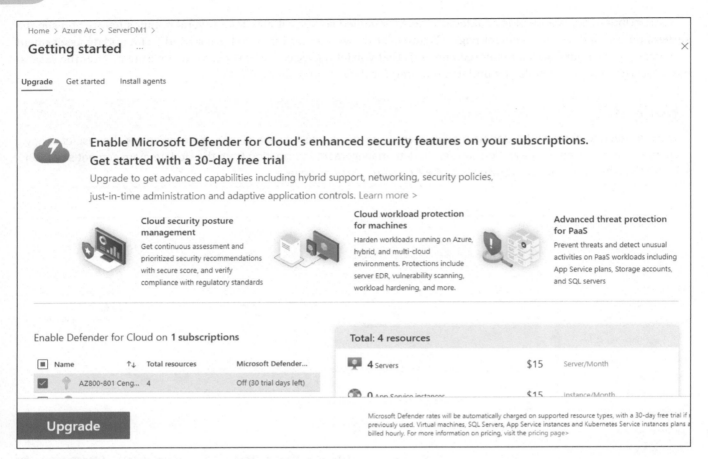

Figure 6-51   Defender for Cloud Getting started page

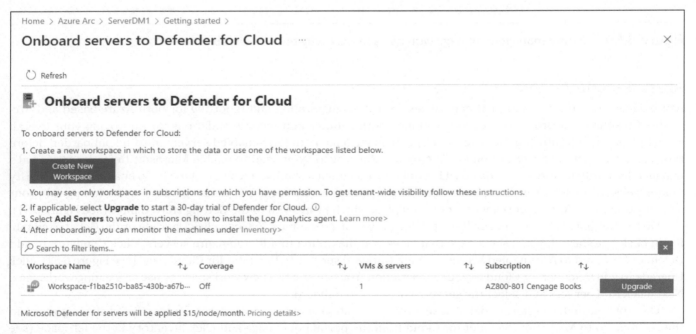

Figure 6-52   Onboard servers for Microsoft Defender for Cloud

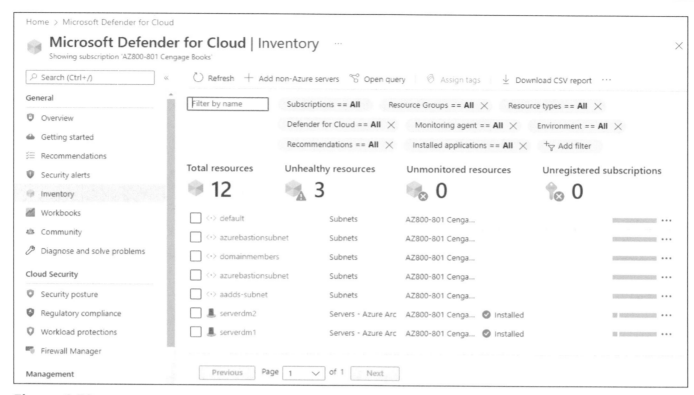

Figure 6-53   Microsoft Defender for Cloud Inventory

Just-in-Time Access to VMs

Another feature of Microsoft Defender for Cloud is just-in-time (JIT) access for VMs. This feature allows administrators to access a VM only by request and within a specified time period. At this writing, only VMs deployed through Azure Resource Manager and AWS EC2 VMs are supported with JIT VM access. JIT access for VMs reduces the attack surface of your VMs by opening remote access ports such as RDP (TCP port 3389) and SSH (TCP port 22), but only by request and only for a specified period of time.

Before you can enable a VM for JIT access, the VM's network interface must be associated with a network security group (NSG). To configure or create an NSG, go to the portal home screen, start typing "network security group" in the search box, and select the Network security groups service. If there are no NSGs, click Create to create one. When you have an NSG, click on it and click Network interfaces in the left pane. You'll see a list of network interfaces associated with the NSG. If the VM you want to configure for JIT access is not listed, click Associate and follow the instructions to associate the VMs. It's important that the NSG is in the same region as the VM with which you want to associate.

When your VM's NIC is associated with an NSG, enable JIT for VMs by going to Microsoft Defender for Cloud and clicking Workload protections in the left pane. Scroll down if necessary under Advanced protection and click Just-in-time VM access. On the Just-in-time VM access page, click Not Configured under Virtual machines and click Enable JIT on VM(s), as shown in Figure 6-54. If you don't see your VM under Not Configured, click Unsupported to see why the VM does not support JIT access. In most cases, it is because the VM is turned off or not associated with an NSG.

When the VM is configured for JIT access, you will see it under Configured. You can request access on the Just-in-time VM access page by selecting a VM and clicking Request access. The Request access page contains the following options (see Figure 6-55):

- The list of ports that were configured when you enabled JIT; you can toggle the list on or off
- The allowed source IP addresses. You can specify the address of the machine you're currently on or an IP address range.
- The amount of time that the VM should be available for access. You can select 1, 2, or 3 hours.

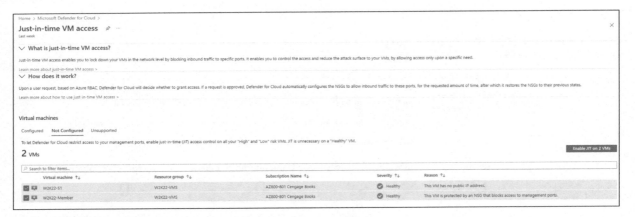

Figure 6-54 Enable JIT VM access

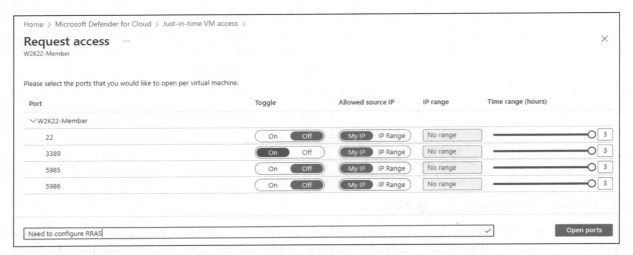

Figure 6-55 Configure ports, IP addresses, and timeframe for JIT access to VMs

You can also request access to a JIT-enabled VM from the Connect page for the VM, where you can connect using RDP, SSH, or Bastion (see Figure 6-56). In this case, the appropriate port is opened for the protocol with which you want to connect, and you can enter the source IP address information.

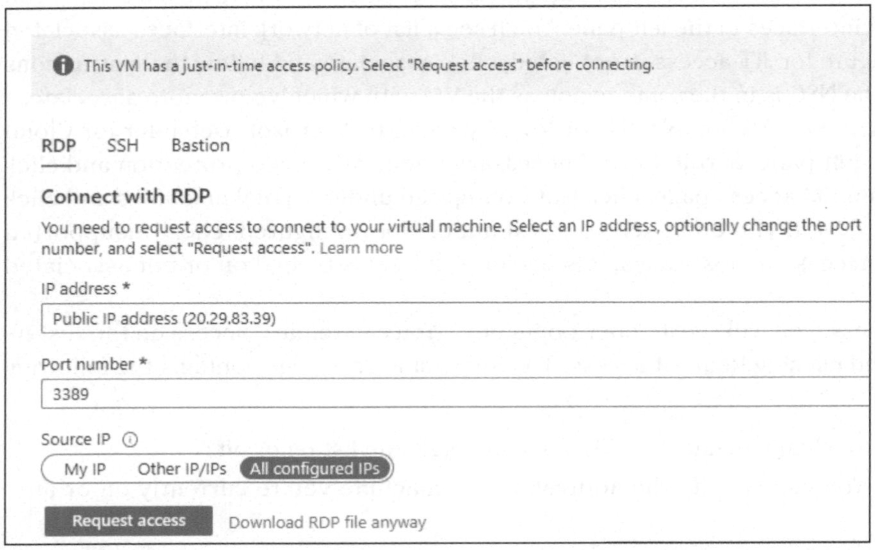

This VM has a just-in-time access policy. Select "Request access" before connecting.

RDP   SSH   Bastion

Connect with RDP

You need to request access to connect to your virtual machine. Select an IP address, optionally change the port number, and select "Request access". Learn more

IP address *

Public IP address (20.29.83.39)

Port number *

3389

Source IP

My IP   Other IP/IPs   All configured IPs

Request access   Download RDP file anyway

Figure 6-56 Request JIT VM access from the Connect page of a VM

Using Runbooks to Manage Azure VMs

A **runbook** is a set of related procedures that are performed to complete a particular task. A runbook can be a physical document or a digital document. In Azure, you can use a runbook with an Automation account to perform repetitive tasks using PowerShell, PowerShell Workflow, or Python. You can automate common tasks performed on VMs, such as starting and stopping the VM, starting and stopping services, and just about any other task that can be performed by a script.

To create a runbook, select an Automation account and click Runbooks under Process Automation in the left pane. You'll see two example runbooks; one uses PowerShell and the other uses Graphical PowerShell (see Figure 6-57). If you click on a runbook, you'll see an overview page. From the Overview page, you can click View to see the contents of the runbook or click Start to execute it.

Figure 6-57   Runbooks

Create a new runbook by clicking Create a runbook and filling in the information, as shown in Figure 6-58. After the runbook is created, an editor opens where you can write code according to the type of runbook you selected.

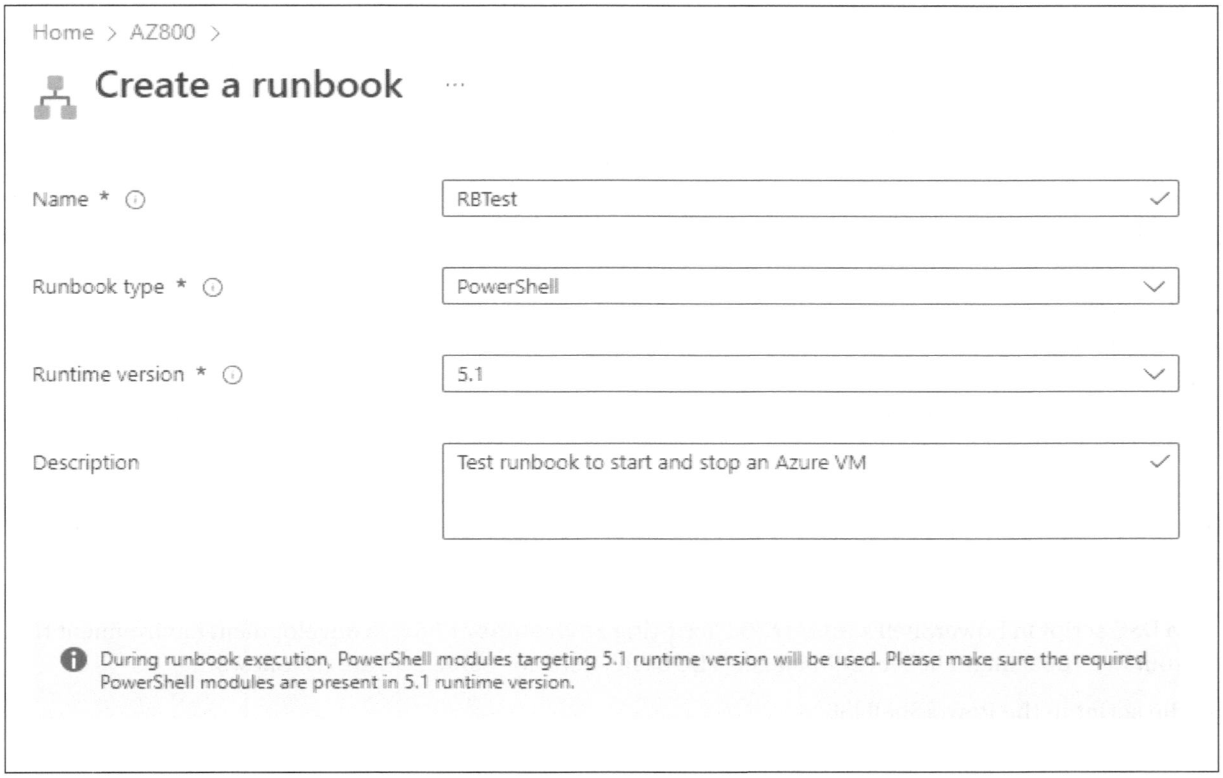

Figure 6-58   Creating a new runbook

Exam Tip ✔

The details of writing code for a runbook are beyond the scope of this book. For the AZ-800 exam, you must be aware of what a runbook is and the process required to create one.

Self-Check Questions

6. You want to manage on-premises servers using Azure tools. What do you need to install on your on-premises servers?

   a. PowerShell remoting
   b. Connected Machine agent

   c. Windows Admin Center
   d. WinRM

7. JIT access to Azure VMs is a feature of which Azure service?

   a. Log Analytics
   b. Azure Active Directory

   c. Azure Automation
   d. Microsoft Defender for Cloud

◉ Check your answers at the end of this module.

Managing Servers with Desired State Configuration

Microsoft Exam AZ-800:

Manage Windows servers and workloads in a hybrid environment.
  • Manage Windows servers and workloads by using Azure services

Starting with PowerShell 4.0 (first appearing in Windows Server 2012 R2), a feature called **Desired State Configuration (DSC)** gives you a way to manage and maintain servers with simple declarative statements. The primary purpose of DSC is to prevent **configuration drift**, which is the term used when a server's configuration is altered over time, whether accidentally or on purpose, but the change is not officially sanctioned by administration. Configuration drift can occur when there are multiple administrators and there is a lack of communication or changes aren't documented.

DSC's declarative syntax makes it possible for you to tell the server how it should be configured without using the actual commands for performing configuration steps. DSC can install or uninstall server roles, start and stop services, configure the registry and file system, and perform other common tasks. DSC can operate in one of two modes:

- *Push mode*—In this mode, a server configuration is manually sent to one or more target servers by an administrator. This mode is best used to test your DSC configuration without having to configure a pull server.
- *Pull mode*—In this mode, instead of DSC configurations having to be sent to remote servers, servers can pull their configurations from a central server by using standard web protocols. This technology eliminates the need to open additional firewall ports.

As mentioned, push mode is a good way to test your DSC configuration without having to set up a DSC pull server. In push mode, you set up the configurations on a desktop computer and manually begin the DSC process by sending configurations to target machines. However, to realize the power of DSC, you set up a pull server, and the target computers check with the server every 15 minutes to see if a configuration is available.

You create a DSC script in PowerShell's **Integrated Scripting Environment (ISE)**, a development environment that you can open from the Tools menu in Server Manager. The basic steps for using DSC are as follows:

1. Create the script in the PowerShell ISE.
2. Run the script to create configuration files called management object files (MOFs).
3. Enter the `Start-DscConfiguration` cmdlet at a PowerShell prompt.

Here's an example of using DSC to check whether the DNS Server role is installed on ServerA and ServerB and then to install the server role if necessary. It also verifies that the Print Spooler service (the service name is Spooler) is set to automatically start and is running.

```
Configuration DNSSpool
{
 Node ServerA, ServerB
 {
 WindowsFeature DNSserver
 {
 Name = "DNS"
Ensure = "Present"
 }
 Service PrintSpooler
 {
 Name = "Spooler"
 StartupType = "Automatic"
 State = "Running"

 }
 }
}
```

Windows Server 2022 comes with DSC version 2 (v2) and lets you automate a variety of configuration tasks on a set of computers using scripts like those in the previous example. Some of the automated tasks include the following:

- Enabling or disabling server roles and features
- Managing services (starting and stopping, for example)
- Retrieving the configuration of a server
- Deploying software
- Managing registry settings
- Managing files and folders
- Managing accounts
- Running PowerShell scripts

The configuration tasks you can perform with DSC are based on DSC resources. To see a list of DSC resources, use the Get-DscResources PowerShell cmdlet. A number of DSC resources are built in to DSC, but you can add more resources, and therefore more configuration tasks, by downloading the DSC Resource Kit available on Microsoft TechNet. In addition to automating server configuration tasks, DSC can determine whether a server still has the desired configuration. If it doesn't, DSC can restore the server to the desired state. For example, if someone changes the configuration of a server, DSC can determine that it has been changed and then change it back.

At the heart of DSC is the **local configuration manager (LCM)**, which is responsible for sending (pushing) and receiving (pulling) configurations, applying configurations, monitoring, and reporting discrepancies between the desired state and current state of a server. When a discrepancy exists (a term referred to as configuration drift or simply drift), DSC is responsible for reapplying the desired configuration to resolve the drift. One major enhancement in DSC v2 is the ability to split a configuration into multiple configuration files. Different people can then create different configurations according to their expertise. Each partial configuration can be used independently or combined with any other partial configuration to configure a server. For example, in DSC v1, if you needed to configure a server as a DHCP, DNS, and file and print server, you would create a single DSC script to be used by each server that required the configuration. If you needed a server with just DHCP and DNS, a different script would be required that excluded the file and print components. With DSC v2, you can create a script for each role and deploy the scripts independently according to how they are needed. For example, you can deploy the DNS, DHCP, and file and print scripts to all servers that need all three components, but deploy only the DNS and DHCP scripts to servers that don't require file and print components.

> **Note 9**
>
> The details of using DSC are beyond the scope of this book, but for a quick primer and examples, take a look at *https://msdn.microsoft.com/en-us/powershell/dsc/overview*.

Implementing DSC on Azure VMs

You can use Azure Automation DSC to prevent configuration drift on Azure VMs. Azure Automation DSC requires an Automation account on Azure. To create an Automation account, sign in to the Azure portal, click Create a resource, and then select IT & Management Tools. From there, select Automation (see Figure 6-59).

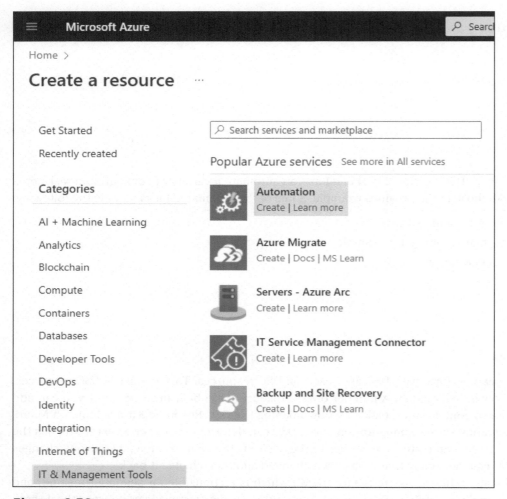

Figure 6-59   Automation resource

You will be prompted to create an Automation account if you don't already have one. Creating an Automation account is similar to creating other resources in Azure. You select the subscription, resource group, and Azure region, you provide a name, and so forth. After you have created the resource, you can begin working with it from the Automation account page (see Figure 6-60).

When you have an Automation account, you can configure DSC for your Azure VMs via PowerShell. On your computer, open a PowerShell prompt and connect to your Azure account with the following cmdlet:

```
Connect-AzAccount
```

You will be prompted for your Azure login credentials. When you are connected to your Azure account, complete the following four steps to implement DSC on an Azure VM:

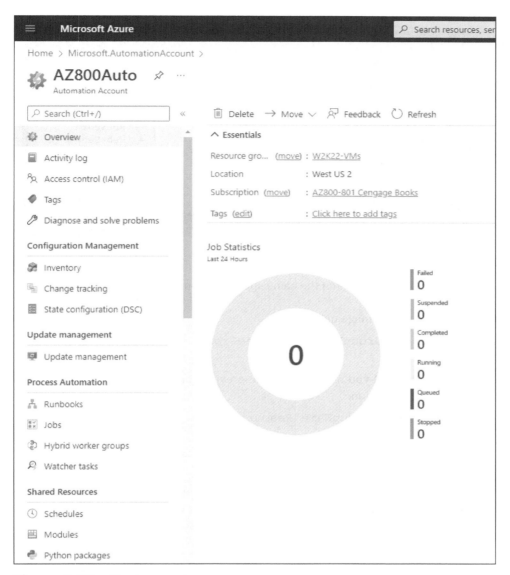

Figure 6-60   The Automation account page

- Upload a DSC configuration file
- Compile the DSC configuration
- Register the VM to use DSC
- Assign a node configuration

Assuming you have already created the DSC file, use the following cmdlet to upload the DSC configuration file to Azure Automation.

```
Import-AzAutomationDscConfiguration  -SourcePath  DSCfilePath  -ResourceGroupName
   ResourceGroup -AutomationAccountName Name -Published
```

In the preceding cmdlet, you need to supply the path to the DSC file, the name of the resource group you selected when you created the Automation account, and the name of the Automation account.

Figure 6-61 shows the PowerShell cmdlet to upload DSC configuration file testdsc.ps1 and the DSC file. The DSC file specifies that VM W2K22-S1 should have the IIS feature installed along with all subfeatures.

The next step is to compile the DSC configuration so it can be assigned to a node (VM) in Azure using the following cmdlet:

```
Start-AzAutomationDscCompilationJob -ConfigurationName ConfigName -ResourceGroupName
   ResourceGroup -AutomationAccountName Name
```

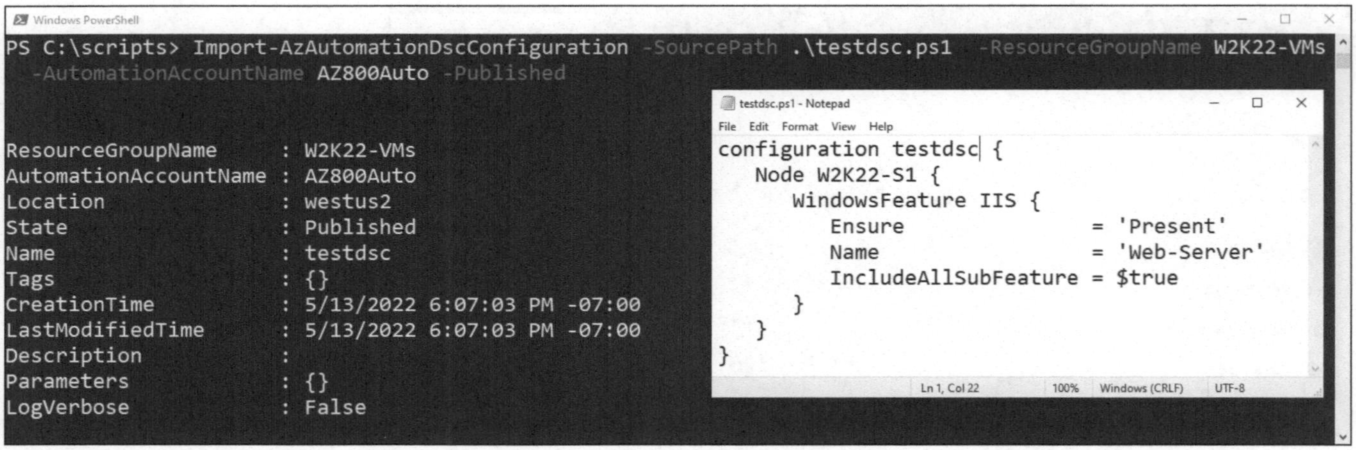

```
Windows PowerShell                                                          —  □  ×
PS C:\scripts> Import-AzAutomationDscConfiguration -SourcePath .\testdsc.ps1 -ResourceGroupName W2K22-VMs
  -AutomationAccountName AZ800Auto -Published


ResourceGroupName      : W2K22-VMs
AutomationAccountName  : AZ800Auto
Location               : westus2
State                  : Published
Name                   : testdsc
Tags                   : {}
CreationTime           : 5/13/2022 6:07:03 PM -07:00
LastModifiedTime       : 5/13/2022 6:07:03 PM -07:00
Description            :
Parameters             : {}
LogVerbose             : False
```

```
testdsc.ps1 - Notepad                          —  □  ×
File  Edit  Format  View  Help
configuration testdsc {
    Node W2K22-S1 {
        WindowsFeature IIS {
            Ensure              = 'Present'
            Name                = 'Web-Server'
            IncludeAllSubFeature = $true
        }
    }
}
                    Ln 1, Col 22    100%   Windows (CRLF)    UTF-8
```

Figure 6-61   Uploading a DSC file to Azure Automation

In the preceding cmdlet, the configuration name must match the name specified in the DSC file, which in Figure 6-61 is testdsc.

The third step is to register the VM you want to manage using DSC.

```
Register-AzAutomationDscNode -ResourceGroupName ResourceGroup -AutomationAccountName
    Name -AzureVMName VMName
```

Finally, you assign a node configuration to the VM you registered in the previous step. First, you need to get the ID of the managed node, and then assign the configuration:

```
$node = Get-AzAutomationDscNode -ResourceGroupName ResourceGroup -AutomationAccountName
    Name -Name VMName
```

```
Set-AzAutomationDscNode -ResourceGroupName ResourceGroup -AutomationAccountName Name
    -NodeConfigurationName NodeConfigName -NodeId $node.Id
```

In the preceding cmdlets, the first cmdlet puts the node object (the VM you will apply the DSC to) in a variable named $node. The second cmdlet applies the DSC configuration to the VM. The -NodeConfigurationName parameter value is a combination of the configuration name and the node name. Given the DSC file in Figure 6-61, that would be testdsc.W2K22-S1.

Exam Tip ✔

You can also configure DSC from the Azure portal by selecting State Configuration (DSC) from the Automation account; however, Microsoft expects you to know how to use PowerShell to perform most configuration tasks.

Caution ❗

When you register the VM using the `Register-AZAutomationDscNode` cmdlet, the VM and the Automation account must be in the same Azure region or the cmdlet will fail. If they are not in the same region, use the `-AzureVMLocation` parameter and specify the region the VM is in.

Self-Check Questions

8. Which DSC operating mode eliminates the need to open additional firewall ports?

    a. Pull mode   c. Anonymous mode
    b. Auto mode   d. Push mode

⊙ Check your answers at the end of this module.

Module Summary

- You need to add roles and features to take advantage of Windows Server 2022's capabilities. You can add and remove roles and features with Server Manager or PowerShell. You can also use PowerShell to query whether a role or feature is installed or available to be installed. You can use PowerShell to act on remote servers by using the `-ComputerName` argument.
- You can add servers to Server Manager and perform most management tasks on remote servers. You can add servers by using Active Directory, DNS, or an import file. Remote computers that aren't domain members must be added to the TrustedHosts file on the managing computer.
- PowerShell remoting allows you to execute PowerShell cmdlets on a remote server. WinRM has a command-line interface for performing a variety of tasks. This feature must be enabled to use PowerShell cmdlets remotely. The `Configure-SMRemoting` command enables and disables WinRM.
- Second-hop remoting is the process of using PowerShell remoting into a server and then using the remote server to execute PowerShell cmdlets on another remote server. You can configure PowerShell second-hop remoting using CredSSP, Kerberos delegation, and JEA.
- JEA is a technology that allows administrators to delegate administrative tasks to other personnel without granting excessive privileges. JEA leverages the principle of least privilege, which states that users and administrators should be given sufficient rights and permissions to perform their jobs, but no more than that.
- You need to configure firewall rules to allow remote management with an MMC. You can use the Windows Firewall with Advanced Security MMC, the `netsh` command, or PowerShell cmdlets to set firewall rules.
- Windows Admin Center provides another way to remotely manage both on-premises and Azure VM servers and client stations. It is a browser-based application that can be downloaded free from the Microsoft Evaluation Center.
- Microsoft Azure provides a host of services for managing Windows servers running in Azure and in your on-premises datacenter. These services include Azure Arc, just-in-time access to VMs, and runbooks for VM task automation.
- Azure Arc is a management platform that allows you to run Azure services on on-premises servers and public clouds using Azure-based tools. Management features include policies, extensions, logs, update management, and security.
- Just-in-time access to VMs allows administrators to access a VM only by request and within a specified time period.
- A runbook is a set of related procedures that are performed to complete a particular task. In Azure, you can use a runbook with an Automation account to perform repetitive tasks using PowerShell, PowerShell Workflow, or Python.
- Desired State Configuration gives you a way to manage and maintain servers with simple declarative statements. The primary purpose of DSC is to prevent configuration drift, which is the term used when a server's configuration is altered over time.

Key Terms

configuration drift
Credential Security Support Provider (CredSSP)
Desired State Configuration (DSC)
Integrated Scripting Environment (ISE)
JEA endpoint
Just Enough Administration (JEA)

Kerberos constrained delegation
local configuration manager (LCM)
onboarding
PowerShell role capability file
principle of least privilege
resource-based constrained delegation

runbook
second-hop remoting
Windows Admin Center
Windows Remote Management (WinRM)

Review Questions

1. Which of the following is a task you should perform before installing server roles and features? (Choose all that apply.)
   a. Set a strong Administrator password.
   b. Make the server a domain member.
   c. Configure static IP addresses.
   d. Make sure security updates are current.

2. Which of the following is true about installing roles and features in Windows Server 2022?
   a. You can't install a server role by using the command line.
   b. All server role installations require a server restart.
   c. You can install more than one role at a time.
   d. Server roles can be installed only on online drives.

3. Which PowerShell command shows a list of installed roles and features?
   a. `Installed-WindowsFeature -Show`
   b. `Get-WindowsFeature | where Installed`
   c. `List-InstalledFeature`
   d. `Show-Features .if. Installed`

4. Which of the following is a method for adding a server to Server Manager? (Choose all that apply.)
   a. Query NetBIOS.
   b. Search Active Directory.
   c. Import a file.
   d. Search DNS.

5. You add a server to Server Manager but see the error message "WinRM Negotiate authentication error." What should you do?
   a. Add the server with different credentials.
   b. Add the server to the TrustedHosts list.
   c. Install .NET Framework 4.5.
   d. Enter the `Configure-SMRemoting` command.

6. You're managing 75 servers from a single Server Manager console and find you're wasting a lot of time scrolling through the list of servers to find the one you want to manage. You have five locations with about 15 servers in each location. What can you do to make it easier to manage these servers in Server Manager?
   a. Create a group in Active Directory.
   b. Use WinRM.
   c. Enable PowerShell remoting.
   d. Create server groups.

7. In Windows Server, what must be running to allow PowerShell remoting?
   a. Windows Firewall
   b. LBFO
   c. Telnet
   d. WinRM

8. You are signed in at the console of a Windows Server 2022 computer named ServerA. You use the `Enter-PSSession` cmdlet to establish a connection to ServerB. While you are connected to ServerB, you enter `Install-WindowsFeature Telnet-Client -ComputerName ServerC`. ServerB and ServerC are both Windows Server 2022 computers. What procedure have you performed?
   a. WinRM jumping
   b. Second-hop remoting
   c. Remote command execution
   d. Kerberos unconstrained delegation

9. Which authentication feature allows you to create a PowerShell session from ServerA to ServerB and execute commands on ServerB that target ServerC by caching credentials on ServerB? Assume all servers are running Windows Server 2022.
   a. Kerberos constrained delegation
   b. Credential Security Support Provider
   c. Kerberos resource-based constrained delegation
   d. Just Enough Administration

10. You need to perform some tasks using PowerShell second-hop remoting. You don't want to incur the security risk that cached credentials create and you want to limit delegation by performing configuration tasks only on the target (second-hop) server. You also want the solution to require the least amount of administrative effort. Which of the following methods should you try?
    a. Kerberos constrained delegation
    b. CredSSP
    c. Kerberos resource-based constrained delegation
    d. Just Enough Administration

11. Which method of allowing PowerShell remote administration best leverages the principle of least privilege?
    a. Credential Security Support Provider
    b. Kerberos unconstrained delegation
    c. Kerberos resource-based constrained delegation
    d. Just Enough Administration

12. What type of file must you create to allow your IT employees to execute specific PowerShell cmdlets that perform administrative tasks?
    a. CredSSP command specification file
    b. PowerShell role capability file
    c. Kerberos resource file
    d. PowerShell session configuration file

13. You have created a file that lists the PowerShell cmdlets and functions users can execute when using PowerShell remoting. What else must you do to complete JEA for PowerShell remoting?

a. Register a JEA endpoint.

b. Create a file with a .psrc extension.

c. Update the $PSVersionTable file.

d. Add hosts to the TrustedHosts list.

14. You right-click a Server Core server in Server Manager and click Computer Management. You see an error indicating that the server can't be managed. What should you do to solve the problem?

a. Run `configure-SMRemoting.exe -Enable` on the local computer.

b. Configure Windows Firewall on the remote computer.

c. Install the GUI on the remote computer.

d. Disable WinRM on the local computer.

15. You want to be able to manage a Server Core computer's firewall by using the Windows Firewall with Advanced Security snap-in. What should you do?

a. On the local computer, disable the Windows Firewall Remote Management rule group.

b. On the remote computer, enter the command `Configure-SMRemoting -ConfigureFirewallRules`.

c. On the remote computer, use the PowerShell command `Set-NetFirewallRule -DisplayGroup "Windows Firewall Remote Management" -enabled True`.

d. On the local computer, enable the COM+ Network Access firewall rule.

16. With which Windows Admin Center installation option do you access the tool using the loopback address of the installation computer, typically when you are managing a small number of servers?

a. Local client   c. Managed server

b. Gateway server   d. Failover cluster

17. When you install Windows Admin Center on Windows Server 2022, what is the default method of deployment?

a. Local client   c. Managed server

b. Gateway server   d. Failover cluster

18. You want to be able to manage Windows Server VMs that run in Azure using Windows Admin Center. You want to use the public IP address of the VMs, and you will install Windows Admin Center in gateway mode on an on-premises server. Which of the following are required? (Choose all that apply.)

a. Azure Active Directory is set up.

b. TCP port 5985 is open for inbound connections.

c. You have created a session configuration file.

d. WinRM is enabled on the VMs.

19. You have a hybrid server infrastructure that includes Windows and Linux servers installed as

VMs in Microsoft Azure and physical and virtual servers running in your on-premises datacenter. You have enjoyed using Azure management tools such as policies, Log Analytics, and Update management to manage your Azure VMs. You want to be able to use the same tools to manage aspects of your on-premises resources. What should you use?

a. Azure Active Directory Domain Services

b. JIT access for VMs

c. Azure Arc

d. Windows Admin Center

20. What must you do before Azure Arc-enabled servers can participate in Security Center?

a. Onboard the servers.

b. Enable JIT access for VMs.

c. Configure JEA.

d. Add them to Windows Admin Center.

21. You want to provide additional security for your Azure VMs by requiring users to request access to a VM before they can manage it using RDP, SSH, or WinRM. The necessary ports will be open for only a specified time period. What should you configure?

a. Azure Arc

b. JIT access for VMs

c. Just Enough Administration

d. Windows Admin Center

22. Which of the following must be set up before you can create and execute runbooks?

a. Automation account

b. Log Analytics

c. Windows Admin Center

d. Azure Arc

23. Which of the following modes does Desired State Configuration operate in? (Choose all that apply.)

a. Push mode   c. State mode

b. Config mode   d. Pull mode

24. Which of the following configuration tasks can be automated when using DSC in Windows Server 2022? (Choose all that apply.)

a. Deploying software

b. Managing disk images

c. Managing registry settings

d. Running PowerShell scripts

25. Which of the following is the last step in configuring DSC for Azure VMs?

a. Registering a VM

b. Assigning a node configuration

c. Compiling a DSC configuration

d. Uploading a DSC configuration

Critical Thinking

The following activities give you critical thinking challenges. Case projects offer a scenario with a problem for which you supply a written solution.

Case Projects

Case Project 6-1: Outfitting a Branch Office with Server Core

You have been supporting CSM Tech Publishing's Windows Server 2016 server network for over a year. The office has two Windows Server 2016 servers running Active Directory and a number of other roles. Management has informed you that a small sales office is opening in the same building three floors up. The sales manager wants to install a sales application on a server located in the sales office. This server will have limited physical security because there's no special room dedicated for it, which means it will be accessible to non-IT personnel and visitors. You're considering installing Windows Server 2016 Server Core on the new server because accessing its console regularly probably won't be necessary, and this server will be managed from one of the other CSM Tech Publishing servers. What are the benefits and drawbacks of using Server Core for this branch office? What should you do to set up this server management environment?

Case Project 6-2: Dealing with Server Core Anxiety

The owner of CSM Tech Publishing was at the new sales office last week. Out of curiosity, he signed in to the server there. The owner is somewhat tech-savvy and has even worked a little with Active Directory in Windows Server 2016. He was shocked when he signed in and didn't see a familiar user interface—only a command prompt. He asked you about this and accepted your explanation of Server Core and why you chose this installation option. However, he was wondering what would happen if you stopped providing support or were unavailable for an extended period, and if your replacement wasn't familiar with Server Core. Write a memo explaining how this situation could be handled easily.

Case Project 6-3: Securing Remote Access to Azure VMs

Your organization has just extended your on-premises datacenter to the Azure cloud. Your supervisor is concerned about access to those VMs through a public IP address. Because the VMs have a public IP address for remote desktop and SSH access, she is concerned that hackers could exploit that access. What is one way to ease her concerns while still maintaining public IP address access to the VMs that will limit the availability of those servers, such that the RDP and SSH services are not always available? Explain.

Case Project 6-4: Ensuring Proper Server Configuration

You are called to consult with an organization that has well over 100 servers, including virtual servers. The manager you spoke with said they are having problems keeping the servers properly configured. Different administrators make changes to the configuration or add and remove services to keep up with user demand. However, the manager finds that changes are not well documented and often cause problems. The manager would like to know if there is a way to automate control of changes to server roles, features, services, and so forth. What Windows Server feature can you suggest and why?

Solutions to Self-Check Questions

Section 6-1: Working with Server Roles and Features

1. Which PowerShell cmdlet lists all roles and features that are both installed and available to be installed?

    Answer: b. `Get-WindowsFeature`

    Explanation: The `Get-WindowsFeature` cmdlet displays a list of features that are currently installed and those that are available to be installed. The `Add-WindowsFeature` cmdlet is used to install new features, not list them. The other choices listed are not valid PowerShell cmdlets.

Section 6-2: Managing Servers Remotely

2. If you want to manage servers remotely using Server Manager on a workgroup computer, what do you need to do for each remote server?

    Answer: d. Add the server name to the TrustedHosts file.

    Explanation: The TrustedHosts file holds a list of computers that your computer trusts for remote management. This procedure is required when the remote server is not a member of a domain.

3. Which of the following is a reason to configure CredSSP?

    Answer: b. To use PowerShell second-hop remoting

    Explanation: CredSSP is an authentication provider tool that caches credentials on the remote server so they can be used to connect to the second-hop server.

Section 6-3: Using Windows Admin Center

4. Which Windows Admin Center installation option should you use to manage a single server from a client web browser?

    Answer: d. Local client

    Explanation: The local client option is usually installed on a Windows 10 or 11 computer to manage local servers in a small environment or for testing.

5. If you want to install Windows Admin Center on an on-premises Windows Server 2022 computer, and you want to manage Azure VMs from a web browser running on Windows 11, what type of installation should you use?

    Answer: a. Gateway server

    Explanation: The gateway server option is installed on a Windows Server computer to allow any client machine that has access to the gateway server to manage all the servers in your enterprise, including server VMs running on Azure.

Section 6-4: Managing Windows Servers with Azure Services

6. You want to manage on-premises servers using Azure tools. What do you need to install on your on-premises servers?

    Answer: b. Connected Machine agent

    Explanation: Before you can start managing physical or virtual servers with Azure Arc, you need to onboard them with the Connected Machine agent. Onboarding is a process that brings a device under a management system; in this case, by installing the Connected Machine agent, you will be able to manage the server using tools in the Azure portal.

7. JIT access to Azure VMs is a feature of which Azure service?

    Answer: d. Microsoft Defender for Cloud

    Explanation: A feature of Microsoft Defender for Cloud is just-in-time (JIT) access for VMs. This feature allows administrators to access a VM only by request and within a specified time period.

Section 6-5: Managing Servers with Desired State Configuration

8. Which DSC operating mode eliminates the need to open additional firewall ports?

    Answer: a. Pull mode

    Explanation: In pull mode, instead of DSC configurations having to be sent to remote servers, servers can pull their configurations from a central server by using standard web protocols. This technology eliminates the need to open additional firewall ports.

Module 7

Configure DNS

Module Objectives

After reading this module and completing the exercises, you will be able to:

1 Describe the structure of Domain Name System

2 Install DNS

3 Configure DNS

4 Create DNS resource records

5 Configure DNS zones

6 Configure DNS server settings

7 Configure DNS security

8 Use Azure DNS

To function correctly, most applications and services that use TCP/IP depend on a service to resolve computer names to addresses and to find computers that offer specific services. In fact, most network systems today would be almost unusable without a name-to-address translation system; without one, users and computers would need to know the address of each computer they communicate with. Because the TCP/IP suite is the default protocol for Windows, Domain Name System (DNS) is the default name resolution protocol for Windows computers. For Windows domain networks, DNS is required for operation because Active Directory depends on it. This module describes the structure of the worldwide DNS system and explains how to configure and maintain DNS in a Windows domain environment.

Table 7-1 describes what you need for the hands-on activities in this module.

Table 7-1   Activity requirements

Activity	Requirements	Notes
Activity 7-1: Resetting Your Virtual Environment	ServerDC1, ServerSA1	
Activity 7-2: Exploring DNS with DNS Manager	ServerDC1	
Activity 7-3: Installing DNS and Creating a New Zone	ServerSA1	
Activity 7-4: Working with Reverse Lookup Zones	ServerSA1	
Activity 7-5: Creating Static DNS Entries	ServerSA1	
Activity 7-6: Creating a Secondary Zone and Configuring Zone Transfers	ServerDC1, ServerSA1	
Activity 7-7: Configuring and Testing Forwarders	ServerDC1, ServerSA1	
Activity 7-8: Working with Root Hints	ServerDC1, ServerSA1	Internet connection required
Activity 7-9: Configuring DNSSEC	ServerDC1	

Introduction to Domain Name System

Microsoft Exam AZ-800:
Implement and manage an on-premises and hybrid networking infrastructure.
- Implement on-premises and hybrid name resolution

Domain Name System (DNS) is a distributed hierarchical database composed mainly of computer name and IP address pairs. A distributed database means that no single database contains all data; instead, data is spread out among many different servers. In the worldwide DNS system, data is distributed among thousands of servers throughout the world. A hierarchical database, in this case, means there's a structure to how information is stored and accessed in the database. In other words, unless you're resolving a local domain name for which you have a local server, DNS lookups often require a series of queries to a hierarchy of DNS servers before the name can be resolved.

The Structure of DNS

To better understand the DNS lookup process, reviewing the structure of a computer name on the Internet or in a Windows domain is helpful. Computer names are typically expressed as *host.domain.top-level-domain*; the *top-level-domain* can be com, net, org, us, edu, and so forth. This naming structure is called the **fully qualified domain name (FQDN)**. The DNS naming hierarchy can be described as an inverted tree with the root at the top (named simply "dot," which is represented with a period), top-level domains branching out from the root, and domains and subdomains branching off the top-level domains (see Figure 7-1).

The entire DNS tree is called the **DNS namespace**. When a domain name is registered, the domain is added to the DNS hierarchy and becomes part of the worldwide DNS namespace. Every domain has one or more servers that are authoritative for the domain, meaning the servers contain a master copy of all DNS records for that domain. A single server can be authoritative for multiple domains.

Each shape in Figure 7-1 has one or more DNS servers managing the names associated with it. For example, the root of the tree has 13 DNS servers called **root servers** scattered about the world that keep a database of addresses of other DNS servers managing top-level domain names. These other aptly named servers are called **top-level domain (TLD) servers**. Each top-level domain has servers that maintain addresses of other DNS servers. For example, the .com

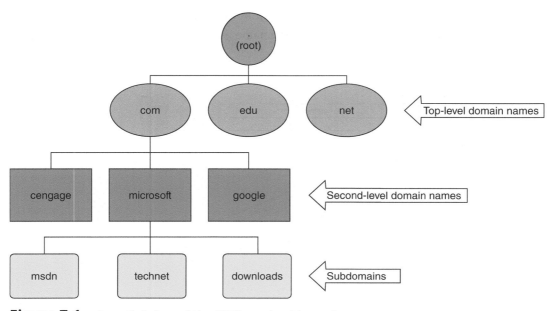

Figure 7-1　A partial view of the DNS naming hierarchy

TLD servers maintain a database containing addresses of DNS servers for each domain name ending with .com, such as *tomsho.com* and *cengage.com*. Each second-level DNS server can contain hostnames, such as www, mail, or server1. **Hostnames** are associated with an IP address, so when a client looks up the name *www.microsoft.com*, the DNS server returns an IP address. Second-level domains can also have subdomains, such as *docs* in *docs.microsoft.com*.

The DNS Database

DNS servers maintain a database of information that contains zones. A **zone** is a grouping of DNS information that belongs to a contiguous portion of the DNS namespace, usually a domain and possibly one or more subdomains. Each zone has a variety of record types called **resource records** that contain information about network resources, such as hostnames, other DNS servers, and domain controllers. Resource records are identified by letter codes. DNS resource records are discussed in more detail later in the "Creating DNS Resource Records" section.

The DNS Lookup Process

When a computer needs to acquire information from a DNS server, such as looking up the IP address for host *www.cengage.com*, it sends a lookup or query to the server. A computer making a DNS query is called a **DNS client** or **DNS resolver**. Two types of DNS queries can be made:

- *Iterative query*—When a DNS server gets an **iterative query**, it responds with the best information it currently has in its local database to satisfy the query, such as the IP address of a host record it retrieves from a local zone file or cache. If the DNS server doesn't have the specific information, it might respond with the IP address of a name server that *can* satisfy the query; this type of response is called a **referral** because the server is referring the DNS client to another server. If the server has no information, it sends a negative response that essentially means "I can't help you." DNS servers usually query each other by using iterative queries.

- *Recursive query*—A **recursive query** instructs the DNS server to process the query until it responds with an address that satisfies the query or with an "I don't know" message. A recursive query might require a DNS server to contact several other DNS servers before it finally sends a response to the client. Most queries made by DNS clients are recursive queries, and DNS servers also use recursive queries when using a forwarder, as discussed later in this module in the "DNS Server Roles" section.

A typical DNS lookup made by a DNS client can involve both recursive and iterative queries. A sample query demonstrating the hierarchical nature of DNS (see Figure 7-2) is outlined in the following steps:

1. A user types "www.microsoft.com" in the web browser's address bar. The computer running the web browser is the DNS client, which sends a recursive query to the DNS server. Typically, this DNS server, called the "local DNS server," is maintained on the local network or at the client's ISP.

2. The local DNS server checks its local zone data and cache. If the name isn't found locally, it sends an iterative query to a DNS root server.

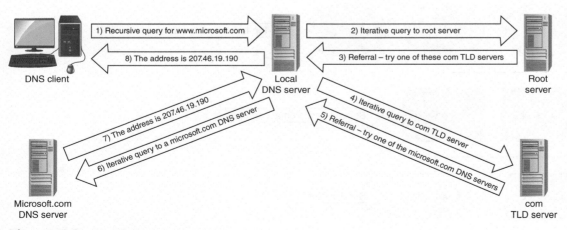

Figure 7-2   A DNS hierarchical lookup

3. The root server sends a referral to the local DNS server with a list of addresses for the TLD servers handling the .com top-level domain.
4. Using the referral information from the root server, the local DNS server sends another iterative query to a .com TLD server.
5. The .com TLD server responds with a referral to DNS servers responsible for the microsoft.com domain.
6. Using the referral information from the TLD server, the local DNS server then sends another iterative query to a microsoft.com DNS server.
7. The microsoft.com DNS server replies with the host record IP address for www.microsoft.com.
8. The local DNS server responds to the client with the IP address for www.microsoft.com.

Thankfully, the process shown in Figure 7-2 doesn't occur with every DNS lookup. Computers cache information they get from DNS and use the information in cache when possible, instead of sending another query to a DNS server. Furthermore, the local DNS server also caches information from other DNS servers that was received as a result of recent lookups. So, the entire eight-step process occurs only when neither the computer doing the lookup nor the local DNS server has a cached copy of the requested name resolution.

To add another wrinkle to the DNS lookup process, DNS clients maintain a text file called Hosts that can contain static DNS entries. In Windows, this file is stored in *%systemroot%*\System32\drivers\etc. By default, it contains only sample entries. In versions of Windows before Windows Server 2008 R2 and Windows 7, it contained records for resolving the local loopback address for both IPv4 and IPv6. These records are now commented out with an explanation that the DNS service handles localhost name resolution. The file's format is simply the IP address and hostname separated by one or more spaces. A typical Hosts file entry looks like this:

```
127.0.0.1 localhost
::1 localhost
```

Note 1

You see these two entries in the Hosts file in Windows Server 2022, but they have the # character in front of them, indicating that they're comments, which means they're ignored by the DNS client.

The entries in the Hosts file are cached at system startup and each time the file is changed. You can add as many entries as you want to this file. Usually, however, it's left as it is because in a dynamic network, static DNS entries are likely to cause more harm than good. Some people use the Hosts file as a sort of web filter. For example, you can add entries to this file for hosts on domains that create pop-up ads and fill your web pages with advertisements. For each entry, simply use the address 127.0.0.1. Unless your computer is also a web server, your browser won't get a response from this address, and the website supplying the ad will be blocked. You can even download a Hosts file that's already loaded with hundreds of entries for well-known web advertisers.

DNS Server Roles

DNS servers can perform one or more of the following roles for a zone:

- *Authoritative server*—An **authoritative server** for a domain holds a complete copy of a zone's resource records.
- *Forwarder*—A **forwarder** is a DNS server to which other DNS servers send requests they can't resolve themselves. It's commonly used when a DNS server on an internal private network receives a query for a domain on the public Internet. The internal DNS server forwards the request recursively to a DNS server connected to the public Internet. This method prevents the internal DNS server from having to contact root servers and TLD servers directly because the forwarder does that on its behalf.
- *Conditional forwarder*—A **conditional forwarder** is a DNS server to which other DNS servers send requests targeted for a specific domain. For example, computers in the csmtech.corp domain might send a DNS query for a computer named server1.csmpub.corp. The DNS server in the csmtech.corp domain can be configured with a conditional forwarder that in effect says, "If you receive a query for csmpub.corp, forward it to the DNS server handling the csmpub.corp domain." Servers that are forwarders or conditional forwarders require no special configuration, but the servers using them as forwarders must be configured to do so.

- *Caching-only server*—A **caching-only DNS server** isn't configured with any zones. Its sole job is to field DNS queries, send iterative queries to upstream DNS servers, or send requests to forwarders, and then cache the results. After the query results are cached, the caching server can respond to a similar query directly, without having to contact other DNS servers. Caching servers are ideal for branch offices because queries from local computers can be forwarded to an authoritative server at a main office.

Self-Check Questions

1. DNS queries can always be resolved by a single query to one server. True or False?

   a. True   **b.** False

2. Which of the following is an example of a top-level domain name?

   a. microsoft   **c.** www

   b. com   **d.** host1

⊙Check your answers at the end of this module.

Activity 7-1

Resetting Your Virtual Environment

Note 2

The activities in this book are based on the use of virtual machines (VMs) in a Windows Server 2022 Hyper-V environment. Other virtualization platforms such as VMware and VirtualBox should work for most activities. See the "Before You Begin" section of this book's preface for more information about using virtualization.

You only need to perform this activity if you are using virtual machines with snapshots and you are performing the activities in this module an additional time. If you are using your virtual machines for the first time, they will already be in the initial configuration state.

Time Required: 5 minutes
Objective: Reset your virtual environment by applying the InitialConfig checkpoint or snapshot.
Required Tools and Equipment: ServerDC1, ServerSA1
Description: Apply the InitialConfig checkpoint or snapshot to ServerDC1 and ServerSA1.

1. Be sure ServerDC1 and ServerSA1 are shut down. In your virtualization program, apply the InitialConfig checkpoint or snapshot to both servers.
2. When the snapshot or checkpoint has been applied, continue to the next activity.

Activity 7-2

Exploring DNS with DNS Manager

Time Required: 15 minutes
Objective: Explore DNS with DNS Manager.
Required Tools and Equipment: ServerDC1
Description: In this activity, you familiarize yourself with the DNS Manager console on a domain controller.

1. Sign in to ServerDC1 as **Administrator**.

(continues)

Activity 7-2 Continued

2. Open Server Manager, click **Tools**, and then click **DNS** to open the DNS Manager console.
3. Click **ServerDC1** in the left pane and double-click to expand **Forward Lookup Zones** in the right pane. Then click **Forward Lookup Zones**. You see a window similar to that in Figure 7-3. Right-click **ServerDC1** in the left pane and click **Properties**. Click the **Forwarders** tab. If a forwarder is listed, it's because Windows installs the DNS server configured for this computer as a forwarder when DNS is installed. If there's a forwarder, click the **Edit** button, click the forwarder address, click **Delete**, and then click **OK**. Examine the other tabs in the Properties dialog box, and then click **Cancel**.

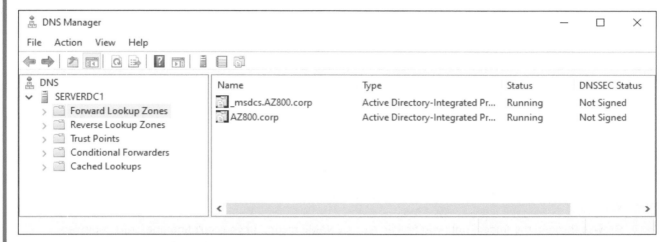

Figure 7-3   The DNS Manager console

4. In the right pane, double-click **AZ800.corp** to see folders and resource records. Scroll to the right, if necessary, to see the Timestamp column. Records that were created dynamically have a timestamp; records created by an administrator or generated by the system are shown as static.
5. The first few entries show "(same as parent folder)" in the Name column, which means they take on the domain's name. If DNS gets a host record query for AZ800.corp without a hostname, it returns the IP addresses shown for the "(same as parent folder)" Host (A) record entry. Double-click the **Start of Authority (SOA)** record. In the AZ800.corp Properties dialog box, review the information available in all the tabs. (The SOA record is discussed in more detail later in the "Start of Authority Records" section.) Click **Cancel**.
6. Double-click the **serverdc1** A record entry. Figure 7-4 shows the Properties dialog box for an A record. You can't change the Host or FQDN fields of an A record, but you can change the IP address. If you make a change, you can click the "Update associated pointer (PTR) record" check box to have the PTR record reflect the address change.
7. Click the **Security** tab. DNS records stored in Active Directory have the same type of permission settings as other Windows objects, including permission inheritance and special permissions. You can assign permissions to users to allow them to manage DNS records, if necessary. Click **Cancel**.
8. Click **View** and then **Advanced** from the DNS Manager menu. The Advanced view shows additional information in DNS Manager, such as the Cached Lookups folder. Click to expand **Cached Lookups** and then the **.(root)** folder, which has subfolders named for TLDs (com, local, net, and so on). Click to expand the **com** folder. Domains you have visited with any computer using this DNS server for DNS lookups have a folder containing A, NS, and other resource records. Cached entries save time and bandwidth because the local DNS server can respond to queries for records it has in its cache.

(continues)

Activity 7-2 Continued

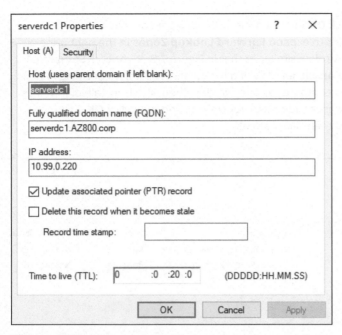

Figure 7-4   The Properties dialog box for an A record

9. Browse through the folders until you find an A or a CNAME record. (If you can't find one, start your web browser and go to *www.microsoft.com* to create a record in the microsoft folder. Close your browser and refresh DNS Manager.) Double-click the **A** or **CNAME** record. In the Properties dialog box, you see a time to live (TTL) value, which tells DNS how long to keep the cached entry. The referring DNS server (an authoritative DNS server for the domain the record came from) sends the TTL value, which prevents a DNS server from caching out-of-date information. Click **Cancel**.

10. Click the **com** folder. You should see several NS entries with names in the Data column, such as a.gtld-servers.net, b.gtld-servers.net, and so on, referred to as "generic top-level domain (GTLD) servers." These servers are responsible for .com domains throughout the Internet. Double-click **a.gtld-servers.net**. Notice that no IP address is associated with the entry. When your DNS server needs to find the address of a .com name server, it must query to find a TLD server's address first. Click **Cancel**.

11. Right-click **Cached Lookups** and click **Clear Cache** to delete the cache. There are no entries in the cache now, except some folders and an entry for localhost. Clear the local DNS cache by opening a command prompt window, typing **ipconfig /flushdns**, and pressing **Enter**. Close the command prompt window.

12. Start your web browser, go to any .com domain, and then exit your web browser. Refresh the DNS Manager console. Under Cached Lookups, click to expand the **.(root)** folder, and then click the **com** folder. You should see the list of GTLD servers and a folder for the domain you visited (possibly more than one folder). Click the **net** folder, and then double-click the **gtld-servers** folder. You see several A records for the GTLD servers listed and AAAA entries with IPv6 addresses. This is where the server caches the IP addresses associated with the GTLD servers.

13. Shut down ServerDC1.

Installing and Configuring DNS

Microsoft Exam AZ-800:
Implement and manage an on-premises and hybrid networking infrastructure.
- Implement on-premises and hybrid name resolution

DNS is an integral part of most network communication sessions between computers. Each time an application communicates with the Internet or another device, it uses DNS to resolve a network device's name to an IP address. A correctly configured and efficiently functioning DNS service, therefore, is essential for a well-functioning network.

Windows domains and Active Directory rely exclusively on DNS for resolving names and locating services. When a workgroup computer attempts to join a domain, it contacts a DNS server to find records that identify a domain controller for the domain. When a member computer or server starts, it contacts a DNS server to find a domain controller that can authenticate it to the domain. When domain controllers replicate with one another and when trusts are created between domains in different forests, DNS is required to resolve names and services to IP addresses.

During Active Directory installation, Windows attempts to find a DNS server; if it's unsuccessful, Windows asks whether you want to install DNS. When a new forest is created, it's best to have Windows install DNS during Active Directory installation because Windows automatically creates all the initial zone records that Active Directory needs. If DNS is installed later, you have to create the zone database manually.

You might need to install DNS manually on a domain controller, member server, or standalone server. In any case, you start by installing the DNS server role with Server Manager or PowerShell. To install DNS with PowerShell, use the following cmdlet:

```
Install-WindowsFeature DNS -IncludeManagementTools
```

If the DNS server is intended to manage domain name services for Active Directory, you should install the DNS server role on a domain controller so that you gain the benefits of Active Directory integration. If you're installing DNS on a domain controller, Windows detects the installation and informs you that DNS zones will be integrated with Active Directory.

After DNS is installed, your first step is usually to create a zone so it can be populated with resource records. If DNS was installed along with Active Directory, the zone representing the domain name is automatically created. In Activity 7-3, you install DNS, create a zone, and populate it with a host record.

After DNS is installed, it's ready to start resolving host and domain names to IP addresses. You don't even have to configure a zone if the DNS server will be a caching-only server. However, in most network environments that have an Internet presence or an Active Directory domain, there are a number of configuration tasks you'll want to undertake. There are three aspects of DNS configuration, as discussed in the following sections:

- DNS zones
- DNS resource records
- DNS server settings

Creating DNS Zones

Although DNS zones are created automatically during Active Directory installation, you might need to create a zone manually in the following situations:

- When you don't install DNS at the time you install Active Directory
- When you install DNS on a server that's not a domain controller
- When you create a stub zone
- When you create a secondary zone for a primary zone
- When you create a primary or secondary zone for an Internet domain

When you create a zone in DNS Manager, you must answer the following questions about it:

- Will it be a forward or reverse lookup zone?
- What type of zone do you want to create: primary, secondary, or stub?
- Should the zone be Active Directory–integrated?
- What's the replication scope of the zone?
- What's the name of the zone?
- How should the zone handle dynamic updates?

Forward and Reverse Lookup Zones

There are two DNS zone categories that define what kind of information is stored in a zone:

- *Forward lookup zone*—A **forward lookup zone (FLZ)** contains records that translate names to IP addresses. The zone name is based on the domain of the resource records it contains. For example, the zone name might be csmtech.corp, and it might contain resource records for www, mail, db-server, vpnserver, and so forth, which are hostnames of computers in the domain. FLZs can contain a variety of resource record types, as discussed later in the "Creating DNS Resource Records" section. Forward lookup zones are used to perform forward lookups, which resolve computer names (FQDNs) to addresses. For example, the following ping command resolves the FQDN to an IP address before the ping program can send a packet to *www.csmtech.corp*:

  ```
  ping www.csmtech.corp
  ```

- *Reverse lookup zone*—A **reverse lookup zone (RLZ)** contains records that map IP addresses to names and is named after the IP network address (IPv4 or IPv6) of the computers whose records it contains. For example, a typical name for an RLZ might be 99.10.in-addr.arpa, and it contains records for computers in the 10.99.0.0/16 subnet. An RLZ is queried when a network application has an IP address for a computer and needs the FQDN for that computer. A simple example of an application that queries an RLZ is ping, as in the following:

  ```
  ping -a 10.99.0.201
  ```

  The -a option in the command tells ping to do a reverse lookup query. If the query is successful, ping displays the FQDN of the computer with IP address 10.99.0.201. This option might be useful if you need to know where packets are coming from and all you have is the IP address of the packet's source. For example, say that your DNS server is sluggish, so you begin to monitor traffic to and from this server. You find that the server is receiving queries from an unknown source. To learn about the domain where these packets are originating, you can do a reverse lookup query with ping -a.

To create one of these zones, right-click the Forward Lookup Zones folder or the Reverse Lookup Zones folder in the DNS Manager console and click New Zone to start the New Zone Wizard.

Zone Type

After you have decided whether to install an FLZ or RLZ and started the New Zone Wizard, you select the type of zone you want to create, as shown in Figure 7-5. As mentioned, a zone is a database containing resource and information records for a domain and possibly subdomains. There are three different zone types:

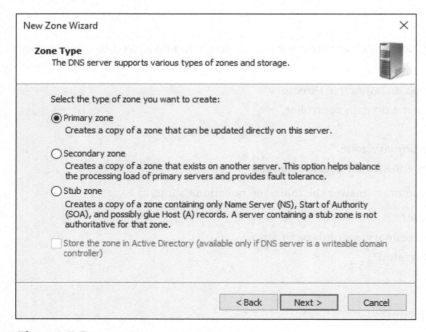

Figure 7-5   Selecting the zone type

- *Primary zone*—A **primary zone** contains a read/write master copy of all resource records for the zone. Updates to resource records can be made only on a server configured as a primary zone server. A primary DNS server is considered authoritative for the zone it manages. A primary zone can be either an Active Directory–integrated zone or a standard zone. If a primary zone is a standard zone, there can be only one server that hosts the primary zone, referred to as the "primary DNS server." If a primary zone is Active Directory–integrated, each DC in the replication scope of the Active Directory partition in which the zone is stored gets a copy of the zone, and changes can be made on any DC that hosts the zone, unless it's a read-only domain controller (RODC).

- *Secondary zone*—A **secondary zone** contains a read-only copy of all resource records for the zone. Changes can't be made directly on a secondary DNS server, but because it contains an exact copy of the primary zone, it's considered authoritative for the zone. A secondary zone can be only a standard zone, not an Active Directory–integrated zone. However, a file-based secondary zone can be created on a standalone server or a DC. Secondary zones are sometimes used to resolve names for domain-based resources outside the domain. For example, if you have two Active Directory forests, Forest1 and Forest2, you can create secondary zones on servers in Forest2 to resolve names for domains in Forest1, and vice versa. Secondary zones are also used in environments without Active Directory, such as for Internet domains and networks that are Linux/UNIX- or macOS-based.

  When you're working with standard zones, a server that holds the primary zone is called the *master DNS server*, and servers that hold secondary zones are called *slave DNS servers*. You must configure zone transfer settings on the master DNS server that holds the primary zone to allow resource records to be transferred or copied to one or more slave DNS servers that hold secondary zones.

- *Stub zone*—A **stub zone** contains a read-only copy of only the SOA and NS records for a zone and the necessary A records to resolve NS records. A stub zone forwards queries to a primary DNS server for the zone for which it holds SOA and NS records, and isn't authoritative for the zone. A stub zone can be an Active Directory–integrated zone or a standard zone.

At the bottom of the Zone Type window, you can choose to integrate the zone with Active Directory if the DNS server is on a writable domain controller. If the box is unchecked, the zone will be stored in a file on the local server.

Zone Replication Scope

If you are creating a zone on a writable domain controller and you chose to integrate the zone with Active Directory, the next option in the New Zone Wizard is to choose the zone replication scope. The **zone replication scope** determines which Active Directory partition the zone is stored in and to which DCs the zone information is replicated (see Figure 7-6). An **Active Directory partition** is a special file that Active Directory uses to store domain information. You can change the replication scope, if necessary, after a zone is created by selecting one of these options:

- *To all DNS servers running on domain controllers in this forest*—Stores the zone in the forest-wide DNS application directory partition called ForestDNSZones. This partition is created when DNS is installed on the first DC in the forest.

- *To all DNS servers running on domain controllers in this domain*—Stores the zone in the domain-wide DNS application directory partition called DomainDNSZones. It's the default option for new zones.

- *To all domain controllers in this domain (for Windows 2000 compatibility)*—Stores the zone in the domain partition, which is used to store most Active Directory objects. DNS zone information is replicated to all other DCs in the domain, regardless of whether the DNS server role is installed. This option is the only one available for Windows 2000 DCs and should be selected if DNS information must be replicated to Windows 2000 DNS servers.

- *To all domain controllers specified in the scope of this directory partition*—A custom DNS application partition must be created before selecting this option, and the partition must use the same name on each DC hosting DNS that should participate in replication. Use this option to limit which DNS servers receive zone data to control replication traffic. By default, this option is grayed out and disabled until you have created a custom DNS application directory partition (discussed next).

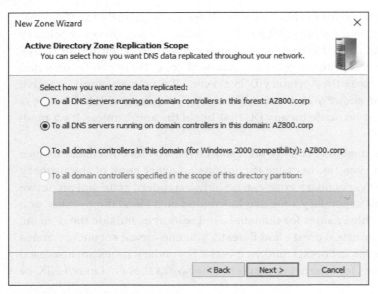

Figure 7-6 Selecting a zone replication scope

Zone Name

The next step is to give the zone a name. For an FLZ, it's the FQDN, such as csmtech.corp. For an RLZ, specify whether it's an IPv4 or IPv6 zone, and then enter the network ID portion of the zone. The zone name is created automatically by using the network ID's octets in reverse order and appending "in-addr.arpa" to the name. For example, if the IP network the RLZ is being created for is 192.168.0.0/24, you enter 192.168.0 in the Zone Name window, and Windows creates a zone named 0.168.192.in-addr.arpa.

Zone File

If you're creating a standard zone, you specify the filename for storing the zone data. The default name is *zonename*.dns, where *zonename* is usually the FQDN. For example, for a zone named csmtech.corp, the zone file name will be csmtech.corp.dns (see Figure 7-7). You can change the name if desired, or you can specify an existing file. If you specify an existing file, DNS will load the zone data in that file.

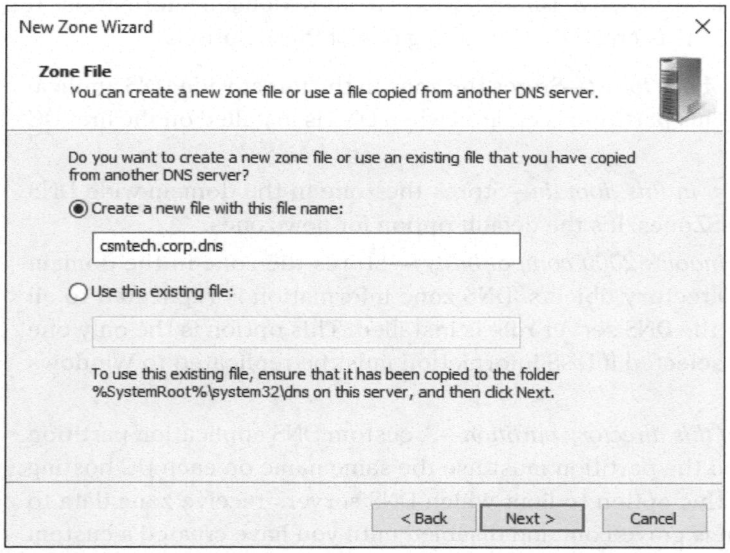

New Zone Wizard	
Zone File You can create a new zone file or use a file copied from another DNS server.	
Do you want to create a new zone file or use an existing file that you have copied from another DNS server?	
⊙ Create a new file with this file name:	
csmtech.corp.dns	
○ Use this existing file:	
To use this existing file, ensure that it has been copied to the folder %SystemRoot%\system32\dns on this server, and then click Next.	
< Back Next > Cancel	

Figure 7-7 Specifying a zone file

Dynamic Updates

The final step in creating a new zone is to select whether and how to use dynamic updates, as shown in Figure 7-8. Dynamic updates can be configured in one of three ways:

- *Allow only secure dynamic updates*—Available only for Active Directory–integrated zones, this option ensures that the host initiating the record creation or update has been authenticated by Active Directory.
- *Allow both nonsecure and secure dynamic updates*—Both authenticated Active Directory clients and non–Active Directory clients can create and update DNS records. This option isn't recommended because it allows rogue clients to create DNS records with false information. A rogue DNS client can impersonate a server by updating the server's A record with its own IP address, thereby redirecting client computers to a fraudulent server.
- *Do not allow dynamic updates*—All DNS records must be entered manually. This option helps secure the environment, but on a network with many hosts that must be accessed by name and on networks using DHCP, it's an administrative nightmare. However, this option does work well for a DNS server that manages names for public resources, such as web and mail servers with addresses that are usually assigned statically and don't change often. This is the default option for a standard zone.

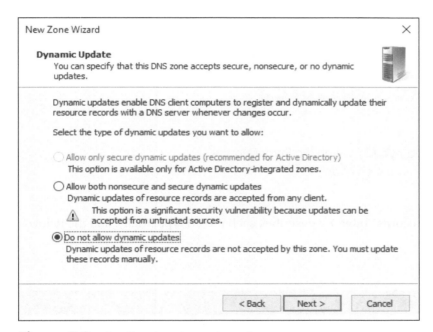

Figure 7-8   Configuring dynamic updates

Configuring DNS with PowerShell

A number of PowerShell cmdlets are available for installing and configuring DNS. The following cmdlets cover installing DNS and creating a new zone:

- `Install-WindowsFeature DNS -IncludeManagementTools`—Installs DNS and the DNS management tools.
- `Add-DnsServerPrimaryZone csmtech.corp -ZoneFile csmtech.corp.dns`—Creates a standard FLZ named csmtech.corp and stores it in a zone file named csmtech.corp.dns.
- `Add-DnsServerPrimaryZone -NetworkID 10.99.0.0/16 -ZoneFile 10.99.in-addr.arpa.dns`—Creates a standard RLZ for network ID 10.10.0.0/16 and stores it in a zone file named `10.99.in-addr.arpa.dns`.

To create secondary or stub zones, the relevant commands are `Add-DnsServerSecondaryZone` and `Add-DnsServerStubZone`. Remember that secondary zones can't be Active Directory–integrated.

Note 3

You can use the command-line tool `dnscmd.exe` to create zones and perform other DNS management tasks. However, this command might be deprecated in the future, and Microsoft recommends using PowerShell to manage DNS from the command line. Remember: To get help and examples for using PowerShell cmdlets, type `get-help CmdletName -detailed` at a PowerShell prompt.

Self-Check Questions

3. What type of zone should be queried if you have an IP address and want to know the hostname?

   a. RLZ
   b. FLZ

   c. Stub
   d. Secondary

4. Which type of zone only contains SOA and NS records?

   a. Primary
   b. Secondary

   c. Stub
   d. Forwarder

⊘Check your answers at the end of this module.

Creating DNS Resource Records

Microsoft Exam AZ-800:
Implement and manage an on-premises and hybrid networking infrastructure.
- Implement on-premises and hybrid name resolution

A DNS zone contains several types of resource records. Table 7-2 describes each record type briefly, and the following sections give you additional information.

Table 7-2   DNS resource record types

Record type (code)	Description
Host (A)	The most common resource record; consists of a computer name and an IPv4 address.
IPv6 Host (AAAA)	Like an A record but uses an IPv6 address.
Canonical Name (CNAME)	A record containing an alias for another record that enables you to refer to the same resource with different names yet maintain only one host record. For example, you could create an A record for a computer named "web" and a CNAME record that points to the A record but allows users to access the host with the name "www."
Pointer (PTR)	Used for reverse DNS lookups. Although DNS is used mainly to resolve a name to an address, it can also resolve an address to a name by using a reverse lookup. PTR records can be created automatically on Windows DNS servers.
Mail Exchanger (MX)	Contains the address of an email server for the domain. Because email addresses are typically specified as *user@domain.com*, the mail server's name is not part of the email address. To deliver a message to the mail server, an MX record query supplies the address of a mail server in the specified domain.
Service Location (SRV)	Allows DNS clients to request the address of a server that provides a specific service instead of querying the server by name. This type of record is useful when an application doesn't know the name of the server it needs but does know what service is required. For example, in Windows domains, DNS servers contain SRV records with the addresses of domain controllers so that clients can request the logon service to authenticate to the domain.

Table 7-2   (continued)

Record type (code)	Description
Start of Authority (SOA)	Less a resource than an informational record, an SOA identifies the name server that's authoritative for the domain and includes a variety of timers, dynamic update configuration, and zone transfer information.
Name Server (NS)	The FQDN of a name server that has authority over the domain. NS records are used by DNS servers to refer queries to another server that's authoritative for the requested domain.

Resource records are added to a zone in one of two ways:

- *Static*—With this method, an administrator enters DNS record information manually. This method is reasonable with a small network of only a few resources accessed by name, but in a large network, creating and updating static records can be an administrative burden. Some records created by the system are also called static records, such as the SOA and NS records created automatically when a zone is created and records created automatically when Active Directory is installed.
- *Dynamic*—Referred to as **Dynamic DNS (DDNS)**, computers in the domain can register or update their own DNS records, or DHCP can update DNS on the clients' behalf when a computer leases a new IP address. Both the client computer and the DHCP server must be configured to use this feature.

Host (A and AAAA) Records

Host records are the most abundant type of record in a typical DNS primary or secondary zone. A **host record** is fairly simple; it consists of a hostname and an IP address. A host record can be an **A record**, meaning it contains an IPv4 address, or an **AAAA record**, which contains an IPv6 address. When you configure a host record, an A or AAAA record is selected automatically, based on the IP address's format. When you create a host record, the only option by default is to update the associated PTR record in the RLZ, if it exists.

There are additional options for host records, however, if you enable the Advanced view setting in DNS Manager. In DNS Manager, click View and then Advanced. If you open the properties of a host record, you see a dialog box similar to that in Figure 7-9. The following list describes the options you see in this figure:

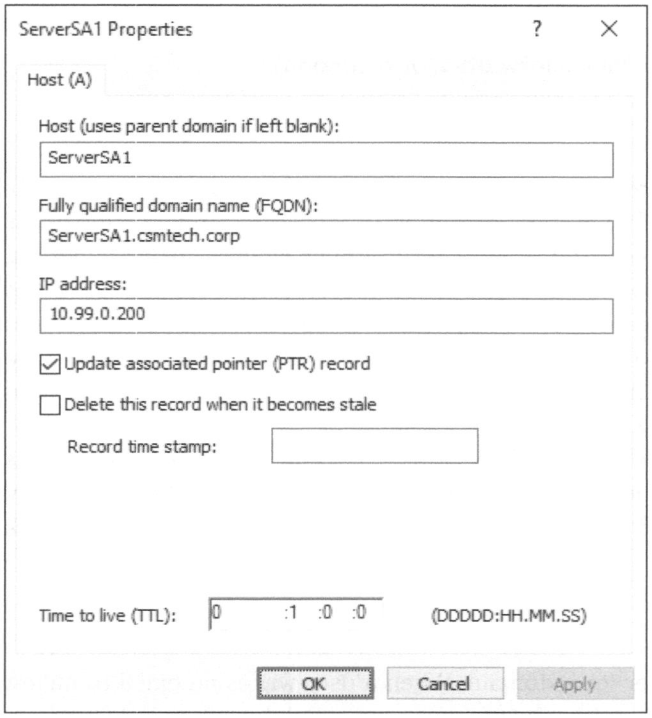

Figure 7-9   Properties of a host record with Advanced view enabled

- *Update associated pointer (PTR) record*—If you enable this option, a PTR record is created or updated in the relevant RLZ, if it's present.
- *Delete this record when it becomes stale*—A stale record hasn't been updated in a period longer than its time to live (TTL) value. This option is set automatically on a dynamic record and can be set manually on a static record. If it's set, stale records are deleted (scavenged) from the database, a process discussed in Module 3.
- *Record time stamp*—For dynamic records, this field shows the date and time the record was created or updated. On static records, it's filled in automatically with the current date and time if the "Delete this record when it becomes stale" option is set and you click Apply in the Properties dialog box.
- *Time to live (TTL)*—The TTL tells the system how long the record should remain in the database after it was created or last updated. The default is 1 hour. This field is relevant only on zones that have scavenging enabled. It works with the "Record time stamp" option. If the actual time and date are past the "Record time stamp" value plus the TTL value, the record is eligible for scavenging.

Canonical Name (CNAME) Records

A **CNAME record** is an alias for another domain name record in the DNS database. It's often used when multiple services are running on the same server and you want users to be able to refer to each service with a different name. For example, you might have an FTP service and a web service hosted on the same server. You can set up DNS records as follows:

Record type	Name	Value
CNAME	www.csmtech.corp	server1.csmtech.corp
CNAME	ftp.csmtech.corp	server1.csmtech.corp
A	server1.csmtech.corp	192.168.0.101

In this example, a reference to *www.csmtech.corp* or *ftp.csmtech.corp* returns server1.csmtech.corp, which returns the IP address 192.168.0.101. A CNAME record must always point to another domain name; it can't point to an IP address. Although a CNAME record can point to another CNAME, it's not recommended, as it can result in circular logic. For example, you could have CNAME record X point to CNAME record Y, which points back to CNAME record X in an unresolvable loop.

You can also create CNAME records that point to records in other domains. For example, you can create a CNAME record with the alias ftp.csmpub.corp that points to *www.csmtech.corp*, as long as the server on which you create the record has a way to resolve ftp.csmpub.corp (from local zone data, a forwarder, or recursion).

Pointer (PTR) Records

As discussed, a **PTR record** is used to resolve a known IP address to a hostname. PTR records are used by some web-based applications that limit their use to specific domains. When the application is accessed, a reverse lookup is performed, and the domain name of the host attempting to access the application is verified against the list of permitted domains. PTR records are also useful for certain applications when only the IP address is known and you want to find the hostname. For example, when you use the `tracert` command to map the route between your computer and a destination, each router along the way replies with its IP address. The `tracert` command can then do a reverse lookup to determine the router's FQDN, which often contains information for determining where the router is located and to which ISP it belongs. PTR records are found only in RLZs.

PTR records have much the same information as a host record, including a timestamp and TTL. When you create a host record, you have the option to create the related PTR record for the host automatically, as long as the RLZ already exists. In addition, you can edit an existing host record and select the "Update associated pointer (PTR) record" check box to create or update the PTR associated with the host.

Mail Exchanger (MX) Records

An **MX record** is used by mail services to find the mail server for a domain. When a user writes an email to mike@csmtech.corp, for example, all that's known from the email address is the recipient name and domain name. However, the mail protocol needs the name of a host in the domain that provides mail services, which is where the MX record comes in. When an outgoing mail server, usually an SMTP server, needs to deliver an email message, it performs a DNS lookup for the MX record for the domain name contained in the email address. The MX record points to an A record (much as a CNAME record does). So, in this example, there might be records in the csmtech.corp zone that look like the following:

Record type	Name	Value
A	mail.csmtech.corp	192.168.0.102
MX	csmtech.corp	mail.csmtech.corp

When a client queries for an MX record for the csmtech.corp domain, the DNS server returns the name of the server (mail.csmtech.corp) and its IP address. The outgoing mail server can then deliver the mail to address 192.168.0.102, which contains a mailbox for the user account mike.

To create an MX record, right-click the zone where you want to create the record and click New Mail Exchanger (MX). There's only one required field: the FQDN of the mail server, which can be a host or CNAME record (see Figure 7-10). The following list explains each option in this figure:

- *Host or child domain*—This field is usually left blank because the parent domain name is most often used. However, you can add a hostname or the name of a child domain. For example, if your primary domain name is csmtech.corp, but you also have mail accounts in a child domain, such as europe.csmtech.corp, you could enter *europe* in this text box.
- *Fully qualified domain name (FQDN)*—This is the name of the domain where you're creating the record. If you enter a value in the "Host or child domain" text box, it's added to the beginning of the default value. For example, if you enter *europe* in the "Host or child domain" text box, this field changes to europe.csmtech.corp. You can't change its contents manually.
- *Fully qualified domain name (FQDN) of mail server*—This is the FQDN of the actual mail server, which is usually a host or CNAME record in the zone. In this example, the mail server is mail.csmtech.corp.

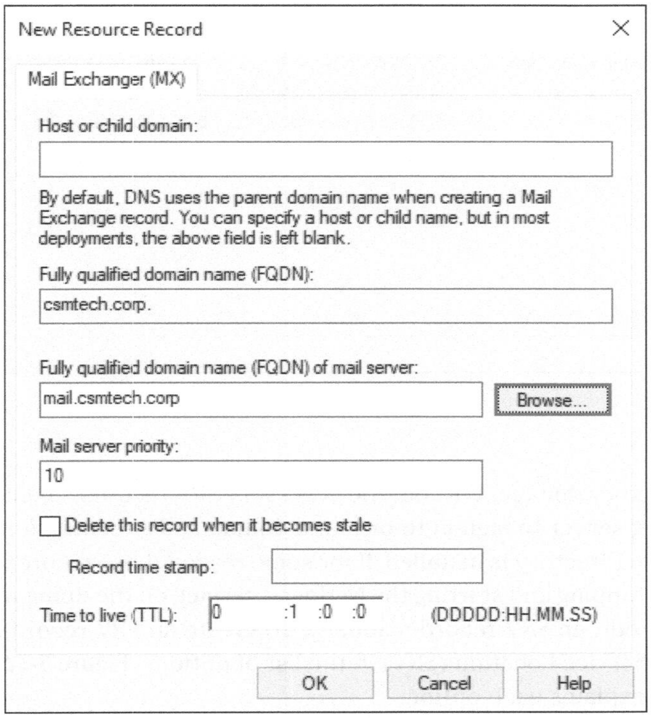

Figure 7-10   Creating an MX record

- *Mail server priority*—If you have multiple mail servers in the zone, you can set a priority in this text box. Lower values have higher precedence. When a client queries for an MX record, the DNS server returns all MX records defined in its database for the zone. The client first tries the MX record with the lowest-priority value. If it gets no response, it tries the next one, and so on. You can set the same priority value on two or more servers for a round-robin type of load balancing, as the equal-priority records are returned to the client in round-robin order. (Round-robin settings are discussed later in this module.)

- The last three fields are for scavenging stale records. Note that these fields can only be seen if the Advanced view is turned on in DNS Manager.

Service Location (SRV) Records

An SRV record specifies a hostname and port number for servers that supply specific services. For example, servers that provide Kerberos authentication or Lightweight Directory Access Protocol (LDAP) services can register an SRV record with a DNS server so that clients requiring these services can find them. SRV records are queried by client computers in the following format:

```
_ServiceName._Protocol.DomainName
```

For example, a client looking for an LDAP (Active Directory) server using the TCP protocol for the csmtech.corp domain sends a query that looks like this:

```
_ldap._tcp.csmtech.corp
```

In DNS Manager, several SRV records are in the _msdcs subdomain created for every Active Directory domain. Figure 7-11 shows DNS Manager with SRV records for the Kerberos, global catalog, and LDAP services in the AZ800.corp domain.

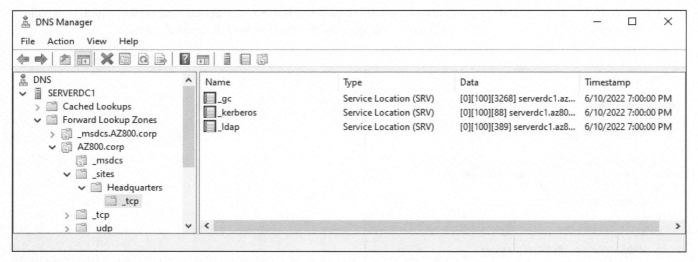

Figure 7-11 SRV records in an Active Directory domain

SRV records are critical to the operation of an Active Directory domain. Without the necessary SRV records, client computers couldn't find a domain controller or global catalog server to sign in to or join a domain. SRV records for Active Directory are usually created automatically when Active Directory is installed. If for some reason these records aren't created or updated correctly, you can register them by stopping and starting the Netlogon service on the domain controller or by restarting the server. You can also create or edit an SRV record manually. To create an SRV record, right-click the zone, click Other New Records, and then click Service Location (SRV) in the list of options. Figure 7-12 shows an SRV record for the LDAP service. The following list explains each option.

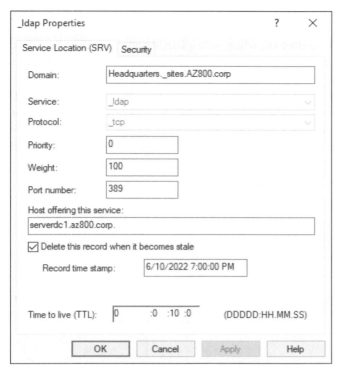

Figure 7-12 An SRV record for the LDAP service

- *Domain*—The name of the domain in which the service is located. This field is filled in for you, and you can't change it.
- *Service*—Choose a service in this list. The name is prefaced with an underscore character, so the Kerberos service, for example, is listed as _kerberos. Services you can choose from are finger, FTP, HTTP, Kerberos, LDAP, MSDCS, NNTP, Telnet, and Whois.
- *Protocol*—The Transport-layer protocol the service uses. The choices are TCP and UDP.
- *Priority*—The priority of this record if more than one server is providing the same service. Lower numbers have higher priority. The default value is 0.
- *Weight*—If two of the same service records have equal priority, the weight value determines which record the host should use. Unlike the priority, where the record with the highest priority (lowest value) is always used, the weight value is used more as a proportion. The higher the weight is, the higher the proportion. So, if there are two records with equal priority, and Record1 has a weight of 40 and Record2 has a weight of 20, Record1 is used twice as often as Record2. Records with equal weight are used equally. The default value is 0.
- *Port number*—This value is filled in automatically with the default port number for the selected service. However, you can change it if the service uses a nonstandard port number.
- *Host offering this service*—The FQDN of the host providing the service, ending with a dot.

Like all record types, if you have the Advanced view setting enabled, you can change the default TTL and select the option to delete the record when it becomes stale.

Note 4

The last two record types from Table 7-2, SOA and NS records, are discussed later in the module in the "Configuring DNS Zones" section.

Creating Dynamic DNS Records

Dynamic DNS records are created and updated by a host computer or, when using DHCP to assign IP addresses, by the DHCP server when an IP address is leased or renewed. When a device is assigned an IP address, it registers its name with the DNS server configured in its IP address settings. If the device has an IPv4 address, an A record is created; if it has an IPv6 address, an AAAA record is created. If the device gets its IP address settings from a DHCP server, the DHCP server can be configured to register the computer's name and address on its behalf. Whenever a computer's IP address changes or it renews its IP address lease from the DHCP server, the DNS records are updated. Each time a dynamic record is created or updated, a time-to-live (TTL) value and timestamp are added to the record. The TTL specifies how long the record should remain in the DNS database. If the record expires, it's deleted from the database.

> **Note 5**
>
> You can also force a Windows client to register its address by using the `ipconfig /registerdns` command.

If a reverse lookup zone exists for the host's IP address, PTR records are created dynamically in the same manner as host records. PTR records can also be created by opening a host record's properties and selecting the "Update associated pointer (PTR) record" check box.

Creating Static DNS Records

Static DNS records are called static because they don't expire. They stay in the DNS database until someone removes them. Unlike dynamically created records, which have a timestamp, static records have no timestamp by default. Static records are created manually by an administrator or automatically by Windows under some circumstances. To create a static record in DNS Manager, you right-click the zone and select the record type. In an FLZ, the most common type of record to create is a New Host record, which can be an IPv4 (A) record or an IPv6 (AAAA) record (see Figure 7-13). Enter a name in the Name text box to create the FQDN automatically. DNS Manager creates an A or AAAA record automatically, depending on whether an IPv4 or IPv6 address is entered. If you select the "Create associated pointer (PTR) record" check box, a PTR record is created when a suitable RLZ exists for the IP address entered.

Figure 7-13 Creating a new host record

To create a PTR record, right-click the RLZ and click New Pointer (PTR). Type the host IP address, and then type in the hostname or browse for one (see Figure 7-14).

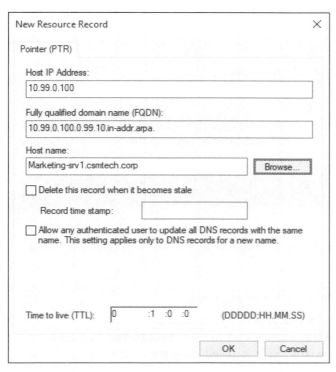

Figure 7-14   Creating a new PTR record

As mentioned, Windows can create a static resource record automatically. When a new zone is created, SOA and NS static records are created for the zone, and in Active Directory–integrated zones, SRV, PTR, and A records are created automatically for domain controllers.

> **Note 6**
>
> Figures 7-13 and 7-14 show the new host record and new PTR record dialog boxes with the Advanced view option set in DNS Manager.

PowerShell Commands for Creating DNS Resource Records

The following PowerShell cmdlets are used to create DNS resource records:

- `Add-DnsServerResourceRecord -A -ZoneName csmtech.corp -Name host1 -IPv4Address 192.168.0.11`—Adds an A record named host1 to the csmtech.corp zone.
- `Add-DnsServerResourceRecord -AAAA -ZoneName csmtech.corp -Name host1 -IPv6Address 2001:DB8::11`—Adds an AAAA record named host1 to the csmtech.corp zone.
- `Add-DnsServerResourceRecord -CName -ZoneName csmtech.corp -Name h1 –HostNameAlias host1.csmtech.corp`—Adds a CNAME (alias) record named h1 with the target host1.csmtech.corp.
- `Add-DnsServerResourceRecord -Ptr -ZoneName 0.168.192.in-addr.arpa -Name 11 -PtrDomainName host1.csmtech.corp`—Adds a PTR record named host1.csmtech.corp with the IP address 192.168.0.11 to the 0.168.192.in-addr.arpa RLZ.

Self-Check Questions

5. What type of resource record will you find in an RLZ?

   a. PTR
   b. A

   c. MX
   d. AAAA

6. Which record type points to another domain name and is considered an alias?

   a. MX
   b. A

   c. CNAME
   d. PTR

◉ Check your answers at the end of this module.

Activity 7-3

Installing DNS and Creating a New Zone

Time Required: 20 minutes
Objective: Install DNS on a standalone server.
Required Tools and Equipment: ServerSA1
Description: In this activity, you install DNS on a standalone server and create a test zone.

1. Start ServerSA1, sign in as **Administrator**, and open Server Manager.
2. Start the Add Roles and Features Wizard. In the Server Roles window, click to select **DNS Server**. Click **Add Features** and accept the remaining default options. When the role is installed, close the wizard.
3. In Server Manager, click **Tools** and then **DNS** from the menu to open DNS Manager. In the left pane, click to expand **ServerSA1** and then click **Forward Lookup Zones**. No zones are listed yet.
4. Right-click **Forward Lookup Zones** and click **New Zone** to start the New Zone Wizard. In the welcome window, click **Next**.
5. In the Zone Type window, notice that the option to store the zone in Active Directory is grayed out because the server isn't a DC. Accept the default **Primary zone** setting, and then click **Next**.
6. Type **testdom1.corp** in the Zone name text box, and then click **Next**. In the Zone File window, accept the default filename **testdom1.corp.dns**; this is the name of the file where the zone data is stored. Click **Next**.
7. In the Dynamic Update window, click the **Allow both nonsecure and secure dynamic updates** option, and then click **Next**. Click **Finish**.
8. In the DNS Manager console, double-click **testdom1.corp** in the right pane. You see two resource records: the SOA record that is created for every zone and an NS record. Double-click the SOA record to open the domain Properties dialog box to the Start of Authority (SOA) tab. Most SOA settings are discussed later in the "Start of Authority Records" section. Click **Cancel**.
9. Double-click the NS record. The Properties box from the previous step appears again, but it opens to the Name Servers tab. Click **Cancel**, and close the DNS Manager console.
10. Now that ServerSA1 is a DNS server, you will change its IP address configuration so that it uses itself for DNS lookups and DNS registration. Open a PowerShell window, type **Set-DNSClientServerAddress Ethernet -ServerAddresses 127.0.0.1**, and press **Enter**.
11. To set the DNS suffix search list for the Ethernet interface to testdom1.corp so that the server registers its name with the zone you just created, type **Set-DnsClient Ethernet -ConnectionSpecificSuffix testdom1.corp -UseSuffixWhenRegistering $true** and press **Enter**.
12. Before you register the name with DNS, type **nslookup ServerSA1.testdom1.corp** and press **Enter**. You see a message that localhost can't find ServerSA1, which means there's no A record yet for ServerSA1.
13. To register the server name with DNS, type **ipconfig /registerdns** and press **Enter**. Try the lookup again by typing **nslookup ServerSA1.testdom1.corp** and pressing **Enter**. The lookup is successful this time. (If it's not, wait a minute and try the command again.)

(continues)

Activity 7-3 Continued

14. Close the PowerShell window. Open the DNS Manager console, click the **testdom1.corp** zone, and click the **Refresh** icon to verify that the A record for ServerSA1 has been created (see Figure 7-15).

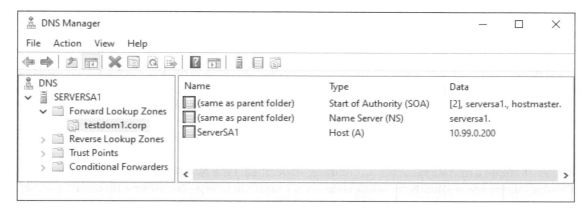

Figure 7-15   DNS Manager with the ServerSA1 host record

15. Stay signed in and continue to the next activity.

Activity 7-4

Working with Reverse Lookup Zones

Time Required: 15 minutes
Objective: Create an RLZ and view its properties.
Required Tools and Equipment: ServerSA1
Description: In this activity, you create an RLZ on ServerSA1 and add a PTR record to it.

1. Sign in to ServerSA1 as **Administrator**, if necessary.
2. Open a PowerShell window. Type **nslookup 10.99.0.200** (the address of ServerSA1) and press **Enter**. You see a response that the address can't be found. Note that nslookup is not a PowerShell cmdlet but can be run from a PowerShell window as well as from a command prompt.
3. To create an RLZ named 0.99.10.in-addr.arpa, type **Add-DnsServerPrimaryZone -NetworkID 10.99.0.0/24 –ZoneFile 0.99.10.in-addr.arpa.dns** and press **Enter**.
4. Open the DNS Manager console, then click to expand **Reverse Lookup Zones** and verify that the zone has been created. (If you don't see it, click the **Refresh** icon in DNS Manager.) Click **0.99.10.in-addr.arpa**. You see the SOA and NS records.
5. You can use `ipconfig /registerdns` on each computer to create PTR records, but there's another method you can use from the DNS Manager console. Click to expand **Forward Lookup Zones**, and then click **testdom1.corp**. Double-click **ServerSA1** in the right pane. Click to select the **Update associated pointer (PTR) record** check box, and then click **OK**.
6. Click the **0.99.10.in-addr.arpa** RLZ in the left pane again. If the PTR record isn't there, click the **Refresh** icon in DNS Manager to see the 10.99.0.200 PTR record.
7. In the PowerShell prompt, type **nslookup 10.99.0.200** and press **Enter** to verify that you can do a reverse lookup. You should get a response with the Name field shown as ServerSA1.testdom1.corp.
8. Stay signed in to ServerSA1 for the next activity.

Activity 7-5

Creating Static DNS Entries

Time Required: 15 minutes

Objective: Create static A, CNAME, and PTR records.

Required Tools and Equipment: ServerSA1

Description: In this activity, you experiment with creating static DNS records using the test zone you created on ServerSA1.

1. On ServerSA1, open the DNS Manager console, if necessary, and click to expand **Forward Lookup Zones**. Right-click **testdom1.corp** and click **New Host (A or AAAA)**.
2. In the New Host dialog box, type **webserver1** in the Name text box and **10.99.0.101** in the IP address text box. Click the **Add Host** button. Click **OK** and then click **Done**.
3. In PowerShell, type **nslookup webserver1.testdom1.corp** and press **Enter**. The name is resolved. Type **nslookup 10.99.0.101** and press **Enter**. The IP address is resolved.
4. Now, you'll create a CNAME resource record using PowerShell. Type **Add-DnsServerResourceRecord –CName –Name www –HostNameAlias webserver1.testdom1.corp –ZoneName testdom1.corp**, and then click **OK**. This command creates an alias named www for the existing host record webserver1.
5. Type **nslookup** www.testdom1.corp and press **Enter**. The command returns the address for webserver1.testdom1.corp and lists the alias name www.testdom1.corp.
6. Now, create a PTR record for the new alias. Type **Add-DnsServerResourceRecord -Ptr -Name 101 -ZoneName 0.99.10.in-addr.arpa -PtrDomainName** www.testdom1.corp and press **Enter**.
7. At the command prompt, type **nslookup 192.168.0.101** and press **Enter**. Because webserver1 also has a PTR record with that address, either the www.testdom1.corp or webserver1.testdom1.corp record is returned. If you repeat the command, the other record will be returned.
8. Stay signed in to ServerSA1 and continue to the next activity.

Configuring DNS Zones

Microsoft Exam AZ-800:

Implement and manage an on-premises and hybrid networking infrastructure.

- Implement on-premises and hybrid name resolution

After a zone is created, you can view and change its properties in DNS Manager by right-clicking the zone and clicking Properties. In the General tab (see Figure 7-16), you can view and change the following options:

- *Status*—Pause a running DNS zone or start a paused DNS zone. When a zone is paused, queries made to it are refused.
- *Type*—Change the zone type (primary, secondary, or stub) and choose whether the zone should be Active Directory–integrated.
- *Replication*—Change the replication scope. (Replication is discussed later.) This button is grayed out for a standard zone.
- *Dynamic updates*—On an Active Directory–integrated zone, choose Secure only, Nonsecure and secure, or None. Standard zones don't have the Secure only option.
- *Aging*—Click this button to configure aging and scavenging options, which specify how often stale resource records are removed from the zone database.

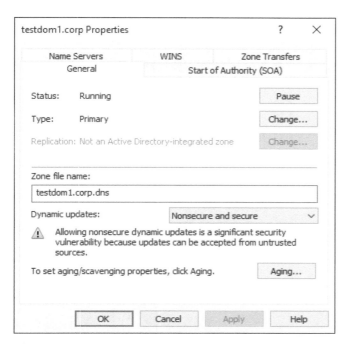

Figure 7-16   A zone's Properties dialog box

Start of Authority Records

The SOA record, found in every zone, contains information that identifies the server primarily responsible for the zone as well as some operational properties for the zone. You can edit the SOA record by double-clicking it in the right pane of DNS Manager after selecting the zone or by viewing the zone's properties and clicking the Start of Authority tab. Shown in Figure 7-17, the SOA record contains the following information:

- *Serial number*—A revision number that increases each time data in the zone changes. This number is used to determine when zone information should be replicated.

- *Primary server*—On a primary Active Directory–integrated zone, this field displays the name of the server where DNS Manager is currently running. For a standard zone, it displays the primary DNS server's name.

- *Responsible person*—The email address of the person responsible for managing the zone. A period rather than an @ sign is used to separate the username from the domain name (according to RFC 1183, which defines DNS resource record types).

- *Minimum (default) TTL*—This setting specifies a default TTL value for zone data when a TTL isn't supplied. The TTL value tells other DNS servers that cache records from this zone how long to keep cached data; it should be adjusted according to how often data in the zone is likely to change. For example, a zone that maintains only static entries for resources that aren't changed, added, or removed can often specify a high TTL value. If a zone maintains dynamic records or records for resources that are going online and offline constantly, this value should be lower. If a redesign of your network will cause many changes to zone data, this value can be lowered temporarily. Then wait until the previous TTL time has elapsed before making the changes. This way, servers caching records that will be changed don't store them very long. The TTL set separately on resource records overrides this default value, which is 1 hour.

The other three fields—Refresh interval, Retry interval, and Expires after—control zone transfers and are discussed later in the section called "Creating Secondary Zones and Configuring Zone Transfers."

Figure 7-17 The Start of Authority (SOA) tab

Name Server Records

NS records specify FQDNs and IP addresses of authoritative servers for a zone. Each zone that's created has an NS record, which points to an authoritative server for that zone. For example, when a primary zone is created, the NS record points to the server it's created on. A typical configuration with Active Directory–integrated zones has an NS record for each domain controller configured as a DNS server in the domain or forest, depending on the scope of zone replication.

NS records are also used to refer DNS queries to a name server that has been delegated authority for a subdomain. For example, .com TLD servers refer queries for resources in the docs.microsoft.com subdomain to a DNS server that's authoritative for the microsoft.com domain. The microsoft.com domain name server can then refer the query to another DNS server that has been delegated authority for the docs subdomain of microsoft.com. Subdomains need not be delegated; they can simply be created under the zone representing their parent domain. If the subdomain has many resources and traffic on it is heavy, however, zone delegation is a wise approach.

An NS record technically consists of just the name server's FQDN, but for the name to be useful, there must be a way to resolve it to an IP address. DNS does this with a **glue A record**, which is an A record containing the name server's IP address. On Windows DNS servers, glue records are created automatically, if possible, by a DNS lookup on the NS record's FQDN; they don't appear as an A record anywhere in the zone database. Figure 7-18 shows the interface for creating and editing NS records. If Windows fails to resolve the name server's FQDN, you can edit the record and add an IP address manually. You can add a TTL value for the record that tells other servers caching the NS record during recursive lookups how long they should keep it in cache. If no value is specified, the default TTL for the domain is used.

Zone Delegation

Zone delegation is transferring authority for a subdomain to a new zone, which can be on the same server or another server. Typically, you use zone delegation when a business unit in an organization is large enough to warrant its own subdomain and has the personnel to manage its own DNS server for the subdomain. Even if the business unit won't be managing the subdomain, delegating the handling of the subdomain to other servers might make sense for performance reasons.

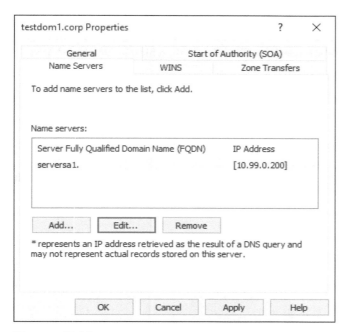

Figure 7-18   The Name Servers tab

When a subdomain has been delegated to a zone on another server, the DNS server hosting the parent zone maintains only an NS record pointing to the DNS server hosting the delegated zone. When the parent DNS server receives a query for the subdomain, it refers the query to the DNS server hosting the subdomain.

Note 7

If IP address changes are made to the name servers hosting the delegated zone, the NS records on the server hosting the parent domain must be updated manually.

Creating Secondary Zones and Configuring Zone Transfers

As mentioned, a secondary zone is a read-only copy of a primary zone. When a secondary zone is created, it must have the same name of an existing primary zone and zone transfers must be configured to load data from the primary zone to the secondary zone. Because secondary zones are read-only, all changes to the zone data occur at the server hosting the primary zone and are subsequently transferred to all secondary zone servers. While only one server can host a primary zone, multiple servers can host secondary zones.

Note 8

Only one server can host a *standard* primary zone. Active Directory-integrated primary zones can be hosted on as many servers as there are domain controllers.

Zone Transfer Settings

A **zone transfer** copies all or part of a zone from one DNS server to another and occurs as a result of a secondary server requesting the transfer from another server. The server requesting the zone transfer is sometimes called the *slave*, and the server providing the zone information is sometimes called the *master*. The master server can host a primary or secondary zone, but the slave server always hosts a secondary zone. Although Active Directory–integrated zones use Active Directory replication to transfer zone information, you can configure standard zone transfers if the target is a standard secondary zone. Zone transfers can be initiated in two ways:

- *Refresh interval*—The Refresh interface is found on the SOA tab of a zone's Properties window. As discussed, a secondary zone server requests zone information from another server (a primary or another secondary master) when the zone's refresh interval expires, which is every 15 minutes by default.

- *DNS notify*—A master server can be configured to send a DNS notify message to secondary servers when zone information changes. The secondary server can then request the zone transfer immediately without waiting for the refresh interval to expire. DNS notify is configured on the Zone Transfers tab, which is discussed next.

Note 9

Zone transfers typically use TCP port 53, and most DNS queries from a client to a server use UDP port 53. If zone transfers must occur through a firewall, be sure to open TCP port 53 to allow master and slave servers to communicate.

Zone transfers are configured in the Zone Transfers tab of a zone's Properties dialog box (see Figure 7-19), which has the following options:

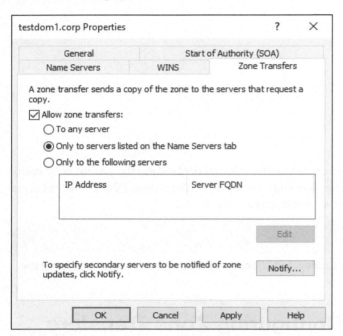

Figure 7-19   The Zone Transfers tab

- *Allow zone transfers*—Selecting this check box enables zone transfers. By default, zone transfers in Active Directory–integrated zones are disabled. In standard zones, zone transfers are enabled for all other name servers listed for that zone. Options for configuring zone transfers are as follows:
  - To any server: Allows any server to request a zone transfer. This option isn't recommended for most environments, as it allows any host to request network information, which is not secure.
  - Only to servers listed on the Name Servers tab: This option is the default for standard zones. By default, no servers are listed on the Name Servers tab except the current server, so zone transfers are not allowed.
  - Only to the following servers: You can specify servers to which zone information can be transferred.
- *Notify*—Clicking this button opens a dialog box where you can specify servers that should receive notifications of changed zone information. By default, the notify option is enabled in standard zones for servers listed in the Name Servers tab.

Note 10

If all zones are hosted on Windows domain controllers and are Active Directory–integrated, there's no need to configure zone transfers because Active Directory replication handles this process.

You configure timing intervals of zone transfers in the Start of Authority tab. There are three timers related to zone transfers:

- *Refresh interval*—Specifies how often a secondary DNS server attempts to renew its zone information. When the interval expires, the server requests the SOA record from the primary DNS server. The serial number in the retrieved SOA record is then compared with the serial number in the secondary server's SOA record. If the serial number has changed, the secondary server requests a new copy of the zone data. After the transfer is completed, the refresh interval begins anew. The default value is 15 minutes. If notification is configured, the DNS server attempts to renew its zone information when it receives a notification and resets the Refresh interval timer.

- *Retry interval*—The amount of time a secondary server waits before retrying a zone transfer that has failed. This value should be less than the Refresh interval timer; by default, the value is 10 minutes. The Retry interval timer begins after the Refresh interval expires if the primary server can't be contacted or the zone transfer fails.

- *Expires after*—The amount of time before a secondary server considers its zone data obsolete if it can't contact the primary DNS server. If the Refresh interval timer expires without a successful zone transfer, this timer begins. If it expires without contacting the primary DNS server or without a successful zone transfer, the DNS server stops responding to queries. This value must be higher than the Refresh interval and Retry interval combined; the default is 1 day. This timer prevents a secondary server from responding to DNS queries with data that might be stale.

Full Versus Incremental Zone Transfers

There are two types of zone transfers: full zone transfers and incremental zone transfers. A full zone transfer was the only transfer method in older DNS versions prior to Windows Server 2003. As DNS databases grew larger and zone files became more numerous and much bigger, incremental zone transfers were defined. Incremental zone transfers can only be used if both the master and slave DNS servers support them.

When a secondary server requests a zone transfer, it can request an incremental transfer. (If the secondary zone is newly configured on the server, it requests a full zone transfer.) If the serial number of the slave's zone is lower than the master's, the master determines the differences between its current zone data and the slave's zone data. The master then transfers only the resource records that have changed. For incremental zone transfers to work, the master must keep a record of incremental changes with each serial number change. For example, if a slave server requests an incremental zone transfer, and its zone serial number is 500 and the master's zone serial number is 502, the master sends all changes that have occurred to the zone between serial number 500 and 502. Even if an incremental transfer is requested, the master can still respond with a full zone transfer if it doesn't support incremental transfers or have enough change history to respond accurately with an incremental transfer.

Note 11

A full zone transfer is often referred to as an AXFR because that's the query code used when the slave DNS server requests the transfer. An incremental zone transfer uses the code IXFR.

Self-Check Questions

7. Which of the following is *not* found in an SOA record?

   a. Serial number
   b. IP address of server

   c. Minimum TTL
   d. Refresh interval

8. Which zone transfer parameter can cause a server to stop responding to queries?

   a. Refresh interval
   b. Retry interval

   c. Expires after
   d. Notify

⦾ Check your answers at the end of this module.

Activity 7-6

Creating a Secondary Zone and Configuring Zone Transfers

Time Required: 15 minutes
Objective: Create a secondary zone and configure zone transfers.
Required Tools and Equipment: ServerDC1 and ServerSA1
Description: In this activity, you create a secondary zone for the Active Directory-integrated primary zone on ServerDC1 and configure zone transfers between ServerDC1 and ServerSA1.

1. Sign in to ServerSA1 as **Administrator** and open the DNS Manager console.
2. Right-click **Forward Lookup Zones** and click **New Zone**. In the New Zone Wizard's welcome window, click **Next**.
3. In the Zone Type window, click the **Secondary zone** option button, and then click **Next**. Type **AZ800.corp** in the Zone name text box, and then click **Next**.
4. In the Master DNS Servers window, type **10.99.0.220** (the address of ServerDC1) in the Master Servers text box, and press **Enter**. You should see that the address is validated. Click **Next**, and then click **Finish**.
5. Sign in to ServerDC1 as **Administrator** and open the DNS Manager console.
6. Click to expand **Forward Lookup Zones**, right-click **AZ800.corp**, and click **Properties**. Click the **Name Servers** tab.
7. Click **Add** and type **ServerSA1** in the Server fully qualified domain name (FQDN) text box. In this case, you do not need the FQDN; the server name will suffice. In the IP Addresses of the NS record box, type **10.99.0.200**, press **Enter**, and then click **OK**.
8. Click the **Zone Transfers** tab. Click the **Allow zone transfers** check box, and then click the **Only to servers listed on the Name Servers tab** option button. Click **Notify**, type **10.99.0.200** in the box under IP Address, and press **Enter**. Click **OK**. Click **OK** again.
9. On ServerSA1 in DNS Manager, click **AZ800.corp** in the left pane and then click the **Refresh** icon in the toolbar. The zone data should have been transferred successfully, and you should see the resource records for AZ800.corp. If you don't see the zone data, click Refresh again after a few moments. If you still don't see zone data, close DNS Manager and re-open it.

Note 12

It can take several minutes before the zone transfer is successful. If you see an error message in the right pane of DNS Manager when you click the AZ800.corp zone on ServerSA1, click Refresh periodically until you see the resource records.

10. Test the zone by opening PowerShell on ServerSA1, typing **nslookup serverdm1.AZ800.corp**, and pressing **Enter**. You should get a successful reply. Close the command prompt window.
11. Continue to the next activity.

Configuring DNS Server Settings

Microsoft Exam AZ-800:
Implement and manage an on-premises and hybrid networking infrastructure.
- Implement on-premises and hybrid name resolution

So far, you have focused on DNS zone creation and configuration—and rightly so because zones are where all the data is and where most DNS configuration takes place. However, you should be familiar with several DNS server settings to configure an optimal DNS environment and solve DNS problems when they occur. These settings are discussed in the following sections:

- Forwarders
- Root hints
- Round robin
- Recursion

DNS Forwarders

Forwarders were defined previously in the "DNS Server Roles" section, but this section goes into more detail on when to configure and use them. Recall how a typical DNS query is processed: A DNS server receives a lookup request from a client and, if it's unable to satisfy the request, a recursive query ensues, starting with a root server. This process works well, but in situations such as the following, referring the query to a forwarder is more efficient:

- *When the DNS server address for the target domain is known*—Suppose a company has a department working on highly confidential research, and this department is segmented from the rest of the network by routers and firewalls. This department maintains its own domain controllers and DNS servers that aren't part of the organization's domain. However, department members often need access to resources on the network servers. In addition, the research department's DNS servers aren't permitted to contact the Internet. For computers in this department network to resolve names for company resources, a forwarder can be configured on its DNS server that points to a company DNS server. The company DNS server not only resolves queries for company domain resources, it also performs recursive lookups for external domains on behalf of the research department's DNS server.

- *When only one DNS server in a network should make external queries*—A network consisting of several DNS servers might want to limit external queries to a single DNS server. This strategy has several benefits. First, network security can be enhanced by limiting exposure to the Internet to only one server. Second, because a single server is making all the queries to Internet domains, overall DNS performance can be enhanced because the server builds an extensive cache of Internet names. To use this strategy, all DNS servers on the network except the actual forwarder should be configured with the forwarder.

- *When a forest trust is created*—Windows requires DNS name resolution between the two forests involved in a trust relationship. Configuring conditional forwarders in the forest root name servers of both forests that point to each other is a good way to accomplish this.

- *When the target domain is external to the network and an external DNS server's address is known*—A company running a small network with limited bandwidth might find that the traffic caused by an internal DNS server's recursive lookups is excessive. The internal DNS server can provide name resolution for all internal resources and forward queries for external names to the DNS server of the company's ISP.

Another type of forwarding is called conditional forwarding. Whereas traditional forwarding means "If you can't resolve the query, forward it to this address," conditional forwarding enables administrators to forward queries for particular domains to particular name servers and all other unresolved queries to a different server.

Configuring Traditional Forwarders

Configuring a traditional forwarder is straightforward. Right-click the server node in DNS Manager, click Properties, and click the Forwarders tab (see Figure 7-20).

After clicking the Edit button, you can enter the IP address or FQDN of DNS servers to which unresolved requests should be sent. If more than one server is specified, they're queried in the order in which they're listed. Additional servers are queried only if no response is received from the first server. By default, the option to use root hints is enabled. If no response is received from any forwarder, the normal recursive lookup process is initiated, starting with a root server. If the "Use root hints if no forwarders are available" check box is cleared and no forwarders respond, the DNS server sends a failure reply to the client.

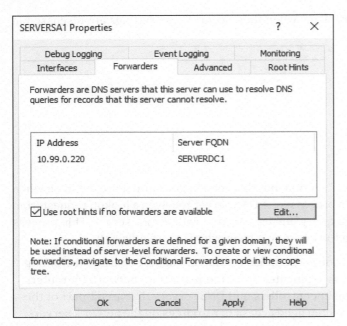

Figure 7-20   Configuring traditional forwarders

Configuring Conditional Forwarders

Conditional forwarders are configured in the Conditional Forwarders node in DNS Manager. To create a conditional forwarder, expand the Conditional Forwarders node, right-click Conditional Forwarders, and click New Conditional Forwarder.

Enter the domain name for which you want to forward queries, and then add IP addresses for DNS servers that are authoritative for the domain. After you enter the IP address, Windows attempts to resolve the IP address to the server's FQDN. You can store the forwarder in Active Directory and have it replicated forest-wide or domain-wide. With forwarders and/or conditional forwarders configured, the DNS server attempts to resolve DNS queries in this order:

1. From locally stored zone resource records
2. From the DNS cache
3. From conditional forwarders (if configured and the domain name matches)
4. From traditional forwarders (if configured)
5. Recursively by using root hints (only if no traditional forwarder is configured)

> **Note 13**
>
> Root hints aren't used if a traditional forwarder is configured and responds because after the forwarder is queried, the recursive lookup process is complete.

Root Hints

Root hints consist of a list of name servers preconfigured on Windows DNS servers that point to Internet root servers, which are DNS servers located on the Internet and managed by the Internet Assigned Numbers Authority (IANA). These servers contain lists of name servers that are responsible for top-level domains. Root hints are configured in the Root Hints tab of a DNS server's Properties dialog box.

The root hints data comes from the Cache.dns file in the *%systemroot%*\System32\DNS folder on a DNS server. Why is this file called the root hints file? As you can imagine, if the file is loaded during DNS installation, its data (root server IP addresses, for the most part) can become obsolete quickly. Instead of using the addresses in Cache.dns to perform recursive lookups, Windows selects one of the addresses randomly to request an up-to-date list of root server addresses. Windows then caches this list to use for queries to TLD servers. The Cache.dns file is also updated with this list. The query for the list of root servers occurs each time the DNS server is started. The root hints file can also be copied from another DNS server by clicking the Copy from Server button in the Root Hints tab. In addition, root hints can be updated through the Windows Update service.

You can configure an internal DNS server as a root server if your network is isolated from the public Internet. You do this by creating an FLZ with the "." name. This server is then considered authoritative for all domains. After you create this root zone, your root hints file is disabled, and you can't create any forwarders. Next, configure your other DNS servers to point to your new root server by removing the existing root hints entries and adding an entry that points to your new root server. If you ever decide to remove the root server, simply delete the root FLZ; Windows prompts you to reload the root hints file.

Round Robin

You can configure load sharing among servers running mirrored services. With a mirrored service, data for a service running on one server is duplicated on another server (or servers). For example, you can set up an FTP server or a web server on servers that synchronize their content with one another regularly. Then configure DNS with multiple A records, using the server's name in both records, but with each entry configured with a different IP address.

For example, suppose you have a web server with the FQDN *www.csmtech.corp* that's heavily used, responding slowly, and dropping connections. You can set up two additional web servers and configure a mechanism for synchronizing files between the servers. Next, you create two additional DNS A records (you already have one for the existing web server) in the csmtech.corp domain that use the same hostname, www, but different IP addresses. The Windows DNS service responds to queries for the www host by sending all three IP addresses in the response but varying the order of IP addresses each time.

This process is called **round robin** because each IP address is placed first in the list an equal number of times. Hosts receiving the DNS response always attempt to use the first address listed. You can improve the results of round-robin DNS by configuring a shorter TTL on the three A records so that remote DNS servers don't cache IP addresses for an extended period. By default, the round-robin option is enabled on Windows DNS servers, but you can disable it in the Advanced tab of the DNS server's Properties dialog box (see Figure 7-21 in the next section).

> **Note 14**
>
> Unlike SRV records that have a weight parameter, you can't change the number of times a particular host record is used in round robin.

Recursive Queries

Recursive queries, used in DNS queries, were defined earlier in "The DNS Lookup Process" section. Typically, resolving DNS queries involves iterative queries to a root server first, then to a TLD server, and finally to an authoritative server for the domain name being resolved. However, a recursive query might involve a forwarder instead, in which the DNS server sends a recursive query to the forwarder. The forwarder resolves the query and responds to the DNS server or performs a recursive query starting with a root server.

Recursion is enabled on Windows DNS servers by default, but there are two ways to change this setting. The first involves configuring forwarders. As shown previously in Figure 7-20, there's the check box "Use root hints if no forwarders are available." If this check box isn't selected, recursion is disabled, but only if forwarders don't respond. The second way to change the setting is the "Disable recursion (also disables forwarders)" option in the Advanced tab of the DNS server's Properties dialog box (see Figure 7-21).

If this check box is selected, the DNS server doesn't attempt to contact any other DNS servers, including forwarders, to resolve a query. For example, you might want to disable recursion when you have a public DNS server containing resource records for your publicly available servers (web, email, and so forth). The public DNS server is necessary to resolve iterative requests from other DNS servers for your public domain, but you don't want unauthorized Internet users using your DNS server to field recursive client requests.

Figure 7-21   The Advanced tab of a DNS server's Properties dialog box

PowerShell Commands for Advanced DNS Server Settings

Table 7-3 lists PowerShell cmdlets you can use to configure some DNS server settings discussed in the preceding sections.

Table 7-3   PowerShell cmdlets for DNS server settings

PowerShell cmdlet	Description	Example
Add-DnsServerForwarder	Adds forwarders to the DNS server's forwarders list	Add-DnsServerForwarder -IPAddress 192.168.0.4
Set-DnsServerForwarder	Changes the settings of an existing forwarder or overwrites the existing list of forwarders	Set-DnsServerForwarder -IPAddress 192.168.0.4
Add-DnsServerRootHint	Adds a root hint to the DNS server	Add-DnsServerRootHint root.mydomain.corp -IPAddress 192.168.0.10
Import-DnsServerRootHint	Imports root hints from another DNS server	Import-DnsServerRootHint serverdm1.testdom1.corp
Set-DnsServerRecursion	Sets the recursion settings for the DNS server	Set-DnsServerRecursion -Enable $true

Self-Check Questions

9. Which setting on a DNS server helps it to contact Internet servers?

   a. Forwarders
   b. Root hints

   c. Round robin
   d. Cache

10. Which DNS server option will prevent the DNS server from contacting other DNS servers?

    a. Conditional forwarders
    b. Round robin

    c. Disable recursion
    d. DNSSEC

◉ Check your answers at the end of this module.

Activity 7-7

Configuring and Testing Forwarders

Time Required: 10 minutes

Objective: Create and test a conditional forwarder and a regular forwarder.

Required Tools and Equipment: ServerDC1 and ServerSA1

Description: In this activity, you create a conditional forwarder on ServerSA1 that forwards queries for the AZ800.corp domain. Then you remove the conditional forwarder and configure a standard forwarder.

1. Make sure ServerDC1 is running. On ServerSA1, open the DNS Manager console, if necessary. First, delete the secondary zone you created earlier by right-clicking **AZ800.corp**, clicking **Delete**, and then clicking **Yes** to confirm.

2. At a PowerShell prompt, type **nslookup ServerDC1.AZ800.corp** and press **Enter**. The lookup is not successful.

3. In DNS Manager, right-click **Conditional Forwarders** and click **New Conditional Forwarder**. The New Conditional Forwarder dialog box opens. In the DNS Domain text box, type **AZ800.corp**. Click in the "IP addresses of the master servers" list box, type **10.99.0.220**, and press **Enter** (see Figure 7-22). If you see a red circle with an X, it should not be a problem as long as the name resolves to ServerDC1. Click **OK**.

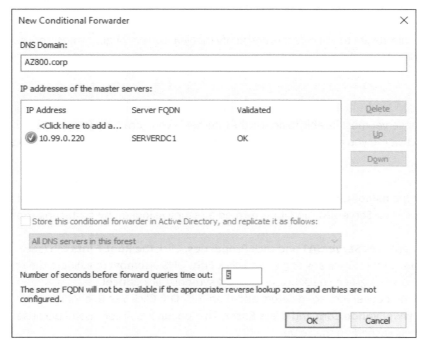

Figure 7-22   Adding a conditional forwarder

(continues)

Activity 7-7 Continued

4. At the PowerShell prompt, type **nslookup ServerDC1.AZ800.corp** and press **Enter**. The lookup is successful.

5. Next, you remove the conditional forwarder using PowerShell. Type **Remove-DnsServerZone AZ800.corp** and press **Enter**. Press **Enter** to confirm. (Note that a conditional forwarder is considered a zone, which is why you used a zone cmdlet to delete it.)

6. Type **nslookup ServerDC1.AZ800.corp** and press **Enter**. The lookup is still successful because the local DNS server cached the information for ServerDC1 from the previous successful lookup. Eventually, the cached information expires, but you delete it in the next step.

7. Type **Clear-DnsServerCache** and press **Enter**. Press **Enter** to confirm. Type **nslookup ServerDC1.AZ800. corp** and press **Enter**. The lookup is no longer successful.

8. To create a standard forwarder, type **Add-DnsServerForwarder 10.99.0.220** and press **Enter**.

9. In DNS Manager, right-click **ServerSA1** in the left pane and click **Properties**. Click the **Forwarders** tab. You see the forwarder you created in Step 8. (If you don't see the forwarder, close the Properties dialog box, click **ServerSA1**, click the **Refresh** icon, and repeat this step.) Click **Cancel**.

10. Type **nslookup ServerDC1.AZ800.corp** and press **Enter**. The lookup is successful. If the lookup is not successful, repeat the lookup several times; it can take a while before the forwarder takes effect. (If the lookup is still not successful, right-click **ServerSA1** in DNS Manager, point to **All Tasks**, and click **Restart**.)

11. To remove the forwarder, type **Remove-DnsServerForwarder 10.99.0.220**, press **Enter**, and press **Enter** again to confirm.

12. Stay signed in and continue to the next activity.

Activity 7-8

Working with Root Hints

Time Required: 15 minutes
Objective: View the root hints file and transfer root hints.
Required Tools and Equipment: ServerDC1, ServerSA1, Internet connection
Description: In this activity, you work with the root hints file. You'll verify that you can contact root servers for DNS lookups and then delete the root hints file, delete the DNS cache, and verify that you can no longer contact root servers for DNS lookups. Finally, you view the contents of the root hints file.

Note 15

In order to perform this activity, your server must be able to access the Internet. If you don't have Internet access, you can still perform the steps of this activity so you are familiar with the root hints file, but attempts to look up Internet names will fail.

1. On ServerSA1, in PowerShell, type **nslookup www.yahoo.com** and press **Enter**. The lookup is successful because root hints are configured on ServerSA1, and it performed a recursive lookup by contacting root servers and then TLD servers.

2. In the DNS Manager console, right-click **ServerSA1** and click **Properties**. Click the **Root Hints** tab (see Figure 7-23). In the list of 13 root servers, click any server and click **Edit**. DNS attempts to validate the root server. If it can be validated, you see a green check box and an OK symbol. Click **Cancel**.

3. Click the **Remove** button until all root servers are deleted, and then click **OK**. Click **Yes** to confirm.

4. In PowerShell, type **nslookup www.yahoo.com** and press **Enter**. The lookup is still successful because the record for www.yahoo.com is cached on the server.

(continues)

Activity 7-8 Continued

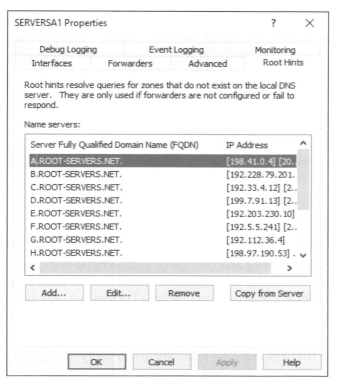

Figure 7-23   Configuring root hints

5. Type **Clear-DnsServerCache** and press **Enter**. Press **Enter** to confirm.
6. Type **nslookup www.yahoo.com** and press **Enter**. The lookup is no longer successful because your server can't contact the root servers.
7. In the DNS Manager console, right-click **ServerSA1** and click **Properties.** Click the **Root Hints** tab, and then click the **Copy from Server** button. In the IP address or DNS name text box, type **10.99.0.220** (the address of ServerDC1), and then click **OK** to repopulate the root server list. Click **OK**.
8. In PowerShell, type **nslookup www.yahoo.com** and press **Enter**. The lookup is successful. (If the lookup times out, try again; DNS must perform the entire recursive lookup process, including loading TLD servers, and this takes some time.)
9. To see the file where root hints are stored, type **notepad c:\windows\system32\dns\cache.dns** and press **Enter** to see the list of root servers.
10. Continue to the next activity.

> **Note** 16
>
> You can also update the root hints file manually by going to *www.internic.net/domain/named.root* and copying the contents of the file there into the cache.dns file.)

Configuring DNS Security

Microsoft Exam AZ-800:
Implement and manage an on-premises and hybrid networking infrastructure.
- Implement on-premises and hybrid name resolution

DNS is a common target for attacks because it figures so prominently in network transactions. The types of attacks on DNS include spoofing, DNS cache poisoning, denial of service, domain registration hijacking, and man-in-the-middle attacks, to name a few. The goal of most of these attacks is to compromise DNS so that users are unable to access network resources or are redirected to a different resource than was intended, often one with nefarious intentions. The techniques discussed in the following sections are steps that most DNS administrators should take to help prevent or at least mitigate the effectiveness of many DNS attacks.

Domain Name System Security Extension

Domain Name System Security Extension (DNSSEC) is a suite of features and protocols for validating DNS server responses. DNSSEC provides DNS clients with three critical methods to ensure that data they receive from DNS queries is accurate and secure:

- *Origin authentication of DNS data*—Verifies that the DNS server replying to a query is authentic
- *Authenticated denial of existence*—Allows verification that a resource record couldn't be found
- *Data integrity*—Verifies that data hasn't been tampered with in transit

With DNSSEC in place, DNS is much less susceptible to spoofing and DNS cache poisoning. DNSSEC can secure zones by using a process called **zone signing** that uses digital signatures in DNSSEC-related resource records to verify DNS responses. By verifying the digital signature, a DNS client can be assured that the DNS response is identical to the information published by the authoritative zone server. Zones that are signed using DNSSEC have the following additional resource records:

- *DNSKEY*—The **DNSKEY** record is the public key for the zone that DNS resolvers use to verify the digital signature in Resource Record Signature records.
- *RRSIG*—A **Resource Record Signature (RRSIG)** key contains the signature for a single resource record, such as an A or MX record. RRSIG records are returned with the requested resource records so that each returned record can be validated.
- *NSEC*—**Next Secure (NSEC)** records are returned when the requested resource record doesn't exist. They're used to fulfill the authenticated denial-of-existence security feature of DNSSEC.
- *NSEC3*—**Next Secure 3 (NSEC3)** records are an alternative to NSEC records. They can prevent zone-walking, which is a technique of repeating NSEC queries to get all the names in a zone. Zones can use NSEC or NSEC3 records but not both.
- *NSEC3PARAM*—**Next Secure 3 (NSEC3) Parameter** records are used to determine which NSEC3 records should be included in responses to queries for nonexistent records.
- *DS*—**Delegation Signer (DS)** records hold the name of a delegated zone and are used to verify delegated child zones.

Zone signing uses public key cryptography. To secure a zone with a digital signature, a key master must be designated. It can be a Windows DNS server that's authoritative for the zone. Two keys must be generated:

- *Key-signing key*—A **key-signing key (KSK)** has a private and public key associated with it. The private key is used to sign all DNSKEY records and the public key is used as a trust anchor for validating DNS responses. A **trust anchor** is usually the DNSKEY for the zone but can also be a DS key for a delegated zone.
- *Zone-signing key*—A **zone-signing key (ZSK)** is a public and private key combination stored in a certificate used to sign the zone. The KSK is used to sign the ZSK to validate it.

Trust anchors are distributed from authoritative DNS servers to nonauthoritative DNS servers that request DNSSEC validation. For example, when a client queries its local DNS server for a record in a zone not held by the local DNS server, the local DNS server must query the authoritative DNS server for that zone. When it does so, if the zone is protected by DNSSEC, the returned record contains the trust anchor (the DNSKEY or DS record) with the necessary public key to validate the record.

> **Note 17**
>
> DNSSEC doesn't provide confidentiality of data; that is, data isn't encrypted, only authenticated.

Validating DNS Responses

When a client requests a resource record from a zone secured with DNSSEC, the following steps take place:

1. A DNS client sends a query to the local DNS server configured in its network interface settings. If the client is DNSSEC aware, that information is included in the query message.
2. The local DNS server sends a query to a root server and top-level domain (TLD) server, as necessary. The message contains information indicating that the DNS server is DNSSEC aware.
3. The local DNS server receives a response containing the IP address of a DNS server authoritative for the zone.
4. The local DNS server sends a query to the authoritative DNS server. The message indicates that the DNS server is DNSSEC aware, and the server can validate signed resource records.
5. The authoritative DNS server returns the resource record information requested plus the RRSIG records needed to validate the response.
6. The local DNS server returns the response to the DNS client with an indication of whether the response was validated.

Configuring DNSSEC

To configure DNSSEC in Windows Server 2022, use the following procedure:

1. In DNS Manager, right-click the zone you want to configure, point to DNSSEC, and click Sign the Zone to start the Zone Signing Wizard. Click Next to begin.
2. You have three options for signing a zone (see Figure 7-24):

   - *Customize zone signing parameters*—Allows you to choose the details for signing the zone, including the DNS server that will serve as the key master and the KSK and ZSK parameters.
   - *Sign the zone with parameters of an existing zone*—Use the zone-signing parameters from an existing signed zone. If you choose this option, click Next and then Finish. Zone signing is complete.
   - *Use default settings to sign the zone*—Default values are configured for zone signing, and you can review them before continuing. If you choose this option, click Next and then Finish.

Figure 7-24   Choosing zone-signing options

3. If you selected "Customize zone signing parameters" in Step 2, continue with the wizard; otherwise, DNSSEC configuration is complete for this zone. The next step is to choose the Key Master. By default, the current DNS server is chosen as the key master, but you can choose another primary server for the zone.

4. Next, you configure parameters for the KSK (see Figure 7-25). You can use the default values or select new values. A globally unique ID (GUID) is generated automatically. You can configure between one and three KSKs.

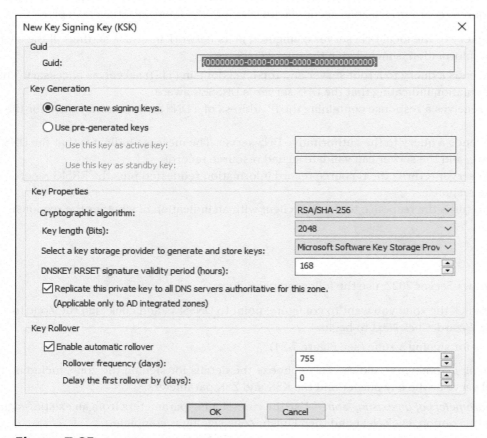

Figure 7-25   Configuring the KSK

5. Next, you configure the parameters for the ZSK; the window looks similar to the one for configuring the KSK.

6. The next step is to select NSEC or NSEC3 for authenticated denial of existence. NSEC3 is the default option.

7. Next, you specify how trust anchors are distributed. Trust anchors aren't required on authoritative DNS servers. You should distribute trust anchors only if other DCs provide nonauthoritative responses for the zone.

8. The last step is to configure signing and polling parameters. You can accept the default settings for most situations. If you don't need to change any default values in the wizard, you could select the option to use the default settings in Step 2.

The DNS Socket Pool

The **DNS socket pool** is a pool of port numbers used by a DNS server for DNS queries. It protects against DNS cache poisoning by enabling a DNS server to randomize the source port when performing DNS queries. **DNS cache poisoning** is an attack on DNS servers in which false data is introduced into the DNS server cache, causing the server to return incorrect IP addresses. At best, this attack keeps clients from accessing requested network resources; at worst, clients are redirected to an attacker's server. If a random source port is chosen from the socket pool, an attacker must successfully guess the source port of a query issued by the server, along with a random transaction ID.

As you've learned, DNS uses recursive queries. A client issues a query for a network resource, such as the *www.cengage.com* host record. The DNS server first looks in its local zone database or cache. If the record can't be found, the DNS server queries other DNS servers until it finds a DNS server that's authoritative for the *cengage.com* zone. This is where DNS cache poisoning comes in. If an attacker knows that the DNS server has requested the record for *www.cengage.com*, it can issue its own response to the query first, providing false information. The DNS server caches the information for *www.cengage.com*, and the current client query and future queries are resolved to the IP address supplied by the attacker.

However, to issue a valid response, the attacker must know what port the DNS server used to issue the query. By default, DNS servers issue queries via UDP port 53. With that knowledge, an attacker can send the response, causing the DNS server to accept the response as though it came from the authoritative server. If the port is randomized, attackers have a much more difficult job because they must guess which port number to use.

Configuring the DNS Socket Pool

By default, a socket pool is enabled on Windows Server 2008 R2 and later servers, but you can configure the socket pool size and excluded port ranges with dnscmd.exe. By default, the socket pool size is 2500 port numbers, but you can increase this value up to 10,000. For example, to change the socket pool size to 5000, enter the following command:

```
dnscmd /Config /SocketPoolSize 5000
```

To exclude a range of ports from 100 to 500 from the socket pool, use the following command:

```
dnscmd /Config /SocketPoolExcludedPortRanges 100-500
```

DNS Cache Locking

DNS cache locking is a DNS security feature that allows you to control whether data in the DNS cache can be overwritten. When a DNS server receives a record as the result of a query to another DNS server, it caches the data. Each cached record has a time to live (TTL) value that tells the server when the record should be deleted from the cache, preventing cached data from becoming stale. Normally, if updated information about the cached record is received, the record can be overwritten. An attacker can falsify update information, causing cached data to be overwritten by the attacker's data, resulting in cache poisoning. Cache locking prevents any updates to a cached record until the TTL expires.

Configuring DNS Cache Locking

DNS cache locking is configured as a percentage of the TTL. For example, if the cache locking value is set to 50, the cached data can be overwritten when the TTL is 50 percent expired. If the cache locking value is 100, the data can never be overwritten. Starting with Windows Server 2008 R2, cache locking is enabled and set at 100 percent by default. To change the cache locking value, use dnscmd.exe. For example, to change the value so that records can be overwritten when the TTL is 75 percent expired, use one of the following two commands. The second command is a PowerShell cmdlet:

```
dnscmd /Config /CacheLockingPercent 75
Set-DnsServerCache -LockingPercent 75
```

> **Note 18**
>
> To see the current cache locking percentage, replace /Config with /Info in the preceding dnscmd command. In PowerShell, use Get-DnsServerCache.

Enabling Response Rate Limiting

A DNS server role feature available starting with Windows Server 2016, **Response Rate Limiting (RRL)** mitigates a type of distributed denial-of-service (DDoS) attack called a DNS amplification attack. A **DNS amplification attack** uses public DNS servers to overwhelm a target with DNS responses by sending DNS queries with spoofed IP addresses. The attacker sends DNS queries to multiple public DNS servers with the spoofed address of the target's system. The DNS servers send the responses to the queries to the target system. Because the query responses look like legitimate data, these types of attacks can be difficult to prevent with firewalls.

RRL examines queries to the DNS server and flags them when a lot of queries received in a short period of time have a similar source address and query parameters. RRL will cause the DNS server to limit the number of responses sent to the same subnet when certain parameters have been met. By default, RRL is disabled, but it can be enabled with the following PowerShell cmdlet and the default parameters:

```
Set-DNSServerRRL
```

A number of parameters can be set to change how RRL flags queries as suspect and begins limiting responses. To see the default values and the status of RRL, use the following PowerShell cmdlet (see Figure 7-26):

```
Get-DNSServerRRL
```

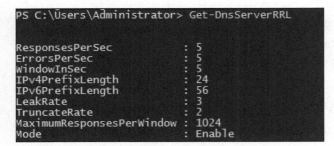

```
PS C:\Users\Administrator> Get-DnsServerRRL

ResponsesPerSec            : 5
ErrorsPerSec               : 5
WindowInSec                : 5
IPv4PrefixLength           : 24
IPv6PrefixLength           : 56
LeakRate                   : 3
TruncateRate               : 2
MaximumResponsesPerWindow  : 1024
Mode                       : Enable
```

Figure 7-26   Viewing the status of Response Rate Limiting

Here are descriptions of some of the RRL parameters you can configure:

- *ResponsesPerSec*—Sets the maximum number of identical responses the DNS server will send a client in one second. The default value is 5.

- *ErrorsPerSec*—Sets the maximum number of error responses the DNS server will send a client in one second. The default value is 5.

- *WindowInSec*—Sets the time period in seconds over which RRL measures and averages queries from the same subnet. If queries from the same subnet occur more frequently, RRL is applied. The default value is 5.

- *IPv4PrefixLength*—Used to set the number of bits to match in the IP address of the query to determine if queries are from the same subnet. The default value is 24. For example, with a value of 24, IP addresses 172.16.1.10 and 172.16.1.100 are considered to be from the same subnet because the first 24 bits of the address match. However, 172.16.1.10 and 172.16.2.10 are considered to be from different subnets. The same description applies to IPv6 addresses but the default value is 56.

- *LeakRate*—When RRL is in effect for a particular query, this value determines how many queries should be dropped before sending a response anyway. This allows the coincidental legitimate query to be responded to amid a flood of spoofed queries. The default value is 3, and the value can range from 2 to 10. A value of 0 disables this feature.

- *Mode*—Possible values are Enable, Disable, and LogOnly. When this parameter is omitted with the `Set-DNSServerRRL` cmdlet, RRL is enabled. Use `-Mode Disable` to disable RRL. Use `-Mode LogOnly` if you want to log RRL information but do not want to prevent DNS from responding when RRL is triggered.

DNS-Based Authentication of Named Entities

DNS-based Authentication of Named Entities (DANE) is a DNS security feature starting with Windows Server 2016 that provides information about the certification authority (CA) used by your domain when a client is requesting DNS information for your domain. This feature prevents man-in-the-middle attacks in which a cached DNS entry for your domain is altered, pointing the client to a server run by the attacker. If the attacker sends a forged certificate from a different CA, the client will reject it. DANE uses Transport Layer Security Authentication (TLSA) records, which you can add to a DNS zone using the `Add-DnsServerResourceRecord` cmdlet with the following syntax:

```
Add-DnsServerResourceRecord -ZoneName AZ800.corp -TLSA -CertificateUsage
  DomainIssuedCertificate
```

This command is not complete because you also need to include certificate data and additional parameters, but those aspects of DANE are beyond the scope of this book. DANE is another security measure available in Windows DNS Server to protect your data and your identity.

Self-Check Questions

11. Which DNSSEC method verifies that data hasn't been tampered with in transit?

    a. Origin authentication

    b. Authenticated denial

    c. Zone spoofing

    d. Data integrity

12. Which DNS server security feature can mitigate a distributed denial-of-service attack called DNS amplification?

    a. Response Rate Limiting

    b. DNS cache locking

    c. DNS socket pool

    d. Zone signing

⊙ Check your answers at the end of this module.

Activity 7-9

Configuring DNSSEC

Time Required: 10 minutes

Objective: Configure DNSSEC.

Required Tools and Equipment: ServerDC1

Description: In this activity, you configure DNSSEC and test it.

1. On ServerDC1, open DNS Manager.
2. Click to expand **Forward Lookup Zones**, and click to select **AZ800.corp**. Then right-click **AZ800.corp**, point to **DNSSEC**, and click **Sign the Zone** to start the Zone Signing Wizard. In the welcome window, click **Next**.
3. In the Signing Options window, leave the default option **Customize zone signing parameters** selected. (Note that you aren't changing any default options, so you could select the "Use default settings" option to sign the zone, but this way you can see the configurable options.) Click **Next**.
4. In the Key Master window, don't change the default option that selects ServerDC1 as the key master. Click **Next**.
5. In the Key Signing Key (KSK) window, read the information about the KSK and then click **Next**. Click **Add**. In the New Key Signing Key (KSK) dialog box, accept the default settings and click **OK**. Click **Next**.
6. In the Zone Signing Key (ZSK) window, read the information about the ZSK and then click **Next**. Click **Add**. In the New Zone Signing Key (ZSK) dialog box, accept the default settings and click **OK**. Click **Next**.
7. In the Next Secure (NSEC) window, accept the default option **Use NSEC3** and then click **Next**.
8. In the Trust Anchors (TAs) window, accept the default option **Enable automatic update of trust anchors on key rollover**, and then click **Next**.
9. In the Signing and Polling Parameters window, accept the default settings and click **Next**. Review the selected options, and then click **Next** and **Finish**.
10. In DNS Manager, click the **Refresh** icon to see the RRSIG, DNSKEY, and NSEC3 resource records that were created.
11. Now you remove DNSSEC. In DNS Manager, right-click **AZ800.corp**, point to **DNSSEC**, and click **Unsign the Zone**. Click **Next** and then **Finish**. Click the **Refresh** icon in DNS Manager to see that the DNSSEC-related records are gone.
12. Close all windows, sign out, and shut down both servers.

Azure DNS

Microsoft Exam AZ-800:

Implement and manage an on-premises and hybrid networking infrastructure.

- Implement on-premises and hybrid name resolution

DNS is a vital networking service, so it's no wonder that Azure has support for the DNS service. Azure DNS comes in two flavors: **Azure DNS zones**, which provide name resolution for public resources such as Internet web servers, and **Azure private DNS zones**, which provide name resolution for internal Azure resources with private IP addresses, such as Azure VMs. The focus in this book and the AZ-800 exam is Azure private DNS zones and how they can work along with on-premises DNS servers.

Azure DNS provides much of the same functionality as the Windows DNS Server role, with support for zones and the most common record types. Because you already know the purpose of DNS and how DNS works, this section focuses on how to implement private DNS zones.

Creating and Testing an Azure Private DNS Zone

To create an Azure private DNS zone, search for "private DNS zones" from the Azure portal home page and click "private DNS zones" in the search results. From the Private DNS zones page, click Create to create a new zone. You'll see a familiar page with instructions to select a subscription and resource group, and then you need to supply a name for the zone and resource group location (see Figure 7-27). At the bottom of Figure 7-27, an information box explains that you can link virtual networks to the private DNS zone after it's been created. Private DNS zones must be linked to one or more Azure virtual networks; only the resources on the linked networks can use the private zone.

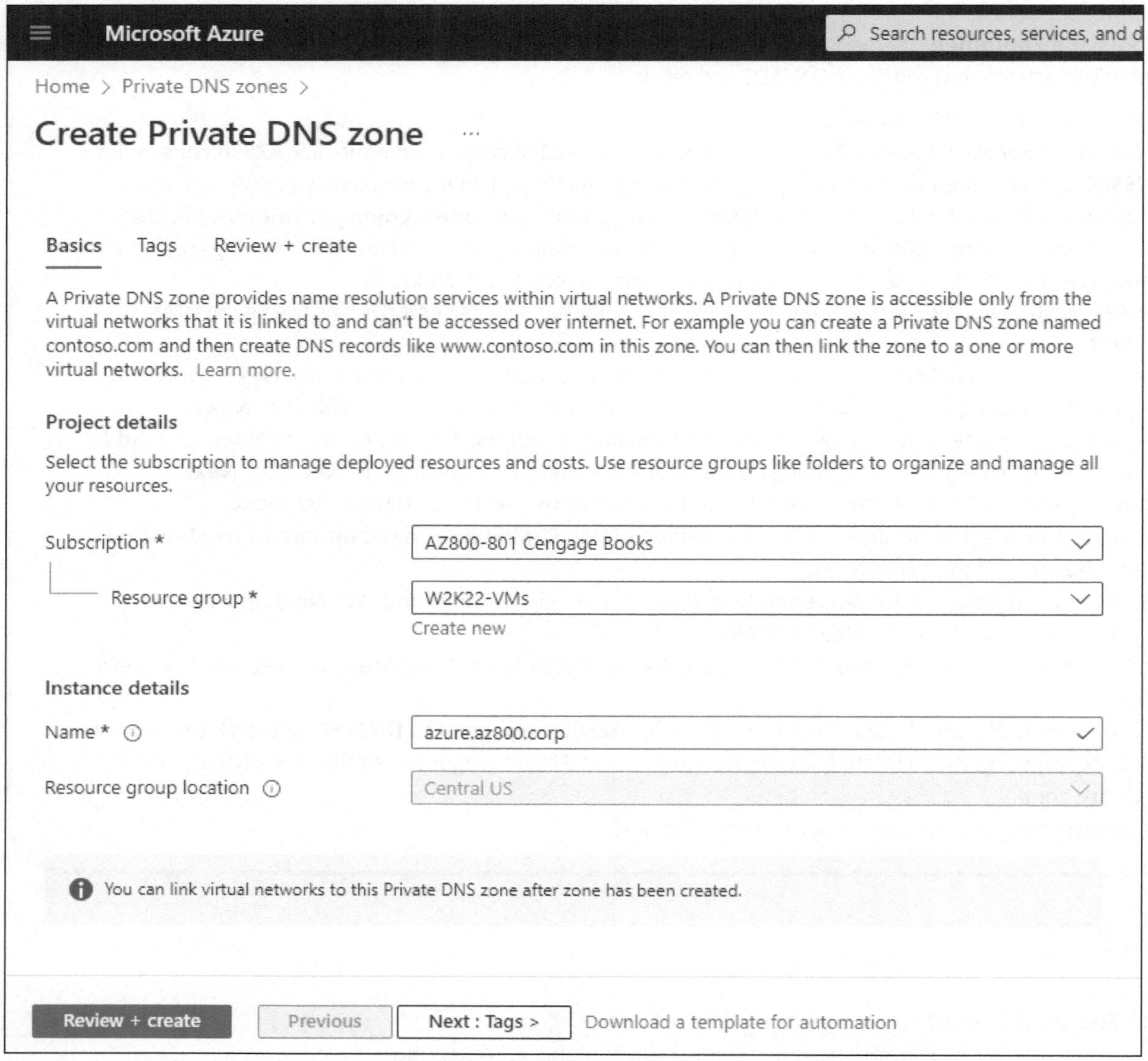

Figure 7-27 Creating a private DNS zone

That's all there is to it. Like all other resources you create in Azure, you can create tags to categorize the resource for billing purposes if you want. Click Review + create; once validated, click Create to create the zone. Zone creation may take a few moments. After deployment is complete, you can click Go to resource to see the Overview page for the new private DNS zone. On the Overview page, you see the details of the SOA record with a default TTL value of 3600 (seconds). If you click on the SOA record, you can edit the TTL and other time-based values.

The next step is to link one or more virtual networks with the zone. If you don't already have virtual networks created, you need to create a virtual network. To link an existing virtual network with the zone, click Virtual network links in the left pane and click Add. Give the link a name and select the subscription and virtual network. If you want records to be automatically created for VMs on the virtual network, click the Enable auto-registration check box (see Figure 7-28). By doing so, any running VMs on the virtual network will have a host record created in the zone automatically.

Exam Tip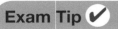

If you have multiple virtual networks with VMs that should use a private zone, you need to create a virtual network link for each virtual network.

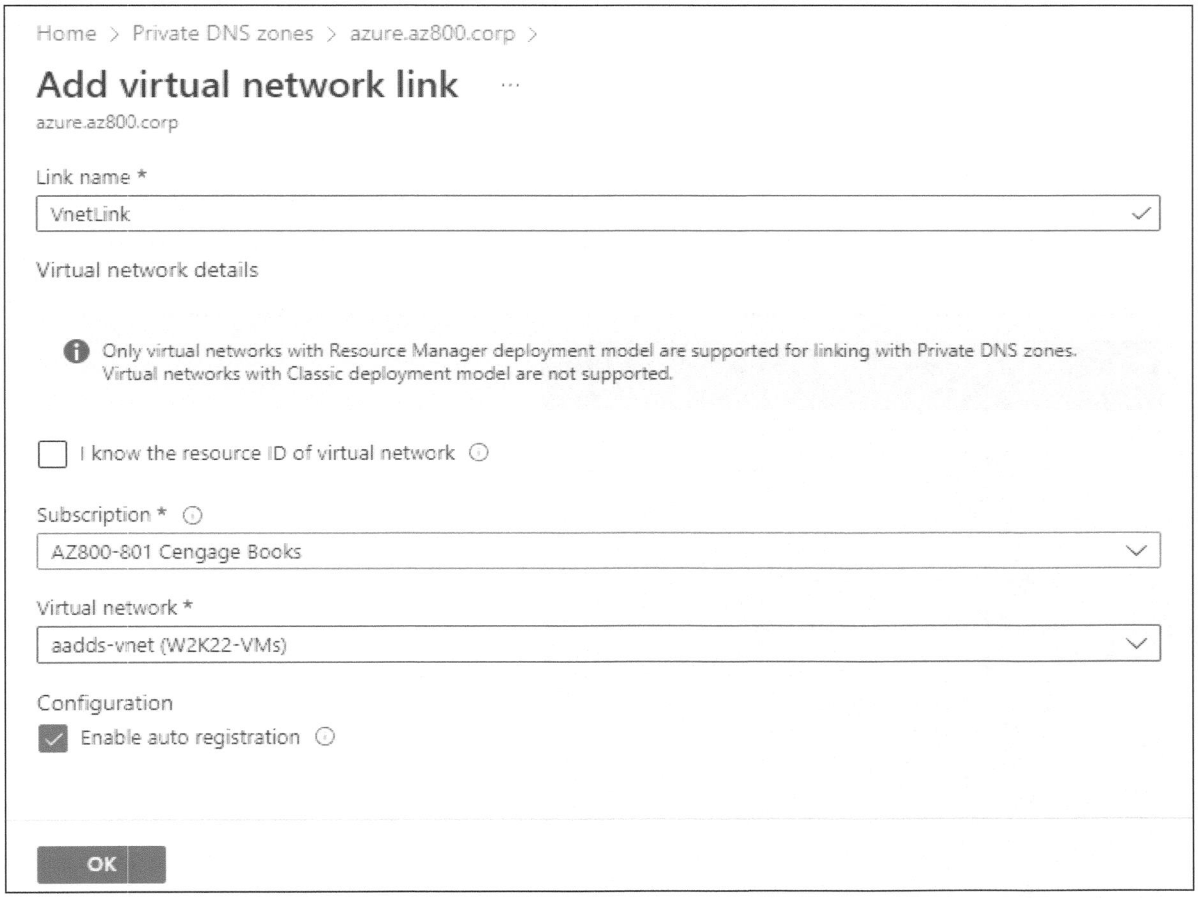

Home > Private DNS zones > azure.az800.corp >

Add virtual network link ⋯
azure.az800.corp

Link name *

    VnetLink   ✓

Virtual network details

ⓘ Only virtual networks with Resource Manager deployment model are supported for linking with Private DNS zones.
   Virtual networks with Classic deployment model are not supported.

☐ I know the resource ID of virtual network ⓘ

Subscription * ⓘ

    AZ800-801 Cengage Books   ⌄

Virtual network *

    aadds-vnet (W2K22-VMs)   ⌄

Configuration
☑ Enable auto registration ⓘ

    OK

Figure 7-28   Adding a virtual network link to the zone

Figure 7-29 shows the zone after two VMs on the virtual network were started and auto-registered. Auto-registration automatically creates an A record for private IPv4 addresses. If your VM also has an IPv6 address, an AAAA record is also created. The records will automatically age out of the DNS zone based on the TTL value, which is set at 10 seconds by default. If a VM is turned off or otherwise stops responding, its DNS record will be removed shortly afterward.

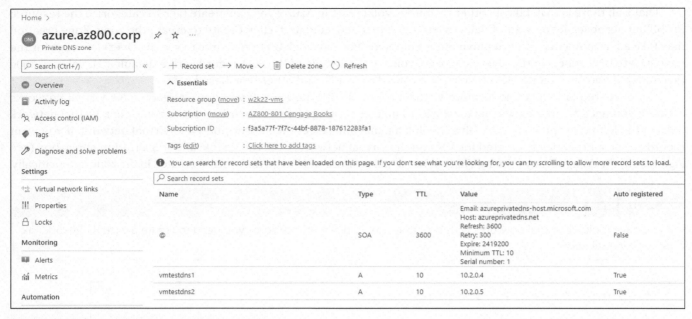

Figure 7-29 The DNS zone with two A records

Testing a Private DNS Zone

You can test DNS on Azure VMs in the same way you would test it on an on-premises computer. For example, you can ping from one VM to another using the VM's computer name or you can use nslookup to verify DNS operation. (If you want to ping, be sure that ping messages are allowed through the Microsoft Defender firewall.) Figure 7-30 shows a PowerShell window on the virtual machine vmtestdns1 using nslookup and ping to verify that DNS is resolving the VM name vmtestdns2.

```
PS C:\Users\gtomsho> nslookup
Default Server:  UnKnown
Address:  168.63.129.16

> vmtestdns2.azure.az800.corp
Server:  UnKnown
Address:  168.63.129.16

Non-authoritative answer:
Name:    vmtestdns2.azure.az800.corp
Address:  10.2.0.5

> exit
PS C:\Users\gtomsho> ping vmtestdns2.azure.az800.corp

Pinging vmtestdns2.azure.az800.corp [10.2.0.5] with 32 bytes of data:
Reply from 10.2.0.5: bytes=32 time<1ms TTL=128
Reply from 10.2.0.5: bytes=32 time<1ms TTL=128
Reply from 10.2.0.5: bytes=32 time<1ms TTL=128
Reply from 10.2.0.5: bytes=32 time<1ms TTL=128

Ping statistics for 10.2.0.5:
    Packets: Sent = 4, Received = 4, Lost = 0 (0% loss),
Approximate round trip times in milli-seconds:
    Minimum = 0ms, Maximum = 0ms, Average = 0ms
PS C:\Users\gtomsho> _
```

Figure 7-30 Testing DNS from an Azure VM

Creating a DNS Record

You can create a new DNS record by going to the zone, clicking + Record set, and filling out the name of the record, record type, TTL, and IP address. Figure 7-31 shows the dialog box for creating a second record for one of the VMs and giving it a different name. This allows the VM vmtestdns2 to be accessed using the name www.azure.az800.corp (for example, if the VM is a web server). After the record is created, you can test it by using ping or nslookup from another VM on the virtual network.

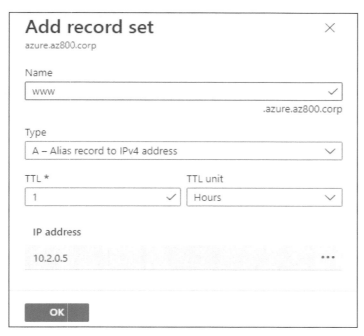

Figure 7-31   Creating a DNS A record

Integrating On-Premises DNS with Azure Private DNS Zones

In a hybrid network infrastructure, you might want to resolve DNS names of VMs running on Azure from your on-premises network and vice versa. If you want on-premises computers to resolve names of Azure VMs, there are a few requirements:

- *Connection to the Azure virtual network*—The on-premises network must be connected to the Azure virtual network. The connection can be via site-to-site or point-to-site VPN, ExpressRoute, or Bastion. Module 9 of this book covers how to implement a site-to-site VPN between your on-premises network and your Azure virtual network.
- *An Azure VM running the DNS server with a forwarder*—Create a VM in Azure on a virtual network that is linked to the Azure private DNS zone (or you can use an existing Windows Server VM). Install the DNS server role and configure a forwarder pointing to 168.63.129.16 (see Figure 7-32). This address is that of the Azure DNS service, which can resolve records in an Azure private DNS zone.

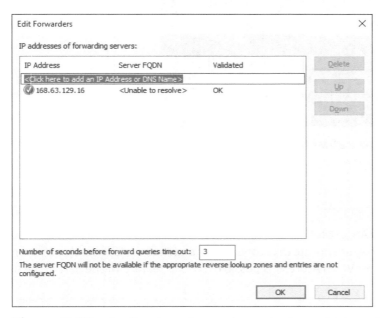

Figure 7-32   Configuring a forwarder to the Azure DNS service

- *DNS configuration on the virtual network*—Configure your virtual network(s) to point to the DNS server VM that has the forwarder configured. In this example, the VM's IP address is 10.2.0.5. Go to the virtual network in the Azure portal and click DNS servers in the Settings section, then select Custom and type the IP address of the DNS server (see Figure 7-33). Now, any devices on the virtual network as well as on-premises devices connected to the Azure virtual network are able to resolve the DNS names of the Azure VMs. Figure 7-34 shows an on-premises Windows 10 computer connected to the Azure network via point-to-site VPN pinging one of the Azure VMs using its DNS name.

Exam Tip ✔

The AZ-800 exam expects you to understand both on-premises DNS and Azure private DNS zones. You should have a solid understanding of DNS forwarders and conditional forwarders and when to use each.

vnetTestDNS | DNS servers
Virtual network
Search (Ctrl+/)
DDoS protection
Firewall
Microsoft Defender for Cloud
Network manager
DNS servers
Peerings
DNS servers
Default (Azure-provided)
Custom
IP Address
10.2.0.5
Add DNS server

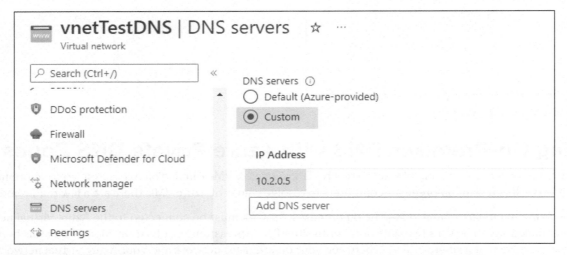

Figure 7-33 Configuring a virtual network with the address of a DNS forwarder

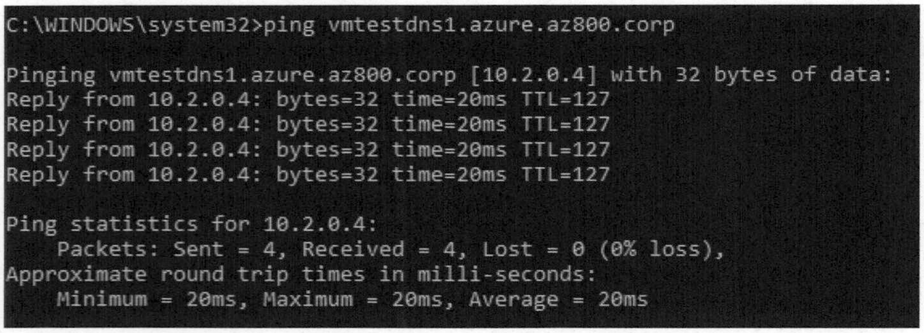

C:\WINDOWS\system32>ping vmtestdns1.azure.az800.corp
Pinging vmtestdns1.azure.az800.corp [10.2.0.4] with 32 bytes of data:
Reply from 10.2.0.4: bytes=32 time=20ms TTL=127
Reply from 10.2.0.4: bytes=32 time=20ms TTL=127
Reply from 10.2.0.4: bytes=32 time=20ms TTL=127
Reply from 10.2.0.4: bytes=32 time=20ms TTL=127
Ping statistics for 10.2.0.4:
Packets: Sent = 4, Received = 4, Lost = 0 (0% loss),
Approximate round trip times in milli-seconds:
Minimum = 20ms, Maximum = 20ms, Average = 20ms

Figure 7-34 Testing DNS resolution of Azure VMs from an on-premises Windows 10 computer

Note 19

As of this writing, Microsoft has announced a new Azure DNS feature, now in preview, called Azure DNS Private Resolver. This feature allows on-premises devices to resolve Azure private DNS zone names and Azure VMs to resolve on-premises DNS zone names without the need for a DNS server VM in Azure. It is possible that this feature will be part of the future AZ-800 exam objectives.

If you need Azure VMs to resolve names on your private on-premises network, you configure a conditional forwarder on the Azure DNS server VM that points to a DNS server on your on-premises network that hosts the zone. The on-premises DNS server must be connected to the Azure network via VPN, ExpressRoute, or Bastion.

Self-Check Questions

13. An Azure private DNS zone can be accessed by all Azure VMs on all virtual networks by default. True or False?

    a. True   **b.** False

14. Which of the following is *not* necessary to allow on-premises computers to resolve names in an Azure private DNS zone?

    a. Connection to the Azure virtual network   **c.** Virtual network DNS configuration
    b. An Azure VM configured with a forwarder   **d.** A DNS server on the on-premises network

    ◉ Check your answers at the end of this module.

Module Summary

- DNS is based on a hierarchical naming structure and a distributed database. DNS names use the structure *host.domain.top-level-domain* or perhaps *host.subdomain.domain.top-level-domain*. This naming structure is the fully qualified domain name (FQDN).
- DNS can be described as an inverted tree with the root domain at the top, top-level domains branching off the root, and domains and subdomains branching off top-level domains. The entire DNS tree is called the DNS namespace. Every domain has one or more authoritative name servers.
- Hostnames are associated with an IP address, so when a client looks up the name *www.microsoft.com*, for example, the DNS server returns an IP address. Second-level domains can also have subdomains, such as *docs* in *docs.microsoft.com*.
- DNS lookups involve iterative and recursive queries. Most lookups start from the DNS resolver with a recursive query to a DNS server. The DNS server satisfies the query or performs a series of iterative queries, starting with a root server.
- DNS servers can perform one or more of the following roles: authoritative server, forwarder, conditional forwarder, and caching-only server.
- A forwarder is a DNS server to which other DNS servers send requests they can't resolve themselves. A conditional forwarder is a DNS server to which other DNS servers send requests targeted for a specific domain.
- DNS is an integral part of most network communication sessions between computers. A properly configured and efficiently functioning DNS, therefore, is essential for a well-functioning network. DNS can be installed automatically during Active Directory installation or as a separate server role.
- You might need to install a new DNS zone manually if the DNS server isn't a DC, when you create a stub zone, when you create a secondary zone, and when you create a zone for an Internet domain.
- A zone can be a forward lookup zone or a reverse lookup zone. FLZs contain host records primarily. Reverse lookup zones contain PTR records.
- DNS databases consist of the following zone types: primary zone, secondary zone, and stub zone. Primary and stub zones can also be Active Directory–integrated zones.
- Resource records can be static or dynamic. There are A, AAAA, CNAME, PTR, MX, NS, SRV, and SOA records.
- Dynamic records are often created with a DHCP server. Static records can be created by using DNS Manager or PowerShell cmdlets.
- SOA records contain information about a zone, including its serial number and timers used for zone transfers.
- NS records specify FQDNs and IP addresses of authoritative servers for a zone. Each zone that's created has an NS record, which points to an authoritative server for that zone.

- There are two types of zone transfer: full zone transfers and incremental zone transfers. Incremental zone transfers can only be used if both the master and slave DNS servers support them.
- Zone delegation is transferring authority for a subdomain to a new zone, which can be on the same server or another server. When a subdomain has been delegated to a zone on another server, the DNS server hosting the parent zone maintains only an NS record pointing to the DNS server hosting the delegated zone.
- Advanced DNS settings include configuring forwarders, root hints, round robin, and recursive queries.
- Domain Name System Security Extension (DNSSEC) is a suite of features and protocols for validating DNS server responses. DNSSEC provides DNS clients with three critical methods to ensure that data they receive from DNS queries is accurate and secure: origin authentication of DNS data, authenticated denial of existence, and data integrity.
- The DNS socket pool is a pool of port numbers used by a DNS server for DNS queries. It protects against DNS cache poisoning by enabling a DNS server to randomize the source port when performing DNS queries.
- DNS cache locking is a DNS security feature that allows you to control whether data in the DNS cache can be overwritten. When a DNS server receives a record as the result of a query to another DNS server, it caches the data.
- A DNS server role feature first available in Windows Server 2016, Response Rate Limiting (RRL) mitigates a type of distributed denial-of-service (DDoS) attack called a DNS amplification attack. Response Rate Limiting examines queries to the DNS server and flags them when a lot of queries received in a short period of time have a similar source address and query parameters.
- DNS-based Authentication of Named Entities (DANE) is a feature starting with Windows Server 2016 that provides information about the certification authority (CA) used by your domain when a client is requesting DNS information for your domain. This feature prevents man-in-the-middle attacks.
- Azure DNS comes in two flavors: DNS zones, which provide name resolution for public resources such as Internet web servers, and private DNS zones, which provide name resolution for internal Azure resources such as Azure VMs.
- To create an Azure private DNS zone, search for "private DNS zones" from the Azure portal home page and click "private DNS zones" in the search results.
- If you want on-premises computers to resolve names of Azure VMs, there are a few requirements: connection to the Azure virtual network, an Azure VM running a DNS server with a forwarder, and DNS configuration on the virtual network.

Key Terms

A record	DNSKEY	recursive query
AAAA record	Domain Name System (DNS)	referral
Active Directory partition	Domain Name System Security	Resource Record Signature (RRSIG)
authoritative server	Extension (DNSSEC)	resource records
Azure DNS zone	Dynamic DNS (DDNS)	Response Rate Limiting (RRL)
Azure private DNS zone	forward lookup zone (FLZ)	reverse lookup zone (RLZ)
caching-only DNS server	forwarder	root hints
CNAME record	fully qualified domain name (FQDN)	root server
conditional forwarder	glue A record	round robin
Delegation Signer (DS)	host record	secondary zone
DNS amplification attack	hostname	stub zone
DNS-based Authentication of Named	iterative query	top-level domain (TLD) server
Entities (DANE)	key-signing key (KSK)	trust anchor
DNS cache locking	MX record	zone
DNS cache poisoning	Next Secure (NSEC)	zone delegation
DNS client	Next Secure 3 (NSEC3)	zone replication scope
DNS namespace	Next Secure 3 (NSEC3) Parameter	zone signing
DNS resolver	primary zone	zone-signing key (ZSK)
DNS socket pool	PTR record	zone transfer

Review Questions

1. Which of the following best describes DNS? (Choose all that apply.)
   a. Hierarchical database
   b. Flat database
   c. Monolithic database
   d. Distributed database

2. Which of the following accurately represents an FQDN?
   a. host.top-level-domain.subdomain.domain
   b. domain.host.top-level-domain
   c. host.subdomain.domain.top-level-domain
   d. host.domain.top-level-domain.subdomain

3. What specific type of DNS query instructs a DNS server to process the query until the server replies with an address that satisfies the query or with an "I don't know" message?
   a. Recursive
   b. Referral
   c. Iterative
   d. Resolver

4. What type of zone should you create that contains records allowing a computer name to be resolved from its IP address?
   a. RLZ
   b. FLZ
   c. Stub
   d. TLD

5. A resource record containing an alias for another record is which of the following record types?
   a. A
   b. CNAME
   c. NS
   d. PTR

6. What type of resource record is necessary to get a positive response from the command `nslookup 192.168.100.10`?
   a. A
   b. CNAME
   c. NS
   d. PTR

7. When a DNS server responds to a query with a list of name servers, what is the response called?
   a. Iterative
   b. Recursive
   c. Referral
   d. Resolver

8. You're scanning the local cache on a DNS client, and you come across the notation `::1`. What does it mean?
   a. The cache is corrupt.
   b. It's the IPv6 localhost address.
   c. It's the link-local address.
   d. It's a reverse lookup record.

9. You have a DNS server outside your corporate firewall that's a standalone Windows Server 2022 server. It hosts a primary zone for your public Internet domain name, which is different from your internal Active Directory domain names. You want one or more of your internal servers to be able to handle DNS queries for your public domain and to serve as a backup for the primary DNS server outside the firewall. Which configuration should you choose for internal DNS servers?
   a. Configure a standard secondary zone.
   b. Configure a standard stub zone.
   c. Configure a forwarder to point to the primary DNS server.
   d. Configure an Active Directory–integrated stub zone.

10. Which of the following is true about stub zones? (Choose all that apply.)
    a. They're authoritative for the zone.
    b. Their records are updated by the primary server automatically.
    c. They can't be Active Directory–integrated.
    d. They contain SOA and NS records.

11. The DNS server at your headquarters holds a standard primary zone for the abc.com domain. A branch office connected by a slow WAN link holds a secondary zone for abc.com. Updates to the zone aren't frequent. How can you decrease the amount of WAN traffic caused by the secondary zone checking for zone updates?
    a. In the SOA tab of the zone's Properties dialog box, increase the minimum (default) TTL.
    b. In the Advanced tab of the DNS server's Properties dialog box, increase the expire interval.
    c. In the SOA tab of the zone's Properties dialog box, increase the refresh interval.
    d. In the Zone Transfers tab of the SOA Properties dialog box, decrease the retry interval.

12. What type of record does DNS create automatically to resolve the FQDN of an NS record?
    a. PTR records
    b. CNAME records
    c. Glue A records
    d. Auto SRV records

13. You want a DNS server to handle queries for a domain with a standard primary zone hosted on another DNS server, and you don't want the server to be authoritative for that zone. How can you configure the server? (Choose two answers.)
    a. Configure a secondary zone on the DNS server.
    b. Configure a stub zone on the DNS server.
    c. Configure a conditional forwarder on the DNS server.
    d. Configure zone hints for the primary zone.

14. You're in charge of a standard primary zone for a large network with frequent changes to the DNS database. You want changes to the zone to be transmitted as quickly as possible to all secondary servers. What should you configure and on which server?

    a. Configure DNS notifications on the primary zone server.

    b. Configure DNS recursion on the secondary zone servers.

    c. Configure round robin on the primary zone server.

    d. Configure a smaller default TTL for the primary zone server.

15. You manage the DNS structure on your network. The network security group has decided that only one DNS server should contact the Internet. Under no circumstances should other servers contact the Internet for DNS queries, even if the designated server is down. You have decided that the DNS server named DNS-Int should be the server allowed to contact the Internet. How should you configure your DNS structure to accommodate these requirements?

    a. On each DNS server except DNS-Int, configure a forwarder pointing to DNS-Int. Configure DNS-Int as a forwarder by enabling forwarded requests in the Forwarders tab of the server's Properties dialog box.

    b. On each DNS server except DNS-Int, configure a root hint to point to DNS-Int and delete all other root hints. Configure a root zone on DNS-Int.

    c. On each DNS server except DNS-Int, configure a forwarder pointing to DNS-Int. Disable the use of root hints if no forwarders are available. No changes are necessary on DNS-Int.

    d. On each DNS server except DNS-Int, open the Advanced tab of the server's Properties dialog box and disable recursion. No changes are necessary for DNS-Int.

16. You have a zone containing two A records for the same hostname, but each A record has a different IP address configured. The host records point to two servers hosting a high-traffic website, and you want the servers to share the load. After some testing, you find that you're always accessing the same web server, so load sharing isn't occurring. What can you do to solve the problem?

    a. Enable the load-sharing option on the zone.

    b. Enable the round-robin option on both A records.

    c. Enable the load-sharing option on both A records.

    d. Enable the round-robin option on the server.

17. Which is the correct order in which a DNS client tries to resolve a name?

    a. Cache, DNS server, Hosts file

    b. Hosts file, cache, DNS server

    c. Cache, Hosts file, DNS server

    d. DNS server, cache, Hosts file

18. You want to verify whether a PTR record exists for the server1.csmtech.corp host, but you don't know the server's IP address. Which of the following commands should you use to see whether a PTR record exists for server1.csmtech.corp?

    a. `ping -a server1.csmtech.corp`, and then `ping IPAddress` returned from the first `ping`

    b. `nslookup server1.csmtech.corp`, and then `nslookup IPAddress` returned from the first `nslookup`

    c. `dnscmd /PTR server1.csmtech.corp`

    d. `dnslint /PTR server1.csmtech.corp`

19. You have delegated a subdomain to a zone on another server. Several months later, you hear that DNS clients can't resolve host records in the subdomain. You discover that the IP address scheme was changed recently in the building that contains the server hosting the subdomain. What can you do to make sure DNS clients can resolve hostnames in the subdomain?

    a. Configure a forwarder pointing to the server that hosts the subdomain.

    b. Edit the NS record in the delegated zone on the parent DNS server.

    c. Edit the NS record in the delegated zone on the DNS server hosting the subdomain.

    d. Configure a root hint pointing to the server that hosts the subdomain.

20. Domain Name System Security Extension (DNSSEC) provides specific features and protocols for validating server responses. Which of the following methods are used by DNSSEC to ensure that data received from DNS queries is accurate and secure? (Choose all that apply.)

    a. Data integrity

    b. Authenticated zone signing

    c. Authenticated denial of existence

    d. Origin authentication of DNS data

21. Which of the following records are returned when the requested resource record doesn't exist and are used to fulfill the authenticated denial-of-existence security feature of DNSSEC?
  a. DNSKEY
  b. Delegation Signer
  c. Next Secure
  d. Zone-signing key

22. Which of the following uses digital signatures contained in DNSSEC-related resource records to verify DNS responses?
  a. Zone signing
  b. Data integrity
  c. Socket pool
  d. Cache locking

23. Which of the following protects against DNS cache poisoning by enabling a DNS server to randomize the source port when performing DNS queries?
  a. Zone signing
  b. Data integrity
  c. Socket pool
  d. Cache locking

24. You have decided that you need to change the setting of an existing DNS forwarder. Which of the following PowerShell cmdlets will allow you to accomplish this task?
  a. `Add-DnsServerForwarder`
  b. `Import-DnsServerForwarder`
  c. `Set-DnsServerRecursion`
  d. `Set-DnsServerForwarder`

25. Which of the following is required to allow on-premises computers to resolve Azure VM names when using Azure private DNS zones?
  a. An on-premises DNS server with a conditional forwarder
  b. An Azure VM running a DNS server with a forwarder
  c. An Azure VM running a DNS server with a conditional forwarder
  d. An on-premises DNS server with a forwarder

Critical Thinking

The following activities give you critical thinking challenges. Case projects offer a scenario with a problem for which you supply a written solution.

Case Projects

Case Project 7-1: Resolving Names of Internet Resources

You have an Active Directory–integrated domain named csmtech.corp with two DCs that are DNS servers. You also have an Internet presence with its own domain name, csmpub.com, and a DNS server that's not part of an Active Directory domain. You want the DCs to be able to resolve the names of csmpub.com resources and to act as backup for the csmpub.com DNS database. What can you do to achieve these goals? Describe the steps you would take.

Case Project 7-2: Restricting Registration

You manage an Active Directory domain named csmtech.corp. The DNS server is a DC for csmtech.corp and hosts a standard primary DNS zone for csmtech.corp. You have noticed resource records in the zone from computers that aren't domain members. What can you do to ensure that only domain members can update resource records in the zone?

Case Project 7-3: Configuring Zones

You have an Active Directory forest named csmtech.corp and two Active Directory domains in the forest named csmpub.corp and csmsales.corp. You want the DNS servers in each domain to be able to handle DNS queries from client computers for any of the other domains. DNS servers in the csmtech.corp and csmpub.corp domains should be authoritative for their own domains and the csmsales.corp domain. However, DNS servers in csmsales.corp should be authoritative only for csmsales.corp.

How should you set up the DNS servers and zones to handle this situation? Explain how the DNS servers in each domain should be configured with zones. Be sure to include information about replication scope and zone types.

Case Project 7-4: Multilevel Domain Names

You have three DNS servers running on standalone servers. DNSS1 hosts the csm.corp zone. It has a delegation for the tech.csm.corp and pub.csm.corp zones that are hosted on DNSS2 and DNSS3, respectively. All three servers can access the Internet and have root hints configured.

You want to be sure that all three DNS servers can resolve hostnames for all three zones and the Internet. What is the most straightforward solution that causes the least amount of configuration?

Solutions to Self-Check Questions

Section 7-1: Introduction to Domain Name System

1. DNS queries can always be resolved by a single query to one server. True or False?

   Answer: b. False

   Explanation: Global DNS information is distributed among thousands of servers throughout the world, so DNS lookups often require a series of queries to a hierarchy of DNS servers before the name can be resolved.

2. Which of the following is an example of a top-level domain name?

   Answer: b. com

   Explanation: Top-level domain names include com, edu, net, gov, and many others. Company names such as Microsoft are second-level domain names. Names such as www and host1 are examples of hostnames.

Section 7-2: Installing and Configuring DNS

3. What type of zone should be queried if you have an IP address and want to know the hostname?

   Answer: a. RLZ

   Explanation: A query to resolve an IP address to a hostname is a reverse lookup; it targets a reverse lookup zone (RLZ).

4. Which type of zone only contains SOA and NS records?

   Answer: c. Stub

   Explanation: Stub zones contain only SOA and NS records and are sometimes used instead of forwarders because the NS records are automatically updated if a name server address changes. Primary and secondary zones usually also contain host records and other DNS records.

Section 7-3: Creating DNS Resource Records

5. What type of resource record will you find in an RLZ?

   Answer: a. PTR

   Explanation: PTR records are found in a reverse lookup zone (RLZ); A, AAAA, and MX records are found in forward lookup zones.

6. Which record type points to another domain name and is considered an alias?

   Answer: c. CNAME

   Explanation: CNAME records are often called Alias records. An alias is a record with a different name that points to an existing record, such as an A or AAAA record.

Section 7-4: Configuring DNS Zones

7. Which of the following is *not* found in an SOA record?

   Answer: b. IP address of server

   Explanation: The SOA record contains a serial number, minimum TTL value, and refresh interval. It contains the hostname of the DNS server but not the IP address.

8. Which zone transfer parameter can cause a server to stop responding to queries?

   Answer: c. Expires after

   Explanation: If the Refresh interval timer expires without a successful zone transfer, the Expires after timer begins. If it expires without contacting the primary DNS server or without a successful zone transfer, the DNS server stops responding to queries.

Section 7-5: Configuring DNS Server Settings

9. Which setting on a DNS server helps it to contact Internet servers?

   Answer: b. Root hints

   Explanation: Root hints consist of a list of name servers preconfigured on Windows DNS servers that point to Internet root servers, which are DNS servers on the Internet. They are managed by the Internet Assigned Numbers Authority (IANA).

10. Which DNS server option will prevent the DNS server from contacting other DNS servers?

    Answer: c. Disable recursion

    Explanation: Recursive queries specify that a DNS server should continue contacting other DNS servers to try to resolve a query. If recursion is disabled, the DNS server will only attempt to resolve a query from its local zone and cache information.

Section 7-6: Configuring DNS Security

11. Which DNSSEC method verifies that data hasn't been tampered with in transit?

    Answer: d. Data integrity

    Explanation: Data integrity verifies that data hasn't been tampered with in transit. Origin authentication verifies that the DNS server replying to a query is authentic. Authenticated denial allows verification that a resource record couldn't be found. Zone spoofing is not a DNSSEC security method.

12. Which DNS server security feature can mitigate a distributed denial-of-service attack called DNS amplification?

    Answer: a. Response Rate Limiting

    Explanation: Response Rate Limiting (RRL) mitigates a type of distributed denial-of-service (DDoS) attack called a DNS amplification attack. DNS cache locking prevents any updates to a cached record until the TTL expires. The DNS socket pool protects against DNS cache poisoning by enabling a DNS server to randomize the source port when performing DNS queries. Zone signing uses digital signatures in DNSSEC-related resource records to verify DNS responses. By verifying the digital signature, a DNS client can be assured that the DNS response is identical to the information published by the authoritative zone server.

Section 7-7: Azure DNS

13. An Azure private DNS zone can be accessed by all Azure VMs on all virtual networks by default. True or False?

    Answer: b. False

    Explanation: Private DNS zones must be linked to one or more Azure virtual networks; only the resources on the linked networks can use the private zone.

14. Which of the following is *not* necessary to allow on-premises computers to resolve names in an Azure private DNS zone?

    Answer: d. A DNS server on the on-premises network

    Explanation: A DNS server on the on-premises network is not required for on-premises computers to resolve names in an Azure private DNS zone; however, the on-premises network must be connected to the Azure network, an Azure DNS server VM must be configured with a forwarder, and DNS must be configured on the virtual network to which the on-premises network is connected.

Module 8

Manage IP Addressing

Module Objectives

After reading this module and completing the exercises, you will be able to:

1   Describe DHCP

2   Install and configure DHCP

3   Configure DHCP server options

4   Configure DHCP high availability

5   Implement IPAM

6   Implement IP addressing in a hybrid environment

Transmission Control Protocol/Internet Protocol (TCP/IP) is the standard networking protocol for all types and sizes of networks. As you have learned, every device on a TCP/IP network needs an IP address to communicate with other devices. Two methods are available for IP address assignment: static and dynamic. Although static IP addressing has its merits, managing static addresses on networks of more than a few dozen computers can descend into chaos quickly.

After Dynamic Host Configuration Protocol (DHCP) has been configured, it relieves many of the administrative headaches of managing static IP addressing on large networks. Small office and home networks typically use a Wi-Fi-enabled router, which is configured to assign an IP address via DHCP to devices that connect to the network. These routers might require little to no configuration because they come configured as a DHCP server. On a larger Windows-based network, however, you want more control over IP addressing and the ability to use features such as authorization and filters to enhance security, reservations, exclusions, IPv6 compatibility, and server policies. Windows Server 2022 has the DHCP Server role with these features and others to give you an enterprise-scale, dynamic IP addressing solution.

This module discusses how DHCP works, and you learn how to install and configure DHCP, including server authorization, scopes, and DHCP options. You also learn about some advanced features, such as reservations, exclusions, server policies, and filters. In addition, you learn how to configure DHCP to work with DNS, DHCP relay, and DHCP high availability. Finally, you'll learn how to resolve IP address issues in hybrid environments.

Table 8-1 describes what you need for the hands-on activities in this module.

Table 8-1   Activity requirements

Activity	Requirements	Notes
Activity 8-1: Resetting Your Virtual Environment	ServerDC1, ServerDM1, Server DM2, ServerSA1	
Activity 8-2: Installing and Authorizing a DHCP Server	ServerDC1, ServerDM1, ServerSA1	
Activity 8-3: Working with Exclusions and Reservations	ServerDC1, ServerDM1, ServerSA1	
Activity 8-4: Configuring DHCP Options	ServerDC1, ServerDM1, ServerSA1	
Activity 8-5: Creating a DHCP Policy	ServerDC1, ServerDM1, ServerSA1	
Activity 8-6: Creating a DHCP Filter	ServerDC1, ServerDM1, ServerSA1	
Activity 8-7: Working with Split Scopes	ServerDC1, ServerDM1, ServerSA1	
Activity 8-8: Configuring DHCP Failover	ServerDC1, ServerDM1, ServerSA1	
Activity 8-9: Uninstalling the DHCP Server Role	ServerDC1, ServerDM1, ServerSA1	
Activity 8-10: Resetting Your Virtual Environment	ServerDC1, ServerDM1, ServerDM2, ServerSA1	
Activity 8-11: Installing DHCP Roles on Managed Servers	ServerDC1, ServerDM2	
Activity 8-12: Installing and Provisioning the IPAM Server	ServerDC1, ServerDM1, ServerDM2	
Activity 8-13: Discovering and Selecting Servers	ServerDC1, ServerDM1, ServerDM2	
Activity 8-14: Creating a Virtual Network and IP Address Space	A web browser with access to the Azure portal	A valid Azure subscription
Activity 8-15: Creating a VM on the Virtual Network	A web browser with access to the Azure portal	A valid Azure subscription

An Overview of Dynamic Host Configuration Protocol

Microsoft Exam AZ-800:
Implement and manage an on-premises and hybrid networking infrastructure.
- Manage IP addressing in on-premises and hybrid scenarios

Dynamic Host Configuration Protocol (DHCP) is a component of the TCP/IP protocol suite, which is used to assign an IP address to a host automatically from a defined pool of addresses. IP addresses assigned via DHCP are leased, not permanently assigned. When a client receives an IP address from a server, it can keep the address until the lease expires, at which point the client can request a new IP address. However, to prevent a disruption in communication, the client attempts to renew the lease when the lease interval is 50 percent expired. DHCP is based on broadcast packets, so there must be a DHCP server or DHCP relay agent in the same subnet as the client. (This topic is discussed later in the "DHCP Relay Agents" section.) Recall that broadcast packets are forwarded by switches but not by routers, so they're heard only by devices on the same LAN. DHCP is a fairly simple protocol, consisting of just eight message types. These message types and the DHCP address assignment and renewal processes are discussed in the following sections.

The DHCP Address Assignment Process

Like most TCP/IP protocols, DHCP is a client/server protocol. A client makes a request for an IP address, and the server responds. The process of a DHCP client requesting an IP address and a DHCP server fulfilling the request is actually a four-packet sequence. All four packets are broadcast packets. DHCP was designed to use broadcast packets because a client that doesn't have an IP address can't be sent a unicast packet; it can, however, receive and respond to a broadcast packet. DHCP uses the UDP Transport-layer protocol on ports 67 and 68. Port 67 is for sending data from the client to the server, and port 68 is for sending data from the server to the client. The four-packet sequence is explained in the following list and illustrated in Figure 8-1:

1. *DHCPDISCOVER*—The client transmits a broadcast packet via UDP source port 68 and UDP destination port 67 to the network, asking for an IP address from an available DHCP server. The client can request its last known IP address and other IP address parameters, such as the subnet mask, router (default gateway), domain name, and DNS server.

2. *DHCPOFFER*—A DHCP server receives the DHCPDISCOVER packet and responds with an offer of an IP address and subnet mask from the pool of addresses, along with the lease duration. The broadcast packet is transmitted via UDP source port 67 and UDP destination port 68. Because the packet is a broadcast, all devices on the subnet get it. The packet contains the MAC address of the client computer that sent the DHCPDISCOVER packet, so other devices disregard it.

3. *DHCPREQUEST*—The client responds by requesting the offered address. Because it's possible that multiple DHCP servers responded to the DHCPDISCOVER, the client might get multiple offers but accepts only one. The DHCPREQUEST packet includes a server identifier, which is the IP address of the server the offer is accepted from. Any other DHCP servers that made an offer see the server identifier and return the offered, but not accepted, IP address to the pool.

4. *DHCPACK*—The server from which the offer was accepted acknowledges the transaction and sends any other requested IP parameters, such as default gateway and DNS server address, to the client. The transaction is now complete, and the client binds the IP address and other parameters to its network interface.

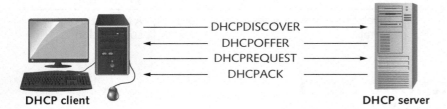

DHCP client   DHCP server

- DHCPDISCOVER
- DHCPOFFER
- DHCPREQUEST
- DHCPACK

Figure 8-1   The packet sequence for DHCP address assignment

DHCP Address Renewal

The DHCPDISCOVER broadcast packet is sent only when the client currently has no IP address configured on the interface from which the packet is transmitted, or after the current address has expired. As mentioned, a client attempts to renew the address lease when it's 50 percent expired. The **lease renewal** process is somewhat different from the DHCPDISCOVER process; because the client already has an IP address and the address of the DHCP server, the client uses unicast packets rather than broadcast packets. A successful renewal is a two-packet sequence:

1. *DHCPREQUEST*—When the lease is 50 percent expired, the client sends a unicast packet to the DHCP server, requesting a lease renewal for its current IP address. If the server doesn't respond, the client retries the renewal request up to three more times—4, 8, and 16 seconds after the first renewal request.

2. *DHCPACK*—If the server responds and can honor the renewal request, the server sends a unicast packet to the client granting and acknowledging the renewal request.

The two-packet sequence for a lease renewal occurs when a server is available to service the request and the server can honor the renewal request. The renewal request might fail in these common situations:

- The server responds but can't honor the renewal. This situation can occur if the requested address has been deleted or deactivated from the scope or the address has been excluded from the scope since the time the client received it. The server sends a DHCPNAK (negative acknowledgment) to the client, which unbinds the address from its network interface and begins the process anew with a broadcast DHCPDISCOVER packet.
- The server doesn't respond. If the server has been taken offline, moved to another subnet, or can't communicate (perhaps because of a hardware failure), the DHCPREQUEST packet can't be serviced. In this case, the following steps occur:

1. The client keeps its current address until 87.5 percent of the lease interval has expired. At that time, the client sends a broadcast DHCPREQUEST requesting a lease renewal from any available DHCP server.
2. There are two possible results from the DHCPREQUEST broadcast:
    - A DHCP server responds to the request. If it can provide the requested address, it replies with a DHCPACK and the address is renewed; otherwise, it replies with a DHCPNAK indicating that it can't supply the requested address. In this case, the client immediately unbinds the address from the network interface and starts the DHCP sequence over, beginning with a DHCPDISCOVER broadcast packet.
    - No DHCP server responds. In this case, the client waits until the lease period is over, unbinds the IP address, and starts the sequence over with a DHCPDISCOVER broadcast packet. If no server responds, a Windows client binds an Automatic Private IP Addressing (APIPA) address to the network interface and sends a DHCPDISCOVER every 5 minutes in an attempt to get a DHCP-assigned address. (Other client OSs might behave differently.) If an alternate IP address configuration has been configured on the interface, it's used instead of an APIPA address, and no further attempts are made to get a DHCP-assigned address until the interface is reset or the computer restarts.

DHCP Messages

You've learned about the most common DHCP message types for lease request and renewal. Table 8-2 describes all the message types exchanged between a DHCP server and client. The first column includes the message type number found in the DHCP packet. Message types that have been covered already are described briefly.

Table 8-2 DHCP message types

Message number	Message name	Description
1	DHCPDISCOVER	Sent by a client to discover an available DHCP server and request a new IP address.
2	DHCPOFFER	Sent by the server in response to a DHCPDISCOVER with an offer of an IP address.
3	DHCPREQUEST	Sent by a client to request a lease on an offered IP address in response to a DHCPOFFER or to renew an existing lease.
4	DHCPDECLINE	Sent by a client in response to a DHCPOFFER to decline an offered IP address. Usually occurs when the client has determined that the offered address is already in use on the network.
5	DHCPACK	Sent by the server to acknowledge a DHCPREQUEST or DHCPINFORM. This message also contains DHCP options requested by the client.
6	DHCPNAK	Sent by the server in response to a DHCPREQUEST. Indicates that the server can't fulfill the request. Usually occurs when a client is attempting a renewal and the requested address is no longer available for lease.

(continues)

Table 8-2 (continued)

Message number	Message name	Description
7	DHCPRELEASE	Sent by a client to release a leased address. Usually occurs when a user runs the `ipconfig/release` command or a command of a similar function. However, it can also occur if a client is configured to release its address when the computer is shut down. (By default, Windows clients don't release an address when they are shut down.)
8	DHCPINFORM	Sent by a client to request additional configuration. The client must already have an IP address and a subnet mask. Can be used by a client that has a static IP address but has been configured to get a DNS address or router address via DHCP.

Self-Check Questions

1. When a DHCP client does not have an IP address, what is the first packet sent by the client in an attempt to request an address?

   a. DHCPREQUEST   **c.** DHCPINFORM
   b. DHCPDISCOVER   **d.** DHCPOFFER

2. After how much of the IP address lease time has expired does a DHCP client first attempt to renew the lease?

   a. 50 percent   **c.** 100 percent
   b. 87.5 percent   **d.** 75 percent

○ Check your answers at the end of this module.

Installing and Configuring DHCP

Microsoft Exam AZ-800:
Implement and manage an on-premises and hybrid networking infrastructure.
• Manage IP addressing in on-premises and hybrid scenarios

The DHCP service is installed as a server role, aptly named DHCP Server. There are no role service components for this server role; the DHCP management tool is the only additional component installed. DHCP Server can be installed by using the Add Roles and Features Wizard via Server Manager or the following PowerShell cmdlet:

```
Install-WindowsFeature DHCP -IncludeManagementTools
```

After you install this role, the DHCP console (see Figure 8-2) is available on the Tools menu in Server Manager. The red down arrow on the IPv4 and IPv6 nodes indicates that the server isn't currently providing services. In a Windows domain network, the DHCP server must be authorized and a scope must be created before the server can begin providing DHCP services. In a workgroup network, authorization is automatic.

DHCP Server Authorization

A DHCP server must be authorized on a domain network before it can begin providing services. **DHCP server authorization** is the process of enabling a DHCP server in a domain environment to prevent rogue DHCP servers from operating on the network. DHCP clients have no way of determining whether a DHCP server is valid. When a client transmits a DHCPDISCOVER packet, any DHCP server receiving the broadcast can respond. The client accepts the first offer it gets that meets the requirements in the DHCPDISCOVER packet. If a rogue DHCP server is installed on a

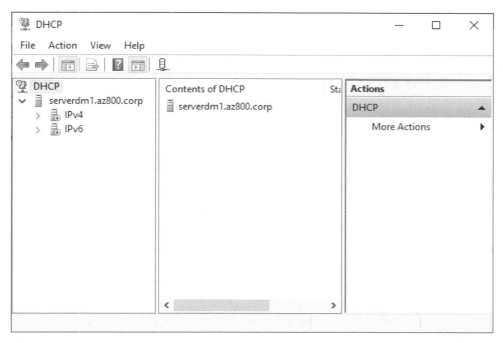

Figure 8-2   The DHCP console

network, whether accidentally or on purpose, incorrect IP address settings could be configured on client computers. These settings likely include the DNS server and default gateway the client uses in addition to the IP address and subnet mask. At best, incorrect IP address settings cause the client to stop communicating correctly. At worst, servers set up by an attacker to masquerade as legitimate network resources can capture passwords and other sensitive information.

On a domain network, a DHCP server can be installed on a domain controller, a member server, or a standalone server. However, for authorization to work correctly, installing DHCP on a standalone server in a domain network isn't recommended. If you use this setup in a network that already has an authorized server, the standalone server can't lease addresses.

After a DHCP server is installed, you authorize it by right-clicking the server name in the DHCP console and clicking Authorize. DHCP server authorization requires Enterprise Administrator credentials, so if you aren't signed in as an Enterprise Administrator (the Administrator account in the forest root domain or a member of the Enterprise Administrators universal group), you're prompted for credentials. To authorize a DHCP server with PowerShell, use the `Add-DhcpServerInDC` cmdlet.

DHCP Scopes

A **DHCP scope** is a pool of IP addresses and other IP configuration parameters that a DHCP server uses to lease addresses to DHCP clients. A scope consists of the following required parameters:

- *Scope name*—A descriptive name for the scope. You can define multiple scopes on a DHCP server, so you might name the scope based on the range of IP addresses in it. For example, a scope that services the 10.99.0.0/24 network might be named "10.99.0-subnet."
- *Start and end IP addresses*—The start and end IP addresses define the address pool. You can't specify a start address that's the network ID or an end address that's the broadcast address for the subnet.
- *Prefix length or subnet mask*—Specify a prefix length or subnet mask that's assigned with each IP address. For example, you can specify 24 for the prefix length or 255.255.255.0 for the subnet mask. Windows fills in the prefix length and subnet mask automatically based on the class of the start and end IP addresses, but you can change this information (see Figure 8-3).
- *Lease duration*—The **lease duration** specifies how long a DHCP client can keep an address. As discussed, a client tries to renew the address long before the lease expires but must release the address if it can't renew the

address before it expires. The lease duration is specified in days, hours, and minutes, with a minimum lease of 1 minute and a maximum lease of 999 days, 23 hours, and 59 minutes. The default lease duration is 8 days. The lease can also be set to unlimited, but this setting isn't recommended because if the client is removed from the network or its NIC is replaced, the address is never returned to the pool for lease to other clients. An unlimited duration can also cause DNS records to become stale when DHCP is configured to update DNS records on behalf of the client.

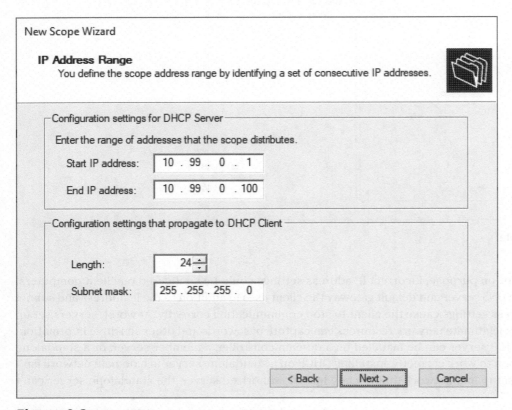

Figure 8-3   Setting the IP address range for a scope

Note 1

The preceding four items are the required DHCP scope options. You can configure other options when you create a scope with the New Scope Wizard or PowerShell or change the scope's properties after it's created.

After a scope is created, you must activate the scope before it can begin serving IP addresses. Until the scope is activated, it will be shown in the DHCP console with a red down arrow. To activate a scope with the DHCP console, simply right-click the scope and click Activate. To activate a scope with PowerShell, use the Set-DhcpServerv4Scope cmdlet with the -State Active parameter.

Exclusion Ranges

A DHCP scope contains a continuous range of IP addresses that are leased to DHCP clients. You might want to exclude certain addresses or a range of addresses from the scope for use in static address assignments. Static addresses are usually assigned to servers, routers, and other critical infrastructure devices to make sure they always have an address that never changes. To avoid IP address conflicts, you need to exclude addresses that are assigned statically. Addresses can be excluded in two ways:

- *De facto exclusion*—You don't actually create an exclusion with this method; you simply set the start and end IP addresses in the scope so that several addresses in the subnet fall outside the scope's range. For example, if you set a scope's start address to 192.168.0.10 and end address to 192.168.0.240 with a 28-bit prefix, you have addresses 192.168.0.1 through 192.168.0.9 and addresses 192.168.0.241 through 192.168.0.254 to use for static address assignments. You might not need to create an exclusion range unless you use all these addresses and require more.

- *Create an exclusion range*—Sometimes a scope is created after static address assignments have been made, and the static addresses occupy several ranges of addresses throughout the subnet (instead of at the beginning or end). For example, if your subnet is 192.168.0.0/24 and you have devices with static addresses in the range 192.168.0.100 through 192.168.0.110, you probably need to create one or more exclusion ranges because these addresses fall right in the middle of the subnet. An **exclusion range** consists of one or more addresses in the scope that the DHCP server doesn't lease to clients. An exclusion range can be created when the scope is created with the New Scope Wizard or afterward by right-clicking the Address Pool node under the scope and clicking New Exclusion Range. In the Add Exclusion dialog box, type the start and end IP addresses. You can exclude a single IP address by specifying only the start address. You can create as many exclusion ranges as you need.

Reservations

A **reservation** is an IP address associated with the MAC address of a DHCP client to ensure that when the client requests an IP address, it always gets the same one, along with any configured options. The IP address in the reservation must fall within the same subnet as the scope and uses the same subnet mask that's configured for the scope. If options are configured for the reservation, they take precedence over options configured at the scope or server level (as discussed later in the "DHCP Options" section). A reservation address can be any address in the subnet defined by the scope's address range and can even be within an exclusion range.

If the IP address you want to use in the reservation is already in use by another DHCP client, the client using the address continues to use it until the client attempts to renew it. You can force the client to release the address and get a different address by entering `ipconfig /release` and `ipconfig /renew` at a command prompt. The client the reservation is made for can be forced to start using the reserved address by entering `ipconfig /renew` at the command prompt, or you can wait until it attempts to renew its current address.

Multiple Subnets, Multiple Scopes

A DHCP scope can service a single subnet. When a DHCP server receives a DHCPDISCOVER message on an interface, it offers an IP address from the scope in which the address pool is in the same subnet as the interface's address. For example, suppose a DHCP server has a single network interface configured for address 192.168.0.1/24. When a DHCPDISCOVER is received on that interface, the server offers an address from the scope containing addresses in the 192.168.0.0/24 network. Likewise, if the DHCP server receives a DHCPREQUEST for a particular IP address, as when a client renews a lease, the server can fulfill the request only if the requested address is on the same subnet as the server's interface and there's a matching scope.

Note 2

You can't create overlapping scopes. In other words, you can't create multiple scopes with address pools in the same subnet. For example, suppose you create a scope with the start address 192.168.0.1, end address 192.168.0.100, and prefix length 24. You can't create another scope with the start address 192.168.0.150 and end address 192.168.0.200 because both address pools are in the 192.168.0.0 subnet.

What do you do when your network has multiple subnets? Because DHCP is based on broadcasts, which can't traverse routers, there are three main methods for handling a network with multiple subnets:

- Configure a DHCP server in each subnet, each configured with a scope to service that subnet.
- Configure a single DHCP server with network interfaces connected to each subnet and scopes defined for each subnet. This setup is shown in Figure 8-4. This method obviously becomes untenable when the number of subnets increases because you need an interface for each subnet.
- Configure DHCP relay agents on subnets that don't have a DHCP server. DHCP relay agents forward DHCP requests to a central DHCP server configured with scopes for each subnet. DHCP relay agents are discussed later in the "DHCP Relay Agents" section.

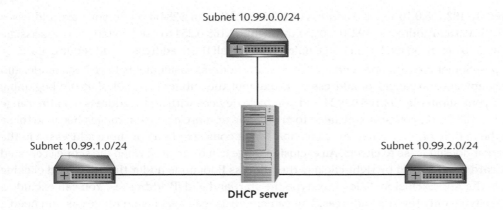

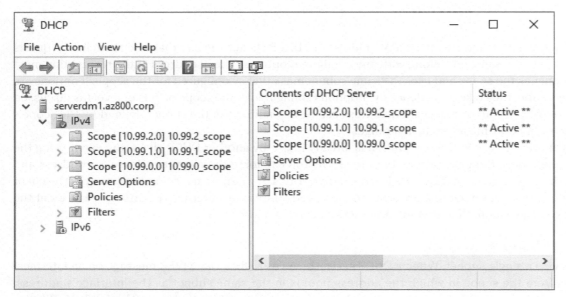

Figure 8-4   A server configured with three scopes

Configuring Superscopes

A **superscope** is a special type of scope consisting of one or more member scopes that allow a DHCP server to service multiple IPv4 subnets on a single physical network. (Superscopes aren't supported in IPv6.) Although it isn't a common configuration for a network, it can and does occur. A superscope directs the DHCP server to draw addresses from all configured scopes, even though it has only a single interface configured for one of the IP subnets. This configuration can be useful if the number of computers on a physical network exceeds the original subnet's size or when a second subnet has been added to a physical network for testing purposes. To configure a superscope, first configure two or more scopes to include in the superscope; each scope that's part of a superscope is referred to as a member scope. Then create the superscope and add the member scopes. Superscopes don't have any DHCP options of their own, and you can't create an IP address pool for a superscope. All IP address pools and options are configured in member scopes. However, you can deactivate a superscope, which deactivates all member scopes as well.

Figure 8-5 is an example of a network with a superscope. Two subnets are configured: 192.168.0.0/24 and 192.168.1.0/24. The router interface is configured with two IP addresses and can route between the two subnets. The DHCP server is configured with a superscope named Superscope1 that has two member scopes, one for each subnet.

You create superscopes in the DHCP console by right-clicking the IPv4 node, clicking New Superscope, and then following the New Superscope Wizard. You can also create a superscope with PowerShell, as in the following example:

```
Add-DhcpServerv4SuperScope -SuperscopeName "NewSuperScope"
  -ScopeID 192.168.0.0,192.168.1.0
```

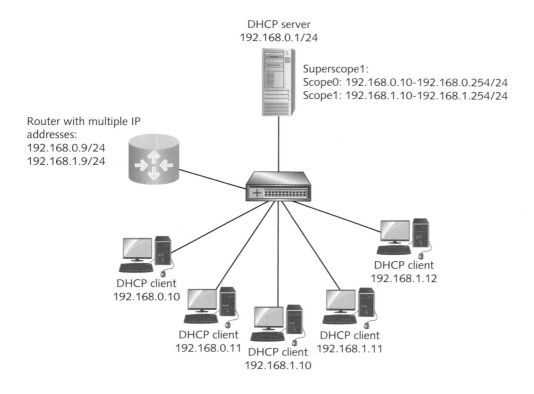

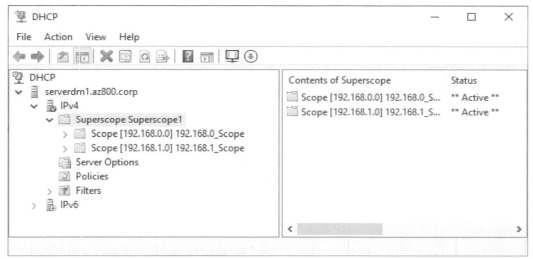

Figure 8-5   A network that uses a superscope

The IP addresses that follow the -ScopeID option are the subnet addresses of the two scopes you want to add to the superscope.

Configuring Multicast Scopes

Most network packets are addressed as unicast packets, meaning a single host is the intended recipient, or as broadcast packets, meaning all hosts on the network should process them. An IPv4 multicast packet is a network packet addressed to a group of hosts listening on a particular multicast IP address. These hosts listening for multicast packets receive and process them while other hosts ignore them. A multicast address doesn't replace a host's regular IP address assignment. The first octet of IPv4 multicast addresses is in the range 224 to 239 and is classified as a class D IP address. Multicast addresses can't be assigned as a host's IP address; instead, a network service or application informs the IP protocol that it wants to "join" a multicast group. By doing so, the network software listens for the specified multicast address in the destination field of packets and processes them rather than ignoring them.

> **Note 3**
>
> Although IPv6 does support multicasting and uses it much more than IPv4 does, there's no support for IPv6 DHCP multicast scopes.

Most multicast applications use a reserved multicast address known by the server running the multicast service and by the clients that might join the multicast group, and there's no need for dynamic multicast address allocation. For example, several routing protocols use multicast addresses to exchange information. Routing Information Protocol version 2 (RIPv2) uses the reserved multicast address 224.0.0.9, and Open Shortest Path First (OSPF) uses addresses 224.0.0.5 and 224.0.0.6. All routers supporting these protocols have these addresses statically assigned, so there's no need to use DHCP for multicast address assignment in these cases. However, if you're using an application that doesn't use a reserved multicast address, you might want to use DHCP to assign multicast addresses temporarily on your network. If you want to reserve an address permanently, you must register it with the Internet Assigned Numbers Authority (IANA).

> **Note 4**
>
> You can find a list of multicast addresses reserved by the IANA for designated purposes at https://www.iana.org/assignments/multicast-addresses/multicast-addresses.xhtml.

A **multicast scope** allows assigning multicast addresses dynamically to multicast servers and clients with the Multicast Address Dynamic Client Allocation Protocol (MADCAP). Typically, a multicast server (MCS) is allocated a multicast address, and multicast clients register or join the multicast group, which allows them to receive multicast traffic from the MCS.

> **Note 5**
>
> All devices using TCP/IP must be assigned a unicast IP address before they can be assigned and begin using multicast addresses.

There are two common ranges of multicast addresses you can use to create a multicast scope:

- *Administrative scopes*—An administrative scope is composed of multicast addresses intended to be used in a private network. This range of addresses is similar to the private unicast IP address ranges beginning with 10, 172.16-172.31, and 192.168. The range most recommended for this purpose is 239.192.0.0/14, which has plenty of addresses for a large enterprise. The range you specify when configuring the multicast scope must contain at least 256 addresses.
- *Global scopes*—In a global scope, the multicast application is used across the public Internet and has the recommended range of 233.0.0.0/24. There's no minimum number of addresses in a global scope.

> **Note 6**
>
> The preceding ranges are recommended. You can use any range of multicast addresses for creating a scope, as long as it doesn't include any addresses reserved by the IANA.

You configure multicast scopes in the DHCP console or with PowerShell cmdlets. You don't configure options for a multicast scope, but you can configure exclusions, and you must specify a lease time. (The default value is 30 days.) The multicast scope consists of start and end IP addresses in the multicast address range, along with a time to live (TTL) value that specifies how many routers a multicast packet can pass through before being discarded. No subnet mask is specified in the scope because multicast addresses are considered secondary addresses, and a host already has a subnet mask assigned along with its unicast IP address.

DHCP Options

An IP address and subnet mask are the minimum settings needed for a computer to communicate on a network. However, almost every network requires a DNS server IP address for name resolution and a default gateway to communicate with other subnets and the Internet. The DHCP server can be configured to send both those addresses to DHCP clients along with the IP address and subnet mask. Many other options can be configured and might be necessary, depending on the network environment. DHCP options can be assigned at the following levels:

- *Server options*—Options configured at the server level affect all scopes but can be overridden by a scope, policy, or reservation option.

- *Scope options*—Scope options affect clients that get a lease from the scope in which the option is configured. Scope options can be overridden by reservation options or DHCP policies.

- *Policy options*—DHCP policies allow an administrator to assign IP address options to clients based on client properties, such as device type, MAC address, or OS. DHCP policies are discussed later in the "Configuring Policies" section. Options specified at the policy level can be overridden only by reservation options.

- *Reservation options*—As discussed, a reservation is an address associated with a computer's MAC address. When the computer with the specified MAC address requests an IP address, the DHCP server offers the reserved address and any configured options, thus ensuring that the computer is always assigned the same IP address settings. Options set on a reservation take precedence over any conflicting options set at any other level.

Common DHCP Options

DHCP options are specified in the format *NNN OptionName*, with *NNN* representing a three-digit number that uniquely identifies the option in the DHCP packet, and *OptionName* being the option's user-friendly name. Some of the most common options include the following:

- *003 Router*—This option is almost always requested by the DHCP client and supplied by the DHCP server because it configures the client's default gateway setting, which is needed for the client to communicate with other networks. This option is usually configured at the scope level because each scope has a different default gateway associated with it. If you have only one scope, you can configure it at the server level. If you use policies or reservations, you can configure the router option at these levels so that selected computers can use a different default gateway than the rest of the scope does, if needed.

- *006 DNS Servers*—This option is often configured as a server option that applies to all scopes because DNS servers often provide services for an entire internetwork. However, if the option is configured on a scope, the scope option takes precedence. The DNS Servers option consists of a list of IP addresses of DNS servers the client can use for name resolution.

- *015 DNS Domain Name*—This option can also be configured as a server or scope option. It provides a domain name, such as csmtech.corp, to DHCP clients. The DNS Domain Name option configures the client domain name, which a client needs when performing a DNS query with a single-label name. For example, if a user types \\Server1 in the Run dialog box, the DNS client attempts to resolve Server1 to an IP address. If no domain name is configured, the client sends the query to the DNS server as just Server1. Without a domain name, the lookup fails. However, if a domain name is configured, the DNS client software adds the domain name to the query so that the actual DNS query is sent as Server1.csmtech.corp. The domain name is also used by the client when registering its computer name with the DNS server. Without a domain name that matches a zone name on the server, the registration fails. Domain members configure their DNS domain names automatically with the name of the domain they're a member of, so this option is unnecessary if all computers receiving DHCP addresses are domain members.

- *044 WINS/NBNS Servers*—This option is used only on networks with Windows Internet Name Service (WINS) servers.

- *046 WINS/NBT node type*—This option is used with option 044 to specify the WINS node type.

Configuring Options

Server options are configured in the DHCP console by right-clicking Server Options under the IPv4 or IPv6 node and clicking Configure Options. The Server Options dialog box has two tabs. The General tab has a list of available options in the upper pane. If you click the check box for an option, the lower pane is enabled so that you can enter information for the selected option. For example, in Figure 8-6, the 003 Router option is selected. For this option, you add one or more router addresses that clients use for their default gateway configuration.

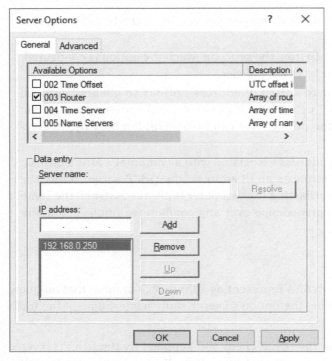

Figure 8-6   The Server Options dialog box

The Advanced tab of the Server Options dialog box has the same list of options as well as a list box to choose the **Vendor Class**, a field in the DHCP packet that device manufacturers or OS vendors use to identify a device model or an OS version. You can use this field to set different DHCP options. Starting with Windows Server 2012, the Vendor Class options should be used only when creating DHCP policies, as discussed later in the "Configuring Policies" section.

Scope and reservation options are set the same way as server options. To configure scope options, click the scope in the DHCP console, right-click Scope Options in the right pane, and click Configure Options. To configure reservation options, right-click a reservation and click Configure Options. You can configure different options for each reservation.

Self-Check Questions

3.   Which part of the DHCP configuration creates a pool of IP addresses that can be leased to clients?

    a. DHCP zone   **c.** DHCP scope

    b. Exclusion ranges   **d.** Reservations

4.   What does a DHCP reservation use to identify a client?

    a. IP address   **c.** DNS name

    b. Computer name   **d.** MAC address

⊙ Check your answers at the end of this module.

Activity 8-1

Resetting Your Virtual Environment

Time Required: 5 minutes

Objective: Reset your virtual environment by applying the InitialConfig checkpoint or snapshot.

Required Tools and Equipment: ServerDC1, ServerDM1, ServerDM2, ServerSA1

Description: Apply the InitialConfig checkpoint or snapshot to ServerDC1, ServerDM1, ServerDM2, and ServerSA1.

1. Be sure all servers are shut down. In your virtualization program, apply the InitialConfig checkpoint or snapshot to all servers.
2. When the snapshot or checkpoint has been applied, continue to the next activity.

Activity 8-2

Installing and Authorizing a DHCP Server

Time Required: 10 minutes

Objective: Install and authorize a DHCP server.

Required Tools and Equipment: ServerDC1, ServerDM1, ServerSA1

Description: In this activity, you install the DHCP Server role on a domain member server and authorize it. Then, you create and configure a DHCP scope.

1. Start ServerDC1 and ServerDM1, if necessary. Sign in to ServerDM1 as **Administrator**.
2. On ServerDM1, open Server Manager and open a PowerShell window. Type **Install-WindowsFeature DHCP -IncludeManagementTools** and press **Enter**.
3. When the DHCP Server installation finishes, click **Tools** and then **DHCP** from the Server Manager menu to open the DHCP console.
4. Click to expand the server node in the left pane. Notice that both the IPv4 and IPv6 nodes display red arrows, indicating that they're currently not enabled because the server is not authorized.
5. To authorize the server, right-click the server node (**serverdm1.az800.corp**) and click **Authorize**.
6. Click the **Refresh** toolbar icon. You see a check mark in a green circle on the IPv4 and IPv6 nodes. If you need to, you can unauthorize a server after it's authorized by right-clicking the server node and clicking Unauthorize. For now, leave the server authorized.
7. To create a scope, click to select the **IPv4** node. Then, right-click **IPv4** and click **New Scope** to start the New Scope Wizard. In the welcome window, click **Next**.
8. In the Scope Name window, type **10.99.0_scope** in the Name text box, add a description if you want, and then click **Next**.
9. In the IP Address Range window, type **10.99.0.1** in the Start IP address text box and **10.99.0.100** in the End IP address text box. In the Length text box, type **24,** and then click **Next**.
10. In the Add Exclusions and Delay window, click **Next**.
11. In the Lease Duration window, type **0** in the Days text box, **1** in the Hours text box, and **0** in the Minutes text box. One hour is a short lease time, but it's adequate for testing. Click **Next**.
12. In the Configure DHCP Options window, click **No, I will configure these options later**, and then click **Next**.
13. In the Completing the New Scope Wizard window, click **Finish**.
14. In the DHCP console, you see the new scope, but a red down arrow indicates that it's not activated. Click the scope you just created. Under it are additional folders that you work with later. Right-click the scope and click **Activate**. The scope is now activated.
15. Start ServerSA1 and sign in as **Administrator**.

(continues)

Activity 8-2 Continued

16. On ServerSA1, open a PowerShell window, type **Set-NetIPInterface -InterfaceAlias Ethernet -Dhcp Enabled**, and press **Enter**. To set the DNS server address for DHCP, type **Set-DnsClientServerAddress -InterfaceAlias Ethernet -ResetServerAddresses** and press **Enter**.

17. Type **ipconfig /all** and press **Enter**. You see that the address 10.99.0.1 with subnet mask 255.255.255.0 was assigned. Look for the line starting with "DHCP Server"; the address is 10.99.0.201, the address of ServerDM1.

18. On ServerDM1, in the DHCP console, click **Address Leases**. You see the address leased to ServerSA1 (see Figure 8-7). If necessary, click the Refresh icon to see the address lease.

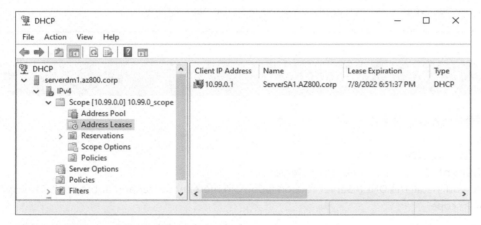

Figure 8-7 Viewing address leases

19. Stay signed in to ServerDM1 and ServerSA1 if you're continuing to the next activity.

Activity 8-3

Working with Exclusions and Reservations

Time Required: 20 minutes

Objective: Create and test exclusion ranges and reservations.

Required Tools and Equipment: ServerDC1, ServerDM1, ServerSA1

Description: In this activity, you create an exclusion range and verify that the address can't be leased. You also create a reservation for ServerSA1 and verify that the reserved address is leased by ServerSA1.

1. On ServerSA1, in a PowerShell window, type **ipconfig /renew** and press **Enter** to get a fresh lease on the IP address. The leased address should still be 10.99.0.1.

2. On ServerDM1, in the DHCP console, click to expand the **10.99.0_scope** you created earlier. Click to select **Address Pool**, right-click **Address Pool**, and click **New Exclusion Range**.

3. In the Start IP address text box, type **10.99.0.1**, and in the End IP address text box, type **10.99.0.5**. Click **Add** and then **Close**. You see the exclusion range with a red × (highlighted in Figure 8-8).

4. On ServerSA1, in the PowerShell window, type **ipconfig /all** and press **Enter**. In the output, look for the "Lease Obtained" and "Lease Expires" lines under the Ethernet connection to see your lease information.

Activity 8-3 Continued

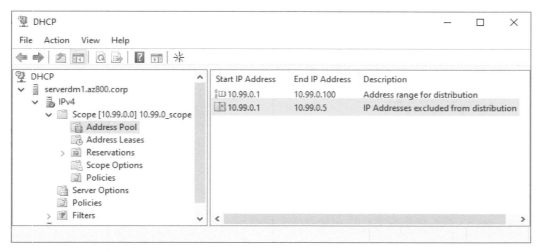

Figure 8-8   An exclusion range

5. Type **ipconfig /renew** and press **Enter**. You'll probably see a message indicating an error while renewing the interface. Because you excluded the address ServerSA1 was using, it was unable to renew the address, but it leased a new one. Type **ipconfig** and press **Enter**. You should see that you now have the address 10.99.0.6.

6. On ServerDM1, click **Address Leases** in the DHCP console. Click the **Refresh** icon to see the new address lease in the middle pane. You see the lease for ServerSA1. In the middle pane, scroll to the right until you see the Unique ID column, which is the MAC address of ServerSA1.

7. You can create a reservation manually or from an existing lease. To create a reservation from ServerSA1's existing lease, right-click the lease in the middle pane and click **Add to Reservation**. You see a message that the lease was converted to a reservation successfully. Click **OK**.

8. In the left pane, click **Reservations**. Right-click the new reservation in the middle pane and click **Properties**. You can change the name of the reservation, change the MAC address, and add a description, but you can't change the IP address. If you need to change the IP address, you must delete the reservation and create a new one. Click **Cancel**.

9. To delete this reservation, right-click it and click **Delete**. Click **Yes** to confirm.

10. To create a reservation manually, you need the MAC address of the computer for which you're creating the reservation. In the PowerShell window, type **ping 10.99.0.6** and press **Enter**. Don't worry if the ping times out.

11. Type **arp –a** and press **Enter** to list the MAC addresses known by ServerDM1. Use your mouse to select the MAC address next to the entry starting with 10.99.0.6 and press **Ctrl+C** to copy it.

12. In the DHCP console, right-click **Reservations** and click **New Reservation**. In the Reservation name text box, type **ServerSA1**. (The reservation name is just a label and doesn't affect a reservation's function.)

13. In the IP address text box, Windows starts the address. Finish it by typing **0.1**. Right-click the MAC address text box and click **Paste** to paste the MAC address of ServerSA1 you copied in Step 11. (See Figure 8-9, although your address will be different from the one in the figure.) Click **Add** and then **Close**. Remember that 10.99.0.1 is in the excluded range you created earlier, but as you see in the next step, reservations still work even if they're in the excluded range.

14. On ServerSA1, type **ipconfig /renew** in the PowerShell window and press **Enter**. An error message is displayed. Type **ipconfig** and press **Enter**. ServerSA1 now has the address 10.99.0.1.

15. Stay signed in to ServerDM1 and ServerSA1 and continue to the next activity.

Activity 8-3 Continued

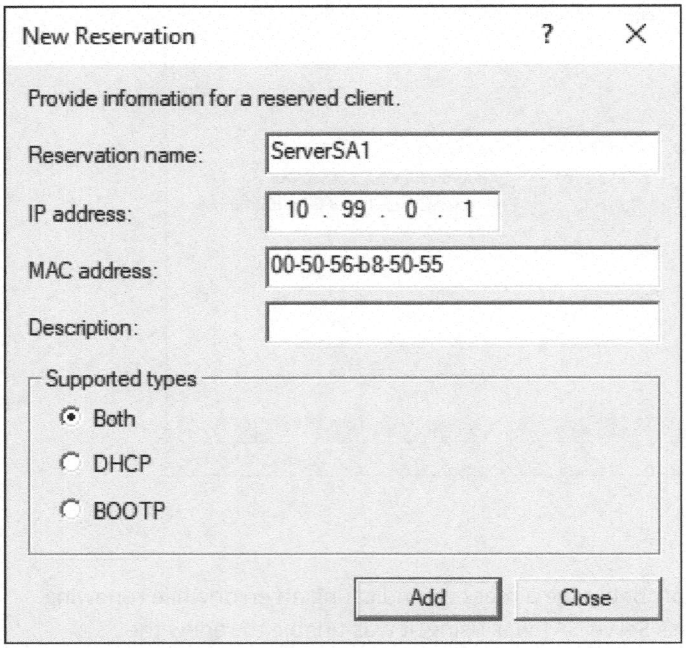

Figure 8-9 Creating a reservation

Activity 8-4

Configuring DHCP Options

Time Required: 10 minutes

Objective: Configure router and DNS server options.

Required Tools and Equipment: ServerDC1, ServerDM1, ServerSA1

Description: You have the scope configured and tested. Now you need to add router and DNS server options so that clients are fully functional. First, you configure the 003 Router and 006 DNS Servers options in the scope, and then you configure a different value for the 006 DNS Servers option in the reservation so that you can see reservation options take precedence over scope options.

1. On ServerDM1, in the DHCP console, click the **10.99.0** scope. In the left pane, right-click **Scope Options** and click **Configure Options**.
2. In the Scope Options dialog box, click the **003 Router** check box. In the lower pane, type **10.99.0.250** (or another value if required for your network) in the IP address text box and click **Add**.
3. In the upper pane, click the **006 DNS Servers** check box. Type **10.99.0.220** in the IP address text box and click **Add**. Windows attempts to validate the address. (If ServerDC1 isn't running, a message states that the address is not a valid DNS address and asks whether you still want to add it. Click **Yes**.) Scroll down until you see **015 DNS Domain Name** and click it. Type **AZ800.corp** in the String value box. Click **OK**.
4. In the DHCP console, double-click **Scope Options** in the left pane. You see the three options you just configured (see Figure 8-10).
5. On ServerSA1, in a PowerShell window, type **ipconfig /renew** and press **Enter**. You see that the default gateway is set to 10.99.0.250. Type **ipconfig /all** and press **Enter**. The DNS Servers line under the Ethernet connection should be set to 10.99.0.220 and the Connection-specific DNS Suffix is set to AZ800.corp.

(continues)

Activity 8-4 Continued

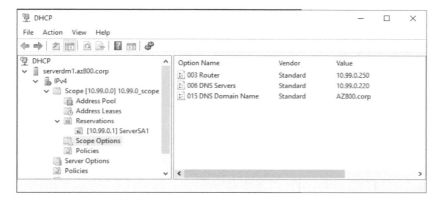

Figure 8-10   Scope options

6. Next, you configure options for the reservation. On ServerDM1, click to expand **Reservations**. Click the **ServerSA1** reservation, then right-click it and click **Configure Options**.
7. Click the **006 DNS Servers** check box. Type **10.99.0.2** in the IP address text box and click **Add**. Click **Yes** in the message box and click **OK**.
8. On ServerSA1, type **ipconfig /renew** and press **Enter**, and then type **ipconfig /all** and press **Enter**. The DNS Servers line under the Ethernet connection should be set to 10.99.0.2 because the reservation option takes precedence over the scope option.
9. On ServerDM1, click **Reservations** in the left pane. Right-click the reservation and click **Delete**. Close the DHCP console.
10. Stay signed in to ServerDM1 and ServerSA1 and continue to the next activity.

DHCP Server Options

Microsoft Exam AZ-800:
Implement and manage an on-premises and hybrid networking infrastructure.
- Manage IP addressing in on-premises and hybrid scenarios

You can perform several DHCP server configuration tasks in the DHCP console. The options you can change depend on whether you right-click the topmost node with the server name or the IPv4 or IPv6 nodes. If you right-click the server node, you see a menu listing the tasks you can perform, most of which are described in the following list:

- *Add/Remove Bindings*—This option is useful on multihomed servers. If the DHCP server has two or more network connections, you might not always want it to respond to DHCP packets from all networks, as when one network is connected to the Internet or a datacenter in which all addresses are statically assigned. You can enable or disable the binding for each interface (see Figure 8-11). When a binding is disabled, it prevents the server from listening for DHCP messages on port UDP 67.
- *Backup*—You can back up the DHCP database, which is stored in *%systemroot%*\System32\dhcp\dhcp.mdb. The backup is stored in *%systemroot%*\System32\dhcp\backup\DhcpCfg by default, but you're prompted to change the path if needed. After you select a path, the DHCP database is backed up, including all scopes, options, exclusion ranges, reservations, and leases.
- *Restore*—If you need to restore a backup of the DHCP database, perhaps after database corruption caused by a system crash, choose this option and the path to the most current backup. When you restore the database, the DHCP server is stopped and restarted after the restore is finished. You should then reconcile the scopes by right-clicking the IPv4 or IPv6 node in the DHCP console and clicking Reconcile All Scopes. You can also reconcile a scope separately by right-clicking it and clicking Reconcile.

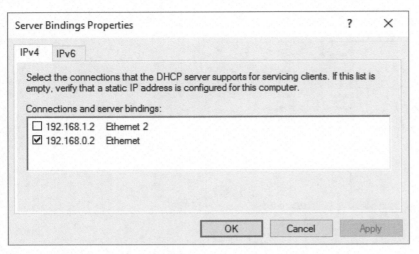

Figure 8-11 The Server Bindings Properties dialog box

- *All Tasks*—If you point to All Tasks, you have the option to start, stop, pause, resume, or restart the DHCP server service.
- *Delete*—Deletes the server from the console but doesn't actually uninstall the DHCP Server role.
- *Refresh*—Refreshes the view.
- *Properties*—Opens the Properties dialog box for the DHCP server, where you can change the default database path and backup path.

The IPv4 and IPv6 nodes have many of the same options, but several are found only in the IPv4 mode. Right-click the IPv4 node to see the menu options described in the following list:

- *Display Statistics*—This option displays statistics about the server and DHCP transactions (see Figure 8-12) that can be useful in troubleshooting problems. For example, a lot of Nacks can indicate an incorrect configuration, such as a corrupt or deactivated scope. A lot of Declines can indicate IP address conflicts. If a DHCP client finds that the leased IP address is in use, it sends a DHCPDECLINE and requests another address.

Server serverdm1.az800.corp Statistics

Description	Details
Start Time	7/5/2022 7:35:45 PM
Up Time	91 Hours, 58 Minutes, 40 Seconds
Discovers	4
Offers	4
Delayed Offers	0
Requests	49
Acks	46
Nacks	3
Declines	0
Releases	0
Total Scopes	1
Scopes with delay configured	0
Total Addresses	95
In Use	1 (1%)
Available	94 (98%)

Refresh   Close

Figure 8-12 Server statistics

- *New Scope*—Starts the New Scope Wizard.
- *New Superscope*—Starts the New Superscope Wizard. This option is available only under the IPv4 node because IPv6 doesn't support superscopes.
- *New Multicast Scope*—Starts the New Multicast Scope Wizard.
- *Configure Failover* and *Replicate Failover Scopes*—These options configure high availability for DHCP services. You can configure fault tolerance and load balancing of DHCP services by allowing two DHCP servers to provide IP address and DHCP option information for the same scopes. The servers replicate configuration and lease information with each other to ensure that both servers have current data for leasing IP addresses to clients. Configuring high availability for DHCP is covered later in this module. Failover isn't an option in IPv6.
- *Define User Classes* and *Define Vendor Classes*—These options are used to define User Class and Vendor Class values that can be used in DHCP policies.
- *Reconcile All Scopes*—If the lease information shown in the DHCP console doesn't seem to reflect the actual client leases or if the database appears corrupted, use this option to try to solve the problem. It attempts to fix inconsistencies between DHCP summary lease information stored in the Registry and detailed lease information stored in the DHCP database. If no problems are found, DHCP reports that the database is consistent. If inconsistencies are found, the inconsistent addresses are listed in the Reconcile All Scopes dialog box. Select the addresses listed and click Reconcile. The reconcile process restores an inconsistent address to the original DHCP client or creates a temporary reservation for the address. When the lease time expires with a temporary reservation or a renewal attempt is made, the address is returned to the scope. This option isn't available for IPv6 scopes.
- *Set Predefined Options*—Using this selection, you can create custom DHCP options. One use is to create the 060 PXEClient option required for some configurations of Windows Deployment Services (WDS), as discussed later in the "Configuring DHCP for PXE Boot" section. Some specialized IP devices, such as Voice over IP (VoIP) phones, might also require custom options.
- *Properties*—This option opens the Properties dialog box for the IPv4 server, as discussed next.

Configuring IPv4 Server Properties

The IPv4 Properties dialog box has these five tabs:

- *General*—Specify statistics and logging parameters (see Figure 8-13). In addition, if you enable the "Show the BOOTP table folder" option, a new folder is added under the IPv4 node in the DHCP console so that you can configure BOOTP support. BOOTP is a remote boot protocol that devices use to boot from an image stored on a server.

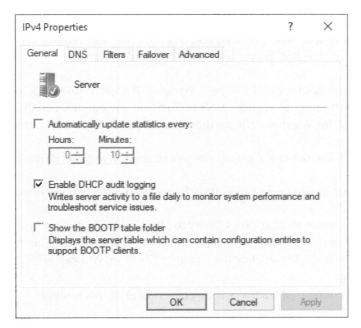

Figure 8-13   The General tab for IPv4 Properties

- *DNS*—Configure how DHCP interacts with a DNS server for making dynamic updates on behalf of DHCP clients (see Figure 8-14). You can configure the following settings:

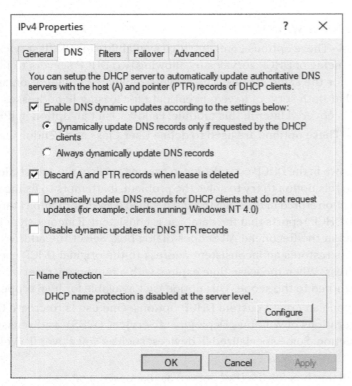

Figure 8-14 The DNS tab for IPv4 Properties

- ○ Dynamically update DNS records only if requested by the DHCP clients: This option is selected by default. When a client leases an IP address or renews a lease and sends option 81 in the DHCPREQUEST packet, the DHCP server attempts to register records dynamically with the DNS server on behalf of the client. Option 81 in the DHCPREQUEST packet contains the client's FQDN. By default, Windows clients configure option 81 so that the client updates its own A record and requests that the server update the PTR record.
- ○ Always dynamically update DNS records: If this option is set, the DHCP server always attempts to register A and PTR records for the client as long as the client supports option 81.
- ○ Discard A and PTR records when lease is deleted: If a lease is deleted and this option is selected (it's selected by default), the DHCP server attempts to contact the DNS server to delete the A and PTR records associated with the lease.
- ○ Dynamically update DNS records for DHCP clients that do not request updates: If a client doesn't support option 81 and this option is set, the server attempts to register DNS records on the client's behalf. (You have to go all the way back to Windows NT 4.0 for Windows clients that don't support option 81, but some modern non-Windows clients may not support it.)
- ○ Disable dynamic update for DNS PTR records: If set, the DHCP server doesn't attempt to register PTR records for DHCP clients.
- ○ Name Protection: Click the Configure button to enable name protection. Name protection is discussed later in the section called "DHCP Name Protection."
- *Filters*—In this tab (see Figure 8-15), you can configure MAC address filters to allow or deny DHCP services to computers based on their MAC addresses. You can only enable or disable the allow or deny list. To configure the lists, you use the Filters node under the IPv4 node. If you click the Advanced button, you can select from a list of hardware types to exempt from filtering.
- *Failover*—Configure and view failover status, if configured. Failover is discussed later in this module.

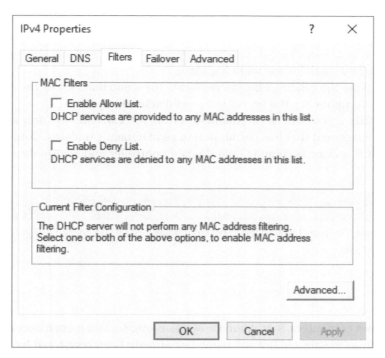

Figure 8-15   The Filters tab for IPv4 Properties

- *Advanced*—In this tab (see Figure 8-16), you configure the following options:

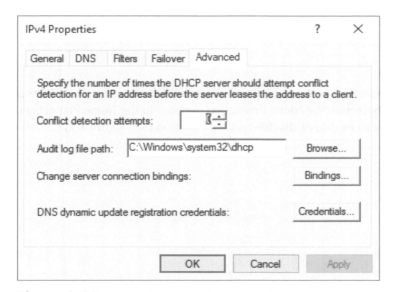

Figure 8-16   The Advanced tab for IPv4 Properties

○ Conflict detection attempts: If enabled, **conflict detection** causes the DHCP server to attempt to ping an IP address before it's offered to a client to make sure the address isn't already in use. Conflict detection attempts can be set between 0 and 5, which specifies how many `ping` packets the server should send before assuming the address isn't in use. By default, conflict detection attempts are set to 0, which disables conflict detection. In most cases, the server never sends a `ping` packet because it must first send an ARP (Address Resolution Protocol) request to get a MAC address, unless it has an entry for the IP address in its ARP cache already. In any case, the DHCP server must time out between attempts before trying another attempt or proceeding with the lease, which slows down the DHCP lease process. Because most client computers perform conflict detection before accepting an offered address, conflict detection should be enabled on the DHCP server only if the server is receiving many DHCPDECLINE messages. After the problem is remedied, conflict detection should be disabled.

- Audit log file path: You can change the default path for the audit log file.
- Change server connection bindings: Clicking the Bindings button performs the same function as the Add/Remove Bindings option you see when you right-click the server node (as discussed earlier).
- DNS dynamic update registration credentials: If you click the Credentials button, you can enter the username, domain name, and password for a domain account that has permission to send dynamic updates. Configuring credentials is needed only if the DHCP service is running on a domain controller and secure dynamic DNS update is enabled.

Note 7

The IPv6 Properties dialog box has only the General, DNS, and Advanced tabs; they have largely the same configuration options as these tabs in the IPv4 Properties dialog box.

DHCP Name Protection

On networks with both Windows and non-Windows computers, a problem known as **name squatting** can occur when a non-Windows computer registers its name with a DNS server, but the name has already been registered by a Windows computer. Name squatting isn't a problem on networks where all computers are members of a Windows domain because Active Directory ensures that all computer names are unique.

DHCP name protection prevents name squatting by non-Windows computers by using a DHCP resource record called Dynamic Host Configuration Identifier (DHCID). It's a resource record used by DHCP and DNS to verify that a name being registered in DNS is from the original computer that registered it if the name already exists. DHCP name protection can be configured at the scope level or the IPv4 and IPv6 server node levels. If it's configured at the IPv4 or IPv6 server level, all the corresponding scopes are configured. Name protection configured at the scope level doesn't affect other scopes.

Configuring DHCP Name Protection

To configure name protection, right-click the scope, IPv4 node, or IPv6 node in the DHCP console and click Properties. Click the DNS tab, and then click the Configure button in the Name Protection section. In the Name Protection dialog box, click the Enable Name Protection check box to enable or disable name protection (see Figure 8-17).

Figure 8-17 Configuring name protection

Configuring Scope Properties

To access a scope's properties, right-click it and click Properties. The Scope Properties dialog box has three tabs:

- *General*—In the General tab (see Figure 8-18), you can change the scope name and the start and end IP addresses, but you can't change the subnet mask (prefix length). You can also change the lease duration, which by default is 8 days. This duration is fine for a typical office environment where the same computers are used each day. Having a long lease duration prevents unnecessary traffic from frequent lease renewals. However, you might want a shorter lease time in a less predictable environment where lots of computers are used for brief periods and then not used again for long periods or ever, as in a testing or training environment that uses a lot of virtual machines (VMs). Another example is a wireless network in a public setting, where mobile devices come and go constantly. You might also set a short lease duration if you're planning to make changes to the IP addressing scheme that require a major scope change. As the time for the change approaches, you can make the lease time shorter and shorter until it's less than a day. You can make the scope change overnight or over a weekend; the short lease time ensures that all clients need to renew their lease within a short period. Renewal requests are denied; instead, clients are assigned addresses from the new scope.

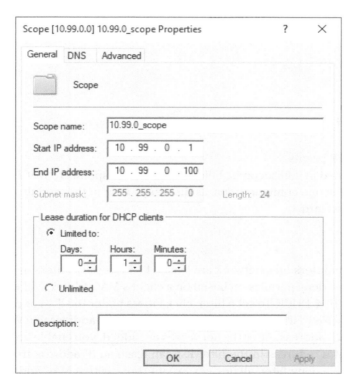

Figure 8-18   The General tab for scope properties

- *DNS*—This tab contains the same dynamic DNS configuration options as the DNS tab in the IPv4 Properties dialog box, as discussed earlier, but it pertains to only a single scope rather than all scopes.
- *Advanced*—Configure which type of clients the server responds to (see Figure 8-19):
  - DHCP: The default setting; the server responds only to DHCP client requests.
  - BOOTP: The server responds to BOOTP clients.

Note 8

If BOOTP or DHCP is selected, you can choose a maximum lease duration for BOOTP clients.

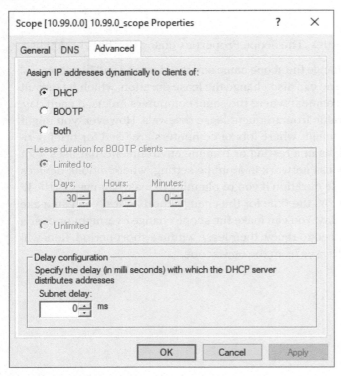

Figure 8-19   The Advanced tab for scope properties

> ○ Both: The server responds to DHCP and BOOTP clients.
> ○ Delay configuration: You can set a delay, specified in milliseconds, before the server responds to DHCPDIS-COVER messages. This option is useful in split scope configurations, as discussed later in the module, and is configured automatically by the split scope wizard.

Configuring Filters

DHCP filters allow administrators to restrict which computers on a network are leased IP addresses. Filters use MAC addresses as the filtering criteria, so it's a simple allow or deny permission based on a client's MAC address. Filters are configured under the IPv4 node and aren't available for IPv6 DHCP. To set a filter, click Filters under the IPv4 node, and then right-click Allow or Deny and click New Filter. In the New Filter dialog box, you add each MAC address you want to allow or deny, along with an optional description for each address. After the addresses are added, you enable the filter.

If you create an allow filter, only a device with a MAC address in the filter list can lease an IP address from the DHCP server. All other devices are denied. If you create a deny filter, all devices except those with a MAC address in the filter list can lease an address from the DHCP server.

You can add addresses to the allow or deny filter from the list of current address leases instead of manually adding each address. To do so, click Address Leases under a scope and select one or more addresses you want to add to a filter. Right-click a selected address, point to Add to Filter, and click Allow or Deny to add the selected addresses to the filter.

Configuring Policies

DHCP policies give administrators more fine-tuned control over address lease options through the use of conditions. A policy contains conditions that specify one or more clients to which IP address settings should be delivered. Conditions can be based on a number of criteria, and more than one criterion can be used in a condition with `AND` and `OR` operators. You can create policy conditions with any combination of the following criteria:

- *Vendor Class*—Defined earlier, the Vendor Class is most often used by device or OS manufacturers to identify a type of device or OS. Vendor Classes can be used to identify VoIP phones, printers, mobile devices, and so forth. For example, you can create the condition "Vendor Class equals Hewlett-Packard JetDirect" to identify all HP printers.

> **Note 9**
>
> Finding the Vendor Class in a device's documentation can be difficult. One way to discover this information is to set up the device on the network, configure it to use DHCP, and then capture the DHCP packets it transmits with a protocol analyzer, such as Wireshark. The Vendor Class is in the DHCPDISCOVER packet in the Option 60 field.

- *User Class*—This is similar to the Vendor Class, except a **User Class** can be a custom value you create on the DHCP server and then configure on a DHCP client. For example, if you have special settings you want the DHCP server to deliver to all computers in the Engineering Department, you can create a User Class named Engineering and then configure the network interface on the relevant computers with this User Class. To configure this User Class on a Windows computer, type `ipconfig /setclassid Ethernet "Engineering"`, which sets the User Class on the Ethernet network connection to Engineering.
- *MAC address*—You can use wildcards with a list of MAC addresses so that you can use the organizationally unique identifier (OUI) part of the MAC address to specify a manufacturer. The OUI is the first 24 bits of a MAC address. For example, you can create the condition "MAC address equals 000F34*" to identify certain types of Cisco routers.
- *Client identifier*—The client identifier (ClientID) is usually the MAC address but can also be the GUID of the NIC on a PXE client.
- *Fully qualified domain name*—An FQDN can be used only to configure DNS-related configuration information, such as dynamic DNS registration. You can use this criterion to match computers based on their FQDNs and use wildcards to group computers based on their hostnames or DNS suffixes. For example, you can create a condition such as "Fully qualified domain name equals *.csmtech.corp," which matches computers with an FQDN ending with csmtech.corp. You can also use this criterion to identify workgroup computers (computers that aren't domain members).
- *Relay agent information*—This criterion is useful when a wireless access point acts as a DHCP relay, sending DHCP requests to the DHCP server on behalf of wireless clients. You can assign wireless clients' IP addresses with a shorter lease time and perhaps a different default gateway and DNS server. To create a condition based on relay agent information (DHCP option 82), you enter a hexadecimal code provided by the relay agent's manufacturer.

Policies can be configured at the server level or the scope level. Scope-level policies take precedence over server-level policies if both are configured and there's a conflict. Server-level policies are limited to assigning DHCP options and lease duration to clients matching the policy conditions. Scope-level policies can also issue IP addresses from a specified range to matching clients. For example, if the scope has the start address 10.99.0.1 and end address 10.99.0.254 with the prefix length 24, the policy can specify that all matching clients are issued an address in the range 10.99.0.100 through 10.99.0.150. To create a policy, just right-click the Policies node under the IPv4 node or the scope and click New Policy to start the DHCP Policy Configuration Wizard. Then follow these steps:

1. Give the policy a name and an optional description.
2. Create one or more conditions that identify devices.
3. Configure settings for the policy, such as the router and DNS servers.
4. Configure additional settings in the policy's Properties dialog box. You can configure a lease time and DNS settings and make changes to other settings that were configured in the wizard.

Configuring DHCP for PXE Boot

If you're using Windows Deployment Services (WDS) to install Windows OSs on computers, you might need to configure DHCP to respond to **Preboot Execution Environment (PXE)** network interfaces. PXE is a network environment built into many network interface cards (NICs) that allows a computer to boot from an image stored on a network server. WDS uses this feature to install the Windows OS remotely. When you configure the WDS role service, the DHCP configuration is often handled by the WDS configuration wizard, but in some circumstances, you need to configure DHCP options manually.

If a Microsoft DHCP server and WDS are on the same server and all potential WDS clients are on the same network as the WDS server, you don't have to change any DHCP settings. However, if the DHCP server is on a different server or a different subnet, you do. Here are the most common setups that require special DHCP configuration:

- *The DHCP server is on a different server or a different subnet from the WDS server*—You must configure two DHCP server options. For Option 066 Boot Server Host Name, you can supply the WDS server's IP address or server name. Option 067 Bootfile Name is the name and path of the boot file that WDS clients need to start remote OS installation.

- *DHCP is installed on the same server as WDS, but it's not a Microsoft DHCP server or the Microsoft DHCP server was installed after WDS was installed*—In this case, you need to configure a predefined DHCP option with code 060. (This option was discussed earlier in the "DHCP Server Configuration" section.) Add the 060 PXEClient option to the DHCP server by right-clicking the IPv4 node in the DHCP console and clicking Set Predefined Options. Click Add, and then fill in the dialog box shown in Figure 8-20. Click OK. In the resulting dialog box, type the WDS server's IP address or name in the String text box, and click OK. Under the IPv4 node, right-click Server Options, click Configure Options, and then click 060 PXEClient to enable the option. When PXE clients request an IP address, this option instructs them to contact the specified WDS server to get their boot configuration.

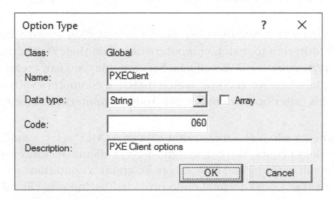

Figure 8-20   Creating the PXEClient option

DHCP Relay Agents

A **DHCP relay agent** is a device that listens for broadcast DHCPDISCOVER and DHCPREQUEST messages and forwards them to a DHCP server on another subnet. You configure a DHCP relay agent on a subnet that doesn't have a DHCP server so that you can still manage DHCP addresses from a central server without having to configure the DHCP server with network interfaces in each subnet. In this setup, a DHCP server is configured on one subnet and has multiple scopes configured, one for each subnet in the internetwork that has DHCP clients (as shown in Figure 8-21). This figure shows three subnets. The DHCP server in the 10.1.1.0/24 subnet has three scopes configured, one for each of the three subnets. When a DHCP client in the 10.1.2.0 or 10.1.3.0 subnet requests an IP address, the DHCP relay agent in the same subnet forwards the request to the DHCP server on the 10.1.1.0 subnet.

The details of the DHCP relay process are as follows:

1. A client on the same subnet as the DHCP relay agent sends a DHCPDISCOVER broadcast requesting an IP address.

2. The relay agent forwards the message to the DHCP server's IP address as a unicast.

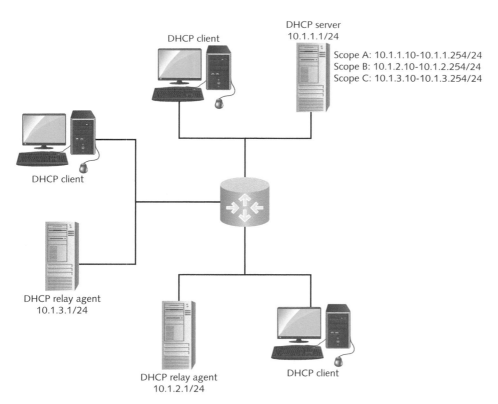

Figure 8-21   DHCP relay agents

3. The DHCP server receives the unicast DHCPDISCOVER. The relay agent's address is contained in the message, so the DHCP server knows to draw an address from the scope matching the relay agent's IP address. For example, if the relay agent has the address 10.1.2.10, the DHCP server looks for a scope containing a range of addresses that includes 10.1.2.10.
4. The DHCP server sends a unicast DHCPOFFER message to the relay agent.
5. The relay agent forwards the DHCPOFFER as a broadcast to the subnet the DHCPDISCOVER was received from. Because the client doesn't yet have an IP address, the agent must forward the DHCPOFFER as a broadcast message.
6. The DHCP client broadcasts a DHCPREQUEST.
7. The relay agent receives the DHCPREQUEST and forwards it to the DHCP server.
8. The DHCP server replies with a DHCPACK to the relay agent.
9. The relay agent forwards the DHCPACK to the client, and the client binds the address to its interface.
10. Renewal requests are unicast packets, so the DHCP client can communicate directly with the DHCP server for renewals.

Installing a DHCP Relay Agent

The DHCP relay agent function is configured as part of the Routing role service under the Remote Access server role. To make a Windows Server 2022 server a DHCP relay agent, follow these steps:

1. Install the Remote Access server role and include the Routing role service.
2. In the Routing and Remote Access console, right-click the server node, click Configure, and click Enable Routing and Remote Access.
3. In the Routing and Remote Access Server Setup Wizard, click Next, and then click Custom configuration.
4. In the Custom Configuration window, click the LAN routing check box (see Figure 8-22). Click Next and then Finish. Click Start service when prompted.

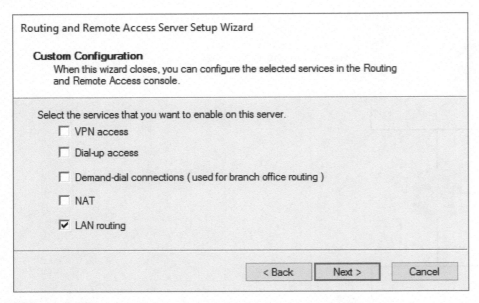

Figure 8-22   The Custom Configuration window

5. In the Routing and Remote Access console, expand the IPv4 node, right-click the General node, and click New Routing Protocol. Click DHCP Relay Agent. If you have more than one interface, you see other options in addition to DHCP Relay Agent. Click OK.
6. In the Routing and Remote Access console, right-click DHCP Relay Agent and click New Interface. Click the interface for which you want the server to provide relay services and click OK. If the server has more than one network connection, you can add interfaces.
7. In the DHCP Relay Properties dialog box, accept the default settings (see Figure 8-23) and click OK.

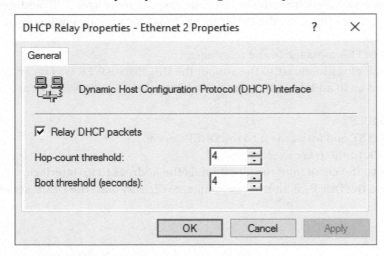

Figure 8-23   Setting DHCP relay properties

8. In the Routing and Remote Access console, right-click DHCP Relay Agent and click Properties. Type the address of the DHCP server to which the relay agent should forward DHCP messages, and then click Add. You can add more than one address if you're using load balancing. Click OK. The relay agent is configured to send DHCP messages to the specified IP address.

Note 10

A DHCP server can't be configured as a DHCP relay agent.

Server Migration, Export, and Import

If you need to migrate the DHCP server role to another server, you can do so fairly easily by exporting the server configuration and database to a file and then importing that file on another server. To migrate a DHCP server from Server1 to Server2, follow these steps:

1. On Server1, create a folder named C:\Export or something similar and then go to that folder. Export the DHCP server configuration and database using one of the following methods:

   - Use the following PowerShell cmdlet:

     ```
     Export-DhcpServer -File Dhcp.xml -Leases
     ```

   - Use the following Command Prompt command:

     ```
     netsh dhcp server export Dhcp.txt all
     ```

2. On Server1, copy the exported file to Server2. For example, use the command `copy dhcp.xml \\server2\c$` to copy the file to the root of the C: drive on Server2.
3. Unauthorize the DHCP server, stop the DHCP service, or uninstall the DHCP Server role on Server1.
4. On Server2, install the DHCP server role and authorize it, if necessary.
5. On Server2, import the exported file using one of the following methods:

   - Use the following PowerShell cmdlet:

     ```
     Import-DhcpServer -File C:\Dhcp.xml -Leases -BackupPath C:\dhcpback
     ```

   - Use the following Command Prompt command:

     ```
     netsh dhcp server import C:\Dhcp.txt all
     ```

6. On Server2, verify that the scope and existing leases were imported and the DHCP service is running.

In the preceding procedure, the `-Leases` option of the PowerShell cmdlet specifies that current lease data should be exported and imported. If you only want to migrate the configuration and scopes, you can omit that option.

Troubleshooting DHCP

DHCP is a generally reliable protocol, but things can and do go wrong from time to time. The following is a list of possible problems, symptoms, and solutions for troubleshooting DHCP:

- *A client is not receiving a DHCP address*—A Windows DHCP client assigns itself an APIPA address in the range 169.254.0.0/16 if no DHCP server responds to its DHCPDISCOVER message. Verify that the DHCP service is running and authorized, that the scope is activated, and that addresses are available in the scope. If the client was recently moved to a different subnet and a reservation exists for the client from the old subnet, its request for an address will be denied because the reservation is for an address in the wrong subnet. In this case, delete the reservation and create a new one.
- *A client is receiving an incorrect DHCP address*—Another DHCP server might be operating on the subnet. Check the IP address of the DHCP server from which the client received the address (run `ipconfig /all` from a command prompt) and verify its identity.
- *IP address conflicts are occurring*—This can happen if there is a rogue DHCP server on the network or if the DHCP database needs to be reconciled. Check server statistics for a high number of Declines, which can be an indication of address conflicts resulting from rogue DHCP servers. Verify the identity of DHCP servers on the network and reconcile all scopes. In addition, look for addresses that are assigned statically. Be sure to create exclusions for statically assigned addresses.
- *The DHCP server service is not starting*—Verify that the server is authorized. Check for a corrupt scope. Reconcile the scope, if necessary. Restore the database from a backup if the scope data appears to be corrupted.

- *No addresses are being leased*—Verify that the DHCP service is running and authorized and that the scope is activated. Verify that addresses are available in the scope. For single-subnet deployments, verify that the scope is in the same subnet as the server's IP address. For DHCPv6, make sure the server has been assigned an IPv6 address with the same prefix as the scope. In multisubnet deployments, make sure the DHCP relay is configured with the correct IP address of the DHCP server. Also, verify the server bindings from the Server Bindings Properties dialog box (shown earlier in Figure 8-11).

DHCP Troubleshooting Tools

There are a number of tools you can use to troubleshoot DHCP. We've discussed some of them, including reviewing DHCP server statistics and reconciling scopes. If you need to see what's happening between your DHCP server and clients, use a third-party protocol analyzer such as Wireshark. Configure the protocol analyzer to capture packets on UDP ports 67 and 68; then, from a client station, issue the `ipconfig /release` and `ipconfig /renew` commands to generate DHCP messages.

Another troubleshooting tool is the built-in DHCP audit logging feature, which is enabled by default (recall Figure 8-13). The logging file shows information about when addresses were leased, renewed, and released, as well as information about DNS updates attempted by the DHCP server. The log also shows when the server was authorized and when the service started and stopped. The log file is a simple text file you can open with Notepad or any text editor; it can be found by default in C:\Windows\System32\dhcp.

Self-Check Questions

5. What should you configure on a multihomed server if you don't want the server to respond to DHCP packets on one or more interfaces?

   a. Bindings   **c.** Options
   b. Exclusions   **d.** Classes

6. How many conflict detections are configured on a DHCP server by default?

   a. 3   **c.** 1
   b. 2   **d.** 0

⊙ Check your answers at the end of this module.

Activity 8-5

Creating a DHCP Policy

Time Required: 10 minutes
Objective: Create a DHCP policy.
Required Tools and Equipment: ServerDC1, ServerDM1, ServerSA1
Description: Suppose you have new Cisco VoIP phones that require different IP address settings from the rest of the devices on the network. You decide to create a policy to deliver different options to these phones. In this activity, you create a new User Class so that you can test the policy with your ServerSA1 computer. In a real situation, the phones would have a defined Vendor Class, so if you were following these steps for actual Cisco IP phones, you would replace User Class with Vendor Class each time you see it in this activity.

1. On ServerDM1, in the DHCP console, click to expand the server node and the **IPv4** node, if necessary.
2. To create a new User Class, right-click the **IPv4** node and click **Define User Classes**. In the DHCP User Classes dialog box, click **Add**. In the New Class dialog box, type **Cisco IP Phone** in the Display name text box and **Cisco Voice over IP phones** in the Description text box.
3. In the lower pane of the New Class dialog box, click in the box under ASCII and type **Cisco IP Phone** (see Figure 8-24). This is the actual Vendor Class ID used by DHCP; the display name might not be the same. Click **OK** and then **Close**.

(continues)

Activity 8-5 Continued

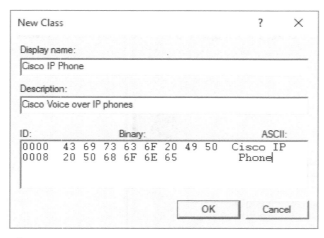

Figure 8-24   The New Class dialog box

4. Under the IPv4 node, right-click **Policies** and click **New Policy**. In the DHCP Policy Configuration Wizard, type **Cisco VoIP Policy** and click **Next**.
5. In the Configure Conditions for the policy window, click **Add**.
6. In the Add/Edit Condition dialog box, click the arrow to see the available criteria in the Criteria list box, and click **User Class**. In the Operator list box, you have the choice of Equals or Not Equals. Leave the default setting **Equals**.
7. In the Value(s) section, click the **Value** list arrow and click **Cisco IP Phone**. Because there might be different models of Cisco IP phones, click the **Append wildcard** check box so that the condition is "User Class Equals Cisco IP Phone*," meaning any string can come after "Phone," and the User Class will match. Click **Add** (see Figure 8-25), and then click **Ok**.

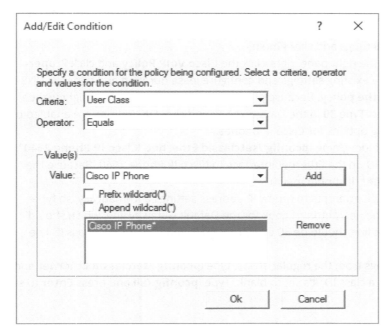

Figure 8-25   Adding a condition

(continues)

Activity 8-5 Continued

8. In the Configure Conditions for the policy window, you see the line "User Class Equals Cisco IP Phone*."
   You can add conditions if needed (see Figure 8-26). Leave the **OR** option button selected and click **Next**.

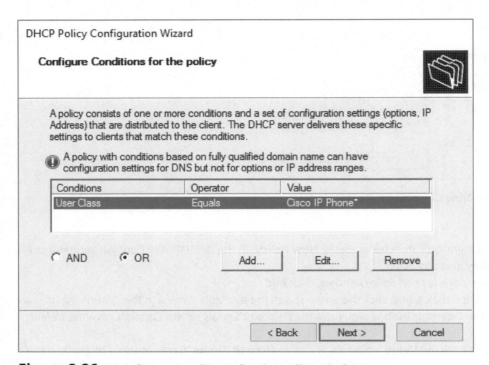

Figure 8-26 Configure Conditions for the policy window

9. In the Configure settings for the policy window, you select the DHCP options you want to apply to the
   selected devices. You might want a different default gateway for these devices, so click the **003 Router**
   check box. Type **10.99.0.251** in the IP address text box and click **Add**. Click **Next**.
10. In the Summary window, check your settings and click **Finish**.
11. Click **Policies** in the DHCP console. In the right pane, right-click the **Cisco VoIP Policy** and click **Proper-
    ties**. In this dialog box, you can change existing settings and configure lease duration and dynamic DNS
    settings. Click **Set lease duration for the policy**. Because phones are on all the time, you might want a
    longer lease duration for these devices. Type **30** in the Days text box and click **OK**. Policies are enabled by
    default, so you're ready to start serving options for Cisco IP phones.
12. On ServerSA1, from the PowerShell window, type **ipconfig /setclassid Ethernet "Cisco IP Phone 2640"**
    and press **Enter** to set the User Class ID on the Ethernet interface to Cisco IP Phone 2640. Because the
    policy specifies to match Cisco IP Phone*, it should match.
13. When you change the class ID on a PC, it attempts to renew IP address settings automatically, so type
    ipconfig /all and press **Enter** to see the new settings. Look for the Default Gateway line, which should
    now be 10.99.0.251. The Lease Expires line should be 30 days from now, and the DHCPv4 Class ID line
    should be set to Cisco IP Phone 2640.
14. To delete the class ID and get IP settings from the regular scope, type **ipconfig /setclassid Ethernet** and
    press **Enter**. Because you didn't enter a class ID, it's set to blank. Type **ipconfig /all** and press **Enter** to see
    that your settings are back to normal.
15. Continue to the next activity.

Activity 8-6

Creating a DHCP Filter

Time Required: 10 minutes
Objective: Create a DHCP filter.
Required Tools and Equipment: ServerDC1, ServerDM1, ServerSA1
Description: In this activity, you configure DHCP Allow and Deny filters. First, you create an Allow filter manually, and then you create a Deny filter from an existing lease.

1. On ServerDM1, in the DHCP console, click to expand the server node and the **IPv4** node, if necessary.
2. In the left pane, click to expand **Filters**. In the left pane, right-click **Allow** and click **New Filter**. In the New Filter dialog box, type **123456789012** in the MAC address text box. In the Description text box, type **Sample filter**, and then click **Add**. Click **Close**.
3. In the left pane, click **Allow** to see the new filter in the middle pane. Notice that the Allow node has a red down arrow, indicating that the filter isn't enabled. You won't test this filter, so you can leave it disabled.
4. Now you'll add a filter from an existing lease. Click to expand the **10.99.0_scope**, and then click **Address Leases**. In the middle pane, right-click the lease for ServerSA1, point to **Add to Filter**, and click **Deny** to add ServerSA1's MAC address to the Deny filter.
5. In the left pane, click the **Deny** filter to see the new entry for ServerSA1. (You might need to click the Refresh icon.) Right-click the **Deny** filter and click **Enable**.
6. On ServerSA1, in the PowerShell window, type **ipconfig /renew** and press **Enter**. After a while, you see an error message that the address couldn't be renewed. Type **ipconfig** and press **Enter**. Because the lease hasn't expired, ServerSA1 still has its IP address. The deny filter keeps clients from getting a new address or renewing an address, but it doesn't prevent them from keeping an address that's already leased.
7. Type **ipconfig /release** and press **Enter**, and then type **ipconfig /renew** and press **Enter**. ServerSA1 is unable to lease an IP address.
8. On ServerDM1, in the DHCP console, right-click the **Deny** filter and click **Disable**.
9. On ServerSA1, type **ipconfig /renew** and press **Enter**. ServerSA1 can lease an address again.
10. Continue to the next activity.

DHCP High Availability

Microsoft Exam AZ-800:
Implement and manage an on-premises and hybrid networking infrastructure.
- Manage IP addressing in on-premises and hybrid scenarios

DHCP is a crucial service in networks that use it. If the DHCP server fails to respond to client requests, clients can't communicate on the network. Microsoft offers the following ways to achieve high availability for DHCP:

- Split scopes
- DHCP failover
- DHCP server cluster
- Hot standby

Using a DHCP server cluster requires a complex network setup, including shared storage for the DHCP database that multiple DHCP servers access. This method works well, but setup and configuration can be difficult, and the shared storage can be a single point of failure. The hot standby method consists of two DHCP servers configured with identical scopes and options. If the primary DHCP server fails, an administrator must manually restore the

DHCP database from backup to the standby server, which might not have the most recent lease data. The following sections cover the most recommended methods for providing DHCP high availability and fault tolerance: split scopes and DHCP failover.

DHCP Split Scopes

A **split scope** is a fault-tolerant DHCP configuration in which two DHCP servers share the same scope information, allowing both servers to offer DHCP services to clients. One server is configured as the primary DHCP server and the other as the secondary. In most cases, the secondary server leases addresses only if the primary server is unavailable. The DHCP Server role has the DHCP Split-Scope Configuration Wizard to automate the process of configuring a split scope. You create a split scope by using the wizard as follows:

1. Install the DHCP Server role on two servers designated DHCP1 and DHCP2 for this example. DHCP1 is the primary DHCP server, and DHCP2 is the secondary.
2. Create a scope on DHCP1, including any options, and activate it.
3. Run the DHCP Split-Scope Wizard on DHCP1. To do so, right-click the scope in the DHCP console, point to Advanced, and then click Split-Scope. The wizard prompts you for the following information:

   - The name or address of the secondary DHCP server.
   - The percentage of split (see Figure 8-27). A typical split percentage is 80/20, meaning the primary server can lease 80 percent of the addresses and the secondary server has 20 percent, but you can configure the split as needed for your environment. If you're configuring the split scope for load balancing rather than fault tolerance, you can set the split to 50 percent.

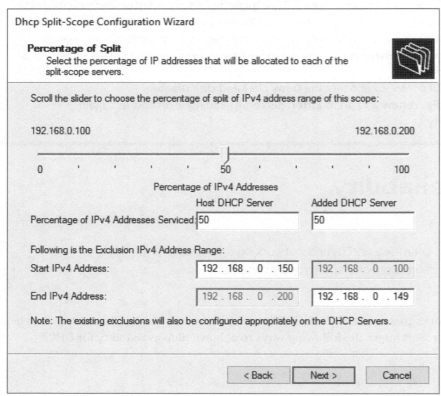

Figure 8-27   Setting the percentage of split

   - Delay in DHCP offer. Specify the number of milliseconds each server should delay between receiving a DHCPDISCOVER and sending a DHCPOFFER. You usually set the primary server for a 0 delay. You want the secondary server to delay long enough that the primary server services most client requests. You might have to adjust this value until you get the intended results. A value of 1000 is a good place to start. If you're configuring a split scope for load balancing, leave the delay at 0 for both servers. Both servers will respond to all requests, but the client will accept only the first response. With the delay set at 0 for both servers and assuming similar load and network conditions, each server should be the first to respond about half the time, which is what you want in a load-balancing arrangement.

4. The wizard creates the scope on the secondary server and creates the necessary exclusion range, according to the split percentage on both servers, to ensure that IP addresses aren't duplicated.
5. Create reservations on both servers. If you're using reservations, you need to create them manually on both servers so that either server can offer reserved addresses; the split scope function doesn't replicate reservations.

One problem with split scopes is that if one DHCP server fails, the lease information it stores is lost. In addition, because the second server has only a portion of the IP addresses available to lease, it could run out of IP addresses before the failed server is back up and running. Both these problems are solved by DHCP failover, as discussed next.

Note 11

Split scopes are an option only on IPv4 scopes, not on IPv6 scopes.

DHCP Failover

DHCP failover allows two DHCP servers to share the pool of addresses in a scope, giving both servers access to all the addresses in the pool. Lease information is replicated between the servers, so if one server goes down, the other server maintains the lease information. Like split scopes, DHCP failover is available only in IPv4 scopes; if you need fault tolerance for IPv6 scopes, you have to use traditional server clustering or hot standby servers. There are two modes for DHCP failover:

- *Load-balancing mode*—With **load-balancing mode**, the default, both DHCP servers participate in address leasing at the same time. You can configure the load-balancing priority if you want one server to service the majority of DHCP clients. If one server fails, the other server takes over all leasing duties, and because the DHCP database is replicated between the servers, no lease information is lost.
- *Hot standby mode*—With **hot standby mode**, one server is assigned as the active server that provides DHCP services to clients while the other server is placed in standby mode. The standby server begins providing DHCP services if the primary server becomes unresponsive.

Because DHCP failover is configured per scope, not per server, you can configure load balancing for one scope and hot standby for another. In addition, with hot standby mode, you can configure one server as the primary server for one scope and the secondary server for another scope.

Caution !

DHCP failover requires close time synchronization between servers. Server clocks should be synchronized within one minute of each other, so make certain all servers use the same reliable time source.

Configuring Load-Balancing Mode

You configure DHCP failover in the DHCP console by right-clicking the IPv4 node or the target scope and then clicking Configure Failover. The Configure Failover Wizard guides you through the process, including whether you want to use load sharing or hot standby mode. In the first window, you choose the scope or scopes on which you want to configure failover. If you configure failover from the IPv4 node, all scopes are listed and selected by default.

Note 12

You can configure DHCP failover with the `Add-DhcpServerV4Failover` PowerShell cmdlet.

Next, you choose the partner server, which must be an authorized server that already has the DHCP Server service configured. If any servers have an existing failover configuration, you can select one from a list.

In the next window, you name the failover relationship and choose whether the failover configuration will be load balancing or hot standby. By default, the relationship name is composed of the names of the servers. Load balancing is the default configuration mode, and you configure the following additional parameters (see Figure 8-28):

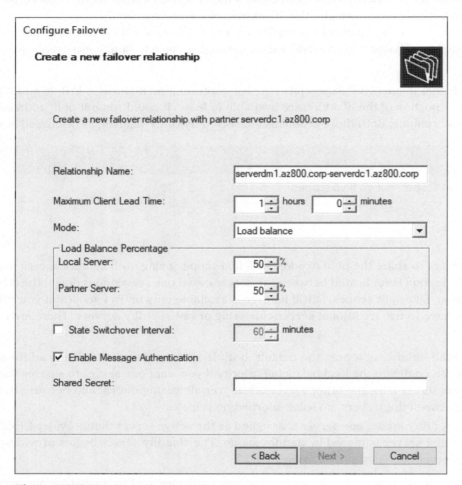

Figure 8-28   Configuring failover parameters

- *Maximum Client Lead Time*—The **maximum client lead time (MCLT)** defines the maximum amount of time a DHCP server can extend a lease for a DHCP client without the partner server's knowledge. It also defines the amount of time a server waits before assuming control over all DHCP services if its partner is in Partner Down state. In Partner Down state, the DHCP server assumes that its failover partner is no longer operational.
- *Load Balance Percentage*—Define the percentage of client requests serviced by each server. The default value is 50 percent for each server.
- *State Switchover Interval*—When a DHCP server loses communication with its partner, it enters the Communication Interrupted state, whereby each server operates independently but assumes the other server is still operational. If the State Switchover Interval option is enabled, you can define the time in which a server transitions from Communication Interrupted state to Partner Down state. By default, this option isn't enabled; an administrator must manually configure Partner Down state.
- *Enable Message Authentication*—To increase security, you can enable authentication between failover partners, an option that is configured by default. If you use this option, you must enter a shared secret on both DHCP servers.

Finally, review the selected options and click Finish to create the failover relationship. After the failover relationship is established, both inbound and outbound rules for TCP port 647 (DHCP Server Failover) are configured on the Windows firewall to allow communication between the two servers.

Configuring Hot Standby Mode

The process for configuring hot standby mode is almost identical to configuring load-balancing mode, with the following exceptions:

- Select the Hot standby option for the failover mode.
- Instead of choosing a load-balancing percentage, specify whether the failover partner is the active server or the standby server, and assign a percentage of addresses reserved for the standby server (see Figure 8-29).

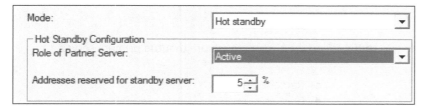

Figure 8-29 Configuring hot standby mode

In hot standby mode, the standby server doesn't normally lease IP addresses. However, if communication between the servers is interrupted, the standby server leases the addresses defined in the "Addresses reserved for standby server" option. If these addresses are exhausted before the MCLT timer has expired, the standby server no longer leases new addresses, but it can continue to renew existing address leases. If the MCLT timer expires and the primary server is in Partner Down state, the standby server takes full control of the address pool.

Editing and Deleting a Failover Configuration

If you need to edit or delete a failover configuration, right-click the IPv4 node in the DHCP console and click Properties. Click the Failover tab (see Figure 8-30). Select the name of the failover relationship and click Edit to edit the failover parameters or Delete to delete the failover relationship. If you delete the failover relationship in a hot standby configuration, the scope is deleted from the standby server but retained on the active server. If you delete a load-balancing configuration, the scope is deleted from the partner server and all addresses are available to the local server.

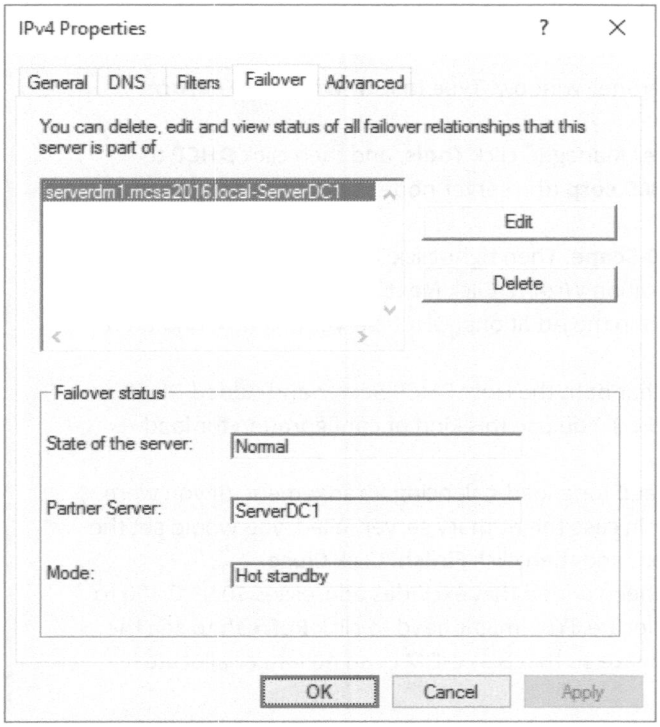

Figure 8-30 Editing or deleting a failover configuration

Note 13

If you view the Failover tab in the Properties dialog box for a scope, you see information about the failover relationship (if any) of that scope, but you can't make changes. Changes must be made in the Failover tab of the IPv4 node's Properties dialog box.

Self-Check Questions

7. In a split scope configuration, what option do you configure on the servers to ensure that the primary server services most client requests?

   a. Bindings
   b. Delay

   c. Percentage
   d. Classes

8. In a DHCP load-balancing failover configuration, what option can you configure if you want one of the servers to service the majority of DHCP requests?

   a. Delay
   b. Split

   c. Percentage
   d. Interval

◉ Check your answers at the end of this module.

Activity 8-7

Working with Split Scopes

Time Required: 10 minutes
Objective: Install a second DHCP server and configure a split scope.
Required Tools and Equipment: ServerDC1, ServerDM1, ServerSA1
Description: You want to work with split scopes, so you install the DHCP Server role on ServerDC1, configure a split scope between ServerDM1 and ServerDC1, and then test it.

1. On ServerDC1, sign in as **Administrator**. Open a PowerShell window. Type **Install-WindowsFeature DHCP -IncludeManagementTools** and press **Enter**.
2. When the DHCP Server installation finishes, open Server Manager, click **Tools**, and then click **DHCP** to open the DHCP console. Click to select **ServerDC1.AZ800.corp** (the server node), then right-click it and click **Authorize**.
3. On ServerDM1, click to select **Scope [10.99.0.0] 10.99.0-Scope**. Then right-click it, point to **Advanced**, and click **Split-Scope** to start the Dhcp Split-Scope Configuration Wizard. Click **Next**.
4. In the Additional DHCP Server window, type **ServerDC1** in the Additional DHCP Server text box, and then click **Next**.
5. In the Percentage of Split window, move the slider so that both the Host DHCP Server and Added DHCP Server text boxes show **50** (see Figure 8-27, shown earlier). You use this kind of configuration for load-balancing DHCP. Click **Next**.
6. In the Delay in DHCP Offer window, leave both values at **0** for a load-balancing arrangement. (If you were more concerned with having a secondary DHCP server in case the primary server failed, you would set the delay for Added DHCP Server to about 1000.) Click **Next**, and then click **Finish**. Click **Close**.
7. Click **Address Pool** to see that an exclusion range has been added that excludes addresses 10.99.0.150 to 10.99.0.200, which are the addresses ServerDC1 will allocate. (You might need to click **Refresh** to see the exclusion range.) Right-click the scope and click **Deactivate** so that ServerDM1 can no longer allocate IP addresses. Click **Yes** to confirm.

(continues)

Activity 8-7 Continued

8. On ServerDC1, open the DHCP console, if necessary. Right-click **10.99.0_scope** and click **Activate**. Click **Address Pool** to see the exclusion range of 10.99.0.100 through 10.99.0.149, the addresses ServerDM1 is configured to allocate.

9. On ServerSA1, open a PowerShell window, type **ipconfig /release** and press **Enter**, and then type **ipconfig /renew** and press **Enter**. You'll see that an address from ServerDC1 was assigned.

10. On ServerDC1, right-click **10.99.0_scope** and click **Delete**. Click **Yes** twice to confirm the deletion. On ServerDM1, delete the exclusion in 10.99.0_scope and reactivate the scope.

11. On ServerSA1, type **ipconfig /release** and press **Enter**, and then type **ipconfig /renew** and press **Enter** so that its address is again leased from ServerDM1.

12. Continue to the next activity.

Activity 8-8

Configuring DHCP Failover

Time Required: 10 minutes
Objective: Configure DHCP failover.
Required Tools and Equipment: ServerDC1, ServerDM1, ServerSA1
Description: In this activity, you configure DHCP failover in hot standby mode.

1. On ServerDM1, in the DHCP console, right-click **10.99.0_scope** and click **Configure Failover** to start the Configure Failover Wizard. In the welcome window, click **Next**.

2. In the Partner Server text box, type **ServerDC1** and click **Next**. The partnership is validated.

3. In the Create a new failover relationship window, type **ServerDM1-ServerDC1-HotStandby** in the Relationship Name text box. Leave the Maximum Client Lead Time set at the default **1 hour**. In the Mode list box, click **Hot standby**.

4. In the Role of Partner Server list box, leave the default setting **Standby**, and leave the default **5%** for the "Addresses reserved for standby server" setting.

5. Click the **State Switchover Interval** check box and leave the default value **60** in the minutes text box. Click to clear the **Enable Message Authentication** check box (see Figure 8-31), and then click **Next**.

6. Confirm the configuration and then click **Finish**. The failover configuration might take several seconds. After it's finished, click **Close**.

7. On ServerDC1, in the DHCP console, click the **Refresh** icon. Click **Address Leases** under 10.99.0_scope. You should see the current address lease for ServerSA1. (If you don't, click the **Refresh** icon.)

8. On ServerSA1, open a PowerShell window, type **ipconfig /release**, and press **Enter**. Verify that the lease is no longer shown on ServerDM1 and ServerDC1. (You probably need to click the **Refresh** icon in the DHCP console on both servers.)

9. On ServerSA1, type **ipconfig /renew** and press **Enter** to lease an address. Verify that the address lease can be seen on both servers, and then close the DHCP console on both servers.

10. Continue to the next activity.

(continues)

Activity 8-8 Continued

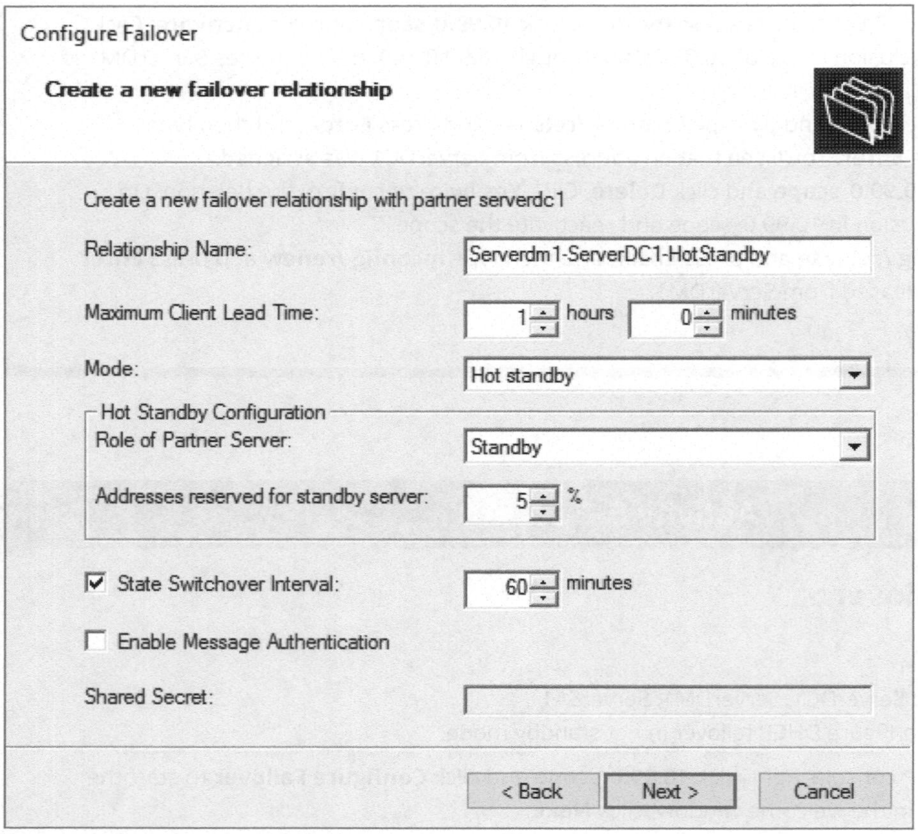

Configure Failover

Create a new failover relationship

Create a new failover relationship with partner serverdc1

Relationship Name: | Serverdm1-ServerDC1-HotStandby

Maximum Client Lead Time: | 1 hours | 0 minutes

Mode: | Hot standby

Hot Standby Configuration
Role of Partner Server: | Standby

Addresses reserved for standby server: | 5 %

☑ State Switchover Interval: | 60 minutes

☐ Enable Message Authentication

Shared Secret: |

< Back | Next > | Cancel

Figure 8-31 Configuring failover

Activity 8-9

Uninstalling the DHCP Server Role

Time Required: 5 minutes
Objective: Uninstall the DHCP server role.
Required Tools and Equipment: ServerDC1, ServerDM1, ServerSA1
Description: You're finished working with DHCP, so you uninstall the server role on ServerDC1 and Server DM1 and set ServerSA1's IP address back to a static address.

1. On ServerDC1, open a PowerShell window, type **Uninstall-WindowsFeature DHCP**, and press **Enter**. On ServerDM1, open a PowerShell window, type **Uninstall-WindowsFeature DHCP**, and press **Enter**.
2. Shut down ServerDM1 and ServerDC1.
3. On ServerSA1, open Network Connections and change the IPv4 address settings for the Ethernet connection as follows:
   IP address: 10.99.0.4
   Subnet mask: 255.255.255.0
   Default gateway: 10.99.0.250
   Primary DNS server: 10.99.0.1
4. Shut down ServerSA1.

IP Address Management

A large enterprise network has thousands of IP addresses in use, usually configured by several DHCP servers, and thousands of hostnames maintained by DNS servers. With so many addresses, hostnames, and servers to manage, IP address management can become unwieldy. **IP Address Management (IPAM)** is a feature in Windows Server that enables an administrator to manage the IP address space. IPAM has monitoring, auditing, and reporting functions to help you manage key server components in an IP network. IPAM handles forest-wide discovery and management of all Microsoft DHCP, DNS, and DC servers, and monitors DHCP scopes and DNS zones throughout the network. You might be able to solve the following problems with IPAM:

* Manual address management with spreadsheets or another custom solution
* Inefficiency in keeping track of and managing multiple DNS and DHCP servers
* Difficulties keeping track of address use across multiple domains and sites
* Global changes to all DHCP scopes across several servers, such as changing a DNS server address
* Problems identifying available IP addresses quickly

This section describes the IPAM infrastructure and shows you how to set up an IPAM solution, including IPAM requirements and installation, server provisioning, and server discovery and selection.

Exam Tip

IP address management is a large topic. This section serves as an introduction to get you started with IPAM and help you understand what you need to know about IPAM for the AZ800 certification exam.

The IPAM Infrastructure

The IPAM infrastructure consists of IPAM servers and managed servers. You can also install the IPAM management console on another server, called an **IPAM client**, so that you can manage the IPAM server remotely. The IPAM client can also be on a computer running a Windows client OS with remote server administration tools installed.

The **IPAM server** discovers servers you want to manage and collects and stores data from IPAM-managed servers in the IPAM database. A **managed server** is a Windows server running one or more of these Microsoft services: DHCP, DNS, or Active Directory. You can install more than one IPAM server on your network, particularly when it includes multiple sites, domains, or forests, and select which servers each IPAM server manages. An IPAM deployment has three topology options:

* *Centralized*—In a **centralized topology**, a single IPAM server is deployed for the entire enterprise (see Figure 8-32). The central server collects information from all managed servers. With this type of topology, the IPAM server should be centrally located with a reliable and high-performance connection to the network. A variation on this topology is to have multiple IPAM servers centrally located, with each IPAM server dedicated to managing a particular type of server. For example, one IPAM server can manage DHCP servers, and another can manage DNS servers.
* *Distributed*—In a **distributed topology**, an IPAM server is deployed at every site in the network. Each server is assigned a group of managed servers in the same site. There's no communication between IPAM servers.

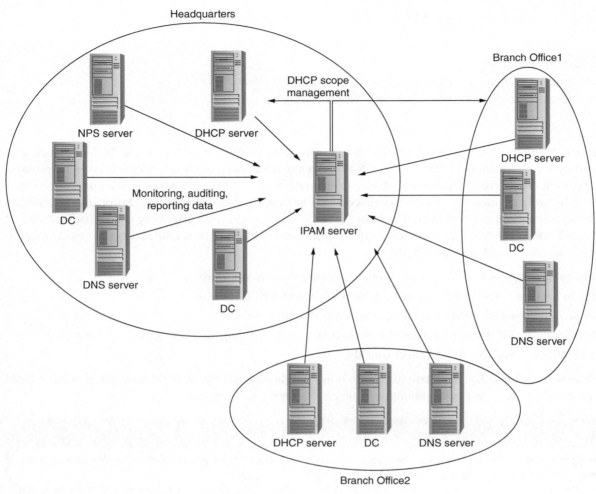

Figure 8-32 A centralized IPAM deployment

- *Hybrid*—Like the centralized topology, in a **hybrid topology**, a single IPAM server collects information from all managed servers in the enterprise; however, an IPAM server is also deployed at key branch locations. You might use this method when you have some large branch locations with IT staff so that they can easily manage servers in their locations. Figure 8-33 shows a hybrid IPAM deployment, with an IPAM server in the headquarters and the larger branch office locations and an IPAM client running the IPAM management console at the headquarters location. In this topology, the IPAM server in the headquarters collects data from servers in all three locations. The IPAM server in the branch office collects data only from servers in that location.

Deploying IPAM

IPAM deployment involves the following steps:

1. Determining the requirements for an IPAM deployment
2. Installing the IPAM Server feature
3. Provisioning the IPAM server
4. Performing server discovery
5. Provisioning IPAM GPOs
6. Selecting servers and services to manage
7. Collecting data from managed servers

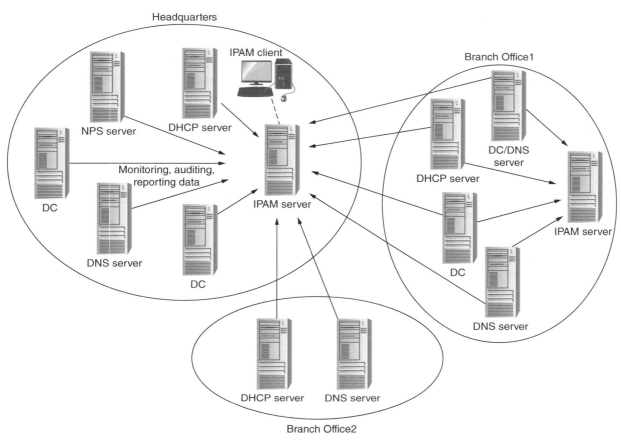

Figure 8-33   A hybrid IPAM deployment

The following sections discuss each of the steps necessary to deploy IPAM.

Meeting IPAM Requirements

Before you deploy IPAM, you should have a good understanding of its requirements and limitations. The following list describes the requirements for the IPAM server, client, and managed servers:

- *IPAM server*—The IPAM server must be running the Standard or Datacenter Edition of Windows Server 2012 or a later version and must be a domain member. The IPAM server can't be a domain controller. IPAM should be the sole server role installed on the server, although IPAM can coexist with other server roles. However, if IPAM is installed on a DHCP server, DHCP server discovery is disabled, which defeats one of the primary purposes of using IPAM.
- *IPAM client*—An IPAM client isn't a necessary component in an IPAM deployment, as you can manage IPAM from the IPAM server. However, if you want to manage IPAM from a different computer, you can install the IPAM management console on a computer running Windows Server 2012 or later or on a Windows client computer running Windows 11, for example, with the Remote Server Administration Tools (RSAT) installed.
- *IPAM managed server*—All servers managed by IPAM must be running Windows Server 2008 or later. In early versions of IPAM, the IPAM server could manage only domain member servers in the same Active Directory forest. Starting with Windows Server 2016, the managed servers can be members of other forests if a two-way trust relationship exists between the forests. As mentioned, IPAM can collect monitoring, reporting, and auditing data from the following services: Active Directory, DHCP, and DNS. IPAM can manage DHCP scopes.

Installing the IPAM Server Feature

IPAM Server is a feature you install with the Add Roles and Features Wizard or the `Install-WindowsFeature` PowerShell cmdlet. If you use the wizard, run it from Server Manager; in the Select Features window, select IP Address Management (IPAM) Server. Group Policy Management and the Windows Internal Database are also required, and you're prompted to include these features in the installation. By default, the IPAM management console is also installed. To install IPAM Server using PowerShell, enter the following command at a PowerShell prompt:

```
Install-WindowsFeature IPAM -IncludeManagementTools
```

If you just want to install the IPAM client feature on a server to manage an IPAM server remotely, open the Select Features window, expand Remote Server Administration Tools, expand Feature Administration Tools, and select IP Address Management (IPAM) Client. Enter the following command at a PowerShell prompt:

```
Install-WindowsFeature IPAM-Client-Feature
```

To install the IPAM feature in a Windows client OS such as Windows 8/8.1 or Windows 10, download the Remote Server Administration Tools from the Microsoft Download Center and follow the installation instructions. Then add the IPAM server to Server Manager; the IPAM console is installed on your Windows client computer.

After IPAM Server is installed, IPAM is added to the left pane in Server Manager. To get started, click IPAM in the left pane of Server Manager. You see a list of IPAM server tasks you can perform (see Figure 8-34). If you're running the management console on the server, the first task, Connect to IPAM server, takes place automatically. Now you're ready to provision the IPAM server.

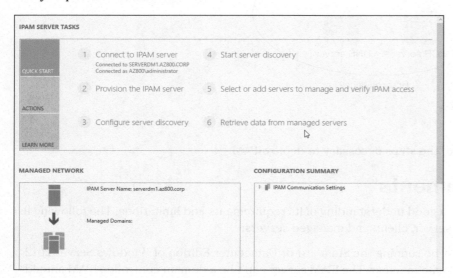

Figure 8-34   The IPAM server management console

IPAM Server Provisioning

The next step is to provision the IPAM server. In the IPAM Server Tasks window (shown in Figure 8-34), click "Provision the IPAM server" to start the Provision IPAM Wizard. The first window gives you information about IPAM and the provisioning process. In the next window, you select the type of IPAM database you want to use (see Figure 8-35). The default option is to use the Windows Internal Database (WID), which stores the database on the Windows system drive in C:\Windows\System32\IPAM\DataBase. Starting in Windows Server 2012 R2, you can use a Microsoft SQL Server database, which must already be installed and running. If you choose to use the WID and later want to migrate the IPAM database to a Microsoft SQL server, you can move the IPAM database with the `Move-IpamDatabase` PowerShell cmdlet.

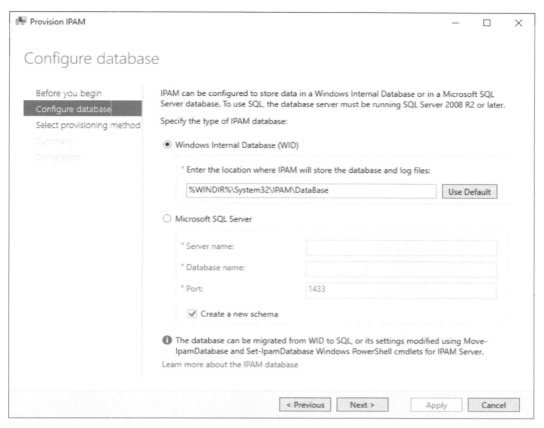

Figure 8-35   Configuring the IPAM database

In the next window, you select the method to provision managed servers. The default and recommended method is to use Group Policy provisioning. **Group Policy provisioning** uses group policies to perform tasks such as creating security groups, setting firewall rules, and creating shares for each IPAM-managed server. **Manual provisioning** requires manually configuring each IPAM server task and managed server. If you choose Group Policy provisioning, you must enter a GPO name prefix, which is used to name the GPOs that are created. For example, if you enter the name prefix IPAMaz800 (see Figure 8-36), the following GPOs are created and linked to the domain object:

- *IPAMaz800_DC_NPS*—This GPO sets the firewall rules and other policies needed for the IPAM server to collect data from domain controllers and NPS servers.
- *IPAMaz800_DHCP*—This GPO sets the firewall rules and other policies needed to collect data from and manage DHCP servers.
- *IPAMaz800_DNS*—This GPO sets the firewall rules and other policies needed for the IPAM server to collect data from DNS servers.

Caution !

If you choose the GPO provisioning method, you can't change to manual provisioning. However, using the `Set-IpamConfiguration` PowerShell cmdlet, you can change from manual to GPO provisioning.

Manual provisioning requires that you perform a number of tasks manually on each managed server:

- Configure security groups
- Create and configure shares
- Set firewall rules

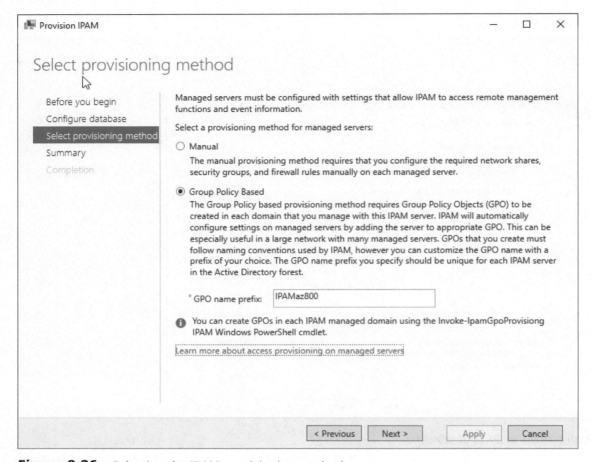

Figure 8-36   Selecting the IPAM provisioning method

GPO-based provisioning performs those tasks using the GPOs created by the provisioning wizard. Clicking Next in the wizard shows a summary of tasks performed by the provisioning process:

- Prepares GPO settings (if GPO-based provisioning was selected) so that an administrator can deploy the IPAM GPOs discussed earlier. GPOs must be deployed by running the `Invoke-IpamGPOProvisioning` PowerShell cmdlet after servers have been discovered and selected.
- Creates the specified database to store IPAM server configuration parameters and collected data.
- Creates scheduled tasks on the IPAM server to discover servers and collect data from managed servers.
- Creates local security groups used to assign IPAM administrator permission.
- Enables the IPAM server to track IP addressing.

Configuring Server Discovery

After the IPAM server has been provisioned, you configure server discovery. From Server Manager, you can get started by clicking IPAM and then clicking "Configure server discovery." In the Configure Server Discovery dialog box, you select the forests and domains where the IPAM server should search for servers to manage. If you're using a distributed IPAM topology, you might want to limit the search to a single domain, but with a central or hybrid topology, you want to select all domains in multiple forests. When you first open the Configure Server Discovery dialog box, you need to click "Get forests" and then close and reopen the dialog box to see a list of forests and domains. You can also choose the server roles the IPAM server should discover. By default, all services are selected (see Figure 8-37). Click OK to close the Configure Server Discovery dialog box.

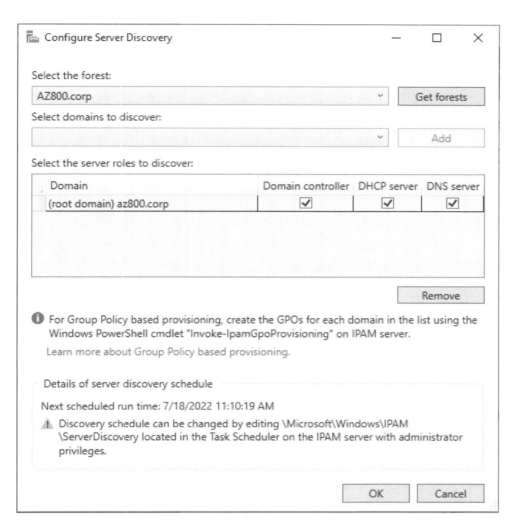

Figure 8-37   Configuring server discovery

After server discovery is configured, click "Start server discovery" in the IPAM Server Tasks window in Server Manager. IPAM probes the network in the specified domains to find servers that run the specified services. Server discovery might take several minutes or longer, depending on the number of domains and servers in the network. A message is displayed in the IPAM Server Tasks window to indicate the status of server discovery. When discovery is finished, servers that have been discovered are listed in the Server Inventory window (see Figure 8-38). Server discovery is scheduled to occur once per day by default and when any new servers are added to the database. DHCP servers must have at least one scope defined, and DNS servers must be authoritative for an Active Directory domain that is included in server discovery.

Note 14

IPAM discovery is not always reliable, so if a server is not discovered or not all services are recognized by the discovery process, you can add a server manually. In the Server Inventory window, click Tasks, click Add Server, and provide the required information, being sure to check the appropriate boxes for the services you want to manage with IPAM.

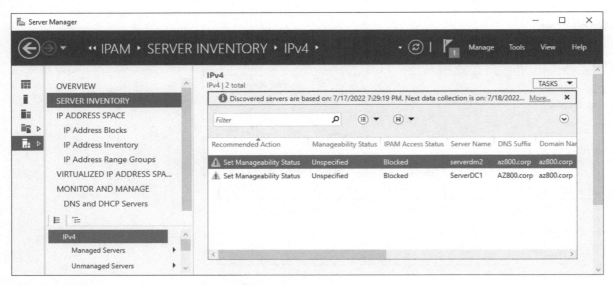

Figure 8-38   The Server Inventory window

Provisioning GPOs

The IPAM server provisioning process doesn't actually create and link the IPAM GPOs to the domain. After the managed servers have been identified, run the following PowerShell cmdlet to provision the GPOs:

```
Invoke-IpamGpoProvisioning –domain yourdomain –GpoPrefixName
    GPOprefix –DelegatedGpoUser IPAMUser
```

In this command, replace *yourdomain* with your domain name. If you're managing multiple domains, run the command for each domain. Replace *GPOprefix* with the prefix specified in the Provision IPAM Wizard. The account running the cmdlet requires domain administrator privileges to create and link the GPOs. The *IPAMUser* specified in the command is a list of users who are delegated permissions to edit the IPAM GPOs later. The *DelegatedGpoUser* parameter isn't required. After running the cmdlet, the three GPOs are created and linked to the domain node of the specified domain.

After provisioning the GPOs, you can open the Group Policy Management console on a DC in the domain to see the IPAM GPOs that have been linked to the domain. You'll see that the security filtering on each GPO is blank, which means the GPOs aren't applied to any servers. The next step in the process, selecting servers to manage, adds the managed server to the security filtering on the GPOs. The `Invoke-IpamGpoProvisioning` cmdlet also creates a universal security group named IPAMUG and adds the computer account of the IPAM server to the group.

Verifying IPAM Server Group Membership

Before the IPAM server can perform management tasks, the following security group memberships should be verified:

- The IPAMUG is created on a domain controller in the domain, and the server computer account on which the IPAM feature is installed is a member of the group. For example, if you installed the IPAM feature on ServerDM1, the ServerDM1 computer account must be a member of the IPAMUG in Active Directory.
- The IPAMUG is a member of the DHCP Users local group on all managed DHCP servers.
- The IPAMUG should be a member of the Event Log Readers local group on all managed DHCP servers and DNS servers. For managed domain controllers, the IPAMUG should be a member of the Event Log Readers Builtin Local group.

> **Note 15**
>
> If the DHCP Users group does not exist, you can create it from an elevated command prompt using the `netsh dhcp add securitygroups` command or the PowerShell cmdlet `Add-DhcpServerSecurityGroup`.

If the IPAMUG group does not exist—for example, because you used manual provisioning—create a universal security group named IPAMUG in the Users folder on a domain controller. Then, add the computer account that is running IPAM to the group. Next, add the IPAMUG group as a member of the DHCP Users and Event Log Readers groups on the managed servers.

After you have verified group memberships, the DHCP server service on all managed DHCP servers must be restarted so the permissions take effect.

Selecting Servers to Manage

As you can see in Figure 8-38, the manageability status of discovered servers is Unspecified, and the IPAM access status is Blocked. To select a server to manage, right-click the server in the Server Inventory window and click Edit Server. In the Add or Edit Server dialog box, you can change the manageability status to Managed if you want this IPAM server to manage the server; otherwise, it should be Unmanaged. You can also choose the services you want to manage on the selected server (see Figure 8-39).

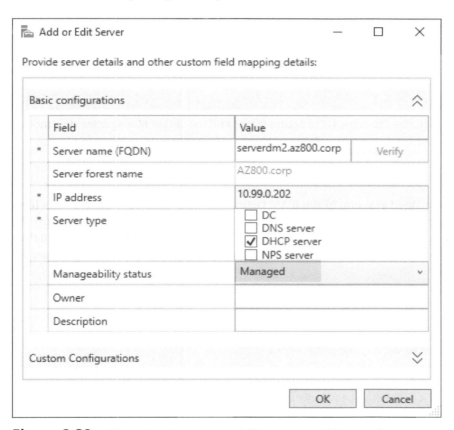

Figure 8-39   Changing the manageability status to Managed

When you set a server's manageability status to Managed, the server account is added to the security filter of the corresponding GPOs (depending on which services the server is running). However, you'll see that the IPAM access status remains in the Blocked state because the GPOs must be applied to each server. You can wait until the servers refresh their computer policies or run `gpupdate /force` at a command prompt on each managed server. After the policies are updated, right-click a server in the Server Inventory window, click Refresh Server Access Status, and then click the Server Manager refresh icon. The IPAM access status should then be Unblocked (see Figure 8-40). Alternatively, you can wait until the IPAM scheduled task automatically refreshes the access status, which is every 15 minutes. IPAM can then collect data from servers and manage DHCP addressing.

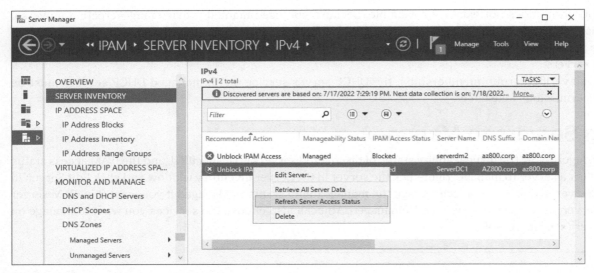

Figure 8-40   Unblocking servers

> **Note 16**
>
> After running `gpupdate` on servers, you might need to refresh the access status and the Server Manager window more than once to see the servers' Unblocked status.

Retrieving Server Data

The next step is to retrieve data from the managed servers. In the IPAM Overview window, click "Retrieve data from managed servers" to begin the process, or in the Server Inventory window, right-click a server and click "Retrieve All Server Data." When data retrieval is finished, you see a message at the top of the window indicating the date and time of the last data collection and the schedule for the next data collection. You're now ready to start using the IPAM server and administering the IP address space.

Self-Check Questions

9. In which type of IPAM topology is an IPAM server deployed at every site?

   a. Centralized

   b. Distributed

   c. Hybrid

   d. Mesh

10. After the IPAM server has been provisioned, you configure server discovery next. True or False?

   a. True

   b. False

   ⊙ Check your answers at the end of this module.

Activity 8-10

Resetting Your Virtual Environment

Time Required: 5 minutes
Objective: Reset your virtual environment by applying the InitialConfig checkpoint or snapshot.
Required Tools and Equipment: ServerDC1, ServerDM1, ServerDM2, ServerSA1
Description: Apply the InitialConfig checkpoint or snapshot to ServerDC1, ServerDM1, ServerDM2, and ServerSA1.

1. Be sure all servers are shut down. In your virtualization program, apply the InitialConfig checkpoint or snapshot to all servers.
2. When the snapshot or checkpoint has been applied, continue to the next activity.

Activity 8-11

Installing DHCP Roles on Managed Servers

Time Required: 10 minutes
Objective: Install DHCP on ServerDC1 and ServerDM2 for management by IPAM.
Required Tools and Equipment: ServerDC1 and ServerDM2
Description: In this activity, you install DHCP on ServerDC1 and ServerDM2. Next, you authorize the server and create and activate a scope on each server. The DHCP servers are only for the purpose of working with IPAM.

1. Start ServerDC1 and ServerDM2. Sign in to both servers as the domain administrator.
2. On ServerDC1, open a PowerShell window, type **Install-WindowsFeature DHCP -IncludeManagementTools**, and press **Enter**. To authorize the server, type **Add-DhcpServerInDC** and press Enter.
3. To create a new scope and activate it, type **Add-DhcpServerV4Scope -Name 192.168.0-Scope -StartRange 192.168.0.100 -EndRange 192.168.0.200 -SubnetMask 255.255.255.0 -State Active** and press **Enter**.
4. Create the necessary DHCP security groups. Type **Add-DhcpServerSecurityGroup** and press **Enter**.
5. On ServerDM2, from the command prompt, type **powershell** and press **Enter**. Type **Install-WindowsFeature DHCP** and press **Enter**. To authorize the server, type **Add-DhcpServerInDC** and press Enter.
6. To create a new scope and activate it, type **Add-DhcpServerV4Scope -Name 192.168.1-Scope -StartRange 192.168.1.100 -EndRange 192.168.1.200 -SubnetMask 255.255.255.0 -State Active** and press **Enter**.
7. Create the necessary DHCP security groups. Type **Add-DhcpServerSecurityGroup** and press **Enter**.
8. Continue to the next activity.

Activity 8-12

Installing and Provisioning the IPAM Server

Time Required: 10 minutes
Objective: Install the IPAM Server feature and provision the IPAM server.
Required Tools and Equipment: ServerDC1, ServerDM1, ServerDM2
Description: In this activity, you install the IPAM Server feature on ServerDM1 and provision the IPAM server using Group Policy provisioning.

1. Make sure ServerDC1 and ServerDM2 are running. Start ServerDM1 and sign in to the domain as **Administrator**.
2. On ServerDM1, open Server Manager, click **Manage**, and then click **Add Roles and Features** from the menu. Click **Next** until you get to the Features window. Click to select **IP Address Management (IPAM) Server** and then click **Add Features**. Click **Next** and then click **Install**. When the installation is finished, click **Close**.

(continues)

Activity 8-12 Continued

3. In Server Manager, click the **IPAM** node in the left pane.

4. In the IPAM Server Tasks window, verify that you see the server name under "Connect to IPAM server." Click **Provision the IPAM server** to start the Provision IPAM Wizard.

5. In the Before you begin window, read the information about IPAM provisioning, and then click **Next**.

6. In the Configure database window, accept the default option of **Windows Internal Database** and click **Next**.

7. In the Select provisioning method window, accept the default option, **Group Policy Based**, and type **IPAMaz800** in the GPO name prefix text box. Click **Next**.

8. In the Summary window, verify the settings. Read the information describing what tasks are performed with Group Policy provisioning. Click **Apply**. When provisioning is finished, read the information under Next steps. You'll perform these steps in the next activity. Click **Close**.

9. In the IPAM Server Tasks window, under Configuration Summary, click to expand **Access Provisioning Method** to see a summary of how IPAM is provisioned, including the names of GPOs to be created. Click the other configuration categories to see IPAM scheduled tasks, IPAM security groups, and IPAM communication settings.

10. Open a PowerShell window. Type **Invoke-IpamGpoProvisioning -Domain az800.corp -GpoPrefixName IPAMaz800** and press **Enter**. You see a message stating that you didn't specify the `-DelegatedGpoUser` parameter, but it's needed only if you want nonadministrator users to be able to edit the IPAM GPOs. Press **Enter** to confirm. If you see a second message about GPO permissions, press **Enter** to confirm until you return to the PowerShell prompt. Close the PowerShell window.

11. On ServerDC1, open Group Policy Management. For each GPO under the domain object whose name starts with IPAMaz800, first click the GPO. Then, in the right pane under Security Filtering, add an entry for **Authenticated Users** if it does not already exist. Do this for all three GPOs. Figure 8-41 shows what Security Filtering should look like when you have finished.

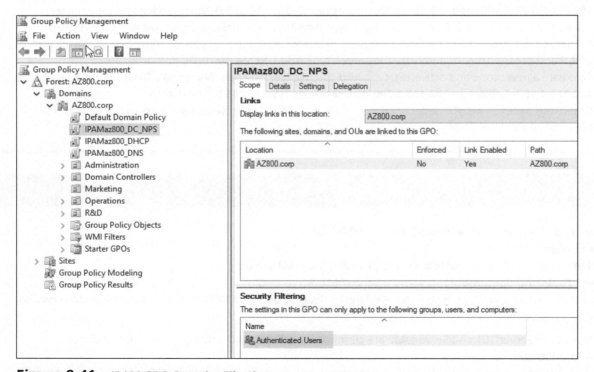

Figure 8-41   IPAM GPO Security Filtering

(continues)

Activity 8-12 Continued

12. On ServerDC1, open **Active Directory Users and Computers** and click **Users**. In the right pane, double-click the **IPAMUG** group that was created. Click the **Members** tab and verify that ServerDM1 is a member. Click **Cancel**. Next, you'll configure group memberships for the managed servers ServerDC1 and ServerDM2.

13. Double-click the **DHCP Users** group. Click the **Members** tab, click **Add**, type **IPAMUG**, and click **Check Names**. Click **OK**. Click **OK** again.

14. In the left pane, click the **Builtin** folder and double-click the **Event Log Readers** group. Click the **Members** tab. If IPAMUG is not already a member, click **Add**, type **IPAMUG**, and click **Check Names**. Click **OK**. Click **OK** again.

15. On ServerDM2, click **Tools** and click **Computer Management**.

16. Click to expand **Local Users and Groups** and click **Groups**. In the right pane, double-click the **DHCP Users** group. Click **Add**, type **IPAMUG**, and click **Check Names**. Click **OK**. Click **OK** again.

17. Double-click the **Event Log Readers** group. Click **Add**, type **IPAMUG**, and click **Check Names**. Click **OK**. Click **OK** again.

18. You need to restart the DHCP service for the new permissions to take effect. Click to expand the **Services and Applications** node and click **Services**. In the right pane, right-click **DHCP Server** and click **Restart**. Close the Computer Management console.

19. On ServerDC1, restart the DHCP service as you did on ServerDM2. Close the Computer Management console.

20. Continue to the next activity.

Activity 8-13

Discovering and Selecting Servers

Time Required: 15 minutes
Objective: Discover and select servers to manage.
Required Tools and Equipment: ServerDC1, ServerDM1, ServerDM2
Description: With IPAM installed and provisioned, you can start server discovery and then select servers to manage. Because you have only one other server, IPAM discovers it, and you select ServerDC1 to manage.

1. On ServerDM1, in Server Manager, click **IPAM** if necessary. In the IPAM Server Tasks window, click **Configure server discovery**. In the Configure Server Discovery dialog box, the forest AZ800.corp is listed. If it's not listed, click **Get forests**, click **OK**, close the Configure Server Discovery dialog box, and open it again. If AZ800.corp is listed already, continue to the next step.

2. Next to the Select domains to discover box (refer to Figure 8-37 shown earlier), click **Add**. By default, the server discovery process will discover servers running the following roles: Domain controller, DHCP server, and DNS server. Click **OK**.

3. In the IPAM Server Tasks window, click **Start server discovery**. You see a message near the top of the window indicating that an IPAM task is running. After a while, you see the message "Discovered servers are based on: *date and time*" (with *date and time* representing the current date and time). When you see this message, click **Select or add servers to manage and verify IPAM access**. You see ServerDC1 and ServerDM2 in the inventory window. The manageability status is Unspecified, and the IPAM access status is Blocked (refer to Figure 8-38 shown earlier).

4. Right-click **ServerDC1** and click **Edit Server**. In the Add or Edit Server dialog box, the DC, DNS server, and DHCP server check boxes are selected in the Server type section. Click the **Manageability status** list arrow and click **Managed**. (Refer to Figure 8-39 shown earlier.) Click **OK**. You see the manageability status is set to Managed, but the IPAM access status is still set to Blocked.

(continues)

Activity 8-13 Continued

5. Repeat Step 4 for ServerDM2. (ServerDM2 only has the DHCP Server check box selected.)
6. On ServerDC1, click **Tools** and then click **Group Policy Management** to open the Group Policy Management console. Click to expand the **Forest** and **Domains** nodes and then click to expand **AZ800.corp**. Click the **Linked Group Policy Objects** tab to see the IPAM GPOs (see Figure 8-42). In the left pane, under AZ800.corp, click each of the IPAM GPOs; you should see that ServerDC1 has been added to the security filtering for each GPO and ServerDM2 has been added to the security filtering for the DHCP GPO. This means the policies specified in those GPOs can be applied to those servers. The policies that are applied are primarily firewall settings that allow the IPAM server (ServerDM1) to manage the selected services.

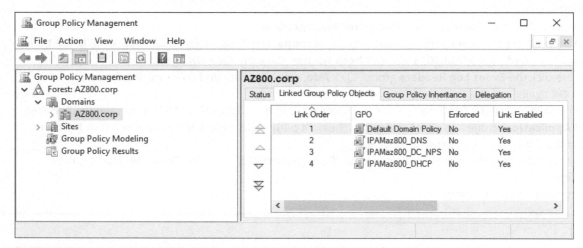

Figure 8-42 Viewing the IPAM GPOs in Group Policy Management

7. Group policies are applied to a computer when the computer starts and every 90 minutes. To make sure the policies are applied immediately, open a command prompt window, type **gpupdate /force**, and press **Enter**. Close the command prompt. Repeat this step for ServerDM2.
8. On ServerDM1, in the IPAM Server Inventory window, right-click **ServerDC1** and click **Refresh Server Access Status**. You see a message that IPAM tasks are running. After you see the "Discovered servers" message, click the **Refresh** icon in Server Manager to refresh the view. If all went well, you should see that the IPAM access status is set to Unblocked, and you'll see a white check mark in a green circle next to the ServerDC1 entry. Repeat this step for ServerDM2. Figure 8-43 shows what the Server Inventory page looks like with both servers being managed.

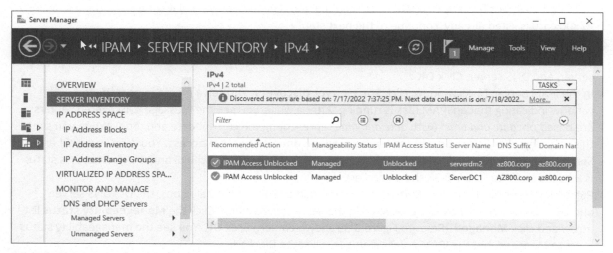

Figure 8-43 IPAM Server Inventory with both servers being managed

(continues)

Activity 8-13 Continued

9. Click **ServerDC1** in the IPAM Server Inventory window, and then scroll down to the Details view. You see detailed status information for the server. If access to the IPAM server is blocked, you can see which service is causing IPAM access to be blocked. For example, if Event Log Access is blocked, the IPAM server needs to be added to the Event Log Readers group on the managed server.

10. Continue to the next activity.

> **Note 17**
>
> If the status for a server remains blocked, verify group memberships as explained earlier. However, it is possible that group memberships are correct but the IPAM access status remains blocked. A common reason for this problem is that the Event Log Access Status for DNS stays blocked; you can check this in the Details view on the Server Inventory page. To solve this problem, you can add the IPAM server computer account to the local Administrators group on the DNS server. If the DNS server is a domain controller, add the IPAM server computer account to the Administrators group in Active Directory.

IP Addressing in Hybrid Environments

> **Microsoft Exam AZ-800:**
> Implement and manage an on-premises and hybrid networking infrastructure.
> - Manage IP addressing in on-premises and hybrid scenarios

Microsoft Azure provides methods to manage IP addresses of network resources on an Azure virtual network. IP addressing in Azure can be static or dynamic, as in an on-premises network. Devices on an Azure virtual network that are configured for dynamic IP address assignment are automatically assigned an IP address from an address space associated with the virtual network, but not using DHCP. Dynamic IP address assignment is done automatically by Azure and is not managed by the Azure user in the same sense that a DHCP server is managed. However, the Azure user can create address spaces and subnets from which the addresses are assigned. This section will go through the steps required to create a virtual network and assign an IP address space and subnets to the virtual network.

Virtual Networks and IP Addresses

An Azure virtual network (often referred to as a Vnet) allows Azure devices to communicate with one another just as a physical network allows physical computers and other devices to communicate with one another. A virtual network is associated with an IP address space that is used for dynamic and static IP address assignment to devices on the virtual network. An **IP address space** is an IP network specified in CIDR notation, such as 10.99.0.0/16. The defined address space determines how many addresses are available to assign to devices. For example, the 10.99.0.0/16 address space has 65534 usable addresses to assign to devices. The address space 192.168.1.0/24 has 254 usable addresses. The concept is similar to a DHCP address pool but the address space is associated directly with the virtual network, not a server on the network. Devices that are configured for dynamic IP address assignment are automatically assigned an address from the address space. You are not limited to a single address space, however, and you can create subnets and allocate portions of an address space to each subnet. This is similar to the concept of a physical switch that can be configured with VLANs to create subnets. However, with a physical switch, you would need to configure a DHCP server (or several DHCP servers) with a pool of IP addresses for each subnet. We'll go through the process of creating a virtual network and then creating an address space and breaking the space into subnets. At the end of this section, you'll have an opportunity to create a virtual network and assign IP addresses in the activities.

Creating a Virtual Network

Like most items in Azure, a virtual network is a resource. You begin the process of creating a virtual network by creating a new resource and then selecting Virtual network as the resource you want to create. The Create virtual network wizard starts. Like other resources, you must choose a subscription, a resource group, and a region. You must also give the virtual network a name. You could stop at this point, create the virtual network, and accept the default assignment of an IP address pool. Or, you could review the default address pool, change it, or delete it and create your own by going to the next tab of the wizard. On the IP Addresses tab, you'll see the default address space Azure has assigned to your virtual network. If the address space isn't suitable, you can delete it and create a new one.

You can also create a new subnet. Most virtual networks will need subnets to partition network traffic. A default subnet is suggested, which you can accept by checking the box (see Figure 8-44).

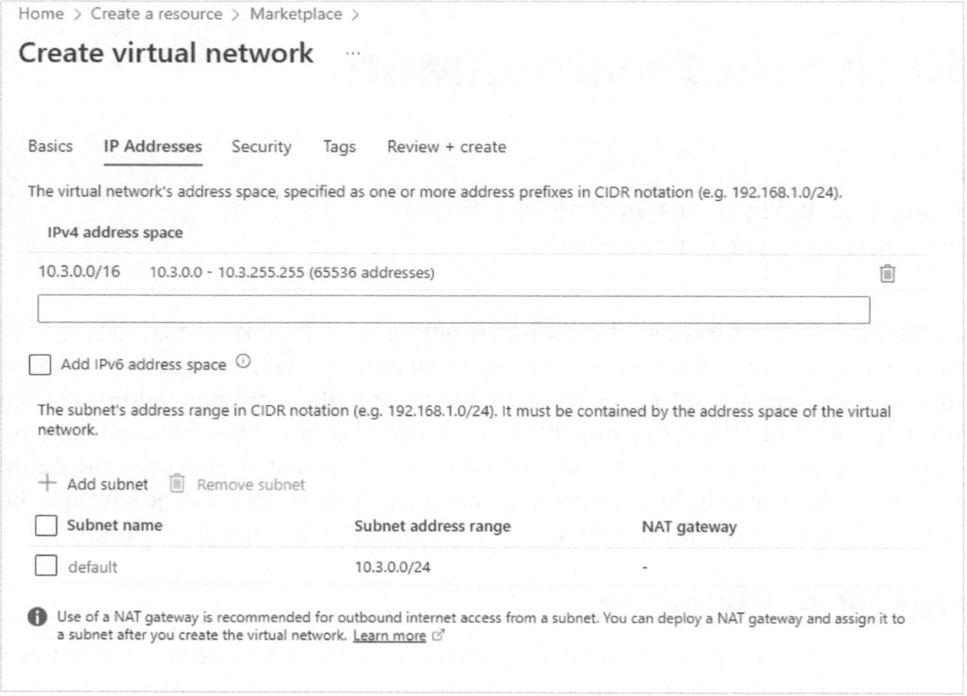

Home > Create a resource > Marketplace >

Create virtual network   ⋯

Basics   **IP Addresses**   Security   Tags   Review + create

The virtual network's address space, specified as one or more address prefixes in CIDR notation (e.g. 192.168.1.0/24).

IPv4 address space

| 10.3.0.0/16   10.3.0.0 - 10.3.255.255 (65536 addresses) | 🗑 |

☐ Add IPv6 address space ⓘ

The subnet's address range in CIDR notation (e.g. 192.168.1.0/24). It must be contained by the address space of the virtual network.

＋ Add subnet   🗑 Remove subnet

☐ Subnet name	Subnet address range	NAT gateway
☐ default	10.3.0.0/24	-

ⓘ Use of a NAT gateway is recommended for outbound internet access from a subnet. You can deploy a NAT gateway and assign it to a subnet after you create the virtual network. Learn more ↗

Figure 8-44   Creating a virtual network—IP addresses

The Security tab lets you enable various features such as BastionHost, DDoS Protection, and Firewall, if desired. Each of these options requires a new subnet within the address space. Some of these options will be explored in more detail in Module 9. Like all resources, you have the option of adding tags that allow you to categorize resources.

Once the virtual network is created, you can add more address spaces, create new subnets, and add or change services such as the BastionHost, DDoS Protection, and Firewall. Be aware, however, that you cannot easily move a virtual machine (VM) from one virtual network to another. To move a VM to a new virtual network, you must create a Recovery Services vault in the region where the VM is located, back up the VM to the Recovery Services vault, stop and deprovision VM, and then restore it from the vault to the new virtual network. Alternatively, you can delete the VM while preserving the NIC and virtual disk and create a new VM from the original VM's virtual disk. Keep in mind that the VM and the virtual network must be located in the same Azure region, and you must have defined at least one subnet on the virtual network to which the VM can be connected.

IP Address Issues in a Hybrid Environment

While there are few problems you are likely to encounter with IP addressing in a hybrid environment, the most likely issue you can run into is an IP address conflict between your on-premises network and the Azure virtual network. This problem can occur if you have a VPN or ExpressRoute connection between the on-premises network and the Azure virtual network because the two networks can communicate with one another. If you have an IP address range that overlaps between the on-premises network and the Azure network, routing may not work properly because a subnet will exist in two physical locations (on-premises and Azure). So, you must be careful to define a unique address space on Azure for each virtual network, with no overlap with your on-premises address spaces.

In addition to avoiding address conflicts between on-premises networks and Azure virtual networks, you must be careful to use IP address ranges for virtual networks only from the following address ranges:

- 10.0.0.0 – 10.255.255.255
- 172.16.0.0 – 172.31.255.255
- 192.168.0.0 – 192.168.255.255
- 100.64.0.0 – 100.127.255.255

While other address ranges may work, it is recommended to use only the previously listed ranges. The following address spaces cannot be used:

- 224.0.0.0 – 239.255.255.255
- 127.0.0.0 – 127.255.255.255
- 169.254.0.0 – 169.254.255.255
- 168.63.129.16 (Azure internal DNS address)

Other restrictions for IP address spaces on an Azure virtual network include the following:

- A virtual network can have a maximum of 3000 subnets.
- Subnets cannot overlap each other.
- The first four addresses and last IP address in each subnet are reserved by Azure. This means that the smallest subnet you can create is with a /29 prefix. A /29 prefix provides eight IP addresses, and because five of them are reserved, only three remain for customer use. In each subnet, the first address is reserved as the subnet identifier or network address, the next address is reserved by Azure for the default gateway, the next two addresses are reserved by Azure to map Azure DNS IP addresses to the virtual network space, and the last address in a subnet is reserved as the subnet broadcast address.
- Broadcast addresses are not supported on Azure virtual networks.

> **Caution** ❗
>
> The following activities will incur charges on your Azure account. If you do not want to incur these charges, do not perform the activities, but instead read through the activities so you understand the process. You may also want to perform the activity simulation associated with these activities.

Self-Check Questions

11. Which of the following is an address range that cannot be used when creating a virtual network?

   a. 10.0.0.0 – 0.255.255.255
   b. 169.254.0.0 – 169.254.255.255
   c. 192.168.0.0 – 192.168.255.255
   d. 172.16.0.0 – 172.31.255.255

12. An address space is specified using IP address/subnet mask notation. True or False?

   a. True
   b. False

⊙ Check your answers at the end of this module.

Activity 8-14

Creating a Virtual Network and IP Address Space

Time Required: 20 minutes
Objective: Create a virtual network and add an IP address space.
Required Tools and Equipment: A web browser with access to the Azure portal
Description: You plan to create virtual machines on Azure. You need to create a virtual network first so you can assign the VMs to the Vnet when you create them.

1. Open a web browser and sign in to the Azure portal.
2. You'll start by creating a new resource that can be deleted at the end of the next activity. From the portal home page, click **Create a resource**.
3. Click the **Search services and marketplace** text box, begin typing **resource group**, and select **Resource group** when you see it in the search results. On the Resource group page, click **Create**.
4. On the Create a resource group page, select the appropriate subscription if necessary, click the **Resource group** box, and type **TestVnetRG**. Select an appropriate region for the resource group and remember which region you selected; you'll need it when you create the virtual network (see Figure 8-45).

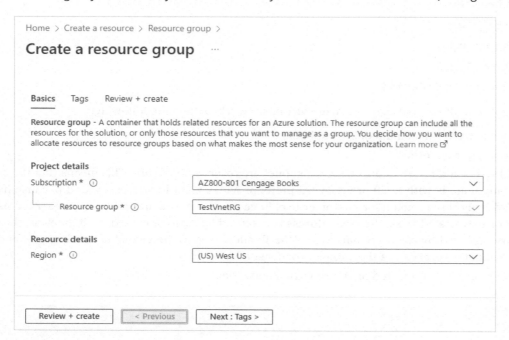

Figure 8-45   Creating a new resource group for the virtual network

5. Click **Review + create** and then click **Create**. Click **Home** at the top of the page and then click **Create a resource**. Click the **Search services and marketplace** text box, begin typing **virtual network**, and select **Virtual network** when you see it in the search results. On the Virtual network page, click **Create**.
6. On the Create virtual network page, select the appropriate subscription if necessary, click the **Resource group** box, and select **TestVnetRG**. Click the **Name** box and type **MyVnet**. The Region box should be populated with the same region (see Figure 8-46) as that for the resource group you created in Step 4.
7. Click the **IP Addresses** tab or the **Next: IP Addresses** button.
8. On the IP Addresses tab, click the **delete** (Trash can) icon next to the default address space. Click the **IPv4 address space** box and type **172.20.0.0/16**.

(continues)

Activity 8-14 Continued

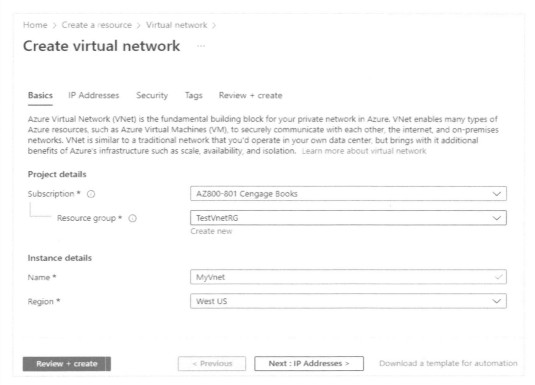

Home > Create a resource > Virtual network >

Create virtual network   ...

Basics   IP Addresses   Security   Tags   Review + create

Azure Virtual Network (VNet) is the fundamental building block for your private network in Azure. VNet enables many types of Azure resources, such as Azure Virtual Machines (VM), to securely communicate with each other, the internet, and on-premises networks. VNet is similar to a traditional network that you'd operate in your own data center, but brings with it additional benefits of Azure's infrastructure such as scale, availability, and isolation. Learn more about virtual network

Project details

Subscription * ⓘ   AZ800-801 Cengage Books   ⌄

　　　Resource group * ⓘ   TestVnetRG   ⌄
　　　　　　　　　　　　　　　　　　　　Create new

Instance details

Name *   MyVnet   ✓

Region *   West US   ⌄

[Review + create]   [< Previous] [Next : IP Addresses >]   Download a template for automation

Figure 8-46   Creating a virtual network—Basics tab

9. Click **Add subnet** to add a subnet. In the pop-up pane on the right, click the **Subnet name** box and type **WebServers**. Click the **Subnet address range** box and type **172.20.1.0/28**. Click the **Services** box and click **Microsoft.Web**. This limits the subnet to only web-related traffic (see Figure 8-47). If the subnet would host general servers or you aren't sure which services would be hosted, you could select all services. Click **Add**.

10. Click the **Security** tab. On this tab, you can enable the network services BastionHost, DDoS Protection, and Firewall. Click **Enable** next to Firewall. You might want to enable the other services, but they come with additional costs.

11. Type **TestVnetFW** in the Firewall name box and type **172.20.2.0/26** in the Firewall subnet address space box. (A /26 prefix is the smallest prefix you can assign to a firewall subnet.) In the Public IP address box, you can select an existing public IP address if one exists, or you can create a new one. Click **Create new**. Type **TestVnetFWIP** in the Name box and click **OK**.

12. Click **Review + create**. Review the settings, which should look similar to those in Figure 8-48. Click **Create**. It will take a few minutes to create the new virtual network.

13. After the virtual network is created, you see an Overview page. Click **Go to resource**. On the MyVnet page, you see all the properties of the virtual network and the options for modifying it. On this page, you can add or change address spaces and subnets, add or change security services, and configure DNS servers, among other options.

14. If you are continuing to the next activity, stay signed in to the Azure portal; otherwise, sign out.

Activity 8-14 Continued

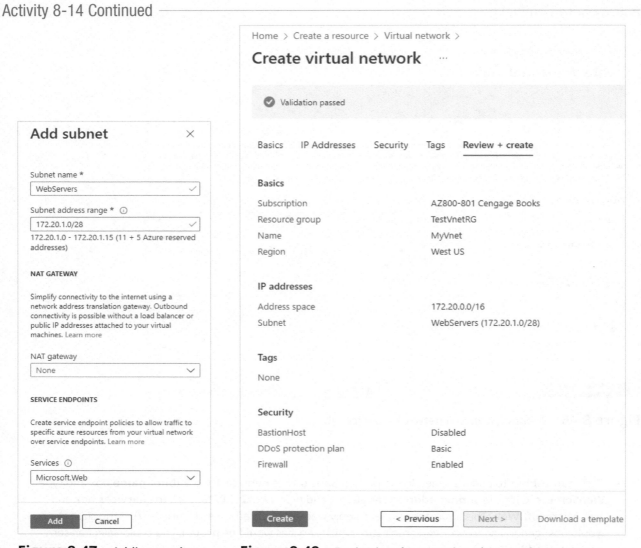

Figure 8-47 Adding a subnet   **Figure 8-48** Reviewing the new virtual network settings

Activity 8-15

Creating a VM on the Virtual Network

Time Required: 20 minutes

Objective: Create a virtual machine and examine the IP address settings.

Required Tools and Equipment: A web browser with access to the Azure portal

Description: You have created a virtual network, and now it is time to populate it with virtual machines. In this activity, you will create a VM and assign it to the virtual network you created in the previous activity.

1. Open a web browser and sign in to the Azure portal, if necessary.
2. From the portal home page, click **Create a resource**. Click **Create** under Virtual machine, which is under Popular Azure Services.
3. Click the **Resource group** box and click **TestVnetRG** (the resource group you created in the previous activity).
4. In the Virtual machine name box, type **TestVnetVM**. In the Region box, select the same region that you used to create the virtual network.

(continues)

Activity 8-15 Continued

5. Click the **Image** box and click **Windows Server 2019 Datacenter – Gen 2**.

6. In the Username box, type **TestAdmin**. In the Password and Confirm password boxes, type **Password1234**.

7. Leave the rest of the fields at their default settings. Scroll up if necessary and click the **Networking** tab.

8. On the Networking tab, verify that **MyVnet** is selected for the Virtual network and that **WebServers** is selected for the Subnet.

9. Leave the rest of the fields at the default settings and click **Review + create**. Review the settings and then click **Create**.

10. It will take a few minutes to create the virtual machine. After it is created, click **Go to resource**.

11. On the TestVnetVM page, notice that the status of the VM is "running." In the Networking section of the VM properties, notice that the Private IP address is set to 172.20.1.4, which is the subnet you created.

12. Click **Connect** and click **RDP**. Click **Download RDP File**. Open the downloaded RDP file and click **Connect** in the dialog box.

13. When you are prompted to enter credentials, click **More choices** and then click **Use a different account**. Type **TestAdmin** in the User name box and **Password1234** in the Password box. Click the **Remember me** box if desired. Click **OK**.

14. In the Remote Desktop Connection dialog box, click the check box and click **Yes**. A new window opens and you are signed in to the virtual machine.

15. Right-click **Start** and click **Windows PowerShell**. Type **ipconfig/all** and press **Enter** to see your IP address configuration.

16. Notice that the address shown is the private IP address, not the public IP address you used to connect via RDP. Also notice that the DNS server address is 168.63.129.16, which is the Azure DNS service address. Right-click **Start**, point to **Shut down or sign out**, and click **Shutdown**. Click **Continue**.

17. Now you will delete the resources you created for these activities. In the Azure portal, click **Home**. Under Resources, click **TestVnetRG**. On the TestVnetRG page, click **Delete resource group**. In the pop-up window, type **TestVnetRG** in the box. Notice that all the resources associated with the resource group will be deleted. Click **Delete**. By deleting all resources, you will not incur any more charges for the VM or the public IP address.

18. Sign out of the Azure portal and close all open windows.

Module Summary

- Dynamic Host Configuration Protocol (DHCP) is a component of the TCP/IP protocol suite that's used to assign an IP address to a host automatically from a defined pool of addresses. IP addresses assigned via DHCP are usually leased, not permanently assigned. DHCP is a client/server protocol.

- The process of a DHCP client requesting an IP address and a DHCP server fulfilling the request is actually a four-packet sequence of broadcasts: DHCPDISCOVER, DHCPOFFER, DHCPREQUEST, and DHCPACK. DHCP uses the UDP Transport-layer protocol on ports 67 and 68. Port 67 is used for sending data from the client to the server, and port 68 is for sending data from the server to the client. There are eight DHCP message types.

- The DHCP service is installed as a server role named DHCP Server; it has no role service components. A DHCP server must be authorized on a domain network before it can begin providing services.

- A DHCP scope is a pool of IP addresses and other IP configuration parameters that a DHCP server uses to lease addresses to DHCP clients. An exclusion range consists of one or more addresses in the scope that the DHCP server doesn't lease to clients. A reservation is an IP address associated with the MAC address of a DHCP client to ensure that when the client requests an IP address, it always gets the same one, along with any configured options.

- A superscope is a special type of scope consisting of one or more member scopes that allow a DHCP server to service multiple IPv4 subnets on a single physical network. A superscope directs the DHCP server to draw addresses from both scopes, even though it has only a single interface configured for one of the IP subnets.

- An IPv4 multicast packet is a network packet addressed to a group of hosts listening on a particular multicast IP address. Multicast DHCP scopes allow assigning multicast addresses dynamically to multicast servers and clients by using the Multicast Address Dynamic Client Allocation Protocol (MADCAP).

- Almost every network requires a DNS server's IP address for name resolution and a default gateway to communicate with other subnets and the Internet. The DHCP server can be configured to send both these addresses to DHCP clients along with the IP address and subnet mask. DHCP options can be assigned at these levels: server, scope, policy, and reservation.

- You can perform several DHCP server configuration tasks in the DHCP console. The options you can change depend on whether you right-click the topmost node with the server name or the IPv4 or IPv6 nodes. Server configuration tasks include adding or removing bindings, backing up and restoring, creating scopes, configuring failover, reconciling scopes, setting predefined options, and configuring properties.

- The IPv4 server properties include statistics and logging parameters, dynamic DNS configuration, filters, conflict detection, and configuration of DNS registration credentials. Configurable scope properties include scope name and address range, dynamic DNS configuration, and DHCP/BOOTP configuration.

- On networks with both Windows and non-Windows computers, a problem known as name squatting can occur when a non-Windows computer registers its name with a DNS server, but the name has already been registered by a Windows computer. DHCP name protection prevents name squatting by non-Windows computers by using a DHCP resource record called Dynamic Host Configuration Identifier (DHCID).

- DHCP filters allow administrators to restrict which computers on a network are leased an IP address based on the client MAC address.

- DHCP policies allow you more fine-tuned control of address lease options than you have with server, scope, and reservation options. Policies can be configured based on criteria such as Vendor Class, User Class, MAC address, client identifier, FQDN, and relay agent information.

- If you're using Windows Deployment Services to install Windows OSs on computers, you might need to configure DHCP to respond to Preboot Execution Environment network interfaces. PXE is a network environment built into many NICs that allows a computer to boot from an image stored on a network server.

- A DHCP relay agent is a device that listens for broadcast DHCPDISCOVER and DHCPREQUEST messages and forwards them to a DHCP server on another subnet. It's configured as part of the Routing role service under the Remote Access server role.

- Windows Server 2022 allows you to migrate the DHCP server role to another server; you can do so easily by exporting the server configuration and database to a file and then importing that file on another server.

- DHCP is a fairly reliable protocol, but at times you may encounter some basic problems. These problems may include a client not receiving a DHCP address, a client receiving an incorrect DHCP address, IP address conflicts, the DHCP server service not starting, and no addresses being leased.

- The DHCP audit logging feature, which is enabled by default, provides a logging file that shows information about when addresses were leased, renewed, and released, as well as information about DNS updates attempted by the DHCP server. The log also shows when the server was authorized and when the service started and stopped.

- Microsoft has several ways to achieve high availability for DHCP: split scopes, DHCP failover, a DHCP server cluster, and hot standby. A split scope is a fault-tolerant DHCP configuration in which two DHCP servers share the same scope information, allowing both servers to offer DHCP services to clients.

- DHCP failover allows two DHCP servers to share the pool of addresses in a scope, giving both servers access to all addresses in the pool. There are two modes for DHCP failover: load-balancing mode and hot standby mode.

- The IPAM server provisioning process doesn't create and link the IPAM GPOs to the domain. You can utilize PowerShell to provision the GPOs. After provisioning the GPOs, you can open the Group Policy Management console on a DC in the domain to see the IPAM GPOs that have been linked to the domain.

- When selecting a server to manage, right-click the server in the Server Inventory window and click Edit Server. In the Add or Edit Server dialog box, you can change the manageability status to Managed if you want the IPAM server to manage the server.

- Once the IPAM server has collected data from selected servers and services, you can start working with IPAM. The IPAM console's navigation pane contains links to several monitoring and management views of your IP address space and DNS zone data.
- Microsoft Azure provides methods to manage IP addresses of network resources on an Azure virtual network. IP addressing in Azure can be static or dynamic, as in an on-premises network.
- An Azure virtual network (often referred to as a Vnet) allows Azure devices to communicate with one another just as a physical network allows physical computers and other devices to communicate with one another.
- While there are few problems you are likely to encounter with IP addressing in a hybrid environment, the most likely issue you can run into is an IP address conflict between your on-premises network and the Azure virtual network.
- You must be careful to define a unique address space on Azure for each virtual network, with no overlap with your on-premises address spaces. In addition to avoiding address conflicts between on-premises networks and Azure virtual networks, you must be careful to use IP address ranges for virtual networks only from the prescribed ranges.

Key Terms

centralized topology	exclusion range	manual provisioning
conflict detection	Group Policy provisioning	maximum client lead time (MCLT)
DHCP failover	hot standby mode	multicast scope
DHCP filters	hybrid topology	name squatting
DHCP name protection	IP Address Management (IPAM)	Preboot Execution Environment (PXE)
DHCP policies	IP address space	reservation
DHCP relay agent	IPAM client	split scope
DHCP scope	IPAM server	superscope
DHCP server authorization	lease duration	User Class
distributed topology	lease renewal	Vendor Class
Dynamic Host Configuration Protocol (DHCP)	load-balancing mode	
	managed server	

Review Questions

1. Which of the following is true about DHCP? (Choose two.)
   a. There are eight message types.
   b. DHCPDISCOVER messages sent by clients traverse routers.
   c. It uses the UDP Transport layer protocol.
   d. An initial address lease involves three packets.

2. You have a DHCP server set up on your network and no DHCP relay agents. You're capturing DHCP packets with a protocol analyzer and see a broadcast packet with UDP source port 68 and UDP destination port 67. Which of the following DHCP message types can the packet be?
   a. A DHCPREQUEST to renew an IP address lease
   b. A DHCPACK to acknowledge an IP address lease request
   c. A DHCPDISCOVER to request an IP address
   d. A DHCPOFFER to offer an IP address lease

3. In the DHCP server's statistics, you notice that a lot of DHCPNAK packets have been transmitted. What's the most likely reason?
   a. You changed the range of addresses in a scope recently.
   b. The DHCP server has been taken offline.
   c. The server is offering a lot of addresses that are already in use.
   d. Client computers are getting multiple offers when they request an address.

4. You have configured your computers with static IP addresses but want them to get the DNS server and default gateway settings via DHCP. What type of DHCP message do you see as a result?
   a. DHCPREQUEST
   b. DHCPRELEASE
   c. DHCPNAK
   d. DHCPINFORM

5. After you install the DHCP Server role on a member server, what must occur before the server can begin providing DHCP services?
   a. Options must be configured.
   b. The server must be restarted.
   c. The server must be authorized.
   d. Filters must be created.

6. Which of the following is a required element of a DHCP scope? (Choose three.)
   a. Subnet mask
   b. Scope name
   c. Router address
   d. Lease duration

7. What's the default lease duration on a Windows DHCP server?
   a. 8 hours
   b. 16 minutes
   c. 8 days
   d. 16 hours

8. What should you define in a scope to prevent the DHCP server from leasing addresses that are already assigned to devices statically?
   a. Reservation scope
   b. Exclusion range
   c. Deny filters
   d. DHCP policy

9. You have four printers that are accessed via their IP addresses. You want to be able to use DHCP to assign addresses to the printers, but you want to make sure they always have the same address. What's the best option?
   a. Create reservations.
   b. Create exclusions.
   c. Configure filters.
   d. Configure policies.

10. You have defined a scope on your DHCP server with the start address 172.16.1.1, end address 172.16.1.200, and prefix length 16. You want to create another scope on the server. Which of the following is a valid scope you can create on this server?
    a. Start address 172.19.1.1, end address 172.19.1.255, prefix length 16
    b. Start address 172.17.1.1, end address 172.17.1.200, prefix length 16
    c. Start address 172.16.2.1, end address 172.19.2.100, prefix length 16
    d. Start address 172.31.1.0, end address 173.31.1.254, prefix length 24

11. What should you create if you need to service multiple IPv4 subnets on a single physical network?
    a. Split scope
    b. Relay agent
    c. Superscope
    d. Multicast server

12. What do you configure if you need to assign addresses dynamically to applications or services that need a class D IP address?
    a. IPv6 relay
    b. Multicast scope
    c. Dynamic scope
    d. Autoconfiguration

13. You want high availability for DHCP services, a primary server to handle most DHCP requests, and a secondary server to respond to client requests only if the primary server fails to respond promptly. The primary server has about 85 percent of the IP addresses to lease, leaving the secondary server with about 15 percent. You don't want the servers to replicate with each other. What should you configure?
    a. Multicast scope
    b. Failover
    c. Superscope
    d. Split scope

14. A subnet on your network uses DHCP for address assignment. The current scope has a start address of 192.168.1.1 and an end address of 192.168.1.200 with the subnet mask 255.255.255.0. Because of network expansion, you have added computers, bringing the total number that needs DHCP for address assignment to 300. You don't want to change the IP addressing scheme or the subnet mask for computers already on the network. What should you do?
    a. Create a new scope with start address 192.168.2.1, end address 192.168.2.200, and a prefix length of 24; add the existing scope and new scope to a superscope.
    b. Add a scope with start address 192.168.1.1, end address 192.168.2.200, and the subnet mask 255.255.255.0. Then delete the existing scope.
    c. Create a new scope with start address 192.168.1.1, end address 192.168.2.200, and prefix length 16.
    d. Add another DHCP server. Using the split scope wizard, split the existing scope with the new server and assign each server 100 percent of the addresses.

15. You want mobile devices on your network to have a shorter lease time than other devices without having a different scope. You don't have detailed information about the mobile devices, such as MAC addresses, because they are employees' personal devices. What DHCP feature might you use to assign a shorter lease to these mobile devices?
    a. Reservation options
    b. Scope options
    c. Policy options
    d. Filter options

16. You have DHCP clients on the network that aren't domain members. You want to be sure these computers can register their hostnames with your DNS servers. Which option should you configure?
    a. 003 Router
    b. 044 WINS/NBNS Servers
    c. 006 DNS Servers
    d. 015 DNS Domain name

17. You want all computers in the Management Department to use a default gateway that's different from computers in other departments. All departments are on the same subnet. What should you do first on the server?
    a. Create a User Class.
    b. Create a new scope.
    c. Create an allow filter.
    d. Create a Vendor Class.

18. You have a DHCP server with two NICs: NIC1 and NIC2. NIC1 is connected to a subnet with computers that use DHCP for address assignment. NIC2 is connected to the datacenter subnet, where all computers should use static addressing. You want to prevent the DHCP server from listening for DHCP packets on NIC2. What should you do?
    a. Configure bindings.
    b. Disable the scope.
    c. Create a filter for NIC2.
    d. Configure failover.

19. You notice that some information shown in the DHCP console for DHCP leases doesn't agree with lease information you see on some client computers where you used `ipconfig /all`. What should you do to make DHCP information consistent?
    a. Back up and restore the database.
    b. Reconcile the scopes.
    c. Create a deny filter for the leases that look wrong.
    d. Delete the dhcp.mdb file and click Refresh.

20. Some of your non-Windows clients aren't registering their hostnames with the DNS server. You don't require secure updates on the DNS server. What option should you configure on the DHCP server so that non-Windows client names are registered?
    a. Dynamically update DNS records only if requested by the DHCP clients.
    b. Always dynamically update DNS records.
    c. Dynamically update DNS records for DHCP clients that do not request updates.
    d. Configure name protection.

21. You're reviewing DHCP server statistics and notice that the server has received many DHCPDECLINE messages. What should you configure on the server to reduce the number of DHCPDECLINE messages?
    a. DHCP policies
    b. Conflict detection
    c. Connection bindings
    d. DNS credentials

22. You have a network of 150 computers and notice that a computer you don't recognize has been leasing an IP address. You want to make sure this computer can't lease an address from your server. What's the best solution that takes the least administrative effort?
    a. Create an allow filter.
    b. Create a new policy.
    c. Create a deny filter.
    d. Create a Vendor Class.

23. Which of the following is a criterion you can use with conditions in DHCP policies? (Choose two.)
    a. Vendor Class
    b. MAC address
    c. OS version
    d. SSID

24. You have noticed that your DHCP service is not starting. You must immediately troubleshoot your DHCP server and determine the cause of the problem as quickly as possible. Which of the following DHCP troubleshooting steps should you perform? (Choose two.)
    a. Reconcile all scopes.
    b. Verify that the scope is not corrupted.
    c. Power cycle the DHCP server immediately.
    d. Verify that the DHCP server is authorized.

25. You want to deploy IPAM in your network. You have four servers running and need to decide on which server you should install the IPAM Server feature. Which of the following server configurations is the best solution?
    a. Windows Server 2022 domain controller
    b. Windows Server 2022 standalone server running DHCP
    c. Windows Server 2022 member server running Web Server
    d. Windows Server 2022 member server running DHCP

26. You recently configured IPAM in your Windows Server 2022 domain. When you view the Server Inventory window, you notice that one DHCP server isn't displayed. This missing server runs Windows Server 2016 in a workgroup configuration and is located in the Engineering Department. Which of the following actions is most likely to display the missing server in the Server Inventory window?
    a. Upgrade the server to Windows Server 2022.
    b. Join the server to the domain.
    c. Configure the server's firewall.
    d. Uninstall DHCP from the server.

27. You have just finished the Add Roles and Features Wizard and clicked the IPAM node in Server Manager. The IPAM Server Tasks window indicates that

you're connected to the IPAM server. What should you do next?

  a. Provision the IPAM server.
  b. Configure server discovery.
  c. Start server discovery.
  d. Select servers to manage.

28. You have decided to manually provision your IPAM managed servers. Which of the following are tasks you must complete on each managed server? (Choose three.)

  a. Configure security groups.
  b. Create and configure shares.
  c. Install an SQL server.
  d. Set firewall rules.

29. Which of the following is true about IP addressing in Azure?

  a. You create an IP address pool and bind it to a VM group.
  b. Each Azure subscription requires a DHCP server.
  c. An IP address space is associated with a virtual network.
  d. You must create a new DHCP server resource for each subnet.

30. Which of the following is true about IP subnets in Azure?

  a. You can create a maximum of 100 subnets per virtual network.
  b. The smallest IP address prefix you can use is /29.
  c. Azure uses the last two addresses of each subnet for internal use.
  d. Broadcast packets on one subnet are forwarded to all other subnets.

Critical Thinking

The following activities give you critical thinking challenges. Case projects offer a scenario with a problem for which you supply a written solution.

Case Projects

Case Project 8-1: Configuring DHCP for a New Subnet

CSM Tech Publishing has expanded its network from one subnet to two subnets and is putting 200 computers on the new subnet, with plans for adding up to 100 more computers over the next few years. Currently, it's using DHCP for the existing subnet and has a scope configured with start address 172.16.1.1, end address 172.16.1.200, and a prefix length of 24. The DHCP server is in the main distribution facility where the router is placed to route between the subnets. The current DHCP server runs Windows Server 2022, is performing well, and has plenty of unused computing resources (CPU, memory, and so forth). You need to configure DHCP for the new subnet at the lowest cost possible. What do you recommend for adding DHCP services to the new subnet? Propose a DHCP configuration and the scope's start address, end address, and prefix length for the new subnet.

Case Project 8-2: Supporting New Mobile Devices

You're called in to consult for a company that's issuing about 100 new wireless mobile devices to selected employees. There are two subnets, each with a DHCP scope that has about 150 unused addresses and an access point that relays DHCP requests from wireless clients to the DHCP server. The mobile devices will be equally distributed between the subnets. Both scopes are served by a dual-homed server. You want these mobile devices to be issued IP addresses using the last 75 addresses of both scopes and to have a shorter lease time for addresses. What do you propose? What information do you need to carry out the proposal?

Case Project 8-3: Implementing IPAM

You're a consultant for a large enterprise that needs a comprehensive IP addressing and DNS management solution for their physical and virtual networks. They have a primary office in Pittsburgh and three branch offices in Allentown, New York, and Phoenix. They only have IT support staff in the branch offices. Their server specialists are located in Pittsburgh. The IT director in Pittsburgh wants to offload some of the IPAM management functions on some of the IT staff without giving them broader domain or forest administrative rights. Which type of IPAM architecture do you recommend? Which features of IPAM are you likely to recommend to address the requirements?

Solutions to Self-Check Questions

Section 8-1: An Overview of Dynamic Host Configuration Protocol

1. When a DHCP client does not have an IP address, what is the first packet sent by the client in an attempt to request an address?

    Answer: b. DHCPDISCOVER

    Explanation: DHCP packets are sent in this order: DHCPDISCOVER, DHCPOFFER, DHCPREQUEST, and DHCPACK.

2. After how much of the IP address lease time has expired does a DHCP client first attempt to renew the lease?

    Answer: a. 50 percent

    Explanation: A DHCP client attempts to renew the lease after it is 50 percent expired. If there is no response, the client tries again at 87.5 percent.

Section 8-2: Installing and Configuring DHCP

3. Which part of the DHCP configuration creates a pool of IP addresses that can be leased to clients?

    Answer: c. DHCP scope

    Explanation: A DHCP scope creates a pool of IP addresses that can be leased to clients. There is no DHCP zone. An exclusion range excludes addresses from the pool, and reservations reserve individual addresses for specific clients.

4. What does a DHCP reservation use to identify a client?

    Answer: d. MAC address

    Explanation: The MAC address of a client is used to create a reservation and to identify a client requesting an IP address.

Section 8-3: DHCP Server Options

5. What should you configure on a multihomed server if you don't want the server to respond to DHCP packets on one or more interfaces?

    Answer: a. Bindings

    Explanation: If the DHCP server has two or more network connections, you might not always want it to respond to DHCP packets from all networks, as when one network is connected to the Internet or a datacenter in which all addresses are statically assigned. You can enable or disable the binding for each interface. If a binding is disabled, that interface will not listen for DHCP packets.

6. How many conflict detections are configured on a DHCP server by default?

    Answer: d. 0

    Explanation: By default, conflict detection is disabled by setting the number of detections to 0.

Section 8-4: DHCP High Availability

7. In a split scope configuration, what option do you configure on the servers to ensure that the primary server services most client requests?

   Answer: b. Delay

   Explanation: The "Delay in DHCP offer" option specifies the number of milliseconds each server should delay between receiving a DHCPDISCOVER and sending a DHCPOFFER. You usually set the primary server for a zero delay.

8. In a DHCP load-balancing failover configuration, what option can you configure if you want one of the servers to service the majority of DHCP requests?

   Answer: c. Percentage

   Explanation: The Load Balance Percentage option defines the percentage of client requests serviced by each server. The default value is 50 percent for each server.

Section 8-5: IP Address Management

9. In which type of IPAM topology is an IPAM server deployed at every site?

   Answer: b. Distributed

   Explanation: An IPAM deployment has three topology options: centralized, distributed, and hybrid. In a distributed topology, an IPAM server is deployed at every site in the network. Each server is assigned a group of managed servers in the same site. There's no communication between IPAM servers.

10. After the IPAM server has been provisioned, you configure server discovery next. True or False?

    Answer: a. True

    Explanation: The next step after provisioning the IPAM server is to discover servers to manage.

Section 8-6: IP Addressing in Hybrid Environments

11. Which of the following is an address range that cannot be used when creating a virtual network?

    Answer: b. 169.254.0.0 – 169.254.255.255

    Explanation: The range 169.254.0.0 – 169.254.255.255 is reserved for automatic IP addressing (APIPA) and cannot be used for a virtual network. All other ranges in the choices are allowed.

12. An address space is specified using IP address/subnet mask notation. True or False?

    Answer: b. False

    Explanation: An address space is specified using CIDR notation. An example in this format is 192.168.1.0/24, where /24 specifies that the first 24 bits of the IP address are the network identifier.

Module 9

Implement Network Connectivity

Module Objectives

After reading this module and completing the exercises, you will be able to:

1 Implement and manage the Remote Access server role

2 Configure the Network Policy Server role

3 Describe Web Application Proxy

4 Implement Azure networking

The old work model of throngs of workers going to an office and staying there from 9 to 5 no longer applies to many businesses. With remote access technology, employees can work from home or on the road and still have access to all the resources and applications they would have while sitting at a desk in the company office. With the Remote Access server role, network administrators can offer options to employees for accessing network resources remotely. The Remote Access server role can also facilitate communication between a main office and a branch office using site-to-site VPN technology. That same technology can be used to seamlessly tie your on-premises datacenter to your Azure resources.

With an abundance of remote access possibilities, security is of utmost concern. The Network Policy Server role addresses many of those concerns by allowing you to create policies and rules that govern remote access. With web-based applications being the norm today, Web Application Proxy, a component of the Remote Access role, makes publishing web applications convenient and secure.

Finally, you'll learn more in this module about implementing Azure networking, including working with Azure Network Adapter, Azure Extended Network, Azure Relay, Azure Virtual WAN, and Azure AD Application Proxy. All are vital tools for making a hybrid computing and network infrastructure work smoothly and efficiently.

Table 9-1 describes what you need for the hands-on activities in this module.

Table 9-1 Activity requirements

Activity	Requirements	Notes
Activity 9-1: Resetting Your Virtual Environment	ServerDC1, ServerDM1, ServerSA1	
Activity 9-2: Installing and Configuring the Remote Access Role	ServerDC1, Server DM1	
Activity 9-3: Creating a VPN Connection and Testing the VPN	ServerDC1, ServerDM1, ServerSA1	
Activity 9-4: Resetting Your Virtual Environment	ServerDC1, ServerDM1, ServerSA1	
Activity 9-5: Installing the NPS and RRAS Server Roles	ServerDC1, ServerDM1	
Activity 9-6: Configuring a RADIUS Server	ServerDC1, ServerDM1, ServerSA1	
Activity 9-7: Creating a VPN Connection and Testing RADIUS	ServerDC1, ServerDM1, ServerSA1	
Activity 9-8: Creating a Connection Request Policy	ServerDC1	
Activity 9-9: Creating a VPN Client Network Policy	ServerDC1	
Activity 9-10: Creating a Shared Secret Template	ServerDC1	

The Remote Access Role

> **Microsoft Exam AZ-800:**
>
> Implement and manage an on-premises and hybrid networking infrastructure.
> - Implement on-premises and hybrid network connectivity

Remote Access is a server role that provides services to keep a mobile workforce and branch offices securely connected to resources at the main office. The Remote Access server role also plays a part in maintaining a hybrid networking infrastructure between on-premises users and resources and Azure cloud resources. Businesses both large and small might use a remote access solution for the following reasons:

- *Work-from-home employees*—Employees' physical locations might not be as important as their ability to produce the required work. In addition, teleconferencing applications can often meet the need for personal interactions among employees and team members.
- *Frequent travelers*—Employees who are on the road a lot, such as salespeople, product support specialists, and people who need to work with customers or products in the field, require up-to-date access to company resources.
- *Business partners*—You might need to provide limited access to the company network (intranet) for partners who need real-time information on inventory and product delivery.
- *Branch offices*—With the widespread availability of high-speed Internet connections, branch offices can often use less expensive but still secure virtual private networks (VPNs) to connect to the main office.
- *Hybrid network connectivity*—This technology connects on-premises datacenter resources and users to Azure computing, storage, and application resources.

No matter how remote access is set up, the goal is usually the same: giving remote users access to network resources in a way that's much like being on the network premises. This includes branch office workers and users accessing

Azure resources within the company network and remotely. The Remote Access server role has several services and tools to help achieve this goal, including the following:

- *Virtual private network*—A VPN uses the Internet to create a secure connection from a client computer or branch office to the company's intranet. VPNs have largely replaced remote dial-in for client computers.
- *Remote dial-in*—This technology is less common today but still used when broadband Internet isn't available. It uses the phone system and modems to connect remotely.
- *Routing*—This service configures a Windows server as a router with support for static and dynamic routing.
- *Network Address Translation (NAT)*—NAT is used with routing to translate private IP addresses to public IP addresses and to facilitate hosts accessing the Internet in a private network.
- *Web Application Proxy*—This service allows remote users to access network applications from any device that supports a web browser.
- *DirectAccess*—Similar to VPNs, DirectAccess provides a more convenient, manageable, and secure remote connection using features available in IPv6.

The Remote Access server role has some additional features, but the ones in the preceding list are the core services for most remote access needs. This book focuses on virtual private networks and Web Application Proxy.

Installing and Configuring the Remote Access Role

The Remote Access server role is installed by using Server Manager or the `Install-WindowsFeature` PowerShell cmdlet. Under the main Remote Access server role, there are three role services to choose from:

- *DirectAccess and VPN (RAS)*—This role service has the features needed for dial-in, VPN, and DirectAccess remote access.
- *Routing*—This role service provides routing and NAT. The Routing role service requires the DirectAccess and VPN (RAS) role service.
- *Web Application Proxy*—This service allows publishing web-based applications for use by clients outside the network.

Virtual Private Networks

A **virtual private network (VPN)** is a connection that uses the Internet to give mobile users or branch offices secure access to a company's network resources on a private network. VPNs use encryption and authentication to ensure that communication is secure and legitimate, so although data travels through the public Internet, the connection remains private—hence the name "virtual private network."

Privacy is achieved by creating a "tunnel" between the VPN client and VPN server. A **tunnel** is a method of transferring data across an unsecured network so that the actual data in the transmission is hidden from all but the sender and receiver. Tunnels are created by encapsulation, in which the inner packet containing the data is encrypted and the outer headers contain the unencapsulated addresses that Internet devices need to route packets correctly. To use a mail delivery analogy, suppose you have an ultra-secure package to deliver, but you must use a courier. In a separate transaction, you deliver a key to the office manager at the package recipient's location. Next, you place the secret package containing the recipient's name in a lockbox. You put the lockbox inside a separate box and address it to the office manager of the company where the recipient works. The courier can read the address on the box, but if it is opened, the package contents can't be accessed without the key to the lockbox. The box is delivered, and the office manager removes the lockbox from the outer box and opens it with the key delivered earlier. The office manager can then deliver the package to the final recipient. In this analogy, the lockbox and outer box make up the VPN tunnel, and the office manager is the VPN server to which messages are delivered.

Figure 9-1 shows a VPN tunnel between a client computer and an intranet. The tunnel connection is made between the client computer and the VPN server. After the VPN server opens the packet, the inner packet is decrypted (unlocked) and delivered to the resource that the client requested. From the client computer's standpoint, access to network resources is little different than if the client were physically connected to the company network. In fact, the

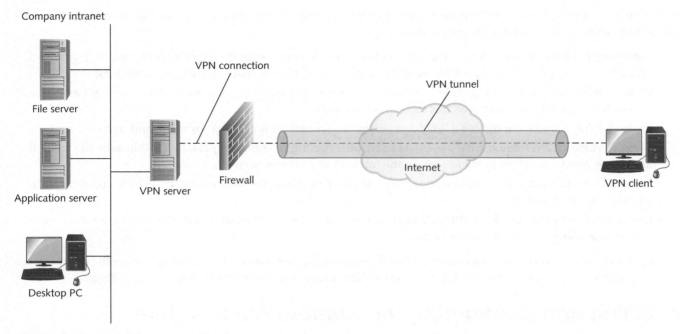

Figure 9-1 A typical VPN connection

VPN network connection on the client OS is assigned an IP address on the network. While Figure 9-1 depicts a client-to-site VPN connection, a site-to-site VPN connection works much the same way and is discussed later in this module.

VPN Tunnel Types

Windows Server 2022 has a VPN server solution with Routing and Remote Access Service (RRAS), a component of the Remote Access server role, and supports three types of VPN tunnels:

- *Point-to-Point Tunneling Protocol (PPTP)*—A commonly used VPN protocol that encapsulates Point-to-Point Protocol (PPP), PPTP uses a modified version of Generic Routing Encapsulation (GRE). The data in encapsulated PPP frames is compressed, encrypted, or both. Frames are encrypted with Microsoft Point-to-Point Encryption (MPPE) by using encryption keys from the authentication process. Authentication uses Microsoft Challenge Handshake Authentication Protocol version 2 (MS-CHAP v2) or Extensible Authentication Protocol-Transport Layer Security (EAP-TLS, which is described later). An advantage of using PPTP is that it is well supported by most OSs and network devices and doesn't require exchanging a preshared key or certificates. Because of its widespread support, this tunnel type is often used when a variety of clients are used to connect to the VPN.

- *Layer 2 Tunneling Protocol with Internet Protocol Security (L2TP/IPsec)*—Developed in cooperation with Cisco Systems and Microsoft, L2TP with IPsec generally provides a higher level of security than PPTP. L2TP doesn't use MPPE for encryption; instead, it uses the encryption technology built into IPsec. IPsec uses Data Encryption Standard (DES) or Triple DES (3DES), using encryption keys generated by the Internet Key Exchange (IKE) process. L2TP/IPsec requires certificates or preshared keys for authentication. Certificates issued both to client and server computers from a public key infrastructure (PKI) is recommended. In addition to securing data through encryption, L2TP/IPsec provides data integrity and identity verification. This tunnel type is most often used when an organization has an established PKI and client computers are members of the organization's network (as opposed to being employee home computers).

- *Secure Socket Tunneling Protocol (SSTP)*—SSTP has the advantage of working behind most firewalls without firewall administrators needing to configure the firewall to allow VPN. It uses the standard TCP port 443 used for Secure Sockets Layer (SSL) communication (HTTPS). SSTP is supported only on Windows clients, starting with Vista SP1, and as a VPN server starting with Windows Server 2008. It requires the VPN server to have a valid digital certificate issued by a certification authority (CA) for server identification. This tunnel type is gaining in popularity because of its ease of use and compatibility with firewalls, but it only works when client computers run Windows Vista SP1 and later versions.

All three types are enabled by default when you configure Windows Server 2022 as a VPN server, so any type of client that tries to connect will be successful as long as each tunnel type is configured correctly. VPN server configuration in Windows Server 2022 is fairly straightforward. After the Remote Access server role is installed, you configure it in the Routing and Remote Access console, which is accessed from the Tools menu in Server Manager.

VPN Requirements

Before you can configure a VPN with RRAS, your server and network must meet the following requirements for the type of VPN you want to set up:

- *Two or more NICs installed on a server*—One NIC is connected to the private network to which you are allowing remote access, and the other is connected to the Internet. The VPN server acts as a router of sorts, receiving traffic from VPN clients on the interface connected to the Internet and routing the traffic to the private network. The VPN server decrypts, authenticates, and validates the traffic as the tunnel type requires before sending it to the private network. Traffic from the private network is received on one or more other NICs and routed to the Internet-connected NIC, where it is made secure for transmission to the VPN client.
- *Correctly configured firewall*—The network firewall must be configured according to the requirements of the VPN tunnel type. When the VPN is configured on the Windows server, Windows configures Windows Firewall for the VPN tunnel type, but the firewall protecting the network must also be configured to allow VPN traffic to reach the VPN server. Firewall configurations are discussed later in this section.
- *Authentication*—Depending on which tunnel types your VPN supports, you might need to configure one or more authentication methods, such as a Remote Authentication Dial-In User Service (RADIUS) server to handle user authentication. RADIUS is a service that's part of the Network Policy Server (NPS) server role, which provides centralized authentication for remote access and wireless clients. (NPS and RADIUS are discussed later in this module.) If the VPN supports SSTP connections, the server must have a digital certificate assigned by a public CA, such as VeriSign. L2TP/IPsec tunnels that don't use preshared keys need both client and server certificates, which can be issued from a Windows-based PKI with Windows Certificate Services.
- *DHCP configuration*—Clients that connect to the VPN server are usually assigned an IP address dynamically. Although the server can be configured with a pool of addresses to assign to clients, a Dynamic Host Configuration Protocol (DHCP) server is recommended for centralized IP address management. When a DHCP server is used, the VPN server requests a small pool of 10 addresses from the DHCP server and then allocates these addresses to clients when they connect. If the VPN server runs out of addresses, it requests another small pool of addresses to lease to clients.

Network Firewall Configuration for a VPN

Configuring the perimeter network firewall is critical for VPN operation. A **perimeter network** is a boundary between the private network and the public Internet. Most resources that are available to the Internet, such as mail, web, DNS, and VPN servers, are located on the perimeter network. Although these resources can be accessed from the Internet, they're still guarded by a firewall to prevent malicious packets from entering the network.

Most firewalls are configured to allow only limited types of incoming traffic. For example, if you have a company web server, the firewall must allow TCP ports 80 and 443 for incoming web traffic to reach the web server. If you're running a DNS server for Internet resources, the firewall must allow UDP port 53 for DNS queries. For VPNs, the firewall must be configured to allow the following types of traffic to the VPN server, according to the VPN tunnel type:

PPTP tunnels

- Inbound destination TCP port 1723 for PPTP maintenance traffic from VPN client to server
- Inbound destination IP protocol ID 47 (GRE) for tunneled data transfers from VPN client to server
- Outbound source TCP port 1723 for PPTP maintenance traffic from VPN server to client
- Outbound source IP protocol ID 47 (GRE) for tunneled data transfers from VPN server to client

L2TP/IPsec tunnels

- Inbound destination User Datagram Protocol (UDP) port 500 for IKE traffic from VPN client to server
- Inbound destination UDP port 4500 for IPsec NAT traversal traffic from VPN client to server

- Inbound destination IP protocol ID 50 for IPsec Encapsulating Security Payload (ESP) traffic from VPN client to server
- Outbound source UDP port 500 for IKE traffic from VPN server to client
- Outbound source UDP port 4500 for IPsec NAT traversal traffic from VPN server to client
- Outbound source IP protocol ID 50 for IPsec ESP traffic from VPN server to client

SSTP tunnels

- Inbound destination TCP port 443 for HTTPS traffic from VPN client to server
- Outbound source TCP port 443 for HTTPS traffic from VPN server to client

VPN Configuration

After meeting the requirements for a VPN server and network, it's time to configure a VPN. If the VPN server is a domain member, its computer account must first be added to the RAS and IAS Servers group in Active Directory. (IAS stands for Internet Authentication Service.) The RAS and IAS Servers group is in the Users folder. When you install the Remote Access server role, the computer on which you are installing it should automatically be added to this group, but it's a good idea to verify it.

Although you can use PowerShell cmdlets to configure RRAS, the following steps use the Routing and Remote Access console. By default, all remote access functions are disabled, as indicated by a red, downward-facing arrow on the server icon. To enable these functions, right-click the server icon and click Configure and Enable Routing and Remote Access. After the Welcome window, the Configuration window gives you the following options for the type of remote access server you want to configure (see Figure 9-2):

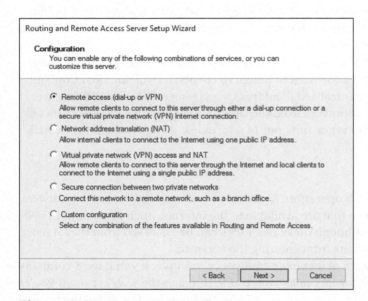

Figure 9-2 The RRAS Configuration window

- *Remote access (dial-up or VPN)*—Configures the server as a VPN server, a dial-up server, or both. Select this option if the server will provide incoming VPN or dial-up services for remote clients but not act as a NAT device for outgoing Internet connections.
- *Network Address Translation (NAT)*—Configures the server as a NAT router to allow computers on the private network to access the Internet with a public IP address.
- *Virtual private network (VPN) access and NAT*—Configures the server as both a remote access (VPN or dial-up) server and a NAT router. This option combines the first two options.
- *Secure connection between two private networks*—Configures the server as a VPN router between two networks, such as between a main office and branch office. With this configuration, all traffic between the two networks is secure, but the server doesn't accept client connections.

- *Custom configuration*—Allows you to manually configure the routing and remote access features you need if one of the standard options doesn't meet your requirements.

For a standard VPN server, select the "Remote access (dial-up or VPN)" option. In the next window, you can choose VPN, dial-up, or both. For a VPN server without dial-up support, select the VPN option. In the VPN Connection window, select the network interface that connects the server to the Internet (see Figure 9-3). This interface must be connected to the Internet and the correct firewall ports must be open to allow VPN traffic to this interface's IP address.

Figure 9-3   The VPN Connection window

In Figure 9-3, the network connections are named descriptively; although this naming convention isn't required, it's a good idea on any computer with multiple network connections. You can rename network connections in the Network Connections window. The "Enable security on the selected interface by setting up static packet filters" option is enabled by default. It prevents the interface connected to the Internet from accepting any traffic that isn't part of a VPN connection. For example, even if the firewall is configured to allow ping packets into the network, the packet filters created by this option deny the packets unless they originate from a VPN client.

Next, you decide how VPN client connections are assigned an IP address when they connect to the VPN (see Figure 9-4):

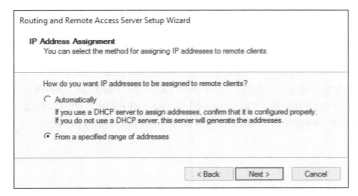

Figure 9-4   The IP Address Assignment window

- *Automatically*—This option is preferred and requires a correctly configured DHCP server on the network. The VPN server gets a pool of 10 addresses at a time to allocate to VPN clients. If the DHCP server is on a different subnet from the VPN client, the DHCP relay agent must be configured. Both IPv4 and IPv6 addresses can be assigned. If you select this option and no DHCP server can be contacted to assign IPv4 addresses, the VPN server assigns APIPA addresses to clients. (APIPA stands for Automatic Private IP Addressing.) If a DHCP server can't be contacted to assign IPv6 addresses, the client uses the IPv6 prefix configured on the VPN server and a locally generated interface ID.

- *From a specified range of addresses*—If no DHCP server is available, choose this option to specify a range of IPv4 addresses for allocating to clients. For IPv6 addresses, only the prefix is assigned by the VPN server; the client uses a locally generated interface ID.

Next, you decide how clients are authenticated to the VPN server and specify whether you want to use RADIUS to handle authentication for client connection requests (see Figure 9-5):

Figure 9-5   Configuring authentication

- *No, use Routing and Remote Access to authenticate connection requests*—With this option, the VPN server authenticates connection requests by contacting a domain controller if the server is a domain member. If it isn't a domain member, it uses accounts from the local SAM database. For security reasons, a domain-joined VPN server isn't recommended.
- *Yes, set up this server to work with a RADIUS server*—Choose this option when there are multiple remote access servers that aren't joined to a domain. A RADIUS server performs centralized authentication, as you learned in Module 7.

After you click Finish in the summary window, you see a message that you must configure the DHCP relay agent. You need to do this only if you configured automatic IP address assignment and the DHCP server isn't on the same subnet as the server's private network connection.

> **Note 1**
>
> Occasionally, RRAS configuration fails, and you will see an error message that RRAS could not start because there's a problem—for example, the Windows Defender Firewall wasn't configured. If this happens, disable RRAS by right-clicking the server node and clicking Disable Routing and Remote Access. After it is disabled, repeat the configuration process.

Finishing VPN Configuration

After you have finished the RRAS Setup Wizard, the VPN server is ready to start accepting VPN client connections. However, first you need to define who's allowed to connect via remote access. By default, all users are denied remote access. There are two ways to allow users to connect via remote access: configuring dial-in settings in user accounts and configuring a network policy in the Network Policy Server (NPS) console.

Configuring Dial-in Settings in User Accounts

If you have only a few users who should be able to access the network remotely, you can configure each user's account properties in Active Directory or Local Users and Groups to allow remote access. In each account's Properties dialog box, click the Dial-in tab (see Figure 9-6). By default, the Network Access Permission attribute is set to "Control access through NPS Network Policy." The NPS Network Policy is configured to deny access to all users by default, so select the Allow access option (highlighted in the figure) to give the user permission to connect remotely via dial-in, VPN, and DirectAccess.

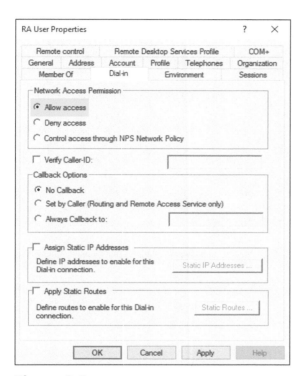

Figure 9-6   Configuring the Network Access
Permission attribute for a user account

The remaining settings on the Dial-in tab are as follows:

- *Verify Caller-ID*—This option is used only for dial-in remote access. When the user attempts to log on, the phone number attempting the remote connection is verified against the phone number entered in the text box by using caller ID. If the number doesn't match or caller ID isn't supported, the connection is denied.
- *Callback Options*—This option is used only for dial-in remote access and by default is set to No Callback. If Set by Caller is selected, the remote access client enters a number, and the server calls the client back to make the connection, thereby saving client phone charges. If Always Callback to is selected, the server attempts to call the number specified to make the connection.
- *Assign Static IP Addresses*—Use this option to assign static IPv4 and IPv6 addresses the client uses for remote access connections rather than dynamic addresses assigned by the VPN server.
- *Apply Static Routes*—Select this option to configure routes the client's connection uses when accessing certain network resources.

VPN Client Configuration

The VPN client is configured by setting up a new connection in the Network and Sharing Center. When you set up a new connection, you choose "Connect to a workplace," and then you have the option to use your existing connection to the Internet or create a dial-up connection. After you choose the connection, you enter the address of the VPN server you'll connect to and enter a name for the connection. You can also create a VPN connection by using the following PowerShell cmdlet in Windows 10, Windows Server 2012 R2, and later versions:

```
Add-VpnConnection -Name "VPN to Work" -ServerAddress
    "203.0.113.1"
```

If you need to set up a VPN connection to several computers in your network, you can do so with group policy preferences. Open a GPO in Group Policy Management Editor and navigate to Computer Configuration, Preferences, and Control Panel Settings. Right-click Network Options, point to New, and click VPN Connection. In the New VPN Properties dialog box, fill in the information shown in Figure 9-7.

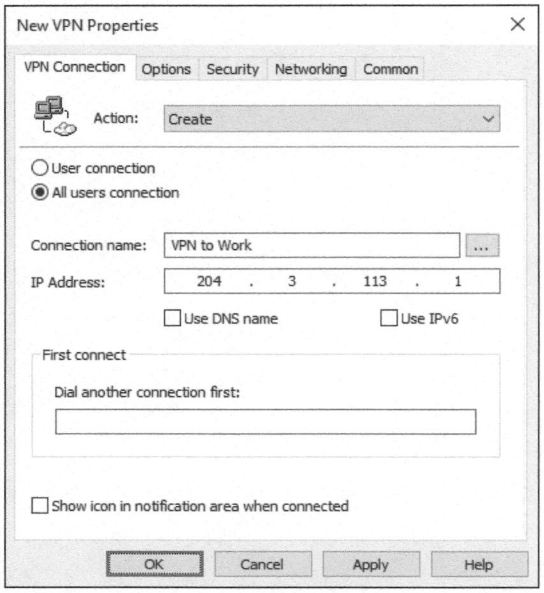

Figure 9-7 Creating a VPN connection with group policy preferences

When you create a VPN connection, the default tunnel type is Automatic. This means the VPN client attempts to make the connection by using each tunneling method until it's successful or the connection fails. You can configure the client to use a particular tunnel type in the connection's properties.

Configuring Remote Access Options

The default settings for VPN and dial-up might be adequate in many circumstances, but you might need to support different OSs and VPN clients over a variety of tunneling methods, which could require security settings other than the defaults. In addition, although RRAS allows multiple tunneling types by default for VPN connections, you might want to restrict connections to a particular tunneling method.

As you've learned, you can configure remote access settings in the properties of a user account, but this method can prove inefficient when many users need remote access permission. Instead, you can allow or disallow remote access to users based on connection-related group policies. The following sections cover tasks you might need to perform after configuring RRAS.

Configuring Remote Access Security

To configure security settings for remote access, right-click the server in the Routing and Remote Access console and click Properties. In the Security tab (see Figure 9-8), you can configure the following settings:

- *Authentication provider*—Choose Windows Authentication or RADIUS Authentication. If you choose Windows Authentication, Windows tries to authenticate users attempting to log on via VPN or dial-in from the local SAM

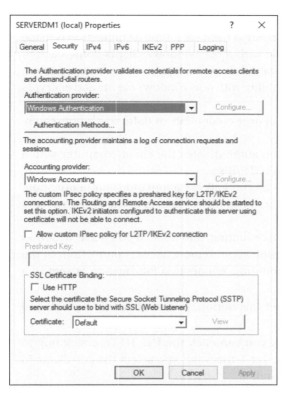

Figure 9-8   Security settings for remote access

account database or a DC. If you choose RADIUS, you must specify which RADIUS servers the RRAS server should use.

- *Authentication Methods*—Whether you're using Windows Authentication or RADIUS Authentication, you can select the authentication methods available to the user account trying to log on. Authentication is attempted by using the enabled methods in the order you see in Figure 9-9:
  - ○ Extensible authentication protocol (EAP): Selected by default, it's the most flexible authentication method because it works with non-Windows clients, and third-party providers can develop custom authentication schemes. EAP is required for the use of smart cards and can be used for biometric authentication.

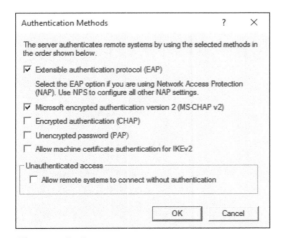

Figure 9-9   Authentication methods

     ○ Microsoft encrypted authentication version 2 (MS-CHAP v2): This mutual authentication protocol encrypts both authentication information and data. A different encryption key is used each time a connection is made and on both ends of the connection. MS-CHAP v2 is compatible with most Windows clients going back to Windows 98. This method has the advantage of being able to prompt the user to change an expired password.

     ○ Encrypted authentication (CHAP): This method provides compatibility with non-Windows clients and encrypts authentication data but not connection data.

     ○ Unencrypted password (PAP): This method has no encryption of user credentials or data, so it's not recommended for most applications.

     ○ Allow machine certificate authentication for IKEv2: This method authenticates the client computer with a digital certificate and can be used only when the tunnel type is L2TP/IPsec.

     ○ Allow remote systems to connect without authentication: This method allows anonymous authentication, meaning no user credentials are required. It should be used only to test other aspects of the remote access connection.

- *Accounting provider*—Options are Windows Accounting, RADIUS Accounting, and none. If you leave Windows Accounting selected (the default option), the server logs information about remote access connections in the log files configured in the Logging tab. If you select RADIUS Accounting, connection information is sent to a RADIUS server for logging.

- *Allow custom IPsec policy for L2TP/IKEv2 connection*—If you select this option, you must supply a preshared key for all connections using the custom IPsec policy.

- *SSL Certificate Binding*—If you're using the SSTP tunneling type, you can click the Use HTTP check box to specify that SSTP should use the same certificate as the HTTP server. Otherwise, you select the certificate in the Certificate drop-down list. The certificate must already be installed.

Configuring Available Tunnel Types

When a VPN client attempts to connect to a VPN, it tries to use each of the tunneling types until it's successful or the connection fails. By default, each tunneling type is enabled in the RRAS service when you configure a VPN, and each type allows up to 128 connections or ports. You can configure the number of ports in the Routing and Remote Access console by right-clicking Ports and clicking Properties. In the Ports Properties dialog box, double-click a tunnel type to see the Configure Device dialog box, where you can change the maximum number of ports (see Figure 9-10). Changing the number of ports to 0 effectively disables the tunnel type. You can also disable inbound remote access connections for that tunnel type, which disables the tunnel type as well.

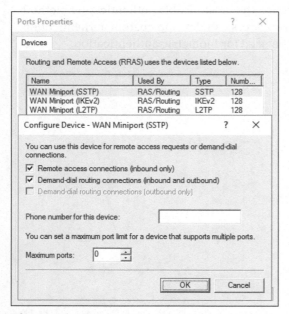

Figure 9-10   Configuring port properties

Configuring a Site-to-Site VPN

A site-to-site VPN securely connects two networks—for example, a branch office and a main office. The VPN tunnel is established between two network devices such as routers or Windows servers configured as VPN servers (see Figure 9-11). Client computers do not run a VPN client, so traffic between the client computers and the router/VPN server is not encrypted; only traffic between the router and VPN servers is encrypted.

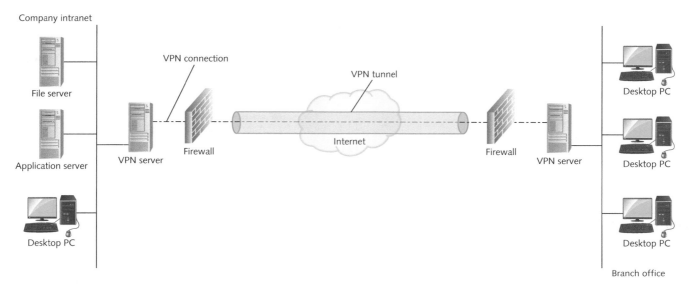

Figure 9-11   A site-to-site VPN

To configure a site-to-site VPN with Windows Server 2022, configure Routing and Remote Access using the "Secure connection between two private networks" option in the Configuration window. In the Demand-Dial Connections window, choose Yes. You will configure the demand-dial connection after the wizard finishes. A **demand-dial interface** is a network connection that is used to establish the VPN connection whenever traffic from the internal network has a destination address of the other network to which you are connecting. To configure the demand-dial interface, follow the Demand-Dial Interface Wizard that is started automatically:

1. On the first screen of the Demand-Dial Interface Wizard, you are prompted to enter the name of the interface. The interface name is usually the name of the router or device you are connecting to. For example, if you are configuring the main office server, you might name the connection BranchOffice (see Figure 9-12). If you are configuring the branch office server, you might name the connection MainOffice.

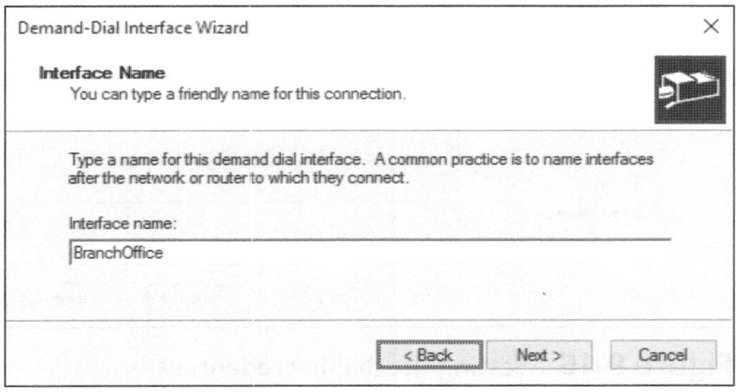

Figure 9-12   Specifying the demand-dial interface name

2. Next, you specify the connection type. You have the option of VPN or PPoE. Choose VPN and click Next.
3. Specify the connection type. You can select Automatic, PPTP, L2TP, or IKEv2 (see Figure 9-13).
4. Next, you enter the host name or IP address of the remote router you are connecting to.
5. In the Protocols and Security window (see Figure 9-14), select "Route IP packets on this interface" and "Add a user account so a remote router can dial in." These options allow the VPN server to act as a router and require authentication with the other network.

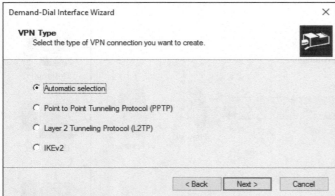

Figure 9-13   Selecting the VPN type

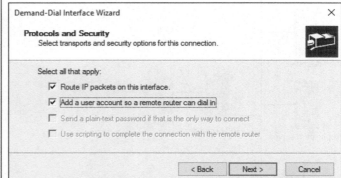

Figure 9-14   Protocols and Security window

6. Next, you configure static routes. A static route specifies the IP network address of the remote network (see Figure 9-15). When a client on the internal network sends a packet to the remote network, the static route activates the demand-dial connection and routes the packet over the VPN. You can add more than one static route.
7. Specify credentials that the remote router will use when connecting to the VPN server you are configuring. The interface name you specified in Step 1 is automatically used and a user account is created with the password you specify in this window (see Figure 9-16).
8. Finally, specify the dial-out credentials, which is the username and password used to connect to the remote router. The credentials configured here must match the dial-in credentials configured on the remote router. For example, if you are configuring the VPN server at the main office, you would assign a username of MainOffice.
9. You must follow the same steps at the remote office, interchanging the dial-in and dial-out credentials.

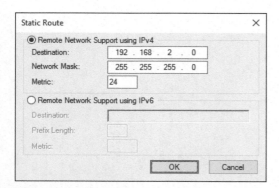

Figure 9-15   Configuring a static route

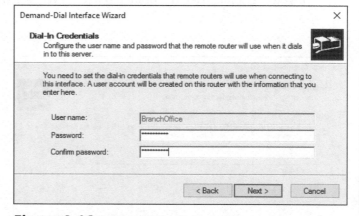

Figure 9-16   Setting the dial-in credentials

After you have completed the preceding steps, you can further configure the demand-dial interface by clicking Network Interfaces in Routing and Remote Access and right-clicking the demand-dial interface (see Figure 9-17). You can configure the credentials, set a demand-dial filter to allow only certain types of traffic to activate the demand-dial interface, and set dial-out hours to restrict when the VPN connection can be used.

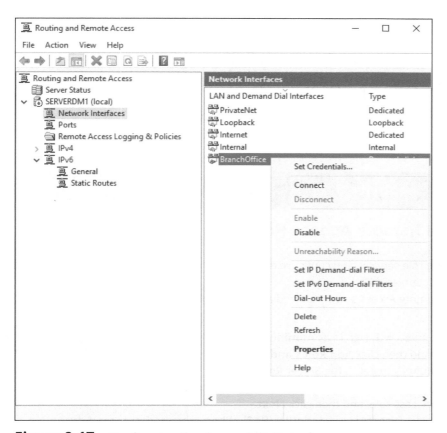

Figure 9-17   Configuring the demand-dial interface

Self-Check Questions

1. Which Remote Access service facilitates access to the Internet when your network is using private IP addresses?

   a. VPN

   b. Remote dial-in

   c. NAT

   d. DirectAccess

2. Which VPN tunnel type uses certificates and TCP port 443?

   a. L2TP/IPsec

   b. SSTP

   c. PPTP

   d. DirectAccess

◉ Check your answers at the end of this module.

Activity 9-1

Resetting Your Virtual Environment

Time Required: 5 minutes
Objective: Reset your virtual environment by applying the InitialConfig checkpoint or snapshot.
Required Tools and Equipment: ServerDC1, ServerDM1, ServerSA1
Description: Apply the InitialConfig checkpoint or snapshot to ServerDC1, ServerDM1, and ServerSA1.

1. Be sure all servers are shut down. In your virtualization program, apply the InitialConfig checkpoint or snapshot to all servers.
2. When the snapshot or checkpoint has been applied, continue to the next activity.

Activity 9-2

Installing and Configuring the Remote Access Role

Time Required: 20 minutes
Objective: Install the Remote Access role and role services and configure a VPN server.
Required Tools and Equipment: ServerDC1, ServerDM1
Description: In this activity, you install the Remote Access server role and associated role services. Then you will configure a VPN server.

1. Start ServerDC1 and ServerDM1. On ServerDM1, sign in as **Administrator**.
2. Open Server Manager, click **Manage**, and then click **Add Roles and Features** from the menu. In the Add Roles and Features Wizard, click **Next** until you get to the Server Roles window.
3. Click **Remote Access**, and then click **Next** twice. In the Remote Access window, read the information that describes the features of the Remote Access role, and then click **Next**.
4. In the Role Services window, click to select **DirectAccess and VPN (RAS)**. When prompted, click the **Add Features** button. Click **Routing** and then click **Next**.
5. In the Web Server Role (IIS) window, read the information and click **Next**. Accept the default role services for the Web Server role, and then click **Next**.
6. Click **Install**. The installation might take a while. When it's finished, click **Close**.
7. The next step is to configure routing and remote access in the Routing and Remote Access console. In Server Manager, click **Tools** and then **Routing and Remote Access** from the menu.
8. In the Routing and Remote Access console, right-click **SERVERDM1 (local)** and click **Configure and Enable Routing and Remote Access**. Click **Next**.
9. In the Configuration window, accept the default setting **Remote access (dial-up or VPN)**, and click **Next**.
10. In the Remote Access window, click **VPN** to configure the server to accept VPN connections, and then click **Next**.
11. In the VPN Connection window, click to select the interface that connects to the Internet. In this case, it's the interface with the IP address 172.31.0.240. Leave the **Enable security on the selected interface by setting up static packet filters** check box selected and click **Next**.
12. In the IP Address Assignment window, click **From a specified range of addresses**, and click **Next**.
13. In the Address Range Assignment window, click **New**. In the Start IP address text box, type **10.99.0.1**, and in the Number of addresses text box, type **10**. Clients that connect to the VPN will be given an address in the specified range so they can access resources on the private network. Click **OK**, and then click **Next**.
14. In the Managing Multiple Remote Access Servers window, accept the default setting **No, use Routing and Remote Access to authenticate connection requests**. Click **Next**, and then click **Finish**.
15. Click **OK** in response to the message about supporting the relaying of DHCP messages. Click **Finish**.
16. Continue to the next activity.

Activity 9-3

Creating a VPN Connection and Testing the VPN

Time Required: 15 minutes

Objective: Create and test a VPN connection.

Required Tools and Equipment: ServerDC1, ServerDM1, ServerSA1

Description: Test the VPN configuration by creating a VPN client connection on ServerSA1 and attempting to connect to the VPN server. For this activity, you'll disable the network interface on ServerSA1 that is connected to the 10.99.0.0/24 network. The second network interface on ServerSA1, with the address 172.31.0.101, will be used to make the VPN connection, as shown in Figure 9-18.

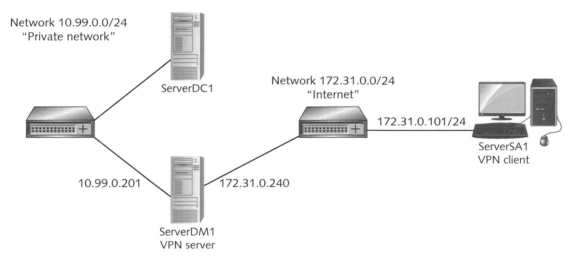

Figure 9-18   Network setup for Activity 9-3

Note 2

In a real VPN scenario, the VPN client and server would be on different subnets. The arrangement in this activity is only meant to illustrate and test a VPN connection.

1. On ServerDM1, right-click **Start** and click **Computer Management**. Click to expand **Local Users and Groups**, right-click **Users**, and click **New User**.

2. In the User name text box, type **VPNTest1**. Type **Password01** in the Password and Confirm password text boxes. Click to clear the **User must change password at next logon** box and click to select the **Password never expires** box. Click **Create** and click **Close**.

3. Double-click **VPNTest1** to open the Properties dialog box. Click the **Dial-in** tab, click **Allow access** in the Network Access Permission section, and then click **OK**. Close Computer Management.

4. On ServerSA1, sign in as **Administrator**. Right-click **Start** and click **Network Connections**. Click **Change adapter options**, right-click **Ethernet0**, and click **Disable**. Verify that Ethernet1 has an IP address of 172.31.0.101 by right-clicking **Ethernet1**, clicking **Status**, and clicking **Details**. Click **Close** twice and close the Network Connections window.

5. Click the network icon on the right side of the taskbar and click **Network & Internet Settings**. Click **VPN** and then click **Add a VPN connection**.

6. In the Add a VPN connection window, fill out the form as shown in Figure 9-19. Click **Save**.

(continues)

Activity 9-3 Continued

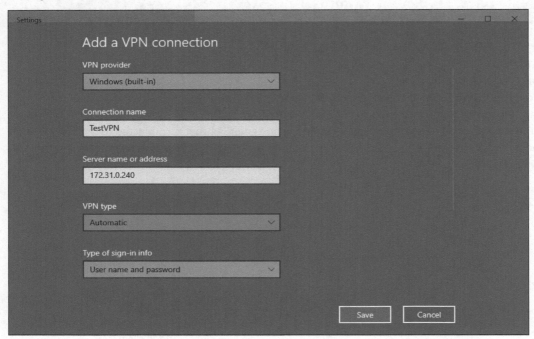

Figure 9-19 Setting up a VPN connection

7. Click **TestVPN** and click **Connect**. When prompted for the username and password, type **serverdm1\vpntest1** for the username, type **Password01** for the password, and click **OK**. You will see the word "Connected" under the TestVPN connection (see Figure 9-20).

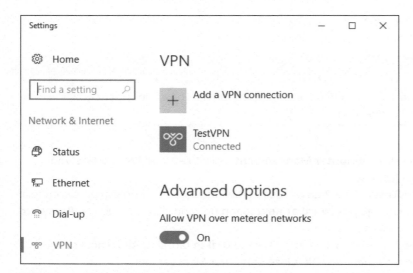

Figure 9-20 Connected to a VPN

8. Open a command prompt. Type **ipconfig** and press Enter. You should see two interfaces: the Ethernet1 interface, which has IP address 172.31.0.101, and the PPP adapter TestVPN with IP address 10.99.0.1 or 10.99.0.2. To verify that you can access resources on the private network, type **ping serverdc1.az800.corp** and press **Enter**. Your pings should be successful. Close the command prompt window.

9. In the Network Connections window, right-click **TestVPN** and click **Connect/Disconnect**. In the Networks panel, click **TestVPN** and click **Disconnect**. Right-click **Ethernet0** and click **Enable** to re-enable the network interface connected to the 10.99.0.0/24 network.

10. Close the Network Connections window and continue to the next activity.

Network Policy Server Overview

Microsoft Exam AZ-800:

Implement and manage an on-premises and hybrid networking infrastructure.

- Implement on-premises and hybrid network connectivity

With Network Policy Server (NPS), a role service of the Network Policy and Access Services (NPAS) server role, you can define and enforce rules that determine who can access your network and how they can access it (via VPN, dial-up, and so forth). Access attempts both successful and unsuccessful can be logged, so NPS has authentication, authorization, and auditing capabilities. The NPS architecture includes three features: RADIUS server, RADIUS proxy, and RADIUS accounting.

The RADIUS Infrastructure

Network Policy Server is Microsoft's implementation of the **Remote Authentication Dial-In User Service (RADIUS)** protocol, a proposed IETF standard that's widely used to centralize authentication, authorization, and accounting to network services. To use NPS, you need to understand the types of messages used in a RADIUS infrastructure carried out in an NPS environment. The following list describes the process and what types of messages are sent:

1. An **access client** (for example, a user on a laptop) makes a connection request to a **network access server (NAS)**, which handles access to a network. An NAS can be, for example, a wireless access point or a VPN server. In the RADIUS infrastructure, an NAS is configured as a RADIUS client.

> **Note 3**
>
> The term "client" can be a bit confusing. Only an NAS that's already part of the network can be a RADIUS client. Devices such as users' desktops, laptops, or mobile devices that are requesting access to the network are called access clients in this context, not RADIUS clients.

2. The RADIUS client sends an Access-Request message, including a username/password combination or a certificate from the user to an NPS server acting as a RADIUS server. This message can include other information about the user, such as the network address.
3. The NPS server evaluates the Access-Request message. This process can include authenticating the username and password (along with other user information) via a domain controller or client certificate.
4. The NPS server can respond with one of three types of messages:

   - *Access-Reject*—The request is rejected, and access is denied to the network or resources.
   - *Access-Challenge*—More information is requested, such as a secondary password or other access code or credential.
   - *Access-Accept*—Access is granted, and authorization is given to certain resources based on defined network policies.

5. The connection is completed, and the NAS sends an Accounting-Request message to the NPS server to be logged. This message is sent to collect information about the user, such as the IP address, the method of connecting to the network, and a session identifier, so that additional information sent can be attributed to this user's connection.
6. The NPS server sends an Accounting-Response message to the NAS to acknowledge that the request was received.
7. During the session, additional Accounting-Request messages are sent with information about the current session. Each Accounting-Request message is acknowledged by an Accounting-Response message.

8. When the user's connection ends, one last Accounting-Request message is sent with information about overall use during the session. This final message is acknowledged by an Accounting-Response message.

A RADIUS proxy can be inserted between network access servers and NPS servers to help manage the load on the NPS servers. The proxy receives the Access-Request and Accounting-Request messages from an NAS and directs them to the NPS server. Figure 9-21 shows the overall RADIUS message flow among access clients, RADIUS clients, RADIUS proxies, and RADIUS servers.

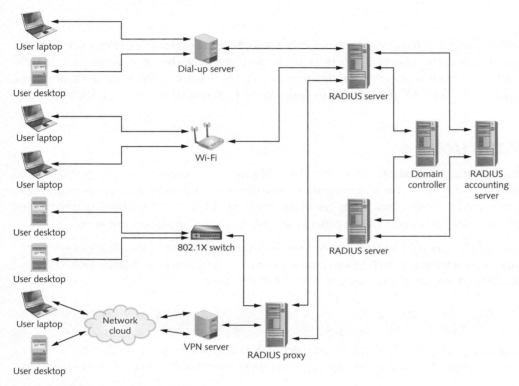

Figure 9-21   RADIUS infrastructure

Installing and Configuring NPS and RADIUS

There are two main reasons you should set up an NPS architecture with RADIUS when you have different connection paths to your network. First, RADIUS centralizes control over authentication and authorization. No matter which path a user takes to access the network, a single point of contact—the NPS server acting as a RADIUS server—handles authenticating the user and determining the level of authorization. Next, standardizing on RADIUS requires all NAS devices to be RADIUS clients so that only one protocol performs authentication and authorization and only one standard configuration process is used, regardless of the kind of device connecting to the network. To begin configuring an NPS/RADIUS environment, you must install the NPS role. To do so, install the Network Policy and Access Services server role from Server Manager or with the following PowerShell cmdlet:

```
Install-WindowsFeature NPAS -IncludeManagementTools
```

After NPS is installed, you can configure the server to be a RADIUS server, RADIUS proxy, or both. In a small environment with few network logon requests, a single RADIUS server is usually sufficient. After you have installed the NPS Server role, you can manage NPS in the Network Policy Server console. You need to configure a couple of settings: which NASs can connect and the authentication method each one uses. NPS gives you the choice of standard or advanced configuration options. The advanced configuration option requires you to set up the components for a RADIUS server or proxy. The standard configuration has wizards to walk you through these policy settings:

- *RADIUS server for Dial-Up or VPN Connections*—This option defines network policies for authenticating and authorizing connections from these RADIUS clients: dial-up or VPN network access servers.

- *RADIUS server for 802.1X Wireless or Wired Connections*—This option defines network policies for authenticating and authorizing connections from these RADIUS clients: wireless access points and authenticating switches.

> **Note 4**
>
> While analog telephone dial-up is no longer a practical method for network communication, the remote access services on Windows Server still support dial-up because digital dial-up technologies such as ISDN and DSL are still in use.

A policy must be defined for each type of RADIUS client, such as VPN NAS, in the NPS console. To create these policies, you need to consider several factors. Just as you want to authenticate clients attempting to access the network, you need to validate communication between a RADIUS client and a RADIUS server or proxy with a **shared secret**, a text string that acts as a password between RADIUS clients, servers, and proxies. Here are a few guidelines for creating shared secrets:

- A shared secret should be at least 22 characters to make guessing it or using brute-force techniques more difficult. It should include uppercase and lowercase letters, numbers from 0 to 9, and symbols such as !, &, and @.
- A shared secret can be up to 128 characters.
- Use a random combination of letters, numbers, and symbols rather than a phrase.

The credentials the NAS passes need to be authenticated. Depending on the type of NAS, two general types of authentication methods are used: password-based and certificate-based. Four password-based methods are supported:

- *Microsoft Challenge Handshake Authentication Protocol*—**Microsoft Challenge Handshake Authentication Protocol (MS-CHAP)** starts with a challenge-response with the access client, and then sends the username and a password with a one-way encryption (meaning the password can't be unencrypted) to be authenticated against the stored credentials.
- *Microsoft Challenge Handshake Authentication Protocol version 2*—**Microsoft Challenge Handshake Authentication Protocol version 2 (MS-CHAP v2)** is an update to MS-CHAP with stronger security. Of the four password-based methods, it's the preferred one.
- *Challenge Handshake Authentication Protocol*—**Challenge Handshake Authentication Protocol (CHAP)** is similar to MS-CHAP, but the password must be able to be unencrypted, making it less secure than MS-CHAP.
- *Password Authentication Protocol*—**Password Authentication Protocol (PAP)** is the least secure method. The password is sent in plaintext, and there's no challenge and response. Because the password could be captured easily, PAP isn't recommended.

The certificate-based authentication method is **Extensible Authentication Protocol (EAP)**. Certificate-based authentication is more secure than password-based methods. Depending on the method you choose, there are two authentication types. The authentication type for EAP is **Transport Layer Security (TLS)**, which is a cryptographic protocol used to encrypt network messages. TLS provides privacy (data encryption), data integrity (detects unauthorized changes in the data), and authentication. Certificates and options for using them are discussed later in the "Using Certificates for Authentication" section.

Protected Extensible Authentication Protocol (PEAP) is a special way to encrypt a password being sent via MS-CHAP v2. With PEAP, you can check the server's certificate for identity verification, but user authentication is still done through passwords.

The groups a user belongs to can control access based on the network policy's access permission setting. With user groups and IP filters, you can create policies that restrict users to using specific protocols and specific servers. Several other authentication settings can be configured. If the client is encrypting its messages to the NAS, you can specify what level of encryption is supported. For example, with an RRAS server, levels such as VPN, Encryption, Strong Encryption, and Strongest Encryption are all supported.

Another part of the network policy is the **realm**. By default, it's the domain where the NPS server is located. If connection requests require authentication from another domain controller, they can be sent to an NPS server acting as a RADIUS proxy, and the realm determines which server the request is routed to.

Although a basic RADIUS infrastructure such as the one you just configured is adequate for most cases, a simple configuration has a few drawbacks. Lack of fault tolerance is the biggest disadvantage. If the one and only RADIUS server goes down, no network connection requests can be authenticated, which makes the network inaccessible to users. To eliminate this single point of failure, you can deploy multiple RADIUS servers. RADIUS clients can be configured to use a primary server and alternates, so if the primary isn't available, the client tries the alternates in turn.

Another concern is the server's load. In a network with hundreds or thousands of requests in extremely short periods, a single RADIUS server could be overwhelmed. One solution is to use RADIUS proxies with multiple RADIUS servers. (Having only one proxy reintroduces the single-point-of-failure problem.) Requests received by a proxy are forwarded to a **RADIUS server group**, composed of one or more RADIUS servers, for handling. In a server group of two or more RADIUS servers, the load can be balanced based on these properties:

- *Priority*—Tells the NPS proxy the order of importance of this server group member when passing on requests. This setting is a nonzero integer (such as 1, 2, or 3). The lower the number, the higher the priority, so servers assigned a priority of 1 get requests first. If the Priority 1 server is unavailable, the request is sent to the Priority 2 server, and so on. Setting just the priority doesn't result in load balancing because the lowest-priority server continues getting requests unless it becomes unavailable. However, a priority of 1 can be assigned to multiple servers, and the Weight setting can be used to force load balancing.
- *Weight*—Determines what percentage of connection requests are sent to a server group member when the priority is the same as other members. This setting is a nonzero integer between 1 and 100. For example, to distribute the load between two servers evenly, you could assign each a priority of 1 and a weight of 50 so that each server gets 50 percent of the connection requests. The sum of all weights in the server group must be 100.
- *Advanced settings*—Determines whether a server group member is unavailable and whether connection requests need to be routed to another server in the group. The settings include the number of seconds a proxy should wait for a response before deciding the request is dropped, the maximum number of requests dropped before the group server is considered unavailable, and the number of seconds between requests before the group server is considered unavailable.

Configuring RADIUS Accounting

RADIUS accounting is essentially a log of the different access and accounting requests and responses sent between RADIUS clients and RADIUS servers, as outlined previously in the section called "The RADIUS Infrastructure." NPS logs requests and responses by using one of these methods:

- *Event logging*—Events that occur while NPS is running are written to event logs.
- *Local text file*—Each user authentication and accounting request is logged to a text file.
- *Microsoft SQL Server XML-compliant database*—Logged data is written to a SQL Server database. Multiple servers can write to a single database. One advantage of this method is that the accounting data is stored in an easily accessible container (a SQL Server database), and the data for multiple systems is combined in this container, which makes reporting more flexible.

The default setting is to log accounting information in a local text file in C:\Windows\System32\LogFiles. You can change this setting in the Network Policy Server console.

Using Certificates for Authentication

The easiest authentication method to set up is password-based. Unfortunately, easy authentication methods often have less security. For stronger security, **certificate-based authentication** is recommended; it uses a certificate (a digital document) containing information that establishes an entity's identity, such as an NPS server or an access client. With this authentication method, a server or client's identity can be verified. You have seen this type of authentication in action on the Internet. When you connect to a website by using https:// in the URL instead of http://, the server is asked for the website certificate to prove that you're connecting to the site you requested. If the server doesn't present the certificate, the connection fails. If the certificate has expired or information such as the requested URL doesn't match what's on the certificate, the connection fails. With NPS, the certificate is presented when the client is attempting to connect, and the server, the client, or both are asked to prove their identity.

Certificates are created and distributed by a **certification authority (CA)**, which is given information that can uniquely identify the server or client. There are two types of CAs: public and private. Examples of public CAs are

VeriSign and Thawte. You purchase certificates from these companies and give them information to prove that you are who you say you are. A private CA, such as Active Directory Certificate Services, allows you to produce as many certificates as you want.

For a certificate to be used for authentication, the CA must be trusted by the client or server. To be trusted, the CA must have a **root certificate** (also called the "CA certificate") in the Trusted Root Certification Authorities certificate store. Think of the root certificate as the master certificate for a CA. After the root certificate is installed, all other certificates from this CA are trusted automatically by the client or server. The process of requesting a certificate, having it approved, and downloading it is called "enrollment." Clients can be enrolled automatically for some certificates in a domain. For example, if the client is a member of the same domain as the CA, the CA certificate is auto-enrolled. Besides the root certificate, there are three other important certificate types:

- *Client computer certificate*—This certificate verifies a client computer's identity to an NPS server. It's enrolled automatically for domain members and imported manually for non-domain members.
- *Server certificate*—This certificate verifies a server's identity to a client. It can be set for auto-enrollment in Active Directory.
- *User certificate*—This certificate can be put on a smart card to verify a user's identity; the smart card reader is attached to the client computer. If you're using smart cards, you don't auto-enroll client computer certificates.

When a certificate is presented for authentication, it must meet these three criteria for authentication to succeed:

- It must be valid (for example, it hasn't expired).
- It must be configured for the purpose it's presented for.
- It must be issued by a trusted CA.

For a client to accept a certificate from an NPS server, the certificate must meet these requirements:

- The subject name can't be blank.
- The certificate is linked to a trusted root CA.
- The purpose of the certificate is server authentication.
- The algorithm name is RSA, and the minimum key size is at least 2048.
- If the subject alternative name (SubjectAltName) extension is used, which allows multiple servers to use the certificate, the certificate must contain the NPS server's DNS name.

You can select certificate-based authentication—EAP—when you're setting the authentication method. EAP requires both the server and the access client to present valid certificates, which is the most secure authentication method. However, in a large organization, maintaining potentially thousands of client certificates can be a daunting administrative job, even with auto-enrollment for new access clients. Selecting PEAP as the authentication method doesn't involve using a client certificate; instead, it uses MS-CHAP v2 for client authentication. It's not as secure, however, as a pure certificate-based authentication method (such as EAP) because users still enter passwords, which can be guessed or stolen. However, PEAP can be configured to require a server certificate. This method protects clients from connecting to a server that's pretending to be the server they want to connect to; also, PEAP encrypts the information it's passing.

Activity 9-4

Resetting Your Virtual Environment
Time Required: 5 minutes
Objective: Reset your virtual environment by applying the InitialConfig checkpoint or snapshot.
Required Tools and Equipment: ServerDC1, ServerDM1, ServerSA1
Description: Apply the InitialConfig checkpoint or snapshot to ServerDC1, ServerDM1, and ServerSA1.

1. Be sure all servers are shut down. In your virtualization program, apply the InitialConfig checkpoint or snapshot to all servers.
2. When the snapshot or checkpoint has been applied, continue to the next activity.

Activity 9-5

Installing the NPS and RRAS Server Roles

Time Required: 10 minutes

Objective: Install Network Policy Server and Remote Access.

Required Tools and Equipment: ServerDC1, ServerDM1

Description: In this activity, you install the Network Policy Server role service and the DirectAccess and VPN Routing and Remote Access role services. Then you configure a VPN server so you can test RADIUS.

1. Start ServerDC1 and ServerDM1. On ServerDC1, log on as **Administrator**, if necessary. Open a PowerShell window.
2. Type **Install-WindowsFeature NPAS –IncludeManagementTools** and press **Enter**. Close the PowerShell window.
3. On ServerDM1, log on as **Administrator**, if necessary. Open a PowerShell window. Type **Install-WindowsFeature DirectAccess-VPN –IncludeManagementTools** and press **Enter**. Close the PowerShell window.
4. On ServerDM1, in Server Manager, click **Tools** and then **Routing and Remote Access** to start the RRAS console.
5. In the Routing and Remote Access console, right-click **ServerDM1** and click **Configure and Enable Routing and Remote Access**. Continue with the Routing and Remote Access Server Setup Wizard, making sure to configure a VPN using the network connection with address 172.31.0.240 as the Internet connection. (If necessary, review the steps in Activity 9-2.) For IP Address Assignment, specify the range 172.31.0.1 to 172.31.0.10. Accept the default selections for the rest of the settings.
6. Continue to the next activity.

Activity 9-6

Configuring a RADIUS Server

Time Required: 15 minutes

Objective: Configure a RADIUS server to authenticate VPN access requests.

Required Tools and Equipment: ServerDC1, ServerDM1, ServerSA1

Description: You want to authenticate and authorize VPN traffic coming into the network, so you need to configure a RADIUS server to accept access requests from VPN clients.

1. On ServerDC1, in Server Manager, click **Tools** and then **Network Policy Server** from the menu to open the Network Policy Server console.
2. In the Standard Configuration section of the Getting Started window shown in Figure 9-22, be sure **RADIUS server for Dial-Up or VPN Connections** is selected in the list box and then click the **Configure VPN or Dial-Up** link to start the corresponding wizard.

(continues)

Activity 9-6 Continued

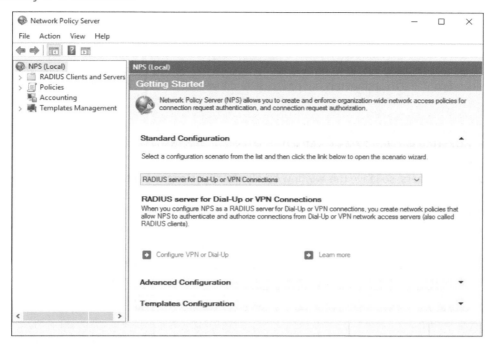

Figure 9-22   Selecting a configuration option for the RADIUS server

3. In the Select Dial-up or Virtual Private Network Connections Type window, click the **Virtual Private Network (VPN) Connections** option button. This option adds text to the Virtual Private Network (VPN) Connections text box that's used as part of the name of all policies created with the wizard. Leave this text as is and click **Next**.

4. In the Specify Dial-Up or VPN Server window, click **Add** to open the New RADIUS Client dialog box. In the Friendly name text box, type **ServerDM1**, and in the Address (IP or DNS) text box, type **10.99.0.201** (see Figure 9-23). You can click the **Verify** button to make sure you entered the correct address. Type **Password01** in the Shared secret and Confirm shared secret text boxes.

Figure 9-23   The New RADIUS Client dialog box

(continues)

Activity 9-6 Continued

> **Note 5**
>
> For the purposes of this activity, you're using a simple password. For a production server, you should use a password that's at least 22 characters and contains a random mix of uppercase and lowercase letters, numbers, and symbols.

5. Click **OK**, and then click **Next** to continue. In the Configure Authentication Methods window, click **Microsoft Encrypted Authentication version 2 (MS-CHAP v2)**, if necessary, and then click **Next**.
6. In the Specify User Groups window, you can add Active Directory user groups that the policy affects. You want this policy to apply to all users, so leave this window blank and click **Next** to continue.
7. In the Specify IP Filters window, you can add IPv4 and IPv6 inbound and outbound filters or select from a template you have created. Filters allow you to restrict remote access to specific source and destination IP addresses and protocols. You do not need to add filters for this activity. Click **Next** to continue.
8. Because the Routing and Remote Access Service supports all three types of encryption (Basic, Strong, and Strongest), all are selected in the Specify Encryption Settings window. The VPN will use the strongest encryption supported by both the client and server. Leave them selected and click **Next** to continue.

> **Note 6**
>
> If you want to connect a non-Microsoft RADIUS client, you need to verify that it supports the encryption type you select.

9. In the Specify a Realm Name window, leave the Realm name text box blank. Your ISP will tell you if a realm name is required for the connection. Click **Next**. In the final window, you see a summary of the settings, including the RADIUS clients and the names of the connection request policy and the network policies to be generated. Click **Finish**.
10. Now you configure Routing and Remote Access to use RADIUS authentication and accounting. On ServerDM1, open the **Routing and Remote Access** console, if necessary.
11. Right-click **SERVERDM1 (local)** in the left pane, click **Properties**, and click the **Security** tab. In the Authentication provider drop-down list, click **RADIUS Authentication** (see Figure 9-24), and then click the **Configure** button to open the RADIUS Authentication dialog box.
12. Click **Add** to open the Add RADIUS Server dialog box (see Figure 9-25). Type **ServerDC1** in the Server name text box, click the **Change** button, and type **Password01** in the New secret and Confirm new secret text boxes.

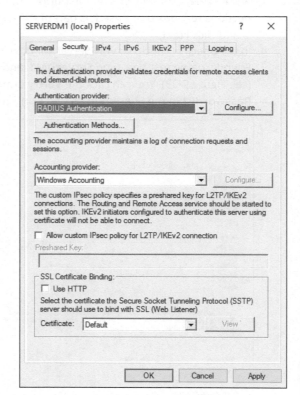

Figure 9-24   Selecting RADIUS Authentication on the Security tab

(continues)

Activity 9-6 Continued

13. Click **OK** three times to return to the Properties dialog box. In the Accounting provider drop-down list, click **RADIUS Accounting**, and then click the **Configure** button to open the RADIUS Accounting dialog box. Repeat Step 12 to add ServerDC1 as the RADIUS Accounting provider. Click **OK** to close the Properties dialog box.

14. You need to restart the RRAS service for the changes to take effect. To do so, in the Routing and Remote Access console, right-click **SERVERDM1 (local)**, point to **All Tasks**, and click **Restart**.

15. Continue to the next activity, where you'll connect to the VPN server to verify that the authentication is working.

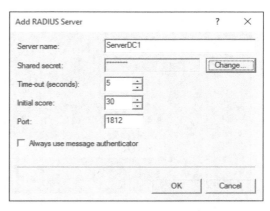

Figure 9-25   The Add RADIUS Server dialog box

Activity 9-7

Creating a VPN Connection and Testing RADIUS

Time Required: 15 minutes

Objective: Create a VPN connection to test RADIUS.

Required Tools and Equipment: ServerDC1, ServerDM1, ServerSA1

Description: Test the VPN and RADIUS configuration by creating a VPN client connection on ServerSA1 and attempting to connect to the VPN server. For this activity, you'll disable the network interface on ServerSA1 that is connected to the 10.99.0.0/24 network. The second network interface on ServerSA1, with the address 172.31.0.101, will be used to make the VPN connection.

1. Create a user on ServerDC1 that will be used to authenticate to the VPN. On **ServerDC1**, in Server Manager, click **Tools** and then **Active Directory Users and Computers**.

2. Click the Users folder and click the User icon on the toolbar. Use the following criteria to create the user:

   Full Name: **VPN Test1**
   User logon name: **VPNTest1**
   Password: **Password01**
   Password never expires: **Checked**

3. Double-click **VPNTest1** to open the Properties dialog box. Click the **Dial-in** tab, click **Allow access** in the Network Access Permission section, and then click **OK**. Close Active Directory Users and Computers.

4. On ServerSA1, log on as **Administrator**. Right-click **Start** and click **Network Connections**. Click **Change adapter options**. Right-click **Ethernet0** and click **Disable**. Verify that Ethernet 1 has an IP address of 172.31.0.101 by right-clicking **Ethernet1**, clicking **Status**, and clicking **Details**. Click **Close** twice and close the Network Connections window.

5. Click the network icon on the right side of the taskbar and click **Network & Internet Settings**. Click **VPN** and then click **Add a VPN connection**.

6. In the Add a VPN connection window, fill out the form as shown in Figure 9-26. Click **Save**.

(continues)

Activity 9-7 Continued

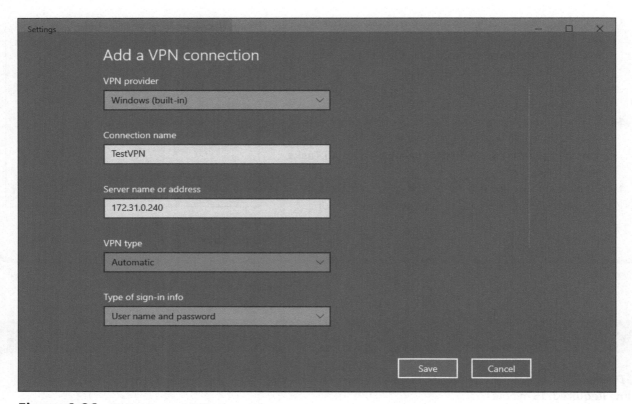

Figure 9-26   Setting up a VPN connection

7. To verify the authentication type, click **Change adapter options**. Right-click **TestVPN** and click **Properties**. Click the **Security** tab. Click **Allow these protocols** and click to select **Microsoft CHAP Version 2**, if necessary (see Figure 9-27). Click **OK**.
8. Right-click **TestVPN** and click **Connect/Disconnect**. In the Networks panel, click **TestVPN** and click **Connect**. When prompted for the username and password, type **az800\vpntest1** for the username, type **Password01** for the password, and click **OK**. You will see the word "Connected" under the TestVPN connection.
9. On ServerDC1, right-click **Start** and click **Event Viewer**. Click to expand **Windows Logs** and click **Security**. In the right pane, look for an event with **Event ID 6272** and double-click it. The event is "Network Policy Server granted access to a user." Scroll down to view more of the event. The NAS shows that the RADIUS client is ServerDM1 (see Figure 9-28). Click **Close** and then close Event Viewer.

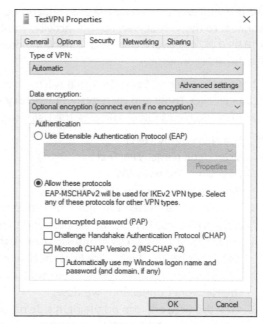

Figure 9-27   Setting the authentication type on the VPN client

(continues)

Activity 9-7 Continued

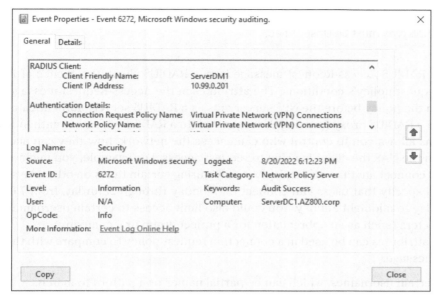

Figure 9-28   Viewing an NPS event

10. On ServerSA1, in Network Connections, right-click **TestVPN** and click **Connect/Disconnect**. In the Networks panel, click **TestVPN** and click **Disconnect**.
11. Close the Network Connections window and continue to the next activity.

Configuring NPS Policies

NPS policies define who can connect to a network, when they can connect, and how they can connect to the network. Two policy types are available:

- *Connection request policies*—Specify which RADIUS servers handle connection requests from RADIUS clients.
- *Network policies*—Specify which users and groups have access, the times they can access the network, and any conditions that apply.

Configuring Connection Request Policies

Connection request policies are used to specify which RADIUS servers perform authentication and authorization of RADIUS clients' connection requests. These policies can also specify which servers RADIUS accounting requests are sent to. They're applied to NPS servers configured as RADIUS servers or RADIUS proxies. Requests are authenticated and authorized by NPS acting as a RADIUS server or forwarded by NPS acting as a RADIUS proxy for authentication and authorization by another RADIUS server, but only if settings in the Access-Request message match at least one of the connection request policies that have been configured. You can define connection request policies for the following NAS types:

- *Unspecified*—Process or forward connection requests from any type of NAS, depending on whether the server receiving the message is configured as a RADIUS server or RADIUS proxy.
- *Remote Desktop Gateway*—Process or forward connection requests from an NAS that's managing connections from Remote Desktop clients.
- *Remote access server (VPN-dial up)*—Process or forward requests from an NAS that's managing dial-up and VPN connections.
- *Vendor specific*—Process or forward requests from an NAS with proprietary RADIUS attributes not included in RFCs 2865 and 2866, which list the standard RADIUS attributes.

Note 7

For a policy to apply to an 802.1x authenticating switch (for example, several types of Cisco switches can act as RADIUS clients) or a wireless access point, the NAS type must be Unspecified.

When a RADIUS server receives a RADIUS Access-Request message from a RADIUS client, the client's attributes are checked against the connection request policy's conditions. The attributes in the Access-Request message must match at least one of the conditions in the policy before the NPS server acts as a RADIUS server (authenticating and authorizing the connection request) or a RADIUS proxy (passing the request on to a RADIUS server for authentication and authorization). Creating conditions allows you to control who can access the network, how they can access it, and when they can access it, based on the NAS the client is using to request access. For example, you might decide that dial-in users should be allowed to connect anytime on Sunday but only during certain times on other days of the week. The condition you set up could specify that users can connect on Monday through Saturday, from 7:00 a.m. to 6:00 p.m., and from midnight Saturday to midnight Sunday. You could also limit access to certain usernames or to usernames starting with certain characters (such as an abbreviation for a project group or a company).

The following groups of condition attributes can be used in a connection request policy to compare with the attributes of the RADIUS Access-Request message:

- *Username*—Restrict access to certain usernames, which can be partial names or a pattern to match.
- *Connection properties*—Restrict access to certain IPv4 or IPv6 addresses, service types, such as PPP or Telnet, and tunnel types such as Point-to-Point Tunneling Protocol (PPTP) or Layer Two Tunneling Protocol (L2TP).
- *Day and time restrictions*—Restrict access to specific days and times.
- *RADIUS client properties*—Specifies information about the RADIUS client, such as phone number, IP address, RADIUS client computer name, and RADIUS client vendor name.
- *Gateway properties*—Specify where a client is connecting from, such as the NAS IP address, or port type (for example, VPN, Ethernet, or cable).

Note 8

In Activity 9-6, you created a connection request policy automatically when you were setting up and configuring a RADIUS server, but you can also add policies after a server has been configured.

Configuring Network Policies

After configuring RADIUS servers and clients defined in connection request policies, you need to specify who can connect to the network and under what conditions. To do this, you create network policies. Connection request policies are specific to an NAS type, but network polices affect all clients who are trying to connect. For these policies, you must configure at least one condition. As with connection request policies, there are groups of conditions for determining access, each with attributes to compare to the incoming request:

- *Groups*—Specify user or computer groups created in Active Directory Domain Services that the client must be a member of to match the policy. Using this condition, you can restrict access to users or computers belonging to a particular Windows group, computers belonging to a particular machine group, or users who are members of a particular user group.
- *Day and time restrictions*—Specify days and times that clients can or can't access the network.
- *Connection properties*—Specify attributes for how the access client is connecting to the network. This condition compares attributes such as the access client's IP address (not the RADIUS client's IP address), the authentication method being used, the framing protocol (for example, PPP), the service being used (such as Telnet or PPTP), and the tunnel type (PPTP or L2TP). This condition could be used to restrict access for clients with a particular IP address yet allow access for other clients using the same NAS.

- *RADIUS client properties*—Specify RADIUS attributes the client must have to match the policy. For example, you could restrict access to RADIUS clients that have a certain IP address or fall in a specified range of addresses.

Note 9

A RADIUS client's IP address isn't the same as an access client's IP address. This condition applies to all access clients connecting via a particular NAS type, such as a VPN server.

- *Gateway*—Specify NAS attributes, such as the phone number, name, IP address, and port type. For example, this condition can limit access to connection requests from an NAS with a particular IP address or clients requesting access via a wireless connection.

In addition to network policy conditions, you can specify network policy constraints. Constraints are similar to conditions, with one major difference. If a condition in a policy isn't met, NPS continues trying to find a match in the remaining conditions. If a constraint doesn't match the connection request, however, no further policies are checked, the request is rejected, and access to the network is denied. You can configure the following constraints, which are found in the Constraints tab of a network policy's Properties dialog box:

- *Authentication method*—The authentication method used when requesting access
- *Idle timeout*—The maximum number of minutes an NAS can be idle before dropping the connection
- *Session timeout*—The maximum number of minutes a user can remain connected to the network
- *Called station ID*—The phone number of the dial-up server (NAS) that access clients use
- *Day and time restrictions*—The schedule of days and times that access is allowed
- *NAS port type*—The allowed access client's media type (such as phone lines or VPNs)

Configuring Network Policies for Virtual Private Networks

VPNs are a common way to access networks remotely and securely. Because VPNs access a network remotely, using a network policy to control how they can access your network is a natural choice. The authentication type for a VPN can be password based or certificate based. Certificate-based methods are more secure, but you must have a valid CA certificate installed on every computer connecting via the VPN and client certificates installed on each computer. Some of the settings made in the Routing and Remote Access console when you configure a network policy are particularly applicable to VPNs:

- *Multilink and Bandwidth Allocation Protocol (BAP)*—Handle connection types that include multiple channels (for example, ISDN). You can adjust how multilink connections are handled and modify BAP parameters to specify when to drop the extra connections.
- *IP filters*—Filter access based on the client computer's IP address. You can permit or disallow packets from a particular address or network and restrict access to certain ports and protocols.
- *Encryption settings*—Specify which encryption strengths you allow. The choices are Basic, Strong, Strongest, and No encryption (not recommended). All are supported by the Routing and Remote Access Service, but some third-party clients might not support them. The connection tries the strongest type first and then moves to the weaker choices if needed.
- *IP settings*—Adjust how IP addresses are assigned to the access client. The choices are "Server must supply an IP address," "Client may request an IP address," "Server settings determine IP address assignment (the default)," and "Assign a static IPv4 address."

Managing NPS Templates

Templates can reduce the amount of work and minimize the chance of error when configuring RADIUS servers and clients. You can use NPS or RADIUS templates to reuse settings on the local server or export settings to other NPS servers. If you have many NPS servers and proxies to manage, templates can save time and prevent configuration errors when you're replacing a server or adding a new one.

> **Note 10**
>
> Template settings apply only when the template is selected and actually applied in a RADIUS configuration; merely creating a template has no effect on a server's configuration.

Templates are in the Network Policy Server console under the Templates Management node. There are four template types:

- *Shared secrets*—Specify a reusable password for validating a connection between RADIUS servers and proxies and NAS servers.
- *RADIUS clients*—Specify reusable RADIUS client settings.
- *Remote RADIUS servers*—Specify reusable RADIUS server settings.
- *IP filters*—Specify reusable lists of the IPv4 and IPv6 addresses of allowed destinations.

Exporting and Importing Templates

NPS can export templates to an XML file that can then be imported to another NPS server, which is particularly useful when you're setting up multiple NPS servers that should be configured the same way (for example, a server group). To export a template, open the Network Policy Server console. Right-click Templates Management and click Export Templates to a File. Select a location for the file, enter a name, and click Save.

To import a template, open the Network Policy Server console. Right-click Templates Management and click Import Templates from a File. Navigate to the XML file, select it, and click Open. You can also click Import Templates from a Computer and enter the name of another NPS server on your network.

Importing and Exporting NPS Policies

After configuring policies and templates, you can back up the entire NPS configuration by exporting it to an XML file. You can keep it to restore the configuration, if needed, or use it to configure other NPS servers in your network. To export an NPS backup file, follow these steps in the Network Policy Server console:

1. In the left pane, right-click the NPS (Local) node and click Export Configuration. In the message box about exporting shared secrets, click the "I am aware that I am exporting all shared secrets" check box, and then click OK.
2. Choose a name and location to save the XML file and click Save.
3. To restore the configuration, right-click the NPS (Local) node and click Import Configuration. Navigate to the XML file and click Open.

To perform this same task from the command line, follow these steps:

1. Open a command prompt window. Type netsh and press Enter. At the netsh prompt, type nps and press Enter.
2. Type export filename=*path**NPSconfig.xml* exportPSK=YES, replacing *path* with the location you specified and *NPSconfig.xml* with a name of your choosing, and press Enter.
3. To import the file on this server or another server, type netsh and press Enter.
4. Type nps and press Enter, and then type import filename="*path**filename*.xml" and press Enter.
5. You get a message that the import was successful. Close the command prompt window.

Self-Check Questions

3. Which of the following is a protocol used to centralize authentication, authorization, and accounting for remote access to network services?

   a. VPN

   b. EAP-TLS

   c. Kerberos

   d. RADIUS

4. Which type of NPS policy specifies which users and groups have access to a network?

   a. Network policies

   b. Group policies

   c. Network connection policies

   d. Account policies

⊙Check your answers at the end of this module.

Activity 9-8

Creating a Connection Request Policy

Time Required: 10 minutes

Objective: Create a connection request policy.

Required Tools and Equipment: ServerDC1

Description: In a previous activity, you created a connection request policy by configuring a RADIUS server with a wizard. In this activity, you create a connection request policy manually.

1. On ServerDC1, open **Network Policy Server**.
2. In the left pane, expand **Policies**, right-click **Connection Request Policies**, and click **New** to start the New Connection Request Policy wizard. Enter **TestCRP** for the name of the policy. Leave **Unspecified** selected in the "Type of network access server" drop-down list and click **Next**.
3. In the Specify Conditions window, click **Add** to open the Select condition dialog box (see Figure 9-29).

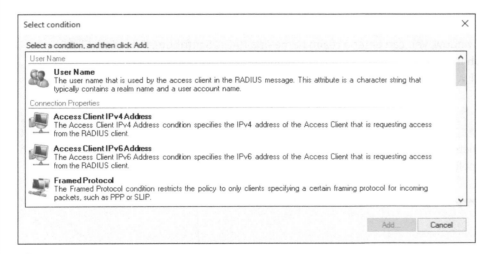

Figure 9-29   The Select condition dialog box

(continues)

Activity 9-8 Continued

4. Scroll down and click **Tunnel Type**, and then click **Add** to open the Tunnel Type dialog box. Click **GRE**, **L2TP**, **PPTP**, and **SSTP** to allow a wide variety of VPN tunnels, and then click **OK**. Click **Next**.

5. In the Specify Connection Request Forwarding window, leave the **Authenticate requests on this server** option selected, and leave the default accounting settings (see Figure 9-30). You can also use this window to forward requests to a RADIUS server group if you want these functions to be performed elsewhere. Click **Next**.

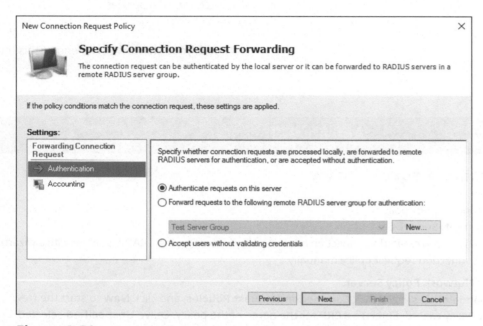

Figure 9-30 The Specify Connection Request Forwarding window

6. In the Specify Authentication Methods window, you can override the authentication methods specified in the network policy, if needed. For this activity, leave the **Override network policy authentication settings** check box cleared and click **Next**.

7. In the Configure Settings window, you can enter a realm name or a RADIUS attribute, if needed. Click **Next**, and then click **Finish** in the Completing Connection Request Policy Wizard window.

8. Continue to the next activity.

Note 11

Policies are processed until a matching one is found. To make sure more specific policies are evaluated, place them higher in the list than general policies.

Activity 9-9

Creating a VPN Client Network Policy

Time Required: 10 minutes
Objective: Create a network policy for VPN clients.
Required Tools and Equipment: ServerDC1
Description: Network policies help determine what resources a client can access in the network. In this activity, you set up a network policy for VPN clients to give only domain users access to network resources.

1. On ServerDC1, open the Network Policy Server console if necessary, expand **Policies**, right-click **Network Policies**, and click **New** to start the New Network Policy wizard.
2. Type **Test VPN Policy** in the Policy name text box, click **Remote Access Server (VPN-Dial up)**, and then click **Next**.
3. In the Specify Conditions window, click **Add** to open the Select condition dialog box. Click **Windows Groups**, and then click **Add** to open the Windows Groups dialog box. Click **Add Groups**, type **Domain Users**, click **Check Names**, and click **OK** twice. Click **Next**.
4. In the Specify Access Permission window, leave the default option **Access granted** selected, and then click **Next**.
5. In the Configure Authentication Methods window, click the **Microsoft Encrypted Authentication version 2 (MS-CHAP v2)**, **User can change password after it has expired**, **Microsoft Encrypted Authentication (MS-CHAP)**, and **User can change password after it has expired** check boxes, if necessary (see Figure 9-31), and then click **Next**.

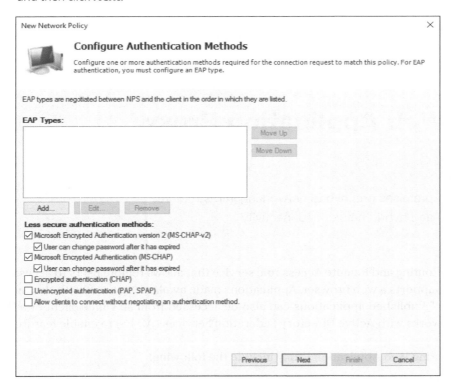

Figure 9-31   Configuring authentication methods

6. In the Configure Constraints window, review the possible options and then click **Next** to go to the Configure Settings window, where you can specify settings such as standard and vendor-specific RADIUS attributes, NAP settings, and RRAS settings. Click **Next**.
7. In the Completing New Network Policy window, click **Finish**.
8. Continue to the next activity.

Activity 9-10

Creating a Shared Secret Template

Time Required: 5 minutes
Objective: Create and apply a shared secret template.
Required Tools and Equipment: ServerDC1
Description: In this activity, you create a template to set the shared secret between ServerDC1 (the RADIUS server) and ServerDM1 (the RADIUS client).

1. On **ServerDC1**, open the Network Policy Server console, if necessary.
2. In the left pane, expand **Templates Management**, right-click **Shared Secrets**, and click **New**.
3. Type **Test Shared Secret** as the template's name and **Password01** in the Shared secret and Confirm shared secret boxes, and then click **OK**.
4. In the left pane, expand **RADIUS Clients and Servers**, and click **RADIUS Clients**. In the right pane, right-click **ServerDM1** (the RADIUS client) and click **Properties**. In the Shared Secret section, click **Test Shared Secret** in the drop-down list (see Figure 9-32), and then click **OK**.
5. Close all open windows (except Server Manager) on all servers.

Figure 9-32 Setting the Shared Secret template

Implementing Web Application Proxy

Microsoft Exam AZ-800:

Implement and manage an on-premises and hybrid networking infrastructure.

- Implement on-premises and hybrid network connectivity

Web Application Proxy (WAP) is a Routing and Remote Access role service that allows remote users to access network applications from any device that supports a web browser. Applications made available to users with this method are said to be "published applications." Published applications can also be accessed from an Office client or a Windows store app. Web Application Proxy works with Active Directory Federation Services (AD FS) to enable features such as single sign-on.

Some requirements for configuring Web Application Proxy include the following:

- A functioning AD FS deployment on the network
- Two NICs installed on the Web Application Proxy server with one NIC accessible to the Internet and the other connected to the private network
- A certificate in the Personal certificate store issued by a certificate authority (CA) that covers the federation service name and another certificate that covers the address of the web application you publish

Here are the basic steps for configuring Web Application Proxy:

1. Install the Remote Access server role and the Web Application Proxy role service.
2. Open the Remote Access Management console from the Tools menu in Server Manager and click Web Application Proxy in the left pane (see Figure 9-33).

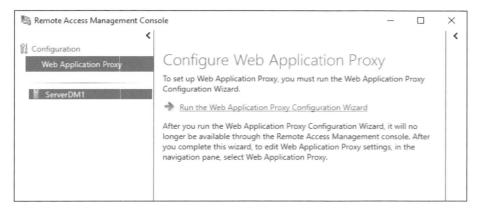

Figure 9-33   The Remote Access Management console

3. Click "Run the Web Application Proxy Configuration Wizard," and then click Next in the Welcome window.
4. In the Federation Server window, enter the fully qualified domain name (FQDN) of the server running AD FS, and enter the credentials of the local administrator account on the federation servers (see Figure 9-34). Click Next.

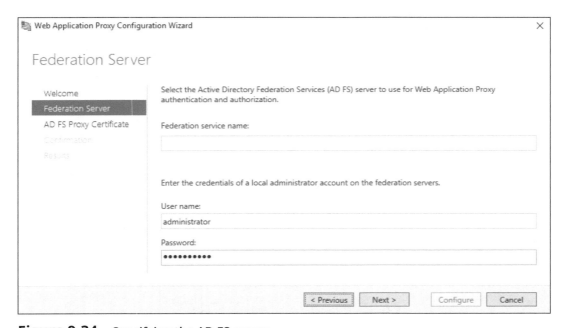

Figure 9-34   Specifying the AD FS server

5. In the AD FS Proxy Certificate window, select the certificate to be used by the AD FS proxy. The certificate must have already been installed in the server's Trusted Root Certification Authorities store. Usually, this is the same certificate used by the AD FS server that you import to the WAP server. Click Next.
6. Click Configure in the Confirmation window.

Publishing Web Apps with WAP

After Web Application Proxy is configured, you can begin publishing applications. To do so, open the Remote Access Management console, click Web Application Proxy, and click Publish in the Tasks pane (see Figure 9-35) to start the Publish New Application Wizard, which guides you through the process.

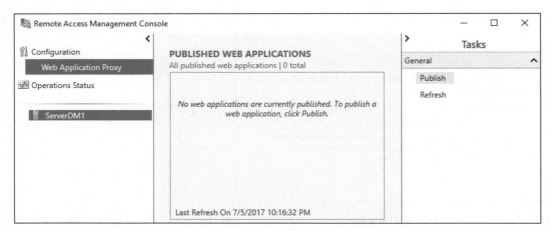

Figure 9-35   Publishing an application with WAP

When publishing a web application, you have two options for preauthentication (see Figure 9-36):

- *AD FS*—With this option, client requests for the application are redirected to the federation server. If AD FS authenticates the user successfully, the request is forwarded to the application server. This option configures WAP as a proxy for AD FS because client requests must first go through the WAP server.
- *Pass-through*—With this option, client requests for the application are sent directly to the application server.

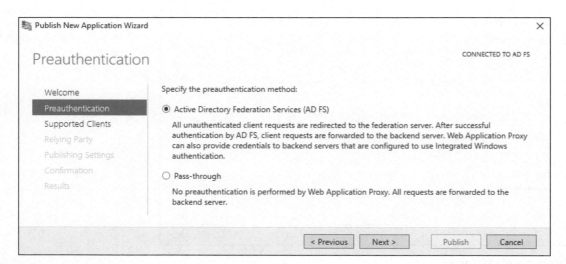

Figure 9-36   Configuring preauthentication

Next, you enter a name for the application, an external URL for users to access the application, a certificate for the application, and the URL of a back-end server (if it's different from the external URL), as shown in Figure 9-37. The external and back-end server URLs must be able to be resolved through DNS to the IP address of the Web Application Proxy server's external interface. You have the option to click "Enable HTTP to HTTPS redirection" so that all URLs entered using HTTP will be automatically changed to HTTPS. This option ensures that users can still access the application even if they omit the "S" in HTTPS for secure transactions.

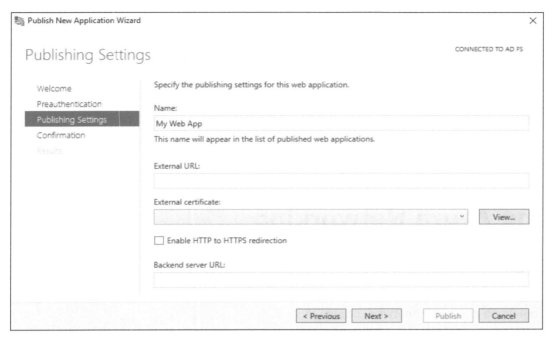

Figure 9-37   Web application publishing settings

Publishing Remote Desktop Gateway Applications

Remote Desktop (RD) Gateway applications are a convenient way for organizations to make applications available to users without having to install the applications on each user's computer. In addition, RD Gateway allows users to access applications with a web browser interface. However, RD Gateway doesn't provide sufficient security by itself to allow users to access the applications remotely. You can use WAP as a front end to RD Gateway using either pass-through preauthentication or AD FS preauthentication. If you decide to use pass-through preauthentication, you can simply publish the application as described in the previous section, choose pass-through preauthentication, and then specify the URL of the RD web server as the External URL.

To use AD FS preauthentication for RD Gateway, you must also create a relying party trust on the AD FS server and specify the URL of the RD Gateway server as the Relying Party Trust identifier. Then, on the WAP server, publish the application, choose AD FS preauthentication, and follow the wizard. When prompted for the relying party, specify the relying party trust you created on the AD FS server (see Figure 9-38).

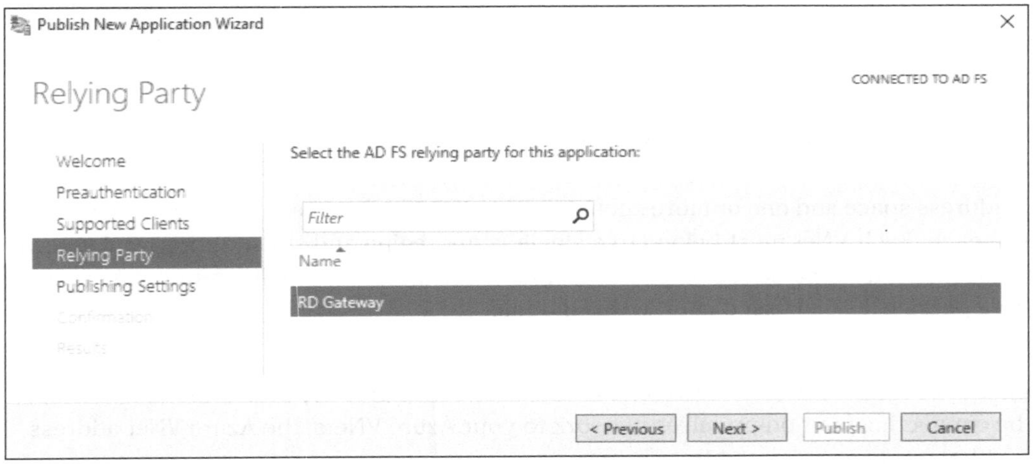

Figure 9-38   Specifying the RD gateway as the relying party for an RD Gateway app

Self-Check Questions

5. Which of the following is *not* a requirement for implementing Web Application Proxy?

    a. A VPN
    b. AD FS
    c. Two NICs
    d. A certificate

○ Check your answers at the end of this module.

Implementing Azure Networking

Microsoft Exam AZ-800:

Implement and manage an on-premises and hybrid networking infrastructure.
- Implement on-premises and hybrid network connectivity

Now that you are familiar with using Windows Server to provide remote access network connectivity for on-premises networks, it's time to turn your attention to Azure networking. Azure networking includes the technologies necessary to allow communication between Azure resources such as Azure VMs, Azure storage, and Azure databases, as well as the technologies needed to allow on-premises resources to communicate with Azure resources.

In this section, we discuss the following Azure networking technologies:

- Azure Virtual Network
- Azure Network Adapter
- Azure Extended Network
- Azure Relay
- Azure Virtual WAN
- Azure AD Application Proxy

Azure Virtual Network Overview

An **Azure Virtual Network (VNet)** provides the basis for communication between Azure resources on the same VNet, between resources on different VNets, and between your on-premises network and Azure resources. VNets allow Azure VMs to communicate with one another, access the Internet, and access your on-premises network. VNets also enable communication between VMs and other resources, such as Azure storage and databases.

An Azure VNet is similar to a virtual network running on a hypervisor such as Microsoft Hyper-V or VMware, or on a traditional physical network; however, VNet has additional benefits such as scalability, reliability, security, and ease of management.

A VNet is composed of an address space and one or more subnets within the address space. There can be multiple address spaces with subnets in each. Each VNet must belong to a single Azure region and subscription, and you can create multiple VNets per region. VNets in the same region can be connected and VNets from different regions can be connected using virtual network peering, as discussed later in this module.

There are a few considerations and limitations when creating and configuring VNets:

- VNet address spaces cannot overlap. If you have two or more VNets, the address spaces must not overlap; in addition, if you will be connecting your on-premises network to your Azure VNets, the Azure VNet address spaces cannot overlap with your on-premises address spaces.
- You can create a maximum of 1000 VNets per region per subscription.
- You can create a maximum of 3000 subnets per address space.

- You can have 500 VNet peerings, which are connections to other VNets.
- You can have 65,536 private IP addresses per VNet.
- The number of public IP addresses varies according to your subscription type. They range from 10 for a free trial subscription to 1000 for an Enterprise Agreement subscription.
- Do not create a subnet that uses the entire address space; this cannot be changed without deleting the subnet. You should leave some address space available for additional subnets.

Creating an Azure Virtual Network

Creating an Azure VNet is a straightforward process, like creating most Azure resources. When you create a VNet, you assign it a name and choose a subscription, resource group, and location (Azure region) for the VNet. A default address space and a subnet will be assigned to the VNet, or you can choose your own address space and subnet. Optionally, you can enable security features such as BastionHost, DDoS protection, and a firewall. At a minimum, enabling the firewall is recommended. You can create a VNet using the Azure portal, PowerShell, or the Azure command-line interface (CLI).

Adding Address Spaces and Subnets to a Virtual Network

An address space and at least one subnet must be defined when you create a VNet, but you can add more address spaces and subnets to a VNet. To add an address space, simply select the VNet in the portal, click Address space in the menu, and type the new address space range. An address space is specified using CIDR notation or "slash" notation: the IP network address followed by a slash and a value for the prefix—for example, 172.16.0.0/16. Figure 9-39 shows the address space 172.16.0.0/16 being added to the existing address space 10.3.0.0/16.

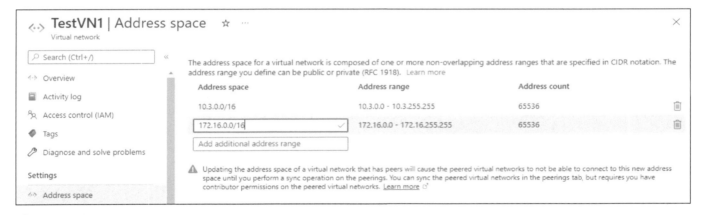

Figure 9-39   Adding another address space to a VNet

To add a subnet to a VNet, go to the Virtual Network page, select Subnets, and click + Subnet or + Gateway subnet. A Gateway subnet is used when a VNet is connected to other networks. When you add a subnet, you are prompted to enter several items of information (see Figure 9-40), some of which are described here:

- *Name*—Provide a descriptive name for the subnet. Usually, you will want to use a name that describes the resources on the subnet, such as WebServers or AppServers. This field is required.
- *Subnet address range*—Enter the subnet address range in CIDR notation. The subnet must not overlap with other subnets and must be contained in the address space. This field is required. The remaining fields can be left at their default settings.
- *Network security group*—A network security group (NSG) is used to filter traffic within the subnet. It contains rules based on a packet's source or destination address, protocol, TCP and UDP ports, and so forth. The rules can specify that matching packets are allowed or denied.
- *Route table*—By default, Azure routes data between subnets within a virtual network and between virtual networks and on-premises networks that are connected. You can alter the default routing by creating a custom route table and associating it with a subnet. You might create a route table to route traffic to a virtual appliance such as a firewall or to an internal load balancer. You might also create a custom route to drop packets addressed to a specific subnet.

Figure 9-40 Adding a subnet to a VNet

- *Services*—The Services option allows you to create a service endpoint that specifies the type of service (Azure Active Directory, web, storage, database, and so forth) contained in the subnet. A VNet **service endpoint** provides secure and optimized access to an Azure service across the Azure backbone network. An endpoint ensures that only your VNets will have access to these resources without requiring a public IP address.

Virtual Network Peering

Azure routes data between subnets within an address space automatically, with no further configuration from the user. However, each VNet is isolated from other VNets, so if you have two or more VNets, the resources in one cannot communicate with resources in another VNet by default. If you need to communicate between VNets, you configure virtual network peering. **Virtual network peering** is an Azure technology that allows you to connect VNets and enable their resources to communicate with one another. Azure supports network peering for VNets within the same region or across regions. When VNets are connected across different regions, it is called **global virtual network peering**. Virtual network peering is a fast, secure technology, as the data never leaves the Microsoft Azure backbone network.

Configure virtual network peering by selecting a VNet in the portal and selecting Peerings from the menu. The second VNet should already be created. Figure 9-41 shows the Add peering dialog box, in which a peering is created between TestVN1 and TestVN2. The options are described in the following list:

- *Peering link name*—Enter the name of the peering link. It's a good idea to have the name describe which VNets are peered.
- *Traffic to remote virtual network*—Select Allow if you want the two VNets to communicate; you might select the Block all traffic option if you want to disable communication temporarily between the VNets.
- *Traffic forwarded from remote virtual network*—Select Allow if you want traffic that originates outside the remote network to enter the VNet you are configuring (TestVN1 in the figure). In Figure 9-41, the remote network is TestVN2.
- *Virtual network gateway or Route Server*—If neither VNet is configured with a gateway or Route Server, choose None. A virtual network gateway allows communication with on-premises networks. A Route Server is used to dynamically exchange routing information in complex on-premises-to-VNet connections.

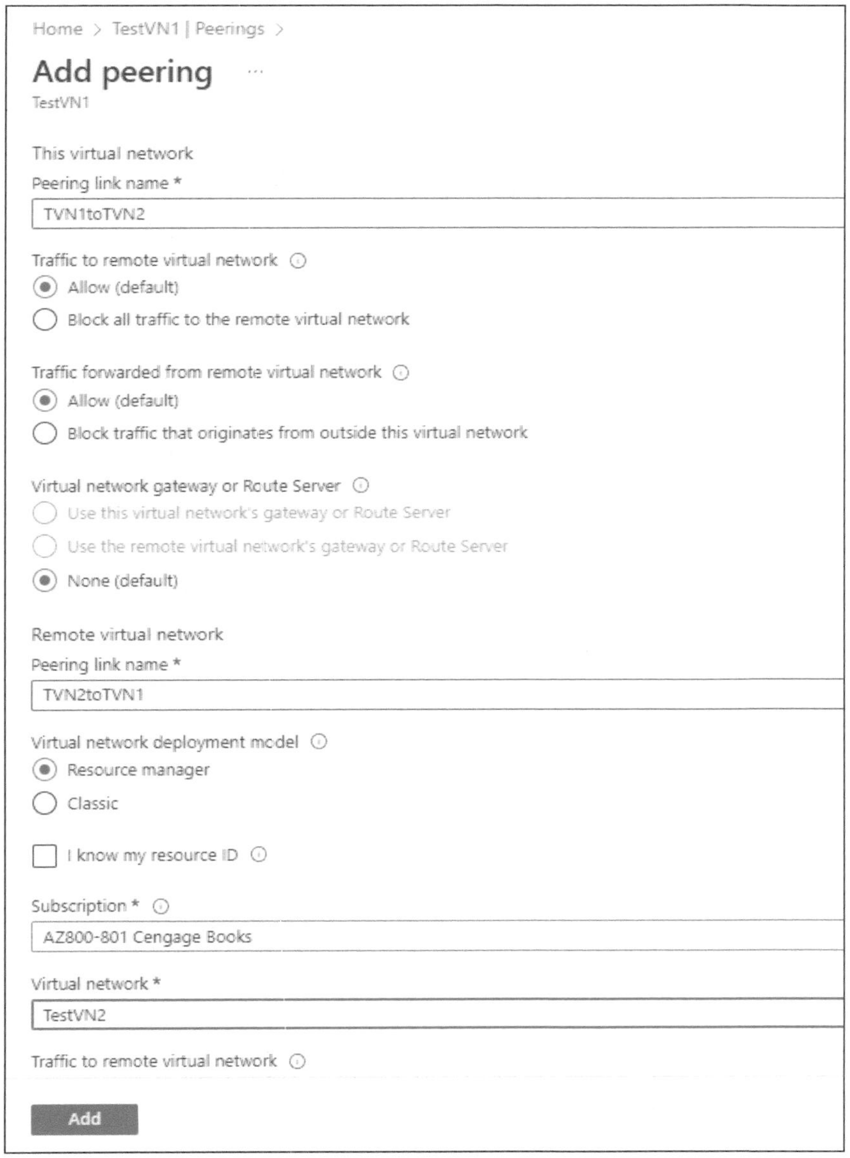

Figure 9-41   Configuring virtual network peering

The remaining options are for the configuration of the remote VNet, which typically mirrors the configuration of the first VNet. The peering link name should be different; for example, in Figure 9-41, the peering link name for TestVN2 is TVN2toTVN1 to describe that the link connects TestVN2 to TestVN1.

After you click Add, the peering is created. When the status shows Connected (see Figure 9-42), the VNets can begin communicating.

Figure 9-42 Peering status is Connected

Azure Network Adapter

Azure Network Adapter is a technology that allows an on-premises server to communicate with an Azure VNet using a point-to-site VPN connection. Azure Network Adapter is useful when you have only a few servers that must communicate with the Azure networks. If you have many servers that must communicate with your Azure network infrastructure, it is better to use a site-to-site VPN, which can connect all the devices in your on-premises network to the Azure network.

To create an Azure network adapter, the following prerequisites must be in place:

- An Azure VNet exists to which the on-premises server will connect. There must be some VNet address space available that has not been assigned to a subnet.
- There are network resources (such as an Azure VM) on the VNet that can be accessed by the on-premises server. You can connect to an Azure VNet that has no resources on it, but there is no point in doing so.
- Windows Admin Center (WAC) must be installed in your on-premises network and must be able to manage the server to which you will add the Azure network adapter.
- WAC must be connected to Azure. If it is not already connected to Azure, you will be prompted to register WAC with Azure when you try to add an Azure network adapter. Module 6 discusses how to connect WAC to Azure.

> **Note 12**
>
> Azure Network Adapter is a relatively new Azure feature that is still in preview mode as of this writing. Azure Network Adapter can be very slow to deploy; in at least one case, it took all night before the adapter was visible in WAC. In addition, the ability to connect to the Azure VNet can be unreliable. A site-to-site VPN might be a better option until the feature is out of preview mode and is more reliable.

The following steps for adding an Azure network adapter to an on-premises server assume that WAC is already connected to Azure.

1. In WAC, select the server you want to connect to an Azure VNet.
2. From the Tools menu on the left, select Networks (see Figure 9-43).

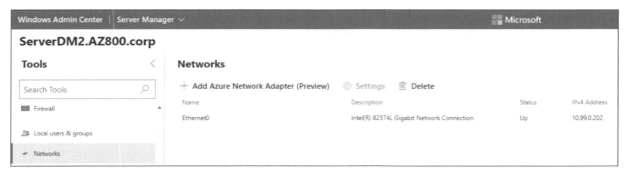

Figure 9-43   Windows Admin Center Networks page

3. Click Add Azure Network Adapter.
4. In the Add Azure Network Adapter dialog box, first select the Azure Subscription and the Azure region of the VNet to which you are connecting. Then, fill in the following values (see Figure 9-44):
   - *Virtual Network*—The VNet you want to connect to.
   - *Gateway Subnet*—If the VNet does not have a gateway already created, specify the subnet address. The subnet address must not overlap existing subnets and must be within the VNet address space. If the gateway does not already exist, it will be created during the process. Creating the gateway can take 30 minutes or more.
   - *Gateway SKU*—The Gateway SKU determines the point-to-site VPN connection limits and maximum throughput of the VPN. To find out more about SKUs, click the information icon.
   - *Client Address Space*—Enter an address range using CIDR notation. The client address space should not overlap with your on-premises network address space or the VNet address space. When the on-premises server connects to the VNet, it will be assigned an IP address from this range.
   - *Authentication Certificate*—The certificate is used by Azure to authenticate the identity of the VPN client. You can use an automatically generated self-signed certificate or an existing certificate. If you use an existing certificate, you will be prompted to upload the root and client certificate files.

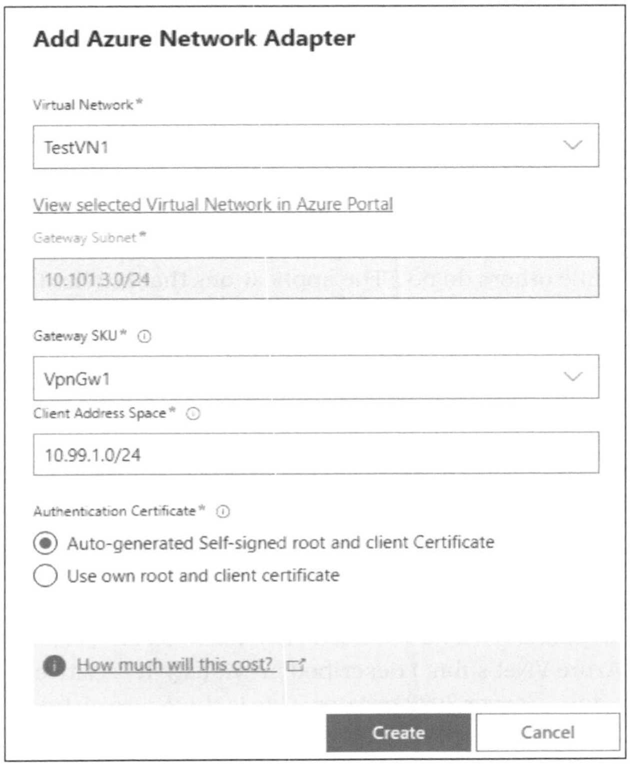

Add Azure Network Adapter

Virtual Network*

TestVN1

View selected Virtual Network in Azure Portal

Gateway Subnet*

10.101.3.0/24

Gateway SKU* ⓘ

VpnGw1

Client Address Space* ⓘ

10.99.1.0/24

Authentication Certificate* ⓘ
- ⦿ Auto-generated Self-signed root and client Certificate
- ◯ Use own root and client certificate

ⓘ How much will this cost? ↗

Create   Cancel

Figure 9-44   Add Azure Network Adapter option

After the information is filled in, click Create. The VNet gateway is created if necessary, and the Azure network adapter is added to the list of network connections on your server (see Figure 9-45).

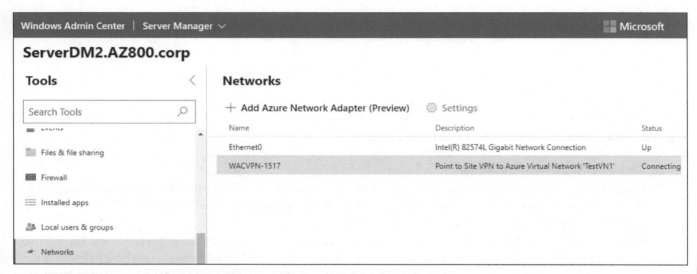

Figure 9-45   The Azure network adapter added to the server in WAC

The Azure network adapter will automatically try to connect to the VNet. You can also select the adapter from the Networks page and click Connect or Disconnect. A new network connection is created on the server. You can connect to the Azure VNet using the network connection, just like you would for a VPN client connection.

When the Azure network adapter connection is made, you can access Azure resources on the VNet as well as resources on other VNets that are peer connected.

Azure Extended Network

The **Azure extended network** is an Azure migration feature that allows you to extend an on-premises subnet into an Azure VNet while allowing the on-premises servers to keep their existing private IP addresses. This feature is most useful when you are migrating some or all of your servers from an on-premises datacenter to the Azure cloud.

For example, you might have a number of on-premises applications that you want to migrate to Azure. You can do a phased migration by extending the network and moving some of the applications to Azure VMs while maintaining the same IP addressing scheme. This way, there is no disruption to user access to the applications and you can test the migration in phases rather than moving everything to Azure at one time. An extended network is also useful when some of the applications require very fast response times while others do not. The applications that require fast response can be kept on-premises while the others can be moved. Finally, compliance requirements may dictate that certain data managed by your applications be kept on site; those applications can remain on-premises while others can be moved to Azure.

An Azure extended network has a number of requirements and components:

- *Azure VNet*—Your Azure VNet must have at least two subnets plus a gateway subnet. One of the subnets must have the same address range as the on-premises network that you want to extend. For example, if you want to extend your datacenter subnet, which is 10.100.1.0/24, your VNet must have an address space such as 10.100.0.0/16 and two subnets such as 10.100.0.0/24 and 10.100.1.0/24 to match your on-premises subnet.
- *Windows Server VM in Azure*—You must create a Windows Server Azure Edition VM with Hyper-V configured for **nested virtualization** (running a hypervisor inside a hypervisor). The VM needs two network interfaces connected to two external virtual switches—one for each Azure VNet subnet described previously. It is critical that you use the Azure Edition of Windows Server and Windows Server 2022 or later. This is the Azure virtual appliance in the extended network configuration.

- *Virtual network gateway*—A virtual network gateway must be configured using a site-to-site VPN or ExpressRoute. This gateway connects the VNet to your on-premises network.
- *A Windows Server 2019 or later VM on-premises*—The on-premises VM can run in any hypervisor as long as nested virtualization is supported. This VM is referred to as a **virtual appliance** in the extended network. At least two network interfaces on the VM are required. The Hyper-V server role must be installed on this VM. This virtual appliance communicates with the Windows Server VM virtual appliance in Azure.
- *A minimum of two on-premises subnets*—Besides the subnet you are extending, you must have one other subnet that doesn't overlap with any on-premises or Azure subnets. The on-premises VM (virtual appliance) must be connected to both subnets.
- *Windows Admin Center*—Windows Admin Center must be connected to Azure and must be managing the virtual appliance VMs.

Note 13

You'll learn more about virtualization, including hypervisors and nested virtualization, in Modules 12 and 13.

When all the prerequisites are met for creating an extended network, add the Extended Network extension in WAC. To do so, go to Settings (using the settings icon in the upper-right corner of WAC), select Extensions, select Azure Extended Network from the list of extensions (see Figure 9-46), and click Install. The extension should only take a few seconds to install.

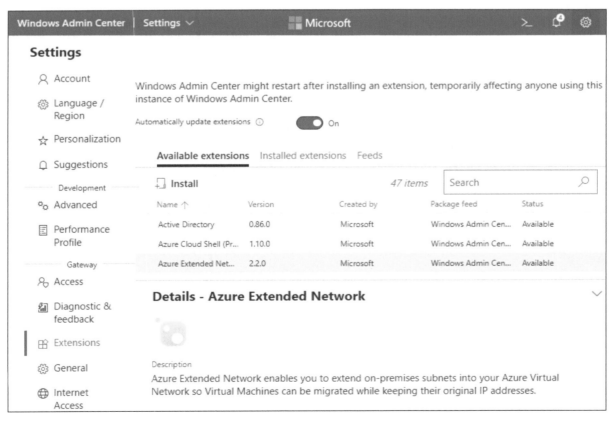

Figure 9-46   Adding the Azure Extended Network extension

After the extension is installed, select the virtual appliance server in WAC and click Azure Extended Network from the Tools menu on the left. Click the Set up button to begin the deployment of the extended network. Read the Overview page, which lists the prerequisites to deploying an extended network. You cannot proceed with the extended network deployment until the prerequisites are met. The following list describes the basic steps to deploy the extended network:

- *Select the subnet that you want to extend*—A list of subnets is retrieved from the virtual appliance through its configured network interfaces.
- *Select the Azure VNet subnet that the on-premises network will extend into*—Select the subscription, resource group, and VNet; the subnet will be selected automatically.
- *Configure the on-premises virtual appliance*—The virtual appliance is referred to as the on-premises extended-network gateway; the IP address information is filled in automatically, so all you need to do is verify that it is correct.
- *Configure the Azure VM*—Select the Azure VM (also referred to as the Azure virtual appliance or Azure extended-network gateway) by selecting the resource group and VM name. The IP address information is filled in automatically for you to review.
- *Select Deploy*—The extended network will take several minutes to deploy. Once deployed, you can begin configuring IP addresses in the extended network subnet that you want to be able to access from the on-premises network. A maximum of 250 IP addresses can be extended. However, you can't extend more IP addresses than the size of the extended network subnet.
- *Begin using IP addresses*—After you have added the IP addresses, you can begin using them by assigning them to VMs on the Azure network. Note that you cannot use the same address on both an on-premises device and an Azure VM. You can add addresses any time up to the maximum allowable amount.

Azure Relay

Azure Relay is an Azure network service that allows you to make your on-premises network services available on the public cloud without firewall configuration changes or VPN configuration. Azure Relay can target a specific application running on a server in your on-premises network without exposing a larger segment of the network to the outside world.

Azure Relay is configured in the Azure portal and works by creating a secure connection to your on-premises application using Transport Layer Security (TLS). The main difference between Azure Relay and a traditional VPN is that a VPN is a general secure channel between networks that can be used by any computer that has access to the VPN. Azure Relay, on the other hand, provides a secure channel only for a single application on the designated server running the application. So, it has a much smaller network footprint for an intruder to try to exploit. The basic steps of how the relay service works are as follows:

1. A connection is established between the on-premises application and the Azure Relay service using an outbound port on the on-premises network and a public IP address assigned to the Azure Relay service. The connection creates a secure bidirectional channel using TLS between the application and the Azure Relay service.
2. A client that wants to access the on-premises application does so by communicating with the Azure Relay service address.
3. The Azure Relay service passes the data on to the on-premises application using the secure channel created in the first step. The client has no knowledge that data is being passed from the Azure Relay service and the on-premises application, and because the channel is created using an outbound port on the on-premises network, no inbound ports on the on-premises firewall need to be opened.

The details for using Azure Relay involve creating a .NET application on an on-premises server, which is beyond the scope of this book. The basic steps for implementing Azure Relay are as follows:

1. Create an Azure namespace that clients will use to access the relay service. In the Azure portal, click Create a Resource. In the search box, type "relay," select Relay in the search results, and click Create. The Create namespace page opens.

2. On the Create namespace page, select the subscription and resource group and then provide a name for the namespace. The name will automatically have the suffix servicebus.windows.net. So, if you type mywebapp for the name, the full namespace will be mywebapp.servicebus.windows.net, which is what clients will use to connect to the on-premises application. Finally, select the location (see Figure 9-47). Click Review + create and then click Create.

3. Create management credentials. This step involves going to the namespace in Azure, selecting Shared access policies from the menu on the left, and creating a key to be used for making a secure connection between the relay and the on-premises application.

4. Next, from the namespace page, select Hybrid Connections or WCF relays depending on whether you are using a .NET application or a Windows Communication Foundation (WCF) application.

5. The details from here differ substantially depending on which method you chose in Step 4. The remaining part of the process involves creating a .NET server application and a client application that will access the server application using the Azure namespace created in Step 2.

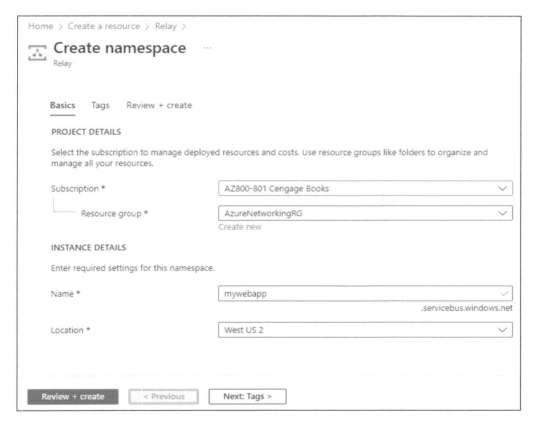

Figure 9-47 Creating a namespace

Note 14

Azure Relay was previously named Service Bus Relay. You can follow an online tutorial about creating an application using Azure Relay at https://docs.microsoft.com/en-us/azure/azure-relay/relay-hybrid-connections-dotnet-get-started.

Azure Virtual WAN

Azure Virtual WAN is an Azure networking service that can act as a central hub for all your Azure network connections, including VNet to VNet, site-to-site and point-to-site VPNs, ExpressRoute VPN, and third-party branch office connectivity. Routing is automatic and uses the Azure backbone for high-performance connectivity between all the network connections you use both within Azure and between your on-premises networks and Azure. You can get an idea of how Azure Virtual WAN connects multiple network types by reviewing Figure 9-48.

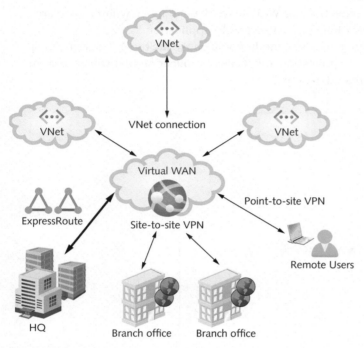

Figure 9-48   Azure Virtual WAN

As you can see from Figure 9-48, Azure Virtual WAN creates a hub and spoke topology in which all connected networks go through the virtual WAN hub (labeled Virtual WAN in the figure). Note that you can also connect virtual WAN hubs in different regions so that networks created in different regions can communicate with each other through the virtual WAN hub (vHub). When you use a virtual WAN (vWAN) with a vHub, you don't need to create separate connections from your on-premises networks (such as ExpressRoute or site-to-site and point-to-site VPNs) to your vNets in Azure. Instead, you connect your vNets and on-premises networks to the vHub, and the vHub routes traffic among all the connected networks. Note that a vHub, like other Azure resources, is located in an Azure region and is the core of your network connectivity in the region. If you have network resources in multiple regions that need the connectivity a vWAN provides, you must create a vHub in each region. You can then connect vHubs together for connectivity across regions.

Creating a Virtual WAN

To configure a virtual WAN, create a new resource in the Azure portal, type "virtual wan" in the search box on the Create a resource page, and press Enter. Select the Microsoft Azure Virtual WAN resource from the Marketplace page (see Figure 9-49) and click Create.

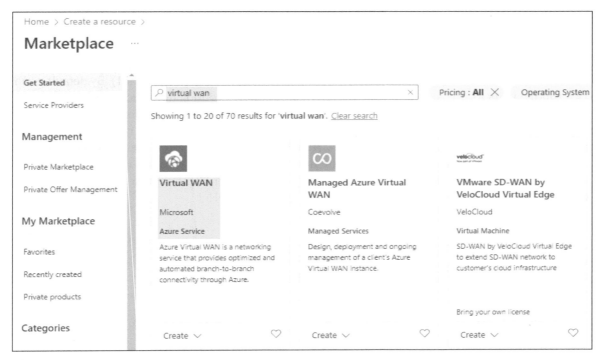

Figure 9-49   Selecting a virtual WAN resource

Choose your subscription, resource group, and region from the Create WAN page (see Figure 9-50) and give your vWAN a name. You also choose the type of vWAN. The choices are Basic and Standard. The basic vWAN only supports site-to-site VPNs, whereas the standard option supports site-to-site and point-to-site VPNs, ExpressRoute, VNets, and vWAN-to-vWAN connectivity across regions.

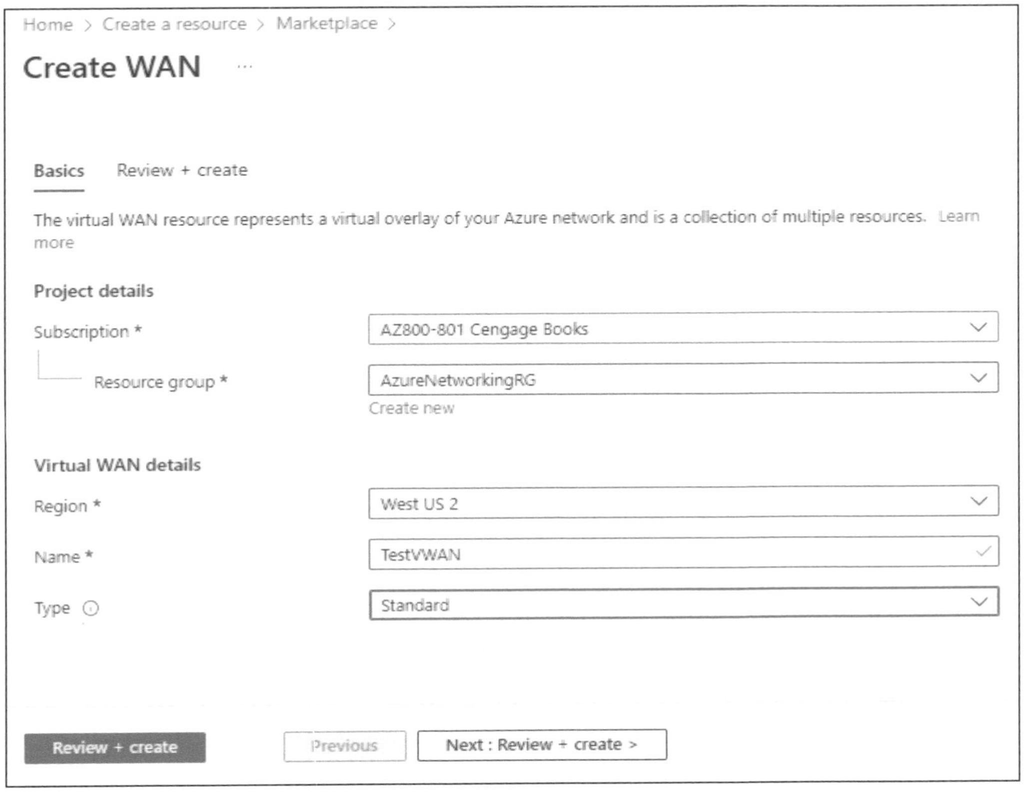

Home > Create a resource > Marketplace >

Create WAN   ...

Basics   Review + create

The virtual WAN resource represents a virtual overlay of your Azure network and is a collection of multiple resources.   Learn more

Project details

Subscription *	AZ800-801 Cengage Books
Resource group *	AzureNetworkingRG

Create new

Virtual WAN details

Region *	West US 2
Name *	TestVWAN
Type ⓘ	Standard

[Review + create]   [Previous]   [Next : Review + create >]

Figure 9-50   Creating a virtual WAN

After the vWAN is created, you add a virtual hub (vHub). From the vWAN page, click Hubs under Connectivity and then click New Hub to open the Create virtual hub page. The subscription and resource group are set to the same settings as the vWAN. Select a region, give your vHub a name, and assign an address space. The address space you assign cannot overlap with the address spaces in existing vNets or on-premises networks that will connect to the vHub. Finally, you select the virtual hub capacity, which is expressed in routing units (see Figure 9-51). By default, each vHub is assigned two routing units for the standard cost of the vHub. Additional routing units incur additional costs. Two routing units provide 3 Gbps of routing throughput among all connected networks and support up to 2000 virtual machines connected to all VNets in the vHub. Each additional routing unit provides an additional 1 Gbps of throughput and 1000 VMs. You can create the vHub at this point or create virtual hub gateways for the on-premises networks that you will connect to the vHub. It is recommended that you create the gateways while creating the vHub, as the process is faster. You can create a site-to-site, point-to-site, or ExpressRoute gateway, depending on the network types you are using to connect to Azure. A gateway is not necessary for connecting vNets to a vHub.

> **Caution** ❗
>
> When you create a virtual hub, you are charged for it even if you don't connect any networks to it.

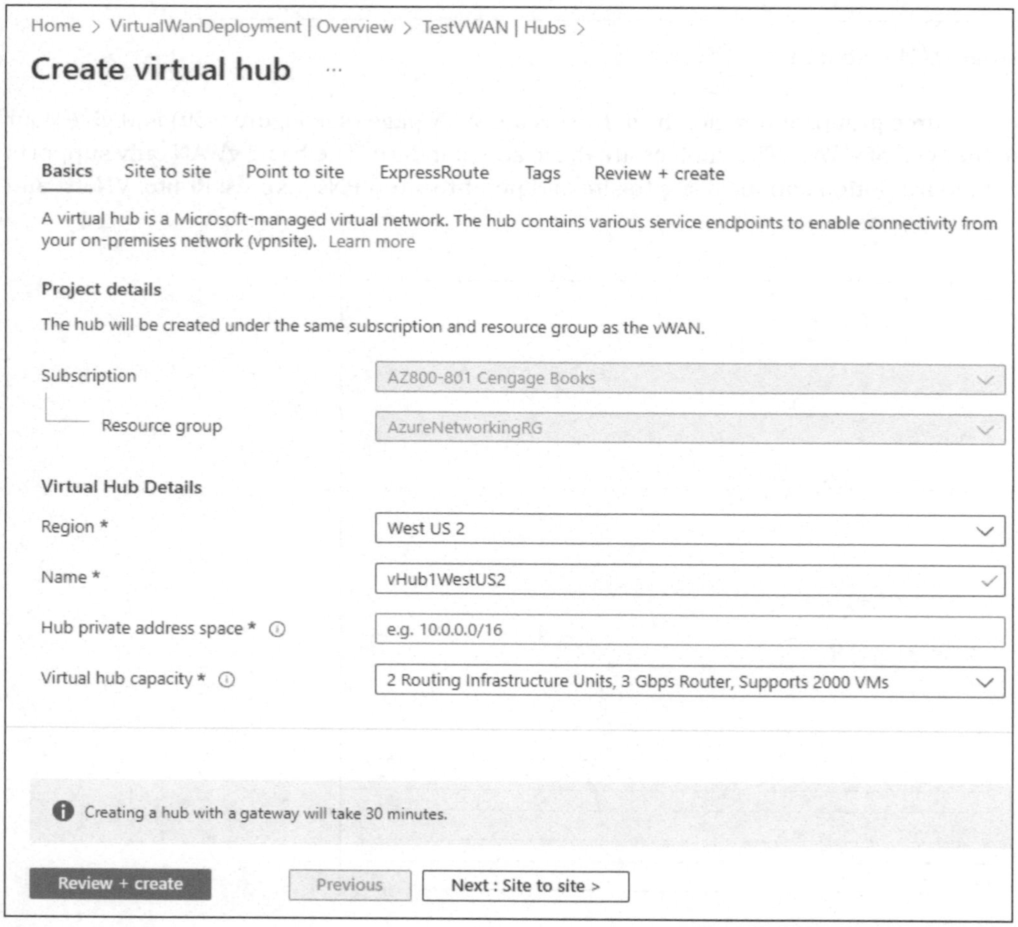

Home > VirtualWanDeployment | Overview > TestVWAN | Hubs >

Create virtual hub   ...

Basics   Site to site   Point to site   ExpressRoute   Tags   Review + create

A virtual hub is a Microsoft-managed virtual network. The hub contains various service endpoints to enable connectivity from your on-premises network (vpnsite). Learn more

Project details

The hub will be created under the same subscription and resource group as the vWAN.

Subscription	AZ800-801 Cengage Books ⌄
└─ Resource group	AzureNetworkingRG ⌄

Virtual Hub Details

Region *	West US 2 ⌄
Name *	vHub1WestUS2 ✓
Hub private address space * ⓘ	e.g. 10.0.0.0/16
Virtual hub capacity * ⓘ	2 Routing Infrastructure Units, 3 Gbps Router, Supports 2000 VMs ⌄

ⓘ Creating a hub with a gateway will take 30 minutes.

[Review + create]   [Previous]   [Next : Site to site >]

Figure 9-51   Creating a virtual hub

With a vHub created and one or more gateways created, you can create new networks or add existing networks to the vHub (see Figure 9-52). The specifics for adding each type of network to a vHub is beyond the scope of this book.

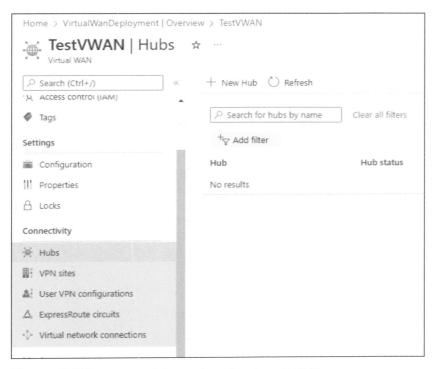

Figure 9-52   Connectivity options for virtual WANs

Azure AD Application Proxy

Azure **AD Application Proxy** provides remote access and single sign-on to on-premises and Azure web applications. AD Application Proxy has two primary components:

- **Application Proxy service**—This component runs in the Azure cloud and allows remote users who have authenticated with Azure AD to access the on-premises web application without requiring on-premises, open firewall ports.
- **Application Proxy connector**—This component runs on-premises and works with the Application Proxy service to provide secure access to the on-premises web application.

When a remote user tries to access the on-premises web application, the following steps occur (see Figure 9-53):

1. The user is prompted to sign in using their Azure AD credentials.
2. The user client device sends the authentication token provided by Azure AD to the Application Proxy service.
3. The Application Proxy service relays the request to the on-premises Application Proxy connector, which can authenticate the user with on-premises Active Directory if you want.
4. The Application Proxy connector forwards the request to the web application.
5. The web application sends a response back to the user via the on-premises Application Proxy connector and the Application Proxy service running in Azure.

As you can see, there is no direct communication from outside the on-premises network with the web application, which limits opportunities for attacks on the web application. This method for providing remote connectivity to an on-premises web application allows secure access with no VPN or firewall configuration requirements at the on-premises network.

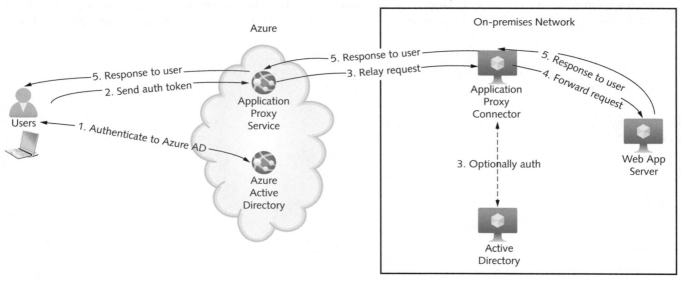

Figure 9-53 Azure AD Application Proxy

Self-Check Questions

6. Which Azure networking technology allows an on-premises server to communicate with an Azure VNet using a point-to-site VPN?

   a. Azure extended network

   b. Azure Relay

   c. Azure AD Application Proxy

   d. Azure Network Adapter

7. Which Azure networking technology provides communication between VNets?

   a. Azure Relay

   b. Azure extended network

   c. Virtual network peering

   d. Azure virtual appliance

○ Check your answers at the end of this module.

Module Summary

- Remote Access is a server role that provides services to keep a mobile workforce and branch offices securely connected to the main office. Services include VPNs, remote dial-in, routing, NAT, Web Application Proxy, and DirectAccess.
- When you install the Remote Access server role, you can install three role services: DirectAccess and VPN, Routing, and Web Application Proxy.
- A VPN is a network connection that uses the Internet to give mobile users or branch offices secure access to a company's network resources on a private network. VPNs use encryption and authentication to ensure that communication is secure and legitimate, so although data travels through the public Internet, the connection remains private.
- Windows Server 2022 supports three tunnel types: PPTP, L2TP/IPsec, and SSTP. After you finish the VPN server configuration, you need to define who's allowed to connect via remote access. You can do this with a user's account settings or by configuring a network policy in the Network Policy Server (NPS) console.

- The VPN client is configured by setting up a new connection in the Network and Sharing Center. When you set up a new connection, you choose "Connect to a workplace," and then you have the option to use your existing connection to the Internet or to create a dial-up connection.
- The default settings for VPN and dial-up might be adequate in many circumstances, but you might need to support different OSs and VPN clients over different tunneling methods, which could require security settings other than the defaults.
- A site-to-site VPN securely connects two networks—for example, a branch office and a main office. The VPN tunnel is established between two network devices such as routers or Windows servers configured as VPN servers.
- Network Policy Server is Microsoft's implementation of the RADIUS protocol, a proposed IETF standard that's widely used to centralize authentication, authorization, and accounting.
- There are two main reasons you should set up an NPS architecture with RADIUS when you have different connection paths to your network. First, RADIUS centralizes control over authentication and authorization. Second, standardizing on RADIUS requires all NAS devices to be RADIUS clients so that only one protocol performs authentication and authorization, and only one standard configuration process is used.
- RADIUS accounting is essentially a log of access and accounting requests and responses sent between RADIUS clients and RADIUS servers.
- For stronger security, certificate-based authentication is recommended; it uses a certificate containing information that establishes an entity's identity. With this authentication method, a server or client's identity can be verified.
- Connection request policies are used to specify which RADIUS servers perform authentication and authorization of RADIUS clients' connection requests. They can also specify which servers RADIUS accounting requests are sent to.
- After configuring RADIUS servers and clients defined in connection request policies, you need to specify who can connect to the network and under what conditions by creating a network policy.
- Templates can reduce the amount of work and minimize the chance of error when configuring RADIUS servers and clients. You can use NPS or RADIUS templates to reuse settings on the local server or export settings to other NPS servers.
- NPS can export templates to an XML file that can then be imported to another NPS server, which is useful when you're setting up multiple NPS servers that should be configured the same way (for example, a server group).
- Web Application Proxy is a Routing and Remote Access role service that allows remote users to access network applications from any device that supports a web browser. Web Application Proxy works with AD FS to enable features such as single sign-on.
- After Web Application Proxy is configured, you can begin publishing applications. To do so, use the Remote Access Management console. When publishing a web application, you have two options for preauthentication: AD FS preauthentication or pass-through preauthentication.
- Azure networking includes the technologies necessary to allow communication between Azure resources such as Azure VMs, Azure storage, and Azure databases, as well as the technologies needed to allow on-premises resources to communicate with Azure resources.
- An Azure Virtual Network (VNet) provides the basis for communication between Azure resources on the same VNet, between resources on different VNets, and between your on-premises network and Azure resources.
- Azure Network Adapter is a technology that allows an on-premises server to communicate with an Azure VNet using a point-to-site VPN connection.
- The Azure extended network is an Azure migration feature that allows you to extend an on-premises subnet into an Azure VNet while allowing the on-premises servers to keep their existing private IP addresses.
- Azure Relay is an Azure network service that allows you to make your on-premises network services available on the public cloud without firewall configuration changes or VPN configuration.
- Azure Virtual WAN is an Azure networking service that can act as a central hub for all your Azure network connections, including VNet to VNet, site-to-site and point-to-site VPNs, ExpressRoute VPN, and third-party branch office connectivity.
- Azure AD Application Proxy provides remote access and single sign-on to on-premises and Azure web applications.

Key Terms

access client
AD Application Proxy
Application Proxy connector
Application Proxy service
Azure extended network
Azure Network Adapter
Azure Relay
Azure Virtual Network (VNet)
Azure Virtual WAN
certificate-based authentication
certification authority (CA)
Challenge Handshake Authentication
 Protocol (CHAP)
demand-dial interface

Extensible Authentication Protocol
 (EAP)
global virtual network peering
Microsoft Challenge Handshake
 Authentication Protocol (MS-CHAP)
Microsoft Challenge Handshake
 Authentication Protocol version 2
 (MS-CHAP v2)
nested virtualization
network access server (NAS)
Password Authentication Protocol (PAP)
perimeter network
Protected Extensible Authentication
 Protocol (PEAP)

RADIUS server group
realm
Remote Access
Remote Authentication Dial-In User
 Service (RADIUS)
root certificate
service endpoint
shared secret
Transport Layer Security (TLS)
tunnel
virtual appliance
virtual network peering
virtual private network (VPN)
Web Application Proxy (WAP)

Review Questions

1. Which of the following is a service provided by the Remote Access server role? (Choose all that apply.)
   a. Network Address Translation
   b. Web Application Proxy
   c. Windows Server Update Services
   d. Internet Information Services

2. Which VPN tunnel type requires the firewall to allow TCP port 443?
   a. PPTP
   b. SSTP
   c. L2TP/IPsec
   d. PPP

3. Which VPN tunnel type uses an Internet Key Exchange?
   a. PPP
   b. PPTP
   c. SSTP
   d. L2TP/IPsec

4. Which tunnel type needs to authenticate client and server computers with a preshared key or a digital certificate?
   a. PPTP
   b. SSTP
   c. L2TP/IPsec
   d. PPP

5. Which of the following needs to be configured on the firewall to allow PPTP VPN connections? (Choose two.)
   a. UDP port 4500
   b. TCP port 1723

   c. IP protocol ID 50
   d. IP protocol ID 47

6. Which remote access configuration option should you choose if you want mobile users to be able to make a secure connection to the main network and allow computers on the private network to access the Internet with a public IP address?
   a. Remote access (dial-up or VPN)
   b. Network Address Translation
   c. VPN access and NAT
   d. Secure connection between two private networks

7. The Network Access Permission attribute for a user account is set to which of the following by default?
   a. Control access through NPS Network Policy
   b. Allow access
   c. Deny access
   d. Control access through Group Policy

8. When you create a VPN connection on a client computer, what's the default tunnel type?
   a. SSTP
   b. PPTP
   c. Automatic
   d. L2TP/IPsec

9. Which authentication method should you choose if users authenticate with smart cards?
   a. MS-CHAP v2
   b. PAP
   c. EAP
   d. RADIUS

10. What should you configure if you want only users who are members of particular groups to be able to connect to the VPN?
   a. Connection request policy
   b. Network policy
   c. Remote authentication rule
   d. Network access rule

11. Remote access is denied to users by default. Which of the following can you do to allow users to connect via remote access? (Choose two.)
   a. Configure settings in the Routing and Remote Access console.
   b. Configure dial-in settings in user accounts.
   c. Configure a network policy in the Network Policy Server console.
   d. Set up a VPN.

12. Which of the following can function as a RADIUS client? (Choose three.)
   a. A VPN server
   b. An unmanaged switch
   c. A wireless access point
   d. A dial-in server

13. Which of the following are options for configuring NPS? (Choose two.)
   a. As a RADIUS server
   b. As a RADIUS client
   c. As a RADIUS proxy
   d. As both a RADIUS client and server

14. What client authentication method can PEAP use?
   a. Passwords
   b. Certificates
   c. Biometrics
   d. None of these methods

15. What criteria can a RADIUS proxy use to determine where to forward a request? (Choose three.)
   a. The priority assigned the server
   b. The weight assigned the server
   c. The availability of the server
   d. The IP address of the server

16. What formats does RADIUS accounting write to? (Choose three.)
   a. Event log
   b. SQL Server
   c. RADIUS accounting format
   d. Text file

17. What do connection request policies specify?
   a. Which RADIUS servers handle connection requests from RADIUS clients

   b. Which users and groups can connect, what times they can access the network, and what conditions apply
   c. Both a and b
   d. None of these

18. What do network policies specify?
   a. Which RADIUS servers handle connection requests from RADIUS clients
   b. Which users and groups can connect, what times they can access the network, and what conditions apply
   c. Both a and b
   d. None of these

19. To make a connection request policy apply to a wireless access point, the NAS type must be set to which of the following?
   a. Wireless access point
   b. 802.11
   c. Unspecified
   d. None of these

20. Which of the following is *not* an NPS template type?
   a. Certificates
   b. Shared secrets
   c. RADIUS clients
   d. Remote RADIUS servers

21. Which of the following is not an encryption setting you can choose when configuring network policies for VPNs?
   a. Basic
   b. Strong
   c. Clear text
   d. No encryption

22. When all NPS policies on an NPS server are exported, what else is exported?
   a. The RADIUS accounting log
   b. Physical device names
   c. Shared secrets
   d. A list of client access devices

23. RADIUS proxies distribute requests equally between servers when which of the following is true?
   a. The load balancing attribute is set.
   b. The servers have the same priority.
   c. Each server has a different weight.
   d. The servers have the same weight and priority.

24. Which of the following is a possible response from an NPS server when evaluating an Access-Request message? (Choose all that apply.)

a. Access-Reject
b. Access-Deny
c. Access-Accept
d. Access-Challenge

25. Which of the following is an authentication type for EAP and is a cryptographic protocol used to encrypt network messages?
a. System Extensible Protocol
b. Transport Layer Security
c. Protected Extensible Authentication Protocol
d. Password Authentication Protocol

26. When a connection request requires authentication from another domain controller and is sent to an NPS server acting as a RADIUS proxy, what specific part of the network policy determines which server the request is routed to?
a. Realm
b. PEAP
c. Priority
d. Weight

27. When a certificate is used for authentication, the certification authority (CA) must be trusted by the client or server. To be trusted, the CA must have which of the following in the Trusted Root Certification Authorities certificate store?
a. Trusted CA
b. CA certificate
c. Client certificate
d. Authenticated certificate

28. Which of the following NPS template types can specify a reusable password for validating a connection between RADIUS servers and proxies and NAS servers?
a. System health agent
b. NPS agent
c. System health validator
d. Shared secrets

29. You are configuring network policies. After you have configured your RADIUS servers and clients, which specific policy will allow you to specify attributes for how the access client is connecting to the network?
a. Day and time restrictions
b. Connection properties
c. RADIUS client properties
d. Gateway properties

30. When a RADIUS server receives a RADIUS Access-Request message from a RADIUS client, which of the following are checked against the connection request policy's conditions?
a. Client's permissions
b. Radius server's attributes
c. Group policies
d. Client's attributes

31. Which of the following are requirements for configuring the Web Application Proxy role service on Windows Server? (Choose two.)
a. The database must be hosted by an external SQL server.
b. You must have a functioning AD FS deployment on the network.
c. Two NICs are needed: one NIC for the Internet and the other connected to the private network.
d. The Web Application Proxy must be installed on a standalone server.

32. What do you use to connect VNets that are in the same region or different regions?
a. Azure Network Adapter
b. Azure Routing and Remote Access
c. Azure Relay
d. Virtual network peering

33. Which of the following are required to use Azure Network Adapter to connect an on-premises server to a VM running in Azure? (Choose two.)
a. VNet peering
b. Windows Admin Center
c. An Azure VNet
d. Nested virtualization

34. Which feature must be enabled on an on-premises server that will act as a virtual appliance in an Azure extended network configuration?
a. Azure Network Adapter
b. Nested virtualization
c. Routing and Remote Access
d. VPN client

35. What type of topology is created when you implement Azure Virtual WAN?
a. Hub and spoke
b. Partial mesh
c. Extended star
d. Point-to-point

Critical Thinking

The following activities give you critical thinking challenges. Case projects offer a scenario with a problem for which you supply a written solution.

Case Projects

Case Project 9-1: Adding a RADIUS Infrastructure

CSM Tech Publishing is growing. To keep building costs down, it's allowing more people to work from home and connect to the network via a VPN. For this reason, the CIO has asked you to propose a RADIUS infrastructure. The users can access most of the resources they could use if they were logged on at the office. The only external access to the network is through a VPN, and the internal infrastructure uses switches that don't perform any kind of authentication. Although not many people are currently working from home, the number is expected to grow quickly if things work out well. Given these considerations, what suggestions should you give the CIO?

Case Project 9-2: Setting Up Remote Access for Contractors

Several new projects are being staffed by outside contractors who will be working on servers in the contractors' office, not in the company building, and will have their own VPN server. The contracting company has informed your company that none of its people will be working weekends. What VPN controls can you set up to minimize contract employees' access to your network?

Case Project 9-3: Determining an Azure Network Solution

CSM Tech Publishing has determined that it wants to dip its toes into the cloud by moving some of its on-premises applications to Azure. You have been asked to come up with a solution that meets the following requirements:

- The migration of existing apps must be tested in phases and there should be little disruption to the existing network infrastructure. The same IP addressing scheme for all apps must be maintained.
- Some apps must stay on-premises due to compliance requirements for customer and vendor data protection.
- Three of the apps are latency-sensitive and may not perform well in the cloud.

What Azure networking technology or technologies do you propose to meet these requirements? Be specific and explain your reasons for the technology or technologies chosen. Describe some of the requirements for implementing the solution.

Solutions to Self-Check Questions

Section 9-1: The Remote Access Role

1. Which Remote Access service facilitates access to the Internet when your network is using private IP addresses?
   Answer: c. NAT
   Explanation: Network Address Translation (NAT) changes private IP addresses to public IP addresses on outgoing packets and public IP addresses back to private IP addresses on incoming packets.

2. Which VPN tunnel type uses certificates and TCP port 443?

    Answer: b. SSTP

    Explanation: Secure Socket Tunneling Protocol uses certificates for authentication and TCP port 443.

Section 9-2: Network Policy Server Overview

3. Which of the following is a protocol used to centralize authentication, authorization, and accounting for remote access to network services?

    Answer: d. RADIUS

    Explanation: Remote Authentication Dial-In User Service (RADIUS) provides centralized AAA services for remote access to networks. A VPN is a virtual private network, EAP-TLS is an authentication protocol, and Kerberos is an authentication protocol used in Windows domains.

4. Which type of NPS policy specifies which users and groups have access to a network?

    Answer: a. Network policies

    Explanation: Network policies are a policy type in NPS that allow an administrator to specify which users and groups can gain remote access to a network.

Section 9-3: Implementing Web Application Proxy

5. Which of the following is *not* a requirement for implementing Web Application Proxy?

    Answer: a. A VPN

    Explanation: Web Application Proxy requires Active Directory Federation Services, a server with two NICs, and a server with a digital certificate issued by a certificate authority. A virtual private network (VPN) is not required.

Section 9-4: Implementing Azure Networking

6. Which Azure networking technology allows an on-premises server to communicate with an Azure VNet using a point-to-site VPN?

    Answer: d. Azure Network Adapter

    Explanation: Azure Network Adapter is a technology that allows an on-premises server to communicate with an Azure VNet using a point-to-site VPN connection. The Azure extended network is an Azure migration feature that allows you to extend an on-premises subnet into an Azure VNet. Azure Relay is an Azure network service that allows you to make your on-premises network services available on the public cloud without firewall configuration changes or VPN configuration. Azure AD Application Proxy provides remote access and single sign-on to on-premises and Azure web applications.

7. Which Azure networking technology provides communication between VNets?

    Answer: c. Virtual network peering

    Explanation: Virtual network peering is an Azure technology that allows you to connect VNets and enable their resources to communicate with one another. Azure Relay is an Azure network service that allows you to make your on-premises network services available on the public cloud without firewall configuration changes or VPN configuration. The Azure extended network is an Azure migration feature that allows you to extend an on-premises subnet into an Azure VNet. The Azure virtual appliance is a VM in an Azure extended network configuration that is connected both to the subnet you are extending and another subnet.

Module 10

Configure Storage and File Services

Module Objectives

After reading this module and completing the exercises, you will be able to:

1 Describe server storage

2 Configure local disks

3 Use virtual disks

4 Describe file sharing

5 Secure access to files with permissions

6 Use File Server Resource Manager

7 Deploy Distributed File System

8 Deploy BranchCache

Configuring a server's storage is usually one of the first tasks you need to perform on a new server after finishing its initial configuration. In the past, server storage was simply a disk controller and one or two hard drives. Now, advanced storage solutions are available to provide fault tolerance and high performance. This module covers the basics of server storage and then explains how to configure local disks. With virtualization becoming such an important part of network environments, it's no surprise that Windows Server 2022 supports creating and mounting virtual disks. This module describes the basic steps needed to work with virtual disks.

After storage is configured, you'll need to configure the storage for use, which often means sharing it with network users and setting permissions. This module discusses a variety of methods for creating and configuring Windows shares and shows you how to properly set permissions to allow users proper access. Because many networks include Linux/UNIX computers, you'll also learn how to configure NFS shares, the native file-sharing protocol for Linux/UNIX operating systems.

Table 10-1 describes what you need to do the hands-on activities in this module.

Table 10-1   Activity requirements

Activity	Requirements	Notes
Activity 10-1: Resetting Your Virtual Environment	ServerSA1, ServerDC1, ServerDM1, ServerDM2	
Activity 10-2: Configuring a New Disk	ServerSA1	
Activity 10-3: Working with Volumes in Disk Management	ServerSA1	
Activity 10-4: Working with Virtual Disks in Disk Management	ServerSA1	
Activity 10-5: Sharing a Folder with Simple File Sharing	ServerSA1	
Activity 10-6: Sharing a Folder with Advanced Sharing	ServerSA1	
Activity 10-7: Creating a Share with File and Storage Services	ServerSA1	
Activity 10-8: Creating a Hidden Share and Monitoring Share Access	ServerSA1	
Activity 10-9: Mapping a Drive	ServerSA1	
Activity 10-10: Examining Default Settings for Volume Permissions	ServerSA1	
Activity 10-11: Experimenting with File and Folder Permissions	ServerSA1	
Activity 10-12: Restricting Access to Subfolders of Shares	ServerSA1	
Activity 10-13: Installing the File Server Resource Manager Role Service	ServerSA1	
Activity 10-14: Creating and Applying a Quota Template	ServerSA1	
Activity 10-15: Creating a File Screen	ServerSA1	
Activity 10-16: Installing the DFS Namespaces and DFS Replication Role Services	ServerDC1, ServerDM1, ServerDM2	
Activity 10-17: Creating a Domain-Based Namespace	ServerDC1, ServerDM1, ServerDM2	
Activity 10-18: Configuring BranchCache on a File Server	ServerDC1, ServerDM1	
Activity 10-19: Configuring BranchCache on a Client	ServerDC1, ServerDM1, ServerDM2	

An Overview of Server Storage

Microsoft Exam AZ-800:

Manage storage and file services.

- Configure Windows Server storage

One of the main reasons networks and servers were invented was to have a centralized repository for shared files. The need for faster, bigger, and more reliable storage is growing as fast as the technology can keep up. Everything is stored on digital media now—documents, email, music, photographs, videos—and this trend is continuing. In addition, people want "instant anywhere" access to whatever they store. Just about every large Internet company has its own version of cloud storage, from Dropbox to iCloud to OneDrive. Dozens of cloud storage services are competing to store your files, and although these services are convenient and seemingly work by magic, they all start with a server and some disk drives. The following sections cover some basics of server storage: what it is, why you need it, and the common methods for accessing storage.

What Is Storage?

Generally speaking, storage is any digital medium to which data can be written and retrieved. Technically, this definition includes random access memory (RAM), but the term *server storage* generally means long-term storage in which data is maintained without a power source. Long-term storage includes the following types of media:

- Hard disk drives
- Solid state drives
- USB memory sticks (flash drives)
- CDs and DVDs
- Magnetic tape
- Secure Digital (SD) cards and Compact Flash (CF) cards

This discussion focuses on server storage, which is based on hard disk drives (HDDs) and solid state drives (SSDs). A **solid state drive (SSD)** uses flash memory and the same type of high-speed interfaces (SATA, SAS) as traditional hard disks. An SSD has no moving parts, requires less power, and is faster and more resistant to shock than an HDD, but the cost is still higher per gigabyte than an HDD. However, because of the speed advantages of SSDs, you'll often find them alongside HDDs in server systems. Most of the discussion of HDD storage also applies to SSDs. As technology progresses and prices drop, you'll see SSDs eventually replace HDDs except in the most storage-centric of applications.

> **Note 1**
>
> Some SSD drives now come with a PCI Express interface that plugs directly into a PCI Express slot. There are other variations of SSDs, such as SATA Express, mSATA, and M.2.

Reasons for Storage

Every computer needs some amount of storage, but servers generally require more than client computers because one of the server's main purposes is to store and serve files. The following list isn't exhaustive, but it covers most uses for storage:

- *Operating system files*—The OS itself requires a good deal of storage. The files that make up the OS include boot files, the kernel, device drivers, user interface files, and all the files for roles and features you can install. Together, they add up to around 9 GB on a server with the GUI installed and approximately 5 GB with Server Core.
- *Page file*—A **page file** is used as virtual memory and to store dump data after a system crash. Its size varies depending on how much RAM is installed, memory use patterns, and other factors. In the past, the page file was set to 1.5 times the amount of installed memory, but this formula is no longer valid. By default, the system manages the page file, which can change size depending on the amount of RAM installed and whether the system has recently crashed.
- *Log files*—The log files you see in Event Viewer and other log files change size dynamically depending on how the system is used. You can use Event Viewer to configure the maximum size of many log files. Be aware that even if you aren't adding any files to the disk where Windows is installed, log files can slowly eat up disk space unless you keep an eye on them.
- *Virtual machines*—If the server is a virtualization server running Hyper-V, you need plenty of space to store files for virtual hard disks. Virtualization technology is one of the largest users of disk space in servers now.

- *Database storage*—If a server is running one or more databases, disk storage requirements vary depending on the size of the databases. Because databases can grow dynamically, it's a good idea to store them on a drive separate from the Windows drive, preferably on a volume that can have its capacity expanded if needed.
- *Multimedia storage*—Graphic, audio, and video files use large amounts of storage. If the organization uses these types of files extensively, their storage requirements must be taken into account.
- *User documents*—If a server is being used to store user files or user profiles, they might be the largest use of disk space. Using disk quotas on servers that store user files is a good idea so that a single user can't monopolize disk space by storing a large collection of movies, for example, on a network server.

When deciding how much disk space you need for a server, you should take all the preceding uses into account. Remember that certain storage uses benefit from being on separate disks from the disk where Windows is stored. This advice is particularly true of the page file and virtual machines, but ideally, the Windows directory should be on a separate drive from most other storage uses.

Storage Access Methods

The discussion on storage access methods revolves around where storage is located in relation to the server. There are three broad categories of storage access methods:

- Local storage and direct-attached storage
- Network-attached storage (NAS)
- Storage area network (SAN)

Local Storage and Direct-Attached Storage

Local storage has been around as long as computers have, but the interfaces to storage media have improved as speed and capacity requirements have grown. Local storage is the focus of this module; disk interface technologies are discussed later in the "Configuring Local Disks" section.

Local storage can be defined as storage media with a direct, exclusive connection to the computer's system board through a disk controller. Local storage is almost always inside the computer's case, attached to a disk controller via internal cables and powered by the computer's internal power supply. The term *local storage* usually refers to HDDs or SSDs instead of CD/DVDs or other types of media. Local storage provides rapid and exclusive access to storage media through ever-faster bus technologies. The downside of local storage is that only the system where it's installed has direct access to the storage medium. Data on disks can be shared through network file sharing, but the system with the installed storage must fulfill requests for shared data.

Direct-attached storage (DAS) is a type of local storage, in that it's connected directly to the server using it. In fact, DAS includes hard drives mounted inside the server case. However, DAS can also refer to one or more HDDs in an enclosure with its own power supply. In this case, the DAS device is connected to a server through an external bus interface, such as eSATA, SCSI, USB, FireWire, or Fibre Channel.

A DAS device with its own enclosure and power supply can usually be configured as a disk array, such as a RAID configuration (discussed later in the "Configuring Local Disks" section). Although most DAS devices provide exclusive use to a single computer, some have multiple interfaces so that more than one computer can access the storage medium simultaneously. Most of the later discussion in the "Configuring Local Disks" section also applies to DAS devices because the computer usually sees an externally attached DAS device as local storage.

Network-Attached Storage

Network-attached storage (NAS), sometimes referred to as a **storage appliance**, has an enclosure, power supply, slots for multiple HDDs, a network interface, and a built-in OS tailored for managing shared storage. An NAS is designed to make access to shared files easy to set up and easy for users to access. Because an NAS is typically dedicated to file sharing, it can be faster than a traditional server in performing this task because a server is often sharing its computing and networking resources among several duties. An NAS shares files through standard network protocols, such as Server Message Block (SMB), Network File System (NFS), and File Transfer Protocol (FTP). Some NAS devices can also be used as DAS devices because they often have USB, eSATA, or other interfaces that can be attached directly to a computer.

Storage Area Network

The most complex type of storage is a **storage area network (SAN)**, which uses high-speed networking technologies to give servers fast access to large amounts of shared disk storage. The storage a SAN manages appears to the server OS as though it's physically attached to the server. However, it's connected to a high-speed network technology and can be shared by multiple servers. The most common network technologies used in SANs are Fibre Channel over Ethernet, iSCSI, and Network File System (NFS) over Ethernet. These technologies are designed to connect large arrays of hard drive storage that servers can access and share. Client computers access shared data by contacting servers via the usual method, and the servers retrieve the requested data from the SAN devices and pass it along to the client computer. Figure 10-1 shows a SAN using Fibre Channel, in which disk arrays are connected to a Fibre Channel switch and servers are connected to the Fibre Channel network as well as to a traditional network. In this arrangement, all servers have access to the storage medium, which can be shared and allocated as needed. SANs are often used by server clusters so that all cluster members have access to shared storage for the purposes of load balancing and fault tolerance.

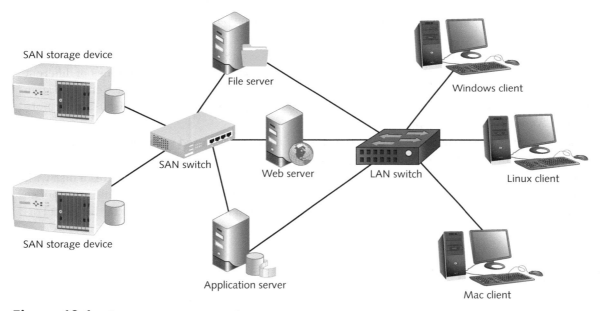

Figure 10-1   A storage area network

Self-Check Questions

1. A page file is used to store pages from document files that are currently being edited by a word processor. True or False?

   a. True **b.** False

2. Which type of storage is shared by multiple servers and can be used in a server cluster?

   a. NAS **c.** SAS
   b. DAS **d.** SAN

○ Check your answers at the end of this module.

Configuring Local Disks

Microsoft Exam AZ-800:

Manage storage and file services.

- Configure Windows Server storage

Configuration of local disks can be divided into two broad categories: physical disk properties and logical properties. Physical disk properties, which must be considered first before purchasing disk drives for a server, involve disk capacity, physical speed, and the interface for attaching a disk to the system. Logical disk properties include its format and the partitions or volumes created on it. Before you get too far into these properties, however, make sure you're clear on disk-storage terminology:

- *Disk drive*—A **disk drive** is a physical component with a disk interface connector (such as SATA or SAS) and a power connector. A mechanical disk drive (usually called an HDD) has one or more circular magnetic platters storing the data's bits and one or more read/write heads—one for each side of the magnetic platters. The platters spin at high speed, and the read/write heads move from the inside of the platter to the outside to read data on the disk. An SSD has a disk interface and power connector but has flash memory chips instead of magnetic platters, and there are no read/write heads or other moving parts. Data on SSDs is accessed in a similar fashion as RAM.

- *Volume*—Before an OS can use a disk drive, a volume must be created on the drive. A **volume** is a logical unit of storage that can be formatted with a file system. A disk drive can contain one or more volumes of different sizes. Disk drive space that hasn't been assigned to a volume is said to be unallocated. Volumes can also span two or more disks in an arrangement called RAID. Volumes, including RAID volumes, are discussed in more detail later in the "Volumes and Disk Types" section.

- *Partition*—This older term means the same thing as *volume*, but a partition is used with basic disks. The term **partition** is still used at times, but in Windows, it has largely been replaced by *volume*.

- *Formatting*—Before an OS can use a volume, the volume must be formatted. **Formatting** prepares a disk with a file system used to organize and store files. There are different format standards, and the format you choose for a disk depends on how the disk will be used. This topic is discussed in more detail later in the "Disk Formats" section.

Disk Capacity and Speed

The disk capacity you need depends entirely on how the disk will be used. Will it be a system disk for storing the Windows OS and related files, a file-sharing disk, a disk storing a database, or maybe one that stores virtual machines? Perhaps you plan to have a combination of uses, but in general, distinct types of data should be kept on separate disks so that you can optimize some of the disk's logical properties for the type of data it will store.

Keep in mind that you might not be basing disk capacity decisions on a single disk because you could be configuring an array of disks in a RAID or using virtual disks with services like Storage Spaces. HDD capacities are now measured in hundreds of gigabytes, with 4 terabytes and larger disks being common. (One terabyte equals 1000 gigabytes.) Disk capacity is fairly inexpensive, and having more than you need is better than having less. Here are some considerations for deciding how much disk capacity to buy and how many disks to use in a server:

- The Windows installation (the volume that stores the \Windows folder) should be on a separate disk from the data to be stored on the server. An SSD is a good candidate for the Windows installation.

- The page file should be on its own disk, if possible. An SSD is also a good candidate for the page file. If a separate disk is impractical, at least try to put the page file on its own volume.

- Take fault tolerance into account by using a RAID, which combines multiple disks to make a single volume so that data stored on the volume is maintained even if an individual disk fails. However, overall storage capacity is diminished.

The speed of HDDs is affected by a number of factors. The disk interface technology is an important performance factor that's discussed next. Other factors include rotation speed and the amount of cache memory installed. The rotation speed of disk platters in HDDs ranges from a low of about 5400 revolutions per minute (rpm) to 15,000 rpm, with speeds of 7200 and 10,000 rpm in between. A server should be outfitted with an HDD that rotates at a minimum of 7200 rpm, but for high-performance applications, look for 10,000 or 15,000 rpm drives.

The amount of cache in an HDD allows the drive to buffer read and write data locally, which speeds overall disk access. Cache sizes of 32 and 64 MB are common for server-class drives, but some very fast drives might have as little as 16 MB. What you're most interested in for disk performance is how fast data can be read from and written to the disk—the data rate. When researching disks for performance factors, look for the sustained data rate the manufacturer claims, which tells you how fast the drive can transfer data for an extended period.

Disk Interface Technologies

The disk interface connects a disk to a computer system, usually with some type of cable. The cable acts as a bus that carries data and commands between the disk and computer. The faster the bus, the faster the system can read from and write to the disk. The most common types of disk interfaces for locally attached disks are SATA, SAS, and SCSI. Each technology has advantages and disadvantages, as discussed in the following sections.

Note 2

You might also hear of parallel ATA (PATA) or Integrated Drive Electronics (IDE) drives that were used on older computers, and Fibre Channel drives on high-end systems. For locally attached drives for servers, the most common by far are SATA and SAS. IDE drives are obsolete, and Fibre Channel drives are most likely to be used in SANs.

Serial ATA Drives

Serial ATA (SATA) drives have replaced parallel ATA (PATA) drives and have several advantages over this older technology, including faster transfer times and smaller cable size. Whereas the PATA interface is limited to about 167 megabytes per second (MB/s), SATA drives boast transfer times up to 6 gigabits per second (Gb/s; 600 MB/s). SATA drives are inexpensive, fast, and fairly reliable. They're a good fit for both client computers and lower-end servers. The SATA standard has evolved from SATA 1.0, supporting transfer speeds of 1.5 Gb/s (150 MB/s), to the current SATA 3.2, supporting speeds up to 16 Gb/s (or 1.6 gigabytes per second, GB/s). However, most readily available devices support SATA 2.0 (3 Gb/s) or SATA 3.0 (6 Gb/s). Even with their high transfer rates, however, SATA drives take a back seat to SAS drives in the enterprise server realm.

SAS and SCSI Drives

Small computer system interface (SCSI) drives were a mainstay in enterprise-class servers for decades, and this drive technology has endured through more than a half-dozen upgrades. The most recent SCSI variation, developed in 2003, is Ultra-640, with up to 640 MB/s transfer rates. SCSI is a parallel technology, like PATA, and has probably reached its performance limits. SCSI, however, has always provided high reliability and enterprise-level command features, such as error recovery and reporting. Its successor is **serial attached SCSI (SAS)**, which maintains the high reliability and advanced commands of SCSI and improves performance, with transfer rates up to 12 Gb/s with SAS-3. SAS has the benefit of having bus compatibility with SATA, so SATA drives can be connected to SAS backplanes. A **backplane** is a connection system that uses a printed circuit board instead of traditional cables to carry signals.

The SAS standard offers higher-end features than SATA drives do. SAS drives usually have higher rotation speeds and use higher signaling voltages, which allow their use in server backplanes. Overall, SAS is considered the more enterprise-ready disk interface technology, but enterprise features come with a price—SAS drives are more expensive than SATA drives. As with many other things, server disk technologies have a tradeoff between performance and reliability versus price.

Volumes and Disk Types

Before data can be stored on a disk drive, space on the drive must be allocated to a volume. On a Windows system, each volume is typically assigned a drive letter, such as C or D. A volume can use some or all of the space on an HDD, or a single volume can span multiple drives. Before you go further, there are two Microsoft-specific volume definitions you need to know:

- *Boot volume*—The **boot volume** is the volume where the \Windows folder is located. It's usually the C drive but doesn't have to be. The boot volume is also called the *boot partition*.
- *System volume*—The **system volume** contains files the computer needs to find and load the Windows OS. In Windows 2008 and later, it's created automatically during installation if you're installing an OS for the first time on the system, and it's not assigned a drive letter, so you can't see it in File Explorer. You can, however, see it in Disk Management (see Figure 10-2). In earlier Windows versions, the system volume was usually the C drive. The system volume is also called the *system partition*.

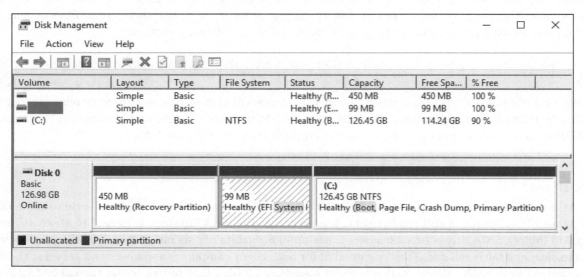

Figure 10-2   Boot and system volumes in Disk Management

In Windows, the types of volumes you can create on a disk depend on how the disk is categorized. Windows defines two disk categories: basic and dynamic. These categories are discussed next.

> **Note 3**
>
> The Windows boot and system volumes can be created only on basic disks.

Basic Disks

As the name implies, a **basic disk** can accommodate only basic volumes, called *simple volumes*. A simple volume is a disk partition residing on only one disk; it can't span multiple disks or be used to create a RAID volume. The volumes on a basic disk are also called *partitions*. The Disk Management snap-in uses both terms in its interface, but the term *partition* is more accurate and distinguishes it from a volume created on a dynamic disk. When Windows detects a new disk drive, it's initialized as a basic disk by default.

You can create a maximum of four partitions on a basic disk. The first three you create with Disk Management are primary partitions. A **primary partition** can be an active partition and can be the Windows system volume. Primary partitions are usually assigned a drive letter but don't have to be, as with the Windows system volume. If you create a fourth partition, it's called an **extended partition**, which can be divided into one or more logical drives, each assigned a drive letter. A logical drive on an extended partition can hold the boot volume, but it can't hold the system volume because it can't be marked as active.

Dynamic Disks

If you need more than a simple volume, you must convert a basic disk to a **dynamic disk**. Volumes created on dynamic disks can span multiple disks and be configured for fault tolerance by using RAID. A dynamic disk can hold the Windows boot or system partition, but only if you convert the disk to dynamic after Windows is already installed on the volume. You can create up to 128 volumes on a dynamic disk.

To convert a basic disk to dynamic in Disk Management, simply right-click the disk and click Convert to Dynamic Disk. Existing volumes on the basic disk are converted to simple volumes on the dynamic disk, and all data on the disk is maintained. You can convert a dynamic disk to basic in the same manner, but you must first delete existing volumes on the dynamic disk, and existing data will be lost.

> **Note 4**
>
> If you attempt to create a volume on a basic disk that isn't supported, Windows prompts you to convert it to dynamic before you can proceed.

Partitioning Methods

Windows offers two methods for partitioning disks. The most common method, **Master Boot Record (MBR)**, has been around since DOS. MBR partitions support volume sizes up to 2 TB. MBR-based disks are compatible with all Windows versions as well as most other OSs. When a disk is initialized in Disk Management, it's initialized as an MBR disk by default.

The second and newer method is **GUID Partitioning Table (GPT)**. GPT disks became an option starting with Windows Server 2008 and Vista. They support volume sizes up to 18 exabytes (EB, a million terabytes); however, Windows file systems currently support volume sizes only up to 256 TB. Starting with Windows Server 2022, new disks are initialized using GPT, but you can select MBR if desired. In Disk Management, you can convert an MBR disk to GPT and vice versa, but you must delete existing partitions first, which erases all data. In addition to larger volume sizes, GPT partitions offer improved reliability in the form of partition table replication (a backup copy of the partition table) and Cyclic Redundancy Check (CRC) protection of the partition table.

> **Note 5**
>
> Systems with an EFI BIOS (virtual machines created in Hyper-V, for example) can only boot to GPT partitions. GPT partitions contain an area on the disk called the *protective MBR*, which is maintained for backward compatibility with disk utilities that work only with MBR disks.

Disk Sector Sizes

The storage space on disk drives is divided into sectors, and sectors are combined by the file system into clusters when the disk is formatted. Sector sizes have traditionally been 512 bytes in length, and sectors are combined into cluster sizes of 4K, 8K, 16K, 32K, or 64K bytes. Windows Server 2022 supports disks with 512 byte sectors, referred to as a Standard Format disk, but Windows Server 2022 also supports Advanced Format disks that use 4096 byte sectors. The larger sector size allows Windows to support much larger volume sizes than previously possible using 512 byte sectors. Windows Server 2022 also supports a hybrid version of Advanced Format disks called 512e drives in which the disk is configured with 4096 byte physical sectors but emulates 512 byte sectors to support systems that can't use 4096 byte sectors. You can view the sector size in use on a drive by typing `fsutil fsinfo sectorinfo` *DriveLetter*: at a command prompt. For example, Figure 10-3 shows the logical sector size as 512 bytes and the physical sector size as 4096 bytes. The command was run on a Hyper-V virtual machine, indicating that Windows formats virtual disks using the larger-size sectors but with 512 byte emulation. In general, if your server application requires very large volumes containing large files, the Advanced Format disk is more efficient, but not all OSs support this type of disk.

```
C:\Windows\system32>fsutil fsinfo sectorinfo h:
LogicalBytesPerSector :                                 512
PhysicalBytesPerSectorForAtomicity :                    4096
PhysicalBytesPerSectorForPerformance :                  4096
FileSystemEffectivePhysicalBytesPerSectorForAtomicity : 4096
Device Alignment :                                      Aligned (0x000)
Partition alignment on device :                         Aligned (0x000)
Performs Normal Seeks
Trim Supported
Not DAX capable
```

Figure 10-3   Checking the sector size

Types of Volumes

A basic disk supports only simple volumes, but you can create several volume types on a dynamic disk, including RAID volumes. **Redundant array of independent disks (RAID)** is a disk configuration that uses space on multiple disks to form a single logical volume. Most RAID configurations offer fault tolerance, and some enhance performance. The following are the types of volumes you can create on a Windows Server system. Some of these volume types are described in the "Storage Spaces" section of Module 11.

- *Simple volume*—A **simple volume**, as mentioned, resides on a single basic or dynamic disk. On a basic disk, a simple volume can be extended (made larger) if unallocated space is available on the disk. A simple volume can also be shrunk on basic or dynamic disks. A simple volume on a dynamic disk can be extended on the same disk or to multiple disks as long as they have unallocated space. A simple volume can also be made into a mirrored volume by using two dynamic disks.

- *Spanned volume*—A **spanned volume** extends across two or more physical disks. For example, a simple volume that has been extended to a second disk is a spanned volume. When the first disk has filled up, subsequent disks are used to store data. Spanned volumes don't offer fault tolerance; if any disk fails, data on all disks is lost. There's also no performance advantage in using a spanned volume.

- *Striped volume*—A **striped volume** extends across two or more dynamic disks, but data is written to all disks in the volume equally. For example, if a 10 MB file is written to a striped volume with two disks, 5 MB is written to each disk. A striped volume can use from 2 to 32 disks. Striped volumes don't offer fault tolerance, but they do have a read and write performance advantage over spanned and simple volumes because multiple disks can be accessed simultaneously to read and write files. A striped volume is also referred to as a *RAID 0 volume*. The Windows system and boot volumes can't be on a striped volume.

- *Mirrored volume*—A **mirrored volume** (or *RAID 1 volume*) uses space from two dynamic disks and provides fault tolerance. Data written to one disk is duplicated, or mirrored, to the second disk. If one disk fails, the other disk has a good copy of the data, and the system can continue to operate until the failed disk is replaced. The space used on both disks in a mirrored volume is the same. Mirrored volumes might have a disk read performance advantage, but they don't have a disk write performance advantage.

- *RAID 5 volume*—A **RAID 5 volume** uses space from three or more dynamic disks and uses disk striping with parity to provide fault tolerance. When data is written, it's striped across all but one of the disks in the volume. Parity information derived from the data is written to the remaining disk. The system alternates which disk is used for parity information, so each disk has both data and parity information. Parity information is used to re-create lost data after a disk failure. A RAID 5 volume provides increased read performance, but write performance is decreased because of having to calculate and write parity information. The Windows system and boot volumes can't be on a RAID 5 volume.

> **Note 6**
>
> Striped, mirrored, and RAID 5 volumes configured in Windows are referred to as *software RAID*. You can also purchase a RAID disk controller that can create RAID disks by using the controller's firmware—called *hardware RAID*. Hardware RAID is done at the disk level, whereas software RAID in Windows is done at the volume level. Hardware RAID typically results in better performance than software RAID. In addition, the restrictions on placing Windows system and boot volumes on RAID volumes apply to software RAID because the OS must be up and running before the RAID is recognized. Hardware RAID configurations don't have these restrictions in most cases. As you'll see in Module 11, you can also use Storage Spaces to create fault-tolerant virtual disk configurations.

Disk Formats

Before you can store data on a volume, it must be formatted with a file system. Formatting creates the directory structure needed to organize files and store information about each file. The information stored about each file depends on the file system used.

A **file system** defines the method and format an OS uses to store, locate, and retrieve files from electronic storage media. Windows supports three file systems for storing files on hard disks: FAT, NTFS, and ReFS. NTFS is by far the most important and is dominant on Windows servers. However, FAT is still found occasionally on workstations and servers, and there are valid reasons to use this file system in certain circumstances. ReFS has limited features compared with NTFS.

Before going into detail on these disk formats, reviewing the components of a file system is helpful. Modern file systems have some or all of the following components:

- *Filenaming convention*—All files stored on a disk are identified by name; the file system defines rules for how to name a file. These rules include length, special characters that can be used (such as $, #, %, &, and !), and case sensitivity (differentiating uppercase and lowercase letters).

- *Hierarchical organization*—Most file systems are organized as an inverted tree structure, with the root of the tree at the top and folders or directories underneath acting as branches. A folder can be empty or contain a list of files and additional folders. In most file systems, folders or directories don't contain the data that makes up the actual file; they contain information about the file along with a pointer to the file's location on the disk. Information for each file is usually called a *directory entry*.

- *Data storage method*—Space on hard disks is divided into one or more partitions, with each partition containing its own file system. A partition is typically divided into 512-byte sectors. The file system groups one or more sectors into blocks or clusters, which are used as the basic unit of storage for file data. These blocks are indexed so that the file data they contain can be retrieved easily. A single file can occupy from one to many thousands of blocks. File systems vary in the methods used for indexing and managing these blocks, which affect the efficiency and reliability of data storage and retrieval.

- *Metadata*—Metadata is information about a file beyond its name and the data it contains. This information is generally stored by the directory or folder with the file's name or in a data structure the directory entry points to. Metadata can include timestamps indicating when a file was created, last changed, and last accessed; descriptive information about the file that can be used in searches; file attributes; and access control lists.

- *Attributes*—Attributes are usually on/off settings, such as Read Only, Hidden, and Compressed. File systems differ in the attributes that can be applied to files and folders.

- *Access control lists (ACLs)*—ACLs determine who can access a file or folder and what can be done with the file (read, write, delete, and so on).

File systems vary in whether and how each component is used. Generally, more advanced file systems have flexible filenaming rules, an efficient method of managing data storage, a considerable amount of metadata, advanced attributes, and ACLs. Next, you examine these file systems more closely.

The FAT File System

The File Allocation Table (FAT) file system consists of two variations: FAT16 and FAT32. The term *File Allocation Table* vaguely describes the structure used to manage data storage. FAT16, usually referred to simply as *FAT*, has been around since the mid-1980s, which is one of its biggest strengths—it's well known and well supported by most OSs. FAT32 arrived on the scene with the release of Windows 95 OSR2 in 1996.

> **Note 7**
>
> A third variation, FAT12, is the original version of FAT developed in the late 1970s. It was limited to use on floppy disks.

The main difference between FAT16 and FAT32 is the size of the disk partition that can be formatted. FAT16 is limited to 2 GB partitions in most implementations (although Windows NT permits partitions up to 4 GB). FAT32 allows partitions up to 2 TB; however, in Windows 2000 and later, Microsoft limits them to 32 GB because the file system becomes noticeably slower and inefficient with larger partition sizes. This 32 GB limitation applies only to creating partitions. Windows can read FAT32 partitions of any size. FAT16 supports a maximum file size of 2 GB, and FAT32 supports files up to 4 GB.

> **Note 8**
>
> The number in FAT versions refers to the number of bits available to address disk clusters. FAT16 can address up to 2^{16} disk clusters, and FAT32 can address up to 2^{32} disk clusters. The number of disk clusters a file system can address is directly proportional to the largest-sized partition it supports.

Already, you can see that FAT has severe limitations in current computing environments. The file size limitation alone prevents storing a standard DVD image file on a FAT file system. The limitations are even more apparent when you consider reliability and security requirements of current OSs. FAT doesn't support file and folder permissions for users and groups, so any user logging on to a computer with a FAT disk has full control over every file on that disk. In addition, FAT lacks support for encryption, file compression, disk quotas, and reliability features such as transaction recovery and journaling, all of which NTFS supports.

You might think FAT isn't good for much, especially compared with the more robust NTFS, but FAT/FAT32 still has its place. It's the only file system option when using older Windows OSs, such as Windows 9x. In addition, FAT is simple and has little overhead, so it's still the file system of choice on removable media, such as flash drives. For hard drives, however, particularly on Windows servers, NTFS is usually the way to go, although some applications benefit from ReFS.

> **Note 9**
>
> Another variation of FAT is exFAT, which has the same features as FAT32 but can be used to format volumes larger than 32 GB, up to a theoretical 64 zettabytes (ZB, a billion terabytes), and file sizes up to 16 EB. When you format a volume larger than 32 GB in Disk Management, exFAT is offered as a format option.

The NTFS and ReFS File Systems

NTFS is a full-featured file system that Microsoft introduced with Windows NT in 1993. Since that time, its features have been expanded to help administrators gain control of ever-increasing storage requirements. NTFS has supported file and folder permissions almost since its inception, which was a considerable advantage over FAT. Many compelling features have been added, particularly starting with Windows 2000:

- *Disk quotas*—Enable administrators to limit the amount of disk space that users' files can occupy on a disk volume. Starting with Windows Server 2008, quotas can also be specified for folders.
- *Volume mount points*—Make it possible to associate the root of a disk volume with a folder on an NTFS volume, thereby forgoing the need for a drive letter to access the volume.

- *Shadow copies*—Enable users to keep historical versions of files so that they can revert a file to an older version or restore an accidentally deleted file.
- *File compression*—Allows users to store documents in a compressed format without needing to run a compression/decompression program to store and retrieve the documents.
- *Encrypting File System (EFS)*—Makes encrypted files inaccessible to everyone except the user who encrypted the file, including users who have been granted permission to the file. EFS protects files even if the disk is removed from the system.

The Resilient File System (ReFS)

The main uses of ReFS are in large file-sharing applications where volumes are managed by Storage Spaces and for storage of virtual disks. Although ReFS is mostly backward compatible with NTFS, it doesn't support file compression, disk quotas, and EFS. Also, Windows can't be booted from an ReFS volume and the boot volume (the volume that contains the \Windows folder) cannot be ReFS-formatted. ReFS can repair minor problems with the file system automatically and supports volume sizes up to 1 yottabyte (YB, a trillion terabytes).

ReFS works with Storage Spaces (discussed in Module 11) to automatically repair disk failure caused by corruption, whether from software or hardware problems. Unlike other fault-tolerant disk options, such as RAID 1 and RAID 5, that can only recover from failures, ReFS can also correct some types of data corruption automatically. This capability, when used with Storage Spaces, allows building highly reliable and scalable disk systems without using RAID disk controllers and the sometimes-wasteful disk allocation schemes that RAID configurations require.

ReFS is now the disk format of choice for storing virtual hard disks for use in Storage Spaces and on Hyper-V servers. ReFS is optimized for creating virtual disk files and moving blocks of data between files. For example, a fixed-size virtual disk of 100 GB can be created on an ReFS volume in a little more than one second. The same operation on an NTFS volume can take several minutes. In addition, operations such as checkpoint merging and other Hyper-V storage operations perform much faster on ReFS.

Because of the features ReFS doesn't support, this file system isn't intended as a replacement for NTFS. ReFS is best for supporting applications that require virtual disks, such as Storage Spaces and Hyper-V, and on volumes for high-availability applications that use very large files but don't require user-specific features, such as disk quotas and EFS.

Preparing a New Disk for Use

Now that you know most of the options for local disk storage in Windows Server 2022, you can work through the process of adding a disk to a working system. Depending on the system, you might be able to add a new HDD to a server while it's powered on, a process called *hot-add* or *hot-swap*. Windows Server supports hot-adding a hard disk as long as the server hardware supports it. Don't attempt to add a disk to a running server unless you know the hardware supports it.

After the HDD has been physically attached to the server and the server is running, you need to use the Disk Management snap-in or File and Storage Services to make the disk accessible. By default, new disks must be initialized and brought online from their initial offline state, as explained in the following steps. After the disk is online and initialized, you can create a volume and format it. In Disk Management, you can convert the disk to dynamic or between MBR and GPT partitioning schemes.

Managing Disks with PowerShell

You may need to manage disks using PowerShell—for example, on a Server Core installation of Windows Server 2022. You can perform all the same tasks on disks using PowerShell as you can using the Disk Management or File and Storage Services GUI tools. To bring a volume online, initialize it, and create a new simple volume formatted as ReFS, follow these steps using PowerShell cmdlets after opening a PowerShell prompt:

1. Get a list of disks. Type the following into PowerShell with no arguments:

```
Get-Disk
```

You'll see a list similar to that in Figure 10-4.

```
PS C:\Users\Administrator> get-disk

Number Friendly Name      Serial Number          HealthStatus      OperationalStatus      Total Size Partition
                                                                                                    Style
------ -------------      -------------          ------------      -----------------      ---------- ---------
0      Msft Virtual Disk                         Healthy           Online                 127 GB GPT
1      Msft Virtual Disk                         Healthy           Offline                 20 GB RAW
2      Msft Virtual Disk                         Healthy           Offline                 15 GB RAW
3      Msft Virtual Disk                         Healthy           Offline                 10 GB RAW
```

Figure 10-4   The results of the `Get-Disk` **cmdlet**

2. In Figure 10-4, notice the Number column, which you will use for subsequent commands. To bring Disk 1 online and initialize it using the GPT partition style, use the following cmdlets:

```
Set-Disk -Number 1 -IsOffline $false
Initialize-Disk -Number 1
```

In the `Initialize-Disk` cmdlet, you can initialize a disk using MBR by including the argument `-PartitionStyle MBR`.

3. Next, create a new partition and assign a drive letter of H:

```
New-Partition -DiskNumber 1 -Size 10GB -DriveLetter H
```

4. Format the volume with the ReFS file system and name it ReFSVol:

```
Format-Volume H -FileSystem ReFS -NewFileSystemLabel ReFSVol
```

Self-Check Questions

3. A volume is similar to a partition; they can both be formatted with a file system. True or False?

   a. True

   b. False

4. Which disk technology is best suited for modern high-end server usage?

   a. IDE

   b. SAS

   c. SCSI

   d. SATA

○ Check your answers at the end of this module.

Activity 10-1

Resetting Your Virtual Environment

Time Required: 5 minutes

Objective: Reset your virtual environment by applying the InitialConfig checkpoint or snapshot.

Required Tools and Equipment: ServerSA1, ServerDC1, ServerDM1, ServerDM2

Description: Apply the InitialConfig checkpoint or snapshot to ServerSA1, ServerDC1, ServerDM1, and ServerDM2.

1. Be sure the servers are shut down. In your virtualization program, apply the InitialConfig checkpoint or snapshot to ServerSA1, ServerDC1, ServerDM1, and ServerDM2.

2. When the snapshot or checkpoint has been applied, continue to the next activity.

Activity 10-2

Configuring a New Disk

Time Required: 10 minutes
Objective: Configure a new disk for use in a server.
Required Tools and Equipment: ServerSA1
Description: You have just installed a new disk in your server, and you need to prepare it for use. First you bring the disk online and initialize it, and then you create a simple volume and format it. You should already have a disk installed in ServerSA1 for use in this activity.

> **Note 10**
>
> The size of your disks may not match the size of the disks in the figures for this activity.

1. Start ServerSA1 and log on as **Administrator**.
2. In Server Manager, click **File and Storage Services**, and then click **Disks** to open the Disks window shown in Figure 10-5.

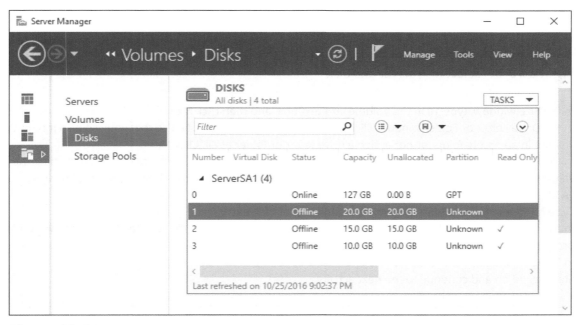

Figure 10-5   The Disks window in File and Storage Services

3. Find the 20.0 GB disk; its status might be Offline. If it is, right-click the disk and click **Bring Online**. In the Bring Disk Online message box, click **Yes**. Repeat this step for the 15.0 GB and 10.0 GB disks, if necessary.
4. Right-click the 20.0 GB disk again and click **Initialize**. In the Initialize Disk box, leave all three disks checked. Notice that the Initialize Disk message indicates the disks will be configured as GPT disks. Click **OK** in the Initialize Disk message box.
5. To create a new volume, right-click the 20.0 GB disk and click **New Volume** to start the New Volume Wizard. Read the information in the Before You Begin window, and then click **Next**.
6. In the Server and Disk window, make sure **ServerSA1** and the 20.0 GB disk are selected (see Figure 10-6), and then click **Next**.

(continues)

Activity 10-2 Continued

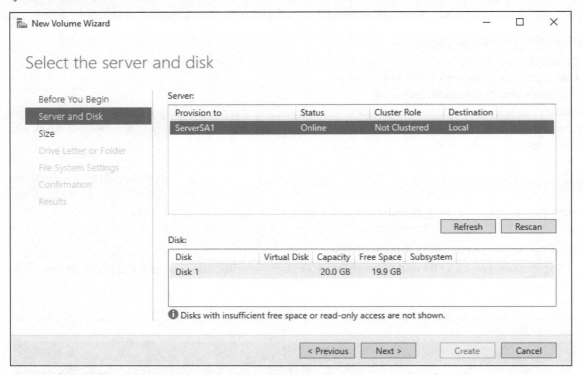

Figure 10-6 Selecting a server and disk

7. In the Size window, type **10** in the Volume size text box, and then click **Next**.
8. In the Drive Letter or Folder window, click **H** in the Drive letter list box. Notice that you can also mount the volume in an empty folder or not assign a drive letter or folder at all. Click **Next**.
9. In the File System Settings window, click the **File system** list arrow to see the options for formatting the volume. File and Storage Services lists only NTFS and ReFS as options. In Disk Management, you also have FAT32 as an option (or exFAT for volumes larger than 32 GB).
10. Type **NTFSvol** in the Volume label text box, and then click **Next**.
11. In the Confirmation window, verify your choices and then click **Create**. The Results window shows your progress. Click **Close** when the process is finished.
12. In Server Manager, click **Volumes** in the left pane to see the new volume.
13. Stay logged on and continue to the next activity.

Activity 10-3

Working with Volumes in Disk Management

Time Required: 10 minutes
Objective: Work with basic and dynamic volumes.
Required Tools and Equipment: ServerSA1
Description: In this activity, you examine options for working with basic and dynamic disks and with ReFS and NTFS volumes.

Note 11

The size of your disks may not match the size of the disks in the figures for this activity.

(continues)

Activity 10-3 Continued

1. Start ServerSA1 and log on as **Administrator**, if necessary.
2. Right-click **Start** and click **Disk Management**. Notice that Disk 0 has three volumes: the Recovery partition, the System partition, and the Boot partition (C:). These volumes contain the Windows OS, so make sure you don't make any changes to Disk 0.
3. Right-click **NTFSvol** and notice the options for working with this volume. Click **Extend Volume**. In the Extend Volume Wizard welcome window, click **Next**.
4. In the Select Disks window, you can add disks to extend to, if any are available. If you do, you're prompted to convert the disk to dynamic because basic disks don't support extending to other disks (disk spanning). In the "Select the amount of space in MB" text box, type **5000**, which makes the total volume about 15 GB. Click **Next**.
5. In the Completing the Extend Volume Wizard window, click **Finish**. The disk is extended to about 15 GB.
6. In Disk Management, right-click **NTFSvol** and click **Shrink Volume** to open the Shrink H: dialog box. In the "Enter the amount of space to shrink in MB" text box, type **5000** and click **Shrink**. The volume goes back to 10 GB.
7. Next, you create an ReFS-formatted volume. Right-click the unallocated space next to NTFSvol and click **New Simple Volume** to start the New Simple Volume Wizard. Click **Next**.
8. In the Specify Volume Size window, click **Next** to accept the default size, which is the remaining space on the disk. In the Assign Drive Letter or Path window, click the selection arrow next to "Assign the following drive letter" and click **I**. Click **Next**.
9. In the Format Partition window, click the selection arrow next to File system and click **ReFS**. In the Volume label box, type **ReFSVol**. Click **Next** and then click **Finish**.
10. Right-click **NTFSvol** and click **Properties**. Review the tabs available to configure the volume. In particular, notice that the General tab has an option to compress the drive and save disk space. Also notice the Quota tab, where you can set file quotas to restrict the amount of space a user's file can occupy on the volume. Click **Cancel** when you are finished exploring the properties of NTFSvol.
11. Right-click **ReFSVol** and click **Properties**. Notice that there is no option to compress the drive on the General tab and there is no Quota tab or Shadow Copies tab because ReFS doesn't support these features. Click **Cancel**.
12. Now, you will create a mirror volume. Right-click **NTFSvol** and click **Add Mirror**. There is only one option for creating the mirror because the 10.0 GB disk is too small. In the Add Mirror window (see Figure 10-7), click **Disk 2** and click **Add Mirror**.

Figure 10-7   Creating a mirror volume

(continues)

Activity 10-3 Continued

13. You see a Disk Management message that the basic disks will be converted to dynamic disks because dynamic disks are required to support a mirror. Click **Yes**. After a pause, you see the mirror. The volume is now shown on Disk 1 and Disk 2 and is displayed in red to indicate it is a mirror (see Figure 10-8). In the top pane of Disk Management, note that the Layout column for NTFSvol changes to Mirror.

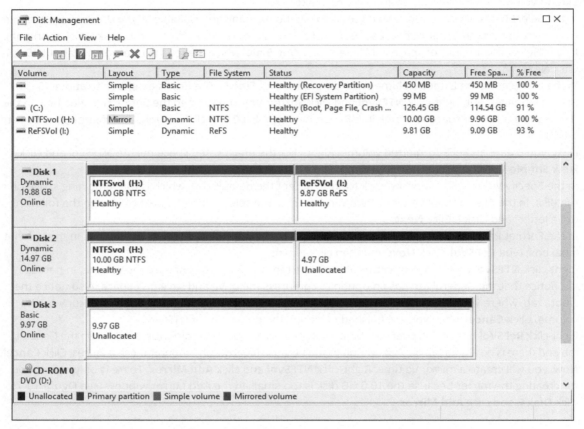

Figure 10-8   A mirror volume in Disk Management

14. Next, you'll create a RAID-5 volume. First, however, you need three disks for a RAID-5 volume, so you must delete the volumes you just created. Right-click **NTFSvol**, click **Delete Volume**, and click **Yes** to confirm. Next, right-click **ReFSVol**, click **Delete Volume**, and click **Yes** to confirm.

15. Right-click **Disk 1**. (This should be the 20.0 GB disk, but a smaller number might be shown.) Click **New RAID-5 Volume** and click **Next**.

16. In the Select Disks window, click **Disk 2**, click **Add**, click **Disk 3**, and click **Add** again (see Figure 10-9). Notice the total size of the RAID-5 volume will be about 20 GB, even though you are using 10 GB of space from each disk. RAID-5 uses the equivalent of the space from one disk for the parity information needed to re-create missing data if a disk fails. Click **Next**.

17. In the Assign Drive Letter or Path window, click the drive letter selection box and click **H**. Click **Nex**t.

18. In the Format Volume window, type **RAID5Vol** in the Volume label box and click **Next**. Click **Finish** and then click **Yes** when prompted to convert basic disks to dynamic. (When you deleted the volumes, the disks were converted back to basic disks.)

19. After a short while, you see the new RAID-5 volume, as shown in Figure 10-10. It will take a while for the volume to synch between the three disks and be formatted.

20. You'll be using these disks for other activities, so delete the RAID-5 volume as you did the other volumes. Close Disk Management.

(continues)

Activity 10-3 Continued

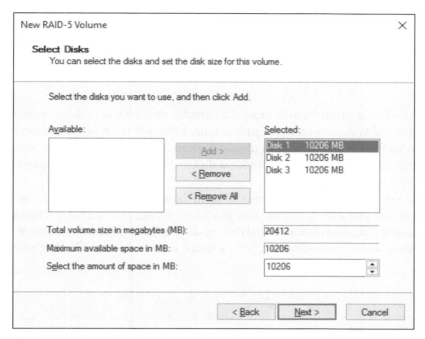

Figure 10-9   Select disks for the RAID-5 volume

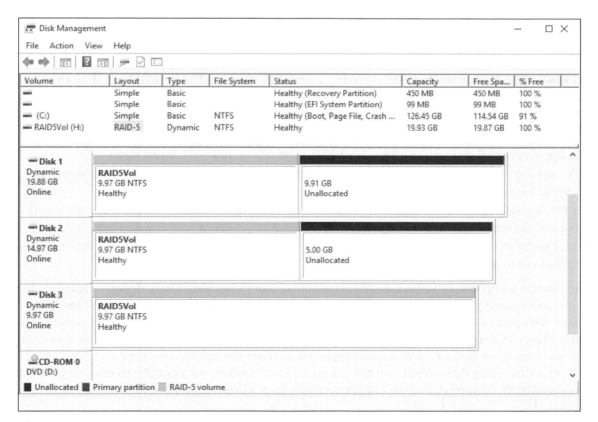

Figure 10-10   A RAID-5 volume in Disk Management

Working with Virtual Disks

Microsoft Exam AZ-800:

Manage storage and file services.
- Configure Windows Server storage

Virtual hard disks (VHDs) are files stored on a physical disk drive that emulate a physical disk but have additional capabilities for virtual machines and general Windows storage applications. VHDs are used by virtual machines running in Hyper-V as the primary storage for the OS and data. On a physical computer, Windows can mount virtual hard disks (VHD or VHDX files) and use them as though they were physical disk volumes. VHDs are also used in Storage Spaces applications to create flexible storage solutions.

You might want to use virtual disks instead of physical volumes to store data. Virtual disks have the advantage of being very portable. Because a virtual disk is just a file on an existing physical volume, you can copy it to any location quickly and easily for the purposes of backing up data on the virtual disk or allowing it to be used by another computer. The Disk Management snap-in has options to create and mount virtual disks, and there are a number of PowerShell cmdlets for working with VHDs.

> **Note 12**
>
> Virtual disks can have a .vhd or .vhdx extension. Windows Server can mount either file type. The VHDX format, introduced in Windows Server 2012 Hyper-V, has more capacity (up to 64 TB), protection from corruption, and performance improvements over the original VHD format.

VHD versus VHDX Format

When you create a virtual disk, you have the option to use the VHD or the VHDX format. The VHD format is the original format used by Hyper-V VMs. You may want to choose this format for backward compatibility with Windows Server 2008. However, for the most features, you should choose the VHDX format. Following is a list of differences between VHD and VHDX:

- VHD supports virtual disks up to 2 TB while VHDX supports up to 64 TB virtual disks.
- VHDX uses a 4096 byte logical sector size, compared to 512 byte sectors used in VHD. As mentioned, a larger sector size improves performance and increases the maximum disk and volume size.
- With VHDX disks, you can store custom metadata about the disk to indicate information such as the OS version or the build number.
- VHDX is resilient to power failures because it tracks updates in the metadata, allowing incomplete writes to be backed out to avoid corruption.

You can convert a VHD disk to VHDX using Hyper-V Manager or PowerShell. Using Hyper-V Manager, click Edit Disk in the Actions pane (see Figure 10-11) to start the Edit Virtual Hard Disk wizard and then select the disk you want to edit. You have the option to compact, convert, or expand the disk (see Figure 10-12). Choose Convert and select the VHDX format. (You can also choose VHD if you want to convert a VHDX disk to a VHD disk.) The conversion process actually copies the original disk to a new file and adjusts the format during the copy process.

To convert a disk using PowerShell, use the `Convert-VHD` cmdlet; for example, to convert a VHD file named Win2K16Boot.vhd to VHDX format, use the following cmdlet from a PowerShell prompt:

```
Convert-VHD -Path D:\Vdisks\Win2k16Boot.vhd -DestinationPath
    D:\Vdisks\Win2k16Boot.vhdx
```

The PowerShell cmdlet determines the format you want to convert to and from by the filename extension (.vhd or .vhdx).

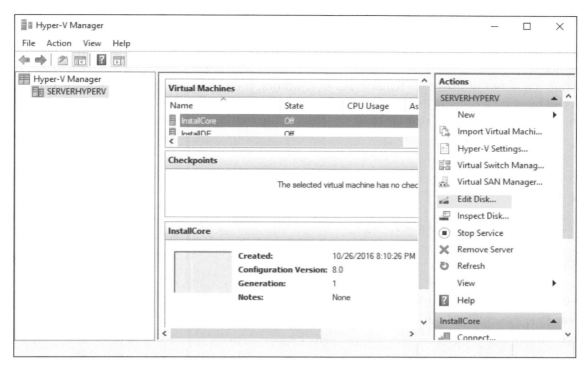

Figure 10-11   Editing a disk in Hyper-V Manager

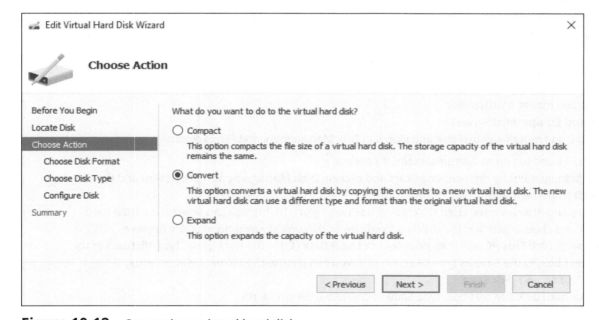

Figure 10-12   Converting a virtual hard disk

Dynamically Expanding and Fixed-Size Disks

One of the benefits of using virtual disks is that they can be created as dynamically expanding or fixed-size disks. A dynamically expanding disk is referred to as a thin provisioned disk and a fixed-size disk is called a thick provisioned disk. A thin provisioned disk takes up little space initially (typically less than 100 MB, depending on the maximum size of the disk) and grows to the assigned maximum size as data is stored on it. When a thick provisioned disk is created, the entire size of the disk is allocated on the host volume. A thick provisioned disk provides better performance because the overhead of expanding the disk is removed and a fixed-size disk will generally occupy contiguous clusters, reducing host disk fragmentation. For production environments that require the fastest disk performance, use thick provisioned disks, but for testing and applications in which speed is not a critical factor, use thin provisioned disks.

While you may find a number of uses for virtual disks in Windows, their most common use is with Storage Spaces and with virtual machines running in Hyper-V; these topics are discussed in Modules 11 and 12, respectively. Next, we turn our attention to other storage topics, including file sharing and securing access to files with permissions.

Self-Check Questions

5. Which of the following is true about virtual disks?

   a. VHD supports higher capacities than VHDX.
   b. VHDX provides fault tolerance in case of power failures.
   c. VHD files cannot be mounted in Windows Server 2022.
   d. Thin provisioned VHDs are faster than thick provisioned VHDs.

6. You can create and mount virtual disks using the Disk Management snap-in. True or False?

   a. True   **b.** False

   ◉ Check your answers at the end of this module.

Activity 10-4

Working with Virtual Disks in Disk Management

Time Required: 10 minutes
Objective: Create and mount a virtual disk.
Required Tools and Equipment: ServerSA1
Description: Create and mount a virtual disk and view it in Disk Management and File Explorer.

1. Start ServerSA1 and log on as **Administrator**, if necessary.
2. Open Disk Management by right-clicking **Start** and clicking **Disk Management**. Click **Action** and then **Create VHD** from the menu.
3. In the Create and Attach Virtual Hard Disk dialog box (see Figure 10-13), you can select the virtual hard disk format and choose whether the disk is a fixed size or dynamically expanding. Click **Browse**.
4. In the left pane, click **This PC** and then double-click **Local Disk (C:)** in the right pane. Type **Virtual1** in the File name text box. In the Save as type selection box, you can choose the format (.vhd or .vhdx). Accept the default option and click **Save**.
5. In the Virtual hard disk size text box, type **5000** to create a 5 GB virtual disk.
6. The virtual hard disk format is VHD by default. Because you're creating a small volume, you can accept this default setting. Click the **Dynamically expanding** option button so that the disk's file size is very small at first and then expands as you add data to it, up to the 5 GB you specified. Click **OK**.
7. When you create a VHD file in Disk Management, it's mounted automatically. The disk should be listed as Disk 4, and its status is Not Initialized. Right-click **Disk 4** and notice the Detach VHD option in the menu. Detaching the disk is the same as unmounting it. Click **Initialize Disk**.
8. In the Initialize Disk dialog box, click **OK**. Your new virtual disk is initialized and ready to have a volume created on it. Notice that the disk icon turns green, indicating it is a virtual disk.

(continues)

Activity 10-4 Continued

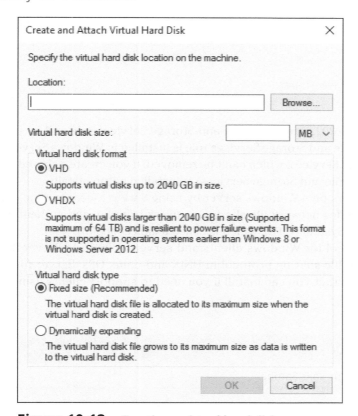

Figure 10-13   Creating a virtual hard disk

9. Right-click the unallocated space of Disk 4 and click **New Simple Volume**. Follow the New Simple Volume Wizard, using the following settings:
Volume size: Use the default size.
Drive letter: Assign drive letter **V:**.
Format: Use the default settings but make the volume label **VirtualVol**.

10. When the volume has finished formatting, you can access it. Right-click the volume and click **Explore**.

11. File Explorer treats the virtual disk and volumes in it like any other disk and volume. In File Explorer, click **Local Disk (C:)**. You should see a file named Virtual1 with a disk icon next to it, indicating a virtual disk. Notice the size of the virtual disk file; it is probably around 60 MB. The size of the file will expand up to the maximum of 5 GB as you add data to it.

12. Now, you will copy a file to V:. Right-click **Start** and click **Command Prompt**. Type **V:** and press **Enter**. You are now on the V: volume. Type **copy c:\windows\explorer.exe** and press **Enter**. Close the command prompt.

13. In File Explorer, click **Local Disk (C:)**. Notice that the size of the Virtual1 file has increased because you have added data to it.

14. Right-click **Virtual1 (V:)** in the left pane of File Explorer and click **Eject** to unmount the disk. The disk is no longer shown in File Explorer or Disk Management.

15. Open File Explorer again and click **Local Disk (C:)**. Right-click **Virtual1** and click **Mount**, or just double-click the file. The volume is mounted again. Dismount the virtual disk again. In File Explorer, delete the Virtual1 file.

16. Close all open windows and shut down ServerSA1.

File Sharing

Microsoft Exam AZ-800:

Manage storage and file services.
- Configure and manage Windows Server file shares

File and print sharing functions in Windows Server 2022 are in the File and Storage Services role and its many role services and related features. As you've seen, the File and Storage Services role is installed in Windows Server 2022 by default, but the only role service installed is Storage Services, which can't be removed. If you create a shared folder on your computer, the File Server role service (under File and Storage Services) is installed automatically.

Windows clients access shared files and printers on a Windows server by using **Server Message Block (SMB)**, a client/server Application-layer protocol that provides network file sharing, network printing, and authentication. A common variation of SMB is Common Internet File System (CIFS), which is called a *dialect* of SMB.

Although SMB is the native file-sharing protocol for Windows clients and servers, Windows Server 2022 also supports **Network File System (NFS)**, the native file-sharing protocol in UNIX and Linux OSs. Server for NFS is a role service found under File and Storage Services that you can install if you need to support clients using the NFS protocol.

Note 13

Linux supports SMB in a variation of the protocol Linux calls Samba.

Creating Windows File Shares

The File Server role service is required if you need to share folders. You can install this role service via Server Manager, or you can simply share a folder to have the role service installed automatically. Folders in Windows Server 2022 can be shared only by members of the Administrators or Server Operators groups.

Sharing files on the network, as you saw in Module 1, isn't difficult in a Windows environment. Nonetheless, you should be familiar with some techniques and options before forging ahead with setting up a file-sharing server. You can use the following methods to configure file and folder sharing in Windows Server 2022:

- *Simple file sharing*—To use simple file sharing, right-click a folder in File Explorer and click Give access to or click Share on the Sharing tab of a folder's Properties dialog box. The File Sharing dialog box (see Figure 10-14) simplifies sharing for novices by using easy-to-understand terms for permissions and by setting file and folder permissions to accommodate the selected share permissions. If you share a file by using this method, the share permissions are set to Full control for the Administrators and Everyone groups. If you choose the Read permission for a specific user or group, the file and folder permissions are set to Read & execute, List folder contents, and Read for the specified user or group. If you choose Read/Write, the file and folder permissions are set to Full control for the specified user.

Note 14

As you'll see later in the module, there are two types of permissions: share permissions are assigned to a shared folder through the Sharing tab of the folder's properties and file and folder permissions are assigned through the Security tab of a file or folder's properties. File and folder permissions are only available on NTFS and ReFS formatted volumes.

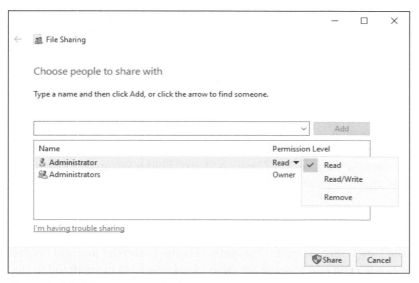

Figure 10-14   Simple file sharing

- *Advanced Sharing dialog box*—To open this dialog box, click Advanced Sharing in the Sharing tab of a folder's Properties dialog box. There are several options in this dialog box (see Figure 10-15):
  - Share this folder: Sharing can be enabled or disabled for the folder by clicking this check box.
  - Share name: The share name is the name users see in the Network folder of File Explorer when browsing the server. To put it another way, the share name is the name you use to access the folder with the UNC path (*server**share name*). You can add or remove share names. A single folder can have multiple share names, each with different permissions, a different number of simultaneous users, and different caching settings.
  - Limit the number of simultaneous users to: In Windows Server 2022, the default limit is 16,777,216, which is practically unlimited. In Windows 10 and Windows 11, the maximum number of users who can access a share is 15.

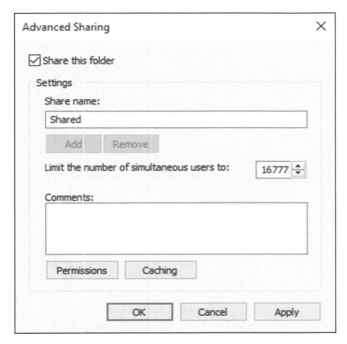

Figure 10-15   The Advanced Sharing dialog box

○ Comments: You can enter a description of the share's contents and settings in this text box.

○ Permissions: Click this button to open the Permissions dialog box discussed later in this module. In Windows Server 2022, folders shared with advanced sharing are configured with the Everyone special identity, which has Read permission by default.

○ Caching: This option controls how offline files are configured. Offline files enable users to disconnect from the network and still have the shared files they were working with available on their computers. When a user reconnects to the network, the offline and network copies of the file are synchronized.

- *Shared Folders snap-in*—You use this component of the Computer Management MMC to monitor, change, and create shares on the local computer or a remote computer. To create a new share, right-click the Shares node under the Shared Folders snap-in and click New Share. The Create A Shared Folder Wizard walks you through the processes of selecting the folder to share or creating a new folder to share, naming the share, configuring offline files, and setting permissions.

- *File and Storage Services*—In Server Manager, click File and Storage Services, and then click Shares. (The File Server role must be installed before you can see the Shares option in File and Storage Services.) Click Tasks and then New Share to start the New Share Wizard. This method is the preferred method for creating and managing shares. Creating shares with File and Storage Services is discussed in more detail in the next section.

Creating Shares with File and Storage Services

You can create shares and set a number of sharing options with the New Share Wizard in the File and Storage Services role. To start the wizard, click File and Storage Services in the left pane of Server Manager, and then click Shares. In the Tasks list box, click New Share. The first window in the File Share Wizard is for setting the share profile (see Figure 10-16), which has five options:

- *SMB Share – Quick*—Creates a standard Windows share with default settings and permissions that you can customize by using the wizard or customize later in the shared folder's properties.

- *SMB Share – Advanced*—Allows you to create a Windows share with advanced options for setting the folder owner, the ability to classify data, and quotas. This option requires the File Server Resource Manager role service.

- *SMB Share – Applications*—Creates a Windows share that's suitable for Hyper-V, databases, and other applications.

- *NFS Share – Quick*—Creates an NFS share for Linux/UNIX clients with standard options.

- *NFS Share – Advanced*—Offers advanced options for creating a Linux/UNIX-style share.

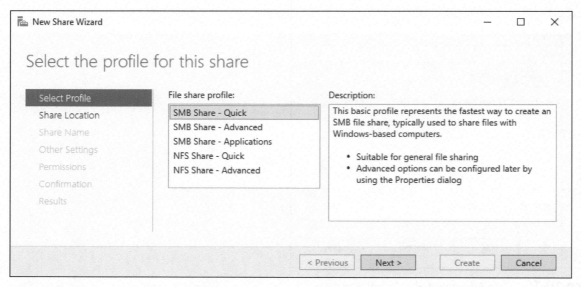

Figure 10-16   Selecting a profile for a share

The next windows described are based on the SMB Share – Quick profile. After selecting the profile, you choose a server and volume for the share's location (see Figure 10-17). By default, the share is created in the \Shares directory, but you can set a custom path.

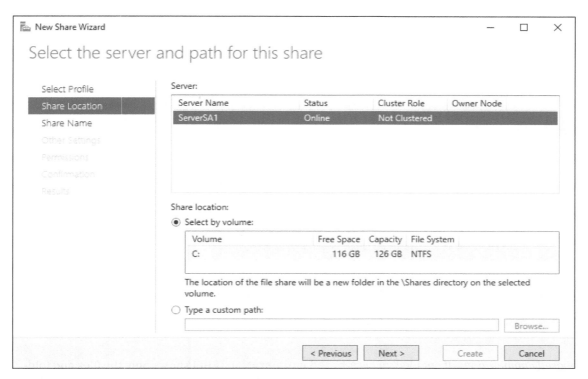

Figure 10-17   Specifying a share location

Next, you specify a share name and then add a description if you want. The local and remote path are displayed, as shown in Figure 10-18.

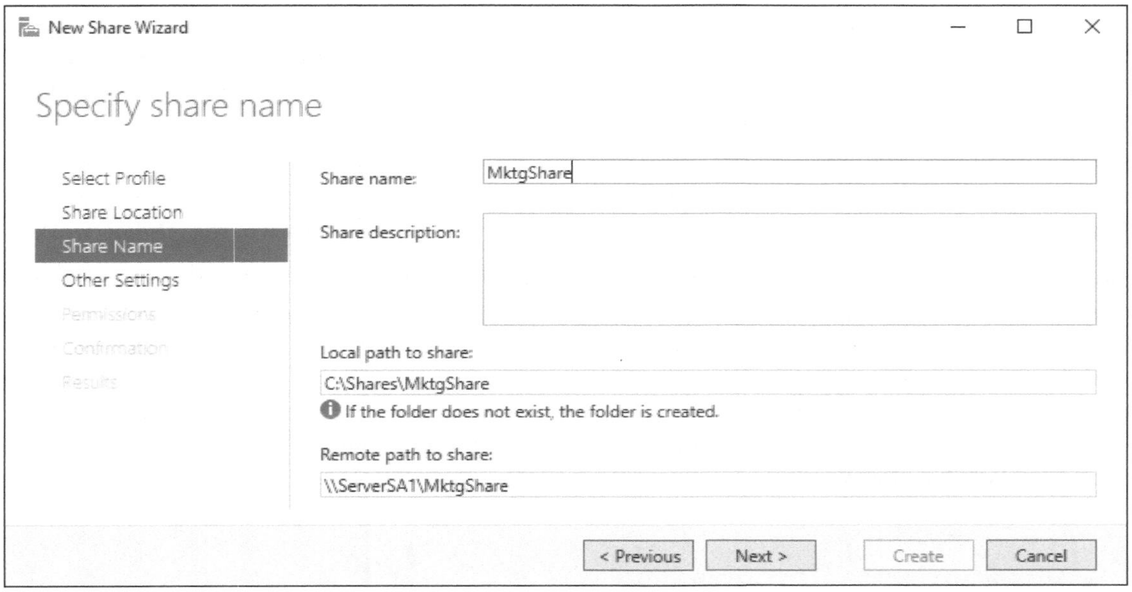

Figure 10-18   Specifying the share name

In the next window, you can set the following additional options for an SMB share (see Figure 10-19):

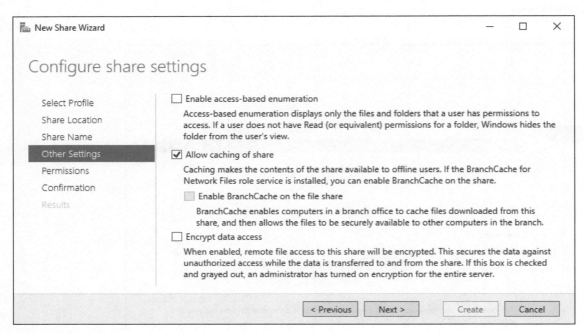

Figure 10-19   Configuring share settings

- *Enable access-based enumeration*—If enabled, **access-based enumeration (ABE)** shows only the files and folders to which a user has at least Read permission. If the user doesn't have at least Read permission, the files and folders in the share are hidden from the user. If ABE isn't enabled, users can still see files and folders they don't have access to but can't open them. ABE is disabled by default.

- *Allow caching of share*—This option enables or disables offline files. **Offline files**, also known as *client-side caching*, is a feature of shared folders that allows users to access the contents of shared folders when not connected to the network. If a file is opened in a share with caching enabled, it's downloaded to the client's local storage so that it can be accessed later, even if the client isn't connected to the network. Later, when the client reconnects, the file is synchronized with the copy on the share. Clients have the capability to always use the locally cached version of files even when connected to the network. This feature can be enabled in Group Policy with the "Configure slow-link mode" policy setting. If caching is enabled and the BranchCache for Network Files role service is installed, the BranchCache feature can also be enabled on the share. Branch-Cache is discussed later in this module.

- *Encrypt data access*—When this feature is enabled, files retrieved from the share are encrypted to prevent someone from using a network sniffer to view the contents of files as they're transferred across the network.

You set permissions for the share in the next window (see Figure 10-20). By default, new share permissions are set to Read Only for everyone, and file and folder permissions are inherited from the parent folder. If you click the Customize permissions button, you can edit permissions in the Advanced Security Settings dialog box. Because it's a shared folder, a new tab is added for managing share permissions.

In the last window, you confirm your choices and create the share. When the new share is created, it's added to the list of shares in File and Storage Services. You can make changes to any settings configured in the New Share Wizard by right-clicking the share and clicking Properties.

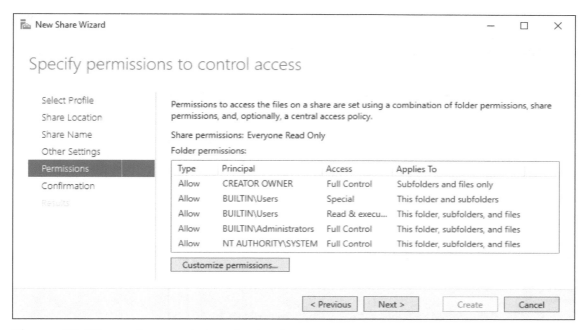

Figure 10-20   Setting permissions for the share

Managing Shares with the Shared Folders Snap-in

You use the Shared Folders snap-in to create, delete, and monitor shares, view open files, and monitor and manage user connections or sessions. To open this snap-in, add it to an MMC or open the Computer Management MMC. The Shared Folders snap-in has the following subnodes:

- *Shares*—In the Shares node (shown in Figure 10-21), you can view all shares, their path on the local file system, and how many clients are currently connected to each share. You can also open the folder on the local file system, stop sharing a folder, and create new shares.

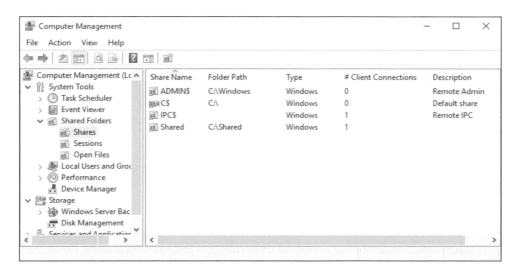

Figure 10-21   The Shares node

- *Sessions*—The Sessions node lists users who currently have a network connection to the server, which client computer they're connected from, how many files they have open, and how long they have been connected (see Figure 10-22). Administrators can select a user and close the session.

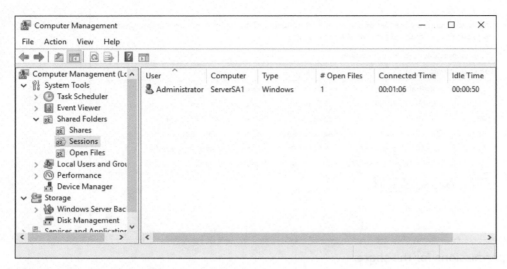

Figure 10-22   The Sessions node

- *Open Files*—The Open Files node lists files that network users have open and identifies which user has opened the file (see Figure 10-23).

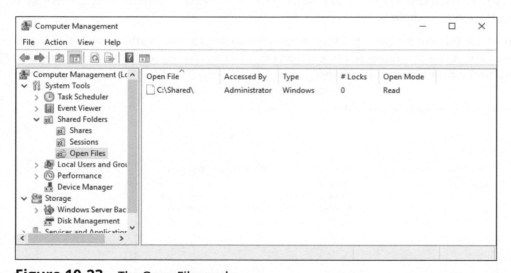

Figure 10-23   The Open Files node

The Shared Folders snap-in is useful for monitoring how much a server's shares are being used and by whom. You can also use this tool to see whether any files are being accessed over the network before shutting down the server or otherwise interrupting server access. You can also check the Idle Time column in the Sessions node to see whether a user is actively using shares on the server (a short idle time) or simply has a share open but hasn't accessed any files for a while (a longer idle time).

You can view and change a share's properties by double-clicking it in the Shares node. You can't change the share's name or the folder location, but you can change the user limit, offline settings, share permissions, and file and folder permissions. In addition, you can publish a share in Active Directory or change the publish options of a published share.

Creating and Managing Shares at the Command Line

Shared folders can be created and managed at the command line with the `net share` command or PowerShell cmdlets. Take a look at the `net share` command first:

- `net share MyDocs=D:\Documents`—Creates a share named MyDocs, using the D:\Documents folder
- `net share MyDocs`—Lists information about the MyDocs share
- `net share MyDocs /delete`—Deletes the MyDocs share
- `net share`—Lists shares on the computer

For more information and examples on using `net share`, type `net share /?` at a command prompt.

Managing and Creating Shares with PowerShell

Several dozen PowerShell cmdlets are available for working with file shares; Table 10-2 lists a few. For details on using a cmdlet, type `get-help` *cmdlet* `-detailed` at a PowerShell prompt. To see a list of all cmdlets related to Windows shares, type `get-command -Module SmbShare` at a PowerShell prompt.

Table 10-2   PowerShell cmdlets for working with file shares

PowerShell cmdlet	Description
`New-SmbShare`	Creates a share
`Get-SmbShare`	Lists shares on the computer
`Remove-SmbShare`	Deletes a share
`Set-SmbShare`	Changes a share's properties
`Get-SmbShareAccess`	Displays permissions for a share
`Grant-SmbShareAccess`	Adds a permission to a share
`Close-SmbOpenFile`	Closes a shared file that a client has open
`Close-SmbSession`	Closes a file share session
`Get-SmbOpenFile`	Displays information about currently open shared files
`New-SmbMapping`	Creates a drive letter mapping to a share
`Remove-SmbMapping`	Deletes a drive letter mapping
`Set-SmbClientConfiguration`	Sets the configuration of a file sharing client
`Set-SmbServerConfiguration`	Sets the configuration of a file sharing server

Take a look at a few examples:

- `New-SmbShare MyDocs D:\Documents`—Creates a share named MyDocs, using the D:\Documents folder
- `Get-SmbShare MyDocs | Format-List -Property *`—Lists detailed information about the MyDocs share
- `Remove-SmbShare MyDocs`—Deletes the MyDocs share
- `Get-SmbShare`—Lists shares on the computer

Default and Administrative Shares

Every Windows OS since Windows NT (excluding Windows 9x and Windows Me) includes **administrative shares**, which are hidden shares available only to members of the Administrators group. On computers that aren't domain controllers, these shares are as follows:

- *Admin$*—This share provides network access to the Windows folder on the boot volume (usually C:\Windows).
- *Drive$*—The *drive* represents the drive letter of a disk volume (for example, C$). The root of each disk volume (except removable disks such as DVDs and floppy disks) is shared and accessible by using the drive letter followed by a dollar sign.
- *IPC$*—IPC means *interprocess communications*. This share is less an administrative share than a system share. It's used for temporary connections between clients and servers to provide communication between network programs.

Domain controllers have all the hidden administrative shares listed previously as well as the following default shares, which aren't hidden but are considered administrative shares:

- *NETLOGON*—Used for storing default user profiles as well as user logon scripts for pre-Windows 2000 clients.
- *SYSVOL*—Used by Active Directory for replication between DCs. Also contains group policy files that are downloaded and applied to Windows 2000 and later clients.

Windows creates administrative shares automatically, and permissions on these shares can't be changed. An administrator can disable sharing on the Admin$ share or a volume administrative share, but the share is re-created the next time the system starts or when the Server service is restarted. The IPC$ share can't be disabled.

> **Note 15**
>
> You can prevent Windows from creating administrative shares automatically by creating the Registry subkey HKEY_LOCAL_MACHINE\SYSTEM\CurrentControlSet\Services\LanmanServer\Parameters\AutoShareServer, setting the value to 0, and restarting the server.

The dollar sign at the end of a hidden share name prevents the share from being displayed in a network browse list. To access a hidden share, you must use the UNC path. For example, entering \\ServerSA1\C$ opens the root of the C drive on Server1. You can create your own hidden shares by simply placing a $ at the end of the share name. Sometimes administrators use hidden shares to prevent users from attempting to access shares they don't need to access or have permission to use.

Accessing File Shares from Client Computers

The file-sharing discussion so far has focused on how to create and manage shared resources. However, for shared resources to be useful, users must know how to access them. You have already seen some access methods in this module's activities. The following methods of accessing shared folders are among the most common:

- *UNC path*—The **UNC path**, which you've seen in examples and activities, uses the syntax *server**share*[*subfolder*][*file*]. The parameters in brackets are optional. In fact, the *share* parameter is optional if all you want to do is list shared resources on a server. Using *server* by itself in a File Explorer window lists all shared folders and printers (except hidden shares) on that server. The disadvantage of this method is that the user must know the server name and share name, and in a network with dozens or hundreds of servers and shares, that might be asking a lot.
- *Active Directory search*—An Active Directory search allows you to search by keyword or simply list all shared folders in the directory. With this method, users don't need to know the hosting server's name. However, shares aren't published to Active Directory automatically, so this method might not find all shared folders on the network.

- *Mapping a drive*—Administrators often set up a logon script or configure a group policy in which a drive letter is mapped to a network folder where users can store documents. Users can also map a drive letter to shared folders that they access often. Users tend to be more comfortable using drive letters to access files in a Windows environment because all their local resources (hard drives, DVD drives, flash drives) are accessed in this manner. Drive letters can be mapped only to the root of the share, as in *server**share*, not to a subfolder of the share, as in *server**share**folder1*.

- *Browsing the network*—You can open the Network node in File Explorer and see a list of all computers found on the network. You can then browse each computer to find the share you want. This method has the advantage of not requiring you to know the server's name. However, starting with Windows Vista, you must enable the Network Discovery feature for your computer to see other computers and for your computer to be seen by other computers. You can enable this feature in the Network and Sharing Center by clicking "Change advanced sharing settings." Browsing a network for shares might be convenient in a small network, but in a large network, you could be browsing for quite a while to find the right computer.

Network File System

Not every network is composed solely of computers running Windows. Some networks include Linux and UNIX computers that use the native file-sharing system, Network File System (NFS). NFS is a file-sharing protocol that allows users to access files and folders on other computers across a network. From a user's standpoint, NFS makes network resources seem to be part of the local file system, much like mapping a drive does for Windows file shares. NFS has both a client and server component; both are installed by default on most Linux and UNIX systems.

Windows Server 2022 supports an NFS server component as a role service under the File and Storage Services role and an NFS client component as a feature. You can install either component or both. The Enterprise Edition of Windows 10 supports an NFS client but not the NFS server component.

Installing and Configuring Server for NFS

You install Server for NFS like any other role service, by using the Add Roles and Features Wizard or the PowerShell cmdlet `Install-WindowsFeature`. After it's installed, a tab named NFS Sharing is added to the Properties dialog box of folders.

The NFS Sharing tab shows the current status of NFS for the folder (whether it is shared by using NFS or not). Clicking the Manage NFS Sharing button opens the NFS Advanced Sharing dialog box shown in Figure 10-24. In the NFS Advanced Sharing dialog box, you can configure the following settings:

- *Share this folder*—When this check box is selected, the folder is shared with NFS.
- *Share name*—Name the share; the default value is the name of the folder.
- *Encoding*—Choose the encoding method, which determines the characters that can be used in file and directory names.
- *Authentication*—Configure Kerberos authentication options and specify whether to allow unmapped user access and anonymous access. If you enable the "No server authentication" option, you can select "Enable unmapped user access." Doing so allows users of Linux and UNIX systems to access the NFS share without authenticating through Active Directory. You can also allow anonymous access.
- *Permissions*—By default, all NFS client computers that request access to the share are allowed Read-Only access. You can change the default access to Read-Write or No Access. You can add client groups and assign each group different access.

You can also configure an NFS share using the New Share Wizard in File and Storage Services from Server Manager. If you configure an NFS share using File and Storage Services, the Server for NFS role is automatically installed.

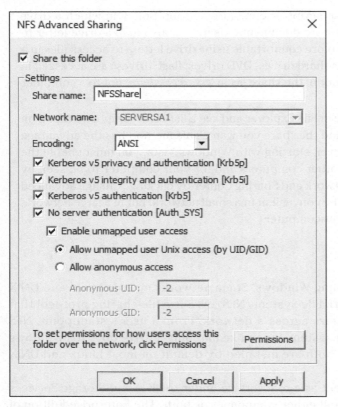

Figure 10-24   The NFS Advanced Sharing dialog box

Self-Check Questions

7.   What protocol does Windows file sharing use by default?

   a. NFS

   b. FTP

   c. SMB

   d. HTTP

8.   Administrative share names on Windows end with a $. What is the purpose of the $ in the share name?

   a. It tells Windows that only administrators may access the share.

   b. It tells Windows to encrypt data in the share.

   c. It makes the share available to the Windows OS, but not to users.

   d. It makes the share hidden in a network browse list.

⊙ Check your answers at the end of this module.

Activity 10-5

Sharing a Folder with Simple File Sharing

Time Required: 10 minutes

Objective: Create a test folder and then share it with simple file sharing.

Required Tools and Equipment: ServerSA1

Description: You understand that there are several ways to create shared folders. You decide to try simple file sharing to see how it sets permissions automatically. Before you create shares, you will create a new volume that will be used for working with shared folders and permissions.

(continues)

Activity 10-5 Continued

1. Log on to ServerSA1 as **Administrator**, if necessary.
2. Open Disk Management and create a 5 GB volume named **TestVol** on the 20.0 GB disk formatted as NTFS. Assign the drive letter H:. Use default settings for all other parameters. (If you need help, review Activity 10-2 for instructions on creating a new volume.)
3. Open File Explorer and create a folder named **TestShare1** on TestVol.
4. Open TestShare1's Properties dialog box and click the **Security** tab. Make a note of the permissions assigned on this folder, and then close the Properties dialog box.
5. Right-click **TestShare1**, point to **Share with**, and click **Specific people** to open the File Sharing dialog box. Notice that the Administrator user and Administrators group already have access.
6. Click the list arrow next to the Add button and click **TestUser** in the list. (You can also create a new user by clicking the "Create a new user" option.) Click the **Add** button. By default, the user has Read permission. Click the list arrow next to Read and click **Read/Write**.
7. Click **Share**. You see a message indicating that the folder is shared. You can email links to the shared folder or copy the links to the Clipboard. You can also click the "Show me all the network shares on this computer" link to open the network browser window for your server. Click **Done**.
8. Open **TestShare1**'s Properties dialog box. Click the **Sharing** tab and then click **Advanced Sharing**.
9. Click **Permissions**. Notice that the Everyone group and Administrators group are assigned Full control to the share, which is the default setting with simple file sharing. Permissions can be restricted by using file and folder permissions through the Security tab. Click **Cancel** twice.
10. In the TestShare1 folder's Properties dialog box, click the **Security** tab. Scroll through the users and groups in the top pane. Notice that TestUser and Administrator were added to the list and that they have Full control permissions. In addition, the CREATOR OWNER user has been removed. However, all other groups and users were maintained. In the real world, this may or may not be what you intended. Simple file sharing is just that—simple—but you might want to exert more control over file sharing.
11. Close all open windows and continue to the next activity.

Activity 10-6

Sharing a Folder with Advanced Sharing

Time Required: 15 minutes

Objective: Create a new folder and share it with advanced sharing.

Required Tools and Equipment: ServerSA1

Description: You're concerned that simple file sharing doesn't always yield the results you want, so you decide to experiment with advanced sharing. You will create a new folder, share it, and assign permissions. The permissions allow all members of the Users group to read files in the share, give all members of the Administrators group full control, and allow TestUser to create new files (with full control over them) and read files created by other users.

1. On ServerSA1, open File Explorer and create a folder named **TestShare2** on TestVol. Open TestShare2's Properties dialog box and click the **Security** tab. Examine the new folder's default permissions. The Users group has Read & execute, List folder contents, and Read permissions. The Administrators group has Full control permission, and the CREATOR OWNER special identity has advanced permissions that give any user who creates or owns a file full control over the file.
2. Click the **Sharing** tab and then click **Advanced Sharing**. Click to select the **Share this folder** check box. Leave the share name as is and then click **Permissions**. By default, the share permission is Allow Read for Everyone.

(continues)

Activity 10-6 Continued

3. In this activity, you don't want everyone to have Read permission, so click **Remove**. Click **Add**, type **Users**, click **Check Names**, and then click **OK**. Next, click **Add**, type **Administrators**, click **Check Names**, and then click **OK** to add the Administrators group.

4. Click **Users** and click the **Full Control** check box in the Allow column. Click **Administrators** and click the **Full Control** check box in the Allow column. Even though the Users group permission is set to Full Control, file and folder permissions will restrict them to Read and Read & execute. Click **OK** twice.

5. Click the **Security** tab. Notice the permissions haven't changed as they did when you used simple file sharing. Click **Edit** and then click **Add**. Type **TestUser** and click **Check Names**. Click **OK**.

6. Click **TestUser**. Notice the permissions for TestUser are set to Read & execute, List folder contents, and Read. Click **Write** in the Allow column, which gives TestUser the ability to create files and make changes to them. Click **OK** and then **Close**.

7. Later in this module, you will learn more about permissions and work with permissions. Close all open windows and continue to the next activity.

Activity 10-7

Creating a Share with File and Storage Services

Time Required: 5 minutes

Objective: Create a share with File and Storage Services.

Required Tools and Equipment: ServerSA1

Description: You want to practice creating shares by using simple and advanced file sharing. In this activity, you use File and Storage Services to create a share.

1. Log on to ServerSA1 as **Administrator**, if necessary.

2. In Server Manager, click **File and Storage Services** and then click **Shares**.

3. Click the **Tasks** list box and click **New Share** to start the New Share Wizard. In the Select Profile window, click **SMB Share – Quick**, and then click **Next**.

4. In the Share Location window, click the **H:** volume in the Select by volume section, and then click **Next**.

5. In the Share Name window, type **NewShare1** in the Share name text box. By default, the local path to the share is set to H:\Shares\NewShare1. You can change the local path, but for now, leave it as is. Click **Next**.

6. In the Other Settings window, read the descriptions for the three options described previously. Leave the default settings and click **Next**.

7. In the Permissions window, review the default permissions. Note that the share permissions are Everyone Read Only, which means that only Read access to the share is allowed for all users. The Folder permissions list the file and folder permissions. By default, Administrators have full control, and Users can read and create files when accessing the folder locally. Click the **Customize permissions** button to open the Advanced Security Settings for NewShare1 dialog box, where you can change the file and folder permissions and share permissions, if necessary. Click **Cancel** and then click **Next**.

8. In the Confirmation window, review your choices and then click **Create**. After the share is created successfully, click **Close**. You see the new share in the list of shares.

9. Close all windows and continue with the next activity.

Activity 10-8

Creating a Hidden Share and Monitoring Share Access

Time Required: 10 minutes

Objective: Create a hidden share and monitor access to shared folders.

Required Tools and Equipment: ServerSA1

Description: You want to be able to keep users from seeing certain shares on the network unless they type the UNC path for the share. You haven't worked with hidden shares yet, so you want to experiment with them. You will create a new folder on TestVol and then share it with the Shared Folders snap-in. You append a $ to the share name so that it's hidden, verify that the share is hidden, and then open it by using the full UNC path. Then you use the Shared Folders snap-in to monitor access to the share.

1. On ServerSA1, open File Explorer and create a new folder on TestVol named **HideMe**.
2. Open Computer Management and click to expand **Shared Folders**.
3. Right-click **Shares** and click **New Share** to start the Create a Shared Folder Wizard. Click **Next**.
4. In the Folder Path window, type **H:\HideMe** in the Folder path text box, and then click **Next**.
5. In the Name, Description, and Settings window, type **HideMe$** in the Share name text box, and then click **Next**.
6. In the Shared Folder Permissions window, click **Administrators have full access; other users have read-only access**, and then click **Finish**.
7. In the Sharing was Successful window, click **Finish**.
8. Right-click **Start**, click **Run**, type **\\ServerSA1**, and press **Enter**. A File Explorer window opens and lists the shares on ServerSA1. The share you just created isn't listed because it's hidden. Close the File Explorer window.
9. Right-click **Start**, click **Run**, type **\\ServerSA1\HideMe$**, and press **Enter**. A window opens and shows the share's contents. A hidden share is hidden in network browse lists, but if you specify the share in a UNC path, it's available to all who have permission.
10. Minimize the File Explorer window and open the Computer Management window. In the left pane, click **Shares** to see the HideMe$ share listed. The Client Connections column displays the number 1 because you currently have the share open.
11. Click **Sessions** to see that the Administrator account has one open file. Click **Open Files** to see the H:\HideMe folder listed as an open file. (Folders are considered files in Windows.) Close Computer Management and File Explorer.

Activity 10-9

Mapping a Drive

Time Required: 10 minutes

Objective: Map a drive letter to a shared folder.

Required Tools and Equipment: ServerSA1

Description: In this activity, you use several methods to map a drive letter to a share. For testing purposes, you will map the drive on the same server where the share is located; you would use the same procedure when accessing the share from another computer.

1. On ServerSA1, right-click **Start**, click **Run**, type **\\ServerSA1**, and press **Enter**.
2. Right-click the **NewShare1** share and click **Map network drive** to open the Map Network Drive dialog box (see Figure 10-25).
3. Click the **Drive** list arrow and click **M:**. By default, the "Reconnect at sign-in" check box is selected, which is what you usually want in this situation. This option means the M drive always connects to this share when the user logs on. For this activity, click to clear the **Reconnect at sign-in** check box. You can also use a different username to access this share, if necessary.

(continues)

Activity 10-9 Continued

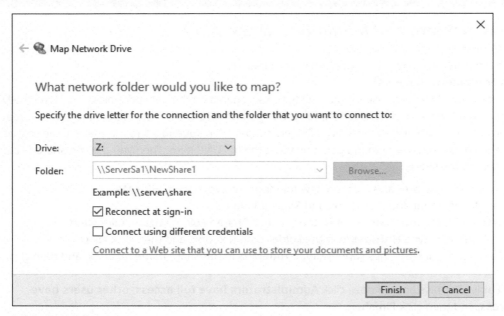

Figure 10-25 The Map Network Drive dialog box

4. Click **Finish**. A File Explorer window opens and shows the contents of the share. Close this window.
5. In the File Explorer window that's still open, click **This PC**. Notice that the M drive is listed under Network Locations, below the "Devices and drives" section. Right-click the **M:** drive and click **Disconnect** to remove the drive mapping.
6. On the File Explorer menu bar, click **Computer** and then click **Map network drive** on the ribbon to open the Map Network Drive window. Click the **M:** drive in the Drive list box. In the Folder text box, type **\\ServerSA1\NewShare1** and then click **Finish**.
7. Disconnect the M drive again, as you did in Step 5.
8. Open a command prompt window. Type **net use m: \\ServerSA1\NewShare1** and press **Enter**. In File Explorer, verify that the drive has been mapped. The net use command is good to use in batch files for mapping drives.
9. At the command prompt, type **net use** and press **Enter** to see a list of mapped drives. Type **net use m: /delete** and press **Enter** to disconnect the M drive again.
10. Close all open windows.

Securing Access to Files with Permissions

Microsoft Exam AZ-800:

Manage storage and file services.

- Configure and manage Windows Server file shares

Sharing files on a Windows server is a fairly straightforward process, but configuring permissions to secure shared files so that only authorized users can access them is a little more complex. There are two modes for accessing files on a networked computer: network (sometimes called *remote*) and interactive (sometimes called *local*). Similarly, there are two ways to secure files: share permissions and file and folder permissions. Share permissions are applied when a user attempts network access to shared files. File and folder permissions always apply, whether file access is attempted interactively or remotely, through a share. That last statement might sound confusing, so take a closer look at how permissions work.

Permissions specify which users can access a file system object (a file or folder) and what users can do with the object if they're granted access. Each file system object has permissions associated with it, and each permission can be set to Allow or Deny. Permissions can be viewed as a gatekeeper to control who has access to files. When you log on to a computer or domain, you're issued a "ticket" containing information such as your username and group memberships. If you attempt to access a file or folder, the gatekeeper examines your ticket, so to speak, and compares your username and group memberships to the file or folder's access list. If neither your username nor your groups are on the list, you're denied access. If you or your groups *are* on the list, you're issued an access ticket that combines all your allowed permissions. You can then access the resource as specified by your access ticket.

That's how the process works when you're attempting interactive access to files. If you're attempting network access, there are two gatekeepers: one that checks your ticket against the share permissions access list and, if you're granted access by share permissions, another that checks your ticket against the file and folder permissions access list. The file and folder permissions gatekeeper is required to examine your ticket only if you get past the share gatekeeper. If you're granted access by share permissions, you're issued an access ticket. Then, if you're granted access by file and folder permissions, you're allowed to keep the access ticket that gives you the least permission between the two.

For example, Sophia is granted Read access by share permissions and Read and Write access by file and folder permissions. Sophia gets to keep only the Read access ticket because it's the lesser of the two permissions. Another example: Neither Sophia nor any of Sophia's groups are on the share permissions access list. There's no need to even examine file and folder permissions because Sophia is denied access at the share permissions gate. As a final example, Sophia is granted Full Control access by share permissions and Modify access by file and folder permissions. Sophia's access ticket provides Modify permission because it allows less access than Full Control.

The general security rule for assigning permissions to resources is to give users the least access necessary for their jobs. This rule is often referred to as the *least privileges principle*. Unfortunately, this axiom can be at odds with another general rule: *Keep it simple*. Sometimes, determining the least amount of access a user requires can lead to complex permission schemes. The more complex a permission scheme is, the more likely it will need troubleshooting, and the more troubleshooting that's needed, the more likely an administrator will assign overly permissive permissions out of frustration.

Note 16

Because FAT volumes don't have permissions, everybody who logs on locally to a computer with a FAT volume has full access to all files on that volume. If a folder is shared on a FAT volume, network users' access is determined solely by share permissions. Only the NTFS and ReFS file systems support file and folder permissions.

Security Principals

Three types of objects, called **security principals**, can be assigned permission to access the file system: users, groups, and computers. A file system object's security settings have three components that make up its **security descriptor**:

- *Discretionary access control list*—A list of security principals with permissions defining access to an object is called a **discretionary access control list (DACL)**. Each entry in the DACL is an **access control entry (ACE)**. A security principal or group not included in the DACL has no access to the object.
- *Object owner*—Typically, the user account that created the object or a group or user who has been assigned ownership of the object is the **object owner**, which has special authority over the object. Most notably, even if the owner isn't in the object's DACL, the owner can still assign permissions to the object.
- *System access control list*—A **system access control list (SACL)** defines the settings for auditing access to an object.

How Permissions Are Assigned

Users can be assigned permission to an object in four different ways:

- The user creates the object. In this case, the user account is granted Full Control permission to the object and all descendant objects and is assigned as owner of the object.
- The user's account is added to the object's DACL. This method is called **explicit permission**.
- A group the user belongs to is added to the object's DACL. This method is also considered explicit permission.
- Permission is inherited from the DACL of a parent object to which the user or group account has been added. This is **inherited permission**.

Effective Permissions

When a user has been assigned permission to an object through a combination of methods, the user's **effective permissions** are a combination of the assigned permissions. For example, if Joe Tech1's account has been added to an object's DACL and assigned the Allow Read permission, and a group that Joe Tech1 belongs to has been added to the same object's DACL and assigned the Allow Write permission, Joe Tech1 has both Read and Write permissions to the object. A user's effective permissions determine the user's effective access to an object.

Share Permissions

Share permissions apply to folders and files accessed across the network. Before a file can be accessed across the network, it must reside in a shared folder or a subfolder of a shared folder. Share permissions are configured on a shared folder and apply to all files and subfolders of the shared folder. These permissions can't be configured on files; file and folder permissions are used for that purpose. There are three share permission levels (see Figure 10-26):

- *Read*—Users can view contents of files, copy files, run applications and script files, open folders and subfolders, and view file attributes.
- *Change*—This level includes all permissions granted by Read, plus permissions to create files and folders, change contents and attributes of files and folders, and delete files and folders.
- *Full Control*—This level includes all permissions granted by Change, plus permissions to change file and folder permissions as well as take ownership of files and folders. (File and folder permissions and ownership are available only on NTFS volumes.)

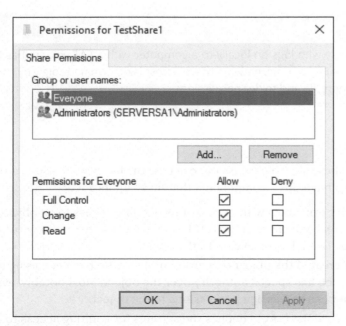

Figure 10-26 Share permission levels

Windows assigns default permissions depending on how a folder is shared, as you have seen. Generally, the default share permission is Read for the Everyone special identity. On FAT volumes, share permissions are the only way to secure files accessed through the network. File and folder permissions protect file accesses via the network and those done interactively.

File and Folder Permissions

File and folder permissions give both network users and interactive users fine-grained access control over folders and files. Unlike share permissions, which can be configured only on a shared folder, file and folder permissions can be configured on both folders and files. By default, when permissions are configured on a folder, subfolders and files in that folder inherit the permissions. However, inherited permissions can be changed when needed, making it possible to have different permission settings on files in a folder.

Permission inheritance defines how permissions are transmitted from a parent object to a child object. In a file system, parent objects can be a volume or folder, and child objects can be folders and files. For example, a folder can be the parent object, and any files it contains, including other folders, are considered child objects. All objects in a volume are child objects of the volume. So, if a user is assigned the Modify permission to a folder, all subfolders and files in the folder inherit the permission, and the user has Modify permission to these objects as well. Permission inheritance and how to change it are discussed later in the "Permission Inheritance" section.

To view or edit permissions on a folder or file, you use the Security tab of the object's Properties dialog box. Unlike share permissions, which have only three permission levels, there are six basic permissions in the Security tab for folders, and five permissions for files. Folders also have 14 advanced permissions, and files have 13. Advanced permissions aren't completely separate from basic permissions, however. Each basic permission is really a grouping of advanced permissions, as you see later.

Basic permissions for folders and files are as follows (see Figure 10-27):

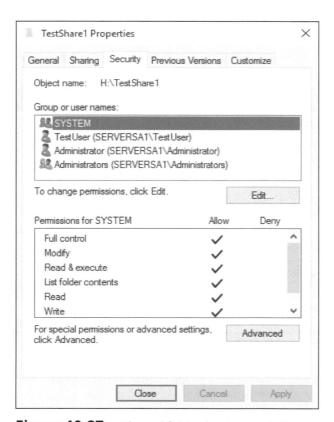

Figure 10-27   File and folder basic permissions

- *Read*—Users can view file contents, copy files, open folders and subfolders, and view file attributes and per-missions. However, unlike the Read permission in share permissions, this permission doesn't allow users to run applications or scripts.
- *Read & execute*—This option grants the same permissions as Read and includes the ability to run applications or scripts. When this permission is selected, List folder contents and Read are selected, too.
- *List folder contents*—This permission applies only to folders and grants the same permission as Read & execute. However, because it doesn't apply to files, Read & execute must also be set on the folder to allow users to open files in the folder.
- *Write*—Users can create and modify files and read file attributes and permissions. However, this permission doesn't allow users to read or delete files. In most cases, the Read or Read & execute permission should be given with the Write permission.
- *Modify*—Users can read, modify, delete, and create files. Users can't change permissions or take ownership. Selecting this permission automatically selects Read & execute, List folder contents, Read, and Write.
- *Full control*—Users can perform all actions given by the Modify permission with the addition of changing per-missions and taking ownership. This permission is very powerful because it gives users complete control over who can access a file or folder as well as take ownership (discussed later in the "File and Folder Ownership" section). Full control should be assigned to non-administrator users only sparingly. In most cases, the Modify permission gives users enough capabilities to interact with the file system.

Basic permissions should work for most situations. Configuring advanced permissions should be reserved for special circumstances. The temptation to configure advanced permissions to follow the least privileges principle can lead to breaking the "keep it simple" rule and result in administrators' and users' frustration. However, if you look at the file and folder permissions Windows sets by default on every volume, you see a few ACEs that use advanced permissions. So, although you don't have to use them often, you need to understand them, particularly to figure out how initial volume permissions are set. Table 10-3 describes each advanced permission and lists which basic permissions include it.

Table 10-3   File and folder advanced permissions

Advanced permission	Description	Included in basic permission
Full control	Same as the standard Full control permission	Full control
Traverse folder/execute file	For folders: Allows accessing files in folders or subfolders even if the user doesn't normally have access to the folder For files: Allows running program files	Full control, Modify, Read & execute, List folder contents
List folder/read data	For folders: Allows users to view subfolders and filenames in the folder For files: Allows users to view data in files	Full control, Modify, Read & execute, List folder contents, Read
Read attributes	Allows users to view file or folder attributes	Full control, Modify, Read & execute, List folder contents, Read
Read extended attributes	Allows users to view file or folder extended attributes	Full control, Modify, Read & execute, List folder contents, Read
Create files/write data	Allows users to create new files and modify the contents of existing files	Full control, Modify, Write
Create folders/append data	Allows users to create new folders and add data to the end of existing files but not change existing data in a file	Full control, Modify, Write
Write attributes	Allows users to change file and folder attributes	Full control, Modify, Write

(continues)

Table 10-3   (continued)

Advanced permission	Description	Included in basic permission
Write extended attributes	Allows users to change file and folder extended attributes	Full control, Modify, Write
Delete subfolders and files	Allows users to delete subfolders and files in the folder	Full control
Delete	Allows users to delete the folder or file	Full control, Modify
Read permissions	Allows users to read file and folder permissions of a folder or file	Full control, Modify, Read & execute, List folder contents, Read, Write
Take ownership	Allows users to take ownership of a folder or file, which gives the user implicit permission to change permissions on that file or folder	Full control

File and Folder Ownership

As mentioned, every file system object (files and folders) has an owner. An object owner is granted certain implicit permissions, regardless of how permissions are set in the object's DACL: viewing and changing permissions for the object and transferring ownership to another user. So, it's possible that users can be file owners but not be able to open the files they own. However, because owners can change permissions on files they own, they can grant themselves the permissions they want.

A user can become the owner of a file system object in three ways:

- *Create the file or folder*—The user who creates a file or folder is automatically the owner.
- *Take ownership of a file or folder*—User accounts with Full control permission or the Take ownership advanced permission for a file or folder can take ownership of the file or folder. Members of the Administrators group can take ownership of all files.
- *Assigned ownership*—An Administrator account can assign another user as the owner of a file or folder.

Permission Inheritance

On an NTFS or ReFS volume, permissions are first set at the root of a volume, and all folders and files in the volume inherit these settings unless configured otherwise.

> **Note 17**
>
> Windows changes the default inheritance settings on many folders created during installation so that they don't inherit all permissions from the root of the volume.

You can change how permission inheritance works by going to advanced settings in the Security tab of a file or folder's Shared Properties dialog box. When you select an ACE and click Edit, you see seven options for how permissions on a folder apply to other objects in the folder, as shown in Figure 10-28.

All basic permissions have the Applies to option set to "This folder, subfolders and files," but there might be reasons to change this default setting. For example, you might want users to be able to create and delete files in a folder but not delete the folder itself. To do this, you could set the standard Read & execute and Write permissions on the folder, and then set the Delete advanced permission to apply to subfolders and files only.

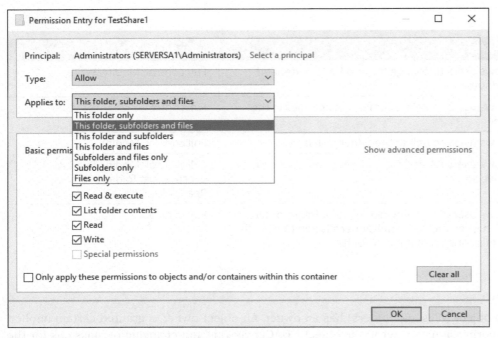

Figure 10-28 Configuring permission inheritance

Subfolders and files are configured to inherit permissions by default; however, permission inheritance can be disabled. If you need to remove permissions from a file or folder, you must disable inheritance first. You can add new ACEs or add permissions to an existing ACE with inheritance enabled, but you can't remove inherited permissions. To disable permission inheritance, open the Advanced Security Settings dialog box for an object (see Figure 10-29) and click the Disable inheritance button. When you disable inheritance, you're prompted to convert the existing inherited permissions into explicit permissions or remove all inherited permissions. In most cases, converting the permissions

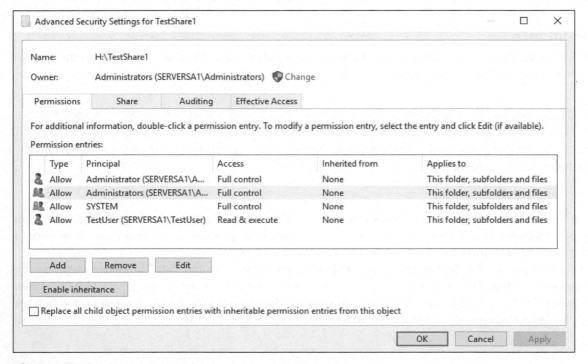

Figure 10-29 The Advanced Security Settings dialog box

is best so that you have a starting point from which to make changes. The "Replace all child object permission entries with inheritable permission entries from this object" option forces the current folder's child objects to inherit applicable permissions. If a child object has inheritance disabled, this option reenables it.

Effective Access

With all the variables involved in permissions, determining what access a user account has to a file or folder isn't always easy, but Windows has a tool called **effective access** to help sort out object access. As shown previously, the Advanced Security Settings dialog box has an Effective Access tab where you can select a user or group to see its access to a file or folder after taking into account sharing permission, file and folder permissions, and group memberships (see Figure 10-30). You can also see which permissions a user or group has. For permissions that aren't granted, the "Access limited by" column specifies whether the limiting factor is share or file and folder permissions.

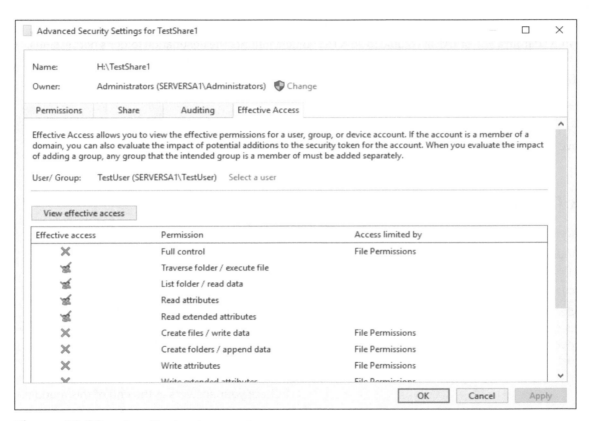

Figure 10-30   The Effective Access tab

Using Deny in an ACE

The Deny permission should be used cautiously and only for exceptions. As stated, if a security principal isn't represented in an object's DACL, it doesn't have access to the object. For this reason, you don't need to add Deny ACEs to every object to prevent users from accessing objects. However, the Deny permission does have its place, usually when an exception is needed. For example, Bill is a member of the Accounting group, which has been given access to the Accounting share so that group members have access to accounting-related files. Bill is a new employee, so until he's fully trained, you don't want him to be able to make changes to files in the share. You can add Bill's user account to the Accounting share's DACL and assign the Deny Delete and Deny Create files/write data permissions to his account. Using Deny in this way enables you to assign broad permissions to groups yet make exceptions for certain group members. Another common use of the Deny permission is to override a permission inherited from a parent object.

As a rule, a Deny permission overrides an Allow permission. For example, a group Joe Tech1 belongs to has been added to an object's DACL and assigned the Allow Full control permission, and Joe Tech1's account has been added to the same object's DACL and assigned the Deny Write permission. In this case, Joe Tech1 could perform all actions on the object that Full control allows, except actions requiring the Write permission. There's an exception to this rule: If the Deny permission is inherited from a parent object, and the Allow permission is explicitly added to the object's DACL, the Allow permission takes precedence in case of a conflict.

Copying and Moving Files and Folders

When you copy or move files and folders within or between volumes, you need to know how the permissions assigned to those files and folders are handled. Here's a list of rules:

- A file or folder copied within the same NTFS volume or to a different NTFS volume inherits permissions from the destination folder. If the destination is the root of the volume, it inherits permissions from the root of the volume.
- A file or folder moved within the same NTFS volume retains its original permissions.
- A file or folder moved to a different NTFS volume inherits the destination folder's permissions.
- A file or folder moved from a FAT or FAT32 volume to an NTFS volume inherits the destination folder's permissions.
- A file or folder moved or copied from an NTFS volume to a FAT or FAT32 volume loses all permission settings because FAT/FAT32 volumes don't support permissions.

Note 18

ReFS volumes behave the same way as NTFS volumes when copying and moving file system objects.

Self-Check Questions

9. What type of account can be assigned permissions to files on a Windows system?

    a. Security principals

    b. Distribution account

    c. Only file owners

    d. Only guest accounts

10. Which of the following is true about copying and moving files and folders on a Windows system?

    a. A file or folder copied within the same NTFS volume retains its original permissions.

    b. A file or folder moved within the same NTFS volume inherits permissions from the new folder.

    c. A file or folder moved to a different NTFS volume inherits the destination folder's permissions.

    d. A file or folder moved or copied from an NTFS volume to a FAT32 volume retains its original permissions.

⊙ Check your answers at the end of this module.

Activity 10-10

Examining Default Settings for Volume Permissions

Time Required: 10 minutes

Objective: Examine default permission settings on a volume.

Required Tools and Equipment: ServerSA1

Description: You want a solid understanding of which permissions are inherited by files and folders created on a new volume, so you will view the default permissions on a volume, create a folder, and see how permissions are inherited.

1. Log on to ServerSA1 as **Administrator**, if necessary.

2. Right-click **TestVol** and click **Properties**. Click the **Security** tab in the Properties dialog box.

3. Click each ACE in the volume's DACL to see the assigned permissions. You might need to scroll the Permission list box to see the Special permissions entry. (If there is a check in the Special permissions row, it means the account has been assigned one or more advanced permissions.)

(continues)

Activity 10-10 Continued

4. Click the **Advanced** button. Notice that the Administrators group and SYSTEM and CREATOR OWNER special identities are granted Full control. Double-click the **CREATOR OWNER** entry. This special identity is given Full control, but only over subfolders and files. This entry ensures that any user who creates a file or folder is granted Full control permission for that object. A user must have at least the Write basic permission to create files and folders. Click **Cancel**.

5. Double-click the **Users** entry with Create files/write data in the Access column. This entry and the Users entry above it allow users to create folders and files, but files can be created only in subfolders. This permission prevents users from creating files in the root of the volume. Click **Cancel**.

6. Double-click the **Everyone** entry. This set of permissions allows the Everyone special identity to read and execute files and view a list of files and folders in the root of the volume. The "Applies to" setting "This folder only" prevents child objects from inheriting these permissions. Click **Cancel** three times.

7. Create a folder named **TestPerm** in the root of the TestVol volume.

8. Open the TestPerm folder's Properties dialog box and click the **Security** tab. Click any ACE in the Group or user names list box. Permissions for the entries are grayed out, meaning you can't change them because they are inherited. Click **Cancel**.

9. Create a text file named **Permfile1** in the TestPerm folder.

10. Open the Permfile1 file's Properties dialog box and click the **Security** tab. Notice that the file inherits the TestPerm folder's permissions except the CREATOR OWNER special identity, which is assigned only to folders, not files.

11. Close all open windows and continue to the next activity.

Activity 10-11

Experimenting with File and Folder Permissions

Time Required: 20 minutes
Objective: Experiment with file and folder permissions.
Required Tools and Equipment: ServerSA1
Description: You're somewhat confused about file and folder permissions, so you will create some files to use in a variety of permission experiments.

1. Log on to ServerSA1 as **Administrator**, if necessary.

2. Open File Explorer and navigate to the **TestPerm** folder you created on the TestVol volume.

3. First, you want to be able to view file extensions in File Explorer so that you can create batch files easily. Click **View** on the toolbar and then click the box next to **File name extensions**. You can now see the .txt extension on the Permfile1 file you created previously.

4. Create a text file called **TestBatch.bat** in the TestPerm folder. When asked whether you want to change the file extension, click **Yes**.

5. Right-click **TestBatch.bat** and click **Edit**. Type **@ Echo This is a test batch file** and press **Enter**. On the next line, type **@ Pause**. Save the file and then exit Notepad. To test your batch file, double-click it. A command prompt window opens, and you see "This is a test batch file. Press any key to continue ... " Press the **spacebar** or **Enter** to close the command prompt window.

6. Open the Properties dialog box for TestBatch.bat, click the **Security** tab, and then click **Advanced**. Click the **Disable inheritance** button. In the message box that opens, click **Convert inherited permissions into explicit permissions on this object**. Notice that the three permissions entries now indicate "None" in the Inherited from column (see Figure 10-31). Click **OK**.

7. On the Security tab for TestBatch.bat, click **Edit**. Click **Users** in the Group or user names list box. In the Permissions for Users list box, click to clear the **Read & execute** check box in the Allow column and leave the **Read** check box selected. Click **OK** twice.

(continues)

Activity 10-11 Continued

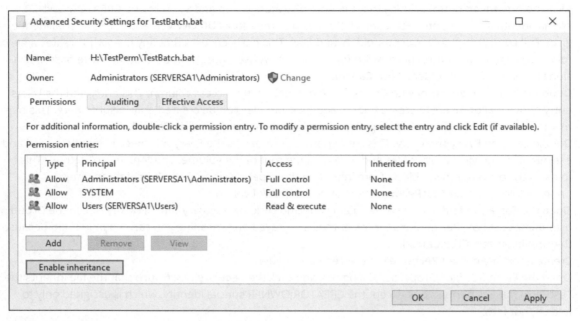

Figure 10-31   Permissions after removing inheritance

8. Log off and log on as **TestUser** with **Password01**. In File Explorer, browse to the **TestPerm** folder on the TestVol volume. Double-click the **TestBatch.bat** file. Read the error message, which indicates that you cannot access the file. The message appears because you are trying to run (execute) the batch file and you no longer have the Read & execute permission. Click **OK**.

9. Right-click **TestBatch.bat** and click **Edit**. Notice that you can still open this file because you have Read permission. Click **File** and then click **Save**. A dialog box opens and asks you to save the file. Click **Save**. When prompted to replace the file, click **Yes**. You see a message that access is denied because you don't have write permission to the file. Click **OK** and exit Notepad.

10. In File Explorer, right-click the right pane and point to **New**. Strangely, the right-click New menu and the Quick Access toolbar menu offer only Folder as an option. However, you can save a file you create in Notepad in this folder.

11. Right-click **TestBatch.bat** and click **Edit**. Click **File** and then **Save As** from the menu. In the Save As dialog box, type **NewBatch.bat** and click **Save**. Exit Notepad.

12. Open the Properties dialog box for NewBatch and click the **Security** tab. Click **TestUser**. This user has been assigned Full control of the file because of the CREATOR OWNER Full control permission on the parent folder. Click **Advanced**. You see TestUser next to Owner. Notice that you can change the owner if you click the Change link.

13. Disable permission inheritance and convert the existing permissions. (Refer back to Step 6 if necessary.) Click **OK** until you get back to the Security tab of the NewBatch file's Properties dialog box.

14. Click **Edit**. Click **TestUser** and then click **Remove**. Click the **Users** entry and then click **Remove**. Only SYSTEM and Administrators are left in the DACL. Click **OK** twice.

15. Double-click **NewBatch**. You see a message that access is denied because you no longer have permission to open or execute this file. Click **OK**. Although you no longer have access to this file, you're still the file owner and can assign yourself permissions.

16. Open the Properties dialog box for NewBatch, click the **Security** tab, and then click **Edit**. Click **Add**. Type **TestUser**, click **Check Names**, and then click **OK**. Click **Full control** in the Allow column in the Permissions for TestUser list box. Click **OK** twice. Double-click **NewBatch** to verify that you can open and execute the file.

17. Log off the system and continue to the next activity.

Activity 10-12

Restricting Access to Subfolders of Shares

Time Required: 20 minutes

Objective: Restrict access to a subfolder of a share.

Required Tools and Equipment: ServerSA1

Description: The Sales Department wants a subfolder of the Marketing share to store sensitive documents that should be available only to users in the Sales Department because some Marketing and Advertising users tend to leak information before it should be discussed outside the company. You could create a new share, but the Sales Department users prefer a subfolder of the existing share. To do this activity, you need to create a couple of groups and some users to put in the groups.

1. Log on to ServerSA1 as **Administrator**.
2. Right-click **Start** and click **Computer Management**. You'll create two users named **Marketing1** and **Sales1**.
3. Click to expand **Local Users and Groups** and then click the **Users** folder. In the Actions pane, click **More Actions** and click **New User**.
4. Type **Marketing1** in the User name text box. Type **Password01** in the Password and Confirm password text boxes. Click to clear **User must change password at next logon** and click **Create**. Repeat this step, replacing Marketing1 with **Sales1**. Click **Close** when finished.
5. In the left pane, right-click **Groups** and click **New Group**. In the Group name text box, type **MarketingG**.
6. Next, users in the Marketing and Sales departments should be added to the MarketingG group. To do this, click **Add**. In the Select Users dialog box, type **Marketing1; Sales1**, click **Check Names**, and then click **OK**. Click **Create** and then **Close**.
7. Create a group named **SalesG** and add the **Sales1** user to the group. Close Computer Management.
8. Open File Explorer. On TestVol, create a folder named **MktgDocs**. In the MktgDocs folder, create a subfolder named **SalesOnly**.
9. Open the Properties dialog box for MktgDocs and click **Sharing**. Click **Advanced Sharing** and then click **Share this folder**. Click **Permissions** and then remove **Everyone** from the DACL.
10. Add the **Users** group to the DACL and give the group **Full control** to the share. You limit access to files and subfolders by using file and folder permissions. Click **OK** until you're back to the MktgDocs Properties dialog box.
11. Click the **Security** tab. Currently, the Users group has Read permission to the folder and the Administrators group has Full control. Click **Advanced**. Click **Disable Inheritance** and then click the **Convert** option. Click **OK**.
12. Click **Edit**, click **Users**, and click **Remove**.
13. Add both the **MarketingG** and **SalesG** groups to the DACL. Click **MarketingG** and click the **Write** check box in the Allow column so that MarketingG has Read & execute, List folder contents, Read, and Write permissions to the folder. Repeat the step for **SalesG**. Click **OK** and then **Close**.
14. In File Explorer, open the **MktgDocs** folder and then open the Properties dialog box for the **SalesOnly** folder. Click the **Security** tab. The SalesOnly folder has inherited permissions from the MktgDocs folder.
15. Disable inheritance on the SalesOnly folder, being sure to convert existing permissions. On the Security tab, click **Edit**. Click **MarketingG** and then click **Remove**. Click **OK** twice.
16. Log off ServerSA1 and log back on as **Sales1**. Open the MktgDocs share by right-clicking **Start**, clicking **Run**, typing **\\ServerSA1\MktgDocs**, and pressing **Enter**. Create a text file in MktgDocs named **Mktg1**.
17. Open the **SalesOnly** folder and create a text file named **SalesDoc**. You have verified that you can create files while logged on as a member of the SalesG group. Open the Properties dialog box for SalesDoc and click the **Security** tab. Note that SalesG and Sales1 are in the DACL. Click **SalesG** and notice that it has Read & execute, Read, and Write permissions. Click **Sales1** and notice that it has Full control because it's the file owner.

(continues)

Activity 10-12 Continued

18. Log off ServerSA1 and log back on as **Marketing1**. Open the MktgDocs share by right-clicking **Start**, clicking **Run**, typing **\\ServerSA1\MktgDocs**, and pressing **Enter**. Create a text file in MktgDocs named **Mktg2**. You have verified that members of the MarketingG group can create files in the MktgDocs share.

19. Try to delete the Mktg1 file that Sales1 created. You can't because you have only Write permission to the file, which doesn't allow you to delete files.

20. Double-click the **SalesOnly** folder. You see a network error message because the Marketing1 user doesn't have access to the SalesOnly folder. Click **Close**.

21. Shut down ServerSA1.

Using File Server Resource Manager

Microsoft Exam AZ-800:

Manage storage and file services.
- Configure and manage Windows Server file shares

A major challenge in network management is the use—or abuse—of storage space. Although storage has become less expensive, it's not free, and filling a volume can have adverse consequences on other processes and system efficiency. Users often need read and write access to file server shares but might not be careful about what, and how much, they save to these shares. Worse, users might not be aware that certain files (such as audio or video files) violate copyright law and could pose a legal risk for the organization. In addition, as the number of files on a network grows, finding files becomes a time-consuming task.

The **File Server Resource Manager (FSRM)** role service has services and management tools for monitoring storage space, managing quotas, controlling the types of files that users can store on a server, creating storage reports, and classifying and managing files. When this role service is installed, you can open the File Server Resource Manager console from the Tools menu in Server Manager. This console contains five tools (see Figure 10-32):

- *Quota Management*—Monitor and create quotas for volumes and folders and apply preconfigured quota templates to volumes and folders.

- *File Screening Management*—Create file screens for volumes and folders to prevent users from storing certain types of files in a volume or folder. For example, if you set up a file screen to keep users from storing audio and video files, a user who attempts to store a blocked file sees an "Access denied" message. File screening can also be set to allow saving the screened file on the volume and sending users an email informing them of violations.

- *Storage Reports Management*—Define use thresholds on volumes and folders; any use above these thresholds generates reports on several possible storage parameters. You can save reports in a variety of formats, including HTML and text.

- *Classification Management*—Categorize files by setting classification properties on files or folders; these additional file attributes are saved as part of a file's metadata. They can be used to search for files based on a certain value or to identify files containing certain types of information. For example, a file can be classified as Sensitive, indicating that it contains information that must be handled discreetly.

- *File Management Tasks*—Use them to act on files based on classification properties and other attributes. For example, files classified as sensitive can be encrypted with EFS, or files can be archived or deleted based on their last accessed date. A host of tasks can be performed, including custom commands.

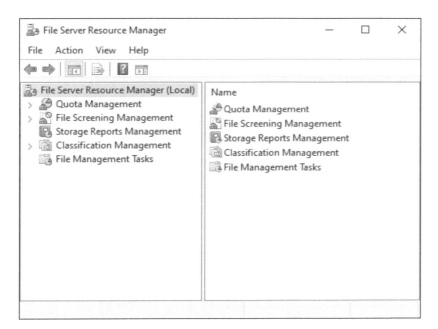

Figure 10-32   The File Server Resource Manager

FSRM Quotas

Simply put, **quotas** are limits on the amount of storage that users have on a volume or in a folder. They differ from NTFS quotas, which limit a user to a specified amount of storage on a volume. Quotas can be hard or soft. **Hard quotas** prevent users from saving files if their files in the target folder already meet or exceed the quota limit. **Soft quotas** alert users when they have exceeded the quota but don't prevent users from saving files.

You can use a predefined quota template or create your own. There are several advantages to using quota templates. For example, you can apply a quota template across different volumes and folders, and a quota template can be applied to volumes and folders to assign quotas automatically to new folders or subfolders. You also have the option of applying changes to a quota to all or some of the volumes or folders that used the quota template previously. You install FSRM in Activity 10-13 and create quota templates in Activity 10-14.

Modifying Quota Templates and Monitoring Quota Use

There are two ways to modify a quota: editing the quota or editing the template from which the quota was generated. In the FSRM console, you can click Quotas under Quota Management and double-click a quota in the middle pane to edit its properties. When you do so, the template from which the quota was created remains unchanged, but the changes affect the quota applied to the folder or volume you're editing. If you change the quota limit or notification threshold and cause the threshold to be exceeded, no notifications are created for existing files. Only attempts to add new files that exceed the threshold generate a notification.

When you edit a quota template, the changes can be applied to all, some, or none of the quotas created from this template. You can configure the following settings:

- *Apply template only to derived quotas that match the original template*—The changes are applied only to quotas that haven't been changed manually since the template was applied.
- *Apply template to all derived quotas*—The template is applied to all quotas generated by the template, even if the quota was changed manually.
- *Do not apply template to derived quotas*—No changes are made to existing quotas.

Often you need to make a quick check on the status of quotas you have set up or get some details on quota use. To review their current status, go to Quota Management in the FSRM console and click Quotas. The center pane lists quotas along with the percentage used and a summary of quota settings. Select a quota in the list to see additional details, including peak use, peak time, and available space. Figure 10-33 shows an example of this simple report.

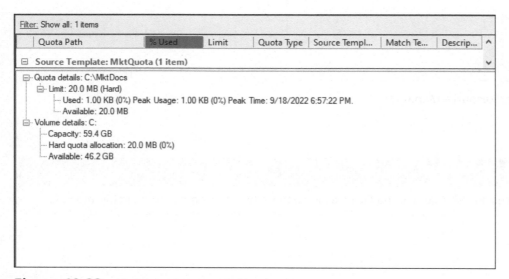

Figure 10-33   Viewing quota use information

Using File Screens

Sometimes it's better not to allow storing certain types of files on a server, even if there's enough space. For example, you might not want users storing their MP3 and video libraries on the company file servers or storing executable files on server shares. **File screens** enable you to monitor and control the types of files allowed on the server. FSRM includes file screen templates you can use as is or as a starting point for more detailed file screens.

To begin controlling the types of files stored on servers, you need to create and apply a file screen. There are two types of file screens. **Active screening** prevents users from saving unauthorized files, and **passive screening** simply monitors and notifies when unauthorized files are saved.

Unfortunately, global restrictions often interfere with real business needs. You can use file screen exceptions, however, to restrict general file types yet allow certain files or folders for special cases. For example, audio and video files might be blocked, but the Human Resources Department might need to show a training video to employees. To create a file screen exception, follow these steps:

1. In the left pane of the File Server Resource Manager console, right-click File Screening Management and click Create File Screen Exception to open the Create File Screen Exception dialog box.
2. Enter the exception path in the text box. The exception applies to the folder you specify and all its subfolders. Then select the file groups to exclude from screening. If necessary, you can create a new file group by clicking Create. When you're finished, click OK to close the dialog box.

To create a file screen template, you follow the same procedure as you do for creating a file screen, but you click Create File Screen Template in the FSRM console. All the options are the same as for creating a file screen, except that you enter a name for the template and don't specify a file screen path.

File Groups

A **file group** is a list of the types of files that define a file screen. For example, you can choose the Compressed Files file group to create a file screen. FSRM includes predefined file groups that should meet most needs, but you might need to create custom file groups or create exceptions to your file screens. To create custom file groups, expand File Screening Management in the left pane of the File Server Resource Manager console and click File Groups. In the center pane, you see a list of predefined file groups. Then follow these steps:

1. In the Actions pane, click Create File Group or right-click File Groups in the left pane and click Create File Group.
2. The Create File Group Properties dialog box opens (see Figure 10-34). Type a name for the file group.
3. In the "Files to include" section, you can add specific filenames or filename patterns by using the * wildcard character (for example, *.mp4 or tmp*.*). After typing an entry, click the Add button to add it to the list. You can add as many filenames as you want.
4. Follow the same procedure in the "Files to exclude" section. After you have entered all the files or file types, click OK to close the dialog box.

Figure 10-34   Creating a custom file group

Exam Tip ✔

The AZ-800 exam objectives expect you to understand how to configure File Server Resource Manager quotas and file screens. There are additional features in FSRM, such as storage reports, file classification management, and file management tasks, but those features are beyond the scope of this book.

Self-Check Questions

11. You can create quotas on folders using Windows File Explorer. True or False?

a. True

b. False

12. If you want to prevent users from saving specific file types to a Windows server, what feature should you use?

a. Hard quotas

b. Active screening

c. Soft quotas

d. Deny permission

○ Check your answers at the end of this module.

Activity 10-13

Installing the File Server Resource Manager Role Service

Time Required: 10 minutes

Objective: Install the File Server Resource Manager role service.

Required Tools and Equipment: ServerSA1

Description: Install the File Server Resource Manager role service and explore some of its features.

1. Log on to ServerSA1 as **Administrator**, if necessary.
2. Open Server Manager and start the Add Roles and Features Wizard. In the Server Roles window, click to expand **File and Storage Services** and **File and iSCSI Services**. Click to select **File Server Resource Manager**. Install the role service with the default settings.
3. After the installation is finished, click **Tools** and then **File Server Resource Manager** in Server Manager.
4. In the left pane, click to expand **Quota Management**. You see two nodes: Quotas and Quota Templates. You use the Quotas node to create custom quotas for folders or volumes. You can also create predefined quotas from the Quota Templates node.
5. In the left pane, click to expand **File Screening Management**. You create file screens to restrict the types of files that users can store on your servers. There are predefined templates for this feature, too.
6. In the left pane, click **Storage Reports Management**. You can create reports for duplicate files, large files, least recently used files, quota use, and many more criteria.
7. In the left pane, click to expand **Classification Management**. You see the Classification Properties and Classification Rules nodes. Click **Classification Properties** to see three predefined classification properties for folders. For files, you create your own properties by clicking Create Local Property in the Actions pane. You can also create classification rules to specify which files the classification properties should be applied to and when.
8. In the left pane, click **File Management Tasks**. You create new file management tasks based on file classification properties and other file attributes.
9. Leave the File Server Resource Manager console open if you're continuing to the next activity.

Activity 10-14

Creating and Applying a Quota Template

Time Required: 10 minutes

Objective: Configure a quota template and apply it to a folder.

Required Tools and Equipment: ServerSA1

Description: In this activity, you configure a quota template and apply it to a folder. You then test the quota and quota notifications by copying files to the folder.

(continues)

Activity 10-14 Continued

1. Sign in to ServerSA1 as **Administrator** and open the File Server Resource Manager console, if necessary.
2. Click to expand **Quota Management**, if necessary. Click **Quota Templates** to see the list of defined templates in the middle pane. Right-click **Quota Templates** and click **Create Quota Template**.
3. In the next dialog box, notice that you can copy settings from an existing template by clicking the Copy button. Type **MktQuota** in the Template name text box and **Quota for Marketing Share** in the Description text box.
4. Set the space limit to **20 MB**. This amount of storage is small by today's standards, but it's suitable for this example. Leave the default option **Hard quota**. See Figure 10-35.

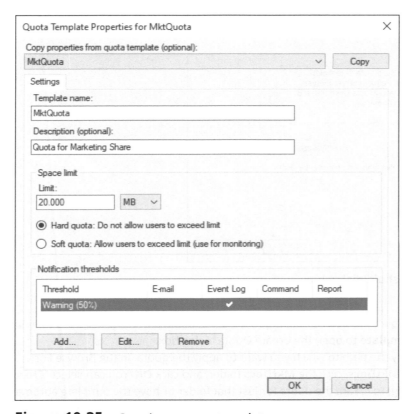

Figure 10-35   Creating a quota template

5. Click the **Add** button to add a notification threshold. In this dialog box, you can generate notifications when the folder or volume use reaches a certain percentage of the quota limit. In the E-mail Message tab, you can send an email to administrators, the user who exceeded the threshold, or both. You can customize the message by adding text with variables, as you can see in Figure 10-36. If you enable any of the email options, the server must be configured with an SMTP email server.
6. Click the **Event Log** tab. Here you can specify the creation of a warning event, which you can customize much like the notification message in the previous step. The event is created in the Application log with event ID 12325 and event source SRMSVC. You view this log with Event Viewer. In the "Generate notifications when usage reaches (%)" text box, type **50**, and click **Send warning to event log** to enable event notifications.
7. Click the **Command** tab, where you can specify that a command or script should run when the threshold is exceeded. For example, you could specify a script that deletes all temporary files.
8. Click the **Report** tab. You can specify how to generate a storage report if the threshold is exceeded and how to email reports to selected administrators, users who exceeded the threshold, or both. Click **Cancel** to return to the previous dialog box. Note that you can create multiple notification thresholds, each with its own notification messages and events. Click **OK**.

(continues)

Activity 10-14 Continued

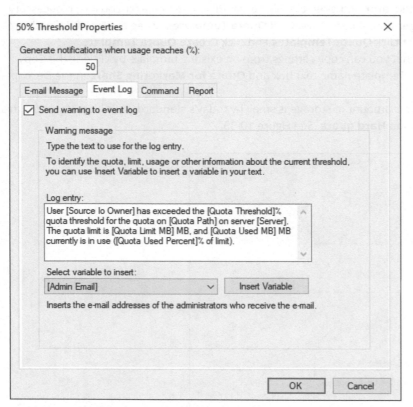

Figure 10-36   The Add Threshold dialog box

9. Now that you have a custom template, you can create a quota from it. Right-click the **MktQuota** template and click **Create Quota from Template** to open the Create Quota dialog box.

10. Click the **Browse** button to specify the path to which you want to apply the quota. In the Browse For Folder dialog box, navigate to **C:\MktDocs**, click the **MktDocs** folder, and click **OK**. You can select "Create quota on path" (the default setting) to create the quota for just that folder or have the template automatically applied to the existing folder and any new subfolders. If you wanted to create a custom quota, you could select "Define custom quota properties." Leave the default settings, as shown in Figure 10-37, and click **Create**.

11. To test the quota, open File Explorer and navigate to **C:\Windows\System32**. Find the **wmp.dll** file, which is a little more than 111 MB, and copy it. (If you can't find this file, another file between 10 and 20 MB will do.) Navigate to **C:\MktDocs** and paste the file. You should have just exceeded the 50 percent threshold. You'll see whether an event was generated in a moment.

12. Rename the file **wmp.dll** to **abc.dll** and paste the wmp.dll file again in the **MktDocs** folder. You see a message that there's not enough disk space in the MktDocs folder, so click **Cancel**. Close File Explorer.

13. In Server Manager, click **Tools** and then **Event Viewer**. Click to expand **Windows Logs** and click **Application**. You should see the warning event with event ID 12325 and event source SRMSVC. Double-click the event to read the details. Click **Close** and close Event Viewer.

14. Open the File Server Resource Manager console, click **Quota Management**, and then click **Quotas**. You should see that C:\MktDocs is at approximately 55 percent of its limit. Right-click the quota for C:\MktDocs and click **Delete** to delete the quota. Click **Yes** to confirm. If you're continuing to the next activity, stay signed in and leave the File Server Resource Manager console open.

(continues)

Activity 10-14 Continued

Figure 10-37   Creating a quota from a template

Activity 10-15

Creating a File Screen

Time Required: 10 minutes
Objective: Create a file screen.
Required Tools and Equipment: ServerSA1
Description: In this activity, you create a file screen that allows you to restrict the types of files users can save in a particular folder. The file screen also alerts you if users attempt to save unauthorized files in the folder.

1. Log on to ServerSA1 as **Administrator** and open the File Server Resource Manager console, if necessary.
2. Click to expand **File Screening Management**, if necessary. Right-click **File Screens** and click **Create File Screen**. In the Create File Screen dialog box, type **C:\MktDocs** in the "File screen path" text box.
3. In the "How do you want to configure file screen properties?" section, the default option enables you to select an existing template. Click the **Define custom file screen properties** option button (see Figure 10-38), and then click the **Custom Properties** button.
4. In the File Screen Properties dialog box, click the **Settings** tab, if necessary. Here you choose active screening or passive screening and select the file groups to block. Accept the default setting, **Active screening**, and click the **Compressed Files** check box in the list of file groups (see Figure 10-39).
5. Click the remaining tabs: **E-mail Message**, **Event Log**, **Command**, and **Report**. You see options similar to the ones available for creating quotas. In the Event Log tab, click to select the **Send warning to event log** option, and then click **OK**. Click **Create** to create the file screen for the MktDocs folder.
6. If you want, you can save a template based on the screen you've created. For this activity, however, click **Save the custom file screen without creating a template** and then click **OK**.

(continues)

Activity 10-15 Continued

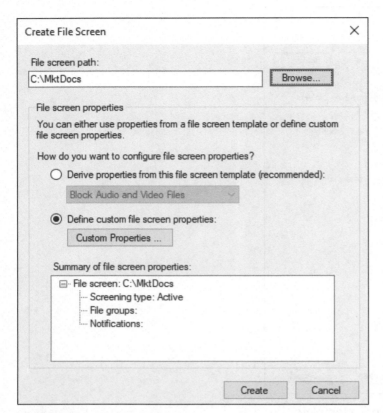

Figure 10-38 The Create File Screen dialog box

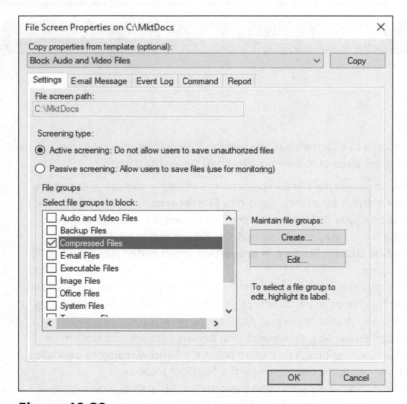

Figure 10-39 Setting custom properties for a file screen

(continues)

Activity 10-15 Continued

7. To test the file screen, open File Explorer and navigate to the **C:\MktDocs** folder. Your file screen prevents storing compressed files, which includes zipped files. Select the file you copied to the folder from the last activity, right-click it, point to **Send to**, and click **Compressed (zipped) folder**. In the message "File not found or no read permission," click **OK**. It's not the most enlightening error message, but it lets you know you can't create the file, so the file screen works.

8. Open Event Viewer from Server Manager, click **Windows Logs**, and then click **Application**. Verify that a warning event was generated based on the attempt to save a compressed file in the MktDocs folder. It will have Event ID 8215.

9. Close File Server Resource Manager. If you're continuing to the next activity, stay signed in.

Using Distributed File System

Microsoft Exam AZ-800:

Manage storage and file services.

- Configure and manage Windows Server file shares

A network can have any number of file servers, each with its own storage. Shares make it easy for users to access parts of this storage, but as the number of servers grows, so does the number of shares, and productivity suffers when users must try to navigate a complex maze of server names and share names. **Distributed File System (DFS)** is a role service under the File and Storage Services role that enables you to group shares from different servers into a single logical share called a **namespace**. Users see each namespace as a share with subfolders, giving them access to files that are actually stored on different servers. The DFS Namespaces role service is used to create and manage these logical shares.

DFS has four main components, shown in Figure 10-40:

- *Namespace server*—A **namespace server** is a Windows server with the DFS Namespaces role service installed.

- *Namespace root*—The **namespace root** is a folder that's the logical starting point for a namespace. It contains one or more folders or folder targets but no files. To access it, you use a UNC path, such as \\Domain1\AllShares or \\DFSServer\AllShares. In Figure 10-40, AllShares is the name of the namespace root. The domain name is used in the UNC path for a domain-based namespace; the server name is used for a standalone namespace. (Domain-based and standalone namespaces are discussed later in the "Creating a Namespace" section.)

- *Folder*—A folder can be used to organize the namespace without containing any actual files, or a folder can contain one or more folder targets. A folder without folder targets simply adds structure to the namespace hierarchy. For example, a folder named Marketing Docs might contain one or more folders with folder targets that are shared folders containing files for the Marketing Department. In Figure 10-40, Share1 and Share2 are folders, and both contain folder targets.

- *Folder target*—A **folder target** is a UNC path that points to a shared folder hosted on a server. A folder can have one or more folder targets. If there's more than one folder target, the files are usually replicated between servers to provide fault tolerance. In Figure 10-40, the folder target for Share1 is \\Server1\Share1, and for Share2, it's \\Server2\Share2. The folder names can be the same as the share name, but they don't have to be.

In Figure 10-40, the two client computers need to know only the name of the namespace server (or the domain name) and the DFS root folder to access Share1 and Share2, even though the shares are actually hosted on Server1 and Server2.

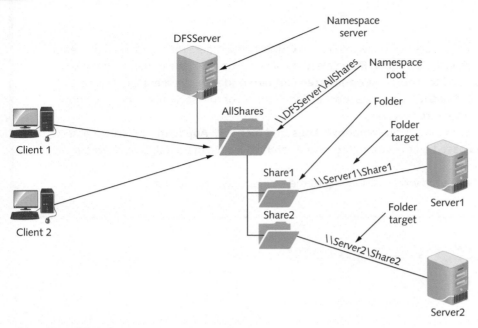

Figure 10-40 Namespace organization

Increasing ease of access, however, increases the consequences of file loss (because more users have access to files) and means files must be more available throughout an organization. Increased loads mean servers might go down, which could make the files stored on them inaccessible to users. One way to help ensure reliable access to files is to use **replication** to make copies of files in different locations, as shown in Figure 10-41. In this figure, the shares are replicated between the two file servers, so if either server becomes unavailable, the files in the shares are still accessible through the other server. There are several ways to use DFS replication, including replicating the entire DFS namespace. In this example, the DFS Replication role service must be installed on Server1 and Server2.

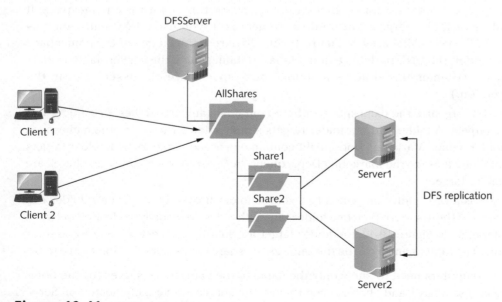

Figure 10-41 DFS replication

Combining these two server roles makes it possible to set up access to files in easy-to-access logical groups and maintain copies of critical files to minimize loss and downtime in case of a server failure. You can also configure them to work together to provide failover and help ensure continuous access for users.

Note 19

DFS replication isn't designed to be a substitute for regular backups, but it can be used to enhance backup effectiveness and efficiency. For example, files can be replicated to a central location where a single backup can be done.

Installing and Configuring DFS

To use DFS namespaces and replication, you must install the DFS Namespaces and DFS Replication role services. In the Add Roles and Features Wizard, these role services are under the File and Storage Services role and the File and iSCSI Services role service. To install DFS Namespaces and DFS Replication using PowerShell, run the following cmdlets in a PowerShell window:

```
Install-WindowsFeature FS-DFS-Namespace -IncludeManagementTools
Install-WindowsFeature FS-DFS-Replication -IncludeManagementTools
```

After installing the two role services, you can manage your namespaces and replication using DFS Management or a number of PowerShell cmdlets. To see a list of PowerShell cmdlets for managing the DFS namespace, use the cmdlet `Get-Command -Module DFSN`. To see a list of PowerShell cmdlets for managing DFS replication, use the cmdlet `Get-Command -Module DFSR`.

Creating a Namespace

After the DFS Namespaces role service is installed, you can begin creating namespaces. Remember, a namespace doesn't actually contain the shares or any files; instead, it's a list of pointers to the shares referred to in the namespace. Review Figure 10-40; the Namespace server doesn't actually host the shares but contains pointers to the shares residing on other servers. To users, however, all the shares appear to reside in one place.

Note 20

The server that hosts the namespace can host some of the shares contained in the namespace.

There are two types of namespaces: domain-based and standalone. The type you choose depends on several factors: whether you're using Active Directory, the availability requirements of the namespace, the number of folders needed in a namespace, and the need for access-based enumeration. Access-based enumeration is a feature of the Windows file system that allows users to see only files and folders in a File Explorer window or in a listing of files from the dir command to which they have been given at least read (or equivalent) permission.

A namespace must be stored somewhere on the network, and the type of namespace determines the storage location. A domain-based namespace enables you to increase its availability by using multiple namespace servers in the same domain. This namespace type doesn't include the server name in the namespace, making it easier to replace a namespace server or move the namespace to a different server. A standalone namespace stores information only on the server where it's created and includes the server name in the namespace. If this server becomes unavailable, the namespace becomes unavailable, too. However, you can improve the availability of a standalone namespace by creating it on a failover cluster.

In organizations with different types of users (for example, mobile and guest users in addition to regular users) and a wide variety of documents and media with varying degrees of sensitivity, being able to control file permissions is crucial. File security in DFS namespaces is managed via the same permissions as those for standard files and folders: share permissions and NTFS permissions. As a general rule, adjusting permissions on shares before configuring DFS is best. However, if multiple servers and folder targets are used with DFS replication, permissions on files and folders are replicated by DFS. During namespace creation, you can specify basic permission settings or set custom permissions that apply to the entire namespace (see Figure 10-42).

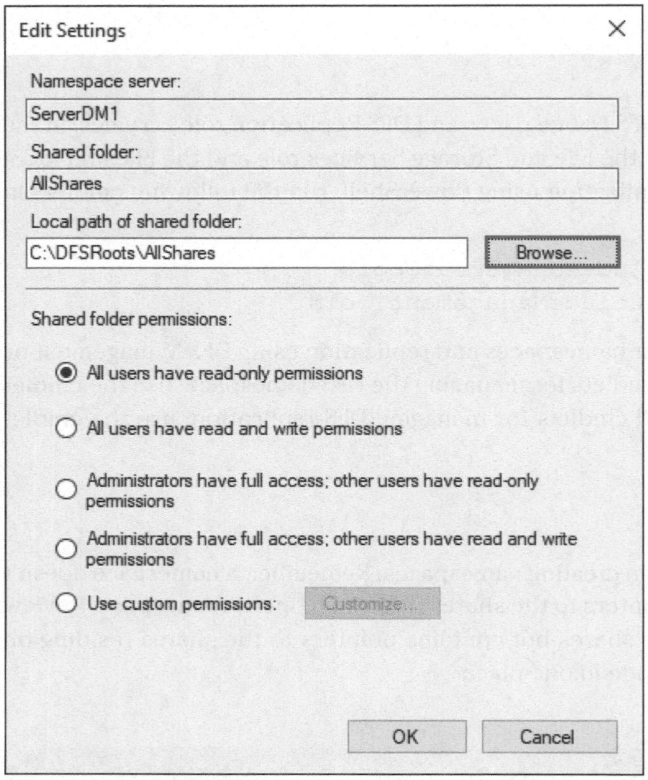

Figure 10-42   Setting namespace permissions

Standalone namespaces in Windows Server 2022 can support up to 50,000 folders and access-based enumeration. The maximum number of folders and support for access-based enumeration depend on whether you choose Windows Server 2008 mode or Windows 2000 Server mode. Windows Server 2008 mode is available if the domain uses the Windows Server 2008 (or later) functional level and if all the namespace servers are running Windows Server 2008 or later. If you choose Windows 2000 Server mode, domain-based namespaces are limited to 5000 folders and don't support access-based enumeration. During namespace creation, you choose the type of namespace you want to create and whether Windows Server 2008 mode is enabled. The latter option is enabled by default (see Figure 10-43).

After a namespace is created, you add folders to the namespace. The folders can be existing shares or you can create new folders and shares from the DFS Management console. To create new folders, click New Folder in the Actions pane to open the New Folder dialog box. You give the folder a name and add one or more folder targets (see Figure 10-44). A folder target is specified using UNC path syntax. You can select an existing share as the folder target or create new shares on remote servers or the local server. In Figure 10-44, a new folder named Marketing was created with a target of \\ServerDM2\MktgDocs. If you specify multiple folder targets for a folder, you would do so for fault tolerance or load sharing and you would want the folder targets to reside on different servers.

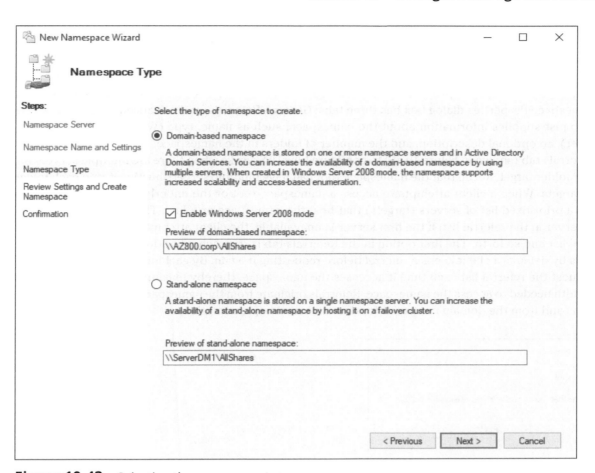

Figure 10-43   Selecting the namespace type

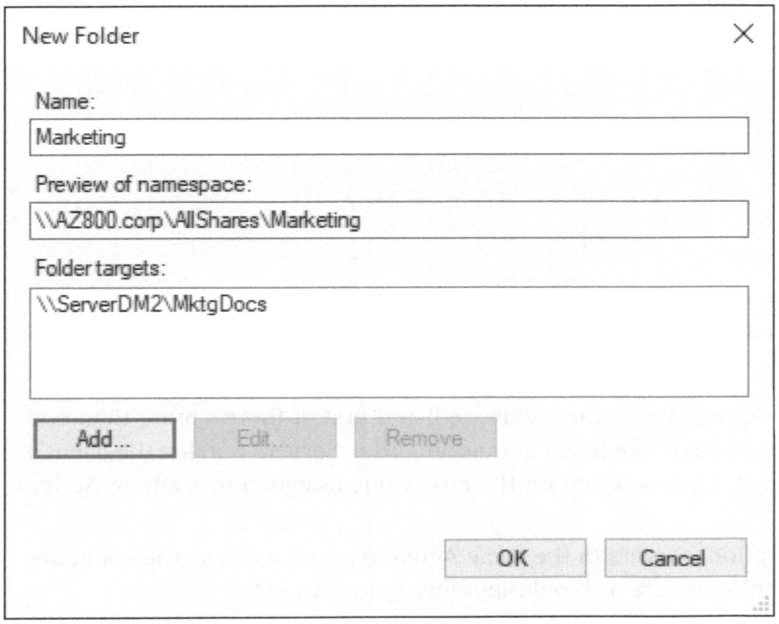

Figure 10-44   Creating a new folder for a namespace

Configuring Referrals and Advanced Namespace Settings

A simple DFS namespace with a single server for hosting the namespace and a single folder target for each folder might not require more configuration. However, if you want to add fault tolerance and load sharing to a DFS namespace, you might want to configure the namespace's properties. To do so, right-click the namespace in DFS Management and click Properties. The namespace Properties dialog box has three tabs: General, Referrals, and Advanced.

The General tab just supplies information about the namespace, such as name, type (Windows Server 2008 or Windows 2000 Server), an optional description, and the number of folders in the namespace.

You use the Referrals tab (shown in Figure 10-45) to configure how DFS works when there are multiple servers for a namespace root or folder target. Recall that the namespace root can have multiple servers hosting it, and each folder can have multiple targets. When a client attempts to access a namespace root or the underlying folders, it receives a **referral**, which is a prioritized list of servers (targets) that host the namespace or folder. The client then attempts to access the first server in the referral list. If the first server is unavailable, the client attempts to access the second server in the referral list and so forth. The first option in the Referrals tab is the cache duration, which is the amount of time (300 seconds by default) a client keeps a referral before requesting it again. By caching the referral, the client doesn't have to request the referral list each time it accesses the namespace, thereby maximizing access speed and reducing the bandwidth needed to access the namespace. Referrals originate from the namespace server for standalone DFS implementations and from the domain controller for domain-based implementations.

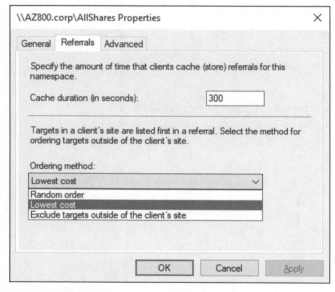

Figure 10-45   Configuring referral settings for a namespace

The next option is the ordering method, which determines the order in which servers are listed in a referral. This option can be set to the following values:

- *Lowest cost*—Servers in the same Active Directory site as the client are listed first. If there's more than one server in the site, servers in the same site as the client are listed in random order. Servers outside the client's site are listed from lowest cost to highest cost. Cost is based on the cost value assigned to a site in Active Directory Sites and Services.

- *Random order*—Similar to the Lowest cost option, servers in the same Active Directory site as the client are listed first. However, servers outside the client's site are ordered randomly, ignoring cost.

- *Exclude targets outside of the client's site*—The referral contains only servers in the same site as the client. If there are no servers in the client's site, the client can't access the requested part of the namespace. This method can be used to ensure that low-bandwidth connections, such as virtual private networks (VPNs), can't access shares containing large files.

The last option in the Referrals tab, under the Ordering method list box, is "Clients fail back to preferred targets." (This list box is not shown in Figure 10-45 because it is covered by the full list of options in the Ordering method list.) The option is important only if referral order has been overridden in the properties of the namespace server or folder target, which essentially configures a preferred target. If the option is selected and the preferred server fails, the client chooses another server from the referral list. If the preferred server comes back online, the client begins using it again.

The Advanced tab has options for configuring polling and access-based enumeration (see Figure 10-46). When namespaces change, changes are reflected instantly in a standalone namespace. If a domain-based namespace changes, however, information must be relayed to all the namespace servers. Namespace changes are first reported to the server in the domain that holds the PDC emulator Flexible Single Master Operation (FSMO) role. Recall that PDC stands for *primary domain controller*. The PDC emulator then replicates this information to all other domain controllers.

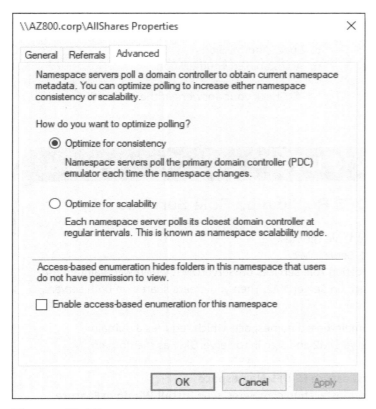

Figure 10-46   Namespace settings for polling and access-based enumeration

By default, namespace servers poll the PDC emulator to get the most current information for a namespace. In DFS configurations with many namespace servers, polling can place a considerable load on the PDC emulator. The more namespace servers there are in a domain, the larger the load on the PDC emulator because of increased polling. If necessary, you can configure polling options to reduce the load on the PDC emulator:

- *Optimize for consistency*—This setting is the default. In a domain with 16 or fewer namespace servers, this method is preferred because namespace servers poll the PDC emulator, which is the first DC updated after a namespace change.
- *Optimize for scalability*—This setting causes namespace servers to poll the nearest DC for namespace changes. This setting reduces the load on the PDC emulator but should be used only when there are more than the recommended 16 namespace servers in the domain. Because there's a delay between the PDC emulator getting a namespace update and the other DCs receiving it, users might have an inconsistent view of a namespace.

The last option in the Advanced tab is for enabling access-based enumeration for the namespace. Making sure only authorized users have access to sensitive data is a concern in most organizations. Restricting permissions on files and folders certainly helps, but to improve security, you can enable access-based enumeration to prevent users from even seeing files and folders they don't have permission to access.

Self-Check Questions

13. The namespace root in DFS is the server that has the DFS Namespaces role service installed. True or False?

    a. True

    b. False

14. Which Windows file system feature allows users to see only files and folders to which they have at least read permission?

    a. Namespace restricting

    b. File screens

    c. Special permissions

    d. Access-based enumeration

⊙ Check your answers at the end of this module.

Activity 10-16

Installing the DFS Namespaces and DFS Replication Role Services

Time Required: 10 minutes

Objective: Install the DFS Namespaces and DFS Replication role services.

Required Tools and Equipment: ServerDC1, ServerDM1, ServerDM2

Description: Install the DFS Namespaces and DFS Replication role services on ServerDM1, which will maintain the namespace, and install just the DFS Replication role service on ServerDM2. Then you create shares on both servers, which will be used in the next activity.

1. Start ServerDC1 because you will be creating a domain-based namespace, which requires a domain controller to be available. Start ServerDM1 and ServerDM2 and sign in to ServerDM1 as the domain **Administrator**.

2. Open a PowerShell window, type **Install-WindowsFeature FS-DFS-Namespace -IncludeManagementTools**, and press **Enter**. After installation completes, type **Install-WindowsFeature FS-DFS-Replication** and press **Enter**.

3. Create a new folder named AcctDocs on ServerDM1 by typing **New-Item c:\AcctDocs -Type Directory** and press **Enter**. Share the folder by typing **New-SmbShare -Name Accounting -Path c:\AcctDocs -FullAccess Administrators -ReadAccess Everyone** and press **Enter**.

4. Open a remote PowerShell session with ServerDM2 by typing **Enter-PSSession ServerDM2** and press **Enter**. Type **Install-WindowsFeature FS-DFS-Replication** and press **Enter**.

5. Create a new folder named MktDocs on ServerDM2 by typing **New-Item C:\MktDocs -Type Directory** and press **Enter**. Share the folder by typing **New-SmbShare -Name Marketing -Path c:\MktDocs -FullAccess Administrators -ReadAccess Everyone** and press **Enter**.

6. Type **Exit-PSSession** and press **Enter**. Continue to the next activity.

Activity 10-17

Creating a Domain-Based Namespace

Time Required: 15 minutes

Objective: Create a domain-based namespace and add shares to it.

Required Tools and Equipment: ServerDC1, ServerDM1, ServerDM2

Description: Use DFS to create a domain-based namespace, and then add several shares from ServerDM1 and ServerDM2 to this namespace. The new namespace allows users to access shared folders from a single location without needing to know the server where the files are stored.

1. Start ServerDC1, ServerDM1, and ServerDM2, if necessary. Sign in to ServerDM1 as the domain **Administrator**, if necessary. Open Server Manager, click **Tools**, and click **DFS Management** from the menu to open the DFS Management console.

2. In the Actions pane, click **New Namespace** to start the New Namespace Wizard.

3. In the Namespace Server window, type **ServerDM1** to specify the server hosting the new namespace, and then click **Next**.

4. In the Namespace Name and Settings window, you specify the name of the namespace you're creating. Type **AllShares** in the Name text box. Users will access the namespace by using the UNC path \\AZ800\ AllShares or \\ServerDM1\AllShares. Click the **Edit Settings** button to change the shared folder location and permissions. By default, the namespace is located at C:\DFSRoots*Namespace* (with *Namespace* representing the name of the namespace). All users have read-only permission by default. You can choose any of the predefined permission settings or create custom permissions. Leave the default settings and click **OK** to close the Edit Settings dialog box. Click **Next** to continue.

5. In the Namespace Type window, you choose a domain-based or standalone namespace. Both types show a preview of the namespace's full name. Notice that for a domain-based type, the name starts with the domain name, and for a standalone type, it starts with the server name. Leave the default settings **Domain-based namespace** and **Enable Windows Server 2008 mode**, and then click **Next**.

6. Verify the settings in the Review Settings and Create Namespace window. (If necessary, you can click the Previous button to change a setting.) If everything is correct, click **Create**.

7. In the Confirmation window, you should see a message indicating success. Click **Close**.

8. In the DFS Management console, click to expand **Namespaces** in the left pane, and then click the **AZ800.corp\AllShares** namespace you created. In the middle pane, you see four tabs. The Namespace tab shows the shares that are members of the new namespace. Because you haven't added any shares, it's empty. Click the **Namespace Servers** tab to see the servers configured with the namespace. More than one server can be configured with the same namespace to provide fault tolerance and load balancing.

9. Now it's time to add some folders to the namespace. You can add existing folders and shares or create new ones. Click the **Namespace** tab. In the Actions pane, click **New Folder**. In the New Folder dialog box, type **Accounting** in the Name text box. This name is what users see when they connect to the namespace; the name can be different from the actual share name. Click **Add**.

10. In the Add Folder Target dialog box, you can enter the folder target with its UNC name or click the Browse button and select the folder target. Click **Browse**.

11. In the Browse for Shared Folders dialog box, the shares on the current server are listed. You can click Browse to choose a different server, select an existing share on the current server, or create a new shared folder. Click **Accounting**, the share you created in Step 9, and click **OK**. Click **OK** again.

12. Back in the New Folder dialog box, notice that the UNC path to the Accounting share is added to the Folder targets list. You can add folder targets to provide fault tolerance. Click **OK**.

13. Now add the share from ServerDM2. Click **New Folder** again in the Actions pane of the DFS Management console. Type **Marketing** in the Name text box and click **Add**. Click **Browse**. In the Browse for Shared Folders dialog box, type **ServerDM2** and click **Show Shared Folders**.

(continues)

Activity 10-17 Continued

14. In the Shared Folders box, click **Marketing** if necessary, and then click **OK**. Click **OK** twice more to return to the DFS Management console, which should now look like Figure 10-47 with both shares listed in the Namespace tab.

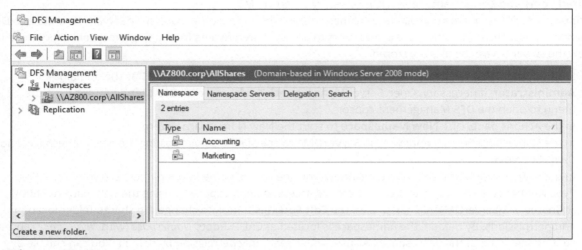

Figure 10-47   A namespace with two shares

15. To see how users would use this feature, right-click **Start**, click **Run**, type **\\AZ800\AllShares**, and press **Enter**. You see both shares, Accounting and Marketing, in File Explorer. Users could also enter the name of the server hosting the namespace, \\ServerDM1\AllShares. A drive letter can be mapped to the namespace, too.

16. Close all open windows and continue to the next activity.

> **Note 21**
>
> Installing the DFS Namespaces role service on ServerDM2 isn't required; a share can be added to a namespace from any server in the domain. Only ServerDM1 requires the DFS Namespaces role service because it's hosting the namespace.

Using BranchCache

Microsoft Exam AZ-800:

Manage storage and file services.
- Configure and manage Windows Server file shares

Sharing files across a WAN link can be slow and sometimes expensive. Organizations with branch offices can solve some problems of sharing files across WAN links by placing traditional file servers in branch offices and using file replication to synchronize files between branch offices and the main office. However, this solution requires servers and someone to maintain servers and file shares, which isn't always practical or economical. **BranchCache** is a file-sharing technology that allows computers at a branch office to cache files retrieved from a central server across a WAN link. When a computer in the branch office requests a file for the first time, it's retrieved from a server in the main office and then cached locally. When a subsequent request for the file is made, only content information is transferred from the server hosting the original file, not actual file contents. This **content information** indicates to the client where the file can be retrieved from the cache in the branch office. The content information that's transferred is very small compared with the original file contents; it can also be used by clients to secure cached information so that it can be accessed only by authorized users.

BranchCache supports content stored on Windows Server 2008 R2 and later servers running the following roles and protocols:

- *File Server role*—A file server sharing files by using the Server Message Block (SMB) protocol
- *Web Server (IIS) role*—A web server using the HTTP or HTTPS protocol
- *Background Intelligent Transfer Service (BITS) feature*—An application server running on a Windows server with BITS installed

BranchCache has two modes of operation, so you can configure it depending on the resources available at a branch office:

- *Distributed*—With **distributed cache mode**, cached data is distributed among client computers in the branch office. Client computers must be running Windows 7 or a later version.
- *Hosted*—With **hosted cache mode**, cached data is stored on one or more file servers in the branch office. Servers operating in this mode must be running Windows Server 2008 R2 or later, and clients must be running Windows 7 or later.

If you have more than one branch office, you can choose the mode that's suitable for each office, but only one mode can be used at each branch office. Figure 10-48 shows a central office with a connection to two branch offices using different BranchCache modes. In the figure, Branch office 1 uses hosted cache mode, in which client PCs access a central BranchCache server to retrieve cached files. Branch office 2 uses distributed cache mode, in which cached files are distributed among all client computers, which retrieve the files from one another. In this case, the content information retrieved from servers in the main office specifies which computer hosts a requested file.

Distributed cache mode is the best solution for small branch offices when having a dedicated server is neither practical nor desirable. Servers require more expertise to maintain and secure and have a higher cost than client computers. When using BranchCache in distributed cache mode, no extra equipment and no additional resources or personnel for server maintenance are necessary.

Hosted cache mode is best for branch offices that already have servers performing other functions, such as a domain controller or a DHCP server. Using hosted cache mode has the following advantages over distributed cache mode:

- *Increased availability of cached files*—In distributed cache mode, if the client that cached the file is turned off, the file is unavailable to other clients. With hosted cache mode, all cached files are stored on servers, which are rarely turned off.
- *Support for multiple subnets*—A larger branch office might have more than one IP subnet. Distributed cache mode works only in a single subnet, so files cached by computers on one subnet aren't available to computers on another subnet. Hosted cached mode works across subnets, so files cached by a server on one subnet are available to client computers on all subnets. You can also deploy multiple servers operating in hosted cache mode, and clients are directed to the server hosting the requested file, even if it's on a different subnet from the client.

When a change is made to a cached file, clients that access the file after the change has occurred must have a way to access the changed content. The fact that a file has changed is reflected in the content information clients retrieve from the server hosting the original file. There are two versions of the content information. Version 1 content information is the original version supported by Windows Server 2008 R2 and later versions and by Windows 7 and later versions. Version 2 content information is supported by Windows Server 2012 and later versions and by Windows 8 and later versions.

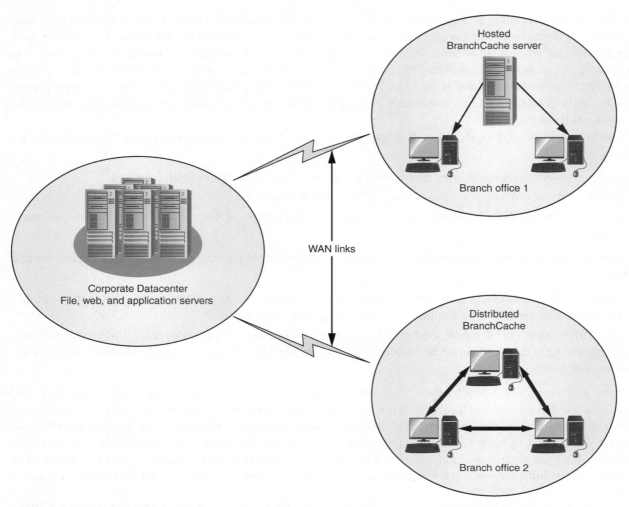

Figure 10-48 BranchCache modes of operation

When a file is changed, some or all of it must be retrieved from the server hosting the original content. With version 1 content information, changes made to a file require the client to retrieve the entire file, starting with the part that changed. With version 2, only the changed part of the file must be retrieved, which saves bandwidth because fewer bytes must be transferred across the WAN link. Version 2 content information can be used only when all devices involved in BranchCache support version 2; otherwise, version 1 is used. This means that the client requesting the file, the local hosted cache server, and the server hosting the original content must all use Windows 8, Windows Server 2012, or a later version of either in order to use version 2 content information.

Note 22

With distributed cache mode, clients using different content information versions can't share cached files with each other.

Installing and Configuring BranchCache

The procedure to install and configure BranchCache depends on the type of content you want to cache and whether you're using hosted or distributed cache mode, as shown in Table 10-4.

Table 10-4   BranchCache installation

Content type	Installed on content server	Hosted cache mode	Distributed cache mode
File server using the SMB protocol	BranchCache for Network Files role service	BranchCache feature on hosting server	Enable BranchCache on client
Web server using HTTP or HTTPS	BranchCache feature	BranchCache feature on hosting server	Enable BranchCache on client
Application server using BITS	BranchCache feature	BranchCache feature on hosting server	Enable BranchCache on client

Note 23

In all cases, BranchCache must be enabled on client computers, whether you're using hosted or distributed cache mode. After you enable BranchCache, you select the cache mode you want the client to use. If no mode is selected, the client uses only locally cached files.

Installing BranchCache on a File Server

To install BranchCache to cache files in shared folders, take the following steps:

1. Install the File Server role service and the BranchCache for Network Files role service on all servers that will host shared folders by using BranchCache. You can use Server Manager or the PowerShell cmdlet:

   ```
   Install-WindowsFeature FS-BranchCache
   ```

2. Configure the Hash Publication for BranchCache group policy (see Figure 10-49), which is located under Computer Configuration, Policies, Administrative Templates, Network, Lanman Server. In most cases, computer accounts for servers using BranchCache for shared folders should be placed in a separate OU in Active Directory. Then, you link a GPO with the policy configured to this OU. The hash publication is part of the content information that allows BranchCache servers to find a file that has been cached on the local servers.

3. Set the BranchCache support tag on each shared folder that should be cached. Click File and Storage Services in Server Manager and click Shares. Right-click the share and click Properties. Click to expand Settings and then click "Enable BranchCache on the file share" (highlighted in Figure 10-50). You can also enable BranchCache in the Shared Folders snap-in in the Computer Management MMC. The share is now ready to be cached with hosted or distributed cache mode.

Installing BranchCache on a Web Server or an Application Server

To install BranchCache on a web server or an application server, you just need to install the BranchCache feature in Add Roles and Features or use the PowerShell cmdlet `Install-WindowsFeature BranchCache`. The Web Server role or an application using BITS takes advantage of the BranchCache service automatically, so no additional configuration on the content server is needed.

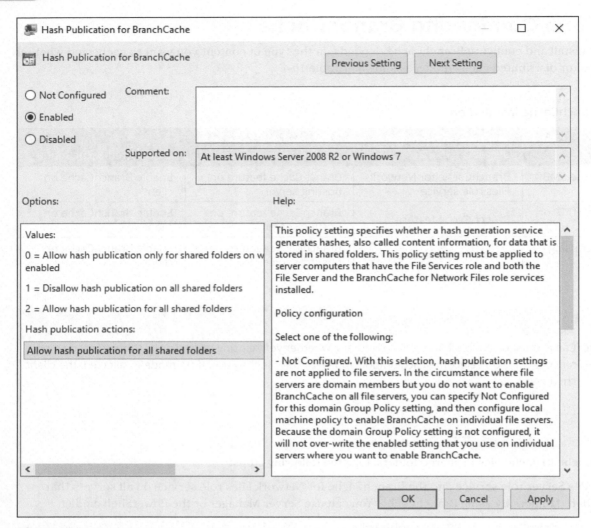

Figure 10-49   Configuring the Hash Publication for BranchCache policy

Configuring a Server for Hosted Cache Mode

If you're using BranchCache in hosted cache mode, you need to configure a server running Windows Server 2008 R2 or a later version. The hosted cache server must be trusted by BranchCache clients, so part of the process involves installing a certificate on the server that's trusted by the BranchCache client computers. This requires issuing a certificate from a Windows server configured as a certification authority (CA) or installing a certificate issued by a third-party CA. The details of working with a CA and issuing a certificate are beyond the scope of this book. The following steps outline the process for installing a hosted cache server:

1. Install the BranchCache feature by using Add Roles and Features or the PowerShell cmdlet `Install-WindowsFeature BranchCache`.
2. Import a certificate that's trusted by the branch office client computers.
3. Link the certificate to BranchCache with the `netsh HTTP ADD SSLCERT` command.
4. Configure BranchCache clients to use BranchCache in hosted cache mode.

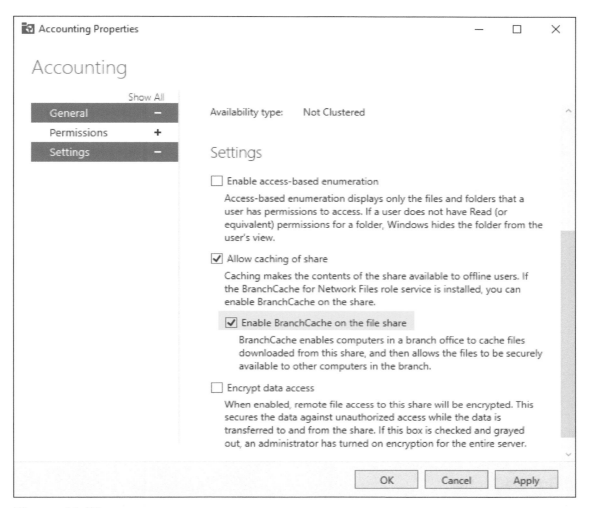

Figure 10-50   Enabling BranchCache on a share

Configuring Clients to Use BranchCache

The BranchCache client feature is built into Windows client OSs that support BranchCache, so no installation is needed. Enabling client computers to use BranchCache is a simple three-step process:

1. To enable BranchCache with a group policy, open a GPO linked to the OU where the branch office computer accounts are located. Navigate to Computer Configuration, Policies, Administrative Templates, Network, BranchCache, and then double-click the Turn on BranchCache policy. Click the Enabled option button.

2. To configure BranchCache clients to use BranchCache in hosted cache mode, open the GPO you used in Step 1 and navigate to the same location. Double-click Set BranchCache Hosted Cache mode and click the Enabled option button. Type the name of the hosted cache server under Options, as shown in Figure 10-51. The name must match the name on the certificate installed on the hosted cache server. If you're using distributed cache mode, enable the Set BranchCache Distributed Cache mode policy instead.

3. To configure Windows Firewall on client computers, use a group policy or the Windows Firewall with Advanced Security console to configure inbound rules that allow the following predefined rules:

   ○ BranchCache – Content Retrieval (uses HTTP)
   ○ BranchCache – Hosted Cache Server (uses HTTPS)
   ○ BranchCache – Peer Discovery (uses WSD): This rule is required only for distributed cache mode.

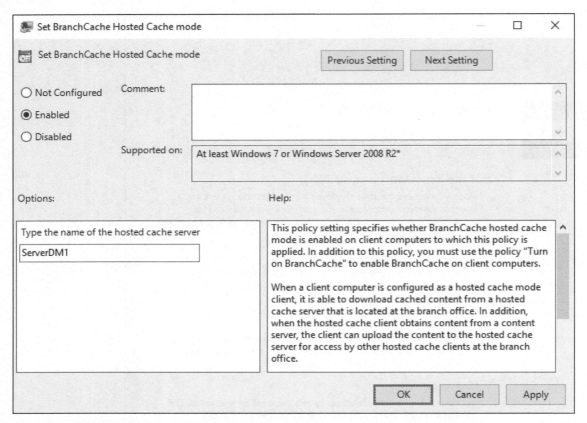

Figure 10-51   Setting BranchCache hosted mode on clients with a group policy

Troubleshooting BranchCache

BranchCache is usually reliable if the underlying network infrastructure is working well and configured correctly. However, configuration errors can occur, especially when it comes to correctly configuring Group Policy. Here are some of the issues to look out for and some of the commands you can use to verify BranchCache operation:

- Some of the BranchCache configuration relies on Windows Active Directory and Group Policy. Ensure that the policies are correctly configured and the GPOs are linked to the correct organizational units where the BranchCache server and client accounts are located.
- Verify correct certificate distribution when using hosted cache mode.
- Verify the firewall settings.
- Verify that all clients are on the same subnet as the BranchCache server.
- Ensure that the `peerdistsvc` service is running on clients and servers when running in distributed caching mode. Use `Get-Service peerdistsvc` in PowerShell.
- Make sure that all clients are using the same caching mode, that caching is enabled, and that the cache is not full. Check these items and the general status of BranchCache using `netsh branchcache show status all` or the PowerShell cmdlets `Get-BCStatus` and `Get-BCDataCache`.
- Be sure to clear application caches such as web browser caches and the Offline Files cache on file servers. In addition, clear the BranchCache cache on all clients using `netsh branchcache flush`. With PowerShell, the equivalent command is `Clear-BCCache`.

Self-Check Questions

15. With hosted mode, BranchCache cached data is stored on file servers in the branch office. True or False?

    a. True   **b.** False

16. What type of information is transferred from the server hosting a file in the main office when a request is made for a file that is already cached on a local BranchCache server?

    a. No information is transferred from the hosting server.
    b. Only changes to the original file are transferred.
    c. Only content information is transferred.
    d. The file header, attributes, and permissions are transferred.

◉ Check your answers at the end of this module.

Activity 10-18

Configuring BranchCache on a File Server

Time Required: 15 minutes
Objective: Configure BranchCache on a file server.
Required Tools and Equipment: ServerDC1, ServerDM1
Description: In this activity, you configure BranchCache on ServerDM1 and enable it on a share.

1. On ServerDM1, open a PowerShell window, type **Install-WindowsFeature FS-BranchCache**, and press **Enter**.
2. On ServerDC1, open a PowerShell window. Create an OU for BranchCache servers by typing **New-ADOrganizationalUnit BCServers** and pressing **Enter**. Move ServerDM1 to the BCServers OU by typing **Get-ADComputer ServerDM1 | Move-ADObject -TargetPath "ou=BCServers,dc=AZ800,dc=corp"** and pressing **Enter**.
3. In Server Manager, click **Tools** and then **Group Policy Management**. Click to expand the forest and domain nodes, right-click the **BCServers** OU, and click **Create a GPO in this domain, and Link it here**.
4. In the New GPO dialog box, type **BranchCache Server** in the Name text box and click **OK**.
5. Click the **BCServers** OU, if necessary. In the right pane, right-click the **BranchCache Server** GPO and click **Edit**. In the Group Policy Management Editor, navigate to **Computer Configuration**, **Policies**, **Administrative Templates**, **Network**, **Lanman Server**.
6. In the right pane, double-click **Hash Publication for BranchCache**. Click the **Enabled** option button and accept the default option **Allow hash publication for all shared folders**. Click **OK**. Close the Group Policy Management Editor and Group Policy Management console.
7. On ServerDM1, in Server Manager, click **File and Storage Services** in the left pane, and then click **Shares**. Right-click **Accounting** and click **Properties**. (You created the Accounting share in Activity 10-16.) Click to expand **Settings**. Click the **Enable BranchCache on the file share** check box, and then click **OK**. Click the **back arrow** in Server Manager twice to return to the Dashboard. BranchCache is now enabled on the server.
8. Continue to the next activity.

Activity 10-19

Configuring BranchCache on a Client

> **Note 24**
>
> Configuring BranchCache in hosted cache mode requires a certificate, so this activity configures your ServerDM1 computer to use distributed mode. There's only one computer, but you'll see how to check the status of BranchCache to know if it's working.

Time Required: 20 minutes
Objective: Configure BranchCache on a client computer with `netsh`.
Required Tools and Equipment: ServerDC1, ServerDM1, ServerDM2
Description: In this activity, you configure BranchCache on a client computer in distributed mode and test it.

1. First, you'll copy some files to the share enabled for BranchCache. On ServerDM1, open a PowerShell window, type **copy c:\windows*.exe c:\acctdocs**, and press **Enter**. It doesn't matter which files you copy; you just need some files large enough to test the cache.
2. Sign in to ServerDM2 as **Administrator**. Because ServerDM2 is a server, not a client OS, you'll first need to install the BranchCache feature. The feature is already installed on Windows clients like Windows 10 Enterprise. Open a PowerShell window, type **Install-WindowsFeature BranchCache**, and press **Enter**.
3. The BranchCache service is named peerdistsvc. Verify that the service is running by typing **Get-Service peerdistsvc** and pressing **Enter**. The Status column should report that the service is Running. Type **Enable-BCDistributed** and press **Enter** to set the mode to distributed.
4. Type **Get-BCStatus** and press **Enter**. You should see output similar to that in Figure 10-52. Type **Set-BCMinSMBLatency 0** and press **Enter** to have BranchCache cache all files, even if there's no delay in retrieving them from the file server. The default latency value is set to 80 ms.

```
PS C:\Users\Administrator> Get-BCStatus

BranchCacheIsEnabled         : True
BranchCacheServiceStatus     : Running
BranchCacheServiceStartType  : Automatic


ClientConfiguration:

    CurrentClientMode          : DistributedCache
    HostedCacheServerList      :
    HostedCacheDiscoveryEnabled : False


ContentServerConfiguration:

    ContentServerIsEnabled : True
```

Figure 10-52   Checking the status of BranchCache on a client

5. Type **copy \\ServerDM1\accounting*.exe** and press **Enter**.
6. Type **Get-BCStatus** and press **Enter**. You should see that the line beginning with "CurrentActiveCache Size" shows a number of bytes in use by the cache. If the value is still 0, wait a while and try the command again. Sometimes it takes a while for the statistics to update. Review the command output to verify that the current status is running and the firewall rules are enabled.
7. Type **PowerShell** and press **Enter**. Type **Get-BCDataCache** and press **Enter**. You see information about the cache, such as the maximum percentage of the volume used by the cache and the current use of the cache.
8. Shut down all servers.

Module Summary

- Storage is any digital medium to which data can be written and later retrieved. Long-term storage includes USB drives, SD cards, CDs/DVDs, magnetic tape, SSDs, and HDDs.

- All computers require at least some storage, but servers usually require more than client computers. Server storage is needed for OS files, page files, log files, virtual machines, database files, and user documents, among others.

- The main methods of storage access are local, DAS, NAS, and SAN. Local storage and DAS are similar, but DAS can also be a separate unit attached through an external interface. NAS is a standalone storage device with a network interface. A SAN is the most complex storage device, using high-speed networking technologies to provide shared storage.

- Configuration of local disks can be divided into two broad categories: physical disk properties and logical properties. Physical properties include disk capacity, rotation speed, and the disk interface technology. SATA and SAS are the most common disk interfaces on servers.

- Disk types include basic disks and dynamic disks. Partitioning types include MBR and GPT. Volume types are simple, spanned, striped, mirrored, and RAID 5. File systems include FAT, NTFS, and ReFS.

- Windows Server can mount virtual disks and use them like regular volumes. Virtual disks are stored as files with a .vhd or .vhdx extension.

- The File Server role service is required to share folders. You can install this role service in Server Manager or you can simply share a folder to have it installed automatically. The SMB protocol is used to access Windows file shares, but Windows also supports NFS.

- There are several ways for client computers to access shared folders: using the UNC path, doing an Active Directory search, mapping a drive, and browsing the network.

- Every recent Windows OS includes administrative shares, which are hidden shares available only to members of the Administrators group. They include Admin$, Drive$, and IPC$; on domain controllers, the NETLOGON and SYSVOL shares are added.

- Network File System (NFS) is a file-sharing protocol that allows users to access files and folders on other computers across a network. Windows Server 2022 supports an NFS server component as a role service under the File and Storage Services role and an NFS client component as a feature.

- Three types of objects can be assigned permission to access the file system: users, groups, and computers. These object types are referred to as security principals.

- Permissions are assigned in four ways: a user creates an object, a user account is added to the DACL, a group the user belongs to is added to the DACL, or permission is inherited. Effective permissions are a combination of assigned permissions.

- There are three share permissions: Read, Change, and Full control. There are six standard permissions: Read, Read & execute, List folder contents, Write, Modify, and Full control. On an NTFS or ReFS volume, permissions are set at the root of a volume first, and all folders and files in that volume inherit these settings unless configured otherwise.

- File Server Resource Manager helps manage file servers through the use of quotas (to limit how much data can be stored) and file screens (to specify what types of data can be stored).

- Quotas can be set manually or a template can be defined and applied. Hard and soft quotas can be defined to restrict creating files beyond the quota and to send a notification.

- File screens can be set manually or a template can be defined and applied. Active and passive screens can be defined to restrict creating certain types of files or to just send a notification.

- Distributed File System is a role service under the File and Storage Services role that enables you to group shares from different servers into a single logical share called a namespace. Users see each namespace as a share with subfolders, giving them access to files that are actually stored on different servers.

- DFS uses two technologies: DFS namespaces and DFS replication. They can be used together to provide fault tolerance and load balancing for files.

- DFS namespaces create a hierarchy of shared folders to provide access to shared files from a single logical reference point across an organization.
- There are two types of DFS namespaces: domain-based and standalone. Domain-based information is stored in Active Directory and namespaces are available even if server names change. Standalone information is stored on the server where it was created.
- Referrals are prioritized lists of folder targets. They can be configured by using lowest cost, using random order, and excluding targets outside the client's site.
- BranchCache is a file-sharing technology that allows computers at a branch office to cache files retrieved from a central server across a WAN link. It supports content stored on Windows Server 2008 R2 and later servers running the File Server role for SMB shares, the Web Server role, and the BITS feature.
- BranchCache has two modes of operation: distributed cache mode and hosted cache mode. Distributed cache mode is the best solution for small branch offices when having a dedicated server is neither practical nor desirable. Hosted cache mode is best for branch offices that already have servers performing other functions, such as a domain controller or a DHCP server.
- The procedure to install and configure BranchCache depends on the type of content you want to cache and whether you're using hosted or distributed cache mode.
- BranchCache is usually reliable if the underlying network infrastructure is working well and configured correctly. However, configuration errors can occur, especially when it comes to correctly configuring Group Policy.

Key Terms

access-based enumeration (ABE)
access control entry (ACE)
active screening
administrative shares
backplane
basic disk
boot volume
BranchCache
content information
direct-attached storage (DAS)
discretionary access control list (DACL)
disk drive
distributed cache mode
Distributed File System (DFS)
dynamic disk
effective access
effective permissions
explicit permission
extended partition
file and folder permissions
file group
file screen
File Server Resource Manager (FSRM)

file system
folder target
formatting
GUID Partitioning Table (GPT)
hard quotas
hosted cache mode
inherited permission
local storage
Master Boot Record (MBR)
mirrored volume
namespace
namespace root
namespace server
network-attached storage (NAS)
Network File System (NFS)
object owner
offline files
page file
partition
passive screening
permission inheritance
permissions
primary partition
quotas
RAID 5 volume

redundant array of independent disks (RAID)
referral
replication
security descriptor
security principal
Serial ATA (SATA)
serial attached SCSI (SAS)
Server Message Block (SMB)
share permissions
simple volume
small computer system interface (SCSI)
soft quotas
solid state drive (SSD)
spanned volume
storage appliance
storage area network (SAN)
striped volume
system access control list (SACL)
system volume
UNC path
virtual hard disk (VHD)
volume

Review Questions

1. Which of the following is an example of long-term storage? (Choose two.)
   a. Magnetic tape
   b. CPU cache
   c. SSD
   d. RAM

2. Which of the following is true about an SSD?
   a. Uses magnetic platters
   b. Has no moving parts
   c. Less expensive than an HDD
   d. Uses EPROM

3. Which of the following is an example of why a server uses long-term storage? (Choose three.)
   a. Page file
   b. Virtual machines
   c. Working memory
   d. Documents

4. You want shared network storage that's easy to set up and geared toward file sharing with several file-sharing protocols. What should you consider buying?
   a. SAN
   b. DAS
   c. NAS
   d. RAID

5. You have four servers that need access to shared storage because you're configuring them in a cluster. Which storage solution should you consider for this application?
   a. NAS
   b. SAN
   c. SCSI
   d. DAS

6. You have installed a new disk and created a volume on it. What should you do before you can store files on it?
   a. Format it.
   b. Partition it.
   c. Initialize it.
   d. Erase it.

7. Which disk interface technology transfers data over a parallel bus?
   a. SATA
   b. USB
   c. SAS
   d. SCSI

8. What's created automatically when you install Windows Server 2022 on a system with a disk drive that has never had an OS installed on it before?
   a. System volume
   b. Dynamic disk
   c. GPT
   d. Extended partition

9. What type of volumes or partitions can be created on a basic disk? (Choose two.)
   a. Spanned volume
   b. Striped partition
   c. Extended partition
   d. Simple volume

10. Which of the following is true about GPT disks?
    a. They support a maximum volume size of 2 TB.
    b. GPT is the default option when initializing a disk in Disk Management.
    c. They use CRC protection for the partition table.
    d. You can't convert a GPT disk to MBR.

11. You have a server with Windows Server 2022 installed on Disk 0, a basic disk. You're using the server to store users' documents. You have two more disks that you can install in the server. What should you do if you want to provide fault tolerance for users' documents?
    a. Convert Disk 0 to dynamic. Create a striped volume using Disk 0, Disk 1, and Disk 2.
    b. Create a RAID 1 volume from Disk 1 and Disk 2.
    c. Convert the new disks to GPT. Create a spanned volume using Disk 1 and Disk 2.
    d. Create a RAID 5 volume from Disk 0, Disk 1, and Disk 2.

12. You need a disk system that provides the best performance for a new application that frequently reads and writes data to the disk. You aren't concerned about disk fault tolerance because the data will be backed up each day; performance is the main concern. What type of volume arrangement should you use?
    a. Spanned volume
    b. RAID 1 volume
    c. RAID 0 volume
    d. RAID 5 volume

13. You need to protect sensitive files from unauthorized users even if the disk is stolen. Which of the following features should you use, and on what file system?
    a. EFS, NTFS
    b. Disk compression, ReFS
    c. Quotas, NTFS
    d. Shadow copies, ReFS

14. You come across a file with a .vhd extension on your server's hard disk. What should you do to see this file's contents?
    a. Right-click the file and click Open.
    b. Open the file in Notepad.
    c. Burn the file to a DVD.
    d. Mount the file.

15. Which type of virtual disk would you create if you needed to use the virtual disk in a production environment that required fast disk performance?
    a. Dynamically expanding
    b. Thin provisioned
    c. Fixed size
    d. Extended FAT

16. Which of the following is a UNIX native file-sharing protocol that is supported by the Windows Server File and Storage Services role?
    a. SMB
    b. FTP
    c. TFTP
    d. NFS

17. Which SMB share option should you enable if you don't want users to see files to which they don't have at least Read permission?
    a. Offline files
    b. Hidden shares
    c. BranchCache
    d. Access-based enumeration

18. Which of the following commands or cmdlets can be used to list the shares on the computer? (Choose two.)
    a. New-SmbShare
    b. Net share
    c. Get-SmbShare
    d. Net disk

19. Which administrative share does Active Directory use for replication?
    a. NETLOGON
    b. SYSVOL
    c. Admin$
    d. IPC$

20. Which of the following is part of a file system object's security settings and defines the settings for auditing access to an object?
    a. DACL
    b. ACE
    c. ACL
    d. SACL

21. Which of the following is not a standard NTFS permission?
    a. Read & execute
    b. Change
    c. Write
    d. List folder contents

22. In which of the following ways can a user become a file's owner? (Choose three.)
    a. Take ownership of the file.
    b. Create the file.
    c. Belong to the File Owner special identity.
    d. Be assigned as the owner by an administrator.

23. Which of the following NTFS permissions allows a user to read, modify, delete, and create files, but does not allow the user to change a file's permissions?
    a. Read & execute
    b. Modify
    c. Write
    d. Full control

24. The Distributed File System role service provides which of the following? (Choose three.)
    a. Access to files across the network
    b. Replacement for regular backups
    c. Copies of files created automatically for redundancy
    d. Fault-tolerant access to files

25. Which of the following is true about DFS namespaces?
    a. Standalone namespaces always use more bandwidth.
    b. Domain-based namespaces remain regardless of the server status where the share resides.
    c. Domain-based namespaces include the current server name for faster name resolution.
    d. Standalone namespaces can't be replicated.

26. Folders added to a namespace can be described as which of the following?
    a. Copies of existing folders
    b. Copies of existing folders that are initially empty
    c. Pointers to existing shared folders
    d. Copied to a staging area automatically

27. In DFS, what are the differences between Windows Server 2008 mode and Windows Server 2000 mode?
    a. Server 2008 mode supports 15,000 folders and access-based enumeration; Server 2000 mode supports 5000 folders.
    b. Server 2008 mode supports 75,000 folders and Server 2000 mode supports 10,000 folders.
    c. There are no differences a user can see.
    d. Server 2008 mode supports 50,000 folders and access-based enumeration; Server 2000 mode supports 5000 folders.

28. Where does a referral originate when a client accesses a DFS namespace?
    a. From the namespace server
    b. From the domain controller
    c. From the namespace server for a standalone type and from the domain controller for a domain-based type
    d. From a cached copy of referrals on the server where the share is located

29. Which of the following BranchCache modes should you install if you don't want to use a dedicated server in a branch office?
    a. Distributed cache mode
    b. Tiered cache mode
    c. Single cache mode
    d. Hosted cache mode

30. Which mode should you configure if you want to support multiple subnets?
    a. Hosted cache mode
    b. Distributed cache mode
    c. Branch cache mode
    d. Tiered cache mode

31. Which of the following roles or protocols can benefit from using the BranchCache role service? (Choose three.)
    a. File Server
    b. Web Server
    c. Network File System
    d. BITS

32. Which of the following scenarios would benefit from selecting a distributed cache mode over a hosted cache mode? (Choose two.)
    a. Small branch office with two dedicated servers
    b. Small branch office with no dedicated server
    c. Additional resources and personnel are not available
    d. Unlimited resources and multiple servers are available

33. What are the two types of quotas you can create with File Server Resource Manager?
    a. Hard and soft
    b. Hard and notify
    c. Limit and notify
    d. Maximum and minimum

34. What are the two types of file screens you can create with File Server Resource Manager?
    a. Hard and soft
    b. Active and passive
    c. Active and notify
    d. Restrict and notify

35. A file screen is used to do which of the following? (Choose two.)
    a. Limit access to certain types of files.
    b. Screen files for malware and viruses.
    c. Analyze file use and restrict use to maximize network bandwidth.
    d. Send a notification about access to certain types of files.

Critical Thinking

The following activities give you critical thinking challenges. Case projects offer a scenario with a problem for which you supply a written solution.

Case Projects

Case Project 10-1: Dealing with a Disk Crash

Last week, a disk containing CSM Tech Publishing's current project manuscripts crashed. Fortunately, there was a backup, but all files that had been added or changed that day were lost. A new disk had to be purchased for overnight delivery, and the data had to be restored. Several days of work time were lost. The owner of CSM Tech wants to know what can be done to prevent the loss of data and time if a disk crashes in the future.

The server currently has two disks installed: one for the Windows boot and system volumes and one for manuscript files. The disk used for manuscript files is about two-thirds full. There's enough money in the budget to purchase up to two new drives if needed. What solution do you recommend, and why?

Case Project 10-2: Creating a Shared Folder Structure

CSM Tech Publishing has asked you to develop a file-sharing system for the company's departments, which include Management, Marketing, Sales, Development, and Editorial. The following are some requirements for the file-sharing solution:

- Management must be able to access all files in all the shares, unless stated otherwise, and must be able to create, delete, and change files.
- The Management Department must have a share that only it can access, and each member of the department must be able to create, delete, and change files in the share.
- Marketing and Sales should have one common folder to which both departments' users have access. Members of both departments should be able to create new files, have full control over files they create, and view and change files created by other group members. They should not be able to delete files created by other members.
- Sales should have its own share that only Sales and Management can access. The Sales users must have full control over all files in the share.
- Development and Editorial have their own shares that only these departments and Management can access. The users from these two departments must have full control over all files in their department shares.
- There should be a public share in which users in the Management Department can create, change, and delete documents, and all other users have the ability only to read the documents.
- There should be a share available to management that no other users can see in a browse list. It contains confidential documents that only selected users in the Management Department can access.
- Users must be able to restore files they accidentally delete and restore an earlier version of a file without having to use a backup program.
- Sales users must be able to access the files in the Sales share when they're traveling, whether they have an Internet connection or not. When Sales users are back in the office, any changed files should synchronize with their mobile devices automatically. All Sales users have a Windows 10 or Windows 11 laptop.
- All users except Management users should be limited to 10 GB of space on the volume that houses shares. Management users should be limited to 50 GB.

Given these requirements, perform the following tasks and answer the following questions:

- Design the folder structure and include information about the permissions (sharing and NTFS) you plan to assign to each share and group of users. Name each share appropriately.
- What tool will you use to create the shares? Why?
- What protocols and technologies (including the file system) will be used to set up these shared folders? Explain the reason for using each protocol or technology.

Case Project 10-3: Managing DFS Referrals

CSM Tech Publishing has expanded dramatically, and suddenly there's heavy file server use. DFS is installed on several file servers and shares are replicated among all the servers. All the file servers are fairly close to clients, and you're adding several more servers in hopes of reducing the load on the existing servers. The number of namespace servers has also expanded. Your initial configuration used default settings for the referral ordering method and polling. Due to heavy server usage and an expanded number of servers, what changes should you consider in your DFS configuration?

Case Project 10-4: Using Advanced File and Storage Features

You're the IT administrator for CSM Tech Publishing. You've just had a meeting with the general manager about a data storage problem the company has been having. You've been asked to find solutions for the following problem:

- Two satellite offices have been complaining about slow access to shared files on the servers at the company's headquarters. One office has about 25 client computers running Windows 11, and there's one server running Windows Server 2022 that provides DHCP and DNS services but isn't heavily loaded. The other office has only four client machines running Windows 10. There's no budget for additional hardware at either location.

What solution do you propose for this problem? Include implementation details.

Solutions to Self-Check Questions

Section 10-1: An Overview of Server Storage

1. A page file is used to store pages from document files that are currently being edited by a word processor. True or False?

   Answer: b. False

   Explanation: A page file is used as virtual memory and to store crash dump information.

2. Which type of storage is shared by multiple servers and can be used in a server cluster?

   Answer: d. SAN

   Explanation: A storage area network (SAN) allows multiple servers to access the storage and is often used in a server cluster. An NAS and DAS are not suitable for cluster storage and SAS is a disk interface technology.

Section 10-2: Configuring Local Disks

3. A volume is similar to a partition; they can both be formatted with a file system. True or False?

   Answer: a. True

   Explanation: The terms *partition* and *volume* are sometimes used interchangeably, and they can both be formatted with a file system. The term *volume* is used more often in modern operating systems.

4. Which disk technology is best suited for modern high-end server usage?

   Answer: b. SAS

   Explanation: Serial Attached SCSI (SAS) is the best technology for server usage; IDE and SCSI are older parallel bus technologies, and SATA is better suited for workstations and low-end servers.

Section 10-3: Working with Virtual Disks

5. Which of the following is true about virtual disks?

   Answer: b. VHDX provides fault tolerance in case of power failures.

   Explanation: VHDX can prevent disk corruption that can occur due to sudden power outages. VHDX supports higher capacities than VHD. VHD and VHDX files can be mounted in Windows Server 2022; thin provisioned VHDs are slower than thick provisioned VHDs due to the time needed to expand the disk dynamically.

6. You can create and mount virtual disks using the Disk Management snap-in. True or False?

   Answer: a. True

   Explanation: The Disk Management snap-in can create virtual disks and mount them.

Section 10-4: File Sharing

7. What protocol does Windows file sharing use by default?

   Answer: c. SMB

   Explanation: Server Message Block (SMB) is the default Windows file-sharing protocol. NFS is the native Linux/UNIX file-sharing protocol, while FTP and HTTP are used to transfer files across networks.

8. Administrative share names on Windows end with a $. What is the purpose of the $ in the share name?

   Answer: d. It makes the share hidden in a network browse list.

   Explanation: The $ at the end of a share name makes the share hidden in a network browse list. Administrative shares have a $ at the end of the name so users cannot see the share, but administrators can still access it if they type the share name in a UNC path. New shares can be created with a $ in the name so users cannot see them.

Section 10-5: Securing Access to Files with Permissions

9. What type of account can be assigned permissions to files on a Windows system?

   Answer: a. Security principals

   Explanation: A security principal is a user, group, or computer account that can be assigned permissions. A distribution account is for mailing lists and cannot be assigned permissions. While file owners and guest accounts can be assigned permissions, they are not the only account types that can be assigned permissions.

10. Which of the following is true about copying and moving files and folders on a Windows system?

    Answer: c. A file or folder moved to a different NTFS volume inherits the destination folder's permissions.

    Explanation: If a file or folder is moved to a different NTFS volume, it inherits the permissions of the destination folder. A file or folder copied within the same NTFS volume inherits the permissions of the destination folder. When a file or folder is moved within the same NTFS volume, it retains its original permissions. FAT32 volumes do not support permissions, so files copied or moved to a FAT32 volume will have no associated permissions.

Section 10-6: Using File Server Resource Manager

11. You can create quotas on folders using Windows File Explorer. True or False?

    Answer: b. False

    Explanation: You can only create quotas on folders using File Server Resource Manager.

12. If you want to prevent users from saving specific file types to a Windows server, what feature should you use?

    Answer: b. Active screening

    Explanation: Active screening allows you to prevent users from saving files of the specified type on a file server. Quotas and permissions do not examine file types.

Section 10-7: Using Distributed File System

13. The namespace root in DFS is the server that has the DFS Namespaces role service installed. True or False?

    Answer: b. False

    Explanation: The namespace root is a folder that is the logical starting point for a namespace, but it may be hosted on a server that does not have the DFS Namespaces role service installed.

14. Which Windows file system feature allows users to see only files and folders to which they have at least read permission?

    Answer: d. Access-based enumeration

    Explanation: Access-based enumeration (ABE) prevents a user from seeing files or folders in File Explorer or in a dir listing unless the user has at least read permissions to the file. If ABE is not enabled, users without read access can still see the file or folder in a listing but cannot open it.

Section 10-8: Using BranchCache

15. With hosted mode, BranchCache cached data is stored on file servers in the branch office. True or False?

    Answer: a. True

    Explanation: In hosted mode, cached data is stored on BranchCache servers in the branch office. In distributed mode, cached data is stored among the BranchCache client computers.

16. What type of information is transferred from the server hosting a file in the main office when a request is made for a file that is already cached on a local BranchCache server?

    Answer: c. Only content information is transferred.

    Explanation: If a file has already been cached by a local BranchCache server, the next time the file is requested, only content information is transferred from the original hosting server in the main office. Content information tells the client where the file can be retrieved from the cache in the branch office.

Module 11

Configure Advanced Storage Solutions

Module Objectives

After reading this module and completing the exercises, you will be able to:

1 Manage Storage Spaces
2 Implement data deduplication
3 Implement Storage Replica
4 Configure SMB Direct and Storage QoS
5 Manage Azure File Sync

You have learned how to configure basic storage solutions with direct attached storage. Many applications require advanced storage solutions to provide fault tolerance and high performance. This module discusses a variety of methods for creating and configuring advanced storage solutions that provide flexibility, high availability, high performance, and fault tolerance. You'll learn how to implement Storage Spaces, a technology based on virtual disks, and how to implement data deduplication and Storage Replica. Data deduplication helps reduce storage requirements by eliminating duplicated data, while Storage Replica provides server-to-server and cluster-to-cluster volume replication for high-availability applications.

Next, you will learn how to improve file-sharing performance with SMB Direct and how to monitor and manage storage performance with Storage QoS. Finally, you will work with Azure File Sync to integrate on-premises storage with Azure cloud storage.

Table 11-1 describes what you need in order to do the hands-on activities in this module.

Table 11-1 Activity requirements

Activity	Requirements	Notes
Activity 11-1: Resetting Your Virtual Environment	ServerDC1, ServerDM1, ServerDM2, ServerSA1	
Activity 11-2: Creating a Storage Space with File and Storage Services	ServerSA1	There must be three unallocated disks installed on ServerSA1
Activity 11-3: Cleaning Up Storage Spaces	ServerSA1	
Activity 11-4: Creating a Storage Space with PowerShell	ServerSA1	There must be three unallocated disks installed on ServerSA1
Activity 11-5: Installing and Configuring Data Deduplication	ServerDC1, ServerDM1	

Storage Spaces

Microsoft Exam AZ-800:
Manage storage and file services.
- Configure Windows Server storage

Storage Spaces, first introduced in Windows Server 2012, provides flexible provisioning of virtual storage. It uses the flexibility available with virtual disks to create volumes from storage pools. A **storage pool** is a collection of physical disks from which virtual disks and volumes are created and assigned dynamically. Volumes created from storage pools can be simple volumes, striped volumes, or fault-tolerant RAID volumes.

Unlike traditional physical disks and volumes created in Disk Management, Storage Spaces can allocate storage by using thin provisioning. **Thin provisioning** uses dynamically expanding disks so that you can provision a large volume, even if you have the physical storage for a volume only half the size. Later, you can add physical disks to the disk pool, and Storage Spaces expands into the additional storage as needed. If the disk pool becomes full, Windows takes it offline to alert you that you need to add physical storage to the pool.

Storage Spaces uses the concept of **just a bunch of disks (JBOD)**, in which two or more disks are abstracted to appear as a single disk to the OS but aren't arranged in a specific RAID configuration. JBOD gives you more flexibility because you can simply add a physical disk to a storage pool, and existing volumes can grow into the new space as needed. You can even add external disks to a pool via an external bus architecture, such as SAS or eSATA. If you use an external disk system, it should be a certified JBOD system, preferably using a SAS disk controller. You can find JBOD systems that are certified specifically for Storage Spaces.

> **Note 1**
>
> Using slower external bus architectures, such as USB, adversely affects your storage solution's overall performance and isn't recommended.

Storage Spaces brings storage flexibility to a Windows server for a fraction of the cost of a traditional storage area network (SAN). Before Storage Spaces, a SAN was the best way to achieve similar storage features and performance. Storage Spaces offers the following features that are usually found only in traditional SAN-based storage arrays:

- *Disk pooling*—A collection of physical disks viewed as a single storage space from which volumes can be provisioned for the server's use.
- *Data deduplication*—A feature that finds data that exists on a volume multiple times and reduces it to a single instance, thereby reducing space used on the volume. Data deduplication is a role service that can be installed and then enabled on volumes separately. For more information, see the "Implementing Data Deduplication" section later in this module.
- *Flexible storage layouts*—Storage Spaces has three storage options, called **storage layouts**:
  - *Simple space*: A **simple space** is a simple volume with no fault tolerance, or **resilience**, as Storage Spaces calls storage that can recover from disk failure. A simple space can use disk striping (RAID 0) if two or more physical disks are available, which provides better performance than a volume on a single disk or a spanned volume. Figure 11-1 shows a simple space using disk striping across two disks. It also shows two files, F1 and F2. F1 is spread across both disks in two parts (F1-a and F1-b). F2 is spread across both disks in four parts (F2-a, F2-b, F2-c, and F2-d).

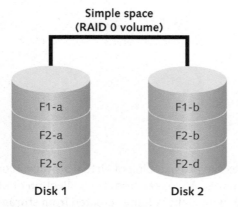

Figure 11-1 A simple space layout using two disks

○ *Mirror space*: A **mirror space** is a resilient storage layout configured as a two-way or three-way mirrored volume. A two-way mirror (RAID 1) requires at least two disks in the storage pool, and a **three-way mirror** requires at least five disks. This resilient storage layout maintains data if one disk fails or two disks fail. If two disks fail, a three-way mirror is needed. Mirror spaces are recommended for all storage applications that require resiliency. Figure 11-2 shows a mirror space with two disks. However, all parts of both files, F1 and F2, are on both Disk 1 and Disk 2, so if one disk fails, the other disk has a complete copy of all the data.

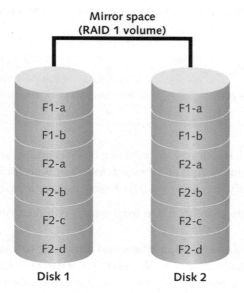

Figure 11-2 A mirror space layout using two disks

○ *Parity space*: A **parity space** is similar to a RAID 5 volume. A parity space can be configured for single parity or dual parity. At least three disks are required for a single parity space, and seven disks are required for a dual parity space. A **dual parity space** can recover from simultaneous failure of two disks. Parity spaces are recommended for archival storage, not standard storage workloads, because calculating parity data somewhat decreases performance. Figure 11-3 shows a parity space with three disks. The same two files are represented in all three disks depicted in the figure, with the files striped across two disks and parity information written to the third disk. The parity information is spread across all three disks. If any disk fails, the parity information on the remaining disks is used to reconstruct missing data from the failed disk.

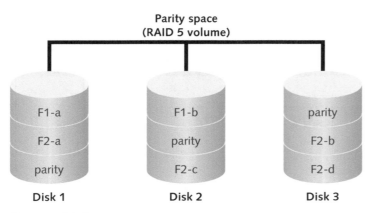

Figure 11-3   A parity space layout using three disks

- *Storage tiering*—Storage tiering combines the speed of SSDs with the low cost and high capacity of HDDs. You can add SSDs to a storage pool with HDDs, and Windows keeps the most frequently accessed data on the faster SSD disks and moves less frequently accessed data to HDDs. This scheme improves performance substantially without the expense of moving all storage to costly SSDs.

Creating Storage Spaces

Storage Spaces is configured with File and Storage Services in Server Manager or with PowerShell cmdlets. (There are more than 70 for working with Storage Spaces.) A storage space has three components:

- *Storage pool*—This storage consists of one or more physical disks with unallocated space. Physical disks available for adding to a storage pool are listed as part of the **primordial pool**. If a disk already has a volume on it, it's still part of the primordial pool, but only the unallocated space is used for a storage pool. A disk added to a storage pool is no longer shown in Disk Management unless it contains a traditional volume. You need two or more physical disks in a pool if you want to create a resilient storage space. Figure 11-4 shows the primordial pool before any storage pools have been created. Available disks are shown in the Physical Disks pane.

Note 2

A disk that has been converted to dynamic isn't listed in the primordial pool and can't be a member of a storage pool.

- *Virtual disks*—You create virtual disks from storage pools and choose the storage layout: simple space, mirror space, or parity space. If you choose a storage layout your pool can't support (for example, choosing a parity layout when you have only two disks in the pool), Storage Spaces prompts you to choose another one. Next, you select the provisioning type: thin provisioning (described previously) or **fixed provisioning**, which allocates all space for the virtual disk from the storage pool immediately. Then you specify the disk size. After a virtual disk is created, it's available in Disk Management like any other disk, and you can perform the usual operations on it. Storage Spaces creates the virtual disk as a GPT disk. Figure 11-5 shows a new storage pool with three member disks and a virtual disk that's been created. The virtual disk is thin-provisioned and uses a parity layout.

Note 3

You might hear the term *LUN* associated with virtual disks in Storage Spaces. An LUN is a logical reference to a unit of storage that could be composed of part of a physical disk or an entire array of disks, which is exactly what a virtual disk is.

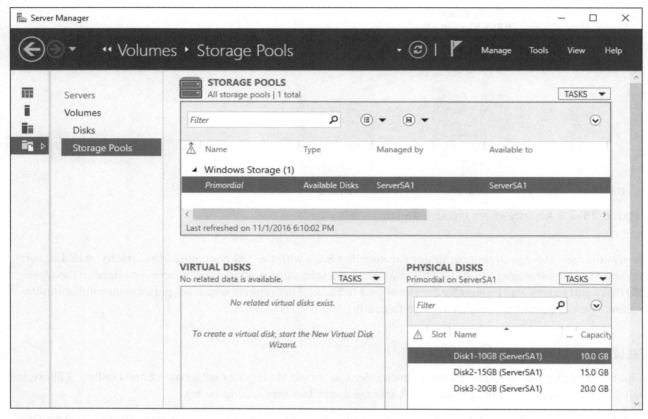

Figure 11-4 The primordial pool

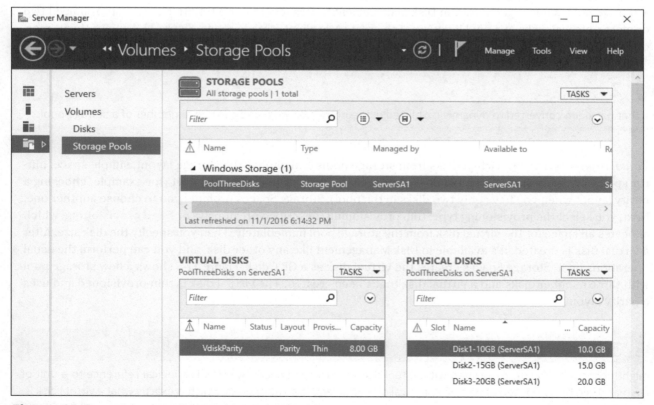

Figure 11-5 A new storage pool and virtual disk

- *Volumes*—After you create a virtual disk, you create volumes. Every volume you create on the disk uses the virtual disk's storage layout and provisioning type. For example, if you create two volumes on a virtual disk with a parity layout, both volumes are parity (RAID 5) volumes. You create a volume on a virtual disk in much the same way as on a traditional disk. You can use File and Storage Services or Disk Management. After a volume is formatted, it's ready to use like any other volume you create. The new volume is available in File Explorer, File and Storage Services, and Disk Management.

Figure 11-6 is a logical view of how these components work. You start with one or more disks that are part of the primordial pool. Next, you create storage pools from one or more of the disks in the primordial pool. In the figure, Pool1 is composed of two disks, and Pool2 is made up of three disks. After a disk is assigned to a pool, it's no longer part of the primordial pool. Two disks labeled "unused" remain part of the primordial pool after Pool1 and Pool2 are created. Two types of virtual disk layouts can be created from Pool1—simple and mirror—because you need at least two disks to create a mirror layout, and a simple layout can be created from any number of disks. You can create any of the three virtual disk layouts from Pool2 because a parity layout requires at least three disks. It's important to understand that you can create more than one virtual disk of any type supported from a pool until you run out of physical disk space in the pool. If you do, you can add disks from the primordial pool to make the pool larger.

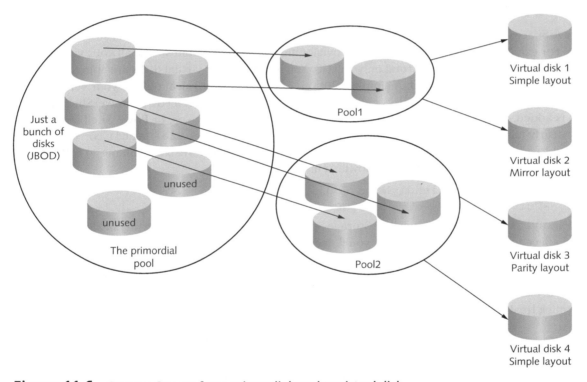

Figure 11-6 Storage Spaces from primordial pool to virtual disk

From the virtual disks, you create volumes (not shown in Figure 11-6). As mentioned, the volumes you create match the virtual disk's layout. You can create multiple volumes from a single virtual disk, as with physical disks.

Creating a Storage Pool and Volume with PowerShell

You use the `New-StoragePool` cmdlet to create a new storage pool in PowerShell. First, you'll need to get information about the physical disks you can add to the pool because this information is needed when you run the `New-StoragePool` cmdlet. For example, if you want to add all disks that are available for pooling, use the following cmdlet:

```
$PoolDisks = Get-PhysicalDisk -CanPool $true
```

The preceding command stores the list of disks that are available for pooling in a variable named `$PoolDisks`. Next, you want to use that variable in the `New-StoragePool` cmdlet to create a pool named `Pool1` and add the disks contained in the `$PoolDisks` variable to the pool. The `New-StoragePool` cmdlet requires the `-StorageSubSystemFriendlyName` parameter; for local storage, you can use `"Windows*"`:

```
New-StoragePool -FriendlyName Pool1 -PhysicalDisks $PoolDisks
    -StorageSubSystemFriendlyName "Windows*"
```

Now that your storage pool is created, you can create a virtual disk and a new volume. To create a virtual disk on Pool1, use the `New-Volume` cmdlet. When you create a new volume in a storage pool, a virtual disk is automatically created to match the volume name, size, and resiliency setting. The following cmdlet creates a volume named Vol1 with a size of 500 GB and assigns drive letter V.

```
New-Volume -StoragePoolFriendlyName Pool1 -FriendlyName Vol1 -Size 500 GB -DriveLetter V
```

By default, the `New-Volume` cmdlet creates a fixed-size virtual disk configured as a mirror and formatted with NTFS. If you only have one disk in the pool, you must specify a resiliency setting of "Simple," as in `-ResiliencySettingName Simple`. To specify a thin-provisioned disk, use the `-ProvisioningType Thin` parameter.

Expanding a Storage Pool

An advantage of Storage Spaces versus traditional storage is the ability to easily expand the amount of storage available for your virtual disks. For example, say you are using thin provisioning and the maximum size of all your virtual disks is 300 GB, but they reside on physical disks that total only 250 GB. You find that your virtual disks are approaching the limit of your physical disks and need to expand. A simple solution: Attach a new physical disk to your server, right-click the pool in Server Manager, and click Add Physical Disk (or use the `Add-PhysicalDisk` PowerShell cmdlet). After a physical disk is added, you can go to Disk Management, File and Storage Services, or PowerShell and expand any volumes that are nearly full. To expand a volume using PowerShell, you use the `Resize-Partition` cmdlet. For example, if you wanted to add a disk to a storage pool with the friendly name Pool1, resize a volume to 800 GB, and map it to the V: drive in the pool, you would use the following cmdlets:

```
Add-PhysicalDisk -StoragePoolFriendlyName Pool1
Resize-Partition -DriveLetter V -size 800 GB
```

However, it's not always as simple as that, because Storage Spaces spreads data among the physical disks that are in the pool. So, to add space to an existing virtual disk, you'll need to add as many physical disks as the virtual disk is currently using. The number of physical disks a virtual disk is using is referred to as **columns**. To see the number of columns a virtual disk is using, use the cmdlet `Get-VirtualDisk | ft FriendlyName, NumberOfColumns` (see Figure 11-7). You can also right-click the virtual disk in the Storage Pools window of File and Storage Services, click Properties, and then click Health to see the physical disks used by the virtual disk (see Figure 11-8).

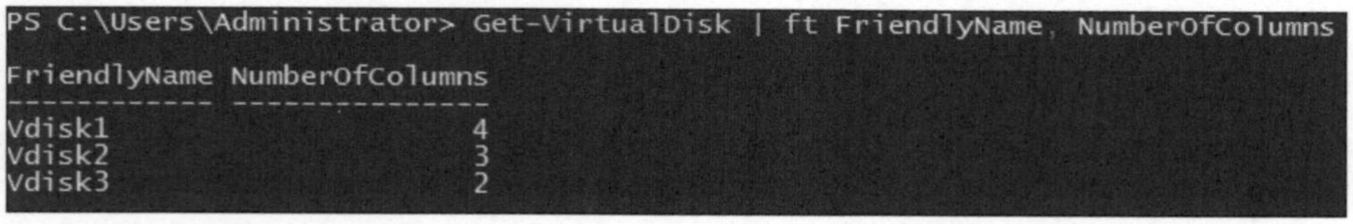

```
PS C:\Users\Administrator> Get-VirtualDisk | ft FriendlyName, NumberOfColumns

FriendlyName NumberOfColumns
------------ ---------------
Vdisk1                     4
Vdisk2                     3
Vdisk3                     2
```

Figure 11-7   Command to show the number of columns a virtual disk is using

Once you know how many physical disks a virtual disk is using, you'll want to add the same number of physical disks to the pool before you can expand the size of the virtual disk and then the volume.

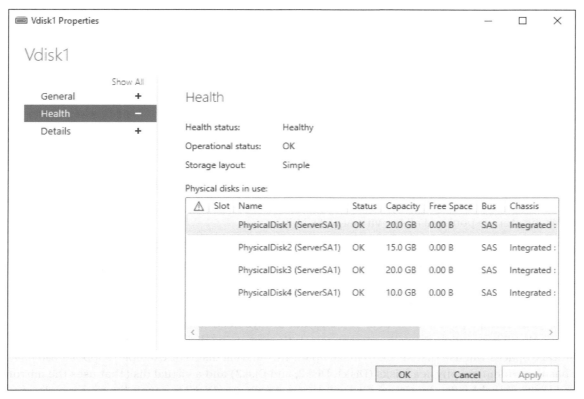

Figure 11-8   Viewing the physical disks in use by a virtual disk

> **Note 4**
>
> When a mirror space is involved, the number of columns doesn't always equal the number of physical disks. To calculate the number of physical disks needed to expand a mirror, multiply the `NumberOfColumns` value by the `NumberOfDataCopies` value. You can see these values by using the `Get-VirtualDisk | fl` command. A mirror space created with two or three disks will typically have one column and two data copies, requiring two disks to expand it. A mirror space created with four or five disks will typically have two columns and two data copies, requiring four disks to expand it.

Replacing a Failed Physical Disk in a Storage Pool

If you are using a mirror or parity space, your volumes can survive a physical disk failure. However, if one of the disks in a storage pool fails or is failing, you'll want to replace it as soon as possible because your system's performance and reliability will be compromised until you do. To replace a failed or failing physical disk from a storage pool, follow these steps:

1. Identify the problem disk. You may need to check the Windows System event log to find the disk ID, or your disk system may have LED indicators to show you that a disk has failed.
2. Replace the failed physical disk.
3. Add the replacement disk to the pool using File and Storage Services or the PowerShell cmdlet `Add-PhysicalDisk`. Make sure the new disk has at least as much space as the disk it is replacing.
4. Retire the old disk. If a disk fails entirely, Storage Spaces will retire it automatically, but if the disk is in the process of failing (read and write errors on a disk indicate imminent failure), you may need to retire it manually. You can view the health of a disk in File and Storage Services by going to Storage Pools, right-clicking

the disk, clicking Properties, and then clicking Health. Or, in PowerShell, type `Get-PhysicalDisk` and look at the `HealthStatus` column. To retire a disk, use the command `Set-PhysicalDisk -FriendlyName` *DiskName* `-Usage Retired`. Alternatively, you can select the physical disk that isn't healthy and use that information in the `Set-PhysicalDisk` command as follows:

```
$BadDisk = Get-PhysicalDisk -HealthStatus Unhealthy
$BadDisk | Set-PhysicalDisk -Usage Retired
```

Note 5

Other values for `-HealthStatus` include Healthy, Unknown, and Warning.

5. Next, you repair the storage pool and all the virtual disks in it:

```
Get-StoragePool -FriendlyName Pool1 | Get-VirtualDisk | RepairVirtualDisk
```

6. Finally, you remove the disk from the storage pool. In the following command, the `$BadDisk` variable was created in step 4:

```
Remove-PhysicalDisk -StoragePoolFriendlyName Pool1 -PhysicalDisks $BadDisk
```

Depending on how your storage pool is allocated, you may not always need to replace a physical disk that has failed. If your storage pool still has sufficient unallocated space on the remaining disks equivalent to the space used on the failed disk, Storage Spaces will use that space to make up for the missing disk. For example, suppose you have a storage pool that has three identical physical disks (Disk1, Disk2, and Disk3) and a virtual disk that uses the mirror layout with Disk1 and Disk2. If Disk1 fails, the virtual disk will automatically use Disk3 to repair the mirror as long as Disk3 has sufficient unallocated space to make up for Disk1. The pool and virtual disk will still have a degraded health status until you retire and remove the failed disk from the pool, but the virtual disk will work.

Disk Allocation Options

When you add a physical disk to a storage space, you have three options for how that physical disk can be used; Storage Spaces refers to this as the allocation type (see Figure 11-9):

- *Automatic*—An **automatic disk** will be used as Storage Spaces sees fit when a virtual disk is created. With automatic allocation, Storage Spaces will attempt to use the optimal number of physical disks (columns) when creating a virtual disk. For example, if you have four physical disks in the pool, all set to Automatic, and you create a simple volume, Storage Spaces will stripe the data across all four physical disks. A disk with Automatic allocation may also be used to automatically repair a resilient volume in the event another disk fails.

- *Hot Spare*—A **hot spare disk** will sit idle until it is needed to repair a volume due to disk failure. If a disk in the pool fails, an appropriate hot spare will automatically be put into service without administrator intervention. When that occurs, the Hot Spare disk will be changed to Automatic allocation.

- *Manual*—With **manual disk** allocation, the administrator chooses which disks will be used when creating a virtual disk. For example, if you have four physical disks in the pool set to Manual allocation when you create a virtual disk with a simple layout, you must choose which disks Storage Spaces should use to create the virtual disk. So, you can choose one disk, two, three, or all four. If you are creating a mirror-layout virtual disk, you must choose at least two disks; if you are creating a parity-layout virtual disk, you must choose at least three disks. This option is not recommended if the pool also has disks that use automatic allocation.

While you can have different disks in the same pool that are allocated as Automatic or Manual (as you saw in Figure 11-9, plus two set as Hot Spare), you can create virtual disks only from physical disks that have the same allocation type. For example, say you have two physical disks in a pool that are allocated as Automatic and two that are allocated as

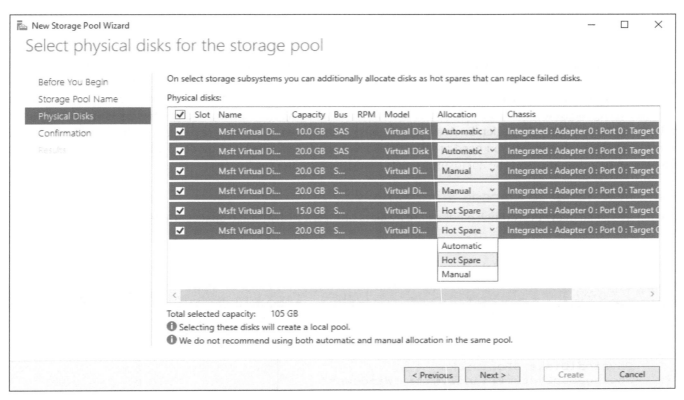

Figure 11-9   Selecting the physical disk allocation type

Manual. When you create a virtual disk, you will have to choose which allocation type to use, and you will be presented with only the disks of that allocation type (see Figure 11-10). So, even though you might have four usable disks in the pool, as shown previously in Figure 11-8, you can only use those of the allocation type chosen for any one virtual disk.

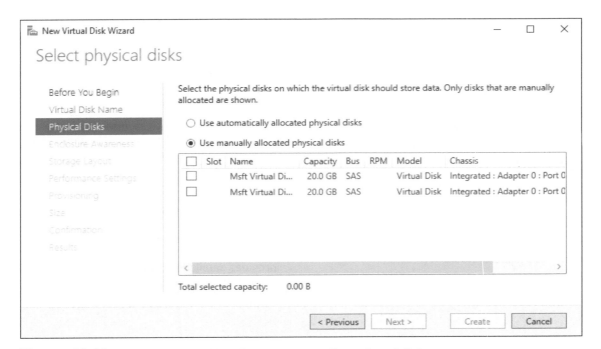

Figure 11-10   Choosing the allocation type to use for a virtual disk

Configuring Enclosure Awareness

As mentioned, you can attach external disk enclosures to a server to expand the amount of available storage and to create additional Storage Spaces. Windows Server has a feature called **enclosure awareness** in which Storage Spaces can place copies of data on separate enclosures, ensuring that if an entire disk enclosure fails, the data is maintained. To use enclosure awareness, you must enable it during the process of creating a virtual disk, either by clicking a check box when using the New Virtual Disk Wizard or in PowerShell by using the -IsEnclosureAware $true parameter in the New-VirtualDisk cmdlet. Enclosure awareness is only relevant if you are using a resilient space such as a mirror space or parity space. You need at least three enclosures, the allocation mode of all disks in each enclosure must be set to automatic, and the enclosures must be certified for Storage Spaces.

Using PowerShell to Manage Storage Spaces

As you have seen, many PowerShell cmdlets are available to work with Storage Spaces. Table 11-2 lists the most common ones.

Table 11-2 PowerShell cmdlets for working with Storage Spaces

PowerShell cmdlet	Function

`$PoolDisks = Get-PhysicalDisk -CanPool $true`
 	
`New-StoragePool -FriendlyName Pool1 -PhysicalDisks $PoolDisks -StorageSubSystemFriendlyName "Windows*"`
	Creates a storage pool: first, gets an array of physical disks that can be pooled, then creates the pool.

`New-VirtualDisk Pool1 -FriendlyName Vdisk1 -Size 100GB -ProvisioningType Thin`	Creates a thinly provisioned virtual disk named Vdisk1 from storage pool Pool1. By default, resiliency is set to "mirror."

`$NewDisk = Get-Disk -FriendlyName Vdisk1`
 	
`Initialize-Disk -InputObject $NewDisk`
 	
`New-Partition -InputObject $NewDisk -AssignDriveLetter -UseMaximumSize`
 	
`Format-Volume -DriveLetter F -FileSystem NTFS`
	Creates a new volume on the virtual disk. First, assigns the disk to a variable using Get-Disk, then initializes the disk, and finally creates the partition and formats it.

`New-Volume -StoragePoolFriendlyName Pool1 -FriendlyName NewVol -DriveLetter F -ProvisioningType Thin ResiliencySettingName Parity -Size 50GB -FileSystem NTFS`	Creates a thinly provisioned virtual disk with parity layout and creates a volume named NewVol in one step, then assigns a drive letter and formats it with NTFS.

`$DisksToAdd = Get-PhysicalDisk -CanPool $True`
 	
`Add-PhysicalDisk -StoragePoolFriendlyName Pool1 -PhysicalDisks $DisksToAdd`
	Adds one or more physical disks to a pool. First, gets all the disks that can be added and then adds them to the pool.

`Set-PhysicalDisk PhysicalDisk6 -Usage ManualSelect`
 	
`Set-PhysicalDisk PhysicalDisk6 -Usage Retired`
	Sets properties of a physical disk. The first cmdlet sets PhysicalDisk6 to Manual allocation. The second cmdlet retires a disk.

`Get-VirtualDisk -FriendlyName Vdisk1`	The first cmdlet displays basic information about virtual disk Vdisk1.The second cmdlet provides detailed information, such as the number of columns used or the sector size.
`Get-Command -Module Storage`	Displays all cmdlets related to storage.

Configuring Tiered Storage

Tiered storage combines the speed of solid state drives (SSDs) with the low cost and high capacity of hard disk drives (HDDs). You can add SSDs to a storage pool with HDDs; if you do, Windows keeps the most frequently accessed data on the faster SSD disks and moves less frequently accessed data to HDDs. This scheme improves performance substantially without the expense of moving all storage to costly SSDs.

To configure tiered storage, you must have at least one SSD and one HDD as part of a Storage Spaces storage pool. You specify tiered storage when you create a virtual disk with the New Virtual Disk Wizard in Storage Spaces. In the Virtual Disk Name window, click the "Create storage tiers on this virtual disk" check box, as shown in Figure 11-11. If Storage Spaces doesn't recognize a disk as an SSD, you can configure it as one with the following PowerShell cmdlet after the disk has been added to a storage pool:

```
Set-PhysicalDisk diskname -MediaType SSD
```

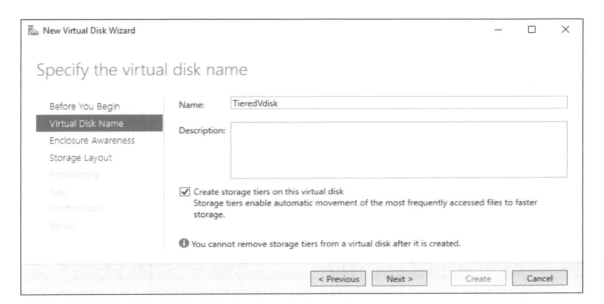

Figure 11-11   Creating a storage tier

Note 6

If you use the preceding PowerShell cmdlet to change the media type of a disk, you might need to click the Refresh button in Server Manager before the disk will be properly recognized as an SSD.

After you select the storage layout and provisioning type (storage tiers require fixed provisioning, so you can't use thin provisioning), you configure the size of the virtual disk and how you want to use the SSDs and HDDs in the tier (see Figure 11-12). Normally, the amount of space you allocate from SSDs is considerably smaller than the space from HDDs. A typical ratio of HDD space to SSD space might be 4 to 1, 5 to 1, or higher. If you need to create more than one virtual disk, you can distribute space from a single SSD among several virtual disks.

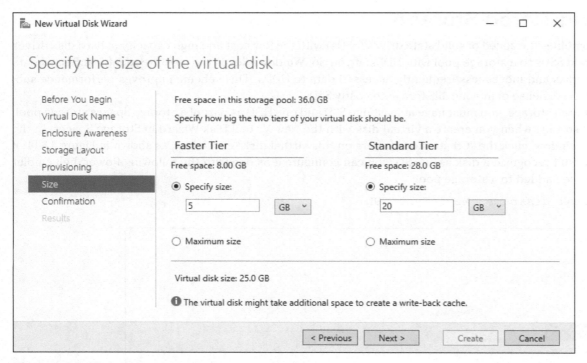

Figure 11-12 Configuring the size of storage tiers

Configuring Tiered Storage with PowerShell

Table 11-3 lists some common commands for configuring tiered storage.

Table 11-3 Tiered storage PowerShell cmdlets

Cmdlet	Description
`Set-PhysicalDisk diskname -MediaType SSD`	Sets the media type of a physical disk in the pool to SSD
`New-StorageTier SSDTier -MediaType SSD`	Creates a storage tier named SSDTier and sets the media type to SSD
`New-StorageTier HDDTier -MediaType HDD`	Creates a storage tier named HDDTier and sets the media type to HDD

`$SSD=Get-StorageTier SSDTier`
`$HDD=Get-StorageTier HDDTier`
 	
`New-VirtualDisk diskname -StorageTiers`
`  $SSD, $HDD -StorageTierSizes 40GB, 200GB`
	Stores information about storage tiers SSDTier and HDDTier in variables named $SSD and $HDD
	
	Creates a virtual disk named diskname and assigns 40 GB to SSDTier and 200 GB to HDDTier

Self-Check Questions

1. Which of the following is a collection of physical disks viewed as a single storage space from which volumes can be provisioned?

   a. Mirror space

   b. Disk pooling

   c. Storage tiering

   d. Fixed provisioning

2. Which of the following combines the speed of SSDs with the high capacity of HDDs?

   a. Enclosure awareness

   b. Parity space

   c. Primordial pool

   d. Tiered storage

Check your answers at the end of this module.

Activity 11-1

Resetting Your Virtual Environment

Time Required: 5 minutes

Objective: Reset your virtual environment by applying the InitialConfig checkpoint or snapshot.

Required Tools and Equipment: ServerDC1, ServerDM1, ServerDM2, ServerSA1

Description: Apply the InitialConfig checkpoint or snapshot to ServerDC1, ServerDM1, ServerDM2, and ServerSA1.

1. Be sure all servers are shut down. In your virtualization program, apply the InitialConfig checkpoint or snapshot to all servers.
2. When the snapshot or checkpoint has been applied, continue to the next activity.

Activity 11-2

Creating a Storage Space with File and Storage Services

Time Required: 20 minutes

Objective: Create a storage pool, virtual disk, and volume with Storage Spaces.

Required Tools and Equipment: ServerSA1, with three unallocated disks installed

Description: In this activity, you create a storage pool, virtual disk, and volume with Storage Spaces. You also see how Disk Management displays physical disks that have been added to a storage pool.

1. Start ServerSA1, and sign in as **Administrator**, if necessary.
2. In Server Manager, click **File and Storage Services**, and then click **Storage Pools**. Click the **Refresh** icon so that the disks are inventoried and displayed correctly. After the screen refreshes (which might take a minute or so), you see the primordial pool and three disks in the Physical Disks pane, as in Figure 11-13.

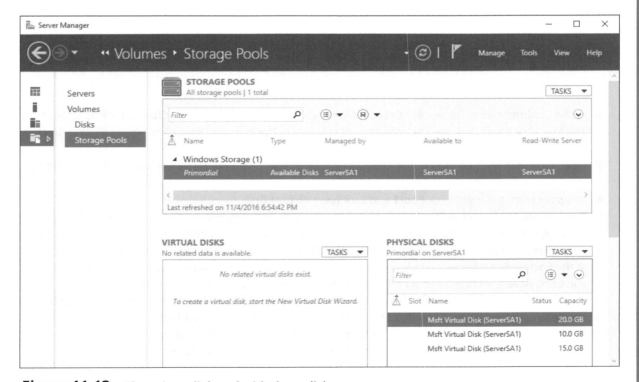

Figure 11-13   The primordial pool with three disks

(continues)

Activity 11-2 Continued

> **Note 7**
>
> If you are using Hyper-V virtual machines, the physical disks will be named Msft Virtual Disk (ServerSA1). If you are using another virtualization platform, the virtual disks will be named something else.

3. Right-click the **Primordial** pool and click **New Storage Pool**. In the Before You Begin window of the New Storage Pool Wizard, read the information and click **Next**.
4. In the Storage Pool Name window, type **Pool1** in the Name text box, and then click **Next**.
5. In the Physical Disks window, click all three check boxes (see Figure 11-14). At the bottom of the window, note the total capacity of the selected disks. You can also use this window to change the allocation type from Automatic to Manual or Hot Spare. Click **Next**.

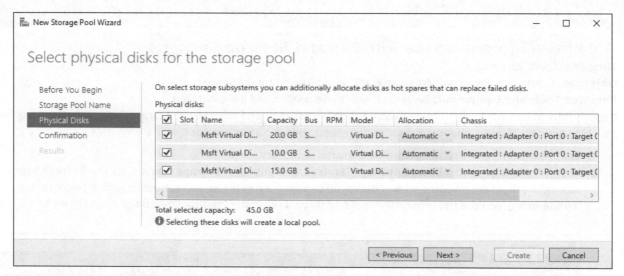

Figure 11-14 Selecting physical disks for a storage pool

6. In the Confirmation window, click **Create**. After the new pool is created, click **Close**. In the Storage Pools window, click **Pool1**. You see the members of the pool in the Physical Disks pane. You no longer see the primordial pool because you don't have more disks available to add to a pool.
7. Open Disk Management and notice that Disk 1, Disk 2, and Disk 3 are no longer shown because they're part of a storage pool. Close Disk Management.
8. In Server Manager, right-click **Pool1** and click **New Virtual Disk**.
9. The Storage Pool window lists only one pool, so click **OK**. Read the information in the Before You Begin window, and then click **Next**. In the Virtual Disk Name window, type **Vdisk1** in the Name text box. The check box for creating storage tiers is unavailable because an SSD isn't part of the pool. Click **Next**.
10. In the Enclosure Awareness window, the option to enable enclosure awareness is unavailable because you don't have a Storage Spaces certified enclosure attached to the server. Click **Next**.
11. In the Storage Layout window (see Figure 11-15), notice that the default option is Mirror. Click each option and read the description. Click **Mirror** in the Layout list box, and then click **Next**.
12. In the Provisioning window, click the **Thin** option button, and then click **Next**.
13. In the Size window, type **10** to create a 10 GB virtual disk, and then click **Next**.

(continues)

Activity 11-2 Continued

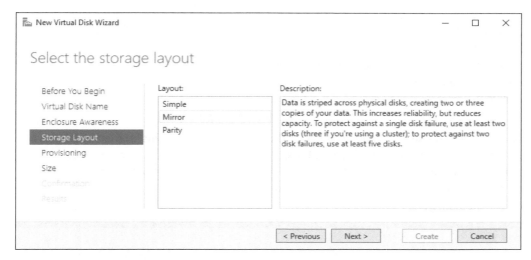

Figure 11-15   Selecting a storage layout

14. In the Confirmation window, verify your choices and then click **Create**. Creating the virtual disk might take a few minutes. Click to clear the **Create a volume when this wizard closes** check box. Click **Close**. The new virtual disk is listed in the Virtual Disks pane (see Figure 11-16).

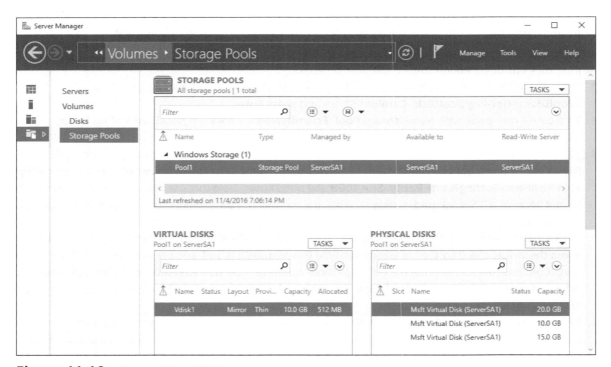

Figure 11-16   A new virtual disk

15. Open Disk Management to see that the new virtual disk is available. Close Disk Management. At this point, you don't need to create a new volume, but you could by following the procedure explained in earlier modules and using either File and Storage Services or Disk Management.

16. In File and Storage Services, right-click **Vdisk1** and click **Properties**. In the Vdisk1 Properties window, click **Health**. You see that all three physical disks are in use.

17. Continue to the next activity.

Activity 11-3

Cleaning Up Storage Spaces

Time Required: 5 minutes
Objective: Delete the virtual disk and storage pool created in the previous activity.
Required Tools and Equipment: ServerSA1
Description: You delete the storage space you created in the previous activity.

1. On ServerSA1, open Server Manager, if necessary.
2. In Server Manager, click **File and Storage Services**, and then click **Storage Pools**. In the Virtual Disks section, right-click **Vdisk1** and click **Delete Virtual Disk**. When prompted to continue, click **Yes**.
3. In the Storage Pools section, right-click **Pool1** and click **Delete Storage Pool**. When prompted to delete the pool, click **OK**. The disks are returned to the primordial pool.
4. Continue to the next activity.

Activity 11-4

Creating a Storage Space with PowerShell

Time Required: 20 minutes
Objective: Create a storage pool, virtual disk, and volume using PowerShell.
Required Tools and Equipment: ServerSA1, with three unallocated disks installed
Description: In this activity, you create a storage pool, virtual disk, and volume with PowerShell.

1. On ServerSA1, open a PowerShell window as follows: Click the **search** icon next to Start, type **power**, and then click **Windows PowerShell** in the search results.
2. You will add all available disks to the pool using the default allocation type of Automatic. Type **$PoolDisks=Get-PhysicalDisk -CanPool $True** and press **Enter**.
3. To create a new pool, type **New-StoragePool -FriendlyName Pool1 -PhysicalDisks $PoolDisks -StorageSubSystemFriendlyName "Windows*"** and press **Enter**.
4. To create a new volume and parity-layout virtual disk, format the volume, and assign a drive letter, type **New-Volume -StoragePoolFriendlyName Pool1 -FriendlyName NewVol -DriveLetter V -ProvisioningType Thin ResiliencySettingName Parity -Size 10GB** and press **Enter**. Note that it was not necessary to specify the format because NTFS is selected by default. When the command is completed, you see information about the new volume.
5. To see information about the new virtual disk, type **Get-VirtualDisk** and press **Enter**. To see more details about the virtual disk displayed in list format, type **Get-VirtualDisk | FL** and press **Enter**. Look for the NumberOfColumns row and see that the disk uses three columns. Type **Get-VirtualDisk | FT FriendlyName, Size, NumberOfColumns** and press **Enter**. This command shows only specific properties of the virtual disk in table format.
6. Type **Get-VirtualDisk | Where-Object -Property OperationalStatus -eq OK** and press **Enter**. Use this cmdlet to see virtual disks according to their operational status. Possible status values include OK, Detached, Degraded, Lost Communication, and Suboptimal. Next, type **Get-VirtualDisk -HealthStatus Healthy** and press **Enter**. The other possible health status values are Unhealthy, Warning, and Unknown.
7. To delete the volume, virtual disk, and storage pool, type **Remove-VirtualDisk NewVol** and press **Enter**. Press **Enter** to confirm. Both the volume and virtual disk are deleted. Type **Remove-StoragePool Pool1** and press **Enter**. Press **Enter** to confirm.
8. Verify that the three disks in Pool1 were returned to the primordial pool and are once again available to be placed in a pool. Type **Get-PhysicalDisk -CanPool $True** and press **Enter**.
9. Shut down ServerSA1.

Implementing Data Deduplication

Microsoft Exam AZ-800:

Manage storage and file services.

* Configure Windows Server storage

The sheer number of files and quantity of data that is stored on servers is staggering. To make matters worse, much of the data stored in those files is duplicated. Data duplication comes from multiple versions of the same file being saved either manually or automatically, through multiple users saving copies of shared files, and from multiple copies of the same email (including attachments like photos) being sent to dozens or even thousands of users. In addition, virtual disks that contain the same operating systems can be up to 95 percent identical.

To cope with duplication and ever-increasing amounts of data, storage systems have gotten bigger and more complex, and developers of storage systems seek to find methods to maximize the use of those systems. One such method is data deduplication. **Data deduplication** is a technology that reduces the amount of storage necessary to store an organization's data. Data deduplication (or dedup, for short) actually consists of multiple techniques for reducing storage requirements, including data compression, which transforms a series of repeated data bytes to just a few bytes, and deduplication, which reduces multiple copies of a file or data block to a single instance of the file or data block. Data deduplication in Windows Server combines both compression and data deduplication.

Windows Server performs data deduplication in a series of steps:

1. The deduplication process scans the volume looking for files that are candidates for deduplication (based on the file age and type).
2. Files are organized into variably sized chunks.
3. Duplicate chunks are identified.
4. A single instance of each duplicate chunk is placed into a chunk store. You have the option of compressing the chunk.
5. The original file chunk in the file system is replaced with a pointer to the chunk in the chunk store (called a **reparse point**).
6. When a reparse point is encountered during file access, the deduplication system redirects the file access to the appropriate chunk in the chunk store.

When to Use Data Deduplication

As mentioned, data is duplicated in a number of ways. You can use data deduplication for a variety of applications, but it cannot be used on operating system volumes such as the Windows boot or system volume. Common uses for data deduplication include the following:

* *File servers*—General-purpose file servers that store user documents, including multimedia files such as video and music files, often hold duplicated data. As the number of users increases, the amount of duplicated data tends to increase as well. This may be particularly true when many users work with copies of the same file, such as in an educational setting where students access and often save assignment and lesson files. Also, if Shadow Copies for shared folders is enabled, where multiple versions of the same file are kept so users can access previous versions, the volumes those shares reside on are good candidates for data deduplication.
* *Backup servers*—Backup sets can have a lot of duplicated data, especially when multiple versions of full backups are kept or with virtualized backups using Microsoft Data Protection Manager, a component of Microsoft System Center.
* *Virtualization servers*—As mentioned, most of the volume that is used to store the OS is identical among multiple virtual machines (VMs). Although you can't run deduplication on the OS volume on the system where

the deduplication feature is installed, you can run deduplication on virtual disks that contain the OS for virtual machines. Data deduplication for virtual desktop infrastructures (VDI) is particularly useful because the virtual disks used by VMs that users access in a VDI environment typically have the same OS and same applications installed.

There are probably many other applications for data deduplication, but it isn't ideal for every situation. For example, database servers such as SQL servers might or might not benefit from data deduplication, depending on the nature of the data stored. If you are unsure whether a particular storage scenario would benefit from data deduplication, you can perform a test using a tool that's included when you install data deduplication. The tool, DDPEval.exe, will evaluate any volumes or network shares you specify *before* you actually enable deduplication. This tool should be run on a test dataset; for example, if you are considering a particular volume for data deduplication, you can restore a backup of that volume to a test server or virtual machine and run the DDPEval.exe tool on the test system. The DDPEval.exe tool generates a report about the amount of data that can be saved if data deduplication is deployed.

Like any optimization tool, there is some overhead with data deduplication. Data deduplication runs periodically and requires server resources, so it might not be a good solution on servers that constantly have a high utilization rate. It works best on servers that have some idle time, such as late at night or on weekends, or on servers that are consistently busy but have moderate processor and disk utilization.

Installing and Using Data Deduplication

Data deduplication can be installed both on physical servers and virtual machines. When you have identified candidates for data deduplication, install the Data Deduplication role service under File and Storage Services (see Figure 11-17) in the Add Roles and Features Wizard.

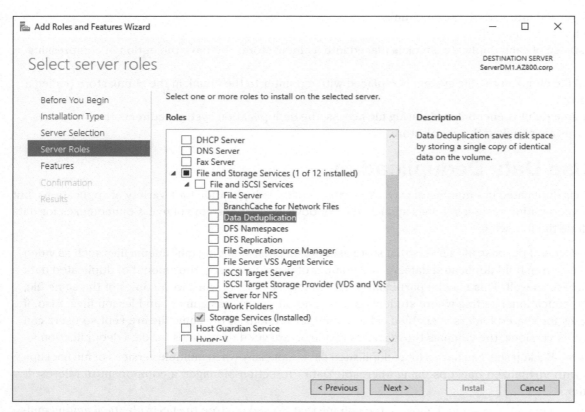

Figure 11-17   Installing Data Deduplication from Server Manager

The requirements and limitations of data deduplication are as follows:

- A physical or virtual machine running Windows Server 2012 or later, with at least one volume that does not contain the operating system. For satisfactory performance, at least 4 GB of RAM is recommended.
- The volume can be partitioned using MBR or GPT but must be formatted using NTFS. Volumes larger than 64 TB are not supported.
- Volumes running deduplication should have at least 10 percent free space.
- The volume can be local storage or part of a Fibre Channel or iSCSI SAN but cannot be a remote volume accessed through Windows file sharing (i.e., a mapped drive). Removable media are not supported. Cluster Shared Volumes (CSVs) are not supported.
- Encrypted files and files smaller than 32 KB are not processed by deduplication. Files up to 1 TB can be processed by deduplication.

Once installed, data deduplication must be enabled on selected volumes. You can enable data deduplication from File and Storage Services in Server Manager or by using PowerShell. In File and Storage Services, you can enable data deduplication when you create a new volume or by right-clicking an existing volume and clicking Configure Data Deduplication. In the Deduplication Settings window (see Figure 11-18), you must choose a usage type for this volume. There are three usage types:

- *General purpose file server*—Data deduplication is optimized for general-purpose files such as documents, graphic files, and video files.
- *Virtual Desktop Infrastructure (VDI) server*— Data deduplication is optimized for virtual machine files, such as virtual disks that are used in VDI.
- *Virtualized Backup Server*—Data deduplication is optimized for files used in virtualized backup applications.

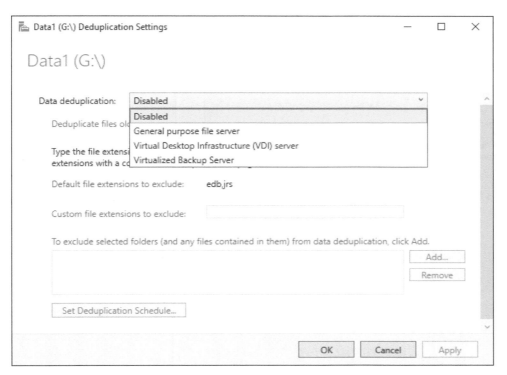

Figure 11-18   Data deduplication settings

After you select the usage type, you choose the age (in days) of files that should be considered for optimization. Only files older than the specified number of days are scanned for duplicate data. The default value is three days. A value of zero will cause deduplication to process all files, regardless of their age.

By default, files with certain extensions are excluded from deduplication, depending on which usage type you choose. The default extensions are listed; you can add more extensions if you want. In addition, you can select folders that should be excluded from deduplication. By default, the entire volume is included.

Finally, you choose the schedule and priority you want for deduplication (see Figure 11-19). By default, deduplication runs in the background on an hourly basis at a low priority and pauses when the system is busy. If you choose Enable throughput optimization, deduplication runs at a normal priority on the schedule you specify. You can also create a second normal priority schedule, if desired. For example, one schedule can run on weekdays starting after midnight, while the other can run on weekends starting in the morning. You can specify how many hours you would like the optimization process to run. You can have both the background optimization and regular priority optimization schedules active, if desired.

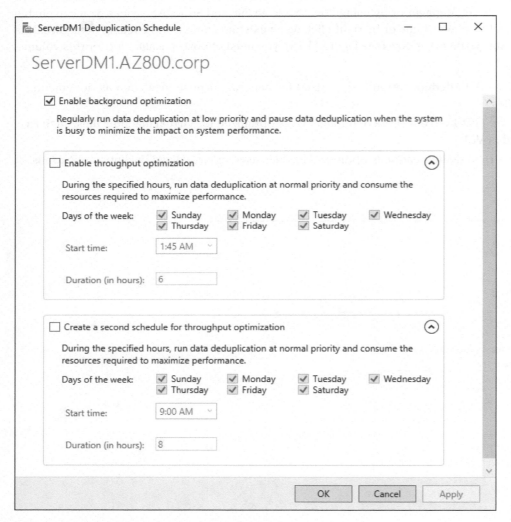

Figure 11-19   Configuring a data deduplication schedule

Configuring Data Deduplication with PowerShell

Configuring data deduplication with PowerShell involves the following two default steps:

- *Install data deduplication*: `Install-WindowsFeature FS-Data-Deduplication`

- *Enable data deduplication on volume H: with the default usage type of general-purpose file server:*
  `Enable-DedupVolume -Volume H:`

Table 11-4 shows examples of various PowerShell cmdlets for configuring different deduplication settings.

Table 11-4   PowerShell cmdlets for configuring data deduplication

PowerShell cmdlet	Function
`Enable-DedupVolume -Volume H:` `  -UsageType HyperV`	Enables deduplication for HyperV usage
`Enable-DedupVolume -Volume H:` `  -UsageType Backup`	Enables deduplication for backup usage
`Enable-DedupVolume -Volume H:` `  -UsageType Default`	Enables deduplication for general file server usage
`Set-DedupVolume H: -MinimumFileAgeDays` `  10`	Sets the minimum age of files that should be deduplicated to 10 days; a value of 0 means all files are processed
`Start-DedupJob H: Optimization`	Starts an optimization deduplication job
`Stop-DedupJob H:`	Stops all deduplication jobs on the volume

`Set-DedupSchedule -Name "WeekendDedup"`
`  -Type Optimization -Start 9:00`
`  -Duration 6 -Days Saturday,Sunday`
	Sets a schedule for deduplication on weekends to last for six hours at normal priority

`Get-Command -Module Deduplication`	Displays all cmdlets related to deduplication

Monitoring Data Deduplication

You can monitor data deduplication in a variety of ways. You can check the status of a running data deduplication job, get information about deduplicated volumes, look at the deduplication schedule, and view the status of deduplication, which gives you an idea of how well deduplication is keeping up with the data on the volume. Data deduplication is performed with the following PowerShell cmdlets:

- `Get-DedupJob`—Displays the status of a running deduplication job, as shown in Figure 11-20.

Figure 11-20   Getting the status of a deduplication job

- `Get-DedupVolume`—Displays the amount of saved space and the percentage of savings on a volume, as shown in Figure 11-21.

Figure 11-21   Getting information about deduplication on a volume

- `Get-DedupSchedule`—Shows the current deduplication schedule, as shown in Figure 11-22. There are three types of deduplication jobs: Optimization, Garbage Collection, and Scrubbing. Optimization scans files and deduplicates data, and it typically runs each hour. Garbage collection frees disk space by removing chunks from the chunk store that are no longer referenced by files. Scrubbing is an analysis of the chunk store log files to look for signs of corruption and make repairs when possible.

```
PS C:\Users\administrator.AZ800> Get-DedupSchedule

Enabled    Type                 StartTime       Days         Name
-------    ----                 ---------       ----         ----
True       Optimization                                      BackgroundOptimization
True       GarbageCollection    2:45 AM         Saturday     WeeklyGarbageCollection
True       Scrubbing            3:45 AM         Saturday     WeeklyScrubbing
```

Figure 11-22 Getting the current deduplication schedule

- `Get-DedupStatus`—Displays the status of deduplication, as shown in Figure 11-23. You can get an idea of how well deduplication is keeping up with the data on a volume by comparing the OptimizedFiles number with the InPolicyFiles number. The InPolicyFiles column shows the number of files that need to be scanned for optimization and the OptimizedFiles column shows the number of files already optimized. If the InPolicyFiles number is rising much faster than the OptimizedFiles number, you may need to run additional optimization jobs to keep up with the workload.

```
PS C:\Users\administrator.AZ800> Get-DedupStatus

FreeSpace    SavedSpace    OptimizedFiles    InPolicyFiles    Volume
---------    ----------    --------------    -------------    ------
19.22 GB     2.16 GB       1164              1164             G:
```

Figure 11-23 Getting the deduplication status

Backing Up and Restoring with Data Deduplication

Data deduplication provides features for backup applications to perform optimized backup and restore operations on enabled volumes. Optimized backups copy optimized files and the chunk store from shadow copies of the volume, which minimizes the backup size and the backup time. A non-optimized backup copies the data on the volume as if data deduplication had not occurred, making the backup much larger and the backup time much longer. Optimized backups offer backup applications the option to perform full or incremental backups. Note that optimized backups can themselves be stored on optimized volumes, further reducing the space needed to store the backups.

Volume restores from optimized backups essentially reverse the process of an optimized backup. Restores can be full-volume restores or selective restores; both should be performed to a newly formatted volume.

Self-Check Questions

3. Which of the following is *not* a candidate for data deduplication?

   a. Operating system volumes
   b. Backup servers

   c. Virtualization servers
   d. Data volumes

4. To optimize efficiency, the deduplication process runs when the system is most busy. True or False?

   a. True
   b. False

○ Check your answers at the end of this module.

Activity 11-5

Installing and Configuring Data Deduplication

Time Required: 10 minutes
Objective: Configure data deduplication.
Required Tools and Equipment: ServerDC1, ServerDM1
Description: In this activity, you install the Data Deduplication role service, create a new volume on ServerDM1, and enable data deduplication on it.

1. Make sure ServerDC1 is running. Start ServerDM1 and sign in as domain administrator.
2. Open a PowerShell window. Type **Install-WindowsFeature FS-Data-Deduplication** and press **Enter**.
3. Open **Disk Management**. On the 20 GB disk, create a new volume named **DataVol** that is formatted with NTFS and assigned the **H:** drive letter. Use the default settings for all other options.
4. In PowerShell, change to the H: drive by typing **h:** and pressing **Enter**. Next, you'll create two folders to store some duplicate files. Type **md data1** and press **Enter**. Type **md data2** and press **Enter**.
5. Next, copy several files to the data1 folder. Type **copy C:\windows\system32*.exe data1** and press **Enter**. Copy the same files to the data2 folder. Type **copy C:\windows\system32*.exe data2** and press **Enter**. The files you copied take about 580 MB of space. You can verify this in File Explorer or by typing **Get-Volume h | fl** and pressing **Enter**. Subtract the SizeRemaining value from the Size value to get the amount of used space.
6. To enable disk deduplication on the volume, type **Enable-DedupVolume –Volume H: -UsageType Default** and press **Enter**.
7. Set the minimum age for deduplication to 0 days. Type **Set-DedupVolume h: -MinimumFileAgeDays 0** and press **Enter**.
8. Start a deduplication job. Type **Start-DedupJob –Volume h: Optimization** and press **Enter**.
9. Check the status of the deduplication job by typing **Get-DedupJob** and pressing **Enter**. If there is no output, the job has already completed.
10. Check the status of deduplication by typing **Get-DedupStatus** and pressing **Enter**. You should see output for how much space was saved and how many files were optimized. Type **Get-DedupVolume** and press **Enter** to see deduplication by volume. The output shows the type of optimization, the amount of saved space, and the percent savings.
11. Close PowerShell. Using Disk Management, delete the H: volume. Shut down all servers.

Storage Replica

Microsoft Exam AZ-800:

Manage storage and file services.
- Configure Windows Server storage

Storage Replica is a Windows Server feature that provides block-level file replication between storage devices, primarily for fault tolerance and disaster recovery. The idea of Storage Replica seems to be at odds with the Data Deduplication service. While data deduplication strives to eliminate duplicate data to free up disk space, the Storage Replica feature creates duplicates of data and uses more disk space. The goal of data deduplication is to reduce duplicated data within a single file system, while Storage Replica's primary goal is to copy data from one server or storage system to another server or storage system for the purposes of fault tolerance, disaster recovery, and load sharing. Storage Replica can be used to replicate data between servers and between server clusters, regardless of whether those servers are in the same room, different buildings, or even different countries.

Block-level replication means that individual data blocks on the disk are copied as they change, as opposed to file-level replication, which replicates entire files as they change. With block-level replication, only the parts of a file that change are replicated, not the entire file. Storage Replica supports local storage such as SAS or SATA disks as well as iSCSI or Fibre Channel-based SAN storage. To ensure consistent data between storage sites, Storage Replica uses log files to back out changes if a failure occurs.

Storage Replica Use Scenarios

Storage Replica supports three primary use scenarios:

- *Server-to-server*—Replication occurs between two servers. Storage can be a Storage Spaces volume with shared SAS storage, locally attached storage, or an iSCSI or Fibre Channel SAN. Replication is configured and managed using PowerShell only.
- *Cluster-to-cluster*—Replication occurs between two clusters. Storage can be a Storage Spaces volume with shared SAS storage, an iSCSI or Fibre Channel SAN, or a Storage Spaces Direct volume. Replication can be configured using PowerShell or Failover Cluster Manager.
- *Stretch cluster*—Replication occurs between two clusters configured as a stretch cluster. A **stretch cluster** is a cluster in which the servers are in different geographical locations. A stretch cluster is primarily used in disaster recovery scenarios; when one location is subject to a natural disaster such as a flood or hurricane, the other location can assume its workload.

Installing and Configuring Storage Replica

Before you implement Storage Replica, you should verify that your servers meet the minimum requirements:

- Each server must have 4 GB of RAM.
- Two CPU cores are needed; on virtual machines, two virtual processors must be assigned to each server.
- Servers should be domain members for automatic Kerberos authentication.
- A 1 Gbps network connection is needed.
- The replication volume must be NTFS or ReFS formatted with GPT partitioning.
- You need a log volume with at least 8 GB of free space. You also need NTFS or ReFS with GPT partitioning. An SSD disk is highly recommended for the log volume.
- Both the replication volume and log volume on each server must have identical sector sizes.
- Replication and log volumes cannot be used to store OS components, including the paging file.

Storage Replica is a Windows Server feature you can install with Server Manager or PowerShell. To install Storage Replica with PowerShell, use the following cmdlet:

```
Install-WindowsFeature Storage-Replica -IncludeManagementTools
```

Be sure to add the `-IncludeManagementTools` option or the PowerShell cmdlets necessary to configure Storage Replica won't be installed. Before implementing Storage Replica, you can test the configuration of your servers using the following cmdlet:

```
Test-SRTopology -SourceComputerName ServerDM1 -SourceVolumeName R: -SourceLogVolumeName L:
    -DestinationComputerName ServerDM2 -DestinationVolumeName R: -DestinationLogVolumeName L:
    -DurationInMinutes 30 -ResultPath C:\temp
```

This cmdlet tests Storage Replica between two servers, ServerDM1 and ServerDM2. The volume to be replicated is the R: drive, and the log volume is the L: drive. The test is run for 30 minutes, and an HTML report is generated and saved in C:\temp.

Note 8

In order to get useful results from `Test-SRTopology`, you should introduce a load on the source storage volume. You can download a utility called Diskspd.exe from Microsoft's Github repository at *https://github.com/microsoft/diskspd.*

To begin replication, you create a partnership between the source and destination computers:

```
New-SRPartnership -SourceComputerName ServerDM1 -SourceVolumeName R: -SourceLogVolumeName
   L: -SourceRGName RG01 -DestinationComputerName ServerDM2 -DestinationVolumeName R:
   -DestinationLogVolumeName L: -DestinationRGName RG02
```

As part of the preceding command, you assign a replication group number using the `-SourceRGName` and `-DestinationRGName` parameters. To check the status of the replication, use the following cmdlet:

`Get-SrGroup`—Shows the status of all running replication groups, as shown in Figure 11-24.

```
PS C:\windows\system32\LogFiles> Get-SRGroup

AllowVolumeResize  : False
AsyncRPO           :
ComputerName       : SERVERDM1
Description        :
Id                 : 6fe11e24-4c68-4398-afe7-bf21c4037877
IsAutoFailover     :
IsCluster          : False
IsEncrypted        : False
IsInPartnership    : True
IsPrimary          : True
IsSuspended        : False
IsWriteConsistency : False
LastInSyncTime     :
LogSizeInBytes     : 8589934592
LogVolume          : l:\
Name               : rg01
NumOfReplicas      : 1
Partitions         : {058fe5d7-860f-4f0f-bca9-f33b660b74b9}
Replicas           : {MSFT_WvrReplica (PartitionId = "058fe5d7-860f-4f0f-bca9-f33b660b74b9")
ReplicationMode    : Synchronous
ReplicationStatus  : ContinuouslyReplicating
PSComputerName     :
```

Figure 11-24 Output of `Get-SRGroup`

To view information about the Storage Replica partnership, enter the following cmdlet:

`Get-SRPartnership`

To remove replication, run the following cmdlets:

`Get-SRPartnership | Remove-SRPartnership`—Run this cmdlet only on the source computer.
`Get-SRGroup | Remove-SRGroup`—Run this cmdlet on the source and destination computers.

Synchronous and Asynchronous Replication

Storage Replica supports two modes of replication:

- *Synchronous replication*—With synchronous replication, an application writes data to the source volume; while the source volume log file is updated, data is written (replicated) to the destination volume and then the destination log file is updated. Only when the destination data has been written and the destination log file has been updated is an acknowledgment sent to the application. This ensures that the data remains in sync with no data loss in the event of a failure at the source site. Synchronous replication requires a very low-latency network connection between source and destination. A connection of 10 Gbps is recommended, but 1 Gbps is required.

- *Asynchronous replication*—This mode replicates data between sites over slower, high-latency networks. With asynchronous replication, there is no guarantee that data will be identical when a failure occurs; however, the amount of unsynchronized data is dependent on the latency of the network. Storage Replica runs continuously, so changes are still replicated as soon as they occur.

Self-Check Questions

5. Which Storage Replica use scenario would you most likely use as a disaster recovery measure when you have servers in different geographical locations?

   a. Server-to-server   **c.** Stretch cluster
   b. LAN-to-LAN   **d.** Cluster-to-cluster

6. With block-level replication, individual data blocks on the disk are copied as they change. True or False?

   a. True
   b. False

⊙ Check your answers at the end of this module.

SMB Direct and Storage QoS

Microsoft Exam AZ-800:

Manage storage and file services.
- Configure Windows Server storage

Server Message Block (SMB), the primary Windows protocol for file sharing, can take advantage of performance technologies such as RSS and SR-IOV. **Receive side scaling (RSS)** is a feature for network drivers that efficiently distributes processing of incoming network traffic among multiple CPU cores. In Windows, the feature is enabled by default, but you might need to enable it on individual network adapters. Without RSS, all incoming network data is processed on the CPU where the network interface card interrupt occurs, potentially leading to an imbalance in CPU usage on systems with multiple CPUs or multiple CPU cores.

Single-root I/O virtualization (SR-IOV) enhances a virtual network adapter's performance by allowing it to bypass the virtual switch software on the hypervisor and communicate directly with the physical hardware, thereby lowering overhead and improving performance.

SMB Direct is a performance technology designed specifically for the SMB protocol. SMB Direct uses the capabilities of a remote direct memory access (RDMA) network adapter, nearly eliminating server processor utilization for data transfers. SMB Direct requires the host network adapter to be RDMA-compatible, which you can check by running the `Get-NetAdapterRdma` cmdlet (see Figure 11-25). The command will list the adapters that support RDMA.

```
PS C:\Users\Administrator> Get-NetAdapterRdma

Name                    InterfaceDescription                    Enabled
----                    --------------------                    -------
vEthernet (Intern-192.... Hyper-V Virtual Ethernet Adapter #2    True
vEthernet (TestingNet1... Hyper-V Virtual Ethernet Adapter       False
```

Figure 11-25   The results of the `Get-NetAdapterRdma` cmdlet

To enable RDMA on an adapter that supports it, use the following PowerShell cmdlet or enable it in the network adapter's properties:

```
Set-NetAdapterRdma "AdapterName" -Enabled $true
```

Storage Quality of Service

Storage Quality of Service (QoS) enables administrators to specify minimum and maximum performance values for virtual hard disks. The maximum specified value actually limits a VM's access to a virtual hard disk to prevent it from consuming too many storage resources, which can affect other VMs' access to storage. Setting a minimum specified value generates a notification if access to a virtual hard disk falls below the specified threshold.

Storage QoS can be set on IDE and SCSI virtual hard disks. In Hyper-V Manager, open a VM's Settings window, click to expand the hard disk where you want to set QoS, and click Quality of Service (see Figure 11-26). Click the "Enable Quality of Service management" check box. You can set minimum and maximum I/O operations per second (IOPS). Each 8 KB of data read or written per second is considered one I/O operation. For example, if you want to be notified when the hard disk falls below 8000 KB of input or output per second, set the minimum to 1000. If you want to prevent the disk from exceeding 80,000 KB per second, set the maximum to 10,000.

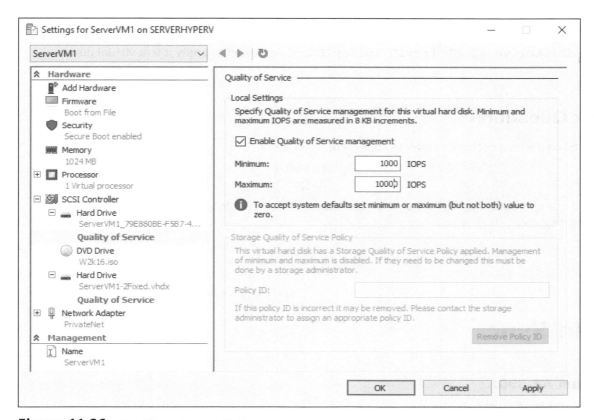

Figure 11-26   Enabling storage QoS

In addition, with Storage QoS enabled, you can monitor storage performance of VMs stored on a Scale-Out File Server cluster. Multiple VMs can be monitored this way from a central location.

Storage QoS Requirements

Storage QoS is used in cluster environments where virtual machine storage is shared. These environments include the following scenarios:

- *Hyper-V is used in a Scale Out File Server*—In this scenario, the VM storage is located on a Scale-Out File Server cluster and Hyper-V is installed on at least one server in a compute cluster.

- *Hyper-V is used with Cluster Shared Volumes*—In this scenario, Hyper-V is running in a failover cluster and is using Cluster Shared Volumes for VM storage.

Storage QoS Policies

Storage QoS policies can be created and applied to individual or multiple virtual disk files. Two types of policies exist: Aggregated policies and Dedicated policies. An **Aggregated policy** applies the minimum and maximum IOPS values to a set of virtual disks working as a whole. In other words, if you apply an Aggregated policy that specifies a minimum 1000 IOPS and maximum 5000 IOPS to five virtual disks, the policy guarantees that the combined minimum of all five virtual disks will be 1000 IOPS and the combined maximum will be 5000. This means that if all five disks have similar I/O requirements, they will get an average of 200 IOPS each at minimum and up to 1000 IOPS each at maximum.

A **Dedicated policy** applies minimum and maximum values to individual virtual disks; for example, if a Dedicated policy with the same limits is applied to five virtual disks, each disk is guaranteed the minimum and maximum IOPS values.

Storage QoS policies can be created using PowerShell; for example, the following cmdlet creates a policy with the minimum and maximum IOPS values of 1000 and 5000, respectively:

```
New-StorageQoSPolicy -Name FileServer -PolicyType Aggregated -MinimumIOPS 1000
   -MaximumIOPS 5000
```

After the policy is created, use the `Get-StorageQoSPolicy` cmdlet to display the policy ID number and then use the `Set-VMHardDiskDrive -QoSPolicyID` *PolicyIDNumber* cmdlet to apply it to a virtual disk.

Self-Check Questions

7. What is required on the host network adapter to implement SMB Direct?
   - **a.** RSS
   - **b.** RDMA
   - **c.** SR-IOV
   - **d.** QoS

8. A dedicated storage QoS policy applies the minimum and maximum IOPS values to a set of virtual disks working as a whole. True or False?
   - **a.** True
   - **b.** False

○ Check your answers at the end of this module.

Azure File Sync

Microsoft Exam AZ-800:

Manage storage and file services.
- Configure and Manage Azure File Sync

Azure File Sync is an Azure service that provides an organization with a cloud-based extension to its on-premises Windows Server file sharing. The service centralizes file sharing in Azure while maintaining the advantages of an on-premises server-based solution: performance, flexibility, and compatibility. Some of the advantages of adding Azure File Sync to your on-premises, Windows Server-based file-sharing solution include the following:

- *Azure cloud backups*—Azure Backup provides automated, centralized backup for SMB shares. Azure Backup integrates with your Windows Server file shares and synchronizes cloud restores with your on-premises servers.
- *Tiering*—Cloud tiering caches the most recently accessed files on local servers, while less frequently accessed files are kept in the cloud.

- *Business continuity*—Azure File Sync, along with Azure Files, provides a number of high-availability options, including no-restore server recovery, warm standby servers, and Windows Clustering. Recovery from server or disk failure traditionally involves component replacement followed by a restore procedure from backup. With Azure File Sync, the replaced device need only be added to the Azure File Sync deployment, which synchronizes the files from the cloud to the new device.
- *Distributed access*—With file servers deployed in each branch office along with Azure File Sync, changes to files in one office are automatically synced to the servers in other offices.

Azure Storage and File Shares

Before you can use Azure File Sync, you need a storage account and an **Azure file share** that will be synced with your on-premises servers. To create an Azure storage account, go to the Azure portal, type "storage account" in the search box, and click Storage accounts in the search results. From the Storage accounts page, click Create and then supply a subscription, resource group, storage account name, and region. The region you select must be the same as the Azure File Sync resource you create, as described in the next section.

You can choose Standard or Premium performance for the storage account and one of four levels of redundancy.

Next, you select advanced options for security, storage protocols, and access tiers. The default settings are acceptable because they meet the requirements for Azure File Sync. Next, you select network options, where you can choose public or private access to your storage endpoints. If you choose public access, your storage endpoints will be available to the public Internet. You also choose either Microsoft network routing or Internet routing. Microsoft network routing is recommended for most applications. Finally, you select data protection options and encryption options. The default settings should suit most scenarios.

After you create a storage account, you can create an Azure file share by going to the storage account and clicking File shares under the Data storage section. You need only supply a name and a tier level. Your tier-level options are as follows:

- *Transaction optimized*—This tier is for transaction-oriented applications that frequently update files as part of their operation—for example, web applications that create or modify customer files.
- *Hot*—This tier is best for general-purpose file sharing, as you might find in an organization that uses word processor, spreadsheet, and presentation files that are stored on a server.
- *Cold*—This tier is best suited for infrequently accessed archival storage.

You can now proceed to mount the file share from a host on your on-premises network. To do so, select the share and click Connect. You will be prompted to select the host OS on which you want to mount the share (Windows, Linux, or macOS). For Windows hosts, you select a drive letter and authentication method. The authentication methods are Active Directory or storage account key; Azure File Sync requires a storage account key. A script is generated that you can download to your host and run from a command prompt. On Windows systems, you can also use File Explorer to mount the share using the UNC path of *storageaccount*.file.core.windows.net*sharename*. Replace *storageaccount* and *sharename* with the name of the storage account and the name of the share, respectively.

> **Note 9**
>
> To mount an SMB share, you must be able to access port 445 through your network firewall. Many organizations block this port. If you cannot access port 445, you must connect to Azure using a VPN or ExpressRoute.

Configuring Azure File Sync

Deploying Azure File Sync has the following prerequisites:

- *An Azure storage account*—The storage account must be configured to allow SMB version 3.1.1, NTLMv2 authentication, and AES-128-GCM encryption. Storage account key access must be enabled.
- *Azure file share*—You must first create an Azure file share in the same Azure region you want to deploy Azure File Sync.

- *Windows Server*—An on-premises Windows Server must be running Windows Server 2012 R2 or a later version. The server can be a virtual or physical server with a minimum of 2 GB of RAM. You will install the Azure File Sync downloadable agent on this server.

The steps required to deploy Azure File Sync are outlined as follows:

1. Create a Storage Sync Service resource in Azure.
2. Install the Azure Storage Sync agent on an on-premises Windows Server.
3. Register the server with the Storage Sync Service.
4. Create a sync group and cloud endpoint.
5. Create a server endpoint.

These steps are detailed in the following sections.

Creating a Storage Sync Service Resource

A **Storage Sync Service resource** is created in the Azure portal and is the link between Azure file shares and your on-premises servers. A trust is created between one or more on-premises servers running the Azure Storage Sync agent and the Storage Sync Service. A server can only be registered to one Storage Sync Service, but multiple servers can be registered to a single Storage Sync Service. In addition, servers can only synchronize with other servers that are registered to the same Storage Sync Service.

To create a Storage Sync Service resource, click Create a resource from the Azure portal home page. Search for Azure File Sync, click Create, and then click Azure File Sync. On the Deploy Azure File Sync page, select a subscription, resource group, name, and region (see Figure 11-27). From the Networking tab, you can choose to allow access to the resource from all networks (the default option) or from private endpoints only. Click Review + Create and then click Create to finish the process.

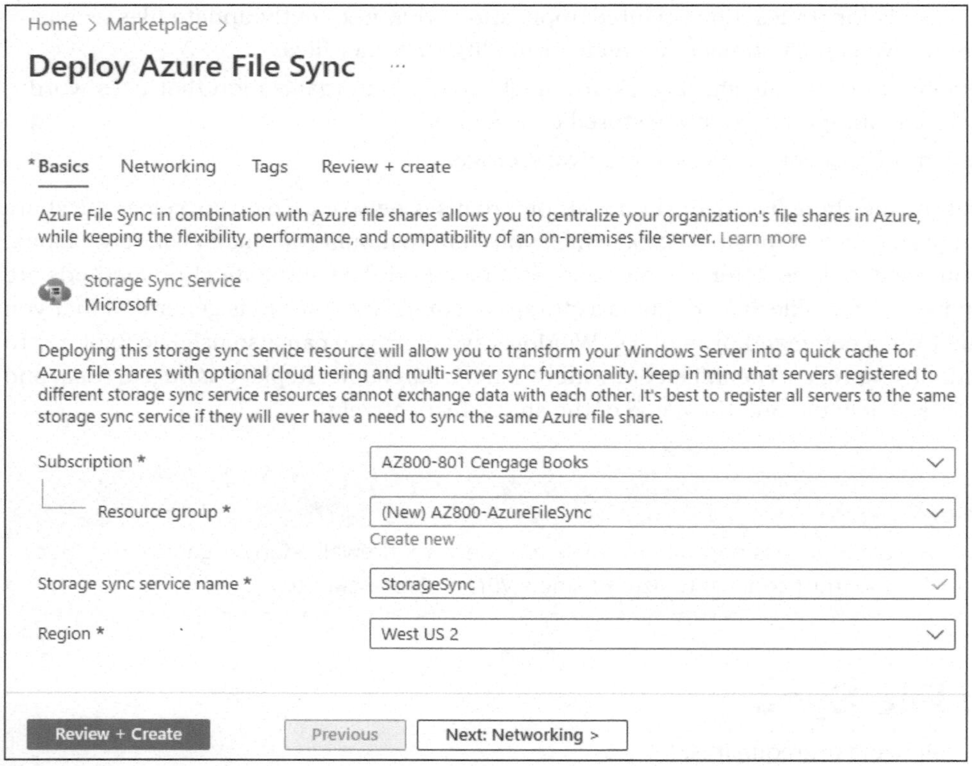

Home > Marketplace >

Deploy Azure File Sync   ...

*Basics   Networking   Tags   Review + create

Azure File Sync in combination with Azure file shares allows you to centralize your organization's file shares in Azure, while keeping the flexibility, performance, and compatibility of an on-premises file server. Learn more

Storage Sync Service
Microsoft

Deploying this storage sync service resource will allow you to transform your Windows Server into a quick cache for Azure file shares with optional cloud tiering and multi-server sync functionality. Keep in mind that servers registered to different storage sync service resources cannot exchange data with each other. It's best to register all servers to the same storage sync service if they will ever have a need to sync the same Azure file share.

Subscription *	AZ800-801 Cengage Books
Resource group *	(New) AZ800-AzureFileSync
	Create new
Storage sync service name *	StorageSync
Region *	West US 2

Review + Create   Previous   Next: Networking >

Figure 11-27   Creating a Storage Sync Service resource

Installing the Azure Storage Sync Agent

After you have created a Storage Sync Service resource, install the **Azure Storage Sync agent** on an on-premises Windows Server that you want to sync with your Azure file shares. Download the agent from the Microsoft Download Center and click the MSI package you downloaded to start the installation. When you download the agent, you may be asked to choose the version of Windows Server you want to use for installation. The file name will be similar to StorageSyncAgent_WS2022.msi for the Windows Server 2022 version of the agent. You can accept most of the default installation options for most installation scenarios. However, you can select the option to automatically update the agent when a new version becomes available and set a day and time to install the update (see Figure 11-28).

At the end of the installation, the agent will check for updates if the option was selected and then start the server registration process with the Azure Storage Sync Service.

> **Note 10**
>
> Before you start the server registration process, turn off IE Enhance Security Configuration on the server in which you are installing the agent. Open Server Manager, click Local Server, and click next to IE Enhance Security Configuration.

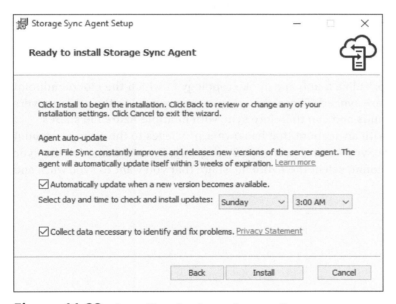

Figure 11-28   Installing the Azure Storage Sync agent

Registering the Server with the Storage Sync Service

You are prompted to choose an Azure environment and sign in to Azure to start the registration process (see Figure 11-29). After you sign in, you are prompted to choose the subscription and resource group you used to create the Storage Sync Service as well as the name of the Storage Sync Service resource you created. Once registration is complete, you are ready to create a sync group and cloud endpoint.

Creating a Sync Group and Cloud Endpoint

A **sync group** specifies the servers and cloud shares that participate in file synchronization. A sync group is composed of an Azure file share, which is referred to as a cloud endpoint, and one or more servers with the Storage Sync Service agent installed that are referred to as **server endpoints**. A **cloud endpoint** is basically a pointer to an Azure file share. A sync group is a one-to-many relationship in which there is always only one cloud endpoint, but there can be one or more server endpoints. For example, if your organization has several branch offices, each with a Windows Server that has the Storage Sync Service agent installed, files that are changed in the cloud or on any of the servers will be synced

Figure 11-29 Registering a server with the Storage Sync service

to all endpoints. A topology with multiple servers works like a hub and spoke topology in which the cloud endpoint (Azure file share) is the hub to which all file changes are synced. These changes are then synced to the other servers in turn. Note that a server can be in multiple sync groups and can therefore sync with multiple Azure file shares.

To create a cloud endpoint, sign in to the portal with an account that has owner privileges to the storage account that contains the Azure file share. Select the Storage Sync service and click Sync group. Enter a name for the sync group, choose the Azure subscription and storage account, select the Azure file share that you want to sync with, and click Create (see Figure 11-30).

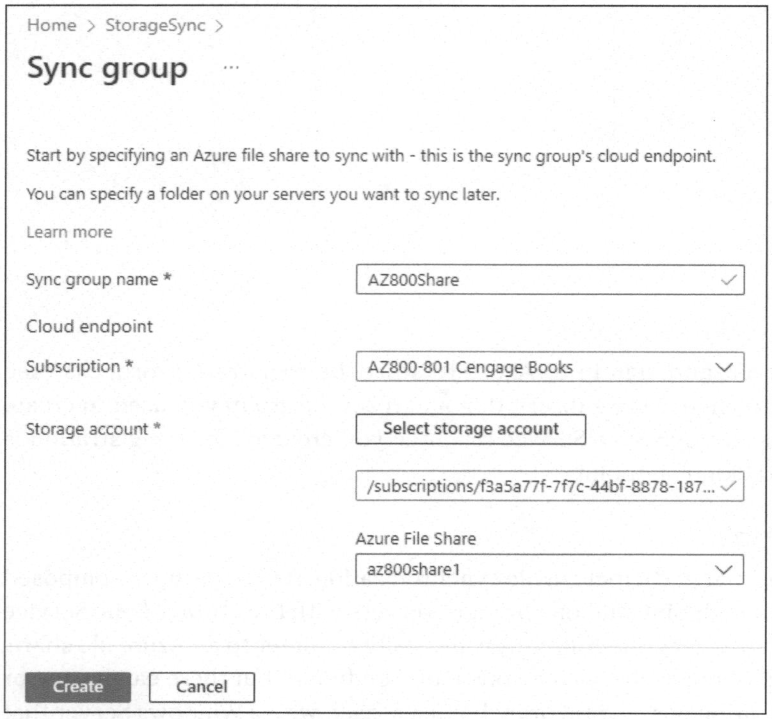

Home > StorageSync >

Sync group ···

Start by specifying an Azure file share to sync with - this is the sync group's cloud endpoint.

You can specify a folder on your servers you want to sync later.

Learn more

Sync group name *   AZ800Share ✓

Cloud endpoint

Subscription *   AZ800-801 Cengage Books ∨

Storage account *   Select storage account

/subscriptions/f3a5a77f-7f7c-44bf-8878-187... ✓

Azure File Share
az800share1 ∨

Create   Cancel

Figure 11-30 Creating a sync group and cloud endpoint

Creating a Server Endpoint

After you create a sync group, you can add one or more server endpoints to the group. Select the sync group, click Add server endpoint, and fill in the following information (see Figure 11-31):

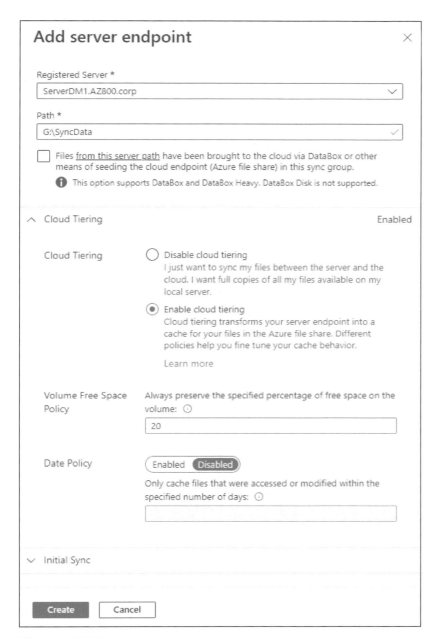

Figure 11-31   Creating a server endpoint

- *Registered Server*—Choose a server that has the Storage Sync agent installed and has been registered.
- *Path*—Choose an absolute local path where you want synced files to be stored on the server—for example, G:\SyncData.
- *Cloud Tiering*—Enable or disable cloud tiering. With cloud tiering enabled, frequently accessed files are stored on the registered server and less frequently accessed files are stored only in Azure. All files are always stored in Azure regardless of the tiering setting, so tiering only affects which files are stored on the registered server. You can choose from one of two policies: Volume Free Space or Date Policy. The Volume Free Space policy allows you to specify the amount of free space on the volume that should be reserved. For example, if the path is G:\SyncData and you select 30 percent for the Volume Free Space policy, files synced to the G: volume can't

take up more than 70 percent of the volume space, leaving at least 30 percent free. The Volume Free Space policy defaults to 20 percent. The Date policy allows you to tier files to Azure if they are not accessed within a specified number of days. So, if you choose 20 days, all files that have not been accessed in the past 20 days will be removed from the on-premises server but will still be accessible in the Azure file share.

- *Initial Sync*—If you are configuring the first server in the sync group, the Initial Sync policy can be configured. You can choose initial upload and initial download behavior. The initial upload policy allows you to merge the files located in the specified server path with existing files in the Azure file share or overwrite files in the Azure file share with the files on the server. The initial download policy allows you to specify how files on the Azure file share are downloaded to the server:
  - *Namespace, then files*—Download the namespace and as much data as will fit on the volume according to the tiering policy, if specified.
  - *Namespace only*—Download only the namespace and retrieve files from the cloud as they are accessed.
  - *Avoid tiered files*—This option is only available if tiering is not enabled. All files are downloaded to the server and no files are tiered to the cloud.

Note that the `namespace` in the preceding list refers to all the names of files and folders stored in the Azure file share. From a user standpoint, all files are seen on the local server, but the file contents may be stored in the cloud (the Azure file share) until the file is accessed. A file is said to be "tiered to the cloud" when the file's contents are in the Azure file share and not on the local server.

Configuring Cloud Tiering and Monitoring Azure File Sync

When you create a server endpoint, you can configure cloud tiering under the Cloud Tiering options; you can change those settings after the endpoint has been created. To begin, go to the Storage Sync service and click the sync group. You will see a page that lists the cloud endpoint and server endpoints for the sync group, along with a graph showing the sync statistics (see Figure 11-32).

Figure 11-32   Sync group status

Click the server endpoint for which you want to configure tiering and expand the Cloud Tiering section. You can enable or disable cloud tiering and configure the tiering policy (see Figure 11-33), as discussed previously in the "Creating a Server Endpoint" section.

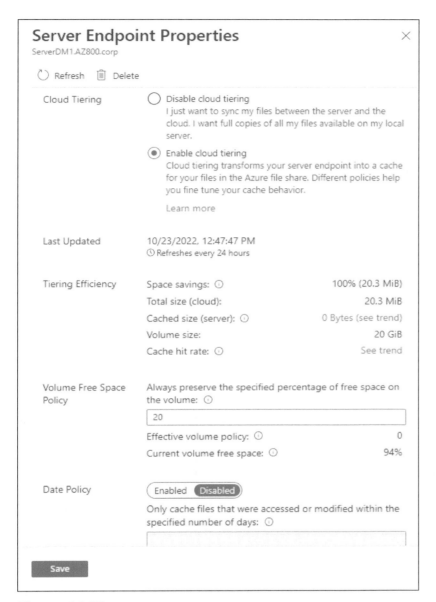

Figure 11-33   Configuring cloud tiering

Monitoring Azure File Sync

There are several ways to monitor various aspects of Azure File Sync, including the following:

- View metrics and alerts in Azure Monitor.
- View the status of sync groups and registered servers.
- Use Windows Server Event Viewer and Performance Monitor.

You can view metrics by selecting the Storage Sync Service in the Azure portal and selecting Metrics under Monitoring from the left menu. Choose the metric from the drop-down menu; for example, select Files Synced to see a graph of the chosen metric (see Figure 11-34).

You can configure alerts by selecting Alerts under Monitoring. Create alert rules based on metrics and log activity. For example, you can create alerts based on the number of files syncing or not syncing or the online status of a

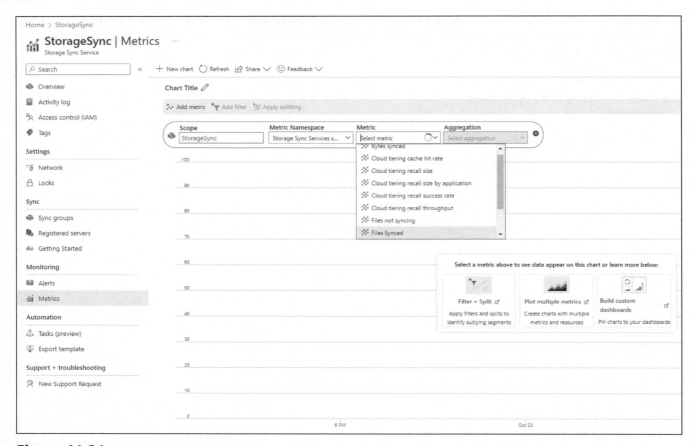

Figure 11-34 Choosing an Azure File Sync metric

server. If an alert is triggered, you define an action that should be taken, such as sending an email or text message or running an automation task.

To see the status of a sync group, select the Storage Sync Service and click Sync groups under Sync from the left menu. Choose the sync group you want to view; you'll see a page similar to that in Figure 11-32.

You can also view the status of registered servers by clicking Registered servers under Sync. The resulting window shows the online status of the server and the last communication with the Storage Sync service (see Figure 11-35).

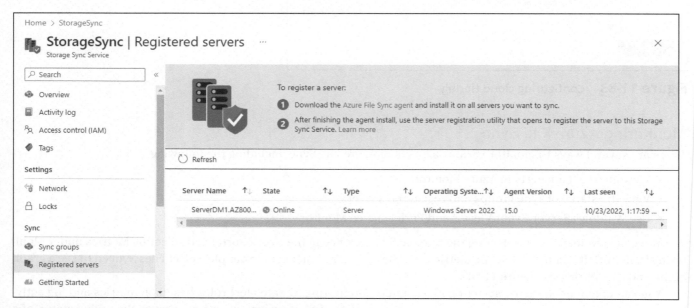

Figure 11-35 Viewing the status of registered servers

The event logs on the registered servers are a source of monitoring information as well. Several events are created by the installed file sync agent. You can view these events by opening Event Viewer and navigating to Applications and Services Logs\Microsoft\FileSync\Agent (see Figure 11-36). There are several categories of log entries; for example, event ID 9102 is created when a sync session completes, and Hresult: 0 indicates a successful sync. For more information on event IDs and their descriptions, refer to *https://learn.microsoft.com/en-us/azure/storage/file-sync/file-sync-monitoring*.

You can monitor a number of performance counters using Windows Server Performance Monitor. These counters can be found in the AFS Bytes Transferred and AFS Sync Operations performance object categories.

Grow with Cengage Unlimited

Performance Monitor is covered in detail in *Guide to Configuring Windows Server Hybrid Advanced Services, Exam AZ-801*.

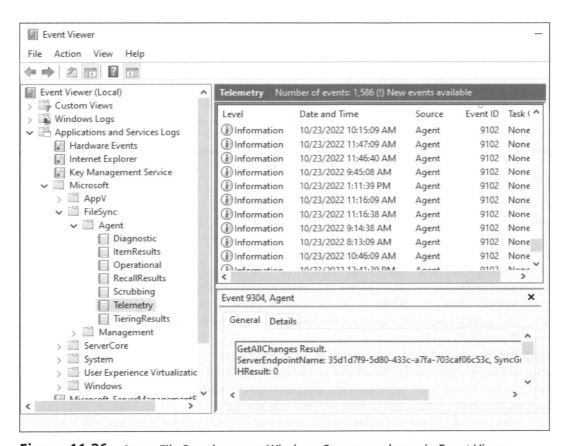

Figure 11-36   Azure File Sync logs on a Windows Server, as shown in Event Viewer

Migrating Distributed File System to Azure File Sync

Distributed File System (DFS) is the fully on-premises distributed file-sharing solution on Windows Server. DFS was described in detail in Module 10. For organizations that want to migrate to a cloud-based distributed file-sharing solution, Azure File Sync supports DFS namespaces and replication. Simply install the Azure Storage Sync agent on one or more DFS namespace servers and configure a sync group that specifies the DFS namespace path as the server endpoint. In most cases, it is recommended that you replace DFS Replication with Azure File Sync, which allows you to uninstall the DFS Replication role on your servers. To replace DFS Replication with Azure File Sync, perform the following steps:

1. Create a sync group that includes the DFS replication servers in your DFS topology.
2. Install the Azure Storage Sync agent on a server that contains all the files in your DFS topology; register that server and create a server endpoint in the sync group. Cloud tiering must be disabled.

3. Wait until all the data from your DFS shares is synced to the Azure file share in the sync group.
4. Install the Azure Storage Sync agent on the remaining DFS servers and disable DFS replication on all servers.
5. Create a server endpoint in the sync group for each of the additional servers.
6. Ensure that syncing works among all servers and the Azure file share.
7. Remove the DFS Replication role on your servers.
8. Enable cloud tiering as desired on your server endpoints.

Self-Check Questions

9. Which of the following is *not* an advantage to using Azure File Sync?

   a. Azure cloud backups
   b. Data deduplication

   c. Tiering
   d. Distributed access

10. To implement Azure File Sync, you should install the Azure Storage Sync agent on an on-premises server after you create a Storage Sync Service resource in Azure. True or False?

    a. True
    b. False

⊙ Check your answers at the end of this module.

Module Summary

- Storage Spaces provides flexible provisioning of virtualized storage by using storage pools. A storage pool is a collection of physical disks from which virtual disks and volumes are created and assigned dynamically. Storage Spaces can allocate storage by using thin provisioning.
- Storage Spaces uses the concept of just a bunch of disks (JBOD), in which two or more disks are abstracted to appear as a single disk to the OS but aren't arranged in a specific RAID configuration.
- Storage Spaces brings storage flexibility to a Windows server. Storage Spaces has three storage options: a simple space, a mirror space, and a parity space. Storage Spaces can be configured with File and Storage Services in Server Manager or with PowerShell cmdlets.
- An advantage of Storage Spaces versus traditional storage is the ability to easily expand the amount of storage available for your virtual disks. Storage Spaces also allows you to replace a failed physical disk in a storage pool.
- Storage Spaces allows you to choose from three allocation types when you add a physical disk to a storage space. You can choose an automatic disk, a hot spare disk, or a manual disk.
- Windows Server 2022 contains a feature called enclosure awareness in which Storage Spaces can place copies of data on separate enclosures, ensuring that if an entire disk enclosure fails, the data is maintained.
- Tiered storage was introduced in Storage Spaces in Windows Server 2012 R2. Tiered storage combines the speed of solid state drives (SSDs) with the low cost and high capacity of hard disk drives (HDDs).
- Data deduplication is a technology that uses multiple techniques to reduce the amount of storage necessary to store an organization's data. Data deduplication can be installed both on physical servers and virtual machines.
- Data deduplication provides features for backup applications to perform optimized backup and restore operations on volumes that have deduplication enabled. Optimized backups copy optimized files and the chunk store from shadow copies of the volume, which minimizes the backup size and the backup time.
- Storage Replica is a Windows Server feature that provides block-level file replication between storage devices, primarily for fault tolerance and disaster recovery.
- Storage Replica supports two modes of replication: synchronous replication and asynchronous replication.
- Server Message Block (SMB) is the primary Windows protocol for file sharing. SMB Direct is a performance technology designed specifically for the SMB protocol that nearly eliminates server processor utilization for data transfers.

- Quality of Service (QoS) in a network enables administrators to specify minimum and maximum performance values for virtual hard disks. Storage QoS can be set on IDE and SCSI virtual hard disks. It is used in cluster environments where virtual machine storage is shared. Storage QoS policies can be created and applied to individual or multiple virtual disk files.
- Azure File Sync is an Azure service that provides an organization with a cloud-based extension to its on-premises Windows Server file sharing. The service centralizes file sharing in Azure while maintaining the advantages of an on-premises server-based solution.
- To deploy Azure File Sync, you need an Azure storage account, an Azure file share, and an on-premises Windows Server.
- When you create a server endpoint, you can configure cloud tiering under the Cloud Tiering options in Azure File Sync; you can change those settings after the endpoint has been created.
- There are several ways to monitor Azure File Sync, including Azure Monitor, sync groups, Windows Event Viewer, and Performance Monitor.
- For organizations that want to migrate to a cloud-based distributed file-sharing solution, Azure File Sync supports DFS namespaces and replication.

Key Terms

Aggregated policy	hot spare disk	SMB Direct
automatic disk	just a bunch of disks (JBOD)	storage layout
Azure file share	manual disk	storage pool
Azure File Sync	mirror space	Storage Quality of Service (QoS)
Azure Storage Sync agent	namespace	Storage Replica
block-level replication	parity space	Storage Spaces
cloud endpoint	primordial pool	Storage Sync Service resource
column	receive side scaling (RSS)	stretch cluster
data deduplication	reparse point	sync group
Dedicated policy	resilience	thin provisioning
dual parity space	server endpoint	three-way mirror
enclosure awareness	simple space	tiered storage
fixed provisioning	single-root I/O virtualization (SR-IOV)	

Review Questions

1. You see something named "primordial" in File and Storage Services. What can you do with it?
   a. Create a storage pool.
   b. Create a virtual disk.
   c. Format it.
   d. Create a new volume.

2. What type of storage layout does Storage Spaces support? (Choose all that apply.)
   a. Simple space
   b. Mirror space
   c. Parity space
   d. Striped space

3. Which of the following is a feature in Storage Spaces that combines the speed of SSDs with the low cost and capacity of HDDs?
   a. JBOD
   b. Thin provisioning

   c. Storage tiering
   d. Resilient spaces

4. Which Windows Server storage feature finds data that exists on a volume multiple times and reduces it to a single instance?
   a. Disk quotas
   b. Storage tiering
   c. Fixed provisioning
   d. Data deduplication

5. Which of the following uses dynamically expanding storage?
   a. Thin provisioning
   b. Primordial pools
   c. Parity volumes
   d. Resilient File System

6. Which of the following refers to the number of physical disks a virtual disk is using and must be considered when you add space to an existing virtual disk?
   a. Parity volumes
   b. Columns
   c. Volumes
   d. Virtual disk

7. Which of the following PowerShell cmdlets allows an administrator to replace a failed disk in a storage pool?
   a. `Get-PhysicalDisk`
   b. `Remove-PhysicalDisk`
   c. `Add-VirtualDisk`
   d. `Add-PhysicalDisk`

8. When you add a physical disk to a storage space, which of the following are allocation types that determine how the new disk will be used? (Choose all that apply.)
   a. Automatic
   b. Manual
   c. Virtual
   d. Hot Spare

9. What feature in Windows Server allows Storage Spaces to place copies of data on separate enclosures, ensuring that if an entire disk enclosure fails, the data is maintained?
   a. Secondary volumes
   b. Enclosure awareness
   c. Disk awareness
   d. Virtual replacement

10. Which of the following physical disk arrangements allows you to set up a tiered storage configuration?
    a. Two SSDs
    b. Three SSDs
    c. Two HDDs
    d. One SSD and two HDDs

11. Which of the following is a valid disk provisioning option when configuring storage tiers?
    a. Virtual provisioning
    b. Thin provisioning
    c. Fixed provisioning
    d. Set provisioning

12. With respect to data deduplication, where does Windows Server place a single instance of duplicated data?
    a. Chunk store
    b. Disk store
    c. Deduplication file
    d. Dedup folder

13. After installing data deduplication, which of the following tools allows you to run a test to determine whether a specific storage scenario would benefit from data deduplication without enabling it on your volume?
    a. DDVol.exe
    b. File manager
    c. DDPEval.exe
    d. SYSEval.exe

14. Which of the following files will *not* be processed by data deduplication? (Choose all that apply.)
    a. A 500 MB file
    b. An encrypted file
    c. A 16 KB file
    d. A video file

15. Which of the following PowerShell cmdlets allows you to view the amount of saved space and percentage of savings on a volume when using data deduplication?
    a. `Get-DedupSchedule`
    b. `Get-DedupStatus`
    c. `Get-DedupJob`
    d. `Get-DedupVolume`

16. Which of the following means that individual data blocks on the disk are copied as they change, as opposed to file-level replication, which replicates entire files as they change?
    a. Volume replication
    b. Storage Replica
    c. Block-level replication
    d. File-level replication

17. Which of the following use scenarios is supported by Storage Replica? (Choose all that apply.)
    a. Stretch cluster
    b. Server-to-server
    c. Cluster-to-server
    d. Cluster-to-cluster

18. What technology enables administrators to specify minimum and maximum performance values for virtual hard disks?
    a. Storage Quality of Service
    b. SR-IOV
    c. Storage Replica
    d. SMB Direct

19. What Windows Server technology nearly eliminates processor utilization for data transfers?
    a. SMB Direct
    b. Storage QoS
    c. Azure File Sync
    d. Receive side scaling

20. What requirement must be met on your host's network adapter if you are planning to implement SMB Direct to reduce server processor utilization for data transfers?
    a. SR-IOV must be enabled.
    b. QoS must be disabled.
    c. QoS must be enabled.
    d. The adapter must be RDMA-compatible.

21. What feature in Azure File Sync keeps the contents of infrequently accessed files in the cloud?
    a. Tiering
    b. Data deduplication
    c. Storage QoS
    d. Namespaces

22. Which of the following is *not* a requirement for deploying Azure File Sync?
    a. Azure file share
    b. Azure storage account
    c. Distributed File System
    d. Windows Server

23. What must be installed on an on-premises Windows server in order to deploy Azure File Sync?
    a. Storage QoS
    b. Storage Sync agent
    c. Storage Sync resource
    d. SMB Direct

24. Which of the following are components of a sync group?
    a. One server endpoint, one or more cloud endpoints
    b. One or more server endpoints, one or more cloud endpoints
    c. Exactly two cloud endpoints and one or more server endpoints
    d. One cloud endpoint, one or more server endpoints

25. What is the first step you should complete when migrating DFS to Azure File Sync?
    a. Create a sync group.
    b. Disable DFS replication.
    c. Enable cloud tiering.
    d. Create a server endpoint.

Critical Thinking

The following activities give you critical thinking challenges. Case projects offer a scenario with a problem for which you supply a written solution.

Case Projects

Case Project 11-1: Creating Flexible Storage

It's been six months since a disk crash at CSM Tech Publishing, and the owner is breathing a little easier because you installed a fault-tolerant solution to prevent loss of time and data if a disk crashes in the future. Business is good, and the current solution is starting to get low on disk space. In addition, other pressing needs might require more disk space, and the owner wants to keep the data on separate volumes. The company wants a flexible solution in which drives and volumes aren't restricted in their configuration, and administrators want to be able to add storage space to existing volumes easily without having to reconfigure existing drives. The company has the budget to add a storage enclosure system that can contain up to 10 HDDs. Which Windows feature can accommodate these needs, and how does it work?

Case Project 11-2: Using Advanced File and Storage Features

You're the IT administrator for CSM Tech Publishing. You've just had a meeting with the general manager about some data storage problems the company has been having. You've been asked to find solutions for the following problems:

- You have a database application that has been exhibiting poor performance caused by latency from the drives it uses for storage. The storage system uses Storage Spaces and consists of four 1 TB HDDs. You have been asked to see what you can do to improve the performance of the storage used by the database application.

You have a limited budget for the project—certainly not enough for a new server but probably enough for some new components.

- You have a file server that is used to store user documents. Many of the documents stored by users are related to projects that several users collaborate on, and many users keep their own copies of the files. In addition, you use Shadow Copies for shared folders so users can easily revert files to previous editions. You also know that many users keep copies of training videos and other multimedia files. You want to reduce the amount of storage being used on your file server without making users change the way they work and store files.

What solutions do you propose for these two file and storage problems? Include implementation details.

Case Project 11-3: File Share Fault Tolerance

CSM Tech maintains a number of file shares on its Windows server computers, using DFS for a centralized namespace and automatic replication for fault tolerance. The general manager has recently taken an interest in using the Azure cloud to augment CSM's on-premises server solution. In particular, she is concerned about disaster recovery in the event the on-premises datacenter becomes disabled. What Azure feature can be used to integrate the on-premises datacenters with the cloud and provide a level of off-site fault tolerance? How does your proposed solution address the concerns of the general manager? How would you implement this solution?

Solutions to Self-Check Questions

Section 11-1: Storage Spaces

1. Which of the following is a collection of physical disks viewed as a single storage space from which volumes can be provisioned?

   Answer: b. Disk pooling

   Explanation: A disk pool is a collection of physical disks viewed as a single storage space from which volumes can be provisioned for the server's use. The process of creating a disk pool is called disk pooling.

2. Which of the following combines the speed of SSDs with the high capacity of HDDs?

   Answer: d. Tiered storage

   Explanation: Tiered storage combines the speed of solid state drives (SSDs) with the low cost and high capacity of hard disk drives (HDDs). When you add SSDs to a storage pool with HDDs, Windows keeps the most frequently accessed data on the faster SSD disks and moves less frequently accessed data to HDDs. This scheme improves performance substantially without the expense of moving all storage to costly SSDs.

Section 11-2: Implementing Data Deduplication

3. Which of the following is *not* a candidate for data deduplication?

   Answer: a. Operating system volumes

   Explanation: Operating system volumes cannot be configured for disk deduplication. Backup servers, virtualization servers, and data volumes on general-purpose servers can all be configured for disk deduplication.

4. To optimize efficiency, the deduplication process runs when the system is most busy. True or False?

   Answer: b. False

   Explanation: Data deduplication is disk access intensive and is most efficient when the system is not busy with other tasks.

Section 11-3: Storage Replica

5. Which Storage Replica use scenario would you most likely use as a disaster recovery measure when you have servers in different geographical locations?

   Answer: c. Stretch cluster

   Explanation: A stretch cluster is a cluster in which the servers are in different geographical locations. A stretch cluster is primarily used in disaster recovery scenarios; when one location is subject to a natural disaster such as a flood or hurricane, the other location can assume its workload.

6. With block-level replication, individual data blocks on the disk are copied as they change. True or False?

   Answer: a. True

   Explanation: Block-level replication means that individual data blocks on the disk are copied as they change, as opposed to file-level replication, which replicates entire files as they change. With block-level replication, only the parts of a file that change are replicated, not the entire file.

Section 11-4: SMB Direct and Storage QoS

7. What is required on the host network adapter to implement SMB Direct?

   Answer: b. RDMA

   Explanation: SMB Direct uses a remote direct memory access (RDMA) network adapter, nearly eliminating server processor utilization for data transfers. SMB Direct requires the host network adapter to be RDMA-compatible.

8. A dedicated storage QoS policy applies the minimum and maximum IOPS values to a set of virtual disks working as a whole. True or False?

   Answer: b. False

   Explanation: A Dedicated policy applies minimum and maximum values to individual virtual disks; for example, if a Dedicated policy with the same limits is applied to five virtual disks, each disk is guaranteed the minimum and maximum IOPS values. An Aggregated policy applies the minimum and maximum IOPS values to a set of virtual disks working as a whole.

Section 11-5: Azure File Sync

9. Which of the following is *not* an advantage to using Azure File Sync?

   Answer: b. Data deduplication

   Explanation: Some advantages of adding Azure File Sync to your on-premises, Windows Server-based file-sharing solution include the following: Azure cloud backups, tiering, business continuity, and distributed access. Data deduplication is not a feature of Azure File Sync.

10. To implement Azure File Sync, you should install the Azure Storage Sync agent on an on-premises server after you create a Storage Sync Service resource in Azure. True or False?

    Answer: a. True

    Explanation: The steps required to deploy Azure File Sync are outlined as follows: Create a Storage Sync Service resource in Azure; install the Azure Storage Sync agent on an on-premises Windows server; register the server; create a sync group; and create a server endpoint.

Module 12

Implement Virtualization with Hyper-V and Azure

Module Objectives

After reading this module and completing the exercises, you will be able to:

1   Install the Hyper-V server role

2   Create and use virtual machines in Hyper-V

3   Manage and configure virtual machines

4   Work with virtual hard disks

5   Use Hyper-V virtual networks

6   Manage advanced virtual network configuration

7   Manage Windows Server VMs on Azure

Virtualization has become a mainstream technology in networks both large and small. Server virtualization can be used to achieve a variety of goals, including consolidating servers, increasing server availability, creating virtual desktops, and isolating applications for testing. For these reasons and more, the Hyper-V role is likely to be a part of most Windows Server deployments.

This module focuses on how to use the Hyper-V server role for a virtualization platform. You learn the requirements for installing Hyper-V and how to install and configure the Hyper-V role. You'll learn how to manage Hyper-V both locally and remotely, create virtual machines (VMs), and manage and optimize VMs. In a hybrid network infrastructure, you may also implement virtual machines in the cloud to augment your on-premises VM solution or even replace it with Azure Virtual Machines. This module expands upon what you have already learned about deploying VMs in Azure and shows you how to manage VM data disks, resize VMs, configure continuous delivery of Azure VMs, and manage connections to Azure VMs from your on-premises network.

Table 12-1 describes what you need for the hands-on activities in this module.

Table 12-1 Activity requirements

Activity	Requirements	Notes
Activity 12-1: Resetting Your Virtual Environment	ServerHyperV	
Activity 12-2: Creating a Virtual Machine	ServerHyperV	
Activity 12-3: Working with Virtual Machines in Hyper-V Manager	ServerHyperV, ServerVM1 virtual machine	
Activity 12-4: Exporting and Importing a VM	ServerHyperV, InstallCore virtual machine	
Activity 12-5: Enabling Enhanced Session Mode	ServerHyperV, ServerVM1 virtual machine	
Activity 12-6: Creating a Dynamically Expanding Virtual Disk	ServerHyperV, ServerVM1 virtual machine	
Activity 12-7: Editing a Virtual Disk	ServerHyperV, ServerVM1 virtual machine	

> **Note 1**
>
> The Hyper-V role is supported on a virtual machine running on a Windows Server Hyper-V host if the host requirements are met. (This process is referred to as nested virtualization.) It's also possible to install and use the Hyper-V role on a virtual machine running in VMware Workstation, but additional configuration steps are necessary. See the lab setup guide in the "Before You Begin" section from the Introduction of this book for details on using Hyper-V in a nested virtualization scenario. Nested virtualization is also covered in Module 13.

Installing Hyper-V

> **Microsoft Exam AZ-800:**
>
> Manage virtual machines and containers.
> - Manage Hyper-V and guest virtual machines

Virtualization creates a software environment to emulate a computer's hardware and BIOS, allowing multiple OSs to run on the same physical computer at the same time. In Windows Server, you use the Hyper-V server role to create this environment. Before jumping into installing Hyper-V, review the following virtualization terms:

- A *virtual machine (VM)* is the virtual environment that emulates a physical computer's hardware and BIOS.
- A *guest OS* is an operating system installed in a VM, in the same way you install an operating system on a physical computer. Hyper-V supports a wide variety of guest OSs, as discussed later in the "Creating Virtual Machines in Hyper-V" section.
- A *host computer* is the computer on which VMs run, and a host OS is the operating system running on the host.
- *Virtualization software* is the software for creating and managing VMs and for creating the virtual environment in which a guest OS is installed. Examples are VMware Workstation, Oracle VirtualBox, and of course Hyper-V.
- The *hypervisor* is the virtualization software component that creates and monitors the virtual hardware environment, which allows multiple VMs to share physical hardware resources. The hypervisor on a host computer acts somewhat like an OS kernel, but instead of scheduling processes for access to the CPU and other devices, it schedules VMs. It's sometimes called the *virtual machine monitor (VMM)*. There are type 1 and type 2 hypervisors. **Type 2 hypervisors** are installed on an OS such as Windows 10 or Linux and use the host OS's resources and drivers. Type 2 hypervisors are best used for testing and development environments. **Type 1 hypervisors** are installed directly on the hardware of the host machine and may coexist with a host OS such as Windows Server, but they do not use the host OS's resources. Type 1 hypervisors are best for running production VMs.

- A **virtual disk** consists of files on the host computer that represent a virtual machine's hard disk.
- A **virtual network** is a network configuration created by virtualization software and used by virtual machines for physical and virtual network communication.
- A **checkpoint** is a partial copy of a VM made at a particular moment; it contains changes made since the VM was created or since the last checkpoint and can be used to restore the VM to its state when the checkpoint was taken. A checkpoint is also referred to as a *snapshot*.

As a type 1 hypervisor, the Hyper-V virtualization environment sits between the hardware and virtual machines. Each virtual machine is a child partition on the system, and Windows Server with Hyper-V installed is the parent or management partition. The Hyper-V management console runs on Windows Server in the parent partition and serves as an interface for managing the VMs running in child partitions, as shown in Figure 12-1.

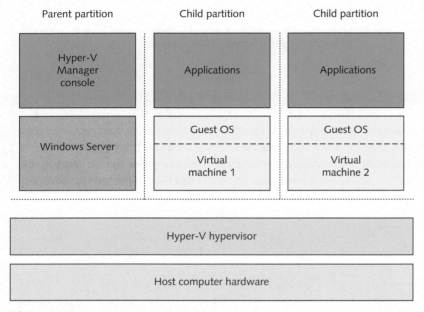

Figure 12-1   The Hyper-V architecture

> **Note 2**
>
> Hyper-V Server, a free download, can be installed on a server without having Windows Server installed. Hyper-V is then managed by another computer running Windows Server.

Figure 12-2 shows the Hyper-V Manager console in Windows Server with two VMs running. At the bottom of the middle pane is a thumbnail of the currently selected VM, which is named ServerVM2. You can double-click the thumbnail to connect to the VM and use it like a physical computer.

Hyper-V is a server role that's installed like any server role in Windows Server, using the Add Roles and Features Wizard in Server Manager or the `Install-WindowsFeature` PowerShell cmdlet. However, unlike some other roles you can install, your host system must meet a few prerequisites before you can install and use Hyper-V:

- Windows Server Standard or Datacenter Edition installed
- A 1.4 GHz or faster 64-bit CPU with virtualization extensions (AMD-V or Intel-VT)
- A CPU that supports Data Execution Prevention (DEP) and second-level address translation (SLAT); SLAT is called Extended Page Tables (EPT) on Intel processors and Nested Page Tables (NPT) on AMD processors
- Virtualization support enabled in the BIOS
- Free disk space at least equal to the minimum requirement for the OS you're going to install as a virtual machine

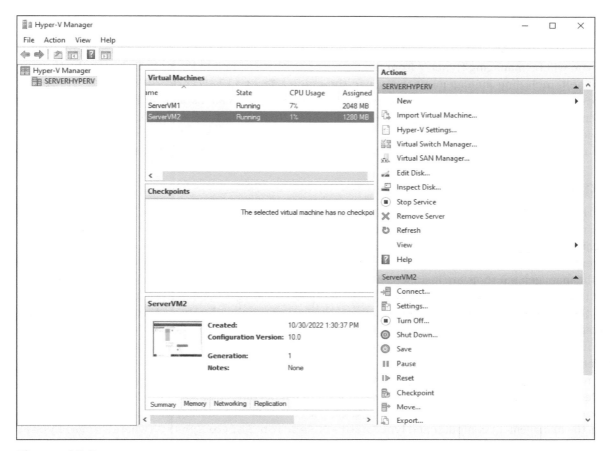

Figure 12-2   The Hyper-V Manager console

- RAM at least equal to the minimum amount required for Windows Server, plus the minimum amount required for the OS you're installing

Note 3

Remember that the amount of space required by a guest OS is no different from the space required of an OS installed on physical hardware.

Note 4

For example, the minimum amount of RAM required by Windows Server 2022 is 1 GB. If you plan to install a Windows Server 2022 guest OS, you need another 1 GB for the guest for a total of 2 GB. For all practical purposes, however, 4 to 8 GB of RAM should be considered the bare minimum amount on a Hyper-V host machine.

After you have an adequately configured system running a 64-bit version of Windows Server, you can install the Hyper-V role. Although you can install Hyper-V on Windows Server running as a virtual machine, you need to perform some additional tasks, as outlined in Module 13 in the "Nested Virtualization" section.

Note 5

To check if your system meets the requirements for Hyper-V, type systeminfo at a command prompt and scroll down to a section labeled Hyper-V Requirements. You'll see the requirements listed and whether your system meets them.

Installing the Hyper-V Role and Management Tools

When you install the Hyper-V role from Server Manager, you are prompted to install the management tools, which you should do if you will be managing Hyper-V from the same server that is running Hyper-V. To install the Hyper-V role from PowerShell, including management tools, use the cmdlet `Install-WindowsFeature Hyper-V -IncludeManagementTools`. If you will be managing Hyper-V remotely, you can install just the management tools on the management computer: `Install-WindowsFeature RSAT-Hyper-V-Tools` installs both the GUI and the Hyper-V module for PowerShell. The cmdlet `Install-WindowsFeature Hyper-V-Powershell` installs only the Hyper-V module for PowerShell.

Managing Hyper-V Remotely

A server running Hyper-V is likely to be resource-intensive, especially if it is running several VMs. Therefore, you might want to consider managing the server remotely so that the management tasks are offloaded to another computer. In addition, you can install Hyper-V Server, which installs directly on the host system without Windows Server. Hyper-V Server requires remote management via PowerShell or the Hyper-V management tools running on another Windows computer. Once the management tools are installed, you can use them to manage Hyper-V remotely. If you install the GUI management tools, you can run Hyper-V Manager, click the Hyper-V Manager node in the left pane, and click Connect to Server in the Actions pane. Then specify the name of the server running the Hyper-V role. Both the Hyper-V host and the management computer must be configured for remote management. As a reminder, you can enable remote management through Server Manager by clicking Local Server and then clicking Remote management or using the PowerShell cmdlet `Configure-SMRemoting`.

To remotely manage Hyper-V using PowerShell, PowerShell remoting must be enabled. By default, PowerShell remoting is enabled on Windows Server 2012 and later versions, but if it becomes disabled, use the PowerShell cmdlet `Enable-PSRemoting` on the computer you want to manage. With PowerShell remoting enabled, you open a PowerShell prompt from the management computer and type `Enter-PSSession` *ServerHyperV* (where *ServerHyperV* is the name of the remote server). If both computers are in the same domain, you do not have to enter credentials. If the remote server is not in a domain or is in a different domain, use the cmdlet `Enter-PSSession ServerHyperV -Credential (Get-Credential)`; you will be prompted for the credentials to sign in to the remote server. However, the remote server must be added to the TrustedHosts list on the management server first. Once you are connected to the remote server, your PowerShell prompt changes by the addition of *[ServerHyperV]* at the beginning of the prompt. From that point, every PowerShell cmdlet you enter is executed on the remote server. To exit the remote PowerShell session, simply type `exit`.

> **Note** **6**
>
> Remote management with PowerShell is not limited to Hyper-V, of course. Once you are connected to the remote server with `Enter-PSSession`, you can manage all aspects of the remote server with PowerShell cmdlets.

Hyper-V Licensing

When you install a guest OS in a virtual machine, you must have a valid license for the guest OS. Windows Server includes licenses for **virtual instances** of Windows Server with the Standard and Datacenter editions:

- Standard Edition includes two licenses for virtual instances of Windows Server on a fully licensed host computer, which means you can install Windows Server as a guest OS on up to two VMs without having to purchase an additional Windows Server license. The version of Windows Server installed on the VMs must be the same as the host computer version.
- Datacenter Edition includes licenses for unlimited virtual instances of Windows Server.

Self-Check Questions

1. A type 2 hypervisor is the best choice for production virtualization environments. True or False?

   a. True   **b.** False

2. Which of the following is *not* a requirement for installing Hyper-V?

   a. Windows Server Standard or Datacenter Edition   **c.** Virtualization extensions

   b. A quad-core processor   **d.** A 64-bit CPU

⊙ Check your answers at the end of this module.

Creating Virtual Machines in Hyper-V

Microsoft Exam AZ-800:

Manage virtual machines and containers.

  • Manage Hyper-V and guest virtual machines

With Hyper-V installed, the Hyper-V Manager console is available in Server Manager's Tools menu. You use it to create and manage virtual machines, configure virtual networks, and configure the Hyper-V server. In addition, there are a number of PowerShell cmdlets for creating and configuring VMs, as discussed later in this section.

To use virtualization, you must create a virtual machine first. In Hyper-V Manager, all tasks related to configuring the Hyper-V server and creating and managing virtual machines are listed in the Actions pane.

Hyper-V VMs consist of these files stored on the Hyper-V server:

- *Configuration file*—This XML file containing the details of a VM's virtual hardware configuration is stored by default in the Virtual Machines folder in *%systemroot%*\ProgramData\Microsoft\Windows\Hyper-V. Each checkpoint created for a VM also has an XML configuration file associated with it; the file is stored by default in the same path in the Snapshots folder. These files have an .xml extension. You can change the path where these files are stored when you create the virtual machine, and you can also change the default path in Hyper-V Settings.

- *Virtual hard disk files*—Each virtual hard disk assigned to a VM has an associated VHD or VHDX file that holds the hard disk's contents. By default, these files are stored in C:\Users\Public Documents\Hyper-V\Virtual hard disks\; they have a .vhd or .vhdx extension. VHDX is the newer and preferred virtual hard disk format. VHDX disks provide better performance than VHD disks and have a 64 TB capacity, compared with 2 TB for VHD disks.

In addition, you might find the following types of files associated with a VM:

- *Differencing or checkpoint files*—These files are similar to virtual hard disk files, but they're associated with a parent VHD or VHDX file and are created when you create a differencing disk or checkpoint. Differencing disks are discussed in the "Working with Virtual Hard Disks" section, and checkpoints are discussed in the "Managing Checkpoints" section later in this module. These files have an .avhd or .avhdx extension, depending on whether they're associated with a VHD or VHDX virtual hard disk.

- *Saved state files*—If you save a VM's state, two files are created. A file with a .bin extension contains the contents of the saved VM's memory, and a file with a .vsv extension contains the saved state of the VM's devices. Both files are in a folder named with the GUID of the VM located where the VM's configuration file is stored.

The process of creating a VM involves just a few general steps:

1. Start the New Virtual Machine Wizard in Hyper-V Manager.
2. Give the new VM a descriptive name.

3. Choose a location for the VM. Storing virtual machines on a hard disk that's separate from your Windows Server installation is usually best. In datacenter applications, VMs are often stored on storage area networks (SANs) for enhanced reliability and management. With this setup, if a host server goes down or is taken out of service for maintenance, another Hyper-V host can be assigned to run its VMs without having to physically move VM files.

4. Choose a generation 1 or generation 2 virtual machine. A generation 1 virtual machine creates a virtual hardware environment compatible with Hyper-V versions before Windows Server 2012. A generation 2 virtual machine requires at least a Windows Server 2012 or Windows 8 guest OS and supports features such as secure boot, PXE boot, and SCSI boot.

5. Assign the amount of memory the VM requires. Memory requirements for virtual machines are typically the same as requirements for installing the OS on a physical computer. With Hyper-V, you can take advantage of dynamic memory allocation, in which the hypervisor allocates only as much memory as the VM needs, up to the maximum specified. The amount of memory assigned to a VM can be changed later, but the VM must be powered off.

6. Configure networking. You have the choice of connecting with an external switch, which uses one of the host network adapters; using a private switch or an internal switch; or leaving the VM disconnected from the network. There are no virtual switches until you create one, which you can do during Hyper-V installation or after installation is complete using Hyper-V Manager or PowerShell. You can change the network connection for a VM at any time, including while the VM is running.

7. Create a virtual hard disk. You can give the virtual disk a name or accept the default, and you can choose the virtual disk's size and location. Putting virtual disk files on a drive separate from the Windows Server host's boot drive results in the best performance. You can also use an existing virtual hard disk or attach a hard disk later.

8. Install an OS. In this step, you can install an OS from media inserted in the host's physical CD/DVD drive (generation 1 VM only), from a CD/DVD image file (an .iso file), from a boot floppy disk image (generation 1 VM only), or over the network by using PXE boot. You can also install an OS later.

Basic Virtual Machine Management with Hyper-V Manager

With Hyper-V, a virtual machine runs in the background until you connect to it in Hyper-V Manager. A running VM doesn't require Hyper-V Manager to be running or even installed, nor does it require anyone to be signed in to the server. Furthermore, you can configure a VM to start and shut down automatically when the host server starts and shuts down. In addition, like any OS, you can manage a VM remotely by using tools such as Remote Desktop, MMCs, and PowerShell if the VM is configured to communicate with the host network.

Hyper-V Manager provides a graphical interface for creating, managing, and interacting with virtual machines. The middle pane shows all installed virtual machines at the top (see Figure 12-3) and displays each VM's name, state, CPU use, assigned memory, uptime, and status. Normally, the Status column doesn't display anything unless you perform a task, such as exporting a VM or creating a checkpoint. When you select a VM, the Checkpoints section shows a list of checkpoints created for it. If you click the VM's name in this section, you see a screenshot of the VM at the time the checkpoint was taken along with the time and date it was taken. The bottom section shows a real-time screenshot of a running VM. When a running VM's screen changes, the screenshot in Hyper-V Manager reflects the change with a slight delay.

Connecting to a virtual machine opens a window that serves as the user interface to the VM and looks similar to a Remote Desktop connection. You can connect to a VM by using any of the following methods:

- Right-click the VM and click Connect.
- Double-click the VM.
- Select the VM and double-click its screenshot in the bottom section.
- Select the VM and click Connect in the Action menu or Actions pane.

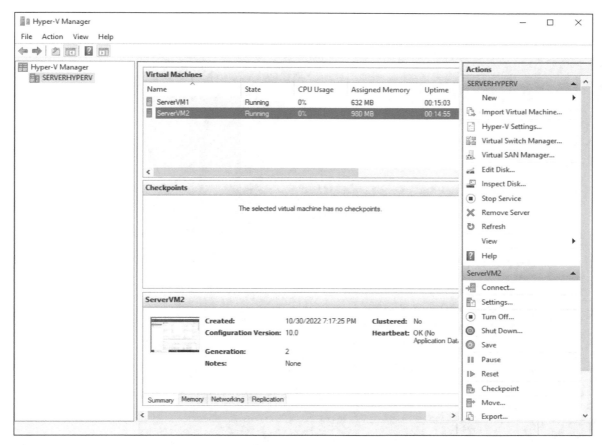

Figure 12-3   Hyper-V Manager showing a virtual machine

After you're connected, you see the Virtual Machine Connection console, shown in Figure 12-4. The toolbar icons from left to right are as follows:

- Ctrl+Alt+Delete (sends a Ctrl+Alt+Delete keystroke combination to the VM)
- Start (starts the VM)
- Turn Off (turns off the VM)
- Shut Down (sends a signal to the OS to perform a shutdown)
- Save (saves the VM's state, similar to Windows hibernation mode)
- Pause (pauses the VM, similar to Windows sleep mode)
- Reset (resets the VM)
- Checkpoint (creates a checkpoint of a VM)
- Revert (reverts to a VM's checkpoint)
- Enhanced session (changes the session mode to enhanced)

Note 7

When you press the Ctrl+Alt+Delete keys while running a virtual machine, the host operating system captures it rather than the guest OS running in the VM. You sometimes need to send a Ctrl+Alt+Delete sequence to a guest OS—for example, when you are signing in to Windows. Instead of using the keystroke combination, you must press the Ctrl+Alt+Delete icon in the Virtual Machine Connection console so that the guest OS responds to it.

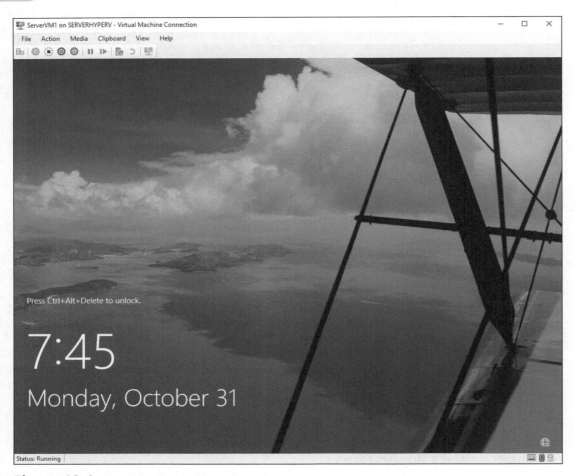

Figure 12-4 The Virtual Machine Connection console

Most options on the toolbar are self-explanatory. Checkpoints are discussed later in the module in the "Managing Virtual Machines" section, and Enhanced Session mode is discussed in the "Enhanced Session Mode" section. You can access all these toolbar options from the Action menu, too. The following list summarizes some tasks you can perform with other menus:

- *File*—Access the VM's settings and exit the VM.
- *Action*—Perform all the actions on the toolbar.
- *Media*—Specify a CD/DVD drive the VM should connect to, specify an .iso file the VM mounts as a virtual CD/DVD drive, or specify a floppy disk image that can be mounted as a virtual floppy disk.
- *Clipboard*—Copy a screenshot of the VM to the Clipboard or paste Clipboard text into the VM. You can also copy and paste between the host computer and virtual machines or between virtual machines.
- *View*—Toggle the display of the toolbar and switch to full-screen mode.
- *Help*—Get help on various topics related to the Virtual Machine Connection console.

If you want to disconnect from a virtual machine, which closes the Virtual Machine Connection console but doesn't shut down the VM, simply click File and then Exit from the menu or close the window.

Advanced VM Creation Methods

Virtual machines can be created by using other methods besides the New Virtual Machine Wizard, including the following:

- Importing an exported VM
- Copying the virtual disk
- Converting a physical machine to a virtual machine (this method is not part of the AZ-800 exam objectives and is not covered in this text)

Exporting VMs

Virtual machines can be exported and then imported to create one or more virtual machines. You can even export a running VM. Because you can export a VM while it's running, this feature allows you to back up a VM by exporting it without first shutting it down. You can use an exported VM as a backup, to move a VM to a different host, or to make a copy of an existing VM. When you choose the Export option for a VM, you're prompted to enter a path for storing the exported VM. You can export the VM to local storage or enter a path to a network share. After a VM is exported, it can be moved to archival storage as a backup, imported on another server running Hyper-V, or imported on the same server. To export a VM using PowerShell, use the `Export-VM` *VMName* `-Path` *C:\ExportVMs* cmdlet, replacing *VMName* and *C:\ExportVMs* with the name of the VM to export and the path where the files should be exported. When you export a VM, it creates a folder with the name of the VM in the specified path and creates three subfolders named Virtual Machines, Virtual Hard Disks, and Snapshots.

Importing VMs

You can import a VM that has been exported or a VM that hasn't been exported. The ability to import a VM that hasn't been exported first can come in handy if, for example, your Hyper-V host suffers a hardware or software failure; you can simply move the hard disk containing VMs to another host and import them in place. When you import a virtual machine, you have three options for the type of import:

- *Register the virtual machine in-place (use the existing unique ID)*—This option registers the exported VM in Hyper-V from its current location. No copy of the exported VM is made. Use this option only if you're restoring a failed or corrupt VM or rebuilding a Hyper-V host, and the files are already where you want them. The advantage of this option is that the import process is fast. Note that you can't import a virtual machine that already exists in Hyper-V. If you need to import a VM that is already in Hyper-V (for example, if it is corrupt or will no longer boot for some reason), you must first delete that VM in Hyper-V Manager or use the "Restore the virtual machine" option discussed next.

- *Restore the virtual machine (use the existing unique ID)*—This option is usually best for restoring VMs from an export intended as a backup. It copies the VM files to their original location on the host, leaving the exported files unchanged and available for future restoration if needed. You can't use this option if the original exported VM is already running on the Hyper-V host, so you must shut it down.

- *Copy the virtual machine (create a new unique ID)*—Use this option to make a copy or clone of a virtual machine and register it in Hyper-V. For example, use this option if you want to use a VM as a template for additional VMs that you can run on the same Hyper-V host or another Hyper-V host. Because a new unique ID is created, the VMs can run on the same Hyper-V host as the exported VM.

> ### Caution ❗
>
> If you import a VM in which the original VM is a member of a domain, you must run Sysprep on the guest OS before you can make it a member of the same domain as the exported VM. For example, say you are running a domain named AZ800.corp and you create a VM named ServerDM1 and export that VM. You then join ServerDM1 to the domain. Next, you import ServerDM1 using the copy option. Next, you change its computer name and try to join it to the AZ800.corp domain. You will get an error indicating that the VM is already a member of the domain. You must first run Sysprep on the imported VM because Sysprep will change the necessary security identifiers within Windows.

To import a VM using PowerShell, use the `Import-VM` *-ImportType* `-Path` *PathtoVM* cmdlet, where *-ImportType* is either `-Register` to register the VM in place or `-Copy` to restore the VM and use the existing unique ID. Use `-Copy -GenerateNewId` to copy the VM and create a new unique ID. *PathtoVM* is the path of the VM configuration file. You need the file name of the configuration file that includes the VM's GUID. The GUID is the unique identifier for the VM, and is 128 bits in length or 32 hexadecimal digits, which is cumbersome to type. However, there is a shortcut as long as there is only one configuration file in the path from which you are importing. First, find out the name of the configuration file by looking in the Virtual Machines folder where you exported the VM. Make a note of the first character of the file name. (It will be a hexadecimal number.) Then, when you type the `Import-VM` cmdlet, type the path to the configuration file, then type only the first character of the file name and press Tab. PowerShell will complete the file name for you. You will see this in action in an activity.

> **Note 8**
>
> By default, when you import a VM with the copy option, it will copy the VM to the default location specified in the Hyper-V settings for virtual machines and virtual hard disks. You can override this using the `-VirtualMachinePath` and `-VhdDestinationPath` parameters.

Copying a Virtual Disk

Copying a virtual disk doesn't actually create a new VM, but it means you don't have to install a guest OS on a new VM you create. The result isn't much different from an export operation followed by an import with the "Copy the virtual machine (create a new unique ID)" option, but the procedure is different:

1. Copy the virtual hard disk from an existing VM to a new folder. Hyper-V virtual hard disks have the extension .vhdx and are usually placed in the location you select when you create a virtual hard disk in the New Virtual Machine Wizard. The VM that's currently using the virtual disk must be shut down before you copy it.

2. Create a virtual machine with the New Virtual Machine Wizard, but in the Connect Virtual Hard Disk window, select the "Use an existing virtual hard disk" option and browse to the copied virtual hard disk. With PowerShell, use the `New-VM` cmdlet, include the `-VHDPath` parameter, and specify the path to the copied VHD.

Because the guest OS is on the virtual hard disk, you have a new VM with the same guest OS as the virtual hard disk. The only real difference between this method and the export/import method is that you must create the virtual machine in the New Virtual Machine Wizard and can change the VM name and configuration there.

Summary of PowerShell Cmdlets for Working with VMs

You can also create and manage VMs with PowerShell cmdlets and create PowerShell scripts to automate VM management. Table 12-2 describes the cmdlets you use most often when working with VMs. To see all cmdlets that work with VMs, use the `Get-Command *-VM*` cmdlet. To see all Hyper-V cmdlets, use the `Get-Command -Module Hyper-V` cmdlet. There are over 200 of them.

Generation 1 and Generation 2 VMs

When you create a VM with the New Virtual Machine Wizard or the `New-VM` PowerShell cmdlet, you have the option of creating a generation 1 or generation 2 VM. Generation 2 VMs are based on revised virtual hardware specifications, so they have enhanced VM capabilities and support for newer standards:

- *Unified Extensible Firmware Interface (UEFI) firmware instead of traditional PC BIOS*—Enhances the VM's hardware environment and removes the 2.2 TB partition limit for the boot volume. Also supports PXE boot with synthetic device drivers as well as booting from a SCSI virtual disk. The guest OS must be 64-bit.

- *Device support*—Removes support for legacy network adapters, IDE controllers, legacy keyboards, and floppy disk controllers. Adds support for booting from software-based devices, using virtual machine bus (VMBus), SCSI devices, and a new software-based DVD drive. Generation 2 VMs don't support booting from a physical DVD device; you must use an ISO file or a network boot to start an installation.

- *Network boot with IPv6*—Generation 1 VMs could network boot with IPv4 only.

- *VHDX-only support*—Generation 2 VMs support only VHDX hard disk files, but you can convert a VHD file to VHDX with the `Convert-VHD` PowerShell cmdlet.

- *GPT boot*—Generation 2 VMs can boot to a boot disk that uses a GUID Partitioning Table (GPT) partitioning scheme.

Table 12-2   PowerShell cmdlets for working with VMs

Cmdlet	Use	Example

New-VM	Create a virtual machine.	To create a VM named VMTest1 with 2 GB of RAM and a blank virtual disk named VMTest1.vhdx stored in the V:\VMs\VMTest1 folder, enter:
		
		`New-VM -Name VMTest1`
		`-MemoryStartupBytes 2GB`
		`-NewVHDPath V:\VMs\VMTest1\`
		`VMTest1.vhdx`

Start-VM	Start a VM.	To start all VMs with a name starting with "VMTest," enter: `Start-VM -Name VMTest*`
Stop-VM	Shut down a VM. Use the -Force option to force the shutdown even if running applications have unsaved data or the screen is locked. Loss of data can result if a running application doesn't automatically save data.	To shut down all VMs with a name starting with "VMTest," enter: `Stop-VM -Name VMTest*`
Get-VM	Display information about a VM. This cmdlet can also be used to pipe information to other cmdlets.	To display a list of running VMs, enter: `Get-VM	Where-Object` `{$_.State -eq 'Running'}`
Suspend-VM	Pause a running VM.	`Suspend-VM -Name VMTest1`
Save-VM	Save the state of a VM.	`Save-VM -Name VMTest1`
Restart-VM	Shut down and restart a VM.	`Restart-VM -Name VMTest1`

Checkpoint-VM	Create a VM checkpoint (snapshot).	To create a checkpoint for VMTest1 named "BeforeInstallingAD," enter:
		
		`Checkpoint-VM -Name "VMTest1"`
		`-SnapshotName "BeforeInstallingAD"`

Restore-VMSnapshot	Restore a VM to a previous checkpoint.	To restore the VMTest1 VM to a snapshot named "BeforeInstallingAD," enter:
		
		`Restore-VMSnapshot -Name`
		`"BeforeInstallingAD" -VMName`
		`VMTest1`

Export-VM	Export a VM.	To export the VMTest1 VM to the V:\VMExport folder, enter:
		
		`Export-VM -Name VMTest1 -Path`
		`V:\VMExport`

Import-VM	Import a VM.	To import the previously exported VMTest1 with the copy and create new ID option, enter:
		
		`Import-VM -Path "V:\VMExport`
		`\VMTest1" -Copy -GenerateNewID`

- *Disk expansion*—A VHDX disk can be expanded while the VM is online, including the boot volume.
- *Reduced attack surface*—By removing legacy devices and adding the secure boot feature, security is improved for generation 2 VMs.
- *Secure boot*—This enhancement prevents unauthorized code from running during a system boot.

There are other changes, but this list contains the most important improvements. Converting a generation 1 VM to generation 2 is possible, but you can't use a generation 2 VM on Hyper-V versions before Windows Server 2012 R2. In addition, generation 2 VMs support only Windows 8 or Windows Server 2012 and later guest OSs.

Self-Check Questions

3. A Hyper-V virtual hard disk can have a VHD or VHDX file. True or False?

    a. True   **b.** False

4. Which virtual machine import option should you choose if you want to restore a corrupt VM without making a copy of the exported files?

    a. Register the virtual machine in-place (use the existing unique ID)
    b. Restore the virtual machine (use the existing unique ID)
    c. Copy the virtual machine (create a new unique ID)
    d. Restore from backup (create a new unique ID)

⊙ Check your answers at the end of this module.

Activity 12-1

Resetting Your Virtual Environment

Time Required: 5 minutes
Objective: Reset your virtual environment by applying the InitialConfig checkpoint or snapshot.
Required Tools and Equipment: ServerHyperV
Description: Apply the InitialConfig checkpoint or snapshot to ServerHyperV.

1. Be sure ServerHyperV is shut down. In your virtualization program, apply the InitialConfig checkpoint or snapshot to ServerHyperV.
2. Close your virtual machine environment.

Activity 12-2

Creating a Virtual Machine

Time Required: 10 minutes
Objective: Create a new virtual machine using PowerShell.
Required Tools and Equipment: ServerHyperV
Description: The Hyper-V role is installed on your server, so you are ready to create a virtual machine using PowerShell.

1. Sign in to ServerHyperV as **Administrator**.
2. Open a PowerShell window. You will create a new virtual machine named VMTest1 with 1 GB of RAM and a 40 GB virtual hard disk located in C:\VMs\VMTest1.

(continues)

Activity 12-2 Continued

3. In PowerShell, type **New-VM VMTest1 –MemoryStartupBytes 1GB –NewVHDPath C:\VMs\VMTest1\VMTest1.vhdx –NewVHDSizeBytes 40GB** and press **Enter**. By default, a generation 1 VM is created unless you specify otherwise using the `–Generation 2` parameter. In addition, a network adapter is created, but it is not connected to a virtual switch.

4. Next, you connect the network adapter to the virtual switch named PrivateNet. Type **Connect-NetworkAdapter VMTest1 –Name "Network Adapter" –SwitchName PrivateNet** and press **Enter**.

5. You need to point the virtual DVD to an ISO file if you want to install an OS on it. Point the DVD drive to an ISO file on the host at the path C:\isos\w2k16.iso. Type **SetVMDvdDrive VMTest1 –Path C:\isos\w2k16.iso** and press **Enter**.

6. To see information about the new VM, type **Get-VM VMTest1** and press **Enter**. You see just a summary of the VM. To see more details, type **Get-VM VMTest1 | fl *** and press **Enter**. That command tells PowerShell to show all the properties of the VM in a list format. The `fl` stands for Format-List and the asterisk (`*`) means all properties are listed. You can also see the VM and its settings in Hyper-V Manager. Open Hyper-V Manager, if desired, and verify that your VM can be seen and managed there.

7. One of the nice things about using PowerShell to manage VMs is that you can get detailed information about VMs and create scripts for a number of management functions. For example, you can start all VMs that are currently turned off. Type **Get-VM | Where-Object {$_.State –eq "Off"} | Start-VM** and press **Enter**. All VMs that are currently off are started. You can access most of the properties of a VM by using the syntax `$_.PropertyName`. For example, in the cmdlet you just entered, the `PropertyName` is `State`.

8. Next, you can stop all the running VMs. Type **Get-VM | Where-Object {$_.State –eq "Running"} | Stop-VM –Force** and press **Enter**. The `–Force` parameter causes the VM to be turned off even if the OS is locked or there is no OS installed.

9. Delete this VM. You will use the premade VM named ServerVM1 for the remainder of the Hyper-V activities. Type **Remove-VM VMTest1 –Force** and press **Enter**. Removing a VM doesn't delete the virtual disk it was using. To delete the virtual disk, just use the `del` command. Type **del C:\VMs\VMTest1\VMTest1.vhdx** and press **Enter**.

10. Stay signed in to ServerHyperV and continue to the next activity.

Activity 12-3

Working with Virtual Machines in Hyper-V Manager

Time Required: 25 minutes

Objective: Explore Hyper-V Manager.

Required Tools and Equipment: ServerHyperV, ServerVM1 virtual machine

Description: In this activity, you work with Hyper-V Manager to become familiar with managing virtual machines in Windows Server. You create a checkpoint, make some changes to the OS, and revert to the checkpoint.

1. Sign in to ServerHyperV as **Administrator**, if necessary.

2. Open Server Manager, click **Tools**, and then click **Hyper-V Manager** from the menu.

3. Right-click the **ServerVM1** virtual machine and click **Connect**.

4. Power on ServerVM1 by clicking the **Start** toolbar icon or clicking **Action** and then **Start** from the menu. While Windows is booting, close the Virtual Machine Connection console. Notice that in Hyper-V Manager, the VM's CPU use changes as Windows boots, and the VM's screenshot in the bottom pane changes periodically.

5. Double-click the VM's screenshot at the bottom of Hyper-V Manager to open the Virtual Machine Connection console for the VM. After Windows finishes booting, click the **Ctrl+Alt+Delete** toolbar icon (the leftmost icon) to send a Ctrl+Alt+Delete keystroke to the VM, and then sign in as **Administrator**.

(continues)

Activity 12-3 Continued

> **Note 9**
>
> To see a description of any toolbar icon, hover your mouse pointer over it.

6. Start Notepad and type your name in a new text document. Don't close Notepad or save the file yet. In the Virtual Machine Connection console menu, click the **Save** toolbar icon or click **Action** and then **Save**.

7. Close the Virtual Machine Connection console. In Hyper-V Manager, notice that the State column for the VM shows Saved (or Saving if it hasn't finished saving). After it has finished saving, open the Virtual Machine Connection console by double-clicking **ServerVM1**. Start the VM by clicking the **Start** toolbar icon. You're right where you left off in Notepad.

8. Save the Notepad file to your desktop as **file1.txt**, and then exit Notepad.

9. Click the **Checkpoint** toolbar icon or click **Action** and then **Checkpoint** from the menu. When you're prompted to enter a name, type **BeforeDeletingFile1**, and then click **Yes**. You see a message titled "Production checkpoint created." Read the information in the message, which informs you that the running application state was not included in the checkpoint. Production checkpoints are a new feature in Windows Server and are discussed later in this module. Click **OK**.

10. After the checkpoint is finished, minimize the VM and note in Hyper-V Manager that the checkpoint is listed in the Checkpoints section. Maximize the VM and delete file1 from your desktop. Empty the Recycle Bin so that you know the file is really gone.

11. Click the **Revert** toolbar icon or click **Action** and then **Revert** from the menu.

12. Click **Revert** when prompted. The VM displays a message that it's reverting and the VM is turned off. Start the VM and log on. When the desktop is displayed again, you should see the Notepad file back on the desktop. Close the Virtual Machine Connection console.

> **Note 10**
>
> The VM was turned off when you reverted the checkpoint because it is a Production checkpoint, which doesn't save the running state of the VM. If it had been a regular checkpoint, the VM would have stayed on and you would have been returned to the running state when you took the checkpoint.

13. In Hyper-V Manager, right-click **ServerVM1** and click **Shutdown**. When prompted, click the **Shut Down** button. The Status column displays "Shutting Down Virtual Machine." Close the Virtual Machine Connection console.

14. After the VM state changes to Off, delete the checkpoint by right-clicking **BeforeDeletingFile1** in the Checkpoints section and clicking **Delete Checkpoint**. Click **Delete** to confirm.

15. Stay signed in to ServerHyperV if you're continuing to the next activity.

Activity 12-4

Exporting and Importing a VM

Time Required: 30 minutes

Objective: Export a VM and then import it using PowerShell.

Required Tools and Equipment: ServerHyperV, InstallCore virtual machine

Description: In this activity, you practice exporting and importing a VM using PowerShell. You will work with the VM named InstallCore because it takes much less time to export and import. Also, it takes less disk space.

(continues)

Activity 12-4 Continued

1. On ServerHyperV, open a PowerShell window.
2. Type **Export-VM InstallCore –Path C:\ExportVMs** and press **Enter**. PowerShell will create the ExportVMs folder for you.
3. When the export has completed, type **dir C:\ExportVMs** and press **Enter**. You see a folder named InstallCore. Type **dir C:\ExportVMs\InstallCore** and press **Enter**. You see the three folders that contain the exported VM. Type **dir "C:\ExportVMs\InstallCore\Virtual Machines"** and press **Enter**. Be sure to include the quotation marks (") because there is a space in the path. You see the two files that have the configuration information of your exported VM. Make a note of the first character of the file name (both file names are the same except for the extension).
4. Now you will import the VM using the following cmdlet. In the path parameter, be sure to use quotation marks, type the first character of the configuration file name in place of the *X*, and press the Tab key where the command shows <Tab> so PowerShell will finish the path with the configuration file name. Type **Import-VM –Copy -GenerateNewID –Path "C:\ExportVMs\InstallCore\Virtual Machines\X<Tab>"** and press **Enter**. Note that had you not included the –GenerateNewID option, you would have received an error about a duplicate identifier.

> **Note 11**
>
> You can use the Tab key in any path when typing PowerShell cmdlets or command prompt commands. Windows will always display the first file or folder name it finds that starts with the character or characters you type. For example, if you type dir c:\ex<Tab>, Windows will complete that part of the path with C:\ExportVMs\, assuming a folder with that name exists.

5. Verify the new virtual machine by typing **Get-VM** and pressing **Enter**. Note that there are now two VMs named InstallCore. Normally, the next thing you would do is rename the imported VM. To do that in PowerShell, you'd need to use the virtual machine ID because you can't distinguish the VMs by name. For now, open **Hyper-V Manager**.
6. The VM you just imported will be listed second because it has a later creation date. To verify, click each VM and look in the bottom pane where the creation date is shown. Delete the second virtual machine named **InstallCore** by right-clicking it and clicking **Delete**. Click **Delete** again to confirm. Note that deleting the VM in Hyper-V only deletes the configuration file, not the virtual hard disk.
7. Stay signed in and continue to the next activity.

Managing Virtual Machines

Microsoft Exam AZ-800:

Manage virtual machines and containers.

- Manage Hyper-V and guest virtual machines

Now that you have a general understanding of how Hyper-V works and how to configure virtual networks and virtual hard disks, this section covers additional features you can use to manage and configure the virtual environment. In particular, you examine the following:

- Virtual machine hardware settings
- Integration Services

- Checkpoints
- Automatic start and stop actions
- Enhanced Session mode

Virtual Machine Hardware Settings

Virtual machines have a number of hardware settings that can be configured. The next module covers working with virtual hard disks and virtual network settings in more detail. In this section, you look at options for changing BIOS settings, modifying the amount of memory allocated to a VM, and configuring virtual processor settings. Most settings can't be changed unless the VM is powered off. All these settings are accessed by right-clicking a VM and clicking Settings.

BIOS and Firmware Settings

The BIOS settings for a generation 1 VM enable you to change the order in which the VM's BIOS searches for boot devices (see Figure 12-5). Click a device in the Startup order list box and click the Move Up and Move Down buttons to change its order. For example, if you already have an OS installed on the VM's hard disk, you might want to set the boot order to list the IDE disk first so that the VM doesn't attempt to boot from a CD.

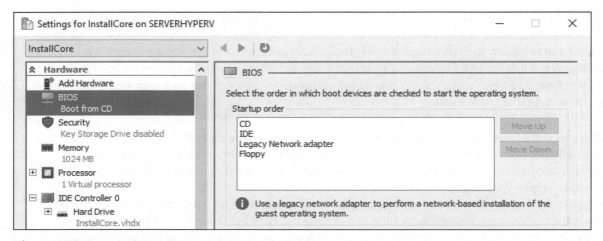

Figure 12-5   BIOS settings for a generation 1 VM

On a generation 2 VM, the hardware category is Firmware instead of BIOS (see Figure 12-6). As with a generation 1 VM, you can set the boot order. By default, a generation 2 VM is set to boot from the network adapter using PXE boot or from the DVD drive if you specified an ISO file to connect to the DVD drive. After Windows is installed, the first entry in the boot order is the Windows boot manager file. Secure Boot is enabled by default and is recommended because it prevents unauthorized code from running at startup. On generation 2 VMs, the only option for disk controllers is SCSI. IDE controllers are not supported.

Security

In the Security settings of a VM (see Figure 12-7), you can enable or disable Secure Boot (generation 2 VMs only) and enable encryption support, which allows you to encrypt the virtual hard disks. A security feature available starting in Windows Server 2016 is Shielded VMs. If you enable shielding, Secure Boot and encryption are automatically enabled. Shielding prevents a compromised or malicious administrator from accessing the data on a VM and allows only specific hosts to run the VM. Specifically, you must deploy the Host Guardian Service (HGS), which sets up a trust relationship between the host and the VM, disallowing other hosts from running the VM and preventing the host from running untrusted VMs. Shielded VMs and the Host Guardian Service are beyond the scope of this book.

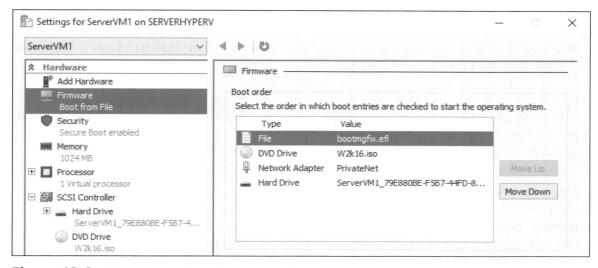

Figure 12-6   Firmware settings for a generation 2 VM

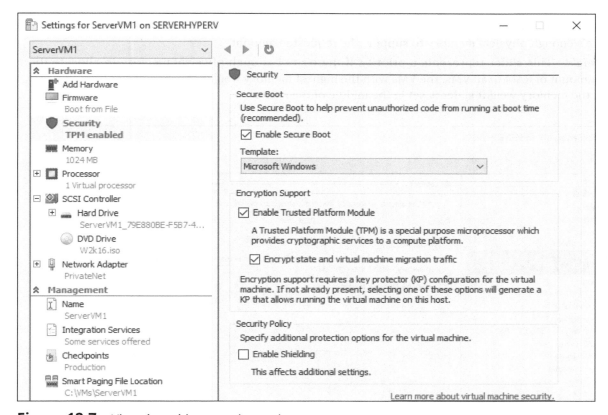

Figure 12-7   Virtual machine security settings

Memory Allocation

When you create a VM, you can configure the amount of memory it's allocated from the host computer, and you can change this amount at any time later while the VM is turned off. The amount of memory you allocate must take into account other VMs running simultaneously and have enough memory left over for the host server. Windows Server running Hyper-V needs about 1 GB of RAM plus 32 MB for each running VM that has been assigned up to 1 GB of RAM. For example, if you plan to run three virtual machines, each with 1 GB of RAM, you need a total of 3 GB for the VMs plus 1 GB and an extra 96 MB (32 MB × 3) for the host, which is a total of slightly more than 4 GB. If the VMs are allocated more than 1 GB, add 8 MB to the host for each additional GB.

Dynamic Memory

Dynamic Memory allows an administrator to set startup, minimum, and maximum memory allocation values for each VM. Hyper-V adjusts the memory allocation for a VM up or down, based on its actual memory needs, between the minimum and maximum values you specify. Dynamic Memory isn't enabled by default; you enable it by choosing Memory in the VM's settings (see Figure 12-8). The following list describes the settings for this feature:

- *RAM*—This setting specifies the amount of RAM allocated to a VM when it starts. When a computer starts, it often consumes more RAM because of all the processes loaded into memory and started. Some processes look for a minimum amount of available RAM when they're started, and if this amount isn't available, they don't start. After all the initial processes have started, the system might require less than the startup RAM.
- *Minimum RAM*—The least RAM the VM can ever be allocated.
- *Maximum RAM*—The most RAM the VM can ever be allocated.
- *Memory buffer*—The amount of extra memory Hyper-V attempts to assign to a VM above the VM's current requirements. For example, if the memory buffer is set to 20 percent and the VM currently needs 1 GB of RAM, Hyper-V attempts to allocate 1 GB plus 20 percent, or 1.2 GB. The memory buffer amount is allocated to a VM only if there's enough physical memory to support the requested amount.
- *Memory weight*—This slider represents a priority. If there's not enough physical memory to allocate the requested amount of RAM to all VMs, the VMs with the highest memory weight are given the highest priority. By default, the memory weight slider is set in the middle of the scale.

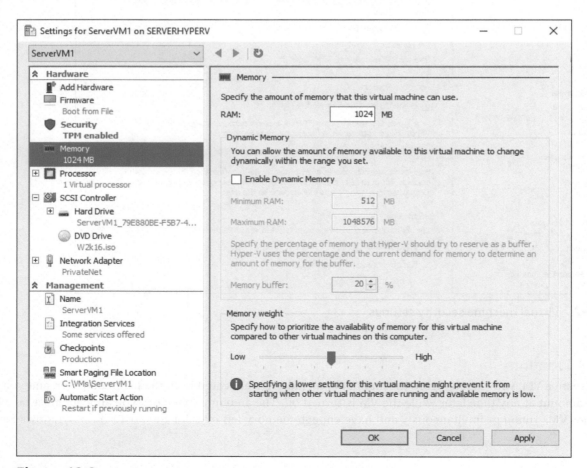

Figure 12-8 Memory settings with Dynamic Memory enabled

Hot-Add Memory

Hyper-V in Windows Server adds the ability to hot-add and remove memory, which is the addition of memory or removal of memory while the VM is running. This feature is only supported on VMs running Windows 10 or Windows Server guest OSs and some distributions of Linux. Furthermore, the VM configuration must be version 8 or later, so VMs created in earlier versions of Hyper-V will not support this feature until you upgrade the configuration.

Smart Paging

Smart paging works with Dynamic Memory. It's a file on the host computer used for temporary memory storage when a sudden surge in memory requirements exceeds the physical amount of memory available. Smart paging is used only when a VM is restarting, there's no available physical memory, and the host can't reclaim any memory from other running VMs. In fact, the smart paging file is created only when it's needed, and it's deleted after the VM no longer needs it. So, this file functions as a type of failsafe measure to bridge the gap between a VM's required startup memory and its minimum memory when physical memory is low.

No configuration is needed for smart paging other than its location on the host, which is C:\ProgramData\Microsoft \Windows\Hyper-V by default. However, the smart paging file should be stored on a non-system disk—in other words, on a different disk from the one holding the \Windows directory.

Virtual Processor Settings

You can adjust how many virtual processors are assigned to the virtual machine. The maximum number of virtual processors you assign can match the total number of physical processors or processor cores installed on the host computer (see Figure 12-9). If you're running a Hyper-V server on a quad-core Xeon, for instance, you can assign up to four virtual processors to each VM. However, if your VMs handle substantial processing workloads, the recommended method is to assign one or more virtual processors to each VM and reserve one physical processor (or processor core) for the host computer. For example, if the host computer has a quad-core processor and you're running three VMs on the host, allocate each VM one virtual processor and reserve one for the host computer. If your VMs aren't carrying substantial processing workloads, you can use more virtual processors than there are physical processors. For instance, you can allocate one virtual processor for each of six VMs when the host has only four physical processor cores.

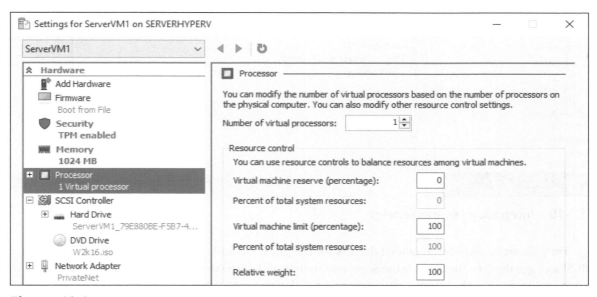

Figure 12-9   Virtual processor settings

The "Resource control" section specifies how host resources are allocated to the VM. In this example, the host has four processors and the VM has been assigned two:

- *Virtual machine reserve (percentage)*—This setting specifies what percentage of the total processing resources allocated to the VM is guaranteed to be available. The default setting is 0. If you change this setting, the "Percent of total system resources" value changes to reflect what percentage of the total host processing power is in reserve for the VM. For example, if the VM has been assigned two virtual processors on a host with four processors, and you reserve 50 percent for the VM, 25 percent of the total host system resources is held in reserve for the VM.

- *Virtual machine limit (percentage)*—This value specifies what percentage of the assigned processing power the VM can use. The default value is 100. If you assign two processors to the VM on a host with four processors, the VM can use 100 percent of the processing power of two processors, which sets "Percent of total system resources" at 50. That leaves 50 percent of the total processing power available for other workloads.

- *Relative weight*—This setting assigns a priority to the VM's access to processing resources when more than one VM is competing for the same resource. The value can range from 1 to 10,000; the higher the value, the higher the VM's priority. The default value is 100. If multiple VMs have the same relative weight value, they get an equal share of the available resources.

Integration Services

The Integration Services section of a VM's settings (see Figure 12-10) indicates which integration services are enabled on a VM. On Windows VMs starting with Windows Server 2008 and Vista, all the services shown in Figure 12-10, except Guest services, are installed by default. You need to manually install integration services only on VMs running OSs before Windows Server 2008/Vista or non-Windows OSs.

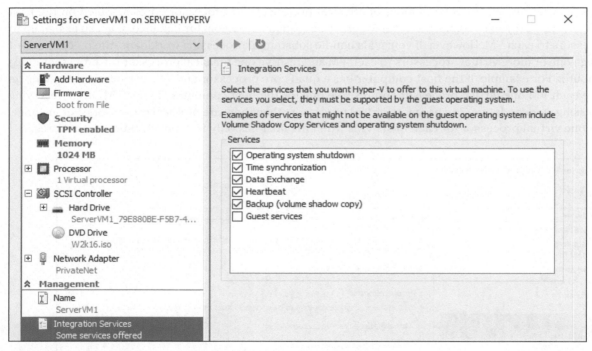

Figure 12-10   Integration Services settings

Integration Services provide enhanced drivers for the guest OS and improve performance and functionality for IDE and SCSI storage devices, network interfaces, and mouse and video devices. The storage controller and network interface drivers included in the integration services are called **synthetic drivers**, and they're optimized for use in the Hyper-V environment. **Emulated drivers**, which are used when integration services aren't installed, are also referred to as legacy drivers.

Enhanced video and mouse drivers in integration services make it easier to use a guest OS's user interface. Without integration services installed, the VM captures the mouse when you click inside the VM window, and you must press Ctrl+Alt+left arrow to release the mouse back to the host OS. With integration services installed, however, you can move the mouse from guest to host freely. Furthermore, if you access the guest OS through Remote Desktop, the mouse isn't functional in the guest OS at all unless integration services are installed.

Aside from enhanced drivers, integration services offer additional options that you can enable or disable in the VM's settings:

- *Operating system shutdown*—Allows you to shut down the VM by clicking the Shutdown button in the Virtual Machine Connection console or in Hyper-V Manager.
- *Time synchronization*—Allows you to synchronize the VM's time with the host. If the VM is a Windows domain controller, however, you shouldn't use this option because domain controllers have their own mechanism for time synchronization.
- *Data exchange*—Allows the VM and host to exchange information by using Registry keys.
- *Heartbeat*—Allows the host machine to detect when the VM has locked up or crashed. The host sends heartbeat messages to the guest VM periodically, and the heartbeat service on the guest VM responds. If it fails to respond, the host machine logs an event.
- *Backup (volume shadow copy)*—Allows host backup programs to use Volume Shadow Copy Service (VSS) to back up VM hard disk files.
- *Guest services*—Allows copying files to a running VM "out of band," meaning without using a virtual network connection. Guest services use the Hyper-V virtual machine bus (VMBus) that all VMs are connected to internally through Hyper-V. By default, guest services are disabled, but after they're enabled, you can use the PowerShell cmdlet `Copy-VMFile` on the host computer to copy files from the host to the VM.

Checkpoints

Checkpoints, as you have seen, allow you to save the state of a VM and return to that state later. In previous versions of Hyper-V, the only configuration option for checkpoints was specifying the path where they are stored. Starting with Windows Server, Hyper-V now has two types of checkpoints (see Figure 12-11):

- **Standard checkpoint**—This is the original type of checkpoint that captures the state of a virtual machine, including the running state, if desired. Standard checkpoints should only be used in development and testing, not on production VMs. They are particularly useful if you need to capture the running state of a VM for troubleshooting purposes or perform what-if scenarios in a lab environment.
- **Production checkpoint**—This new type of checkpoint is supported for production virtual machines and uses backup technology in the guest OS to create the checkpoint. Production checkpoints do not save the running state of a virtual machine, but they can be created while the VM is running. If you apply a production checkpoint to a running VM, the VM will be shut down and you must restart it. Production checkpoints can only be created on a VM running a supported OS. If you try to create a production checkpoint on a VM that does not support them, a standard checkpoint will be created instead.

Managing Checkpoints

Checkpoints make working with VMs more flexible than working with physical machines. You can use checkpoints to revert a VM to a previous state, which allows you to explore what-if situations and recover from installations and configurations that have gone wrong. You can create up to 50 checkpoints per VM and revert a VM to any saved checkpoint. This feature is particularly useful in testing and lab environments because you can reset a VM to its original state with the click of a button. Production checkpoints can be safely used on production VMs.

When you create a checkpoint, either two or three files are created, depending on whether the VM is running at the time:

- *Configuration file*—This file contains configuration information about the checkpoint (such as the path to the checkpoint virtual disk file) and the virtual machine configuration. Any changes to the virtual machine configuration are recorded in the configuration file, including network, memory, device, and storage settings. This file is stored in the checkpoint file location path specified for the virtual machine in a folder named Snapshots.
- *Automatic virtual hard disk (AVHD or AVHDX) file*—A virtual disk file with the .avhd or .avhdx extension is created for each virtual disk attached to the VM. All changes made to any of the virtual disks are stored in this file. The file links back to the original virtual disk (VHD or VHDX), which remains unchanged until the checkpoint is deleted. This file is stored in the same folder as the original virtual hard disk file.

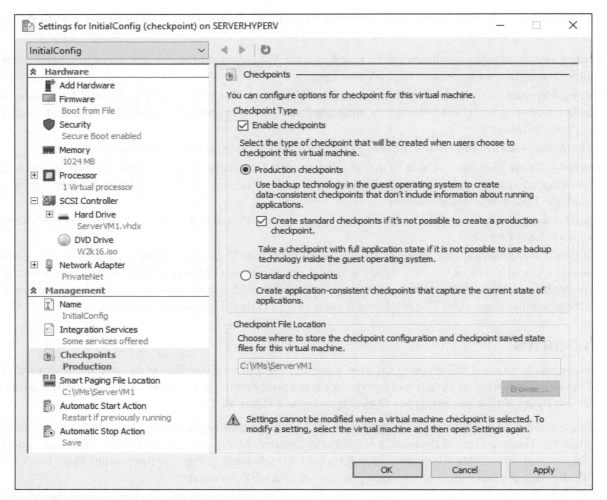

Figure 12-11 Configuring checkpoints

- *Saved state file*—If the virtual machine is running when a standard checkpoint is created, the contents of the virtual machine's memory is saved. This file can be quite large, depending on how much memory the VM is currently using. This file doesn't apply to production checkpoints because they do not save the running state of a VM. This file is stored in the same location as the checkpoint configuration file.

You need to be aware of some issues with checkpoint storage:

- By default, checkpoints are stored in the C:\ProgramData\Microsoft\Windows\Hyper-V\Snapshots folder. Because this location is on the host's system volume (where the C:\Windows folder is stored), however, you might want to relocate the checkpoints folder to a different disk, if possible, for performance reasons. You can change the checkpoint storage location for each VM in the Hyper-V Manager Settings window or change the default location for all VMs in Hyper-V Settings by specifying the default location where virtual machine configuration files are stored.
- After a checkpoint is created for a VM, you can't change the checkpoint location for that VM, but each VM can have a different checkpoint location.
- You should always use Hyper-V Manager to delete checkpoints. Checkpoint files shouldn't be deleted manually unless the VM has been deleted because the files must be merged with the original hard disk file.
- If you create a standard checkpoint while a VM is running, the amount of space required for the checkpoint includes the amount of memory allocated to the VM, which substantially increases the total amount of space the checkpoint needs. Ideally, create checkpoints while the VM is shut down to reduce the disk space used.

Some additional cautions apply to checkpoints:

- Checkpoints decrease a VM's disk performance, so use them only as necessary and delete checkpoints that are no longer needed.
- Checkpoints must be deleted before expanding a disk.
- Checkpoints can't be used with pass-through or differencing disks. Pass-through and differencing disks are discussed later in this module.

Reverting to and Applying Checkpoints

There are two ways to use a saved checkpoint: revert and apply. Reverting to a checkpoint returns the VM to its state when the *most recent* checkpoint was taken. The Revert option is available in the Actions pane of Hyper-V Manager when a VM is selected and no checkpoints are currently selected. If you click the Revert option in the Actions pane, the VM is reverted to the last checkpoint made.

The Apply option is available when a checkpoint is selected in the Checkpoints section. Selecting the most recent checkpoint and applying it has the same effect as the Revert option. However, if you select an earlier checkpoint and apply it, a new checkpoint subtree is created, as shown in Figure 12-12. Checkpoint3 was applied in the figure, and the VM is now in the state it was in when Checkpoint3 was taken, as indicated by the Now arrow. Checkpoint2 and Checkpoint4 are still available but represent a different checkpoint subtree than Checkpoint3. Because Hyper-V allows you to skip back and forth in time, so to speak, you can test several application scenarios with the ability to return to an initial state or any one of several configurations. Just be aware that the more checkpoints and checkpoint subtrees a VM has, the more resources are used by the host computer, so be sure to delete checkpoints and checkpoint subtrees when they are no longer needed.

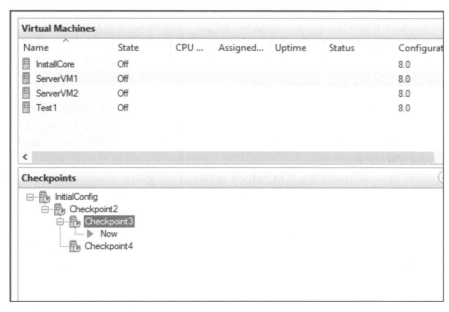

Figure 12-12   After applying a checkpoint

Automatic Start and Stop Actions

You use automatic start actions and automatic stop actions to specify how a VM should behave when the host computer starts and shuts down. The options for automatic start actions are as follows (see Figure 12-13):

- *Nothing*—The VM doesn't start when the host computer starts.
- *Automatically start if it was running when the service stopped*—If the VM was running when the host machine (or Hyper-V service) was last running, it starts when the host starts. If the VM wasn't running previously, it's not started. This option is the default start action and should be used with production VMs.

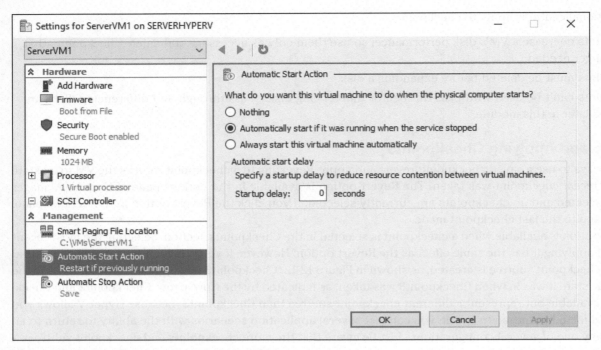

Figure 12-13 Automatic start action settings

- *Always start this virtual machine automatically*—The VM always starts when the host starts.
- *Startup delay*—If multiple VMs are set to start when the host starts, you might want to set a startup delay of different lengths for each VM to prevent resource contention. Also, if the services of one VM depend on another VM, you can set the delay time to ensure that the VMs start in the correct order.

The options for automatic stop actions are as follows (see Figure 12-14):

- *Save the virtual machine state*—The VM's state is saved when the host is shut down, which is similar to hibernate mode for a desktop computer. When the VM restarts, it picks up where it left off. This option is the default stop action, but it's not recommended for domain controllers. Be aware that the same amount of disk space is reserved as the amount of memory the VM uses.
- *Turn off the virtual machine*—This option powers down the VM, which is like pulling the power cord on a physical machine. It's not recommended unless the VM doesn't support shutdown, but even then, the save option is preferable.
- *Shut down the guest operating system*—The VM's OS undergoes a normal shutdown procedure as long as Integration Services are installed and shutdown is supported by the guest OS. This option is recommended for domain controllers, other VMs that run server roles, and applications that synchronize with other servers.

Enhanced Session Mode

Enhanced Session mode is a feature that improves interaction and device redirection between the host computer and the Virtual Machine Connection console. It provides most of the same functions as a Remote Desktop connection without the need for a network connection to the guest OS.

A regular session, called a "basic session" in Hyper-V, redirects only screen, mouse, and keyboard I/O from the guest to the Virtual Machine Connection console. An enhanced session offers these additional redirected resources and features:

- Audio redirection
- Printer redirection
- USB devices and smart cards

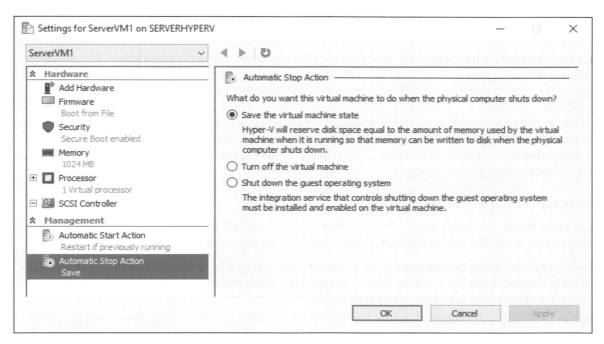

Figure 12-14 Automatic stop action settings

- Drives
- Some plug-and-play devices
- Display configuration
- Copy and paste of Clipboard data, files, and folders

With Enhanced Session mode enabled, the first thing you notice is that when you try to connect to a Virtual Machine Connection console, a message box prompts you to select the display configuration. If you click the Show Options button, you see the dialog box shown in Figure 12-15.

You can click the Local Resources tab to choose which resources from the VM should be redirected to the host computer. For example, you can use a printer connected to the host computer from the guest OS or play audio files on the guest through the host computer's speakers. You also have access to the Clipboard so that you can copy and paste text and files between the host and guest.

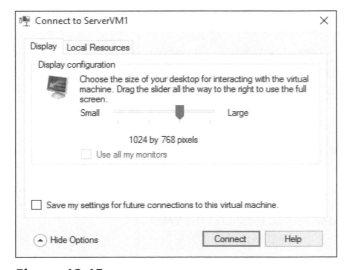

Figure 12-15 Enhanced Session mode settings

> **Note 12**
>
> To copy and paste files between the host and guest, you must use the traditional copy-and-paste method; you can't drag and drop files between host and guest.

You can also redirect drives so that files on the host computer are available to the VM. If you do, a new drive icon is displayed in File Explorer on the guest OS. For example, if you redirect the C drive on the ServerHyperV host, a new icon named "C on ServerHyperV" is listed under Devices and drives in File Explorer on the guest OS. The VM now has access to files on the C drive of the host computer.

Enabling Enhanced Session Mode

To use Enhanced Session mode, you must enable it in Hyper-V Manager and on the guest OS. By default, Enhanced Session mode is enabled on guest OSs that support it. However, verify the following:

- Remote Desktop Services must be running on the guest OS. This service is running by default, but you can verify it or start it if necessary in the Services MMC. Selecting the "Allow remote connections to this computer" option in the System Properties dialog box isn't necessary.
- You must sign in to the guest OS with an account that's a member of the local Administrators or remote Desktop Users group.

To enable Enhanced Session mode, open Hyper-V Manager, click Hyper-V Settings, and then click Enhanced Session Mode Policy. In the right pane, click Allow enhanced session mode (see Figure 12-16). To configure Virtual Machine Connection to use Enhanced Session mode, click Enhanced Session Mode in the left pane under User and click "Use enhanced session mode," which is enabled by default. To enable it on the VM, start the VM and click Connect when prompted. In the Hyper-V connect window, you'll see that the Session mode icon is now enabled and the VM is running in Enhanced Session mode. Click the Session mode icon between the enhanced and basic session modes. To enable Enhanced Session mode using PowerShell, use the `Set-VMHost -EnableEnhancedSessionMode $true` cmdlet on the Hyper-V host.

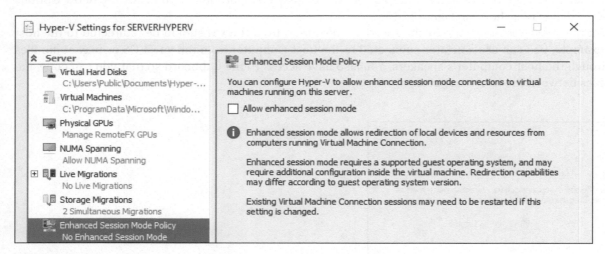

Figure 12-16 Enabling Enhanced Session mode in Hyper-V Manager

When Enhanced Session mode is enabled, you must enter your sign-in credentials each time you connect to the VM console using the virtual machine connection. Essentially, each time you close the virtual machine connection, the VM goes to the lock screen and you must enter your password when you reconnect the VM.

Discrete Device Assignment

Another feature in Windows Server Hyper-V is the ability to give a VM exclusive access to hardware devices on the host computer, a feature called **Discrete Device Assignment (DDA)**. With DDA, the VM has direct access to the device, bypassing the Hyper-V hypervisor, which increases performance. Only PCI Express (PCIe) devices are supported; the most likely candidates for this type of access are SSD drives that plug directly into the PCIe, and graphics processing units (GPUs). The details of using DDA are beyond the scope of this book, but the basic steps are as follows:

1. Disable the device on the host computer using Device Manager or the `Disable-PnPDevice` cmdlet.
2. Dismount the device from the host computer using the `Dismount-VMHostAssignableDevice` cmdlet.
3. Attach the device to the VM using the `Add-VMAssignableDevice` cmdlet.

Managing Windows VMs with PowerShell Direct

PowerShell Direct allows management of a running Hyper-V Windows VM from a Hyper-V host PowerShell prompt. Previously, a VM and host computer had to have a working network connection and valid remote management settings in order to perform management of the VM from the host. With PowerShell Direct, you simply use the `Enter-PSSession -VMName` *VMToManage* cmdlet and provide proper credentials for the VM. From there, all cmdlets you type in PowerShell are executed on the virtual machine. To exit to the host PowerShell session, type `Exit-PSSession`. You can also run a PowerShell script that is located on the host. For example, if you have a script named VMScript.ps1, you can run it on a VM named VMServer1 from the Hyper-V host by entering `Invoke-Command -VMName VMServer1 -FilePath C:\Scripts\VMScript.ps1`. The ability to manage VMs using PowerShell Direct greatly simplifies the process. PowerShell Direct only works with Windows 10, Windows Server 2016, and newer VMs running on Hyper-V hosts. Also, you must be logged in to the host computer as a Hyper-V administrator.

Managing Linux VMs with SSH Direct

PowerShell Direct works only with Windows guest OSs. For similar functionality when using Linux-based VMs, you can use a tool called SSH Direct that in turn uses a tool called HVC. HVC is an executable program that provides an SSH connection from a Hyper-V host computer to a VM running Linux with the SSH service configured and running. Note that, just like PowerShell Direct, a network connection between the host and VM is not necessary. To use HVC, type `hvc ssh` *VMname* at a Windows command prompt or PowerShell prompt. To get help using SSH Direct, type `HVC ssh` and press Enter. Like PowerShell Direct, SSH Direct requires a Windows 10, Windows Server 2016, or newer guest OS to be running on a Hyper-V host.

Self-Check Questions

5. A generation 1 VM is required if you want to boot using UEFI. True or False?

   a. True
   b. False

6. Which Hyper-V virtual machine feature provides temporary storage when a sudden surge in memory requirements exceeds the physical memory available?

   a. Hot-add memory
   b. Smart paging
   c. Dynamic memory
   d. Shielded VMs

⊙ Check your answers at the end of this module.

Activity 12-5

Enabling Enhanced Session Mode

Time Required: 10 minutes
Objective: Enable Enhanced Session mode in Hyper-V Manager and connect to a VM with this mode.
Required Tools and Equipment: ServerHyperV, ServerVM1 virtual machine
Description: You want your guest OS to have access to files on the host computer and be able to copy and paste files between the host and guest OS, so you enable Enhanced Session mode in Hyper-V Manager.

1. Sign in to ServerHyperV as **Administrator** and open Hyper-V Manager if necessary.
2. Click **Hyper-V Settings** in the Actions pane. In the left pane, under Server, click **Enhanced Session Mode Policy**. By default, this mode is disabled. In the right pane, click **Allow enhanced session mode**.
3. In the left pane, under User, click **Enhanced Session Mode**. In the right pane, the "Use enhanced session mode" check box is selected by default. With this setting, Enhanced Session mode will be enabled when you connect to a VM. Click **OK**.
4. In Hyper-V Manager, right-click **ServerVM1** and click **Connect**. Hover your mouse pointer over the icon on the far-right side of the toolbar. This is the Enhanced Session mode button. Click the **Start** button in the Virtual Machine Connection console to start ServerVM1.
5. You see the Connect to ServerVM1 dialog box. You are prompted to set the display configuration. If necessary, adjust the display settings by using the slider. Click the **Show Options** button to see the Local Resources tab and additional options.
6. Click the **Local Resources** tab, and then click the **More** button. Click to expand **Drives**, click **Local Disk (C:)**, and click **OK**. Click **Connect**.
7. Sign in to ServerVM1 as **Administrator**. Open File Explorer, click **This PC** in the left pane, and click the **C on ServerHyperV** icon. You see the contents of the C drive on ServerHyperV.
8. Next, you'll copy and paste a file from the ServerHyperV host to the ServerVM1 VM. On ServerHyperV, right-click the desktop, point to **New**, and click **Text Document**. Right-click the file and click **Copy**.
9. On ServerVM1, right-click the desktop and click **Paste** to copy the file from ServerHyperV to ServerVM1.
10. Shut down ServerVM1 and close the connection window. Next, disable Enhanced Session mode using PowerShell. On ServerHyperV, open a PowerShell prompt, type **Set-VMHost -EnableEnhancedSessionMode $false**, and press **Enter**.
11. Close the PowerShell window and continue to the next activity.

Working with Virtual Hard Disks

Microsoft Exam AZ-800:

Manage virtual machines and containers.

- Manage Hyper-V and guest virtual machines

As you've learned, a virtual hard disk is a file on the host computer with a .vhd or .vhdx extension. From a VM's standpoint, a virtual hard disk is no different from a physical hard disk. However, from the perspective of an IT manager using Hyper-V, virtual hard disks are more flexible than physical disks. Virtual hard disks can be one of three types:

- *Fixed size*—The full amount of space required for a fixed-size disk, as the name implies, is allocated on the host's storage when the virtual disk is created. **Fixed-size disks** are recommended when the VM needs to run disk-intensive applications (which have a lot of disk I/O operations) because performance is slightly better than with dynamically expanding disks. It is not necessary to perform the extra step of expanding the size of the disk when disk writes are performed.

- *Dynamically expanding*—The virtual hard disk file grows as data is written to it, up to the size you specify when the disk is created. The dynamic aspect of this type of disk goes only one way; the file doesn't shrink when data is deleted from the virtual disk. This option saves host disk space until the disk grows to its maximum size, but at the expense of performance. **Dynamically expanding disks** are slower than fixed-size disks, and there are some concerns about host disk fragmentation when using them. However, with the VHDX format, Microsoft has made strides toward performance parity between fixed-size and dynamically expanding disks. Unless the VM is running disk-intensive applications, dynamically expanding disks are a good choice. Additionally, VMs that use dynamic disks can be backed up faster because VHDX files are usually smaller than fixed-disk files.

> ### Note 13
> Although dynamically expanding virtual disks do not dynamically shrink as data is deleted, you can edit the disk and compact it to reclaim host disk space. Editing virtual disks is discussed in the next section.

- *Differencing*—A **differencing disk** uses a parent/child relationship. A parent disk is a dynamically expanding or fixed-size disk with an OS installed, possibly with some applications and data. It becomes the baseline for one or more child (differencing) disks. A VM with a differencing disk operates normally, but any changes made to its hard disk are made only to the differencing disk, leaving the parent disk unaltered. The parent disk shouldn't be connected to a VM because it must not be changed in any way. With differencing disks, several VMs can be created by using the parent disk as the baseline but using only the additional host disk space of the differencing disk. Differencing disks are an ideal way to provision (make available) several VMs quickly without having to install an OS and applications or copy an entire virtual disk. Differencing disks work like dynamically expanding disks, in that they start very small and grow as data is written to them. All child disks must use the same format (VHD or VHDX) as the parent disk.

Creating and Modifying Virtual Disks

Virtual disks can be created when a VM is created or with the New Virtual Hard Disk Wizard. During VM creation, the disk is created as a dynamically expanding disk, but you can change it to a fixed-size disk later. When you use the wizard, the first thing you do is choose the disk format, for which you have the following options (see Figure 12-17):

- *VHD*—This is the original virtual disk format; it provides backward compatibility with virtual machines created in OSs prior to Windows Server 2012. The VHD format supports virtual disks of up to 2 TB.
- *VHDX*—This is the default option, supporting virtual disks up to 64 TB. The VHDX format also provides resiliency to problems that might occur due to unexpected power failures or host system crashes. This format can only be used on VMs created in Windows Server 2012 or later versions.
- *VHD Set*—A new feature starting with Hyper-V in Windows 10 and Windows Server 2016, a **VHD set** is a shared virtual hard disk used with virtual machine cluster configurations, where multiple VMs have access to the same virtual hard disk for fault tolerance and load-balancing applications. Shared VHDX-format virtual hard disks are supported in earlier versions of Hyper-V, but they cannot be resized or migrated to other hosts. In addition, backups of VMs using shared VHDX files are not supported. VHD sets remove these limitations of shared VHDX files. Shared virtual disks are discussed in more detail later in this module.

After you select the format of a virtual disk, you choose the disk type, as shown in Figure 12-18 and discussed earlier in this section. Dynamically expanding is the default choice and is recommended for most applications.

The next step is to specify a name for the virtual disk file and the location on the host where it is stored. Virtual disks are created in a default location (C:\Users\Public Documents\Hyper-V\Virtual hard disks\) unless you specify a different path or change the default location in Hyper-V settings. You can view and change the default location by clicking Hyper-V Settings in the Actions pane of Hyper-V Manager. You can also specify a shared folder to store the virtual disk using the UNC path of the share.

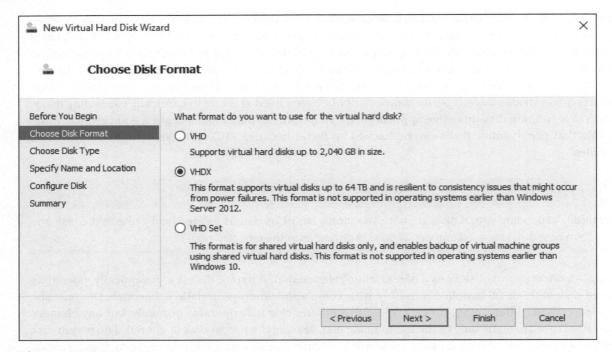

Figure 12-17 Choosing the virtual disk format

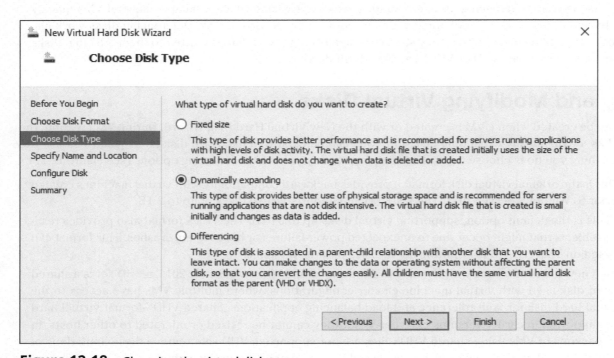

Figure 12-18 Choosing the virtual disk type

The last step is to specify the size of the virtual disk, as shown in Figure 12-19. On this screen, you can choose one of three options:

- *Create a new blank virtual hard disk*—With this option, simply specify the size of the virtual disk in gigabytes (GB).
- *Copy the contents of the specified physical disk*—With this option, you can convert a physical disk to a virtual disk. This option comes in handy when you want to convert the disks on a physical computer to virtual disks. To do so, attach the physical disk from the computer you want to convert to the Hyper-V host computer and select this option.

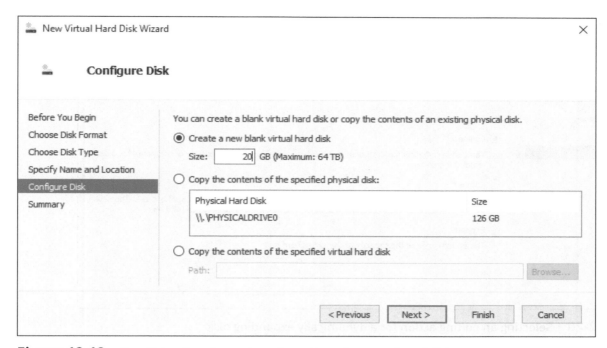

Figure 12-19   Specifying the size and configuration of a new virtual disk

- *Copy the contents of the specified virtual hard disk*—This option copies the contents of an existing virtual disk to a new virtual disk. This option comes in handy if the source disk is fragmented because the copy operation will copy files from the source to contiguous blocks on the destination virtual disk, thus defragmenting the data in the process. You can also copy data from a VHD disk to a VHDX disk or from a dynamic disk to a fixed-size disk (and vice versa), thereby eliminating conversion steps.

After a virtual disk is created, you can attach it to a new or existing VM.

Modifying a Virtual Disk

One thing that makes virtual disks so flexible is the ability to modify certain aspects of them. There are several PowerShell cmdlets for modifying a virtual hard disk, or you can use the Edit Virtual Hard Disk Wizard in Hyper-V Manager. To start this wizard, click Edit Disk from the Actions menu. After selecting the virtual hard disk you want to edit, you can select actions that vary depending on the type of disk you select. Figure 12-20 shows the options for dynamically expanding and fixed-size disks. These three options, as well as three additional disk editing options, are described next:

- *Compact*—Reduces the size of a dynamically expanding disk by eliminating the space used by deleted files.
- *Convert*—Converts a dynamically expanding disk to a fixed-size disk, and vice versa. You can also change the format from VHD to VHDX and vice versa. Note that converting a disk creates a new virtual disk and does not delete the original disk.
- *Expand*—Allows you to make a fixed-size or dynamically expanding disk larger. After you expand the disk, you can use Disk Management or diskpart.exe in Windows to extend the volume to use the additional space.
- *Shrink*—Allows you to make a fixed-size or dynamically expanding disk smaller. Before you can shrink a virtual disk, you must first use the Shrink Volume feature in Disk Management or diskpart.exe to shrink the volume to a size equal to or less than the size you want.
- *Merge*—This option is available only for differencing disks. You can merge a differencing disk's contents into its parent disk or merge the differencing disk with the parent disk to create a new disk while leaving the original parent disk unchanged.
- *Reconnect*—Reconnects a differencing disk with its parent disk.

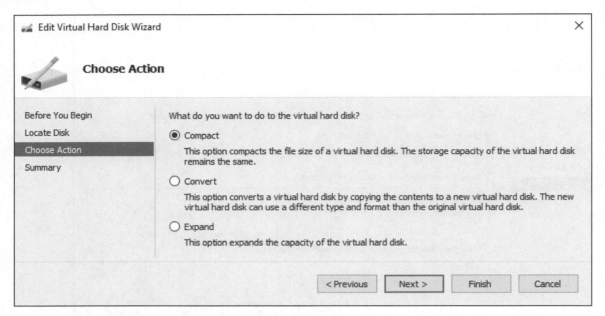

Figure 12-20   Selecting an editing action for a dynamically expanding disk

Note 14

You can expand or shrink a virtual disk when the virtual machine is running or shut down; however, you cannot convert or compact a virtual disk that is attached to a running virtual machine.

A little explanation is needed for a few of these disk-editing tasks. When you convert a dynamic disk to a fixed-size disk, a new fixed-size virtual disk is created, and you supply a new name. After the conversion is finished, you disconnect the original dynamic disk from the VM and connect the new fixed-size disk. Alternatively, you can rename the dynamic disk (or delete it), and then assign the new fixed-size disk the same name as the original dynamic disk. With this method, the VM connects to the new fixed-size disk automatically when you restart it. For example, if the original dynamically expanding disk is named ServerVM1.vhdx, you can name the new fixed-size disk ServerVM1fixed.vhdx when you do the conversion. When the conversion is finished, rename ServerVM1.vhdx as ServerVM1dyn.vhdx and rename ServerVM1fixed.vhdx as ServerVM1.vhdx.

Here's an important consideration to keep in mind before you edit a disk that is connected to a virtual machine: No checkpoints can be associated with the VM attached to the virtual disk you're expanding.

Note 15

If you rename the fixed-size disk instead of connecting the new fixed-size disk in the VM's settings, you must make sure the VM has at least Modify permissions to the new virtual hard disk. In most cases, the Authenticated Users group is assigned the Modify permission automatically, which is adequate, but if the VM fails to start and displays an "Access denied" error, check the permissions for the .vhdx file.

Pass-Through Disks

A **pass-through disk** isn't a virtual disk; it's a physical disk in the offline state that's attached to the host. It can be connected to a VM only if it has been set to offline status. If you have an offline physical disk on the host, you can attach it to a VM in the VM's Settings window (see Figure 12-21). If the disk already has data on it, the data is retained and available to the VM.

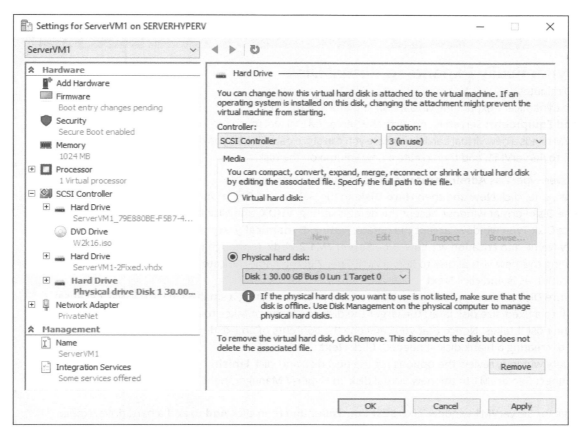

Figure 12-21   Adding a pass-through disk to a VM

From the VM's standpoint, a pass-through disk works just like a virtual disk, except you can't use any disk-editing options on it, you can't take checkpoints, and you can't use a differencing disk with it. A pass-through disk has modest performance advantages over virtual disks, but unless you really need the extra bit of performance, a pass-through disk's lack of flexibility makes it less attractive as a VM storage option. Pass-through disks do have an advantage over VHD disks because VHD disks are limited to 2 TB. However, the VHDX format doesn't have the 2 TB limitation, so using pass-through disks is a benefit only when direct access to the physical drive improves performance. Some applications that might benefit from the VM using a pass-through disk include SQL servers and high-performance cluster servers.

Note 16

For high-performance disk storage, many administrators prefer using SAN storage through Fibre Channel or iSCSI instead of pass-through disks.

Self-Check Questions

7.   Dynamically expanding disks provide better performance than fixed-size disks. True or False?

   a. True   **b.** False

8.   Which virtual hard disk type should you use if you want multiple VMs in a cluster configuration to have access to the same data?

   a. Dynamic   **c.** VHD set
   b. VHDX   **d.** Differencing

● Check your answers at the end of this module.

Activity 12-6

Creating a Dynamically Expanding Virtual Disk

Time Required: 20 minutes
Objective: Create a dynamically expanding virtual disk and attach it to a VM.
Required Tools and Equipment: ServerHyperV with the ServerVM1 virtual machine
Description: Your VM needs a new virtual hard disk where you can store data files, so you create a dynamically expanding virtual disk, attach it to ServerVM1, and then create a new volume on the disk.

1. Sign in to ServerHyperV as **Administrator** and open Hyper-V Manager.
2. In the Actions pane, click **New** and then **Hard Disk**. In the Before You Begin window, click **Next**.
3. In the Choose Disk Format window, accept the default setting, **VHDX**, and click **Next**.
4. In the Choose Disk Type window, accept the default setting, **Dynamically expanding**, and click **Next**.
5. In the Specify Name and Location window, type **ServerVM1-2.vhdx**. (Although the name isn't critical, you will be attaching this new virtual disk to ServerVM1. The -2 in the name indicates it's the second disk.) Leave the location as is and click **Next**.
6. In the Configure Disk window, type **5** in the **Size** text box. You're creating a small 5 GB virtual disk because you convert it to a fixed-size disk later; the larger the disk, the longer it takes to convert and the more storage on the host it takes. Notice that you can copy the contents of an existing physical disk or virtual disk instead of creating a blank disk, if needed. Click **Next**.
7. In the Summary window, review the options for the new disk and click **Finish**.
8. Next, you connect ServerVM1 to the new virtual disk. In Hyper-V Manager, right-click **ServerVM1** and click **Settings**.
9. In the Settings for ServerVM1 window, click **SCSI Controller** and then click **Add** to add a hard drive. Notice that you can create a new virtual disk now, but because the disk you want is already created, click **Browse**. Click **ServerVM1-2** and click **Open**. Click **OK**.
10. In Hyper-V Manager, double-click **ServerVM1** and click the **Start** icon. Log on to **ServerVM1**, open File Explorer, and click **This PC**. The new virtual disk isn't shown because you need to initialize it and create a new volume first.
11. On ServerVM1, right-click **Start** and click **Disk Management**. Right-click **Disk 1** and click **Online** to bring the disk online. Right-click it again and click **Initialize Disk**. Click **OK**.
12. Right-click the **Unallocated** box next to Disk 1 and click **New Simple Volume**. Finish the New Simple Volume Wizard by naming the volume **TestVol** and accepting the default settings for the other options. After the disk is finished formatting, close Disk Management.
13. In File Explorer, you should see the new volume with drive letter E assigned. (If you see a message that you need to format the disk, click **Cancel**.) Create a folder on the E drive and then create a text file in this folder.
14. Shut down ServerVM1. Stay signed in to ServerHyperV and continue to the next activity.

Activity 12-7

Editing a Virtual Disk

Time Required: 15 minutes
Objective: Edit a virtual disk with Hyper-V Manager.
Required Tools and Equipment: ServerHyperV with the ServerVM1 virtual machine
Description: In this activity, you convert a dynamically expanding disk to a fixed-size disk and then expand and shrink the disk.

(continues)

Activity 12-7 Continued

1. Sign in to ServerHyperV as **Administrator** and open Hyper-V Manager, if necessary.
2. Right-click **ServerVM1** and click **Settings**. In the left pane, click the **ServerVM1-2.vhdx** hard disk under SCSI Controller, and in the right pane, click **Edit**.
3. In the Locate Disk window, read the information about editing virtual hard disks. Note that editing differencing disks, disks with checkpoints, and disks involved in replication might result in data loss. Click **Next**.
4. In the Choose Action window, click the **Convert** option button, and then click **Next**. In the Choose Disk Format window, accept the default setting, **VHDX**, and click **Next**.
5. In the Choose Disk Type window, click **Fixed size** and then click **Next**. In the Configure Disk window, leave the current path and type **ServerVM1-2Fixed** at the end of it. (The .vhdx extension will be added automatically.) Click **Next**.
6. In the Summary window, click **Finish**. The conversion takes a few minutes.
7. When the conversion is finished, click **Browse** in the Settings for ServerVM1 window. The fixed-size disk is shown with a size of about 5 GB. Click **ServerVM1-2Fixed** and click **Open** to attach this disk to ServerVM1. Click **OK**.
8. In Hyper-V Manager, double-click **ServerVM1** and click the **Start** icon. Log on to ServerVM1 and open File Explorer. Explore the E drive to verify that the files you created in the previous activity are still there.
9. Close File Explorer and open Disk Management by right-clicking **Start** and clicking **Disk Management**. Notice that there is no unallocated space on Disk 1.
10. In Hyper-V Manager, right-click **ServerVM1** and click **Settings**. Click **Hard Drive ServerVM1-Fixed** under SCSI Controller and click **Edit** in the right pane to open the Edit Virtual Hard Disk Wizard.
11. In the Locate Virtual Hard Disk window, click **Next**. In the Choose Action window, the only option is Expand because you can't convert a virtual disk that is attached to a running VM. Click **Next**.
12. In the Configure Disk window, type **7** in the New size box and click **Next**. In the Summary window, click **Finish**.
13. In the Settings window, click **OK**. Open the ServerVM1 connection window. Disk Management should still be open. You see that there is now 2 GB of unallocated space on Disk 1.
14. Right-click **TestVol** and click **Extend Volume**. Accept the default options to extend the volume to the maximum size of about 7 GB. You have successfully expanded the virtual disk and extended the volume to occupy the additional space.
15. Now you'll shrink the volume and then shrink the virtual disk. Right-click **TestVol** and click **Shrink Volume**. In the "Enter the amount of space to shrink in MB" box, type **5000** to shrink the volume by 5 GB. Click **Shrink**.
16. In Hyper-V Manager, open the Settings window for ServerVM1, click the hard drive, and click **Edit**. Click **Next**.
17. Because the volume is not occupying all the available space on the virtual disk, you have the option to shrink the virtual disk and reclaim disk space on the host. Click **Shrink** and click **Next**. The minimum size you can shrink the volume is 3 GB, so type **3** in the New size box and click **Next**. Click **Finish**.
18. Click **OK** to close the Settings window.

Hyper-V Virtual Networks

Microsoft Exam AZ-800:

Manage virtual machines and containers.
- Manage Hyper-V and guest virtual machines

Hyper-V virtual machines are used for a variety of reasons, and how a particular VM is used typically dictates how you configure the VM's network connection. VMs are connected to a virtual network through a Hyper-V virtual switch created in Hyper-V Manager or with a PowerShell cmdlet. Each virtual switch you create is a separate virtual network. You can create three types of virtual switches and, by extension, virtual networks: external, internal, and private.

To create, delete, and modify virtual switches in Hyper-V, click Virtual Switch Manager in the Actions pane or use the PowerShell cmdlets listed when you enter Command *-VMSwitch*. The following sections describe the types of virtual networks you can create.

External Virtual Switches

An **external virtual switch** binds a virtual switch to one of the host's physical network adapters, allowing virtual machines to access a LAN connected to the host. During installation of the Hyper-V role, you have the option of creating an external virtual switch by binding one or more of the host's physical adapters to a virtual switch. Only one external switch can be created per physical network adapter. When a VM is connected to an external switch, it acts like any other device on the LAN. For example, the VM can get an IP address from a DHCP server on the external network and use the network's default gateway to access other networks and the Internet.

You use an external virtual switch when external computers must have direct access to the VM or when the VM must have access to external network resources, such as when a VM is configured as a web server, DNS server, or domain controller.

Note 17

You can use a wired or wireless NIC to bind to an external switch. However, when you bind a wireless NIC, Hyper-V creates an additional network bridge adapter on the host computer.

If you're using external virtual switches, having more than one physical NIC installed on the host computer is highly recommended. This way, you can dedicate one of the NICs to host communication, and the other NIC or NICs can be bound to external virtual switches.

When a NIC is designated for use in an external virtual switch, Windows binds the Hyper-V Extensible Virtual Switch protocol to the physical NIC and unbinds all other protocols. This process creates a virtual switch through which VMs and the host can communicate with the physical network and each other. A new virtual network adapter (virtual NIC) is created on the host computer that has all the usual protocol bindings enabled. The VMs configured to use the external virtual switch are bound to the virtual NIC, which communicates through the virtual switch.

To help you understand virtual networks better, Figure 12-22 shows a host computer without any virtual networks configured, and Figure 12-23 shows the host and virtual machines connected to an external virtual network. In Figure 12-23, the host's physical NIC is bound only to the Hyper-V Extensible Virtual Switch protocol and has a physical connection to the external network. The host's physical NIC has a virtual connection to the virtual switch and facilitates communication between VMs and the external network. The new virtual NIC created on the host has all the usual network protocol bindings (Client for Microsoft Networks, File and Printer Sharing for Microsoft Networks, TCP/IP, and so forth), allowing host applications and protocols to communicate through the virtual switch with the external network and VMs.

Internal Virtual Switches

An **internal virtual switch** allows virtual machines and the host computer to communicate with one another but doesn't give VMs access to the physical network. An internal switch isn't bound to any of the host's physical NICs. When an internal virtual switch is created, a new virtual NIC is created on the host computer that's bound to the name of the new internal virtual switch. The new virtual NIC allows the host computer to communicate with the VMs on that internal switch. A virtual switch is created, but it's internal to Hyper-V and therefore can't be seen on the host computer. By default, the new virtual NIC attempts to get an address via DHCP, but because it doesn't have a connection to the physical network, it's assigned an APIPA address. Any VMs connected to the internal switch are also assigned an APIPA address if you don't assign a static IP address. Figure 12-24 shows how an internal virtual switch works. The difference

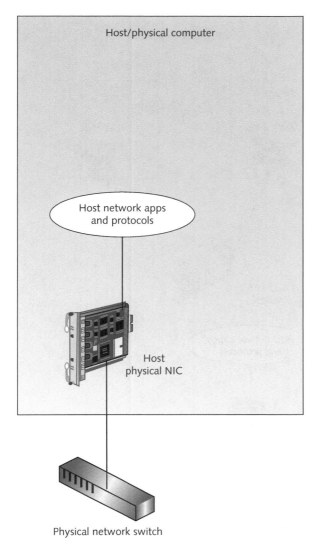

Figure 12-22 A host computer with no virtual networks configured

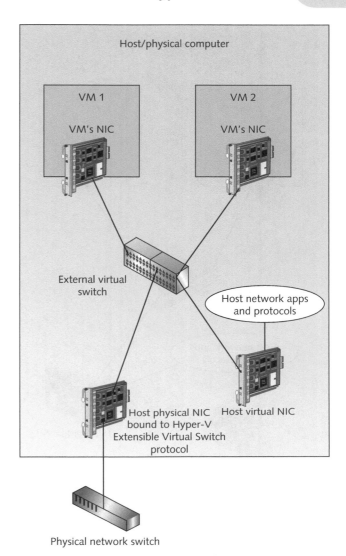

Figure 12-23 A host and VM connected through an external virtual network

between an external and internal virtual switch is that the host virtual NIC doesn't have a connection to the physical network switch, which prevents VMs from communicating with the physical network. In addition, the host physical NIC and host virtual NIC have all the normal bindings, allowing network applications and protocols to communicate with both NICs. Only the host can communicate with the virtual machines.

An internal virtual switch is used when devices on the physical network don't need direct access to the VMs, and vice versa. Examples include test and lab environments where you want VMs to be isolated from the physical network but you still want to communicate with VMs from the host. You can also use an internal virtual switch to isolate applications from the external network but allow communication between the networks by using a virtual machine configured as a router. This configuration is discussed later in the section called "Communicating Between Hyper-V Switches."

Private Virtual Switches

A **private virtual switch** isn't much different from an internal virtual switch, except that the VMs connected to the private virtual switch can't communicate with the host computer. Creating a private virtual switch doesn't create a network connection on the host computer because there's no connection between the host computer and the VMs. Figure 12-25 shows this configuration. Notice that there's no virtual NIC on the host in this configuration because there's no communication between the host and the VMs.

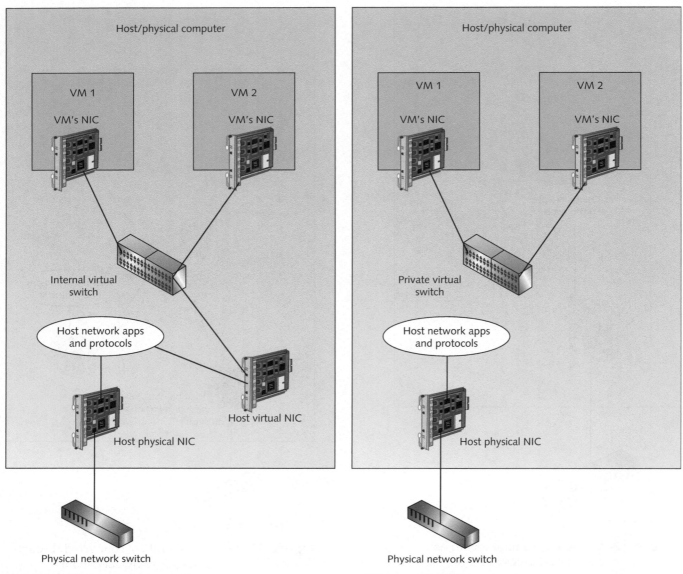

Figure 12-24 An internal virtual network

Figure 12-25 A private virtual network

A private virtual switch is used when you want to isolate the VMs connected to the network from all outside communication. You might use this setup as a domain testing environment or a development network in which you need to isolate virtual network traffic.

Communicating Between Hyper-V Switches

What if you want to isolate VMs in their own private network, but you want them to be able to access other private networks or an external network? With a physical network, you do this by creating subnets and using a router to route traffic between them. Hyper-V virtual networks are no different. You can do this in two different ways:

- Create an external virtual switch and a private virtual switch, and then configure one VM with two NICs and have one NIC connected to each virtual switch (see Figure 12-26). You can configure a Windows server as a network router by installing the Remote Access role and installing the Routing role service. This VM can route packets between the private switch and the external switch.
- Create an internal virtual switch and enable routing on the host machine so that it routes between the internal and physical switches (see Figure 12-27).

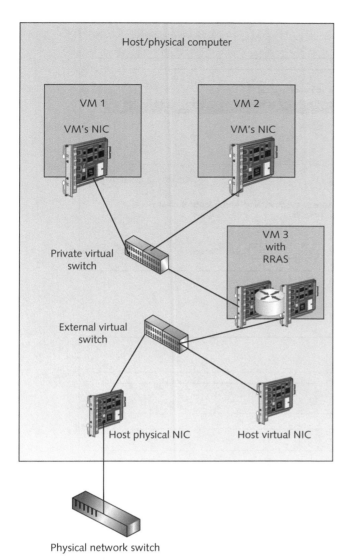

Figure 12-26 Routing between a private virtual switch and an external virtual switch

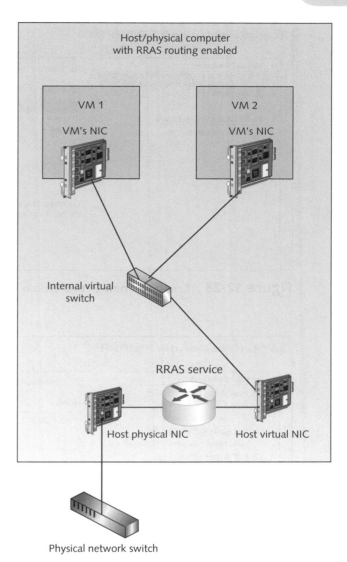

Figure 12-27 Routing between an internal network and the physical network

Creating a Virtual Switch

You create a virtual switch in Hyper-V Manager by clicking Virtual Switch Manager in the Actions pane. From this window, you can edit an existing virtual switch or create a new virtual switch. Choose External, Internal, or Private and click Create Virtual Switch (see Figure 12-28). It doesn't matter much what you choose here because you'll be able to change it on the next screen.

In the Virtual Switch Properties window (see Figure 12-29), give the virtual switch a name. It's a good idea to provide a descriptive name so you'll know later how the virtual switch is being used. Then, you have the following options to configure the switch.

- *Connection type*—This is where you choose whether the switch should be External, Internal, or Private. If you choose External, you choose the physical network adapter on the virtual switch's host system. If you choose External network, you also have the following choices:
  - ○ *Allow management operating system to share this network adapter*—If your host computer only has one physical network adapter, you must choose this option. Ideally, you clear this option to isolate the host OS traffic from virtual machine traffic and dedicate a network adapter on the host for the management operating system.

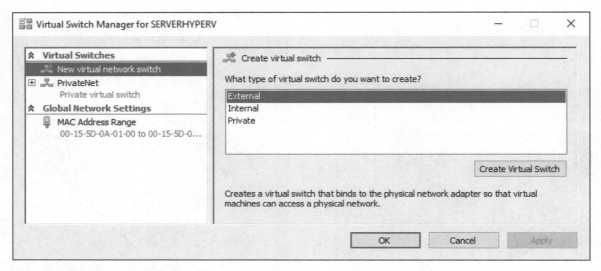

Figure 12-28   Creating a new virtual switch

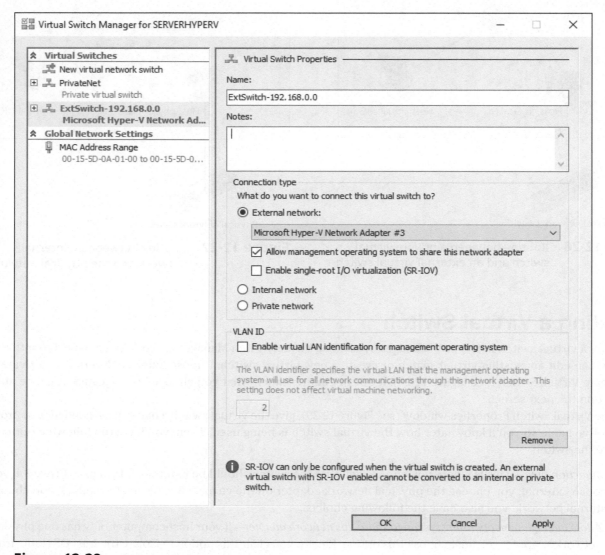

Figure 12-29   Virtual switch properties

○ *Enable single-root I/O virtualization (SR-IOV)*—This feature provides enhanced performance but requires support from the host NIC. You should leave this option unselected unless you know your hardware supports it. If you enable SR-IOV on the virtual switch, you'll also want to enable it on the network adapter of virtual machines that connect to the switch. You cannot change the SR-IOV setting after the switch is created. If you need to enable it or disable it later, you will have to delete the virtual switch and re-create it.

• *VLAN ID*—This setting isolates traffic between the management OS and virtual machines. You set the VLAN identifier to correspond with the VLAN identifier configured on the physical switch. The host machine's virtual NIC used for management is placed on the specified VLAN, but VM traffic is not affected. Enabling VLAN identification is available for external or internal networks but not private networks. Configuring VLANs for VMs is discussed later in this module in the section titled "Adding and Removing Virtual Network Interface Cards."

Configuring MAC Addresses

Every network adapter must have a unique MAC address on the network, and the network adapters on VMs are no different. Because the network adapter on a VM is virtual and therefore can't have a true burned-in address, Hyper-V must assign a MAC address to each network adapter connected to a virtual network, using a pool of addresses it maintains. When a new network adapter is connected to a virtual network, a MAC address is assigned dynamically to the adapter from the pool. The MAC address pool contains 256 addresses by default, but this number can be changed. To view or change the MAC address pool in Hyper-V Manager, click Virtual Switch Manager and then click MAC Address Range in the left pane (see Figure 12-30).

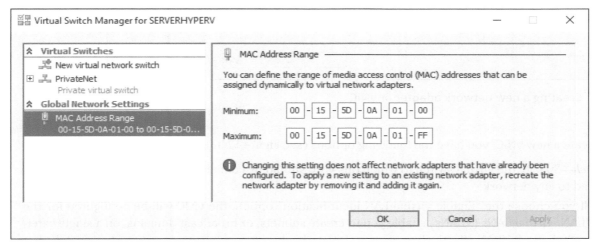

Figure 12-30   The MAC address pool

If you want to expand or change the pool, be aware that the first three bytes are the organizationally unique identifier (OUI) assigned to Microsoft and shouldn't be changed. The fourth and fifth bytes are the hexadecimal equivalent of the last two octets of the MAC address of the server's physical NIC. To expand the pool, changing the second-to-last byte of the maximum address is best. For example, in Figure 12-30, if you change the 01 to 02 in the Maximum text boxes, your range of available addresses is now 00-15-5D-0A-01-00 to 00-15-5D-0A-02-FF, doubling the number of addresses from 256 to 512. If you have more than one Hyper-V server on the network and are connecting VMs to an external network, you must be careful that you don't overlap the MAC address range with another server's range. The problem with overlapping ranges is important only if the VMs are connected to the external network. To view or change the assigned MAC address to a VM's network adapter, open the VM's settings, click to expand the network adapter, and then click Advanced Features.

Adding and Removing Virtual Network Interface Cards

Once you have virtual switches created, you can configure VMs to connect to them. To do so, you need at least one virtual network interface card (vNIC) on a VM. A vNIC is created when you create a VM; you have the option during VM creation to attach it to a virtual switch. You can also add a vNIC to a VM after it is created. To add a vNIC, select the VM in Hyper-V Manager, click Settings in the Actions pane, and click Add Hardware. In the right pane, choose Network Adapter and click Add (see Figure 12-31).

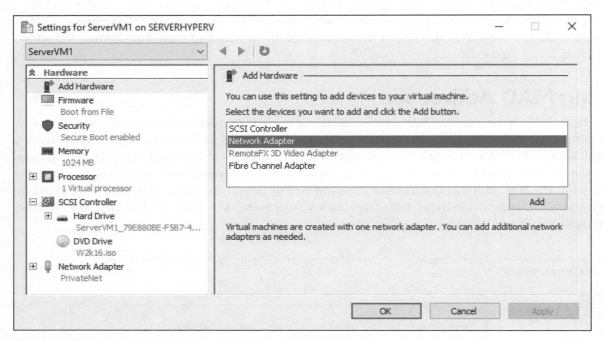

Figure 12-31   Creating a new network adapter or vNIC

When you create a new vNIC, you have the following options (see Figure 12-32).

- *Virtual switch*—Specify the virtual switch to which this vNIC should be connected. You can also leave the vNIC unconnected to any network.
- *VLAN ID*—If you choose the "Enable virtual LAN identification" option, the vNIC will be configured for the specified VLAN. Virtual LANs (VLANs) enable you to create subnets, or broadcast domains, on a single external virtual switch. Each VLAN effectively creates an isolated network, much like a private virtual switch. The physical NIC on the host must support VLANs (also called "VLAN tagging") for this option to work. When you enable VLAN identification, you choose an ID number, which is the VLAN identifier configured on the physical network switch. All VMs that share a VLAN ID can communicate with one another as though they were on the same subnet. The machines sharing a VLAN ID must be configured with IP addresses that have a common network ID. Machines with different VLAN IDs can't communicate directly with one another but can communicate if a router is configured to route between the VLANs. The primary reason for configuring VLANs on virtual machines is to allow VMs that are connected to the same virtual switch to be isolated from one another on separate broadcast domains. You configure a router to route between VLANs just as you configure one to route between separate virtual networks, as discussed earlier in this module.
- *Bandwidth Management*—If you enable bandwidth management, you can specify the minimum and maximum bandwidth (in Mbps) available to the vNIC. For example, if you have three VMs connected to an external virtual switch that is mapped to a 100 Mbps physical NIC on the host, you could configure the maximum bandwidth on each VM to about 33 Mbps so that each VM has equal bandwidth but no VM can monopolize the link. Or, perhaps one VM must always have at least 20 Mbps of bandwidth available; if so, set the minimum bandwidth for this VM to 20 and leave the maximum bandwidth at 0. A value of 0 means unrestricted.

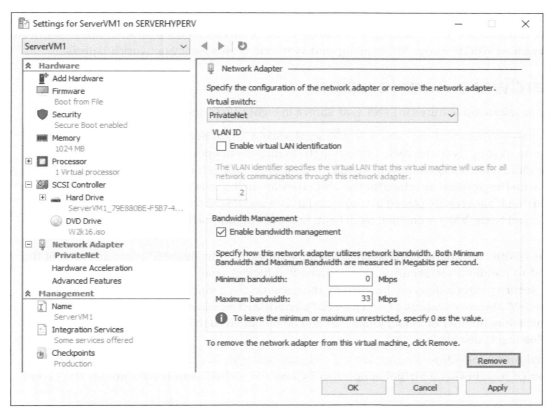

Figure 12-32   Configuring a vNIC

Note 18

The terms *virtual network interface card (vNIC)* and *virtual network adapter* are equivalent. Microsoft uses the latter term in many of its commands and management consoles but uses *vNIC* in much of its documentation.

Self-Check Questions

9. An external virtual switch binds the virtual switch to a physical network adapter. True or False?

   a. True   **b.** False

10. Which virtual switch setting can isolate traffic between the management OS and virtual machines?

   a. Connection type   **c.** SR-IOV

   b. MAC address pool   **d.** VLAN ID

◉ Check your answers at the end of this module.

Advanced Virtual Network Configuration

Microsoft Exam AZ-800:

Manage virtual machines and containers.

- Manage Hyper-V and guest virtual machines

Aside from connecting a VM's network adapter to a virtual switch, you might need to perform other configuration tasks related to a VM's network connections. The following sections cover these advanced configuration tasks: hardware acceleration on vNICs, advanced vNIC features, NIC teaming, and synthetic versus legacy network adapters.

Virtual NIC Hardware Acceleration

There are three hardware acceleration features for vNICs, as shown in Figure 12-33 and described here:

- *Virtual machine queue*—**Virtual machine queue (VMQ)** accelerates vNIC performance by delivering packets from the external network directly to the vNIC, bypassing the management operating system. VMQ is enabled or disabled on each vNIC. When VMQ is enabled, a dedicated queue is created for the vNIC on the physical NIC. When packets arrive on the physical interface for the vNIC, they are delivered directly to the VM. In contrast, when VMQ is not enabled, packets are placed in a common queue and distributed to the destination vNIC on a first-come, first-served basis. VMQ is enabled by default, but must be supported by the physical NIC on the host computer.

- *IPsec task offloading*—With this option enabled (the default setting), the physical NIC controls much of the processing required to handle IPsec security associations. If sufficient resources are not available on the physical NIC, IPsec security associations are handled by the guest OS. To configure IPsec task offloading with PowerShell, use `Set-VMNetworkAdapter -IpsecOffloadMaximumSecurityAssociation` *Max*, where *Max* is the maximum number of associations that can be offloaded to the physical NIC. If *Max* is set to zero, IPsec task offloading is disabled.

- *Single-root I/O virtualization (SR-IOV)*—**Single-root I/O virtualization (SR-IOV)** enhances the virtual network adapter's performance by allowing a virtual adapter to bypass the virtual switch software on the parent

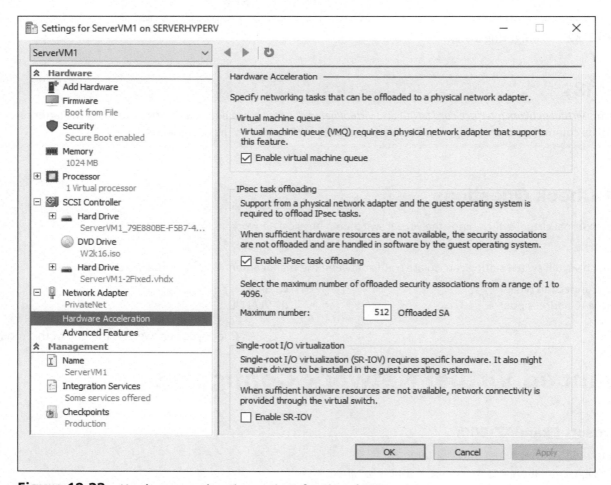

Figure 12-33 Hardware acceleration options for virtual NICs

partition (the Hyper-V host) and communicate directly with the physical hardware, thereby lowering over-head in addition to improving performance. The performance advantage is most obvious on high-speed NICs, such as 10 GB Ethernet and higher. SR-IOV must be supported by a PCI Express NIC installed on the host, and installing drivers on the guest OS might be necessary. If you enable SR-IOV but resources to support it aren't available, the virtual network adapter connects by using the virtual switch as usual. You must also enable SR-IOV in the Virtual Switch Manager when you create the external virtual switch. If you enable SR-IOV and it's supported, you can check Device Manager on the VM and see the actual NIC make and model listed under network adapters. When using adapters for which SR-IOV is not enabled or not supported, you see only the Microsoft Hyper-V network adapter.

Configuring vNICs with Advanced Features

In the Advanced Features dialog box for a network adapter (see Figure 12-34), you can configure the following features and security options:

- *MAC address*—By default, network adapters are assigned a MAC address dynamically, but you can assign a static MAC address if necessary. You must be careful not to duplicate a MAC address, and changing the OUI portion of the address isn't recommended. If you do change it, make sure bit 2 of the first byte is set, indicating

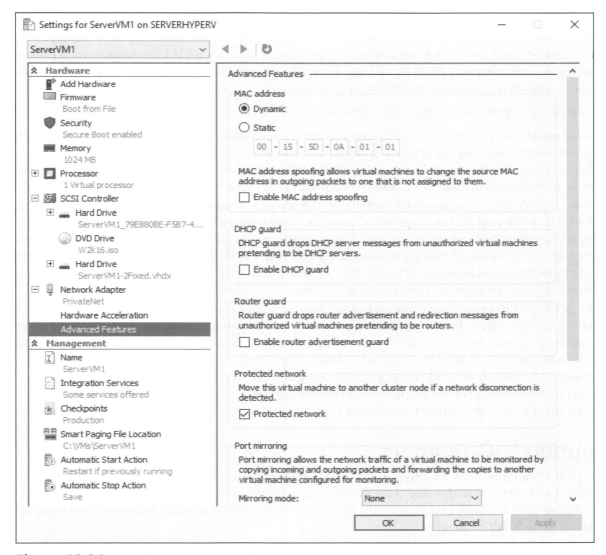

Figure 12-34   Configuring advanced features for a virtual network adapter

that the address is locally administered and doesn't contain an OUI. For example, you can change the first byte to 02. You might want to use a static MAC address if the VM moves between host computers and you want its MAC address to remain the same. For example, if you're using DHCP reservations, the reservation is based on the MAC address, so the VM's MAC address must stay the same for the reservation to work.

- *Enable MAC address spoofing*—If this option is enabled, the VM can change the source MAC address on outgoing packets, and the virtual switch is allowed to "learn" addresses other than the one assigned to the virtual adapter. This feature makes the virtual network less secure, but it might be necessary for network load balancing and clustering.

- *DHCP guard*—This option prevents a VM from acting as a DHCP server. With this option enabled, if the VM sends a DHCP server message on the specified interface, the virtual switch will drop the packet. This option is most useful when your Hyper-V servers are operating in a multitenant environment in which multiple clients are using VMs hosted on your servers and you have little control over what services they may install. Essentially, the option prevents a VM from becoming a rogue DHCP server. It is recommended that this option be enabled on all VMs except actual DHCP servers. To enable the option on all adapters on all VMs running on a host, use the following PowerShell cmdlet on the Hyper-V host:

```
Get-VM | Set-VMNetworkAdapter -DhcpGuard On
```

To allow DHCP packets to be transmitted from a VM named MyDHCPServer that is a legitimate DHCP server, use the following cmdlet:

```
Set-VMNetworkAdapter -VMName MyDHCPServer -DhcpGuard Off
```

- *Router guard*—Similar to the DHCP guard option, this option prevents a VM from sending router advertisements and redirection messages to other VMs. To enable and disable this feature using PowerShell, you use commands similar to those for using the DHCP guard option:

```
Get-VM | Set-VMNetworkAdapter -RouterGuard On
```

- *Protected network*—This feature is enabled by default. If Hyper-V detects that the VM's network adapter has become disconnected from the network, it attempts to move the VM to another server where the network is available. This option is applicable only on Hyper-V failover clusters. Uncheck this option if you don't want a VM to be moved automatically to another cluster node in the event the network connection fails.

- *Port mirroring*—Traffic from the virtual switch port the adapter is connected to is copied and sent to another VM's virtual switch port for the purposes of monitoring and capturing network traffic. Port mirroring can be configured as None, Source, or Destination. The None setting disables port mirroring on the vNIC. Use the Source setting if you want incoming and outgoing network traffic to be monitored. Use the Destination setting if you want monitored traffic to be sent to the vNIC. Typically, you would have a network monitoring or protocol analyzer application running on the VM that is configured as Destination.

- *Device naming*—This option (not shown in Figure 12-34, but shown later in Figure 12-37) allows the name of the virtual network adapter to be available to the guest OS. When you create a network adapter using PowerShell, you can assign it a descriptive name because the default name is just Network Adapter. This name is usually only available on the host machine in Hyper-V Manager or in PowerShell cmdlets. However, with Device naming enabled, the name is available in the guest OS using the Get-NetAdapterAdvancedProperty cmdlet or from the Advanced tab of the adapter's properties in Network Connections. This feature allows you to better correlate the network adapter you see from the host computer with the network adapter in the guest OS.

Configuring NIC Teaming

NIC teaming allows multiple network interfaces to work in tandem to provide increased bandwidth, load balancing, and fault tolerance. Another term for this is **load balancing and failover (LBFO)**. You can create a NIC team with a single network interface, but most of the utility of a NIC team comes from having more than one in the team. Windows Server supports up to 32 NICs in a team.

Let's consider how NIC teaming provides load balancing. **Load balancing** distributes traffic between two or more interfaces, providing an increase in overall network throughput a server is able to maintain. A basic example illustrates the concept. Suppose two client stations are each transferring a 100 MB file to a share on a Windows server. A server with a single NIC operating at 100 Mbps could transfer both files in about twenty seconds (10 seconds for each file). A server with a two-NIC team will load-balance the data from the two clients, with each NIC able to transfer data at 100 Mbps, totaling 200 Mbps, cutting the total transfer time in half.

Let's look at an example of how to use NIC teaming for fault tolerance, or failover. **Failover** in this context is the ability of a server to recover from network hardware failure by having redundant hardware that can immediately take over for a device failure. Suppose you have a server that must be highly available. A server with a single NIC that is connected to a switch becomes unavailable if the switch or the NIC fails. However, with a NIC team configured to provide failover, you can connect one NIC to one switch and the other NIC to another switch. If one NIC or switch fails, the other NIC takes over, maintaining server availability.

You can configure NIC teaming on a Hyper-V host server and allow the VMs running on the host to benefit from the NIC team, or you can configure NIC teaming in the guest OS of a VM to provide a dedicated NIC team for that particular VM.

You configure NIC teaming using Server Manager or PowerShell. The process is the same whether you configure it on a physical computer or a virtual machine; however, there are additional considerations when you configure NIC teaming on a VM, as described later. From Server Manager, click Local Server. In the left column of the Properties page, you'll see a link for NIC Teaming, which is disabled by default. Clicking the link brings you to the NIC Teaming configuration page, as shown in Figure 12-35.

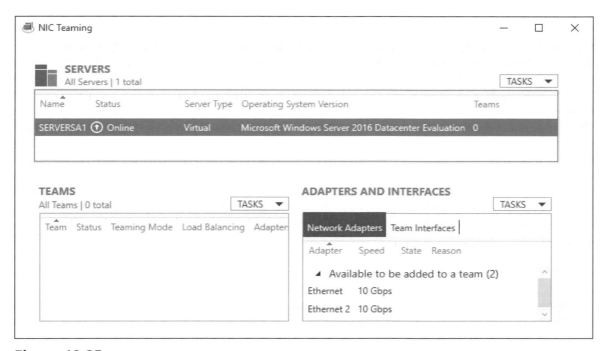

Figure 12-35   NIC teaming configuration

In Figure 12-35, you see three panes, which have the following functions:

- *Servers*—This pane shows the available servers for which you can manage NIC teaming. You add servers to this list in a manner similar to adding servers to Server Manager—by clicking Tasks and Add Servers. The Servers pane also shows you if the server is a physical or virtual server and displays the number of NIC teams defined.
- *Teams*—This pane lists the current NIC teams, their mode and status, and which network adapters are part of the team. You can create or delete a NIC team by clicking Tasks.
- *Adapters and Interfaces*—This pane shows you the list of network adapters available to be added to a NIC team. You can add an interface to an existing team or add an adapter to a new team.

From PowerShell, you can list, create, remove, rename, and set properties of a team using the following commands:

- `Get-NetLbfoTeam`—Shows a list of NIC teams on the server.
- `New-NetLbfoTeam`—Creates a new NIC team and adds network adapters to the team; you can set the properties of the team if you want.
- `Remove-NetLbfoTeam`—Deletes a team.
- `Rename-NetLbfoTeam`—Renames a team.
- `Set-NetLbfoTeam`—Sets the properties of an existing team.

To get help for using any of these PowerShell commands, open a PowerShell prompt and type `get-help` followed by the command.

NIC Teaming Modes

When you create a new NIC team, you can configure the teaming mode and the load-balancing mode (see Figure 12-36):

- *Teaming mode*—There are three teaming modes:
  - Switch Independent—This is the default mode and the only mode available for virtual machines. Using Switch Independent mode, you connect the NICs in a team to separate switches for fault tolerance. The switches are unaware that a connected NIC is part of a team; the server provides all the teaming functions. You can also connect the NICs to the same switch. Switch Independent mode allows you to configure fault tolerance in one of two ways: Active or Standby. The Active option makes all NICs active, which means you get the benefit of the bandwidth from all NICs in the team. If a NIC fails, the others continue to run. The Standby option lets you choose an adapter that remains in standby mode until there is a failure. Upon failure, the NIC in standby mode becomes active. The default setting is Active.

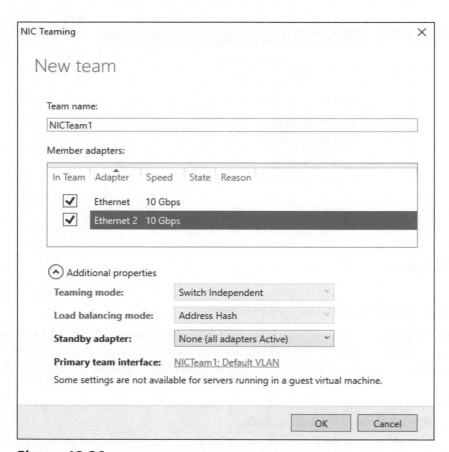

Figure 12-36   Configuring NIC teaming modes

○ Static Teaming—This mode, also called Switch Dependent mode, is primarily used for load balancing. All NICs are connected to one switch and the switch participates in the NIC teaming process. You must use a switch that supports IEEE 802.3ad, which is a standard that defines link aggregation. The switch must be manually configured to identify ports to which members of a switch team are connected. The switch load-balances network traffic between the switches.

○ LACP—Link Aggregation Control Protocol (LACP), defined in IEEE 802.1ax, allows a switch to automatically identify ports to which a team member is connected and dynamically create a team. You must use a switch that supports LACP and enable the protocol before it can be used.

- *Load balancing mode*—The load-balancing mode determines how the server load-balances outgoing data packets among the NICs in the team. There are three options:

○ Address Hash—This mode uses an algorithm based on properties of the outgoing packet to create a hash value. The hash value is then used to assign the packet for delivery using one of the NICs in the team. This is the only load-balancing mode available when configuring NIC teaming on a virtual machine.

○ Hyper-V Port—This method is used when the team members are connected to a Hyper-V switch. Each virtual NIC is associated with only one team member at system startup. This method works well to evenly distribute the load among NICs in the team if a number of virtual machines are running.

○ Dynamic—This is the default mode on physical computers. In this mode, traffic is evenly distributed among all team members, including from virtual NICs. A potential problem with the Address Hash and Hyper-V Port modes is that a NIC in the team could be overwhelmed when there are very large traffic flows involving a single NIC, even if the other NICs had unused capacity. This mode balances large flows of traffic over multiple NICs, thereby providing even distribution of traffic among all team members.

NIC Teaming on Virtual Machines

As mentioned, you can configure NIC teaming on VMs as well as on physical computers. On VMs, you use the same procedure as on physical computers, but for the most reliability, you should enable the feature first in the network adapter's Advanced Features dialog box (shown in Figure 12-37). If you don't enable it, you can still create a NIC team in the VM's guest OS, but if one of the physical NICs in the team fails, the team stops working instead of providing failover protection. NIC teaming can be configured only on vNICs connected to an external virtual switch.

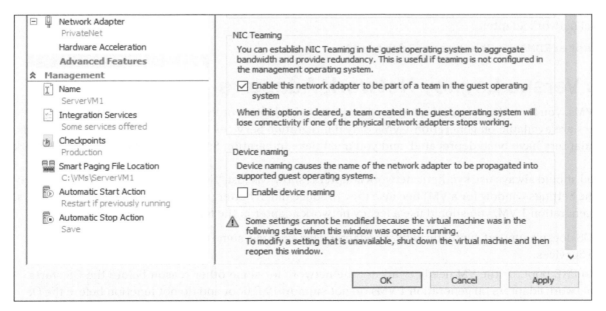

Figure 12-37   Enabling NIC teaming on a VM's network adapter

If you have already configured NIC teaming on the Hyper-V host server, configuring it on VMs running on the host isn't necessary. Any VM connected to an external virtual switch that's mapped to the host's NIC team gets the benefits of NIC teaming on the host. However, if you want a VM to have a dedicated NIC team, you should configure NIC teaming on the VM, too. In this case, NIC teaming must be enabled on each virtual network adapter that's part of the team, and each virtual network adapter must be connected to a separate external virtual switch. You can have NIC teams configured on the host computer and on VMs, but they must use separate physical NICs. That is, the NICs on the host that are part of a NIC team can't be used in a NIC team on a VM, and vice versa. Likewise, an external virtual switch can be mapped only to a NIC team on the host or to a physical NIC on the host; it can't be mapped to a NIC that's a member of a NIC team. You must plan physical and virtual network configurations carefully to be sure you have enough physical NICs to accommodate the host's physical network needs and the virtual network needs.

Note 19

Although NIC teaming on physical computers can use up to 32 NICs in a team, Microsoft supports VM NIC teams with only two team members. You can create a team with more members, but it's not officially supported.

Implementing Switch Embedded Teaming

Switch Embedded Teaming (SET) is a feature that allows up to eight identical physical adapters on the host system to be configured as a team and mapped to a virtual switch. The virtual switch can control all the physical adapters simultaneously, providing fault tolerance and load balancing. SET is targeted for enterprise servers with very fast NICs—10 Gb and faster. The physical NICs can be connected to the same or different physical switches to provide additional fault tolerance. To configure SET, you simply create a new virtual switch and specify the network adapters that should be members, as in the following cmdlet:

```
New-VMSwitch -Name SETSwitch1 -NetAdapter
    Ethernet1,Ethernet2 -EnableEmbeddedTeaming $true
```

Next, you add the virtual network adapters that will communicate through the SET-enabled switch:

```
Add-VMNetworkAdapter -SwitchName SETSwitch1 -Name Adapter1
```

SET supports remote direct memory access (RDMA) on virtual network adapters, which provides additional performance benefits. You must enable RDMA on the virtual network adapter created on the host system. The adapter will always be named vEthernet (*VirtualAdapterName*), where *VirtualAdapterName* is the name assigned when you created the virtual network adapter.

```
Enable-NetAdapterRDMA "vEthernet (Adapter1)"
```

Synthetic Versus Legacy Network Adapters

On generation 1 VMs, you have the option of using synthetic network adapters or legacy network adapters. **Synthetic network adapters** are available on generation 1 VMs only if Integration Services is installed. On generation 2 VMs, legacy network adapters have been deprecated, and you must have Integration Services installed to add a network adapter.

In general, you should always use synthetic network adapters (shown as just "Network Adapters" in the Add Hardware section of the Settings window for a VM) because they produce much better performance than legacy adapters. However, with a generation 1 VM, you should use a legacy network adapter in the following situations:

- The guest OS doesn't support synthetic network adapters; for example, some non-Windows OSs don't support Integration Services.
- You need to PXE boot, or the VM needs to access the network for some other reason before the OS starts. Synthetic network adapters on generation 1 VMs do not support PXE boot and do not function before the OS starts.

Note that generation 2 VMs don't support legacy network adapters, and the synthetic adapters on generation 2 VMs do support PXE boot, so there's no reason to use a legacy adapter. However, generation 2 VMs support only Windows Server 2012/R2 and later versions as well as 64-bit versions of Windows 8/8.1 and later editions. So, for older VMs, you might want to install a legacy network adapter on the VM for PXE boot and then replace it with a synthetic network adapter after the OS is installed.

Self-Check Questions

11. When VMQ is enabled, packets are placed in a common queue. True or False?

    a. True   **b.** False

12. Which virtual NIC setting allows a VM to see the network traffic that is addressed to another VM?

    a. Protected network   **c.** Router guard
    b. Port mirroring   **d.** MAC address spoofing

○ Check your answers at the end of this module.

Managing Windows Server VMs on Azure

Microsoft Exam AZ-800:

Manage virtual machines and containers.

- Manage Azure virtual machines that run Windows Server

You have already seen how to create and deploy a VM in Azure as well as manage aspects of an Azure network and network services. This section begins with an overview of Azure VMs and then discusses specific management tasks you can perform once an Azure VM running Windows Server is deployed:

- Manage Azure VMs
- Manage Azure VM data disks
- Resize Azure VMs
- Configure VM connections

Managing Azure VMs

When you create a VM in Hyper-V on an on-premises server, you have full control over the virtual hardware settings, including memory, OS and data disks, and network interfaces. When you deploy an Azure VM, you choose from a list of configuration options that determine the VM size, which in turn specify the speed and number of processors, RAM amount, number of network adapters, and maximum number of data disks. VMs are also categorized according to tier level:

- *Basic tier*—Used for standalone servers (not part of a high-availability configuration) that are deployed for development and testing purposes, because there is no service level agreement (SLA) that guarantees availability. Basic-tier servers range from A0 (single CPU core and data disk, 768 MB of RAM) to A4 (8 CPU cores, 16 data disks, and 14 GB of RAM).
- *Standard tier*—Offers high availability and load balancing, high-performance storage options, and a variety of CPU, data disk, networking, and memory configurations. Standard-tier VMs are recommended for production workloads, and there are a number of size options to choose from to meet most performance and storage needs.

VM sizes in the standard tier are organized into a number of categories. There are general-purpose servers intended for low-end databases or web servers; high-performance computing options intended for applications that require the fastest processing speeds; and several categories optimized for security, memory, computing, or storage. In addition, you can select generation 2 VMs that use the UEFI boot architecture and support VMs of up to 12 TB.

Note 20

You can learn more about VM sizes and how they are identified at *https://azure.microsoft.com/en-us/pricing/details/virtual-machines/series/*.

Managing Azure VM Data Disks

Azure VMs are built with three categories of disk storage:

- *Operating system disk*—A maximum 2 TB disk holds the OS and is designated as drive C on Windows VMs.
- *Data disks*—The number of data disks you can attach to a VM is dependent on the VM size. A data disk can have a capacity of up to 32 TB. On Windows, you can assign a drive letter starting with F or mount a disk into an empty folder.
- *Temporary disk*—Only one temporary disk per VM is allowed, and it is assigned drive letter D on Windows systems. Unlike OS and data disks, which are stored in Azure storage, temporary disks are stored on the system hosting the VM. These disks hold nonpersistent data such as the paging file, so the data is deleted when the VM is turned off or rebooted.

When you create a VM in Azure, the VM size you select determines the attributes of the OS and temporary disks, so most of your storage customization is in the number and type of data disks you attach to the VM.

You can create a data disk in an Azure storage account or when you create a virtual machine. If you create a data disk in a storage account, you can attach it to a VM during VM creation or afterward. In any case, you have the following data disk options:

- *Standard HDD*— Best for infrequently accessed bulk storage, such as file archiving and backup, or any type of storage that does not require high performance.
- *Standard SSD*—Good for applications such as web servers or development and testing servers.
- *Premium SSD*—Best for applications that require high-performance data access.
- *Ultra disk*—The highest-performing storage option, ultra disks are SSDs that are ideal for transaction-intensive applications and high-performance databases. Ultra disks cannot be used as OS disks and do not support disk encryption.

> **Note 21**
>
> All of the preceding disk types except ultra disks support disk encryption.

Attaching and Detaching a Data Disk

Data disks can be attached and detached from a virtual machine. Using the Azure portal or Azure PowerShell, a data disk that is created in a storage account can be later attached to a VM that is running or turned off. You can also use the Azure portal or Azure PowerShell to detach a data disk from a VM while the VM is running or turned off.

To attach a data disk using the portal, select the VM, select Disks under Settings, and click Attach existing disks under Data disks. You can also create a new data disk and attach it (see Figure 12-38). To detach a disk from a VM, follow the same procedure and select X on the far-right side of the entry for the data disk you want to detach.

To attach a data disk using Azure PowerShell, use the Add-AzVMDataDisk cmdlet. After you have run the cmdlet, you must run the Update-AzVM cmdlet to update the VM and apply the changes.

Use the Remove-AzVMDataDisk cmdlet to detach a disk; again, be sure to run the Update-AzVM cmdlet.

Expanding a Data Disk

A data disk attached to a VM can be expanded, providing additional storage space. You can expand the disk without downtime in most cases. You cannot expand an Ultra or Premium SSD v2 disk without first stopping and deallocating the VM. To expand a data disk, select the VM, select Disks, and click the name of the disk. Under Settings, select Size + Performance and then select the new size for the disk from the available size options, which range from 32 GB to 32767 GB. You can also expand an OS disk up to 4 TB, but the VM must be stopped and deallocated first.

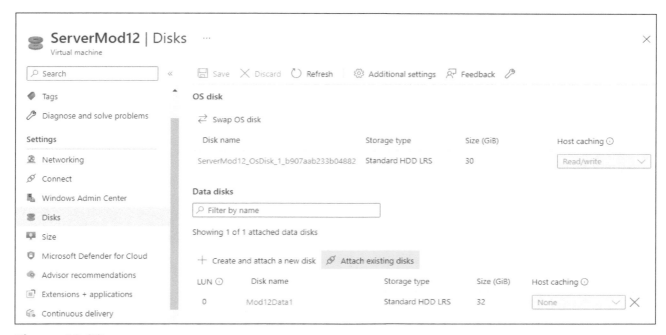

Figure 12-38   Attaching a data disk

Sharing a Data Disk

A shared disk is a data disk that can be attached to multiple VMs at the same time, allowing you to deploy VMs configured in a cluster for fault tolerance and load balancing. You can share most disk types except for standard HDDs. You can enable sharing when you create a disk or after the disk is created. When you create a new data disk, enable sharing by going to the Advanced tab and clicking Yes next to Enable shared disk. You set the Max shares value to two or more, which specifies how many VMs can be attached to the disk (see Figure 12-39). To enable sharing on an existing disk, select the disk, click Configuration under Settings, click Yes next to Enable shared disk, and set the Max shares value. The disk can't be attached to a VM when you enable sharing. To enable sharing with PowerShell, use the following commands:

```
$diskconfig = Get-AzDisk -DiskName "SharedDisk"
$diskconfig.maxShares = 2
Update-AzDisk
```

In the `Update-AzDisk` cmdlet, you need to specify the resource group, the disk name, and the disk configuration variable. After sharing is enabled, attach the disk to the VMs in the usual way.

Resizing an Azure VM

If you create an Azure VM and its properties as defined by its size do not meet your computing needs, you can resize the VM. Resizing a VM changes the number and type of processors and the amount of memory allocated to the VM. You can resize a VM using the portal by selecting the VM and clicking Size under Settings. If the VM is running, you may not see all available sizes; stopping the VM may provide more choices. After you have selected the new size, click Resize at the bottom of the window (see Figure 12-40); a running VM will reboot with the new size settings. Keep in mind that resizing a VM may also change the number and type of data disks that can be attached to the VM. This point can be important to keep in mind if you are choosing a smaller VM size.

Note 22

A VM with a local temp disk can only be revised to a size that can accommodate the local temp disk. A VM with no local temp disk can only be revised to a size that does not have to account for a local temp disk.

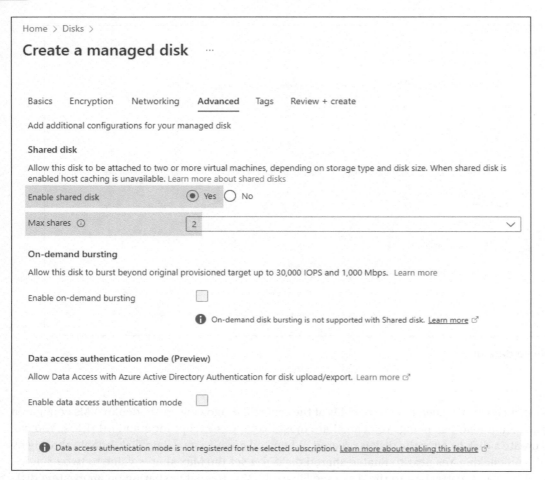

Figure 12-39   Configuring disk sharing

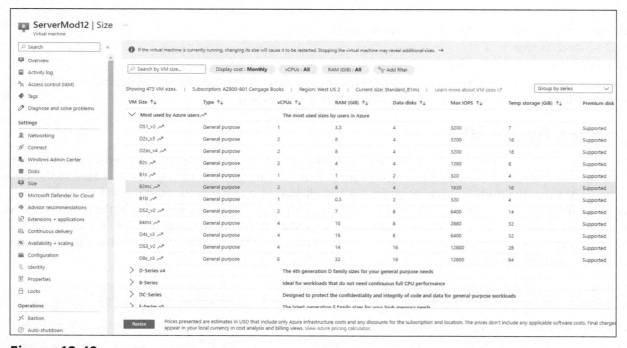

Figure 12-40   Resizing a VM

Configuring VM Connections

After you have created and deployed a virtual machine, you need to access it so you can configure it, install server roles, and perform other management tasks. There are a number of options for connecting to a VM, including the following:

- *Using a public IP address*—When you create a VM, you can configure certain ports to be open and available through a public IP address (see Figure 12-41). Two of the ports provide remote management access: RDP on port 3389 and SSH on port 22. While both protocols provide some level of security, it is not advisable to leave those ports open for an extended period of time. If you do choose to make those ports available through a public IP address, it is advisable to configure firewall rules to allow only the public IP addresses from which you will be accessing the server. Further, you should configure Just-in-Time VM access so that the ports are only open when requested by an authorized administrator. Just-in-Time VM access was discussed in Module 6.

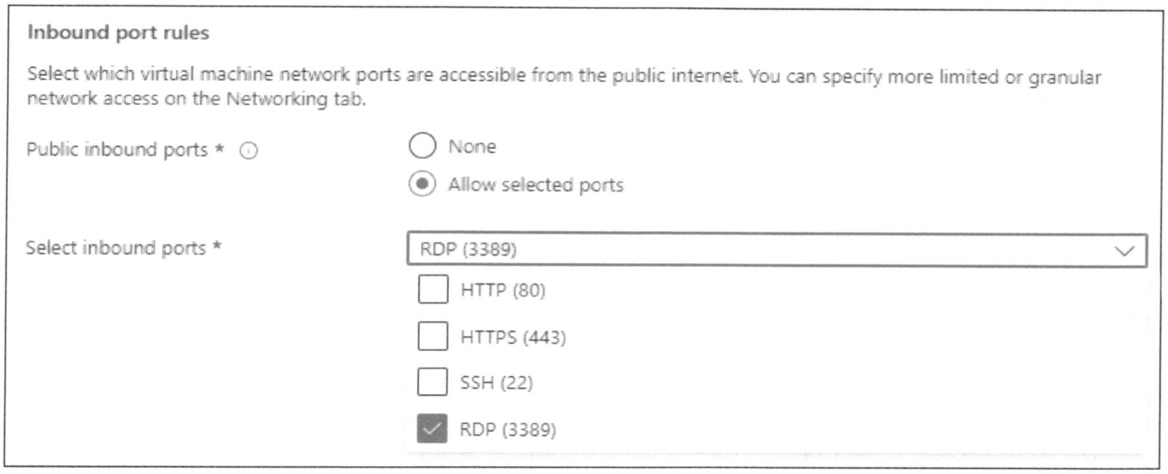

Inbound port rules

Select which virtual machine network ports are accessible from the public internet. You can specify more limited or granular network access on the Networking tab.

Public inbound ports * ⓘ

    ◯ None

    ◉ Allow selected ports

Select inbound ports *

    | RDP (3389) ⌄ |

    ☐ HTTP (80)

    ☐ HTTPS (443)

    ☐ SSH (22)

    ☑ RDP (3389)

Figure 12-41   Enabling public IP address access when creating a VM

- *VPN*—You can implement a host-to-site VPN or site-to-site VPN to the virtual network (Vnet) the VM is on so that you don't need to open remote access ports on a public IP address. VPNs were discussed in Module 9. By using this option, your connection is encrypted from the management station or on-premises network to the Vnet and you can use RDP or SSH access to the VM via its private IP address.
- *ExpressRoute*—If you already have an Azure ExpressRoute connection from your on-premises network to your Azure network, you can simply use RDP or SSH access to a VM with the VM's private IP address. ExpressRoute is a costly solution; it requires third-party WAN providers instead of an ISP because it does not use the Internet for connectivity. ExpressRoute should be used to manage Azure VMs only if it is already part of your hybrid Azure/on-premises solution.
- *Azure Bastion*—Azure Bastion is an easy, secure solution to Azure VM remote management. Once it is enabled on a Vnet, you can access a VM using RDP or SSH and a standard web browser such as Microsoft Edge or Chrome. Azure Bastion does not require the VM to have a public IP address. Your browser connects to a public IP address but the RDP or SSH traffic from the client to the Azure VM is encapsulated and encrypted inside a Bastion packet that routes the packet to the appropriate VM once it reaches the Azure network. To configure Azure Bastion, go to the Azure portal, select the Vnet on the VM you want to manage, choose Settings, and then select Bastion. As long as the Vnet has sufficient address space for Azure Bastion to create a new subnet with a /26 prefix, you can select Deploy Bastion (see Figure 12-42) to automatically create a new subnet named AzureBastionSubnet and configure it with default settings. It will take several minutes for Azure Bastion to be deployed. You can also configure Bastion manually if you want to choose the name, tier, and public IP address name. You can manage either two VMs (Bastion Basic tier) or up to 50 VMs (Bastion Standard tier) on a single Azure Bastion subnet, depending on the service tier you select. Once it's deployed, you can connect to a VM on a Bastion-enabled Vnet by selecting a running VM in the portal, clicking Connect, and then selecting

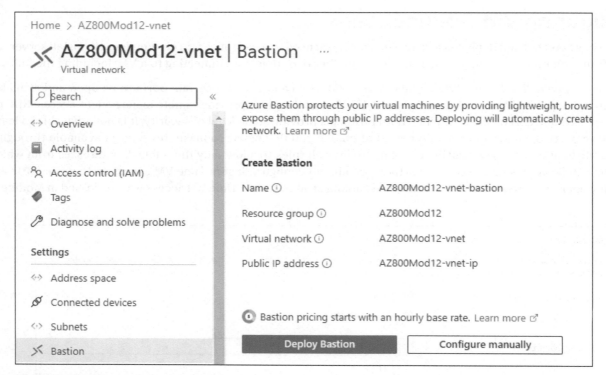

Figure 12-42 Deploying Azure Bastion

Bastion. You will be asked to enter a username and password that has permissions to connect to the VM, and then you will see a browser window with the VM desktop. Azure Bastion does include an hourly cost for the service plus an hourly cost per VM, as well as a fee for outbound data transfers, so the cost must be factored into whether you want to use this convenient and secure solution to manage your VMs. In many cases, you may want to set up Azure Bastion after new servers have been deployed so you can do initial configuration tasks conveniently and then delete the Bastion service after initial configuration has been completed. You can redeploy Bastion again later if necessary.

Note 23

As of this writing, the Azure Bastion Basic service costs $0.19 per hour and the Standard service costs $0.29 per hour. Each VM instance beyond the default of two VMs costs an additional $0.14 per hour.

Self-Check Questions

13. Basic-tier Azure VMs cannot be used in a high-availability configuration. True or False?

    a. True
    b. False

14. Which Azure disk type cannot be used as an OS disk?

    a. Standard HDD
    b. Standard SSD
    c. Premium SSD
    d. Ultra disk

⦿ Check your answers at the end of this module.

Module Summary

- The Hyper-V virtualization environment sits between the hardware and virtual machines. Each virtual machine is a child partition on the system, and Windows Server with Hyper-V installed is the parent or management partition. The Hyper-V management console runs on Windows Server in the parent partition and serves as an interface for managing the VMs running in child partitions.

- Hyper-V is installed as a server role in Windows Server 64-bit versions of the Standard and Datacenter editions. The CPU on the host machine must be 64-bit and support virtualization extensions, such as AMD-V or Intel-VT. Standard Edition includes a license for two virtual instances of Windows Server, and Datacenter Edition includes unlimited virtual instances of Windows Server.

- Hyper-V allows a virtual machine to run in the background until you connect to it in Hyper-V Manager. A running VM doesn't require using Hyper-V Manager, nor does it require anyone to be signed in to the server. You can manage a VM remotely by using tools such as Remote Desktop and MMCs if the VM is configured to communicate with the host network.

- Virtual machines can be exported and then imported to create one or more virtual machines. You can even export a running VM. You can import a VM that has been exported or a VM that hasn't been exported.

- Virtual machines created with the New Virtual Machine Wizard can be created as a generation 1 or generation 2 VM. Generation 2 VMs are based on revised virtual hardware specifications; they have enhanced VM capabilities and support for newer standards.

- Many aspects of a VM's physical environment can be configured, including BIOS settings, memory allocation, and virtual processor settings. Hyper-V in Windows Server adds the ability to hot-add and remove memory, which is the addition of memory or removal of memory while the VM is running.

- Checkpoints allow you to save the state of a VM and return to that state later. Standard checkpoints enable you to revert a VM to a previous state; they should not be used on production VMs. Production checkpoints are a new type of checkpoint that supports production virtual machines and uses backup technology in the guest OS to create the checkpoint.

- A VM's software environment can be enhanced by installing Integration Services, which includes enhanced drivers for disk, network, display, and mouse devices. Automatic start and stop actions can be configured to determine what actions the VM should perform when the host computer is shut down and started.

- Enhanced Session mode is a feature that improves interaction and device redirection between the host computer and the Virtual Machine Connection console.

- Discrete Device Assignment (DDA) is a feature in Windows Server Hyper-V that allows a VM exclusive access to hardware devices on the host computer.

- A virtual hard disk is a file on the host computer with a .vhd or .vhdx extension. Virtual hard disks are more flexible than physical disks. Three types of virtual hard disks can be created: dynamically expanding, fixed size, and differencing. A fourth type of hard disk, called a pass-through disk, can be attached to a VM; it's an offline physical disk attached to the host.

- Virtual disks can be created when a VM is created or with the New Virtual Hard Disk Wizard. During VM creation, the disk is created as a dynamically expanding disk, but you can change it to a fixed-size disk later. When you use the wizard, the first thing you do is choose the disk format. The virtual disk can be formatted as VHD, VHDX, or a VHD set.

- There are three types of virtual networks: external, internal, and private. External networks connect the VM to the host's physical network, and internal networks allow VMs to communicate only with one another and the host. Private networks allow communication only between the VMs connected to them. More than one private and internal network can be created on a host.

- You create a virtual switch in Hyper-V Manager by clicking Virtual Switch Manager in the Actions pane. From this window, you can edit an existing virtual switch or create a new virtual switch. Choose External, Internal, or Private. Then you can configure the switch with the following options: Connection type, Allow management operating system to share this network adapter, Enable single-root I/O virtualization, and VLAN ID.

- A network adapter on a VM is virtual and cannot have a true burned-in address. Hyper-V must assign a MAC address to each network adapter connected to a virtual network, using a pool of addresses it maintains. When a new network adapter is connected to a virtual network, a MAC address is assigned dynamically to the adapter from the pool. The MAC address pool contains 256 addresses by default.

- There are three hardware acceleration features for vNICs: Virtual machine queue, IPsec task offloading, and Single-root I/O virtualization (SR-IOV). In the Advanced Features dialog box for a network adapter, you can configure the following features and security options: MAC address, Enable MAC address spoofing, DHCP guard, Router guard, Protected network, Port mirroring, and Device naming.

- NIC teaming allows multiple network interfaces to work in tandem to provide increased bandwidth, load balancing, and fault tolerance. You can create a NIC team with a single network interface, but most of the utility of a NIC team comes from having more than one in the team. Windows Server supports up to 32 NICs in a team. There are three teaming modes: Switch Independent, Static Teaming, and LACP.

- Load balancing distributes traffic between two or more interfaces, providing an increase in overall network throughput a server is able to maintain. The load-balancing mode determines how the server load-balances outgoing data packets among the NICs in the team. There are three options: Address Hash, Hyper-V Port, and Dynamic.

- When using generation 1 VMs, you have the option of using synthetic network adapters or legacy network adapters. Generation 2 VMs don't support legacy network adapters, and the synthetic adapters on generation 2 VMs do support PXE boot, so there's no reason to use a legacy adapter.

- When you deploy an Azure VM, you choose from a list of configuration options that determine the VM size, which in turn specify the speed and number of processors, RAM amount, number of network adapters, and maximum number of data disks. VMs are also categorized according to tier level: basic or standard.

- Azure VMs are built with three categories of disk storage: OS disk, data disks, and temporary disk. When you create a VM in Azure, the VM size you select determines the attributes of the OS and temporary disks, so most of your storage customization is in the number and type of data disks you attach to the VM.

- You have the following data disk options: Standard HDD, Standard SSD, Premium SSD, and Ultra disk. Data disks can be attached and detached from a VM, and they can also be expanded.

- A shared disk is a data disk that can be attached to multiple VMs at the same time, allowing you to deploy VMs configured in a cluster for fault tolerance and load balancing. You can share most disk types except for standard HDDs.

- If you create an Azure VM and its properties as defined by its size do not meet your computing needs, you can resize the VM. Resizing a VM changes the number and type of processors and the amount of memory allocated to the VM.

- After you have created and deployed a virtual machine, you need to access it so you can configure it, install server roles, and perform other management tasks. There are a number of options for connecting to a VM, including using a public IP address, VPN, ExpressRoute, and Azure Bastion.

Key Terms

checkpoint	internal virtual switch	synthetic driver
differencing disk	load balancing	synthetic network adapter
Discrete Device Assignment (DDA)	load balancing and failover (LBFO)	type 1 hypervisor
Dynamic Memory	NIC teaming	type 2 hypervisor
dynamically expanding disk	pass-through disk	VHD set
emulated drivers	private virtual switch	virtual disk
Enhanced Session mode	production checkpoint	virtual instance
external virtual switch	single-root I/O virtualization	virtual machine queue
failover	(SR-IOV)	(VMQ)
fixed-size disk	smart paging	virtual network
Integration Services	standard checkpoint	virtual processor

Review Questions

1. Which of the following is described as a partial copy of a VM made at a specific moment?
   a. Virtual instance
   b. Differencing disk
   c. Hypervisor
   d. Checkpoint

2. You have just purchased and installed Windows Server Standard Edition. How many virtual instances of Windows Server can you run on a fully licensed host computer without purchasing an additional Windows Server license?
   a. One virtual instance
   b. Two virtual instances
   c. Three virtual instances
   d. Unlimited virtual instances

3. You have just placed a new Windows Server with Hyper-V server into production; this server is the management partition. Which of the following best describes a new virtual machine installed on this system?
   a. Parent partition
   b. Secondary partition
   c. Child partition
   d. Virtual partition

4. You have just purchased a server with Windows Server Datacenter Edition installed. The server has 4 GB of RAM, a 1000 GB hard disk, and an Intel 2.4 GHz Xeon processor with Intel-VT. You plan to install the Hyper-V server role on this server and run two Windows Server VMs, each with a 2 GB RAM allocation. You have discovered, however, that the server does not work for this purpose. What should you do?
   a. Install more RAM.
   b. Install a bigger hard disk.
   c. Install Standard Edition.
   d. Upgrade the processor.

5. You created a VM running Windows Server and some applications. You want to create a second VM quickly that has the same configuration options and installed applications as the first one. You plan to use this second VM on the same Hyper-V server as the first. You want good disk performance from both VMs. What should you do?
   a. Create a VM with a differencing disk. Assign the first VM's virtual disk as the parent disk; the first VM will continue to use its original virtual disk.
   b. Export the first VM and import it with the "Copy the virtual machine" option to create the second VM.

   c. Create a VM. Create a checkpoint of the first VM. Copy and rename the checkpoint file and use it for the second VM's virtual hard disk.
   d. Export the first VM and import it using the "Register the virtual machine in place" option. Use the imported VM as the second virtual server.

6. To remotely manage Hyper-V using PowerShell, PowerShell remoting must be enabled. By default, PowerShell remoting is enabled on Windows Server 2012 and later versions. However, if it becomes disabled, which of the following PowerShell cmdlets will allow you to remotely manage Hyper-V using PowerShell?
   a. `Configure-PSRemoting`
   b. `Enable-PSRemoting`
   c. `Enable-SMRemoting`
   d. `Configure-SMRemoting`

7. You are creating a new VM in Hyper-V on a Windows Server computer. Your new VM will use Windows 11 and support the use of PXE boot. Which hardware generation type should you select when creating the new VM?
   a. Generation 1
   b. Generation 1 or generation 2
   c. Generation 2
   d. Generation 3

8. Your network has had long power outages that have caused Hyper-V servers to shut down after the UPS battery has drained. When power returns, the Hyper-V servers restart automatically, but the VMs don't start. You need to make sure the VMs start when the host starts. What should you do?
   a. Change the VMs' BIOS settings.
   b. Write a script on the host that starts the VMs automatically when the host starts.
   c. Reinstall Integration Services.
   d. Change the automatic start action setting on the VMs.

9. Checkpoints for your test VMs are taking up too much space on the host's system disk. You have two test VMs running, each with one checkpoint to represent the baseline testing environment. You're finished with your current testing and are ready for another round of testing, but you want to make sure your checkpoints are stored on another volume. What should you do?

a. In Hyper-V Manager, change the checkpoints' path in the Settings window to point to the other volume; the checkpoints are moved automatically.

b. Use File Explorer to move the checkpoint files from their current location to the other volume.

c. Shut down the VMs. Apply the checkpoint to each VM and delete all checkpoints in Hyper-V Manager. Change the path of the checkpoint files to the other volume and create a new checkpoint for each VM.

d. In each VM's settings, change the checkpoint path. Apply the checkpoint and then create a new checkpoint for each VM. Delete the old checkpoints in File Explorer.

10. Which of the following is true if you enable shielding and create a shielded VM in Windows Server? (Choose two.)

a. Secure Boot is automatically disabled.

b. Secure Boot is automatically enabled.

c. Encryption is automatically enabled.

d. Encryption is automatically disabled.

11. You have four checkpoints of a VM. You want to return the VM to its state when the second checkpoint was taken. Which checkpoint option should you use?

a. Apply

b. Save

c. Select

d. Revert

12. You are configuring four VMs on a Hyper-V server. One of the virtual machines needs to be assigned a new relative weight value to allow it to have priority to the shared processing resources among the four VMs. All four VMs are currently set to the default relative weight of 100. What relative weight value can you use to configure the VM that needs priority to the shared processing resources?

a. 10

b. 200

c. −1

d. 0

13. You want to allow your VM the ability to copy files to a running VM without using a virtual network connection. Which of the following integration services should you enable in the VM's settings?

a. Guest services

b. Data exchange

c. Heartbeat

d. Time synchronization

14. You solved the problem with VMs not starting when the host restarts, but now you notice that VMs take a long time to start when the host starts. On some

hosts, you have as many as six VMs. You also find that the VM running an application server can't initialize correctly because the VM running DNS isn't available immediately. What can you do to improve the VMs' startup times and solve the application server problem?

a. Set a virtual machine priority in Hyper-V's Settings window, making sure the priority value on the DNS server is highest.

b. Set a startup delay for each VM, making sure the delay for the DNS server is less than that of the application servers.

c. Change the BIOS settings of the DNS server to use the Quick Boot option.

d. Assign more virtual processors to the VMs you want to start faster.

15. You currently have four VMs running on a Hyper-V server. You need to increase the amount of memory to VM4 so that you can install a new application. You're running low on physical memory. You tried to allocate less memory to the other three VMs to free up memory, but after you did so, they wouldn't start. What can you do that doesn't involve installing additional physical memory on the host or changing the configuration of the guest OSs?

a. Enable Dynamic Memory on all the VMs and set the startup memory higher than the minimum memory.

b. Configure integration services on all four VMs.

c. Uninstall server roles on the guest OSs until you have enough free memory for VM4.

d. Enable memory QoS on the other three VMs and set a maximum IOPS for their memory use.

16. You're using a VM with a Windows 11 guest OS to run applications that you want isolated from the host computer and the LAN. However, you want to be able to print from the VM to the printer connected to your host and copy files between the host and guest OS. What can you enable to accomplish this task?

a. Enable Enhanced Session mode in Hyper-V and verify that Remote Desktop Services is running on the guest.

b. Create shares on the host and VM to transfer files back and forth, and install a printer driver on the guest OS.

c. Connect the VM running Windows 11 to an external virtual switch.

d. Install Integration Services on the Windows 11 guest OS and enable the device-sharing and file-sharing options.

17. You currently have an application server VM running on your Windows Server Hyper-V server.

Your application server VM's performance would benefit greatly if the host machine's SSD drives could be accessed by allowing the application server VM to bypass the Hyper-V hypervisor. What feature in Windows Server Hyper-V can give your application server VM exclusive access to hardware devices on the host computer?

a. Hyper-V Manager
b. Authorization Manager
c. Virtual Device Assignment
d. Discrete Device Assignment

18. Which of the following PowerShell cmdlets will allow the management of a running Hyper-V VM named VMTestServer from a Hyper-V host PowerShell prompt?

a. `Get-PSSession -VMName VMTestServer`
b. `Enter-Session -VM VMTestServer`
c. `Enter-PSSession -VMName VMTestServer`
d. `Enter-PSSession -VM VMTestServer`

19. Hyper-V will allow you to use three different types of virtual disks. Which of the following is not a virtual disk type found in Hyper-V?

a. Dynamically expanding
b. Fixed size
c. Differencing
d. Pass-through

20. Which of the following virtual disk formats is a shared virtual hard disk used with virtual machine cluster configurations where multiple VMs have access to the same virtual hard disk for fault tolerance and load-balancing applications?

a. VHD plus
b. VHDX
c. VHD set
d. VHDX HA

21. What virtual disk option can be selected to allow a differencing disk's contents to be incorporated into its parent disk or combine the differencing disk with the parent disk to create a new disk while allowing the original disk to be unchanged?

a. Compact
b. Convert
c. Shrink
d. Merge

22. A system administrator needs to create a high-performance SQL server. What type of disk configuration will allow the administrator to connect an offline physical disk from the host machine to a VM to maximize the VM's performance?

a. Pass-through disk
b. Expanded disk
c. Fixed-size disk
d. Host-based disk

23. A virtual switch with the host's physical NIC bound to the Hyper-V Extensible Virtual Switch protocol is called which of the following?

a. External virtual switch
b. Private virtual switch
c. Hosted virtual switch
d. Internal virtual switch

24. You have three VMs that must communicate with one another and with the host computer but not be able to access the physical network directly. What type of virtual network should you create?

a. Private
b. Internal
c. Hosted
d. External

25. Your Hyper-V server has a single disk of 300 GB being used as the system disk and to host a dynamically expanding disk for a Windows Server VM. The VM's virtual disk has a maximum size of 200 GB; it is currently 80 GB and growing. You have only about 30 GB of free space on the host disk. You have noticed disk contention with the host OS, and the constant need for the virtual disk to expand is causing performance problems. You also have plans to install at least one more VM. You have installed a new 1 TB hard disk on the host, and you want to make sure the VM doesn't contend for the host's system disk and the expansion process doesn't hamper disk performance. What should you do?

a. Create a new fixed-size disk on the new drive. Use the Disk Management MMC on the VM to extend the current disk to the new fixed-size disk.
b. Shut down the VM. Convert the dynamically expanding disk to a fixed-size disk, being sure to place the fixed-size disk on the new host drive. Connect the VM to the fixed-size disk in place of the dynamically expanding disk. Delete the old virtual disk.
c. Shut down the VM. Create a new fixed-size disk on the new drive. Copy the contents of the dynamically expanding disk to the new fixed-size disk. Connect the VM to the fixed-size disk in place of the dynamically expanding disk. Delete the old virtual disk.
d. Create a new fixed-size disk on the new drive. Add the fixed-size disk to the VM as a new disk. On the VM, create a new volume on the new disk and begin saving files to the new volume.

26. You're working with a Windows Server VM in Hyper-V. You have decided that you are going to accelerate the vNIC's performance by delivering packets from the external network directly to the vNIC. What virtual NIC feature would you enable?
    a. IPsec task offloading
    b. Virtual machine vNIC priority
    c. Virtual machine queue
    d. Single-root I/O virtualization

27. Which of the following vNIC configuration options will allow the VM to change the source MAC address on outgoing packets and allow the virtual switch to learn addresses other than the one assigned to the virtual adapter?
    a. DHCP guard
    b. Port mirroring
    c. Device naming
    d. MAC address spoofing

28. You have just installed a VM named VM5 running an application that requires the best possible network performance when communicating with resources on the physical LAN. The host has four NICs. One NIC is dedicated to the host computer, and two are bound to two virtual switches used by four other VMs on the system. One of the NICs is currently unused. What network configuration should you use that wouldn't disturb the current VM's network configuration?
    a. Connect VM5 to an internal network and run RRAS on the host server.
    b. Connect the four existing VMs to a private network, create a NIC team on the host server, and bind the NIC team to a virtual switch for VM5 to use.
    c. In Virtual Switch Manager, bind the unused NIC to an external virtual switch and enable SR-IOV. Connect VM5's virtual network adapter to that virtual switch and enable SR-IOV on the virtual network adapter.
    d. Create a NIC team in VM5, using all four NICs on the host. Turn on virtual network adapter sharing so that the NICs can be used for the team and the other two virtual switches.

29. You currently have four VMs running on a Hyper-V server. You would like to use NIC teaming. Which of the following NIC teaming modes can be used with your virtual machines?
    a. Switch Independent
    b. Static Teaming
    c. LACP
    d. Dynamic

30. Which of the following load-balancing modes available in Hyper-V allows each virtual NIC to be associated with only one team member at system startup?
    a. Hyper-V Port
    b. Static load balancing
    c. Dynamic
    d. Address Hash

31. You want to create an Azure VM that supports the UEFI boot architecture. Which option should you choose?
    a. Basic-tier VM
    b. Standard-tier VM
    c. Generation 1 VM
    d. Generation 2 VM

32. Which of the following is *not* a category of disk storage on Azure VMs?
    a. OS disk
    b. Fixed-size disk
    c. Data disk
    d. Temporary disk

33. You are creating an Azure VM that requires high-performance access to storage. The data kept on the server will be sensitive, so the storage option you select must support encryption. Which disk type should you choose for a data disk on this VM?
    a. Standard SSD
    b. Ultra disk
    c. Standard HDD
    d. Premium SSD

34. Which of the following commands enables sharing on an Azure data disk?
    a. `$diskconfig.maxShares = 2`
    b. `$vm.diskSharesEnabled = $True`
    c. `$diskconfig.maxVMs = 2`
    d. `$vm.sharedDisks = $True`

35. You have created a new Azure VM with Windows Server installed and you want to connect to it and install server roles using Server Manager. Which option should you choose if you want to access the Windows Server desktop using a web browser that is secure and requires the least administrative effort?
    a. Assign a public IP address and enable RDP.
    b. Create a site-to-site VPN and install VNC.
    c. Enable Azure Bastion on the Vnet.
    d. Install ExpressRoute and enable RDP.

Critical Thinking

The following activities give you critical thinking challenges. Case projects offer a scenario with a problem for which you supply a written solution.

Case Projects

Case Project 12-1: Devising a Hyper-V Solution

You want to optimize your datacenter using Hyper-V virtualization. You have targeted four servers with quad-core processors that are old and taking up quite a bit of space. You want to implement the functions of these four servers using virtual machines. Two servers are running Windows Server 2016 and two are running Windows Server 2022. Each of the four servers has two disks, one for the Windows OS and the other for data storage. The OS volume is using about 100 GB of space on each server and the data volume is a 1 TB volume, with each server using about half the available space. You need to devise a plan to deploy each of the four servers as a virtual machine. Create a plan that details the host server hardware and software configuration (what edition of Windows Server should be installed, what server roles, etc.) and the virtual machine configuration. What are some of the questions that you must answer to implement your plan? What are some of the options for transferring the function of each server to a virtual machine?

Case Project 12-2: Choosing a Virtual Disk Configuration

You have two Windows Server 2022 computers with the Hyper-V role installed. Both computers have two hard drives, one for the system volume and the other for data. One server, named HyperVTest, will be used mainly for testing and what-if scenarios, and its data drive is 1 TB. You estimate that you might have 8 or 10 VMs configured on HyperVTest, with two or three running at the same time. Each test VM has disk requirements ranging from about 100 GB to 200 GB. The other server, named HyperVApp, runs in the datacenter with production VMs installed. Its data drive is 2 TB. You expect two VMs to run on HyperVApp, each needing about 300 GB to 500 GB of disk space. Both are expected to run fairly disk-intensive applications. Given this environment, describe how you would configure the virtual disks for the VMs on both servers.

Case Project 12-3: Choosing a Virtual Network Configuration

You're setting up a test environment that involves two subnets with three Windows Server 2022 servers on each subnet. The servers are running broadcast-based network services, such as DHCP. The host computer is attached to the production network, so you must prevent any conflicts. You want the two subnets to be able to communicate with one another. The test environment consists of a single Windows Server 2022 machine running Hyper-V. Describe how you plan to configure the virtual network.

Case Project 12-4: Working with Azure VMs

You want to configure a Windows Server solution in Azure to run a cloud web application. This is your first foray into using Azure VMs to augment your on-premises solution. Your solution requires high availability and load balancing and will run a back-end database that requires very fast access to storage. Consider how this VM should be configured, taking into account VM tier level and disk storage type. You want a simple, secure solution to use RDP access into your servers and perform configuration tasks from any computer you might be using, whether at home, on-premises, or from your laptop in other locations. Write a detailed description of the VM configuration you propose, and justify your choices. Also explain how you will connect to perform management and configuration tasks.

Solutions to Self-Check Questions

Section 12-1: Installing Hyper-V

1. A type 2 hypervisor is the best choice for production virtualization environments. True or False?

   Answer: b. False

   Explanation: There are type 1 and type 2 hypervisors. Type 2 hypervisors are installed on an OS like Windows 10 or Linux and use the host OS's resources and drivers. Type 2 hypervisors are best used for testing and development environments. Type 1 hypervisors are installed directly on the hardware of the host machine and may coexist with a host OS such as Windows Server, but they do not use the host OS's resources. Type 1 hypervisors are best for running production VMs.

2. Which of the following is *not* a requirement for installing Hyper-V?

   Answer: b. A quad-core processor

   Explanation: The CPU requirements for Hyper-V are to use a 1.4 GHz or faster 64-bit unit with virtualization extensions (AMD-V or Intel-VT). The CPU must support Data Execution Prevention (DEP) and second-level address translation (SLAT). There is no requirement for the number of cores.

Section 12-2: Creating Virtual Machines in Hyper-V

3. A Hyper-V virtual hard disk can have a VHD or VHDX file. True or False?

   Answer: a. True

   Explanation: Each virtual hard disk assigned to a VM has an associated VHD or VHDX file that holds the hard disk's contents. VHDX is the newer and preferred virtual hard disk format, but either format can be used.

4. Which virtual machine import option should you choose if you want to restore a corrupt VM without making a copy of the exported files?

   Answer: a. Register the virtual machine in-place (use the existing unique ID).

   Explanation: Use the "Register the virtual machine in-place" option only if you're restoring a failed or corrupt VM or rebuilding a Hyper-V host, and the files are already where you want them.

Section 12-3: Managing Virtual Machines

5. A generation 1 VM is required if you want to boot using UEFI. True or False?

   Answer: b. False

   Explanation: A generation 2 VM uses UEFI firmware instead of the traditional BIOS found on generation 1 VMs.

6. Which Hyper-V virtual machine feature provides temporary storage when a sudden surge in memory requirements exceeds the physical memory available?

   Answer: b. Smart paging

   Explanation: Smart paging works with Dynamic Memory. It's a file on the host computer used for temporary memory storage when a sudden surge in memory requirements exceeds the physical amount of memory available.

Section 12-4: Working with Virtual Hard Disks

7. Dynamically expanding disks provide better performance than fixed-size disks. True or False?

   Answer: b. False

   Explanation: Dynamically expanding disks are slower than fixed-size disks, and there are some concerns about host disk fragmentation when using them.

8. Which virtual hard disk type should you use if you want multiple VMs in a cluster configuration to have access to the same data?

   Answer: c. VHD set

   Explanation: A VHD set is a shared virtual hard disk used with virtual machine cluster configurations, where multiple VMs have access to the same virtual hard disk for fault tolerance and load-balancing applications.

Section 12-5: Hyper-V Virtual Networks

9. An external virtual switch binds the virtual switch to a physical network adapter. True or False?

    Answer: a. True

    Explanation: An external virtual switch binds a virtual switch to one of the host's physical network adapters, allowing virtual machines to access a LAN connected to the host.

10. Which virtual switch setting can isolate traffic between the management OS and virtual machines?

    Answer: d. VLAN ID

    Explanation: The VLAN ID setting isolates traffic between the management OS and virtual machines. You set the VLAN identifier to correspond with the VLAN identifier configured on the physical switch. The host machine's virtual NIC used for management is placed on the specified VLAN, but VM traffic is not affected.

Section 12-6: Advanced Virtual Network Configuration

11. When VMQ is enabled, packets are placed in a common queue. True or False?

    Answer: b. False

    Explanation: When VMQ is enabled, a dedicated queue is created for the vNIC on the physical NIC. When packets arrive on the physical interface for the vNIC, they are delivered directly to the VM. In contrast, when VMQ is not enabled, packets are placed in a common queue and distributed to the destination vNIC on a first-come, first-served basis.

12. Which virtual NIC setting allows a VM to see the network traffic that is addressed to another VM?

    Answer: b. Port mirroring

    Explanation: With port mirroring enabled, traffic from the virtual switch port the adapter is connected to is copied and sent to another VM's virtual switch port for the purposes of monitoring and capturing network traffic. Port mirroring can be configured as None, Source, or Destination.

Section 12-7: Managing Windows Server VMs on Azure

13. Basic-tier Azure VMs cannot be used in a high-availability configuration. True or False?

    Answer: a. True

    Explanation: Basic-tier VMs are for standalone servers (not part of a high-availability configuration) that are deployed for development and testing purposes. Standard-tier VMs offer high availability and load balancing, high-performance storage options, and a variety of CPU, data disk, networking, and memory configurations.

14. Which Azure disk type cannot be used as an OS disk?

    Answer: d. Ultra disk

    Explanation: The highest-performing storage option, ultra disks are SSDs that are ideal for transaction-intensive applications and high-performance databases. Ultra disks cannot be used as OS disks and do not support disk encryption.

Module 13

Implement Advanced Virtualization

Module Objectives

After reading this module and completing the exercises, you will be able to:

1 Configure nested virtualization

2 Configure VM groups and Hyper-V scheduling

3 Implement high availability with Hyper-V

4 Implement Windows containers

5 Manage Windows containers

Continuing with our discussion of Hyper-V and virtualization, this module covers nested virtualization, which allows you to work with Hyper-V in a virtual machine and implement Hyper-V containers. You'll learn how to properly configure your Hyper-V host to enable nested virtualization. Next, you'll learn how to configure virtual machine groups and Hyper-V scheduling, tools that help you fine-tune resource utilization on your Hyper-V host machines.

You'll learn how to implement high availability at the Hyper-V host level, which is referred to as highly available or clustered virtual machines. You'll also learn how to implement high availability at the guest OS level, which is called guest clustering. Finally, you learn about containers and the open source container management environment called Docker. Containers are likely to be deployed in highly virtualized environments and cloud computing environments, but they might also be useful to administrators of moderately sized datacenters.

Table 13-1 describes what you need for the hands-on activities in this module.

Table 13-1 Activity requirements

Activity	Requirements	Notes
Activity 13-1: Resetting Your Virtual Environment	ServerHyperV	
Activity 13-2: Deploying a Process Isolation Container	ServerHyperV	Internet access is required
Activity 13-3: Deploying a Hyper-V Isolation Container	ServerHyperV	
Activity 13-4: Managing Container Images	ServerHyperV	
Activity 13-5: Working with Container Networks	ServerHyperV	

Nested Virtualization

Microsoft Exam AZ-800:

Manage virtual machines and containers.
- Manage Hyper-V and guest virtual machines

Nested virtualization is the ability to run a hypervisor inside another hypervisor. For example, if you have a physical server running Hyper-V and you install a virtual machine (VM) in Hyper-V and then install Hyper-V on the virtual machine, you are running nested virtualization. You are not limited to Hyper-V; for example, nested virtualization can be implemented with VMware and other virtualization platforms. However, this discussion focuses on implementing nested virtualization in Hyper-V on Windows Server. Nested virtualization in Hyper-V is supported only in Windows 10, Windows Server 2016, and newer versions of each OS. Likewise, both the host machine and the virtual machine must be running Windows 10, Windows Server 2016, or newer versions. To configure nested virtualization, take the following steps:

1. Install Hyper-V on Windows Server, Windows 10, or Windows 11. (You can also use Hyper-V Server.) The host computer must have an Intel processor that includes the VT-x virtualization extensions and extended page tables (EPT) technology, which is also known as second level address translation (SLAT).
2. Create a VM and install a supported guest OS. Turn off the VM.
3. On the physical Hyper-V host, run this cmdlet: `Set-VMProcessor -VMName VirtualMachine -ExposeVirtualizationExtensions $true`, where `VirtualMachine` is the name of the VM you created in step 2.
4. Configure MAC address spoofing on the virtual NIC of the physical Hyper-V host. You can do that in Hyper-V Manager or by using the following cmdlet: `Set-VMNetworkAdapter -VMName VirtualMachine -MacAddressSpoofing On`.
5. Start the virtual machine and install Hyper-V. Now you can create VMs in Hyper-V running in the VM.

There are a few caveats with nested virtualization that you should be aware of. The VM that is running Hyper-V cannot use dynamic memory while Hyper-V is running. You can enable dynamic memory, but it will have no effect; you must turn off the VM to adjust its memory. Therefore, you should disable dynamic memory on the Hyper-V VM. In addition, you cannot live-migrate a VM that is running Hyper-V. **Live migration** is a feature that allows you to move a running VM to another Hyper-V host with no downtime.

Self-Check Questions

1. Nested virtualization in Hyper-V is only available on Windows Server 2022 and newer versions of Windows Server. True or False?

   a. True

   b. False

2. Which of the following is true about nested virtualization?

   a. You need to run PowerShell commands on the VM to enable nested virtualization.

   b. It requires a quad-core processor.

   c. The nested VM cannot use dynamic memory.

   d. You can live-migrate a VM that is running Hyper-V.

   ⊙ Check your answers at the end of this module.

Configuring VM Groups and Hyper-V Scheduling

Microsoft Exam AZ-800:

Manage virtual machines and containers.

- Manage Hyper-V and guest virtual machines

You have learned that you can configure how much of the host computer's resources a single VM can use by adjusting the amount of memory, configuring the memory weight, and adjusting the number and weight of virtual processors. Very often, a group of VMs might be working together to perform a task or may be dedicated to a particular department. In such a situation, you may want to configure the amount of host resources a group of VMs can use as a whole. Hyper-V provides features that do just that: VM resource controls, or specifically, VM CPU groups.

Another tool that a Hyper-V administrator has for fine-tuning VM processor usage is hypervisor scheduler types, which determine how Hyper-V schedules virtual processors on the underlying host's logical processors. To better understand CPU groups and Hyper-V scheduler types, keep the following definitions in mind:

- **Physical processor**—This is the physical chip that usually plugs into a socket on a physical host computer's system board. Most modern physical processors used in servers have several logical processors.
- **Logical processor**—Each physical processor has one or more logical processors determined by the number of CPU cores and whether **simultaneous multithreading (SMT)** is supported. SMT is the ability of a processor core to run two segments, or threads, of program code simultaneously. A physical processor that has four cores and no hyperthreading will have four logical processors. A physical processor with four cores and hyperthreading will have eight logical processors.
- **Virtual processor**—A virtual processor is assigned to a virtual machine running on a hypervisor such as Hyper-V. A virtual processor can be assigned to any logical processor on the host machine. For example, if a VM is allocated two virtual processors on a host that has eight logical processors, the virtual processors may be scheduled on logical processors 3 and 7, on 0 and 5, or any other combination of two logical processors. The scheduling assignment can change based on the availability of logical processors at any given time.

VM CPU Groups

VM CPU groups allow you to better manage host CPU resources shared among the guest VMs running on the Hyper-V host. VM CPU groups allow you to do the following:

- Create groups of VMs for which you can specify maximum host CPU usage across the entire group. This capability effectively allows you to create service classes for VMs running particular guest OSs, executing specific tasks, or belonging to a particular department or user.
- Specify the host CPUs that a VM group can run on so VM groups can be isolated from each other with respect to the host CPUs they are using. You can also isolate host OS CPU usage from guest VM CPU usage, thus ensuring that VMs running in a particular VM group do not have to share CPU usage with the Windows Server parent partition.

VM CPU groups cannot be created or managed using Hyper-V Manager or PowerShell; rather, the Hyper-V Host Compute Service (HCS) is used by way of a command-line utility called cpuGroups.exe. This utility is not preinstalled on Windows Server and must be downloaded from the Microsoft Download Center. CpuGroups.exe is a standalone program that does not require installation; simply place the file in a folder on the Hyper-V host system and open a command prompt in the folder. You can see the CPU topology that shows the number of logical CPUs by running the following cmdlet:

```
CpuGroups GetCpuTopology
```

When you run the preceding command, you will see output similar to that in Figure 13-1. The following list describes each column shown in the figure.

- *LpIndex*—The logical processor number, starting with 0. The system where the command was run has four logical processors numbered 0–3.
- *NodeNumber*—The NUMA node number to which the logical processor is bound. Non-uniform memory access (NUMA) is a memory architecture for multiprocessor systems.
- *PackageID*—The physical processor number, starting with 0. This system has only one physical processor.
- *CoreID*—The CPU core identifier. This value may or may not correspond with the LpIndex; in Figure 13-1, each logical processor maps to one CPU core. However, in multithreaded systems, where each core has two threads, each core will have two logical processors associated with it.
- *RootVpIndex*—Specifies whether the Windows Server host OS can use the logical processor. Hyper-V creates a root partition for the host OS to run in. A logical processor that has a RootVpIndex value of 0 or more indicates that the host OS can use that processor for its computing needs; a value of –1 indicates that only VMs can use that logical processor. This setting allows you to isolate the processor usage of the host OS so VMs won't have to share processor time with the host OS.

```
C:\Tools>CpuGroups.exe getcputopology
LpIndex NodeNumber PackageId CoreId RootVpIndex
------- ---------- --------- ------ -----------
      0          0         0      0           0
      1          0         0      1           1
      2          0         1      2           2
      3          0         1      3           3
```

Figure 13-1   The output of the `CpuGroups`
`GetCpuTopology` command

Creating VM CPU Groups

Before you can utilize the benefits of VM CPU groups, you need to create one or more groups. To create a group, you use the `CpuGroups CreateGroup` command. Here is an example of using the command:

```
CpuGroups CreateGroup /GroupID:6a3433f4-5626-40e8-a9b9-000000000001
    /GroupAffinity:0,1
```

In the preceding command, the `GroupID` needs additional explanation. The first part of this value (up to the series of 0s) is taken from the properties of the computer. You'll find this value by opening Device Manager (see Figure 13-2), expanding Computer, right-clicking the item under Computer, clicking Properties, and then clicking the Details tab. From the drop-down box, look for a property near the end of the list that has an 8-digit hexadecimal number, followed by three 4-digit numbers and then a 12-digit number. You use only the 8-digit number and the three 4-digit numbers in the `GroupID` followed by a custom 12-digit number, as in the example. This number (excluding the 12-digit number you create) will be the same for similar hardware platforms. For example, the number will be identical for all ACPI x64-based PC devices, so you must be sure that the 12-digit value you add to it is unique for each group you create. For example, if you create a second group, use 000000000002 for the last 12 digits.

The `GroupAffinity` parameter specifies which logical processors can be used by the VMs that are assigned to the group.

After you have created a group that specifies the logical processors the group can use, you might want to set the maximum amount of CPU the group can use:

```
CpuGroups SetGroupProperty /GroupID:6a3433f4-5626-40e8-a9b9-000000000001
    /CPUCap:32768
```

In this command, the `CPUCap` parameter specifies the percentage of the logical CPUs the VMs in the group can use. Values range from 0 to 65,536, where 0 is 0 percent and 65,536 is 100 percent. A value of 32,768 caps the VMs at 50 percent of the total CPU usage among the logical CPUs assigned to the group. (In this case, the group was assigned logical CPUs 0 and 1 by the `GroupAffinity` parameter when the group was created.)

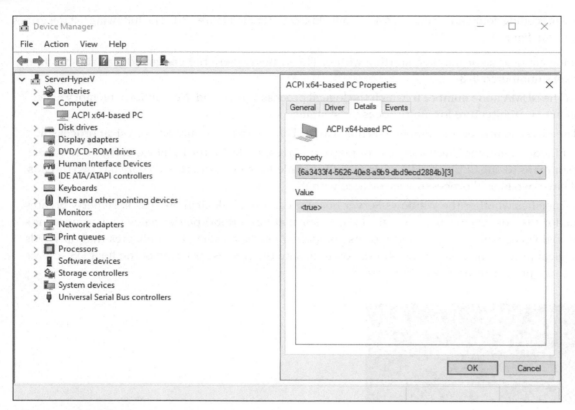

Figure 13-2   Finding the group ID prefix

Last, you need to assign VMs to the group:

```
CpuGroups SetVMGroup /VMName:ServerVM1 /GroupID:6a3433f4-5626-40e8-a9b9-000000000001
```

You need to run the preceding command for each VM you want to assign to the group. Note that a VM can only be assigned to one group.

To display all the groups and the VMs assigned to them, use the following command:

```
CpuGroups GetVMGroup
```

Figure 13-3 shows the output of the command. It shows ServerVM1 as a member of the group specified by the group ID. ServerVM2 is also listed, but the group ID is all 0s, which indicates that it's not assigned to any groups.

Figure 13-3   The output of the `CpuGroups GetVMGroup` command

Configuring Hyper-V Scheduler Types

The Hyper-V scheduler determines how and when CPU resources are allocated to VMs that are running and have work to do. A Hyper-V administrator can select the hypervisor scheduler type that best suits the needs of the VMs deployed on the Hyper-V host. There are two scheduler types from which an administrator can choose: classic and core. These types are described in the following sections.

Classic Scheduler

The **classic scheduler** was the default scheduler for all Windows Server versions from the inception of Hyper-V in Windows Server 2008 through Windows Server 2016. It was the only scheduler available until Windows Server 2016. This scheduler uses a round-robin method of scheduling VMs to run on all virtual processors across the system.

If SMT is enabled, VM virtual processors are scheduled to run on any available thread on a logical processor core. This means that two VMs could be running on a single processor core, one on each of the two threads of the core.

Core Scheduler

The **core scheduler**, available as an alternative to the classic scheduler since Windows Server 2016, is available only on systems that support SMT. The core scheduler ensures that the virtual processors of a VM will always be scheduled on the same core. For example, on a host system that supports two threads per core, the threads on a VM's virtual processor will be assigned to the same core on the physical host processor. On a non-SMT VM, the virtual processor will use one thread on the physical core, leaving one thread idle. Therefore, when choosing the core scheduler, the VMs should all be configured to support SMT and get the most out of the host processors. This method also provides a security boundary between VMs because no two VMs will share the same processor core, and the method delivers performance consistency because VMs do not have to share a core.

To summarize, the benefits of using the core scheduler include the following:

- *Simultaneous multithreading*—This feature provides similar multithreading performance advantages as a non-virtualized processor environment.
- *Performance consistency*—Because a VM doesn't need to share a CPU core with another VM, performance metrics are consistent.
- *Workload isolation*—This feature prevents side-channel snooping attacks, a sophisticated type of attack that gathers information from a computer chip based on timing, power monitoring, and electromagnetic radiation.

Because of the benefits offered by the core scheduler, Microsoft uses it on Azure virtualization hosts and has made it the default scheduler on Windows Server 2019 and newer versions of Hyper-V. However, despite its advantages, if a virtual processor does not support SMT, the overall performance of the host system could be reduced because the VM will run on one thread while the other thread on a core will remain idle. By default, VMs that are created in Windows Server 2019 and newer versions (VM version 9.0 or later) have SMT enabled, assuming the host processor supports SMT. For VMs created in earlier versions of Hyper-V, such as those created in Windows Server 2016, SMT will be disabled. Updating a VM to version 9.0 does not automatically enable SMT. A VM property named HwThreadCountPerCore determines SMT status according to the following values:

- 0—The VM will inherit SMT status from the host system; this value is only valid on systems newer than Windows Server 2016.
- 1—The VM does not support SMT.
- 2—The VM supports two threads per core. Values greater than 2 are supported if the host physical processor supports more than two threads per core, but the typical number is 2.

The PowerShell command to see the SMT settings for a virtual machine is:

```
(Get-VMProcessor -VMName <VMName>).HwThreadCountPerCore
```

The PowerShell command to set the SMT status is:

```
Set-VMProcessor -VMName <VMName> -HwThreadCountPerCore <0, 1, 2>
```

In the preceding commands, the parameters in angle brackets should be replaced by the appropriate value.

Self-Check Questions

3. You create VM CPU groups using Hyper-V Manager. True or False?

    a. True   **b.** False

4. What command displays the CPU topology on a Hyper-V host system?

    a. `CpuGroups GetCpuTopology`
    b. `Get-CpuTopology`
    c. `List-CpuGroups -CpuTopology`
    d. `netsh -CPU Topology`

⊙ Check your answers at the end of this module.

Implementing High Availability with Hyper-V

Microsoft Exam AZ-800:

Manage virtual machines and containers.

- Manage Hyper-V and guest virtual machines

The use of virtual machines has become standard practice both in small and large organizations. Because so many organizations depend on virtual servers for enterprise applications, being able to provide high availability to the Hyper-V hosts that run them has become paramount. This section describes the steps for configuring high availability and disaster recovery options in Hyper-V and for configuring monitoring and guest clusters on highly available virtual machines. You also learn about another high-availability option for VMs that doesn't involve server clusters: Hyper-V Replica.

Configuring Highly Available Virtual Machines

A **highly available virtual machine** (also known as a *clustered virtual machine*) allows you to make applications and services highly available simply by installing them on a virtual machine residing on a Hyper-V server configured for high availability. In other words, configuring each application or service for high availability isn't necessary because the VM it's running on is highly available. To configure a highly available VM, you need to create a failover cluster on two or more host computers running the Hyper-V role. In addition, it's best to use cluster shared volumes (CSVs) to store the highly available VMs because multiple VMs hosted by different Hyper-V servers can be put on the same CSV. If you use traditional shared storage, each node in the cluster requires a separate volume for its hosted VMs. Before creating a highly available VM, you should perform the following tasks:

- Verify that you have two host computers that meet the requirements for the Hyper-V role and the Failover Clustering feature.
- Be sure all host computers are members of the same domain.
- Install the Hyper-V role and Failover Clustering feature on all servers participating in the failover cluster.
- Configure the shared storage that the failover cluster will use.
- In Hyper-V Manager, configure the virtual networks that the VMs will use.
- Validate the failover cluster configuration by running the Validate a Configuration Wizard in the Failover Cluster Manager.
- Create the failover cluster.
- Add storage to a cluster shared volume if you're using CSVs (recommended).

> **Note 1**
>
> A CSV is a storage option in a failover cluster in which all cluster nodes have access to the shared storage for read and write access.

Creating a Highly Available VM

You can create a highly available VM directly in the Failover Cluster Manager, which configures a VM for high availability automatically. In the Failover Cluster Manager, click the Roles node, and in the Actions pane, click Virtual Machines and then New Virtual Machine to start the New Virtual Machine Wizard. The first window prompts you to choose the target cluster node to host the VM (see Figure 13-4). From that point, the New Virtual Machine Wizard runs normally as though you had started it in Hyper-V Manager.

In the Specify Name and Location window, you must select the option "Store the virtual machine in a different location." If you're using a CSV, select one of the virtual disk volumes in the C:\ClusterStorage folder (see Figure 13-5).

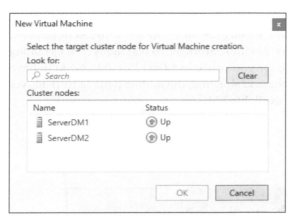

Figure 13-4   Choosing a target cluster node

Figure 13-5   Choosing shared storage for the VM

If you're using traditional shared storage, specify the shared storage currently owned by the target cluster node you selected.

After you specify the location, continue with the New Virtual Machine Wizard as usual. You need to select the following options for the new VM:

- *Specify the generation*—You can choose generation 1 or 2. Generation 2 VMs offer some advanced features and are recommended.
- *Assign memory*—Choose the right amount of memory for applications the VM will run.
- *Configure networking*—You should have created the virtual switches earlier; select one from the available choices.
- *Configure the virtual hard disk*—Be sure the path to the virtual hard disk points to the shared storage location—for example, C:\ClusterStorage\Volume1 if you're using CSVs. You can also attach a hard disk later or use an existing virtual hard disk. In any case, the virtual disk must be on shared storage.
- *Install an operating system*—You can specify a path to installation media or install an OS later.

The wizard creates the VM and configures it for high availability automatically. A report is generated so that you can see whether there were any errors or warnings in configuring the VM for high availability. The Roles node in the

Failover Cluster Manager shows the highly available VM and its current status (see Figure 13-6). If you click the VM, you can manage it in the Failover Cluster Manager. You can test failover by using the Move option in the Actions pane, which enables you to choose Live Migration, Quick Migration, or Virtual Machine Storage. To test failover of a running VM, choose Live Migration. You can specify which node to fail over to, or you can select Best Possible Node to have the cluster service choose for you. The status of the live migration process is shown in the middle pane of the Failover Cluster Manager. If the live migration is successful, you have a highly available VM.

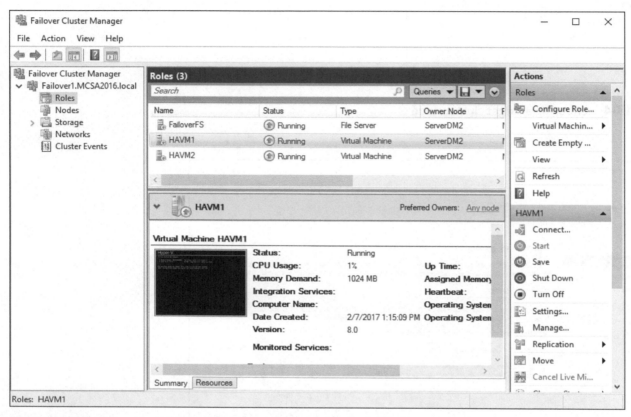

Figure 13-6   Two highly available VMs in Failover Cluster Manager

Configuring an Existing VM for High Availability

If the VM you want to configure for high availability already exists, you can move it to shared storage using the Move option in Hyper-V Manager and configure it for high availability in the Failover Cluster Manager. Click Configure Role in the Actions pane to start the High Availability Wizard. In the Select Role window, click Virtual Machine. You see a list of VMs you can configure for high availability. Select one or more of the VMs and continue with the High Availability Wizard.

Using Drain on Shutdown

What happens if you shut down a Hyper-V host that's configured in a cluster hosting one or more VMs? The best way to shut down a node in a Hyper-V cluster is to place it in maintenance mode by pausing it and selecting Drain Roles. Doing so signals the cluster that the host will be unavailable, and the VMs are migrated automatically to another node in the cluster. To pause a node, right-click it in the Failover Cluster Manager, point to Pause, and click Drain Roles (see Figure 13-7). Then you can take the node offline for maintenance or for other reasons. When you resume the node, you can choose Fail Roles Back if you want the VMs (and any other clustered roles that were running on the server when it was paused) to be migrated back to that node.

Look back at Figure 13-6, where both VMs were running on ServerDM2. In Figure 13-7, ServerDM2 is paused and the roles are drained. Now take a look at Figure 13-8, where both VMs were automatically live-migrated to ServerDM1.

Suppose, however, that you simply shut down a clustered Hyper-V server without pausing it first. In Windows Server 2012, the state of running VMs is saved, the VMs are moved, and then the VMs are resumed on another

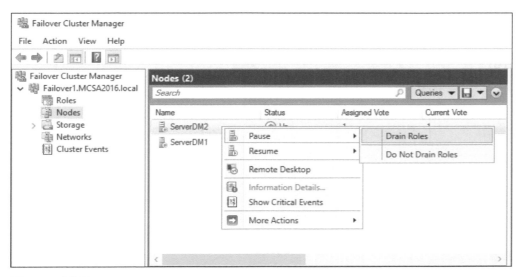

Figure 13-7   Draining roles on a Hyper-V cluster

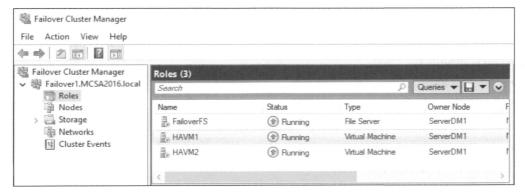

Figure 13-8   VMs were migrated to ServerDM1

cluster node. This process results in downtime for VMs that are moved. Windows Server 2012 R2 introduced the **drain on shutdown** feature, which drains roles automatically and live-migrates the VMs to another cluster node before the Hyper-V server shuts down. Drain on shutdown is enabled by default on Windows Server 2012 R2 and later versions.

Implementing Node Fairness

Node fairness is a failover cluster feature that helps optimize usage of failover cluster node members. VMs hosted on clustered Hyper-V servers can move from node to node based on system reboots and maintenance operations, resulting in unbalanced distribution of VMs throughout the cluster. Node fairness attempts to identify Hyper-V nodes that are hosting a disproportionate number of VMs and redistribute VMs to other nodes that are underutilized. Live migration is used for VM movement, so no downtime is incurred. Node fairness works with other failover tuning features, such as fault domains. The two most important factors used for evaluating a node's load are:

- CPU utilization
- Memory utilization

Node fairness is enabled by default and can be configured using Failover Cluster Manager from the Balancer tab on the Properties page of the cluster (see Figure 13-9). As you can see from the figure, there are two modes and three Aggressiveness levels. You can configure load balancing to work only when a node initially joins the cluster or to always work (the default value).

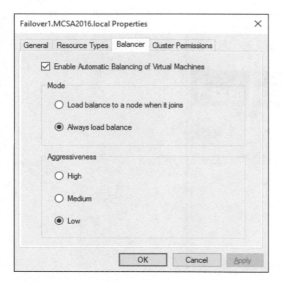

Figure 13-9   The Balancer tab of a cluster's
Properties page

To configure this setting with PowerShell, you modify the `AutoBalancerMode` property of the cluster. The `AutoBalancerMode` property can have three possible values:

- 0—Automatic load balancing is disabled.
- 1—Load balance to a node when it joins.
- 2—Always load balance (the default setting).

To configure the `AutoBalancerMode` property, use the following PowerShell cmdlet, where *value* is 0, 1, or 2:

`(Get-Cluster).AutoBalancerMode = value`

The three Aggressiveness settings are described as follows:

- *Low*—Nodes are moved when the host is 80 percent loaded or more. This is the default setting.
- *Medium*—Nodes are moved when the host is 70 percent loaded or more.
- *High*—Nodes are moved when the host is 60 percent loaded or more.

Using PowerShell, the Aggressiveness setting is configured with the `AutoBalancerLevel` property of a cluster. The `AutoBalancerLevel` property has three possible values to determine the Aggressiveness setting: 1 is Low, 2 is Medium, and 3 is High.

To configure the `AutoBalancerLevel` property, use the following PowerShell cmdlet where *value* is 1, 2, or 3:

`(Get-Cluster).AutoBalancerLevel = value`

Implementing VM Resiliency

Many features of a failover cluster are designed to prevent or reduce downtime in the event of a catastrophic failure; however, failures are sometimes transient and short-lived. Aggressive reaction to such failures sometimes causes more harm than good. Many of the failures are caused by problems with communication between cluster nodes. When cluster nodes fail to communicate, the cluster takes action, assuming a node has failed or gone offline. If the communication failure is temporary, it might be better to simply wait until the problem is resolved rather than have the cluster go into failover mode. To this end, Windows Server has cluster node and VM states to make highly available VMs more resilient to transient failures:

- *Unmonitored*—This is a state that applies to a highly available VM running on a clustered Hyper-V host. In this state, the VM is no longer monitored by the cluster service.
- *Isolated*—This is a state that applies to a clustered Hyper-V node. When the node is in this state, it is removed from active membership in the cluster but continues to host the VM role.

- *Quarantined*—This is a state that applies to a clustered Hyper-V node. The VMs hosted by the node are drained and the node will not be able to rejoin the cluster for a period of two hours by default. Quarantine occurs when a node leaves a cluster three times within an hour due to a communication failure or other failure.

These states are used in the following way: When a transient communication failure occurs between clustered Hyper-V nodes, a node hosting VMs is placed in the Isolated state and removed from active cluster membership. The VMs that the node is hosting are placed in the Unmonitored state and are no longer monitored by the cluster service.

If a node in the Isolated state has even more communication problems within 4 minutes (the default setting), the VMs are migrated to another cluster node. The isolated node is placed in the Down state. If the node is placed in the Isolated state three times within an hour, it is put in the Quarantined state and remains there for two hours by default.

Resiliency is enabled by default, but you can configure various resiliency settings to change the default values using PowerShell. You change the resiliency settings by changing a cluster property in a manner that is similar to configuring node fairness. The following cluster properties apply to resiliency and are changed using `(Get-Cluster).`*`ClusterProperty`* `=` *`value`*, where *`ClusterProperty`* is the setting described in the following list:

- `QuarantineDuration`—Sets the number of seconds that a node remains in quarantine. The default value is 7200 (two hours). The range is 0 to 0xffffffff. A value of 0xffffffff (or –1) means the node will remain in quarantine indefinitely until brought online manually.
- `QuarantineThreshold`—Determines the number of failures within a one-hour period before a node is placed in the Quarantined state. The range is 0 to 3.
- `ResiliencyLevel`—A value of 2 is the default and specifies that resiliency is always used in the event of node failure. A value of 1 specifies that resiliency is only used when the cause of the failure is known. The range is 1 to 2.
- `ResiliencyDefaultPeriod`—Specifies the number of seconds that nodes can remain in the Isolated state. The default value is 240 (4 minutes). The range is 0 to 0xffffffff. This setting applies to all nodes in a cluster. A value of 0 means the node will not go into the Isolated state.
- `ResiliencyPeriod`—Similar to `ResiliencyDefaultPeriod` but applies to a particular cluster node instead of all nodes in the cluster. Use `(Get-Cluster "Node Name").ResiliencyPeriod =` *`value`* to set this property.

Another aspect of VM resiliency is VM storage resiliency. In Windows Server 2016 and newer versions, a highly available VM that loses access to its storage will be placed in a Paused-Critical state. If the problem is resolved within 30 minutes, the VM resumes running from the same state it was in before being paused. This feature requires that the VM's storage is on a CSV. You can configure storage resiliency using PowerShell cmdlets. To enable storage resiliency, use the following command:

```
Set-VM VMName -AutomaticCriticalErrorAction Pause
```

To disable storage resiliency, replace `Pause` with `None` in the preceding cmdlet.

The following cmdlet specifies the amount of time a VM can remain in the Paused-Critical state before being powered off. A value of 0 powers off the VM immediately; the maximum value is 24 hours (1440 minutes).

```
Set-VM VMName -AutomaticCriticalErrorActionTimeout Minutes
```

Configuring Virtual Machine Monitoring

Virtual machine monitoring enables you to monitor resources, applications, and services running on highly available VMs. If a resource fails, the cluster node can take actions to recover, such as attempting to restart a service or moving the resource to another cluster node. VM monitoring has the following prerequisites:

- The guest OS and Hyper-V host must be running at least Windows Server 2012.
- The guest OS must be a member of the same domain as the Hyper-V host.
- The user managing the cluster must be a member of the local Administrators group in the VM's guest OS.

To configure VM monitoring, you need to enable the Virtual Machine Monitoring firewall rule on each guest to be monitored. To do so, open Windows Firewall from Control Panel and click "Allow an app or feature through Windows Firewall." Then click to select the Virtual Machine Monitoring rule, making sure the Domain check box is selected (see Figure 13-10).

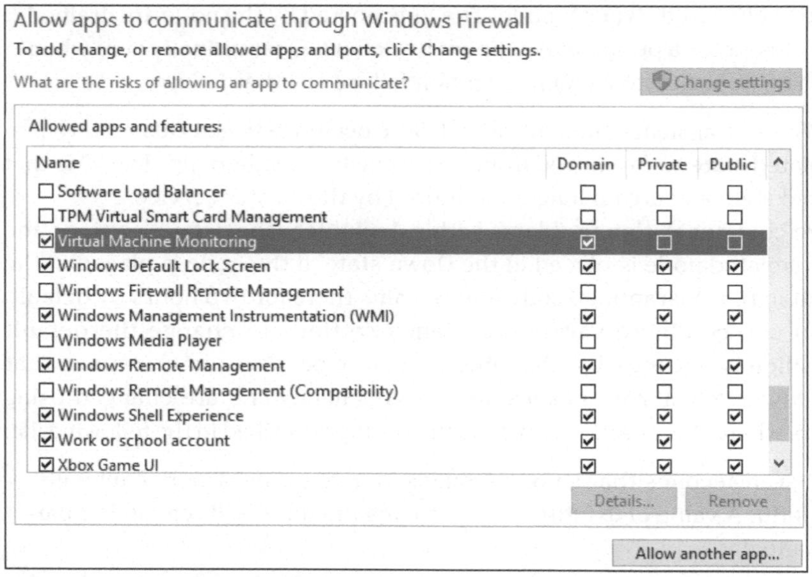

Figure 13-10 Enabling the Virtual Machine Monitoring firewall rule

In the Failover Cluster Manager on a VM's host machine, click Roles, right-click the VM you want to monitor (the guest OS must be running), point to More Actions, and click Configure Monitoring. In the list of services that's displayed, click to select each one you want to monitor.

If a service being monitored has failed, a service restart is attempted up to two times by default. If the service fails to start after the second restart attempt, an event with ID 1250 is generated in the System log and the VM is restarted. If another failure occurs, the VM is moved to another cluster node and started. This behavior is the default action for a failed service. You can change the failure response policy by selecting the VM in the Failover Cluster Manager and clicking the Resource tab at the bottom of the Roles pane. Then right-click the VM and click Properties to open the VM's Properties dialog box. In the Policies tab (see Figure 13-11), you can choose whether

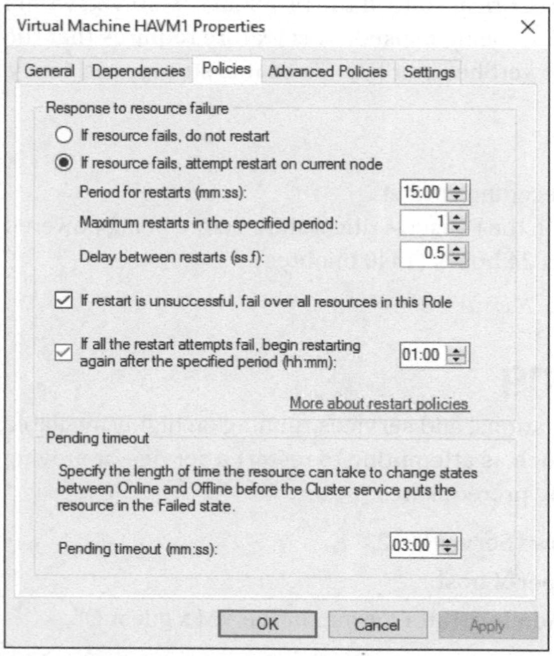

Figure 13-11 Configuring VM failure response policies

to perform a restart and specify the time between restart attempts. In the Advanced Policies tab, you can select which cluster hosts can be owners of the resource and select the resource health check intervals. Use the Settings tab to determine the actions to take if the virtual machine stops and whether automatic recovery is enabled for the virtual machine.

Configuring Guest Clustering

Guest clustering is different from a highly available or clustered VM in that it requires two or more VMs with a guest OS installed and configured for failover clustering. A highly available VM requires configuring the Hyper-V host server with the Failover Clustering feature, but in a guest cluster, the failover clustering occurs in the VM's guest OS. Each application that requires high availability must be configured in the guest OS with the Failover Cluster Manager. The benefits of using guest clustering as opposed to a clustered VM are as follows:

- *Monitoring clustered resources in the guest OS*—A clustered VM can fail over only to another Hyper-V server if the entire VM or host OS fails, but a guest cluster monitors each clustered resource, such as applications, services, network, and storage, and can initiate recovery or failover if a failure is detected.
- *Hyper-V host optimization*—VMs participating in a guest cluster can be moved easily between Hyper-V hosts to optimize Hyper-V host resource use.
- *Host failure protection*—VMs participating in a guest cluster can reside on multiple Hyper-V hosts so that clustered applications and services are protected from VM failure as well as host failure. In addition, the Hyper-V hosts can be configured in a failover cluster, adding resiliency for highly available applications.

Ideally, the VMs in a guest cluster are on separate Hyper-V servers so that if the Hyper-V host fails, the cluster can continue to function. However, you can run a guest cluster on a single Hyper-V cluster to provide some fault tolerance and for testing purposes. If you choose a single Hyper-V server to host the cluster, each cluster node should be connected to a separate virtual network assigned to its own physical NIC. In addition, each VM participating in the cluster should be stored on a separate physical disk on the host or on a shared virtual hard disk (as described later). These measures provide cluster fault tolerance in case of component failure on the Hyper-V host.

To create a guest cluster, you follow the same basic procedure as for creating a failover cluster with physical hosts, and the same prerequisites apply. For example, for domain-based clusters, all the guest OSs must belong to the same Active Directory domain, and shared storage must be available to all cluster nodes. Shared storage can be provided by a SAN using iSCSI or Fibre Channel, as with a physical host cluster. Starting in Windows Server 2012 R2, a guest cluster can use a shared virtual hard disk instead of traditional SAN storage.

The following steps explain how to configure a two-node guest cluster running Windows Server 2016 or a newer version and using a two-node Hyper-V failover cluster:

1. Configure the Hyper-V failover cluster, as described earlier in the section titled "Configuring Highly Available Virtual Machines." The Hyper-V failover cluster can use a CSV or a scale-out file server for shared storage.
2. Create two highly available virtual machines.
3. Install Windows Server on both virtual machines.
4. Join each VM to an Active Directory domain.
5. Install the Failover Clustering feature on both VMs.
6. Make sure both VMs have access to the shared storage.
7. Create the failover cluster and add both VMs to the cluster.

Configuring a Shared Virtual Hard Disk

You can avoid having to configure traditional SAN storage for the guest cluster by using a shared virtual hard disk (shared VHDX), which is a virtual disk created in shared storage on the Hyper-V cluster (see Figure 13-12). Using a shared VHDX is a good solution for applications running on the guest cluster, such as file sharing and database applications. In these applications, the shared folders or database files are stored on the shared VHDX. In Figure 13-12, two Hyper-V nodes make a cluster using a CSV. A VM runs on each Hyper-V node, making a guest cluster that is using a shared VHDX for shared storage.

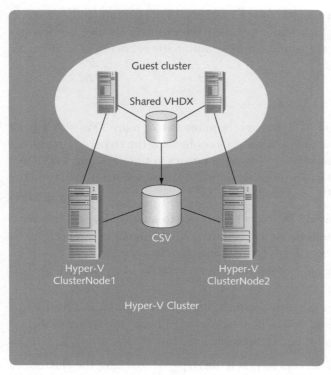

Figure 13-12 A guest cluster using a shared VHDX
for cluster storage

To use a shared VHDX for a guest cluster, you need to make sure the following requirements are met:

- You have configured a Hyper-V failover cluster, as described earlier in the section called "Configuring Highly Available Virtual Machines." The Hyper-V hosts must be running Windows Server 2012 R2 or a later version.
- You're using cluster shared volumes or a share on a scale-out file server to store the virtual hard disk.
- The shared VHDX must be connected to a virtual SCSI controller and be in the VHDX format. The shared VHDX can be a fixed-size or dynamically expanding disk, but not a differencing disk.

To create a shared VHDX for a guest cluster, configure the VM from Failover Manager by clicking the Roles node, clicking the VM, and then clicking Settings. Click SCSI Controller, click Shared Drive, and then click Add (see Figure 13-13). In the Shared Drive dialog box, click New to start the New Virtual Hard Disk Wizard.

Follow the wizard as usual, but in the Choose Disk Format window, note that you have the option to use VHDX or VHD Set. **VHD Set** is a new option and is designed specifically for shared virtual hard disks. It enables backup of virtual machine groups and online disk resizing. VHD Set is the default option, but you can choose VHDX for backward

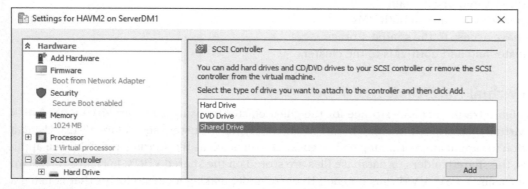

Figure 13-13 Adding a shared drive to a VM in a guest cluster

compatibility with Windows Server 2012/R2 VMs (see Figure 13-14). In the Specify Name and Location dialog box, be sure to navigate to C:\ClusterStorage\Volume1 (or the appropriate CSV) so the shared VHDX is stored on the host's CSV. After you have created a shared VHDX on one VM, you can add the shared VHDX to other VMs in the guest cluster.

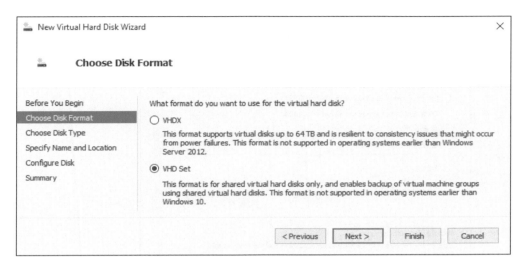

Figure 13-14   Selecting the disk format for a shared VHDX

Configuring Hyper-V Replica

Hyper-V Replica periodically replicates changes in a VM to a mirror VM hosted on another Hyper-V server. It works over a regular IP network and can be enabled on standalone servers or servers in a failover cluster. There are no domain requirements, so the Hyper-V servers might or might not be members of a domain or can even be members of different domains. In addition, the Hyper-V servers can be at the same site or at different sites, so you can continue VM operation easily if a single server goes down or an entire site suffers a catastrophic failure. There are no shared storage requirements, so there's no need to configure a SAN or cluster. In fact, a VM with a shared VHDX cannot be replicated.

Replication occurs asynchronously, so although the replica VM is always in operational condition, its state might lag behind the original VM by a few seconds to a few minutes, depending on the settings and connection speed between hosts. You can configure encryption so that the data transfer between hosts is secure, and you can configure compression to reduce bandwidth requirements.

Hyper-V Replica can also be used for site-level disaster recovery if your organization maintains a hot backup site, a location that duplicates much of the main site's IT infrastructure and can be switched to if a disaster occurs at the main site. With Hyper-V Replica operating between these sites, your VMs can be running at the hot backup site immediately. Minimal data loss occurs because the replica VMs lag behind the primary VMs by only a few seconds or minutes.

> **Note 2**
>
> Hyper-V Replica will work between Windows Server 2016 Hyper-V hosts and Windows Server 2016 and newer Hyper-V hosts; however, you cannot replicate between Windows Server 2016 and earlier versions of Hyper-V.

To configure Hyper-V Replica, follow these steps:

1. Enable replication on the Hyper-V server to receive replicated VMs. In the Settings window of Hyper-V Manager, click Replication Configuration in the left pane, and click "Enable this computer as a Replica server" (see Figure 13-15). The Hyper-V server you enable replication on is called the replica server. Note that if the Hyper-V server is a member of a failover cluster, the option to enable replication in Hyper-V Manager is disabled; you need to configure replication settings in the Failover Cluster Manager console.

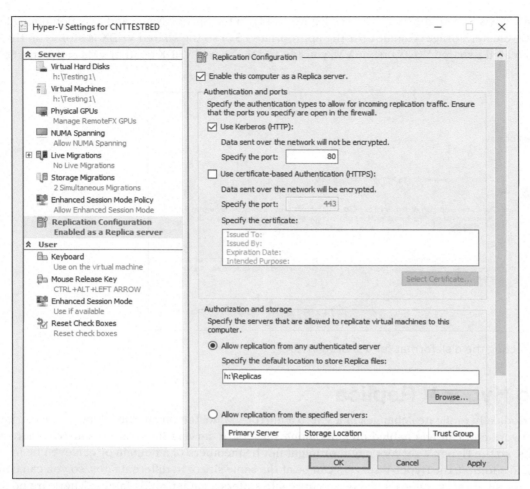

Figure 13-15 Enabling replication in Hyper-V Manager

2. Select the authentication method. You can select Kerberos authentication, but data transfers aren't encrypted with this authentication method. (Kerberos authentication uses port 80 by default, but you can change the port.) You can also select certificate-based authentication, which encrypts data transfers over HTTPS. You should choose certificate-based authentication if the two Hyper-V servers aren't members of the same forest.

3. Specify servers that can replicate to this server and the storage location. You can allow any server that authenticates to replicate to this server or select specific servers. If you select specific servers, you can specify a different storage location for each one. After you finish configuring replication, you're prompted to configure the firewall.

4. Configure firewall rules to allow replication. Create a new inbound firewall rule on the replication server that enables the predefined Hyper-V Replica HTTP Listener (TCP-In) rule.

5. Configure each VM you want to replicate on one or more source servers that you want to replicate to the replica server. These steps are explained in the next section.

Enabling Replication on a Virtual Machine

Before a VM can be replicated to the replica server, replication must be configured in the VM's settings. Follow these steps:

1. In Hyper-V Manager, click the VM you want to enable replication for, and in the Actions pane, click Enable Replication. The Enable Replication Wizard begins.

2. In the Specify Replica Server window, type the name of the replica server or click Browse to select one.

3. In the Specify Connection Parameters window, you choose the authentication method and whether to compress network data (see Figure 13-16). The authentication method must match the authentication method on the replica server.

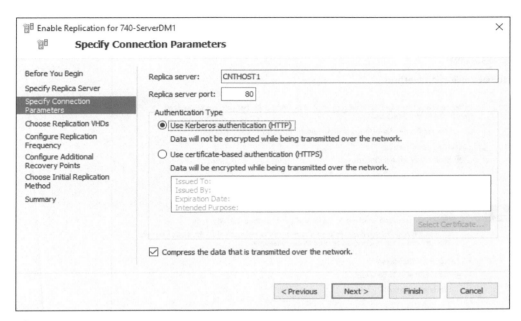

Figure 13-16   Configuring connection parameters

4. In the Choose Replication VHDs window, exclude the virtual disks that shouldn't be replicated. By default, all virtual disks are replicated, but you can deselect any that shouldn't be.
5. In the Configure Replication Frequency window, you specify how often changes to the VM should be checked and replicated. The default frequency is 5 minutes; you can also choose 30 seconds or 15 minutes.
6. In the Configure Additional Recovery Points window, you configure options for recovery points. A **recovery point** is a checkpoint that can be generated automatically so you can revert to an earlier server state if there's an unplanned failover and the VM is in an unworkable state. You can maintain only the most recent recovery point, or you can have hourly recovery points generated. If you choose hourly recovery points, you can specify how many hours of coverage to maintain, as shown in Figure 13-17.

Figure 13-17   Configuring recovery points

7. In the Choose Initial Replication Method window, you can send the initial replica over the network or export a copy of the VM to external media. If the VM is very large or the replica server is located across a low-bandwidth link, using external media might be the best option. The initial replica copy requires the most bandwidth; from then on, only changes are replicated. You can also start the replication immediately or at a scheduled date and time (see Figure 13-18).

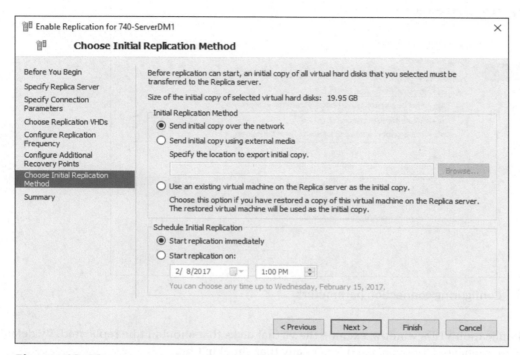

Figure 13-18   Specifying the initial replication method

8. When you have finished configuration and replication begins, you're prompted to configure the network connection settings on the replicated VM if the virtual networks on the source and destination Hyper-V server don't match. When replication begins, check the status by clicking the VM. In the Actions pane, click Replication and then View Replication Health. The following are additional options on the Replication menu in the Actions pane from the replica VM side (not the original VM):

- *Failover*: This option should be used when the primary VM fails. If the primary VM is still running, this option won't work.
- *Test Failover*: Verify the replica's health so that you know it will work in an actual failover. The original VM continues to work normally.
- *Pause Replication*: Pause the replication process.
- *Extend Replication*: This option is discussed later in the section titled "Configuring Hyper-V Extended Replication."
- *Import Initial Replica*: This option is available only if you specified using external media for initial replication.
- *Remove Replication*: This option stops replication but doesn't delete the replica VM.

From the source Hyper-V server, the replication actions you can perform on a replicated VM include the Pause Replication, Remove Replication, and View Replication Health options already discussed. In addition, you have the Planned Failover option. A planned failover is initiated only on the source Hyper-V server. It should be used when you need to take the source server down for maintenance or when you know a service outage is imminent because of a planned power outage or a coming storm.

Configuring Hyper-V Replica Broker

Hyper-V Replica Broker is used to configure Hyper-V Replica between failover cluster nodes. You configure it by adding the Hyper-V Replica Broker role in the Failover Cluster Manager console. Then right-click the role in the Failover Cluster Manager console and click Replication Settings to enable and configure Hyper-V Replica. The process is similar to using Hyper-V Manager, as described earlier.

Configuring Hyper-V Extended Replication

Extended replication is used to replicate a replica. This feature, which you can think of as a "backup of a backup," gives you a third location from which to run a VM. If there's a catastrophic failure at your primary site, your backup site can begin running replicated VMs, and your extended replica site is already configured to act as a backup if your backup site goes offline.

After the initial replication between the original VM and the first replica server is finished, you can configure extended replication. On the replica server in Hyper-V Manager, click the replica VM on the replica server, click Replication in the Actions pane, and click Extend Replication. The process is nearly identical to configuring replication on the original VM, except the replication frequency is limited to 5 minutes or 15 minutes, with no 30-second option. Of course, you need to enable replication on another Hyper-V server and specify that server as the replica server.

Self-Check Questions

5. A highly available virtual machine is a VM that runs on a highly available Hyper-V server. True or False?

   a. True

   b. False

6. Which Hyper-V feature will automatically move a VM to another Hyper-V node if the Hyper-V server it's running on is shut down without being paused first?

   a. Node fairness

   b. Virtual machine monitoring

   c. Drain on shutdown

   d. Guest clustering

   ◉ Check your answers at the end of this module.

Windows Containers

Microsoft Exam AZ-800:

Manage virtual machines and containers.
  • Create and manage containers

A **container** is a software environment in which an application can run but is isolated from much of the rest of the operating system and other applications. Containers are still a type of virtualization, but whereas Hyper-V virtualizes the hardware environment, allowing multiple OSs to coexist on the same host, containers virtualize parts of the operating system, allowing containerized applications to have their own copy of critical OS structures such as the registry, file system, and network configuration while sharing the kernel, the host hardware, and possibly some runtime libraries. This is called **namespace isolation**. In this context, a **namespace** is all the parts of the OS an application can see and interact with, such as the file system and network. The host OS only lets the application running in a container see what it needs to run. The containerized application can't see other applications or the resources being used by other applications, so it can't interfere with them. That's how a container achieves namespace isolation. Further, the host OS can constrain the container to limit its host resource usage. For example, a container can be restricted to a certain percentage of the CPU, so even if the containerized application uses 100 percent of the CPU, it's only using 100 percent of the restricted amount. If a container is constrained to 20 percent of the host CPU, that's the most it can use, even if it is using 100 percent from the application's perspective.

If namespace isolation doesn't provide sufficient isolation, you can deploy a Hyper-V container in which each container has its own copy of the kernel and OS instance. There are two types of containers supported by Windows Server:

- *Process isolation containers*—A **process isolation container** is an application environment in which the processes running in the container share host OS and kernel resources with other Windows Server containers and the host OS, but the container has its own copy of user mode data structures such as the registry, file system, and network configuration. Process isolation containers were referred to as Windows Server containers in Windows Server 2016.
- *Hyper-V isolation containers*—A **Hyper-V isolation container** is an application environment that provides OS and kernel isolation like a traditional VM but is not managed by Hyper-V Manager.

After an application is containerized, you have the option of deploying it as a Windows Server container or as a Hyper-V container; in the case of a Hyper-V container, the VM is created and managed automatically. A Windows Server container has the benefit of very fast deployment compared to a Hyper-V container, but Hyper-V containers provide greater isolation.

A third deployment option is deploying containers in a Hyper-V virtual machine. In this scenario, the virtual machine is the container host, and your physical host system must support nested virtualization because the Hyper-V role is installed in the virtual machine. All of these scenarios are explored starting with the next section.

> ### Note 3
>
> Containers are supported by Windows 10 and newer versions and by Windows Server 2016 and newer versions; however, Windows 10 and newer versions support only Hyper-V containers.

The benefit of containers compared to full virtual machines is that containers use resources more efficiently while still providing much of the application isolation provided by VMs. Because multiple containers running on the same host share some of the host computer's resources, such as the kernel, deploying containerized applications uses less memory, disk space, and CPU compared to deploying each application in its own virtual machine. However, containers deployed on a host must all use the same base OS that is installed on the host computer, whereas each virtual machine has its own OS that can be different from the host OS and from other VMs' operating systems.

Certainly, containers are not a replacement for virtual machines, but there are some scenarios in which you might want to consider containers rather than virtual machines:

- When you want to deploy similar applications that use the same OS kernel
- When you want to package an application for fast deployment without worrying about dependencies and resource conflicts
- When an application consists of several lightweight components, or microservices, that can be easily scaled by adding more containers

Containers are ideal for cloud providers that deploy Software as a Service (SaaS) applications, where a single app can be deployed multiple times for multiple customers on a single host system. Each instance of the application runs independently of the other, and each instance cannot affect the behavior of other instances. For example, if one instance of the application experiences a corrupted data structure, the other instances will continue to run unaffected.

Deploying Windows Containers

Windows containers can be deployed on Windows Server with Desktop Experience and on Windows Server Core. They can be deployed both on physical computers and virtual machines as process isolation containers or Hyper-V isolation containers. Although the details of deploying and working with containers differ in the following scenarios, all deployments require the same basic steps:

- Configure the host OS as a container host
- Install Docker on the container host

- Install a base operating system
- Create a process isolation container or Hyper-V isolation container
- Manage container networking, data volumes, and resources

The following sections cover how to implement these steps in various scenarios, including deploying containers on Windows Server 2022 with Desktop Experience and Server Core.

Implementing Containers on Windows Server

The steps for implementing containers on Windows Server with Desktop Experience and Server Core are the same, except that you can use Server Manager to install the Containers feature on Desktop Experience. We'll use command-line tools, which work for either installation of Windows Server. The first thing you need to do is install the Containers feature using PowerShell. Because the server requires a restart after installing the Containers feature, add the -Restart option:

```
Install-WindowsFeature Containers -Restart
```

If you will be deploying Hyper-V containers or deploying containers inside VMs, you also need to install the Hyper-V role.

Installing Docker on a Windows Server Container Host

Docker is open source software that has been used for years in the Linux environment to implement containers. Rather than reinvent the wheel, Microsoft adapted Docker to the Windows environment. Docker is not part of Windows, so it can't be installed as a role or feature; you need to install it using PowerShell package management with the following cmdlets. The first cmdlet installs the Docker package management module and the second one installs Docker.

```
Install-Module DockerMsftProvider –Repository PSGallery –Force
Install-Package Docker –ProviderName DockerMsftProvider
```

You might be prompted to install the NuGet provider after you enter the first command, and you will be asked if you want to trust the DockerDefault package after you enter the second command. Respond with Y for Yes in both cases. Next, you need to restart the computer. After the computer restarts, you can confirm that the Docker service is running with Task Manager (see Figure 13-19). The Docker service is represented by the dockerd.exe file, which was installed with the Docker package. The Docker service is also called the Docker daemon in the Linux world.

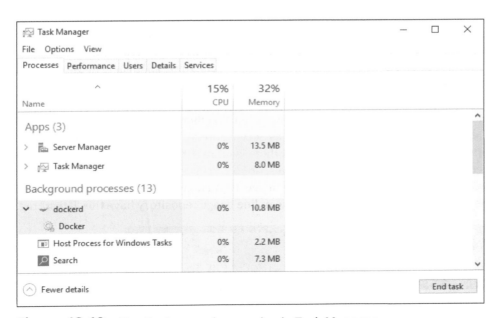

Figure 13-19   The Docker service running in Task Manager

Note 4

You can learn more about Docker and Microsoft at *https://www.docker.com/partners/microsoft*.

Installing a Base Operating System

The next step in deploying a container is to install a base operating system image using the Docker client. The Docker client is the executable file docker.exe that was installed with the Docker package. You install a base operating system image from the Docker Hub repository, which is a collection of Docker images maintained in the cloud. To some extent, the base operating system you can deploy in a container depends on the OS running on the container host. As long as the base image OS kernel matches the host OS kernel, you can install the following base images in a container; they are listed here from smallest footprint to largest footprint:

- *Nano Server*—A very lightweight version of Windows Server that has a limited user interface and small footprint. Nano Server was developed to run applications that use the .NET core and other open source development frameworks. However, it lacks management features such as PowerShell and Windows Management Instrumentation (WMI). This image is just under 300 MB.
- *Server Core*—Windows Server without the GUI and a smaller application programing interface (API); also, it lacks support for some Windows Server roles, role services, and features. This image is about 5 GB.
- *Windows Server*—Has full Windows API support and provides support for all Windows Server roles; lacks only some core Windows libraries such as the GDI library. However, it provides GPU hardware acceleration if required by your applications.
- *Windows*—The largest of the base images and includes most of the Windows core libraries that Server Core and Windows Server images may lack. If you try to run your application on Server Core or Windows Server and it fails dependency checks, try this image.

Note 5

To see the full list of roles and features missing from Windows Server Core, go to *https://learn.microsoft.com/en-us/windows-server/administration/server-core/server-core-removed-roles*.

To download a Server Core image, run the following command from a PowerShell or command prompt:

```
docker pull mcr.microsoft.com/windows/servercore:ltsc2022
```

In this command, the `pull` argument means to download the image, and `mcr.microsoft.com/windows/servercore` specifies that the image provider is Microsoft and the image name is windows/servercore. The `:ltsc2022` is an image tag that specifies the long-term service contract edition of Windows Server 2022. There may be several versions of an image; a **tag** is a way of differentiating them. If you wanted to download a Windows Server 2019 image, you would change the tag to `:ltsc2019`. If you knew of other tags, you could specify the appropriate tag after the colon. Figure 13-20 shows the results of the `docker pull` command while the file is downloading. By default, images are tagged as "latest," but when an image is created, you can specify a name such as ServerCore20221121 if you want to be more descriptive. You can also provide a specific date or other information. If there is more than one image, you can include the `-a` option in the `docker pull` command to download all the images, or you can specify a particular tag name by adding `:Tag` after the image name, where *Tag* is the tag assigned to the image. If you don't specify a tag, an image with a tag of "latest" will be used. As of this writing, no Microsoft images in the online image repository have the "latest" tag.

```
PS C:\Users\Administrator> docker pull mcr.microsoft.com/windows/servercore:ltsc2022
ltsc2022: Pulling from windows/servercore
97f65a0ec59e: Downloading [==>                                    ]  61.08MB/1.437GB
ebccc55a1542: Downloading [==>                                    ]  58.38MB/986.9MB
```

Figure 13-20 Using Docker to pull an image from a repository

If you want to download an image from the general Docker repository but don't know the exact name of the image you want to download, you can use the `docker search` command, as shown in Figure 13-21. The command in the figure tells the Docker client to search for images that contain the keyword "servercore." As you can see, there are a number of images, many of them prebuilt for specific applications.

```
PS C:\Users\Administrator> docker search servercore
NAME                                            DESCRIPTION                                  STA
sourcetechab/servercorenet4                     Windows Server Core 1809 + Net Fw 4          1
dockercontainerteam/servercore                  docker tag <Containerosimage> servercore     0
wakeupgoogle/servercore                                                                      0
yunfandev/servercore                                                                         0
rikka4chan/servercore-python                    Windows Server Core 1809 with Python install… 0
docker4dotnet/servercore                                                                     0
jasperd/servercore                                                                           0
uatdascoe/servercore_jdk8                       uatdascoe/servercore_jdk8                    0
accupara/servercore                                                                          0
dkuchna2/servercoreiis-1803withjsoncompression  includes asp.net 4.5 application development… 0
zxliu/servercorebuild                                                                        0
sourcetechab/servercorenet4msmq                 Windows Server Core 1809 + Net Fw 4 + msmq    0
dkuchna2/servercoreiiswithjsoncompression                                                    0
hymsdocker/servercorewithdrives                 windows docker image with D: and F: drives    0
rafiq1983/servercoreiis                                                                       0
agentpanda/servercore                                                                        0
dockerserver123/servercore                      servercoreimages                             0
mahige/servercore-with-iis                                                                    0
joaquinkot/servercorebase                       Windows/ServerCore image plus .Net core 2.2 … 0
pheonix25/servercore-seq                        Docker image based off Windows Server Core, … 0
mydockercity/servercorewithdrives               A new image based on servercore adding two a… 0
itresourse/servercore                                                                         0
bsantamaria/servercore-git-wix-dotnet                                                         0
sachinnagar/servercore-go-cygwin                                                              0
sigrd/servercore-ignition                                                                     0
```

Figure 13-21   Using Docker to search for images

After images are downloaded, you can list them using the `docker images` command, as shown in Figure 13-22. Two images have been downloaded: servercore and nanoserver.

```
PS C:\Users\Administrator> docker images
REPOSITORY                                TAG       IMAGE ID       CREATED       SIZE
mcr.microsoft.com/windows/servercore      ltsc2022  5b48538011db   12 days ago   5.28GB
mcr.microsoft.com/windows/nanoserver      ltsc2022  a1cc73b9ec99   12 days ago   297MB
PS C:\Users\Administrator>
```

Figure 13-22   Using Docker to list images

Creating a Process Isolation Container

With an image downloaded, you create a container using the `docker run` command. The `docker run` command starts a container based on a specified image and runs a command or application. For example, you could start the container and have it execute a PowerShell script or a command prompt command. You can also run the container interactively, allowing you to type commands at a PowerShell prompt or command prompt running in the container, for example. The following command uses `docker run` to start an interactive PowerShell session.

```
docker run -it --name ContainerTest
    mcr.microsoft.com/windows/servercore:ltsc2022 powershell
```

In the preceding command, the `-it` option specifies an interactive (`-i`) session with a terminal (`-t`) window. The `--name` option assigns a name to the container. If you omit this option, Docker assigns a random name to the container using two words separated by an underscore. The `mcr.microsoft.com/windows/servercore` parameter specifies the image to load, and `powershell` is the command to run. The result of running this command is a PowerShell prompt running inside the container. To exit and return to the host OS, simply type `exit`. When you exit an interactive container, the container stops. To start and reconnect to the container, use the following commands. The first command restarts the container named ContainerTest and the second command reconnects you to the container:

```
docker start ContainerTest
docker attach ContainerTest
```

When you are connected interactively to a container with a PowerShell prompt, you can type PowerShell and command prompt commands normally. For example, in Figure 13-23, the `Get-ComputerInfo | findstr "Windows"` and `ipconfig` commands have been run in the container. The first command shows you that Server Core is running (the host is running Desktop Experience) and the second command shows the IP address configuration on the container, which is quite different from the IP configuration of the host computer. Network configuration of containers is discussed later in the module.

```
Windows PowerShell
Copyright (C) Microsoft Corporation. All rights reserved.

Install the latest PowerShell for new features and improvements! https://aka.ms/PSWindows

PS C:\> Get-ComputerInfo | findstr "Windows"
WindowsBuildLabEx                       : 20348.859.amd64fre.fe_release_svc_prod2.220707-1832
WindowsCurrentVersion                   : 6.3
WindowsEditionId                        : ServerDatacenter
WindowsInstallationType                 : Server Core
WindowsInstallDateFromRegistry          : 11/5/2022 2:50:41 PM
WindowsProductId                        : 00454-60000-00001-AA703
WindowsProductName                      : Windows Server 2022 Datacenter
WindowsRegisteredOrganization           :
WindowsRegisteredOwner                  :
WindowsSystemRoot                       : C:\Windows
WindowsVersion                          : 2009
OsName                                  : Microsoft Windows Server 2022 Datacenter
OsSystemDirectory                       : C:\Windows\system32
OsWindowsDirectory                      : C:\Windows
PS C:\> ipconfig

Windows IP Configuration


Ethernet adapter vEthernet (Ethernet):

   Connection-specific DNS Suffix  . :
   Link-local IPv6 Address . . . . . : fe80::e939:19:c56d:4e8%44
   IPv4 Address. . . . . . . . . . . : 172.20.155.3
   Subnet Mask . . . . . . . . . . . : 255.255.240.0
   Default Gateway . . . . . . . . . : 172.20.144.1
```

Figure 13-23 Running commands in a container

If you want to see all the containers on the host as well as their status, run the `docker ps -a` command on the host computer. In Figure 13-24, two containers exist: ContainerTest2, which is currently running, and ContainerTest, which has been exited. The `-a` option in `docker ps -a` means to list all containers, including those that are not running.

```
PS C:\Users\Administrator> docker ps -a
CONTAINER ID   IMAGE                                              COMMAND        CREATED          STATUS                    PORTS     NAMES
11600b9bf2aa   mcr.microsoft.com/windows/servercore:ltsc2022      "cmd"          9 seconds ago    Up 7 seconds                        ContainerTest2
5b100488b6c1   mcr.microsoft.com/windows/servercore:ltsc2022      "powershell"   17 minutes ago   Exited (0) 8 minutes ago            ContainerTest
PS C:\Users\Administrator>
```

Figure 13-24 Listing containers on the host

You can also create a container without starting it using the `docker create` command. It uses the same options as the `docker run` command and has an initial status of Created.

Creating a Hyper-V Isolation Container

The previous section showed how to create a process isolation container. Creating a Hyper-V isolation container is not much different. Aside from the Containers feature, your host computer must also have the Hyper-V role installed. The only real difference is that you specify the `--isolation=hyperv` option in the `docker run` command as follows:

```
docker run -it --isolation hyperv --name HyperVContainer
    mcr.microsoft.com/windows/servercore powershell
```

It takes a little longer to start a Hyper-V container than a process isolation container, but you otherwise won't notice any difference between them. Of course, there is a difference in terms of resource usage and isolation because the Hyper-V container doesn't share the Windows kernel and other resources with the host.

Note 6

If you don't use the `--isolation` parameter when you create a container, it defaults to process isolation; however, you can use the `--isolation=process` parameter if desired.

Implementing Containers in a Virtual Machine

Up to now, we've been discussing how to implement containers on a physical host computer. You can implement containers in a Hyper-V virtual machine using the same procedures discussed earlier. The only difference is that if you want to create a Hyper-V container running in a virtual machine, the virtual machine must be configured for nested virtualization.

Managing Daemon Startup Options

When you first install Docker using the `Install-Package` cmdlet, the Docker daemon (service) starts automatically after you restart the computer. The default startup options probably work for most scenarios, but there are a number of configurable options. The Docker daemon configuration is stored in a file named daemon.json and is located in C:\ProgramData\docker\config. By default, this file doesn't exist, so the daemon starts with default options. You can create the file with a simple text editor like Notepad using the following format:

```
{
"optionName": optionParameters
"optionName": optionParameters
"optionName": optionParameters
}
```

You replace *optionName* and *optionParameters* with the option names and parameters you want to use. The option name must be enclosed in quotes, and option parameters that take a string value must also be enclosed in quotes. There are over two dozen options you can configure in the Windows Docker implementation. You need to add options only to the configuration file that you want to change. Any options not included in the file use the default value. An example daemon.json file might look like the following:

```
{
"bridge":"none"
"graph":"f:\\docker\images"
"group":"dockerAdmins"
"hosts":["tcp:0.0.0.0:2375"]
}
```

Note 7

Before any daemon startup options can take effect, you must stop and restart the Docker service using the `Restart-Service docker` command.

Here is a brief description of what each of the options does:

- `bridge`: When set to "none", this option tells Docker not to configure a default NAT network. By default, a container is configured with an IP address in the range of 172.16.0.0 through 172.31.0.0 with a default subnet mask of 255.255.240.0, and network address translation (NAT) is used to allow the container access to the external network. If the `"bridge": "none"` option is included, you must manually create a network using the `docker network create` command discussed later.
- `graph`: Sets the path where Docker will store images and containers. By default, the path is C:\ProgramData\docker. In the example, the path is set to F:\\docker\images. (Note that this option requires a double backslash (\\) after the drive letter.)

- `group`: By default, only members of the Administrators group can use Docker. Use this option to specify another group that can use Docker, such as dockerAdmins in the example.
- `hosts`: Configures Docker to accept remote connections on a specific port. By convention, port 2375 is used for unsecure connections and port 2376 is used for secure connections.

Note **8**

For a list of all Docker daemon options available in Windows, see *https://docs.microsoft.com/en-us/virtualization /windowscontainers/manage-docker/configure-docker-daemon*.

Self-Check Questions

7. A process isolation container provides both OS and kernel isolation. True or False?

    a. True   **b.** False

8. What command will reconnect to an interactive container?

    a. `docker run`   **c.** `docker connect`

    b. `docker attach`   **d.** `docker start`

⊙ Check your answers at the end of this module.

Activity 13-1

Resetting Your Virtual Environment

Time Required: 5 minutes
Objective: Reset your virtual environment by applying the InitialConfig checkpoint or snapshot.
Required Tools and Equipment: ServerHyperV
Description: Apply the InitialConfig checkpoint or snapshot to ServerHyperV.

1. Be sure ServerHyperV is shut down. In your virtualization program, apply the InitialConfig checkpoint or snapshot to ServerHyperV.
2. Close your virtual machine environment.

Activity 13-2

Deploying a Process Isolation Container

Time Required: 20 minutes
Objective: Deploy a process isolation container.
Required Tools and Equipment: ServerHyperV, Internet access
Description: Install the Containers feature, install Docker, and download a Nano Server container image from the Microsoft repository. Then deploy a container using the downloaded image.

1. On ServerHyperV, open a PowerShell window.
2. Type **Install-WindowsFeature Containers –Restart** and press **Enter**. The Containers feature is installed and the computer restarts. After the computer restarts, sign in and open a PowerShell window.
3. Type **Install-Module DockerMsftProvider –Repository PSGallery –Force** and press **Enter**. If you are prompted to install the NuGet provider, press **Enter** to confirm.

(continues)

Activity 13-2 Continued

4. Type **Install-Package Docker –ProviderName DockerMsftProvider** and press **Enter**. When prompted to install software from DockerDefault, press **Y** and press **Enter**. Docker is now installed but the service is not running.

5. Type **Restart-Computer** and press **Enter**. When the computer restarts, sign in and open a PowerShell prompt. To verify that Docker is running, type **Get-Service docker** and press **Enter**. You should see that the status is Running.

6. Now you need to install a base operating system by downloading one from the Microsoft Docker repository. You'll use the `docker.exe` command for most of the next steps. Type **docker pull mcr.microsoft.com/windows/nanoserver:ltsc2022** and press **Enter**. It may take several minutes for the download to complete, depending on the speed of your Internet connection. The total download size for a nanoserver image is about 300 MB.

7. When the download is complete, you can verify the images on your local computer by typing **docker images** and pressing **Enter**. To search for nanoserver images on Docker Hub, type **docker search nanoserver** and press **Enter**. You see a listing of images that contain the keyword *nanoserver*.

8. Now it's time to run your first container. Type **docker run -it --name NanoP mcr.microsoft.com/windows/nanoserver:ltsc2022 cmd** and press **Enter**. After a short time, your prompt will change to C:\> and you'll be connected to the container running a command prompt.

9. The nanoserver image can't run PowerShell, and many commands and programs that are in the servercore image are not available in the nanoserver image, including systeminfo.exe and notepad.exe. Aside from the lack of programs in the nanoserver image, there is little to indicate you are running a nanoserver image. However, the nanoserver image has a default user name of ContainerUser, whereas the servercore image has a default user of ContainerAdministrator. To see the default user, type **set** and press **Enter**. You'll see a list of environment variables. Near the end of the list is the USERNAME variable, which is set to ContainerUser.

10. Check your IP address configuration by typing **ipconfig /all** and pressing **Enter**. You'll see output similar to Figure 13-25. Notice that the IP address is in the range from 172.16.00 to 172.31.0.0. (It's 172.18.86.2 in the figure.) This tells you that the default NAT network is being used for this container. Type **ping 10.99.0.10** (the address of the Hyper-V host) and press **Enter** to verify that you can access the host network.

```
C:\Windows\System32>ipconfig /all

Windows IP Configuration

    Host Name . . . . . . . . . . . . : 2b66cc82e486
    Primary Dns Suffix  . . . . . . . :
    Node Type . . . . . . . . . . . . : Hybrid
    IP Routing Enabled. . . . . . . . : No
    WINS Proxy Enabled. . . . . . . . : No

Ethernet adapter vEthernet (Ethernet):

    Connection-specific DNS Suffix  . :
    Description . . . . . . . . . . . : Hyper-V Virtual Ethernet Container Adapter
    Physical Address. . . . . . . . . : 00-15-5D-CD-0C-B0
    DHCP Enabled. . . . . . . . . . . : No
    Autoconfiguration Enabled . . . . : Yes
    Link-local IPv6 Address . . . . . : fe80::749e:f18a:acc0:5994%37(Preferred)
    IPv4 Address. . . . . . . . . . . : 172.18.86.2(Preferred)
    Subnet Mask . . . . . . . . . . . : 255.255.240.0
    Default Gateway . . . . . . . . . : 172.18.80.1
    DNS Servers . . . . . . . . . . . : 172.18.80.1
                                        172.31.1.206
    NetBIOS over Tcpip. . . . . . . . : Disabled
```

Figure 13-25   `ipconfig` in a container

11. Type **exit** and press **Enter** to return to the host PowerShell prompt. Type **ipconfig** and press **Enter**. Notice that a new network adapter has been created on the host named vEthernet (nat) with the IP address 172.18.80.1, which is the default gateway setting for the container. The host is used as the default gateway so the container can access the host's network.

(continues)

Activity 13-2 Continued

12. Type **docker ps –a** and press **Enter** to see running containers. The status of the NanoPS1 container is Exited, which means that while the container is loaded, it's not running.

13. Type **docker start NanoP** and press **Enter**. Make sure the capitalization in NanoP matches the actual container name; container names are case sensitive in Docker. Type **docker ps** and press **Enter**. (You don't need the –a option because it is only required to list containers that aren't running as well as running containers.) Notice the status is Up.

14. Type **docker attach NanoP** and press **Enter** to connect to the container again. Type **exit** and press **Enter** to return to the host.

15. Continue to the next activity.

Activity 13-3

Deploying a Hyper-V Isolation Container

Time Required: 20 minutes
Objective: Deploy a Hyper-V isolation container.
Required Tools and Equipment: ServerHyperV
Description: Deploy a Hyper-V container using the Nano Server image.

1. On ServerHyperV, open the PowerShell prompt, type **docker create -it --isolation hyperv --name NanoH mcr.microsoft.com/windows/nanoserver cmd**, and press **Enter**. This creates the container and loads it but doesn't start it. The container digest ID is displayed if the command is successful.

2. Because the container is not started, you are still at the host computer's PowerShell prompt. Type **docker ps –a** and press **Enter**. You see two containers, one with the status Created and the other with the status Exited. Start the NanoP container by typing **docker start NanoP** and pressing **Enter**.

3. Start the NanoH container by typing **docker start NanoH** and pressing **Enter**. Notice that it takes considerably longer to start the Hyper-V isolation container.

4. Type **docker ps** and press **Enter**. Both containers have the status Up.

5. The NanoP container is running as a process isolation container and the NanoH container is running as a Hyper-V isolation container, but how can you tell? Type **docker inspect NanoP | findstr Isolation** and press **Enter**. You see a single line of output that reads `"Isolation": "process",`.

6. Type **docker inspect NanoH | findstr Isolation** and press **Enter**. You see a single line of output that reads `"Isolation": "hyperv",`. Type **docker inspect NanoH** and press **Enter** to see detailed information about the container, including the network settings, volumes, and memory settings.

7. Type **docker stop NanoP NanoH** and press **Enter** to stop both containers. Type **docker rm NanoP NanoH** and press **Enter** to remove both containers. Type **docker ps -a** and press **Enter** to confirm that no containers are loaded.

8. Continue to the next activity.

Managing Windows Containers

Microsoft Exam AZ-800:

Manage virtual machines and containers.
- Create and manage containers

So far, you've learned about basic container implementation on Windows Server using Docker. This section examines additional container configuration and management tasks using Docker as well as PowerShell. You'll also look at configuring Docker daemon startup options, managing container networking, and managing volumes and resources. Finally, you'll see how to create and manage container images using a variety of tools.

Managing Containers with the Docker Daemon

The docker.exe program is the primary tool for working with containers. You have learned how to download a container image from the Microsoft repository using docker pull and how to deploy a container using docker run. We'll look at some more common tasks you might perform while working with containers and the associated Docker command.

Working with Containers

After you have deployed a container using docker run or docker create, there are several commands you can use to interact with and manage the container. The following list describes the commands you have already used and some additional commands that you are likely to use when working with containers.

Note 9

To get help on using any Docker command, type docker *command* --help, where *command* is run, create, or start, for example.

- docker create: Create a container but don't start it. The container will have a status of Created. The syntax for using it is docker create --name ContainerName Repository:tag command. If you don't specify a name, a random name using two words separated by an underscore will be created; for example, Docker created a container name of gracious_sutherland in response to a recent docker create command.
- docker run: Create a container and start it with the specified command, if included. The container will have a status of Up as long as it continues to run or Exited if it runs the command and exits. The syntax for using the command is the same as for the docker create command.
- docker ps: This command lists running containers along with extensive information about them, including the container ID, the image that's running, such as nanoserver or windowsservercore, the command or app that is running in the container, when the container was created, and its current status. You'll use the docker ps command to see a list of running containers, and you can use the name of a container to perform additional Docker commands on it. By default, docker ps shows only running containers. The -a option lists all containers, including stopped containers.
- docker rm: This command deletes a container. You can use the name of the container or the container ID, as in docker rm ContainerTest2. A container must first be stopped, as indicated by the status "Exited" in the docker ps -a command, before it can be deleted. If the container cannot be stopped for some reason, you can use the -force option in the command.
- docker stop: This command stops a running container. Again, you can use the name or ID of the container.
- docker start: This command starts a container that is loaded but has a status of Exited or Created. After running this command, the container has a status of Up.
- docker restart: This command stops a running container and then starts it again. If the container is already stopped, this command will start it.
- docker attach: This command connects you to a container that was created to run in interactive mode. The container must be running. For example, if you exit a container or you have created a container using docker create, first run docker start and then run docker attach to begin or resume an interactive session.
- docker exec: This command executes a command in a running container. For example, if you wanted to see the IP configuration of a running container named ContainerTest2 without entering an interactive session, you could use this command: docker exec ContainerTest2 ipconfig. The output of the command is displayed, but you resume your prompt on the container host, as in Figure 13-26.

```
PS C:\Users\Administrator> docker exec ContainerTest2 ipconfig

Windows IP Configuration


Ethernet adapter vEthernet (Ethernet):

   Connection-specific DNS Suffix  . :
   Link-local IPv6 Address . . . . . : fe80::ec15:f66b:f0f:5f1a%37
   IPv4 Address. . . . . . . . . . . : 172.18.88.231
   Subnet Mask . . . . . . . . . . . : 255.255.240.0
   Default Gateway . . . . . . . . . : 172.18.80.1
```

Figure 13-26 Results of the `docker exec` command

- `docker --help`: This command lists all the Docker commands, along with brief descriptions.
- `docker command --help`: Use this command to get help for using any Docker command. Replace *command* with `run`, `create`, or `start`, for example.

> **Note 10**
>
> Docker comes from the Linux world, where, unlike Windows, everything is case sensitive. For example, ContainerTest2 is different from containertest2 when using Docker. Command options are also case sensitive, so `docker RM` won't work because the `rm` option must be lowercase.

Working with Container Images

This section looks at a few management tasks you can perform on container images using the Docker program:

- Listing container images
- Tagging container images
- Committing changes to images
- Removing images

Listing Container Images

After you have worked with container images for a while, you may have collected a few of them. To see a list of images that are available on the local computer, use the following command:

`docker images`

The `docker images` command lists the repository name, tag, image ID, when it was created, and the size of the image (see Figure 13-27). You can use the results of the command to select an image when creating an image using `docker run`. To differentiate similar images in the `docker run` command, you can specify the image ID or you can specify the tag, as in `docker run mcr.microsoft.com/windows/servercore:GTTest`. If you don't specify a tag, the "latest" tag is assumed as the default. If you have many images, you can include the repository name in the command to list only the images in a specific repository, as in: `docker images mcr.microsoft.com/windows/nanoserver`. That command will list only the nanoserver images.

```
PS C:\Users\Administrator> docker images
REPOSITORY                                TAG         IMAGE ID       CREATED        SIZE
mcr.microsoft.com/windows/server          ltsc2022    a4b9814cae23   2 weeks ago    12.4GB
mcr.microsoft.com/windows/servercore      GTTest      5b48538011db   2 weeks ago    5.28GB
mcr.microsoft.com/windows/servercore      ltsc2022    5b48538011db   2 weeks ago    5.28GB
mcr.microsoft.com/windows/nanoserver      20231203    a1cc73b9ec99   2 weeks ago    297MB
mcr.microsoft.com/windows/nanoserver      ltsc2022    a1cc73b9ec99   2 weeks ago    297MB
```

Figure 13-27 Output of the `docker images` command

Tagging Container Images

As mentioned earlier, a tag is a way to differentiate multiple versions of the same image. You can tag an image when it is created (for example, using the `docker build` command discussed later), but you can also create a new tag for an existing image. For example, to create a new tag for the `mcr.microsoft.com/windows/nanoserver:ltsc2022` image, you would use the following command:

```
docker tag mcr.microsoft.com/windows/nanoserver:ltsc2022
    mcr.microsoft.com/windows/nanoserver:20231203
```

The `docker tag` command doesn't actually change the tag on the existing image; it creates a duplicate entry, almost like a file shortcut. As you can see from Figure 13-28, the image ID of the nanoserver image is the same for both "ltsc2022" and "20231203." It's the same image, just with two different tags.

```
PS C:\Users\Administrator> docker tag mcr.microsoft.com/windows/nanoserver:ltsc2022 mcr.microsoft.com/windows/nanoserver:20231203
PS C:\Users\Administrator> docker images
REPOSITORY                              TAG        IMAGE ID      CREATED       SIZE
mcr.microsoft.com/windows/server        ltsc2022   a4b9814cae23  2 weeks ago   12.4GB
mcr.microsoft.com/windows/servercore    GTTest     5b48538011db  2 weeks ago   5.28GB
mcr.microsoft.com/windows/servercore    ltsc2022   5b48538011db  2 weeks ago   5.28GB
mcr.microsoft.com/windows/nanoserver    20231203   a1cc73b9ec99  2 weeks ago   297MB
mcr.microsoft.com/windows/nanoserver    ltsc2022   a1cc73b9ec99  2 weeks ago   297MB
```

Figure 13-28   Tagging an image

When you use `docker tag`, you can also change the repository name, which again acts like a shortcut. So, for example, the following command changes the repository name to "core" and gives the image the tag "20231203." This way, you can refer to the image when performing other tasks, such as `docker run`, using the shorter name.

```
docker tag mcr.microsoft.com/windows/servercore:ltsc2022 core:20231203
```

To create a container from the image, you can simply use the following command:

```
docker run core:20231203
```

Committing Changes to Images

You can create a new image from changes you make in a container. For example, suppose you deploy a container image using the following command:

```
docker create --name corePS core:20231203 powershell
```

The image is loaded and is ready to run PowerShell. Suppose you will frequently use this image. You can essentially save this container as a new image with the `powershell` command already integrated into the image by using the following command:

```
docker commit corePS coreps:20231203
```

This command creates a new image in the coreps repository with the tag "20231203" (see Figure 13-29). Again, if you don't specify a tag, "latest" is used. If you then run the image using `docker run -it coreps:20231203`, a container running PowerShell is started. Before you run `docker commit`, the container must not be running (in the Up state); it can be in the Exited or Created state. If you run `docker images` after running `docker commit`, you will see a new image listed with the repository name you specified. The size of the image will be shown as roughly the same size or much larger than the original image, but don't be fooled. When you commit an image, only the changes to the original image are actually saved, but the `docker images` command reports the total size, which includes the original image plus any saved changes.

```
PS C:\Users\Administrator> docker commit corePS coreps:20231203
sha256:40f2b98325306e265f905bf252ad1afe5cfdfc1d5b0cb4935086f3d022d19d54
PS C:\Users\Administrator> docker images
REPOSITORY                              TAG        IMAGE ID      CREATED         SIZE
coreps                                  20231203   40f2b9832530  3 seconds ago   5.28GB
mcr.microsoft.com/windows/server        ltsc2022   a4b9814cae23  2 weeks ago     12.4GB
core                                    20231203   5b48538011db  2 weeks ago     5.28GB
mcr.microsoft.com/windows/servercore    GTTest     5b48538011db  2 weeks ago     5.28GB
mcr.microsoft.com/windows/servercore    ltsc2022   5b48538011db  2 weeks ago     5.28GB
nano                                    20231203   a1cc73b9ec99  2 weeks ago     297MB
mcr.microsoft.com/windows/nanoserver    20231203   a1cc73b9ec99  2 weeks ago     297MB
mcr.microsoft.com/windows/nanoserver    ltsc2022   a1cc73b9ec99  2 weeks ago     297MB
```

Figure 13-29   The results of the `docker commit` command

Removing Images

If you are finished using an image or you want to delete specific image tags, use the `docker rmi` command. If multiple images have the same ID but different tags, this command simply removes the instance of the image specified. If it is the last instance of the image, the image is deleted. For example, if you have two instances of the image of nanoserver, one with the tag "ltsc2022" and the other with the tag "20231203," you can delete the former with the following command:

```
docker rmi nanoserver:ltsc2022
```

After running the command, Docker will respond with "Untagged: nanoserver:ltsc2022." If you are deleting the last instance of the same image, Docker will print a second line of output similar to "Untagged: nanoserver@sha256:*32byteidentifier*," where *32byteidentifier* is the full 32 byte (256 bit) image identifier in hexadecimal.

Implementing Container Networks

Docker configures the container network using **network address translation (NAT)**. NAT is a process in which the IP addresses in a packet are translated to different addresses when the packet leaves or enters a network. With NAT, a network that uses private IP addresses can access the public Internet. By default, the container network uses an IP address in the range from 172.16.0.0 to 172.31.0.0 and assigns a subnet mask of 255.255.240.0. This is the default setting, which can be changed using the daemon configuration file and when creating a container. To illustrate this, Figure 13-30 shows the `ipconfig` command being executed on a container. Next, the `ipconfig` command is executed on the host computer. In the figure, the container's network adapter is named vEthernet (Ethernet), which is the default name given to a container's network adapter. The name vEthernet indicates that it is a virtual network adapter. Notice that the host computer has two network adapters: Ethernet adapter vEthernet and vEthernet (nat). The first adapter is the adapter connected to the host network, and vEthernet (nat) is the virtual adapter used to communicate between the host and the container. The host in this case is a Hyper-V server that is itself a virtual machine, so its adapter is also a virtual adapter.

```
PS C:\Users\Administrator> docker exec NanoTest ipconfig

Windows IP Configuration


Ethernet adapter vEthernet (Ethernet):

   Connection-specific DNS Suffix  . :
   Link-local IPv6 Address . . . . . : fe80::3dc7:8f5c:ec24:76e8%37
   IPv4 Address. . . . . . . . . . . : 172.18.91.149
   Subnet Mask . . . . . . . . . . . : 255.255.240.0
   Default Gateway . . . . . . . . . : 172.18.80.1
PS C:\Users\Administrator> ipconfig

Windows IP Configuration


Ethernet adapter vEthernet (Intel(R) 82574L Gigabit Network Connection - Virtual Switch):

   Connection-specific DNS Suffix  . :
   Link-local IPv6 Address . . . . . : fe80::87e:1c26:a096:c217%10
   IPv4 Address. . . . . . . . . . . : 10.99.0.10
   Subnet Mask . . . . . . . . . . . : 255.255.255.0
   Default Gateway . . . . . . . . . : 10.99.0.250

Ethernet adapter vEthernet (nat):

   Connection-specific DNS Suffix  . :
   Link-local IPv6 Address . . . . . : fe80::cd02:18f9:5b9a:a1ac%32
   IPv4 Address. . . . . . . . . . . : 172.18.80.1
   Subnet Mask . . . . . . . . . . . : 255.255.240.0
   Default Gateway . . . . . . . . . :
PS C:\Users\Administrator>
```

Figure 13-30 IP address settings on a container and the host

The vEthernet adapter on the container has an address of 172.18.91.149 and a default gateway address of 172.18.80.1. The address of vEthernet (nat) on the host is 172.18.80.1, making the host computer the default gateway for the container. When the container wants to communicate with the host network, it sends packets to the host's vEthernet (nat) adapter, which then performs a NAT operation on the packet's source address. The source address is translated to the host's primary adapter address, which in this case is 10.99.0.10. This allows the container to communicate with the host network and any networks the host is able to reach.

> **Note 11**
>
> The host also acts as the container's DNS server. When the host receives DNS lookups from the container, it passes those requests along to the DNS server configured in its IP address settings.

Configuring a NAT Network

You can change the default network settings by configuring the daemon.json file discussed earlier. If you want to use a different address for the NAT network, you can add an entry to the daemon.json file and then restart the docker service. For example, to change the default network to 10.10.10.0/24, enter the following:

```
{
"fixed-cidr":"10.10.10.0/24"
}
```

After you edit the daemon.json file, you must stop the Docker service, remove the default network, and restart the service from a PowerShell prompt as follows:

```
Stop-Service docker
Get-ContainerNetwork | Remove-ContainerNetwork
Start-Service docker
```

Any containers that were running when you stopped the service will need to be started again using docker start. The containers will now use the network specified in the daemon.json file.

As mentioned, you can also disable automatic network creation by adding the "bridge":"none" entry to the daemon.json file. If you do so, you need to create a network manually using the docker network command.

Port Mapping with NAT Networks

With a NAT network, devices on the host network cannot initiate communication with the container because its IP address is translated by the host computer. Port mapping allows the container host to forward packets for specific applications to containers hosting those applications. For example, if a container is hosting a web server, you would need the host to forward TCP ports 80 and 443 to the container using the following command:

```
docker run -p 80:80 -p 443:443 nanoserver
```

Notice in the preceding command that the -p option is used twice. You can use it as many times as necessary— once for each port you want to map. The parameter after the -p option is the *host port number:container port number*. The *host port number* is the port number with which external devices will attempt to contact the container, and the *container port number* is the port number on which the container service is listening. In the preceding example, they are the same port number, but they don't have to be. For example, you could use 8008:80, which means the host will forward packets addressed to port 8008 to port 80 on the container. Container port mappings are shown in the PORTS column of the docker ps output, or you can use the docker port *ContainerName* command.

Deploying Other Network Types

Aside from NAT networks, Docker supports transparent and layer 2 bridge networks. A **transparent network** connects containers to the same network as the host, so a container's network adapter will have an IP address in the same IP subnet as the host's network adapter. This allows the container to communicate with devices on the host network without the address having to be translated. To create a transparent network named Tran1 that uses a DHCP server that's already configured on the host network, use the following command:

```
docker network create -d transparent Tran1
```

Next, you need to connect containers to the network. You can connect a new container to the network using the `docker run` or `docker create` command by adding the option `--network Tran1`, as in this example:

```
docker run --network Tran1 nanoserver
```

If you want to connect an existing container named ContainerTest1 to the Tran1 network, make sure the container is stopped first and run the following command:

```
docker network connect Tran1 ContainerTest1
```

The container will get its IP address configuration from a DHCP server running on the host network. If you don't have a DHCP server on the host network, you can create a static transparent network and assign a static IP address to a container. To create a static transparent network named TranStatic with a network ID of 192.168.0.0/24 and a default gateway address of 192.168.0.250, use the following command:

```
docker network create -d transparent --subnet 192.168.0.0/24 --gateway
    192.168.0.250 TranStatic
```

Next, create a container and assign it a static IP address and DNS server address; the default gateway will be automatically assigned:

```
docker run --network TranStatic --ip 192.168.0.101 --dns
    192.168.0.200 microsoft/nanoserver
```

> **Note 12**
>
> In the preceding `docker run` commands, you can add options such as `-it` and `--name` as well as any other options `docker run` accepts.

A **layer 2 (L2) bridge network** is similar to a transparent network, but the container shares a MAC address with the container host. L2 bridge networks support only static addressing, and the container has a unique IP address in the same subnet as the host virtual adapter that is created when you created the L2 bridge network. These types of networks are useful for advanced container deployment in private and public clouds when the container is running on a VM. When you create an L2 bridge network, you must specify the subnet and gateway in a similar manner to creating a static transparent network, as follows:

```
docker network create -d l2bridge --subnet 192.168.0.0/24 --gateway
    192.168.0.250 BridgeNet1
```

Working with Container Data Volumes

Data that is created while the container is running and then stored on its virtual volumes is not saved when a container is deleted using `docker rm`. Each time a container is created, it starts fresh with no carryover from the previous time it was run. This is called **stateless operation**. You can save changes to the container with the `docker commit` command, but that saves the current state of the container as a new image. What if you want a container image to simply maintain data that is created or changed on its volumes between run times without having to commit changes and create a new image? You can do this by specifying a folder on the host computer and mapping it to a folder in the container. What's more, multiple containers can have access to the same data on the host volume, and you can assign containers read or read/write access to the data.

The following command maps a folder called C:\HostData on the container host to the C:\ContainerData folder on a new container. The `-v` option specifies the volume mapping. By default, mapped volumes are read/write, but you can add `:ro` after the container folder name to make it read only.

```
docker run -v c:\HostData:c:\ContainerData nanoserver
```

After running this command, any data that is created in c:\HostData on the host computer will be seen in the c:\ContainerData folder in the container, and vice versa. You can deploy additional containers with mappings to the same folder on the host, and all containers plus the host will have access to the same data.

Managing Container Resources

Resource control is one of the big advantages of using containers to run applications instead of running them directly on the host computer. As with a virtual machine, you can constrain, or limit, how much of a particular resource a container can utilize, including CPU, memory, and block I/O. To limit CPU resources, there are a number of options you can specify when the container is created using `docker run` or `docker create`:

- `--cpu-percent`—This Windows-only option specifies the percentage of the CPU a container may use. For example, if this value is set to 20, the container may use up to 20 percent of the host computer's CPU.
- `--cpu-count`—This Windows-only option limits the number of CPUs available to the container.
- `--cpu-shares`—This option specifies the proportion of the CPU a container can use relative to other containers running on the same host. The default value is 1024. If you set this value to 0, the system will use the default value of 1024, so if you use this option, set a value higher or lower than 1024. For example, if you have three containers running and you want ContainerA to get half of the available CPU time and the other two to share the remaining half, you can set ContainerA's `cpu-shares` value to 2048 and leave the others at the default value of 1024. ContainerA will take 50 percent of the CPU time and the other two will share the remaining half at 25 percent each. This option can also be expressed as `-c`.
- `--cpuset-cpus`—This option specifies which CPUs or CPU cores a container can use in a multiprocessor or multicore system. CPUs are specified with a starting index value of 0. For example, if you want to limit the container to using only the first and second core on a 4-core CPU, you can use `0,1` or `0-1`.

To see all the options for constraining CPU use, type `docker run --help | findstr cpu`.
Some of the options for constraining memory include the following:

- `--memory`—Specifies the maximum amount of memory a container can use. Use the suffix b, k, m, or g to specify units in bytes, kilobytes, megabytes, or gigabytes, respectively. For example, to limit a container to using 2 MB, specify the option `--memory 2m`. This option can also be expressed as `-m`.
- `--kernel-memory`—Specifies the amount of kernel memory a container can use, with a minimum allowed value of 4 MB. This option uses the same units as `--memory`.
- `--memory-reservation`—Specifies a "soft" memory limit to allow a certain amount of memory to be reclaimed by the host system if needed. This limit must be less than the value specified by the `--memory` option. For example, if you create a container with `--memory 400m` and `--memory-reservation 300m`, the host system can reclaim the difference between the 400m and 300m, ensuring that the container has at least 300m to work with.
- `--memory-swap`—Specifies the amount of virtual memory (swap file) the container can use. This value must be specified as the value of `--memory` plus the amount of virtual memory you want the container to use. For example, if you create a container with `--memory 400m` and `--memory-swap 1000m`, the container can use up to 600m of virtual memory (the difference between `--memory-swap` and `--memory`). If this value is not specified, the system can use up to twice the amount of `--memory` as virtual memory. For example, if you create a container with `--memory 400m` and don't specify `--memory-swap`, the container can use up to 800m as virtual memory. A `--memory-swap` value of `-1` means the container can use unlimited virtual memory.

Managing Container Images with Dockerfile and Microsoft Azure

As you have seen, you can download container images from a repository, and you can deploy containers using those images. You can create new container images from deployed containers using the `docker commit` command and you can manage images using the `docker` command or PowerShell. In this section, you learn how to create new images using Dockerfile and how to manage images stored online using Docker Hub and Microsoft Azure.

Creating Container Images with Dockerfile

Dockerfile is a feature of Docker in which you specify properties of a container image using a text file called a dockerfile and then use the `docker build` command to create the new image using the specifications in the file.

A dockerfile consists of a series of commands in which each command is followed by one or more arguments. The commands are executed by the `docker build` command or `Build-ContainerImage` PowerShell cmdlet, and the result is a container image. Table 13-2 lists the most common Dockerfile commands, descriptions of each, and examples of their usage. The commands are customarily written in uppercase, but they need not be. The table lists the commands in alphabetical order, but the sample dockerfile shown later lists a more typical order for the commands. Not all commands need to be used in a dockerfile.

Table 13-2   Dockerfile commands

Command	Example	Description
ADD	`ADD http://example.com/file.pdf c:/files/`	Copies files and folders from the host or remote computer to the container image; local paths and URLs can be used as the source
CMD	`CMD powershell`	Specifies a command to run when the container is started
COPY	`COPY C:/files/*.txt C:/Textfiles/`	Copies files or folders from the host to the container; COPY and ADD are similar but ADD has more options, including copying files from URLs
FROM	`FROM microsoft/nanoserver`	Specifies the base image to use for the container
RUN	`RUN md C:/SharedVol`	Executes a command and creates a new layer to be added to the image
USER	`USER containeradmin`	Sets the user name when running the container image and any CMD or RUN commands

Note 13

In a dockerfile, file paths must use forward slashes (/) instead of backslashes (\).

The following is a basic dockerfile that creates a new image based on the Server Core image. It installs the DNS server role in the container, creates a new zone, adds a PowerShell script to the container, and runs the script. When the container is run, PowerShell is started. Lines that contain the hash or pound sign (#) are comments for documentation.

```
# Dockerfile to create a container image with DNS installed with the az800.local zone
# Base image
FROM mcr.microsoft.com/windows/servercore:ltsc2022
# install DNS using PowerShell
RUN powershell -Command Install-WindowsFeature dns -IncludeManagementTools
RUN powershell -Command Add-DnsServerPrimaryZone az800.local -ZoneFile az800.local.dns
# Copy the myscript.ps1 Powershell script file to the container and then run the script
ADD myscript.ps1 C:/scripts/myscript.ps1
RUN powershell -executionpolicy bypass C:/scripts/myscript.ps1
CMD powershell
```

After you create the file, save it with the name "dockerfile" and no extension in a new folder. From the command prompt or PowerShell prompt, change to the folder where you saved the file and run the following command:

```
docker build -t dnscore .
```

In the previous command, the `-t` option specifies the image name to be saved (in this case, `dnscore`) and the "." specifies that the dockerfile is in the current folder. When you run the container with the `-it` option, you are placed in a PowerShell prompt, where you can verify that the DNS Server service is running by executing the `Get-Service DNS` cmdlet.

Managing Container Images Using Microsoft Azure

In an earlier module, you learned about Microsoft Azure storage as a method for providing a failover cluster witness. You can also host containers in Azure with Azure Container Service. The Azure Container Service is primarily focused on deploying clusters of virtual machines that are configured to run containerized applications. Azure Container Service uses the familiar Docker container format so your containers can run in the Azure cloud or on a traditional host computer.

As with Azure storage, you need an Azure subscription to use Azure Container Service. When you are logged on to Azure, click the Marketplace and then click Containers to search for existing containers you can deploy or to create new containers using Azure Container Service (see Figure 13-31). Because Docker is open source, there are a variety of preconfigured containers running in different environments that you can try, including those running in Windows and different distributions of Linux. When you deploy a container in Azure, you are actually deploying a virtual machine that has the Containers feature and Docker already installed. Of course, with Azure, you can also deploy a traditional VM and manually install the Containers feature and Docker if you want. Either way, storage and management of the VM and container is through Microsoft Azure. Virtual machines and containers you deploy in Microsoft Azure are fully compatible with your local computing environment as well.

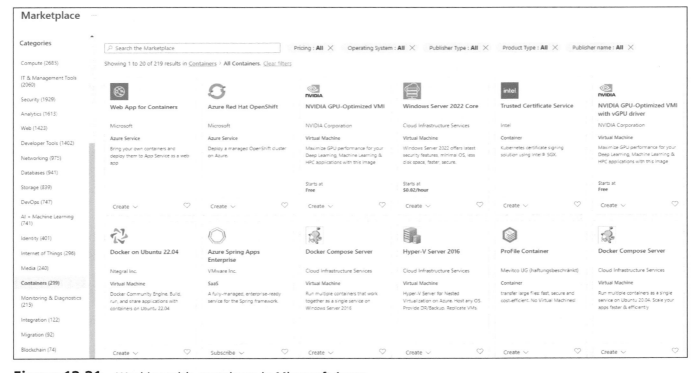

Figure 13-31   Working with containers in Microsoft Azure

Self-Check Questions

9. PowerShell is the primary tool for working with containers. True or False?

   a. True

   b. False

10. What command deletes a docker container?

    a. `docker del`

    c. `Remove-Container`

    b. `docker rm`

    d. `Delete-Image`

Check your answers at the end of this module.

Activity 13-4

Managing Container Images

Time Required: 20 minutes
Objective: Manage container images.
Required Tools and Equipment: ServerHyperV
Description: Work with container images using the `docker tag`, `docker commit`, and `docker rmi` commands.

1. On ServerHyperV, open a PowerShell prompt, type **docker run -it --name Nano mcr.microsoft.com/ windows/nanoserver:ltsc2022 cmd**, and press **Enter**.
2. You're connected to the container at a command prompt. Type **md docs** and press **Enter** to create a new folder in the container.
3. Type **cd docs** and press **Enter**. Now you will create a couple of files. Nano Server isn't equipped with a text editor, but there are other ways to create files. Type **echo Creating file 1 > file1.txt** and press **Enter**. Type **echo Creating file 2 > file2.txt** and press **Enter**. Type **dir** and press **Enter** to see that the files are created.
4. Type **exit** and press **Enter** to return to the host.
5. Type **docker commit Nano nano:cmd** and press **Enter**. This creates a new image based on the running container Nano. The image is saved in a repository named nano with a tag of cmd to indicate that the command prompt is running.
6. Type **docker images** and press **Enter**. You see the new image.
7. Create a new container from the saved image. Type **docker create -it --name NanoNew nano:cmd** and press **Enter**. The image is created, and it will run the command prompt when it starts.
8. Type **docker start NanoNew; docker attach NanoNew** and press **Enter**. You can run multiple commands on one line when they're separated by a semicolon. You are now attached to NanoNew.
9. Type **dir docs** and press **Enter**. You see the files you created earlier. Remember, you can create new images that are based on existing containers. The state of the container, such as startup commands, files, and network settings, is saved in the new image.
10. Type **exit** and press **Enter** to return to the host.
11. Type **docker rm NanoNew Nano** and press **Enter** to remove both containers from memory.
12. Type **docker tag nano:cmd nano:withDocs** and press **Enter**. This adds a tag named withDocs to the image. Type **docker images** and press **Enter**. Notice that the two nano images have the same image ID, which means they are the same image but with different tags.
13. Type **docker tag nano:cmd mynanoimage** and press **Enter**. Type **docker images** and press **Enter**. Now there are three images with the same image ID but with different repository names or tags. They are all the same image, just different shortcuts pointing to the same image. Also notice that the new image has the default tag of "latest" because you didn't specify a tag.
14. Type **docker rmi mynanoimage** and press **Enter**. The output of the command is Untagged: mynanoimage:latest. If you don't specify a tag, "latest" is assumed. Type **docker images** and press **Enter** to see that the image is gone. Type **docker rmi nano:withDocs** and press **Enter**. The output of the command is Untagged: nano:withDocs, which means the withDocs tag was removed from the image.
15. To see details about an image, including its "parent" images (the image or images it was created from), type **docker image inspect nano:cmd** and press **Enter**. You see a lot of output, but toward the top, you see a line named Parent, which tells you the image ID from which the image was created if it was created from an existing image. In the ContainerConfig section, you see the image name from which the image was created (**mcr.microsoft.com/windows/nanoserver:ltsc2022**) and the command the image runs on startup.
16. Continue to the next activity.

Activity 13-5

Working with Container Networks

Time Required: 20 minutes

Objective: Work with container networks.

Required Tools and Equipment: ServerHyperV

Description: In this activity, you work with container networks. You create a static transparent network and deploy a container with a static IP address.

1. On ServerHyperV, open a PowerShell prompt, type **docker network create -d transparent --subnet 192.168.100.0/24 --gateway 192.168.100.250 TranStatic**, and press **Enter**. This creates a static transparent network named TranStatic and assigns a default gateway.
2. Type **docker create –it --name Nano --network TranStatic --ip 192.168.100.1 nano:cmd** and press **Enter**.
3. Type **docker start Nano** and press **Enter**. Type **docker exec Nano ipconfig** and press **Enter**. This command tells the container to execute the ipconfig command. You see that the address of the container is 192.168.100.1 with a default gateway of 192.168.100.250.
4. Type **docker stop Nano** and press **Enter**.
5. Type **docker rm Nano** and press **Enter**.
6. Sign out or shut down the computer.

Module Summary

- Nested virtualization is the ability to run a hypervisor inside another hypervisor. Nested virtualization in Hyper-V is only supported in Windows 10, Windows Server 2016, and later versions of each.
- VM CPU groups allow you to better manage host CPU resources shared among the guest VMs running on the Hyper-V host. The Hyper-V Host Compute Service is a command-line utility used to manage VM CPU groups.
- A Hyper-V administrator can select the hypervisor scheduler type that best suits the needs of the VMs deployed on the Hyper-V host. There are two scheduler types from which an administrator can choose: classic and core.
- The classic scheduler uses a round-robin method of scheduling all VMs to run across all virtual processors. The core scheduler ensures that the virtual processors of a VM will always be scheduled on the same core.
- A highly available virtual machine (also known as a clustered virtual machine) allows you to make applications and services highly available simply by installing them on a virtual machine residing on a Hyper-V server configured for high availability.
- Node fairness is a failover cluster feature that helps optimize usage of failover cluster node members. Node fairness attempts to identify Hyper-V nodes that are hosting a disproportionate number of VMs and redistribute VMs to other nodes that are underutilized.
- Windows Server has cluster node and VM states to make highly available VMs more resilient to transient failures. These VM states are unmonitored, isolated, and quarantined.
- Virtual machine monitoring allows you to monitor resources, applications, and services running in highly available VMs. If a resource fails, the cluster node can take actions to recover.
- Guest clustering is different from a highly available or clustered VM in that a guest cluster requires two or more VMs with a guest OS installed and configured for failover clustering.
- Hyper-V Replica periodically replicates changes in a VM to a mirror VM hosted on another Hyper-V server. It works over a regular IP network and can be enabled on standalone servers or servers in a failover cluster.
- Windows Server supports containers, a software environment in which an application can run but is isolated from much of the rest of the operating system and other applications.

- Containers are a type of virtualization, but containers virtualize parts of the operating system, allowing containerized applications to have their own copy of critical OS structures such as the registry, file system, and network configuration while sharing the kernel, the host hardware, and possibly some runtime libraries. This is called namespace isolation.
- Windows Server supports two types of containers. A process isolation container is an application environment in which the processes running in the container share host OS and kernel resources with other Windows Server containers and the host OS, but the container has its own copy of user mode data structures such as the registry, file system, and network configuration. A Hyper-V isolation container is an application environment that provides OS and kernel isolation like a traditional VM but is not managed by Hyper-V Manager.
- Docker is open source software that has been used for years in the Linux environment to implement containers. Microsoft adapted Docker to the Windows environment. Docker is not part of Windows, so it can't be installed as a role or feature; you need to install it using PowerShell package management.
- To deploy a container, you install a base operating system image using the Docker client. The Docker client is the executable file docker.exe that was installed with the Docker package. You install a base operating system image from the Docker Hub repository, which is a collection of Docker images maintained in the cloud.
- After you have downloaded an image, you can create a container by using the `docker run` command. The `docker run` command starts a container based on a specified image and runs a command or application.
- Docker configures the container network using network address translation (NAT). With NAT, a network that uses private IP addresses can access the public Internet. With a NAT network, devices on the host network cannot initiate communication with the container because its IP address is translated by the host computer. Port mapping allows the container host to forward packets for specific applications to containers hosting those applications.
- Resource control is one of the big advantages of using containers to run applications instead of running them directly on the host computer. As with a virtual machine, you can constrain, or limit, how much of a particular resource a container can utilize, including CPU, memory, and block I/O.
- Dockerfile is a feature of Docker in which you specify properties of a container image using a text file called a dockerfile and then use the `docker build` command to create the new image using the specifications in the file.

Key Terms

classic scheduler	layer 2 (L2) bridge network	replica server
container	live migration	shared virtual hard disk (shared VHDX)
core scheduler	logical processor	
Docker	namespace	simultaneous multithreading (SMT)
Dockerfile	namespace isolation	stateless operation
drain on shutdown	nested virtualization	tag
guest clustering	network address translation (NAT)	transparent network
highly available virtual machine	node fairness	VHD Set
hot backup site	physical processor	virtual machine monitoring
Hyper-V isolation container	process isolation container	virtual processor
Hyper-V Replica	recovery point	VM CPU group

Review Questions

1. What do you need to enable on a Hyper-V VM so that the VM can run the Hyper-V server role?
   a. VM CPU groups
   b. Process isolation
   c. Nested virtualization
   d. Multithreading

2. What can you configure on a Hyper-V server that allows you to specify which CPUs on a host can be used by VMs?
   a. VM CPU groups
   b. Process isolation
   c. Nested virtualization
   d. Multithreading

3. How many logical processors are there on a CPU that supports two-segment SMT and has six cores?
   a. 9
   b. 24
   c. 6
   d. 12

4. Which of the following is the start of the command to create a VM CPU group?
   a. `New-CPUGroup -GroupID`
   b. `cpugroups creategroup /GroupID:`
   c. `Create-VMCPUGroup -GroupID`
   d. `addgroup /VMCPU /GroupID:`

5. Which of the following is *not* a benefit of using the core scheduler in Hyper-V?
   a. SMT performance improvement
   b. Consistent VM performance
   c. Faster storage access
   d. Workload isolation

6. What value of the VM property HwThreadCountPerCore means that the VM does not support SMT?
   a. −1
   b. 0
   c. 1
   d. 2

7. Which of the following is true about a clustered virtual machine? (Choose two.)
   a. You need to have shared storage available to the VM's guest OS.
   b. You need two or more host computers running Hyper-V.
   c. All host computers should be members of the same domain.
   d. CSVs aren't recommended for shared storage.

8. If you're using cluster shared volumes for highly available VMs, which of the following is a likely path for storing the VM files?
   a. \\Server\SharedVM
   b. D:\
   c. C:\ClusterStorage
   d. FTP:\\Server

9. After reviewing system performance data, you have noticed that some virtual machines hosted on clustered Hyper-V servers are currently distributed throughout the cluster in an unbalanced configuration. What feature in Windows Server Hyper-V will allow you to optimize your cluster node members for better performance?
   a. Node sync
   b. Node fairness
   c. Performance cluster
   d. VM CPU groups

10. Which of the following VM states, with respect to a clustered Hyper-V node, allows the node to be removed from active membership in the cluster but continue to host the VM role?
    a. Quarantined
    b. Monitored
    c. Isolated
    d. Unmonitored

11. In a Hyper-V server, what specific state will a high-availability VM be placed in if it has lost access to its storage?
    a. Paused-Critical
    b. Isolated
    c. Quarantined
    d. Paused

12. What feature in Hyper-V causes a highly available VM to be live-migrated automatically if the host it's running on is shut down?
    a. Cluster shared volume
    b. Authoritative restore
    c. Dynamic witness
    d. Drain on shutdown

13. Which of the following is true about Hyper-V Replica? (Choose two.)
    a. The Hyper-V servers need to be members of the same domain.
    b. The Hyper-V servers can be located in different sites.
    c. Replication must be configured on the VM.
    d. The Hyper-V servers must be members of a cluster.

14. What do you configure to enable Hyper-V Replica between failover cluster nodes?
    a. Replica Broker
    b. Drain on shutdown
    c. Extended replication
    d. VHD Set

15. Containers only allow an application to see and interact with certain parts of an operating system. Which of the following terms best describes the parts of the OS an application can see and interact with?
    a. Namespace
    b. Container
    c. Isolation
    d. Docker

16. Which of the following is an application environment that provides OS and kernel isolation like a traditional VM but is not managed by Hyper-V Manager?
    a. Process isolation container
    b. Hyper-V isolation container
    c. Nano Server container
    d. Isolated container

17. Which of the following open source software projects has been adapted by Microsoft to implement containers within the Windows environment?
    a. Linux
    b. Hadoop
    c. Vagrant
    d. Docker

18. What specific command can be used to create a container after you have selected and downloaded an image from the Docker Hub repository?
    a. `Create-Container`
    b. `docker run`
    c. `New-Container`
    d. `docker attach`

19. You have recently decided that you would like to delete a Docker container named AppTest. What command will delete the AppTest container after you have verified that the container has been stopped?
    a. `docker rm AppTest`
    b. `docker -del AppTest`
    c. `Delete-Container AppTest`
    d. `Remove-Container AppTest`

20. You are editing and testing an existing container image and have decided you would like to be able to differentiate between multiple versions of the same image. What can be used to do this?
    a. Shortcut
    b. Label
    c. Commit
    d. Tag

21. You have just been assigned the task of configuring your Docker containers to stop using NAT, the default container network configuration. The containers should be able to communicate with devices on the host network without the network addresses having to be translated or sharing the host's MAC address. What type of container network should you implement?
    a. Transparent
    b. Static
    c. Layer 2 (L2) bridge
    d. Dynamic

22. Which of the following options can be run with the `docker run` or `docker create` command to specify the proportion of the CPU a container can use relative to other containers running on the same host?
    a. `--cpu-percent`
    b. `--cpu-shares`
    c. `--cpuset-cpus`
    d. `--cpuset-count`

23. You need to limit the amount of memory a container may use to 3 megabytes. Which of the following options can be run with the `docker run` or `docker create` command to specify that 3 megabytes are the maximum amount of memory the container can use?
    a. `--memory-limit 3m`
    b. `--memory 3m`
    c. `--memory-swap 3m`
    d. `--memory-reservation 3m`

24. What feature of Docker allows you to specify properties of a container image using a text file?
    a. Containerfile
    b. Dockeredit
    c. Dockerfile
    d. Containeredit

25. What should you configure to allow the container host to forward packets for specific applications to containers hosting those applications?
    a. Transparent network
    b. daemon.json
    c. Application tags
    d. Port mapping

Critical Thinking

The following activities give you critical thinking challenges. Case projects offer a scenario with a problem for which you supply a written solution.

Case Projects

Case Project 13-1: Setting Up a Guest Cluster

You have three Hyper-V servers, and you're currently running four VMs on each server for a total of 12 VMs. You want to be sure that if a Hyper-V server fails or you need to take one down for maintenance, the VMs will continue to run. Describe the configuration you plan to use, including options for shared storage.

Case Project 13-2: Configuring a Container Network

You are beginning to implement containers. In your testing, you have used the default network configuration for the containers you have deployed. Now it's time to begin using the containers in your production network. Your physical network is using a variety of IP networks, including some in the range 172.16.0.0/12. You want to use NAT for your container network, but you want to be sure there is no chance of address conflicts between your container networks and physical networks. What should you do?

Solutions to Self-Check Questions

Section 13-1: Nested Virtualization

1. Nested virtualization in Hyper-V is only available on Windows Server 2022 and newer versions of Windows Server. True or False?

    Answer: b. False

    Explanation: Nested virtualization in Hyper-V is supported in Windows 10, Windows Server 2016, and newer versions of each OS.

2. Which of the following is true about nested virtualization?

    Answer: c. The nested VM cannot use dynamic memory.

    Explanation: The VM that is running Hyper-V cannot use dynamic memory while Hyper-V is running. You can enable dynamic memory, but it will have no effect; you must turn off the VM to adjust its memory.

Section 13-2: Configuring VM Groups and Hyper-V Scheduling

3. You create VM CPU groups using Hyper-V Manager. True or False?

    Answer: b. False

    Explanation: VM CPU groups cannot be created or managed using Hyper-V Manager or PowerShell; rather, the Hyper-V Host Compute Service (HCS) is used by way of a command-line utility called cpuGroups.exe.

4. What command displays the CPU topology on a Hyper-V host system?

    Answer: a. CpuGroups GetCpuTopology

    Explanation: Using this command, you can see the CPU topology that shows the number of logical CPUs.

Section 13-3: Implementing High Availability with Hyper-V

5. A highly available virtual machine is a VM that runs on a highly available Hyper-V server. True or False?

    Answer: a. True

    Explanation: A highly available virtual machine (also known as a *clustered virtual machine*) allows you to make applications and services highly available simply by installing them on a virtual machine residing on a Hyper-V server configured for high availability.

6. Which Hyper-V feature will automatically move a VM to another Hyper-V node if the Hyper-V server it's running on is shut down without being paused first?

    Answer: c. Drain on shutdown

    Explanation: The best way to shut down a node in a Hyper-V cluster is to place it in maintenance mode by pausing it and selecting Drain Roles. Windows Server 2012 R2 introduced the drain on shutdown feature, which drains roles automatically and live-migrates the VMs to another cluster node before the Hyper-V server shuts down. Drain on shutdown is enabled by default on Windows Server 2012 R2 and later versions.

Section 13-4: Windows Containers

7. A process isolation container provides both OS and kernel isolation. True or False?

   Answer: b. False

   Explanation: A Hyper-V isolation container provides OS and kernel isolation; a process isolation container shares OS and kernel resources with other containers and the host OS.

8. What command will reconnect to an interactive container?

   Answer: b. `docker attach`

   Explanation: If you exit an interactive container, the container stops; to start and reconnect to the container, use `docker start` *ContainerName* followed by `docker attach` *ContainerName*.

Section 13-5: Managing Windows Containers

9. PowerShell is the primary tool for working with containers. True or False?

   Answer: b. False

   Explanation: Docker is the primary tool for working with containers.

10. What command deletes a docker container?

    Answer: b. `docker rm`

    Explanation: The `docker rm` command removes a docker container from memory. A container must first be stopped, as indicated by the status "Exited" in the `docker ps -a` command, before it can be deleted.

Appendix A

Microsoft Exam AZ-800 Objectives Mapped to Modules

These tables provide a complete list of the latest Microsoft exam AZ-800 certification exam objectives as of February 1, 2023. For your reference, the following sections and tables list each exam objective, the modules and sections that explain the objective, and the percentage of the exam that will cover each certification domain.

Deploy and Manage Active Directory Domain Services (AD DS) in On-Premises and Cloud Environments—30% to 35% of Examination

Deploy and Manage AD DS Domain Controllers

Objective	Module	Section
Deploy and manage domain controllers on-premises	2	The Role of a Directory Service
	2	Installing Active Directory
	5	Configuring Multidomain Environments
	5	Configuring Multiforest Environments
Deploy and manage domain controllers in Azure	5	Working with Domain Controllers in Azure
Deploy read-only domain controllers (RODCs)	5	Configuring Read-Only Domain Controllers
Troubleshoot Flexible Single Master Operation (FSMO) roles	5	Working with Operations Master Roles

Configure and Manage Multisite, Multidomain, and Multiforest Environments

Objective	Module	Section
Configure and manage forest and domain trusts	2	Working with Forests, Trees, and Domains
	5	Active Directory Trusts
Configure and manage AD DS sites	2	Working with Forests, Trees, and Domains
	5	Understanding and Configuring Sites
Configure and manage AD DS replication	2	Working with Forests, Trees, and Domains
	5	Active Directory Replication

Create and Manage AD DS Security Principals

Objective	Module	Section
Create and manage AD DS users and groups	3	Managing User Accounts
Manage users and groups in multidomain and multiforest scenarios	3	Managing User Accounts
	3	Managing Group Accounts
Implement group managed service accounts (gMSAs)	3	Working with Service Accounts
Join Windows Server to AD DS, Azure AD DS, and Azure AD	3	Working with Computer Accounts

Implement and Manage Hybrid Identities

Objective	Module	Section
Implement Azure AD Connect	3	Using Active Directory in a Hybrid Environment
Manage Azure AD Connect Synchronization	3	Using Active Directory in a Hybrid Environment
Implement Azure AD Connect cloud sync	3	Using Active Directory in a Hybrid Environment
Integrate Azure AD, AD DS, and Azure AD DS	3	Using Active Directory in a Hybrid Environment
Manage Azure AD DS	3	Using Active Directory in a Hybrid Environment
Manage Azure AD Connect Health	3	Using Active Directory in a Hybrid Environment
Manage authentication in on-premises and hybrid environments	3	Using Active Directory in a Hybrid Environment
Configure and manage AD DS passwords	3	Using Active Directory in a Hybrid Environment
	3	Managing User Accounts

Manage Windows Server by Using Domain-Based Group Policies

Objective	Module	Section
Implement Group Policy in AD DS	2	Introducing Group Policies
	4	Group Policy Objects
	4	Group Policy Settings
	4	Working with Administrative Templates
	4	Group Policy Processing
Implement Group Policy Preferences in AD DS	2	Introducing Group Policies
	4	Configuring Group Policy Preferences
Implement Group Policy in Azure AD DS	4	Implementing Group Policy in Azure AD DS

Manage Windows Servers and Workloads in a Hybrid Environment—10% to 15% of Examination

Manage Windows Servers in a Hybrid Environment

Objective	Module	Section
Deploy a Windows Admin Center gateway server	6	Using Windows Admin Center
Configure a target machine for Windows Admin Center	6	Using Windows Admin Center
Configure PowerShell remoting	6	Managing Servers Remotely
Configure CredSSP or Kerberos delegation for second-hop remoting	6	Managing Servers Remotely
Configure JEA for PowerShell Remoting	6	Managing Servers Remotely

Manage Windows Servers and Workloads by Using Azure Services

Objective	Module	Section
Manage Windows Servers by using Azure Arc	6	Managing Windows Servers with Azure Services
Assign Azure Policy Guest Configuration	6	Managing Windows Servers with Azure Services
Deploy Azure services using Azure Virtual Machine extensions on non-Azure machines	6	Managing Windows Servers with Azure Services
Manage updates for Windows machines	6	Managing Windows Servers with Azure Services
Integrate Windows Servers with log analytics	6	Managing Windows Servers with Azure Services
Integrate Windows Servers with Azure Security Center	6	Managing Windows Servers with Azure Services
Manage IaaS virtual machines (VMs) in Azure that run Windows Server	6	Managing Windows Servers with Azure Services
Implement Azure Automation for hybrid workloads	6	Managing Windows Servers with Azure Services
Create runbooks to automate tasks on target VMs	6	Managing Windows Servers with Azure Services
Implement DSC to prevent configuration drift in IaaS machines	6	Managing Servers with Desired State Configuration

Manage Virtual Machines and Containers— 15% to 20% of Examination

Manage Hyper-V and Guest Virtual Machines

Objective	Module	Section
Enable VM enhanced session mode	12	Creating Virtual Machines in Hyper-V
	12	Managing Virtual Machines
Manage VMs using PowerShell remoting, PowerShell Direct, and HVC.exe	12	Managing Virtual Machines
Configure nested virtualization	13	Nested Virtualization
Configure VM memory	12	Creating Virtual Machines in Hyper-V
	12	Managing Virtual Machines
Configure Integration Services	12	Managing Virtual Machines
Configure Discrete Device Assignment	12	Managing Virtual Machines
Configure VM resource groups	13	Configuring VM Groups and Hyper-V Scheduling
Configure VM CPU groups	13	Configuring VM Groups and Hyper-V Scheduling
Configure hypervisor scheduling types	13	Configuring VM Groups and Hyper-V Scheduling
Manage VM checkpoints	12	Managing Virtual Machines
Implement high availability for virtual machines	13	Implementing High Availability with Hyper-V
Manage VHD and VHDX files	10	Working with Virtual Disks
	12	Working with Virtual Hard Disks
Configure a Hyper-V network adapter	12	Hyper-V Virtual Networks
Configure NIC teaming	12	Advanced Virtual Network Configuration
Configure Hyper-V switches	12	Hyper-V Virtual Networks

Create and Manage Containers

Objective	Module	Section
Create Windows Server container images	13	Windows Containers
Manage Windows Server container images	13	Managing Windows Containers
Configure container networking	13	Managing Windows Containers
Manage container instances	13	Managing Windows Containers

Manage Azure Virtual Machines That Run Windows Server

Objective	Module	Section
Manage data disks	12	Managing Windows Server VMs on Azure
Resize Azure virtual machines	12	Managing Windows Server VMs on Azure
Configure continuous delivery for Azure virtual machines	12	This feature is deprecated as of March 31, 2023, and is not covered
Configure connections to VMs	12	Managing Windows Server VMs on Azure
Manage Azure virtual machine network configuration	12	Managing Windows Server VMs on Azure

Implement and Manage an On-Premises and Hybrid Networking Infrastructure— 15% to 20% of Examination

Implement On-Premises and Hybrid Name Resolution

Objective	Module	Section
Integrate DNS with AD DS	7	Introduction to Domain Name System
	7	Installing and Configuring DNS
Create and manage zones and records	7	Installing and Configuring DNS
	7	Creating DNS Resource Records
Configure DNS forwarding/conditional forwarding	7	Configuring DNS Server Settings
Integrate Windows Server DNS with Azure DNS private zones	7	Azure DNS
Implement DNSSEC	7	Configuring DNS Security

Manage IP Addressing in On-Premises and Hybrid Scenarios

Objective	Module	Section
Implement and manage IPAM	8	IP Address Management
Implement and configure the DHCP server role (on-premises only)	8	An Overview of Dynamic Host Configuration Protocol
	8	Installing and Configuring DHCP
Resolve IP address issues in hybrid environments	8	IP Addressing in Hybrid Environments
Create and manage scopes	8	Installing and Configuring DHCP
	8	DHCP Server Options
Create and manage IP reservations	8	Installing and Configuring DHCP
Implement DHCP high availability	8	DHCP High Availability

Implement On-Premises and Hybrid Network Connectivity

Objective	Module	Section
Implement and manage the Remote Access role	9	The Remote Access Role
Implement and manage Azure Network Adapter	9	Implementing Azure Networking
Implement and manage Azure Extended Network	9	Implementing Azure Networking
Implement and manage Network Policy Server role	9	Network Policy Server Overview
Implement Web Application Proxy	9	Implementing Web Application Proxy
Implement Azure Relay	9	Implementing Azure Networking
Implement site-to-site virtual private network (VPN)	9	The Remote Access Role
Implement Azure Virtual WAN	9	Implementing Azure Networking
Implement Azure AD Application Proxy	9	Implementing Azure Networking

Manage Storage and File Services— 15% to 20% of Examination

Configure and Manage Azure File Sync

Objective	Module	Section
Create Azure File Sync service	11	Azure File Sync
Create sync groups	11	Azure File Sync
Create cloud endpoints	11	Azure File Sync
Register servers	11	Azure File Sync
Create server endpoints	11	Azure File Sync
Configure cloud tiering	11	Azure File Sync
Monitor File Sync	11	Azure File Sync
Migrate DFS to Azure File Sync	11	Azure File Sync

Configure and Manage Windows Server File Shares

Objective	Module	Section
Configure Windows Server file share access	10	File Sharing
Configure file screens	10	Using File Server Resource Manager
Configure File Server Resource Manager (FSRM) quotas	10	Using File Server Resource Manager
Configure BranchCache	10	Using BranchCache
Implement and configure Distributed File System (DFS)	10	Using Distributed File System

Configure Windows Server Storage

Objective	Module	Section
Configure disks and volumes	10	An Overview of Server Storage
	10	Configuring Local Disks
	10	Working with Virtual Disks
Configure and manage Storage Spaces	11	Storage Spaces
Configure and manage Storage Replica	11	Storage Replica
Configure data deduplication	11	Implementing Data Deduplication
Configure SMB Direct	11	SMB Direct and Storage QoS
Configure Storage Quality of Service (QoS)	11	SMB Direct and Storage QoS
Configure file systems	10	Configuring Local Disks
	10	Securing Access to Files with Permissions

Glossary

A record   A resource record in a DNS zone that consists of a hostname and an IPv4 address. It is also called a host record.

AAAA record   A resource record in a DNS zone that consists of a hostname and an IPv6 address. It is also called a host record.

access-based enumeration (ABE)   A feature of a file share that shows only files and folders to which a user has at least Read permission.

access client   A user or device attempting access to a network.

access control entry (ACE)   An entry in a discretionary access control list (DACL) that includes a security principal object and the object's assigned permissions. *See also* discretionary access control list (DACL).

Active Directory   The Windows directory service that enables administrators to create and manage users and groups, set network-wide user and computer policies, manage security, and organize network resources.

Active Directory Administrative Center (ADAC)   A GUI tool for managing Active Directory objects and accounts that is built on top of Windows PowerShell.

Active Directory Domain Services (AD DS)   The Windows directory service that enables administrators to create and manage users and groups, set network-wide user and computer policies, manage security, and organize network resources.

Active Directory partition   A special file that Active Directory uses to store domain information.

Active Directory replication   The transfer of information between all domain controllers to make sure they have consistent and up-to-date information.

Active Directory Users and Computers (ADUC)   A GUI tool for managing Active Directory objects and accounts.

active screening   A type of file screen that prevents users from saving unauthorized files.

AD Application Proxy   An Azure technology that provides remote access and single sign-on to on-premises and Azure web applications.

administrative shares   Hidden shares created by Windows that are available only to members of the Administrators group; they include the root of each volume, the \Windows folder, and IPC$. Hidden shares' names end with a dollar sign.

administrative template files   XML-formatted text files (with an .admx extension) that define policies in the Administrative Templates folder in a GPO. Custom ADMX files can also be created.

ADMX central store   A centralized location for maintaining ADMX files so that when an ADMX file is modified from one domain controller, all DCs receive the updated file.

Aggregated policy   A storage QoS policy that applies the minimum and maximum IOPS values to a set of virtual disks working as a whole.

application directory partition   An Active Directory partition that applications and services use to store information that benefits from automatic Active Directory replication and security.

Application Proxy connector   An Azure AD Application Proxy component that runs on-premises and works with the Application Proxy service to provide secure access to the on-premises web application.

Application Proxy service   An Azure AD Application Proxy component that runs in the Azure cloud and allows remote users who have authenticated with Azure AD to access the on-premises web application without requiring on-premises open firewall ports.

assigned application   An application package made available to users via Group Policy that places a shortcut to the application in the Start screen. The application is installed automatically if a user tries to run it or opens a document associated with it. If the assigned application applies to a computer account, the application is installed the next time Windows boots.

attribute value   Information stored in each attribute. *See also* schema attribute.

authentication   A process that confirms a user's identity; the account is assigned permissions and rights that authorize the user to access resources and perform certain tasks on the computer or domain.

authoritative server   A DNS server that holds a complete copy of a zone's resource records (typically a primary or secondary zone).

automatic disk   An option in Storage Spaces that attempts to use the optimal number of physical disks (columns) when creating a virtual disk.

automatic site coverage   A feature in which each domain controller advertises itself by registering SRV records in DNS in sites that don't have a DC if the advertising DC has the lowest-cost connection to the site.

Azure Active Directory (AAD)   An Azure service for managing authentication and access to applications and other resources in the Azure cloud.

Azure Active Directory DS (AADDS)   An Azure service that is a close cousin to on-premises Windows Active Directory, with support for Group Policy, organizational units (OUs), Kerberos, and domain joining, among other features typically found on Windows Active Directory.

Azure AD Connect   A tool that you install on an on-premises Windows Active Directory domain member or domain controller and that synchronizes Windows Active Directory users, groups, and contacts with Azure AD.

Azure AD Connect cloud sync   A more lightweight version of Azure AD Connect sync because the configuration and provisioning information is done in the cloud rather than primarily on the on-premises servers. *See* Azure AD Connect.

Azure DNS zone   A DNS zone created in Azure that provides name resolution for public resources.

Azure extended network   An Azure migration feature that allows you to extend an on-premises subnet into an Azure VNet while allowing the on-premises servers to keep their existing private IP addresses.

Azure file share   A named location in an Azure storage account that stores files accessible to Azure users and that can be mounted on a Windows server or synced to a server using Azure File Sync.

Azure File Sync   An Azure service that provides an organization with a cloud-based extension to its on-premises Windows Server file sharing.

Azure Network Adapter   An Azure technology that allows an on-premises server to communicate with an Azure VNet using a point-to-site VPN connection.

Azure private DNS zone   A DNS zone created in Azure that provides name resolution for internal Azure resources with private IP addresses, such as Azure VMs.

Azure Relay   An Azure network service that allows you to make your on-premises network services available on the public cloud without firewall configuration changes or VPN configuration.

Azure Storage Sync agent   The software installed on an on-premises server that works with Azure File Sync to synchronize files between the server and an Azure file share.

Azure Virtual Network (VNet)   An Azure technology that provides the basis for communication between Azure resources on the same VNet, between resources on different VNets, and between your on-premises network and Azure resources.

Azure Virtual WAN   An Azure networking service that can act as a central hub for all your Azure network connections, including VNet to VNet, site-to-site and point-to-site VPNs, ExpressRoute VPN, and third-party branch office connectivity.

B

backplane   A connection system that uses a printed circuit board instead of traditional cables to carry signals.

basic disk   A traditional Windows or DOS disk arrangement in which the disk is partitioned into primary and extended partitions. A basic disk can't hold volumes spanning multiple disks or be part of a RAID.

Bastion host   A method for connecting to an Azure VM using the VM's private IP address with no requirement for RDP; the VM user interface is rendered in a standard web browser window.

batch file   A text file containing a series of commands that's saved with a `.bat` extension.

block-level replication   A Windows Server feature that provides file replication for individual data blocks between storage devices, primarily for the purpose of fault tolerance and disaster recovery.

boot volume   The volume where the \Windows folder is located; it is usually the C drive, but it doesn't have to be. Also referred to as the "boot partition."

BranchCache   A file-sharing technology that allows computers at a branch office to cache files retrieved from a central server across a WAN link.

bridgehead server   A DC at a site that the Inter-Site Topology Generator designates to replicate a directory partition with other sites.

built-in user account   A user account created by Windows automatically during installation.

C

caching-only DNS server   A DNS server with no zones. Its sole job is to field DNS queries, send iterative queries to upstream DNS servers, or send requests to forwarders, and then cache the results.

centralized topology   An IPAM deployment option that has a single IPAM server for the entire enterprise. *See also* IP Address Management (IPAM).

certificate-based authentication   An authentication method that uses a certificate instead of a password to establish an entity's identity.

certification authority (CA)   An entity that issues digital certificates used for authentication.

Challenge Handshake Authentication Protocol (CHAP)   An authentication protocol that uses a series of challenges and responses to verify a client's identity.

checkpoint   A partial copy of a virtual machine made at a specific moment; it is used to restore the VM to its state when the checkpoint was taken. Also called a snapshot.

child domain   A domain that shares at least the top-level and second-level domain name structure as an existing domain in the forest; also called a subdomain.

classic scheduler   The default scheduler for all Windows Server versions from the inception of Hyper-V in Windows Server 2008 through Windows Server 2016; it uses a round-robin method of scheduling VMs to run on all virtual processors across the system.

cloud computing   A collection of technologies for abstracting the details of how applications, storage, network resources, and other computing resources are delivered to users.

cloud endpoint   A component of a sync group that specifies the Azure file share an on-premises server syncs with. *See also* sync group.

CNAME record   A record containing an alias for another record that enables you to refer to the same resource with different names yet maintain only one host record.

column   A reference to the number of physical disks a virtual disk is using.

conditional forwarder   A DNS server to which other DNS servers send requests targeted for a specific domain.

configuration drift   A process that occurs when a server's configuration is altered over time, whether accidentally or on purpose, and the change is not officially sanctioned by administration.

configuration partition   An Active Directory partition that stores configuration information that can affect the entire forest, such as details on how domain controllers should replicate with one another.

conflict detection   A DHCP server property that causes the DHCP server to attempt to ping an IP address before it's offered to a client to make sure the address isn't already in use.

connection object   An Active Directory object created in Active Directory Sites and Services that defines the connection parameters between two replication partners.

constrained delegation   A type of delegation that limits delegation to specific services running on specific computers. *See also* Kerberos delegation.

contact   An Active Directory object that usually represents a person for informational purposes only, much like an address book entry.

container   A software environment in which an application can run but is isolated from much of the rest of the operating system and other applications.

content information   A message transferred from a BranchCache server to a client that indicates to the client where the file can be retrieved from the cache in the branch office. *See also* BranchCache.

core scheduler   A Hyper-V scheduler alternative to the classic scheduler that ensures the virtual processors of a VM will always be scheduled on the same core.

Credential Security Support Provider (CredSSP)   An authentication provider tool that caches credentials on a remote server so they can be used to connect to a second-hop server.

D

data deduplication A technology that reduces the amount of storage necessary to store an organization's data.

Dedicated policy A storage QoS policy that applies minimum and maximum values to virtual disks; if a Dedicated policy with the same limits is applied to five virtual disks, each disk is guaranteed the minimum and maximum IOPS values.

delegated administrator account A user account that has local administrative rights and permissions to the RODC, similar to members of the local Administrators group on a member computer or standalone computer.

delegation of control In the context of Active Directory, the process of a user with higher security privileges assigning authority to perform certain tasks to a user with lesser security privileges; it is typically used to give a user administrative permission for an OU.

Delegation Signer (DS) A DNSSEC record that holds the name of a delegated zone and is used to verify delegated child zones. *See also* Domain Name System Security Extension (DNSSEC).

demand-dial interface A network connection that is used to establish the VPN connection whenever traffic from the internal network has a destination address of the other network to which you are connecting.

Desired State Configuration (DSC) A feature that allows you to manage and maintain servers with simple declarative statements.

DHCP failover A feature in Windows Server that allows two DHCP servers to share the pool of IP addresses in a scope, giving both servers access to all addresses in the pool.

DHCP filters A DHCP server feature that allows administrators to restrict which computers on a network are leased IP addresses.

DHCP name protection A feature in DHCP that prevents name squatting by non-Windows computers by using a DHCP resource record called Dynamic Host Configuration Identifier (DHCID). *See also* name squatting.

DHCP policies A feature in Windows Server that gives administrators more fine-tuned control over IP address lease options through the use of conditions based on criteria.

DHCP relay agent A device that listens for broadcast DHCPDISCOVER and DHCPREQUEST messages and forwards them to a DHCP server on another subnet.

DHCP scope A pool of IP addresses and other IP configuration parameters from which a DHCP server leases addresses to DHCP clients.

DHCP server authorization The process of enabling a DHCP server in a domain environment to prevent rogue DHCP servers from operating on the network.

differencing disk A dynamically expanding virtual disk that uses a parent/child relationship; the parent disk is a dynamically expanding or fixed-size disk with an OS installed and possibly some applications and data. The differencing disk is a child of the parent. Changes are made only to the differencing disk; the parent disk remains unaltered.

direct-attached storage (DAS) A storage medium directly connected to the server using it. DAS differs from local storage in that it includes externally connected HDDs in an enclosure with a power supply.

directory partition A section of an Active Directory database stored on a domain controller's hard drive. These sections are managed by different processes and replicated to other domain controllers in an Active Directory network.

directory service A database that stores information about a computer network and includes features for retrieving and managing that information.

Directory Services Restore Mode (DSRM) A boot mode used to perform restore operations on Active Directory if it becomes corrupted or parts of it are deleted accidentally.

Discrete Device Assignment (DDA) A feature in Windows Server Hyper-V that gives a VM exclusive access to hardware devices on the host computer.

discretionary access control list (DACL) A list of security principals; each has permissions that define access to an object. *See also* security principal.

disk drive A physical component with a disk interface connector (such as SATA or SCSI) and a power connector.

distributed cache mode   A BranchCache mode of operation in which cached data is distributed among client computers in the branch office. *See also* BranchCache.

Distributed File System (DFS)   A role service under the File and Storage Services role that enables you to group shares from different servers into a single logical share called a namespace.

distributed topology   An IPAM deployment option that places an IPAM server at every site in a network. *See also* IP Address Management (IPAM).

distribution group   A group type used when you want to group users together, mainly for sending emails to several people at once with an Active Directory–integrated email application, such as Microsoft Exchange.

DNS amplification attack   A type of DDoS attack that uses public DNS servers to overwhelm a target with DNS responses by sending DNS queries with spoofed IP addresses.

DNS-based Authentication of Named Entities (DANE)   A feature starting with Windows Server 2016 that provides information about the certification authority (CA) used by your domain when a client is requesting DNS information for your domain.

DNS cache locking   A DNS security feature that allows you to control whether data in the DNS cache can be overwritten.

DNS cache poisoning   An attack on DNS servers in which false data is introduced into the DNS server cache, causing the server to return incorrect IP addresses.

DNS client   A computer making a DNS query.

DNSKEY   The public key for the zone that DNS resolvers use to verify the digital signature in Resource Record Signature (RRSIG) records.

DNS namespace   The entire DNS tree that defines the structure of the names used to identify resources in network domains. It consists of a root name (defined as a period), top-level domains, second-level domains, one or more subdomains (optional), and hostnames, all of which are separated by periods.

DNS resolver   *See* DNS client.

DNS socket pool   A pool of port numbers used by a DNS server for DNS queries to protect against DNS cache poisoning. *See also* DNS cache poisoning.

Docker   Open source software that is used in the Linux and Windows environments to implement containers.

Dockerfile   A feature of Docker in which you specify properties of a container image using a text file called a dockerfile.

domain   The core structural unit of Active Directory; it contains OUs and represents administrative, security, and policy boundaries.

domain controller   A Windows server that has Active Directory installed and is responsible for allowing client computers access to domain resources.

domain directory partition   An Active Directory partition that contains all objects in a domain, including users, groups, computers, and OUs.

domain GPO   A Group Policy object stored in Active Directory on domain controllers. It can be linked to a site, a domain, or an OU and affect users and computers whose accounts are stored in those containers.

domain local group   A group scope that's the main security principal recommended for assigning rights and permissions to domain resources.

Domain Name System (DNS)   A distributed hierarchical database composed mainly of computer name and IP address pairs.

Domain Name System Security Extension (DNSSEC)   A suite of features and protocols for validating DNS server responses.

domain naming master   A forest-wide FSMO role that manages adding, removing, and renaming domains in the forest.

domain user account   A user account created in Active Directory that provides a single logon for users to access all resources in the domain for which they have been authorized.

downlevel user logon name   The user logon name field defined in a user account object that's used for backward compatibility with OSs and applications that don't recognize the UPN format.

drain on shutdown   A feature in Windows Server Hyper-V that drains roles automatically and live-migrates VMs to another cluster node before the Hyper-V server shuts down.

dual parity space   A parity space that can recover from simultaneous failure of two disks.

dynamic disk   A disk arrangement that can hold up to 128 volumes, including spanned volumes, striped volumes, and RAID volumes.

Dynamic DNS (DDNS)   A DNS name-registering process whereby computers in the domain can register or update their own DNS records.

Dynamic Host Configuration Protocol (DHCP)   A component of the TCP/IP protocol suite used to assign an IP address to a host automatically from a defined pool of addresses.

Dynamic Memory   A Hyper-V feature that allows an administrator to set startup, minimum, and maximum memory allocation values for each VM.

dynamically expanding disk   A virtual hard disk in which the .vhd file is very small when created but can expand as additional space is needed, up to the maximum size specified when creating the disk.

E

effective access   The access a security principal has to a file system object when taking sharing permissions, NTFS permissions, and group memberships into account. *See also* security principal.

effective permissions   The combination of permissions assigned to an account from explicit and inherited permissions; they determine an account's effective access to an object. *See also* effective access.

emulated drivers   Legacy drivers installed on a VM that are used when Integration Services aren't installed.

enclosure awareness   A resiliency feature of Storage Spaces that associates each copy of file data with a particular JBOD enclosure so that if an enclosure goes offline, the data is retained in another enclosure.

Enhanced Session mode   A Hyper-V feature that provides improved interaction and device redirection between the host computer and the guest OS.

exclusion range   A range of IP addresses in the scope that the DHCP server doesn't lease to clients.

explicit permission   A permission assigned by adding a user's account to an object's DACL.

ExpressRoute   A technology that provides a secure connection between your on-premises datacenter and the Microsoft Azure virtual network. ExpressRoute does not use the public Internet and therefore requires a third-party provider that supports ExpressRoute.

extended partition   A division of disk space on a basic disk that must be divided into logical drives; it can't be marked as active and can't hold the Windows system volume.

Extensible Authentication Protocol (EAP)   A certificate-based authentication method.

extension   An item in a Group Policy Object (GPO) that allows an administrator to configure a policy setting.

external trust   A one-way or two-way nontransitive trust between two domains that aren't in the same forest.

external virtual switch   A virtual switch in which one of the host's physical network adapters is bound to the virtual network switch, allowing virtual machines to access a LAN connected to the host.

F

failover   The ability of a server to recover from network hardware failure by having redundant hardware that can immediately take over for a device failure.

file and folder permissions   The permissions that give network users and interactive users fine-grained access control over folders and files.

file group   A list of the types of files that define a file screen. *See also* file screen.

file screen   A part of File Server Resource Manager that enables you to monitor and control the types of files allowed on the server.

File Server Resource Manager (FSRM)   A role service that has services and management tools for monitoring storage space, managing quotas, controlling the types of files that users can store on a server, creating storage reports, and classifying and managing files.

file system   The method and format an OS uses to store, locate, and retrieve files from electronic storage media.

filtered attribute set   A collection of attribute data configured on the schema master; it is used to specify domain objects that aren't replicated to RODCs, thereby increasing the security of sensitive information.

fixed provisioning   A method of creating virtual disks that allocates all space for the virtual disk from the storage pool immediately.

fixed-size disk   A virtual hard disk in which the disk's full size is allocated on the host system when it's created.

Flexible Single Master Operation (FSMO) role   A specialized domain controller task that handles operations that can affect the entire domain or forest. Only one domain controller can be assigned a particular FSMO role.

folder redirection   A Group Policy feature that allows an administrator to set policies that redirect one or more folders in a user's profile directory.

folder target   A UNC path that points to a shared folder hosted on a server.

forest   A collection of one or more Active Directory trees. A forest can consist of a single tree with a single domain, or it can contain several trees, each with a hierarchy of parent and child domains.

forest root domain   The first domain created in a new forest.

forest trust   A trust that provides a one-way or two-way transitive trust between forests, which enables security principals in one forest to access resources in any domain in another forest.

forest-wide authentication   A property of a forest trust for granting users in a trusted forest access to the trusting forest.

formatting   The process of preparing a disk with a file system used to organize and store files.

forward lookup zone (FLZ)   A DNS zone containing records that translate names to IP addresses, such as A, AAAA, and MX records. It's named after the domain whose resource records it contains.

forwarder   A DNS server to which other DNS servers send requests they can't resolve themselves.

fully qualified domain name (FQDN)   The full domain name for a host that specifically identifies it within the hierarchy of the Domain Name System. The FQDN includes all parts of the name, including the top-level domain.

G

global catalog partition   An Active Directory partition that stores the global catalog, which is a partial replica of all objects in the forest. It contains the most commonly accessed object attributes to facilitate object searches and user logons across domains.

global catalog (GC) server   A DC configured to hold the global catalog. Every forest must have at least one GC server. GCs facilitate domain-wide and forest-wide searches and logons across domains, and they hold universal group membership information.

global group   A group scope used mainly to group users from the same domain who have similar access and rights requirements. A global group's members can be user accounts and other global groups from the same domain. *See also* group scope.

global virtual network peering   A type of virtual network peering in which VNets are connected across different regions. *See also* virtual network peering.

glue A record   An A record used to resolve the name in an NS record to its IP address.

GPO enforcement   A setting on a GPO that forces inheritance of settings on all child objects in the GPO's scope, even if a GPO with conflicting settings is linked to a container at a deeper level.

GPO filtering   A method used to change the default inheritance settings of a GPO.

GPO scope   A combination of GPO linking, inheritance, and filtering that defines which objects are affected by the settings in a GPO.

group managed service account (gMSA)   A specially configured managed service account that provides the same functions as an MSA but can be managed across multiple servers. *See also* managed service account (MSA).

Group Policy Container (GPC)   A GPO component that's an Active Directory object stored in the System\Policies folder. The GPC stores GPO properties and status information but no actual policy settings.

Group Policy Object (GPO)   A list of settings that administrators use to configure user and computer operating environments remotely through Active Directory.

group policy preferences   A feature of Group Policy that contains settings organized into categories, which enables administrators to set up a baseline computing environment yet still allows users to make changes to configured settings.

Group Policy provisioning   A method of provisioning IPAM that uses the Group Policy tool to perform tasks such as creating security groups, setting firewall rules, and creating shares for each IPAM-managed server. *See also* IP Address Management (IPAM).

Group Policy Template (GPT)   A GPO component that's stored as a set of files in the SYSVOL share. It contains all the policy settings that make up a GPO as well as related files, such as scripts.

group scope   A property of a group that determines the reach of a group's application in a domain or a forest—for example, which security principals in a forest can be group members and to which forest resources a group can be assigned rights or permissions.

group type   A property of a group that defines it as a security group or a distribution group.

guest clustering   A clustering feature that requires two or more VMs with a guest OS installed and configured for failover clustering; the failover clustering occurs in the VM's guest OS.

guest OS   The operating system running in a virtual machine installed on a host computer. *See* virtual machine (VM).

GUID Partitioning Table (GPT)   A disk-partitioning method that supports volume sizes up to 18 exabytes.

H

hard quotas   Limits on the amount of storage that users have on a volume or in a folder; hard quotas prevent users from saving files if their files in the target folder already meet or exceed the quota limit.

hash   A process that takes a string of characters, such as a password, and runs them through a mathematical formula to create a new string of characters. There is no encryption key involved, so a hash cannot be reverse-encrypted.

highly available virtual machine   A virtual machine that allows you to make applications and services highly available by installing them on a VM residing on a Hyper-V server configured for high availability.

host computer   The physical computer on which virtualization software is installed and virtual machines run.

host record   A resource record in a DNS zone that consists of a hostname and an IP address. It is also called an A record or AAAA record depending on whether the IP address is IPv4 or IPv6.

hosted cache mode   A BranchCache mode of operation in which cached data is stored on one or more file servers in the branch office. *See also* BranchCache.

hostname   An assigned name associated with an IP address, so that when a client looks up the name *www.microsoft.com*, for example, the DNS server returns an IP address.

hot backup site   A location that duplicates much of the main site's IT infrastructure and can be switched to if a disaster occurs at the main site.

hot spare disk   An option for a physical disk in Storage Spaces that allows the disk to sit idle until it is needed to repair a volume due to disk failure.

hot standby mode   A DHCP failover mode in which one server is assigned as the active server to provide DHCP services to clients and the other server is placed in standby mode. *See also* DHCP failover.

hybrid cloud   The extension of private cloud resources into the public cloud with common management tools.

hybrid topology   An IPAM deployment option that has a single IPAM server collecting information from all managed servers in the enterprise and has IPAM servers at key branch locations. *See also* IP Address Management (IPAM).

Hyper-V isolation container   An application environment that provides OS and kernel isolation like a traditional VM but is not managed by Hyper-V Manager.

Hyper-V Replica   A feature in Windows Server Hyper-V that periodically replicates changes in a VM to a mirror VM hosted on another Hyper-V server.

hypervisor   The virtualization software component that creates and monitors the virtual hardware environment, which allows multiple virtual machines to share physical hardware resources.

I

infrastructure as a service (IaaS)   A category of cloud computing in which a company can use a provider's computing power, storage, and infrastructure services as its needs demand; IaaS is also called "hosted infrastructure."

infrastructure master   A domain-wide FSMO role that's responsible for making sure changes made to object names in one domain are updated in references to these objects in other domains.

inherited permission   A permission that comes from an object's parent instead of being assigned explicitly. *See also* explicit permission.

Install from Media (IFM)   An option when installing a DC in an existing domain; much of the Active Directory database contents are copied to the new DC from media created from an existing DC.

Integrated Scripting Environment (ISE)   A PowerShell development environment that helps in creating PowerShell scripts.

Integration Services   A software package installed on a VM's guest OS that includes enhanced drivers for the guest OS and improves performance and functionality for IDE and SCSI storage devices, network interfaces, and mouse and video devices. It also integrates the VM with the host OS better to provide services such as data exchange, time synchronization, and OS shutdown.

internal virtual switch   A virtual switch that isn't bound to any of the host's physical NICs. However, a host virtual NIC is bound to the internal virtual switch, which allows virtual machines and the host computer to communicate with one another, but VMs can't access the physical network.

intersite replication   An Active Directory replication that occurs between two or more sites.

intrasite replication   An Active Directory replication between domain controllers in the same site.

IP Address Management (IPAM)   A feature in Windows Server that enables an administrator to manage the IP address space; IPAM has monitoring, auditing, and reporting functions to help manage DHCP and DNS.

IP address space   An IP network specified in CIDR notation, such as 10.99.0.0/16. The defined address space determines how many addresses are available to assign to devices.

IPAM client   A Windows computer with the IPAM management console installed; typically used for remote management. *See also* IP Address Management (IPAM).

IPAM server   A Windows Server member server with the IPAM Server feature installed. *See also* IP Address Management (IPAM).

item-level targeting   A feature of group policy preferences that allows an administrator to target specific users or computers based on criteria.

iterative query   A type of DNS query to which a DNS server responds with the best information it has to satisfy the query. The DNS server doesn't query additional DNS servers in an attempt to resolve the query.

J

JEA endpoint   An administrative paradigm that represents a set of users, a list of tasks they can perform, and resources to which they have access; it is defined by creating a PowerShell session configuration file. *See also* Just Enough Administration (JEA).

just a bunch of disks (JBOD)   A disk arrangement in which two or more disks are abstracted to appear as a single disk to the OS but aren't arranged in a specific RAID configuration.

Just Enough Administration (JEA)   A technology that allows administrators to delegate administrative tasks to other personnel without granting excessive privileges. JEA leverages the principle of least privilege, which states that users and administrators should be given sufficient rights and permissions to perform their jobs, but no more than that. *See also* principle of least privilege.

K

Kerberos constrained delegation   A Windows authentication feature that allows an application running on one server to access resources hosted on a remote server.

Kerberos delegation   A feature of the Kerberos authentication protocol that allows a service to impersonate a client, relieving the client from having to authenticate to more than one service.

key-signing key (KSK)   A DNSSEC key that has a private and public key associated with it. The private key is used to sign all DNSKEY records and the public key is used as a trust anchor for validating DNS responses. *See also* Domain Name System Security Extension (DNSSEC).

Knowledge Consistency Checker (KCC)   A process that runs on every domain controller to determine the replication topology.

L

layer 2 (L2) bridge network   A network that is similar to a transparent network, but the container shares a MAC address with the container host.

leaf object   A type of Active Directory object that doesn't contain other objects and usually represents a security account, network resource, or Group Policy Object (GPO).

lease duration   A parameter of a DHCP IP address lease that specifies how long a DHCP client can keep an address.

lease renewal   The process of a DHCP client renewing its IP address lease by using unicast DHCPREQUEST messages.

Lightweight Directory Access Protocol (LDAP)   A protocol that runs over TCP/IP and is designed to facilitate access to directory services and directory objects. It's based on a suite of protocols called X.500, developed by the International Telecommunications Union.

live migration   An application or service installed on two or more servers participating in a failover cluster; also called a clustered service.

load balancing   A feature of NIC teaming that distributes traffic between two or more interfaces, providing an increase in overall network throughput a server is able to maintain.

load balancing and failover (LBFO)   A network interface configuration that allows multiple network interfaces to work in tandem to provide increased bandwidth, load balancing, and fault tolerance. Also called *NIC teaming*.

load-balancing mode   The default DHCP failover mode, in which both DHCP servers participate in address leasing at the same time from a shared pool of addresses. *See also* DHCP failover.

local configuration manager (LCM)   A configuration manager responsible for sending (pushing) and receiving (pulling) configurations, applying configurations, monitoring, and reporting discrepancies between the desired state and current state of a server.

local GPO   A Group Policy Object stored on local computers that can be edited by the Group Policy Object Editor snap-in.

local group   A group created in the local SAM database on a member server or workstation or a standalone computer.

local storage   Storage media with a direct and exclusive connection to the computer's system board through a disk controller.

local user account   A user account defined on a local computer that's authorized to access resources only on that computer. Local user accounts are mainly used on standalone computers or in a workgroup network with computers that aren't part of an Active Directory domain.

logical processor   A processing unit within a physical processor, determined by the number of cores and threads within the physical processor.

loopback policy processing   A Group Policy setting that applies user settings based on the GPO whose scope the logon computer (the one the user is signing in to) falls into.

M

managed policy setting   A type of group policy setting whereby the setting on the user or computer account reverts to its original state when the object is no longer in the scope of the GPO containing the setting.

managed server   A Windows server running one or more of these Microsoft services: DHCP, DNS, or Active Directory.

managed service account (MSA)   A service account that enables administrators to manage rights and permissions for services, with password management handled automatically.

manual disk   An option for a physical disk in Storage Spaces that allows an administrator to choose which disks will be used when creating a virtual disk.

manual provisioning   A method of provisioning IPAM that requires configuring each IPAM server task and managed server manually.

Master Boot Record (MBR)   A disk-partitioning method that supports volume sizes up to 2 TB.

maximum client lead time (MCLT)   The maximum amount of time a DHCP server can extend a lease for a DHCP client without the partner server's knowledge. It also defines the amount of time a server waits before assuming control over all DHCP services if its partner is in Partner Down state.

member server A Windows server that's in the management scope of a Windows domain but doesn't have Active Directory installed.

Microsoft Challenge Handshake Authentication Protocol (MS-CHAP) Microsoft's implementation of CHAP, used to authenticate an entity (for example, a user attempting access to the network). *See also* Challenge Handshake Authentication Protocol (CHAP).

Microsoft Challenge Handshake Authentication Protocol version 2 (MS-CHAP v2) An authentication protocol used to authenticate a user or server. This newer version of MS-CHAP is more secure. *See also* Microsoft Challenge Handshake Authentication Protocol (MS-CHAP).

Microsoft Software Installation (MSI) file A collection of files gathered into a package with an `.msi` extension that contains the instructions Windows Installer needs to install an application.

mirror space A resilient storage layout in Storage Spaces that is similar to a RAID 1 volume. It can be configured as a two-way or three-way mirrored volume. *See also* three-way mirror.

mirrored volume A volume that uses space from two dynamic disks and provides fault tolerance. Data written to one disk is duplicated, or mirrored, to the second disk. If one disk fails, the other disk has a good copy of the data, and the system can continue to operate until the failed disk is replaced. A mirrored volume is also called a "RAID 1 volume."

multicast scope A type of DHCP scope that allows assigning multicast addresses dynamically to multicast servers and clients by using Multicast Address Dynamic Client Allocation Protocol (MADCAP).

multimaster replication The process for replicating Active Directory objects; changes to the database can occur on any domain controller and are propagated, or replicated, to all other domain controllers.

multitenant A software architecture in which a single instance of a program, service, or database serves multiple customers, with the primary advantage of fewer required computing resources.

MX record A type of DNS resource record that is used to resolve a domain name in an email address to the IP address of a mail server for that domain.

N

name squatting A DNS problem that occurs when a non-Windows computer registers its name with a DNS server, but the name has already been registered by a Windows computer.

namespace A single logical share formed by a group of shares from different servers. Also, the parts of the operating system an application can see and interact with, such as the file system and network. In the context of Azure File Sync, a list of files and folders on a server endpoint that are part of an Azure File Sync sync group. The namespace is only a list of file names, whereas the contents of the files may be located on the Azure file share.

namespace isolation An isolated environment that allows containerized applications to have their own copy of critical OS structures such as the registry, file system, and network configuration while sharing the kernel, the host hardware, and possibly some runtime libraries.

namespace root A folder that's the logical starting point for a namespace.

namespace server A Windows server with the DFS Namespaces role service installed.

nested virtualization A configuration that allows you to run a hypervisor within a hypervisor.

network access server (NAS) A protocol-specific device that aids in connecting access clients to the network.

network address translation (NAT) The process whereby the IP addresses in a packet are translated to different addresses when the packet leaves or enters a network. With NAT, a network that uses private IP addresses can access the public Internet.

network-attached storage (NAS) A storage device that has an enclosure, a power supply, slots for multiple HDDs, a network interface, and a built-in OS tailored for managing shared files and folders.

network client The part of the OS that sends requests to a server to access network resources.

network connection The network interface, network protocol, and network client and server software working together on a Windows computer.

Network File System (NFS) The native file-sharing protocol in UNIX and Linux OSs; also supported by Windows Server.

network interface   The network interface card and the device driver software working together.

network protocol   Software that specifies the rules and format of communication between devices on a network.

network server software   The part of the OS that receives requests for shared network resources and makes these resources available to a network client.

Next Secure (NSEC)   A DNSSEC record that is returned when the requested resource record does not exist. *See also* Domain Name System Security Extension (DNSSEC).

Next Secure 3 (NSEC3)   An alternative to NSEC records. NSEC3 can prevent zone-walking, which is a technique of repeating NSEC queries to get all the names in a zone. *See also* Next Secure (NSEC).

Next Secure 3 (NSEC3) Parameter   DNSSEC records used to determine which NSEC3 records should be included in responses to queries for nonexistent records. *See also* Next Secure 3 (NSEC3).

NIC teaming   A network interface configuration that allows multiple network interfaces to work in tandem to provide increased bandwidth, load balancing, and fault tolerance. Also called *load balancing and failover (LBFO)*.

node fairness   A failover cluster feature in Windows Server that helps optimize usage of failover cluster node members.

NT File System (NTFS)   A file system used on Windows OSs that supports compression, encryption, and file and folder permissions.

O

object   In Active Directory, a grouping of information that describes a network resource, such as a shared printer, or an organizing structure, such as a domain or OU.

object owner   Typically, the user account that created the object or a group or user who has been assigned ownership of the object. An object owner has special authority over that object.

offline domain join   A feature that allows a running computer or offline virtual disk to join a domain without contacting a domain controller.

offline files   A feature of shared folders that allows users to access the contents of shared folders when not connected to the network; also called "client-side caching."

onboarding   A process that brings a device under a management system; in the context of Azure Arc, onboarding is accomplished by installing the Connected Machine agent and allowing the server to be managed using tools found in the Azure portal.

one-way trust   A trust relationship in which one domain trusts another, but the reverse is not true.

operations master   An Active Directory domain controller with sole responsibility for certain domain or forest-wide functions.

organizational unit (OU)   An Active Directory container used to organize a network's users and resources into logical administrative units.

P

page file   A system file in Windows used as virtual memory and to store dump data after a system crash.

parameter   An input to a command or PowerShell cmdlet.

parity space   A resilient storage layout in Storage Spaces that is similar to a RAID 5 volume and requires at least three disks.

partition   A logical unit of storage that can be formatted with a file system; it is similar to a volume but used with basic disks.

passive screening   A type of file screen that monitors and notifies when unauthorized files are saved.

pass-through disk   A physical disk attached to the host system that's placed offline so that it can be used by a VM instead of or in addition to a virtual disk.

Password Authentication Protocol (PAP)   An authentication protocol that uses passwords sent in plaintext to authenticate an entity.

password writeback   A feature that allows password changes made on Azure AD to be synchronized back to the on-premises Active Directory.

PDC emulator   A domain-wide FSMO role that processes password changes for older Windows clients (Windows 9x and NT) and is used during logon authentication.

perimeter network   A boundary between the private network and the public Internet where most resources available to the Internet, such as mail, web, DNS, and VPN servers, are located.

permission inheritance   A method for defining how permissions are transmitted from a parent object to a child object.

permissions   A property of the file system that specifies which users can access a file system object (a file or folder) and what users can do with the object if they're granted access.

physical processor   The physical chip that usually plugs into a socket on a physical host computer's system board.

platform as a service (PaaS)   A category of cloud computing in which a customer develops applications with the service provider's development tools and infrastructure; PaaS is also called "hosted platform." After applications are developed, they can be delivered to the customer's users from the provider's servers.

PowerShell   A command-line interactive scripting environment that provides the commands needed for most management tasks in a Windows Server 2022 environment.

PowerShell role capability file   A text file used for PowerShell Just Enough Administration that specifies which cmdlets and functions users can run.

Preboot Execution Environment (PXE)   A network environment built into many NICs that allows a computer to boot from an image stored on a network server.

primary partition   A division of disk space on a basic disk used to create a volume. It can be assigned a drive letter, be marked as active, and contain the Windows system volume.

primary zone   A DNS zone containing a read/write master copy of all resource records for the zone; the primary zone is authoritative for the zone.

primordial pool   A collection of physical disks available to be added to a storage pool.

principle of least privilege   A security best practice that states users and administrators should be given sufficient rights and permissions to perform their jobs, but no more than that.

private cloud   A cloud computing service provided by a company's internal IT department. *See* cloud computing.

private virtual switch   A virtual switch with no host connection to the virtual network, thereby allowing VMs to communicate with one another. However, there's no communication between the private virtual network and the host.

process isolation container   An application environment in which the processes running in the container share host OS and kernel resources with other Windows Server containers and the host OS, but the container has its own copy of user mode data structures such as the registry, file system, and network configuration.

production checkpoint   A checkpoint that is supported for production virtual machines and uses backup technology in the guest OS to create the checkpoint.

Protected Extensible Authentication Protocol (PEAP)   A certificate- and password-based authentication method designed to protect EAP messages by encapsulating them in a secure encrypted tunnel and using MS-CHAP v2 for user authentication. *See also* Extensible Authentication Protocol (EAP).

PTR record   A type of DNS resource record that is used to resolve a known IP address to a hostname.

public cloud   A cloud computing service provided by a third party. *See* cloud computing.

published application   An application package made available via Group Policy for users to install by using Programs and Features in Control Panel. The application is installed automatically if a user tries to run it or opens a document associated with it.

Q

quotas   Limits on the amount of storage that users have on a volume or in a folder.

R

RADIUS server group   A group of RADIUS servers configured to accept authentication and authorization requests from a RADIUS proxy. *See also* Remote Authentication Dial-In User Service (RADIUS).

RAID 5 volume   A volume that uses space from three or more dynamic disks and uses disk striping with parity to provide fault tolerance. When data is written, it's striped across all but one of the disks in the volume. Parity information derived from the data is written to the remaining disk and used to re-create lost data after a disk failure.

read-only domain controller (RODC)   A DC that stores a read-only copy of the Active Directory database but no password information. Changes to the domain must be made on a writeable DC and then replicated to an RODC, which is called unidirectional replication.

realm The Active Directory domain where a RADIUS server is located.

realm trust A trust used to integrate users of other OSs into a Windows domain or forest; it requires the OS to be running a Kerberos v5 or later authentication system that Active Directory uses.

receive side scaling (RSS) A feature for network drivers that efficiently distributes processing of incoming network traffic among multiple CPU cores.

recovery point A checkpoint that can be generated automatically so you can revert to an earlier server state if there's an unplanned failover and the VM is in an unworkable state.

recursive query A query that the DNS server processes until it responds with an address that satisfies the query or with an "I don't know" message. The process might require the DNS server to query several additional DNS servers.

redundant array of independent disks (RAID) A disk configuration that uses space on multiple disks to form a single logical volume. Most RAID configurations provide fault tolerance, and some enhance performance.

referral A response to an iterative query in which the address of another name server is returned to the requester. Also, the process of sending a request for information about an object to DCs in other domains until the information is found.

relative identifier (RID) A unique value that is combined with a domain identifier to form the security identifier for an Active Directory object. *See also* security identifier (SID).

Remote Access A server role that provides services to keep a mobile workforce and branch offices securely connected to resources at the main office.

Remote Authentication Dial-In User Service (RADIUS) An industry-standard client/server protocol that centralizes authentication, authorization, and accounting for a network.

reparse point Metadata associated with a file that is used by a particular application or service that accesses the file.

replica server In the Hyper-V Replica feature, the Hyper-V server where replication is enabled.

replication Making copies of files in different locations, which helps ensure reliable access to files.

replication partner A domain controller configured to replicate with another domain controller.

reservation An IP address associated with a DHCP client's MAC address to ensure that when the client requests an IP address, it always gets the same one, along with any configured options.

resilience Another term for fault tolerance; indicates a disk arrangement's capability to maintain data if a disk fails.

resource-based constrained delegation A variation of Kerberos constrained delegation in which delegation of authentication is configured on the second-hop remote server; it is considered more secure than CredSSP because credentials are not stored on any of the remote servers.

resource forest An Azure AD DS forest type that only synchronizes users and groups created in Azure AD and does not include those synced from on-premises Active Directory.

Resource Record Signature (RRSIG) A key containing the signature for a single resource record, such as an A or MX record.

resource records Data in a DNS database that contains information about network resources, such as hostnames, other DNS servers, and services; each record is identified by a letter code.

Response Rate Limiting (RRL) A DNS server role feature starting with Windows Server 2016 that mitigates a type of distributed denial-of-service (DDoS) attack called a DNS amplification attack.

reverse lookup zone (RLZ) A DNS zone containing PTR records that map IP addresses to names; it's named with the IP network address (IPv4 or IPv6) of the computer whose records it contains.

RID master A domain-wide FSMO role that's responsible for issuing unique pools of RIDs to each DC, thereby guaranteeing unique SIDs throughout the domain.

right A setting that specifies what types of actions a user can perform on a computer or network.

role services   Services that can be installed in Server Manager to add functions to the main role. *See also* server role.

root certificate   A certificate establishing that all other certificates from a CA are trusted; also called a "CA certificate."

root hints   A list of name servers preconfigured on Windows DNS servers that point to Internet root servers, which are DNS servers located on the Internet and managed by IANA.

root server   A DNS server that keeps a database of addresses of other DNS servers managing top-level domain names.

round robin   A method of responding to DNS queries when more than one IP address exists for the queried host. Each IP address is placed first in the list of returned addresses an equal number of times so that hosts are accessed alternately.

runbook   A set of related procedures that are performed to complete a particular task; in Azure, you can use a runbook with an Automation account to perform repetitive tasks using PowerShell, PowerShell Workflow, or Python.

S

scalability   The ability to add storage, computing, or other resources quickly and easily.

schema   Information that defines the type, organization, and structure of data stored in the Active Directory database.

schema attribute   A category of schema information that defines what type of information is stored in each object.

schema class   A category of schema information that defines the types of objects that can be stored in Active Directory, such as user or computer accounts.

schema directory partition   A directory partition containing the information needed to define Active Directory objects and object attributes for all domains in the forest.

schema master   A forest-wide FSMO role that's responsible for replicating the schema directory partition to all other domain controllers in the forest when changes occur.

script   A series of commands that have been saved in a text file to be repeated easily at any time.

secondary zone   A DNS zone containing a read-only copy of all resource records for the zone.

Changes can't be made directly on a secondary DNS server, but because it contains an exact copy of the primary zone, it's considered authoritative for the zone.

second-hop remoting   The process of using PowerShell to connect to a remote server and then execute commands on a third server. The third server in this case is the second hop.

Security Accounts Manager (SAM) database   A database on domain member and workgroup computers that holds the users and groups defined on the local computer.

security descriptor   A file system object's security settings, composed of the DACL, owner, and SACL. *See also* discretionary access control list (DACL) and system access control list (SACL).

security filtering   A type of GPO filtering that uses permissions to restrict objects from accessing a GPO.

security group   A group type that's the main Active Directory object administrators use to manage network resource access and grant rights to users. *See also* group type.

security identifier (SID)   A numeric value assigned to each object in a domain that uniquely identifies the object; it is composed of a domain identifier, which is the same for all objects in a domain, and an RID. *See also* relative identifier (RID).

security principal   An object that can be assigned permission to access the file system; it includes user, group, and computer accounts.

selective authentication   A property of a forest trust that enables administrators to specify users who can be granted access to selected resources in the trusting forest.

self-service password reset (SSPR)   An Azure AD feature that allows Azure users who have accounts in Azure AD to reset or change their password and unlock their account without intervention from an administrator.

Serial ATA (SATA)   A common disk interface technology that's inexpensive, fast, and reliable, with transfer speeds up to 6 Gb/s; it is used both in client computers and low-end servers and replaces the older parallel ATA (PATA) technology.

serial attached SCSI (SAS)   A serial form of SCSI with transfer rates up to 12 Gb/s; the disk technology of choice for servers and high-end workstations. *See also* small computer system interface (SCSI).

server endpoint   An element of a sync group that specifies an on-premises server and a path to a folder that stores synchronized files from an Azure file share.

server features   Components you can install that provide functions to enhance or support an installed role or add a standalone feature.

Server Message Block (SMB)   A client/server Application-layer protocol that provides network file sharing, network printing, and authentication.

server operating system   An OS designed to emphasize network access performance and run background processes rather than desktop applications.

server role   A major function or service that a server performs.

service account   A user account that Windows services use to log on with a specific set of rights and permissions.

service endpoint   An address that provides secure and optimized access to an Azure service across the Azure backbone network.

service principal name (SPN)   A name that uniquely identifies a service instance to a client.

share permissions   The permissions applied to shared folders that protect files accessed across the network; the only method for protecting files on FAT volumes.

shared secret   A text string known only to two systems trying to authenticate each other.

shared virtual hard disk (shared VHDX)
A virtual hard disk configured on a VM in a guest cluster that's used for shared storage among VMs in the guest cluster instead of traditional SAN storage.

shortcut trust   A manually configured trust between domains in the same forest for the purpose of bypassing the normal referral process. *See also* referral.

SID filtering   An option that causes a trusting domain to ignore any SIDs that aren't from the trusted domain.

simple space   A simple volume created in Storage Spaces that has no fault tolerance.

simple volume   A volume that resides on a single basic or dynamic disk.

simultaneous multithreading (SMT)   The ability of a processor core to run two segments, or threads, of program code simultaneously.

single-root I/O virtualization (SR-IOV)
An advanced feature in Hyper-V that enhances a virtual network adapter's performance by allowing it to bypass the virtual switch software on the parent partition (the Hyper-V host) and communicate directly with the physical hardware.

single sign-on (SSO)   A process in which you sign in to a network using a set of credentials that are recognized by other entities and applications so you don't have to enter your credentials multiple times.

site   In Active Directory, a physical location in which domain controllers communicate and replicate information regularly.

site link   A component of a site that is needed to connect two or more sites for replication purposes.

small computer system interface (SCSI)
An older parallel bus disk technology still used on some servers; it has reached its performance limits at 640 MB/s transfer rates.

smart paging   A Hyper-V feature that uses a file on the host computer for temporary memory storage when a sudden surge in memory requirements exceeds the physical amount of memory available.

SMB Direct   A performance technology designed specifically for the Server Message Block (SMB) protocol that uses an RDMA-capable network adapter, nearly eliminating server processor utilization for data transfers.

soft quotas   Limits on the amount of storage that users have on a volume or in a folder; soft quotas alert users when they have exceeded the quota but don't prevent users from saving files.

software as a service (SaaS)   A category of cloud computing in which a customer pays for the use of applications that run on a service provider's network; SaaS is also called "hosted applications."

solid state drive (SSD)   A type of storage medium that uses flash memory, has no moving parts, and requires less power than a traditional HDD. It is faster and more shock resistant than a traditional HDD but costs more per gigabyte and doesn't have as much capacity as an HDD.

spanned volume   A volume that extends across two or more physical disks; for example, a simple volume that has been extended to a second disk is a spanned volume.

special identity group   A group whose membership is controlled dynamically by Windows and doesn't appear as an object in Active Directory Users and Computers or Active Directory Administrative Center; it can be assigned permissions by adding it to resources' DACLs.

split scope   A fault-tolerant DHCP configuration in which two DHCP servers share the same scope information, allowing both servers to offer DHCP services to clients.

staged installation   An RODC installation method that doesn't require domain administrator credentials; a regular user at a branch office can perform the installation. Called *delegated installation* in Windows Server 2008.

standalone server   A Windows server that isn't a domain controller or a member of a domain.

standard checkpoint   A checkpoint that captures the state of a virtual machine, including the running state, if desired. Standard checkpoints should not be used in production VMs.

Starter GPO   A GPO template that can be used as a baseline for creating new GPOs, much like user account templates.

stateless operation   An operation state that allows a container to start fresh and not carry over information from the previous time it was run.

storage appliance   A storage device that has an enclosure, a power supply, slots for multiple HDDs, a network interface, and a built-in OS tailored for managing shared storage.

storage area network   A storage technology that uses high-speed networking technologies to give servers fast access to large amounts of shared disk storage.

storage layout   The method used to create a virtual disk with Storage Spaces; the three options are simple space, mirror space, and parity space. *See also* Storage Spaces.

storage pool   A collection of physical disks from which virtual disks and volumes are created and assigned dynamically.

Storage Quality of Service (QoS)   A technology that enables administrators to specify minimum and maximum performance values for virtual hard disks.

Storage Replica   A Windows Server feature that provides block-level file replication between storage devices, primarily for the purpose of fault tolerance and disaster recovery.

Storage Spaces   A feature in Windows Server 2022 that provides flexible provisioning of virtualized storage.

Storage Sync Service resource   An Azure resource that links an Azure file share with an on-premises server for the purpose of syncing files using Azure File Sync.

stretch cluster   A cluster in which the servers are in different geographical locations. A stretch cluster is primarily used in disaster recovery scenarios.

striped volume   A volume that extends across two or more dynamic disks, but data is written to all disks in the volume equally. Striped volumes don't offer fault tolerance, but they do have a read and write performance advantage over spanned and simple volumes because multiple disks can be accessed simultaneously to read and write files. Also called a RAID 0 volume.

stub zone   A DNS zone containing a read-only copy of only the zone's SOA and NS records and the necessary A records to resolve NS records. A stub zone forwards queries to a primary DNS server for that zone and is not authoritative for the zone.

superscope   A special type of scope consisting of one or more member scopes; it allows a DHCP server to service multiple IP subnets on a single physical network.

sync group   A component of Azure File Sync that specifies the servers and cloud shares that participate in file synchronization. A sync group is composed of an Azure file share, which is referred to as a cloud endpoint, and one or more server endpoints. *See also* server endpoint.

synthetic driver   A driver installed on a VM with Integration Services that's optimized for use in the Hyper-V environment.

synthetic network adapter   A network adapter that uses synthetic drivers in Hyper-V and offers much better performance than legacy network adapters. *See also* synthetic driver.

system access control list (SACL)   A list that defines the settings for auditing access to an object.

system volume   A volume that contains files the computer needs to find and load the Windows OS.

SYSVOL folder   A shared folder that stores information from Active Directory that's replicated to other domain controllers.

T

tag   A way to differentiate multiple versions of the same image.

thin provisioning   A method of allocating disk space for a virtual disk in which the physical disk space is not allocated for a volume until it's actually needed. The virtual disk expands dynamically and uses space from the storage pool as needed until it reaches the specified maximum size.

three-way mirror   A resilient storage layout that requires at least five disks; it maintains data if two disks fail.

tiered storage   A feature of Storage Spaces that combines the speed of solid state drives with the low cost and high capacity of hard disk drives.

top-level domain (TLD) server   A DNS server that maintains addresses of other DNS servers that are authoritative for second-level domains.

transitive trust   A trust relationship based on the transitive rule of mathematics; therefore, if Domain A trusts Domain B and Domain B trusts Domain C, then Domain A trusts Domain C.

transparent network   A network that connects containers to the same network as the host, so a container's network adapter will have an IP address in the same IP subnet as the host's network adapter.

Transport Layer Security (TLS)   A cryptographic protocol used to encrypt messages over a network.

tree   A grouping of domains that share a common naming structure.

trust anchor   A DNSKEY that is typically used for a zone but can also be a DS key for a delegated zone. Public keys are used as trust anchors for validating DNS responses.

trust relationship   An arrangement that defines whether and how security principals from one domain can access network resources in another domain.

tunnel   A method of transferring data across an unsecured network so that the data is hidden from all but the sender and receiver.

two-way trust   A trust in which both domains in the relationship trust each other, so users from both domains can access resources in the other domain.

type 1 hypervisor   Virtualization software that creates and monitors the virtual hardware environment and is installed directly on the hardware of the host machine.

type 2 hypervisor   Virtualization software that creates and monitors the virtual hardware environment, is installed on an operating system, and uses the host OS's resources and drivers.

U

UNC path   The format used to specify a shared folder on a remote Windows computer. It uses the syntax *server**share*[*subfolder*][*file*]. The parameters in brackets are optional.

unidirectional replication   A replication method used with RODCs in which Active Directory data is replicated to the RODC, but the RODC doesn't replicate the data to other domain controllers.

universal group   A group scope that can contain users from any domain in the forest and be assigned permission to resources in any domain in the forest. *See also* group scope.

universal group membership caching
A feature that stores universal group membership information retrieved from a global catalog server so that it doesn't have to be contacted for each user logon.

unmanaged policy setting   A type of group policy setting that persists on the user or computer account, meaning it remains even after the computer or user object falls out of the GPO's scope.

UPN suffix   The part of the user principal name (UPN) that comes after the @.

urgent replication   An event triggering immediate notification that a change has occurred instead of waiting for the normal 15-second interval before replication partners are notified.

User Class   A custom value you create on the DHCP server and then configure on a DHCP client; used much like the Vendor Class value.

user forest   An Azure AD forest type in which all objects in Azure AD and all user accounts in on-premises Active Directory are synchronized.

user principal name (UPN)   A user logon name that follows the format *username@domain*. Users can use UPNs to sign in to their own domain from a computer that's a member of a different domain.

V

variable   A temporary storage location that holds values, whether numeric, strings, or objects.

Vendor Class   A field in the DHCP packet that device manufacturers or OS vendors can use to identify a device model or an OS version.

VHD Set   A shared virtual hard disk used with virtual machine cluster configurations where multiple VMs have access to the same virtual hard disk for fault tolerance and load-balancing applications.

virtual account   A simple type of service account that doesn't need to be created, deleted, or managed by an administrator.

virtual appliance   A VM in an Azure extended network configuration that is connected to both the subnet you are extending and another subnet. If the virtual appliance is in the on-premises network, it communicates with another virtual appliance in the Azure network.

virtual desktop infrastructure (VDI)   A sector of private cloud computing in which users access their desktops through a private cloud; the OS and applications run on servers in a corporate datacenter rather than on the local computer.

virtual disk   Files stored on the host computer that represent a virtual machine's hard disk.

virtual hard disk (VHD)   A file stored on a physical disk drive that emulates a physical disk but has additional capabilities for virtual machines and general Windows storage applications.

virtual instance   An installation of Windows Server in a Hyper-V virtual machine.

virtual machine (VM)   The virtual environment that emulates a physical computer's hardware and BIOS.

virtual machine monitoring   A feature of Windows Server Hyper-V that allows you to monitor resources, applications, and services running on highly available VMs. *See also* highly available virtual machine.

virtual machine queue (VMQ)   A feature of virtual network interfaces (vNICs) that accelerates vNIC performance by delivering packets from the external network directly to the vNIC.

virtual network   A network configuration created by virtualization software and used by virtual machines for network communication.

virtual network peering   An Azure technology that allows you to connect VNets, which allows the resources on the VNets to communicate with one another.

virtual private network (VPN)   A network connection that uses the Internet to give mobile users or branch offices secure access to a company's network resources on a private network.

virtual processor   A processor assigned to a virtual machine running on a hypervisor such as Hyper-V.

virtualization   A technology that uses software to emulate multiple hardware environments, allowing multiple operating systems to run on the same physical server simultaneously.

virtualization software   The software for creating and managing virtual machines and creating the virtual environment in which a guest OS is installed.

VM CPU group   A Hyper-V feature that allows you to better manage host CPU resources shared among the guest VMs running on the Hyper-V host.

volume   A logical unit of storage that can be formatted with a file system.

W

Web Application Proxy (WAP)   A Routing and Remote Access role service that allows remote users to access network applications from any device that supports a web browser. Applications made available to users with this method are said to be "published applications."

Windows Admin Center   A browser-based application that provides a method to remotely manage both on-premises and Azure VM servers and client stations.

Windows domain   A group of Windows computers that share common management and are subject to rules and policies that an administrator defines.

Windows Remote Management (WinRM)   A Windows feature that provides a command-line interface for performing a variety of remote management tasks.

Windows Server Hybrid Infrastructure   The Microsoft paradigm for the hybrid cloud in which Windows Server computing and storage resources running in the on-premises datacenter are linked with resources running in the Microsoft Azure cloud. This paradigm provides central management over both on-premises resources and Azure cloud-based resources.

Windows workgroup   A small collection of Windows computers whose users typically have something in common, such as the need to share files or printers with each other. No computer has authority or control over another. Logons, security, and resource sharing are decentralized. Also called a peer-to-peer network.

WMI filtering   A type of GPO filtering that uses queries to select a group of computers based on certain attributes, and then applies or doesn't apply policies based on the query's results.

Z

zone   A grouping of DNS information that represents one or more domains and possibly subdomains.

zone delegation   The transfer of authority for a subdomain to a new zone, which can be on the same server as the parent zone or on another server.

zone replication scope   A scope that determines which Active Directory partition the zone is stored in and to which DCs the zone information is replicated.

zone signing   A DNSSEC feature that uses digital signatures in DNSSEC-related resource records to verify DNS responses. *See also* Domain Name System Security Extension (DNSSEC).

zone-signing key (ZSK)   A public and private key combination stored in a certificate used to sign the zone.

zone transfer   An operation that copies all or part of a zone from one DNS server to another and occurs as a result of a secondary server requesting the transfer from another server.

Index

A

AAAA record, 377–378
AAD. *See* Azure Active Directory (AAD)
AADDS. *See* Azure Active Directory Domain Services (AADDS)
access-based enumeration (ABE), 574, 607, 608, 611
access client, 505
access control entry (ACE), 97, 588
  defined, 585
  using Deny in, 591–592
access control lists (ACLs), 557
Account tab, for user account properties, 107–108
ACE. *See* access control entry (ACE)
ACLs. *See* access control lists (ACLs)
Active Directory, 11
  configuring sites, 250–252
  configuring trusts, 287–295
  container objects, 57–58
  definition of, 38
  designing domain structure, 74–77
  directory partitions, 70
  domain administrator, 92
  domain controllers, 236–237
  features, 39–40
  hierarchical database, 39
  inside, 54–56
  installing, 44–54
  intersite replication, 259–261
  intrasite replication, 255–258
  leaf object, 58–60
  locating objects, 60–68
  logical structure, 40–44
  managing replication, 263–264, 267–268
  operations master roles, 70–71
  physical structure, 40
  Recycle Bin, recovering objects with, 60
  replication, 69–70, 254–268
  review, 236–237
  schema, 56–57
  in Server Core, 49–51
  trust relationships, 72, 283–287
  using PowerShell to view FSMO roles, 71–72

Active Directory Administrative Center (ADAC), 54, 55, 103, 239
Active Directory database, 56
Active Directory domain. *See* domain
Active Directory Domain Services (AD DS), 9, 11, 44. *See also* Active Directory
  defined, 39
  deploy and manage, 787–788
  features, 39–40
Active Directory Federation Services (AD FS)
  preauthentication, for RD Gateway, 525
  Web Application Proxy works with, 522
Active Directory forest, 42–43
  adding tree to existing, 275–276
  characteristics, 72–73, 281–282
  forest root domain, 73–74
  global catalog server, importance of, 73
  installing new domain in existing, 48–49
  multiforest environments, 281–283
Active Directory object
  defined, 56
  icons in, 57
  permissions, 96–101
  schema classes, attributes, and, 56–57
Active Directory partition, 373
Active Directory Recycle Bin, 60
Active Directory replication, 40
Active Directory search, 578
Active Directory site, 40
Active Directory Sites and Services
  automatic site coverage, 251
  bridgehead servers, 248–249
  global catalog, 250
  managing replication with, 264
  moving DCs between, 251–252
  site link, 248–249
  SRV record registration, 250–251
  subnets, 247–248, 252–254
  understanding and configuring, 246–254
  universal group membership caching, 250
Active Directory tree, 42, 43, 74, 275–276

Active Directory Users and Computers (ADUC), 41, 56, 239
  advanced features option in, 97–98
  defined, 103
active screening, 598
ADAC. *See* Active Directory Administrative Center (ADAC)
Address Resolution Protocol (ARP), 439
address space, adding to virtual network, 527–528
AD DS. *See* Active Directory Domain Services (AD DS)
administrative scopes, 428
administrative shares, 578
administrative template files
  ADMX central store, 199
  computer configuration settings, 197–198, 202–203
  defined, 196
  filters, working with, 199–200, 203–204
  migrating, 201
  user configuration settings, 198–199, 203
  using custom, 200–201
administrator-created service accounts, 130–131
ADMX central store, 199
ADUC. *See* Active Directory Users and Computers (ADUC)
Advanced Sharing dialog box, 571
advanced storage solutions
  Azure File Sync, 660–670
  implementing data deduplication, 649–655
  SMB Direct, 658–659
  Storage Quality of Service, 659–660
  Storage Replica, 655–658
  storage spaces, 633–648
aggregated policy, 660
application directory partition, 70
application efficiency, multiple sites, 246
Application Proxy connector, 539
Application Proxy service, 539
application server, installing BranchCache on, 617–618
A record, 377–378, 438
assigned application, 80, 191

asynchronous replication, 658
attributes, file system, 557
attribute value, 56
authentication
  efficiency, 246
  forest-wide, 290
  methods, 497–498
  provider, 496–497
  selective, 290
  trust level, 291
  user accounts, 59
  VPN, 491
Authentication tab, 293
authoritative server, 367
automatic disk, 640
Automatic Private IP Addressing
    (APIPA), 421, 494
automatic site coverage, 251
automatic virtual hard disk (AVHD)
    file, 697
Azure Active Directory (AAD), 136–137
  accounts, working with, 137–140
  Azure AD Connect (*See* Azure AD
    Connect)
  defined, 136
  groups, creating, 139–140
  implementing, 158–161
  self-service password reset, 145–148
  user accounts, creating, 138–139
Azure Active Directory Domain
    Services (AADDS), 136,
    153–154
  Azure Windows Server VM to, 157
  default containers in, 157
  group policies in, 224–226
  implementing, 155–156
Azure AD Application Proxy, 539–540
Azure AD Connect
  cloud sync, 149–154
  defined, 140
  health of, 148–149
  installing, 141–145, 162–163
Azure AD Connect cloud sync
  defined, 149
  features, 150
  implementing, 150–154
Azure AD Connect Health, 148–149
Azure Arc
  Azure Security Center, 349–351
  defined, 341
  extensions, 345–346
  Log Analytics, 347–348
  managing Windows servers with,
    343–349
  onboarding Windows servers for,
    341–343

policies, 344–346
  Update management, 347–349
Azure Automation, 356–358
Azure Bastion, 731, 732
Azure cloud backups, 660
Azure Container Service, 779
Azure DNS zones, 406
Azure domain controller, 295–296
Azure ExpressRoute, 731
Azure extended network, 532–534
Azure file share, 661
Azure File Sync
  cloud tiering, 666–667
  configuring, 661–666, 792
  defined, 660
  migrating distributed file system
    to, 669–670
  monitoring, 667–669
  storage and file shares, 661
Azure network adapter, 530–532
Azure networking
  Azure AD Application Proxy,
    539–540
  Azure extended network, 532–534
  Azure network adapter, 530–532
  Azure Relay, 534–535
  Azure virtual network, 526–530
  Azure virtual WAN, 536–539
  implementation, 526–540
Azure Policy, 344
Azure Policy Guest Configuration, 344
Azure private DNS zones
  creating and testing, 406–409
  defined, 406
  integrating on-premises DNS with,
    409–411
Azure Quickstart Center, 27
Azure Relay, 534–535
Azure Security Center, 349–351
Azure Storage Sync agent, 663
Azure virtual machine (Azure VM),
    224, 532, 533–790
  accessing, 28
  with Admin Center Gateway, 336–337
  Azure private DNS zone, 409–411
  configuring connections, 731–732
  creating, 27–28
  data disks, 728–730
  implementing DSC on, 356–358
  just-in-time (JIT) access for, 351–352
  managing, 727
  resizing, 729, 730
  runbooks to manage, 353
Azure virtual network (Vnet)
  adding address spaces and
    subnets to, 527–528

creating and configuring, 526–527
  defined, 526
  and IP addresses, 473–474
  service endpoint, 528
  virtual network peering, 528–530
Azure virtual WAN (vWAN)
  creating, 536–539
  defined, 536
Azure VM. *See* Azure virtual machine
    (Azure VM)
Azure Windows Server VM, to
    AADDS, 157

B

Background Intelligent Transfer
    Service (BITS), 198, 615
backplanes, 553
backup servers
  data deduplication, 649
  virtualized, 651
basic disk, 554–555
basic-tier VMs, 727
Bastion host, 157
batch file, 192
BIOS settings, for VMs, 692
BITS. *See* Background Intelligent
    Transfer Service (BITS)
blocking GPO inheritance, 213–214
block-level replication, 656
boot volume, 554
BranchCache
  configuring clients to use,
    619–620, 622
  content information, 615
  defined, 614–615
  installing and configuring,
    617–619, 621
  modes of operation, 616
  troubleshooting, 620
bridgehead servers, 248–249, 259
built-in Administrator account,
    102–103
Builtin folder, default groups in,
    119–120
built-in Guest account, 103
built-in service accounts, 130, 131
built-in user accounts, 59, 102
business continuity, 661

C

CA. *See* certification authority (CA)
caching-only DNS server, 368
canonical name (CNAME)
    records, 378
centralized topology, 459, 460

certificate-based authentication,
508–509
certification authority (CA), 404, 490,
508–509, 618
Challenge Handshake Authentication
Protocol (CHAP), 507
checkpoints
configuration, 697, 698
defined, 678
files, 681
managing, 697–699
production, 697
reverting and applying, 699
standard, 697
child domains, 42, 379
classic scheduler, 746–747
classification management, FSRM, 596
client computers, accessing file
shares from, 578–579
client identifier (ClientID), 443
cloud computing, 13
attributes of, 25–26
public *vs.* private cloud, 14
virtualization, 13–14
cloud endpoint, 663–664
cloud tiering, 660, 665–667
clustered virtual machine. *See* highly
available virtual machine
cluster shared volumes (CSVs),
748, 755
cluster-to-cluster replication, 656
CNAME record, 378
columns, 638
command line, creating and managing
shares at, 577
comma separated value (CSV)
file, 138
Common Internet File System
(CIFS), 570
computer accounts
changing default location, 125
creating, 124–126
disabling, 127
joining domain, 125–126
managing, 127
offline domain join, 126
working with, 124–129
computer configuration node, GPO,
79–80
conditional forwarder, 367, 394
configuration drift, 354
configuration file, 681, 697
configuration partition, 70
conflict detection, 439–440
connection object, 256–257, 265–266
constrained delegation, 135

Kerberos, 320
resource-based, 320–321
contacts, 110
container
base operating system installation,
764–765
create and manage, 790
Daemon startup options
management, 767–768
data volumes, 776
defined, 761
deploying, 762–763
with Docker Daemon, 771–772
Hyper-V isolation container,
766, 770
implementing in virtual
machine, 767
implementing on Windows Server,
763–767
network address translation,
774–776, 781
process isolation container,
765–766, 768–770
resource control, 777
types of, 762
working with, 771–772
container images
committing changes to images, 773
with Dockerfile, 777–778
listing, 772
managing, 780
Microsoft Azure, 779
removing images, 774
tagging, 772–773
container objects
defined, 57
domain objects, 58
folder objects, 58
organizational units, 57–58
content information, 615
core scheduler, 747
cpuGroups.exe, 744
Credential Security Support Provider
(CredSSP), 319, 320
CSV file. *See* comma separated value
(CSV) file
CSVs. *See* cluster shared volumes
(CSVs)
Cyclic Redundancy Check (CRC), 555

D

DACL. *See* discretionary access
control list (DACL)
DAP. *See* Directory Access Protocol
(DAP)
data access encryption, 574

database storage, 550
data deduplication
backing up and restoring with, 654
configuring with PowerShell,
652–653
defined, 633, 649
implementing, 649–655
installing and using, 650–653, 655
monitoring, 653–654
when to use, 649–650
Data Encryption Standard (DES), 490
Data Execution Prevention (DEP), 678
data storage method, 557
DC. *See* domain controller (DC)
DDNS. *See* dynamic DNS (DDNS)
dedicated policy, 660
default containers, in AADDS, 157
default groups
in Builtin folder, 119–120
special identity groups,
121–122
in Users folder, 120–121
in Windows domain, 119–123
default shares, 578
delegated administrator account,
238–239
delegated installation, RODC,
239–241
delegation of control, 95–96
Delegation Signer (DS) records, 400
demand-dial interface, 499–501
Deny permission, 591–592
Desired State Configuration
(DSC), 306
on Azure VMs, 356–358
defined, 354
local configuration manager, 355
modes, 354
steps for, 354
desktop operating systems, server
operating systems *vs.,* 3
device driver software, 10
device naming option, 722
DFS. *See* Distributed File System
(DFS)
DFSR. *See* Distributed File System
Replication (DFSR)
DHCP. *See* Dynamic Host
Configuration Protocol
(DHCP)
DHCP failover
defined, 453
editing and deleting configuration,
455, 457–458
hot standby mode, 453, 455
load-balancing mode, 453–454

DHCP filters, 442, 451
DHCP name protection, 440
DHCP policies, 442–443, 448–450
DHCP relay agent
    defined, 444
    installing, 445–446
    procedural steps, 444–445
DHCP scope, 423–426
DHCP server authorization, 422–423
DHCP server options, 429
    filters, 442, 451
    IPv4 Properties, 437–440
    listing tasks, 435–437
    migration, export, and import, 447
    name protection, 440
    policies, 442–443, 448–450
    for PXE boot, 443–444
    relay agent, 444–446
    scope properties, 441–442
    troubleshooting, 447–448
differencing disk, 681, 705
DirectAccess, 489
direct-attached storage (DAS), 550
Directory Access Protocol (DAP), 39
directory entry, 557
directory partitions, 70
directory service
    defined, 39
    role of, 39–44
Directory Services Restore Mode
        (DSRM), 45–46
Discrete Device Assignment (DDA), 703
discretionary access control list
        (DACL), 96, 215, 217, 293,
        585, 591
disk allocation, in storage pool,
        640–641
disk drive, 552
Disk Management, 9
disk pooling, 633
disks. *See* local disks
distributed access, 661
distributed cache mode, 615
Distributed File System (DFS),
        199, 246
    defined, 605
    installing and configuring, 607, 612
    migrating to Azure File Sync,
        669–670
    namespace, 605–612
    replication, 606, 612
Distributed File System Replication
        (DFSR), 177
    with Azure File Sync, 669–670
    defined, 261
    upgrading, 262–263

distributed topology, 459
distribution group, 110, 113–114
DNS. *See* Domain Name System (DNS)
DNS amplification attack, 403
DNS-based Authentication of Named
        Entities (DANE), 404
DNS cache locking, 403
DNS cache poisoning, 402
DNS client, 366
DNSKEY record, 400
DNS namespace, 365
DNS resolver, 366
DNSSEC. *See* Domain Name System
        Security Extension (DNSSEC)
DNS socket pool, 402–403
Docker
    defined, 742, 763
    installing on Windows Server
        container host, 763
Docker daemon, 763
    with container images, 772–774
    managing containers with, 771–772
    managing startup options, 767–768
Dockerfile
    commands, 778
    container images with, 777–778
    defined, 777
domain, 41, 42. *See also* domain
        controllers (DCs)
    installing additional domain
        controllers in, 48
    internal *vs.* external, 274
    replication between, 73, 282
    SRV records in, 380
    structure, designing, 74–77
    trusts between, 73, 282
domain administrator account, 103
domain-based namespace, 607,
        613–614
domain controllers (DCs)
    administrative shares, 578
    in Azure, 295–296
    defined, 9, 40, 235
    installing additional, in
        domain, 48
    installing with Install from Media,
        51–52
    multidomain environments,
        273–281
    operations master roles, 268–273
    read-only domain controllers,
        237–246
    understanding and configuring
        sites, 246–254
    writeable, 242
domain directory partition, 70

DomainDNSZones, 373
domain GPOs, 175–177
domain-linked GPOs, 213
domain local group, 115
Domain Name System (DNS), 289,
        316, 321
    Azure DNS zones, 406
    Azure private DNS zones,
        406–411
    conditional forwarders, 394
    configuring security, 399–405
    configuring zones, 386–392
    creating resource records,
        376–386
    creating zones, 371–375
    database, 366
    defined, 364, 365
    with DNS Manager, 368–370
    dynamic DNS records, 382
    forwarders, 393–394, 397–398
    installing and configuring, 370–376,
        384–385
    lookup process, 366–367
    notify message, 390
    with PowerShell, 375
    read-only, 243
    records, 438
    recursive queries, 395–396
    root hints, 394–395, 398–399
    round robin, 395
    server, 45, 46, 367–368, 438
    server settings, 392–399
    static DNS records, 382–383, 386
    structure of, 365–366
    tab, 441
    traditional forwarders, 393–394
Domain Name System Security
        Extension (DNSSEC), 400–402,
        405
domain naming master, 70, 269
domain objects, 58
domain user accounts, 59, 102
domain-wide FSMO roles, 268
downlevel user logon name, 104
drain on shutdown, 750–751
DSC. *See* Desired State Configuration
        (DSC)
DSRM. *See* Directory Services Restore
        Mode (DSRM)
dual parity space, 634
dynamically expanding disk, 567–568,
        705
dynamic disk, 555
dynamic DNS (DDNS), 377, 382
Dynamic Host Configuration Identifier
        (DHCID), 440

Dynamic Host Configuration Protocol (DHCP), 321, 355, 418
address assignment process, 420–422
address renewal, 420–421
configuration, 491
configuring multicast scopes, 427–428
configuring superscope, 426–427
defined, 419
exclusion ranges, 424–425, 432–434
failover, 453–458
filters, 442, 451
high availability, 451–458
hot standby mode, 455
installing and configuring, 422–435
load-balancing mode, 453–454
on managed servers, 469
messages, 421–422
multiple subnets, multiple scopes, 425–426
name protection, 440
on network, 493
options, 429–430, 434–435
policies, 442–443, 448–450
relay agent, 444–446
reservation, 425, 432–434
scope, 423–426
server authorization, 422–423, 431–432
server options, 435–451
split scope, 452–453, 456–457
troubleshooting, 447–448
dynamic memory, 694

E

EAP. *See* extensible authentication protocol (EAP)
EAP-TLS. *See* Extensible Authentication Protocol-Transport Layer Security (EAP-TLS)
effective access, 591
effective permissions, 586
emulated drivers, 696
enclosure awareness, 642
encrypted authentication (CHAP), 498
Encrypting File System (EFS), 559
enhanced session mode, 700–702, 704
Ethernet adapter vEthernet, 774
exclusion ranges, 424–425, 432–434
explicit permission, 586
ExpressRoute, 296
extended page tables (EPT), 678, 743
extended partition, 555

extensible authentication protocol (EAP), 497–498, 507, 509
Extensible Authentication Protocol-Transport Layer Security (EAP-TLS), 490
extensions
Azure VM, 345–346
defined, 79, 188
external trust
configuring, 291
defined, 287
external virtual switch, 712

F

failover, 723
File Allocation Table (FAT) file system, 557, 558, 592
file and folder permissions, 584–585
advanced permission, 588–589
basic permissions, 587–588
copying and moving, 592
defined, 587
Deny permission, 591–592
effective access, 591
ownership, 589
permission inheritance, 587, 589–591
subfolders, 590, 595–596
file and printer sharing, 9
File and Storage Services
creating shares with, 572–575, 583
creating storage space with, 645–647
data deduplication, 651
file group, 599
file management tasks, 596
filenaming convention, 557
File Replication Service (FRS), 177, 261, 262
file screening management, 596
file screens, 598–599, 603–605
File Server Resource Manager (FSRM)
defined, 596
file screens, 598–599, 603–605
quotas, 597–598, 600–603
role service, 596, 600
tools, 596
file servers
data deduplication, 649
general purpose, 651
installing BranchCache on, 617
role, 615
file sharing, 570
accessing from client computers, 578–579, 583–584

BranchCache, 614–622
browsing the network, 579
at command line, creating and managing, 577
creating Windows, 570–572
default and administrative shares, 578, 583
Distributed File System, 605–614
with File and Storage Services, 572–575, 583
File Server Resource Manager, 596–605
mapping drive, 579, 583–584
Network File System, 579–580
with permissions, securing access to files, 584–596
with shared folders snap-in, 575–577, 580–582
file system
defined, 557
File Allocation Table, 558
NTFS, 558–559
ReFS, 559
filtered attribute set, 242
firewalls, control traffic through, 261
firmware settings, for VMs, 692
fixed provisioning, 635
fixed-size disk, 567–568, 704
Flexible Single Master Operation (FSMO) roles, 70, 268, 611
best practices with, 269–270
domain naming master, 269
infrastructure master, 270
managing, 270–271
PDC emulator, 269
RID master, 269
schema master, 269
seizing, 271
transferring, 270–271, 273
using PowerShell to view, 71–72
folder, namespace, 605
folder objects, 58
folder redirection, 193–194, 196
folder target, 605
ForestDNSZones, 373
forest root domain, 73–74
forest trust
configuring, 289–291
creating and testing, 294–295
defined, 285, 286
forest-wide administrative accounts, 72, 282
forest-wide authentication, 290
forest-wide FSMO roles, 268
formatting, local disks, 552

forwarders
    conditional, 394
    configuring and testing, 397–398
    defined, 393
    DNS server, 367
    traditional, 393–394
forward lookup zone (FLZ), 372
FQDN. *See* fully qualified domain
        name (FQDN)
FRS. *See* File Replication Service
        (FRS)
FSMO roles. *See* Flexible Single
        Master Operation (FSMO)
        roles
FSRM. *See* File Server Resource
        Manager (FSRM)
fully qualified domain name (FQDN),
        44, 287, 365, 372, 379, 381, 388,
        395, 443
full zone transfer, 391

G

general purpose file server, 651
General tab, for user account
        properties, 106–107
Generation 1 VMs, 686, 688, 692
Generation 2 VMs, 686, 688, 692, 693
Generic Routing Encapsulation
        (GRE), 490
Global administrator account,
        150, 151
global catalog (GC), 45, 250, 282
    partition, 70
    server, 72, 236
global group, 115–117
globally unique ID (GUID), 258,
        402, 685
global scope, 428
global virtual network peering, 528
glue A record, 388
gMSA. *See* group managed service
        account (gMSA)
GPC. *See* group policy container
        (GPC)
GPMC. *See* Group Policy Management
        console (GPMC)
GPME. *See* Group Policy Management
        Editor (GPME)
GPO. *See* Group Policy Object (GPO)
GPO enforcement, 214, 215
GPO filtering
    defined, 215
    security filtering, 215–217, 221–223
    WMI filtering, 217–219
GPO scope, 78, 212–213

GPP CSE. *See* Group Policy
        Preferences Client Side
        Extensions (GPP CSE)
GPT. *See* group policy template (GPT)
graphical user interface (GUI),
        307–311
graphics processing units
        (GPUs), 703
group accounts
    converting group scope, 118–119
    default groups in Windows
        domain, 119–123
    group scope, 114–118
    group types, 113–114
    managing, 113–123
    nesting groups, 118
group managed service account
        (gMSA), 130, 133, 134, 151, 323
group policies
    adding custom administrative
        template to, 201
    administrative templates, working
        with, 196–204
    applying, 80–86
    in Azure AD DS, 224–226
    computer configuration node,
        79–80
    defined, 171
    Group Policy Object, 78–79,
        172–188
    preferences, 204–211
    processing, 212–224
    replication, 261–262
    settings, 188–196
    user configuration node, 80
group policies preferences
    applied, 205
    configuring and testing, 209–211
    creating, 206–208
    defined, 204
    item-level targeting, 207–208, 211
group policy container (GPC),
        175–177, 183–185, 261, 262
Group Policy Management console
        (GPMC), 177, 213, 214, 262
Group Policy Management Editor
        (GPME), 177, 199–200
Group Policy Object (GPO)
    configuring and testing, 186–187
    creating and linking, 172,
        177–181, 185
    defined, 78, 172
    domain, 175–177
    domain-linked, 213
    editing an existing, 178–180
    enforcement, 214, 215

filtering, 215–219
group policy container, 175–177,
        183–185
group policy template, 175–176,
        183–185
inheritance, 172, 213–214,
        220–221
local, 173–174, 182–183
loopback policy processing,
        219–220, 223–224
OU-linked, 213
precedence, 212–213
provisioning method, 463–464,
        466–467
replication, 172, 177
scope, 172, 212–213
site-linked, 212
Starter, 180–181, 187–188
status, 214–216
Group Policy Preferences Client Side
        Extensions (GPP CSE), 205
Group Policy provisioning, 463
group policy template (GPT), 175–
        176, 183–185, 261, 262
group scope
    converting, 118–119
    defined, 114
    domain local group, 115
    global group, 115–117
    local group, 117–118
    membership and resource
        assignment, 114
    universal group, 116–117
group types
    converting, 114
    defined, 114
    distribution groups, 113–114
    security groups, 113–114
guest clustering, 755–757
guest OS, 13, 677
guest virtual machines, 790
GUI. *See* graphical user interface
        (GUI)
GUID. *See* globally unique ID (GUID)
GUID Partitioning Table (GPT), 555

H

hard disk drives (HDDs), 549, 553,
        559, 643, 728
hard quotas, 597
hardware acceleration, for VNICs,
        720–721
hardware RAID, 557
hash process, 141
HDDs. *See* hard disk drives (HDDs)
hierarchical organization, 557

highly available virtual machine
    configuring existing, 750
    creating, 748–750
    defined, 748
    using drain on shutdown, 750–751
host computer, 13, 677
Host Compute Service (HCS), 744
host domain, 379
hosted cache mode
    configuring server for, 618–619
    defined, 615
Host Guardian Service (HGS), 692
hostnames, 366
host record, 377–378
hot-add/hot-swap process, 559
hot-add memory, 695
hot backup site, 757
hot spare disk, 640
hot standby mode, 453
    configuring, 455
    defined, 453
HVC tool, 703
hybrid cloud, 14
hybrid networking infrastructure, 791
hybrid topology, 460–461
Hyper-V
    architecture, 678
    and cloud computing, 13–14
    configuring MAC addresses, 717
    configuring scheduler types, 746–747
    creating virtual machines in,
        681–691
    creating virtual switch, 715–717
    external virtual switch, 712
    guest clustering, 755–757
    Hyper-V Replica, 757–761
    implementing high availability
        with, 748–761
    installing, 677–681
    internal virtual switch, 712–713
    isolation container, 766, 770
    licensing, 680
    managing virtual machines,
        691–704
    nested virtualization, 743
    node fairness, 751–752
    private virtual switch, 713–714
    remote management, 680
    switches, communicating between,
        714–715
    with virtual hard disks, 704–711
    virtual machine management with,
        682–684, 790
    virtual network interface card,
        718–719
    virtual networks, 711–719

hypervisor, 14, 677–678
Hyper-V Replica
    Broker, 761
    configure steps, 757–758
    defined, 757
    enabling replication on VM,
        758–760
    extended replication, 761
Hyper-V Replica HTTP Listener (TCP-
    In) rule, 758
Hyper-V virtual machine bus
    (VMBus), 697

I

IFM. See Install from Media (IFM)
IKEv2, 498
incremental zone transfer, 391
infrastructure as a service (IaaS)
    model, 26
infrastructure master, 70, 270
inherited permission, 586
Initial Sync policy, 666
Install from Media (IFM), 51–52
instance name, SPN, 132
Integrated Scripting Environment
    (ISE), 354
integration services, 696–697
interactive mode, 584
internal virtual switch, 712–713
Internet Assigned Numbers Authority
    (IANA), 428
Internet Authentication Service (IAS)
    Servers, 492
Internet Key Exchange (IKE), 490
intersite replication, 69, 259–261
Inter-Site Topology Generator (ISTG),
    249–250, 259
intersite transport protocols, 260
intrasite replication, 69
    checking replication status, 258
    connection object, 256–257, 265–266
    Knowledge Consistency Checker,
        255–256
    urgent replication, 257–258
IP addresses
    DHCP (See Dynamic Host
        Configuration Protocol
        (DHCP))
    in hybrid environments, 473–479
    IPAM, 459–473
    virtual network and, 473–474,
        476–479
IP Address Management (IPAM)
    configuring server discovery,
        464–466
    defined, 459

deployment, 460–461
discovering and selecting servers,
    471–473
infrastructure, 459–460
installing and provisioning server,
    469–471
installing DHCP roles, 469
provisioning GPOs, 466–467
requirements and limitations, 461
retrieving server data, 468
server feature, installing, 462
server group membership,
    466–467
server manageability, 467–468
server provisioning, 462–464
IP address space, 473, 476–478
IPAM. See IP Address Management
    (IPAM)
IPAM client, 459, 461
IPAM server, 459, 461
IPsec task offloading, 720
IPv4 multicast packet, 427
IPv4 server properties, 437–440
isolated state, 753
ISTG. See Inter-Site Topology
    Generator (ISTG)
item-level targeting, 207–208, 211
iterative query, 366

J

JEA. See Just Enough Administration
    (JEA)
JEA endpoint, 322
just a bunch of disks (JBOD), 633
Just Enough Administration (JEA)
    configuring, 321–322
    defined, 319, 321
    deployment requirements, 321,
        330–332
    endpoint and session
        configuration, 322–324
just-in-time (JIT) access, for VMs,
    351–352

K

KCC. See Knowledge Consistency
    Checker (KCC)
KDS. See Key Distribution Services
    (KDS)
"keep it simple" rule, 585
Kerberos authentication, 380, 758
Kerberos constrained delegation, 320
Kerberos delegation, 134–135,
    319, 320
Key Distribution Services (KDS), 134

key-signing key (KSK), 400–402
Knowledge Consistency Checker
(KCC), 69, 70, 249, 255–256,
258, 259
KSK. *See* key-signing key (KSK)

L

layer 2 (L2) bridge network, 776
Layer 2 Tunneling Protocol with
Internet Protocol Security
(L2TP/IPsec) tunnels, 490–492
LDAP. *See* Lightweight Directory
Access Protocol (LDAP)
leaf object
computer accounts, 59
contact, 59
defined, 58
groups, 59
printer, 59, 60
shared folder, 59, 60
user accounts, 58–59
lease duration, 423–424
lease renewal process, 420
least privileges principle, 585
legacy network adapters, 726
Lightweight Directory Access
Protocol (LDAP), 39, 236, 250,
380, 381
Link Aggregation Control Protocol
(LACP), 725
link status, 214–215
live migration, 743
load balancing, 722–723
load balancing and failover (LBFO), 722
load-balancing mode, 725
configuring, 453–454
defined, 453
local Administrator account, 102
local configuration manager
(LCM), 355
local disks
capacity and speed, 552–553
disk formats, 557
FAT file system, 558
interface technologies, 553–554
logical disk properties, 552
NTFS file system, 558–559
physical disk properties, 552
with PowerShell, 559–560
preparing new disk for use, 559,
561–562
ReFS file system, 559
sector sizes, 555–556
virtual hard disks, 566–569
volumes and disk types, 554–557,
562–565

local DNS server, 366, 367, 401
local GPOs, 173–174, 182–183
local group, 117–118
Local Group Policy Editor, 173
local storage, 550
local user account, 59
Log Analytics, Azure Arc, 347–348
log files, 549
logical processor, 744
loopback policy processing, 219–220,
223–224
L2TP/IPsec tunnels. *See* Layer 2
Tunneling Protocol with
Internet Protocol Security
(L2TP/IPsec) tunnels

M

MAC address, 443
on virtual network, 717, 721, 722
mail exchanger (MX) records, 378–380
mail servers, 380
managed policy setting, 189
managed server, IPAM, 459, 461
managed service account (MSA)
defined, 130
working with, 132–134
management object files (MOFs), 354
manual disk, 640
manual provisioning, 463
Master Boot Record (MBR), 555
maximum client lead time (MCLT), 454
Member of tab, for user account
properties, 109–110
member server, 9
memory allocation, virtual machines,
693–694
metadata, 557
Microsoft 365 group, 139
Microsoft Azure, 26–27
managing container images
using, 779
Microsoft Challenge Handshake
Authentication Protocol (MS-
CHAP), 507
Microsoft Challenge Handshake
Authentication Protocol
version 2 (MS-CHAP v2),
490, 507
Microsoft encrypted authentication
version 2 (MS-CHAP v2), 498
Microsoft Management Console
(MMC), 7–8, 324
Microsoft Point-to-Point Encryption
(MPPE), 490
Microsoft Software Installation (MSI)
file, 189

mirrored volume, 556
mirror space storage layouts, 634
MMC. *See* Microsoft Management
Console (MMC)
MSA. *See* managed service account
(MSA)
Multicast Address Dynamic
Client Allocation Protocol
(MADCAP), 428
multicast scopes, 427–428
multicast server (MCS), 428
multidomain environments
adding subdomain, 274–275
adding tree to an existing forest,
275–276
configuring alternative UPN suffix,
276–277
reasons for, 274
multiforest environments, 281–283
multimaster replication, 69
multimedia storage, 550
multitenant service, 136
MX records. *See* mail exchanger (MX)
records

N

name server (NS) records, 388, 389
namespace, 666, 761
configuring referrals and advanced
settings, 610–612
creating, 607–609
defined, 605
domain-based, 607, 613–614
organization, 606
standalone, 607, 608
namespace isolation, 761
namespace root, 605
namespace server, 605
name squatting, 440
Name Suffix Routing tab, 292–293
Nano Server, 764
NAS. *See* network access server
(NAS); network-attached
storage (NAS)
NAT. *See* network address translation
(NAT)
.NET application, 534, 535
Nested Page Tables (NPT), 678
nested virtualization, 532, 743
nesting groups, 118
network access server (NAS), 505
network address translation (NAT),
489, 492, 767
adapters, 774–775
configuring, 775
defined, 774

layer 2 (L2) bridge network, 776
    port mapping with, 775
    transparent network, 775–776
network-attached storage (NAS),
        550–551
network client, 11
network connection, 9, 10
network connectivity
    Azure networking implementation,
        526–540
    Network Policy Server, 487, 505–522
    Remote Access server role, 488–504
    Web Application Proxy, 522–526
Network File System (NFS)
    file sharing, 579–580
    installing and configuring server
        for, 579–580
network firewall configuration, for
        VPN, 491–492
network interface, 10
network interface cards (NICs), 10,
        443, 491, 712, 713. *See also* NIC
        teaming
network mode, 584
Network Policy and Access Services
        (NPAS) server, 505
Network Policy Server (NPS), 487, 494
    certificate-based authentication,
        508–509
    installing and configuring,
        506–508, 510
    RADIUS, 505–508
network protocol, 11
network security group (NSG), 351
network server software, 11
Next Secure 3 (NSEC3) Parameter
        records, 400
Next Secure 3 (NSEC3) records, 400
Next Secure (NSEC) records, 400
NFS. *See* Network File System (NFS)
NICs. *See* network interface cards
        (NICs)
NIC teaming
    defined, 722
    functions, 723
    modes, 724–725
    Switch Embedded Teaming, 726
    on virtual machines, 725–726
node fairness, 751–752
non-uniform memory access
        (NUMA), 745
NPS. *See* Network Policy Server (NPS)
NPS Network Policy, 495
NT Directory Service (NTDS), 250
NT File System (NTFS), 7, 557–559,
        589, 592

O
object owner, 96, 585
offline domain join, 126
offline files, 574
onboarding
    defined, 341
    Windows servers, for Azure Arc,
        341–343
one-way trust, 284
on-premises, implement and
        manage, 791
Open Files node, 576
Open Shortest Path First (OSPF), 428
operating system (OS) files, 549
operations masters, 73, 282
    best practices, 268–270
    defined, 70
    domain naming master, 269
    infrastructure master, 270
    managing, 270–271
    PDC emulator, 269
    RID master, 269
    roles, 70–71
    rules for, 268–269
    schema master, 269
    seizing, 271
    transferring, 270–271
ordering method, 610–611
organizationally unique identifier
        (OUI), 443, 717
organizational units (OUs), 41, 42,
        57–58
    Active Directory object
        permissions, 96–101
    benefits of, 93
    delegation of control, 95–96
    permission inheritance in,
        96–97
    single-level and multilevel
        structure, 94
    top-level structure, 93–94
    working with, 93–101
OU-linked GPOs, 213

P
page file, 549
parallel ATA (PATA), 553
parameter, 12
parity space storage layouts,
        634, 635
partition, local disks, 552, 555
passive screening, 598
pass-through disk, 708–709
Password Authentication Protocol
        (PAP), 507

Password Replication Policy (PRP),
        242–243, 245–246
password settings object (PSO), 274
password writeback, 141
PCI Express (PCIe) devices, 703
PDC emulator. *See* primary domain
        controller (PDC) emulator
perimeter network, 491
permission inheritance, 96–97, 587
permissions, 59
    assigned, 586
    defined, 585
    file and folder, 585, 587–594
    security principals, 585–586
    share permissions, 584–587,
        595–596
    volumes, 592–594
physical processor, 744
platform as a service (PaaS)
        model, 26
pointer (PTR) record, 378, 438, 382
Point-to-Point Protocol (PPP), 490
Point-to-Point Tunneling Protocol
        (PPTP) tunnels, 490, 491
policies, Azure Arc, 344–346
policy options, DHCP, 429
port mapping, with NAT
        networks, 775
port mirroring, 722
port number, SPN, 132
PowerShell, 11–13
    configuring data deduplication
        with, 652–653
    configuring tiered storage
        with, 644
    creating storage pool and volume
        with, 637–638
    creating storage space with, 648
    data deduplication, 651
    Hyper-V remote management, 680
    Just Enough Administration, 319,
        321–324, 330–332
    to manage storage spaces, 642
    managing and creating shares
        with, 577
    managing disks with, 559–560
    managing server roles with, 312
    remote management, 318–319,
        330–332
    remote server administration tools
        (RSAT), 320
    scripts, 192
    staged RODC installation with, 241
    Storage Replica, 656
    to view FSMO roles, 71–72
    Windows Admin Center, 333, 334

PowerShell cmdlets
    configuring data deduplication, 653
    conversion process, 566, 567
    creating DNS resource records, 383
    DNS server settings, 396
    installing and configuring DNS, 375
    monitoring data deduplication,
        653–654
    storage spaces, 642
    tiered storage, 644
    working with file shares, 577
    working with VMs, 686, 687
PowerShell Direct, managing
        Windows VMs with, 703
PowerShell role capability file, 321, 322
Preboot Execution Environment
        (PXE), 443–444
primary domain controller (PDC)
        emulator, 257, 269, 611
primary partition, 554
primary zone, 373
primordial pool, 635–637
principle of least privilege, 321
private cloud, 14
private virtual switch, 713–714
process isolation container, 765–766,
        768–770
production checkpoint, 697
Profile tab, for user account
        properties, 109
Protected Extensible Authentication
        Protocol (PEAP), 507
protected network, VM, 722
PRP. *See* Password Replication Policy
        (PRP)
PTR record. *See* pointer (PTR) record
public cloud, 14
public IP address, 731
public key infrastructure (PKI), 490
published application, 80, 191
PXE. *See* Preboot Execution
        Environment (PXE)

Q

quarantined state, 754
quota management, FSRM, 596
quotas, 597–598, 600–603

R

RADIUS server. *See* Remote
        Authentication Dial-In User
        Service (RADIUS) server
RADIUS server group, 508
RAID. *See* redundant array of
        independent disks (RAID)

RAID 5 volume, 556, 557
RAS. *See* Remote Access server (RAS)
RDC. *See* remote differential
        compression (RDC)
read-only DNS, 243
read-only domain controller
        (RODC), 45
    changing to standard DC, 272
    defined, 236, 237
    installation, 237–239, 244–245
    read-only DNS, 243
    replication, 242–243
    staged installation, 239–241
realm network policy, 507
realm trust
    configuring, 291
    defined, 287
receive side scaling (RSS), 658
recovery point, 759
recursive query
    defined, 366
    in DNS, 395–396
redundant array of independent disks
        (RAID), 552, 556, 559
referrals
    configuring, 610–612
    defined, 284, 366, 610
ReFS. *See* Resilient File System (ReFS)
relative identifier (RID), 71, 258,
        269, 296
Remote Access server (RAS)
    configuring security settings,
        496–498
    defined, 488
    installing and configuring, 489, 502
    services and tools, 489
    virtual private network, 489–496,
        503–504
Remote Authentication Dial-In User
        Service (RADIUS) server, 491,
        494, 496–498
    accounting, 508
    defined, 505
    infrastructure, 505–506
    installing and configuring, 506–508,
        510–513
    testing, 513–515
Remote Desktop (RD) Gateway
        applications, 525
remote dial-in technology, 489
remote differential compression
        (RDC), 177, 262
remote direct memory access
        (RDMA), 658, 659
remote management
    enabling and disabling, 318

Just Enough Administration,
        321–324
    PowerShell, 318–319, 330–332
    second-hop remoting, 319–321
    Windows Firewall for, 324–326
Remote Procedure Call (RPC), 260
remote server administration tools
        (RSAT), 320, 461
reparse point, 649
replica server, 757
replication
    defined, 606
    between domains, 73
    efficiency, 246
replication partner, 70
reservation, 425, 432–434
    options, DHCP, 429
resilience, 633
resiliency, implementing VM, 752–753
Resilient File System (ReFS), 557,
        559, 589
resource-based constrained
        delegation, 320–321
resource control, 777
resource forest, 156
resource records
    CNAME record, 378
    defined, 366
    DNSKEY record, 400
    DS records, 400
    dynamic DNS records, 382
    host record, 377–378
    MX record, 378–380
    NSEC3PARAM records, 400
    NSEC records, 400
    NSEC3 records, 400
    PTR record, 378
    RRSIG records, 400
    SRV record, 380–381
    static DNS records, 382–383, 386
    types, 376–377
Resource Record Signature (RRSIG)
        record, 400
Response Rate Limiting (RRL),
        403–404
reverse lookup zone (RLZ), 372, 385
RID master, 269
rights, 59
RIPv2. *See* Routing Information
        Protocol version 2 (RIPv2)
RLZ. *See* reverse lookup zone (RLZ)
RODC. *See* read-only domain
        controller (RODC)
RoleDefinitions, 323
role services, 4
root certificate, 509

root hints, 394–395, 398–399
root servers, 365
round robin, 395
Routing and Remote Access Service (RRAS), 490, 492, 498, 510, 522
Routing Information Protocol version 2 (RIPv2), 428
routing service, 489
RRAS. See Routing and Remote Access Service (RRAS)
RunAsVirtualAccount, 323
RunAsVirtualAccountGroups, 323
runbook, 353

S

saved state files, 681, 698
scalability, 25
schema, 56–57, 281
schema attribute, 56, 57
schema classes, 56, 57
schema directory partition, 70
schema master, 70, 269
scope-level policies, 443
scope options, DHCP, 429
scope properties, 441–442
scripts, 192
secondary zone, 373
    creating, 389–392
second-hop remoting, 319–321
second level address translation (SLAT). See extended page tables (EPT) technology
Secure Sockets Layer (SSL), 490
    certificate binding, 498
Secure Socket Tunneling Protocol (SSTP) tunnels, 490, 492, 498
Security Accounts Manager (SAM) database, 102
security descriptor, 585
security filtering, 215–217, 221–223
security groups, 113–114, 139
security identifier (SID), 71, 269
security principals, 585–586
security settings, for VMs, 692, 693
selective authentication, 290
self-service password reset (SSPR), 145–148
serial ATA (SATA), 553
serial attached SCSI (SAS), 553
Server Core, 764
    installing Active Directory in, 49–51
    special considerations for, 326
server endpoints
    creating, 665–666
    defined, 663

server features, 4
server-level policies, 443
Server Manager, 6–7
    adding servers to, 316–317, 327–329
    IPAM, 462
    using groups, 317
Server Message Block (SMB), 570, 658
server operating systems, 3
    vs. desktop operating systems, 3
    hardware/software configuration, 3
server role, 4, 5
server storage
    configuring local disks, 552–565
    description of, 549
    reasons for, 549–550
    storage access methods, 550–551
    virtual hard disks, 566–569
server-to-server replication, 656
service accounts
    administrator-created, 130–131
    built-in, 130, 131
    defined, 129
    Kerberos delegation, 134–135
    managed service account, 132–134
    service principal name, 132
    working with, 129–136
service endpoint, 528
service level agreement (SLA), 727
service location (SRV) records, 380–381
service name, SPN, 132
service principal name (SPN), 132
service type, SPN, 132
Sessions node, 576
shared folders snap-in, managing shares with, 575–577, 580–582
shared secret, 507, 522
shared virtual hard disk (shared VHDX), 755–757
share permissions, 584–587
Shares node, 575
shortcut trust
    configuring, 287–289
    defined, 285, 286
SID filtering, 293–294
Simple Mail Transport Protocol (SMTP), 260
simple space storage layouts, 633, 634
simple volume, 556
simultaneous multithreading (SMT), 744, 747
single-domain environment, 273–274
single-root I/O virtualization (SR-IOV), 658, 717, 720–721
single schema, 72
single sign-on (SSO), 136
site link, 248–249

bridges, 260–261
    creating, 266
site-linked GPOs, 212
site-to-site VPN, 499–501
small computer system interface (SCSI) drives, 553
smart paging, 695
SMB Direct, 658–659
SMB Share, 572–574
SMT. See simultaneous multithreading (SMT)
soft quotas, 597
software as a service (SaaS) model, 26
software-defined storage (SDS), 14
software installation policies, 189
    advanced application deployment options, 190–191
    for computers, 190, 195
    for users, 191
software RAID, 557
solid state drive (SSD), 549, 552, 643, 728
spanned volume, 556
special identity groups, 121–122
split scope, 452–453, 456–457
SRV record registration, 250–251
SSD. See solid state drive (SSD)
SSH Direct, 703
SSL. See Secure Sockets Layer (SSL)
SSPR. See self-service password reset (SSPR)
SSTP tunnels. See Secure Socket Tunneling Protocol (SSTP) tunnels
staged installation, RODC, 239–241
standalone namespace, 607, 608
standalone server, 9
standard checkpoint, 697
standard-tier VMs, 727
Starter GPO, 180–181, 187–188
start of authority (SOA) records, 387, 389
stateless operation, 776
static DNS records, 382–383, 386
static teaming teaming mode, 725
storage appliance, 550
storage area network (SAN), 551, 633, 682
storage layouts, 633–634
storage pool
    defined, 633, 635
    disk allocation options, 640–641
    expanding, 638–639
    replacing failed physical disk in, 639–641
Storage Quality of Service (QoS)

defined, 659
policies, 660
requirements, 659–660
Storage Replica
asynchronous replication, 658
defined, 655
installing and configuring,
656–657
synchronous replication, 657
use scenarios, 656
storage reports management, FSRM,
596
storage spaces, 14
cleaning up, 648
creating, 635–638
creating with PowerShell, 648
defined, 633
enclosure awareness, 642
features, 633–635
with File and Storage Services,
645–647
just a bunch of disks, 633
storage pool, 638–641
tiered storage, 643–644
Storage Sync Service resource
creating, 662
defined, 662
registering server with, 663, 664
storage tiering, 635
stretch cluster replication, 656
striped volume, 556
stub zone, 373
subdomains. *See also* child domains
adding, 274–275
installing, 278–279
removing, 279–281
subnets, 247–248, 252–254
adding to virtual network,
527–528
multiple, 425–426
superscope, 426–427
switch independent teaming
mode, 724
sync group, 663–664
synchronous replication, 657
synthetic drivers, 696
synthetic network adapters, 726
system access control list (SACL),
96, 585
system partition. *See* system volume
system volume, 554
SYSVOL folder, 46
SYSVOL replication
Distributed File System
Replication, 262–263
Group Policy object, 261–262

T

tags, 764
target server, staged RODC
installation with, 241
thin provisioning, 14, 633
three-way mirror, 634
tiered storage, 643–644
time to live (TTL) value, 378, 382, 387,
428
top-level domain (TLD) server,
365–366, 388, 395, 401, 403
traditional forwarders, 393–394
TranscriptDirectory, 323
transitive trust, 284–285
Transmission Control Protocol/
Internet Protocol (TCP/IP), 418
transparent network, 775–776
Transport Layer Security (TLS), 507, 534
Transport Layer Security
Authentication (TLSA)
records, 404
Triple DES (3DES), 490
troubleshooting BranchCache, 620
troubleshooting DHCP, 447–448
trust anchor, 400, 402
trust relationship
Authentication tab, 293
between domains, 73
configuring, 287–295
defined, 72, 283
external trust, 287
forest trust, 285, 286, 289–291
General tab, 292
Name Suffix Routing tab, 292–293
one-way trust, 284
realm trust, 287
reviewing, 288
shortcut trust, 285–289
SID filtering, 293–294
transitive trust, 284–285
two-way trust, 284
tunnel
defined, 489
types, 490–491, 498
two-way trust, 284
type 1 hypervisors, 677–678
type 2 hypervisors, 677

U

UNC path. *See* Universal Naming
Convention (UNC) path
unencrypted password (PAP), 498
unidirectional replication, 242
Unified Extensible Firmware Interface
(UEFI), 686

universal group, 116–117
universal group membership caching,
117, 250
Universal Naming Convention (UNC)
path, 176, 578, 605
unmanaged policy setting, 189
unmonitored state, 753
Update management, Azure Arc,
347–349
UPN. *See* user principal name (UPN)
UPN suffix, 276–277
urgent replication, 257–258
user accounts
Account tab, 107–108
built-in Administrator account,
102–103
built-in Guest account, 103
configuring dial-in settings in, 495
contacts, 110
creating and modifying, 103–105
creating Azure AD, 138–139
disabling, 105
distribution group, 110
domain, 102
functions, 101
General tab, 106–107
managing, 101–113
Member Of tab, 109–110
Profile tab, 109
properties, 106–110
User Class, 443
user configuration node, GPO, 80
user documents, server storage, 550
user forest, 156
user principal name (UPN), 103
alternative suffix, 276–277
defined, 73
Users folder, default groups in,
120–121

V

variable, 12
Vendor Class, 430, 442
vEthernet (nat), 774–775
VHD. *See* virtual hard disk (VHD)
VHD set, 705, 756
VHDX format, virtual hard disk *versus,*
566–567
virtual accounts, 134
virtual appliance, 533
virtual desktop infrastructure (VDI)
server, 14, 650, 651
virtual disks
columns, 638
copying, 686
defined, 678

physical disks in, 638, 639
storage pools, 635, 636
virtual hard disk (VHD), 308
    creating and modifying, 705–708,
        710
    defined, 566
    in disk management, 568–569
    dynamically expanding disk,
        567–568
    editing, 710–711
    files, 681
    fixed-size disk, 567–568
    pass-through disk, 708–709
    types, 704–705
    versus VHDX format, 566–567
virtual instances, of Windows
        Server, 680
virtualization, 13–14, 676
    data deduplication, 649–650
    Hyper-V (*See* Hyper-V)
    nested, 743
    technology, 549
virtualization software, 13, 677
virtualized backup server, 651
virtual LANs (VLANs), 718
virtual machine monitor (VMM), 677
virtual machine queue (VMQ), 720
virtual machines (VMs), 13, 441, 549,
        676, 677. *See also* Hyper-V
    automatic start and stop actions,
        699–700
    on Azure, managing Windows
        Server on, 727–732
    BIOS and firmware settings, 692
    checkpoints, 697–699
    copying virtual disk, 686
    creating in Hyper-V, 681–691
    Discrete Device Assignment, 703
    dynamic memory, 694
    enabling replication on, 758–760
    enhanced session mode, 700–702,
        704
    exporting, 685, 690–691
    generation 1/generation 2, 686, 688
    guest clustering, 755–757
    hardware settings, 692–696
    highly available virtual machine,
        748–751
    hot-add memory, 695
    Hyper-V manager, management
        with, 682–684, 689–690
    implementing containers in, 767
    implementing resiliency, 752–753
    importing, 685–686, 690–691
    integration services, 696–697
    managing, 691–704, 790

managing Linux with SSH Direct,
        703
memory allocation, 693–694
monitoring, 753–755
nested virtualization, 743
NIC teaming on, 725–726
node fairness, 751–752
PowerShell Cmdlets working with,
        686, 687
with PowerShell Direct, 703
security settings, 692, 693
shared VHDX, 755–757
smart paging, 695
on virtual network, 474, 478–479
virtual processors, 695–696
VM CPU groups, 744–745
virtual network interface card (vNIC)
    adding and removing, 718–719
    configuring with advanced
        features, 721–722
    hardware acceleration for,
        720–721
    legacy network adapters, 726
    NIC teaming, 722–726
    synthetic network adapters, 726
virtual network peering, 528–530
virtual networks, 678
    advanced configuration, 719–727
    configuring MAC addresses, 717
    creating virtual switch, 715–717
    external virtual switch, 712
    Hyper-V switches, communicating
        between, 714–715
    internal virtual switch, 712–713
    private virtual switch, 713–714
virtual private network (VPN), 488,
        731
    client configuration, 495–496, 521
    configuration, 492–496
    configuring remote access options,
        496–498
    configuring site-to-site, 499–501
    creating and testing connection,
        503–504, 513–515
    defined, 489
    network firewall configuration for,
        491–492
    requirements, 491
    tunnel method, 489–490
    tunnel types, 490–491, 498
virtual processors, 695–696, 744
virtual switch
    communicating between Hyper-V,
        714–715
    creating, 715–717
    external, 712

internal, 712–713
    private, 713–714
virtual WAN hub (vHub), 536, 538, 539
VisibleCmdlets, 321
VisibleExternalCommands, 322
VisibleFunctions, 322
VisibleProviders, 322
VLAN identifier, 717
VM CPU groups, 744–745
VMs. *See* virtual machines (VMs)
vNIC. *See* virtual network interface
        card (vNIC)
volume, disk drive
    boot, 554
    defined, 552
    storage pools, 637
    system, 554
    types of, 556
VPN. *See* virtual private network (VPN)
VT-x virtualization extensions, 743

W

WAC. *See* Windows Admin Center
        (WAC)
WAP. *See* Web Application Proxy
        (WAP)
WDS. *See* Windows Deployment
        Services (WDS)
Web Application Proxy (WAP), 489
    configuring, 522, 523
    defined, 522
    publishing Web apps with,
        524–525
    Remote Desktop Gateway
        applications, 525
Web server, installing BranchCache
        on, 617–618
Windows 10, 703, 705
Windows 11, 3, 461
Windows 2000/Windows NT
        domain, 287
    installing Windows Admin Center
        on, 333–334
Windows Admin Center (WAC), 306,
        530, 531, 533, 534
    defined, 332
    installing Gateway, 335–340
    installing on Windows 11,
        333–334
    methods, 332–333
Windows Communication Foundation
        (WCF) application, 535
Windows containers. *See* container
Windows Deployment Services
        (WDS), 443, 444

Windows domain
    default groups in, 119–123
    defined, 9
Windows firewall, for remote
        management, 324
    rules with command line, 325–326
    rules with Desktop Experience,
        324–325
    Server Core, 326
Windows Internal Database (WID), 462
Windows Management Framework
        (WMF) 5.1, 321
Windows Management
        Instrumentation (WMI), 318
Windows networking
    domain model, 9
    network client, 11
    network interface, 10
    network protocol, 11
    network server software, 11
    workgroup model, 9
Windows Remote Management
        (WinRM), 318
Windows Server
    Azure Arc, 341–351
    with Azure services, 340–354
    with Desired State Configuration,
        354–358
    GUI, managing roles in, 307–311
    in hybrid environment, 789
    implementing containers on,
        763–767
    installing and removing server
        roles with, 313–314
    just-in-time (JIT) access for VMs,
        351–352
    PowerShell, managing roles with,
        312, 315
    remote management, 316–332
    roles and features, 307–315
    runbooks, to manage Azure
        VMs, 353

storage and file services, 792
Windows Admin Center,
        332–340
Windows Server 2003, 316
Windows Server 2008, 608
Windows Server 2008 R2, 60, 130, 134,
        341, 615
Windows Server 2012, 461, 615, 753
Windows Server 2012 R2, 341,
        751, 755
Windows Server 2016, 321, 404, 461,
        692, 705, 747, 753, 755
Windows Server 2019, 317
Windows Server 2022, 2, 3, 316,
        317, 491, 499, 555, 559,
        570, 579
    Active Directory Domain
        Services, 11
    cloud computing, 13–14
    core technologies, 5–25
    Disk Management, 9
    file and printer sharing, 9
    Hyper-V, 13–14
    Microsoft Management Console,
        7–8
    NT File System, 7
    PowerShell, 11–13
    roles and features, 4–5
    Server Manager, 6–7
    Storage Spaces, 14
    Windows networking, 9–11
Windows Server hybrid
        infrastructure, 25
    agility, 26
    Azure VM, 27–33
    cloud models, 26
    latest technologies, 26
    Microsoft Azure, 26–27
    scalability, 25
Windows workgroup model, 9
WinRM. *See* Windows Remote
        Management (WinRM)

WMI. *See* Windows Management
        Instrumentation (WMI)
WMI filtering, 217–219
Workloads, in hybrid environment, 789
writeable DC, 242

Z

zone
    configuring DNS, 386–392
    configuring zone transfers,
        389–392
    creating DNS, 371–375
    creating secondary zones,
        389–392
    defined, 366
    dynamic updates, 375
    file, 374
    forward lookup zones, 372
    key-signing key, 400
    name, 374
    NS records, 388, 389
    primary, 373
    replication scope, 373–374
    resource records, 376–386, 400
    reverse lookup zone, 372, 385
    secondary, 373
    SOA record, 387–388
    stub, 373
    types, 372–373
    zone delegation, 388–389
    zone-signing key, 400
zone delegation, 388–389
zone replication scope,
        373–374
zone signing, 400
zone-signing key (ZSK), 400–402
zone transfer
    configuring, 389–392
    defined, 389
    full *versus* incremental, 391
    settings, 389–391
ZSK. *See* zone-signing key (ZSK)

ISBN-13: 978-0357511817
ISBN-10: 0357511816

90000

9 780357 511817